THIRD EDITION

Lifespan Development

Megan Clegg Kraynok
Ohio Northern University

Kelvin L. Seifert—Emeritus
The University of Manitoba

Robert J. Hoffnung—Emeritus
University of New Haven

Michele Hoffnung—Emerita
Quinnipiac University

To our families

*Joseph Kraynok, Melanie and Christopher Clegg, and
Sue and Jim McDonough*   **m.c.k.**

Elizabeth Katherine and Michael David Seifert   **k.l.s.**

*Isaac and Naomi Hoffnung and Archer, Forest, and
Kailey Burbank*   **r.j.h.**

*Jeremy, Samuel, Lalo, and Pia Garskof and Arthur and
Oscar Aucoin*   **m.h.**

Lifespan Development, 3rd Edition, Kraynok, Seifert, Hoffnung. Hoffnung

Cover photos: Shutterstock.com
(Main Image) Cienpies Design
(Top Panel Image) YanLev
(Middle Panel Image) vitstudio
(Bottom Panel Image) CHAINFOTO24

Paperback (black/white): ISBN–13: 978-1-942041-21-4
ISBN–10: 1-942041-21-7
Paperback (color): ISBN–13: 978-1-942041-23-8
ISBN–10: 1-942041-23-3
Loose leaf version (B/W): ISBN–13: 978-1-942041-22-1
ISBN–10: 1-942041-22-5
Online version: ISBN–13: 978-1-942041-24-5
ISBN–10: 1-942041-24-1

Copyright © 2017 by Academic Media Solutions. All rights reserved.

No part of this work may be reproduced or transmitted in any form or by any means, electronic or mechanical, including photocopying and recording, or by any information storage or retrieval system without the prior written permission of the publisher.

Printed in the United States of America by Academic Media Solutions

Brief Contents

Special Features xi
Preface xii
About the Authors xvi

PART 1 Beginnings 1
1. Studying Lifespan Development 3
2. Theories of Development 31
3. Genetics, Prenatal Development, and Birth 59

PART 2 The First Two Years of Life 101
4. Physical and Cognitive Development in the First Two Years 103
5. Psychosocial Development in the First Two Years 147

PART 3 Early Childhood 179
6. Physical and Cognitive Development in Early Childhood 181
7. Psychosocial Development in Early Childhood 217

PART 4 Middle Childhood 255
8. Physical and Cognitive Development in Middle Childhood 257
9. Psychosocial Development in Middle Childhood 293

PART 5 Adolescence 331
10. Physical and Cognitive Development in Adolescence 333
11. Psychosocial Development in Adolescence 375

PART 6 Early Adulthood 417
12. Physical and Cognitive Development in Early Adulthood 419
13. Psychosocial Development in Early Adulthood 465

PART 7 Middle Adulthood 499
14. Physical and Cognitive Development in Middle Adulthood 501
15. Psychosocial Development in Middle Adulthood 537

PART 8 Late Adulthood 569
16. Physical and Cognitive Development in Late Adulthood 571
17. Psychosocial Development in Late Adulthood 609

PART 9 Endings 653
18. Dying, Death, and Bereavement 655

Glossary G-1
References R-1
Author/Name Index I-1
Subject Index I-9

Contents

Special Features xi
Preface xii
About the Authors xvi

PART 1 Beginnings 1

1 Studying Lifespan Development 3
The Nature of Lifespan Development 4
   Multiple Domains of Development 5
   Development from a Lifespan Perspective: The Example of Jodi 6
Why Study Development? 10
Focusing On . . . *Wanted: A Child and Family Policy* 11
The Life Course in Times Past 11
   Early Precursors to Developmental Study 12
   The Emergence of Modern Developmental Study 12
Lifespan Perspectives on Human Development 13
   Continuity Within Change 13
   Lifelong Growth 14
   Changing Meanings and Vantage Points 15
   Developmental Diversity 16
Methods of Studying Lifespan Psychology 16
   The Scientific Method 17
A Multicultural View: *Street Children: Comparing Paraguay and North America* 18
   Researching Questions about Causality 18
   Researching Questions about Association 23
Working with *Marsha Bennington, Speech-Language Pathologist: Communication Difficulties Across the Lifespan* 24
Ethical Constraints on Studying Development 27
Strengths and Limitations of Developmental Knowledge 29

2 Theories of Development 31
The Nature of Developmental Theories 32
   What Is a Developmental Theory? 32
   How Do Developmental Theories Differ? 33
Psychodynamic Developmental Theories 35
   Freudian Theory 35
Focusing On . . . *Erik Erikson's Identity Crisis: An Autobiographical Perspective* 37
   Erikson's Psychosocial Theory 37
   Applications of Psychodynamic Developmental Theories Throughout the Lifespan 40
Behavioral Learning and Social Cognitive Learning Developmental Theories 40
   Behavioral Learning Theories 40
   Social Cognitive Learning Theory 42
   Applications of Learning Theories Throughout the Lifespan 43
Cognitive Developmental Theories 43
   Piaget's Cognitive Theory 44
   Neo-Piagetian Approaches 45
   Information-Processing Theory 45
   Applications of Cognitive Developmental Theories Throughout the Lifespan 47
Contextual Developmental Theories 48
   Applications of Contextual Developmental Theories Throughout the Lifespan 48
A Multicultural View: *Street Children: Comparing Paraguay and North America* 49
   Ethological Theory 50
Adulthood and Lifespan Developmental Theories 50
   Normative-Crisis Model of Development 51
   Timing-of-Events Model 52
Working with *Jeffrey Friedman, Clinical Social Worker: The Value of Developmental Theory for Helping Children, Adolescents, and Their Families* 54
Developmental Theories Compared: Implications for the Student 54

3 Genetics, Prenatal Development, and Birth 59
Mechanisms of Genetic Transmission 60
   The Role of DNA 60
   Meiosis and Mitosis 60
Individual Genetic Expression 62
   Genotype and Phenotype 62
   Dominant and Recessive Genes 62
   Transmission of Multiple Variations 62
   Polygenic Transmission 64
   The Determination of Sex 64
Genetic Abnormalities 65
   Disorders Due to Abnormal Chromosomes 65
   Disorders Due to Abnormal Genes 69
Genetic Counseling and Prenatal Diagnosis 70
Relative Influence of Heredity and Environment 71
Focusing On . . . *Technological Alternatives to Natural Conception* 72
   Key Concepts of Behavior Genetics 72
A Multicultural View: *Cultural Difference and Genetic Counseling* 74

Adoption and Twin Studies 74
Cautions and Conclusions about the Influence of Heredity and Environment 76

Prenatal Development and Birth 76

Stages of Prenatal Development 76
Conception 76
The Germinal Stage (First Two Weeks) 77
The Embryonic Stage (Third Through Eighth Weeks) 78
The Fetal Stage (Ninth Week to Birth) 79
The Experience of Pregnancy 80

Prenatal Influences on the Child 81
Harmful Substances, Diseases, and Environmental Hazards 82
Maternal Age and Physical Characteristics 86
Prenatal Health Care 87

Working with Katie Glover, OB-GYN Nurse Practitioner: Preparing for Childbirth 88

Birth 89
Stages of Labor 90
Childbirth Settings and Methods 91
Problems During Labor and Delivery 94
Faulty Passenger 95
Birth and the Family 97

Looking Back/Looking Forward 97

PART 2 The First Two Years of Life 101

4 Physical and Cognitive Development in the First Two Years 103

PHYSICAL DEVELOPMENT 105
The Newborn 105
The First Few Hours 105
Is the Baby All Right? The Apgar Scale 105
Size and Bodily Proportions 106

Growth in Infancy 106
Physical Growth 106
Brain Growth 107

Infant States: Sleep and Arousal 109
Sleep 109

Focusing On . . . Sudden Infant Death Syndrome 110
Parents' Response to Infant Sleep and Arousal 111
States of Arousal 112

Sensory Acuity 113
Visual Acuity 113
Auditory Acuity 114
Tactile, Taste, and Olfactory Acuity 114

Motor Development 115
The First Motor Skills 115
Cultural and Sex Differences in Motor Development 118

Nutrition During the First Two Years 119
Breast Milk Versus Formula 119
Poor Nutrition 120
Overnutrition 121

Impairments in Infant Growth 121
Low-Birth-Weight Infants 121
Failure to Thrive 122
Infant Mortality 123

COGNITIVE DEVELOPMENT 123

Studying Cognition and Memory in Infants 124
Arousal and Infants' Heart Rates 124
Recognition, Memory, and Infant Habituation 125

Infant Perception and Cognition 126
Visual Perception in Infancy 126
Auditory Perception in Infancy 128
Coordination of Sensory Information 129

Cognitive Change During Infancy: Piaget's Stage Theory 130
Stages of Sensorimotor Intelligence 130
Assessment of Piaget's Theory of Infant Cognition 134

Behavioral Learning in Infancy 136
Operant Conditioning 136
Imitation 137

Language Acquisition 138
Phonology 140
Semantics and First Words 140
Influencing Language Acquisition 141

A Multicultural View: Cognitive Effects of Talking to Infants: A Cross-Cultural Perspective 142

Working with Gillian Luppiwiski, Infant Care Provider: Fostering Infants' Thinking 144

The End of Infancy 144

5 The First Two Years: Psychosocial Development 147

Early Social Relationships 148
Transition to Parenthood 149
Caregiver-Infant Synchrony 150
Social Interactions with Other Family Members 151
Interactions with Nonparental Caregivers 153
Interactions with Peers 154

Emotions and Temperament in Infancy 156
Emotions in Infancy 156
Temperament 158

Attachment Formation 160
Phases of Attachment Formation 161
Assessing Attachment: The "Strange Situation" 162
Consequences of Different Attachment Patterns 163

A Multicultural View: Cross-Cultural Variations in Attachment 164
Influences on Attachment Formation 165

Focusing On . . . Family-Leave Policies in the United States and Europe 167

Working with Rachelle Turner, Infant Day-Care Coordinator: Understanding Infant Social Development 168
Long-Term and Intergenerational Effects of Attachment 170

Toddlerhood and the Emergence of Autonomy   171
   Sources of Autonomy   172
   Development of Self   173
   Development of Competence and Self-Esteem   174
Looking Back/Looking Forward   175

PART 3   Early Childhood   179

6   Physical and Cognitive Development in Early Childhood   181

PHYSICAL DEVELOPMENT   182
   Influences on Normal Physical Development   182
   Genetic Background   183
   Nutritional Needs During the Preschool Years   184
The Connection Between Health and Poverty   184
   Bladder Control   185
Focusing On . . . *Reforming Children's Health Care*   186
Motor Skill Development   187
   Fundamental Motor Skills   187
   Fine Motor Coordination: The Case of Drawing Skills   189
   Gender Differences in Physical Development   190
   Variations in Motor Skill Development   191
The Impact of Children's Growth on Adults   192
   Effects of Appearance   192
   Effects of Motor Skills   192
   Effects of Differences in Families   194
COGNITIVE DEVELOPMENT   195
Thinking Among Preschoolers   195
   Piaget's Preoperational Stage   195
   Symbolic Thought   196
   Egocentrism in Preschool Children   197
   Other Aspects of Children's Conceptual Development   197
   Cognition as Social Activity   199
   Neostructuralist Theories of Cognitive Development   201
Language Acquisition in the Preschool Years   201
   The Nature of Syntax   202
   Beyond First Words: Semantic and Syntactic Relations   202
   Mechanisms of Language Acquisition   204
   Innate Predisposition to Acquire Language: LAD   206
   Parent-Child Interactions   207
Language Variations   207
   Gender Differences in Language   208
   Socioeconomic Differences in Language   208
   Language of Deaf and Hearing-Impaired Children   209
Working with *Carolyn Eaton, Preschool Teacher: Introducing Sign Language to Young Children*   210
   Language Deficits or Language Differences?   210
Early Childhood Education   211
   Early Education and Cognitive Theories of Development   212
   Effectiveness of Early Childhood Education   212
   Cultural Diversity and Best Practice in Early Education   213
A Multicultural View: *Parents' Beliefs about Intelligence: A Cross-cultural Perspective*   214
From Preschooler to Child   215

7   Psychosocial Development in Early Childhood   217

Relationships with Family   218
   Relationships with Parents   218
   Patterns of Parental Authority   219
Focusing On . . . *Extended Family Supports for Child-Rearing*   220
   Relationships with Siblings   223
Relationships in an Expanding Social World   225
   Empathy and Prosocial Behavior   226
   Conflict and Aggression   228
   Responding to Aggressive Behavior   231
   The Effects of Media on Preschoolers' Development   232
Play in Early Childhood   234
   The Nature of Play   235
   Theories of Play   235
   Cognitive Levels of Play: Developmental Trends   237
   Other Influences on Play and Friendship   238
   Social Levels of Play   239
   Play and Friendship in Early Childhood   241
Working with *Javier Hernandez, Preschool Program Coordinator: Play and Friendships Among Preschoolers*   242
Gender Development   244
   Learning Gender Schema   245
   Influences on Gender Development   246
   Androgyny   247
Child Abuse and Maltreatment   248
   Causes   248
   Consequences   249
A Multicultural View: *The Cultural Context of Child Abuse and Neglect*   250
   Treatment and Prevention   251
Looking Back/Looking Forward   252

PART 4   Middle Childhood   255

8   Physical and Cognitive Development in Middle Childhood   257

PHYSICAL DEVELOPMENT   258
   Trends and Variations in Height and Weight   259
   Motor Development and Athletics in Middle Childhood   260
A Multicultural View: *Dieting in Cross-Cultural Perspective*   261
   Physical Effects of Early Athletics   262
   Psychological Effects of Early Athletics   263
Health and Illness in Middle Childhood   264
   Social Influences on Illness   265

Attention Deficit Hyperactivity Disorder 265
Sleep 267

COGNITIVE DEVELOPMENT 267

Piaget's Theory: Concrete Operational Skills 268
Conservation in Middle Childhood 268
Conservation Training 269
Piaget's Influence on Education 270

Information-Processing Skills 271
Memory Capacity 271
Difficulties with Information Processing: Learning Disabilities 273

Working with Terry Wharton, Special Education Teacher: Giving Children a Second Chance to Learn 276

Language Development in Middle Childhood 277
Bilingualism and Its Effects 277

Defining and Measuring Intelligence 279
Psychometric Approaches to Intelligence 280

Information-Processing Approaches to Intelligence 281
The Triarchic Theory of Intelligence 281

Focusing On . . . Gifted Students: Victims or Elite? 282
Sociocultural Approaches to Intelligence 285

School Influences 286
Participation Structures and Classroom Discourse 286
Social Biases That Affect Learning 288
The Impact of Assessment 288

The Changing Child: Physical, Cognitive, and Social 290

9 Psychosocial Development in Middle Childhood 293

Psychosocial Challenges of Middle Childhood 294
The Challenge of Knowing Who You Are 294

The Sense of Self 295
The Development of Self in Childhood 295
Processes in Constructing a Self 297

The Age of Industry and Achievement 298
Latency and the Crisis of Industry 298
Achievement Motivation 299

Family Relationships 300
The Quality of Parenting and Family Life During Middle Childhood 301
The Changing Nature of Modern Families 301

A Multicultural View: Parental Expectations and Academic Achievement 302
Divorce and Its Effects on Children 302

Focusing On ... The Quality of Parenting and Family Life During Middle Childhood 304
The Effects of Work on Families 308
Other Sources of Social Support 311

Peer Relationships 312
What Theorists Say about Peer Relationships 313
The Functions of Friends 313
The Functions of Other Peers 314
Influences on Peer Group Membership 314

Popularity and Rejection 318
Conformity to Peers 321
School Influences on Peer Relations 322

Death, Loss, and Grieving During the School Years 323

Working with Lisa Truong, Fourth-Grade Teacher: Reducing Gender Role Stereotyping in Play 324
The Process of Grieving for a Childhood Loss 324
Children's Understanding of Death 326

Looking Back/Looking Forward 327

PART 5 Adolescence 331

10 Physical and Cognitive Development in Adolescence 333

PHYSICAL DEVELOPMENT 335

Growth in Height and Weight 335

Puberty 337
The Development of Primary Sex Characteristics 337
The Development of Secondary Sex Characteristics 337
Hormonal Changes: Physical and Social Consequences 338
Psychological Effects of Physical Growth in Adolescence 339

Health in Adolescence 341
Causes of Death Among Adolescents 341
Health-Compromising Behaviors 342
Adolescent Brain Development 350

Focusing On . . . Female Athletes and Eating Disorders 351

COGNITIVE DEVELOPMENT 353

Beyond Concrete Operational Thinking 353
Possibilities Versus Realities 354
Scientific Reasoning 354
Logical Combination of Ideas 355
Cognitive Development Beyond Formal Thought 355

Working with Jerry Acton, Math and Science Teacher: Blending the Social and Emotional with the Cognitive 356
Implications of the Cognitive Developmental Viewpoint 356

Moral Development: Beliefs about Justice and Care 357
Kohlberg's Six Stages of Moral Judgment 358
Issues in the Development of Moral Beliefs about Justice 360
Gilligan's Ethics of Care 361
The Ethics of Care During Adolescence 362
The Development of Social Cognition 363

Information-Processing Features of Adolescent Thought 364
Improved Capacity to Process Information 364
Expertise in Specific Domains of Knowledge 366

Contents vii

The Influence of School 367
   Cognitive Effects of Schooling 367
   Social Effects of Schooling 369
A Multicultural View: *Cross-cultural Misunderstandings in the Classroom* 370

11 Psychosocial Development in Adolescence 375

Theories of Identity Development 376
   Ruthellen Josselson: Individuation and Identity Development 376
   Erik Erikson: The Crisis of Identity Versus Role Confusion 377

Family Relationships During Adolescence 381
   Relationships with Parents 381
A Multicultural View: *Differing Cultural Views of Delinquency* 388
   Divorce, Remarriage, and Single Parenthood 388

Social Relationships During Adolescence 391
   Friendship 391
   Peer Groups 394
   Adolescents in the World of Work 397

Focusing On . . . *Can Parents Influence Their Adolescent's Choice of Peer Group?* 398

Sexuality During Adolescence 399
   Sexual Experience 399
   Sexual Orientations 402
   Sex and Everyday Life 403

Special Problems of Adolescence 403
   Adolescent Pregnancy and Parenthood 403
Working with *Janet Whallen, Nurse Practitioner: Helping Pregnant Teenagers* 406
   Teenage Depression and Suicide 408
   Juvenile Delinquency 410

Looking Back/Looking Forward 412

PART 6 Early Adulthood 417

12 Physical and Cognitive Development in Early Adulthood 419

PHYSICAL DEVELOPMENT 420

Physical Functioning 420
   Growth and Height and Weight 420
   Strength 421
   Brain Development 422
   Age-Related Changes 422

Health in Early Adulthood 424
   Health-Promoting Behaviors 424
   Health-Compromising Behaviors 429

Working with *Daniel Longram, Case Manager: Helping Families Cope with AIDS* 433

Stress 434
   Stress and Health 435
   The Experience of Stress 435

Focusing On . . . *How Does Stress Relate to Women's Employment?* 436

Sexuality and Reproduction 438
   The Sexual Response Cycle 438
   Sexual Attitudes and Behaviors 439
   Common Sexual Dysfunctions 440
   Infertility 442
   Reproductive Technologies 443

Adult Choices 444

COGNITIVE DEVELOPMENT 444

Postformal Thought 445
   Critiques of Formal Operations as the Final Stage of Cognitive Development 445

Development of Contextual Thinking 446
   Schaie's Stages of Adult Thinking 447
   Contextual Relativism 448

A Multicultural View: *Moral Orientation in the United States and China* 450

Adult Moral Reasoning 450
   Context and Moral Orientation 452
   Development of Faith 453

College 454
   Who Attends College? 456
   Women and Racial/Ethnic Minorities 456

Work 457
   Transition to Work 458
   Gender, Race, Sexual Orientation, Gender Identity, and SES in the Workplace 458

Growth and Change 462

13 Psychosocial Development in Early Adulthood 465

Theories of Adult Development 466
   Timing of Events: Social Clocks 467
   Crisis Theory: George Valliant and the Grant Study 468
   Crisis Theory: Daniel Levinson's Seasons of Adult Lives 470
   Do Women Have the Same "Seasons"? 470
   Crisis Theory: Erik Erikson's Intimacy Versus Isolation 471

Intimate Relationships 472
   Friendship 473
   Love 475

Working with *Marilyn Kline, Suicide Hot Line Worker: Helping Individuals Through Crises* 476
   Mate Selection 479

Marriage, Divorce, Remarriage, and Singlehood 480
   Marital Satisfaction 481

A Multicultural View: *Cross-Cultural Similarities in Spouse Abuse* 482
   Divorce 484
   Remarriage 485
   Singlehood 486
   Cohabitation 487

Parenthood 488
   Transition to Parenthood 489
   Single Parenthood 492
   Stepparent/Blended Families 492
   Child Free 493

Focusing On . . . *The Effects of Growing Up with Same-Sex Parents* 494

Looking Back/Looking Forward 496

PART 7 Middle Adulthood 499

14 Physical and Cognitive Development in Middle Adulthood 501

PHYSICAL DEVELOPMENT 502

The Biology of Aging 502

Physical Functioning in Middle Adulthood 503
 Strength 503
 External and Internal Age-Related Changes 504

Health in Middle Adulthood 506
 Health and Health-Compromising Behaviors 507

Focusing On . . . *The Gender Gap in Life Expectancy* 508
 Breast Cancer 509
 Prostate Cancer 510
 Health and Inequality 511

Reproductive Change and Sexuality 512
 Menopause 513
 The Male Climacteric 516
 Sexuality in Middle Adulthood 517

COGNITIVE DEVELOPMENT 518

Intelligence in Middle Adulthood 519
 Does Intelligence Decline with Age? 519
 Schaie's Sequential Studies 520
 Fluid and Crystallized Intelligence 522

Practical Intelligence and Expertise 525
 Solving Real-World Problems 525
 Becoming an Expert 527

The Adult Learner 528
 Adult Education 528
 Returning to College 529

Working with *Caroline Singer, Associate Dean of Continuing Education: Counseling Students Returning to College* 530

Working in Middle Adulthood 531
 Age and Job Satisfaction 532
 Racial and Ethnic Minorities 532
 Gender 533
 Sexual Orientation and Identity 533
 Unemployment and Underemployment 533

Change and Growth 534

15 Psychosocial Development in Middle Adulthood 537

A Multiplicity of Images of Middle Age 538

Crisis or No Crisis? 539
 Normative Crisis Models: Midlife Crisis 541
 No Crisis 542
 Normative Personality Change 543

Marriage and Divorce 543
 Long-Term Marriage 543
 The Family Life Cycle 545

Focusing On. . . *The Effects of Middle-Aged Adult Children's Problems on Older Parents* 546
 Same-Sex Marriage 548
 Midlife Divorce 548

Family Relationships 550
 Delayed Parenthood 550
 Adolescent Children 550
 Young Adult Children 551

Working with *Joan Stone, Victim Advocate: Helping Victims of Abusive Family Relationships* 552
 Grandparenting 554

A Multicultural View: *Diversity in Intergenerational Families* 555
 Aging Parents 556
 Siblings 558

Bereavement 560
 Mourning for One's Parents 560
 Bereavement and Growth 561
 Reactions to Grief 561

Leisure 562

Preparing for Late Adulthood 564
 Wills and Advance Directives 564
 Retirement Planning 565

Looking Back/Looking Forward 566

PART 8 Late Adulthood 569

16 Physical and Cognitive Development in Late Adulthood 571

PHYSICAL DEVELOPMENT 572

Longevity 572
 Mortality 573
 Life Expectancy 575
 Theories of Aging 575

A Multicultural View: *The Mortality Crossover* 576

Physical Functioning in Late Adulthood 578
 Slowing with Age 579
 Skin, Bone, and Muscle Changes 579
 Cardiovascular System Changes 580
 Respiratory System Changes 581
 Sensory System Changes 581
 Changes in Sexual Functioning 583

Focusing On . . . *Older Adults Have Healthier Lifestyles Than Young and Middle-Aged Adults* 584

Health Behaviors in Late Adulthood 584
 Diet 584
 Exercise 586
 Sleep 587
 Alcohol Consumption 588
 Prescription Drugs 589

Chronic Illnesses 589
 Gender Differences 590
 Cardiovascular Disease 590
 Cancer 591
 Arthritis 593

COGNITIVE DEVELOPMENT 593
Wisdom and Cognitive Abilities 594
  Cognitive Mechanics 594
  Cognitive Pragmatics 595
  Cognitive Plasticity and Training 597
The Aging Brain 599
  Brain Changes 599
  Vascular Neurocognitive Disorder 600
  Alzheimer's Disease 601
Mental Health and Aging 603
Working with *Mark John Isola, Therapeutic Recreation Director: Helping Alzheimer's Patients and Their Families* 604
Work and Retirement 606

17 Psychosocial Development in Late Adulthood 609
Aging and Ageism 610
Personality Development in Late Adulthood 610
  Continuity and Change in Late Life 611
  Integrity Versus Despair 613
  Theories of Successful Aging 613
Retirement 616
  What Is Retirement? 616
  Well-Being in Retirement 618
Marriage and Singlehood 619
  Spouses as Caregivers 619
  Widowhood 623
Focusing On . . . *The Double Standard of Sexuality in Late Adulthood* 624
  Dating and Remarriage 624
  Older Lesbians and Gay Men 626
  Ever-Single Older Adults 627
Relationships with Family and Friends 628
  Siblings 629
  Adult Grandchildren 631
  Great-Grandchildren 632
  Friends 632
  Fictive Kin 633
  Childlessness 634
  Internet and Social Media Use 634

Problems of Living: The Housing Continuum 634
  Independent Living 635
  Assisted Living 637
Working with *Louise Staley, Community Worker: Helping Holocaust Survivors in Late Adulthood* 638
  Long-Term Care 638
  Control over Living Conditions 640
Interests and Activities 642
  Community Involvement 643
  Religion and Spirituality 645
A Multicultural View: *Men and Grief* 646
Looking Back/Looking Forward 648

PART 9 Endings 653

18 Dying, Death, and Bereavement 655
Attitudes Toward Death 656
Facing One's Own Death 658
  Death Acceptance 659
Focusing On . . . *How Children Understand Death* 662
  Late-Life Suicide 664
  The Dying Process 666
  The Good Death 667
Caring for the Dying 668
  Terminal Care Alternatives 669
  Assisted Suicide 672
Bereavement 673
  Grief 673
Working with *Susan Gardner, Social Worker: Helping the Dying and Bereaved* 674
  Funeral and Ritual Practices 677
  Mourning 679
  Support Groups 681
  Recovery 682
Looking Back 683

Glossary G-1
References R-1
Author/Name Index I-1
Subject Index I-9

Special Features

"Working with..." Interviews
Chapter

1. Marsha Bennington, Speech-Language Pathologist: Communication Difficulties Across the Lifespan 24
2. Jeffrey Friedman, Clinical Social Worker: The Value of Developmental Theory for Helping Children, Adolescents, and Their Families 54
3. Katie Glover, OB-GYN Nurse Practitioner: Preparing for Childbirth 88
4. Gillian Luppiwiski, Infant Care Provider: Fostering Infants' Thinking 144
5. Rachelle Turner, Infant Day-Care Coordinator: Understanding Infant Social Development 168
6. Carolyn Eaton, Preschool Teacher: Introducing Sign Language to Young Children 210
7. Javier Hernandez, Preschool Program Coordinator: Play and Friendships among Preschoolers 242
8. Terry Wharton, Special Education Teacher: Giving Children a Second Chance to Learn 276
9. Lisa Truong, Fourth-Grade Teacher: Reducing Gender Role Stereotyping in Play 324
10. Jerry Acton, Math and Science Teacher: Blending the Social and Emotional with the Cognitive 356
11. Janet Whallen, Nurse Practitioner: Helping Pregnant Teenagers 406
12. Daniel Longram, Case Manager: Helping Families Cope with AIDS 433
13. Marilyn Kline, Suicide Hot Line Worker: Helping Individuals Through Crises 476
14. Caroline Singer, Associate Dean of Continuing Education: Counseling Students Returning to College 530
15. Joan Stone, Victim Advocate: Helping Victims of Abusive Family Relationships 552
16. Mark John Isola, Therapeutic Recreation Director: Helping Alzheimer's Patients and Their Families 604
17. Louise Staley, Community Worker: Helping Holocaust Survivors in Late Adulthood 638
18. Susan Gardner, Social Worker: Helping the Dying and Bereaved 674

A Multicultural View
Chapter

1. Street Children: Comparing Paraguay and North America 18
2. Street Children: Comparing Paraguay and North America 49
3. Cultural Difference and Genetic Counseling 74
4. Cognitive Effects of Talking to Infants: A Cross-Cultural Perspective 142
5. Cross-Cultural Variations in Attachment 164
6. Parents' Beliefs about Intelligence: A Cross-cultural Perspective 214
7. The Cultural Context of Child Abuse and Neglect 250
8. Dieting in Cross-Cultural Perspective 261
9. Parental Expectations and Academic Achievement 302
10. Cross-cultural Misunderstandings in the Classroom 370
11. Differing Cultural Views of Delinquency 388
12. Moral Orientation in the United States and China 450
13. Cross-Cultural Similarities in Spouse Abuse 482
15. Diversity in Intergenerational Families 555
16. The Mortality Crossover 576
17. Men and Grief 646

Focusing On
Chapter

1. Wanted: A Child and Family Policy 11
2. Erik Erikson's Identity Crisis: An Autobiographical Perspective 37
3. Technological Alternatives to Natural Conception 72
4. Sudden Infant Death Syndrome 110
5. Family-Leave Policies in the United States and Europe 167
6. Reforming Children's Health Care 186
7. Extended Family Supports for Child-Rearing 220
8. Gifted Students: Victims or Elite? 282
9. The Quality of Parenting and Family Life During Middle Childhood 304
10. Female Athletes and Eating Disorders 351
11. Can Parents Influence Their Adolescent's Choice of Peer Group? 398
12. How Does Stress Relate to Women's Employment? 436
13. The Effects of Growing Up with Same-Sex Parents 494
14. The Gender Gap in Life Expectancy 508
15. The Effects of Middle-Aged Adult Children's Problems on Older Parents 546
16. Older Adults Have Healthier Lifestyles Than Young and Middle-Aged Adults 584
17. The Double Standard of Sexuality in Late Adulthood 624
18. How Children Understand Death 662

Preface

When we began planning this third edition of *Lifespan Development*, our conversations kept coming back to the idea of continuity and change—for in a sense, that is what revising a text is all about. You will find many continuities between this edition and previous editions. However, there is also a great deal of new information and current research. Our major goal of this revision was to maintain and strengthen the text's lifespan perspective. To achieve this goal, we have reorganized our presentation throughout the text to emphasize four lifespan themes:

- *Continuity Within Change*, which looks for continuities in the person that may be hidden by more obvious long-term changes of maturation and evolving life circumstances;
- *Lifelong Growth*, which focuses on the potential for growth at all stages of development—in adulthood as well as in childhood and adolescence;
- *Changing Meanings and Vantage Points*, which considers how universal experiences, such as work, play, love, and sex, take on different meanings at different stages of development; and
- *Developmental Diversity*, which notices differences created by genetic, social, and cultural circumstances within the search for general trends and patterns through the lifespan.

In this edition, you will find these themes introduced in Chapter 1, mentioned throughout the text as we focus on specific stages of development, and highlighted at the end of each part in a special section called "Looking Back/Looking Forward." This feature revisits the four lifespan themes in relation to a hinge issue that appeared in that part. The thematic orientation of this edition is designed to help students appreciate the complex combination of continuity and change from birth to death that constitutes lifespan development.

While the strengthened lifespan perspective is the most obvious change in this edition, we have also broadened our range of examples and applications to increase its relevance to the wide range of students who come to the lifespan course from many departments and are headed for a wide range of occupational and family roles. We realize that they will be educators, health professionals such as occupational and physical therapists, and nurses, social workers, parents, and family members, all roles requiring an understanding of human development. We have revised our book with this in mind. We believe that lifespan psychology is relevant to current career and social issues that all adults face. It is especially relevant to those who will work or live with children, adolescents, or older adults. We see personal involvement as positive and include a wide range of examples that will enable most readers to find themselves, and people they know, in the story of lifespan development.

Content and Organization

Part 1, "Beginnings," introduces our lifespan themes and discusses the field of human development, key theories, genetics, prenatal development, and birth. Some of the changes we have made in this portion of the book include Chapter 1 reorganized to highlight the key themes of lifespan development as they are emphasized in this book. In Chapter 2, a new "Applications Throughout the Lifespan" section following each major set of developmental theories helps students see how theories can be used. Chapter 3 includes an extensive reorganization of "Prenatal Influences on the Child," grouping the coverage of harmful substances, domestic violence, maternal age, and prenatal health care. We have also expanded our coverage of contraceptive choices, family planning, and abortion in the United States and worldwide.

Parts 2 through 8 are then organized chronologically: the first two years, early childhood, middle childhood, adolescence, early adulthood, middle adulthood, and late adulthood. Within each age period, we focus in one chapter on physical and cognitive development and in the other on psychosocial development. Although we frequently point out the interrelatedness of these three domains, we give each separate attention as well. Part 9 explores the topics of dying, death, and bereavement. Content changes in Parts 2 through 9 include these highlights:

- A new section examining sleep has been added to each age period.
- Each of the chapters covering psychosocial development from adolescence to late life includes discussion of gay and lesbian issues.
- Chapter 12 has coverage of changes that occur in the brain during emerging and young adulthood.
- Chapter 13 includes discussion of emerging adulthood as a period of the lifespan.

- Discussions of psychosocial development in Chapters 13, 15, and 17 now include more theories relevant to women.
- Coverage of sexuality in middle and late adulthood in Chapters 14 and 16 has been expanded.
- We have expanded the coverage of euthanasia and end-of-life preferences in Chapter 18 and integrated information about death, loss, and bereavement of children and adolescents as well as adults.

In addition to specific content changes, we have included multicultural coverage throughout the text as well, as in the special "Multicultural View" boxes, and increased integration of practical information, cultural information, and career ideas with research information.

We have also made the organization more parallel throughout the book. In the chapters on physical and cognitive development, for example, we cover systemic change, health and health-compromising behaviors, cognition, moral development, school, and work in the same order in each stage's comparable chapters. Likewise, the chapters on psychosocial development move from discussions of theories of personality development to discussions of the family sphere to relationships in the wider world. For students, this parallelism reinforces continuities from stage to stage and will make it even easier for instructors who prefer to organize their courses topically rather than chronologically to use the book in their own way. For instance, one could teach the child and adolescent portions chronologically and the adult portion topically by first assigning the physical development portions of Chapters 12, 14, and 16, then the cognitive portions, and finally the psychosocial chapters, 13, 15, and 17.

Tools to Enhance Learning

For a textbook to be effective, it must be read. With this in mind, we continued to hold ourselves to high standards for clear, good writing. This text is approachable, filled with real-life examples that can engage students in the issues of human development and illustrations that reinforce key concepts.

A Critical Approach to Research We base our presentation on a firm understanding of current research in the field, balancing the inclusion of classic and recent studies. Yet the book is not so data driven as to be too technical for students new to the issues. Numerous hypothetical and real-life examples balance our research-based discussions. Since research findings do not always agree with one another, this book focuses both on what we know and on how we came to know it. We want students to understand how the data behind the conclusions were generated and to be able to raise questions about the validity, reliability, and generalizability of research findings. We introduce methodological concerns in Chapter 1. In addition, we present critiques of studies as we discuss them (such as limitations of the Grant Study in Chapter 16) and periodically describe methods where they will have the most meaning (such as "Studying Cognition and Memory in Infants" in Chapter 4's discussion of cognitive development during the first two years and the comparison of "Cross-Sectional Versus Longitudinal Studies" in Chapter 15's discussion of "Does Intelligence Decline with Age?").

Rich Illustration Program Numerous graphs, figures, and tables reinforce the text discussions by providing a visual guide to key concepts. These have been updated to reflect the latest demographic data. Captions to line art and photos emphasize critical points and provide additional pedagogical support. We carefully selected photographs to reinforce our emphasis on diversity in culture, race and ethnicity, gender, and socioeconomic status.

Improved Learning Aids As in the previous editions, chapters open with outlines and focusing questions. New to this edition, we organize our end-of-chapter summaries around the focusing questions that appeared in the beginning of the chapter to highlight the conceptual connections among topics in each main section. Key terms lists again serve as pedagogical supports by reinforcing the important themes, ideas, and concepts in each chapter. We have added a margin glossary to this edition to further support student learning of key terms. In addition to assisting in the mastery of content, these aids encourage students to develop their personal perspectives about lifespan psychology and its practical applications.

Special Features

Looking Back/Looking Forward New to this edition, a greatly expanded section at the end of each part examines a hinge issue in light of the four themes of the book: Continuity Within Change, Lifelong Growth, Changing Meanings and Vantage Points, and Developmental Diversity. The hinge issues are as follows: genetic inheritance after "Beginnings"; attachment after the "First Two Years"; friendship after "Early Childhood"; family after "Middle Childhood"; parent-child relationships after "Adolescence"; intimacy after "Early Adulthood"; work after "Middle Adulthood"; problems of living after "Late Adulthood"; and the concept of the good death after "Death, Loss, and Bereavement." These sections reinforce the lifespan themes by approaching key concepts from a fresh angle and linking them to earlier developmental periods and those yet to come.

What Do You Think? In this edition, we continue to have questions designed to stimulate reflection and discussion about the issues and concepts of development, located at the end of each major section throughout every chapter. "What Do You Think?" questions also appear at the end of the "Working With" and "Focusing On" boxes to reinforce the connections between the box and the main text. While addressed directly to the student, the "What Do You Think?" questions can also serve as a basis for class activities and discussion. Many encourage collaboration among classmates and can be used as group assignments.

"Working With" Interviews As in the previous editions, each chapter includes an interview with someone who works in the field discussing the practical application of developmental issues featured in that chapter. Robert Hoffnung's interview with a psychiatric social worker appears in Chapter 2 to enhance the discussion of psychoanalytic theory. Kelvin Seifert's new interview about teaching high school mathematics and its relationship to cognitive development in adolescence appears in Chapter 10. Michele Hoffnung's new interview with a community worker who helps Holocaust survivors appears in Chapter 17 to enhance our discussion of religion and spirituality in late adulthood. Interviews enable students to see the relationship between the theoretical and the practical. "What Do You Think?" questions follow the interviews to stress the connections with the text. The interviews also provide occupational examples for students who are considering possibilities for their futures. For a complete list of featured careers and topics, see page xi.

A Multicultural View Again in this edition, a boxed insert in each chapter highlights an issue of development from a cross- or multicultural perspective. While this perspective is a consistent aspect of the text, we use the boxes to focus on issues of particular interest. Topics new to this edition include a comparison of street children in Paraguay and North America (Chapter 1), a cross-cultural look at delinquency (Chapter 11), and a comparison of Japanese and North American definitions of death (Chapter 18). A revised discussion of cross-cultural similarities in spouse abuse appears in Chapter 13. A complete list of these boxes appears on page xi.

Focusing On Each chapter's "Focusing On" box expands the discussion in the text by highlighting a significant and timely issue and includes "What Do You Think?" questions to enhance the connections among the box, the chapter, and students' experiences. See page xi for a full list.

Online and in Print

Student Options: Print and Online Versions

This third edition of *Lifespan Development* is available in multiple versions: online, in PDF, and in print as either a paperback or loose-leaf text. The content of each version is identical.

The most affordable version is the online book, with upgrade options including the online version bundled with a print version. What's nice about the print version is that it offers you the freedom of being unplugged—away from your computer. The people at Academic Media Solutions recognize that it's difficult to read from a screen at length and that most of us read much faster from a piece of paper. The print options are particularly useful when you have extended print passages to read.

The online edition allows you to take full advantage of embedded digital features, including search and notes. Use the search feature to locate and jump to discussions anywhere in the book. Use the notes feature to add personal comments or annotations. You can move out of the book to follow Web links. You can navigate within and between chapters using a clickable table of contents. These features allow you to work at your own pace and in your own style, as you read and surf your way through the material. (See "Harnessing the Online Version" for more tips on working with the online version.)

Harnessing the Online Version

The online version of *Lifespan Development*, third edition, offers the following features to facilitate learning and to make using the book an easy, enjoyable experience:

- *Easy-to-navigate/clickable table of contents*—You can surf through the book quickly by clicking on chapter headings, or first- or second-level section headings. And the Table of Contents can be accessed from anywhere in the book.

- *Key terms search*—Type in a term, and a search engine will return every instance of that term in the book; then jump directly to the selection of your choice with one click.

- *Notes and highlighting*—The online version includes study apps such as notes and highlighting. Each of these apps can be found in the tools icon embedded in the Academic Media Solutions/Textbook Media's online eBook reading platform (http://www.academicmediasolutions.com).

- *Upgrades*—The online version includes the ability to purchase additional study apps and functionality that enhance the learning experience.

Instructor Supplements

In addition to its student-friendly features and pedagogy, the variety of student formats available, and the uniquely affordable pricing options that are designed to provide students with a flexibility that fits any budget and/or learning style, *Lifespan Development*, third edition, comes with the following teaching and learning aids:

- *Test Item File*—The Test Bank includes 100 multiple-choice and three essay questions per chapter. Each multiple-choice question is keyed to a learning objective and a text page number, and it is identified as requiring factual, applied, or conceptual knowledge. Emphasis is on providing a wealth of applied and conceptual questions. The essay questions include sample response guides.

- **Computerized Test Bank**—These test items give instructors the flexibility to generate tests electronically, edit test items, or add their own.
- **Instructor's Manual**—An enhanced version of the book offering assistance in preparing lectures, identifying learning objectives, developing essay exams and assignments, and constructing course syllabi.
- **PowerPoint Presentations**—Key points in each chapter are illustrated in a set of PowerPoint files designed to assist with instruction. In addition, all of the chapter figures are included for further ease with instruction.

Student Supplements and Upgrades (Additional Purchase Required)

- **Lecture Guide**—This printable lecture guide is designed for student use and is available as an in-class resource or study tool. Note: Instructors can request the PowerPoint version of these slides to use as developed or to customize.
- **Study Guide**—The student Study Guide contains learning objectives, a chapter overview and outline, a fill-in review of key terms and concepts, and two sets of multiple-choice practice questions—one set tests the student's factual knowledge and the other tests applied knowledge. The multiple-choice answer key explains why each option is correct or incorrect, a feature particularly appreciated by students. A printable version of the online study guide is available via downloadable PDF chapters for easy self-printing and review.
- **Online Video Labs**—A collection of high-quality, dynamic, and sometimes humorous video segments (contemporary and classic) that are produced by a variety of media from both academic and entertainment sources accessed via the web. Organized by chapter, each video segment illustrates key topics/issues discussed in that specific chapter. Each video segment is accompanied by a student worksheet, which consists of a series of discussion questions that help students connect the themes presented in the video segment back to a key topic discussed in that specific chapter. Instructors are provided with suggested answers for each worksheet (nonopinion-based questions).

Acknowledgments

Our text benefits from the constructive suggestions and thoughtful reactions offered by reviewers of the various iterations of this text, and we are very appreciative of their help. In particular, we offer our continued gratitude to

Mark B. Alcorn, *University of Northern Colorado*

Nancy Ashton, *Stockton State College*

Robert Bohlander, *Wilkes University*

Lanthan D. Camblin, *University of Cincinnati*

Peter N. Carswell, *Asheville-Buncombe Technical Community College*

Elaine Cassel, *Lord Fairfax Community College*

Stewart Cohen, *University of Rhode Island*

K. Laurie Dickson, *Northern Arizona University*

Bettye S. Elmore, *Humbolt State University*

Dale D. Grubb, *Baldwin Wallace University*

Carol Flaugher, *State University of New York, Buffalo*

Karen Holbrook, *Frostburg State University*

Debra Hollister, *Valencia Community College*

Linda Keefauver, *University of Wyoming, Laramie*

K.C. Kirasic, *University of South Carolina*

Joseph C. LaVoie, *University of Nebraska–Omaha*

Linda Lebie, *Lakeland Community College*

Amy J. Malkus, *Washington State University*

Robert H. Poresky, *Kansas State University*

Mary Kay Reed, *York College of Pennsylvania*

Minakshi Tikoo, *Kansas State University*

Julia Wallace, *University of Northern Iowa*

We wish to thank the individuals who participated in the "Working With" interviews. Thanks also to the staff at Academic Media Solutions (AMS) who worked with us to publish this new edition of *Lifespan Development*: Daniel C. Luciano, president/founder of AMS, Victoria Putman of Putman Productions, and Charles Hutchinson for copyediting. We also thank Dr. Dale D. Grubb (Baldwin Wallace University) for his contribution in early stages of this revision, and Dr. Anthony DiBiasio (Baldwin Wallace University) who assisted us with Chapters 10 and 11 as we developed the manuscript. We thank our families and friends for the support they provided as we worked on this book, as well as the many stories from their lives that serve as examples throughout the text.

About the Authors

As developmental psychologists, college professors who teach adolescents and adults of many ages, and parents who have seen our children through many stages of development (some as far as early adulthood), the authors bring to this project a shared interest in human development as well as training and interests that complement each other. Megan's teaching covers each age period of the lifespan and focuses on adolescence, emerging adulthood, and late life as well as health psychology and sleep; her research is focused on improving sleep among college students and older adults. Kelvin's teaching has focused on early childhood and learning theory; his recent research is on children's cognition, although his earlier research looked at gender issues in early childhood teacher education. Robert has taught about childhood, adolescence, and lifespan development; he has also done clinical work with children, adolescents, adults, and families. Michele's teaching has been in the areas of research methods, psychology of women, and adult development; her recent research has focused on gender issues, motherhood, and balancing career and motherhood during adulthood.

Megan Clegg Kraynok is an Associate Professor of Psychology at Ohio Northern University in Ada, Ohio. She earned her B.A. at West Virginia Wesleyan College, her M.S. at the University of Pittsburgh, and her Ph.D. at West Virginia University. She has published articles on sleep among adolescents, emerging adults, and new parents, and has co-authored chapters on mental health and aging.

Kelvin Seifert is Professor Emeritus of Educational Psychology at the University of Manitoba. He received his B.A. at Swarthmore College and his Ph.D. at the University of Michigan. He is author of *Educational Psychology* (1991) and has published research on gender issues in early childhood education as well as on teachers' and parents' beliefs about children and their development.

Robert Hoffnung is Professor Emeritus of Psychology at the University of New Haven and Associate Clinical Professor of Psychiatry at the Yale University School of Medicine. He received his B.A. at Lafayette College, his M.A. at the University of Iowa, and his Ph.D. at the University of Cincinnati. He has published articles on educational, developmental, and mental health interventions with children, adolescents, and families.

Michele Hoffnung is Professor Emerita of Psychology at Quinnipiac University. She received her B.A. at Douglass College and her Ph.D. at the University of Michigan. She is editor of *Roles Women Play: Readings Towards Women's Liberation* (1971) and author of *What's a Mother to Do? Conversations About Work and Family* (1992) and numerous articles and essays.

Beginnings

PART 1

Chapter 1
Studying Lifespan Development

Chapter 2
Theories of Development

Chapter 3
Genetics, Prenatal Development, and Birth

Source: Sunny Studio–Igor Yaruta/Shutterstock.com.

As individuals grow from infancy into childhood, and from childhood into adolescence and adulthood, they change in some ways while remaining the same in others. Some changes may be small and fleeting, whereas others are profound and long lasting. Among the constancies, some (like your shoe size) matter little to personal identity, whereas others (like your gender) matter a lot. The mix of change and constancy is the subject of this book and of the field known as *lifespan developmental psychology*.

The study of lifespan development offers much insight into human nature—why we are what we are and how we became that way. Because describing development is a complex task, this book begins with three chapters that orient you to what lies ahead. The first two chapters explain just what development is and describe some of the most important tools of lifespan developmental psychology, namely the methods and theories that guide our understanding of the developmental changes that occur from conception through old age. The third chapter describes the genetic basis of human life and the three major events that occur at the beginning of the lifespan: conception, prenatal development, and birth. After completing these three chapters, you will be ready to begin exploring the main focus of lifespan development: people changing and growing throughout their lives.

Studying Lifespan Development

CHAPTER 1

Source: Monkey Business Images/Shutterstock.com.

Chapter Outline

The Nature of Lifespan Development
Why Study Development?
The Life Course in Times Past
Lifespan Perspectives on Human Development
Methods of Studying Lifespan Psychology
Ethical Constraints on Studying Development
Strengths and Limitations of Developmental Knowledge

Focusing Questions

- What in general is lifespan development?
- Why is it important to know about development?
- How has society's view of childhood changed over time?
- What general issues are important in lifespan psychology?
- How do developmental psychologists go about studying development across the lifespan?
- What ethical considerations should guide the study of development?

What do you remember from your past? When thinking back, each of us remembers different details, but we all experience a paradoxical quality about personal memories; when comparing the past and the present, we feel as though we have changed, yet also stayed the same. As a preschooler, for example, one of the authors (Kelvin Seifert) had trouble tying his shoelaces. Now, as an adult, he can tie laces easily, but he has to admit that he has never enjoyed or excelled at tasks calling for delicate or precise physical skills. In this small way, Kelvin has both changed and stayed the same. You yourself may have experienced this same dual quality. As a schoolchild, perhaps you loved spelling "bees" or contests. Now, as an adult, you no longer participate in spelling contests and have lost some of your childhood ability to figure out and remember truly unusual spellings. But perhaps you note, too, that you can still spell better than many adults of your age, and you seem to have a general knack for handling verbal information of other kinds—like computer programming languages—without getting mixed up. Or imagine another example: As a teenager you may have constantly wondered whether you would ever overcome shyness and be truly liked and respected by peers. As an adult, in contrast, you finally believe you have good, special friends; but maybe you also have to admit that it took effort to become sociable enough to acquire them.

Continuity in the midst of change marks every human life. Sometimes changes seem more obvious than continuities, such as when a speechless infant becomes a talkative preschooler, or when a dedicated homemaker of thirty becomes a successful, paid professional at age fifty. Other times continuities seem more obvious than changes, such as when a sixty-year-old still feels like a ten-year-old whenever he visits his older adult parents. But close scrutiny of examples like these suggests that both factors may be operating, even when one of them is partially hidden. The sixty-year-old feels like a child again, but at the same time feels different from that child. The fifty-year-old professional is now preoccupied with her job, but she still cares deeply about her family. It takes both continuity and change to be fully human; I must be connected to my past somehow, but also neither locked into it nor fully determined by it.

The Nature of Lifespan Development

development Long-term changes in a person's growth, feelings, patterns of thinking, social relationships, and motor skills.

This book is about continuity and change throughout the lifespan. Sometimes these processes are called human **development,** although this term is sometimes used to emphasize changes, rather than constancies, in physical growth, feelings, and ways of thinking. As we will see in later chapters, a focus on change may indeed be appropriate at certain points in a person's life. A girl undergoing her first menstrual period, for example, may experience a number of important changes at the same time, and rather suddenly: her body begins looking different, she begins thinking of herself differently, and other people begin treating her differently. But at other periods, continuity dominates over change. As a young adult settles in a job and family, for example, life may seem rather stable from day to day, month to month, or even year to year. Because this book explores the entire life course (from "cradle to grave," so to speak), it will make the most sense to keep both factors in mind—both continuity *and* change—without emphasizing one over the other in advance. When we speak of **lifespan development** in this book, therefore, we will mean the mix of continuities and changes that occur throughout a person's life, from birth to death.

lifespan development The broad changes and continuities that constitute a person's identity and growth from birth to death.

Note that both continuities and changes can take many forms. Changes can be relatively specific, such as when an infant takes her first unassisted step. Others can be rather general and unfold over a long time, such as when an older, middle-aged adult gradually becomes more aware of his growing wisdom. The same can be said of continuities. Some last for only a short time compared to the decades-long span of life: a twelve-year-old who enjoys a certain genre of music, for example, is likely to become a sixteen-year-old who enjoys the same genre of music but not necessarily a thirty-year-old who does. Other continuities seemingly last a lifetime: an extroverted teenager—one who seeks and enjoys social companionship—is likely to still seek and enjoy companionship as a forty-year-old and even as an eighty-year-old.

These examples may make the notion of lifespan development seem very broad, but note that not every change or continuity is truly "developmental," and some human developments are easily overlooked or discounted. Think about the impact of the weather. A sudden cold snap makes us behave differently: we put on warmer clothing and select indoor activities over outdoor ones. A continuous spell of cold weather, on the other hand, creates constancy in behavior: we wear the same type of clothing for a period of time and engage in the same (indoor) set of activities repeatedly. In

Development occasionally involves rapid, visible changes, such as learning to walk without assistance. Development also includes continuity over time, such as a decades-long love of art.
Sources: (*left*) Artgo/Shutterstock.com, (*right*) Rehan Qureshi/Shutterstock.com.

both cases, our behavior does not qualify as "development" because it is triggered by relatively simple external events and has no lasting impact on other behaviors, feelings, or thinking.

But true human development sometimes also can occur, yet be overlooked or dismissed as something other than development. Personal identity or sense of "self" is an example. A concept of who "I" am always seems to be with me, and often it seems so constant that I ignore it, making it "part of the woodwork" of my mind. This is likely true for you, too; your sense of who "you" are probably seems consistent or familiar to you. This fact is so much a part of our lives that it is easy to overlook its importance or to notice changes in our self-concepts when they occur. Yet for each of us, identity evolves and changes as we grow older, and the changes affect our actions and feelings differently when they occur.

Multiple Domains of Development

As these examples suggest, human development can take many forms. For convenience of discussion, this book distinguishes among three major types, or **domains,** of development: physical, cognitive, and psychosocial. The organization of the book reflects this division by alternating chapters about physical and cognitive changes with chapters about psychosocial changes. The domain of **physical development,** or biological change, includes changes in the body itself and how a person uses his or her body. Some of these changes may be noticeable to a casual observer, such as the difference in how a person walks when she is two years old, twenty years old, and eighty years old. Others may be essentially invisible without extended observation or even medical investigation, such as the difference in the ability to hear between a forty-year-old and his seventy-five-year-old father. Like other forms of development, physical changes often span very long periods—literally years or even decades—though not always. For example, changes in height and weight occur rather rapidly during the early teenage years but extremely slowly during middle age.

Cognitive development involves changes in methods and styles of thinking, language ability and language use, and strategies for remembering and recalling information. We tend to think of these abilities and skills as somewhat isolated within individuals; a person is said to "have" a good memory, for example, as if he or she carries that skill around all the time and can display it anywhere with equal ease, no matter what the situation. As later chapters will sometimes point out, however, thinking of cognitive development in this way may be more convenient than accurate: memory, language, and thinking are all heavily dependent on supports (and impediments) both from other people and from circumstances. A child learns to read more easily, for example, if parents and teachers give lots of personal support for her efforts. In this sense cognitive changes of reading "belong" to the helpful adults as well as to the child who acquires them, and the changes are best understood as partially physical and social in nature, and not merely cognitive.

domain A realm of psychological functioning.

physical development The area of human development concerned primarily with physical changes such as growth, motor skill development, and basic aspects of perception.

cognitive development The area of human development concerned with cognition; involves all psychological processes by which individuals learn and think about their environment.

Chapter 1 Studying Lifespan Development

psychosocial development The area of human development concerned primarily with personality, social knowledge and skills, and emotions.

Psychosocial development is about changes in feelings or emotions as well as changes in relations with other people. It includes interactions with family, peers, classmates, and coworkers, but also includes a person's personal identity, or sense of self. Because identity and social relationships evolve together, we often discuss them together in this book. And, as already pointed out, they also evolve in combination with physical and cognitive changes. A widower who forms satisfying friendships is apt to feel more competent than one who has difficulty doing so, and he is even likely to stay healthier as well. Each domain—physical, cognitive, and psychosocial—influences each of the others.

Figure 1.1 shows some major landmarks of development in each of the three domains during a few selected stages of development. It also hints at some of the connections among specific developments, both between domains and within each single domain. Attachment to caregiver(s), for example, is noted as emerging during infancy; early attachment patterns set the stage for the kinds of friendships and romantic relationships that develop during childhood, adolescence and adulthood. Retirement is noted as happening in late adulthood. This change in social circumstances is sometimes (but certainly not always) accompanied by declines in health or physical strength—though which change causes which is not always clear. In addition to these examples from Figure 1.1, numerous other relationships exist between and within domains of development. In later chapters we will point these out more explicitly wherever appropriate. Meanwhile, to get a better sense of what development from a lifespan perspective means, consider a more extended, complete example.

Development from a Lifespan Perspective: The Example of Jodi

So far, though we have talked about the importance of relationships among various forms of development, our examples have been a bit diverse and fragmented. How would developments tie together in the life of a real person? What relationships among them could we see then? These are not simple questions to answer fully, but you can begin to get partial answers by considering a child whom one of the authors knew personally: Jodi.

FIGURE 1.1
Selected Landmarks of Development

Development is a continual unfolding and integration of changes in all domains, from birth until death. Changes in one domain often affect those in another domain, and changes that occur in earlier stages of life can influence those that occur during later stages.

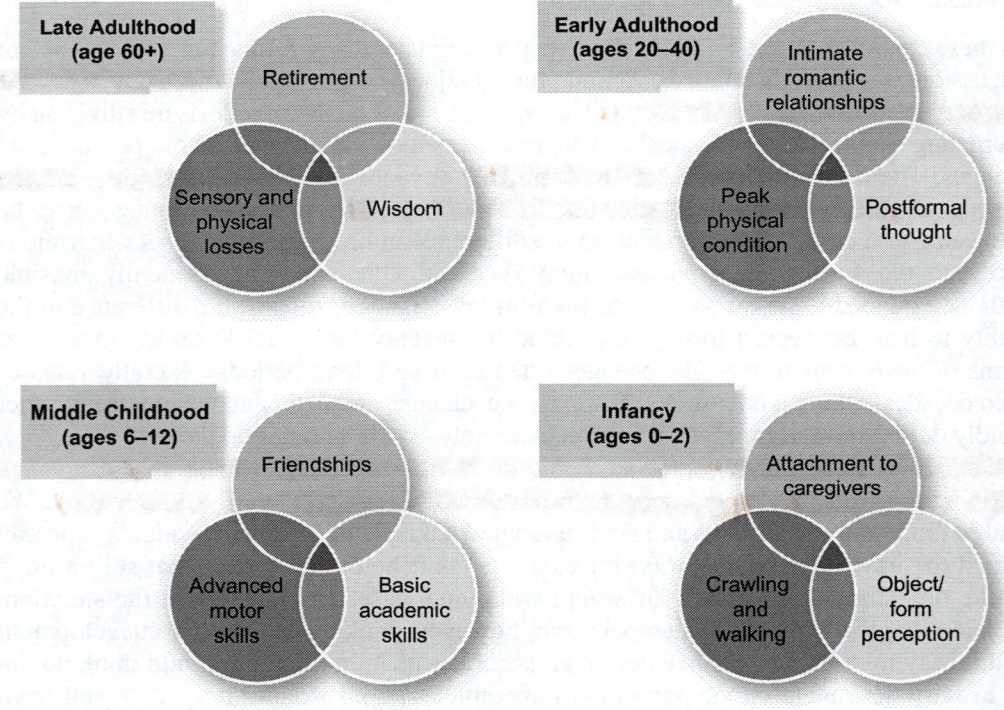

Key: For each age group, the Venn diagram represents the intersection of physical (bottom-left circle), cognitive (bottom-right), and social (top) domains of development.

6   Part 1   Beginnings

When Jodi was four, one of her brothers died. Roger had been 2-1/2 years older, a friendly kid and a decent sibling. Jodi played with him more than with her sister and other brother, who were both older than Roger. He died suddenly one winter from complications of chicken pox. The doctors said he may have reacted to the aspirin he had taken for his fever. The doctors said you weren't supposed to give aspirin to children, but Jodi didn't know that, and apparently her parents didn't know it either.

For a few years after that, they were a three-child family "with a hole in the middle," said Jodi to her best friend, where Roger was supposed to be. It was not ideal for Jodi, but it was tolerable: she didn't have the playmate she used to have, but she did have her family ("What's left of it!") and her friends from school. Life got back to normal—sort of.

When Jodi was nine, her parents adopted another child, a boy of twelve, about the same age Roger would have been had he lived. Frank had lived in numerous foster care homes, some of which had not been happy experiences for him. In two homes the discipline had been extremely strict, but it was hard for Jodi to know this because Frank did not tell her as much as he told the social workers or his new adopted parents, and her parents did not say much about Frank's past. In fact, Frank said little to Jodi about anything; he seemed distinctly cool toward all three of his new siblings—except for his periodic visits to Jodi's room at night. The first time it happened, Jodi was startled out of her sleep: Frank was standing by her bed and demanded that she take off her nightgown. That was all for that time. But he came back every few weeks, each time asking for more than the time before and threatening to hurt her badly if she revealed "our secret."

So Jodi learned not to sleep deeply. She also learned to avoid being alone in the house with Frank. In high school and college, she learned to avoid talking to boys a lot, except in a joking way and in the presence of others. In class she learned to look interested in what the instructors said even though she often was "sleeping inside," as she put it. So Jodi learned a lot from Frank, though not things she wanted to learn and not things most of her classmates were learning.

Jodi's story shows several things about human development over the lifespan. It shows, for example, that the domains of development all unfold together. Jodi's thoughts and feelings about Frank occurred in the context of physical changes happening to herself. Being physically older or younger may not have protected her from abuse, but it probably would have altered the experience, both in impact and in quality.

Jodi's story also suggests the importance of unique, personal experiences when exploring human development in general. Some things about Jodi may always be unique because of her encounters with Frank; she may always be a bit mistrustful of boys and men, for example. But other things about Jodi can be understood as examples of human changes that are universal or nearly universal. In experiencing abuse, for example, Jodi responds to gender role differences that pervade nearly all societies; in most societies, women enjoy less power than men do.

From the point of view of lifespan development, Jodi's story also raises questions about continuity and change across wide ranges of time. We are left wondering whether Jodi's initial responses to abuse will persist throughout her life. Assuming she will be cautious about men even as a thirty-year-old adult, will she still be cautious as a sixty-year-old? After so many years go by, society itself may develop new attitudes about the significance of childhood abuse, just as society already has done in the past few decades. How will Jodi respond to those changes, still decades away, when she becomes an older adult?

To help organize thinking about developmental questions like these, the developmental psychologist Urie Bronfenbrenner has originated a widely used framework for thinking about the multiple influences on individuals (Bronfenbrenner, 1989, 2005; Garbarino, 1992a). He describes the context of development as *ecological systems,* which are sets of people, settings, and recurring events that are related to one another, have stability, and influence the person over time. Figure 1.2 and Table 1.1 illustrate Bronfenbrenner's ecological systems.

FIGURE 1.2
Bronfenbrenner's Ecological Systems for Developmental Change

As shown here, Bronfenbrenner describes human development as a set of overlapping ecological systems. All of these systems operate together to influence what a person becomes as he or she grows older. In this sense, development is not exclusively "in" the person but is also "in" the person's environment. In addition to the systems pictured here, a fifth system, the *chronosystem,* refers to changes in the ecological systems over a person's lifetime and over the course of human history.

Source: Adapted from Garbarino (1992a).

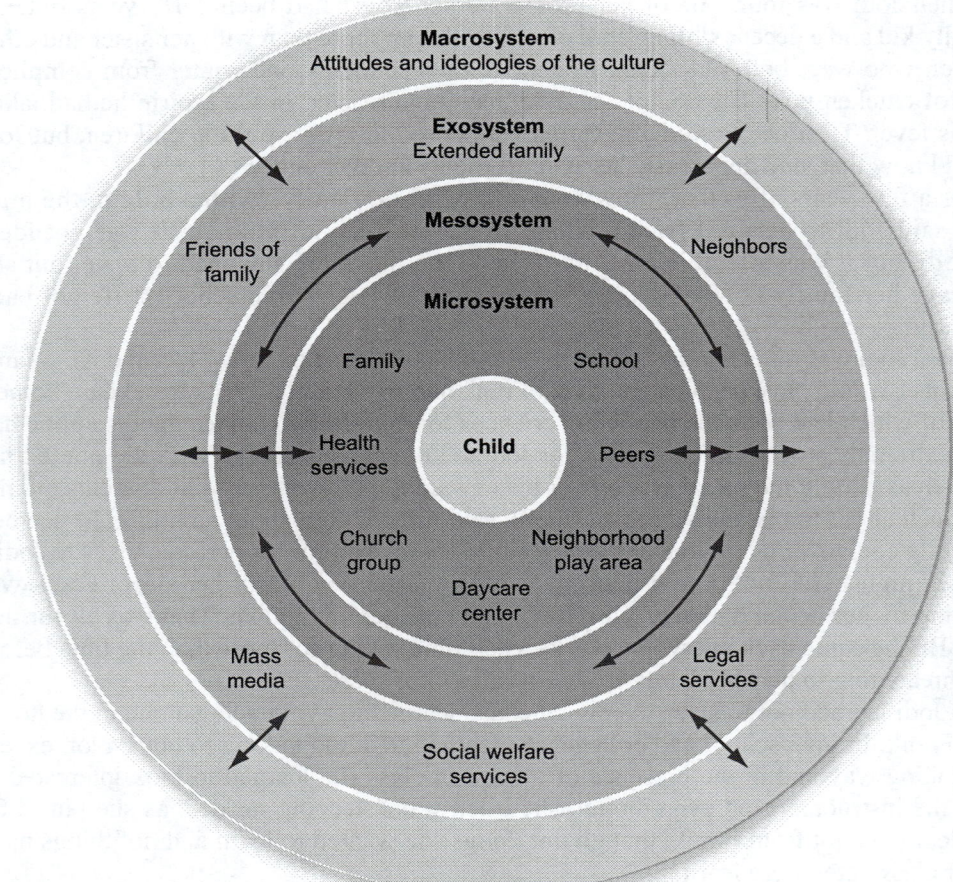

1. The *microsystem* refers to situations in which the person has face-to-face contact with influential others. For Jodi, the microsystem consists of her immediate family (though note that the membership of this family changed over time) as well as her teachers and peers at school.

2. The *mesosystem* refers to the connections and relationships that exist between two or more microsystems and influence the person because of their relationships. An example would be the contacts between Jodi's parents and the social workers responsible for Frank's adoption: their contacts led them (perhaps wrongly) to withhold information about Frank from Jodi.

3. The *exosystem* consists of settings in which the person does not participate but still experiences decisions and events that affect him or her indirectly. An example in Jodi's case might be the medical system, which either lacked the knowledge needed to save Roger at the time of his death or had been organized in a way that interfered with communicating needed medical knowledge to Jodi's parents.

4. The *macrosystem* is the overarching institutions, practices, and patterns of belief that characterize society as a whole and take the smaller micro-, meso-, and exosystems into account. An example that affected Jodi was gender role: a widespread belief that men should dominate women may have contributed to Frank's coercive actions against Jodi, as well as to Jodi's caution with boys and men as she got older.

5. The *chronosystem* (not depicted in Figure 1.2) can be best thought of as a quality of all of the ecological systems: they change over time. During the course of one's lifetime, specific aspects of each person's micro-, meso-, exo-, and macrosystems will change, as will their impact on the individual's development. In Jodi's case, if

Part 1 Beginnings

TABLE 1.1 Ecological System Levels

Ecological Level	Definition	Examples	Issues Affecting the Individual
Microsystem	Situations in which the person has face-to-face contact with influential others	Family, school, peer group, church, workplace	Is the person regarded positively? Is the person accepted? Is the person reinforced for competent behavior? Is the person exposed to enough diversity in roles and relationships? Is the person given an active role in reciprocal relationships?
Mesosystem	Relationships between microsystems; the connections between situations	Home–school, workplace–family, school–neighborhood	Do settings respect each other? Do settings present basic consistency in values?
Exosystem	Settings in which the person does not participate but in which significant decisions are made affecting the individuals who do interact directly with the person	Spouse's place of employment, local school board, local government	Are decisions made with the interests of the person in mind? How well do social supports for families balance stresses for parents?
Macrosystem	"Blueprints" for defining and organizing the institutional life of the society	Ideology, social policy, shared assumptions about human nature, the "social contract"	Are some groups valued at the expense of others (e.g., sexism, racism)? Is there an individualistic or a collectivistic orientation? Is violence a norm?
Chronosystem	Changes in all of the ecological systems over the course of a person's development and over the course of human history.	The developmental impact of certain events will vary depending upon their timing during one's development, and elements of the ecological systems can change from one generation to the next.	What elements of the ecological systems are most impactful on an individual's development, given that individual's age? What factors will greatly influence the development of children born in 2010? How do those factors compare to ones that were present in 1960?

Frank's actions occurred when Jodi was 19 instead of just 9 years old, the events might have played-out very differently. Additionally, over the course of human history, these same ecological systems have undergone significant changes. Today we have a heightened awareness about the developmental consequences of child maltreatment as compared to what we knew a few decades ago.

In the pages ahead we will keep in mind these multiple systems, such as those implied by Jodi's story, as well as the importance both of long-term developments during adulthood and of historical changes. Only in this way will we be able to convince you that lifespan developmental psychology has something to say about particular human lives: about how you, I, or a friend of yours changes and grows and what those changes may signify for our lives as a whole. In taking this perspective, we do not wish to imply that shorter-term changes do not matter. What happened to Jodi at age nine, for example, mattered greatly to her at age ten. We do, however, want to emphasize that developmental changes often have consequences that are more than short term, and that the consequences are not necessarily identical or even similar to each other. Jodi's response to abuse one month or one year after the experience may—or may not—be the same as her response many years later. We encourage you to think of her story as a reminder of these complexities.

Why Study Development?

Knowing about human development can help you in five major ways:

1. Allow you to form realistic expectations for others;
2. Help you respond appropriately to the actions of others;
3. Enable you to distinguish between normative and non-normative behavior in others;
4. Provide insights into yourself; and
5. Inform and enhance your professional advocacy for others.

Each of these benefits is described in more detail below.

First, knowledge about human development can give you realistic expectations for children, adolescents, and adults. Developmental psychology tells you, for example, when infants usually begin talking and when schoolchildren tend to begin reasoning abstractly. It also describes the issues faced by parents—and grandparents, for that matter. Admittedly, it often gives such information only as averages or generalities: when a "typical" person acquires a particular skill, behavior, or emotion. Nonetheless, the averages can help you know what to expect from specific individuals.

Second, knowledge of development can help you respond appropriately to a person's actual behavior. If a preschool boy tells his mother that he wants to marry her, should she ignore his remark or make a point of correcting his misconception? If a father is worried about his older-adult mother's complaints about health, should he actively intervene in her medical decisions or learn to have faith in her ability to deal with them herself? Developmental psychology can help answer such questions by indicating the sources and significance of many patterns of human thought, feelings, behavior, and growth.

Third, knowledge of development can help you recognize the wide range of normal behaviors, and thus when departures from normal are truly significant. If a child talks very little by age two, should her parents and doctors be concerned? What if he still does not talk much by age four? If a fifty-year-old breadwinner reports feeling a lot less ambitious at work than he did when younger, are his feelings unusual or typical? We can answer these questions more easily if we know both what *usually* happens and what *can* happen to people as they move through life. Lifespan psychology will help by placing particular behaviors in a broader context, one that (like Bronfenbrenners' framework pictured in Figure 1.2) calls attention to the many simultaneous influences on every person's life. As we will see in the chapters ahead, this perspective leads to the conclusion that the importance of any particular behavior depends not just on the age of the person doing it but on the place of the behavior in the overall life of the person.

Fourth, studying development can help you understand yourself. Developmental psychology makes explicit the process of psychological growth, processes that each of us may overlook in our personal, everyday lives. Even more important, it can help you make sense out of your own experiences, such as whether it really mattered that you reached puberty earlier (or later) than your friends did.

Finally studying development can make you a more professional advocate for the needs and rights of people of all ages, whether young, old, or in between. By knowing in detail the capacities of people of diverse ages and backgrounds, you will be in a good position to persuade others of their importance and value. All of us, including most readers of this book, have a common stake in making our society a more humane place to live. Yet, as the "Focusing On" feature indicates, we as a society can do a better job of supporting human development than we in fact have done.

> **Focusing On...**
>
> ### Wanted: A Child and Family Policy
>
> Parents generally do value their children, want the best for them, and make sacrifices on their behalf. In spite of this support, though, the lives of children are often difficult:
>
> - According to a recent report on child well-being from UNICEF (UNICEF Office of Research, 2013), more than 20 percent of all children in the United States under age seventeen live in families that are officially poor. This is more than twice the rate of poverty in Canada and about eight times the rate of poverty in Finland. In fact, among the world's developed countries, only Romania has a higher rate of child poverty than the United States.
>
> - While rates of immunization have increased worldwide during the past decade, a significant proportion of children have failed to receive routine immunizations against polio, measles, and other childhood diseases. The United States ranks much lower than many other developed countries, and three of the wealthiest countries in the UNICEF study—Austria, Canada, and Denmark—have the lowest rates of immunization (ranging from 81–88% of children under the age of two). Greece and Hungary reported the highest rates of childhood immunizations (both at 99% of children under age two).
>
> - About a third of all children living today will eventually experience the divorce of their parents, with all of the stress it brings (Hetherington, 1995). One of the stresses will be poverty, because the parent who usually has major custody, the mother, tends to earn much less than the father.
>
> - In the United States, on average, an infant is born into poverty every twenty-nine seconds, a child is physically punished in school every thirty seconds, and a child is killed by a firearm every three hours (Children's Defense Fund, 2012).
>
> A major reason these problems exist is that the United States lacks a comprehensive, integrated set of policies for caring for its children. Programs to remedy social problems have tended to focus on problems selectively rather than recognizing the impact of one problem on another. School programs to assist with learning difficulties, for example, tend to work with children individually, even though health, nutrition, illness, and family disruptions contribute to learning difficulties in major ways. A more effective approach is to provide a set of related and coordinated services to support families: pediatric care, combined with special help at school and a supportive social worker or nurse to visit parents at home to provide encouragement and information. When Victoria Seitz and Nancy Apfel tried this approach with some low-SES families, they found improvements in cognitive abilities not only for the children originally at risk but also for their siblings who had not even been a focus of the intervention (Seitz & Apfel, 1994)!
>
> Such combined approaches to children's welfare may look expensive and difficult when organized as special demonstration projects, but experience in other developed countries suggests that costs decrease markedly when implemented universally and that organizational problems can in fact be solved (Chafel, 1993; U.S. General Accounting Office, 1993). The real challenge, it seems, may be political: enlisting the support of leaders in government and business to develop comprehensive policies for children, and thereby ensuring the future of society.
>
> ### What Do You Think?
>
> Suppose child care were made universally available in the United States and Canada as it currently is in certain European nations. What effect would this policy have on children's development? What effect would it have on their families? Would your feelings about universal child care depend on the age of the children?

The Life Course in Times Past

Until just a few hundred years ago, children in Western society were not perceived as full-fledged members of society or even as genuine human beings (Ariès, 1962). During medieval times, infants tended to be regarded rather like talented pets: at best interesting and even able to talk, but not creatures worth caring about deeply. Children graduated to adult status early in life, around age seven or eight, by taking on major, adultlike tasks for the community. At that time, children who today would be attending second or third grade might have been caring for younger siblings, working in the fields, or apprenticed to a family to learn a trade.

Because children took on adult responsibilities so soon, the period we call *adolescence* was also unknown. Teenagers assumed adult roles. Although these roles often included marriage and childrearing, most people in their teens lived with their original families, helping with household work and with caring for other people's children until well into their twenties.

> **What Do You Think?**
>
> What do you hope to gain by studying lifespan development (besides a college credit, of course!)? Take a minute to think about this question—maybe even jot down some notes about it. Then share your ideas with two or three classmates. How do they differ?

The concept of childhood as a distinct period in a person's life is a relatively new invention. Prior to the 19th century, children were expected to assume responsibilities and contribute to the household in important ways as soon as they were able, much like the girl in the picture who is delivering milk. From the 19th century to the present, childhood has increasingly been viewed as a time for play and the acquisition of skills and knowledge that will serve them later in life, as seen in the picture of the girl who is drawing with colored pencils while in school.
Sources: (top) Chippix/Shutterstock.com, (bottom) Olesya Feketa/Shutterstock.com.

Although this may all seem harsh by modern, middle-class standards, it was not necessarily bad in the context in which it occurred. Historians and sociologists have pointed out that children and youth did have to work, but they tended to do only tasks for which they were capable, and they earned modest respect (if not wealth) from the community because they made true economic contributions to it (Hareven, 1986; Sommerville, 1990)—an advantage modern children experience much less often. Adults at that time also showed more awareness of the profound differences among children in their formative, childhood experiences. The modern tendency to view all children as innocent and needing protection has also led, ironically, to much more uniform views about the nature of childhood and insensitivity to the impact of culture and economic class (Hendrick, 1997; Seifert, 2000).

Early Precursors to Developmental Study

Why did awareness of childhood as a special time of life eventually emerge? Society was becoming less rural and more industrialized. During the eighteenth century, factory towns began attracting large numbers of workers, who often brought their children with them. "Atrocity stories" became increasingly common: reports of young children in England becoming caught and disabled in factory machinery and of children being abandoned to the streets. Partly because of these changes, many people became more conscious of childhood and adolescence as unique periods of life, periods that influence later development. At the same time, they became concerned with arranging appropriate, helpful experiences for children.

Without a doubt, the change in attitudes eventually led to many social practices that we today consider beneficial to children and youth. One positive gain was compulsory education, instituted because children needed to be prepared for the adult world rather than simply immersed in it. Another was the passage of laws against child labor to protect children from physical hardships of factory life and make it less tempting for them to go to work instead of to school.

But these gains also had a dark side. Viewing children as innocent also contributed to increasing beliefs that children are incompetent, their activities are unimportant, and the people who care for children deserve less respect than other people. That is why, it was argued, children cannot do "real" work and why they need education (Cannella, 1997). And viewing them as innocent contributed to the idea that children are essentially passive and lacking in opinions and goals worth respecting; that is why, it was thought, adults have to supervise them in school and pass laws on their behalf (Glauser, 1997; Kitzinger, 1997). These were early signs of what later came to be called *ageism*, a prejudice against individuals based on their age, which eventually also affect social attitudes about adults as well—and especially older adults.

The Emergence of Modern Developmental Study

During the nineteenth and twentieth centuries, the growing recognition of childhood led to new ways of studying children's behavior. One of these was the *baby biography*, a detailed diary of a particular child, usually the author's own. One of the most famous English baby biographies was written and published by Charles Darwin (1877) and contained lengthy accounts of his son Doddy's activities and accomplishments. The tradition of rich description continued in the twentieth century with Arnold Gesell, who observed children at precise ages doing specific things, such as building with blocks, jumping, and hopping (Gesell, 1926). After studying more than five hundred children, Gesell generalized standards of normal development, or **norms**—behaviors typical of children at certain ages. Although the norms applied primarily to white, middle-class children and to specific situations and abilities, they gave a wider-ranging picture of child development than was possible from baby biographies alone.

The method of descriptive observation in developmental research has persisted into the present. An influential observer in this century has been Jean Piaget, who described many details of his own three children's behavior, as well as that of adolescents (Piaget, 1963). Others have provided sensitive commentary on adulthood, some (but not all) of it based on descriptive commentary; for example Bernice Neugarten (1967) has studied the lives of middle-aged adults from a number of perspectives. These works have begun to answer questions about the nature of human development and the influences on it at different points in the lifespan. However, these observations and studies have also created some new issues that have become fundamental to current research and thinking in the field.

norms Behaviors typical at certain ages and of certain groups; standards of normal development.

Lifespan Perspectives on Human Development

As we mentioned earlier, this book is about human development, and in particular about *lifespan development*, the study of continuity and change from birth to death. As the term implies, lifespan development is not confined to any one period of life, such as childhood, adolescence, or adulthood (sometimes psychologists call these by more specific names like *child psychology, the psychology of adolescence,* or *the psychology of adulthood*). Lifespan psychology shares with these other fields of developmental study a commitment to understanding how human beings think, feel, and act at different ages. It also shares a commitment to systematic study of the human condition, a commitment that we will look at more closely later in this chapter. But it also differs from other fields of developmental study in four distinct ways: (1) in dealing with the issue of human continuity and change, (2) in viewing the interplay between lifelong growth and (eventual) decline, (3) in comparing how basic events of life change in meaning at different ages and when viewed by different individuals, and (4) in noting (and respecting) the wide diversity among individuals and the sources of that diversity. These themes are summarized in Table 1.2 and will come up repeatedly in the chapters ahead. To get an initial idea of what they mean, let us look briefly at each of them now.

Continuity Within Change

Because lifespan psychology deals with longer periods of time than other forms of developmental psychology, it encounters more examples of apparent discontinuity in people's lives. A child who, at age two, protested bitterly over the slightest separation from her mother is now, at age thirty-five, very securely attached to her parents. The boy who, at

TABLE 1.2 Lifespan Perspectives on Human Development

Issue	Key Question
Continuity within change	How do we account for underlying continuity in qualities, behaviors, and skills in spite of apparent change?
Lifelong growth	What is the potential for growth—emotional, cognitive, and physical—throughout the lifespan?
Changing meanings and vantage points	How do key life events change in meaning across the lifespan and as a result of changing roles and experiences?
Developmental diversity	What factors create differences in individuals' development across the lifespan?

> **What Do You Think?**
>
> What are the merits and problems of descriptive study of human beings? One way to find out is for you and two or three classmates to make separate written observations of the "same" events. Visit a place with people in it (e.g., your student union, a store, or even your developmental psychology classroom), and separately write about what you see one particular person doing. Afterward, compare notes. How similar are your observations? How do they differ?

age eight, enjoyed identifying and drawing flowers denies any interest in "sissy stuff" at age sixteen; then, at age sixty, he returns to these interests. Each of these transformations has taken years, even decades, to occur. It is the lifespan perspective—the comparisons among widely differing periods of life—that makes change seem more frequent and obvious. Such changes would be less obvious if development were studied over shorter periods of time. The child who protests separation at age two is still likely to protest at age three, at least somewhat. However, changes in the child's reactions to separation from her parents should be quite apparent a few years later.

One challenge of lifespan psychology is to identify the factors that underlie developmental changes that occur over the very long periods with which it deals. In essence, the field looks for the continuities hidden within long-term changes. Lifespan psychology asks, "Who is the person underlying long-term changes, and how does he or she direct and influence the changes?" Consider the thirty-five-year-old who protested over separation at age two but now enjoys a secure relationship with her parents. Is there an underlying continuity between her behavior at two and her behavior at thirty-five? Perhaps a connection exists, but is implicit: when, as a two-year-old, she cried at her mother's departure, maybe she was not just complaining about being "abandoned" but also expressing the strength of her attachment. Perhaps her tantrums over separation even showed her commitment to the relationship, both to her mother and to herself. And her protests actually may have reflected a high comfort level, rather than a low one, in her bond to her mother, showing her confidence that she would not be punished for expressing her opinion! Later, at thirty-five, she is in a better position to express her strong attachment directly, particularly because she no longer feels that separations and reunions are completely out of her control. Across the three decades of her life, what was continuous was strong attachment; what was discontinuous or changeable was the way the attachment was expressed.

Lifelong Growth

This theme of lifespan psychology highlights the potential for growth at all ages, including not only childhood and adolescence but also adulthood and most of old age. Growth can occur in many areas of living, although it is not inevitable. For example, the psychologist William Damon has explored the development of moral goals in a series of research studies from infancy through middle age (Damon, 1996). By "moral goals" he refers to the formation of a sense of right and wrong, as well as the disposition to act on this sense. He points out that a moral sense is never formed completely, but deepens steadily throughout the lifespan. Note in the following developmental sequence how developmental growth in one's moral sense is based upon borrowing and incorporating ideas and commitments from all of a person's previous experiences.

- During infancy and the early preschool years, moral goals depend heavily on a child's ability to *empathize* (actually feel what someone else feels) and to *sympathize* (be aware of another's feelings even though not experiencing the other's feelings directly). Empathy and sympathy direct many actions of preschoolers; a three-year-old might, for example, hand a favorite teddy bear to a crying playmate.

- During the elementary school years, children use empathy and sympathy to develop moral concepts—ideas about equity and fairness—but their opinions at this age may not necessarily translate into action consistent with their beliefs. For example, a ten-year-old will have definite personal opinions about how to distribute a reward of candy to group members when they have worked on a common project. Damon argues that elementary-aged children have not yet linked their moral goals with their self-concepts or self-identifies. So at this age it is possible to believe one thing about morality (e.g., "pay according to effort") but do another (e.g., "pay equally to all").

- In adulthood, however, moral goals gradually become reconciled with self-identity—though only a minority do so completely (Colby & Damon, 1992). Who "I" am is increasingly defined by what I believe to be right and wrong, or good and bad. Aligning my "self" with moral ideas leads to stronger commitments to actions that embody these ideals (Damon, 2008). If I believe in a certain method of payment for group work, as in the example above, I am likely to say so. At the same time, the increasing sophistication of my thinking means I may also balance self-assertion against other moral commitments, such as not offending others unnecessarily—a demonstration of empathy and sympathy. The result is less "verbal hypocrisy," as seen during childhood, but also less predictability and more diversity of both belief and action in adulthood.

From birth through late life, moral goals and moral thinking grow continuously while also changing character: from an exclusive basis in intuitions (empathy and sympathy), to distinct verbal beliefs, to beliefs and actions partially reconciled with a sense of self. The moral complexities of adulthood are based on the abilities to empathize and sympathize—the abilities developed initially in infancy and the preschool years.

Changing Meanings and Vantage Points

By nature, lifespan psychology deals with key events and themes of life from a number of different lenses. Work, play, love, sex, death, and the family: these and other universal experiences mean different things as a person ages and mean different things depending on a person's current roles and responsibilities. Parenthood takes on new forms and significance, for example, as children grow older; it means one thing to an expectant mother or a young father of an infant but something quite different to an elderly parent whose children have children of their own. Parenthood also looks quite different to a child in a family compared to the parents themselves or to other relatives.

Lifespan psychologist Jacqueline Goodnow illustrated the extent of such differences in perspective using one type of work, everyday household chores (Goodnow, 1996). Most families, whatever their size and composition, work out understandings about which family member should do which chores. Whether or not the work is divided equally, the arrangement itself is supposed to be known and agreed on by all. Goodnow points out, however, that this ideal is rarely achieved fully. An "official" division of household labor may really be understood or accepted only by the parents, or even just by one parent (most often the mother). Multiple, competing views of "who should do what" are common. Other family members (such as children) may have their own ideas about how much housework they ought to do and about which particular jobs reasonably belong to each person. Furthermore, the multiple views are also likely to change over time. One reason is that children grow and therefore acquire new housekeeping skills, engage in activities that make new housekeeping demands (like hosting friends as they get older), or leave home altogether. The other reason is that parents also grow and change their own activities and obligations; a parent may start working or get a divorce, for example, and the new conditions will alter the parent's view of what housework really needs doing and by whom. The result of these factors is twofold: in most families conflict about housework is likely at least some of the time, and any current conflict is likely to disappear eventually, to be replaced by other disagreements about housework. It is still the same housework, but people's views of it change.

Developmental Diversity

Like other forms of developmental study, lifespan psychology searches for general trends and patterns that account for important changes during childhood, adolescence, and adulthood. But lifespan psychology is also likely to note *differences* in patterns of development: differences created both by individual experiences and by social and cultural circumstances (Baltes & Staudinger, 1996). The "A Multicultural View" feature, for example, describes the experience of street children in Paraguay, noting how the circumstances in Paraguay modify the impact of life on the street in that society compared to more economically developed societies such as the United States and Canada. In Paraguay, a child who lives on the street some of the time is not necessarily cut off from the support of family or other responsible adults. And not all street children live in the street full time; in fact, most do so only for limited periods. The effect of street life on children's development is therefore more variable; sometimes, in fact, street life creates a more positive context for growing up than staying in school, which costs money and often does not lead to employment later in life.

The diversity among street children in Paraguay suggests the importance of attending to diversity in development in general, and to diversity among North American children in particular. Just as in Paraguay, being a street child in the United States or Canada may be a different experience and hold different significance depending on a child's circumstances, such as the quality of prior family relationships, the resources available to the child and to the family, and the like. Understanding the developmental impact of life on the street requires taking these differences into account.

Diversity occurs not only within cultures and societies but also between cultural groups within a society. In North American society, for example, cultural differences can influence the supports for and expectations of a child in major ways. Patricia Greenfield demonstrated such influence in a research study of routine parent-teacher conferences between Anglo teachers and Hispanic mothers (Greenfield, 1995). Greenfield observed and analyzed the conferences in terms of differences in personal and family values expressed or implied during the conferences. During the conferences, the Anglo teachers uniformly sought to highlight the individual achievements of the child ("Carmen is doing well with her spelling"). But many of the Hispanic mothers preferred to direct the conversation toward how the child fit into the family and into the classroom group ("Carmen is such a help to me and so friendly"). The parents' remarks reflected differences in general cultural values—the Anglo parents valuing independence somewhat more, but the Hispanic parents (sometimes) valuing *inter*dependence more. The result was frustration with the conference on the part of both teachers and parents and less effective support for the children in their efforts to succeed socially and academically.

Yet even among these parents and teachers, there were differences: some parents and teachers adjusted to each other's conversational priorities, regardless of ethnic background. This adjustment was fortunate because chronic miscommunication among caregivers—and the subsequent less effective support—can impair a child's social and cognitive development in the long term.

Methods of Studying Lifespan Psychology

As a field of study, lifespan psychology bases its knowledge on systematic research, study, or investigation of continuity and change in human beings. The methods used are quite diverse, but all bear some relationship to the **scientific method,** procedures to ensure objective observations and interpretations of observations. As noted in this section, the scientific method allows for considerable variety in how research studies might be conducted. In fact, it is more accurate to speak of many scientific methods rather than just one.

An important issue in lifespan psychology has to do with accounting for the diversity among individuals, families, and communities. Are there principles that hold true for all people—including this Amish family and this African American family—regardless of circumstances?
Sources: (top) Ralph R. Echtinaw/Shutterstock.com, *(bottom)* Dragon Images/Shutterstock.com.

scientific methods General procedures of study involving (1) formulating research questions, (2) stating questions as a hypothesis, (3) testing the hypothesis, and (4) interpreting and publicizing the results.

> **What Do You Think?**
>
> A psychologist once said that "every parent believes in nurture until they have their *second* child." What do you think she was getting at with this comment? If you happen to be a parent of at least two children, share your opinion of the comment with a classmate who is not a parent or with one who is a first-time parent. And vice versa: if you've raised no children, or only one, compare your opinions to those of a second- or third-time parent.

The Scientific Method

Due to their adherence to the scientific method, all scientific research studies have a number of qualities in common, whatever their specific topic. For various practical reasons, the qualities cannot always be realized perfectly, but they form ideals to which to aspire (Cherry, 1995; Levine & Parkinson, 1994). The procedures are as follows:

1. *Formulating research questions.* Research begins with questions. Sometimes these questions refer to previous studies, such as when a developmental psychologist asks, "Are Professor Deepthought's studies of thinking consistent with studies of thinking from less developed countries?" Other times they refer to issues important to society, such as "What factors keep older adults from becoming depressed?" This part of the research process is similar to the reflection and questioning often engaged in by parents, teachers, nurses, and other professionals concerned about human growth and development.

2. *Stating questions as hypotheses.* A **hypothesis** is a statement that expresses a research question precisely. In making a hypothesis out of the earlier question regarding older adults, a psychologist needs to be more specific about the terms *older adult* and *depressed.* How old does a person really have to be to qualify as an *older adult*? What exactly is meant by the term *depressed*? After the terms of the question are clarified, the hypothesis is usually stated as an assertion that can be tested ("A network of friends keeps older adults from becoming depressed"), rather than as a question ("Does a network of friends keep older adults from becoming depressed?").

3. *Testing the hypothesis.* Having phrased a research question as a hypothesis, researchers can conduct an actual study about it. As the next section describes further, they can do this in a number of ways. The choice of method usually depends on the type of research question being asked, as well as convenience or efficiency, ethics, and scientific appropriateness. No research method is perfect, although some are more suited for particular research questions than others.

4. *Interpreting and publicizing the results.* After conducting the study itself, psychologists have a responsibility to report its outcomes to others by presenting them at conferences and publishing them in journal articles. Their reports should include reasonable interpretations or conclusions based on the results and enough details to all other psychologists to replicate (or repeat) a study themselves to test the conclusions. In practice, the limits of time (at a conference presentation) or space (in a journal) sometimes compromise this ideal.

hypothesis A precise prediction based on a scientific theory; often capable of being tested in a scientific research study.

There is a wide range of ways to carry out these steps, each with its own strengths and limitations. Viewed broadly, psychological studies can be organized into two groups based upon the type of research questions that the studies are designed to address: studies that attempt to answer questions about *causality*, and studies that attempt to answer questions about *association*. Researchers that ask questions about causality focus on how changes in one variable cause changes in another, while researchers who pose questions

> ### A Multicultural View
>
> **Street Children: Comparing Paraguay and North America**
>
> Like all countries of Latin America, Paraguay contains children and youths who are popularly call "street children." They are a serious concern for the authorities in this country, as indeed they are everywhere, including in North America. Who are the street children, and what do they need? The sociologist and social worker Benno Glauser investigated these questions in Paraguayan society, using interviews and case studies of street children and their families. He was surprised to find it was not at all clear what street children have in common with one another or what they therefore needed (Glauser, 1997). The ambiguities he encountered have implications for how we should think about and deal with street children in more developed societies such as the United States or Canada.
>
> In Paraguay, political leaders, social workers, and other makers of public opinion used the term "street children" to refer to youngsters in cities who lacked a home or family, spent nights on the street, and either begged or worked at various semilegal or illegal activities to get money for food. Yet Glauser found that real street children were much more diverse than this definition implies. Some still slept with their families, for example, and usually spent days on the street only to attend to a job (e.g., selling flowers). Some deliberately slept out, but only occasionally or for selected periods because of their employment (e.g., giving street directions to tourists for money could be done only in the tourist season).
>
> Some never saw their parents but slept in the home of another relative or some other responsible adult. And some (a minority) fit the definition of the authorities: they never saw family or relatives, banded together with other homeless children for mutual protection, and always slept on the street. This last group was much more vulnerable to physical abuse, more likely to become sick, and more likely to become involved in criminal and other illicit activities (e.g., drugs or child prostitution). This finding has been confirmed by other research on street children (Campos et al., 1994).
>
> Unfortunately, as Glauser discovered, the authorities tended to treat all street children as if they belonged to this last group and, therefore, were all in need of rather heavy-handed protection from abuse, disease, and poverty. Policies and actions favored (1) interrupting children's economic activities (e.g., washing car windshields at street corners), (2) moving children out of sight by having police pick them up and take them to more remote areas of the city, and (3) encouraging children to attend school and their caregivers to support children's attendance. Most of these actions proved either inappropriate or ineffective. Usually, for example, a child's job was not a "hobby" in spite of its informal status. Poor families often needed the child's income, or at least needed the child not to be an economic burden on the family. So parents and other relatives did not regret a child working. In

about association focus on identifying relationships (i.e., "covariations" or "correlations") between variables. Different methods are then employed by researchers to seek answers to these two types of questions. These methods vary in the length of time required to complete the study, the extent of intervention and control exercised by the researcher, and the sampling strategies used to recruit participants. The methodologies often get combined in various ways, depending on the questions the studies are investigating. Table 1.3 summarizes the various possible methods and is helpful in reviewing the explanations given in the sections that follow.

Researching Questions about Causality

- What is the effect of video game violence on aggressive behavior?
- What are the effects of age on children's abilities to interpret emotions?
- What are the long-term effects of a preschool program for low-income children on academic achievement and occupational success?
- What are the effects of aging on the cognitive abilities of older adults?

Each of the above questions addresses important cause-and-effect relationships. To clearly and convincingly answer these questions and others like them, researchers must conduct experiments.

> **A Multicultural View**
>
> **Street Children: Comparing Paraguay and North America** *continued*
>
> fact, they often believed that a job developed character and a sense of responsibility. School, on the other hand, was widely regarded as a bad investment among poor families because it led to few jobs and cost money for tuition once a child moved beyond the earliest grades (schoolchildren, in fact, often felt *more* rather than less pressure to work simply to pay the cost of education). And removing children from sight, as the police frequently did, accomplished little in the long term. Children simply walked back to their workplace or living places and began again—though often after experiencing humiliation at the hands of the police. For two reasons, in fact, Glauser suspected that Paraguayan policies and practices regarding street children were serving the interests not of the children but of well-off adults. The first was the emphasis by the police (and other leaders of society) on simply getting street children out of sight, a strategy all too common in some America communities as well (Vissing, 1996). The second was the neglect of children who might need protection and help but are "hidden" from public view, such as unpaid child servants, child prostitutes, or child soldiers in the Paraguayan army. These groups were at least as common as street children but were ignored in all public discourse.
>
> The Paraguayan experience has two important implications about street children in more economically developed countries such as the United States. One implication is about diversity: it is likely here, as in Paraguay, that "street children" come in different types, from those who merely work the street during the day, to those who sleep there intermittently, to those who live there essentially full time. All may need protection, though not necessarily to the same extent or in the same way. As in Paraguay, street children do not necessarily lose touch totally with parents, other relatives, or other responsible adults. Alternative living arrangements (e.g., a foster home) may—or may not—be better for a child in any particular case, especially for children who already receive significant, though partial, care from their biological parents or other close relatives.
>
> A second point is that in a developed country such as the United States, we understandably hope that school is a more productive investment than may be the case in Paraguay. Here, police and social workers may be more justified in encouraging street children to attend school than they are in less developed countries. But such reasoning may be more hope than reality even in the United States, where living conditions for poor families sometimes approach Third World conditions in spite of proximity to wealth, and where schools face tremendous educational challenges as a result (Dalglish, 1998; Kozol, 1991, 1995). Children of industrialized nations, or at least some of them, may not be so very different from children of developing nations.

Experimental Studies

If a researcher was interested in determining if playing violent video games causes an increase in aggressive behavior, the researcher could manipulate the level of violence in video games to which two groups of players are exposed—one group of participants plays a violent video game and another group plays a nonviolent video game. In order to ensure that the results from the study reflect only the effects of the level of violence in the video games, all other potential variables must be kept constant. For example, the two groups of video game players should be equivalent with respect to age, sex, level of education, familiarity with video games, etc. The conditions under which each group plays the video games should be the same as well: each group should play the games for the same amount of time and in the same kind of environment. Lastly, the researcher needs to be able to systematically and accurately measure the level of aggression each player exhibits after playing the video games. An **experimental study** just like this was conducted by Hasan, Bègue, Scharkow and Bushman (2013) that involved two groups of college students who played either violent or nonviolent video games twenty minutes a day for three consecutive days. After each video game session, the level of aggression of the players was assessed by measuring the duration and volume of a blast of loud noise to which the players subjected a *confederate* (someone working with the experimenter who was pretending to be a participant in the study). The results were clear: college students who played the violent video games were far more likely to subject a confederate to louder and longer blasts of noise than college students who

<u>experimental study</u> A study in which circumstances are arranged so that just one or two factors or influences vary at a time.

Chapter 1 Studying Lifespan Development

TABLE 1.3 Methods of Studying Human Development

Research Question	Method	Description
Question about Causality	Experimental study	Observes persons where circumstances are carefully controlled so that just one factor varies at a time
	Cross-sectional study	Observes persons of different ages at one point in time
	Longitudinal study	Observes same group(s) of persons at different points in time
	Sequential studies	Observes persons from different cohorts at the same *and* different points in time.
Question about Association	Naturalistic study	Observes persons in naturally occurring situations or circumstances
	Correlational study	Observes tendency of two behaviors or qualities of a person to occur or vary together; measures this tendency statistically
	Survey	Brief, structured interview or questionnaire about specific beliefs or behaviors of large numbers of persons
	Interview	Face-to-face conversation used to gather complex information from individuals
	Case study	Investigation of just one individual or a small number of individuals using a variety of sources of information

played nonviolent video games. The significant differences between the two groups grew larger after each day's video game session. Figure 1.3 illustrates the observed pattern of aggression.

Because this study was an experiment, Hasan and his colleagues held constant all the factors that might influence aggressive behavior *except* video game content, the one they were studying. This deliberately varied factor is often called the **independent variable**. The factor that varies as a result of the independent variable—in this case, the level of aggression exhibited toward another person—is often called the **dependent variable**.

The experimental method also requires making decisions about the population, or group, to which the study refers. When every member of the population has an equal chance of being chosen for the study, the people selected comprise a **random sample**. If not everyone in a population has an equal chance of being chosen, the sample is said to be *biased*. Investigators can never be completely sure they have avoided systematic bias in selecting individuals to study, but they can improve their chances by defining the population they are studying as carefully as possible and then selecting participants only from that population. When Hasan (2013) and his research team studied the effects of violent video games on college students, for example, the population to which they limited their observations consisted only of young adults who were attending college, and sampled students from this population at random. Interpretations of their results therefore apply only to this population of young adults. In later studies, they (or other investigators) could sample other populations, such as persons of other ages or cultural backgrounds.

independent variable A factor that an experimenter manipulates (varies) to determine its influence on the population being studied.

dependent variable A factor that is measured in an experiment and that *depends on*, or is controlled by, one or more independent variables.

random sample In research studies, a group of individuals from a population chosen such that each member of the population has an equal chance of being selected.

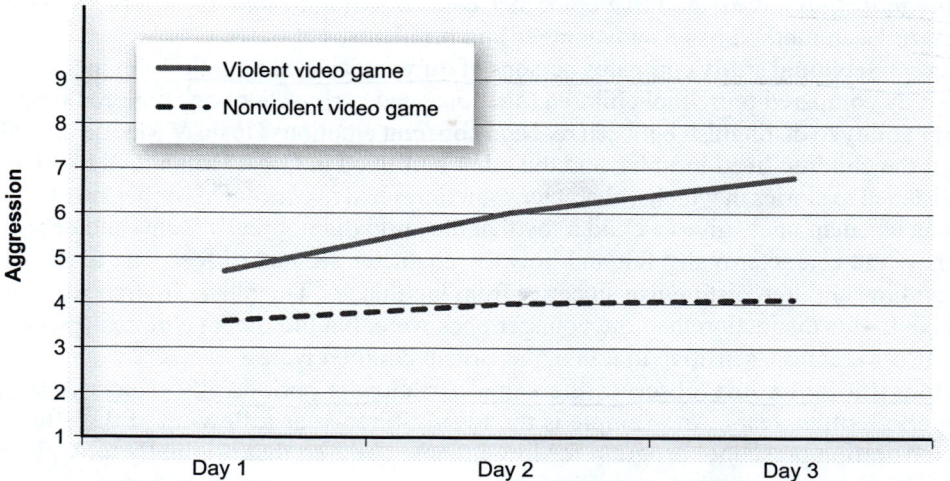

FIGURE 1.3
Effects of Violent and Nonviolent Video Games on Aggression Over Time

Exposure to video games for 20 minutes during three consecutive days resulted in significantly higher rates of aggression in college students who played violent video games compared to those who played nonviolent video games.
Source: Adapted from Hasan, Bègue, Scharkow, and Bushman (2013).

Experimental studies incorporate a number of precautions to ensure that their findings have **validity,** meaning they measure or observe what they intend to measure. One way to improve validity is to observe not one but two sample groups, one an experimental, or treatment, group and the other a control group. The **experimental group** receives the treatment, or intervention related to the purposes of the experiment. The **control group** experiences conditions that are as similar as possible to the conditions of the experimental group, but without experiencing the crucial experimental treatment. Also, to ensure that the experimental and control groups are comparable prior to receiving any treatment or intervention, participants are usually *randomly assigned* to each group. Comparing the results of the two groups helps to explicitly establish the effects of the experimental treatment.

Because of its logical organization, the experimental method often gives clearer results than other types of studies do. But because people sometimes do not behave naturally in experimental situations, one criticism of the experimental method is that its results can be artificial.

Another limitation to the experimental method is that participants cannot always be randomly assigned to the experimental and control groups. This is frequently the case when researchers are seeking the answers to causal questions involving variables like gender, ethnicity, marital status, and age. With each of these variables, participants are already in a group (for example, male or female, single or married, child or adult, etc.); random assignment to these groups is not possible. This poses a challenge when researchers try to produce clear and compelling answers to questions like "What are the effects of age on self-esteem in elementary-aged children?" or "What are the effects of gender on the life satisfaction of retired adults?" Because participants cannot be randomly assigned to experimental and control groups with these kinds of variables—often called "participant variables" because they describe characteristics of certain types of participants—researchers cannot be sure whether the results of their studies are caused by the variable that defines the groups (that is, the participant variable) or by some other variable. In other words, it is impossible to conduct true experiments if the independent variable is a participant variable. Instead, when researchers ask such causal questions, they must conduct **quasi-experiments.**

Quasi-experimental Studies

In general, quasi-experimental studies represent a large variety of studies that share a common feature: members of pre-existing groups are selected for comparison. Of particular interest to developmental psychologists are quasi-experiments that address causal questions pertaining to changes (or continuities) in people over time. Quite often, *age* is employed as a way to quantify time or to categorize participants. Developmental psychologists can either compare people of different ages at one point in time (called a *cross-sectional study*) or compare the same people at different times as they get older (called a

validity The degree to which research findings measure or observe what is intended.

experimental group In an experimental research study, the group of participants who experience the experimental treatment while in other respects experiencing conditions similar or identical to those of the control group.

control group In an experimental research study, the group of participants who experience conditions similar or identical to the experimental group, but without experiencing the experimental treatment.

quasi-experiments Experiments where participants cannot be randomly assigned to the experimental and control groups; instead, members of pre-existing groups are selected for comparison (for example, males versus females, young adults versus older adults, or private school students versus public school students).

Chapter 1 Studying Lifespan Development

longitudinal study). A method that combines elements of both time frames is the *sequential study*. Each method has its advantages and problems.

cross-sectional study A study that compares individuals of different ages at the same point in time.

A **cross-sectional study** compares persons of different ages at a single point in time. One such study compared preschool children (age four) and early-school-age children (age six) on their ability to distinguish between real and apparent emotions (Joshi & MacLean, 1994). Half of the children lived in India, and the other half lived in Great Britain. All of the children listened to stories in which a character sometimes had to conceal his or her true feelings (such as when an uncle gives a child a toy that the child did not really want) and described both how the character really felt and how the character seemed to feel. The results shed light on how children distinguish sincerity from tactfulness. The older children were more sensitive to this distinction than the younger ones were, but the Indian children (especially girls) also were more sensitive to it than the British children were.

longitudinal study A study of the same individuals over a relatively long period, often months or years.

A **longitudinal study** observes the same participants periodically over a relatively long period, often years. An example is the twenty-three-year follow-up of the effects of a demonstration preschool program for low-income children that originally took place in 1967. The four-year-old "graduates" of the program were assessed every few years following the program until they were all twenty-seven years old (Schweinhart et al., 1993; 1999). Researchers gathered interviews, school achievement test results, and reports from teachers and (later) employers and compared them to results from an equivalent group of four-year-olds who had been identified at the time of the program but did not participate in it. The results are gratifying: the graduates have succeeded in school and employment better than the nongraduates and cost taxpayers less by needing less public aid and fewer medical and other services. Cross-sectional and longitudinal studies both have advantages and limitations. Cross-sectional studies can be completed more quickly, but they do not guarantee to show actual change *within* individuals. In the study of children's knowledge of emotions, for example, the fact that older children were more knowledgeable does not ensure that each *individual* child becomes more knowledgeable. It shows only an average trend for the group; in certain individuals, knowledge of emotions may improve little as they get older, or even decrease, whereas other individuals may experience a huge leap in knowledge! Why these differences in individual change occur remains a question—and an urgent one if you work with people as a teacher, a nurse, or a counselor. See, for example, the experiences described in the interview with Marsha Bennington, speech-language pathologist in the "Working With" feature.

cohort In developmental research, a group of subjects born at a particular time who therefore experience particular historical events or conditions.

From the perspective of lifespan psychology, however, a more serious limitation of cross-sectional studies is their inability to distinguish among **cohorts**, or groups of people born at the same time and therefore having undergone similar developmental experiences. For example, a cohort of children born in 1930 shared experiences of less education and less comprehensive health care than a cohort born in 1960. As a result of this difference, comparing their abilities and health cross-sectionally in the 1990s may make the

Longitudinal studies are well-suited for studying long-term constancy and change in individuals. How are people the same after several years of maturing, and how are they different?
Source: Lyudmyla Kharlamova/Shutterstock.com.

older cohort (the ones born in 1930) appear less intellectually able and less healthy. A cross-sectional study may leave the impression that differences in the cohorts reflect true developmental change instead of the effects of being born earlier in the century. Cross-sectional studies always contain this ambiguity, especially when they compare groups that differ widely in age, as is common in studies of adulthood.

Longitudinal studies do not eliminate the ambiguity created by historical changes in cohorts, but they at least reveal more truly "developmental" change because they show the steps by which particular individuals or groups actually change over time. But in doing so, they pose a practical problem: by definition, longitudinal studies take months or even years to complete. Over this time, some of the original participants may move away or die and stop participating, which is known as attrition, investigators may become hopelessly bogged down with other work and fail to complete the original study, or government funding to support the work may disappear prematurely. Given these problems, psychologists have conducted cross-sectional studies much more often than longitudinal studies, despite the latter's special value. The dilemmas and ambiguities posed by time frames can be partially solved by **sequential studies,** which combine elements of cross-sectional and longitudinal studies. In sequential research, at least two cohorts are observed longitudinally and comparisons are made both within each cohort across time and between the cohorts at particular points in time. This approach provides information about actual developmental changes within individuals, but also about historical differences among cohorts that might create the impression of truly developmental changes.

sequential study Research in which at least two cohorts are compared both with each other and at different times.

A good example of sequential research is the work by K. Warner Schaie (1994; 2013) studying changes in cognitive abilities of adults (see Chapter 14's discussion of cognitive development in middle adulthood for more details about this research). A variety of earlier, cross-sectional research suggested that adults' general reasoning ability *decreases* with age—for example, that older adults score lower than younger ones on tests of general academic intelligence. Schaie's sequential research, however, modified this picture substantially. By testing several successive cohorts of young adults and then testing each cohort again at a later age, Schaie found that (1) many cognitive skills do not decline with age, particularly if they are used on a daily basis; (2) earlier cohorts generally achieved lower scores than later cohorts on tests of cognitive abilities; and (3) some individuals showed more decline with age than did others. None of these findings would have resulted from either a cross-sectional or a longitudinal study alone.

Researching Questions about Association

- How is time spent at home related to the level of stress experienced by adolescents and their parents?
- How is bed-wetting related to the social stressors faced by young children?
- How are stereotypes based on race or ethnicity related to actual academic performance?
- How is bilingualism related to the reading abilities of 11-year-olds?

Notice how these questions about association differ from the earlier questions about causation. Questions about association do not imply a causal connection between two variables; they simply suggest that a relationship of some kind exists between two variables. Also, there is no implied order or sequencing of events in questions of association as there is in questions of causation. Researchers can investigate questions about association using a wide variety of research methodologies, often described as "observational methods." Researchers can either observe and note the behaviors of people directly in a variety of settings (for example, in classrooms, on playgrounds, at movie theaters, or in laboratory settings) or they can ask people to observe and report on their own behaviors by asking them to respond to a set of questions. The various methods for researching questions about association are reviewed next.

Chapter 1 Studying Lifespan Development

WORKING WITH   Marsha Bennington, Speech-Language Pathologist

Communication Difficulties Across the Lifespan

Marsha Bennington works as a speech-language pathologist for a school district and in private practice. She thus sees individuals who range widely in age, from early childhood through adulthood. She talked, among other things, about how speech and language needs change across the course of development.

Kelvin: *Speech-language pathologists used to be called "speech therapists," right? Why the name change?*

Marsha: Our clientele has changed. We see people from a greater variety of language backgrounds now. Classrooms include more kids with disabilities, and more infants with medical problems at birth survive into adulthood, thanks to modern medicine. Our work is more diverse than it used to be, and the label "speech therapy" doesn't really describe it any more.

Kelvin: *What do you mean?*

Marsha: We address more than just speech problems. People may face an underlying inability to communicate and have a lot of difficulty with syntax or word choice. They might have trouble with reading, which really grows out of problems with focusing attention or with connecting printed and spoken language. We don't just deal with young children who mispronounce specific sounds—who say /t/ for /k/, for example.

Kelvin: *Sounds like your job is as much about "cognition" as it is about speech.*

Marsha: You're right, although even "cognition" may be narrowing it down too much. Motor skills can play a role, as can people's attitudes and feeling or their parents' attitudes and support. It depends on the individuals' particular needs and on their age.

Kelvin: *Are the problems you see in young children different from those of older kids or adults you work with?*

Marsha: You can't overgeneralize, but there do seem to be differences. A "typical" referral from a kindergarten or first-grade teacher tends to be specifically speech related. A child may articulate certain sounds incorrectly—*wun* instead of *run*—or a child may have some disfluency, that is, "stutter." I do see some young children with underlying language problems—constant syntax errors and trouble with finding words—but not many at this age.

Kelvin: *Does this balance change among older students?*

Marsha: It does change. By the upper elementary grades, students are most likely initially referred to me because they're having trouble with reading. By this age, reading can become a real effort because it depends so much on fluent speech. If your spoken sound or your spoken syntax isn't "standard," it's hard to decipher written sounds or sentences.

Kelvin: *What do you do in these cases?*

In naturalistic research, psychologists study human behavior as it normally occurs in everyday settings. What could be learned from observing these children playing with blocks together?
Source: Dragon Images/Shutterstock.com.

Naturalistic Studies

Naturalistic studies purposely observe behavior as it normally occurs in natural settings, such as at home, at school, or in the workplace. Reed Larson and Maryse Richards (1994) used this strategy to explore the daily emotional lives of parents in their forties and fifties and their adolescent children. For several weeks, each member of the family carried an electronic pager that beeped at random intervals to remind the person to report on his or her current moods and activities by telephoning a prearranged number. In every other respect, however, the family members engaged in their normal daily activities—school, job, homemaking, or whatever. The researchers discovered many interesting facts about individuals' responses to family life. Being at home *relieved* stress for midlife fathers ("Then I can relax"), for example, but often *created* it for midlife mothers ("Home is my 'second job'"). Teenage children felt far more hassled by small daily chores than their parents realized ("They don't notice it when they overdo the reminders about chores").

A particular strength of naturalistic research is that researchers observe naturally occurring or genuine behavior in settings that are a normal part of the participants' day. Naturalistic research does not face the criticism often levied at experimental research due to the experi-

24   Part 1   Beginnings

> **WORKING WITH** Marsha Bennington, Speech-Language Pathologist
>
> **Communication Difficulties Across the Lifespan** *continued*
>
> **Marsha:** It depends! I might work on a child's oral language to build awareness of syntax or of phonological difficulties. But by the time a child is in fourth or fifth grade, strategies to compensate for reading difficulties may help more. I might encourage the child to listen carefully to the teacher's oral directions or to ask for them both orally and in writing.
>
> **Kelvin:** *Does that become more of a problem in high school and beyond?*
>
> **Marsha:** Well, adolescence can aggravate a person's self-consciousness, and any speech or language problems only add to it. The older kids I see definitely need reassurance to boost their motivation and confidence. They've started to learn to hide their problem from others, and that usually means they avoid reading and writing, avoid speaking in class, that sort of thing.
>
> **Kelvin:** *What happens after high school? The bigger world after graduation must pose challenges.*
>
> **Marsha:** It's fair to say that *every* transition poses a challenge: home to kindergarten, elementary to high school, high school and beyond. A teenager may have functioned all right in high school, thanks to some help from the speech-language pathologist, but find that her first job requires more language skills than she expected. So back she comes for more help . . . [pauses and frowns]
>
> **Kelvin:** *Except?*
>
> **Marsha:** Except that help for adults, once they're not in school, can be hard to find and too expensive for many to afford.
>
> **What Do You Think?**
>
> 1. Marsha described changes in the sorts of problems people of different ages bring to her. Do you think these should be called "developmental" changes, even though she is really talking about cross-sectional comparisons among age groups? Compare your opinion with that of a classmate.
>
> 2. Try retelling Marsha's comments form a more longitudinal (versus cross-sectional) perspective. Do they seem more or less true to life from this perspective? This question would make a good topic for an in-class debate if you and/or your instructor can organize one. In formulating your opinions, though, remember that you are talking about the development of a human *problem*, not about the normative course of development.
>
> 3. Given your ideas from questions 1 and 2, how helpful do you think the concept of "lifespan development" is for a speech-language pathologist? Would it be more or less helpful for a regular classroom teacher?

ment's dependence on highly controlled (and thereby, contrived) testing environments, but naturalistic observational research does run a greater risk of generating ambiguous results.

Correlations

Whether they are using naturalistic or more controlled research environments, most research studies look for correlations among variables. A **correlation** is a systematic relationship, or association, between two behaviors, responses, or human characteristics. When two variables tend to change in the same direction—both variables increase together or decrease together—the relationship is called a *positive correlation*; when they tend to change in opposite directions, it is called a *negative correlation*. The ages of married spouses are a positive correlation: older husbands tend to have older wives (though not strictly so). The age of a child and the frequency of bed wetting is a negative correlation: the older the child, the less frequent the bed wetting (though again, not strictly so).

When correlated factors can be expressed numerically, psychologists use a particular statistic, the *correlation coefficient* (abbreviated r), to indicate the degree of relationship between two behaviors or characteristics. The correlation coefficient is calculated in such a way that its value always falls between +1.00 and −1.00. The closer to +1.00 the value, the more positive

naturalistic study A study in which behavior is observed in its natural setting.

correlation An association between two variables in which changes in one variable tend to occur with changes in the other. The association does not necessarily imply a causal link between the variables.

the correlation; the closer to −1.00 the value, the more negative the correlation. Correlations near 0.00 indicate no systematic relationship between behaviors or characteristics, or an essentially random relationship. For various reasons, psychologists tend to consider correlations above +0.70 or below −0.70 as strong ones and those between +0.20 and −0.20 as weak ones.

When you read or talk about correlations, it is important to remember that correlations by themselves do not indicate whether one behavior or characteristic causes another; they indicate only that some sort of association exists between the two. The distinction is illustrated in Figure 1.4, which graphs the number of baby pictures taken versus the weight of the mother taking the photos. While the graph shows an inverse correlation—heavier mothers take fewer pictures—this does not mean that taking baby pictures is a good way to lose weight. In other words, there is no causal relation between the two. More likely, the correlation reflects the influence of a third factor that has an impact on both behaviors.

Surveys

Developmental studies vary in how many people researchers collect information about or observe. The size of the group studied is called the research **sample**. At one extreme are large-scale **surveys** in which large numbers of people are asked to respond to specific questions. Grace Kao (1995) used this method to examine patterns of school achievement among Asian American youth. She was particularly interested in a common stereotype of Asian youngsters as "model students," the belief that they excel academically. Using survey responses from about fifteen hundred Asian American students, parents, and teachers, as well as from about twenty-five thousand white counterparts, Kao compared family incomes, educational levels, and ethnic backgrounds with academic achievement. She found that the stereotype of the model student is rather misleading. Academic success varies substantially among particular Asian ethnic groups. It also depends more heavily on how much time and money particular parents invest in education for their particular children than on the educational, financial, or ethnic backgrounds of the family as such. In these ways, the Asian American students were no different from their white counterparts.

These conclusions seem especially persuasive because of the rather large sample of families on which they are based—an advantage of the survey method. But the method also has limitations. Survey questions tend to be "cut and dried" to ensure that the responses can be compared among large numbers of respondents. They tend not to explore subtleties of thinking or the reasons people have for taking certain actions or holding certain beliefs. Did some of Kao's Asian American families invest more in education because their culture encourages them to do so or because they anticipated discrimination due to

sample Size of the group studied for research purposes.

survey A research study that samples specific knowledge or opinions of large numbers of individuals.

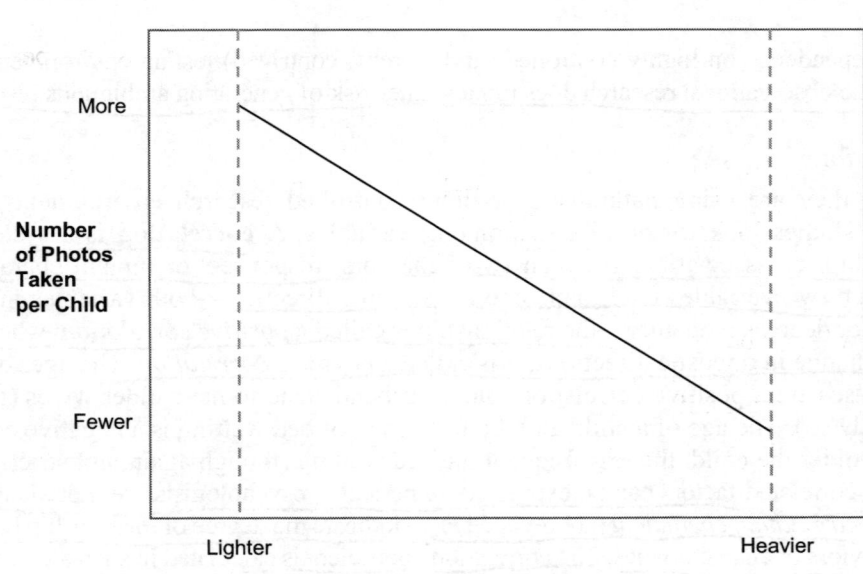

FIGURE 1.4
Correlation Is Not Causation

The number of pictures taken of an infant correlates with the weight of the child's mother, with heavier mothers taking fewer pictures. But this does not mean that gaining weight *causes* mothers to stop taking pictures or that taking pictures causes mothers to gain weight. More likely a third factor, such as the number of previous children to whom the mother has given birth, causes both factors separately.

their ethnic background and regarded education as insurance against the negative effects of such discrimination? To answer questions such as these, researchers need methods that invite respondents to comment more fully, such as interviews and case studies.

Interviews

A research study that seeks complex or in-depth information may use **interviews**, or face-to-face directed conversations. Because they take time, interview studies usually focus on a smaller number of individuals than surveys do, perhaps several dozen or so. Carol Gilligan and her colleagues used interviews to learn more about how teenage girls cope with the stresses of dealing with gender role expectations as they grow up under different conditions (Brown & Gilligan, 1992; Taylor et al., 1995). Some interviews involved girls who were attending a private girls' boarding school and were from economically well-off families; others involved girls who were attending a public high school in a racially mixed, lower-income community. The interview format allowed Gilligan to explore the girls' perspectives in depth and to find out when and how differences in their circumstances influenced their development as young women. As it turned out, economic and family supports did matter, but not always as Gilligan expected. A constant challenge for all girls was to find and remain true to their own perspective (or "voice," as Gilligan termed it). Doing so sometimes proved harder for well-off girls than for lower-income girls, though not necessarily.

interview A face-to-face, directed conversation used in a research study to gather in-depth information.

Case Studies

When a study uses just one or a few individuals, it is called a **case study**. In general, a case study tries to pull together a wide variety of information and observations about the individual case and then present the information as a unified whole, emphasizing relationships among specific behaviors, thoughts, and attitudes in the individual. An example is a study by Robert Jimenez, Georgia Garcia, and David Pearson (1995) comparing the language skills and knowledge about reading of just three eleven-year-old children: one proficiently bilingual Hispanic student, one proficiently monolingual white student, and one modestly bilingual Hispanic student. Each child was interviewed at length about her perceptions of her own skills with each language. Each was also invited to "think aloud" while reading samples of text in each language (that is, the child told about her thoughts as she read along). Because of the time taken with each individual, the investigators were able to discover important subtleties about how each student read. The proficient bilingual reader, for example, thought of *each* language as an aid to understanding the other language, whereas the less fluent bilingual reader believed simply that her Spanish assisted her English.

case study A research study of a single individual or small group of individuals considered as a unit.

By its nature, a case study can explore an aspect of human development, looking for new or unexpected connections among behaviors, needs, or social relationships. This is the most common use of case studies. A second use is to confirm whether connections previously found in experimental studies actually occur in everyday, nonexperimental situations, even when conditions are not carefully controlled. The second use resembles the naturalistic studies described earlier in this section.

Ethical Constraints on Studying Development

Sometimes, ethical concerns influence the methods researchers can use to study a particular question about development. Take the question of punishments administered by parents: what kinds of punishment are most effective, and for what reasons? For ethical reasons, we may be unable to experiment with certain aspects of this problem directly. Observing parents actually scolding and reprimanding their children would require delicacy at best. At worst, if the punishment became severe or physical, ethics might require our active intervention simply to protect the child from abuse.

For ethically sensitive questions, we may instead have to satisfy ourselves with less direct but more acceptable methods of study. We can interview a variety of parents about the methods of punishment they use, or we can ask experts who work directly with families what methods they think parents typically use. A few courageous families might allow us to observe their

> **What Do You Think?**
>
> Are some methods of developmental study inherently more effective than others? Try answering this question by organizing a multisided debate. Pick a successful developmental study (you can use any of the ones described in this chapter, for example), and assign each of three or four debating teams to design and argue the merits of some *alternative* method of studying the same question. In a second round of the debate, each team can try to refute the arguments of any of the other teams. Remember: there will be more than two sides to this discussion!

daily activities, with the understanding that we are interested in observing how they punish their children. But by being volunteers, these few families may not represent other families very well.

Generally, research about human beings faces at least three ethical issues: confidentiality, full disclosure of purposes, and respect for the individual's freedom to participate (American Psychological Association, 1992; 2010). In developmental psychology, all of these issues are complicated when the subjects are naturally vulnerable—when they are young, disabled, or older adults.

1. *Confidentiality.* If researchers collect information that might damage individuals' reputations or self-esteem, they should take care to protect the identities of the participants. Observing parents' methods of managing their children might require this sort of confidentiality. Parents may not want just anyone to know how much and how often they experience conflicts with their children. Similar concerns might influence research on teachers' methods of classroom management or caregivers' styles of caring for elderly people. In such cases, investigators should not divulge the identities of participants in a study without their consent, either during the conducting of the study or afterward when the results are published.

2. *Full disclosure of purposes.* Participants in a study are entitled to know the true purposes of any research study in which they participate. Most of the time, investigators understand and follow this principle carefully. But at times it can be tempting to mislead participants. In studying professionals' techniques for working with multiply handicapped adults, for example, researchers may suspect that stating this research purpose honestly will cause certain professionals, as well as the people under their care, to avoid participation. Investigators may suspect that telling the truth about the study will make the participants distort their behavior, hiding their less desirable behaviors and conflicts. In this sort of study, therefore, it might seem that intentional deception would produce more complete observations and in this sense make the research more "scientific." But investigators would purchase this benefit at the cost of their long-run reputations with participants. Purposeful deception may sometimes be permissible, but only when no other method is possible and when participants are fully informed after the study of the deception and its reasons.

3. *Respect for individuals' freedom to participate.* As much as possible, research studies should avoid pressuring individuals to participate. This may not be as simple as it first appears. Because psychologists have a relatively high status in society, some people may be reluctant to decline an invitation from them to participate in "scientific research." Investigators therefore may have to bend over backward to assure some individuals that participation is indeed voluntary. Researchers cannot simply assume that every potential participant automatically feels free to decline if approached. After all, who wants to feel like they're interfering with the progress of science?

informed consent
An agreement to participate in a research study based on understanding the nature of the research, protection of human rights, and freedom to decline to participate at any time.

When all three principles are closely followed, they allow for what psychologists call **informed consent**: the people or groups being studied understand the nature of the research, believe their rights are being protected, and feel free to either volunteer or refuse to participate. Informed consent, therefore, forms a standard, or ideal, for research to aim for and one that most studies do in fact approximate.

> **What Do You Think?**
>
> Why do you think ethics has become a bigger concern for developmental research in the past three decades? Brainstorm as many ideas about this as you can: have people changed, or research projects, or the conditions of modern life, or . . . ?

As the preceding discussion indicates, however, consent that is completely informed may prove difficult to achieve in some cases. This is especially so for research on vulnerable populations, such as children, people with certain disabilities, older individuals, or members of cultural groups who do not speak the native language. These people tend to depend on the goodwill and wisdom of others, including researchers themselves, to explain the purposes of a study and keep their best interests in mind. In studying an adult who speaks little English, for example, investigators may well wonder whether he fully understands the purposes of a study, even when those purposes are explained. Even if the person does understand, does he feel truly free to participate or decline? Or does he, as an individual, simply assume he must cooperate with whatever investigators request?

In studying children in particular, the developmental levels of the participants should influence the way investigators resolve ethical issues (Thompson, 1990). As a rule, children understand the purposes of a research project less well than do adults. Therefore, what the child will be experiencing during the study should be described at an appropriate level, and if the child is old enough to make decisions about participation, researchers should attain assent, or their agreement to participate. Moreover, it is critical that the parents are thoroughly informed and give consent for their child's participation. Children also are more vulnerable to stressful research procedures, such as experimentation with the effects of personal criticism. Older children and adults, on the other hand, are more prone to self-consciousness and are more likely to detect—and survive—implied personal criticisms. Thus, investigators need to be more careful in studying problems that might shame a person publicly (such as by asking, "How often do you cry?" or "What problems have you had because your parents are divorced?").

Wherever possible, the right to decide about whether to participate in a research study rests with the individual, provided he or she understands the nature of the study and feels truly free to decline participation. When these conditions hold only partially, such as with a child who speaks limited English, parents or other legal guardians share the ultimate right to decide whether the child should participate. When the conditions do not hold at all, such as with infants or adults with little or no language ability, parents and guardians essentially take over the right to decide about participation.

Strengths and Limitations of Developmental Knowledge

As this chapter has demonstrated, lifespan development has to be studied in particular ways and with certain limitations in mind. Because time is a major dimension of development, its impact must be approached thoughtfully. Yet the very nature of time poses real problems for studying at least some major questions. Especially when studied across the lifespan, people may "take too long" to develop within the time frame available to study them. Also, because lifespan psychologists deal with people, they must treat participants with respect and abide by the usual standards of decency and consideration for human needs. Finally, when dealing with especially vulnerable people, lifespan psychologists must take extra care to determine the true best interests of individuals who participate in studies, even when those participants do not know what they are being asked to do or do not feel free to refuse even when they do know.

Lest these limitations sound overly discouraging, be assured that in spite of them, lifespan psychologists have accumulated considerable knowledge about people of all ages in recent decades and continue to do so. The remaining chapters of this book should make that point amply clear. Lifespan psychology may not have definitive answers for all important questions about human nature, but it does have the answers for a good many.

Chapter Summary

- **What in general is lifespan development?** Lifespan development concerns continuities and changes in a person's long-term growth, feelings, and patterns of thinking. It occurs in several domains: physical, cognitive, and psychosocial. The domains of development interact in many ways, and individuals always develop as whole persons rather than in separate parts.
- **Why is it important to know about development?** Studying development can help you develop appropriate expectations about human behavior and its changes. It can help you respond appropriately to individuals' behavior and recognize when unusual behaviors are cause for concern. Studying development can also give you self-knowledge and understanding of your past.
- **How has society's view of childhood changed over time?** Until just a few hundred years ago, childhood and adolescence were not regarded as distinct periods of life. Social changes, including the industrial revolution, led to awareness of children's unique needs and vulnerability, but also contributed to modern (and mistaken) views of children as incompetent, passive, and unimportant. In the nineteenth and twentieth centuries, the first research studies of children consisted of baby biographies and structured observations of children at specific ages.
- **What general issues are important in lifespan psychology?** Lifespan psychology shares much with other forms of developmental study. However, it also has a distinctive emphasis on four themes: (1) continuity within change, (2) lifelong growth, (3) changing meanings and vantage points, and (4) diversity among individuals.
- **How do developmental psychologists go about studying development across the lifespan?** Research about developmental psychology tries to follow the scientific method: formulating research questions, stating them as hypotheses, testing the hypotheses, and interpreting and publicizing the results. Developmental research tends to focus either on questions about causality—studied by using experimental or quasi-experimental methods—or questions about association—studied by using observational designs, including naturalistic observation, correlational designs, surveys, interviews, or case studies. Cross-sectional studies compare individuals of different ages at one point in time. Longitudinal studies observe human change directly by following the same individuals over relatively long periods of time. Naturalistic methods observe individuals in natural contexts as much as possible. Experimental methods try to control or hold constant extraneous conditions while varying only one or two specified variables. Surveys, interviews, and case studies each sample different numbers of people and provide different levels of context in their information.
- **What ethical considerations should guide the study of development?** Ethical considerations guide how development can be studied, sometimes ruling out certain studies altogether. Generally, studies are guided by principles of confidentiality, full disclosure of purposes, and respect for the individual's freedom to participate. Research about children and vulnerable adults should strive for informed consent from participants and their parents or guardians. The specific ethical concerns in studying development depend on the age or developmental level of the individuals studied, as well as on the content of the study itself.

Key Terms

case study (p. 27)
cognitive development (p. 5)
cohort (p. 22)
control group (p. 21)
correlation (p. 25)
cross-sectional study (p. 22)
dependent variable (p. 20)
development (p. 4)
domain (p. 5)
experimental group (p. 21)

experimental study (p. 19)
hypothesis (p. 17)
independent variable (p. 20)
informed consent (p. 28)
interview (p. 27)
lifespan development (p. 4)
longitudinal study (p. 22)
naturalistic study (p. 25)
norms (p. 13)
physical development (p. 5)

psychosocial development (p. 6)
quasi-experiment (p. 21)
random sample (p. 20)
sample (p. 26)
scientific method (p. 16)
sequential study (p. 23)
survey (p. 26)
validity (p. 21)

Theories of Development

CHAPTER 2

Source: Sunny Studio/Shutterstock.com.

Chapter Outline

The Nature of Developmental Theories

Psychodynamic Developmental Theories

Behavioral Learning and Social Cognitive Learning Developmental Theories

Cognitive Developmental Theories

Contextual Developmental Theories

Adulthood and Lifespan Developmental Theories

Developmental Theories Compared: Implications for the Student

Focusing Questions

- What are developmental theories, and how are they useful?
- How have psychodynamic theories influenced thinking about development?
- How have developmental theories based on learning theories contributed to our understanding of developmental change?
- How do cognitive developmental theories help us to understand changes in thinking and problem solving throughout the lifespan?
- How have contextual approaches to development broadened our view of developmental change?
- How do adult developmental changes differ from child and adolescent changes?
- How does comparing developmental theories help us to understand developmental change?

When Elizabeth, age three, began nursery school, she cried and screamed every day when her mother left her. "Home!" and "Mama!" were the only words she seemed able to produce between sobs, which continued for much of each morning. Her concerned teachers met to discuss what to do about Elizabeth.

"It's best to ignore the crying," said one teacher. "If you give her lots of special attention because of it, you will reinforce the crying, and she'll just keep going longer."

"But we can't just ignore a crying child," said another. "This is a new and strange situation, and her crying shows that she's feeling insecure and abandoned. Look at her! She needs comfort and emotional support so that she can feel safer and more secure. At least give her a hug!"

"I think she's unsure whether her mother really will come back for her," said a third teacher. "Maybe we can find ways to help her understand and remember our daily routine here."

The teachers decided to follow all of this advice. They agreed not to fuss too much over Elizabeth's tears and to give her lots of comfort and support when she was not crying. They also helped Elizabeth draw a picture chart of the daily schedule and tape it to her cubbyhole. Finally, they talked with her mother about what they had observed and the solutions they were trying.

How well did their approaches work? Elizabeth stopped crying—more quickly, in fact, than any of the teachers had expected. Although all three teachers agreed that Elizabeth clearly was happier and more at ease, no one was sure exactly how or why the change had come about.

A second question we might ask is: How might the theories we will encounter in this chapter (and throughout this text) help us understand the developmental changes we will see in Elizabeth as she moves through early childhood into the school years? What will she be like as a teenager, a young adult, and beyond? In what ways will developmental theories help us—and Elizabeth and her family—better anticipate and understand these changes? In this chapter, we explore the nature of developmental theories, with a special emphasis on their applications to the developmental changes that take place over the course of an individual's lifespan.

The Nature of Developmental Theories

Each of Elizabeth's teachers' approaches reflects a different set of ideas and beliefs about children and their development. Whether they know it or not, most people—teachers, parents, grandparents, students, and even children themselves—are guided by "informal theories" of human development. And while the preceding example focuses on early childhood, informal theories of development are used to understand older children, adolescents, and adults as well, as we will see shortly.

What Is a Developmental Theory?

As we point out in Chapter 1, *lifespan development* refers to long-term changes and continuities that occur during a person's lifetime and the patterns of those changes. Theories are useful because they help us organize and make sense of large amounts of sometimes-conflicting information about development. For example, how do we decide whether day care is good for children, and, if so, what type of day care is developmentally best? What about day care for older adults? For that matter, how do we make developmental sense out of different approaches to parenting, family life, or education at various points in the lifespan? In contrast to informal theories, the more formal developmental theories we will discuss in this chapter attempt to provide clear, logical, and systematic frameworks for describing and understanding the events and experiences that make up developmental change and discovering the principles and mechanisms that underlie the process of change.

What qualities should a good theory ideally have? A good theory should:

1. be *internally consistent,* meaning its different parts fit together in a logical way;

2. *provide meaningful explanations* of the actual developmental changes we are interested in, be they changes in children's thinking with age or the long-range effects of divorce on their social adjustment;

3. be *open to scientific evaluation* so that it can be revised or discarded if new or conflicting evidence appears or if a better theory is proposed;
4. *stimulate new thinking and research;* and finally,
5. *provide guidance* to parents, professionals, and other interested individuals in their day-to-day work with children, adolescents, and adults.

How Do Developmental Theories Differ?

Although all developmental theories explore the human experience at various points across the lifespan, they also differ in some important ways. In this chapter, we look at how each theory addresses basic questions about human development: To what degree is a given developmental change due to maturation (nature), and to what degree is it due to experience (nurture)? Is development a continuous process or a series of discontinuous stages? Finally, does the individual take an active or a passive role in his or her development? We can use these three questions to identify how a developmental theory is classified. Much like Elizabeth's teachers at the beginning of the chapter had different ways of explaining behaviors, developmental psychologists tend to use different worldviews to understand development. Some theories are *organismic*—focusing on the individual as the source of change. Some theories are *mechanistic*—focusing on the world as the source of change. And some theories are *interactionist*—focusing on how individuals impact their environment, which, in turn, impacts the individual. You can how these different groups of theories address the three developmental questions in Table 2.1.

Many motor skills, such as jumping rope or riding a bike, develop in predictable sequences or stages.
Source: bibiphoto/Shutterstock.com.

Maturation or Experience?

Theories differ in the importance they assign to nature and nurture as causes of developmental change. *Maturation* refers to developmental changes that seem to be determined largely by biology because they occur in all individuals relatively independently of their particular experiences. Examples of maturational changes include growth in height and weight and increases in the muscle coordination involved in sitting up, walking, and running. Examples of changes due to experience, or *nurture*, include increasing skill in playing baseball, basketball, or tennis, which clearly seems to be due mostly to formal and informal learning. But for many developmental changes, the relative contributions of maturation and experience are less clear. Talking is a good example. To what degree do all children learn to talk regardless of their particular learning experiences? How much does their talking depend on their particular experiences in the family, community, and culture in which they grow up?

Continuous or Discontinuous?

Developmental theories also differ about whether developmental change is a *continuous* process, consisting of many small, incremental changes like a ramp, or *discontinuous*,

TABLE 2.1 How Developmental Theories Are Classified

Classification	Maturation or Experience?	Continuous or Discontinuous?	Active or Passive?
Organismic	Maturation	Discontinuous	Active
Mechanistic	Experience	Continuous	Passive
Interactionist	Both	Continuous	Active

Chapter 2 Theories of Development

composed of a smaller number of distinct *stages* like steps. Theorists such as Erik Erikson and Jean Piaget assume developmental change occurs in distinct, discontinuous stages. All individuals follow the same sequence, or order. Each successive stage is *qualitatively* unique from all other stages, is increasingly complex, and integrates the developmental changes and accomplishments of earlier stages. These are organismic theories.

Erikson's theory, for example, assumes an infant must first master the crisis of *trust versus mistrust;* that is, she must come to trust her caregiver's ability to meet her needs. Only then can she move on to tackle the crisis that defines the next stage, *autonomy versus shame and doubt. Autonomy* refers to a person's capacity to be independent and self-directed in his or her activities. Similarly, mastery of the crisis of *intimacy versus isolation* during early adulthood prepares an individual for the crisis of *generativity versus stagnation* that occurs during middle adulthood. These and other stages of development proposed by Erikson are discussed later in the chapter.

Learning theories, on the other hand, see development as a relatively smooth and continuous process. The development of trust and autonomy or of more sophisticated thinking and problem-solving skills is thought to occur through the numerous small changes that unfold as a child interacts with his environment. These theories focus on *quantitative* change and are mechanistic in nature.

Still other theories view developmental change as a sequence of more rounded, overlapping slopes, rather than as one continuous incline or a series of sharply defined stages, and are considered interactionist theories.

Active or Passive?

Developmental theories also differ in their view of how actively individuals contribute to their own development. For instance, behavioral learning theorists believe developmental change is caused by events in the environment that stimulate individuals to respond, resulting in the learned changes in behavior that make up development. Theorists who are interested in how thinking and problem-solving abilities develop, such as Jean Piaget, propose that such changes depend on the person's active efforts to master new intellectual problems of increasing difficulty. Likewise, Erik Erikson's theory of identity development proposes that an individual's personality and sense of identity are strongly influenced by his or her active efforts to master the psychological and social conflicts of everyday life.

A person's choice to enroll in college is a good example of the active role of an individual in his or her own development.
Source: auremar/Shutterstock.com.

> **What Do You Think?**
>
> One of the three developmental questions asks whether developmental change occurs in stages or is a continuous process. How might different answers to this question affect how parents raise their children? How might they affect how teachers educate their students?

Psychodynamic Developmental Theories

Psychodynamic theorists believe development is an active, dynamic process that is influenced by both a person's inborn, biological drives and his or her conscious and unconscious social and emotional experiences. According to Sigmund Freud, a child's development is thought to occur in a series of stages. At each stage, the child experiences unconscious conflicts that he must resolve to some degree before going on to the next stage. Other influential psychodynamic approaches, such as that of Erik Erikson, place less emphasis on biological drives and unconscious conflict. Erikson focuses more on the development of a sense of identity as a result of important social, emotional, and cultural experiences.

Freudian Theory

Sigmund Freud (1856–1939) was the originator of *psychoanalysis*, the approach to understanding and treating psychological problems on which psychodynamic theory is based. Much of Freud's formal theory is outdated. However, his ideas continue to influence our understanding of personality development, including such areas as early infant-caregiver attachment, diagnosis and treatment of childhood emotional disorders, adolescent identity formation, and the long-range consequences of divorce.

The Three-Part Structure of Personality

Freud described each individual's personality as consisting of three hypothetical mental structures: the id, the ego, and the superego.

The **id**, which is present at birth, is unconscious. It impulsively tries to satisfy a person's inborn biological needs and desires by motivating behaviors that maximize pleasure and avoid discomfort with no regard for the realities involved. In this view, the newborn infant is all id, crying for food and comfort but having no idea of how to get them because she cannot distinguish between wishful fantasy and reality.

The **ego** is the largely rational, conscious, problem-solving part of the personality. It is closely related to a person's sense of self. The ego functions according to the *reality principle,* a process by which the infant learns to delay his desire for instant satisfaction and redirect it into more realistic and appropriate ways to meet his needs. This involves a shift of psychological energy from fantasy to the real parents and other caregivers who can in fact meet the infant's needs. Thus, a hungry infant shifts from imagining that the wish for food will satisfy her hunger to a more realistic focus on anticipating the appearance of her parent or other caregiver, who will feed her. An infant's developing ego, or sense of self, is based on her internalized mental images of her relationships with these caregivers.

The **superego** is the moral and ethical component of the personality. It develops at the end of early childhood. The superego includes the child's emerging sense of *conscience,* or right and wrong, as well as the *ego-ideal,* an idealized sense of how he should behave. The superego acts as an internalized, all-knowing parent. It punishes the person for unacceptable sexual or aggressive thoughts, feelings, and actions with guilt and rewards him for fulfillment of parental standards with heightened self-esteem. The superego can sometimes be overly moralistic and unreasonable, but it provides the individual with standards by which to regulate his moral conduct and take pride in his accomplishments.

id In Freud's theory, the part of an individual's personality that is present at birth, unconscious, impulsive, and unrealistic, and that attempts to satisfy a person's biological and emotional needs and desires by maximizing pleasure and avoiding pain.

ego According to Freud, the rational, realistic part of the personality; coordinates impulses from the id with demands imposed by the superego and by society.

superego In Freud's theory, the part of personality that acts as an all-knowing, internalized parent. It has two parts: the conscience, which enforces moral and social conventions by punishing violations with guilt; and the ego-ideal, which provides an idealized, internal set of standards for regulating and evaluating one's thoughts, feelings, and actions.

Chapter 2 Theories of Development 35

Stages of Psychosexual Development

Freud believed development occurs through a series of *psychosexual* stages. Each stage focuses on a different area of the body that is a source of excitation and pleasure. At each stage, developmental changes result from conflicts among the id, ego, and superego. These conflicts can threaten the person's ego, or sense of self. Pressures from the id push the person to act impulsively to achieve immediate pleasure; pressures from the ego encourage her to act more realistically by delaying satisfaction until it can be attained; and pressures from the superego push her to meet standards of moral behavior and achievement that may be overly strict or unrealistically high. Freud's psychosexual stages and the developmental processes that occur are summarized in Table 2.2.

The ego uses defense mechanisms to protect itself from such conflicts. *Defense mechanisms* are unconscious distortions of reality that keep conflicts from the ego's (self's) conscious awareness. One such defense mechanism is *repression,* in which unacceptable feelings and impulses are forced from memory and forgotten. Another is *projection,* in which a person's conflict-producing feelings, such as feelings of aggression, are mistakenly attributed to another person.

According to Freud, unresolved id-ego and superego-ego conflicts can lead to a *fixation,* or a blockage in development. Fixation can also result from parenting that is not appropriately responsive to a child's needs. For example, overindulgence during the oral stage (see Table 2.2) may result in excessive dependence on others later in life. On the other hand, infants who experience severe deprivation and frustration of their needs may later feel they have to exploit or manipulate others to meet their needs. In this view, an individual's personality traits reflect the patterns typical of the stage at which a fixation occurred.

TABLE 2.2 Freud's Psychosexual Stages and Developmental Processes

Psychosexual Stage	Approximate Age	Description
Oral	Birth–1 year	The mouth is the focus of stimulation and interaction; feeding and weaning are central.
Anal	1–3 years	The anus is the focus of stimulation and interaction; elimination and toilet training are central.
Phallic	3–6 years	The genitals (penis, clitoris, and vagina) are the focus of stimulation; gender role and moral development are central.
Latency	6–12 years	A period of suspended sexual activity; energies shift to physical and intellectual activities.
Genital	12–adulthood	The genitals are the focus of stimulation with the onset of puberty; mature sexual relationships develop.

Developmental Processes

Development occurs through a series of psychosexual stages. In each stage, the child focuses on a different area of her body, and how she invests her libido (sexual energy) in relationships with people and things reflects the concerns of her current stage. New areas of unconscious conflict among the id, ego, and superego, the three structures of personality, also occur. Conflicting pressures from the id to impulsively achieve pleasure, from the ego to act realistically by delaying gratification, and from the superego to fulfill moralistic obligations and to achieve idealistic standards all threaten the ego. The ego protects itself by means of unconscious defense mechanisms, which keep these conflicts from awareness by distorting reality.

> **Focusing On . . .**
>
> ### Erik Erikson's Identity Crisis: An Autobiographical Perspective
>
> *How do theorists' own life experiences influence their theories of development? Here is what Erik Erikson has written about his own identity crises and how they influenced his developmental theory.*
>
> Erik Erikson was born in 1902 and died in 1994. He grew up in southern Germany with his mother, who was Danish, and her husband, a German pediatrician. Erikson recalls that "all through my earlier childhood, they kept secret from me the fact that my mother had been married previously; and that I was the son of a Dane who had abandoned her before my birth" (E. Erikson, 1975, p. 27).
>
> As Erikson entered puberty and adolescence, identity conflicts intensified. "My stepfather was the only professional man in an intensely Jewish small bourgeois family, while I . . . was blond and blue-eyed, and grew flagrantly tall. Before long, then, I was referred to as a 'goy' [outsider] in my stepfather's temple, while to my schoolmates I was a 'Jew.' . . . Although during World War I, I tried desperately to be a good German chauvinist, [I] soon became a 'Dane' when Denmark remained neutral" (pp. 27, 28).
>
> During this period, Erikson decided he would be an artist and a writer, rejecting his family's more middle-class values and expectations. He spent most of his time traveling, painting, writing, occasionally taking art classes, and teaching art. In looking back at these years, Erikson said that he now considered them an important part of his training (pp. 25, 26).
>
> In fact, it was not until Erikson was almost thirty and moved to Austria that his career as a psychoanalyst and developmental theorist really began. His training in psychoanalysis was conducted by Anna Freud, who accepted him as a student after observing his work with children as a teacher in a small private school. After studying and practicing psychoanalysis in Vienna, Erikson was forced to leave Austria by the rise of Hitler. He emigrated to the United States, where he lived and worked the rest of his life.
>
> Erikson achieved his outstanding accomplishments as a teacher, scholar, and therapist without the benefit of even a college degree, much less any other professional credentials. In the 1930s, Erikson worked as a psychoanalyst with children and debated whether to return to school for a professional degree. Instead, he accepted a research appointment at Yale Medical School and the Yale Institute of Human Relations, where he worked with an interdisciplinary team of psychologists, psychiatrists, and anthropologists and conducted field studies of the Sioux tribe of Native Americans in South Dakota.
>
> In the 1940s, Erikson moved to California to study the life histories of children living in Berkeley and then the lives of the Yurok Indians. He joined the faculty of the University of California at Berkeley in the early 1950s but was soon fired because of his opposition to the Korean War and his refusal to sign a "loyalty oath," part of the fanatical anticommunist crusade of Senator Joe McCarthy. Erikson was reinstated as politically dependable, but resigned in support of others who were not rehired. Erikson says of this experience, "As I think back on that controversy now, it was a test of our American identity; for when the papers told us foreign-born among the non-signers to 'go back where we came from,' we suddenly felt quite certain that our apparent disloyalty to the soldiers in Korea was, in fact, quite in line with what they were said to be fighting for. The United States Supreme Court has since confirmed our point of view" (pp. 42–43).
>
> Erikson wrote this about that period: "It would seem almost self-evident now how the concepts of 'identity' and 'identity crisis' emerged from my personal, clinical, and anthropological observations in the thirties and forties. I do not remember when I started to use these terms; they seemed naturally grounded in the experience of emigration, immigration, and Americanization. . . . I will not describe the pathological side of my identity confusion, which included disturbances for which psychoanalysis seemed, indeed, the treatment of choice. . . . No doubt, my best friends will insist that I needed to name this crisis and to see it in everybody else in order to really come to terms with it in myself" (pp. 26, 43).
>
> **What Do You Think?**
> In what ways did Erikson's life experiences and the time and places in which he lived influence his developmental theory? What aspects of your own experiences and the time and places you have lived are likely to be important in shaping your own ideas about developmental continuity and change?

Erikson's Psychosocial Theory

Erik Erikson (1902–1994) grew up in Europe. He studied psychoanalysis with Freud's daughter, Anna, who strongly influenced his ideas about personality development. The "Focusing On" feature describes the relationship between Erikson's life and his theory. In Erikson's view, personality development is a *psychosocial* process, meaning internal psychological factors and external social factors are both very important. Developmental changes occur throughout a person's lifetime and are influenced by three interrelated

Chapter 2 Theories of Development

forces: (1) the individual's biological and physical strengths and limitations; (2) the person's unique life circumstances and developmental history, including early family experiences and degree of success in resolving earlier developmental crises; and (3) the particular social, cultural, and historical forces at work during the individual's lifetime (for example, racial prejudice, poverty, rapid technological change, or war).

Psychosocial Stages of Development

Erikson proposed that development occurs in a series of eight stages, beginning with infancy and ending with old age. Each stage is named for the particular *psychosocial crisis*, or challenge, that every individual must resolve to be able to move on to the next stage. Successful mastery of the psychosocial crisis at a particular stage results in a personality strength, or *virtue*, that will help the individual meet future developmental challenges (Erikson, 1982; Miller, 2011). Table 2.3 summarizes Erikson's stages and developmental processes.

Stage 1: Trust versus Mistrust The earliest basic trust is indicated by the infant's capacity to sleep, eat, and excrete in a comfortable and relaxed way. Parents who reliably ensure daily routines and are responsive to their infant's needs provide the basis for a trusting view of the world. The proper ratio, or balance, between trust and mistrust leads to the development of hope. *Hope* is the enduring belief that one's wishes are attainable. Failure to develop such trust may seriously interfere with a child's sense of security and compromise her ability to master successfully the challenges of the stages that follow.

For this school-age youngster, learning new skills is part of mastering Erikson's developmental crisis of industry versus inferiority, while for his grandfather, sharing his lifelong love of chess is one way of mastering the crisis of ego integrity versus despair.
Source: Rus Limon/Shutterstock.com.

TABLE 2.3 Erikson's Psychosocial Stages and Developmental Processes

Psychosocial Stage	Approximate Age	Description (Virtue Attained)
Trust versus mistrust	Birth–1 year	Focus on oral-sensory activity; development of trusting relationships with caregivers and of self-trust (hope)
Autonomy versus shame and doubt	1–3 years	Focus on muscular-anal activity; development of control over bodily functions and activities (will)
Initiative versus guilt	3–6 years	Focus on locomotor-genital activity; testing limits of self-assertion and purposefulness (purpose)
Industry versus inferiority	6–12 years (latency period)	Focus on mastery, competence, and productivity (competence)
Identity versus role confusion	12–19 years (adolescence)	Focus on formation of identity and coherent self-concept (fidelity)
Intimacy versus isolation	19–25 years (early adulthood)	Focus on achievement of an intimate relationship and career direction (love)
Generativity versus stagnation	25–50 years (adulthood)	Focus on fulfillment through creative, productive activity that contributes to future generations (care)
Ego integrity versus despair	50 and older	Focus on belief in integrity of life, including successes and failures (wisdom)

Developmental Processes

Development of the ego, or sense of identity, occurs through a series of stages, each building on the preceding stages and focused on successfully resolving a new psychosocial crisis between two opposing ego qualities. No stage is fully resolved, and more favorable resolution at an earlier stage facilitates achievement of later stages.

Stage 2: Autonomy versus Shame and Doubt This stage occurs during the toddler and preschool years. *Autonomy* refers to a child's capacity to be independent and self-directed in his activities and ability to balance his own demands for self-control with demands for control from his parents and others. *Shame* involves a loss of self-respect due to a failure to meet one's own standards (M. Lewis, 1992). A successful outcome for this stage is the virtue *of will*, the capacity to freely make choices based on realistic knowledge of what is expected and what is possible.

Stage 3: Initiative versus Guilt This stage occurs during the preschool years. *Initiative* combines autonomy with the ability to explore new activities and ideas and to purposefully pursue and achieve tasks and goals. *Guilt* involves self-criticism due to failure to fulfill parental expectations. This crisis often involves situations in which the child takes on more than she can physically or emotionally handle, including the powerful sexual and aggressive feelings children often act out in their play. If the child is treated respectfully and helped to formulate and pursue her goals without feeling guilty, she will develop the virtue of *purpose* in her life.

Stage 4: Industry versus Inferiority As a child leaves the protection of his family and enters the world of school, he must come to believe in his ability to learn the basic intellectual and social skills required to be a full and productive member of society and to start and complete tasks successfully. The virtue of *competence* is the result. A failure to feel competent can lead to a sense of inferiority. The child who consistently fails in school is in danger of feeling alienated from society or of thoughtlessly conforming to gain acceptance from others.

Stage 5: Identity versus Role Confusion This stage coincides with the physical changes of *puberty* and the psychosocial changes of adolescence. *Identity* involves a reliable, integrated sense of who one is based on the many different roles one plays. *Role confusion* refers to a failure to achieve this integration of roles. During this stage, teenagers undergo reevaluation of who they are in many areas of identity development, including the physical, sexual, intellectual, religious, and career areas. Frequently conflicts from earlier stages resurface. A successful resolution of this crisis is the development of the virtue *of fidelity,* the ability to sustain loyalties to certain values despite inevitable conflicts and inconsistencies. Failure to resolve this crisis may lead to a premature choice of identity, a prolonged identity and role confusion, or choosing a permanently "negative" identity that may be associated with delinquent and antisocial behavior. We take a closer look at identity development during adolescence in Chapter 11.

Erikson's final three stages focus on development during adulthood, a topic we discuss more fully at the end of the chapter.

Stage 6: Intimacy versus Isolation Successful resolution of this stage results in the virtue of being able to experience *love*. The young adult, as we will see in Chapter 13, must develop the ability to establish close, committed relationships with others and cope with the fear of losing her own identity and separate sense of self that such intense intimacy raises.

Stage 7: Generativity versus Stagnation This stage occurs during middle adulthood. Successful resolution brings the virtue of *care,* or concern for others. *Generativity* is the feeling that one's work, family life, and other activities are both personally satisfying and socially meaningful in ways that contribute to future generations. *Stagnation* results when life no longer seems purposeful. We look more closely at this crisis in Chapter 15.

Stage 8: Ego Integrity versus Despair This stage occurs during late adulthood, as we will see in Chapter 17. Successful resolution brings the virtue *of wisdom. Ego integrity* refers to the ability to look back on the strengths and weaknesses of one's life with a sense of dignity, optimism, and wisdom. It is in conflict with the despair resulting from health problems, economic difficulties, social isolation, and lack of meaningful work experienced by many older persons in our society.

> **What Do You Think?**
>
> Erikson proposed that cultural and social forces play a major role in developmental change. With this in mind, how might growing up as a male versus a female of your own racial and ethnic background influence how an adolescent deals with the crisis of identity versus role confusion? Compare your conclusions with those of several classmates.

According to Erikson, psychosocial conflicts are never fully resolved. Depending on his or her life experiences, each individual achieves a more or less favorable ratio of trust to mistrust, industry to inferiority, ego integrity to despair, and so on. Therefore, conflicts from earlier stages may continue to affect later development. Moreover, some stages might happen "early," based on life course. For example, a young adult diagnosed with cancer might experience issues of generativity and ego integrity versus despair at a much younger age than is typical.

Applications of Psychodynamic Developmental Theories Throughout the Lifespan

Even young infants participate actively in their own development.
Source: Oksana Kuzmina/Shutterstock.com.

attachment An intimate and enduring emotional relationship between two people, such as infant and caregiver, characterized by reciprocal affection and a periodic desire to maintain physical closeness.

As we will see in the chapters on psychosocial development throughout this text, psychodynamic theories help us understand the formation of **attachments**, the strong and enduring emotional bond that develops between an infant and his or her caregivers during the infant's first year of life (Chapter 5), the development of autonomy and self-control during infancy and toddlerhood (Chapter 5), and the development of intimate relationships during adolescence and adulthood (Chapters 11 and 13). These theories alert us to the social and emotional importance of early childhood play (Chapter 7) and help us deal with death, loss, and grieving during middle childhood (Chapter 9) and with eating disorders, depression, and delinquency during adolescence (Chapters 10 and 11). Erikson's psychosocial theory will help us see that resolving the crisis of *identity versus role confusion,* which is a major task of adolescence, has its origins in earlier experiences and continues through late adulthood, when the crisis of *ego integrity versus despair* must be negotiated (Chapter 17).

Behavioral Learning and Social Cognitive Learning Developmental Theories

Learning is generally defined as relatively permanent changes in the capacity to perform certain behaviors that result from experience. According to the learning theories, the learning experiences that occur over a person's lifetime are the source of developmental change. Thus, changes in existing learning opportunities or the creation of new ones can modify the course of an individual's development.

Behavioral Learning Theories

The behavioral learning theories of Pavlov and Skinner have provided key concepts for understanding how learning experiences influence development and for helping individuals learn new, desirable behaviors and alter or eliminate problematic behaviors.

Pavlov: Classical Conditioning

classical conditioning According to Pavlov, learning in which a neutral stimulus gains the power to bring about a certain response by repeated association with another stimulus that already elicits the same response.

Ivan Pavlov (1849–1936) was a Russian scientist who first developed his behavioral theory while studying digestion in dogs. In his well-known experiments, Pavlov rang a bell just before feeding a dog. Eventually the dog salivated whenever it heard the bell, even if it received no food. Pavlov called this process **classical conditioning**. The food served as the *unconditioned stimulus*, and the salivation to the food was the *unconditioned response.* Over repeated pairings with the bell (a *neutral stimulus*) being presented before the food,

Part 1 Beginnings

those two experiences essentially became intertwined so that, eventually, the dogs began salivating when they heard the bell, even when the food was not present. When the formerly neutral stimulus—the bell—caused a response, it was then considered a *conditioned stimulus*, and the salivation to the bell was then considered the *conditioned response*.

Through the processes involved in classical conditioning, reflexes that are present at birth may help infants to learn about and participate in the world around them. For example, conditioning of the sucking reflex, which allows newborn infants to suck reflexively in response to a touch on the lips, has been reported using a tone as the conditioned stimulus (Lipsitt & Kaye, 1964). Other stimuli, such as the sight of the bottle and the mother's face, smile, and voice, may also become conditioned stimuli for sucking and may elicit sucking responses even before the bottle touches the baby's lips. Although even newborns' behavior may be classically conditioned as early as the first two days of life (Fifer et al., 2009), it cannot be reliably observed over a wide range of reflexes until about six months of age (Lipsitt, 1990). Figure 2.1 illustrates the process of classical conditioning.

Skinner: Operant Conditioning

B. F. Skinner (1904–1991) is best known for his learning theory, which is also known as **operant conditioning**. This theory is based on a simple concept called **reinforcement**, the process by which the likelihood that a particular response will occur again increases when that response is followed by a certain stimulus. *Positive reinforcement* occurs when, following a particular response (a baby saying "da-da"), a rewarding stimulus (his father smiling and saying "good boy!") is added that strengthens the response and increases the likelihood that it will recur under similar circumstances. *Negative reinforcement* also strengthens a response and increases the chance of its recurrence, but does so by removing an undesirable or unpleasant stimulus following the occurrence of that response. Consider Sarah, a four-year-old who has been crying

operant conditioning According to Skinner, a process of learning in which a person or an animal increases the frequency of a behavior in response to repeated reinforcement of that behavior.

reinforcement According to Skinner, any stimulus that increases the likelihood that a behavior will be repeated in similar circumstances.

Illustration of Classical Conditioning

BEFORE CONDITIONING:

(A) Place a nipple in baby's mouth:

Touch of nipple (US) — — — —elicits — — — — — > Sucking reflex (UR)

(B) Show baby a bottle with a nipple:

 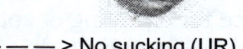

Sight of bottle — — — — —elicits — — — — — > No sucking (UR)
with nipple (CS)

DURING CONDITIONING:

(C) Show baby the a bottle and place its nipples in baby's mouth. Repeat a number of times:

Touch of nipple (US) — — — —elicits — — — — — > Sucking reflex (UR)

(paired with)

Sight of bottle — — — —elicits — — — — — > Sucking reflex (UR)
with nipple (CS)

AFTER CONDITIONING

(D) Show baby the bottle with nipple:

 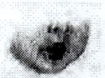

Sight of bottle — — — —elicits — — — — — > Sucking reflex (UR)
with nipple (CS)

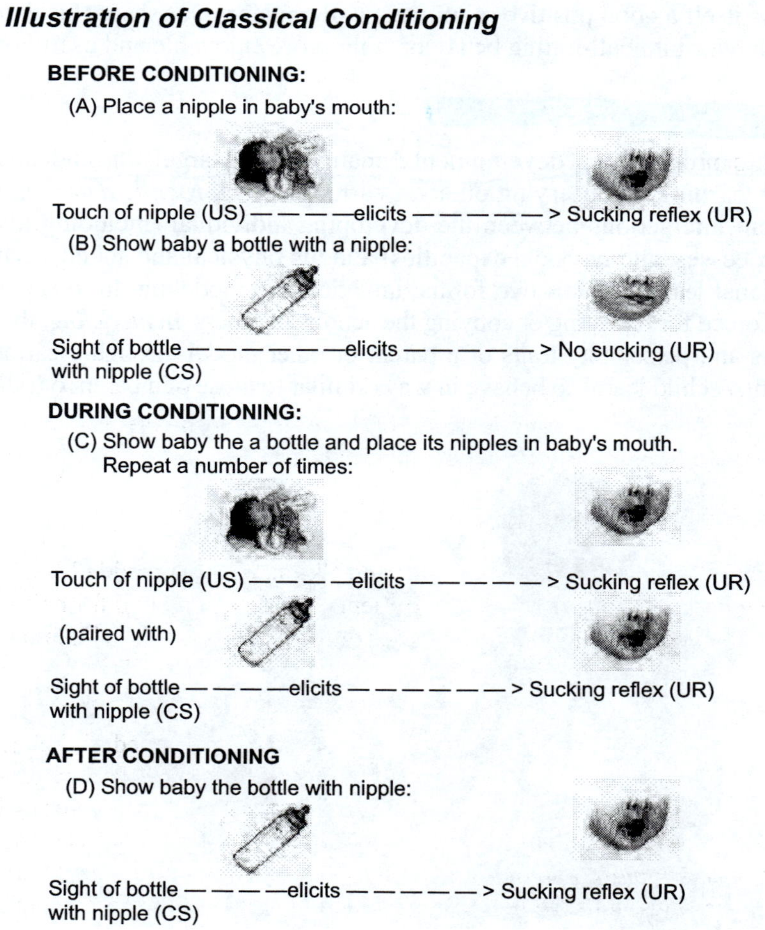

FIGURE 2.1

Illustration of Classical Conditioning

In this example, the nipple in the baby's mouth is an unconditioned stimulus (US), which with no prior conditioning brings about, or elicits, the sucking reflex, an unconditioned response (UR). (a) The nipple in the mouth elicits a sucking reflex. (b) The sight of a bottle is a neutral stimulus (NS) and has no effect. (c) Once the sight of the bottle (NS) is repeatedly paired with the nipple in the mouth (US), the sight of the bottle becomes a conditioned (learned) stimulus (CS), which now elicits sucking, the conditioned response (CR).

Chapter 2 Theories of Development

and misbehaving at the dinner table. By quieting down once she gets her parents' attention, she may actually be negatively reinforcing (increasing) her parents' attention-giving responses by removing the unpleasant stimulus of crying and misbehaving. Furthermore, Sarah's parents are providing positive reinforcement in the form of attention for crying and misbehaving at the dinner table.

Punishment weakens or suppresses a behavioral response by either adding an unpleasant stimulus (a *positive punishment*) or removing a pleasurable one (a *negative punishment*) following the response's occurrence. Taking away television privileges (negative punishment) and adding an extra chore (positive punishment) following a child's misbehavior are both forms of punishment. *Extinction* refers to the disappearance of a response when a reinforcer that was maintaining a behavior is removed. Often, before the undesirable behavior reduces in the face of extinction, the person will actually increase the behavior in an attempt to elicit a response. This is known as an *extinction burst*. Frequently, the best way to extinguish an undesirable response is to ignore it, even in the face of an extinction burst, and reinforce an alternative, more desirable response. For example, at the grocery store, Bea cries for potato chips. To calm Bea down, Amal buys her chips (positively reinforcing the behavior of crying). During their next trip to the grocery store, Bea cries for chips again. Amal ignores her crying daughter, so Bea begins to scream (an extinction burst). Amal is faced with a difficult decision: If she gives in now, she has just positively reinforced a worse behavior. If Amal continues to ignore the behavior, Bea will eventually stop, at which time Amal can praise Bea for being good (positive reinforcement).

Shaping occurs when a child learns to perform new responses not already in his repertoire, or "collection." This is achieved by starting with an existing response and then modifying, or shaping, it by reinforcing small changes that bring it closer and closer to the desired behavior. Consider a dad who wishes to teach his seven-year-old daughter to hit a ball with a bat. Because she already can swing a bat, careful encouragement (a good positive reinforcer) for better and better swings and eventually for actually making contact with the ball (which is itself a good positive reinforcer) will transform, or shape, his daughter's bat-swinging behavior into ball-hitting behavior, a far more enjoyable and useful one.

Social Cognitive Learning Theory

Albert Bandura proposes that developmental change occurs largely through **observational learning**, or learning by observing others. Learning is *reciprocally determined*, meaning it results from interactions between the developing individual (including his behaviors, cognitive processes, and physical capacities) and his physical and social environment.

Observational learning takes two forms: imitation and modeling. In *imitation*, a child is directly reinforced for repeating or copying the actions of others. In *modeling*, the child learns the behaviors and personality traits of a parent or other model through vicarious (indirect) reinforcement. A child learns to behave in ways similar to those of a parent or other model by

punishment According to Skinner, any stimulus that temporarily suppresses the response that it follows.

observational learning The tendency of a child to imitate or model behavior and attitudes of parents and other individuals.

Observational learning likely plays an important role as these children learn to prepare dough.
Source: Margarita Borodina/Shutterstock.com.

> **What Do You Think?**
>
> Think of some examples of developmental changes in a young child's behavior that might be accurately explained using behavioral learning theories. Then think of an example of a developmental change that does not seem to fit the behavioral model.

merely observing the model receiving reinforcement for his or her actions. How influential the model will be depends on a variety of factors, including the model's relationship to the child, his or her personal characteristics, and how the child perceives the model (Bandura, 1989; Miller, 2011). Children's levels of cognitive development strongly influence their ability to observe, remember, and later perform in ways similar to the models they have watched.

The social cognitive learning approach has been useful in explaining gender development, the development of aggression, and the developmental impact of television and other media. It has also been useful to counselors and therapists who work with problems in the parent-child relationship and with children experiencing a variety of behavioral and adjustment difficulties in both outpatient and residential treatment settings.

Applications of Learning Theories Throughout the Lifespan

Pavlov's and Skinner's behavioral learning theories have proved particularly useful in helping to understand development from infancy through adolescence. For example, to study the development of object perception among young infants, classical conditioning has been used to teach infants to respond to different stimuli by sucking on a pacifier. Operant conditioning and observational learning have guided the study of cognitive development during the first two years (Chapter 4) and helped to explain the development of autonomy in infancy and toddlerhood (Chapter 5). **Behavior modification**, a specific set of techniques based on operant conditioning and social cognitive learning, has been essential in helping school-age children and their families deal with *attention deficit hyperactivity disorder (ADHD)* (Chapter 8) and in helping adolescents with eating disorders and delinquent behavior (Chapters 10 and 11). Both behavioral and social cognitive learning theories can help to explain how language is acquired during early childhood (Chapter 6). Social cognitive learning theories help us to understand the role of vicarious (indirect) reinforcement and self-reinforcement in early childhood play, and the limitations of using spanking and other forms of punishment during early childhood (Chapter 7).

behavior modification
A body of techniques based on behaviorism for changing or eliminating specific behaviors.

Cognitive Developmental Theories

In this section, we discuss three theoretical approaches to cognitive development: Piaget's cognitive theory, neo-Piagetian theories, and information-processing theory. All of these theories share a strong focus on how thinking and problem-solving skills develop and how such cognitive activities contribute to the overall process of development.

According to Piaget, children think in qualitatively different ways as they develop. As illustrated in the two photos, very young children usually think about objects and experiences by looking and touching, whereas many adolescents can plan and reason abstractly.
Sources: (left) Ami Parikh/Shutterstock.com; *(right)* Golden Pixels LLC/Shutterstock.com.

Chapter 2 Theories of Development

Piaget's Cognitive Theory

Jean Piaget (1896–1980) was one of the most influential figures in developmental psychology. Just as Freud's ideas radically changed thinking about human emotional development, Piaget's ideas have changed our understanding of the development of human thinking and problem solving, or *cognition*.

Key Principles of Piaget's Theory

Piaget believed thinking develops in a series of increasingly complex stages, or periods, each of which incorporates and revises those that precede it. Table 2.4 summarizes Piaget's cognitive stages and developmental processes. We look at his theory in greater detail in the chapters on cognitive development in childhood and adolescence.

What exactly makes a person develop from one stage of thinking and problem solving to the next? Piaget believed three processes are involved: (1) direct learning, (2) social transmission, and (3) maturation.

Direct learning results when a person actively responds to and interprets new problems and experiences based on patterns of thought and action he already knows. Piaget called these existing patterns *schemes*. A **scheme** is a systematic pattern of thoughts, actions, and problem-solving strategies that helps the individual deal with a particular intellectual challenge or situation. According to Piaget, an infant's first understanding of the world is based on a limited number of *innate schemes* made up of simple patterns of unlearned reflexes that are inherited at birth, such as sucking, grasping, and looking. These schemes rapidly change as the infant encounters new experiences through the complementary processes of *assimilation* and *accommodation*.

Assimilation is the process by which an infant interprets and responds to a new experience or situation in terms of an existing scheme. For example, a two-month-old baby who is presented with a bottle for the first time understands what is needed to suck from the bottle based on her existing sucking scheme for her mother's breast. The infant has assimilated a new situation, sucking from a bottle, into her existing scheme for sucking. As children grow older, schemes involve increasingly complex mental processes.

scheme According to Piaget, a behavior or thought that represents a group of ideas and events in a person's experience.

assimilation According to Piaget, a method by which a person responds to new experiences by using existing concepts to interpret new ideas and experiences.

TABLE 2.4 Piaget's Cognitive Stages and Developmental Processes

Cognitive Stage	Approximate Age	Description
Sensorimotor	Birth–2 years	Coordination of sensory and motor activity; achievement of object permanence
Preoperational	2–7 years	Use of language and symbolic representation; egocentric view of the world
Concrete operational	7–11 years	Solution of concrete problems through logical operations
Formal operational	11–adulthood	Systematic solution of actual and hypothetical problems using abstract symbols

Developmental Processes

The earliest and most primitive patterns, or schemes, of thinking, problem solving, and constructing reality are inborn. As a result of both maturation and experience, thinking develops through a series of increasingly sophisticated stages, each incorporating the achievements in preceding stages. These changes occur through the processes of assimilation, in which new problems are solved using existing schemes, and accommodation, in which existing schemes are altered or adapted to meet new challenges. Together, these processes create a state of cognitive balance, or *equilibrium,* in which the person's thinking becomes increasingly stable, general, and harmoniously adjusted to the environment.

For example, a preschooler sees a truck but calls it a "car" because the concept of *car* is already well established in his thinking. In **accommodation**, a child changes existing schemes, or ways of thinking, when faced with new ideas or situations in which the old schemes no longer work. Instead of calling a truck by the wrong name, the preschooler searches for a new name and begins to realize that some four-wheeled objects are not cars.

According to Piaget, development results from the interplay of assimilation and accommodation, a process called *adaptation*. **Adaptation** results when schemes are deepened or broadened by assimilation and stretched or modified by accommodation.

Social transmission, Piaget's second explanation for development, is the process through which one's thinking is influenced by learning from social contact with and observation of others rather than through direct experience. *Physical maturation*, Piaget's third explanation for developmental change, refers to the biologically determined changes in physical and neurological development that occur relatively independently of specific experiences. For example, a child must reach a certain minimal level of biological development to be able to name an object.

Although research at least partially supports many of Piaget's ideas, it has found a number of shortcomings. One problem is how to explain why, in many instances, children master tasks that are logically equivalent at very different points in their development. It is also hard to explain why a child's cognitive performances on two logically similar tasks are often very different. A third problem is that Piaget's exclusive emphasis on the predetermined "logical" aspects of children's thinking often does not match the actual thought processes children appear to use and largely ignores the social, emotional, and cultural factors that influence the process (Case, 1992; Rogoff & Chavajay, 1995). Finally, Piaget's theory fails to recognize that cognitive development continues after adolescence, as we will see in Chapter 13. Some of these issues are discussed in the "A Multicultural View" feature later in the chapter.

Neo-Piagetian Approaches

Neo-Piagetian theories are new or revised models of Piaget's basic approach. Robbie Case, for example, proposes that cognitive development results from increases in the child's *mental space*, that is, the maximum number of schemes the child can apply simultaneously at any given time. During early childhood, most cognitive structures are rather specific and concrete, such as drawing with a pencil, throwing a ball, or counting a set of objects. As the structures guiding these actions become coordinated with one another, they form new, more efficient, higher-level cognitive structures, which in turn begin to be coordinated with other, similar structures. Thus, a child's ability to use increasingly general cognitive structures enables him to think more abstractly. Different forms of the same logical problem may require different processing skills and capacities. As a result, a child's performance on two logically similar tasks may differ significantly, and mastery of each task may occur at very different points in her development (Case, 1991b, 1991c, 1991d).

Kurt Fischer, another neo-Piagetian theorist, accepts Piaget's basic idea of stages, but uses specific *skills* instead of *schemes* to describe the cognitive structures children use in particular problem-solving tasks or sets of tasks. The breadth of a skill is determined by both the level of maturation a child's central nervous system has reached and the range of specific learning environments to which the child has been exposed (Fischer, 1994; Fischer & Pipp, 1984a, 1984b). Thus, the type of support a child receives from parents, teachers, and others in the environment plays an important role in skill acquisition. Case's "breadth of skill" idea has much in common with Lev Vygotsky's "zone of proximal development," discussed later in this chapter.

Information-Processing Theory

Another alternative to Piaget's cognitive theory is **information-processing theory**, which focuses on the precise, detailed features or steps involved in mental activities (Klahr, 1989; Seifert, 1993). Like a computer, the mind is viewed as having distinct parts that make unique contributions to thinking in a specific order.

---

accommodation According to Piaget, the process of modifying existing ideas or action-skills to fit new experiences.

adaptation Piaget's term for the process by which development occurs; concepts are deepened or broadened by assimilation and stretched or modified by accommodation.

information-processing theory Explanations of cognition that focus on the precise, detailed features or steps of mental activities. These theories often use computers as models for human thinking.

Key Principles of Information-Processing Theory

Figure 2.2 shows one information-processing model of human thinking. According to this model, when a person tries to solve a problem, she first takes in information from her environment through her senses. The information gained in this way is held briefly in the *sensory memory,* the first memory store. The sensory memory records information as it originally receives it, but the information fades or disappears within a fraction of a second unless the person processes it further.

Information to which a person pays special attention is transferred to *short-term memory (STM),* the second memory store. The short-term memory corresponds roughly to "momentary awareness," or whatever the person is thinking about at a particular instant. Short-term memory is often called "working memory" because this is the memory store where information is being acted upon. The short-term/working memory can hold only limited amounts of information—in fact, only about seven pieces of it at any one time. After about twenty seconds, information in short-term/working memory is either forgotten or processed further. At this point, it moves into *long-term memory (LTM),* the third memory store. So if you remember what you had for breakfast this morning, information about the taste and smell of your cereal entered your sensory memory for a brief moment. Some of that information was transferred to your short-term/working memory, and then some of that information was transferred to your long-term memory, where it stayed until you read the beginning of the previous sentence, which queued retrieval back into your short-term/working memory.

Information can be saved permanently in long-term memory. But doing so requires various cognitive strategies, such as rehearsing information repeatedly or organizing it into familiar categories. Unlike short-term/working memory, long-term memory probably has unlimited capacity for storage of new information, as demonstrated by a small number of individuals with highly superior autobiographical memory who can remember immense detail from their own past (LePort et al., 2012). The problem for most people comes in retrieving information, which requires that we remember how it was stored in the first place.

Developmental Changes in Information Processing

As children grow older, they experience several cognitive changes that allow them to process information more efficiently and comprehensively. The most important developmental change in information processing is the acquisition of control processes. *Control processes* direct an individual's attention toward particular input from the sensory register and guide the response to new information once it enters short-term memory. Usually control processes organize information in short-term memory. Sometimes control processes also relate

FIGURE 2.2
An Information-Processing Model of Learning

Information from the environment first enters the sensory memory. With the aid of control processes, it is then transferred to short-term/working memory, where it is either forgotten or processed further, and then to long-term memory, where it is stored for future use.

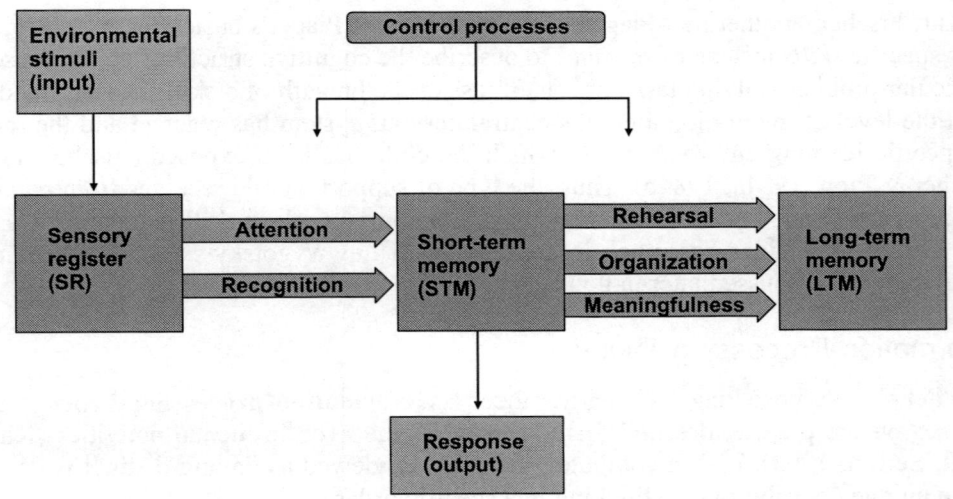

An Information-Processing Model of Learning

information in STM to previously learned knowledge from LTM, such as when a teenager hears a song on the radio and notes its similarity to another song heard previously.

As children grow older they develop **metacognition**, an awareness and understanding of how thinking and learning work. Metacognition assists learning in a number of ways. First, it allows a person to assess how difficult a problem or learning task will be and to plan appropriate ways to approach it. More specifically, metacognition involves knowledge of self, knowledge of task variables, and knowledge of which information-processing strategies are effective in which situations (Forrest-Pressley et al., 1985).

In addition to metacognition, children acquire many other kinds of knowledge. Some children gradually become comparative experts in particular areas, such as math, sports, or getting along with peers. *Knowledge base* refers to children's current fund of knowledge and skills in various areas. A child's knowledge base in one area makes acquiring further knowledge and skills in the same area easier because the child can relate new information to prior information more meaningfully. Metacognition and an expanding knowledge base contribute to cognitive development throughout the lifespan.

According to many information-processing theorists, changes in the knowledge base are not general, stage-like transformations such as those proposed by Piaget (Chi et al., 1989). Instead, they are specialized developments of expertise based on the gradual accumulation of specific information and skills related to a field, including information and skills related to how knowledge in the field is organized and learned efficiently. A very good chess player is an expert in chess but is not necessarily advanced in other activities or areas of knowledge. Her skill probably reflects long hours spent in one major activity: playing chess games. Each hour of play enables her to build a larger knowledge base about chess; memories of board patterns, moves, and game strategies that worked in the past.

> **metacognition** Knowledge and thinking about cognition, how learning and memory operate in everyday situations, and how one can improve cognitive performance.

Applications of Cognitive Developmental Theories Throughout the Lifespan

Piaget's cognitive theory and the more recent Neo-Piagetian approaches have provided the central conceptual framework for understanding the development of thinking and problem solving throughout the lifespan. In Chapter 4, for example, Piaget's theory will help explain sensorimotor development during the first two years, and a "Working With" interview with Gillian Luppiwiski, an infant care provider, will discuss how cognitive theory can be used to foster thinking and intellectual development in infants. Cognitive theory will also help explain the development of symbolic thought and language among preschoolers (Chapter 7) and how growth in thinking and problem-solving abilities affects relationships with peers in middle childhood (Chapter 9). In Chapter 10, we will see how cognitive theory is used to design programs to foster critical thinking among adolescents; to better understand *adolescent egocentrism, imaginary audience,* and *personal fable;* and to understand moral development and the ethics of care during adolescence.

Cognitive developmental theories have been increasingly helpful in explaining intellectual functioning during early, middle, and later adulthood. In Chapter 12 we will explore the question of whether cognitive development culminates *informal operational thinking,* Piaget's fourth and final stage, or *a fifth stage of cognitive development* is needed to capture the ability to define new problems in *new and often contradictory ways* that develops during the adult years.

We will also explore Warner Schaie's contextual theory, which suggests that at different periods of adulthood, adults use their knowledge in different ways that depend on their changing patterns of commitments to work, family, and community life. We will also discover that during middle adulthood, *crystallized intelligence*, which includes learned cognitive processes and abilities such as vocabulary, general information, and word fluency, improves with age, *while fluid, intelligence*, the ability to process new information in novel situations, peaks during adolescence and decreases with age for most people (Chapter 14). Finally, we will see how in later adulthood, *cognitive mechanics*—intellectual problems in which culture-based knowledge and skills such as reading, writing, language comprehension, and professional skills are primary—can help people in their seventies maintain and even improve their memory (Chapter 16).

> **What Do You Think?**
>
> How might the cognitive approach be useful to an elementary school math teacher who is preparing lesson plans? Would this theoretical approach be of any use in a health education class?

Contextual Developmental Theories

Contextual approaches view development as a process of reciprocal, patterned interactions between the individual and his or her physical and social environment. A leading example of this approach is the ecological systems theory of Urie Bronfenbrenner. As we saw in Chapter 1, *ecological systems theory* proposes that a person's development is influenced by four interactive and overlapping contextual levels:

1. the *microsystem*—the face-to-face physical and social situations that directly affect the person (family, classroom, workplace);
2. the *mesosystem*—connections and relationships among the person's microsystems;
3. the *exosystem*—the settings or situations that indirectly influence the person (spouse's place of employment, the local school board, the local government); and
4. the *macrosystem*—the values, beliefs, and policies of society and culture that provide frameworks, or "blueprints," for organizing one's life and indirectly influence the person through their effects on the exosystem, mesosystem, and microsystem.

Another interesting example of contextual theory was developed by the Russian psychologist Lev Vygotsky (1896–1934). Vygotsky was interested in how changing historical and cultural contexts within which children's activities occur influence their cognitive development. According to Vygotsky, higher mental functions grow out of the social interactions and dialogues that take place between a child and parents, teachers, and other representatives of the culture. Through these interactions, children internalize increasingly mature and effective ways of thinking and problem solving. Some of these changes occur through discoveries that the child initiates on her own (Karpov & Haywood, 1998).

Many developmental tasks, however, occur in what Vygotsky called the *zone of proximal development*. The **zone of proximal development** refers to the range of tasks that a child cannot yet accomplish without active assistance from parents and others with greater knowledge, and the framework of support and assistance is called *scaffolding* (Blanck, 1990; Rogoff, 1990; Wertsch, 1989). See the "A Multicultural View" feature for a discussion of culture and cognitive development.

Glen Elder (1998), a pioneer in the study of development over the life course, suggests that education, work, and family create the **social trajectories**, or pathways, that guide individual development. Important life transitions, such as school entry, marriage, and the birth of a child, give these social trajectories distinctive shape and meaning for each individual. Historical changes, such as wars, economic depressions, and technological innovations, shape the social trajectories of family, education, and work, which in turn influence individual development. Though individuals are able to select the paths they follow by asserting their *human agency*, or free will, these choices are not made in a social vacuum and depend on the opportunities and constraints of social structure and culture, which themselves change over time (Elder, 1998; Hernandez, 1997; Coll et al., 1996).

Applications of Contextual Developmental Theories Throughout the Lifespan

Contextual theories have become increasingly useful in understanding how individual development over the life course is influenced by and interacts with the changing life contexts in which development occurs. The discussion of Jodi and her multiple contexts of

---

zone of proximal development According to Vygotsky, the level of difficulty at which problems are too hard for children to solve alone but not too hard when given support from adults or more competent peers.

social trajectory The pathway or direction that development takes over an individual's life course, which is influenced by the school. work, family, and other important social settings in which he or she participates.

> **A Multicultural View**
>
> ### Street Children: Comparing Paraguay and North America
>
> According to Lev Vygotsky's theory, cognitive development is largely "context specific," meaning it must be understood in terms of the particular social, cultural, and historical processes of people's everyday experiences (Vygotsky, 1978; Wertsch, 1985). Individuals growing up in different societies, cultures, and historical periods are likely to display differences in how they think and solve problems and in how cognitive development occurs. This view is very different from that of Jean Piaget, who believed cognitive development is largely "universal," meaning all individuals progress through the same developmental stages at approximately the same ages relatively independently of their particular situations and experiences.
>
> Research based primarily on observations of children from Western industrialized societies, where formal schooling is heavily stressed, has generally supported Piaget's ideas. Studies of children growing up in other societies and cultures, however, have been more consistent with Vygotsky's views. Children growing up in cultures with little formal schooling have been found to take much longer to achieve the *concrete operational stage* of thinking and appear unable to achieve the *formal operational stage* of thinking, Piaget's final stage (Rogoff & Chavajay, 1995). Michael Cole, a pioneer in studying culture and cognitive development, concluded that the superior performance of children who had formal schooling was due to the common structure and activities of schooling and tests of cognitive development rather than to the effects of schooling on children's thinking (Cole, 1990).
>
> Performance on tasks that require participants to classify test items into categories is one good example. Whereas individuals from Western countries typically classify test items based on their type (for example, putting animals in one group, food items in another, and tools in a third), individuals in many other nations sort the same items based on their function (for example, putting a hoe with a potato because a hoe is used to dig up a potato) (Rogoff & Chavajay, 1995).
>
> Logical tasks that require a person to draw conclusions based on abstract, hypothetical reasoning rather than on direct personal experience are another example. Nonliterate individuals who are able to make excellent logical judgments when dealing with the immediate, practical problems of their everyday life experiences may, for cultural reasons, be unwilling to demonstrate similar reasoning abilities in situations that are not culturally familiar. The following example, taken from an interview with a nonliterate Central Asian peasant, illustrates this point:
>
> *Interviewer:* In the Far North, where there is snow, all bears are white. Novaya Zemlya is in the Far North and there is always snow there. What color are the bears there?
>
> *Peasant:* ... We always speak of only what we see; we don't talk about what we haven't seen.
>
> *Interviewer:* But what do my words imply?
>
> *Peasant:* Well, it's like this: our tsar isn't like yours, and yours isn't like ours. Your words can be answered only by someone who was there, and if a person wasn't there, he can't say anything on the basis of your words.
>
> *Interviewer:* But on the basis of my words—in the North, where there is always snow, the bears are white—can you gather what kind of bears there are in Novaya Zemlya?
>
> *Peasant:* If a man was sixty or eighty and had seen a white bear and had told me about it, he could be believed, but I've never seen one, and hence, I can't say. (Luria, 1976, pp. 108–109, quoted in Rogoff & Chavajay, 1995, p. 861)
>
> Differences in performance of common cognitive tasks may also reflect cultural differences in how a problem is defined and how it should be solved (Goodnow, 1976). European Americans, for example, believe intelligence involves technical rather than social skills. Kipsigis (Kenyan) parents include responsible participation in family and social life in their definition. For the Ifaluk of the western Pacific, intelligence means not only having knowledge of good social behavior but also performing it. Ugandan villagers associate intelligence with being slow, careful, and active, whereas westernized groups associate it with speed (Rogoff & Chavajay, 1995).
>
> Future research will provide additional evidence regarding the social and cultural contexts of cognitive development.

development in Chapter 1 is an excellent illustration of how Urie Bronfenbrenner's ecological systems theory helps us understand individual development. Ecological systems theory has been especially useful for understanding the multiple factors and contexts involved in divorce, teen parenthood, and juvenile delinquency and for designing programs to assist troubled adolescents and to prevent those problems from occurring (Chapter 11).

Similarly, the future developmental changes that Elizabeth, the preschooler discussed at the beginning of this chapter, is likely to experience illustrate Glen Elder's ideas about *social trajectories*. For example, entry into first grade, transitions to middle school, high school, and college, entering the world of work, getting married, and having a child are all likely to be important steps in the pathways that will help give her long-term development distinctive meaning and form. At the same time, political, economic, and technological changes in society will influence Elizabeth's family, education, and work, which in turn will influence her behaviors and the particular directions her developmental choices take. Although Elizabeth will have considerable potential to assert her agency and freely choose the paths she will follow, such life choices will not be made in a social vacuum and will also depend on the opportunities and constraints that she encounters.

Vygotsky's sociocultural approach and his concept of *zone of proximal development* help us to understand the development of problem-solving skills and intelligence during middle childhood (Chapter 8). Contextual cognitive approaches such as Schaie's stages of adult thinking have highlighted how cognitive development is organized by external psychosocial contexts, including the demands of work and family, rather than by internal organizing structures. As discussed earlier in this chapter, these theories focus on how adults use their knowledge at different periods of adulthood, such as for achieving specific personal goals in young adulthood.

Ethological Theory

Ethological theory has played an important role in studying the contribution of differences in *temperament* that are observable at birth to development through childhood and adolescence. It has also contributed to the study of the important role *attachment* plays in the development of relationships from early infancy through the life course, a topic we noted in our earlier discussion of lifespan applications of psychodynamic theory.

The ethological approach attempts to apply the principles of evolutionary biology and ethology to behavioral and psychological characteristics (Ainsworth & Bowlby, 1991; Leckman & Mayes, 1998). This approach has its roots in *ethology,* the study of various animal species in their natural environments. Ethology emphasizes the ways widely shared species behaviors evolved through the process of natural selection and adaptation to different developmental contexts to ensure species survival. Developmental ethologists are interested in how certain behavioral and psychological traits or predispositions that appear to be widely shared among human beings may have developed to help ensure the evolutionary survival of the human species.

An underlying assumption is that just as human evolution has imposed certain constraints on our physical development, it may have influenced the range and nature of our behavioral development. Developmental ethologists also attempt to understand how individual differences in traits such as aggressiveness, shyness, competitiveness, and altruism reciprocally interact with the social context to mutually influence development.

One area of ethological interest has been the study of infant emotions and *temperament,* relatively enduring individual differences in infant responsiveness and self-regulation that appear to be present at birth. (See Chapter 5 for a discussion of temperament.) A second important application is the study of infant-caregiver *attachment,* the mutually reinforcing system of physical, social, and emotional stimulation and support between infant and caregiver. This pattern of attachment behaviors has also been observed in other species, and ethologists presume it has survival value for humans as well (e.g., Bowlby, 1948). (See Chapter 5 for a discussion of attachment.) Attachment has importance throughout the lifespan and is discussed again in Chapters 13, 15, and 17 on psychosocial development in adulthood.

Adulthood and Lifespan Developmental Theories

In this section, we look at two theoretical approaches that focus on development during adulthood and across the entire lifespan: the *normative-crisis model* (also called the *stage-theory model)* and the *timing-of-events model.* As we will see, though these two models differ in important ways, they share the assumption that the process of individual developmental change does not end with adolescence but continues throughout a person's adulthood and old age, that is, throughout the life cycle.

> **What Do You Think?**
>
> To what degree does your informal theory of development include the different developmental contexts proposed by the theorists discussed in this section? Are there any you would add? Any you would delete?

Normative-Crisis Model of Development

The **normative-crisis model** of development assumes developmental change occurs in distinct stages that all individuals follow in the same sequence. Each successive stage is qualitatively unique from all other stages, is increasingly complex and more fully developed, and integrates the changes and accomplishments of earlier stages. This model generally presumes that developmental stages are at least in part influenced by biologically driven maturational changes.

Erik Erikson's psychosocial theory, discussed earlier in this chapter, is a good example. The crisis of *intimacy versus isolation*, which occurs during early adulthood, is discussed more fully in Chapter 13; the crisis of *generativity versus stagnation* during middle adulthood is covered in Chapter 15; and the crisis of *integrity versus despair* of late adulthood is discussed in Chapter 17. Here we will briefly look at two other normative-crisis views of adult development: George Vaillant's *adaptive mechanism* approach and Daniel Levinson's *seasons of adult lives* approach. We will look more closely at these other theories of adult development in Chapters 13 and 15.

The normative-crisis lifespan model shares with psychodynamic theories a focus on the importance of impulses within the individual that lead to developmental change. Although the number and content of developmental periods or stages differ for each theory, each approach views a given developmental period as focused on an internally motivated crisis. In Erikson's theory, for example, the crisis of early adulthood involves the need for intimacy to overcome isolation; in middle adulthood, it concerns the need to experience generativity rather than stagnation; and in late adulthood, the crisis involves the need for integrity to overcome the despair associated with the losses of old age and the awareness of one's mortality.

normative-crisis model Explanations that view developmental change in terms of a series of distinct periods or stages that are influenced by physical and cognitive performance.

George Vaillant: Styles of Adult Coping

Based on a long-term, longitudinal study of a sample of 268 men, George Vaillant concluded that development is a lifelong process that is influenced mainly by relationships with others and by the adaptive mechanisms, or *coping styles*, that people used to deal with life events. Mature coping styles include sublimation, the redirecting of anxiety and unacceptable impulses toward acceptable goals, and altruism, the offering of help and support to others with no expectation of personal gain. According to Vaillant, the use of mature coping styles increases with age and is most likely to occur among individuals who have healthy brains and have experienced long-term, loving relationships (Vaillant, 1977; Vaillant & Vaillant, 1990), a finding confirmed with samples that included women and more socioeconomic and racial diversity than the original sample (Cramer, 2003). Table 2.5 summarizes Vaillant's developmental periods.

Daniel Levinson: Seasons of Adult Lives

Based on his biographical study of the lives of forty men between ages thirty-five and forty-five from a variety of backgrounds, Levinson identified three eras, or "seasons," in male adult life: (1) *early adulthood,* (2) *middle adulthood,* and (3) *late adulthood.* During each era, a new "life structure" is established that reflects the person's significant relationships with others and the desires, values, commitment, energy, and skills invested in them. The life structure evolves through a relatively orderly sequence during the adult years. Changes occur within each period, and each era brings transitions that provide an opportunity to reassess and improve on the preceding era (Levinson, 1986).

Chapter 2 Theories of Development

TABLE 2.5 George Vaillant's Phases of Adult Development

Phase	Approximate Age	Description
Age of establishment	20–30	Increasing autonomy from parents; marriage, parenthood, and establishing more intimate friendships
Career consolidation	20–40	Consolidating and strengthening marriage and career; devotion to hard work and career advancement
Midlife transition	40–50	Painful reassessment and reordering of the experiences of adolescence and young adulthood; heightened self-awareness and exploration of forgotten "inner self" opening the way for achieving greater generativity
Midlife	50 and older	Leaving behind compulsive involvement with occupational apprenticeships; becoming increasingly self-reflective, nurturant, and expressive

Table 2.6 presents Levinson's three eras of adult development. In Chapters 13 and 15, we will take a more detailed look at his theory and assess its relevance for adult development among women.

Timing-of-Events Model

timing-of-events model Explanations that view developmental change in terms of important life events such as marriage and parenthood that people are expected to complete according to a culturally determined time table.

The **timing-of-events model** of development views *life events* as markers, or indicators, of developmental change. Life events may be normative or nonnormative. *Normative life events* are transitions that follow an age-appropriate social timetable; individuals create an internalized *social clock* that tells them whether they are "on time" in following that schedule (Neugarten, 1968). Normative life events include work, marriage, and parenthood during early adulthood, career advancement in middle adulthood, and physical decline, retirement, and widowhood during late adulthood.

Many life events, however, are nonnormative and less predictable. A *nonnormative life event* occurs at any point in time in a person's life and may include normative events that occur "off time," such as marrying "late," being widowed as a young adult, or returning to college in middle adulthood. Because of its focus on the importance of external contexts

Marriage represents an important normative event in the lives of a couple and in the lives of their parents and other family members.
Source: Monkey Business Images/Shutterstock.com.

Part 1 Beginnings

TABLE 2.6 Daniel Levinson's Eras of Adult Development

Era	Phase	Approximate Age	Description
Childhood and Adolescence (birth–17)			
Early Adult Era (17–45)	Early adult transition	17–22	Reassessing preadulthood and preparing for early adulthood
	Early life		Entering the adult world and building a first life structure structure. Novice phase: forming and living out the dream of adult accomplishment; forming mentor relationships; developing an occupation; forming love relationships. marriage, and family
	Age 30 transition	28–33	Reassessing and improving early life structure; transition may be smooth or painful
	Culminating life structure	33–40	Settling down: building a second adult life structure. Establishing occupational goals and plans for achieving them; becoming one's own person: achieving greater independence and self-sufficiency
	Midlife transition	40–45	Completing early adulthood and preparing for middle adulthood. Reappraising past progress toward achieving the dream; revising the dream and changing lifestyle around the themes of a new life structure. Midlife individuation through better resolving polarities of young/old, destruction/creation, masculine/feminine, attachment/separateness
Middle Adult Era (40–60)	Early life structure	45–50	Entering middle adulthood. Making and committing to new choices and building a life structure around them
	Age 50 transition	50–55	Modifying and improving the entry life structure
	Culminating life structure	55–60	Completion of middle adulthood
Late Adult Era (60 and older)	Late adult transition	60–65	Preparation for late adulthood

and conditions, the timing-of-events model has helped us to understand variations in adult development that are not adequately accounted for by the normative-crisis model and has drawn our attention to the developmental importance of social expectations and context in childhood and adolescence as well (Elder, 1998; Lerner, 1996).

The timing of events model also reflects an awareness of two important ways in which the capabilities, life experiences, and developmental changes of adulthood tend to differ from those of childhood and adolescence. First, the changes during the adult years appear to be less closely tied to the substantial and predictable physical and cognitive maturational changes that characterize childhood and adolescence; rather, they seem to be more closely linked to the major social and psychological conditions, events, and experiences that adults encounter, many of which are considerably less predictable. Second, the physical, cognitive, and psychosocial competencies of adults allow them to play a much more active and self-conscious role in directing their own development through the decisions and choices they make. For example, individual decisions about whom (and when) to marry, whether or not to have children, where to live, what type of work to do, and what social, political, religious, and lifestyle commitments to pursue can all significantly affect development.

> **WORKING WITH** Jeffrey Friedman, Clinical Social Worker
>
> ### The Value of Developmental Theory for Helping Children, Adolescents, and Their Families
>
> Jeffrey Friedman, a clinical social worker, specializes in child development. He was interviewed in his office at a community mental health center, where he helps children, adolescents, and families with their developmental problems and consults with pediatricians about the developmental problems they encounter in their practices.
>
> **Robert:** *Do you find developmental theories useful in your work?*
>
> **Jeffrey:** They help a lot if you use them in a practical way and don't treat them like cookbook recipes to follow in every case. Theories also help me to avoid mistakes. They add things that I couldn't figure out from my own experience and common sense. They correct myths about people that most of us are taught to believe. Sometimes they remind me to keep the whole person in mind when I am focused on a single pressing problem, and sometimes they help me to divide a big, vague problem into small, discrete parts that are easier to work with.
>
> **Robert:** *That's very interesting. How did this come about?*
>
> **Jeffrey:** Before I had studied development, when I spent time with children, I assumed that they thought the same way adults do, because I couldn't remember how I thought when I was their age. Reading the work of theorists who studied children closely and working under the guidance of teachers who applied these theories has helped me to understand better the peculiar ways in which children think about and experience the world.
>
> **Robert:** *Could you give an example?*
>
> **Jeffrey:** Think of the way a child conceptualizes death. When a child talks about her uncle dying and being buried, you might assume that she kind of knows what death is. If you haven't read somebody's discussion about children's understanding of death, it probably wouldn't occur to ask the child what she meant so that you could help her feel better about it. Because if you *did* ask her, she might very well have told you that they're going to plant her uncle in the ground, and next spring he's going to grow up like some flower and she'll have him back again.
>
> **Robert:** *Or she might think that her uncle went to sleep, but since she doesn't understand the difference between death and sleep, could be terrified that if she goes to sleep, she might also die.*
>
> **Jeffrey:** Exactly.
>
> **Robert:** *How do you apply theories when you're working with children and their families?*
>
> **Jeffrey:** Intimate love relationships involving parents, children, other family members, and very close friends turn out to be central to a person's psychological and social well-being. Unlike more casual or superficial relationships, which we can understand intuitively pretty well, more intense love relationships are often impossible to understand based solely on what a person consciously thinks and feels about them. You find people in these family relationships all tied up in knots, doing things they don't expect or even want to do, feeling things they don't want to feel. For children, the feelings and experiences of their primary caregivers turn out to have an enormous impact on development.
>
> **Robert:** *As I recall, you once worked with a group of children whose problems in their relationships with their parents were so severe that they actually stopped growing. What was this problem called?*
>
> **Jeffrey:** It's called psychosocial dwarfism. I'm glad that you remembered that, because it's a very dramatic instance of how psychological theory helped to explain a very perplexing disorder!
>
> **Robert:** *How so? Can you give me some details?*
>
> **Jeffrey:** They were young kids, mostly six, seven, and eight years old and some as old as ten or eleven. They all were extremely small, and most were two or three years below the normal height and weight for children their age. They were also

Developmental Theories Compared: Implications for the Student

We have reached the end of our review of several of the most important theories in developmental psychology. What conclusions might we draw? In what ways are these theories useful as we investigate lifespan development in the remainder of this book? As we suggested at the beginning of this chapter, theories are useful because they help us systematically organize and make sense of large amounts of sometimes inconsistent information about lifespan develop-

> **WORKING WITH** Jeffrey Friedman, Clinical Social Worker
>
> **The Value of Developmental Theory for Helping Children, Adolescents, and Their Families** *continued*
>
> intensely angry and unhappy and were doing poorly both at home and in school. People thought they were so small for their age because of malnutrition.
>
> **Robert:** *Was that the problem?*
>
> **Jeffrey:** Well, no. Their metabolism and growth hormones were highly abnormal, although the glands that produced the growth hormones were fine—and when the children were given growth hormones, they didn't grow. But when these children were put in the hospital and separated from their families, a surprising thing happened: their mental and physical conditions improved dramatically. They immediately started to grow, gaining on average almost a centimeter a month. When the children were returned home to their families, we were in for another surprise. Their mental states again deteriorated and the growth stopped completely.
>
> **Robert:** *What were their parents like?*
>
> **Jeffrey:** They weren't physically abusive, neglectful, or anything like that. In fact, they loved their children very much. Most were middle class people who lived in nice houses and had good jobs. Often they had other children who were doing just fine. As we got to know the parents better, though, we discovered that in every case at least one parent bad very disturbed ways of thinking about their child—ways of thinking that they had hidden even from themselves.
>
> **Robert:** *Are you talking about their "internal working models"?*
>
> **Jeffrey:** Yes, the working models or mental portraits that these parents held about their dwarfed children were severely defective. Developmental theory helped me to appreciate how, in the context of intense love relationships, patterns of thoughts and feelings that parents are barely aware of can profoundly affect the psychosocial, physical, and cognitive well-being and development of their own children. Over time, I came to recognize the disturbed and irrational feelings that the parents were expressing indirectly to their children. One parent thought the child had demons in him and that God has somehow arranged things so the child was punishing the parent for things the parent had done wrong earlier in life, things the parent thought were horrible. Once the theory helped me to discover what was hidden, I could then help the parent and the child understand what was going on, so they could start to improve the situation. Although it took many months, once the quality of these parent-child relationships improved, the psychological adjustment of the children also improved. They all grew up to be individuals of normal height and weight.
>
> **Robert:** *Are similar problems in the parent-child relationship found in other instances?*
>
> **Jeffrey:** Yes, they are. Frequently, the physical and sexual abuse of children by parents and others who are very close to them arises from problems in the enduring patterns of thoughts and feelings that people have about their children. To understand those disturbed relationships and their impact on children's minds and bodies—and to know how best to improve things—you need developmental theories to help you understand the people involved, the factors in the situation, and the way they interact to affect a particular child and his or her family.
>
> **What Do You Think?**
>
> 1. Why does Jeffrey Friedman believe that developmental theory is essential to understanding and helping individuals and their families?
> 2. What are your views of the differences between children's ways of thinking and those of adults? How has developmental theory influenced those views?
> 3. What are your thoughts about the discussion of psychosocial dwarfism? In what way were you surprised about the power of mental life to influence development? In what way were you not surprised?

ment. Theories also stimulate new thinking and research and guide parents, professionals, and laypersons in their day-to-day involvements with children, adolescents, and adults. In this chapter's "Working With" interview, a clinical social worker discusses this issue.

Although each theory we've explored in this chapter has significantly expanded knowledge in its particular area of focus, none should be thought to provide a complete explanation of development. Taken together, the theories are complementary and can be used in conjunction with one another to provide a comprehensive view of lifespan development. Table 2.7 summarizes the main features and key concepts for each theoretical approach discussed.

TABLE 2.7 Developmental Theories Compared

Theoretical Approach I	Main Focus	Key Concepts	Basic Assumptions
Psychodynamic			
Freud	Personality (social, emotional)	Id, ego, superego; psychosexual conflict; defense mechanisms	This broadly focused stage theory assumes a moderate role for maturation, a strong role for experience, and a moderately active developmental role for the individual.
Erikson	Personality (social, emotional, identity)	Lifespan development, psychosocial crises	This broadly focused stage theory assumes a weak to moderate role for maturation, a strong role for experience, and a highly active role for the individual.
Behavioral Learning			
Pavlov, Skinner	Learning specific, observable responses	Classical and operant conditioning, extinction, reinforcement, punishment	These narrowly focused, process-oriented theories assume a weak role for maturation, a strong role for experience, and a highly active role for the developing individual.
Social Cognitive Learning			
Bandura	Learning behavior, cognitive response patterns, social roles	Imitation, social learning, modeling, cognitive learning, reciprocal determinism, skills, capabilities	This moderately focused, process-oriented theory assumes a weak role for maturation, a strong role for experience, and a highly active role for the developing individual.
Cognitive			
Piaget	Cognitive (thinking, problem solving)	Schemes, assimilation, accommodation, equilibrium, mental space, routinization of schemes	This moderately focused stage theory assumes a strong role for maturation, a moderate role for experience, and a moderately active role for the developing individual.
Case, Fischer	Cognitive (problem-solving skills and capabilities)	Skill acquisition, optimal level of performance, higher-level skills	These moderately focused, process-oriented theories assume a moderate role for both maturation and experience and a highly active role for the developing individual.
Information processing	Cognitive (steps and processes involved in problem solving and other mental abilities)	Sensory register, short-term memory (STM), long-term memory (LTM), metacognition, knowledge base, control processes	This narrowly focused, process-oriented theory assumes a strong role for maturation, a moderate role for experience, and a highly active role for the developing individual.
Contextual			
Bronfenbrenner	Contextual (interactive contextual influences)	Ecological contexts; microsystem, ecosystem, mesosystem, macrosystem	This broadly focused, process-oriented theory assumes a strong role for maturation, a moderate role for experience, and a highly active role for the developing individual.
Vygotsky	Contextual (cultural/historical influences)	Dialogues, zone of proximal development	This moderately focused, process-oriented theory assumes a weak role for maturation, a strong role for experience, and a highly active role for the developing individual.
Elder	Individual change within changing social and historical contexts	Education, work, and family forming social trajectories (pathways) that guide development	This broadly focused, process-oriented theory assumes a weak role for maturation, a strong role for experience, and a highly active role for the developing individual.
Adult and Lifespan Development			
Normative crisis	Personality (social, behavior, life structure, coping mechanisms)	Adult development; mechanisms (Vaillant); eras, transitions, and live structures (Levinson)	These moderately focused stage theories assume a weak role for maturation, a strong role for experience, and a highly active role for the developing individual.
Timing of events	Personality (social, behavior, life structure)	Adult development, normative and nonnormative events, social clock	These broadly focused, process-oriented theories assume a weak role for maturation, a strong role for experience, and a highly active role for the developing individual.

> **What Do You Think?**
>
> Remember three-year-old Elizabeth at the beginning of this chapter? Now that you have learned more about theories of development, which theory (or theories) do you think is most useful in understanding her situation and helping her adjust to her first days of nursery school? Why?

Theories help us understand and actively participate in our own development. Theories can also broaden and deepen our understanding of ourselves, the factors influencing our development, and the choices we have. They can help us better understand how our family dynamics and relationships may have influenced our current personalities and our struggles with issues such as identity, intimacy, gender role, and sexuality.

However, uncritical reliance on theories poses several pitfalls. Because theories guide and direct our perceptions of and thinking about people, reliance on a given theory may lead us to focus on certain aspects of development, make certain assumptions, and draw conclusions about development that are consistent with the theory but not necessarily accurate. For example, overreliance on Piaget's cognitive approach may lead a teacher to underestimate the contributions of social and emotional factors to a child's academic difficulties. Similarly, parents who interpret their child's irresponsible behavior in terms of psychological conflict may overlook the fact that the same behavior is frequently modeled and reinforced by the child's older sibling. Finally, the emphasis many developmental theories place on shared or even universal developmental trends may underestimate the role of individual differences in life conditions, events, and personal choices people face throughout their lives.

As you read the chapters that follow, notice that the theories are applied selectively based on the ages and developmental issues being discussed. We encourage you to refer back to this chapter whenever you have questions about the material and to make your own judgments about which theory (or theories) fits best. Finally, keep an eye on how your own theories of development change as you read the book and talk with your instructor and classmates. By the end of the course, if not sooner, you are likely to have a much clearer idea of your preferred theoretical orientation(s), as well as a much clearer perspective of what development is all about.

Chapter Summary

- **What are developmental theories, and how are they useful?** Theories are useful in organizing and explaining the process of development and in stimulating and guiding developmental research, theory, and practice. Theories differ in the degree to which they emphasize maturation versus experience, continuous versus stage-like development, and the individual's active versus passive participation.

- **How have psychodynamic theories influenced thinking about development?** Freud's and Erikson's theories see development as a dynamic process that occurs in a series of stages, each involving psychological conflicts that the developing person must resolve. According to Freud, personality development is energized by the conflicting functions of the id, ego, and superego. Erikson's theory outlines eight developmental stages that encompass the entire lifespan; by resolving the basic crisis of each stage—such as trust versus mistrust in infancy or intimacy versus isolation in young adulthood—the developing person attains what Erikson terms a *virtue*. Thus, for instance, the infant who resolves the trust/mistrust crisis attains the virtue of hope; the young adult who resolves the intimacy/isolation crisis attains love. Psychodynamic theories help us to understand the importance of attachment in intimate relationships throughout life and to conceptualize the process of identity formation in adolescence and adulthood, to name just two lifespan applications.

- **How have developmental theories based on learning theories contributed to our understanding of developmental change?** Pavlov's theory emphasizes learning through classical conditioning as the main process through which developmental changes occur. Skinner's operant conditioning theory emphasizes the influence of reinforcement, punishment, extinction, and shaping on developmental change. Bandura's social cognitive theory emphasizes reciprocal and interactional processes involving direct, observational learning, modeling, and vicarious reinforcement. Learning theories have applications across the lifespan, particularly in helping us to understand the influence of learning on development and helping individuals modify or eliminate problematic behavior and learn new, desirable behaviors.

- **How do cognitive developmental theories help us to understand changes in thinking and problem solving throughout the lifespan?** Piaget's theory explains the underlying structures and processes involved in the development of children's thinking and problem solving. Piaget suggested that thinking develops in a series of increasingly complex and sophisticated stages, each of which incorporates the achievements of those preceding it. The developing person achieves new ways of thinking and problem solving through the joint processes of assimilation (fitting a new scheme into an existing one) and accommodation (changing an existing scheme to meet the challenges of a new situation). Neo-Piagetian theorists Robbie Case and Kurt Fischer emphasize the role of mental space, skills acquisition, and information-processing capacity in cognitive development. Information-processing theory focuses on the steps involved in thinking. Information is stored in the sensory register, then in short-term memory, and finally in long-term memory. As people grow older, they experience cognitive changes in control processes, metacognition, and their knowledge bases. Cognitive theories help us to understand and foster intellectual development, problem-solving abilities, and critical thinking skills throughout the lifespan.

- **How have contextual approaches to development broadened our view of developmental change?** Bronfenbrenner's ecological systems theory proposes that the microsystem, microsystem, exosystem, and macrosystem form interactive and overlapping contexts for development. Vygotsky emphasizes the contribution of history and culture to development, which takes place within a child's zone of proximal development. Elder suggests that education, work, and family create the social trajectories, or pathways, that guide individual development. Etiological theory focuses on the developmental roles of behavioral dispositions and trails, such as temperament and attachment, that are thought to have evolutionary survival value for the human species. These theories are very useful in explaining how development throughout the life course interacts with and is influenced by the context in which that development occurs.

- **How do adult developmental changes differ from child and adolescent changes?** Normative-crisis theories focus on fairly predictable changes that occur over the lifespan, particularly during the adult years. Timing-of-events theory emphasizes the role of both normative and nonnormative transitions in an individual's life course and how social expectations may be internalized in a "social clock" against which we judge our own development.

- **How does comparing developmental theories help us to understand developmental change?** Although developmental theories differ in both focus and explanatory concepts, together they provide a comprehensive view of the process or developmental change. By systematically organizing what we already know about development and proposing explanations that can lie tested through formal and informal observations, developmental theories are so useful for experts and non-experts alike that they are well worth the effort required to understand them.

Key Terms

accommodation (p. 45)
adaptation (p. 45)
assimilation (p. 44)
attachment (p. 40)
behavior modification (p. 43)
classical conditioning (p. 40)
ego (p. 35)

id (p. 35)
information-processing theory (p. 45)
metacognition (p. 47)
normative-crisis model (p. 51)
observational learning (p. 42)
operant conditioning (p. 41)
punishment (p. 42)

reinforcement (p. 41)
scheme (p. 44)
social trajectory (p. 48)
superego (p. 35)
timing-of-events model (p. 52)
zone of proximal development (p. 48)

Genetics, Prenatal Development, and Birth

CHAPTER 3

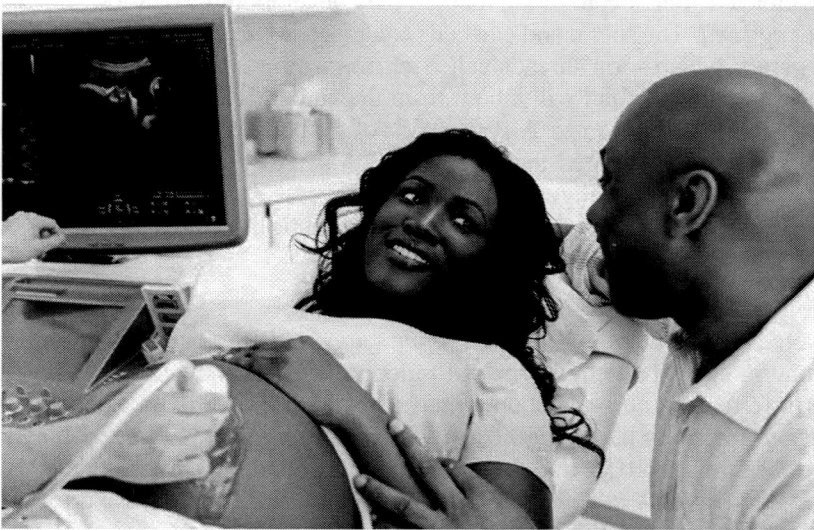

Source: Monkey Business Images/Shutterstock.com.

Chapter Outline

Mechanisms of Genetic Transmission
Individual Genetic Expression
Genetic Abnormalities
Genetic Counseling and Prenatal Diagnosis
Relative Influence of Heredity and Environment
PRENATAL DEVELOPMENT AND BIRTH
Stages of Prenatal Development
Prenatal Influences on the Child
Birth
Looking Back/Looking Forward

Focusing Questions

- How does inheritance work?
- How are genetic differences usually transmitted from one generation to the next?
- How can experts help parents discover and respond to potential genetic problems?
- How do heredity and environment jointly influence development?
- What important developmental changes occur during prenatal development?
- What risks do a mother and baby normally face during pregnancy, and how can they be minimized?
- What happens during the birth process, what difficulties may occur, and how are they handled?

Inheritance affects a vast number of human qualities, from the color of our eyes and how tall we are to more complex characteristics, such as athletic ability, intelligence, and temperament. We begin this section by describing the basic biological processes involved in human reproduction and how genetic information from two parents is combined and conveyed to their children. Next, we discuss genetic abnormalities. Then we address an issue that psychologists have found especially

sperm Male gametes, or reproductive cells; produced in the testicles.

ovum The reproductive cell, or gamete, of the female; the egg cell.

gene A molecular structure, carried on chromosomes, containing genetic information; the basic unit of heredity.

chromosome A threadlike, rod-shaped structure containing genetic information that is transmitted from parents to children; each human sperm or egg cell contains twenty-three chromosomes, and these determine a person's inherited characteristics.

zygote The single new cell formed when a sperm cell attaches itself to the surface of an ovum (egg).

important: the relationship between heredity and environment and how both contribute to individual development over the lifespan. Finally, we describe ways to use knowledge of these relationships to benefit parents, their children, and their children's children.

Mechanisms of Genetic Transmission

The process by which genetic information is combined and transmitted begins with *gametes,* the reproductive cells of a child's parents. In the father, the gametes are produced in the testicles, and each is called a **sperm** cell. In the mother, they develop in the ovaries, and each is called an **ovum**, or *egg cell.* The sperm and egg cells contain genetic information in molecular structures called **genes**, which form threads called **chromosomes**. Thus, the chromosomes contain the genetic material the child will inherit from the parent. Each human sperm or egg cell contains twenty-three chromosomes. All other cells of the body contain forty-six chromosomes and approximately one hundred thousand genes. A single chromosome may contain as many as twenty thousand genes. Figure 3.1 shows pictures, or *karyotypes,* of the chromosomes for a normal human male. Figure 3.2 illustrates the genetic structures involved.

The Role of DNA

The genes themselves are made of *DNA (deoxyribonucleic acid),* the complex protein code of genetic information that directs the form and function of each body cell as it develops. DNA shares this information at conception, when a sperm from the father penetrates an egg from the mother, releasing their chromosomes, which join to form a new cell called a **zygote**. To accomplish this, reproductive cells, or gametes, divide by a process called *meiosis* and recombine into a zygote at conception. All of the other cells that make up a unique human being will develop from this original zygote through a simple division of their genes, chromosomes, and other cellular parts by means of a process called *mitosis.*

Meiosis and Mitosis

Meiosis involves the following steps. First, the twenty-three chromosomes of the egg or sperm) cell duplicate themselves. Then they break up into smaller pieces and randomly exchange segments of genetic material with one another. Next, the new chromosome pairs divide to form two separate cells. Finally, the two new cells divide again. Each of the four new cells contains a unique set of genetic material in its twenty-three chromosomes, *one-half* the usual number of chromosomes carried by all other cells. This ensures that the new, single-cell zygote that forms during conception will contain the normal forty-six chromosomes: twenty-three chromosomes from the egg and twenty-three from the sperm. Figure 3.3 illustrates the process of meiosis for sperm cells. The process for egg cells is the same.

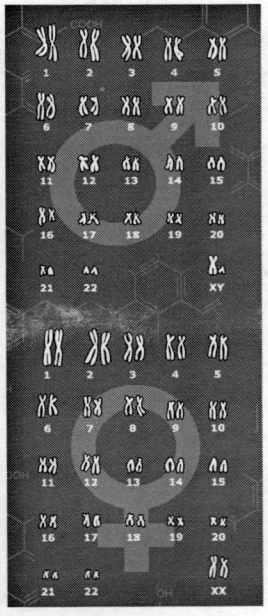

FIGURE 3.1

Chromosomes for the Normal Human Male and Female

This karyotype depicts the twenty-two pairs of chromosomes and the two sex chromosomes for the normal human male (top) and normal human female (bottom). The twenty-third pair of chromosomes determines whether the human will be male (XY) or female (XX).

Source: YKh/Shutterstock.com.

| The human body contains 100 trillion cells. | There is a **nucleus** inside each human cell (except red blood cells). | Each nucleus contains 46 **chromosomes**, arranged in 23 pairs. | One **chromosome** of every pair is from each parent. | The chromosomes are filled with tightly coiled strands of DNA. | **Genes** are segments of DNA that contain instructions to make proteins—the building blocks of life. |

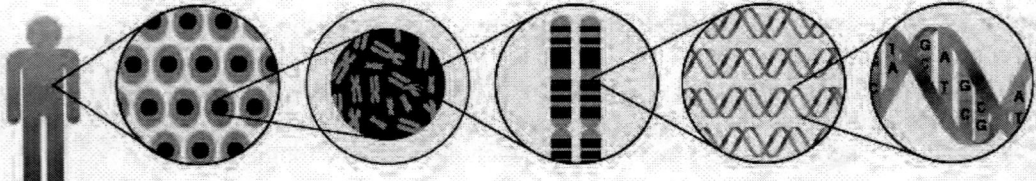

FIGURE 3.2 Genetic Structures

The Process of Meiosis for Sperm Cells

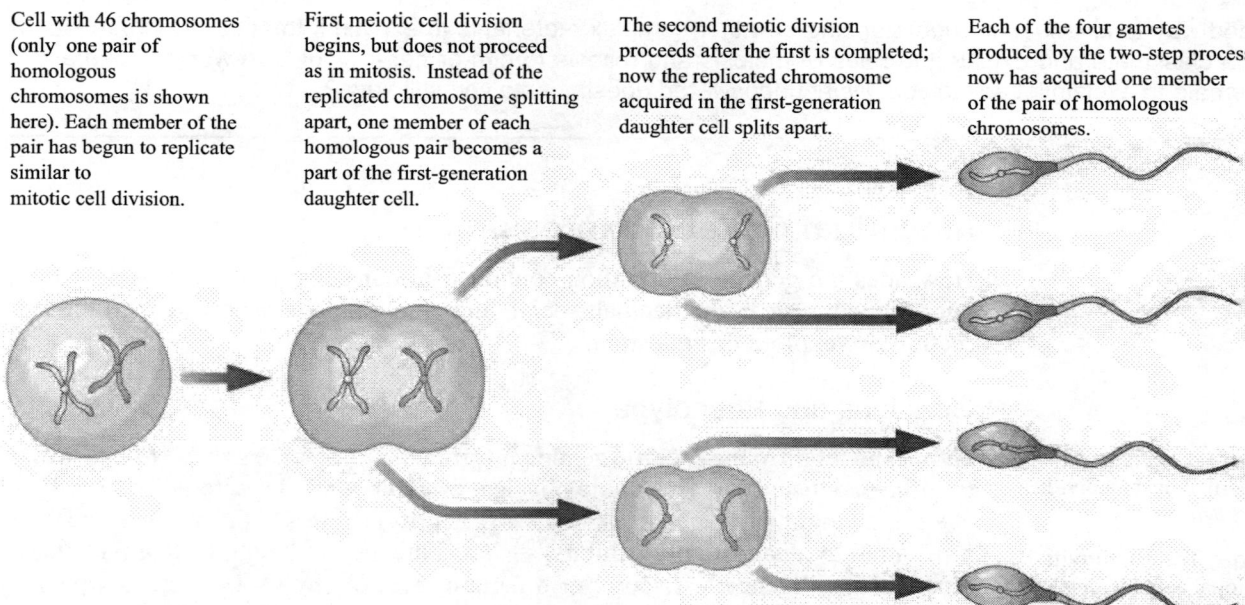

FIGURE 3.3 The Process of Meiosis for Sperm Cells

As meiosis begins, DNA replicates. However, before the replicated arms split apart, one member of each pair of chromosomes moves to become part of each first-generation daughter cell. Once the first generation of daughter cells is established, the DNA copies itself and then splits as part of the second meiotic division. Thus, one copy of one member of the pair of chromosomes is contributed to each second-generation daughter cell. These two successive divisions produce four cells, each with twenty-three chromosomes.

Once the zygote forms, it and all of its descendants divide through the process of mitosis. Mitosis involves the following steps. First, the twenty-three pairs of chromosomes of a cell form a duplicate set. Next, the two sets of chromosomes move to opposite sides of the cell. Finally, a new wall forms between them, resulting in two new, identical cells, each containing the same unique set of chromosomes, genes, and DNA-based genetic code that will help guide the new organisms development. Figure 3.4 depicts the process of mitosis.

The Process of Mitosis

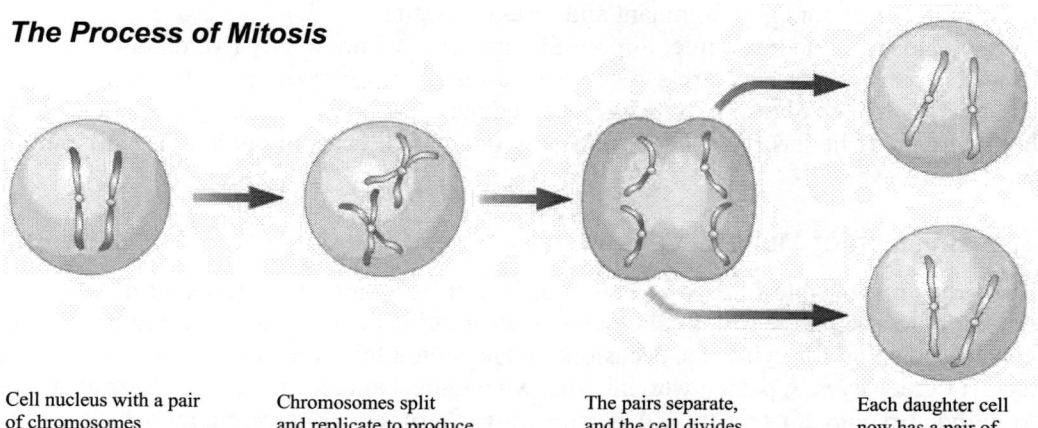

FIGURE 3.4
The Process of Mitosis

Mitotic cell division produces nearly all the cells of the body except the gametes. During mitosis, each chromosome replicates to form two chromosomes with identical genetic blueprints. As the cell divides, one member of each identical pair becomes a member of each daughter cell. In this manner, complete genetic endowment is replicated in nearly every cell of the body.

Chapter 3 Genetics, Prenatal Development, and Birth

> **What Do You Think?**
>
> A good way to check your understanding of rather complex material is to explain it to another person. Team up with a classmate and explain the roles of meiosis and mitosis to him or her in your own words. Then ask your classmate to explain it back to you. What unanswered questions do you still have?

Individual Genetic Expression

How does the genetic information contained in our cells influence the development of our unique physical, intellectual, social, and emotional characteristics? In the following section, we explore this question.

Genotype and Phenotype

genotype The set of genetic traits inherited by an individual. See also *phenotype*.

phenotype The set of traits an individual actually displays during development; reflects the evolving product of genotype and experience. See also *genotype*.

Genotype refers to the specific genetic information a person inherits that has the potential to influence his or her observable physical or behavioral characteristics or traits such as eye color, height, intelligence, or shyness. **Phenotype** refers to the physical and behavioral traits an individual actually exhibits, such as blue eyes; a height of five feet, ten inches; a certain intelligence test score; or a certain level of shyness. A person's phenotype is always the product of the interactions of that person's genotype with the environmental influences that occur from the formation of the first cell at conception onward.

In some cases, there is a close match between a person's original genotype and the phenotype that results. For example, inheriting genes for blue eyes generally results in actually having blue eyes. In other cases, phenotype does not coincide so closely with genotype. Two newborn infants may have inherited the identical genotype for weight at the time of conception, but one may end up heavier (or lighter) than the other because of differences in prenatal nutrition as well as diet and exercise during infancy and childhood. On the other hand, children with different genotypes for weight may end up the same weight (the same phenotype), one through dieting and the other simply by eating whatever she wanted.

Dominant and Recessive Genes

dominant gene In any paired set of genes, the gene with greater influence in determining characteristics that are physically visible or manifest.

recessive gene In any paired set of genes, the gene that influences or determines physical characteristics only when no dominant gene is present.

Genes are inherited in pairs, one from each parent. Some genes are dominant and others are recessive. A **dominant gene** will influence a child's phenotype even if it is paired with a recessive gene. A **recessive gene**, however, must be paired with another recessive gene to be able to influence the phenotype. If it is paired with a dominant gene, its influence will be controlled or blocked. More than one thousand human characteristics appear to follow the dominant-recessive pattern of inheritance (McKussick, 1988, 1995). Table 3.1 lists a number of common dominant and recessive traits.

Eye color is a good example. Suppose human eyes came in only two colors, blue and brown. Because blue eyes are a recessive trait and brown eyes are a dominant trait, a child's eyes will be blue only if he has received the appropriate blue-producing gene from both parents. If he has received it from only one parent or from neither, he will end up with brown eyes.

Transmission of Multiple Variations

allele One of several alternative forms of a gene.

The genes responsible for eye color—and, in fact, for many other traits—often take on two or more alternative forms called **alleles**. In addition to alleles for blue and brown, the gene responsible for eye color occasionally takes on a third allele, which often leads to hazel or green eyes. A person who inherits two identical alleles for a particular trait is said to be *homozygous* for that trait. A person who inherits two different alleles for the trait is said to be *heterozygous* for that trait. In the case of eye color, a heterozygous person (one brown and one blue/hazel/green allele) will therefore show the phenotype of the

TABLE 3.1 Some Common Dominant and Recessive Traits

Dominant Trait	Recessive Trait	Dominant Trait	Recessive Trait
Brown eyes	Gray, green, hazel, or blue eyes	Short fingers	Fingers of normal length
Hazel or green eyes	Blue eyes	Double-fingers	Normally jointed fingers
Normal vision	Nearsightedness	Double-jointedness	Normal joints
Farsightedness	Normal vision	Type A blood	Type O blood
Normal color vision	Red-green color blindness	Type B blood	Type O blood
Brown or black hair	Blond hair	Rh positive blood	Rh negative blood
Nonred hair	Red hair	Normal blood clotting	Hemophilia
Curly or wavy hair	Straight hair	Normal red blood cells	Sickle-cell disease
Full head of hair	Baldheadedness	Normal protein metabolism	Phenylketonuria (PKU)
Normal hearing	Some forms of congenital deafness	Normal physiology	Tay-Sachs disease
Normally pigmented skin	Albino (completely white) skin	Huntington disease	Normal central nervous system functioning in adulthood
Facial dimples	No dimples	Immunity to poison ivy	Susceptibility to poison ivy
Thick lips	Thin lips		

Note: Many common traits show dominant or recessive patterns. Also, a pattern sometimes may be dominant with respect to one trait but recessive with respect to another.

dominant allele and thus have brown eyes. Only a person who is homozygous will display the phenotype of one of the recessive alleles and have blue or hazel eyes. From a genetic standpoint, there are three times as many ways to have brown eyes as there are to have blue/green ones. Figure 3.5 illustrates this example.

Keep in mind, however, that although all of the patterns of inheritance for dominant and recessive traits are possible, each genotype will not necessarily occur in each family, since genes are inherited randomly. In Figure 3.5 (example 1), for instance, although it is possible

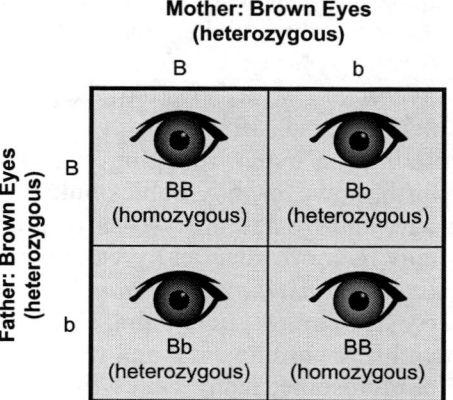

Example 1: Both parents heterozygous

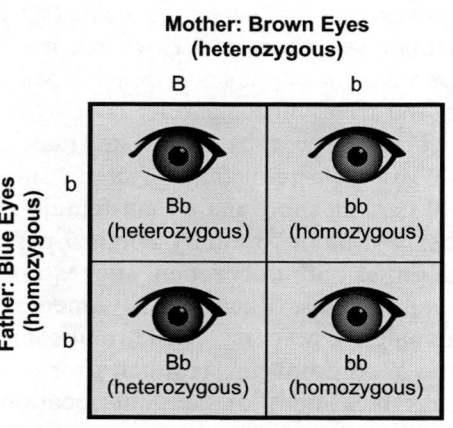

Example 2: One parents heterozygous and one parent homozygous

FIGURE 3.5
Genetic Transmission of Eye Color

Example 1: Three out of four offspring will have brown eyes, and one out of four will have blue eyes. *Example 2:* Two out of four offspring will have brown eyes, and two out of four will have blue eyes.

Key: B = gene for brown eyes, which is dominant for eye color
b = gene for blue eyes, which is recessive for eye color

Chapter 3 Genetics, Prenatal Development, and Birth

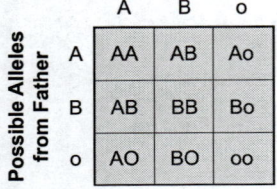

FIGURE 3.6
Inheritance of Blood Type

In blood type inheritance, both A and B alleles are dominant, and the O allele is recessive. Therefore, the following proportions of blood types are likely to occur in the general population: Type A (AA or Ao): 3/9; Type B (BB or Bo): 3/9; Type AB: 2/9; Type O (oo): 1/9.

that the parents will have children with the eye color genotypes of BB, Bb, bB, or bb, all of their children may in reality be BB or bb. Thus, the increased probability of a particular genotype, such as Bb, does not mean that genotype will definitely be seen. In contrast, in the genetic transmission of a sex-linked trait such as hemophilia (discussed shortly), all daughters in a given family are carriers and all sons are affected (see Figure 3.7).

Many genes have more than two alleles. As a result, the traits they govern can vary in more-complex ways. The four major human blood types, for example, are based on three alleles of the same gene. Two of these alleles, type A and type B, are dominant forms, and the O allele is recessive. Figure 3.6 illustrates how these three alleles for blood type can combine in six possible ways but produce only four blood types, A, B, O, and AB. The AB blood type is an example of *codominance,* a situation in which the characteristics of both alleles are independently expressed in a new phenotype rather than one or the other being dominant, or as a mixture of the two. Because each blood type has a unique chemistry that allows it to mix only with certain other blood types, determining the compatible blood genotype is very important for people who receive blood transfusions.

Polygenic Transmission

Unlike eye color and blood type, which can vary only in a limited number of qualitatively distinct ways, the inheritance of most physical traits (including height, weight, hair and skin color, and complex personality) and behavioral traits (such as intelligence, shyness, alcoholism, and depression) do not fit the simple single-gene model just described. These traits are called *polygenic,* meaning they involve *many* genes, each with small effects, as well as environmental influences. In all of these cases, children show a marked tendency to have a phenotype that is intermediate between those of their parents, and for the most part the exact mechanisms of inheritance for such traits are still unknown (Owen & McGuffin, 1994).

Because polygenic phenotypes vary by small degrees, environment can influence them in relatively important ways. An overweight person can become more slender through a change in diet, for example, and a shy person can learn to be more outgoing. Such experiences matter less for traits that are simply transmitted by a single gene; there is no way to change eye color, even though you can cover your irises with tinted contact lenses.

The Determination of Sex

Whether a person becomes male or female depends on events at conception. All ova, or egg cells, contain a single X chromosome, whereas a sperm cell may contain either an X or a Y. If a Y-bearing sperm happens to fertilize the egg, a male (XY) zygote develops; if the sperm is X-bearing, a female (XX) zygote develops (see Figure 3.1).

During the first several weeks following conception, both male and female embryos possess a set of bisexual gonadal (sex) tissues, meaning they can develop either male or female sex structures. However, between the fourth and eighth weeks, gonadal tissue develops into testes or ovaries depending on the presence or absence of a small section of the Y chromosome, referred to as *TDF* or *testis-determining factor.* Ova fertilized by a Y-bearing sperm have TDF, and male embryos result (Page et al., 1987).

More Y sperm than X sperm succeed in fertilizing the ovum, resulting in about 30 percent more male than female zygotes. By birth, however, boy babies outnumber girl babies by only about 6 percent on average, and by age thirty-five, women begin to outnumber men, suggesting that males may be more genetically vulnerable than females. Much of this vulnerability is related to *sex-linked transmission.* Unlike females, who carry XX chromosomes, males carry XY chromosome pairs. Because the Y chromosome is much shorter than its matching X chromosome and therefore may lack many of the gene locations of the X chromosome, many genes from the mother may not be matched or counteracted with equivalent genetic material from the father. As a result, genetic abnormalities on the single, complete X chromosome are more likely to result in phenotypic abnormalities in males than in females. Table 3.2 lists a number of **sex-linked recessive traits,** abnormalities that are transmitted on the single, complete X chromosome.

sex-linked recessive traits
Recessive traits resulting from genes on the X chromosome.

TABLE 3.2 Sex-Linked Recessive Traits

Condition	Description
Colorblindness	Inability to distinguish certain colors, usually reds and greens
Hemophilia	Deficiency in substances that allow the blood to clot; also known as bleeder's disease
Muscular dystrophy	Weakening and wasting away of muscles, beginning in childhood (Duchenne's form)
Diabetes (two forms)	Inability to metabolize sugars properly because the body does not produce enough insulin
Anhidrotic ectodermal dysplasia	Lack of sweat glands and teeth
Night blindness (certain forms)	Inability to see in dark or very dim conditions
Deafness (certain forms)	Impaired hearing or total hearing loss
Atrophy of optic nerve	Gradual deterioration of vision and eventual blindness

Note: All of the above traits are carried by the X chromosome, and all are recessive. As a result, they occur less often in females than in males.

One such trait is *hemophilia,* an inability of the blood to clot and therefore to stop itself from flowing. Because clotting is so slow, internal bleeding can at times be life threatening (American College of Obstetricians and Gynecologists [ACOG], 1990; McKussick, 1995). Because the gene for hemophilia is located on the X chromosome, a female carrier is protected by having a normal gene on her second X chromosome. Each of her children will have a fifty-fifty chance of inheriting the abnormal gene. Daughters who get the gene will be carriers, like their mother, while sons will develop hemophilia because they lack a second X chromosome to counteract the gene's effects. Figure 3.7 illustrates this effect.

Most human characteristics that have been studied follow the pattern of dominant-recessive and codominant inherence, and in most instances, a gene that has been inherited influences development in the same manner whether it was contributed by the biological mother or father. However, geneticists have discovered a new mode of inheritance called **genetic imprinting**, in which genes are chemically marked, or *imprinted,* such that the member of the chromosome pair contributed by either the father or the mother is activated, regardless of its genetic makeup. This imprint is most often temporary and may disappear in the next generation (Cassidy, 1995).

genetic imprinting A mode of inheritance in which genes are chemically marked so that the number of the chromosome pair contributed by either the father or the mother is activated, regardless of its genetic makeup.

Genetic Abnormalities

Once in a while, genetic reproduction goes wrong. Sometimes too many or too few chromosomes transfer to a newly forming zygote. Sometimes the chromosomes transfer properly but carry particular defective genes that affect a child physically, mentally, or both. The changes almost always create significant disabilities for the child, if they do not prove fatal. Table 3.3 lists some common genetic abnormalities and the risk of their presence at birth.

Disorders Due to Abnormal Chromosomes

Most of the time, inheriting one too many or one too few chromosomes proves fatal. In a few cases, however, children with an extra or a missing chromosome survive past

TABLE 3.3 Risk of Selected Genetic Disorders

Disorder	Description	Risk of Having a Fetus with the Disorder — Overall	With One Affected Child
Chromosomal			
Down syndrome	Extra or translocated twenty-first chromosome. Symptoms include almond-shaped eyes, round head, stubby hands and feet, abnormalities of the heart and intestinal tract, facial deformities, and vulnerability to disease. Most children with Down syndrome live until middle adulthood, but about 14 percent die by age one and 21 percent die by age ten.	1/700	1–2 percent
Klinefelter syndrome (XXY)	At least one extra chromosome, usually an X. Affected individual is phenotypically male, but has small testes and is sterile.	1/500 men	N/S[1]
Fragile X syndrome	The most common inherited form of intellectual disability. Caused by an abnormal gene on the bottom end of the X chromosome. Causes spectrum of learning difficulties ranging from mild problems to severe intellectual disability.	1/4,000 male births 1/8,000 female births	N/S[1]
Turner syndrome (XO)	Affects only females born with a single X in the sex chromosome. Are very short as adults, "webbed" necks and ears set lower than usual; fail to develop secondary sexual characteristics; problems with spatial judgment, memory, and reasoning.	1/2,500 women	N/S[1]
Dominant Gene			
Polydactyly	Extra fingers or toes. One of the most common anomalies affecting the hands or feet. Correctable by surgery.	1/300–1/100	50 percent
Achondroplasia	Rare disorder of the skeleton; most common form of dwarfism; afflicted person has shorter than normal arms and legs, large head, physical developmental delays, normal intelligence and lifespan.	1/40,000–1/15,000	50 percent
Huntington disease	Usually first affects people in their thirties and forties; gradual deterioration of the central nervous system, causing uncontrollable movements, mental deterioration, and death.	1/15,000	50 percent
Recessive Gene			
Cystic fibrosis	The most common genetic disease among white persons of Northern European descent. Abnormally thick mucus clogs the lungs, causing serious difficulties in breathing and digestion, delayed growth and sexual maturation, high vulnerability to infection, and shortened life expectancy.	1/2,500 white persons (risk of being a carrier is 1/25)	25 percent
Sickle-cell disease	Abnormal, sickle-shaped red blood cells clog blood vessels, reducing blood supply and causing pain. May cause increased bacterial infections and degeneration of brain, kidneys, liver, heart, spleen, and muscles. Shortened lifespan.	1/500 African Americans (risk of being a carrier is 1/12)	25 percent
Tay-Sachs disease	Found mostly in persons of Eastern European Jewish descent. Chemical imbalance of central nervous system. Symptoms first occur at six months of age, progressively causing severe intellectual disability, blindness, seizures, and death by third year due to lowered resistance to disease.	1/3,000 Eastern European Jews (risk of being a carrier is 1/30–1/300)	25 percent

birth and even live fairly normal lives. It is estimated that approximately one in every 156 births in Western countries involves a chromosomal abnormality (Milunsky, 1992). One such example is Down syndrome. Persons with Down syndrome usually have three number 21 chromosomes instead of two.

TABLE 3.3 Risk of Selected Genetic Disorders *continued*

		\multicolumn{2}{c}{Risk of Having a Fetus with the Disorder}
Disorder	Description	Overall	With One Affected Child
X Linked			
Hemophilia	Lack of substance needed for blood clotting. Risk of life-threatening internal bleeding; risk of AIDS from transfusions.	1/5,000 male babies	50 percent for boy, 0 percent for girl
Multifactorial			
Congenital heart disease	Structural and/or electrical abnormalities of the heart; most common type of birth defect in the United States. May respond to medication or corrective surgery performed after birth.	1/125	2–4 percent
Neural tube defect	Serious birth defect of the spine and brain in which the tube enclosing the spine fails to close completely or normally; significant cause of infant mortality and childhood morbidity worldwide. Brain may be absent or underdeveloped (anencephaly), or spinal cord and nerve bundles may be exposed. Death or severe intellectual disability or other long-term problems for children who survive.	1–2/1,000	2–5 percent
Cleft lip/cleft palate	Gap or space in lip or hole in roof of mouth. May cause difficulties in breathing, speech, hearing, and eating. Corrective surgery at birth can repair most clefts.	1/600	2–4 percent

[1]No significant increase.

Sources: ACOG (1995); CDC, (2011b); Diamond (1989); Hagerman (1996); LPCH (2013); NICHD (2012); NHGRI (2010); Selekman (1993); Stratford (1994); USNLM (2012; 2013); Yale School of Medicine (2013).

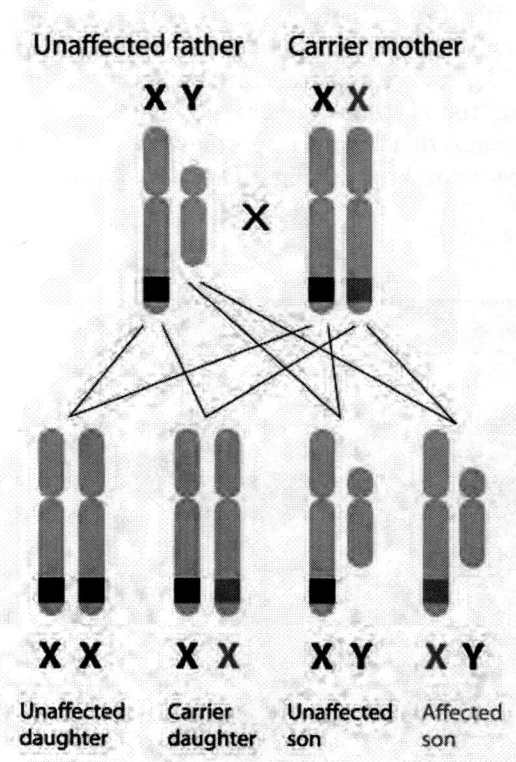

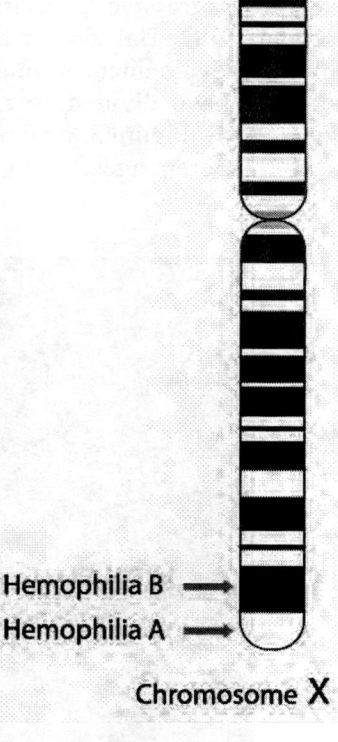

FIGURE 3.7
Inheritance of Hemophilia, a Sex-linked Disorder

In this example of the inheritance of hemophilia, the mother is a carrier of the disease. Each daughter has a 50 percent chance of inheriting a pair of normal chromosomes and a 50 percent chance of being a carrier like her mother. However, she herself will not be affected by the disorder because her second X chromosome protects her. Each son has a 50 percent chance of being healthy and a 50 percent chance of inheriting the abnormal chromosome and acquiring hemophilia. This is because, as a male, his second sex chromosome is a Y, which does not protect him from the disorder.
Source: Alila Medical Media/Shutterstock.com.

Chapter 3 Genetics, Prenatal Development, and Birth

> **What Do You Think?**
>
> Now that you know how eye color and blood type are inherited, see if you can figure out how you inherited *your* eye color. How about your blood type?

Down Syndrome

Down syndrome A congenital condition that causes intellectual disability.

Down syndrome is also called *trisomy 21* because it is generally caused by an extra twenty-first chromosome or the translocation, or transfer, of part of the twenty-first chromosome onto another chromosome. People with this disorder have almond-shaped eyes, round heads, and stubby hands and feet. Many also have abnormalities of the heart and intestinal tract, and facial deformities. They also show greater than usual vulnerability to a number of serious diseases, such as leukemia. Most children with Down syndrome live until middle adulthood, but about 14 percent die by age one and 21 percent die by age ten. The rate of infant mortality among children with Down syndrome is eight times higher than the infant mortality rate of children without Down syndrome (Goldman, Urbano, & Hodapp, 2011).

Although children with Down syndrome achieve many of the same developmental milestones as normal children, as they get older, they fall developmentally farther and farther behind and never "catch up" with their peers. By adulthood, most individuals with Down syndrome plateau at a level of cognitive functioning that is now described as "moderate intellectual disability." They are able to learn and follow simple routines and hold routine jobs, but because they are easily confused by change and have difficulty in making important decisions usually cannot live independently and require extensive, ongoing support from their families and community service programs (Sloper et al., 1990; Stratford, 1994).

Down syndrome is much more frequent in babies of mothers over age thirty-five and among older fathers. As women grow older, they experience longer exposure to environmental hazards, such as chemicals and radiation, that may affect their ovaries. In addition, because a woman's ova are formed before she is born, they are likely to undergo progressive deterioration with age (Baird & Sadovnick, 1987; Feinbloom & Forman, 1987; Halliday et al., 1995). As we will see in Chapter 14's discussion of physical development in middle adulthood, older fathers are at risk because their sperm cells have divided so many times that many opportunities for errors exist (Angier, 1994). Figure 3.8 summarizes the risk of having a Down syndrome baby for women of different ages.

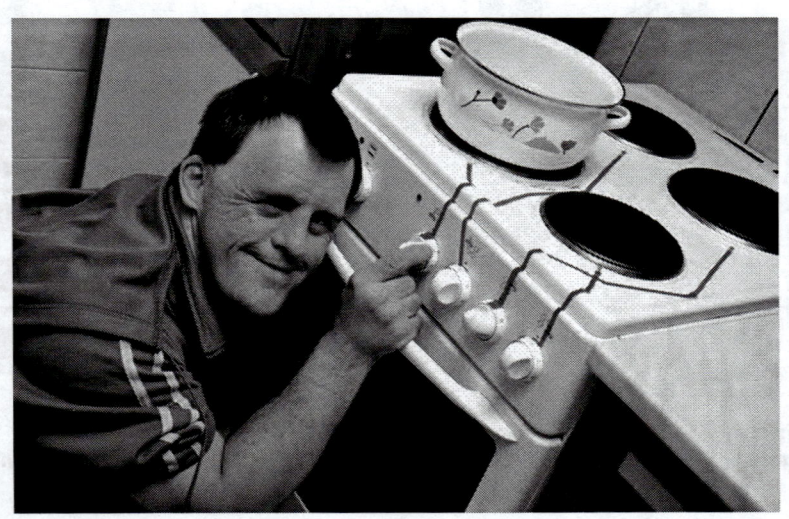

Individuals with Down syndrome, like this man, learn very slowly. But with special educational help and proper support (like the labeled stove in the photo), they can lead satisfying lives.
Source: Marcel Jancovic/Shutterstock.com.

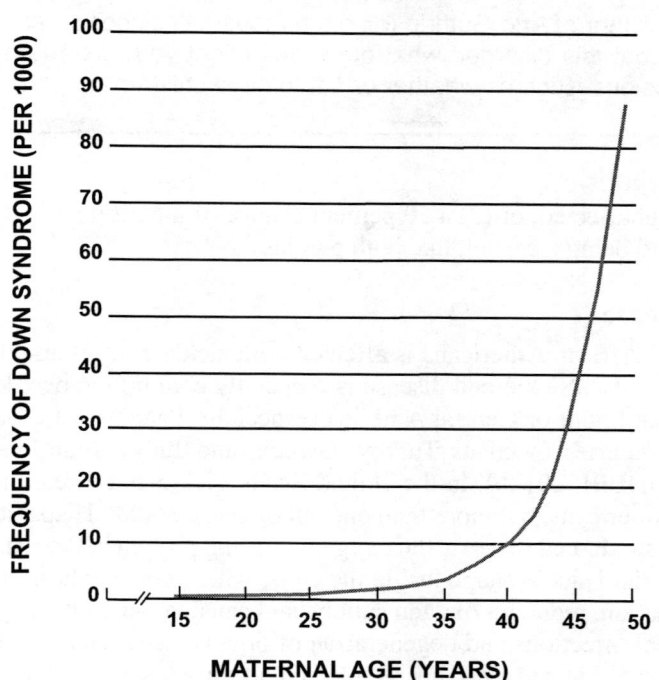

FIGURE 3.8
Relationship between Maternal Age and the Incidence of Down Syndrome

As women get older, their chances of giving birth to a baby with Down syndrome increase. At maternal age twenty-one, one in every 1,500 babies is born with Down syndrome. At maternal age thirty-four, one in every 746 babies is born with Down syndrome, increasing to 1 in 150 babies by maternal age 39. By maternal age forty-nine, one in ten babies is born with Down syndrome.

Disorders Due to Abnormal Genes

Even when a zygote has the proper number of chromosomes, it may inherit specific genes that can create serious medical problems for the child after birth. In many cases, these problems prove lethal. In others, genetic diseases are at least manageable, if not curable.

As Table 3.3 shows, there are four main types of genetic disorders: dominant gene disorders, recessive gene disorders, X-linked disorders, and multifactorial gene disorders.

Dominant Gene Disorders

Dominant gene disorders require only one abnormal gene from either parent to affect a child. When one parent has a dominant gene disorder, each child has a 50 percent chance of inheriting the dominant abnormal gene for the disorder—thereby acquiring the disorder—and a 50 percent chance of inheriting a pair of recessive genes and being unaffected.

Huntington disease is a dominant gene disorder that results in a gradual deterioration of the central nervous system, causing uncontrollable movements and mental deterioration. Typically, it does not appear until affected people are in their thirties or forties, and it always proves fatal. Before that age, people usually have no way of knowing whether they will get the disease (ACOG, 1995; Halliday et al., 1995; USNLM, 2013).

Researchers have identified specific sections of the human genome that are exclusively linked to Huntington disease. The gene for the disorder appears to be located on chromosome four in the *HTT* gene, which is involved in the production of a protein called "huntingtin." A genetic blood test for Huntington disease can detect the *HTT* mutation and, therefore, can accurately diagnose the condition, but an understanding of how the gene actually causes the disease and treatments remain elusive (Horgan, 1993; USNLM, 2013).

Recessive Gene Disorders

Recessive gene disorders can occur when the fetus inherits a pair of recessive genes, one from each parent. When both parents are carriers of a recessive gene disorder, each child faces the following possibilities: (1) a 25 percent chance of inheriting the pair of recessive genes required to have the disorder; (2) a 25 percent chance of inheriting a pair of dominant

Chapter 3 Genetics, Prenatal Development, and Birth

> **What Do You Think?**
>
> Woody Guthrie, the famous folk singer and father of Arlo Guthrie (also a famous folk singer), died of Huntington disease. Based on your new knowledge about this disorder, what questions might you ask Arlo about how his genetic inheritance has affected his life decisions, such as whether or not to have children?

genes and being unaffected; or (3) a 50 percent chance of inheriting one dominant and one recessive gene and being a carrier, like both parents.

Sickle-Cell Disease

About one in 500 African Americans is affected with sickle-cell disease, and about one in twelve is a carrier of it. Sickle-cell disease is especially common in people whose families come from Africa, South or Central America (especially Panama), the Caribbean islands, Mediterranean countries (such as Turkey, Greece, and Italy), India, and Saudi Arabia (ACOG, 1995; NHLBI, 2012b). In the United States, sickle-cell disease is most prevalent among African Americans, but more than one out of every 36,000 Hispanic Americans also suffer from it. In **sickle-cell disease**, the oxygen-carrying protein in the red blood cells takes on an abnormal, rigid sickle shape inside the cells, which get caught in the blood vessels, cutting off circulation, reducing oxygen supply, and causing pain. Other symptoms include increased bacterial infections and degeneration of organs that need a great deal of oxygen, including the brain, kidneys, liver, heart, spleen, and muscles. Individuals who are *heterozygous*, meaning they carry just one abnormal sickle-cell allele along with one dominant, nonsickle-cell allele, show a few signs of sickle-cell disease but also a strong immunity to malaria. Most live normal lives, but when deprived of sufficient oxygen, such as during intense physical exercise or at high altitudes, the sickling of their red blood cells can be triggered, causing pain. Individuals avoid sickle-cell disease completely by having two dominant genes or suffer badly from it because they have two recessive genes.

Although no cure exists for this disease, infants with sickle-cell disease must be given daily doses of antibiotics beginning at two months of age to reduce the chance of infection. Blood transfusions, pain medications, fluids, and hydroxyurea—a medication that stimulates the production of fetal hemoglobin, a type produced by babies that does not sickle—are also commonly used to treat sickle-cell disease. In the past, the majority of victims died before age twenty, and few lived past age forty (Diamond, 1989; Selekman, 1993). Enhanced medical care now enables people with sickle-cell disease to live to age fifty and beyond (USNLM, 2013).

Multifactorial Disorders

Multifactorial disorders result from a combination of genetic and environmental factors. The incidence of these disorders varies widely in different parts of the world, largely because of the great differences in existing environmental conditions. Table 3.3 describes a number of these disorders.

Genetic Counseling and Prenatal Diagnosis

Some genetic problems can be reduced or avoided with the help of genetic counseling. Couples likely to benefit from counseling include those who may carry genetic disorders, know of relatives with genetic disorders, or belong to an ethnic group at risk for a particular disorder, such as African Americans, who are at risk for sickle-cell disease. More immediate signs of genetic risk include the birth of an infant with some genetic disorder or the spontaneous abortion of earlier pregnancies. Table 3.4 presents guidelines for determining who should seek prenatal genetic counseling.

Genetic counselors use potential parents' medical and genetic histories and tests to help couples estimate their chances of having a healthy baby and discuss alternatives

sickle-cell disease
A genetically transmitted condition in which a person's red blood cells intermittently acquire a curved, sickle shape. The condition sometimes can clog circulation in the small blood vessels.

TABLE 3.4 Who Should Seek Prenatal Counseling?

1. Couples who already have a child with some serious defect such as Down syndrome, spina bifida, congenital heart disease, limb malformation, or intellectual disability
2. Couples with a family history of a genetic disease or intellectual disability
3. Couples who are blood relatives (first or second cousins)
4. African Americans, Ashkenazi Jews, Italians, Greeks, and other high-risk ethnic groups
5. Women who have had a serious infection early in pregnancy (rubella or toxoplasmosis) or who have been infected with HIV
6. Women who have taken potentially harmful medications early in pregnancy or habitually use drugs or alcohol
7. Women who have had X rays taken early in pregnancy
8. Women who have experienced two or more of the following: stillbirth, death of a newborn baby, miscarriage
9. Any woman thirty-five years or older

Source: Adapted from Feinbloom & Forman (1987, p. 129) and Simpson, Holzgreve, & Driscoll (2012).

from which a couple can choose. One obvious alternative is to avoid conception completely and, perhaps, to adopt a baby. A second is to take the risk in the hope of conceiving a healthy baby. Modern methods of prenatal diagnosis can now be used to detect genetic disorders after conception but before birth, allowing the parents the choice of terminating pregnancy during the first trimester if a serious problem is detected. In addition, medical intervention early in infancy may help repair damage caused by a genetic disorder, depending on its severity. Finally, *preimplantation diagnosis,* which refers to a variety of methods to screen ova (eggs) and early embryos *before* they are implanted into the uterus, are being developed as an alternative to prenatal screening, which can be used only after a pregnancy has been established (see the "Focusing On" feature).

Most methods of preimplantation diagnosis use *in vitro* or "test tube" fertilization to identify the presence of recessive genes for hereditary and genetic conditions by selecting for fertilization only those eggs that appear to be free of abnormalities. Proponents of this method believe it is a more suitable option for couples who are opposed to abortion or may have difficulty deciding to terminate a pregnancy in which the fetus may be at risk. Some critics have questioned the accuracy of the method. Others are concerned that techniques designed solely to screen embryos based on carefully considered and ethically acceptable medical reasons, will be used as a new form of *eugenics* to engineer "better babies," based on beliefs or prejudices about which human qualities are desirable and which are not, thus limiting the gene pool on which human diversity depends (Hubbard, 1993; Pappert, 1993).

Table 3.5 describes current diagnostic techniques to screen for genetic disorders. In addition, medical intervention early in infancy may help repair damage caused by a genetic disorder, depending on the severity.

Differences in cultural beliefs and expectations can affect who receives genetic counseling and the forms it takes. The "A Multicultural View" feature discusses this issue.

Relative Influence of Heredity and Environment

Untangling the effects of heredity, or nature, from those of environment, or nurture, has become the special focus of behavior genetics. *Behavior genetics* is the scientific study of how genetic inheritance *(genotype)* and environmental experience jointly influence physical and behavioral development *(phenotype).*

Focusing On...

Technological Alternatives to Natural Conception

Earlier in this century, the only alternative for couples who were infertile was to adopt a child or to remain childless. But today's medical techniques offer a growing number of alternative options. These **assisted reproductive technologies (ARTs)** vary in practicality and popularity, but from a strictly medical standpoint, they all work fairly reliably. We will focus on two procedures that account for 97 percent of all pregnancies involving ARTs.

Artificial (donor) insemination (DI) is used in cases where infertility is caused by problems in sperm quality or production. In this procedure, fresh or previously frozen sperm from a donor are inserted into the woman's vagina and held in place for a few hours. While in most cases the donor is anonymous, he can also be a friend or a relative. Artificial insemination is safe and easy to carry out and induces pregnancy as effectively as does normal intercourse between fertile partners—a 20 percent success rate in any one month (Liebmann-Smith, 1993; Silber, 1991). A controversial application of artificial insemination is *surrogate mothering,* in which sperm from the future father are inserted into the womb of a woman who agrees (usually for a fee) to give up the baby once it is born.

In vitro fertilization (IVF) is used if both eggs and sperm are normal and infertility is caused by blocked fallopian tubes that cannot be surgically repaired. With IVF, ovulation is induced with medications that cause multiple eggs to be produced. With the aid of a laparoscope and ultrasound, one or more eggs are then removed through the woman's vagina under local anesthesia. They are either mixed in a laboratory dish with sperm from the male and are allowed to fertilize in an incubator, or more commonly, a single sperm can be injected directly into the egg. Two days later, the fertilized egg or embryo is transferred back into the woman's uterus through her vagina. Additional embryos can be frozen (cryopreserved) for future use. With IVF, fertilization rates are high, although birth rates resulting from this procedure vary, depending on age: Approximately 45 percent of women under the age of thirty-five who experience IVF deliver babies, and this percentage declines steadily to under 5 percent for women over the age of forty-four (Centers for Disease Control and Prevention—Division of Reproductive Health, 2011a).

What are the experiences of families with children conceived by the new reproductive technologies? In a recent European study that compared families with a child conceived by IVF or DI with families whose children were conceived naturally or adopted, Susan Golombok and her associates found no group differences in the quality of children's emotions, behavior, or overall relationships with their parents (Golombok et al., 2006; MacCallum, Golombok, & Brinsden, 2007). Mothers of IVF and DI children, in fact, showed greater warmth toward and deeper emotional involvement with their children, and both mother-child and father-child interactions were more positive. At least for the families studied, genetic ties appeared to be less important for family functioning than a strong desire to become a parent.

What Do You Think?

If now (or in the future) you and your partner wished to have a child but were unable to do so by normal conception, what reservations might you have about using the new technological alternatives? Have the results of Susan Golombok's study influenced your thinking?

---

assisted reproductive technology (ART) Any infertility treatment in which fertilization of the egg occurs outside of the womb.

Key Concepts of Behavior Genetics

Every characteristic of an organism is the result of the unique interaction between the organism's genetic inheritance and the sequence of environments through which it has passed during its development. For some traits, variations in environment have minimal effect. Thus, once the genotype is known, the eventual form or phenotype of the organism is pretty well specified. For other traits, knowing the genetic makeup may be a poor predictor of the eventual phenotype. Only by specifying both the genotype and the environmental sequence can the character, or phenotype, of the organism be predicted.

Range of Reaction

range of reaction The range of possible phenotypes that an individual with a particular genotype might exhibit in response to the particular sequence of environmental influences he or she experiences.

Range of reaction refers to the range of possible phenotypes an individual with a particular genotype might exhibit in response to the specific sequence of environmental influences he or she experiences (Turkheimer & Gottesman, 1991). For example, if three infants start life with different genetic inheritances (genotypes) for intelligence—one low, one middle, and one high—the different levels of intelligence they actually develop (phenotypes), as measured by IQ tests, will depend on how well each child's intellectual development is nurtured by his or her experiences from conception onward, including the conditions created by the

TABLE 3.5 Conditions That Prenatal Diagnosis Can Detect

Procedure	Timing	Conditions Detected
Ultrasound	Throughout pregnancy	Pregnancy; multiple pregnancies; fetal growth and abnormalities, such as limb defects; tubal (ectopic) pregnancy; atypical fetal position
Amniocentesis	15–17 weeks	Chromosomal disorders, such as Down syndrome; neurological disorders; gender of the baby
Chorionic villus sampling (CVS)	11–12 weeks	Tests for most of the same genetic disorders as amniocentesis but is less sensitive to more subtle abnormalities
Fetoscopy	18th week	Used to confirm results from a prior prenatal test or to assess the severity of a disability already identified
Maternal serum alpha-fetoprotein (MSAFP)	15–18 weeks	Various problems, including neural tube defects and Down syndrome; positive first test is followed by additional testing, such as ultrasound and amniocentesis
Percutaneous umbilical blood sampling (PUBS)	18–36 weeks	Down syndrome, neural tube defects, Tay-Sachs disease, cystic fibrosis, sickle-cell disease; gender of the fetus; fetal infections, such as rubella, toxoplasmosis, or AIDS

Sources: ACOG (1995); D'Alton & DeCherney (1993); Feinbloom & Formtin (1987); Weiacker & Steinhard (2010).

child's family, school, and community. Thus, in an enriched environment, the child with low genetic endowment may achieve an IQ that is actually equal to (or even higher than) that of the child with a middle-range endowment who grows up in a restricted or below-average environment. Nevertheless, the first child cannot be expected to achieve an IQ score equal to that of children with high genetic endowment, because this is beyond the upper limit of that child's range of reaction, that is, the highest level of intellectual functioning possible for that child. Figure 3.9 illustrates range of reaction for intelligence. Theorists such as Robert Sternberg (1988) and Howard Gardner (1990), however, believe intelligence consists of several different factors or dimensions, and thus range of reaction may differ according to which aspect of intelligence is being measured. We will look more closely at these theories when we examine cognitive development in middle childhood in Chapter 8.

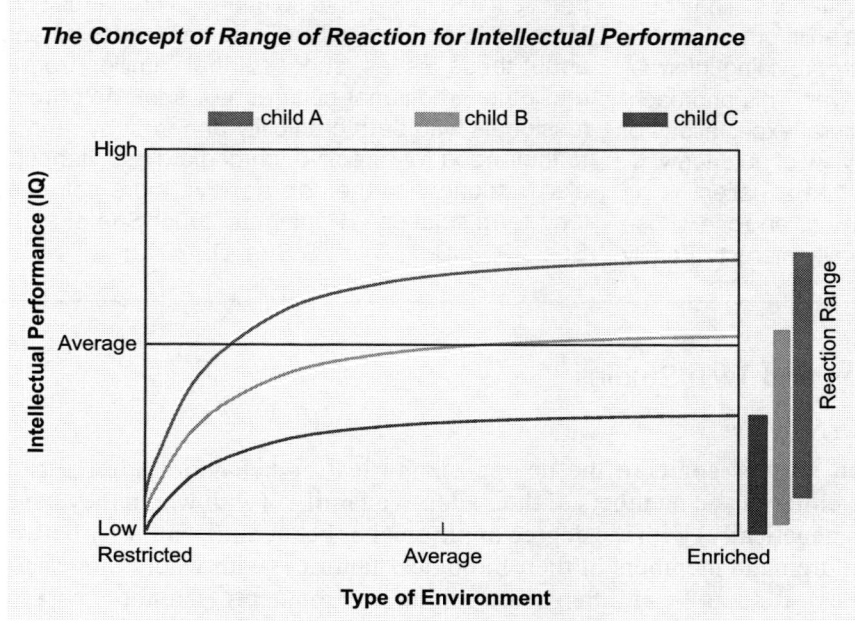

FIGURE 3.9
Range of Reaction for Intellectual Performance

Range of reaction refers to the range of possible phenotypes as a result of different environments interacting with a specific genotype. As this figure shows, while intellectual performance will be impaired or facilitated for all children, depending on whether the environment is restricted, average, or enriched, the range of potential intellectual performance in reaction to different environments will be limited by the child's genetic inheritance for intelligence.
Source: Adapted from Turkheimer & Gottesman, 1991.

Chapter 3 Genetics, Prenatal Development, and Birth

> **A Multicultural View**
>
> ### Cultural Difference and Genetic Counseling
>
> The growing Asian American populations in the Western world tends to use genetic counseling infrequently (Yu, 2012). Reasons for this include lack of information, misperceptions about such services, language and cultural barriers, and cultural attitudes that strongly discourage seeking outside help for family problems.
>
> In traditional Asian cultures, the family is the most important social unit. It is a source of material, social, and emotional support for its members and is responsible for maintaining the cultural and religious traditions that connect the present generation with past and future ones. The personal decisions and actions of an individual regarding pregnancy and genetic counseling reflect not only on herself but on her *nuclear family* (spouse and children), her *extended family* (parents, siblings, and other relatives), and *past and future generations* of her family (Chan, 1991; Wang & Marsh, 1992). John Roland, a psychologist who has studied personality development in India and Japan, believes that in addition to an *individual* and a *spiritual* sense of self, individuals growing up in such traditional societies develop a *powerful familial* self. Within this sense of self, a person experiences himself as an inseparable part of the family unit and one whose actions will be largely determined by family needs and expectations (Roland, 1988).
>
> Three other areas of cultural difference are important for genetic counselors to understand: (1) *collective versus personal autonomy,* (2) *shame and stigma,* and (3) *directive versus nondirective authority* (Wang & Marsh, 1992).
>
> ### Collective Versus Personal Autonomy
>
> A belief in *personal autonomy* is a cornerstone of Western genetic counseling, which views the patient as a self-determining individual who is largely free from the external control of family and other outside influences. The counselor's goal is to help the patient make an informed, autonomous decision about what is best by providing information in a nondirective and value-free way. This approach, however, frequently conflicts with cultural expectations of Asian patients, who hold a *collective* view of autonomy.
>
> *Collective autonomy* presumes that a patient is an inseparable part of the traditional family unit and one whose actions will be largely determined by family interests. Family roles and responsibilities are rigidly and hierarchically defined based on generation, age, and gender, with the father occupying a position of unquestioned leadership and authority. This pattern serves to minimize family conflict by allowing little room for individuality and independence on the part of its members and to maintain family harmony and further the family's welfare and reputation (Roland, 1988; Wang & Marsh, 1992).
>
> ### Shame and Stigma
>
> In traditional Asian culture, which places tremendous importance on daughters being successful in finding a marriage partner, infertility is viewed as a handicapping stigma that will make a young woman unmarriageable and bring shame to herself and her family. Such problems are therefore managed within the family. To seek outside help from a genetic counselor would be a public admission of failure (Paniagua, 2005; Sue & Zane, 1987; Wang & Marsh, 1992).
>
> ### Directive Versus Nondirective Authority
>
> A *nondirective approach to authority* is a second cornerstone of genetic counseling that directly conflicts with the cultural expectations of Asian patients. This approach assumes the patient is responsible for making her own decisions and should not be influenced by the counselor's own views and values. In contrast, the *directive approach* assumes that as an expert authority, the counselor should provide the patient with clear and highly structured guidance about what he should do.
>
> The directive approach is much more consistent with the authority relations and role expectations in Asian families. It therefore is more likely to relieve high levels of anxiety, shame, and doubt by providing practical and immediate solutions to problems (Wang & Marsh, 1992). Stanley Sue, who has written extensively about these issues, suggests that families from Asian and other traditional cultures will seek help from professionals who earn credibility and trust by responding to their need for directive, immediate assistance, while also working with them to achieve more self-directed, long-term solutions (Paniagua, 2005; Sue et al., 1994; Sue, 1998; Sue, D.W., & Sue, D., 2012).

Adoption and Twin Studies

Adoption Studies

adoption study A research method for studying the relative contributions of heredity and environment in which genetically related children reared apart are compared with genetically unrelated children reared together.

Adoption studies compare the degree of physical or behavioral similarity between adoptive children and members of their adoptive families (with whom they have little in common genetically) with the degree of physical or behavioral similarity between these same children and members of their biological families (with whom they share half of their genes). If adoptive children share similar environments (but not genes) with their

> **What Do You Think?**
>
> Do modern medical techniques unwittingly perpetuate several hereditary disorders by using heroic measures to keep alive severely impaired newborns who in the past might have died? If so, does this practice pose an ethical problem?

adoptive family members, differences in trait similarity to their adoptive versus biological relatives should tell something about the influence of their genetic differences. For example, if the IQ scores of adopted children correlated more highly with the IQ scores of their biological families than with those of their adoptive families, we might conclude that heredity—nature—made a strong contribution to intelligence. However, if the IQ scores of these adoptive children were significantly higher (or lower) than those of their biological parents, this might also indicate the influence of family circumstances and other environmental factors—nurture.

Twin Studies

Twin studies compare pairs of *identical twins* raised in the same family with pairs of *fraternal twins* (50 percent shared genes) raised in the same family. Because identical twins have the exact same genetic makeup, greater similarity between identical twins than between fraternal twins on a trait such as intelligence probably would reflect the influence of heredity.

Twin Adoption Studies

Twin adoption studies compare pairs of identical twins who are raised apart since birth in different environments. Twin adoption studies provide the most effective method for understanding the gene-environment relationship in humans. If we could study identical twins who inherit exactly the same genes but are raised in truly different family environments, we would be able to separate the relative contributions of heredity and environment. The catch is to find twins who are growing up in adoptive

twin study A research method for studying the relative contributions of heredity and environment in which the degree of similarity between genetically identical twins (developed from a single egg) is compared with the similarity between fraternal twins (developed from two eggs).

twin adoption study Research that compares twins reared apart with unrelated persons reared together.

Shared genes or shared experiences? Studies comparing identical twins with fraternal twins raised in the same family can help to determine the influences of heredity and environment on the development of a variety of characteristics.
Source: MJTH/Shutterstock.com.

Chapter 3 Genetics, Prenatal Development, and Birth

families. An additional problem is that adoptive families are most frequently chosen with the goal of offering twins similar socioeconomic, cultural, and religious conditions and experiences, raising the question of how different their adoptive family environments really are.

Linkage and Association Studies

Linkage and association studies allow researchers to identify *polymorphisms,* certain segments of human DNA that are inherited together in a predictable pattern—as genetic markers for the genes near which they are located. *Linkage studies* seek to discover polymorphisms that are coinherited, or "linked," with a particular trait in families unusually prone to that trait. This was the case in the discovery of a genetic marker for Huntington disease, and for fragile X syndrome, which were described earlier in this chapter. *Association studies* compare the relative frequency of polymorphisms in two populations, one with the trait and one without it (Hagerman, 1996; Horgan, 1993).

Cautions and Conclusions about the Influence of Heredity and Environment

Though substantial evidence exists that genetic inheritance plays at least a moderate role in differences in physical, intellectual, and personality traits, it is likely that such differences are influenced by *both* heredity and environmental experience. Currently, however, there is a growing trend toward minimizing environmental contributions in favor of *genetic determinism,* a belief that most, if not all, human characteristics, from intellectual functioning to gender roles and career choice, are determined primarily by genes. This tendency may in part be a reaction to *environmental determinism,* an equally simplistic view that sees experience as the central or sole cause of developmental change and dismisses the possibility that genes may also make a significant contribution. It may also reflect the explosive growth in biotechnology and the overly optimistic view it appears to have generated.

Neither biogenetic nor environmental determinism can ever lead to an adequate understanding of human development. Rather, human development is always the product of multiple levels of biological and environmental influences and human agency—the self-determining choices that each individual makes.

PRENATAL DEVELOPMENT AND BIRTH

From the moment of conception, a child becomes a biological entity. How do microscopic cells become people? In the following sections, we look at the events and processes that occur from conception through birth and how they may affect later development. We also look at certain risks and problems of prenatal development and of birth and their long-term impact on the child.

Stages of Prenatal Development

Prenatal development begins with conception and continues through discrete periods, or stages. The first is the **germinal stage**, or *period of the ovum,* which occurs during the first two weeks of pregnancy; the second is the **embryonic stage**, which lasts from the third week to the eighth week; and the third is the **fetal stage**, which lasts from the eighth week until birth.

Conception

Conception normally occurs when one of the approximately 360 million sperm contained in the *semen,* which the father has ejaculated into the mother's vagina during intercourse, swims through the *cervix* (opening of the uterus) into the fallopian tube and successfully attaches itself to the surface of an ovum, or egg, released from one of

---

germinal stage The stage in prenatal development that occurs during the first two weeks of pregnancy; characterized by rapid cell division. Also called the *period of the ovum.*

embryonic stage The stage in prenatal development that lasts from week 2 through week 8.

fetal stage The stage in prenatal development that lasts form the eighth week of pregnancy until birth.

conception The moment at which the male's sperm cell penetrates the female's egg cell (ovum), forming a zygote.

> **What Do You Think?**
>
> Based on what you have just read, how do you view the relationship between genes and environment? To what degree do you believe most or all of human development will someday be explainable in terms of genetics? Where, in your judgment, does human agency or free will fit in?

the woman's ovaries (Wilcox et al, 1995). (See Figure 3.11.) As noted in the "Focusing On" feature and in Chapter 12's discussion of physical development in early adulthood, some couples have difficulty conceiving through intercourse. In such cases, various technological alternatives exist to join sperm and egg. Once it becomes attached, the sperm gradually penetrates the egg. Within a few hours, the walls of the sperm cell and the *nucleus,* or center, of the egg cell both begin to disintegrate. In this process, as Figure 3.10 shows, the sperm and egg cells each release their chromosomes, which join to form a new cell called a *zygote* (Wilcox et al., 1995).

At this point, the zygote is still so small that hundreds of them could fit on the head of a pin. Yet it contains all of the necessary genetic information in its DNA molecules to develop into a unique human being.

The Germinal Stage (First Two Weeks)

The newly formed zygote now begins to divide and redivide to form a tiny sixteen-cell sphere called a morula, which between days three and four postconception begins to travel down the fallopian tube to the uterus. At five days postconception, the mass of cells, a *blastocyst,* differentiates into three layers. The *ectoderm* (upper layer) later develops into the epidermis, or outer layer of skin, nails, teeth, and hair, as well as the sensory organs and nervous system. The *endoderm* (lower layer) becomes the digestive system, liver, pancreas, salivary glands, and respiratory system. The *mesoderm* (middle layer) develops somewhat later and becomes the dermis (inner layer of skin), muscles, skeleton, and circulatory and excretory systems. In a short time the *placenta, umbilical cord,* and *amniotic sac* (discussed shortly) also will form from blastocyst cells.

After a few more days—about one week after conception—implantation occurs. During *implantation,* the blastocyst buries itself like a seed in the wall of the uterus. The fully implanted blastocyst is now referred to as the *embryo.* Figure 3.11 illustrates the changes that occur during the germinal stage of prenatal development.

Gametes and Zygote

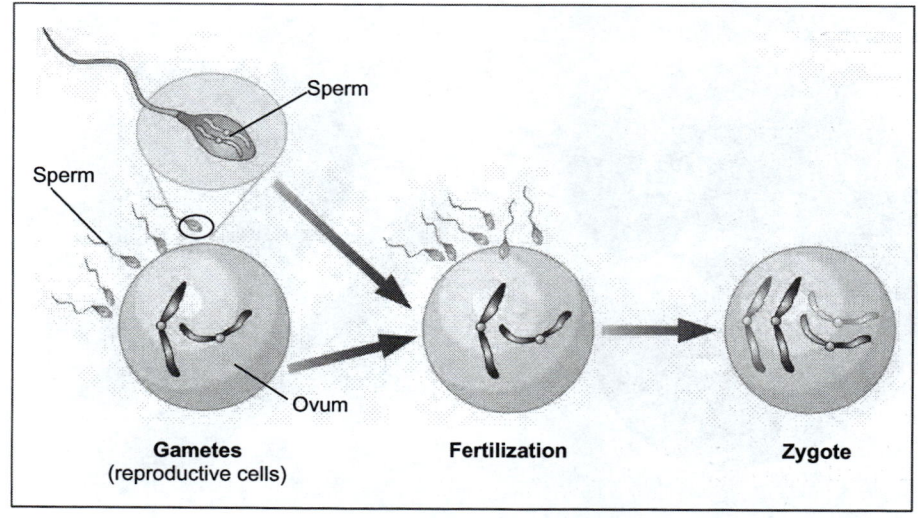

FIGURE 3.10
Gametes and Zygote

Each gamete, whether sperm or ovum, contains twenty-three single chromosomes. (Two chromosomes are shown in each gamete here for ease of illustration.) At fertilization, sperm and ovum combine to form a zygote with forty-six chromosomes in twenty-three pairs. (Two pairs are shown here.) In each pair, one chromosome is from the mother, and one is from the father.

FIGURE 3.11
The Germinal Stage of Prenatal Development

The sperm and ovum join to form a single-celled *zygote*, which then divides and re-divides to become a multicelled *blastocyst*. The blastocyst buries, or *implants*, itself in the uterine wall. The fully-implanted blastocyst is now called an *embryo*.

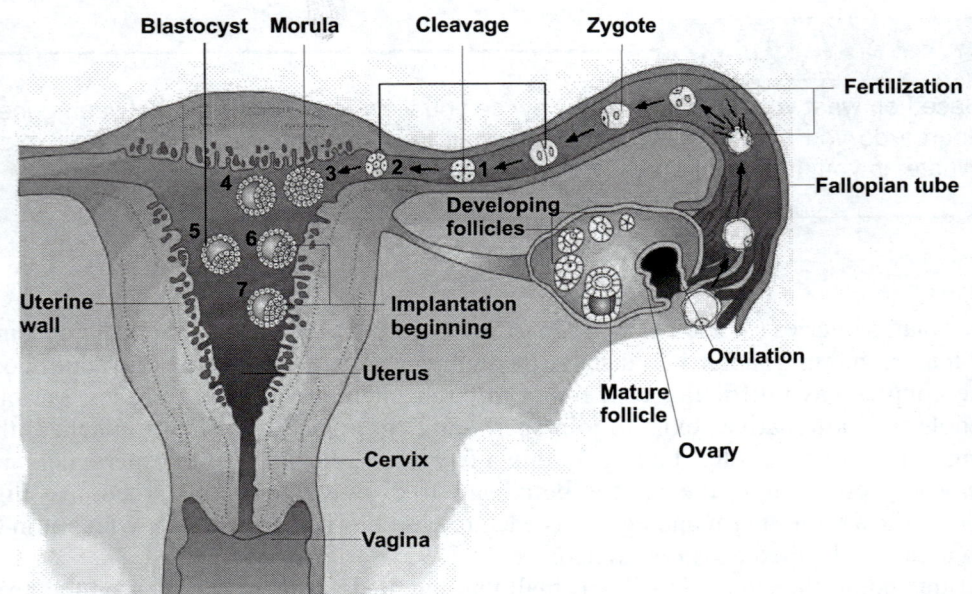

The Embryonic Stage (Third Through Eighth Weeks)

Growth during the embryonic stage (and the fetal stage that follows) occurs in two patterns: a *cephalocaudal* (head-to-tail) pattern and a *proximodistal* (near-to-far, from the center of the body outward) pattern. Thus, the head, blood vessels, and heart—the most vital body parts and organs—begin to develop earlier than the arms, legs, hands, and feet. The three-dimensional renderings shown here and also in Figure 3.12 (upper portion) later in the chapter illustrate these changes.

At *three weeks*, the head, tail, brain, and circulatory system begin to develop and the heart has begun beating. At *four weeks*, the embryo is little more than an inch long. The beginnings of a spinal cord, arms, and legs are evident, a small digestive system and a nervous system have developed, and the brain has become more differentiated (P. Harris, 1983). During *week five*, hands and lungs begin to form. During *week six*, the head grows larger, the brain becomes more fully developed, and hands, legs, and feet become more fully formed. During *week seven*, muscles form and the cerebral cortex begins to develop.

placenta An organ that delivers oxygen and nutrients from the mother to the fetus and carries away the fetus's waste products, which the mother will excrete.

While these developments are taking place, a placenta forms between the mother and the embryo, the **placenta** is an area on the uterine wall through which the mother supplies oxygen and nutrients to the embryo and the embryo returns waste products from her

The embryonic period is characterized by remarkable differentiation and specialization as most of the body's tissues, organs, structures, and systems begin to develop, and some even become functional. The three-dimensional rendering on the left illustrates an embryo at four weeks, while the image on the right shows the embryo just one month later (at eight weeks).
Source: Sebastian Kaulitzki/Shutterstock.com.

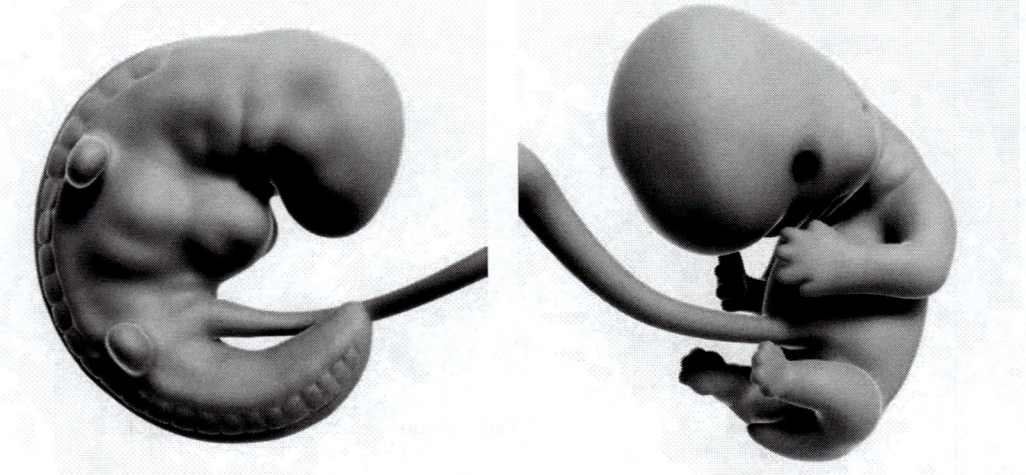

Part 1 Beginnings

bloodstream. In the placenta, thousands of tiny blood vessels from the two circulatory systems intermingle. Although only minute quantities of blood can cross the separating membranes, nutrients pass easily from one bloodstream to the other through a process called *osmosis*. Although many toxic chemicals and drugs in the mother's system do not spread easily by osmosis, others do. As we discuss later, seemingly harmless chemicals sometimes prove devastating to the embryo.

The **umbilical cord** connects the embryo to the placenta. It consists of three large blood vessels, one to provide nutrients and two to carry waste products into the mother's body. The cord enters the embryo at a place that becomes the baby's belly button, or navel, after the cord is cut following birth.

By the end of the eighth week, an **amniotic sac** has developed. The amniotic sac is a tough, spongy bag filled with salty fluid that completely surrounds the embryo, protects it from sudden jolts, and maintains a stable temperature. The embryo floats gently in this environment until birth, protected even if its mother goes jogging, sits down suddenly, or shovels heavy snow.

umbilical cord Three large blood vessels that connect the embryo to the placenta, one to provide nutrients and two to remove waste products.

amniotic sac A tough, spongy bag filled with salty fluid that surrounds the embryo, protects it from sudden jolts, and maintains a stable temperature.

The Fetal Stage (Ninth Week to Birth)

At about *eight weeks* of gestation, the embryo develops its first bone cells, which marks the end of differentiation into the major structures. At this point, the embryo acquires a new name, *the fetus*, and begins the long process of developing relatively small features, such as fingers and fingernails and eyelids and eyebrows. Their smallness, however, belies their importance. For example, the eyes undergo their greatest growth during this stage of development. The fetus's newly developing eyelids fuse shut at about ten weeks and do not reopen until the eyes themselves are essentially complete, at around sixteen to twenty weeks postconception.

Not only the eyes but most other physical features become more adult looking during this period and more truly human in proportion (P. Harris, 1983). The head becomes smaller relative to the rest of the body (even though it remains large by adult standards), partly because the fetus's long bones, the ones supporting its limbs, begin growing significantly. Thus, its arms and legs look increasingly substantial.

By *twelve weeks*, the fetus is about three inches long and able to respond reflexively to touch. By *sixteen weeks*, it has grown to about 4.5 inches in length. If its palm is touched, it exhibits a grasp reflex by closing its fist; if the sole of its foot is touched, its toes spread

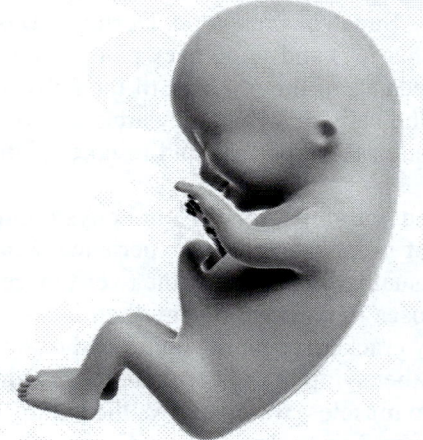 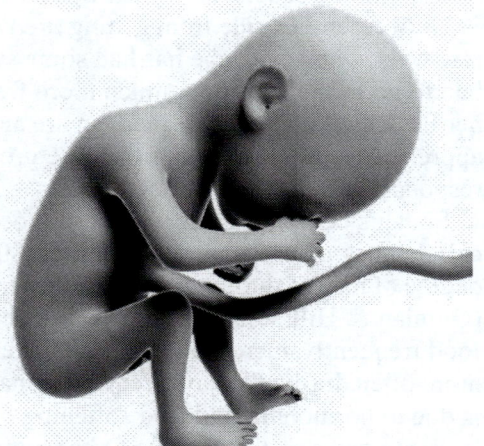 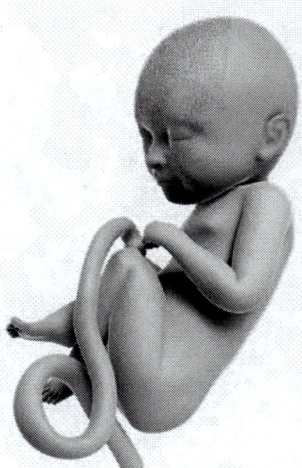

The fetal period is characterized by rapid growth. The three-dimensional renderings depict a fetus at three months *(left)*, six months *(middle)*, and nine months *(right)*. What these renderings cannot easily convey is the actual growth in length and weight during the fetal period. The fetus at three months typically weighs about 0.5 ounce and is just over two inches in length; the fetus at six months averages 1.3 pounds and is nearly twelve inches in length; the fetus at nine months averages 7.5 pounds and is about twenty inches in length.
Source: Sebastian Kaulitzki/Shutterstock.com.

(Babinski reflex); and if its lips are touched, it responds with a sucking reflex. In addition, the fetal heartbeat can now be heard through the wall of the uterus.

Between the *fourth* and *fifth months* (sixteen to twenty weeks), hands and feet become fully developed, eyes can open and close, hearing is present, lungs become capable of breathing in and out, and nails, hair, and sweat glands develop. Around the sixteenth week, most pregnant women feel *quickening,* the movement of the fetus inside the womb. Fetal movements appear to grow progressively stronger and more frequent from eighteen weeks on, reaching a maximum between twenty-eight and twenty-nine weeks, after which they diminish somewhat until delivery (Primeau, 1993).

By the beginning of the *seventh month,* the fetus is about sixteen inches long and weighs approximately three to five pounds. It is able to cry, breathe, swallow, digest, excrete, move about, and suck its thumb. The reflexes mentioned earlier are fully developed. Because of these capacities, the fetus is said to have attained *age of viability*, meaning it could survive if born at this point.

By the *eighth month,* the fetus weighs between five and seven pounds and has begun to develop a layer of body fat that will help it to regulate its body temperature after birth, and by *nine months* it has achieved its full birth weight. Toward the end of nine months, the average baby is about 7.5 pounds and almost twenty inches long. Growth in size stops, although fat continues to be stored, heart rate increases, and internal organ systems become more efficient in preparation for birth and independent life outside the womb.

The developing fetus is also responsive to stimuli in the external environment, such as sound and vibration (Kisilevsky et al., 1992). For example, newborn infants have been found to show preferences for stories and rhymes read aloud to them during the final six weeks of pregnancy (DeCasper et al., 1994), and intrauterine sounds, such as a mother's heartbeat, have been found to soothe newborns (Ullal-Gupta et al., 2013).

The Experience of Pregnancy

Sudah is nearing the end of her pregnancy—just eight weeks to go! She has been careful to eat a good, balanced diet and has gained about twenty-four pounds, which her doctor says is fine for her size and weight. Lately, her belly feels like a basketball, and she sometimes worries whether Dan, her husband, still finds her attractive and whether she will ever get her prepregnancy figure back. During the first two months of pregnancy, Sudah felt nauseous a lot of the time and found it hard to keep food down. She found that eating small amounts of food (especially plain crackers) throughout the day helped, as did resting more frequently—which was hard to do because she was still working full time.

Until recently, aside from getting tired more easily, Sudah has felt good. During the last few weeks, however, she has had some swelling in her legs and some back pain, and has had to go to the bathroom much more frequently because of the pressure of the baby on her bladder. Although she and Dan are anxious for the baby to arrive, they are somewhat apprehensive about whether they are grown up enough to be parents and to take on the responsibilities of parenthood.

Sudah's complaints are typical of those associated with the hormonal and physiological changes of pregnancy. More than 80 percent of pregnant women experience some degree of nausea during the first trimester, but this usually disappears by the twelfth week (Quinlan & Hill, 2003). Strategies for relieving nausea include eating small amounts of food frequently, increasing protein intake, eating dry crackers or plain yogurt, and resting more often during the day. Frequent urination is another symptom of early pregnancy and is due to hormonally induced softening of the pelvic muscles, which allows the enlarged uterus to press on the bladder. Other symptoms include fatigue, headaches, dizziness and fainting, constipation, leg cramps, heartburn, shortness of breath, swelling of legs, hands, or face, varicose veins, and backache (Davis, 1993).

In addition to the influence of hormonal changes, some of these symptoms are due to weight gain during pregnancy. Both a woman's weight before pregnancy and her weight gain during pregnancy influence the baby's birth weight. Current recommendations from the Institute of Medicine (2009) and the American College of Obstetricians and Gynecologists (ACOG, 2013) are as follows:

- Women who are underweight (body mass index [BMI] less than 18.5) before pregnancy should gain between twenty-eight and forty pounds during pregnancy,
- women of normal weight (BMI of 18.5–24.9) should gain between twenty-five and thirty-five pounds,
- women who are overweight (BMI of 25–29.9) should gain between fifteen and twenty-five pounds, and
- women who are obese (BMI of 30 and greater) prior to pregnancy should gain between eleven and twenty pounds.

More-exact recommendations for weight gain should result from consultations early in their pregnancy between pregnant women and their health care providers. Why is there so much emphasis on weight gain during pregnancy? Because the amount of weight gained during pregnancy has significant effects on the present and future health of the mother and her infant. Where does the weight gain go? The increased size of the uterus, breast tissue, blood volume, body fluid, and extra fat to prepare the woman to produce milk for breast feeding all contribute to the additional pounds (ACOG, 1995).

Pregnancy is a powerful experience that can dramatically affect how both the mother and the father feel about themselves and each other. For most prospective parents, it raises the question "Am I ready to be emotionally and economically responsible for this baby?" Couples who are experiencing pregnancy together may wonder, "How will having a baby affect our relationship with each other?" We will take a closer look at these questions in Chapter 13's discussion of psychosocial development in early adulthood. See the interview with Katie Glover for a nurse-practitioner's observations regarding pregnancy and preparation for childbirth.

Prenatal Influences on the Child

As we have noted, physical structures develop in a particular sequence and at precise times. Psychologists and biologists sometimes call such regularity *canalization*. **Canalization** refers to the tendency of genes to narrowly direct or restrict growth and development of particular physical and behavioral characteristics to a single (or very few) phenotypic outcomes and to resist environmental factors that push development in other directions (McCall, 1981).

Typically, prenatal development is a highly reliable process, so prospective parents generally worry much more than they need to about whether their baby will be "all right." In fact, 97 percent of human infants are perfect at birth, and of the 3 percent who are not, half have only minor defects such as hammertoes, extra fingers or toes, or birthmarks (CDC, 2008; Guttmacher & Kaiser, 1984).

canalization The tendency of many developmental processes to unfold in highly predictable ways under a wide range of conditions.

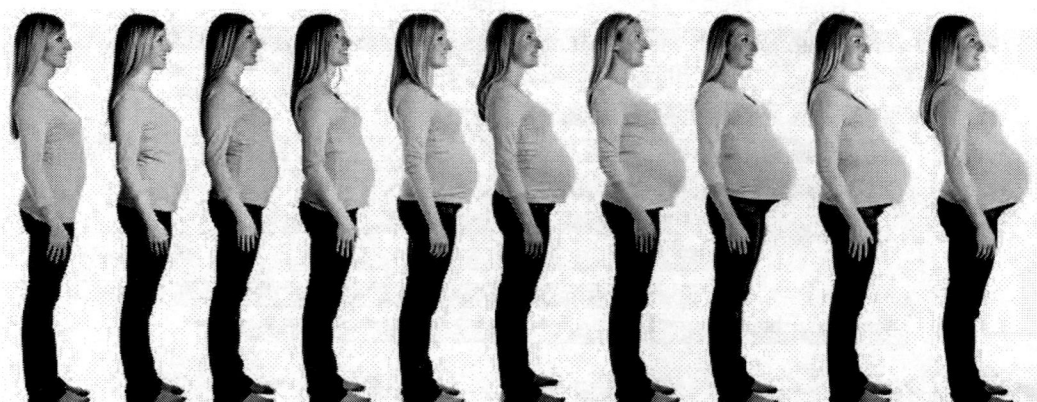

In addition to the visible signs of pregnancy, expectant mothers often experience a series of aches and pains associated with the changes in their bodies during pregnancy. Headaches and backaches are common, as are cramps in the legs and pain in the lower abdomen as ligaments and muscles are stretched.
Source: mathom/Shutterstock.com.

> **What Do You Think?**
>
> For those of you who have already experienced pregnancy, what was it like? For those of you who haven't, what do you imagine the experience might be like for you? How has what you have read so far in this chapter influenced your views about pregnancy?

However, certain conditions can interfere with even the highly canalized processes of fetal development. These conditions are sometimes called *risk factors*. Risk factors increase the chance that the future baby will have medical problems but do not guarantee that these problems will actually appear. Risk factors include the mothers biological characteristics, including age and physical condition, and exposure to diseases, drugs, chemicals, stress, and other environmental hazards during pregnancy.

Harmful Substances, Diseases, and Environmental Hazards

As the complex sequence of prenatal growth proceeds, the timing of the development of each new organ or body part is especially important. **Critical period** refers to a time-limited period during which certain developmental changes are highly vulnerable to disruption. This "window of opportunity" is dictated by complex genetic codes in each cell *and* by the particular set of prenatal conditions that must be in place for each change to occur. If development is disturbed or blocked during a critical period, the changes that were scheduled to occur may be disrupted or prevented from occurring at all. Figure 3.12 shows the critical periods in human development.

Especially during the early weeks of its life, development of the embryo is particularly vulnerable to disruption if it is exposed (through the mother) to certain harmful substances called *teratogens*. A **teratogen** is any substance or other environmental influence that can interfere with or permanently damage an embryo's growth. Named after an ancient Greek word meaning "monster-creating," teratogens can result in serious physical malformations and even in the death of the embryo. Teratogens are most harmful if exposure occurs during the critical or sensitive period for the particular physical change

critical period Any period during which development is particularly susceptible to an event or influence, either negative or positive.

teratogen Any substance that can harm the developing embryo or fetus.

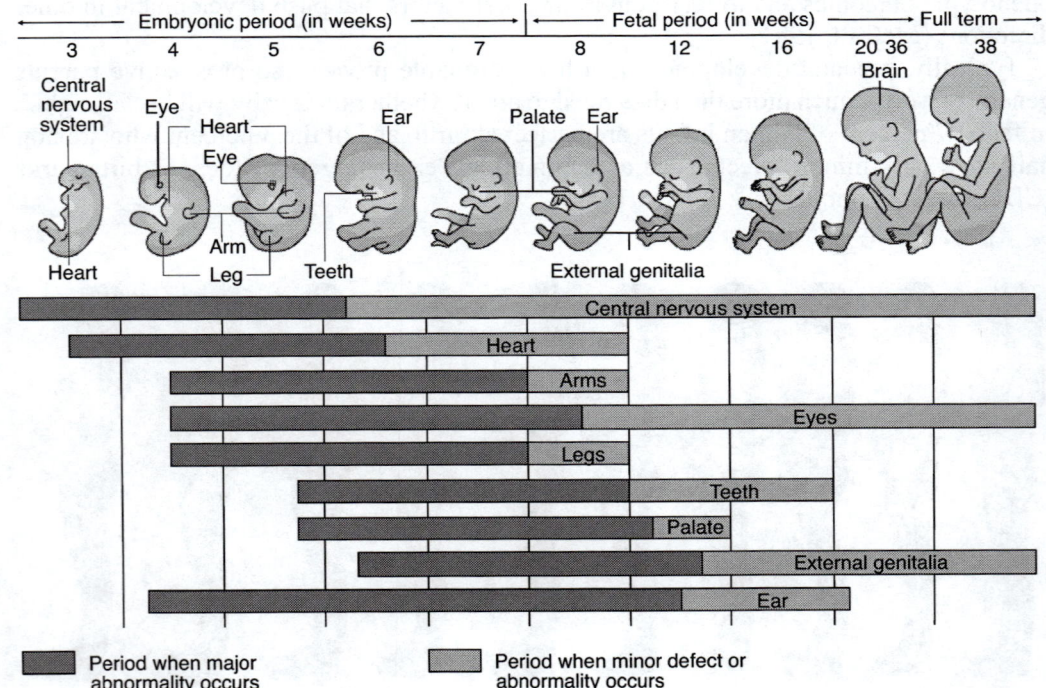

FIGURE 3.12
Timing and Effects of Teratogens During Sensitive or Critical Periods

This figure illustrates the sensitive or critical periods in human prenatal development. The dark band indicates highly sensitive or critical periods; the light band indicates stages that are less sensitive to disruption caused by teratogens. Note that each structure has a critical period during which its development may be disrupted.

Part 1 Beginnings

to occur. Teratogens include many *medicinal and nonmedicinal drugs; other chemicals; diseases* (viruses and bacteria); and certain *other harmful environmental influences*, such as radiation. Teratogens can be contracted from a variety of sources, including from other individuals who have communicable diseases, from drugs, from ingesting foods that have been contaminated, and from exposure to chemicals, X rays, and radioactivity in the workplace and in nonwork environments.

Several factors influence a teratogen's effects. The first is the *timing of exposure*. The nine months of pregnancy generally are divided into three *trimesters*, each lasting three months. Disruptions during the first trimester, when the critical periods for embryonic and fetal development occur, are most likely to result in spontaneous abortion or serious birth defects. During the third week, for example, teratogens can harm the basic structures of the heart and central nervous system that are just beginning to form. The effects of exposure in the second and third trimesters generally are less likely to be as severe.

The impact of a teratogen is also influenced by the *intensity and duration of exposure*. For example, the higher the dose (intensity) and the longer the exposure to a harmful drug such as alcohol or cocaine, the greater the chance that the baby will be harmed and that the harm will be more severe than if dose and duration are less. The *number of other harmful influences* that are also present also makes a difference. The greater the number, the greater the risk. Finally, the *biogenetic vulnerability of mother and infant* will influence a teratogen's effects. Mothers and their infants will differ in the degree to which they will be affected by exposure to a particular type and level of teratogen. For example, whereas heavy and prolonged drinking is likely to affect almost all babies, very moderate drinking may cause considerable harm for one infant but no measurable harm for another.

Medicinal Drugs

Medical science has developed countless drugs with highly beneficial effects, from curing illness to relieving pain. Yet a medication with positive effects overall may negatively affect fetal development if taken during pregnancy. A drug called *thalidomide* is a dramatic example of how such damage can occur. It also illustrates the political, economic, and social policy implications of new medical and scientific discoveries that affect human growth and development.

Thalidomide is a seemingly harmless sedative that during die late 1950s and early 1960s was widely prescribed for calming nerves, promoting sleep, and reducing morning sickness and other forms of nausea dining the early weeks of pregnancy. Although it was advertised as being completely safe, between 1958 and 1962 thousands of babies were born with birth defects that included missing, shortened, or misshapen arms and legs, deafness, severe facial deformities, seizure disorders, dwarfism, and brain damage. Not until 1961 was the drug banned in the United States, in part because the effects of teratogens were less understood then and because the federal Food and Drug Administration (FDA) was under political pressure from the drug industry to keep thalidomide on the market (Stout, 1993). It is estimated that currently there are about eight thousand thalidomide-affected adults and that twice that many babies were stillborn (dead at birth) or died shortly afterward because of defects caused by thalidomide (HHS, 2005; Stout, 1993).

Teratogenic drugs pose an even greater developmental risk in developing countries in South America, Africa, and Asia, where drugs are less strictly regulated than in the United States. In Brazil, one of the world's largest producers of thalidomide, the drug is used to help treat the symptoms of leprosy, which afflicts almost 300,000 people in that country. This has led to a growing number of birth defects in babies born to mothers with leprosy who have taken the drug because they are not aware of its effects (Gorman, 1993; Vianna et al., 2011).

Unfortunately, the damage done by toxic drugs or chemicals does not always show itself as obviously or as soon as in the case of thalidomide. For about twenty-five years following World War II, another drug, *diethylstilbestrol (DES)*, was taken by 3 million to 6 million pregnant women with histories of spontaneous abortions to prevent miscarriages. The drug was especially useful during the early months, when miscarriages occur most often. At birth, the babies of women who took DES seemed perfectly normal, and they remained so throughout childhood. As they became young adults, however, abnormal development of vaginal cells and structural abnormalities of the uterus were found in all female babies who had been exposed, and about one in one thousand eventually developed cancer of the vagina or of the cervix. The sons of DES mothers developed abnormalities in the structure of their reproductive organs and had a higher than usual rate of testicular cancer. Even the daughters who did not get cancer had significantly more problems than usual with their own pregnancies, including higher rates of spontaneous abortion and stillbirth as well as more minor problems, and they had them whether or not their families had histories of difficult births. As most of the individuals exposed to DES before birth are now reaching midlife, there is growing evidence of increased risk for autoimmune disorders such as pernicious anemia, myasthenia gravis (a nerve-muscle disorder), serious intestinal disorders, and multiple sclerosis as a result of DES damage to the immune system (Brody, 1993). DES support networks and social action groups for affected individuals and families have been formed in both Canada and the United States (Linn et al, 1988; Sato, 1993).

Nonmedicinal Drugs

Not surprisingly, drugs such as *heroin, cocaine, alcohol,* and *tobacco* also affect the fetus. Table 3.6 summarizes their effects.

Many babies born to mothers who consume alcohol during pregnancy display fetal alcohol effects (FAEs), and the most severely affected babies exhibit a cluster of defects known as *fetal alcohol syndrome (FAS)*. These two effects represent two points on what is a continuum of alcohol-related teratogenic effects called *fetal alcohol spectrum disorders (FASD)* (Riley, Infante, & Warren, 2011). *Fetal alcohol effects* refer to a set of symptoms that include lower birth weight, lack of responsiveness and arousability, and increased occurrences of heart and respiratory abnormalities in infants. These infants achieve lower mental development scores at eight months and at four years and have higher rates of learning disabilities (Barr et al., 1990; Streissguth et al., 1989, 1995). Longitudinal studies show that problems with vigilance, attention, and short-term memory may be found in adolescents who experienced exposure to alcohol prenatally (Streissguth et al., 1995).

Symptoms of **fetal alcohol syndrome (FAS)** include central nervous system damage and physical abnormalities of the heart, head, face, and joints; intellectual disability and/or behavioral problems, such as hyperactivity and poor impulse control; and impaired growth and/or failure to thrive (Riley et al., 2011). Babies of heavy drinkers, particularly in the last three months of pregnancy, are at much greater risk for these problems. It is estimated that 50 to 75 percent of infants born to chronically alcoholic women may be affected (Barr et al., 1990; Blackman, 1990).

Even moderate daily drinking during pregnancy (two ounces of hard liquor, nine ounces of wine, or two beers) is associated with an increase in these disorders. The chance of fetal alcohol effects in the infant of a mother who consumes more than four drinks daily is estimated to be about 33 percent and about 10 percent for a woman who consumes between two and four drinks per day. However, drinking alcohol at lower levels (less than one drink per day) *may* be safe, as women who consumed less than one drink per day during pregnancy had children who did not differ from abstainers on measures of attention difficulties, behavioral problems, or learning disabilities when those children were fourteen years old (O'Callaghan et al., 2007). The difficulty in determining a "safe" level of alcohol consumption for pregnant women is due to women varying significantly in the quantity of alcohol their bodies can metabolize and in the rate at which their bodies metabolize alcohol (Burd, Blair, & Dropps, 2012). The less alcohol metabolized by the mother's body, the greater the quantity of alcohol exposed to the embryo or fetus, which is why current American Academy of Pediatrics (AAP) guidelines state that no amount of alcohol consumption is safe (AAP, 2015).

Maternal Diseases

Exposure of a pregnant woman to certain viral, bacteriological, and parasitic diseases can adversely affect her baby's development. Table 3.6 summarizes the teratogenic effects of exposure to selected diseases and drugs during pregnancy. In addition, some diseases can

---

fetal alcohol syndrome (FAS) A congenital condition exhibited by babies born to mothers who consumed too much alcohol during pregnancy. They do not arouse easily and tend to behave sluggishly in general; they also have distinctive facial characteristics.

TABLE 3.6 Teratogens and Their Effects

Teratogen	Effects
Drugs	
Medicinal Drugs	
Thalidomide	Birth defects, such as missing, shortened, or misshapen arms and legs, deafness; severe facial deformities; seizure disorders; dwarfism; brain damage; fetal/infant death
Diethylstilbestrol (DES)	*Grown daughters:* Vaginal and cervical cancer; spontaneous abortions and stillbirth; autoimmune disorders, such as pernicious anemia, myasthenia gravis (a nerve-muscle disorder), intestinal disorder, multiple sclerosis
	Grown sons: Abnormalities in reproductive organs, testicular cancer
Nonmedicinal Drugs	
Heroin	Withdrawal symptoms, including vomiting, trembling, irritability, fever, disturbed sleep, an abnormally high-pitched cry; delayed social and motor development
Cocaine	Miscarriage or premature delivery, low birth weight, irritability, respiratory problems, genital and urinary tract deformities, heart defects, central nervous system problems
Marijuana	Tremors and startles among newborns; inattention, impulsivity, memory deficits, and blunted academic achievement during childhood
Alcohol	*Fetal alcohol effects (FAEs):* Lower birth weight, lack of responsiveness and arousability, heart rate and respiratory abnormalities, delayed cognitive development, learning disabilities
	Fetal alcohol syndrome (FAS): Central nervous system damage; heart defects; small head; distortions of joints; abnormal facial features; intellectual disability; behavioral disorders, such as hyperactivity and poor impulse control; impaired growth and/or failure to thrive
Tobacco	Spontaneous abortion, prematurity, fetal/infant death, reduced birth weight, poorer postnatal adjustment
Maternal Diseases	
Rubella	*First trimester:* Blindness, deafness, heart defects, damage to central nervous system, intellectual disability
	Second trimester: Problems with hearing, vision, and language
Syphilis and gonorrhea	Fetal death, jaundice, anemia, pneumonia, skin rash, bone inflammation, dental deformities, hearing difficulties, blindness
Genital herpes	Disease of skin and mucous membranes, blindness, brain damage, seizures, and developmental delay
Cytomegalovirus	Jaundice, microcephaly (very small head), deafness, eye problems, increased risk for severe illness and infant death
AIDS	Abnormally small skull; facial deformities; immune system damage; enlarged lymph glands, liver, and spleen; recurrent infections; poor growth; fever; brain disease; developmental delay; deteriorated motor skills
Toxoplasmosis	Spontaneous abortion, prematurity, low birth weight, enlarged liver and spleen, jaundice, anemia, congenital defects, intellectual disability, seizures, cerebral palsy, retinal disease, blindness

be directly transmitted from mother to fetus, often with devastating consequences; these include syphilis and gonorrhea.

A pregnant woman with untreated syphilis can transmit the disease to her fetus. In 25 percent of cases, death of the fetus results, usually during the second trimester. An additional 25 percent of infected fetuses die soon after birth. Of those who survive, about

25 percent show symptoms such as jaundice, anemia, pneumonia, skin rash, and bone inflammation (Blackman, 1990). Fetuses that contract gonorrhea in the birth canal may later develop eye infections or become blind. It is now standard practice to put drops of silver nitrate or penicillin in newborns' eyes to protect them against these conditions, because gonorrhea may be present in the mother without obvious symptoms. HIV, which leads to pediatric AIDS, can also be directly transmitted from mother to fetus.

Pediatric AIDS

Of the approximately four million babies born in the United States each year, 100 to 200 will have HIV, the virus associated with the development of AIDS, numbers that represent a 90 percent reduction in rates of pediatric AIDS in the past twenty years (EGPAF, 2013; Lee, 1995; Task Force on Pediatric AIDS, 1989). About three-fourths of AIDS cases in children involve perinatal (at the time of birth) transmission from an infected mother to her child, either through the placenta or through contact with HIV-contaminated blood at the time of delivery (American Academy of Pediatrics, 1991; EGPAF, 2013). Children from predominantly low-socioeconomic-status families make up three-quarters of all pediatric AIDS cases in the United States, although they account for only one-fourth of all American children. Because AIDS has an incubation period of up to five years in adults, pregnant women may be unaware that they have the virus or that it can be transmitted to their offspring. Although most children infected *perinatally* show symptoms before age one, some children who are infected may live for years without symptoms. Because newborns retain the protective antibodies they receive from their mothers for several months after birth, testing a newborn for HIV antibodies can give accurate information only about the mother (Lee, 1995; Richter, 1993).

Research indicates that when antiretroviral drugs are administered to AIDS-infected women during late pregnancy, administered intravenously during labor, and given intravenously to their newborns immediately after delivery, the risk of having an HIV-infected baby can be reduced by about 4 percent) (DGHA, 2013).

Pediatric AIDS is a worldwide problem, especially in sub-Saharan Africa, where 91 percent of the 3.4 million children living with HIV worldwide reside (WHO, 2013). Pregnant women in this and other impoverished regions of the world typically do not have access to the three most effective strategies to reduce mother-child transmission of HIV/AIDS: (1) administration of antiretroviral medications given to expectant mothers and then to their infants, (2) the use of cesarean deliveries or "C-sections" for AIDS-infected mothers, and (3) substitution of infant formula for breast milk (Sullivan, 2003).

Environmental Hazards

Currently the majority of women in the United States are employed outside the home, and most women who are employed when they become pregnant continue working throughout their pregnancies. Many of the environmental hazards to pregnant women and their babies are encountered in the workplace. These include (1) physical hazards such as noise, radiation, vibration, stressful physical activity, and materials handling; (2) biological hazards such as viruses, fungi, spores, and bacteria; (3) chemical hazards such as anesthetic gases, pesticides, lead, mercury, and organic solvents; and (4) radiation (Bernhardt, 1990). A mother's age and physical characteristics may also cause complications during pregnancy, as we will see in the next section.

Maternal Age and Physical Characteristics

Healthy women over age thirty-five are not at significantly greater risk for any of these complications than are younger women, although they are at greater risk for infertility and for having a child with Down syndrome (ACOG, 1995). Very young mothers, especially those in their early teens, are at significantly greater risk of having low-birth-weight infants, stillbirths, or problems during delivery. This is partly because teenage mothers have not completed their own growth, so their bodies are unable to meet the extra nutritional demands of a developing fetus. Teenage mothers are more likely to be poor and less likely to get adequate prenatal care and have the maturity of judgment to adapt their lifestyles to the demands of pregnancy (Fraser, Brockert & Ward, 1995; Coley & Chase-Lansdale, 1998).

The United States has the highest rate of teenage pregnancy of all industrialized countries (Lawson & Rhode, 1993; Martin et al., 2013). Pregnant teenagers are much less likely than pregnant adults to maintain nutritious diets and get adequate prenatal care during pregnancy, and they are more likely to suffer complications and experience prolonged and difficult labor. Babies born to teenagers are more likely to be premature and suffer from low birth weight and its associated problems (see Chapter 4). They also have higher rates of neurological defects, have higher mortality rates during their first year, and are more likely to encounter developmental problems during the preschool and school years. We look more closely at the causes and consequences of teenage pregnancy in Chapter 11.

Prenatal Health Care

Adequate early prenatal care is critical to infant and maternal health, and mothers who begin prenatal care early in pregnancy have improved pregnancy and newborn outcomes, including decreased risk of low birth weight and preterm delivery. The quality of prenatal care is strongly influenced by the woman's life circumstances. Race and socioeconomic status, two factors that are closely linked in our society, play a major role. In 2008, for example, only 77 percent of white mothers and 60 percent of African American mothers began care in the first trimester. Seven percent of all mothers delayed care until the last trimester or received no care at all. These mothers were most likely to be teenagers, be unmarried, have less than twelve years of education, and already have three or more children (C. Lewis, 1993; HHS, 2011). Although the risk of problems increases the later prenatal care is begun, by far the worst outcomes occur for mothers receiving no care at all.

How can the prenatal care of high-risk mothers be improved? The *Prenatal/Early Infancy Project* conducted by David Olds and his colleagues is one promising answer to this question (Olds, 1997). Beginning in the second trimester of pregnancy, program nurses made regular home visits during which they provided education about diet and weight gain; the effects of cigarettes, alcohol, and drugs; signs of pregnancy complication; the importance of regular rest, exercise, and personal hygiene; preparation for labor and delivery and early care of the newborn; effective use of the health care system; planning for subsequent pregnancies; returning to school; and finding employment. Nurses also educated mothers about early infant temperament and how to promote infants' social, emotional, and cognitive development. Finally, nurses helped mothers expand their informal support network to include husbands, boyfriends, and other family and friends and to develop reliable, ongoing relationships with their pediatricians and other health and human service providers. Participation in the program lasted for two years, and a follow-up study was conducted when the children were four years old.

The percentage of low-birth-weight babies decreases the earlier prenatal care begins and the more years of education the mother has. Percentages of low-birth-weight infants are higher for African Americans (versus whites) among mothers who began prenatal care at the same time and had similar levels of education.

Pregnant women who participated in the program made more use of formal services, experienced greater informal social support, made more improvements in their diets, and reduced their smoking compared to similar women not in the program. Very young teenagers in the program showed a significant improvement in their babies' birth weights and a reduction in preterm deliveries. After delivery, these women displayed higher levels of infant and child care and made better use of health and social services. There was also a 75 percent reduction in verified cases of child abuse and neglect and a 42 percent decrease in subsequent pregnancies among low-socioeconomic-status unmarried women in the program (Olds, 1997).

Diet and Nutrition

For mothers with poor diets, rates of prematurity and infant mortality are higher, birth weights are lower, and the risk of congenital malformations increases (Salisbury & Robertson, 2013). Nutritionally deprived infants are less responsive to environmental

WORKING WITH Katie Glover, OB-GYN Nurse Practitioner

Preparing for Childbirth

Katie Glover was interviewed in her office at the primary health care clinic where she works. Despite her hectic schedule, Katie has a relaxed and unhurried manner. She has a three-year-old son and is currently seven months pregnant. Our interview focused on preparation for childbirth.

Rob: *What advice do you give pregnant women about their nutrition?*

Katie: Pregnant women need three to four glasses of milk a day and should increase consumption of fruits and vegetables, which many people don't eat regularly. As a bottom line, we recommend a balanced diet plus a few extra calories and vitamin supplements. We also recommend a twenty-five-to-thirty-pound weight gain over the course of a pregnancy, depending on the woman's size, build, and weight.

Rob: *Why do you recommend weight gain?*

Katie: If you figure the average baby weighs roughly 6.5 to 7.5 pounds and the average placenta weighs maybe three to five pounds, and add the extra fluid a woman retains and extra subcutaneous fat her body stores as added protection, that's about twenty to twenty-five pounds right there.

Rob: *How do weight gain and other changes of pregnancy affect women?*

Katie: They certainly change their body image. How a woman feels about that directly relates to how she feels about being pregnant. Someone who's thrilled about pregnancy will be happy to see her belly getting bigger. Someone who resents the pregnancy is likely to have a harder time with her body's changes. It's not just that her breasts are getting larger or her stomach is getting bigger. She can't run up and down the stairs as easily, and she can't find a comfortable position to sleep in. Pregnancy gets in the way of your life. You have to alter how you move and how you eat and how often you go to the bathroom—day and night. When all you really want is a good eight hours of sleep, you may start wondering if it's all worth it!

Rob: *Pregnancy can be stressful, then.*

Katie: Yes. In a way, pregnancy is a crisis. How a person copes with that crisis has a lot to do with her feelings about being pregnant as well as what her social and emotional support system is like. If her partner, parents, or friends provide good, solid support and appreciation for what she's experiencing, pregnancy is likely to be a more positive experience than if she doesn't have such support.

Rob: *What preparation for childbirth do you offer your patients?*

---

stimulation and are irritable when aroused. Malnourished infants are found to have a significantly reduced number of brain cells, especially when the malnutrition occurred during the last trimester or during the first three months following birth (Lozoff, 1989). What constitutes a nutritious diet during pregnancy? As Katie Glover mentions in the "Working With" feature, pregnant women should increase consumption of fruits, vegetables, and calcium-rich and folate-rich foods and strive to eat a balanced diet overall. Chapter 12's discussion of health-promoting behaviors describes a balanced diet.

Infants born to undernourished or poorly nourished mothers not only exhibit immediate effects of their nutritional deprivation, but several long-term studies reveal that they are also at risk for developing cardiovascular disease, type 2 diabetes, and metabolic and endocrine diseases later in life (Salisbury & Robertson, 2013). Evidence is accumulating that permanent adaptations are made in structure, physiology, and metabolism *in utero* in response to inadequate nutritional supply. This response, called "fetal programming" by Barker and his colleagues (Godfrey & Barker, 2001), predisposes the infant to the adult diseases previously mentioned.

Stress and Health

Stress refers to chronic feelings of worry and anxiety. Women who experience severe and prolonged anxiety just before or during pregnancy are more likely to have medical complications and give birth to infants with abnormalities than women who do not. Emotional stress has been associated with greater incidence of spontaneous abortion, difficult

> **WORKING WITH** Katie Glover, OB-GYN Nurse Practitioner
>
> ### Preparing for Childbirth *continued*
>
> **Katie:** Most medical practices encourage some kind of childbirth classes. Classes typically cover the various stages of pregnancy, physiological and psychological changes a woman might experience, changes in the couple's relationship. We talk about labor and what the hospital will be like. We talk about the different kinds of pain medications that might be offered, their effects, and the risks and benefits. Most classes also teach basic relaxation and breathing techniques, which are very important. Knowing what to expect and how to deal with the anxiety and pain can really help make labor a more positive experience.
>
> **Rob:** *How do you feel about birth clinics and home deliveries?*
>
> **Katie:** For many people who don't want to give birth in a hospital, a birth center is ideal, whether it's freestanding or directly attached to a hospital. It offers a little more freedom of movement, a little more comfort, a different atmosphere, and reassurance that medical backup is available if needed, including quick transfer to a fully equipped hospital. Of course, parents who come to a birth center should be carefully screened beforehand for any potential medical complications.
>
> **Rob:** *What about home birth?*
>
> **Katie:** I think it's a good option for the very small percentage of people who are truly suited for it.
>
> **Rob:** *Why is that?*
>
> **Katie:** It takes a very high level of commitment to arrange a home birth. Real problems can arise if it's not something both partners agree on and believe in deeply. If both partners are always there for each other, if the home situation is a nice, clean, supportive place, and if a pediatrician and a well-trained, experienced obstetrician or midwife and good emergency medical backup are available, then go for it!
>
> ### What Do You Think?
> 1. Katie suggests that pregnancy is a type of crisis and that how a woman copes with it will depend on her attitudes toward pregnancy and the social support she receives. How might this knowledge be used to design programs to help pregnant teenagers cope better with the "crisis" of pregnancy?
> 2. How might a woman's pregnancy affect the father and other family members?
> 3. Katie discusses alternatives to hospital birth. What additional information might you need to consider these alternatives for yourself?

labor, premature birth and low birth weight, newborn respiratory difficulties, and physical deformities (Littleton, Bye, Buck, & Amacker, 2010; Norbeck & Tilden, 1983; Omer & Everly, 1988). We will take a closer look at the role of stress when we discuss physical development in early adulthood in Chapter 12.

Birth

After thirty-eight weeks in the womb, the fetus is considered to be "full term," or ready for birth. At this point, it will weigh around 7.5 pounds, but it can weigh as little as 5.75 pounds or as much as ten pounds and still be physically normal. The fetus measures about twenty inches or so at this stage, almost one-third of its final height as an adult.

During the final weeks, the womb becomes so crowded that the fetus assumes one position more or less until birth. This orientation is sometimes called *fetal presentation*. **Fetal presentation** (or *orientation*) refers to the body part of the fetus that is closest to the mother's cervix. The most common fetal presentation, and the most desirable one medically, is head pointing downward (called a *cephalic presentation*). Two other presentations also occur: feet and rump first (*breech presentation*) or shoulders first (*transverse presentation*). These two orientations used to jeopardize an infant's survival, but modern obstetric techniques have greatly reduced their risk.

Most fetuses develop normally for the usual thirty-eight to forty weeks and face their birth relatively well prepared. When the labor process begins, it too usually proceeds normally.

fetal presentation Refers to the body part of the fetus that is closest to the mother's cervix; may be head first (cephalic), feet and rump first (breech), or shoulders first (transverse).

> **What Do You Think?**
>
> If good prenatal diet and health care are so closely related to healthy prenatal and postnatal development, why don't all expectant mothers follow nutritious diets and receive good health care? How can adequate health care be made available to all pregnant women?

The uterus contracts rhythmically and automatically to force the baby downward through the vaginal canal (see Figure 3.13). The contractions occur in a relatively predictable sequence of stages, and as long as the baby and mother are healthy and the mother's pelvis is large enough, the baby usually is out within a matter of hours.

Stages of Labor

It is common for the mother to experience "false labor," or *Braxton-Hicks contractions,* in the last weeks of pregnancy as the uterus "practices" contracting and relaxing in preparation for actual labor. These contractions do not open the cervix as real labor contractions do.

Labor consists of three stages. The *first stage of labor,* which lasts from the first true contraction until the cervix (the opening of the uterus) is completely open, or *dilated* to 10 centimeters (4.5 inches), is the longest stage. It usually begins with relatively mild and irregular contractions of the uterus. As contractions become stronger, more regular, and more frequent, *dilation,* or widening, of the cervix increases until there is enough room for the baby's head to fit through. As it stretches and dilates, the cervix also becomes thinner, a process referred to as *effacement.*

Toward the end of this first stage of labor, which may take from eight to twenty-four hours for a first-time mother, a *period of transition* begins. The cervix approaches full

FIGURE 3.13
The Process of Delivery

The labor and delivery process occurs in three stages, including active labor, birth, and delivery of the afterbirth. The stages vary in their duration, but the labor and delivery process for first-time mothers usually lasts between twelve and eighteen hours.

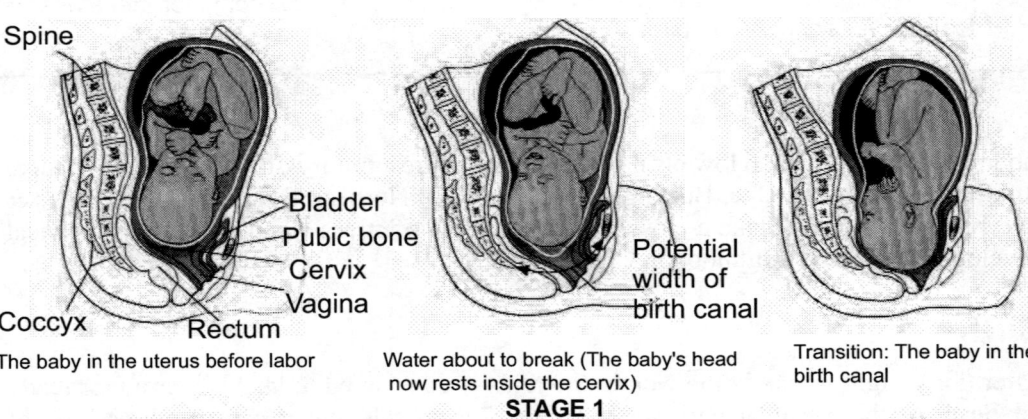

STAGE 1

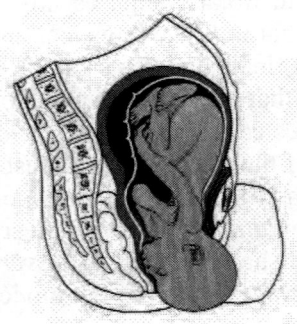

The baby about to be born

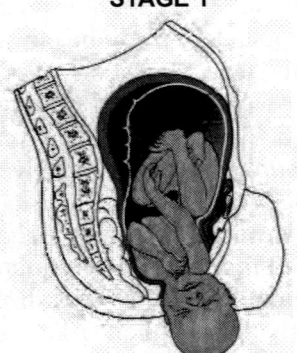

The head rotates sideways after it emerges

STAGE 2

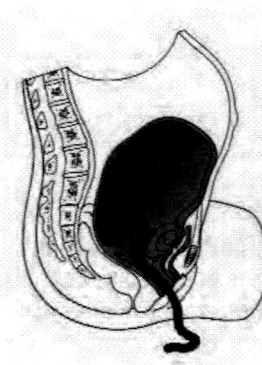

The delivery of the placenta

STAGE 3

90 Part 1 Beginnings

dilation, contractions become more rapid, and the baby's head begins to move into the birth canal. Although this period generally lasts for only a few minutes, it can be the most intense and challenging one because contractions become stronger and more deeply felt, lasting from forty-five to ninety seconds each. Managing each contraction involves a great deal of concentration and energy; women typically use the period between contractions to catch their breath and prepare for the next contraction. During transition, a woman often experiences a variety of physical changes, including trembling, shaking, leg cramps, nausea, back and hip pain, burping, and perspiring, and tends to be preoccupied with feelings of pain, pressure, and hoped-for relief (McKay, 1993).

The *second stage of labor* ranges from complete dilation of the cervix to birth. Contractions continue but may be somewhat shorter, lasting forty-five to sixty seconds. Although the baby now has only a few more inches to move down the vagina to be born, the process can be slow, usually lasting between one and two hours for a first baby and less than a half-hour for women who have previously given birth. Although dilation is complete, for most women the reflexive urge to push the baby out by bearing down full strength usually develops toward the end of this stage, and often becomes irresistible. When a woman first begins to push, she may be uncoordinated and need to learn to push "with" the contraction and rest in between. How hard she pushes will depend on the strength of the contractions, which varies throughout labor. If a woman doesn't feel the urge to push, guidance from a partner can help, particularly if she had an epidural block or other local anesthetic that interferes with her bearing-down reflex.

During the *third stage of labor,* which lasts between five and twenty minutes, the afterbirth, which consists of placenta and umbilical cord, is expelled. Contractions still occur but are much weaker, and the woman may have to push several times to deliver the placenta. The medication Pitocin, a synthetic version of oxytocin, is frequently given to help the placenta to detach from the side of the uterus. Putting the baby to the mother's breast also can help because stimulation of the nipple naturally releases oxytocin (McKay, 1993).

Childbirth Settings and Methods

Until the 1800s, births in the United States generally took place in the woman's home. Usually it was attended by midwives, friends, neighbors, and family members and was viewed as a natural process rather than as a medical procedure. The **midwife** was a woman experienced in pregnancy and childbirth who traditionally served as the primary caregiver during pregnancy, childbirth, and the month or so following birth. During the 1800s, political and social factors and the emergence of medicine as a scientifically based and politically powerful profession led to the replacement of midwives by physicians as the chief birth attendants. In the 1900s, delivery moved to the hospital, where it was increasingly treated as a medical rather than a naturally occurring community event (Bogdon, 1993; Steiger, 1993).

midwife The person, usually a woman, who is the primary caregiver to a woman during pregnancy, childbirth, and the month or so following delivery.

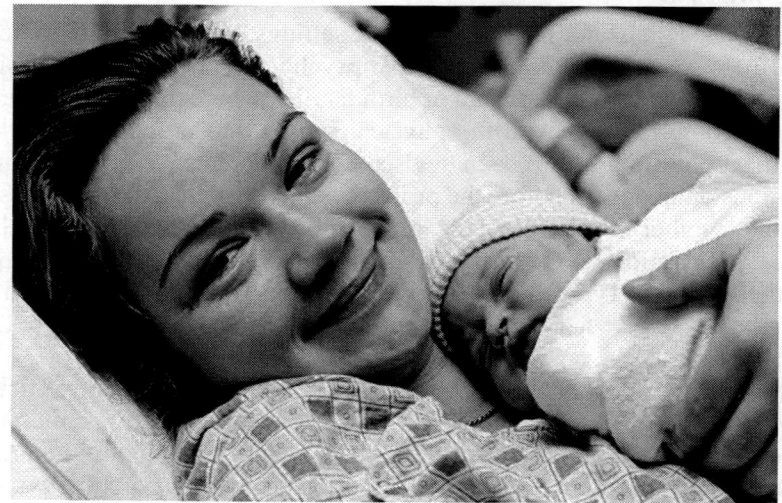

After all the hard work of labor, a baby! No matter how exhausted she may feel, a mother is usually glad to see her new child, especially once reassured that it is healthy.
Source: Mikhail Tchkheidze/Shutterstock.com.

Chapter 3 Genetics, Prenatal Development, and Birth

These changes brought the benefits of modern medical technology to the birth process and resulted in decreased mortality rates for mothers and their babies, particularly in the case of high-risk pregnancies. However, they also shifted the birth process from being a natural event controlled by the pregnant woman, her family, her friends, and the community to a medical event controlled by physicians. As a result, all babies and their mothers were exposed to the risks associated with hospital-based medical practices, including overreliance on medication and on procedures such as episiotomies and caesarian sections (discussed a bit later).

Hospital Births

Currently 98.2 percent of all births in the United States occur in hospitals under the supervision of a physician; the remaining 1.8 percent of births occur at home or in a birth center. In recent years, the maternity wards of many hospitals have modified their environments to be more comfortable and supportive of pregnant women and their families. A growing number of hospitals now have *birthing rooms* with more comfortable furniture, muted colors and lighting, soft music, and facilities for *rooming in* that allow mother and baby to stay together until both are ready to leave the hospital. By the late 1970s, the majority of husbands were attending the birth (Simkin, 2007), and most hospitals now encourage a partner to be present during the delivery because it shortens the duration of labor somewhat and enhances the mother's satisfaction with the birth process (Hodnett et al., 2007).

Nonhospital Settings

Freestanding birth centers (FBCs) are nonhospital facilities organized to provide family-centered maternity care for women who are judged to be at low risk for obstetrical complications (Rooks et al., 1989). Equipped and staffed to handle all but the most serious medical emergencies and designed like simple but comfortable hotels, birth centers encourage the active involvement of the mother, her family, and her friends in a birth process that minimizes technical intervention deemed to be medically unnecessary and physiologically and psychologically stressful in low-risk deliveries (Eakins, 1993).

Home birth is another alternative to hospital birth available for low-risk pregnancies. In a typical home birth, normal daily activities continue through the first stage of labor. When contractions increase, the nurse-midwife or physician is called to monitor the labor. Backup arrangements with a doctor or hospital generally are in place should they be needed, and women planning on home birth are carefully screened to minimize last-minute complications requiring hospital equipment or procedures. In addition to the widely held view that hospitals are the place of choice for birth, difficulty in obtaining malpractice insurance and resistance by the medical profession are major barriers to widespread acceptance of home birth.

Prepared Childbirth

The majority of hospitals and nonhospital birth settings offer programs to help women and their partners prepare for the physical and psychological experience of birth. These include preparatory visits to the hospital or birth facility, where pregnant women and their partners can become familiar with the physical setting and procedures. Various methods of **prepared childbirth** have been devised to help parents rehearse, or simulate, the actual sensations of labor well before the projected delivery date. Although these methods differ from one another in certain details, all generally emphasize educational, physical, and emotional preparation for the birth process and active involvement of the mother and father (or other partner). Typically, they encourage the mother to find a coach (often her spouse or a relative) to give her personal support during labor (Lamaze, 1970; Livingston, 1993a, 1993b, 1993c).

The earliest proponent of prepared or "natural" childbirth was Grantly Dick-Read, an English physician who believed that the pain women experience during childbirth was not natural but due to a combination of fear and tension caused by cultural ignorance of the birth process and by the isolation and lack of emotional and social support women receive

prepared childbirth A method of childbirth in which parents have rehearsed or simulated labor and delivery well before the actual delivery date.

during labor and in hospital delivery rooms (Livingston, 1993a.). The Read method consisted of educating women about the physiology of labor and training them in progressive relaxation techniques to reduce tension, fatigue, and pain. Read also encouraged obstetricians and nurses to be more patient and to rely less heavily on medication in the birth process.

Currently the most widely used approach to prepared childbirth in the United States is the Lamaze method, which was originated in the Soviet Union; brought to France in the 1950s by Fernand Lamaze, the head of a maternity hospital; and then popularized in the United States by Marjorie Karmel, an American who had given birth to her first child at Lamaze's hospital in France and wanted to use the method for the birth of her second child in the United States. The Lamaze method differs from the Read approach in that it strongly encourages the active participation of *both* mother and father (or labor partner) during the weeks preceding delivery and during the delivery itself (Livingston, 1993b; Lothian & DeVries, 2005). The Lamaze method encourages labor either without drugs or with minimal drugs and stresses the importance of birth as a natural, shared, emotional experience (Livingston, 1993b; Lothian & DeVries, 2005).

Women who have participated in Lamaze and similar childbirth approaches report more favorable attitudes toward labor and delivery, less discomfort and stress during the birth process, less reliance on medication, and more sensitive interaction with the newborn baby (Cogan, 1980; Lindell, 1988). A father's involvement in preparing for and participating in the delivery process has been found to positively influence his experience of birth, his behavior toward mother and baby during delivery, and his relationship to his new infant (Hoffnung, 1992; Markman & Kadushin, 1986).

Another widely used method of natural childbirth was introduced by Robert Bradley, an American obstetrician who modified Read's technique. Bradley's husband-coached childbirth method stresses the importance of the father as comforter, supporter, and caregiver before and during the delivery. Bradley also emphasizes relaxation and controlled breathing in a calm, quiet, physically comfortable environment (Livingston, 1993c).

Modern Midwives and Doulas

Throughout human history and around the world, midwives have helped other women give birth. As we saw earlier, doctors largely replaced midwives in the United States in the nineteenth and early twentieth centuries, but in recent years, midwifery has been on the rise. Today, midwives in the United States are trained and licensed to give care and advice to women during pregnancy, labor, and the postpartum period, to conduct deliveries, and to care for newborn infants. Midwives also provide counseling and education not only to women giving birth but to the family and community as well, helping them with prenatal education and preparation for parenthood, family planning, and child care (Davis, 1987; Steiger, 1993).

Pregnant women and their partners/birth coaches attend a childbirth preparation class together. These kinds of classes reduce the stress and discomfort of childbirth, lead to less reliance on pain medication during the birth process, and have even been found to reduce the duration of labor and delivery.
Source: Monkey Business Images/Shutterstock.com.

Two kinds of midwives practice in the United States. *Direct-entry midwives* (DEMs) are self-trained or have learned midwifery skills through apprenticeship to individual practicing midwives. *Certified nurse-midwives* (CNMs) are registered nurses (RNs) with additional hospital and academic training in obstetrics. Direct-entry midwives practice mainly at home births and at privately run, freestanding birth centers, but generally are not licensed to assist in hospital deliveries. Certified nurse-midwives are licensed to practice in a wide variety of settings, including hospitals, freestanding birth centers, and home births, and generally work under the supervision of a physician. Midwives historically have played an important role in poor, rural areas, particularly in the rural South, where a longstanding tradition of midwife-assisted births exists among African American women who were denied access to medical care through segregation and economic discrimination (Holmes, 1993; Steiger, 1993). In 2010, midwives assisted in about 8 percent of all births in the United States (ACNM, 2012). Today, the demographics of women choosing to have a CNM attend their birth are similar to those of national demographics, with more women in New Mexico, the Northeast, and Oregon choosing CNM-assisted birth (Declercq, 2012).

The term *doula* applies to an individual who cares for the new mother, especially when breast feeding begins after the baby is born. Like midwives, doulas have helped with the birth process around the world since the beginning of human history. Doulas do not deliver babies, but may assist a mother and midwife in the process. Depending on the culture, the role of doula may be filled by one or more relatives or friends or, at times, by a midwife. The use of doulas has increased over the last decade in the United States. Research suggests that women who receive social and emotional support from doulas have shorter labors, fewer labor and delivery complications, fewer caesareans, and less use of painkillers or artificial oxytocin; they also appear better able to cope with the demands of motherhood (Gilbert, 1998; Raphael, 1993; Scott, Klaus, & Klaus, 1999).

Medicinal Methods During Delivery

Despite adequate psychological preparation, most mothers feel some pain during labor contractions. Under good conditions, many mothers can endure this pain until the baby is delivered. But if labor takes an unusually long time or a mother finds herself less prepared than she expected, pain-reducing drugs such as narcotics or other sedatives can make the experience bearable. But such medications must be used cautiously. Most pain relievers cross the placenta and therefore can seriously depress the fetus if given at the wrong time or in improper amounts.

During the final stages of delivery, two other forms of pain relief are available. Doctors may inject a sedative into the base of the woman's spine. The two most common of these procedures are an *epidural* and a *dual spinal-epidural (or "walking epidural")*. They allow the mother to remain awake and alert during the final stages of labor, but they may impede her ability to help in the delivery process by regulating her own contractions. Epidurals have also been found to lengthen the duration of labor by two to three hours (Cheng, Schaffer, Nicholson, & Caughey, 2014). Nitrous oxide, which dentists commonly use, also has been used to take the edge off the pain of the peak contractions, while allowing the mother to remain conscious.

Giving a mother a general anesthetic before delivery removes all pain, of course, but both mother and child may take a long time to recover from it. Due to the heightened risk to the mother and newborn, general anesthetics are used in less than 1 percent of deliveries. In addition to the physical risks posed by general anesthetics, the bonding between mother and child may be delayed while both are recovering from the effect of the anesthesia. Table 3.7 lists the major types of medications used during labor and delivery, their administration, and their effects (Feinbloom, 2000).

Problems During Labor and Delivery

Interference with labor and delivery can occur in three ways: through *faulty power* in the uterus, a *faulty passageway* (the birth canal), or a *faulty passenger* (the baby itself). These problems actually interconnect in various ways, but it is convenient to distinguish among them (Buckley & Kulb, 1983).

TABLE 3.7 Major Medications During Childbirth and Their Effects on the Baby

Type	Administration	Positive Effects for Mother	Negative Effects for Baby
Analgesics	By injection (in controlled doses) during the first stage of labor to reduce pain	Reduces pain, causes some drowsiness and euphoria (sense of well-being and tranquility); women participate in labor and delivery	May cause drowsiness and decreased responsiveness for first few hours after birth or longer; naloxone hydrochloride (Narcon) can be used to reverse these effects
Local anesthesia—spinal	By injection into spinal canal in controlled doses when cervix is fully dilated (beginning of second stage of labor); numbs sensory and motor nerves so that mother's pelvic area and legs cannot move voluntarily	Mother can remain awake and aware during labor and delivery; can be used for either vaginal or caesarean birth; is highly effective in eliminating pain	No negative effects reported
Local anesthesia—epidural	By injection during active phase of first stage of labor to numb sensory nerves after their exit from spinal canal	Pain and sensations are generally eliminated; mother is awake; some voluntary movement is preserved, although it is less effective because a woman's sense of position and tension is blocked by the medication	No negative effects reported
General anesthesia	A mixture of nitrous oxide and oxygen is inhaled; is less commonly used than blocking agents	Easily administered, rapid onset of effect; anesthetic of choice in emergencies in which time is critical and baby must be delivered quickly	Decreased alertness and responsiveness following birth

Source: Feinbloom (2000).

Faulty Power

Sometimes the uterus does not contract strongly enough to make labor progress to a delivery. The problem can occur at the beginning of labor or develop midway through a labor that began quite normally, especially if the mother tires after hours of powerful contractions. In many cases, the doctor can strengthen the contractions by giving the mother an injection of a synthetic version of the hormone oxytocin called "Pitocin." Such *induced labor*, which occurs in about 5 percent of all deliveries, must be monitored carefully so that the artificial contractions it stimulates do not harm both baby and mother by forcing the baby through the canal before the canal is ready (WHO, 2011).

Faulty Passageway

Sometimes the placenta partially or completely covers the cervix and blocks the baby from moving down the birth canal during labor. This condition, called *placenta previa*, which occurs in approximately one out of 200 pregnancies, is usually detected early in the third trimester of the pregnancy and causes intermittent bleeding and occasional cramping (USNLM, 2012). If left untreated, it may leave the fetus somewhat undernourished, because it prevents sufficient blood from reaching it. Sometimes it blocks a normal delivery entirely so that the baby must be delivered by caesarean section (ACOG, 1995).

Faulty Passenger

Usually a baby enters the birth canal head first, but occasionally one turns in the wrong direction during contractions. A *breech presentation*—with the bottom leading—is risky for the baby because its spine can be broken if a contraction presses it too hard against the mother's pelvis. Or the baby may not get enough oxygen because it cannot begin breathing on its own until after its nose comes out. In some cases, a skilled midwife or a doctor can deliver a breech baby with no problem, but if the baby is stuck partway out of the vagina, medical staff may use *forceps* or *ventouse* (vacuum-assisted delivery) to pull it the rest of the way out. In most cases, breech babies are either turned to the right position during delivery or delivered surgically by caesarean section.

A small but significant proportion of babies are simply too big to pass through the mother's pelvis and vaginal canal, a problem sometimes called *cephalopelvic disproportion (CPD)*—literally, a disproportion of the head and pelvis. If the mismatch is too severe and threatens the life of mother or child, the doctor may interrupt the labor and deliver the baby surgically.

Caesarean Section

Caesarean section, or *C-section,* is a procedure used in cases where the baby cannot be safely delivered through the vagina and therefore has to be removed surgically. Techniques for this surgery have improved substantially over the past decades. The operation now takes only about half an hour, most of which is devoted to sewing the mother up after getting the baby out. The number of C-sections for live births, is currently at about one in three births (Martin et al., 2013). This rate increased from 26 to 36 percent between 2003 and 2009, with the most common reason cited as "nonreassuring fetal status," a term that refers to changes in fetal heart rate, and a diagnosis that some suggest is overused, accounting for the concerning increase in C-sections (Barber et al., 2011; Morrison, 1998). Many experts and parent advocates remain concerned that the rates are too high and reflect medical practices that are not in the best interests of mothers and their babies (ACOG, 1995; Taffel, 1993).

Both supporters and critics of caesarean birth agree there are a number of good reasons to select a caesarean birth as the safest way to deliver a baby. These include the problems of placenta previa and cephalopelvic disproportion (CPD) already noted, as well as prolapsed cord, where the umbilical cord cuts off the baby's oxygen; unusual positions of the baby that make vaginal delivery impossible; severe fetal distress that cannot be corrected; and active herpes, where the baby may be infected through vaginal birth.

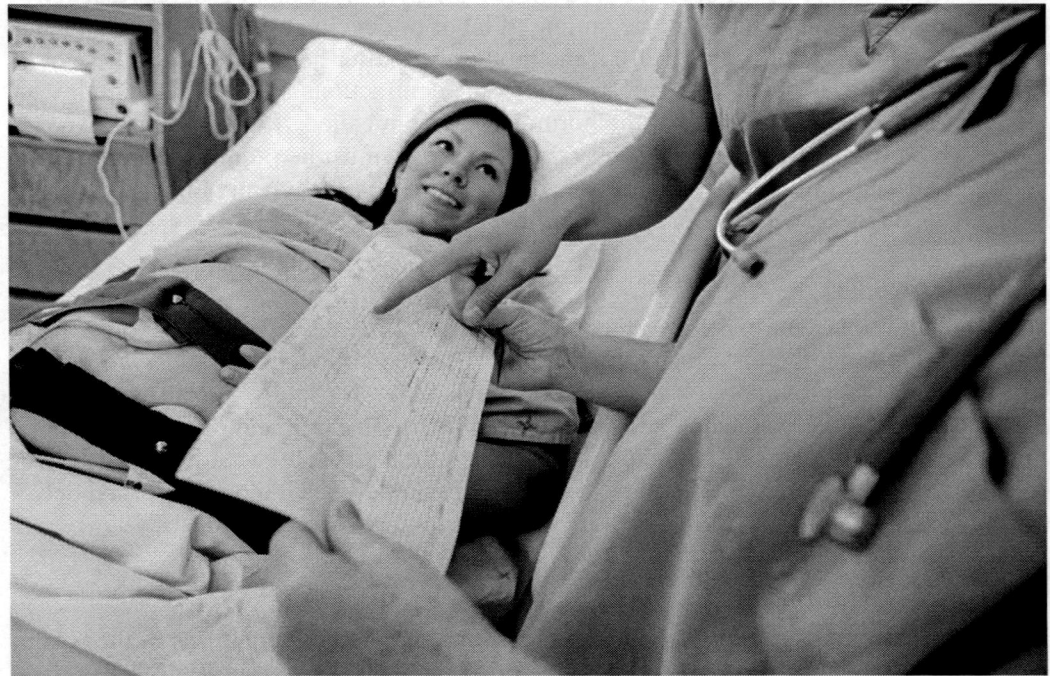

Nurses discussing a fetal monitoring report from the external monitor that is strapped to the expectant mother's abdomen.
Source: Tyler Olson/Shutterstock.com.

Fetal Monitoring

Most hospitals and birthing centers use *electronic fetal monitoring* to record uterine contractions and the fetal heart rate. Uterine contractions are externally measured by a pressure gauge strapped to the mother's abdomen that electronically represents changes in the shape of the uterus on graph paper. Fetal heart rate can be picked up by an *external* ultrasound monitor placed on the abdomen over the uterus or *internally* by a wire, leading through the vagina and screwed into the fetus's scalp, that records more subtle electrical changes in the fetus's heart.

Although internal fetal monitoring is extremely helpful in high-risk and emergency situations, experts have questioned its routine use for low-risk deliveries. Some have suggested that the procedure may itself contribute to fetal (and maternal) distress. In addition, the mother must lie in bed for as long as the wires are attached (USNLM, 2013). Experts have also noted that by shifting the center of focus from the experience of mother and baby to readouts from the equipment, "high-tech" births may reduce certain aspects of clinical awareness that are central to good obstetric care (Davis-Floyd, 1986).

Birth and the Family

For most families, the arrival of a new baby brings many changes, and it takes some time to adjust. For first-time parents, learning to care for a new baby and rearranging family schedules to provide the almost constant attention a newborn requires are very big challenges, to say the least. The arrival of a new baby can be particularly difficult for parents who lack the economic resources, knowledge, and social and emotional support that are so important in adjusting to the complicated demands of caring for a new baby. We will look at these and related issues in Chapter 13's coverage of psychosocial development in early adulthood. Having a baby that is low birth weight or other problems can be particularly traumatic. Though it is unwise to generalize too broadly, adolescent parents, single parents, and parents who are educationally and economically disadvantaged are more likely to find parenthood difficult.

Nevertheless, the great majority of births in this country occur without significant problems and to families whose economic, social, and psychological resources enable them to become effective parents. For women (and their partners) who receive good preparation and training for the birth process and obtain adequate social and emotional support from family, friends, and culture, birth is likely to be a very positive and welcome event.

For parents who already have children, a newcomer to the family also creates stresses. Children naturally worry they will lose their special place in the family and the exclusive attention they enjoy once the newcomer arrives. Involving the child in the preparation for birth, for the period when the mother is in the hospital, and for the changes that will occur with the new arrival are all important ways to help a child adjust to the changes. Talking to the child about these things and listening carefully to his or her questions and concerns are particularly important. Especially with preschoolers, providing concrete information about birth, newborn babies and what they are like, and the specific changes that will occur in the family before and after the baby's birth can help allay their fears.

After the new baby arrives home, parents can do a number of things to assist the adjustment process. Giving the older child lots of verbal reassurance helps, but concrete actions often speak louder than words. One strategy is to give the child an important role in the event by providing special activities, asking friends and family members to bring a gift for the child as well as for the new baby, and including the child in daily activities with the new infant. High priority should also be placed on continuing routine activities with the older child and ensuring that each parent spends lots of special time just with him or her.

Looking Back/Looking Forward

Although we are just beginning our exploration of development over the lifespan, let's use the four main lifespan themes discussed in Chapter 1 to review where we have been and where we are going.

> **What Do You Think?**
>
> How might the process of birth vary depending on a family's circumstances such as age, marital status, income, race, and culture? To explore this question, have yourself and several classmates play the roles of expectant parents from different life circumstances. What did you discover?

- **Continuity within change**—On the one hand, the physical processes involved in genetic transmission, conception, prenatal development, and birth involve enormous and rapid changes. In just nine months or so, genetic material provided by the parents at conception transforms itself into a zygote, an embryo, a fetus, and finally a newborn infant. Though the changes we have discussed are primarily physical, we will see shortly that the newborn is exquisitely prepared for the impressive cognitive and psychosocial changes that will follow. We will also see that the physical changes exhibit a high degree of continuity with the past. Because the complex processes involved in conception and prenatal development are highly canalized, they tend to work very well most of the time, ensuring that physical development proceeds according to longstanding patterns and norms. In addition, significant continuity is ensured through each parent's contribution of genetic material and associated characteristics to the unique genotype of the child. The continuities and changes that occur vividly illustrate the developmental themes of experience and process or stage discussed in Chapter 2.

- **Lifelong growth**—Genetics, prenatal development, and birth are an important part of the groundwork for lifelong growth. The amazing growth in complexity and size that occurs prenatally provides the lifelong basis for the equally amazing changes in the physical, cognitive, and psychosocial domains that occur from birth onward. During infancy, childhood, adolescence, and the adult years, elaboration and growth will occur in all three domains, although not necessarily at the same rates in each. Though physical and cognitive growth will be most rapid through adolescence, important changes in this domain will continue to affect growth throughout the lifespan. In the chapters that follow, we will discover that despite certain physical and cognitive declines in the adult years, many important areas of cognitive and psychosocial functioning continue to grow. Even at the earliest periods of development, we can see the importance of lifespan theoretical approaches for understanding development.

- **Changing meanings and vantage points**—During pregnancy and the months immediately following birth, the meanings of events are almost entirely in the minds of family members and other caregivers of the newborn. But as a combination of maturation, experience, and eventually awareness and self-determination lead the development of the infant through early, middle, and later childhood, adolescence, and adulthood, meanings and vantage points will change substantially, not only for the developing child but also for parents, siblings, and friends, who themselves are changing due to their own developmental experiences. The excitement of an infant's first steps, first words, or first friendship will give way to the excitement of the preschooler's growing athletic, verbal, and interpersonal skills. Similar changes will occur throughout the lifespan.

- **Developmental diversity**—As we have seen in this chapter, the unique genetic inheritance of each new human being at conception provides the earliest basis for the developmental diversity that will follow. Even identical twins who share the same genotype will show subtle differences based on different prenatal experiences, such as where each is located in the womb and how easy or difficult their delivery is. Similarly, subtle differences in temperament may be present at birth, and although the times of their births will be similar, the order of their births is likely to contribute to diversity in their development. As physical, cognitive, and psychosocial development progress through childhood, adolescence, and adulthood, the opportunities for diversity continue to expand, aided to a significant degree by the expanding range of experiences that become available and by the capacity all individuals have to self-determine their own development through their own choices. Differences in families, culture, ethnicity, race, gender, religion, socioeconomic status, and other life circumstances also play an important role. If two so-called "identical twins" are raised under very different life circumstances, they will still display striking phenotypical commonalities due to their shared genotypes, yet they will also be strikingly different based on their different environments, experiences, and personal choices.

Chapter Summary

- **How does inheritance work?** Genetic information is contained in a complex molecule called *deoxyribonucleic acid (DNA)*. Reproductive cells, or gametes, divide by a process called *meiosis* and recombine into a zygote at conception. Meiosis gives each gamete one-half of its normal number of chromosomes; conception brings the number of chromosomes up to normal again and gives the new zygote an equal number of chromosomes from each parent. Other body cells produce new tissue through division of their genes, chromosomes, and other cellular parts by means of a process called *mitosis*.

- **How are genetic differences usually transmitted from one generation to the next?** A person's genotype is the specific pattern of genetic information inherited in his or her chromosomes and genes at conception. A person's phenotype is the physical and behavioral traits the person actually shows during his or her life. Phenotype is the product of the interactions of genotype with environment. Although most genes exist in duplicate, some, called *dominant genes*, may actually influence the phenotype if only one member of the pair occurs. Recessive genes do not influence the phenotype unless both members of the pair occur in a particular form. Many traits are polygenic, meaning they are transmitted through the combined action of several genes. Sex is determined by one particular pair of chromosomes, called the X and Y chromosomes, and a testis-determining factor (TDF) located on a small section of the Y chromosome.

- **How can experts help parents discover and respond to potential genetic problems?** Some genetic abnormalities, such as Down syndrome (trisomy 21), occur when an individual inherits too many or too few chromosomes. Others occur because particular genes are defective or abnormal even though the chromosomes are normal. Examples include Huntington disease, sickle-cell disease, and fragile X syndrome. Genetic counseling can provide parents with information about how genetics influences the development of children and about the risks of transmitting genetic abnormalities from one generation to the next. Personal circumstances and cultural differences in beliefs and expectations must be considered in helping couples reach informed decisions about pregnancy.

- **How do heredity and environment jointly influence development?** According to behavioral geneticists, every characteristic of an organism is the result of the unique interaction between the genetic inheritance of the organism and the sequence of environments through which it has passed during its development. The concept of range of reaction describes the strength of genetic influence under different environmental conditions. Studies of identical twins and of adopted children suggest that heredity and environment operate jointly to influence developmental change. Linkage and association studies use repeated DNA segments called *polymorphisms* as genetic markers to locate abnormal genes. Neither biogenetic nor environmental determinism is likely to give us adequate understanding of human development, which is the product of genes, environment, and individual choice.

- **What important developmental changes occur during prenatal development?** Prenatal development begins with conception, in which a zygote is created by the union of a sperm cell from the father and an egg cell, or ovum, from the mother. It consists of discrete periods, or stages. The germinal stage occurs during the first two weeks following conception; the zygote forms a blastocyst, which differentiates into three distinct layers and then implants itself on the uterine wall to form the embryo. During the embryonic stage, weeks three through eight, the placenta and umbilical cord form and the basic organs and biological systems begin to develop. During the fetal stage, week nine until the end of pregnancy, all physical features complete their development. The experience of pregnancy includes dramatic changes in a woman's physical functioning and appearance, as well as significant psychological changes as prospective parents anticipate the birth of the baby.

- **What risks do a mother and baby normally face during pregnancy, and how can they be minimized?** Although prenatal development is highly canalized, there are critical periods—particularly during the first trimester—when embryonic development is highly vulnerable or at risk for disruptions from teratogens, substances or other environmental influences that can damage an embryo's growth. Teratogenic effects depend on the timing, intensity, and duration of exposure, the presence of other risks, and the biological vulnerability of baby and mother.

Risk factors for prenatal development include both medicinal and nonmedicinal drugs, such as heroin, cocaine, alcohol, and tobacco; diseases such as syphilis, gonorrhea, and AIDS; physical and biological characteristics of the mother; and physical, biological, and chemical environmental hazards.

Adequate prenatal nutrition and health care for the mother and her developing baby is associated with successful pregnancy, a normal birth, and healthy neonatal development.

- **What happens during the birth process, what difficulties may occur, and how are they handled?**

Labor occurs in three distinct but overlapping stages. The first stage, during which uterine contractions increase in strength and regularity and the cervix dilates sufficiently to accommodate the child's head, takes from eight to twenty-four hours (for a first-time mother). The second stage, when the dilation of the cervix is complete and the birth itself takes place, lasts from 60 to 120 minutes. The third stage, during which the placenta is delivered, lasts only a few minutes.

Nonhospital birth centers and home births are two alternatives to hospital-based births. Prepared childbirth is now widely used in both hospital and nonhospital birth settings to help women actively and comfortably meet the challenges of giving birth. Many babies are now delivered by midwives, who provide caregiving to women during pregnancy, childbirth, and the weeks following delivery. Doulas do not deliver babies, but help the mother during birth and with her newborn. Pain-reducing medications can make the experience of childbirth more comfortable, but in recent years have been used more cautiously because of their potentially adverse effects on the recovery of both infant and mother.

Problems during labor and delivery can include insufficient uterine contractions, or faulty power; a faulty passageway caused by blockage of the birth canal; and a faulty passenger, which may occur if the baby's physical position or large head prevents the completion of the journey through the birth canal. When vaginal delivery is not feasible, the physician may perform a caesarean section to deliver the baby surgically.

Learning to care for a new baby is a welcome challenge for most new parents, but it may be especially difficult for adolescent parents, single parents, and parents who are educationally and economically disadvantaged.

Key Terms

adoption study (p. 74)
allele (p. 62)
amniotic sac (p. 79)
assisted reproductive technology (ART) (p. 72)
canalization (p. 81)
chromosome (p. 60)
conception (p. 76)
critical period (p. 82)
dominant gene (p. 62)
Down syndrome (p. 68)
embryonic stage (p. 76)

fetal alcohol syndrome (FAS) (p. 84)
fetal presentation (p. 89)
fetal stage (p. 76)
gene (p. 60)
genetic imprinting (p. 65)
genotype (p. 62)
germinal stage (p. 76)
midwife (p. 91)
ovum (p. 60)
phenotype (p. 62)
placenta (p. 78)
prepared childbirth (p. 92)

range of reaction (p. 72)
recessive gene (p. 62)
sex-linked recessive traits (p. 64)
sickle-cell disease (p. 70)
sperm (p. 60)
teratogen (p. 82)
twin adoption study (p. 75)
twin study (p. 75)
umbilical cord (p. 79)
zygote (p. 60)

The First Two Years of Life

PART **2**

Chapter 4
Physical and Cognitive Development in the First Two Years

Chapter 5
The First Two Years: Psychosocial Development

Source: CroMary/Shutterstock.com.

As parents and other proud relatives keep discovering, infants grow and change more rapidly than the rest of us. Every few weeks, or sometimes even in a matter of days, infants seem to do something new. In just months, they are able to smile, sit, and babble. In just a few more months, they begin acquiring language, show signs of make-believe play, and take their first tentative steps. They go from smiling at any human face, to preferring their parents' familiar faces, to crying and showing distress at the sight of strangers.

These miracles invariably impress caregivers—provided, of course, that the caregivers are receiving the support they need to nurture infants. In reality, the infant is not the only person who is learning and changing. Parents are changing, too, as a result of witnessing and supporting the baby's emerging talents. For example, as they watch their baby grow, they revisit their relationships with their own parents and begin seeing those relationships with new breadth and wisdom. We take a close look at these experiences in Part 6 on early adulthood. For now, we look at infancy in terms of the individual child.

Physical and Cognitive Development in the First Two Years

CHAPTER 4

Source: Fernando Cortes/Shutterstock.com.

Chapter Outline

PHYSICAL DEVELOPMENT
Growth in Infancy
Infant States: Sleep and Arousal
Sensory Acuity
Motor Development
Nutrition During the First Two Years
Impairments in Infant Growth
COGNITIVE DEVELOPMENT
Studying Cognition and Memory in Infants
Infant Perception and Cognition
Cognitive Change During Infancy: Piaget's Stage Theory
Behavioral Learning in Infancy
Language Acquisition
The End of Infancy

Focusing Questions

- What do infants look like when they are first born? How do we know if they are healthy?
- How much do children grow during infancy?
- What changes occur in the brains of infants?
- How do infants' sleep and wakefulness patterns change as infants get older?
- What motor skills evolve during infancy?
- What do infants need nutritionally?
- What factors can impair growth during infancy?
- How do infants' senses operate at birth?
- How can infant cognition be studied?
- Do infants see and hear in the same way adults do?
- How do thinking and learning change during infancy?
- What phases do infants go through in acquiring language?

Anne was looking at the journal she had kept about her daughter since Michelle was seven months old.

- April 9: For two weeks, she has been sleeping through the night! Maybe it helped to start nursing her just before bedtime—but it's so hard to tell. She is starting to enjoy bedtime stories, too; babbles at the book and points at the pictures.

- June 10: Michelle has been crawling all over—mostly after the dog. Gets mad, cries when Huggins walks away; struggles to crawl after him; but then forgets all about him.

- August 10: Here's Michelle's latest words: "dada" (daddy), "tigg'n" (Tigger, the cat), "buh" (book). Maybe not polished English, but she's getting there. At this rate, I'm going to lose track of her full vocabulary soon.

As Anne can attest, during the first months of life a baby's behaviors evolve rapidly. In this chapter, we trace some of these changes through the first two years of life. We begin by discussing young infants' physical growth: what they look like, how they sleep, hear, and see, and what behaviors they can already perform at birth. We also look at variations in growth and in infants' nutritional needs in the first months of life. In the second part of the chapter, we take a second look at infants' development, this time from a cognitive perspective. We explore infants' perceptions and representations of their surroundings and how they learn from their world even before they learn to speak. Finally, we consider one of the most universal yet remarkable of all human accomplishments: the acquisition of language.

As we will see, when compared to other parts of the lifespan, physical and cognitive development during infancy show more obvious growth and more discontinuity, but less diversity. Growth occurs now as at no other time of life! Babies change daily, putting on pounds and inches and acquiring new skills. "You can almost *see* them grow," said one mother. Growth—both physical and psychological—continues throughout life, but never in quite such an obvious way as in infancy. Sometime during adulthood, in fact, physical aging may seem to reverse the trend toward growth. A man or woman who gained several inches and pounds in a year as an infant may now actually shrink a little in height and weight in later years. (Whether such changes are anything to worry about, however, is another question, which we return to in Chapters 12 through 18 on adulthood.

The very speed of infant growth creates important *dis*continuities: a child who cannot talk at six months, for example, is well on her way to talking at eighteen months. To parents, the speechless six-month-old and the speaking eighteen-month-old can seem worlds apart. Discontinuities related to normal aging happen to adults as well, but generally not as suddenly, and more often in social than in cognitive activities. For example, a woman of thirty whose priorities are her children discovers that her priorities are work and career at fifty. She feels like a "different woman" as a result.

Not only does the degree of discontinuity differ between adults and infants, but its character differs as well. Discontinuities that adults experience are more likely a result of unusual or nonnormative experiences. Dreaded disease strikes; a child is saved from an abusive parent by a caring social worker or teacher; the right (or wrong) person is chosen as a spouse. All of these are life-changing events, but none happens universally. Nonnormative experiences not only create discontinuities in the lives of individual adults but also contribute to developmental diversity among them. In this regard, adults differ importantly from infants, who experience discontinuity normally and universally rather than unusually and individually. As we will see, babies also show diversity. Not every infant acquires language, for example, in quite the same sequence or with the same timing. But compared to the important developments of adulthood, infant developments are among the most predictable of the lifespan, both in timing and in nature. It is possible to predict within a few months either way, for example, when most infants will take their first step or speak their first word. Such accurate predictions are rarely possible for adults.

PHYSICAL DEVELOPMENT

The Newborn

As we saw in the last chapter, birth continues rather than initiates physical development. Most organs have already been working for weeks, or even months, prior to this event. The baby's heart has been beating regularly, muscles have been contracting sporadically, and the liver has been making its major product, bile, which is necessary for normal digestion after birth. Even some behaviors, such as sucking and arm stretching, have already developed. Two physical functions, however, do begin at birth: breathing and ingestion (the taking in of foods). These fundamental physical functions constitute the basic physical continuities that must last a lifetime. The baby's heart is the same one that will be beating eighty years and more than two billion heartbeats later; her lungs and stomach will grow larger, but they will be the same lungs and stomach taking in oxygen and food decades later when she has become elderly.

The First Few Hours

When first emerging from the birth canal, the newborn infant (also called a **neonate**) definitely does not resemble most people's stereotypes of a beautiful baby. No matter what his race, his skin often looks rather red. If born a bit early, the baby may also have a white, waxy substance called *vernix* on his skin, and his body may be covered with fine, downy hair called *lanugo*. If the baby was born vaginally rather then delivered surgically, his head may be somewhat elongated or have a noticeable point on it; the shape comes from the pressure of the birth canal, which squeezes the skull for several hours during labor. Within a few days or weeks, the head fills out again to a more rounded shape, leaving gaps in the bones. The gaps are sometimes *called fontanelles*, or "soft spots," although they are actually covered by a tough membrane that can withstand normal contact and pressure. The gaps eventually grow over, but not until the infant is about eighteen months old.

neonate A newborn infant.

Is the Baby All Right? The Apgar Scale

The **Apgar Scale** (named after its originator, Dr. Virginia Apgar) helps doctors and nurses to decide quickly whether a newborn needs immediate medical attention. The scale consists of ratings that are simple enough for non-specialists to make, even during the distractions surrounding the moment of delivery (Apgar, 1953). To use it, someone present at the delivery calculates the baby's heart rate, breathing effort, muscle tone, skin color, and reflex irritability and assigns a score of zero to two on each of these five characteristics. Babies are rated one minute after they emerge from the womb and again at five minutes. For each rating, they can earn a maximum score of two, for a total possible score of ten, as Table 4.1 shows. Most babies earn eight, nine, or ten points, at least by five minutes after delivery. A baby who scores between five and seven points at one minute is given immediate special medical attention, which usually includes

Apgar Scale A system of rating newborns' health immediately following birth based on heart rate, strength of breathing, muscle tone, color, and reflex irritability.

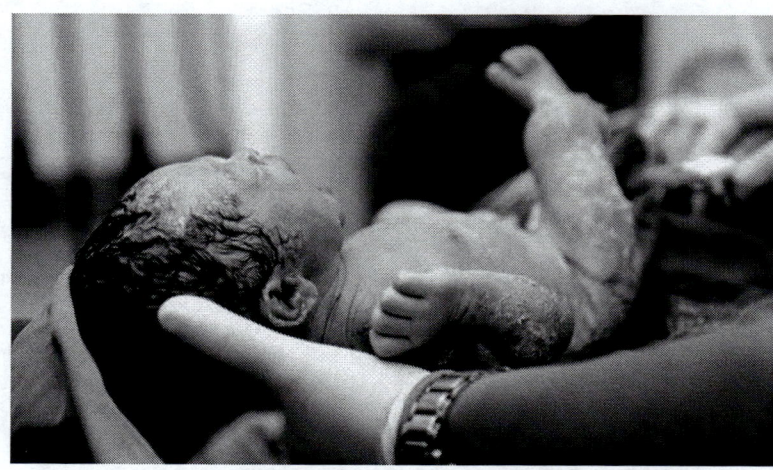

This neonate was delivered moments before the photo was taken. Notice the vernix coating much of the newborn's body.
Source: Napong/Shutterstock.com.

an examination by a pediatrician while oxygen is held under the baby's nose, and is then carefully observed to make sure that the Apgar scores increase to between eight and ten points at the five-minute retest. Monitoring continues during the next few hours and days for any problems that may develop (American Academy of Pediatrics, 2013a; Brazelton & Nugent, 1997).

Size and Bodily Proportions

A newborn baby weighs about 7.5 pounds and measures about twenty inches lying down. Her length matches her adult size more closely than her weight does: her twenty inches represent more than one-quarter of her final height, whereas her 7.5 pounds amount to only a small percentage of her adult weight.

Babies' proportions and general physical appearance may have psychological consequences by fostering *attachments*, or bonds, with the people who care for them (see Chapter 5, "Psychosocial Development in the First Two Years"). Such bonds promote feelings of security. The cuteness of infants' faces in particular seems to help. No matter what their racial or ethnic background, most babies have unusually large foreheads, features that are concentrated in the lower part of the face, eyes that are large and round, and cheeks that are high and prominent. A pattern of babyish features occurs so widely among animals, in fact, that biologists who study animal behavior suspect it has a universal and genetically based power to elicit parental or nurturing responses among adult animals (Archer, 1992; Lorenz, 1970). Mother in some species of ducks, for example, take care of baby ducks even when the babies are not their own. Among human parents and children, attachments may start with this sort of inherent attraction of parents to infants, though, of course, it deepens as additional personal experiences accumulate across the lifespan.

Growth in Infancy

Infants experience a remarkably high rate of growth—they gain height and weight more rapidly during their first two years than at any other point during their post-birth lifetimes. And while increases in height and weight will be clearly evident and frequently measured by pediatricians (because gains in height and weight are indicative of the infant's overall health), less visible growth in the brain will also produce dramatic changes in the infant.

Physical Growth

While actual gains in height and weight can vary from infant to infant, on average, infants double their weight from 7.5 pounds at birth to about 15 pounds by the age of five months, and

Two adorable brown bear cubs.
Sources: (top) Alena Ozerova/Shutterstock.com; (bottom) Voldymyr Burdiak/Shutterstock.com.

TABLE 4.1 The Apgar Scale

Characteristic	Score 0	1	2
Heart rate	Absent	Less than 100 beats per minute	More than 100 beats per minute
Efforts to breathe	Absent	Slow, irregular	Good; baby is crying
Muscle tone	Flaccid, limp	Weak, inactive	Strong, active motion
Skin color	Body pale or blue	Body pink, extremities blue	Body and extremities pink
Reflex irritability	No response	Frown, grimace	Vigorous crying, coughing, sneezing

Source: Apgar (1953).

> **What Do You Think?**
>
> What do you think attracts parents to their newborn children? Explore this question with the parents of a physically handicapped infant. How did they feel about their child (and about themselves) when the child was born?

triple their weight to about 22 pounds by their first birthday (see Figure 4.1). Weight is gained less rapidly during the second year of life, with the average twenty-four-month-old weighing about 28 pounds, approximately four times the weight of a newborn. Young infants tend to have a plump, soft look that results from the accumulation of fat. Body fat helps the infant maintain a constant body temperature. By their first birthday, infants will have lost much of their "baby fat," a trend that continues until puberty (Fomon & Nelson, 2002).

Infants also gain height, adding approximately ten inches (twenty-five centimeters) to their newborn length of twenty inches (fifty centimeters) by their first birthday, and will continue to get taller during their second year, achieving an average height of about thirty-four inches (eighty-six centimeters) by their second birthday, which is roughly half of their adult height (see Figure 4.1). Body proportions are also changing during the first two years, revealing differences in growth for various parts of the body. At birth, the baby's head accounts for one-quarter of the newborn's total height. In other words, the head is more developed than the torso and limbs. By age two, the head accounts for one-fifth of the total height, as growth of the torso and limbs proceeds at a greater rate than the growth of the head. By adulthood, the head will account for approximately one-eighth of the total height of the average adult.

Brain Growth

While the head may not be growing as rapidly as the rest of the body, significant development is occurring in the brain and central nervous system during the first two years of life. The **central nervous system** consists of the brain and nerve cells of the spinal cord, which together coordinate and control the perception of stimuli, as well as motor

central nervous system The brain and nerve cells of the spinal cord.

Height and Weight Growth During the First Two Years

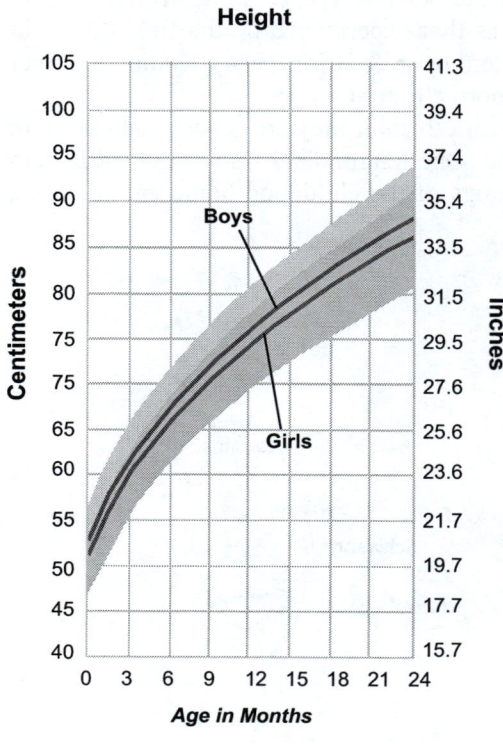
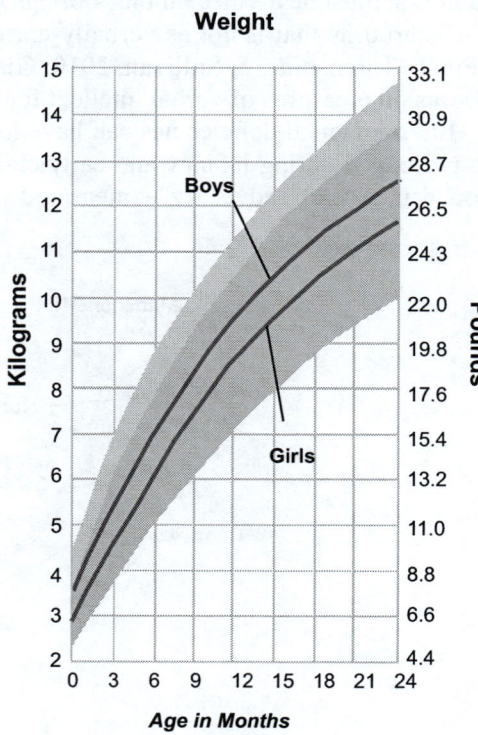

FIGURE 4.1
Growth Curves for the First Two Years

During infancy, rapid gains in height (left chart) and weight (right chart) are evident. On average, boys are slightly taller and heavier than girls are, but differences are minimal and are often overshadowed by increasing variability in height and weight within groups of boys and girls.

Chapter 4 Physical and Cognitive Development in the First Two Years

responses of all kinds. The more complex aspects of this work are accomplished by the brain, which develops rapidly from just before birth until well beyond a child's second birthday. In fact, it will be at least two decades until the brain is fully mature (Stiles & Jernigan, 2010). At seven months past conception, the baby's brain weighs about 10 percent of its final adult weight, but by birth, it has more than doubled to about 25 percent of final adult weight. By the child's second birthday, the brain has tripled to about 75 percent of its final adult weight (Freund et al., 1997).

Most of this increase results not from increasing numbers of nerve cells, or **neurons**, but from the development of a denser, or more fully packed, brain. This happens in two ways. First, the neurons generate many new dendritic fibers that connect them with one another in a process called **synaptogenesis** (see Figure 4.2). At birth, very few neuronal connections or *synapses* exist, but by age two, each neuron may be connected to hundreds or even thousands of other neurons. Growth of the dendrites is the primary reason why brain weight triples from birth to age two (Johnson, 2010). New synapses are formed in response to every experience the child has; in fact, during infancy, more synapses are formed than are necessary, a phenomenon described rather colorfully as **transient exuberance**, due to the temporarily rapid and overproductive nature of synaptogenesis at this time. Because more synapses form in response to every experience during infancy and childhood than are needed, many of these synapses are never used again. Consistent with the adage "use it or lose it," unused synapses are eliminated in a process called **synaptic pruning**. When redundant and unused synapses and neurons are eliminated, the nervous system functions more efficiently.

An important consequence of the transient exuberance that occurs during infancy is that it heightens the **plasticity** of the brain, which is the degree to which the brain reacts to experiences with the environment. Plasticity plays a central and often protective role in infant development. If an infant is raised in an enriched environment that provides lots of stimulation and nurturance, the production of synapses is amplified. However, if the infant is raised in an environment with little stimulation, the brain responds by forming and retaining fewer synapses. We can illustrate this with an explanation that is often offered for the superior verbal abilities of firstborn children when compared to their laterborn siblings. Firstborn children, at least until the second child is born, are the recipients of all of their caregivers' attention. This verbally enriched and supportive environment leads to the proliferation of synapses in the regions of the brain responsible for language—areas of the cerebral cortex in the left hemisphere of the brain. Parental attention must be divided among siblings when laterborns arrive, creating an environment for laterborns that is not as verbally-enriched as that experienced by the firstborn child (Frank, Turenshine, & Sullivan, 2010; Glass, Neulinger, & Brim, 1974), leading to lower scores on measures of verbal intellect for laterborn children.

Environmental deficiencies can have long-term effects if they are severe and exposure is prolonged during infancy and early childhood. One longitudinal study in Great Britain found that "early adversity"—measured by ratings of the childhood home environment,

---

neurons Nerve cell bodies and their extensions or fibers.

synaptogenesis The forming of connections or *synapses* between neurons.

transient exuberance The rapid but temporary increase in the rate of synaptogenesis and, hence, the number of synapses formed between neurons during infancy.

synaptic pruning The process through which unused synapses and neurons are eliminated.

plasticity The degree to which a developing structure or organ (like the brain) can be influenced by the environment.

FIGURE 4.2
Anatomy of a Typical Human Neuron

This illustration shows the typical structures of a human nerve cell, including dendrites through which information typically enters the cell, the cell body, the axon covered by a myelin sheath, and the axon terminals through which nerve impulses are passed to adjacent neurons.
Source: Designua/Shutterstock.com.

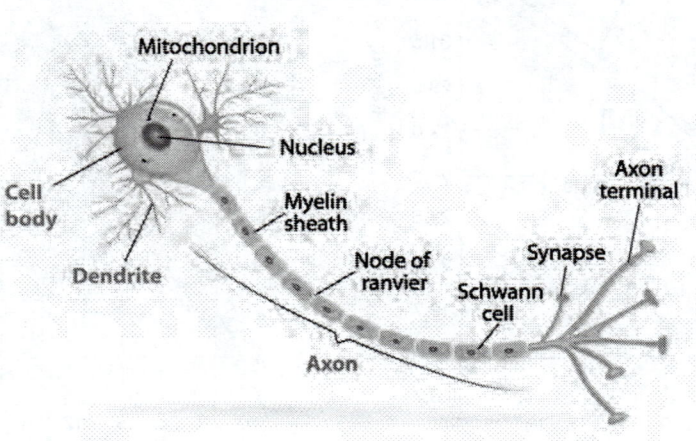

> **What Do You Think?**
>
> Do you think that everyone grows at the rates described? Did you? What factors might lead to more or less growth during infancy? If possible, find out how tall you were on your second birthday and multiply that figure by two. How close is that number to your current height? Why might the numbers be different?

including cleanliness, age, state of repair, and crowdedness, along with ratings of hygiene and cleanliness of the children themselves (prior to age four)—was associated with lower scores on a variety of cognitive measures through childhood and adolescence that persisted into middle adulthood (Richards & Wadsworth, 2004). However, plasticity serves in a protective capacity as well, as indicated in infants who suffered left-hemisphere strokes. After an intervention that included intense verbal stimulation, the right hemisphere assumed control of verbal comprehension and production, and language was able to develop normally (Rowe et al., 2009). The plasticity of the brain is greatest during infancy and early childhood, when the rates of synaptogenesis and synaptic pruning are highest.

An additional, important change in the brain during infancy that has a great impact on development is **myelination,** a process in which certain brain cells called *glia* produce fatty sheathing, or *myelin,* that gradually encases the neurons and their fibers. The myelin serves to protect and insulate the axons of neurons, allowing them to conduct neural impulses much more quickly. Myelination occurs rapidly during infancy and childhood, and then continues at a slower rate until about age thirty (Taylor, 2006).

myelination The process through which myelin covers the axon of some neurons.

An important function of the brain is to control infants' states of sleep and wakefulness. The brain regulates the amount of stimulation infants experience, both externally and internally. Thus, periodic sleep helps infants to shut out external stimulation and thereby allows them to obtain general physical rest. And, somewhat paradoxically, sleep may provide the opportunity for the brain to stimulate itself.

Infant States: Sleep and Arousal

Perhaps one of the biggest surprises for first-time parents is how little time they actually have to interact with their newborn babies while the babies are alert and responsive. Also, the sometimes irregular sleep patterns of newborns can prove to be both physically and emotionally challenging for parents. These challenges are compounded when new parents receive conflicting information about how to help their babies sleep better or longer when they seek advice on the subject.

Sleep

In the days immediately after birth, newborns sleep an average of sixteen hours per day, although some sleep as little as eleven hours a day and others as much as twenty-one (Michelsson et al., 1990). By age six months, babies average just thirteen or fourteen hours of sleep per day, and by twenty-four months, only eleven or twelve. But these hours still represent considerably more sleeping time than the six to eight hours typical for adults.

As Figure 4.3 shows, newborns divide their sleeping time about equally between relatively active and quiet periods of sleep. The more active kind is named **REM sleep,** after the "*r*apid *e*ye *m*ovements," or twitchings, that usually accompany it. In the quieter kind of sleep, **non-REM sleep,** infants breathe regularly and more slowly, and their muscles become much limper. It takes approximately sixty minutes for an infant to cycle through REM and non-REM sleep, as compared to a ninety-minute cycle for adults.

REM sleep A relatively active period of sleep, named after the rapid eye movements that usually accompany it. See also *non-REM sleep*.

non-REM sleep A relatively quiet, deep period of sleep. See also *REM sleep*.

Unfortunately for parents, a baby's extra sleep time does not usually include long, uninterrupted rest periods, even at night. In the first few months, it is more common for the baby to waken frequently—often every two or three hours—but somewhat unpredictably. Studies of brain development suggest that much of the unpredictability may result from the physical immaturity of the baby's nervous system: his brain may have frequent, accidental "storms"

Focusing On...

Sudden Infant Death Syndrome

Each year, about one out of every two thousand young infants dies during sleep for no apparent reason. Doctors call this phenomenon **sudden infant death syndrome (SIDS)**, or "crib death." The problem is most frequent among infants between ages two months and four months, although SIDS can affect babies as young as one month and as old as one year. Even though the rate of SIDS has been reduced by 50 percent since 1994, it is the leading cause of death among infants who survive the first few weeks after delivery (AAP Task Force on SIDS, 2011).

SIDS is disturbing because it is so mysterious. Typically, parents put a seemingly healthy baby down to sleep as usual, but when they come in to get her up again, they discover she is dead. Sadly, because the baby had exhibited no health problems, the parents often blame themselves for the death, suspecting that somehow they neglected their child or hurt him in some way (Kaplan, 1995). Even more unfortunately, friends and relatives often concur in blaming the parents, simply because they can think of no other way to explain SIDS. Other obvious causes simply do not happen. The baby does not choke, vomit, or suffocate; she just stops breathing.

What causes SIDS? One theory is that SIDS is an exaggerated form of normal *sleep apnea,* temporary cessations of breathing during sleep (Hunt, 1992). Another theory suggests that SIDS occurs primarily at a special transition in development, just when inborn reflexive control of breathing begins to fade in importance but before infants have firmly established voluntary control of breathing. For most infants, this transition occurs at about two to four months of age, just when SIDS strikes most often. A third theory suggests that SIDS infants suffer from heart problems: their nervous systems may fail to prompt regular, strong heartbeats and in essence cause them to suffer a heart attack. Unfortunately, no clear evidence points to any of these alternative explanations. Recent neuroscience research suggests that prenatal exposure to nicotine appears to alter receptors in the brain stem that play a role in the governance of certain autonomic functions (like heart rate and respiration). In preterm infants, prenatal exposure to nicotine impairs their recovery from *hypoxia*—low levels of oxygen in the blood—that might result from an obstruction, like a soft blanket, pillow, or stuffed animal, interfering with their supply of oxygen (AAP Task Force on SIDS, 2011).

If medical researchers could identify a basic cause, they would help future infants at risk for SIDS. Those babies could wear monitors that would indicate interruptions in breathing (if lungs are the problem) or heart rate (if that is the problem) and prompt parents or medical personnel to give the baby immediate, appropriate help. But so far, the use of monitors has not been practical on a widespread scale because they can be cumbersome, cause a lot of unnecessary alarm, and occasionally fail to function properly.

Medical research has identified several factors that make a particular family or infant more likely to experience SIDS (American Academy of Pediatrics, 2013b; Byard & Cohle, 1994). Very young mothers and fathers (younger than twenty years) stand a greater chance of having a SIDS infant, as do mothers who smoke cigarettes or have serious illnesses during pregnancy. Mothers who are poorly nourished during pregnancy also carry more risk than mothers who keep reasonably well

sudden infant death syndrome (SIDS)
An unaccountable death of an infant in its sleep. Also known as *crib death*.

FIGURE 4.3
Developmental Changes in Sleep Requirements

Sleep changes in nature as children grow from infancy to adulthood. Overall, they sleep less, and the proportion of REM (rapid-eye-movement) sleep decreases sharply during infancy and childhood.

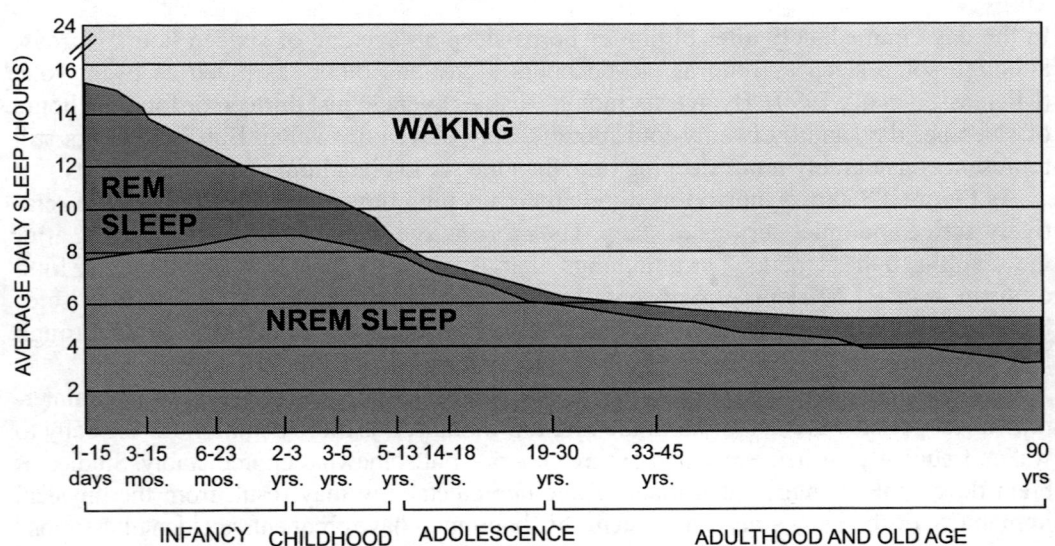

Focusing On...

Sudden Infant Death Syndrome *continued*

nourished. Infants who begin daycare before four months of age also appear to be at higher risk for SIDS. Preliminary data indicate that 20 percent of SIDS deaths occur when the infants are being cared for someone other than a parent, and one-third of those deaths occurred during the first week of day care. But certain babies also are at greater risk for SIDS independent of their parents' qualities or behaviors. Boys die of SIDS more often than girls do, for example, and infants born small (less than seven pounds) die more often than larger infants do. These relationships do not mean, however, that being a boy or being small actually *causes* SIDS; they imply only that for reasons still not understood, SIDS seems to strike boys and small infants more frequently.

Even taken together, these factors do not predict SIDS very accurately. The vast majority of high-risk infants do not die, whereas some infants with few risk factors die from SIDS. This circumstance creates problems in translating the studies of risk factors into concrete recommendations for medical personnel and parents because taking the risk indications too literally can arouse fears in parents unnecessarily. The most useful recommendations tend to be valid for all families, whether or not they are at risk for SIDS (Carroll & Siska, 1998). For example, the American Academy of Pediatrics (2013b) offers the following recommendations as part of their safe sleep policy for all children:

- Infants should sleep on their backs until age one for every sleep; sleep positioners like foam wedges or rolled blankets designed to encourage side-sleeping should not be used.

- Consider the use of pacifiers for naptime and nighttime sleep.

- Infants should sleep on a firm surface that is covered by a fitted sheet.

- Soft objects, loose bedding, bumper pads, top sheets or blankets, and stuffed animals should not be in the baby's sleep area.

- Specifically designed sleep clothing (e.g., sleepers, snug-fitting pajamas) should be used instead of blankets.

- The temperature in the room should be comfortable for a lightly clothed adult.

- Never allow smoking in rooms where babies sleep.

These are good pieces of advice for everyone, but unfortunately, they do not guarantee complete protection from SIDS. For parents whose babies do die, many hospitals and communities have created support groups in which couples can share their grief and come to terms with it.

What Do You Think?

If you were counseling a parent who lost a baby to SIDS, what would be your most important concern? What might you say to the parent? What might you also say to a relative of the parent who suspects that neglect may have caused the death?

---

of impulses because it is not yet fully formed (Fransson et al., 2009; Sheldon et al., 1992). In most cases, the irregularities pose no problem to an infant, though as the "Focusing On" feature describes, in some children irregularities of neural activity may be related to "crib death," or sudden infant death syndrome, in a very small percentage of infants. Once a baby's sleep begins to consolidate into longer periods of wake and sleep, these periods have a tendency to "drift" so that a baby who is mostly sleeping through the night one week may be awake most of the night a few weeks later (Kaltman & Engelmann, 1953; Par melee et al., 1964).

Parents' Response to Infant Sleep and Arousal

The unpredictability of infants' sleep can create chronic sleep deprivation in many parents; as a group, in fact, parents of infants and toddlers—along with older teenagers—are among the most sleep-deprived people in society (Coren, 1996). Research has demonstrated that new mothers obtain about seven hours of sleep each day, which is not significantly less than the average adult gets (Mongtomery-Downs et al., 2010). So why are new parents so much more tired than the rest of us? When babies wake up to be fed or changed, parents' sleep cycles are interrupted, causing sleep fragmentation similar to various sleep disorders (Insana & Montgomery-Downs, 2013; Montgomery-Downs et al.,

2010). In fact, there is evidence that new fathers may be sleepier than new mothers are; most men do not get paternity leave and, therefore, cannot "make up" for disrupted sleep with daytime napping (Insana & Montgomery-Downs, 2013). Parents' fatigue is aggravated by living arrangements common in modem Western society. Unlike in many non-Western societies, where babies often sleep in the same bed the mother does, infants in our society are often "stationed" in an adjoining room, or at least in a separate bed across the room—an arrangement that makes assisting the baby more disruptive. Furthermore, many non-Western households may have a number of adults or older relatives regarded as capable of calming a baby at night. In our society, in contrast, a household commonly has only two adults, or even just one. The scarcity of "qualified" helpers places a disproportionate burden of nighttime child care on parents, and eventually contributes to fatigue.

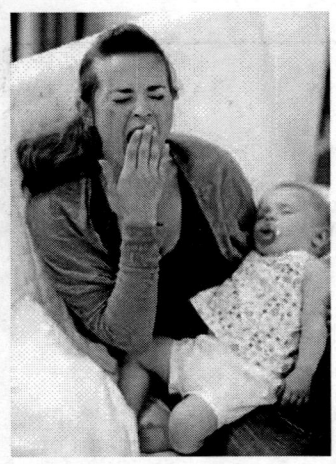

Infants spend more time sleeping than doing anything else. Unfortunately, their sleep may not occur at night, so chronic sleep deprivation and sleep fragmentation is a real problem for most parents, particularly primary caregivers. If possible, it is helpful for the caregiver to nap at the same time as the baby. However, because of discrepancies in the time it takes infants (sixty minutes) and parents (ninety minutes) to complete a sleep cycle, even this is not optimal.
Source: Alliance/Shutterstock.com.

The cure for nighttime fussiness eventually depends on physical maturation, but parents can also influence their infant's sleep patterns by developing regular (though not rigid) times for and methods of waking, feeding, and sleeping that involve the infant. One study found that infants change toward more adultlike levels of wakefulness and sleep within six weeks after arriving home, provided routines are (relatively) regular (Bamford et al., 1990; Rivkees, 2003). Another found that regularity offers dividends later in childhood: comparisons of Dutch and American families found fewer sleep problems among the young children of Dutch families, whose culture encourages regularity of daily routines more strongly than North American society does (Harkness & Keefer, 1995).

The advice to strive for (relatively) regular routines is widely supported among parent advice experts, but note that it makes assumptions about families that are not always true. In some families, routines cannot be made regular because of competing pressures from other children, because of exhaustion from work or from earlier ill-timed wakings or feedings, or because the family has only one parent. Under these conditions, parents need additional support from friends, extended family, or social service workers. They cannot do it all themselves.

States of Arousal

As Table 4.2 shows, infants exhibit various states of arousal, from sleep to full wakefulness. As they get older, their patterns of arousal begin to resemble those of older children (Ferber & Kryger, 1995). The largest share of time, even among older infants, goes to the most completely relaxed and deepest form of sleep.

TABLE 4.2 States of Arousal in Infants

State	Behavior of Infants
Non-REM sleep	Complete rest; muscles relaxed; eyes closed and still; breathing regular and relatively slow
REM sleep	Occasional twitches, jerks, facial grimaces; irregular and intermittent eye movements; breathing irregular and relatively rapid
Drowsiness	Occasional movements, but fewer than in REM sleep; eyes open and close; glazed look; breathing regular, but faster than in non-REM sleep
Alert inactivity	Eyes open and scanning; body relatively still; rate of breathing similar to drowsiness, but more irregular
Alert activity	Eyes open, but not attending or scanning; frequent, diffuse bodily movements; vocalizations; irregular breathing; skin flushed
Distress	Whimpering or crying; vigorous or agitated movements; facial grimaces pronounced; skin very flushed

Source: Ferber and Kryger (1995).

> **What Do You Think?**
>
> How do parents deal with differences in children's sleep patterns? Ask a classmate or friend who is a parent of more than one child, or ask your own parent(s) how he or she responded to sleep differences in the children as infants. Combine your information with that of several other classmates. Do you see any trends?

Obviously, a fully alert state is a time when babies can learn from their surroundings, but it may not be the only time. During REM sleep, infants' heart rates speed up in reaction to sounds, suggesting that infants may process stimulation even while asleep. But the meaning of a faster heart rate is ambiguous: changes in it may also show neural *dis*organization or an inability to shut out the world. Babies who are born prematurely confirm this possibility because they show more variability in heart rate than full-term babies when they hear sounds in their sleep (Spassov et al., 1994).

In addition to responding to external stimulation during REM sleep, the brains of infants also appear to be engaging in self-stimulation (Roffwarg, Muzio, & Dement, 1966) in this sleep phase. For quite some time, researchers have been wondering what is occurring in the minds of infants during REM sleep—are they dreaming? While this question has not been answered definitively, the brain-wave patterns of young infants in REM sleep differ from those of adults who are dreaming, suggesting that infants are not dreaming, or at least they are not dreaming in the same way that adults dream. However, at about three or four months of age, the brain-wave patterns of infants in REM sleep become similar to those of adults who are dreaming (Zampi, Fagioli, & Salzarulo, 2002).

Sensory Acuity

If you have not spent much time around infants, you may share William James' (1890) conclusion that "the baby, assailed by eyes, ears, nose, skin, and entrails at once, feels it all as one great blooming, buzzing confusion" (p. 462). William James was trained as a physician and was a professor of philosophy at Harvard University during the late nineteenth and early twentieth centuries. His writings on the intersection of physiology and philosophy helped to establish and shape the new discipline of psychology. James was pondering what parents have questioned for ages: how can infants, new to this world and with no knowledge or point of reference with which to interpret their experiences, interpret the information flooding their senses? What do they sense, and what is their understanding of it? Are they truly confused amidst the blooming buzz of sensory signals? Since James' 1890 description of infants, more than a century of research that utilized new methodologies and technologies revealed some surprising capabilities regarding the sensory acuity of infants.

Visual Acuity

Infants can see at birth, but they lack the clarity of focus or *acuity* (keenness) characteristic of adults with good vision. When looking at stationary contours and objects, newborns see more clearly at short distances, especially at about eight to ten inches—about the distance, incidentally, between a mother's breast and her face. Their vision is better when tracking moving objects, but even so their overall vision is rather poor until about one month of age (Seidel et al., 1997).

Visual acuity improves a lot during infancy, but it does not reach adult levels until the end of the preschool years. An older infant (age one to two) often has 20/30 or 20/40 vision, meaning he can see fine details at twenty feet that adults can see at thirty or forty feet. This quality of vision is quite satisfactory for everyday, familiar activities; in fact, many adults can see no better than this, without even realizing it. But this level of visual acuity does interfere with seeing distant objects.

Color vision also improves dramatically during the few months after birth. Specialized neurons called cones that are located in the retina at the back of the eye enable humans to see color, but these cones are immature at birth (Kellman & Arterberry, 2006). One-month-old infants can distinguish between black, red, and white, and their attention is drawn to bold, high-contrast color patterns. By approximately four months of age, their ability to see colors, including soft pastels and subtle differences between hues, is similar to that of adults (Franklin, Pilling, & Davies, 2005).

Auditory Acuity

Auditory acuity refers to sensitivity to sounds. Infants can hear at birth, but not as well as adults. Any sudden loud noise near an infant, such as that caused by dropping a large book on the floor, demonstrates she can hear. Such a sound produces a dramatic startle reaction, called a *Moro reflex:* The neonate extends her limbs suddenly, sometimes shakes all over, and may also cry. Not all noises produce this reaction; pure tones, such as the sound of a flute, cause relatively little response. Complex noises containing many different sounds usually produce a stronger reaction; a bag of nails spilling on the floor, for example, tends to startle infants reliably.

Regardless of the type of sound, infants tend to exhibit a preference for higher-pitched sounds than lower tones. This fact has sometimes led some experts to suggest that infants have a "natural" preference for female—that is, high-pitched—human voices. Studies of voice preferences, however, have not confirmed this possibility consistently, probably because newborns' range of special sensitivity lies well above the pitch of even female voices and because male and female voices usually are more similar in overall quality than gender stereotypes suggest. Instead, it is more accurate to say that infants prefer sounds in the middle range of pitches, which is the range most similar to human voices, male or female. Recent research on infant auditory preferences has indicated that infants exhibit a distinct preference for human speech sounds over other human and non-human vocalizations (Shultz & Vouloumanos, 2010), especially those that are expressed in higher pitches (Fernald & Kuhl, 1987).

Tactile, Taste, and Olfactory Acuity

Newborns and infants are sensitive to touch (i.e., *tactile acuity*), as all caregivers who have comforted a crying baby by wrapping the child in a blanket or by cradling the child in their arms can attest. Also, as will be addressed in the next section, infants respond reflexively to physical contact—turning toward a touch on the cheek or closing their hands around objects that touch their palms—abilities that are present at birth (Futagi, Toribe, & Suzuki, 2009).

Can infants feel pain? This question has been the focus of much debate during the past few decades, but an increasing body of behavioral and neurological evidence seems to indicate that they can (Warnock & Sandrin, 2004; Williams et al., 2009). The degree to which infants experience pain is still being researched and is complicated by the subjective nature of the perception of pain. For example, in one study involving a control group of newborns whose heels were pricked, the newborns cried loudly in response to the pain-inducing prick. However, an experimental group of newborns who were first given a drop of sucrose before receiving the heel prick exhibited little response to the prick (Harrison et al., 2010).

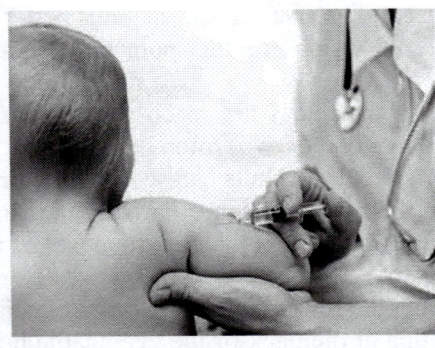

Can infants feel pain? Any parent who has taken a baby to the doctor for a vaccination *(left photo)* can attest that their baby feels pain *(right photo)*.

Sources: *(left)* Dmitry Naumov/Shutterstock.com; *(right)* Piotr Marcinski/Shutterstock.com.

> **What Do You Think?**
>
> Do parenting books agree with our comments that young infants have the use of vision and hearing? That babies can feel pain and have very well-developed senses of taste and smell? Check the comments made in two or three books about the capabilities of newborn babies. Do they seem consistent, or at least not *in*consistent?

As for taste and smell (technically called "olfaction"), infants reveal well-developed acuity, even prior to birth. Preferences for sweet tastes have been demonstrated by fetuses who swallow more frequently after an artificial sweetener has been added to their amniotic fluid (Booth et al., 2010). Infants smile and lick their lips when presented with sweet substances (Steiner et al., 2001), and they pucker and grimace when presented with sour or bitter substances (Kaijura, Cowart, & Beauchamp, 1992). Researchers have argued that infant preferences for sweet tastes may have evolutionary survival advantages, as breast milk tends to be sweet (Liem & Mennella, 2002). Infants also respond with facial expressions that suggest pleasure or disgust when presented with pleasant and unpleasant smells, and by four days after birth, they can discriminate between their own mother's breast smell and that of another lactating mother, keeping their heads turned toward pads with their own mother's scent (Porter & Reiser, 2005).

Given the remarkable sensory acuity of infants, parents may be partly right when they claim their newborn child recognizes them even from birth. What parents may be noticing is their newborn's immediate responsiveness to sights, sounds, smells, taste, and touch. They are right to exclaim over it: by taking an interest in the environment, infants create conditions where they can begin organizing (or *perceiving*) stimuli and attaching meanings to them. As we will see in the next section of this chapter, certain kinds of lines, shapes, and contours are especially interesting to a young infant. So are certain kinds of sounds. Fortunately for the development of family ties, parents are able to provide many of the most interesting sights and sounds with their own faces and voices; and partly in this way, attachments between parents and children are born.

Motor Development

Infants begin life with more than two dozen inborn reflexes, or automatic responses to specific stimuli. Table 4.3 summarizes the most important ones. A few reflexes, such as sucking, clearly help the baby to adapt to the new life outside the womb. Others look more like evolutionary vestiges of behaviors that may have helped earlier versions of *Homo sapiens* to cope, for example, by clinging to their mothers at the sound of danger. A few reflexes, such as blinking, breathing, and swallowing, persist throughout a person's life, but most reflexes disappear from the infant's repertoire during the first few months. Their disappearance, in fact, helps doctors to judge whether a baby is developing normally. Newborn reflexes that persist over many months may suggest damage to the nervous system or generally impaired development (El-Dib et al., 2012; Menkes, 1994).

reflex An involuntary, automatic response to a stimulus. The very first movements or motions of an infant are reflexes.

The First Motor Skills

Motor skills are voluntary movements of the body or parts of the body. They can be grouped conveniently according to the size of the muscles and body parts involved. *Gross motor skills* involve the large muscles of the arms, legs, and torso. *Fine motor skills* involve the small muscles located throughout the body. Walking and jumping are examples of gross motor skills, and reaching and grasping are examples of fine motor skills.

Viewed broadly, the sequence in which skills develop follows two general trends. The **cephalocaudal principle** ("head to tail") refers to the fact that upper parts of the body become usable and skillful before lower parts do. Babies learn to turn their heads before learning to move their feet intentionally, and they learn to move their arms before they

motor skills Physical skills using the body or limbs, such as walking and drawing.

cephalocaudal principle The tendency for organs, reflexes, and skills to develop sooner at the top (or head) of the body and later in areas farther down the body.

Chapter 4 Physical and Cognitive Development in the First Two Years

TABLE 4.3 Major Reflexes in Newborn Infants

Reflex	Description	Development	Significance
Survival Reflexes			
Breathing reflex	Repetitive inhalation and expiration	Permanent, although becomes partly voluntary	Provides oxygen and expels carbon dioxide
Rooting reflex	Turning of cheek in direction of touch	Weakens and disappears by six months	Orients child to breast or bottle
Sucking reflex	Strong sucking motions with throat, mouth, and tongue	Gradually comes under voluntary control	Allows child to drink
Swallowing reflex	Swallowing motions in throat	Permanent, although becomes partly voluntary	Allows child to take in food and to avoid choking
Eyeblink reflex	Closing eyes for an instant ("blinking")	Permanent, although gradually becomes voluntary	Protects eyes from objects and bright light
Pupillary reflex	Changing size of pupils: smaller in bright light and bigger in dim light	Permanent	Protects against bright light and allows better vision in dim light
Primitive Reflexes			
Moro reflex	In response to a loud noise, child throws arms outward, arches back, then brings arms together as if to hold something	Arm movements and arching disappear by six months, but startle reaction persists for life	Indicates normal development of nervous system
Grasping reflex	Curling fingers around any small object put in the child's palm	Disappears by three months; voluntary grasping appears by about six months	Indicates normal development of nervous system
Tonic neck reflex	When laid on back, head turns to side, arm and leg extend to same side, limbs on opposite side flex	Disappears by two or three months	Indicates normal development of nervous system
Babinski reflex	When bottom of foot stroked, toes fan and then curl	Disappears by eight to twelve months	Indicates normal development of nervous system
Stepping reflex	If held upright, infant lifts leg as if to step	Disappears by eight weeks, but later if practiced	Indicates normal development of nervous system
Swimming	If put in water, infant moves arms and legs and holds breath	Disappears by four to six months	Indicates normal development of nervous system

proximodistal principle Growth that exhibits a near-to-far pattern of development, from the center of the body outward.

learn to move their legs. The **proximodistal principle** ("near to far") refers to the fact that central parts of the body become skillful before peripheral, or outlying, parts do. Babies learn to wave their entire arms before learning to wiggle their wrists and fingers. The former movement occurs at the shoulder joint, near the center of the body, and the latter occurs at the periphery.

Gross Motor Development in the First Year

Almost from birth, and before reflex behaviors disappear, babies begin doing some things on purpose. By age four weeks or so, most babies can lift their heads up when lying on their stomachs. At six or seven months, many babies have become quite adept at using their limbs; they can stick their feet up in the air and "bicycle" with them while a parent struggles valiantly to fit a diaper on the moving target. At ten months, the average baby can stand erect, but only if an adult helps. By their first birthday, one-half of all babies can dispense with this assistance and stand by themselves without toppling over immediately (Savelsbergh, 1993). By age seven months, on the average, babies become able to locomote, or move around, on their own. At first, their methods are crude and slow; a baby might simply pivot on her stomach, for example, to get a better view of something interesting. Consistent movement in one direction develops soon after this time, although the movement does not always occur in the direction the baby intends!

Reaching and Grasping

Even newborn infants will reach for and grasp objects they can see immediately in front of them. They often fail to grasp objects successfully; they may make contact with an object but fail to enclose it in their fingers. This early, crude reaching disappears fairly soon after birth, only to reappear at about four or five months of age as two separate skills, reaching and grasping (Pownall & Kingerlee, 1993). During their second year, infants gain increased control over the movements of their fingers, producing a *pincer grasp* in which the thumb and forefinger are brought together to pick up small objects. These skills soon serve infants in many ways. For example, by their second birthday most babies can turn the pages in large picture books one at a time, at least if the paper is relatively indestructible. But they can also point at the pages without grasping for them. The pincer grasp also allows for improved self-feeding with their hands, fingers, and ultimately, utensils (Ho, 2010).

Walking

A reasonably predictable series of events leads to true walking in most children; Figure 4.4 describes some of these milestones. While the development of walking, overall, tends to follow a progression of "stages," on any given day, infants will exhibit creativity and resourcefulness when it comes to their mobility, so caregivers should not be alarmed if their own infant moves around a room in a manner that is unconventional (Adolph, 2008). By about twelve to thirteen months, most children take their first independent steps. Well before two years, they often can walk not only forward but backward or even sideways. Some two-year-olds can even walk upstairs on two feet instead of on all fours. Usually, they use the wall or a railing to do so. Usually, too, coming downstairs proves more difficult than going up; one solution is to creep down backward, using all four limbs.

The toddler on the left is watching his older, preschool-aged sister use a pincer grasp to perform a more precise operation using the toy tools on the workbench.
Source: Glenda/Shutterstock.com.

Chapter 4 Physical and Cognitive Development in the First Two Years

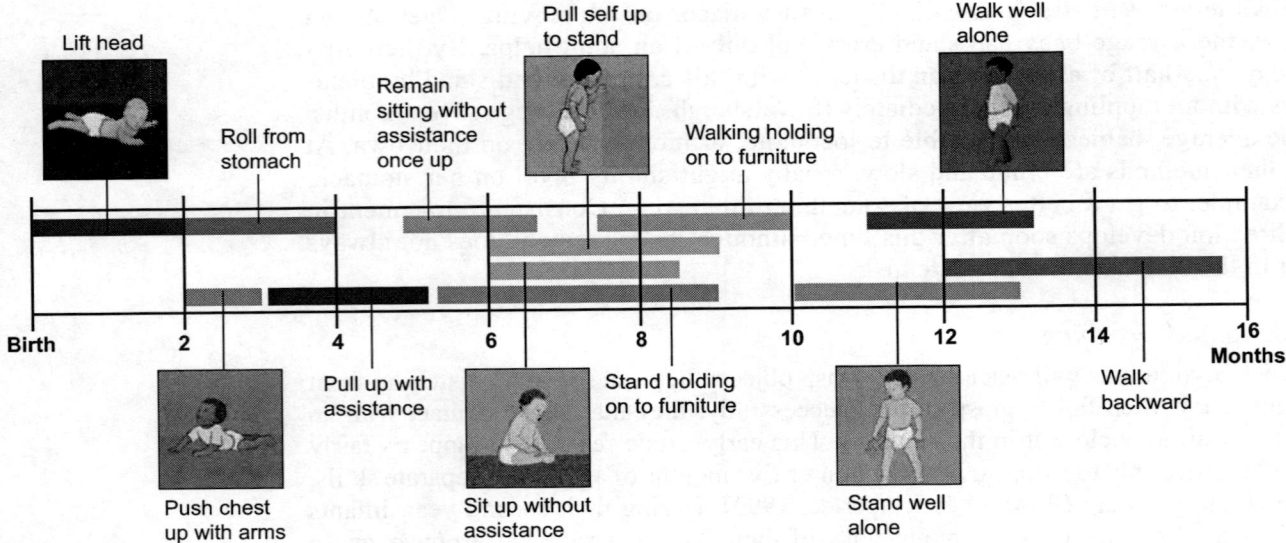

FIGURE 4.4 Milestones of Motor Development

Walking alone is one of the major physical achievements of the first year of life. Quite a few other physical skills usually develop prior to walking, as the figure shows. Note, though, that skills appear at different times for different individuals. Some skills may even appear "out of sequence" in some children.

Cultural and Sex Differences in Motor Development

Differences in motor development exist among cultures and between the sexes, though they are not always large or dramatic. Certain African cultures, for example, give their infants unusually frequent chances to sit upright and to practice their "walking" reflex when held at a standing position by adults and older children (LeVine, 1994; Munroe et al., 1981). These opportunities seem to stimulate toddlers in these societies to learn to walk earlier and better than North American toddlers do. Early walking, in turn, may prove especially valuable in these societies, which do not rely heavily on cars, bicycles, or other vehicles that make walking less important. Yet, early walking may also be a genetic trait (at least partially) for these groups; without comparable training in reflex walking for North American infants, there is no way to be sure.

Yet differences in motor skills do not always appear where we might expect. Take the Navaho and Hopi tribes, whose infants spend nearly all of their first year bound and swaddled tightly to a flat board, with their arms and legs extending straight down along their bodies (J. Whiting, 1981; van Sleuwen, 2007). Apparently as a result, Navaho and Hopi toddlers do tend to acquire walking a little later than Anglo-American children do. But they do not show delays in other skills inhibited by swaddling—notably, reaching and grasping—and the deficit in walking disappears by the end of the preschool years in most cases (Connelly & Forssberg, 1997).

Culture aside, do boys and girls differ, on average, in motor development? The answer depends on distinguishing what infants *can* do from what they typically *do* do. What they can do—their competence—has relatively little relationship to their sex. Girl and boy babies sit upright at about the same age, for example, and stand and walk at about the same time. Similar equality exists for all of the motor milestones of infancy.

How infants use their time is another matter. Almost as soon as they can move, boys show more activity than do girls. The trend begins even before birth, when male fetuses move about in their mothers' wombs more than do female fetuses (Moore & Persaud, 1998). After birth, the trend continues: girls spend more time using their emerging fine motor skills. Of course, the differences in use of time may stem partly from parents' encouragement (praise) for "gender-appropriate" behaviors. Given the young age of the children, though, and the fact that activity actually precedes birth, part of the difference must come from genetic endowment: an inborn tendency to be more (or less) active.

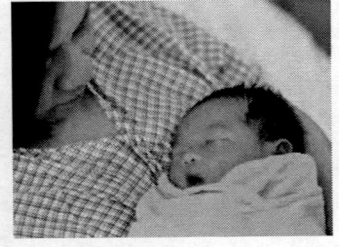

Swaddling infants, as has been done with this Asian baby girl, is practiced in many cultures. Swaddling tends to slow motor development at first, but not permanently. It may also allow caregivers to carry infants with them during daily activities—a circumstance that could make the skills of vocalizing less urgent to develop.
Source: szefei/Shutterstock.com.

Part 2 The First Two Years of Life

> **What Do You Think?**
>
> If motor skills develop partly through learning, why not just deliberately teach infants to walk? What do you think would be the result of doing so? Do similar considerations apply for certain other important developments in infancy?

It is important to note that whatever their source, sex differences in infants' motor development are only averages and, in any case, rather slight. As groups, boys and girls are more alike than different, and numerous individual boys are less active than numerous individual girls, despite "average" behavior. As a practical matter, it is therefore more important for parents and teachers to respond to the qualities of the individual children for whom they are responsible than to stereotypical "gender" averages.

Nutrition During the First Two Years

As obvious as it sounds, the physical developments in infancy depend on good nutrition throughout the first two years. Like adults, babies need diets with appropriate amounts of protein, calories, and specific vitamins and minerals. For various reasons, however, infants do not always get all the nutrients they need. Often poverty accounts for malnutrition: parents with good intentions may be unable to afford the right foods. In other cases, conventional eating practices interfere: despite relatively expensive eating habits, such as going to fast-food restaurants, some families may fail to provide their children with a balanced diet.

Compared with older children, infants eat less in overall or absolute amounts. A well-nourished young baby in North America might drink somewhat less than one liter (about .95 quarts) of liquid nourishment per day. This amount definitely would not keep an older child or a young adult well nourished, although it might prevent starving. In proportion to their body weight, however, infants need to consume much more than older children or adults do. For example, every day a three-month-old baby ideally should take in more than two ounces of liquid per pound of body weight, whereas an eighteen-year-old needs only about one-third of this amount (Queen & Lang, 1993). If adolescents or young adults drank in the same proportion to their body' weights, they would have to consume six quarts of liquid per day. That is equivalent to twenty-five cups per day, or about one cup every forty-five minutes during waking hours!

Breast Milk Versus Formula

Someone (usually parents) must provide for an infant's comparatively large appetite. Whenever breastfeeding is possible, health experts generally recommend human milk as the sole source of nutrition for at least the first six months or so of most infants' lives and as a major source for at least the next six months. In some cases, of course, this recommendation proves difficult or impractical to follow. Babies who need intensive medical care immediately after birth cannot be breast-fed without special arrangements. Some women have difficulty producing milk. Also, for one reason or another, some women may choose not to breast-feed, for example, if they are taking medications that might be passed on to the baby, Also, for one reason or another some women choose not to breast-feed. For example, if a woman is taking medications that might be passed on to the baby or if job situations make breastfeeding difficult she may choose to not breast-feed. For these infants, formulas can be either safer or more convenient.

Why do pediatricians recommend breastfeeding? First, human milk seems to give young infants more protection from diseases and other ailments. Second, human milk matches the nutritional needs of human infants more closely than formula preparations do, and the makeup of human milk changes over time to meet infant nutritional needs; in particular, it contains more iron, an important nutrient for infants. Third, breastfeeding better develops the infant's jaw and mouth muscles because it requires stronger sucking motions than bottle feeding does and because it tends to satisfy infants' intrinsic needs for sucking better than a bottle does. Fourth, breastfeeding may encourage a healthy emotional relationship

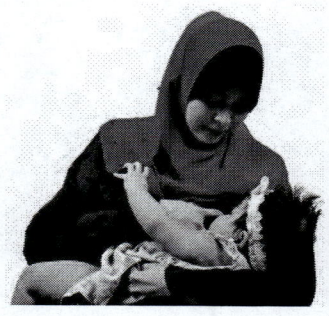

In recent decades, increasing numbers of mothers have chosen to breast-feed their babies, as recommended by most pediatricians. For a significant number of parents and infants, however, partial or complete bottle-feeding remains a valuable option—for example, if fathers wish to be involved in feeding or if the mother's work schedule makes breastfeeding difficult.
Source: Ery Azmeer/Shutterstock.com.

between mother and infant, simply because it involves a lot of close physical snuggling (La Leche League International, 1991). Breastfeeding also provides benefits to mothers: it is less expensive than formula, and it aids in postpartum weight loss, helps reduce risk for postpartum hemorrhaging, and has been linked to a reduced risk for breast, ovarian, and uterine cancer later in life (Dermer, 2001).

After about six months, infants can be introduced gradually to solid foods such as strained cereals and strained fruits. As babies become tolerant of these new foods, parents can introduce others that sometimes require a more mature digestive system, such as strained meats and cooked eggs. Overall, the shift to solid foods often takes many months to complete (see Table 4.4 for guidelines about how to do this). As it occurs, parents must begin paying more attention to their baby's overall nutritional needs because many solid foods lack the broad range of nutrients that breast milk and formula provide.

Poor Nutrition

Often, North American diets fail to provide enough of three specific nutrients: vitamin A, vitamin C, and iron. Prolonged deficiencies of vitamins A and C seem to create deficits in motor ability and deficiency of iron appears to lead to deficits in cognitive performance (Black et al., 2011; Pollitt, 1995). For about 4 to 5 percent of infants, these nutritional deficiencies are serious and require immediate remedy. For another group of about the same size, the nutritional deficiencies are less severe but are still a cause for concern. In developing countries worldwide, approximately one in three children suffers from severe malnutrition (UNICEF, 2009). If undernourishment is prolonged, it may produce a condition called **stunting**, which, as the term implies, results in stunted growth—specifically, falling below the fifth percentile in height for one's age when compared to typical growth norms (Abukabar et al., 2010).

Even when undernourished infants appear healthy and "bright," they may be at risk for later developmental problems because poorly nourished families often experience other serious deprivations, such as poor sanitation, inadequate health care, and lack of educational opportunities. Under these conditions, it may not take much to turn mild undernourishment into severe malnutrition and thus reduce cognitive and motor performance to below satisfactory levels.

stunting Being excessively short in stature—falling under the fifth percentile for height for one's age—caused by chronic undernourishment.

TABLE 4.4 Changing Nutritional Needs During Infancy

Age	Parents May Begin
Birth–4 months	Complete diet of breast milk or baby formula
4–6 months	Puréed single-grain cereal, preferably iron-fortified; begin with one to two teaspoons and work up to one-half cup, twice per day
5 months	100 percent fruit juices; could be diluted; one-half cup serving per day
6–8 months	Puréed vegetables or fruit, one at a time; begin with one to two teaspoons and work up to one-fourth to one-half cup per serving, twice per day
	"Finger" foods (e.g., chopped banana, bits of dry cereal)
10–12 months	Puréed meats or poultry, beginning with one to two teaspoons and working up to one-fourth to one-half cup per serving, three-to four times per day
	Soft but chopped foods (e.g., lumpy potatoes)
	Whole milk, one-half cup per serving, four to five times per day.
24 months	Low-fat milk, one-half cup per serving, four to five times per day.

Source: Adapted from the International Food Information Council, 1993, and the USNLM, 2011.

> **What Do You Think?**
>
> If you (or a partner) were expecting a child, would you prefer that the baby be breast-fed or bottle-fed? Discuss this question with a classmate of the *same* sex; then compare your responses with those of a classmate of the *opposite* sex. Do your responses differ?

Overnutrition

In affluent, calorie-loving societies such as our own, the problem often is not lack of food but getting too much of calorie-rich, nutrient-poor foods. Social circumstances make it difficult for parents to keep convenience food and "junk" food from their children (or to avoid it themselves!). Food manufacturers and fast-food restaurants have discovered that foods sell better if they contain high amounts of fat, sugar, and salt, and low amounts of fiber—all of which are violations of well-established nutritional guidelines (Wootan & Liebman, 1998). The short-term result during infancy can be **overnutrition**: too many calories, too much of the wrong nutrients, and not enough of other nutrients. The longer-term result can be to establish food preferences that may create health risks when the infant becomes a child and later an adult. A toddler who eats too much ice cream and chips may be "cute"; an adult who does so experiences greater risk for heart problems, diabetes, and certain forms of cancer (Bronner, 1997).

overnutrition Diet that contains too many calories and is therefore unbalanced.

Note that although overnutrition can increase an infant's weight, weight itself is not a cause for *medical* concern in infancy as long as the baby is only moderately above (or below) the average. Infants born bigger or heavier than usual tend to have diets relatively higher in calories. They also tend to drink more milk (via either breast or bottle) and other liquids than usual, and to shift earlier to solid foods. Some parents fear that heavier infants are prone to becoming overweight or obese as children or adolescents, but the evidence for this is inconclusive; some researchers have found that weight in infancy correlated little with weight in childhood and even less with weight in adulthood (Williams & Kimm, 1993). However, other researchers have found significant correlations between weight statuses during infancy (e.g., "overweight" or "obese") with weight statuses during childhood or adolescence (Gunnarsdottir & Thorsdottir, 2003; Harrington et al., 2010; Zhang et al., 2013). Parents sometimes feel concerned about a heavy infant for essentially social and psychological reasons: the paradox of a society that makes overnutrition too easy is that it also values thinness in physical appearance too much. As an infant grows into a child and then an adolescent, he or she will inevitably be affected by the social value placed on thinness. We discuss the results of this development in Chapter 8, in conjunction with discussing extremely overweight (or *obese*) children. In the meantime, though, it will be the child's parents who worry about weight on the child's behalf.

Impairments in Infant Growth

Within broad limits, healthy infants grow at various rates and become various sizes, and most of the time the differences are no cause for concern. But a small percentage do not grow as large as they should, beginning either at birth or a bit later during infancy. When a baby's size or growth is well below normal, it *is* a major cause for concern, both for the infant and for the infant's parents. At the extreme, it can contribute to infant mortality.

Low-Birth-Weight Infants

A small percentage of newborns are considered **low-birth-weight** infants if they are born weighing less than 2,500 grams, or about 5.5 pounds. The condition can result from several factors. One of the most common causes is malnourishment of the mother during pregnancy. But other harmful practices, such as smoking cigarettes, drinking alcohol, or taking drugs, also can depress birth weight. Mothers from certain segments of the population, such

low birth weight A birth weight of less than 2,500 grams (about 5.5 pounds).

Chapter 4 Physical and Cognitive Development in the First Two Years

as teenagers and those from very low-SES backgrounds, are especially likely to give birth to low-birth-weight babies, most likely because of their own poor nourishment or their lack of access to good prenatal care. But even mothers who are well nourished and well cared for sometimes have infants who are smaller than is medically desirable. Multiple births (e.g., wins, triplets) usually result in small babies; so do some illnesses or mishaps, such as a serious traffic accident that causes damage to the placenta.

Consequences for the Infant

When birth weight is very low (less than 2,500 grams), infants' reflexes tend to be a bit sluggish, weak, and poorly organized (Brooten, 1992). Such infants do not startle as reliably or grasp as automatically and strongly at objects. Their muscles often seem flabby or overly relaxed. After delivery, the infants must cope with many tasks for which they are inadequately prepared physically, including breathing and digesting food. They also have trouble regulating their own sleep to keep it peaceful, sustained, and smooth.

Neurological limitations often can persist for the first two or three years of life, causing the baby to develop specific motor skills a bit later than other infants. A four-month-old baby who is small due to being born two months preterm, for example, in many ways resembles a two-month-old born at full term; both infants have lived eleven months from conception. Some of the delay may reflect stresses associated with early birth (such as parents' overprotectiveness) rather than the physical effects of early birth as such. Unless they are extremely small, though, most low-birth-weight infants eventually develop into relatively normal preschoolers (Goldson, 1992). This conclusion was supported by a sophisticated study of monozygotic and dizygotic twins in addition to single births that allowed the researchers to control for maternal, environmental, and genetic factors (Datar & Jacknowitz, 2009). The results revealed very small consequences of low birth weight on cognitive and motor development at age two for most of the children in the study, but negative effects on growth were still evident at age two.

Consequences for the Parents

Although low birth weight can worry parents, the condition does not impair relationships with a child in the long term unless the parents are also under additional stresses elsewhere in their lives (Gross et al., 1997). In the short-term, though, low-birth-weight infants lack responsiveness, and initially need intensive care. These circumstances can create distance between parents and child at a time when parents want very much to reach out (literally and figuratively) and connect with their newborn. As the more mature members of the relationship, most parents are capable of understanding the reasons for the distance and of delaying their expectations for response from their child. The reflexive "social smile" normally shown at around two months, for example, may not come until age three or four months. If other stresses of life get in the way, though, waiting for the infant to finally "act normally" may be difficult or even impossible. Poverty, preexisting family conflicts, medical problems of parents, and the like put parents of low-birth-weight infants somewhat more at risk and in need of additional support from professionals, family members, and friends.

Failure to Thrive

An infant or a preschool child who fails to grow at normal rates for no apparent medical reason suffers from a condition called **failure to thrive**. About 6 percent of North American children exhibit this condition at one time or another, although not necessarily continuously (Cole & Lanham, 2011; Woolston, 1993). In some ways, the condition resembles malnutrition, especially when it occurs in developing nations. Failure-to-thrive and malnourished children both develop motor and cognitive skills more slowly than usual; both experience higher rates of school failure and learning disabilities; and both are more likely to live in disadvantaged circumstances and to have parents who are enduring physical or emotional stress.

At one time, professionals tended to attribute failure to thrive to lack of nurturing and love between parent and child. A more complex picture may be closer to the truth: failure

failure to thrive A condition in which an infant seems seriously delayed in physical growth and is noticeably apathetic in behavior.

to thrive may have many sources, both physical and psychological, and depend on both the child and the environment. Consider this pattern: An infant has a genetically quiet, slow-to-respond temperament, making it more difficult for her mother to establish emotional contact. If the mother also is experiencing a number of other stresses (low income, illness, or disapproval of the new baby from others), the relationship between mother and infant is put at risk. A vicious cycle may develop of poorly timed feedings and ineffective efforts to nurture the infant, who persistently resists the mother's love and even her food. Parents in this situation often can benefit from professional help and support in learning new patterns of interacting with their babies.

Infant Mortality

In the past several decades, health care systems in North America and around the world have substantially improved their ability to keep infants alive. The **infant mortality rate**, the proportion of babies who die during the first year of life, has declined steadily during this century. In 1950 in the United States, about twenty-nine out of every one thousand infants died; six decades later, this number was fewer than six out of every one thousand infants (CDC, 2012a). The averages conceal wide differences within society, some of which are listed in Table 4.5. In fact, there is also variability within the United States: infant mortality rates are higher in poorer states, like Mississippi, with a rate of nine out of every one thousand births, than in Massachusetts, with a rate of four out of every one thousand (United Health Foundation, 2016). Families with very low incomes are about twice as likely to lose an infant as families with middle-level incomes. Likewise, African-American families are twice as likely as white families to lose an infant, perhaps because of the historical correlation of race with income level and access to health care in American society. The strongest correlate with mortality is not race, however, but level of family income. As a rule of thumb, infants born to families with lower incomes are much more likely to die than infants born to families with higher incomes. Though this trend may be easy to believe when comparing poor with middle-income families, it actually holds for the full range of income in society (Finch, 2003; Pritchett, 1993). That is, infants born to middle-income families are *also* more likely to die than infants born to extremely wealthy families. The pattern holds no matter what the race or ethnic background of the child.

On average, infant mortality rates in the United States and Canada are two or three times lower than those in many less developed countries. Even so, infant mortality in the United States actually is *higher* than in numerous other developed nations, including Canada, Japan, Sweden, France, and Great Britain (Central Intelligence Agency, 2013). Cross-cultural investigations of infant mortality rates in European countries have given further clues about the reasons for the relatively high U.S. rate and have suggested ways to improve it. The research overwhelmingly indicates that parents need social supports as much as they need access to basic medical services and knowledge. Most European countries provide pregnant mothers with free prenatal care, for example, and also protect women's right to work during and after pregnancy. Pregnant women get special, generous sick leave, get at least four months of maternity leave *with pay*, and are protected from doing dangerous or exhausting work (such as night shifts). Policies such as these communicate support for pregnant mothers and their spouses in ways not currently available in the United States.

infant mortality rate The frequency with which infants die compared to the frequency with which they live.

COGNITIVE DEVELOPMENT

While infants are growing physically, they are also thinking: noticing the world around them, organizing their impressions, and even remembering their experiences. Although these activities are often called "cognitive development," "cognition," or simply "thinking," psychologists frequently classify them according to their mental complexity. **Perception** is the less complex process and refers to the brain's immediate or direct organization and interpretation of sensations. Perceptual processes occur when an infant notices that a toy car is the same car no matter which way she orients it. **Cognition** is the more complex

perception The neural activity of combining sensations into meaningful patterns.

cognition All processes by which humans acquire knowledge; methods for thinking or gaining knowledge about the world.

Chapter 4 Physical and Cognitive Development in the First Two Years

TABLE 4.5 Infant Mortality in Selected Nations

Nation	Infant Mortality (per 1,000 live births)	Nation	Infant Mortality (per 1,000 live births)
Japan	2.2	New Zealand	4.7
Singapore	2.6	Canada	4.8
Sweden	2.7	Greece	4.9
Hong Kong	2.9	**United States, whites**	**5.1**
Italy	3.3	Hungary	5.2
France	3.3	Guam	5.6
Finland	3.4	**United States, average**	**6.0**
Norway	3.5	Poland	6.3
Germany	3.5	Chile	7.2
Spain	3.6	Russia	7.2
Czechoslovakia	3.7	**United States, nonwhites**	**11.4**
Netherlands	3.7	Saudi Arabia	15.1
Ireland	3.8	China	15.2
Switzerland	3.8	Mexico	16.3
Israel	4.0	Morocco	25.5
Denmark	4.1	South Africa	42.1
Austria	4.2	India	44.6
Belgium	4.2	Afghanistan	119.4
Australia	4.5		
United Kingdom	4.5		

Sources: CDC (2012a); Central Intelligence Agency (2013).

process and refers to thinking and other mental activities. It includes reasoning, attention, memory, problem solving, and the ability to represent objects and experiences. Infants engage in both cognition and perception, even as newborns. As we will see, the distinction between them often is blurred, with each process often supporting the other. What infants see and hear depends on what they think and vice versa—just as for adults.

Studying Cognition and Memory in Infants

How can we know whether an infant, who cannot even talk, is actually noticing sights and sounds, organizing information about them, and remembering them? Psychologists have developed two main strategies: studying changes in infants' heart rates and studying infants' tendency to *habituate* to, or get used to, novel stimuli.

Arousal and Infants' Heart Rates

One way to understand an infant's cognition is to measure his heart rate (HR) with an electronic heart rate monitor attached to his chest. The changes in HR are taken to signify variations in the baby's arousal, alertness, and general contentment.

> **What Do You Think?**
>
> It is tempting for parents to blame themselves if their child is born with low birth weight. What would you say to a parent who reacted this way? Would you say essentially the same things to a parent whose child showed failure to thrive?

Psychologists who study infants make this assumption because among adults, HR varies reliably with attention and arousal. Typically, HR slows down, or decelerates, when adults notice or attend to something interesting but not overly exciting, such as reading the newspaper. If adults attend to something *very* stimulating, their HRs speed up, or accelerate. Watching a lab technician draw blood from your own arm, for example, often causes your HR to speed up. On the whole, novel or attractive stimuli produce curiosity and a slower HR, whereas potentially dangerous or aversive stimuli produce defensiveness, discomfort, and a faster HR, at least among adults.

Very young infants, from one day to a few months old, show similar changes, but we need to take several precautions when we study their HRs. For one thing, observations of infants' attention should be made when infants are awake and alert, and, as we already pointed out, newborn babies often spend a lot of time being drowsy or asleep. Many stimuli that lead to deceleration in adults or older children lead to acceleration in infants. Many one-month-olds show a faster HR at familiar sights, such as their mothers, even though the infants may look as though they are just staring calmly into space. Despite these problems, however, studies of HR have provided a useful way to measure infants' attention, perception, and memory.

Recognition, Memory, and Infant Habituation

Although infants cannot describe what they remember, they often indicate recognition of particular objects, people, and activities. Familiar people, such as mothers, bring forth a special response in one-year-olds, who may coo suddenly at the sight of them, stretch out their arms to them, and even crawl or walk to them if they know how. Less familiar people, such as neighbors or the family doctor, tend not to produce responses such as these and may even produce active distress, depending on the age of the infant.

Babies' responses to the familiar and the unfamiliar offer infant psychologists a second way to understand infant perception and conceptual thought. Psychologists study infants' tendency to get used to and therefore ignore stimuli as they experience them repeatedly; the tendency is often called **habituation** by psychologists (Mazur, 1994). One habituation strategy repeatedly offers a baby a standard, or "study," stimulus—a simple picture to look at or a simple melody to hear. Like most adults, the baby attends to the study stimulus carefully at first, but on subsequent occasions, gradually pays less attention to it. In fact, you have likely habituated to the room where you are reading this: You "tune out" the hum of your refrigerator or the sound of your air conditioner or heater until it is mentioned. As this happens, the baby is said to be *habituating* to the stimulus. After the baby has become habituated, the investigators present the original study stimulus along with a few other stimuli. If the baby really recognizes the original, she probably will attend to the others *more* because they are comparatively novel. Her HR will slow down as well.

habituation The tendency to attend to novel stimuli and ignore familiar ones.

This method has shown that young babies recognize quite a lot of past experiences. One classic habituation study found that four-month-old girls recognized a familiar visual pattern among three others that differed from the original (McCall & Kagan, 1967). Another found habituation even in newborns: they "noticed" when a light brush on their cheeks changed location, as revealed by changes in their HRs (Kisilevsky & Mnir, 1984). Sometimes, too, recognition persists for very long periods. Three-month-olds, it seems, can still recognize a picture or a toy two weeks after they first see it, as long as the objects are presented in a familiar context the second time—a performance that matches adults' recognition memory (Hayne et al., 1991).

> **What Do You Think?**
>
> Talk to a parent (preferably of an infant) about when he or she felt sure of being recognized. Do the parent's experiences suggest that infants do remember their parents? Do infants' signs of recognition apply only to their primary caregiver, or do they extend to other relatives?

Habituation is important not only because it provides a way to study infants' learning and development but also because it suggests that infants have memories well before they acquire language. And habituation has interesting, though speculative, implications for parent-child relationships: it suggests that young babies may begin recognizing their parents quite quickly—perhaps as quickly as the habituation psychologists have observed in laboratory experiments. Parents may not simply be imagining it, that is, when they become convinced that their baby responds differently or more fully to them than to other adults; the child may really be doing so even at just a few weeks of age.

Infant Perception and Cognition

It might seem as if infants should be better at *perception* than at *cognition* because perception involves more direct, automatic organization of sensations and requires less cognitive maturity. This hypothesis may indeed be true, but the evidence for it is surprisingly ambiguous. What *is* clear is that whatever "thinking" (or cognition) infants do does not involve language to the extent that it does in children and adults, simply because infants are only beginning to acquire language skills. If we are to see signs of infant thinking, furthermore, we should look at those behaviors infants already show, such as directing their eyes (and ears) or changing their heart rates. If we broaden our notion of cognition to include these nonverbal signs of thinking, infants show not only perception of their world but cognition about it as well. This is true even during their first year, before they understand or speak even a single word. In some situations, even six-month-olds seem to "reason" and solve problems. To see what we mean, let us look at the two most important senses—vision and hearing—and at how infants make use of both to perceive and to conceive of the world.

Visual Perception in Infancy

Given that children can see almost from birth, what do they notice? What, that is, do they perceive? Some of the earliest research on this question stirred up a lot of interest because it

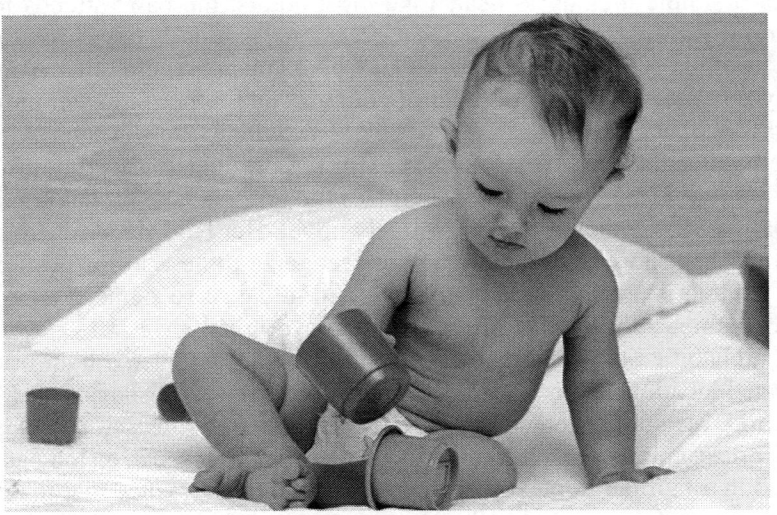

Young infants concentrate longer on certain shapes and contours, even when these are not part of a human face. Newborns are especially attracted to contours and to patches of light and dark. A few months later, they prefer complex patterns over simpler ones and curved lines over straight ones. Such changes are one reason (among many) why a baby's interest in crib toys changes over time.
Source: Vasina Natalia/Shutterstock.com.

seemed to show that infants, even those just two days old, could discriminate between human faces and abstract patterns and that they looked at faces longer than at either patterned disks or plain, unpatterned disks (Fantz, 1963). The researchers presented infants with various combinations of these stimuli side by side and carefully observed which object the babies spent the most time looking at. At all ages studied (birth to six months), the infants showed a clear preference: they stared at a picture of a human face almost twice as long as at any other stimulus picture. Young infants, it seemed, were inherently interested in people.

More recent studies of visual preferences, however, have qualified this conclusion substantially (Yonas, 1988). It is not the humanness of faces that infants enjoy looking at but their interesting contours, complexity, and curvature. Newborns are particularly attracted to contours, or the edges of areas of light and dark. But such edges can be provided either by the hairline of a parent's head or by a properly constructed abstract drawing. When infants reach age two or three months, their perceptual interest shifts to complexity and curvature. At this age, infants look longer at a pattern of many small squares than at one containing just a few large squares. They also look longer at curved lines than at straight ones. Interestingly, research with young infants has also found that infants prefer to look at attractive, rather than unattractive faces (Slater et al., 2000). Attractive faces tend to possess greater symmetry to the contours of their features and are, to infants (and we suspect, adults) more visually-engaging. This same preference for attractive faces has even been demonstrated when three- and four-month-old infants were presented with attractive and unattractive cat faces (Quinn et al., 2005). The complexity, curvature, symmetry, and contours of *any* attractive face seem to draw our attention during infancy, but our attention is captured by other stimuli in our visual field as well.

Object Perception

A more complex form of perception—one that is a step closer to cognition—is *object constancy*, the perception (or is it a "belief"?) that an object remains the same despite constant changes in the sensations it sends to the eye. A baby's favorite toy duck never casts exactly the same image on her retina from one second to the next. The image continually varies depending on its distance and its orientation, or angle of viewing. Somehow, the baby must learn that this kaleidoscope of images really refers to only one constant duck— that the duck always *is* the same but keeps *looking* different.

In general, research on infant perception suggests that infants begin perceiving objects as constant very early indeed (Granrud, 1993, 2006). Consider the development of *size constancy*, the perception that an object stays the same size even when viewed from different distances. In a typical study, newborn babies are conditioned to suck on pacifiers at the sight of a cube of some specified size and placed at some precise distance. During conditioning training, sucking at the sight of cubes of other sizes or distances is deliberately *not* reinforced so that the sucking provides an indicator of the baby's recognition of an object of a particular size and at a given distance.

Later the conditioned infants are shown several cubes of different sizes and placed at different distances. The test cubes include one that casts an image exactly the size of the original but is in fact *larger and farther away*. Typically, the babies are not fooled by this apparent identity of retinal images. They prefer to look at the original cube regardless of its distance; that is, they suck on their pacifiers more vigorously while looking at the original cube than while looking at any substitute. Apparently, they know when an object really is the same size and when it only looks the same size.

Depth Perception

Depth perception refers to a sense of how far away objects are or appear to be. Infants begin acquiring this kind of perceptual skill about as soon as they can focus on objects at different distances, at around two or three months of age. This conclusion is suggested by research that has developed out of the now classic experiment with the visual cliff (Gibson & Walk, 1960). In its basic form, the **visual cliff** consists of a table covered with strong glass under which is a textured surface with colored squares. Part of the textured

visual cliff The classic laboratory setup of a ledge covered by a sheet of glass; used to test the acquisition of depth perception. Young babies crawling on the glass discriminate between the two sides of the "cliff."

surface contacts the glass directly, and another part is separated from it by several feet. Visually, then, the setup resembles the edge of a table, but the glass provides ample support for an infant, even in the dropped-off area. A baby who is placed onto it will seem to float in midair.

On this apparatus, even babies just two months old discriminate between the two sides of the visual cliff. They find the deep side more interesting, as suggested by the extra time they take to study it. Young babies show little fear of the deep side, judging either by their overt behavior or by their heart rates, which tend to decrease during their investigations of the cliff. This finding implies they are primarily curious about the cliff rather than fearful of it.

Babies old enough to crawl, however, show significant fear of the visual cliff. Their heart rates increase markedly, and they will not crawl onto the deep side despite coaxing from a parent and the solid support they feel from the glass. Why the change? Perhaps infants' crawling skills allow them to perceive distances more accurately than before, because the motion of crawling causes faraway objects (including the deep side of the cliff) to move less than nearby objects (such as the shallow side). Perhaps, too, infants old enough to crawl are also old enough to focus their eyes more accurately on each side of the cliff, a physical skill that provides further perceptual information about the difference in distance of the two sides (Kermoian & Campos, 1988).

Anticipation of Visual Events

Even closer to deliberate cognition than perception of contours, objects, and depth are infants' anticipations of visual events that have not yet occurred. Signs of "looking forward" to an interesting sight are visible by observing a child's eye movements carefully. Infant psychologists have developed infrared video cameras to assist with this task, as well as a modified form of the habituation procedure, called a *visual expectation paradigm,* designed to elicit (or encourage) eye movements by the child. Typically, the infant sits in front of a large computer screen, which displays a series of interesting drawings at different locations (usually simply to the left or right) on the screen. Meanwhile, a video camera films the baby's eye movements as he directs his gaze toward the drawings. By linking the camera with the computer, it is possible to determine whether the child's eyes change direction *following* the appearance of a picture at a new location or actually *precede* or anticipate its appearance.

This procedure shows clearly that infants as young as two months do not merely follow but often anticipate the locations of pictures, and in this sense develop expectations about the environment that "foresee the future" (Canfield et al., 1997). Their anticipations, furthermore, show a variety of rule-governed qualities. By one year of age, for example, infants anticipate the location that portrays numerical sequences; they look for the spot where one more of a set will be displayed rather than a spot that will display some other number of items (Canfield & Smith, 1996). Their anticipations suggest that infants "think" in some way about what they see (engage in cognition) and do not merely register what they see automatically (engage simply in perception). In the scanning of interesting visual patterns and contours mentioned earlier, for example, they may be forming rudimentary generalizations, or rules, about what they see, such as where precisely to look to see another friendly smile.

In general, visual expectations become faster and more reliable as infants get older—most likely because they acquire more knowledge about objects and eventually learn to represent the objects mentally. Research on visual expectations also shows individual differences among infants, with some anticipating events faster, more reliably, and at earlier ages than others do (Haith et al., 1997). In at least two ways, then, infants' visual thinking resembles other forms of lifespan development: it shows continuity combined with change, and it shows diversity in developmental patterns and sequences.

Auditory Perception in Infancy

Infants respond to sounds even as newborns. But what do they perceive from sounds? What sense do they make of the sounds they hear? These questions are important, because infants' ability to discriminate among sounds makes a crucial difference in their acquisition of language, as discussed later in this chapter.

Discriminating Between Sounds

In a variety of important and surprising ways, infants reveal their abilities to discriminate between different types of sounds. For example, by five months of age, infants react more to speech sounds that they hear repeated often—like their own name—than to other speech sounds. Even when similar-sounding words are used as distracters, infants can detect their own names (Mandel, Jusczyk, & Pisoni, 1995). By their first birthday, infants can separate the speech from different talkers and attend to one speaker who has mentioned the infant's name (Newman, 2005), a phenomenon that you may recognize as the "cocktail party effect," where you hear your name mentioned by someone in a room filled with people having numerous conversations. Long before they have any sense of the meanings of words, infants develop expectations regarding the rhythms, segmentation, and cadence of spoken language (Minagawa-Kawai et al., 2011), revealing remarkable perceptual abilities that prepare them for their later mastery of language.

Infants possess some impressive music perception abilities as well. Infants have a preference for melodies that are "melodic" rather than those that are dissonant (Trainor & Heinmiller, 1998), and they can distinguish between music from their own culture and music from another, showing a distinct preference for music from their own culture (Soley & Hannon, 2010). When presented with a collection of classical music excerpts, nine-month-old infants can readily distinguish between "happy" (major key, faster tempo) and "sad" (minor key, slower tempo) music, revealing a preference for happy music (Flom & Pick, 2012). And finally, two- and three-day-old infants can do what appears to mystify many adults: they can find the beat in music! When researchers played two measures of various rock-drum rhythms to newborns, the brain-wave patterns of the babies changed when the downbeat was occasionally omitted (Winkler et al., 2009). Likewise, adults who were asked to move to the music either stumbled or their movements became syncopated when the downbeat was omitted. Given that two- and three-day-old newborns have not had much time to be exposed to music, the researchers argued that humans must have some kind of innate ability to detect regular patterns of sound in music.

Localization of Sounds

Infants just two months old can locate sounds, as suggested by the fact that they orient their heads toward certain noises, such as a rattle (Morrongiello, 1994). But they often take much longer to respond than do older children or adults. Instead of needing just a fraction of a second, as adults do, full-term infants require an average of two to three seconds before orienting toward ("looking at") a sound that occurs off to one side. Infants born one month preterm require even more time to respond. These delays may explain why pediatricians and others used to believe that newborn infants could not hear: the sounds they offered to the babies, such as a single hand clap, may not have lasted long enough for the infants to respond.

Although infants can locate sounds, their skill at doing so is somewhat limited. They are better able to locate relatively high-pitched sounds, such as those made by a flute or a small bird, than low-pitched sounds, such as that made by a foghorn (Spetner & Olsho, 1990). In their first efforts to turn their heads, very young babies (one or two months old) act more as though head turning is a reflex than a search for something to see (Morrongielo, 1994). The behavior does not habituate, meaning that a young baby is just as likely to turn toward a sound after many presentations as he was after the first presentation. Also, the behavior occurs even in the dark, when there is no chance to actually see the source of a sound. Only by age five or six months do these reflexive qualities change: by that age, babies habituate quickly to repeated presentations and search only in the light, when there is something to see. In these ways, then, hearing and vision have become coordinated, but it has taken several months of learning for the change to occur.

Coordination of Sensory Information

The localization of sounds suggests that even very young babies coordinate what they see with what they hear; they seem to use sound to direct their visual gaze. But is this what really happens? Do we process different sensory signals separately and then somehow merge them to form our "perception" of an object? For example, upon

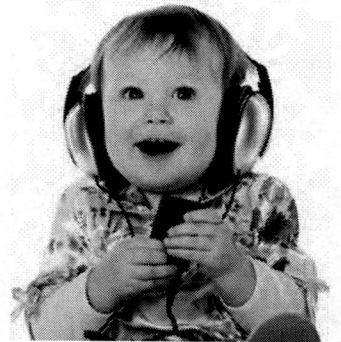

The infant in the photo is responding to music that, judging by her smile, she finds pleasing. The music is most likely melodic, played by instruments common in her culture, and its tempo is probably upbeat.
Source: Ipatov/Shutterstock.com

Chapter 4 Physical and Cognitive Development in the First Two Years

> **What Do You Think?**
>
> Do these impressive perceptual abilities mean that infants can think? And, if so, do they think in similar ways as adults? How might their thinking change as they get older? Do children simply learn "more" as they get older, or do they learn differently?

entering the lobby of a movie theater, do you smell a pleasant aroma, hear popping noises, and see bags full of small, white, irregular-shaped objects and then conclude that it must be popcorn? (Just to be sure, you should probably eat some as well to confirm that it is light, crunchy-ish, buttery, and salty.) Or, do you sense all of this information concurrently and quickly arrive at a "popcorn perception"? Researchers have questioned the nature of infant perception, and several studies have suggested that infants, like adults, integrate various channels of sensory information in a process called **intermodal perception**. In addition to localizing sounds (demonstrating an integration of the visual and auditory senses), one-month-old infants are also able to recognize by sight objects that they had previously put in their mouths but had not before seen, revealing the integration of their tactile and visual senses (Schweinle & Wilcox, 2004). And by eight months of age, infants can match an unfamiliar speaker's face with the correct voice when the choices for faces and voices vary with respect to age and sex (Patterson & Werker, 2002)—and remember, these infants aren't speaking yet! Intermodal perception enables infants to efficiently learn about their physical and social environments, coordinating information from various sensory channels so that they have a fuller understanding of the world in which they are functioning.

intermodal perception The coordination and integration of multiple channels of sensory information.

Cognitive Change During Infancy: Piaget's Stage Theory

The two preceding sections highlighted continuities between infants' and adults' cognitive abilities. Infants can perceive object constancies, anticipate what they are about to see, locate sounds, and categorize certain experiences—all abilities that they share with adults. Most of the research cited is framed by some version of information-processing theory, the approach described in Chapter 2 (and elsewhere in this book) that emphasizes the importance of organizing specific input so that it becomes more meaningful, much as a computer is sometimes thought to do.

Yet infants obviously do not think "just like adults." For one thing, they use little or no language to assist in solving problems. Proud parents notwithstanding, they often also seem slow and error prone in figuring things out. Their skills are still limited and seem worlds away from the cognitive behaviors of older children or adults. How do they transform their budding infant skills into the comparatively smooth expertise of an adult? And during infancy, in particular, how does the transformation begin?

Stages of Sensorimotor Intelligence

Jean Piaget, whose approach was described in Chapter 2, offers one of the most complete descriptions and explanations of cognitive development available (Piaget, 1963). According to Piaget, infants begin life thinking in terms of *sensory* perceptions and *motor* actions, by doing things to and with the objects around them. Piaget called this activity **sensorimotor intelligence**. He identified stages during infancy that mark significant developments in sensorimotor intelligence, as summarized in Table 4.6.

sensorimotor intelligence According to Piaget, thinking that occurs by way of sensory perceptions and motor actions; characteristic of infants.

In general, the stages of infant cognition show two trends. First, infants show a trend toward symbolic thinking. Instead of needing to handle a toy car to understand it, an infant becomes increasingly able to visualize, or think about, a car without actually touching or seeing one. This ability becomes very strong by the end of the first two years of life; to Piaget, it helps mark the end of infancy. Changes in infants' toys reflect this developmental trend, as indicated in Table 4.7.

TABLE 4.6 Some Features of Infant Cognition According to Piaget

Stage	Age	Characteristics
1: Early reflexes	Birth–1 month	Reliance on inborn reflexes to "know" the environment; assimilation of all experiences to reflexes
2: Primary circular reactions	1–4 months	Accommodation (or modification) of reflexes to fit new objects and experiences; repeated actions focusing on infant's own body
3: Secondary circular reactions	4–8 months	Repeated actions focusing on objects; actions used as means toward ends, but haphazardly; early signs of object permanence
4: Combined secondary circular reactions	8–12 months	Deliberate combinations of previously acquired actions (or schemes); A-not-B error; early signs of sense of time
5: Tertiary circular reactions	12–18 months	Systematic application of previously acquired actions (or schemes); well-organized investigation of novel objects, but always overt
6: The first symbols	18–24 months	First symbolic representations of objects; true object permanence; deferred imitation

Source: Piaget (1963).

Second, infants form cognitive structures that Piaget called *schemes*. In relation to infants, **schemes** are organized patterns of actions or concepts that help the baby to make sense out of and adapt to the environment. Schemes develop well before infants can represent objects or events through language or motor skills. A newborn baby's initial grasping motions constitute an early scheme, as do her earliest sucking motions. Eventually, as described shortly, internal, or mental, concepts and ideas develop out of such patterns of behavior. These too are sometimes called *schemes* (or sometimes *schemas* or *schemata*);

scheme According to Piaget, a behavior or thought that represents a group of ideas and events in a person's experience.

TABLE 4.7 Toys That Support Cognitive Development in Infancy

As infants get older, their toys tend to involve more complex motor skills, as well as language and make-believe. Can you see how these trends are reflected in these lists?

Birth–2 Months	6–12 Months	12–24 Months
Mobile in crib	Squeeze toys	Dolls, especially large ones
Rattle	Nested plastic cups	Toy telephone
	Boxes with lids	Puzzles (5–10 pieces)
	Soft ball	Vehicles (cars, boats, train)
	Stuffed animals	Sandbox, shovel, and pail
	Pots and pans	Water toys (cups, funnel, etc.)
	Picture books (especially cloth or cardboard)	Picture books with simple words

Chapter 4 Physical and Cognitive Development in the First Two Years

assimilation According to Piaget, a method by which a person responds to new experiences by using existing concepts to interpret new ideas and experiences.

accommodation According to Piaget, the process of modifying existing ideas or action-skills to fit new experiences.

but Piaget himself more often called cognitive structures and patterns that develop later by names such as *operations* or *systems,* depending on their exact nature (Miller, 2011).

As we discuss more fully in Chapter 2, Piaget argued that sensorimotor intelligence develops by means of two complementary processes—assimilation and accommodation. **Assimilation** consists of interpreting new experiences in terms of existing schemes. A baby who is used to sucking on a breast or bottle may use the same action on whatever new, unfamiliar objects he encounters, such as a rubber ball or his own fist. **Accommodation** consists of modifying existing schemes to fit new experiences. After sucking on a number of new objects, an infant may modify this action to fit the nature of each new object; she may chew on some new objects (her sweater) but not on others (a plastic cup).

The interplay of assimilation and accommodation leads to new schemes and eventually to the infant's ability to symbolize objects and activities. Let us see how Piaget believed this transition occurs.

Stage 1: Early Reflexes—Using What You Are Born With (Birth to One Month)

According to Piaget, cognitive development begins with reflexes, those simple, inborn behaviors that all normal babies can produce at birth. As it happens, the majority of such reflexes remain just that—reflexes—for the individual's entire life; sneezing patterns and blinking responses, for example, look nearly the same in adults as they do in infants. But a few are notable for their flexibility, chiefly sucking, grasping, and looking. These behaviors resemble reflexes at birth, but they quickly begin to be modified in response to experiences such as sucking on the mother's breast, on toys, and on the child's own hand. They give infants a repertoire from which to develop more complex skills, and their susceptibility to influence makes them especially important to cognitive development during infancy.

Stage 2: Primary Circular Reactions—Modifying What You Are Born With (One to Four Months)

Soon after the baby begins modifying his early reflexes, he begins to build and differentiate action schemes quite rapidly. In fact, within a month or so he sometimes repeats them endlessly for no apparent reason. Because of its repetitive quality, Piaget calls this behavior a **circular reaction**. The baby seems to be stimulated by the outcome of his own behavior, so he responds for the mere joy of feeling himself act. At this point, the circular reactions are called *primary circular reactions,* because they still focus on the baby's own body and movements. Waving an arm repeatedly constitutes a primary circular reaction; so does kicking again and again.

circular reaction Piaget's term for an action often repeated, apparently because it is self-reinforcing.

During this period, the young infant practices his developing schemes widely, and the behaviors rapidly become less reflexive. The baby may shape his mouth differently for sucking his fist and for sucking his blanket. In this sense, he begins to recognize the objects all around him, and implicitly, he also begins to remember previous experiences with each type of object. But this memory has an automatic or object-focused quality, unlike the large variety of more conscious memories children have later in life.

Stage 3: Secondary Circular Reactions—Making Interesting Sights Last (Four to Eight Months)

As they practice their first schemes, young infants broaden their interests to include objects and events immediately around them. Shaking her arm, for example, no longer captivates a baby's attention for its own sake; she has become too skilled at arm shaking for it to do so. Now a behavior such as this becomes useful rather than interesting. A baby at this stage may accidentally discover that shaking her arm will make a mobile spin over her head in her crib, or create an interesting noise in a toy she happens to be holding, or make parents smile with joy. In all these cases, shaking an arm becomes a means to other ends. Once primitive means are discovered, a baby at this stage will repeat a useful procedure endlessly to sustain and study the interesting results.

To differentiate this new orientation from the earlier one, Piaget called such repetitions *secondary circular reactions:* repetitions motivated by external objects and events. Secondary circular reactions create two parallel changes in the child's motor schemes. On the one hand, the infant uses existing schemes even more widely than before. She tries to suck on more and more of the toys that come her way. On the other hand, she begins to discover that schemes can be combined to produce interesting results. She may happen to reach toward an object (one scheme) and discover that doing so makes it possible to grasp the object (another scheme). At first, the combination occurs accidentally; but once it does occur, the baby at this stage can produce the new combination of schemes deliberately on future occasions.

Secondary circular reactions also implicitly show that the infant is now acquiring at least a hazy notion of **object permanence**, a belief that objects exist separately from her own actions and continue to exist even when she cannot see them. By stage 3, she will look for an object briefly even after it disappears. Naturally, her searching skills leave something to be desired, so it helps if the hidden object is actually partly visible and within easy reach; a toy duck's tail should stick out from under a blanket if that is where the toy is hidden. But the first signs of symbolic thought are there, because the infant must have some *idea* of the toy duck if she is going to bother searching for it.

object permanence
According to Piaget, the belief that people and things continue to exist even when one cannot experience them directly; emerges around age two.

Stage 4: Combined Secondary Circular Reactions—Deliberate Combinations of Means and Ends (Eight to Twelve Months)

At this stage, instead of just happening on connections among schemes by accident, the infant intentionally chooses to use a scheme as a means toward an end. In stages 1 and 2, he may have developed separate schemes for opening his mouth and for chewing food. In stage 3, he may have accidentally discovered that the first scheme is a means toward the other: mouth opening is a means toward eating. Now, in stage 4, the baby starts using this means-end connection purposefully. Like a young bird in a nest, he opens his mouth to "produce" food to chew. Of course, he may eventually discover that the connection does not always work: sitting with his mouth wide open may sometimes produce no food at all or occasionally produce bad-tasting medicine instead of good-tasting food.

At this stage, too, the infant still lacks alternatives to the single-purpose, fragmented schemes he has developed so far. As he encounters the limitations of these schemes, he gradually modifies and expands (or accommodates, as Piaget would say) his initial schemes that connected means with ends. He may learn to open his mouth at the sight of some foods but not others. He may also add other behaviors to the mouth-opening scheme, such as pointing to favorite foods, thereby turning the original scheme into a more general food-requesting scheme. As these accommodations occur, the infant moves into the next stage of cognition.

Stage 5: Tertiary Circular Reactions—Active Experimentation with Objects (Twelve to Eighteen Months)

At stage 5, the infant deliberately varies the schemes for producing interesting results, or ends. Previously, at stage 4, she could intentionally combine schemes, but only one pair at a time and only if an appropriate situation for using the combination happened to occur. Now, in dealing with a new object, the baby can run through a repertoire of schemes in a trial-and-error effort to learn about the object's properties. Piaget called the variations *tertiary circular reactions,* meaning third-level circular reactions, to distinguish them from the simpler forms of repetition that dominate the earlier stages.

These variations in behavior, however, are still organized largely by trial and error rather than by systematic plans. Given a rubber ball, for example, some babies may try dropping it from different heights and onto different objects. But no matter how delighted these infants are with the results of these variations, they will not think to vary the dropping conditions carefully or experimentally. Such actions require planning and consequently also require considerably more ability to represent objects and situations than the infant has yet developed.

Playing peek-a-boo becomes popular with babies as they approach their first birthday. Even though the mother disappears for a moment, the baby seems to believe that she still exists behind the tree, as shown by the baby's delight when she reappears.
Source: Serg Salivon/Shutterstock.com.

Stage 6: The First Symbols—Representing Objects and Actions (Eighteen to Twenty-Four Months)

At this stage, the motor schemes the child previously explored and practiced overtly begin to occur symbolically. For the first time, the infant can begin to envision, or imagine, actions and their results without actually having to try them out beforehand.

Consider a stage 6 child who wants a favorite toy that is just barely out of reach on a high shelf. Near the shelf sits a small stool that she has played with numerous times. How to get the toy? Earlier in infancy, the baby might simply have stared and fussed and eventually either given up or cried. At this later stage, things are quite different. The baby surveys the situation, observes the stool, and pauses briefly. Then, with a purposeful air, she places the stool under the toy, climbs up, and retrieves the toy. What is important here is the lack of false starts or, conversely, the presence of only a single, correct attempt. The infant may succeed even though she never before used the stool to reach high-up objects. According to Piaget, trial and error is no longer the method of choice; now the infant tries out solutions mentally to envision their results.

Skill with mental representations makes true object permanence possible. A child at the end of infancy will search for a toy even after it has been fully hidden and even if it was hidden without her witnessing the act of hiding. If a ball disappears behind a bookcase, she will go around to the other side to look for it. She will search appropriately, even though she cannot know in advance exactly where behind the bookcase the ball will turn up. In the ball-and-blanket situation described earlier, the child can now play more complex games of hide-and-seek. She usually looks first under the blanket where the toy disappeared; if she fails to find it there, she will search under any and all other blankets and sometimes even under the table and in the experimenter's pockets. Relatively extensive search is made possible in part by the child's new conviction that toys and other objects have a permanent existence independent of her own activities with them. In other words, they do not just disappear.

All of these behaviors depend on the child's ability to form and maintain representations (thoughts or memories) of the relevant experiences, which later become available for expression again. As we will see, representational skill proves crucial in early childhood. It contributes to children's play, because much play involves re-enactment of previous experiences and roles. It makes possible much language development, because the child must learn to use words and expressions when they are appropriate and not just at the time she hears them uttered. And it makes possible the first real self-concept, because sooner or later the child realizes that he too has a (relatively) permanent existence akin to the permanence of all the things and people in his life, whether toys, pet dogs, or parents.

Assessment of Piaget's Theory of Infant Cognition

Piaget's theory stimulated considerable study of infant cognition from the 1960s through the 1980s. A lot of the research has confirmed the main features of the theory, whereas other research has called attention to additional aspects of infancy that at least complicate Piaget's original presentation, if they do not contradict it outright. Here, for example, are two of the main criticisms of the theory and a sample of the research they have inspired.

Motor Versus Cognitive Limitations

Some infant psychologists question Piaget's account because they believe his stages confuse a child's motor abilities with cognitive or thinking abilities (Meltzoff et al., 1991). Object permanence, for example, implicitly depends on a child's capacity to conduct a manual search: to walk around the room, lift and inspect objects, and the like. Perhaps younger infants "lack" classic object permanence, this argument goes, simply because they lack motor skills or at best use them only clumsily.

To test this possibility, psychologists have designed new tests of object permanence that require only visual search rather than motor coordination (Baillargeon, 1993; Hespos & Baillargeon, 2001). In one experiment, infants were habituated to (repeatedly shown) the sight of a toy car sliding down an inclined track from the left and then rolling off to the right, as shown in Figure 4.5. In the middle of this track was a small screen concealing the middle portion of the track and obstructing a view of the car for part of its trip along the track. Dur-

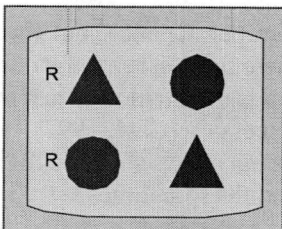
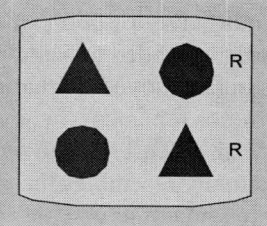
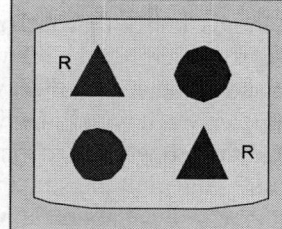

Phase 1: Here, the infant must discriminate the dimension of color. Red shapes are rewarded but blue are not—provided that the child looks at the red ones.

R = Rewarded

Phase 2 Reversal Shift: In phase 2 with a reversal shift, the infant must still discriminate the *same* dimension, but a different value of the dimension. Color is still rewarded, but now it is the color blue instead of red.

Phase 2 Non-Reversal Shift: In phase 2 with a *non*-reversal shift, the infant must discriminate a *new* dimension in order to be rewarded in this case the dimension of shape. Triangles are now rewarded, regardless of color.

FIGURE 4.5

Evidence of Object Permanence in Infants

First, the infant becomes habituated to watching a car roll down a track, behind a screen, and out the other side. In one test condition, a toy mouse is placed behind the tracks but is hidden while the car rolls past. In the other test condition, the mouse is placed on the tracks but is secretly removed after the screen is in place so that the car seems to roll "through" the mouse. Infants stare longer at the second impossible event, suggesting that they already "believe in" object permanence.

Source: Baillargeon (1991).

ing habituation, the babies watched the car slide down the ramp, behind the screen, and out the other side. Between car trips, the screen was lifted temporarily to show that there was nothing behind it that might affect the car's movements.

After the infants had gotten used to seeing this setup and watching the car disappear and reappear predictably, they were shown one of two test events. In the first event, the screen was lifted and a toy mouse was placed directly behind the tracks. Then the screen was lowered, and the car made its usual run down the ramp and out the right side of the screen. This was called the "possible test event." The second test event was the same, except that the toy mouse was placed directly *on* the tracks. Then the screen was lowered, the car was released, it disappeared behind the screen, and—surprise!—it reappeared out the right side of the screen anyway, even though the mouse had been placed on the tracks. This was called the "impossible test event." In reality, the experimenters secretly removed the toy mouse before the car could hit it, using a hole concealed in the back of the test apparatus.

Under these conditions, infants as young as three-and-a-half months looked significantly longer at the *im*possible test event than at the possible test event. The most plausible interpretation is that the impossible event violated assumptions the infants made about the permanence of objects: they seemed to assume the toy mouse should cause a collision, presumably because they believed it continued to exist behind the screen even when they could not see it. They also seemed to assume objects retain their usual physical properties even when invisible—that the car could not simply pass through the mouse, for example, just because it was hidden.

This evidence of early object permanence, though, does not mean young infants are now ready to reason about hidden objects in the ways older children or adults do. If a preschool child experienced the experiment just described, he or she would very likely suspect a trick of some sort and consciously puzzle over what the trick might be. The three- or four-month-old infant still has much developing to do before being able to do this kind of thinking. By requiring manual search skills, though, Piaget's tasks may have delayed children from displaying their pre-existing object permanence until rudimentary reasoning skills had become established. Hence, Piaget's assertion that full object permanence (the stage 6 described earlier) involves conscious problem solving: a deliberate search for the object.

The Effects of Memory

Considerable evidence suggests that memory affects infants' performance on many cognitive tasks more than Piaget thought. Imposing slight delays—just a few seconds—when an infant searches for an object lowers success rates much more for younger infants than for older ones (Baillargeon, 1993). Much of the change may reflect younger infants' difficulties in attending to and retaining relevant cues about the object to be searched for. Younger babies seem to remember less of what they are looking for.

These trends imply that infants may have a notion of object permanence, but find it demanding to remember the relevant facts needed to search: where they last saw the object and when and whether the object was in fact moved. Perhaps infants use memory when they can but supplement it with Piagetian motor schemes whenever necessary (Case, 1992). If an infant cannot recall where a toy is hidden, at least she can reenact the means she used to find it in the past. This multiple strategy actually resembles the way adults sometimes search for a lost object: if you cannot recall where you left it, you may retrace your steps up to the time you remember seeing it last—in essence, using an action scheme.

Motor skill and memory limitations can affect the appearance of competence not only in infants but in adults as well. By showing that the limitations happen to infants, the research once again strengthens the idea of continuity in development (that infants resemble adults) and weakens the idea of change (that infants are somehow different from adults). It also suggests that the "belief in object permanence" that Piaget identified may mean something different to a young infant than to an older one. For a three- or four-month-old, an "object" is anything that remains visible when tracked with the eyes and whose movements meet reasonable expectations when tracked. For an eighteen-month-old, an "object" is whatever becomes visible when sought with the hands or feet, and meets expectations to reappear after a reasonable physical search. We will see that still later in life, the concept of "object" changes meaning again, sometimes even referring to thoughts rather than things. But that is a story for later, when we discuss adolescent thought in Chapter 10.

Behavioral Learning in Infancy

In addition to the cognitively oriented research described in the preceding sections, other research on infant learning has attempted to identify specific behaviors of infants and the relationship of the behaviors to their causes and consequences. In essence, this is the point of view of *behaviorism,* described in Chapter 2 as well as earlier in this chapter when we looked at heart rate and habituation studies. Framing infants' behaviors as examples of conditioning and of imitation often has been helpful for understanding how they learn, because infants seem to do a lot of both.

Operant Conditioning

When an infant participates in psychological research using operant conditioning, she gets a reward, or positive reinforcement, if she performs some simple action or set of actions. By turning her head, for example, she may get to see an interesting toy or picture. In this case, the reinforcement is viewing the interesting toy, and head turning becomes the learned, or conditioned, behavior. Such actions tend to be performed more often than actions that are not reinforced.

As the examples of research in this chapter show, infants are quite capable of learning through operant conditioning. Newborns will learn to suck on their hands longer if doing so yields a tiny amount of sugar water delivered through a tube in the corners of their mouths. Or they will learn to blink their eyes more often if doing so causes a pleasant voice to speak or a melody to play. One reason infants seem to learn to breast-feed so easily is the strong reinforcement the behavior brings in the form of mother's milk and being touched and held closely.

Infants are predisposed to learn these particular behaviors. All examples of operant conditioning in infants rely on those few behaviors that young babies already exhibit, which are mainly their inborn reflexes. By nature, reflexes occur easily—in fact, almost *too* easily. As parents often discover, any slight provocation, such as a touch on the baby's cheek, can stimulate sucking movements in young babies. Such readiness to respond creates confusion about when infant responses really constitute learning rather than general excitement. For example, when do sucking movements show true operant learning: a specific behavior performed more often because a particular reinforcement results from

> **What Do You Think?**
>
> Between about eight and twelve months of age, many babies show distress at separations from their primary caregiver (usually the mother). Some psychologists suggest that the distress is a partial result of their budding belief in object permanence. Do you think this might be true? How you might explain your position to a new parent who is concerned about her baby's distress?

it? And when do sucking movements simply amount to a reflex that is itching to occur, so to speak, and would occur in response to almost any stimulus?

The confusion between learning and excitement diminishes as babies grow older because they acquire behaviors that are more truly voluntary. Even as babies get older, however, they acquire many behaviors, both desirable and regrettable, through what appears to be operant conditioning. A six- or nine-month-old will babble longer and more frequently if parents smile and express praise when he does so. A twelve-month-old will learn to wave good-bye sooner and more frequently if reinforced with praise or encouragement. And a two-year-old may learn to scream at her older sibling when she wants a toy the older child has because her screaming has been inadvertently reinforced: it causes the older child to simply abandon the toy, or it summons a parent who assumes (not always accurately) the older child somehow caused the screaming.

Of course, these are primarily immediate, short-term effects, and they sometimes differ from long-term effects of reinforcement. An example often important to parents is crying: will picking up the baby to quiet his crying actually reinforce him for crying in the long term? Conditioning theory would predict that it would, but most research on the impact of crying has found that fast, sensitive responses to crying actually lead to *less* crying (St. James-Roberts et al., 1993; St. James-Roberts, 2007). The quieting, though, is not reliable in the short term, but may take many months to become a definite, obvious response to being picked up. This delay suggests that decreases in crying may be a product of an interaction between sensitive caregiving and neurological maturation (St. James-Roberts, 2007). Nevertheless, this long delay between increased comforting and decreased rates of crying may cause parents a lot of worry about whether they are "spoiling" their child by responding to her crying.

Imitation

A second key aspect of infant learning is imitation. As make-believe play demonstrates, children obviously learn to imitate at some point in development. But exactly how early, and by what processes? Early research on these questions generally suggested that infants

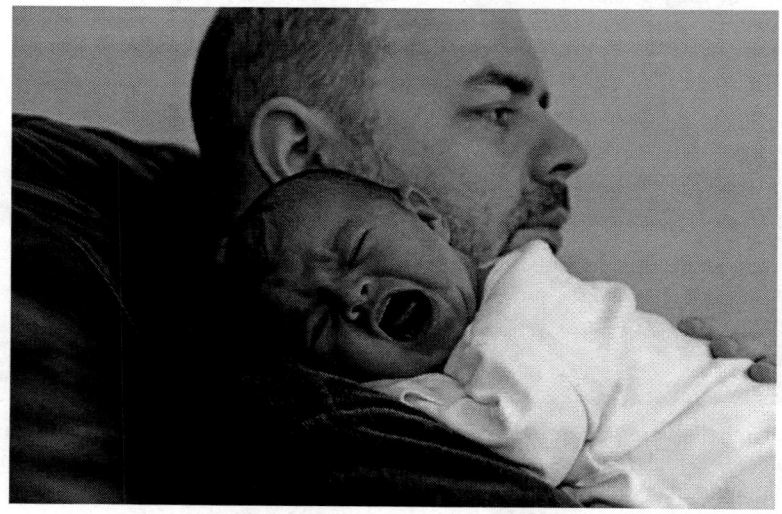

Should parents comfort a crying baby, or will this reinforce the baby for crying, resulting in more frequent crying? Research indicates that, over time, fast and sensitive parental responses to crying reduce the frequency and duration of crying.
Source: Jo Tunney/Shutterstock.com.

can engage in different kinds of imitation at different points during infancy (Piaget, 1962). It found that infants imitated actions they could literally see themselves perform (for example, in a mirror) sooner than those they could observe only in a model. Much research over the past two decades confirms this hypothesis. Imitating a hand gesture such as waving, for example, proves easier than imitating an unusual face made by an adult (Meltzoff & Kuhl, 1994). Also, deferred imitation may not appear until close to a child's second birthday; by that time, the child can imitate a gesture an entire day after seeing a model perform it.

Despite their preference for visible actions, infants sometimes imitate actions that are relatively invisible to themselves. One-week-old babies tend to stick out their tongues in imitation of adults and wiggle their fingers after seeing adults model this behavior. Distinguishing voluntary imitation from general, automatic excitement, however, remains a problem, as it does with other studies of very young babies. One research study highlighted this ambiguity especially well. It showed babies pictures of human faces depicting various emotions (Kaitz et al., 1988). Although the babies responded with emotional facial expressions of their own, their expressions did not match those in the pictures. In fact, the emotions on the babies' faces were hard to classify at all; they just looked "wrought up" at the sight of expressive human faces. However, recent neuroscience research utilizing more sensitive measures of brain-wave activity in various regions—and, in some cases, in specific neurons—of the brain has revealed the presence of what are being called "mirror neurons," neurons that fire either when an action is being performed *or* being observed. For example, when infants see an adult who is waving, the motor cortex in the infants' brains becomes active—the same area of the motor cortex that is active when the infants are actually waiving. This same neurological response occurs with facial expressions—whether infants are watching an adult smile or are smiling themselves, the same areas of their brains are active (Del Guidice, Manera, & Keysers, 2009). Even though young infants may not be able to accurately imitate the facial expression of others, the activity of mirror neurons and the feedback they receive through their interactions with others play important roles in their development of social relationships and their understanding of the emotional states in others (Lepage & Théoret, 2007).

Language Acquisition

When Michael, the son of one of the authors, was an infant, he went through several phases in using language. At twelve weeks, Michael made open-mouthed, cooing noises when he was feeling content. Sometimes these sounds were vaguely similar to ordinary vowel sounds, but they seemed to vary unpredictably. Michael cooed a lot in the morning when he first woke up, which pleased his father and mother.

By six months, Michael had added consonant sounds to his vocalizations to produce complicated babbling noises. His most productive time for this activity continued to be

As this trio of photos indicates, learning through imitation progresses from repeating an infant's own actions observed in a mirror *(left)* to repeating actions initiated by others *(middle)*. Toddlers can even imitate more complicated sequences of behaviors, as the boy who is pretending to do work with mom on her laptop is demonstrating *(right)*.
Sources: (left) Dmitry Kalinovsky/Shutterstock.com ; *(middle)* Yanik Shauvin/Shutterstock.com; *(right)* iofoto/Shutterstock.com.

> **What Do You Think?**
>
> Shift your focus from infants to mothers for a moment. How do you suppose *mothers* might become conditioned to breastfeeding, either positively or negatively? Think about "what's in it" for them, as well as what hassles breast-feeding can create. If possible, talk to a breast-feeding mother about her experiences.

the morning, although he "said" quite a lot whenever he was feeling generally content. Certain sounds seemed to be favorites: *da* and *gn*. Sometimes Michael repeated these and other sounds—*da, da, da, da*. His father thought Michael repeated sounds when he was feeling especially happy.

At fifteen months, Michael could produce about six words, but he did not pronounce them as adults would. The family cat was *dat;* his favorite food, yogurt, sounded like *yugun;* and airplanes were simply *der!* (as in "Look there!"). He seemed to understand dozens of words and sentences, although it was hard to be sure because he probably picked up clues about meaning from the behavior of his parents. When Michael was tired one day, he came immediately when his mother said, "Come sit here" in a sympathetic tone of voice. But when she said the same thing in a cross tone of voice the next day, he looked at her with an impish smile and went the other way.

One day close to his second birthday, Michael sat "reading" a children's book to himself. Occasionally, real phrases could be heard ("bug ate leaf), but mostly Michael sounded as though he were mumbling or talking in the next room. When he finished, he walked to the kitchen and phrased a three-word question: "What's for lunch?"

As these examples show, language is a fundamental feature of development throughout the lifespan. It adds greatly to a person's ability to learn about new people, objects, and events. It provides a way to express feelings more precisely. And it allows a person to participate, through verbal dialogue, more fully in his or her family and community. These benefits begin appearing during infancy as soon as language begins to develop, which is usually around a child's first birthday. They increase as the child gets older and develops more skill with language. Some aspects of language, in fact, continue to improve well into adulthood; vocabulary, for example, increases in size into middle age and beyond. So do some of the more subtle uses of language, such as when to say what, and to whom. We often think of these skills simply as "tact" or diplomacy.

But the major challenge, and one that takes considerable attention and energy from an infant, is acquiring language in the first place. Language acquisition partly involves mastering its structures—its sounds and organization, for example—but partly also involves learning how language is used—its purposes and conversational conventions. Infants begin on both projects immediately. Stated more precisely, infants begin doing all of the following simultaneously:

- They learn the sounds of the language (its *phonology).*
- They learn its words (its *lexicon).*
- They learn the meanings of words *(semantics).*
- They learn the purposes and ways in which words and sentences normally get used in conversation *(pragmatics).*
- They piece together the organization of words into sentences and connected discourse *(syntax).*

Even though infants make progress in all of these areas, we focus on phonology, lexicon, and semantics in this chapter because these are the key "tasks" of language acquisition in infancy. We will discuss pragmatics and syntax in Chapter 6 in connection with cognitive development during early childhood.

Phonology

phonemes Sounds that combine with other sounds to form words.

Every language uses a finite number of **phonemes**, or sounds that speakers of the language consider distinctive and that combine to make the words of the language. English has about forty-one phonemes; other languages have more or fewer than this number. In acquiring language, infants must be sensitive to phonemes and ignore any meaningless variations. Although the task may seem demanding, it actually proves surprisingly easy, even for a baby—so easy, in fact, that some language specialists suspect human beings are genetically and physiologically predisposed toward noticing phonemic differences (Archibald, 1995; Telkemeyer et al., 2009).

babbling Infant vocalizations produced prior to acquiring language and without verbally meaningful intent.

Although skill at producing phonemes takes longer to develop, it too seems to be biologically influenced. Sometime between four and eight months of age, infants begin **babbling** in increasingly complex ways. They apparently do so for the sole reward of hearing themselves vocalize, a form of play with sound and an example of a Piagetian primary circular reaction.

What suggests that babbling is motivated intrinsically? The most important evidence is the fact that all physically normal infants begin babbling at approximately the same age (about six months), regardless of the culture or language to which they are exposed. Furthermore, an observational study of deaf infants found the babies "babbling" with their hands. These infants could not babble orally, but they had been exposed to American Sign Language and were observed to make repetitive hand gestures analogous to the oral babbling of hearing infants (Pettito & Marentette, 1991).

Despite this finding, most research suggests a significant influence on babbling by parents and other members of an infant's language community. Although the study on deaf infants observed a type of babbling in these babies, the fact that the babbling was gestural rather than oral suggests that the infants' language environment influenced the form their babbling took (Takei, 2001). Other research on deaf infants has confirmed this conclusion. Contrary to a long-held belief, deaf infants may *not* babble orally in the same way that hearing infants do; rather, they typically begin oral babbling some months later. In some cases, deaf infants babble only if they hear sound that is amplified, such as through a hearing aid (Marschark, 1993). Interestingly, the patterns of sounds that hearing and hearing-impaired infants produce are quite similar at first (Iyer & Oiler, 2008), diverging when hearing infants begin to narrow their speech sounds to those that occur in their native language, a change that occurs a month or so prior to the production of their first words.

Semantics and First Words

semantics The purposes and meanings of a language.

The **semantics** (or meanings) of a language, and of words in particular, are never mastered fully, even by adults. To test this idea on yourself, scan any page of a large, unabridged dictionary and see how far you go before you encounter an unfamiliar word. Most people, it seems, never learn even a majority of the words or terms in their native language. This is because words get much of their meanings from the real world rather than from other words. Most of us simply do not live long enough to encounter all of these relationships with the real world.

What words do children use first? On the whole, they prefer nominals—labels for objects, people, and events—much more than other kinds of words, such as verbs or modifiers (Hart, 1991). Among nominals, they are most likely to name things that are used frequently or that stand out in some way. The child's own mother or father therefore may be named early, but not always as early as the parents expect. *Dog* may appear as an early word more often than *sun* or *diaper* does, even though children probably experience the latter two objects more frequently than they do dogs.

Other research has found that children vary in how much they emphasize different language functions in their first utterances (Bloom, 1993). Most children have a *referential style,* meaning their first words refer to objects and objective events—*car, book,* and so on. Others have an *expressive style,* using words to express feelings and relationships—*hello* and *goody!* During the second year of life, infants with a referential style tend to make more rapid advances in vocabulary and to develop more elaborate and precise use of syntax (or grammar). The differences seem to be influenced by infants' families, though not in a direct way. Research has found that infants who develop secure attachments to their primary caregivers (in the sense developed by Mary Ainsworth (1979) and discussed in Chapter 5) tend to acquire a referential style of communicating compared to infants with less secure attachments (Meins, 1997). Why might this link occur? Infancy researchers are not sure, but have suggested that it has something to do with the secure child's being more prepared to explore the environment—and confident enough to leave the proximity of parents and familiar surroundings to do so. As a result, the child encounters more new objects and experiences, as well as more people who are somewhat *un*familiar with his language. Therefore, compared to a less adventurous child, he has a greater need to acquire a large vocabulary and more varied means of expression. However, one must be cautious when making generalizations about this finding because cultural differences can influence the kinds of words that infants learn and use (Tardiff et al., 2008),

Influencing Language Acquisition

Just how do parents and other adults actually affect infants' language development? This question has important implications for parents and other caregivers of young children, and research has begun to provide at least some of the answers.

Parental Influences

Even when infants are very young, parents often talk to them as though they were full-fledged adult partners in a conversation (though not equally in all cultures; see the "A Multicultural View" feature). Consider this mother speaking to her three-month-old child:

> **Mother:** How is Kelsey today? *(pause)* How are you? *(pause)* Good, you say? *(pause)* Are you feeling good? *(pause)* I'm glad for that. *(pause)* Yes, I am. *(pause)* What would you like now? *(pause)* Your pacifier? *(pause)* Um? *(pause)* Is that what you want? *(pause)* Okay, here it is.

By asking questions in this "conversation," the mother implies that Kelsey is capable of responding, even though her infant is much too young to do so. Furthermore, the mother leaves pauses for her baby's hypothetical responses. Observations of these kinds of pauses show that they last just about as long as in conversations between adults (Haslett, 1997); it is as though the mother is giving her baby a turn to speak before taking another turn herself. When her child remains silent, the mother even replies on her behalf. In all these behaviors, the mother teaches something about turn talking in conversations, and she expresses her faith that the infant eventually will learn these conventions herself.

When infants finally begin speaking, parents continue this strategy. At the same time, however, they also simplify their language significantly. They speak in shorter sentences, although not as short as the child's, and use simpler vocabulary, although less restricted than the child's (Bryant & Barrett, 2007; Gallaway & Richards, 1994). These extra strategies help to teach a new lesson, namely that words and sentences do in fact communicate and that language is more than interesting noises and babbling. By keeping just ahead of the infant's own linguistic skills, parents can stimulate the further development of language.

This style is called **infant-directed speech**, or *caregiver speech,* meaning a dialect or a version of language characteristic of parents talking with young children. In addition to shorter sentences and simpler vocabulary, caregiver speech has several unique features. It tends to unfold more slowly than speech between adults and to use a higher and more variable, or singsong, pitch; it generally contains unusually strong emphasis on keywords ("Give me your *cup"*). Parents speaking to infants also tend to repeat or paraphrase themselves more than usual ("Give me the cup. The cup. Find the cup, and give it.").

Research shows clearly that parents' conversations with babies are extremely important to the infants' development. The Harvard Preschool Project, a longitudinal study conducted at Harvard University, observed the contacts between parents and their infants that occurred naturally in the families' own homes (White, 1993). At various intervals, the infants were assessed for both intelligence and social skills. When the assessments were correlated with the results of the home observations, one result stood out clearly: the most intellectually and

infant-directed speech The style or register of speech used by adults and older children when talking with a one- or two-year-old infant.

A Multicultural View

Cognitive Effects of Talking to Infants: A Cross-Cultural Perspective

Although the text implies strong support for mothers' talking with their infants, a different impression of this practice occurs if you view it in a cross-cultural context. Then the frequent one-way "conversations" and direct gazing between mother and baby seem a bit less natural or inevitable and even a bit strange.

In North America, the practice is widely regarded as a positive experience: talking with and gazing at a nonverbal infant increases in frequency until the child begins producing her own language, around the first birthday, and cuddling and holding close decrease at the same time. Parents are even given professional assistance when these changes in interaction do not occur (Yoder & Warren, 1993)! Mothers themselves believe that talking with and gazing at infants stimulates infants' intellectual competence.

Research evidence seems to support the mothers' belief. Children who have verbally interactive mothers during infancy do show better language comprehension as four-year olds and do show higher competence at solving simple problems involving both verbal and nonverbal reasoning (Samter & Haslett, 1997). But there is contrary evidence as well. In, China, for example, mothers talk to infants relatively little but cuddle and hold them relatively a lot (Ho, 1994). Yet Chinese culture values education success and Chinese children perform well in school.

The fact is that the effects of maternal talk on infants are not clear. But it is probably not a matter of stimulating thinking and language development, as many mothers themselves might believe. Maternal talk probably is much too complex for a two- or three-month-old infant to learn by hearing it directly. Instead of providing a language model directly, therefore, early verbal interaction may serve other purposes in infants' development: maybe it simply reflects the mother's general interest in and responsiveness to her child. Parents who enjoy talking to their babies as newborns are likely to still enjoy talking to them several years later, when the babies have become capable of learning and using language more effectively. If so, the relationship between early talk and later competence is a good example of a *correlation* (an association) that is not also a *cause*. In that case, too, North American mothers could (in theory) talk with their newborns a good deal less in the earliest months and still expect the babies to end up with good language skills eventually! This would be true, though, only if a mother were responsive and caring throughout the child's infancy and only if the mother did begin interacting verbally as soon as the infant showed signs of actually understanding and using language. This development pattern in fact describes mother-infant relationship in China to a certain extent (though not perfectly).

These ideas remain speculation, though, because mothers' language practices cannot, and probably should not, be manipulated simply to explore their effects on children. In any society, parents need to interact with their babies in ways they consider natural. But comparing cultural beliefs can nonetheless give clues about the deeper, less obvious effects of particular culture practices (Greenfield, 1994). Mother-infant "conversations" are a good example of a culture-bound practice virtually all parent advice books urge parents to talk with their babies. Yet in doing so, the books join parents in assuming a particular cultural value: that skillful oral expression is desirable and should be encouraged as much as possible.

Constant close contact between caregiver and infant, as between this mother and her child, may encourage more nonverbal communication and result in infants who fuss relatively little. Crying and fussing, which we associate with infancy in our society, may actually be a precursor to verbal communication, which parents encourage in North American society.
Source: wong sze yuen/Shutterstock.com.

socially competent infants had parents who directed large amounts of language at them. The most competent babies received about twice as much language as the least competent infants in this study did. But the most competent infants also stimulated interactions with their parents, primarily by procuring various simple kinds of help, such as in pouring a glass of juice or placing the final block on a tower. These "services" probably benefited the infants by offering many opportunities for parents to talk with them ("Shall I put the block on top?").

Influences of Professional Caregivers

Language acquisition can also be supported by other adults who interact with infants extensively—notably, professional caregivers in family childcare or infant-care centers. Their forms of influence parallel those of parents (Chorale et al., 1993). *Contingent dialogue* (extending the child's verbal initiatives), for example, can easily take place at an infant care center: a toddler may name objects in the room ("Book!") or pictures displayed on the wall ("Cat!"), and the caregiver can extend those early initiatives into longer dialogues ("Yes, it's a pretty cat. Do you like cats?"). Gillian Luppiwiski's conversation with Jocelyn about Play-Doh, described in the "Working With" feature, is another example. *Contextual dialogue* (familiar language routines or rituals) can also occur: a caregiver and child may engage in predictable exchanges in preparing to go home each day ("Have you found your coat?" "Now zip it up"). To succeed, these dialogues must be simplified; that is, they should rely on infant-directed or "caregiver" speech that takes the infant's early stage of language into account. Table 4.8 lists some additional ways caregivers can assist in language development.

But important differences also exist between professional caregiver influences and parent influences. One concerns intensity and frequency: caregivers usually do not see a particular infant or toddler for as many hours as a parent does, nor do they develop relationships as emotionally intense as those of parents. Another difference concerns cultural expectations: it is common for caregivers (but rare for parents) to come from a cultural or language background that differs from the children's background. The gap can create confusion and misunderstanding between caregiver and child or between caregiver and parent. If a caregiver and a child speak different primary languages, one may lack facility with some of the words and expressions needed to communicate with the other.

Overall, parents and other caregivers constitute a much more positive than negative influence on language development. Given their importance to the process, it should not be surprising that nearly all children acquire high verbal competence in just a few years. Language acquisition is "over determined": society supports language learning in so many ways that if a child fails to experience that support in one way, she or he is likely to experience it in some other way. So most of us do learn to talk!

TABLE 4.8 Interactions That Support Language Development

Interaction	Purpose
Sitting on the floor with infant and reading books, telling stories, or singing songs	Builds trust; models interesting activities using language
Holding infant close, looking into infant's face, smiling, and talking to infant	Builds trust; models dialogue or conversation
Responding to infant's first words and gestures using caregiver's own words and gestures	Encourages dialogue and conversation; shows respect for infant's language initiatives
Offering simple choices to infant verbally ("Do you want to paint or to play outside?")	Stimulates infant to attend to language; calls attention to relationship between language and actions
Encouraging infant (especially if a toddler) to express desires and resolve differences using words ("What do you want to do?")	Encourages child to practice language; demonstrates power of verbal expression
Distress	Whimpering or crying; vigorous or agitated movements; facial grimaces pronounced; skin very flushed

WORKING WITH Gillian Luppiwiski, Infant Care Provider

Fostering Infants' Thinking

Gillian Luppiwiski worked as a caregiver in an infant daycare center for ten years prior to this interview. She made numerous comments about her work: the changes she sees in the babies as they grow, the responses of mothers and fathers, the interest that even infants and toddlers show in one another. When I asked her to comment on infants' thinking abilities, she began talking about their language and problem solving behaviors and about how she and other caregivers support it.

Kelvin: *What do you notice most about these children when you're working here?*

Gillian: They change so much! Like day and night. Last fall Jocelyn could hardly move; she got so frustrated watching the older children walk around! But now she's all over the place, into *everything*—and happy as a lark.

Kelvin: *Can you figure out what she thinks about? Does it even make sense to ask about her "thoughts"?*

Gillian: Oh, yes. Like when we get out the Play-Doh, and she starts using it—poking it with her fingers, talking about it. She just started naming it, you know; she says "doh" and looks at you with a smile. And "wed" when it's red. That's her favorite color.

Kelvin: *So her language is developing.*

Gillian: Yes, and the Play-Doh helps with that. It gives her something to talk about. We support her comments, saying things like "That's right! We've got red Play-Doh today."

Kelvin: *What about other times? Even when she's not talking, does it seem like Jocelyn's "thinking"?*

Gillian: Definitely! Take the climber: she loves to climb up there and sit with Joel. That teaches her about space and depth, but she learns more by *doing* it than by talking about it. Shelley (another caregiver) might talk about it, comment on it verbally when she sees Jocelyn climbing. But Jocelyn mainly learns it by doing it.

Kelvin: *Do you ever "teach" them anything directly?*

Gillian: We don't so much teach them as make it possible for them to learn. That's how I'd put it. Shelley or I might put out a few puzzles one day, and talk with a child when she chooses to work on one—encourage her to persist in putting it together, maybe give a hint or two, but not do it for her.

Or the other day, Danny started getting out *all* the trucks! He lined them all up with the big ones at one end and the smaller ones at the other end. Sorted them! It was great to see. He needed help, though, in finding enough room to do this without tripping over Jocelyn and the others. He commented on the lineup: "All the trucks!" And so did I, by challenging him gently: "Are you sure have them *all*?"

Kelvin: *So he was grouping? Classifying things?*

Gillian: Yes. In his own way, his own two-year-old way. "Developmentally appropriate practice"—that's what educators are always talking about. That's what makes us a real *infant* center, and different from a preschool center. We try to provide developmentally appropriate things and support the children for using them.

What Do You Think?

1. Considering what Gillian said, how important is an infant care center for fostering a child's thinking ability? How does it compare to experiences that an infant or toddler might have at home?
2. Gillian says, "We don't so much teach them as make it possible for them to learn." How comfortable are you with this idea? Can it apply to working with older children (preschoolers, school-age adolescents) or only to infants and toddlers? Consult with a few classmates about this question; what do they think about it?
3. At times, Gillian seems to equate language development with cognitive development. Is there some way to distinguish these two processes in an infant center? Brainstorm an example or two of how you might do this if you were a caregiver.

The End of Infancy

During the first two years of life, infants become much more like individuals than they are on the day they are born. By their second birthday, they walk about, grasp at objects, and direct their attention toward particular people and activities. These physical skills facilitate certain cognitive activities, such as searching for objects that an infant "knows" exist even though he cannot see them.

> **What Do You Think?**
>
> Find out, if you can, the words you produced first as an infant and the setting in which you produced them. Pool your results with a few classmates. Are there any features common to either the words or the settings?

The language skills that develop at the same time, in turn, contribute to the formation of social skills and relationships, as we will see in the next chapter. By age two, a child knows, and can say, who her parents and siblings are. She can also begin expressing her feelings about these people verbally: whether she is happy or sad, angry or fearful, likes someone or not. In the next chapter, we take a closer look at these social changes, which have a basis in the physical and cognitive developments of infancy.

Chapter Summary

- **What do infants look like when they are first born? How do we know if they are healthy?** The average newborn has rather red-looking skin, is often covered with a waxy substance, and has a skull somewhat compressed on the top. The health of newborns born in hospitals is assessed quickly after delivery with the Apgar Scale. The average newborn at full term weighs about 7½ pounds. Regardless of cultural background, the newborn's bodily proportions make the infant look appealing to adults and may foster the formation of attachments with adults.
- **How much do children grow during infancy?** Infants grow very rapidly during the first two years of life, tripling their weight by their first birthday and adding approximately 50 percent to their length by this same time. The torso and limbs of infants grow more rapidly than their heads, enabling their bodies slowly "catch up" to the advanced development of their heads.
- **What changes occur in the brains of infants?** The brains of infants gain mass rapidly during infancy due to important changes in the neurons and to infants' experiences with their environments. Neurons become myelinated, which improves their efficiency, and they form many new synapses as infants have new experiences and acquire new skills. The efficiency of the nervous system is enhanced by the synaptic pruning process that eliminates redundant or unused synapses.
- **How do infants' sleep and wakefulness patterns change as infants get older?** Infants sleep almost twice as much as adults do, but the amount of sleep gradually decreases as they get older. The interruptions in their sleep contribute to fatigue in their parents.
- **What motor skills evolve during infancy?** Infants are born with a number of innate reflexes, but quickly develop certain motor skills during the first year, including reaching, grasping, and walking. Motor skills develop differently depending on cultural background, biological sex, and social gender roles.
- **What do infants need nutritionally?** Infant need more protein and calories per pound of body weight than older children do. Compared to formula and bottle feeding, breastfeeding has a number of practical and psychological advantages. After weaning from breast or bottle, infants need a diet rich in protein and calories. Most North American families can provide these requirements, but many cannot. A common problem in North American diets is overnutrition, which can create health risks in the long term.
- **What factors can impair growth during infancy?** One of the most important impairments to early growth is low birth weight, because the condition leads to difficulties with breathing, digestion, and sleep, and impairs normal reflexes. The problems low-birth-weight infants experience can sometimes put stress on their relationships with parents, but not necessarily. For a variety of reasons, infants sometimes fail to thrive normally. Infant mortality has decreased in the recent past, but in the United States, it is still higher than it should be.
- **How do infants' senses operate at birth?** At birth, infants already can see and hear, but with less accuracy or acuity than adults do. They have well-developed senses of taste, smell, and touch, and infants demonstrate the ability to combine information from multiple senses to better allow them to function in their environments.
- **How can infant cognition be studied?** Infants' arousal and attention can be studied by noting changes in their heart rates. Infants' recognition and memory of familiar things can be studied by observing their habituation to stimuli, or tendency to attend to novel stimuli and ignore familiar ones.

- **Do infants see and hear in the way adults do?** *Perception* refers to the immediate organization of sensations. *Cognition* refers to the processes by which perceptions are organized, and it often happens deliberately. Studies of visual perception suggest that infants under six months of age perceive a variety of patterns, including those usually found on a human face. Young infants, including newborns, show object constancy in visual perception, as well as visual anticipation of events. Infants also show sensitivity to depth, as indicated in the visual cliff experiments. Infants can localize sounds to some extent at birth, but do not do so accurately until about six months of age. Categorical thought can be demonstrated during infancy by using the reversal shift procedure.

- How do thinking and learning change during infancy? Piaget has proposed six stages of infant cognitive development during which infants' schemes become less egocentric and increasingly symbolic and organized. Research on Piaget's six stages generally confirms his original observations, but it also raises questions about the effects of motor skills and memory on infants' cognitive performance. Like older children and adults, infants can learn through behavioral conditioning and imitation. Behavioral learning tends to be ambiguous in infants less than three months old because it is difficult to distinguish true learning from general, automatic excitement.

- **What phases do infants go through in acquiring language?** Babbling begins around six months of age and becomes increasingly complex until it disappears sometime before the infant's second birthday. Infants show important individual differences in their selection of first words, but generally they use words for objects in their environment that are distinctive in some way. Adults influence language acquisition mainly through modeling simplified utterances, recasting their infants' own utterances, and directing considerable language at the child as she or he grows. Professional caregivers influence language acquisition in ways similar to parents, but they must also recognize the potential effects of cultural gaps between caregiver and child.

Key Terms

accommodation (p. 132)
Apgar Scale (p. 105)
assimilation (p. 132)
babbling (p. 140)
central nervous system (p. 107)
cephalocaudal principle (p. 115)
circular reaction (p. 132)
cognition (p. 123)
failure to thrive (p. 122)
habituation (p. 125)
infant-directed speech (p. 141)
infant mortality rate (p. 123)
intermodal perception (p. 130)

low birth weight (p. 121)
motor skills (p. 115)
myelination (p. 109)
neonate (p. 105)
neurons (p. 108)
non-REM sleep (p. 109)
object permanence (p. 133)
overnutrition (p. 121)
perception (p. 123)
phonemes (p. 140)
plasticity (p. 108)
proximodistal principle (p. 116)
reflex (p. 115)

REM sleep (p. 109)
scheme (p. 131)
semantics (p. 140)
sensorimotor intelligence (p. 130)
stunting (p. 120)
sudden infant death syndrome (SIDS) (p. 110)
synaptic pruning (p. 108)
synaptogenesis (p. 108)
transient exuberance (p. 108)
visual cliff (p. 127)

The First Two Years: Psychosocial Development

CHAPTER 5

Source: Andy Dean Photography/Shutterstock.com.

Chapter Outline
Early Social Relationships
Emotions and Temperament in Infancy
Attachment Formation
Toddlerhood and the Emergence of Autonomy
Looking Back/Looking Forward

Focusing Questions

- What emotional capabilities does an infant have? How do differences in infants' temperaments affect their social development?
- In what ways is a newborn infant capable of participating in the social world? How does caregiver-infant synchrony expand an infant's social capabilities?
- What experiences enable infants to develop secure emotional attachments with their caregivers? What are the consequences of different attachment patterns?
- Why is autonomy so central to development during toddlerhood? What parenting qualities contribute to its successful development?

Even as a newborn, Alberto was an easy baby to feed and comfort. He was also very active and responsive to the sights and sounds in his environment. Even when tired or overstimulated by the people around him, he seemed able to calm himself with just a little help from his caregiver. When he was five weeks old, Alberto just loved attention. His smiles and excitement were irresistible, and he responded to anyone who paid attention to him—from his parents to his older brother and sisters to Luisa, the family dog. However, a special mutual responsiveness seemed to be present whenever Alberto interacted with his mother, Maria, or his father, José. With either of them, Alberto's smiles, sounds, and movements seemed so highly in tune with theirs that they appeared to be having a real conversation.

By the time Alberto was four months old, he began to show a preference for his mother and his oldest sister, Lydia, who helped Maria care for him. When he saw or heard either of them, he became especially happy, active, and noisy, which caused some jealousy among other family members.

Between ages nine and eleven months, Alberto's preferences for specific people became much stronger and more obvious. He clearly preferred his mother to any other adult and responded to his sister Lydia more than to any of the other children. Now able to crawl, he tried to follow his mother wherever she went, and he cried when she left the room. During this period, he also began to do something he had never done before: he sometimes became upset when unfamiliar people visited, even if they were friendly to him.

By the time he was almost two, Alberto was walking and talking well, had begun toilet training, and could do many things himself. He continued to be an active and happy child, but sometimes he became frustrated and upset if he did not succeed at a task. Fortunately, talking to him and giving him just the right amount of helpful guidance usually worked. Although he still demanded a good deal of attention from his mother and still preferred to play with Lydia, he rarely got upset when other family members cared for him. He also seemed quite happy to socialize with almost all friendly visitors, even those he had never met before.

These changes in Alberto are typical of some of the important psychosocial changes that occur during infancy. From the moment of birth, infants differ in their temperament—their characteristic activity levels and stylistic patterns of responding to the people and events in their new environment. As we will see in this chapter, temperamental differences in infants and how well they fit with the temperaments and expectations of their parents, other family members, and society may influence development not only in infancy but through childhood, adolescence, and adulthood as well. And although infants highly depend on their caregivers to meet their needs, they are anything but passive. Infants become active, sophisticated observers and participants in their own psychosocial development.

As an infant grows older, she comes to form close and enduring emotional attachments with the important people in her life and sometimes shows her concerns about them very dramatically. She wails when a strange nurse approaches her in the doctor's office, and she greets her mother or father warmly when one of them "rescues" her from the nurse. Secure attachment relationships, such as those developing between Alberto and his mother and other caregivers, are likely to provide an important basis for successful psychosocial development throughout life. As we will see shortly, the security of an individual's attachment relationships in infancy is an important predictor of relationships as an older child and adolescent, in romantic relationships, and in relationships with the person's own children and grandchildren. A baby may participate in relationships in more subtle ways, such as attending closely to older brothers and sisters while they play—more closely than her siblings attend to her. At times, she may express her needs or feelings in ways that confound the people around her; for example, she may refuse particular foods when a parent offers them but take them happily from a baby sitter.

These behaviors convey two major tasks of psychosocial development in infancy: the development of *trust* and *autonomy*. Infants learn what to expect from the important people in their lives. They develop strong feelings about whom they do (and do not) like to be with and what foods they prefer. The conflicts of trust versus mistrust and autonomy versus shame and doubt, which we examined in Chapter 2, intertwine closely during their first two years, although many observers of children believe trust develops earlier than autonomy does (Erikson, 1963; Maccoby, 1980; Stern, 1985a).

In this chapter, we first discuss the importance of emotions and temperament in infancy. Next, we explore the essential role of early social interactions and attachments in the development of a sense of basic trust (versus mistrust) and in the achievement of autonomy (versus shame and doubt). We examine the ways in which attachments form. Finally, we look at the emergence of self-knowledge and self-awareness during later infancy and toddlerhood.

Early Social Relationships

Infants seem to have a natural tendency to be social participants. Not only do newborns show preferences for their mothers' voices shortly after birth (Purhonen et al., 2004);

Every member of a family has unique ways of interacting with a new child.
Source: AmiParikh/Shutterstock.com.

some evidence also suggests that their perception of speech can be influenced by prenatal exposure to their mothers' speech (DeCasper & Spence, 1986; DeCasper et al., 1994; Granier-Deferre et al., 2011). Immediately after birth, infants are capable of many social responses. For example, a newborn will turn his head toward the sound of a human voice and actively search for its source and will pause regularly in his sucking pattern for human voices but not for similar, nonhuman tones.

Transition to Parenthood

Parent-child relationships begin even before a child is born. Almost as soon as pregnancy is confirmed, parents form *images* of what their child will be like and of how they as parents will respond and cope with this new human presence (Galinsky, 1987). Expecting parents often experience both excitement and fear, the precise mix depending on how much support they have for becoming parents as well as the history of support, or lack thereof, that they had for being children themselves years ago. Even after the baby is born, these images can influence the parents' internal experiences and expectations regarding a child, although this "mental portrait" is now subject to continual revision based on the parents' ongoing interactions and experiences with their baby (Anderson, 1996; Ferholt, 1991; Innamorati et al., 2010; Stern, 1995, 2004).

As we will see in Chapter 13's discussion of psychosocial development in early adulthood, having a child, particularly if it is the first, represents a major life transition that is accompanied by personal, familial, social, and, for many people, professional changes. For most parents, having a child leads them to become less concerned about themselves and more concerned with the well-being of others and about the future as embodied in their child. This shift away from self-centeredness usually comes at some emotional cost, however. During the first two years of rearing an infant, many mothers find themselves removed from much of their normal contact with other adults to devote themselves to infant care, and fathers report working harder at their jobs (Bronstein, 1988; Cowan et al., 1991; Hyman, 1995).

To accommodate the additional family tasks involved in caring for a new infant, the division of roles between husband and wife tends to become more traditional, regardless of the wife's employment, educational level, pre-existing arrangements, or beliefs about gender roles. Social and emotional patterns between parents also appear to change, as reflected in significant decreases in shared leisure and sexual activities, in fewer positive interactions with each other, and in decreased marital satisfaction and greater marital conflict (Levy-Shiff, 1994; Monk et al., 1996; Shapiro et al., 2000; Vandell et al., 1997).

To better understand these changes, Rachel Levy-Shiff (1994) studied marital adjustment in 102 couples from diverse sociocultural backgrounds from pregnancy through the first eight months following the birth of their first child. She found that higher levels of *paternal involvement* with the baby, especially to caregiving, was the most important factor in maintaining marital satisfaction for *both* spouses at a time when opportunities to spend time together in leisure and sexual activities are greatly reduced due to the demands of infant care. Levy-Shiff suggests that during the transition to parenthood, men and women must first solve the internal and interpersonal dilemmas of reorganizing their lives to adjust to the new demands and responsibilities of child-rearing. In most families, the birth of a first child results in gender roles becoming more differentiated and traditional, with women assuming both the main responsibilities for childcare and most of the housework. The physical and emotional drain new mothers experience may lead them to feel resentment toward their husbands because of "overload" and because of unfulfilled prenatal expectations that caring for the new baby would be more fully shared.

Similarly, in a recent longitudinal study, mothers' expectations regarding the role of the father played a significant role in not only the satisfaction that husbands and wives felt in their roles as parents but also in the effectiveness of the child-rearing each provided (Schoppe-Sullivan & Mangelsdorf, 2013). What has become very apparent is that the quality of the parenting partnership established between mothers and fathers—optimally resulting in **coparenting**—has significant developmental implications for both the parents and their children. Coparenting is comprised of four main elements (Feinberg, 2003):

coparenting A parenting partnership in which child-rearing goals, strategies, and responsibilities are shared.

- *Type of behavior exhibited between parents*—Warm and cooperative ("supportive") behavior is clearly preferable to hostile, critical, and competitive ("undermining") behavior.

- *Division of labor regarding child-rearing*—Childcare responsibilities should be shared in a manner that is satisfactory to both parents.

- *Family management*—Decisions about how the family relates to others outside of the family and how family members relate to each other should be made jointly.

- *Parenting practices*—Parents should be in agreement regarding the adoption and development of moral values, the behavioral expectations they have for their children, and the means by which they shape and enforce those behaviors (e.g., discipline techniques).

Fathers who are more involved in coparenting and sharing housework demonstrate that they are not just husbands but also good friends who are committed to meeting their partners' needs in ways that are caring and fair. It is also likely that such shared involvement increases a husband's empathy and appreciation for his wife's experience. Such participation reduces the guilt he would feel if he failed to actively share these new responsibilities. Interestingly, by freeing up their wives' time and conveying a spirit of cooperativeness, husbands create opportunities for more high-quality time with their wives, the lack of which is a major cause of dissatisfaction for many new fathers (Belsky et al., 1995; Levy-Shiff, 1994; Shapiro et al., 2000; Vandell et al., 1997). And to be clear, mothers did not necessarily expect an equal sharing of parenting responsibilities with their husbands. What was important was for the mothers and fathers to communicate effectively and to fulfill each other's expectations in their roles as parents. Under these circumstances, parenting satisfaction and the effectiveness of coparenting were heightened for both parents (Feinberg, 2003.) The transition to parenthood is the start of a lifelong process that we will discuss throughout this book.

Caregiver-Infant Synchrony

Frequently the social interactions between parent (or other caregiver) and infant involve a pattern of close coordination and teamwork in which each waits for the other to finish before beginning to respond. This pattern of closely coordinated interaction is called

caregiver-infant synchrony. Recall the description of Alberto at the beginning of this chapter. Even infants only a few weeks old are able to maintain and break eye contact with their mothers at regular intervals and to take turns with them in making sounds and body movements. Furthermore, videotape studies reveal that mother and baby have "conversations" that resemble adult dialogue in many ways, except for the child's lack of words (De Wolff & van IJzendoorn, 1997; Fish et al., 1993; Stern, 1992).

Until an infant is several months old, responsibility for coordinating this activity rests with the caregiver. But after a few months, the baby becomes capable of initiating social interchanges and influencing the content and style of her caregiver's behavior. Some of this continuity is created by the baby rather than the mother. The smiles, gazes, and vocalizing of a friendly infant prove hard for her mother to resist, and after several months of experience with such a baby, the mother becomes especially responsive to her infant's communications, further reinforcing the baby's sociable tendencies. During the infant's second year, parent and baby use gestures such as pointing, vocalizing, and alternating their gaze between objects and their partner to coordinate and sustain periods of joint attention and maintain each other's interest. High levels of joint attention and reciprocal turn taking in parent-infant interaction, sometimes referred to as *coregulation,* reflect sensitive parenting and help children to become socially competent in relationships with family members and peers (Aureli & Presaghi, 2010; Moore & Denham, 1995; Raver, 1996).

As we will see shortly, a good caregiver-infant temperament "fit" and a well-developed capacity for caregiver-infant synchrony both contribute in important ways to the establishment of the high-quality caregiver-infant relationships that serve as the basis for healthy development (Evans & Porter, 2009). Caregiver-infant relationships that lack the mutual awareness and responsiveness that make synchrony possible may reflect child-rearing difficulties and can place an infant at risk for developmental problems. Studies of interactions between depressed mothers and their infants, for example, have found that mothers' negative moods influence their babies' moods and can affect their longer-term relationships and vulnerability to depression later in life (Letourneau et al., 2011; Moore & Dunham, 1995; Nolen-Hoeksema et al., 1995; Radke-Yarrow et al., 1993).

Social Interactions with Other Family Members

Although infants may interact more with their mothers than with anyone else, they actually live in a network of daily social relationships in which a number of other people make at least minor—and sometimes major—contributions to their social lives. Fathers often belong to this network, and so do siblings and grandparents. How do a baby's contacts with these people compare to those with his or her mother?

caregiver-infant synchrony Patterns of closely coordinated social and emotional interaction between caregiver and infant.

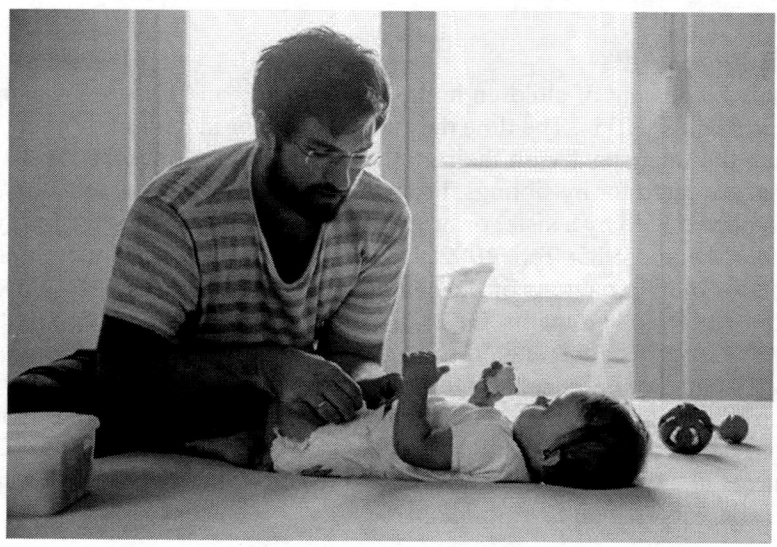

Sharing childcare and household tasks helps all parents with the transition to parenthood.
Source: zeljkodan/Shutterstock.com.

Father-Infant Interactions

Fathers have become increasingly involved in the care of infants and young children, spending around two or three hours per day compared to nine hours for mothers (Yeung et al., 2001). In some cases, fathers assume the role of primary caregiver, reversing the traditional expectations that fathers should set personal and professional goals over investing time and care in their children and the paternal role (Garbarino, 1993; Geiger, 1996; Hyman, 1995). As with mothers, fathers' success at maintaining high levels of caregiver-infant synchrony is related to the goodness of fit between their stress levels, personality characteristics, attitudes, and expectations, and the characteristics and needs of their babies (Bridges et al., 1997; Lundy, 2002; Noppe et al., 1991). In an interesting naturalistic study of fathers' interactions with their infants, Anju Jain, Jay Belsky, and Keith Crnic (1996) observed four groups of fathers: caregivers, playmates-teachers, disciplinarians, and disengaged fathers. Caregivers and playmate-teacher fathers were more educated, had more prestigious occupations, were better adjusted emotionally, more able to rely on others, and experienced fewer daily hassles than the disciplinarian and disengaged fathers.

Although mothers and fathers engage in similar forms of play with their infants, their styles differ. Play episodes with fathers tend to have sharper peaks and valleys: higher states of excitement and more sudden and complete withdrawals by the baby. Fathers tend to jostle more and talk less than mothers do, and they roughhouse more and play ritual games such as peek-a-boo less. These differences in style also appear in middle childhood, and such playful interactions may help prepare infants for future play with peers of both genders (Lamb & Lewis, 2003; Parke et al., 1988).

How do we explain these differences? Past experience with infants, the amount of time routinely spent with young children, demanding work schedules, and fathers' expectations about the stresses and responsibilities of parenting may all play a role. When researchers compared fathers who served as primary, full-time caregivers with fathers who took the more traditional secondary-caregiver role, they found differences in how the two groups played with their infants. Primary-caregiver fathers acted very much like mothers, smiling more and imitating their babies' facial expressions and vocalizations more than secondary-caregiver fathers did. However, almost all of the fathers were quite physical when interacting with their infants (Field, 1987; Geiger, 1996; Noppe et al., 1991; Paquette et al., 2003). These findings suggest that "cohort" effects may be at work here. (*Cohort effects* refer to developmental changes shared by individuals growing up in a particular place or under a specific set of historical circumstances.) As successive generations of fathers assume greater involvement in the care of infants due to changing societal and cultural conditions and expectations, differences in how fathers and mothers interact with their babies will likely decrease, although the rough-and-tumble aspect of the father-child relationship appears to be an enduring one (Paquette, 2004).

Interactions with Siblings

Approximately 80 percent of children in the United States and Europe grow up with siblings (Krieder & Ellis, 2011). The time they spend together in their early years frequently is greater than the time spent with their mothers or fathers (Noller, 2005). In many cultures, children are cared for by siblings. From age one or two they are fed, comforted, disciplined, and played with by a sister or brother who may be only three or four years older (Cicirelli, 1994; Dunn, 1985; Teti, 1992; Updegraff et al., 2011). Firstborn children are likely to monitor the interactions of their mother and the new baby very closely and try to become directly involved themselves. Children as young as eighteen months attempt to help in the bathing, feeding, and dressing of their sibling. At times, they also try to tip over the baby's bath, spill things, and turn the kitchen upside down when they feel jealous of their mother's attention to the new baby. Conflict between siblings is most likely to occur when parents are seen as giving preferential treatment to one child (Dunn et al., 1994; Stewart et al., 1987) or when children feel jealous when their siblings are interacting with their parents (Kolak & Volling, 2010).

In talking to their younger siblings, children make many of the same adjustments their parents do, using much shorter sentences, repeating comments, and using lots of action-getting techniques (baby talk, or "parentese"). In turn, infants tend to respond to their siblings in much the same way they do to their parents. But they also quickly learn the ways siblings differ from parents, particularly young siblings. Because younger children lack their parents' maturity and experience, they are less able to focus consistently on meeting the baby's needs rather than their own. For example, a four-year-old who is playing with his eight-month-old sister may not notice that she is becoming overstimulated and tired and needs to stop. On another occasion, he may become jealous of the attention she is getting and "accidentally" fall on her while giving her a hug. If parents (and other caregivers) keep in mind the needs and capabilities of each of their children and provide appropriate supervision, interactions with siblings are likely to benefit the development of both their new infant and his or her brothers and sisters. Secure infant-mother attachment and warmth toward each child is associated with positive relationships between siblings, while parental coldness is associated with sibling conflicts, possibly because children use their models of attachment with parents in other relationships (Volling & Belsky, 1992). It is important to note that parent attachment may be different with different siblings, and sibling attachment is also highly dependent on sibling responsiveness over time (Whiteman, McHale, & Soli, 2011).

Grandparents

For the majority of well-functioning families, and in most cultural groups in North America, grandparents become welcome companions for the new child (Nicholson & Zeese, 2008; Werner, 1991), as well as secondary sources of practical advice and childcare. This is especially true when the grandparents live geographically close to the parents, they are relatively young and in good health, and the family itself belongs to a cultural group (such as Mexican Americans) that values the participation of the extended family in raising children (Ramirez, 1989; Slomin, 1991). In some circumstances, grandparents become the primary caregivers for their child's infant (Strom et al., 1995). We will look at the importance of grandparenting and the variety of grandparenting styles in Chapter 15, where we examine psychosocial development in middle adulthood.

Interactions with Nonparental Caregivers

In recent decades, caregiving has become increasingly important in the lives of preschool children because many more mothers have returned to working outside the home, even before their children have begun public school. In 2007, just over 63 percent of all mothers

For many families, grandparents play an important role in dealing with the transition to parenthood.
Source: Paul Hakimata Photography/Shutterstock.com.

with children less than six years of age worked outside the home, a number that increased to approximately 77 percent for mothers of school-aged children (HHS, 2009). (We will take a closer look at changes in the nature of families and family life when we discuss psychosocial development in early adulthood in Chapter 13.) All of these parents require suitable, high-quality care for their children for either all or part of the day. The arrangements they actually make depend on the age of the child, on their own preferences (usually family-like settings), and on the kinds of services available in the community. Among all parents who work at least part time or more, about 42 percent arrange for a relative to come into the home or take the child to the relative's home (Laughlin, 2013). Another 11 percent arrange for a nonrelative to care for the child in the child's home or, more commonly, in the caregiver's home.

Approximately 24 percent of infants, toddlers, and preschoolers are cared for in licensed infant and toddler childcare centers and in family day-care homes. (If you have been adding the percentages of children being cared for by relatives, nonrelatives, and day-care center staff, you have probably noticed that the numbers do not sum to 100 percent. This is because a sizable proportion of infants, toddlers, and preschoolers whose parents work have no single or consistent caregiving arrangement.) Figure 5.1 summarizes current childcare arrangements for children under two years of age. In addition to good physical facilities and developmentally appropriate programs, high-quality care for infants is best ensured by employing caregivers who are well trained and supervised and responsive to the physical, cognitive, social, and emotional needs of infants and their families (Scarr, 1998). For parents who are considering day care for their infant, knowing what to look for in a center is extremely important. Table 5.1 presents guidelines for choosing infant day care. Additional discussion of early childhood education and developmentally appropriate practices with preschoolers is found in Chapter 6.

Interactions with Peers

Young babies show considerable interest in other infants, and in much the same ways, they show interest in their parents: by gazing, smiling, and cooing. Sociability of this kind develops with peers at the same time and at the same rate that it does with parents. When given the choice, infants often prefer playing with their peers to playing with their mothers. In play situations, infants more frequently look at and follow their peers, and toddlers are more likely to talk with, imitate, and exchange toys with their peers than with their mothers. Peers also support the autonomy of the toddler from the mother and offer the

Infants show considerable interest in interacting with other infants. When given the opportunity, they may prefer playing with their peers more than their parents.
Source: Pavel L Photo and Video/Shutterstock.com.

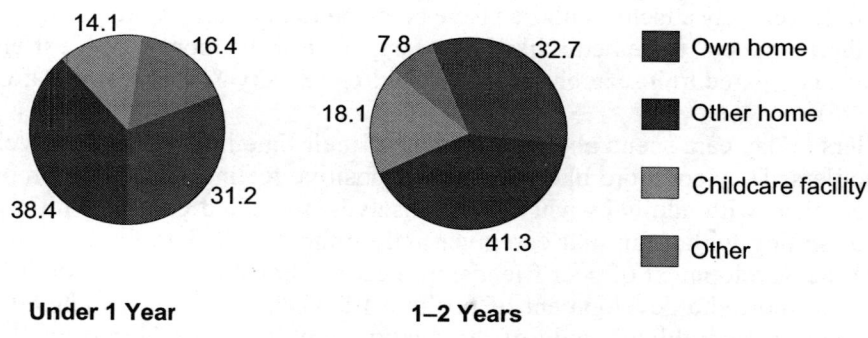

FIGURE 5.1
Current Childcare Arrangements for Working Mothers with Children under One Year and with Children Between One and Two Years

The majority of infants and toddlers whose mothers work are cared for in their own or another home. Somewhat more toddlers than infants go to childcare facilities. Infants are more likely than toddlers are to be cared for in "other" situations, such as accompanying their parents to work.

toddler an alternative source of stimulation and comfort (Chadwick et al., 2004; Hartup, 1989; Rubenstein & Howes, 1983).

Parents, teachers, and other adults play a major role in the development of relationships with peers during toddlerhood, through their relationships with their toddlers, through direct instruction about social interactions, and by providing their toddlers with appropriate opportunities to be with peers in extended family, play-group, and day-care situations (Fagot, 1997; Howes et al., 1994; Parke et al., 1994). Not surprisingly, the quality of infant-parent attachment appears to be related to young children's behavior with peers.

TABLE 5.1 Guidelines for Choosing a Good Infant Day-Care Program

- Children are most likely to thrive intellectually and emotionally in programs that offer a balance between structured educational activities and an open, free environment.

- The caregiving environment should provide ample physical space (at least twenty-five square feet per child) and a variety of materials and activities to foster sensorimotor, social, and cognitive development.

- If the facility includes a playground, the equipment should be safe, clean, age-appropriate and inspected regularly. The playground should also be built on an impact-cushioning surface, be enclosed by a fence, and be monitored at all times when children are using it.

- Cleanliness and safety standards should be high: The day-care facility should be clean, diaper-changing practices should be sanitary, immunization records for all enrolled children should be current, harmful and toxic substances should be stored securely, first-aid kits should be available and staff should be trained to provide first aid.

- Class size should be small (fewer than ten children) and should include children within a two-year age range. Small centers (fewer than thirty children) usually have better staff-child ratios than centers with more children.

- The interaction style of the caregiver is a key aspect of quality care. The caregiver should be actively involved but not restrictive with the children. The caregiver should also be responsive and offer positive encouragement.

- Caregivers who have training in child development and continuing opportunities for education are most likely to provide high-quality care.

- The individual characteristics of the child should be taken into account. Some children will probably do well in a program that balances structure and openness; others may profit from either more structure or a more flexible and relaxed program.

- High staff-child ratio and low staff turnover is important. Research shows, for example, that when the staff-child ratio is at least one to three for infants, one to four for toddlers, and one to nine for preschoolers, the quality of caregiving and of children's activities within the center are both good.

Sources: Adapted from Clarke-Stewart et al. (1994); Clarke-Stewart & Allhusen (2002); National Resource Center for Health and Safety in Child Care (2013).

For example, securely attached children have been found to receive more positive contact from unfamiliar peers, to be better liked by peers, and to have more positive friendships with peers, compared to insecurely attached children (Belsky & Cassidy, 1994; Cassidy et al., 1996).

Toddlers in day care spend about 25 percent of their time interacting positively with other toddlers. They are more likely to express positive feelings and play competently with peers than with adults or when by themselves. Repeated contact with a peer in a familiar setting with a familiar caregiver and minimal adult interference appears to facilitate the development of peer friendship. Peer relationships during toddlerhood in turn may promote the development of positive friendships later in childhood (Engle et al., 2011). A longitudinal study of the quality of children's relationships between infancy and nine years of age found that children's formation of close friendships as toddlers predicted their positive ratings of their friendship quality as nine-year-olds (Howes et al., 1998).

In conclusion, although infants' social interactions with their parents generally are their most important early social experiences, interactions with other family members, nonfamily caregivers, and peers also contribute to their social development. The quality and developmental impact of experiences with siblings and peers will reflect, to some extent, the degree to which parental supervision of such contacts considers the needs of both the baby and the other children.

Emotions and Temperament in Infancy

The healthy cries of a newborn infant make it clear that infants are capable of feeling and expressing their emotions even at birth. During the first three months, infants spend about two hours crying during a typical day. And while most developmental experts recommend that caregivers respond quickly and consistently to the cries of infants (Cong et al., 2002), the ability to successfully console crying babies is often dependent upon correctly interpreting the reasons for their distress. Healthy babies produce four types of cries—the basic hunger cry, the angry cry, the pain cry, and the fussy irregular cry—all of which provide their caregivers with useful information about their physiological states of discomfort (Soltis, 2004; St. James-Roberts & Halil, 1991). Over time, as infants gain better control over their crying, it serves to convey a wider range of messages to their caregivers (Barr, 1995; Green et al., 1998). In the following sections, we discuss the role of early emotions and *temperament*—the infant's characteristic way of feeling and responding.

Emotions in Infancy

Though researchers have long recognized changes in infants' crying, smiling, frustrations, and fear of strangers and novel stimuli, there is now a growing appreciation of the range and complexity of infant emotions (Barrett, 2005; Messinger, 2002). For example, videotape studies reveal that an infant only a few weeks old is able to produce facial expressions corresponding to the range of adult emotional states, even though the infant's expressions of emotion, particularly negative emotions, do not always result from the same events that typically produce them in adults. Similarly, while physiological aspects of emotion, such as changes in heart rate, can be reliably measured, their relationships to specific emotions are not always clear (Camras et al., 1993; Oster et al., 1992). One reason for this lack of specificity is that babies' expectations and understandings appear to play an important role in their emotional reactions. For example, an incongruous stimulus, such as a mother's face covered with a mask, will produce a fear response in some situations but smiling and laughter in others.

While researchers still disagree about the earliest age at which particular emotions are present, they generally agree that most babies can reliably express basic joy and laughter by three or four months, fear by five to eight months, and more complex emotions such as shame, embarrassment, guilt, envy, and pride during toddlerhood (Barrett, 2005; Izard,

> **What Do You Think?**
>
> What advice would you give to prospective parents about maternal employment and childcare arrangements for infants? How will (or do) your own childcare arrangements differ from those of your parents?

1994; Izard & Malatesta, 1987; Kochanska et al., 1998; Lewis, 1992; Weinberg & Tronick, 1994). Table 5.2 shows the approximate ages at which certain infant emotions appear.

Expressions of emotion play an important role in development by providing vital information to infants and their caregivers about ongoing experiences and interactions. Caregivers "read" these messages and use them to guide their actions in helping the infant to fulfill his needs. Very young infants also appear to be sensitive to the positive and negative emotions of their caregivers; they are quite capable of responding to adult fears and anxieties. Recent research indicates that they react in kind to those emotions expressed by their peers and siblings as well (Brownell et al., 2010). These responses are likely based on cues similar to those adults use, such as slight variations in voice quality and touch, as well as variations in facial expression and body language (Grossman, 2010). As they get older, infants display these feelings with increasing frequency and predictability (Eisenberg et al., 1995; Tronick, 1989).

Another important change in an infant's emotional life during the first year is the baby's growing ability to regulate her own expressive behaviors and associated emotional states, especially negative ones. These *self-directed regulatory behaviors* include looking away, self-comforting, and self-stimulation. These behaviors allow the infant to control her negative feelings by shifting her attention away from a disturbing event or by substituting positive for negative stimuli. This helps the infant adjust her emotional state to a comfortable level at which she can successfully maintain interaction with her surroundings (Buss & Goldsmith, 1998; Gianino & Tronick, 1988; Grolinck et al., 1996). During the second year, increases in the capacity for emotional self-regulation also reflect her growing ability to respond to the feelings and needs of others through helping, sharing, and providing comfort (Zahn-Waxier et al., 1992). Claire Kopp (1982, 1989) has proposed that the modulation, or self-regulation, of behavior develops over a series of five successive phases. Table 5.3 describes these phases. As we will see in later chapters, emotional regulation continues to play an important developmental role in childhood and adolescence (Berger, 2011; Caspi et al., 1995; Eisenberg et al., 1997).

TABLE 5.2 Development of Infant Emotions

Approximate Age (in months)	Emotion
0–1	Social smile
3	Pleasure smile
3–4	Wariness
4–7	Joy, anger
4	Surprise
5–9	Fear
17	Guilt, embarrassment
18	Shame

Sources: Barrett (2005); Izard (1994); Lewis (1992).

TABLE 5.3 Development of Behavioral Self-Regulation (modulation) During Infancy: Phases of Self-Regulation

Approximate Ages	Phases	Features	Cognitive Requisites
Birth to 2–3 months	1. Neurophysiological modulation	Modulation of arousal, activation of organized patterns of behavior	
3–9 months+	2. Sensorimotor modulation	Change ongoing behavior in response to events and stimuli in environment	
12–18 months+	3. Control	Awareness of social demands of a situation and initiate, maintain, cease physical acts, communication, etc. accordingly; compliance, self-initiated monitoring	Intentionality, goal-directed behavior, conscious awareness of action, memory of existential self
24 months+	4. Self-control	As above; delay upon request; behave according to social expectations in the absence of external monitors	Representational thinking and recall memory, symbolic thinking, continuing sense of identity
36 months+	5. Self-regulation	As above; flexibility of control processes that meet changing situational demands	Strategy production, conscious introspection, etc.

Source: Kopp (1982), p. 202, Table 2.

Temperament

temperament Individual differences in quality and intensity of emotional responding and self-regulation that are present at birth, are relatively stable and enduring over time and across situations, and are influenced by the interaction of heredity, maturation, and experience.

Temperament refers to an individual's consistent pattern or style of reacting to a broad range of environmental events and situations. Most researchers agree that differences in primary reaction tendencies such as sensitivity to visual or verbal stimulation, emotional responsiveness, and sociability appear to be present at birth, prior to any significant interaction with the external environment. However, researchers disagree on how much such differences are due solely to genetic inheritance and how much they reflect prenatal influences and more subtle environmental experiences during and shortly after birth (Kagan & Snidman, 1991; Kagan et al., 1995; Rothbart, 1989). Parents certainly report differences in their newborn infants' temperaments. The parents of baby Alberto and his sister Lydia, for example, clearly remember that unlike Lydia, who was a fussy and somewhat difficult baby to care for and comfort during her first few months, Alberto was a very easy baby.

In a now classic study of temperament, Alexander Thomas and Stella Chess used parents' reports of differences in their babies on the following nine dimensions: (1) activity level (2) rhythmicity (regularity of eating, sleeping, and elimination), (3) approach-withdrawal to or from novel stimuli and situations, (4) adaptability to new people and situations, (5) emotional reactivity, (6) responsiveness to stimulation, (7) quality of mood (positive or negative), (8) distractibility, and (9) attention span (Thomas & Chess, 1977, 1981). They found three general patterns of temperament.

Easy babies (40 percent of the sample) showed mostly positive moods, regular bodily functions, and good adaptation to new situations. *Difficult babies* (10 percent) displayed negative moods, irregular bodily functions, and high stress in new situations. *Slow-to-warm-up babies* (15 percent) resembled the difficult ones but were less extreme; they were moody and relatively unadaptable, but did not react vigorously to new stimuli. Finally, *mixed-pattern babies* (35 percent) did not fall neatly into any of the first three groups.

Because the original classification of temperaments was based solely on parents' reports, which sometimes can be unreliable, other studies have used two additional measures of temperament: multiple behavior ratings (by pediatricians, nurses, teachers, and other individuals familiar with the child) and direct observation of the child. These studies have confirmed earlier findings of temperamental differences at birth (Huang & Rothbart, 2002; Plomin, 1989; Seifer et al., 1994).

Classifying babies by temperamental pattern has been helpful in predicting problems for children who are difficult or slow to warm up, but not for the majority of children whose temperaments are less extreme. For example, newborn infants whose biological rhythms are irregular, who experience discomfort during feeding and elimination, and who do not communicate their needs clearly often are difficult for their parents and are more likely to experience problems in developing close relationships with them. This is particularly true when mothers have little or no help and emotional support from relatives and friends in caring for their difficult babies, although parenting can improve when such emotional support is made available (Crockenberg & McCluskey, 1986; Kerr et al., 1994; van den Boom & Hoeksma, 1994).

How stable are early differences in temperament? Predictions of later temperament based on temperamental differences among newborns are not very reliable, although predictions based on differences observed toward the end of the first year are somewhat better (Carlson et al., 1995; Gunnar et al., 1995; Kagan & Snidman, 1991; Little et al., 2006; Rothbart & Ahadi, 1994). This may in part reflect the influence of experience and context on temperament. In most cases, the degree to which an infant's early temperamental style contributes to personality development is likely to be influenced by how good *a fit* exists between her temperamental style and the attitudes, expectations, and responses of her parents and other caregivers. For example, an infant who is very active and demanding is more likely to maintain that temperament if these qualities are consistent with his parents' expectations and responses than would be the case if his parents expected him to be more passive and less demanding (Rickman & Davidson, 1995).

In the last two decades, researchers have begun to think of temperamental differences in infancy more broadly, as early-appearing behavioral styles that may influence social and personality development and psychological adjustment in childhood, adolescence, and adulthood (Caspi & Silva, 1995; Hartup & van Lieshout, 1995; Lengua et al., 1998; Little et al., 2006; Newman et al., 1997; Rothbart & Ahadi, 1994). For example, Denise Newman and her colleagues found that temperamental differences observed in children at age three were linked to interpersonal functioning in four important social contexts as young adults: at work, at home, with a special romantic partner, and in the wider social network. Based on behavioral observations of each child in an individual testing session, children were divided into five temperamental groups. Children who were judged to be temperamentally well adjusted, reserved, or confident at age three displayed a normal range of adjustment in all four social contexts as young adults. Children who were temperamentally inhibited as three-year-olds had lower levels of social support but normal adjustment in romantic relationships and at work as adults. Children who had been temperamentally undercontrolled (who had difficulty regulating their emotional states) at age three, reported lower levels of adjustment and greater interpersonal conflict in all four social contexts as young adults (Newman et al., 1997).

Infants vary in temperament, as can be seen by the difficult and more easygoing babies pictured here. These variations may impact long-term development.
Source: (top) szefei/Shutterstock.com; *(bottom)* Flashon Studio/Shutterstock,com.

The long-term developmental effects of temperamental traits such as shyness appear to be influenced by many factors, including culture, gender, and historical period. Margaret Kerr and her colleagues compared the results of a study of how childhood shyness among Swedish eight- to ten-year-olds influenced the timing of marriage, parenthood, and career success at age thirty-five with the results of a similar longitudinal study of American children conducted in Berkeley, California, a generation earlier (Caspi et al., 1988; Kerr et al., 1996). Both American and Swedish men who were shy as children married and became fathers later than men who had no history of childhood shyness. American men who had been shy as boys began stable careers later, resulting in lower career achievement and less career stability by middle adulthood than those who were not shy as children. For Swedish men, however, childhood shyness had no effect on educational attainment, occupational stability, or income during adulthood. Both American and Swedish women who had been shy as young children married and became mothers at the same age as girls with no history of shyness. Childhood shyness was associated with lower levels of educational

Chapter 5 The First Two Years: Psychosocial Development

> **What Do You Think?**
>
> What advice would you give to parents about how to respond to differences in their children's temperaments? What have you noticed about temperamental differences among members of your own family?

achievement than nonshy peers for Swedish women but not for American women. Further research is needed to determine to what degree these differences were due to culture, gender, and the different historical periods in which the two studies were conducted.

Attachment Formation

attachment An intimate and enduring emotional relationship between two people, such as infant and caregiver, characterized by reciprocal affection and a periodic desire to maintain physical closeness.

Attachment refers to the strong and enduring emotional bond that develops between infant and caregiver during the infants first year of life. This relationship is characterized by reciprocal affection and a shared desire to maintain physical closeness (Ainsworth & Bowlby, 1991; Main, 1995).

The concept of attachment has been most strongly influenced by the etiological perspective (see Chapter 2) and, to a lesser extent, by the psychoanalytic approach. In the etiological view, the ties between infant and caregiver develop from the activation of a biologically based motivational system that is an inherited adaptation of human evolution. This system helped ensure survival by protecting infants from environmental dangers. Because the nature of the child-caregiver relationship is widely viewed as being central to successful child development, studies of attachment have come to play an important role in developmental theory. Although attachment cannot be observed directly, it can be inferred from a number of commonly observed infant behaviors that help establish and maintain physical closeness with caregivers. Three of these behaviors—crying, cooing, and babbling—are *signaling behaviors;* four others—smiling, clinging, nonnutritional sucking, and following—are *approach behaviors.* Although researchers do not agree as to whether these *specific* attachment behaviors are biologically inherited, many believe that the tendency to seek and maintain physical closeness with caregivers is biologically determined and essential to infant survival in much the same way food is.

working models Internalized perceptions, feelings, and expectations regarding social and emotional relationships with significant caregivers based on experiences with those caregivers.

Another influence has been the work of theorists who emphasize the importance of **working models**, or internalized perceptions, feelings, and expectations regarding social and emotional relationships with significant caregivers (Biringen, 1994; Mahler, et al., 1994). For example, Margaret Mahler proposes that during the first three years of life, children go through four phases in developing a psychological sense of self. A newborn infant begins life in an *autistic phase,* meaning that she is self-absorbed and has little psychological awareness of the world around her. Next, during the *symbiotic phase,* the infant experiences herself as being completely connected with and dependent on her primary caregiver, rather than as a psychologically separate person. During the *separation-individuation phase,* she begins to develop a separate sense of self. Finally, during the *object constancy phase,* the infant achieves a more stable sense of self based on her increasing ability to form reliable mental representations of her primary caregivers (called *objects*) and their responses to her (Mahler et al., 1975).

Currently most developmental psychologists believe attachment relationships develop over time as a cumulative product of the infant's repeated experiences in interaction with her main caregivers during the first two years. They also believe attachment involves a highly mutual and interactive partnership between caregiver and child, both of whom have strong, although unequal, needs to achieve physical and emotional closeness with each other. This view is influenced by discoveries about the interactive nature of social relations between infants and their caregivers (Belsky, 1996; Insabella, 1993).

According to attachment theory, once attachment with the mother (or other primary caregiver) is established, the infant uses her as a *secure base* from which to explore the environment. As the infant gradually increases his distance from the mother, the *attach-*

ment behavioral system and accompanying feelings of fear and anxiety are more likely to be activated, and the infant begins to seek proximity (closeness) to the caregiver once again. This pattern is also activated when the infant encounters dangers such as strangers, darkness, or animals approaching. The balance between activation of the attachment system and activation of exploratory behaviors varies with the particular context and developmental level of the child (Biringen, 1994).

Phases of Attachment Formation

John Bowlby believes that attachments develop in a series of phases determined partly by cognitive changes (described in the previous chapter) and partly by interactions that appear to develop quite naturally between infants and their caregivers (Ainsworth & Bowlby, 1991; Bowlby, 1969). Table 5.4 presents these four phases. Note that *separation anxiety*, an infant's disturbance at being separated from her caregiver, and *stranger anxiety*, a wariness and avoidance of strangers, appear near the beginning of phase 3. The achievement of object permanence (see Chapter 2) is thought to be an important basis for separation anxiety and attachment development. *Stranger anxiety* is exhibited by many infants between six and nine months of age and often continues through the first year. It is thought to be tied to an infant's increasing ability to recognize and distinguish between familiar and unfamiliar people and to actively make sense of his interpersonal world. Whether or not a particular infant becomes wary of strangers and the strength of the reaction may vary with his temperament, the familiarity of the setting, the friendliness of the stranger, the caregiver's reaction, and how accustomed the child is to meeting strangers (Dickstein & Parke, 1988; Mangelsdorf et al., 1995).

Attachment—the tendency of young infants and their caregivers to seek physical and emotional closeness—provides an important basis for achieving secure and trusting relationships during childhood and throughout life.
Source: michaeljung/Shutterstock.com.

TABLE 5.4 Four Stages of Attachment Formation

Phase 1: Indiscriminate Sociability (birth–2 months)

Responds actively with cries, smiles, coos, and gazes to promote contact and affection from other people; uses limited attachment behaviors less selectively than when older.

Phase 2: Attachments in the Making (2–7 months)

Increasing preference for individuals most familiar and responsive to needs; preferences reinforce parents' affection; accepts certain forms of attention and care from comparative strangers; tolerates temporary separations from parents.

Phase 3: Specific, Clear-cut Attachments (7–24 months)

Preferences for specific people become much stronger due to ability to represent persons mentally (Piaget's fourth stage of sensorimotor development; see Chapter 6); ability to crawl and walk enables toddler to seek proximity to and use caregiver as a safe base for exploration; increasing verbal skills allow greater involvement with parents and others; both *separation anxiety*—an infant's disturbance at being separated from the caregiver—and *stranger anxiety*—a wariness and avoidance of strangers—appear near the beginning of this phase.

Phase 4: Goal-coordinated Partnerships (24 months onward)

By age two, increasing representational and memory skills for objects and events; growing ability to understand parental feelings and points of view and to adjust his or her own accordingly; growing capacity to tolerate short parental absences and delays and interruptions in parents' undivided attention makes possible cooperation with others to meet needs; changing abilities are related to secure attachment relationships grounded in a sense of basic trust.

Source: Bowlby (1969).

Separation anxiety, which generally appears between nine and twelve months, involves displays of fear, clinging, crying, and related distress when an infant's parent or other caregiver leaves her (recall Elizabeth's protest when left at nursery school by her mother in Chapter 2). Separation anxiety appears to be related to how well the infant is prepared for the parents' departure and to her past experiences with separation. However, the responsiveness of the caregiver she is left with may be most important, especially for infants who *are temperamentally reactive to separation* (Gunnar et al., 1992).

Assessing Attachment: The "Strange Situation"

The most widely used method for evaluating the quality of attachment to a caregiver is called the **Strange Situation (SS)**. Originally developed by Mary Ainsworth for infants who are old enough to crawl or walk, the procedure consists of eight brief social episodes with different combinations of the infant, the mother, and an unfamiliar adult (Ainsworth et al., 1978). It presents the infant with a cumulative series of stressful experiences: being in an unfamiliar place, meeting a stranger, and being separated from the caregiver (see Table 5.5).

Based on the infants' patterns of behavior in the Strange Situation, Ainsworth and her colleagues identified three main groups. Most of the infants studied (approximately 65 to 70 percent) displayed a **secure attachment** pattern. When first alone with their mothers, they typically played happily. When the stranger entered, they were somewhat wary but continued to play without becoming upset. But when they were left alone with the stranger, they typically stopped playing and searched for or crawled after their mothers; in some cases, they cried. When the mothers returned, the babies were clearly pleased to see them and actively sought contact and interaction, staying closer to them and cuddling more than before. When left alone with the stranger again, the infants were easily comforted; although they showed stronger

Strange Situation (SS) A widely used method for studying attachment; confronts the infant with a series of controlled separations and reunions with a parent and a stranger.

secure attachment A healthy bond between infant and caregiver. The child is happy when the caregiver is present, somewhat upset during the caregiver's absence, and easily comforted upon the caregiver's return.

TABLE 5.5 Episodes in the Strange Situation (SS)

Episode	Duration	Events	Observed Attachment Behaviors
1	30 seconds	Parent and infant enter the room with the experimenter.	
2	3 minutes	Parent is seated; baby plays with toys and explores the room.	Parent as a secure base
3	3 minutes	A stranger enters room, sits down, talks with parent.	Reaction to unfamiliar adult
4	3 minutes	Parent leaves infant alone with stranger, who responds to the baby and offers comfort if baby is upset.	Separation anxiety
5	3 minutes	Parent returns, greets (comforts) baby; stranger leaves room.	Reaction to reunion
6	3 minutes	Parent leaves baby alone in room.	Separation anxiety
7	3 minutes	Stranger again enters the room and offers comfort to the baby.	Reaction to being comforted by a stranger
8	3 minutes	Parent returns; stranger leaves; parent greets/comforts baby and tries to interest her in toys.	Reaction to reunion

Source: Ainsworth et al., (1978).

signs of distress, they quickly recovered from the upset by actively seeking contact with their mothers on their return.

The second group of infants (about 10 percent) were classified as displaying an **anxious-resistant attachment** or *ambivalent* pattern. They showed some signs of anxiety and, even in the periods preceding separation, stuck close to their mothers, and explored only minimally. They were intensely upset by separation. When reunited with their mothers, they actively sought close contact with them but at the same time angrily resisted the mothers' efforts to comfort them by hitting them and pushing them away. They refused to be comforted by the stranger as well.

The third group of infants (about 20 percent) displayed an **anxious-avoidant attachment** pattern. They initially showed little involvement with their mothers, treating them and the stranger in much the same way. They rarely cried when separated and, when reunited, showed a mixed response of low-level engagement with their mothers and a tendency to avoid them.

A fourth category, **disorganized-disoriented attachment**, has also been investigated. This pattern, which was not included in earlier studies because coding procedures were not available, indicates the greatest degree of insecurity. When reunited with their parent, these infants exhibit confused and contradictory behaviors. They may be unresponsive and turn away when held, display "frozen" postures, and cry out unexpectedly after being comforted (Lyons-Ruth & Block, 1996; Lyons-Ruth et al., 1997; Main & Solomon, 1990).

All four attachment patterns have been studied in many other countries. In all cases, around 60 to 65 percent of the children are reported to be securely attached, whereas rates of insecure attachment are much more variable (van IJzendoorn & Kroonenberg, 1988). The "A Multicultural View" feature discusses cross-cultural variations in attachment.

Consequences of Different Attachment Patterns

Secure attachment early in infancy benefits babies in several ways during their second year of life. Securely attached toddlers tend to cooperate better with their parents than other babies do (Londerville & Main, 1981). They comply better with rules such as "Don't run in the living room!" and they are also more willing to learn new skills and try new activities their parents show them (such as when a parent says, "Sit with me for a minute and see how I do this"). When faced with problems that are too difficult for them to solve, toddlers who are securely attached are more likely than others to seek and accept help from their parents. At age five, these children tend to adapt better than other children to changes in preschool situations (Arend et al., 1979; Matas et al., 1978; Slade, 1987), and college students who demonstrate secure attachments tend to be more adaptable, manage stress better, and have better interpersonal skills than their nonsecurely attached peers (Hamarta, Deniz, & Saltali, 2009).

Less securely attached infants may not learn as well from their parents. Anxious-resistant infants often respond with anger and resistance to their parents' attempts to help or teach them. Such babies may at times invest so much time and energy in conflicts that they are unable to benefit from their parents' experience and to explore their environment. Given a roomful of toys and a mother who has recently returned from an absence, for example, a child may use up a lot of time alternating between being angry at and snuggling with his mother instead of getting on with his play. Anxious-avoidant infants do not have this particular problem, but because of their tendency to avoid interaction with their parents, they also miss out on parental efforts to teach or help them and ultimately may discourage parents from even trying to help (Behrens, Hesse, & Main, 2007; Matas et al., 1978; Stevenson-Hinde & Verschueren, 2002).

The disorganized-disoriented attachment pattern generally is found in seriously disturbed caregiving situations where interactions between mothers and their infants are inconsistent, and out of tune with or inappropriately responsive to the infant's physical, social, and emotional needs. Parents who display disorganized-disoriented attachment behaviors may think of and interact with their infants in inappropriate ways. For instance, they may display role reversal, where the parent inappropriately expects to be cared for by her infant, or they may respond to their infants in overly intrusive, withdrawing, or rejecting ways. An infant's

---

anxious-resistant attachment An insecure bond between infant and caregiver in which the child shows signs of anxiety preceding separation, is intensely upset by separation, and seeks close contact when reunited while at the same time resisting the caregiver's efforts to comfort.

anxious-avoidant attachment An insecure bond between infant and caregiver in which the child rarely cries when separated from the caregiver and tends to avoid or ignore the caregiver when reunited.

disorganized-disoriented attachment This pattern indicates the greatest degree of insecurity between infant and parent. When reunited with the parent, the infant exhibits confused and contradictory behavior, including unresponsiveness, turning away when held, frozen postures, and unexpected cries after being comforted.

A Multicultural View

Cross-Cultural Variations in Attachment

Almost all infants become attached to their parents in some way. However, the patterns by which they do so vary around the world. Studies on the Strange Situation report that whereas 65 to 70 percent of children studied appear to be securely attached, rates of insecure attachment are much more variable (Super & Harkness, 2010; van IJzendoorn & Krooneuherg, 1988). Among infants from northern Germany, for example, anxious-avoidant attachment patterns occur twice as often as they do among North American infants. Among infants from Japan, on the other hand, anxious-resistant responses occur approximately three times as often as they do in the United States, while anxious-avoidant attachment is virtually nonexistent (Bretherton & Waters, 1985; Takahashi, 1990). Similar patterns were found among Korean children (Jin et al., 2010).

These variations result partly from differences in cultural values around the world and partly from the child-rearing practices these values foster. In northern Germany, people value personal independence especially strongly (Grossmann et al., 1985; Super & Harkness, 2010) and believe children should obey parents more consistently than is usually expected in North America. As a result, infants need to learn not to make excessive demands on parents; they must minimize crying and fussing and do without extra bodily contact. During early infancy, mothers entourage these qualities by remaining relatively unresponsive to their infants' moment-by-moment behavior. Thus, in northern Germany, unresponsiveness may not signify personal rejection of the child as much as a desire to raise a good citizen. The results show up in the Strange Situation as anxious-avoidant attachment: a larger than usual number of young children seem indifferent when reunited with their mothers.

Child-rearing practices probably also influence the attachment responses of Japanese children. Separations between Japanese infants and their mothers are quite rare by North American standards. Most Japanese infants have very little experience with strangers. Typically they are left alone or with another adult only two or three times per month on average, usually someone already intimate with the child, such as the father or a grandparent (Mikaye et al., 1985). Their extreme protests to the Strange Situation resemble the anxious-resistant pattern of crying, anger, fear, and clinging when the mother returns. Korean mothers were more likely to stay near their children after the reunion period even after the children had calmed (Jin et al., 2012). As with the German infants, however, it is more likely that these behaviors represent the fulfillment of typical cultural practices rather than failures in child-rearing.

Some researchers have also noted that distribution of attachment types may vary within as well as across cultures. In a study of infants from southern Germany, the distribution of attachment types did not differ significantly from those reported for infants in the United States (Grossmann & Grossmann, 1990; van IJzendoorn & Kroonenberg, 1988). Studies of attachment among Israeli infants raised in kibbutz communities provide further evidence of cultural differences in attachment within a particular society. Kibbutz children were raised in communal peer groups by *metapelot* (nurse/educators), spending regular time with their families during evenings, weekends, and holidays. Kibbutz infants successfully formed attachments to both their parents and their communal caregivers, but a larger proportion displayed insecure attachment patterns compared to Israeli infants raised in the city or infants raised in the United States.

This difference appears to be related to kibbutz sleeping arrangements, which differ among kibbutz communities. When Abraham Sagi and his colleagues compared infants from kibbutz infants' houses with home-based sleeping arrangements with infants who slept in their infants' houses (communal sleeping arrangements), they found that although the two groups did not differ in temperament or life events, only 48 percent of the infants with communal sleeping arrangements were rated as securely attached to their mothers compared to 80 percent of the infants who slept at home. These researchers conclude that although group care and multiple caregiving of high quality did not necessary interfere with the formation of close relationships between parents and children or with the development of social skills, it appears that the sleeping arrangements in the kibbutz communities did (Aviezer et al., 1994; Sagi et al., 1995, 1997).

Cultural values and practices, however, cannot explain all the differences. Even in northern Germany, for example, many babies become securely attached even though their mothers follow culturally approved practices of aloofness. In Japan, some infants become anxious-resistant even though their mothers follow essentially Western child-rearing styles, which include considerable experience with baby sitters and other nonparental caregivers. Observations of these babies in their homes suggest that they were born with somewhat irritable or fussy temperaments, which may predispose them to becoming anxious-resistant despite their mothers' practices.

On balance, attachment seems to result from the combination of several influences, including cultural values, inborn temperament, and the child-rearing practices of the particular family. The developmental meaning of attachment may vary too. What looks like an attachment failure for one child may be a success for another, depending on the circumstances.

attempts to communicate or modify this behavior are often ignored or overridden, leading to the disorganized-disoriented infant attachment behaviors noted earlier. Disorganized-disoriented infant attachment behavior increases with the severity of family risk factors and places infants at risk for future problems, such as aggression, conduct disorder, anxiety, difficulty interacting with peers, and other developmental difficulties (Kerns & Brumariu, 2014; Lyons-Ruth & Block, 1996; Lyons-Ruth et al., 1997; Main & Solomon, 1990).

Differences in attachment appear to persist even into the preschool years. One study found that children rated as securely attached at age one seemed more likely to seek attention in positive ways in nursery school at age four (Sroufe et al., 1983). When they needed help because of sickness or injury, or just wanted to be friendly, they found it easy to secure attention by approaching their teachers fairly directly, and they seemed to enjoy the attention when they received it. Anxious-avoidant or anxious-resistant infants tended to grow into relatively dependent preschool children. They sought help more frequently but seemed less satisfied with what they got. However, methods of seeking attention differed between these two groups. Anxious-resistant children showed signs of chronic complaining or whining, whereas anxious-avoidant children tended to approach their teachers very indirectly, literally taking a zigzagging path to reach them. Having done so, they typically waited passively for the teachers to notice them. As noted earlier, disorganized-disoriented infants are often at risk for developmental difficulties.

Attachment is not limited to the periods of infancy and early childhood. We will discuss the long-term and intergenerational effects of attachment later in this chapter.

Influences on Attachment Formation

So far, we have emphasized the general aspects of attachment. In this section, we discuss some of the factors that appear to influence the quality of attachment between infants and their mothers, as well as other important caregivers.

The Role of the Mother

A major determinant of individual differences in attachment is the quality of the infant-mother relationship during the child's first year. A mother's capacity to respond sensitively and appropriately to her infant and to feel positively about him and his strengths and limitations appears to be more important than the amount of contact or caregiving. Mothers of securely attached infants are more responsive to their babies' crying, more careful and tender in holding them, and more responsive to their particular needs and feelings during both feeding and nonfeeding interactions than are mothers of less securely attached infants (Ainsworth, 1994; DeWolff & van IJzendoorn, 1997; Posada & Kaloustian, 2010).

Differences in infant temperament are likely to affect the mother-infant relationship and the quality of attachment. Infants with irritable temperaments tend to receive less maternal involvement, which in turn may negatively influence the quality of attachment. With appropriate interventions, however, such negative cycles may be interrupted.

In one study of the influence of temperament and mothering on attachment, Dymphna van den Boom (1994) helped mothers to respond to their temperamentally difficult six-month-old infants in more sensitive and developmentally appropriate ways by adjusting their behaviors to the infants' unique cues. Mothers gained practice in imitating their infants' behaviors and repeating their own verbal expressions. They also learned to notice when their infants were gazing at them and when they were not and to coordinate the pace and rhythm of their own behavior with those of their infants. Mothers who received such help were found to be significantly more responsive, stimulating, visually attentive, and able to regulate their infants' behavior than a similar group of mothers who did not get assistance. Infants of these mothers had higher scores on sociability, self-soothing, and exploration, cried less often, and at twelve months of age were much more likely to be securely attached.

Being securely attached herself makes the mother more likely to have a child who is securely attached. The quality of the mother-child relationship is influenced by the mother's *working models*—her perceptions, expectations, and assumptions about her infant, herself, and their relationship. Past mother-infant interactions, the mother's memories of her own childhood, and similar factors also may play a significant role in mother-child attachment relationships (Bretherton, 1997; Mahler et al., 1975; Posada & Kaloustian, 2010; Stern, 1985b; van IJzendoorn & Bakermans-Kranenberg, 1997). A mother's capacity to establish and maintain a secure attachment relationship with her infant is also influenced by her socioeconomic status (SES), which affects her ability to focus on her infant rather than on finding housing, food, work, and other necessities.

The Role of the Father

Although children are most likely to form strong attachment relationships with their mothers, who most often are their primary caregivers, they may form equally strong attachments with their fathers. Studies of father-infant attachment in the United States and other countries suggest that the processes involved are similar and that fathers display the same range of attachment relationships mothers do, and most studies have found no differences in most babies' preferred attachment figures during their first two years (Lamb, 1997; van IJzendoorn & De Wolff, 1997). It is worth noting that when fathers utilize poor parenting practices, their children are more likely to demonstrate insecure attachment, though no significant impact was found on attachment for fathers engaging in good parenting, suggesting that the quality of father-child interactions are particularly important (Brown et al., 2007).

As we pointed out earlier in the chapter, however, fathers and mothers interact with their infants somewhat differently. Fathers generally are more vigorous and physical in their interactions, and mothers are quieter and more verbal. Such differences in the quality of mother-infant versus father-infant attachment relationships are likely to reflect gender-related differences in caregiving opportunities, experiences, and expectations, as well as gender-related differences in the current division of childcare and other household responsibilities within the family (Akande, 1994; Brown, Mangelsdorf, & Neff, 2012; Ferketich & Mercer, 1995; Owen & Cox, 1997; Volling & Belsky, 1992).

For example, Geoffrey Brown and his colleagues (2012) found that the security of father-infant attachment at three years can be predicted from attachment at thirteen months—specifically, the quality of their interactions, the father's attitudes and sensitivity toward the infant, and the amount of time spent with the infant. In addition, research by Nathan Fox and his colleagues (1991) found that the security of attachment to one parent also appears to be closely related to the security of attachment to the other parent. Thus, an infant with a secure (or insecure) attachment to her mother is likely to have the same quality of attachment to her father.

Overall, the better the psychological and social adjustment and life circumstances of the infant and his parents, the greater the probability of a secure attachment. For example, fathers of secure infants tend to be more extroverted and agreeable than fathers of insecure infants, to have more successful marriages, and to experience more positive emotional spillover between work and family (Belsky, 1996). Chronic marital conflict before and after the birth of a child can interfere with sensitive, involved parenting and thereby predict insecurity in attachment relationships, particularly for fathers. An infant's ongoing exposure to parents who are upset

Day care, even for infants and toddlers, has few negative effects on children as long as the care is of high quality and parents feel satisfied.
Source: Dmitri Maruta/Shutterstock.com.

> **Focusing On...**
>
> ### Family-Leave Policies in the United States and Europe
>
> In 1993, the United States enacted its first national Family and Medical Leave Act, guaranteeing up to twelve weeks of *unpaid* leave per year to any worker who is employed for at least twenty-five hours per week at a company with more than fifty employees. Family leaves are allowed after the birth of a child or an adoption to care for a child, spouse, or parent with a serious health condition, as well as for a health condition that makes it impossible for the worker to perform a job. After the leave, the worker is assured of his or her old job or an equivalent position (Hyde et al., 1996).
>
> How does U.S. family-leave policy compare with that in other countries? Most industrialized countries have much more generous policies than those in the United States, providing not only more extended leaves of absence so that working parents can take care of their young children but also financial support for part or all of the leave period (Frank & Zigler, 1996; Kamerman, 1991). In almost every country in the world, one parent can take a paid infant care leave supported by the employer or a social insurance fund. If both parents choose to continue to work, they are guaranteed access to high-quality day care for their child. In Sweden, the mother and the father split up to sixteen-month paid leave to stay home with a new infant, and both parents are required to take off a minimum of three months.
>
> In France, working mothers are entitled to 100 percent reimbursement for four months through the social security system and then up to two more years of unpaid leave with a job guarantee. In Germany, a parent taking a leave of absence from work is entitled to 2/3 of their salary for up to fourteen months. German women may also take off the last 6 weeks of their pregnancy, and there are limits on the types of work, hours of work, and timing of work expecting and nursing mothers are permitted to do.
>
> It seems evident that while the twelve weeks of unpaid leave provided by the U.S. family-leave policy was a step in the right direction, policies in Europe go much farther in helping parents to directly meet the needs of their babies without undue economic hardship and risk to their jobs.
>
> In a review of research on the impact of the Family and Medical Leave Act, Christopher Ruhm (1997, 2000) found that because the leaves are short and unpaid and only half of the workforce is eligible under the law, it has had little impact. Women are more likely than men to work for smaller companies that are exempt from the law, and women who have less education and make less money are the least likely to take full advantage of leave time (American Institutes for Research, 2013). Ruhm suggests that coverage of more workers, extension of the number of weeks of leave allowed, and payment during all or part of the leave would greatly increase the benefit to families and children (Ruhm, 2000). When considering financial and health costs and benefits to employers, families, and society at large, having a longer, *paid* leave would easily outweigh the temporary financial burden to companies or the government (Bartick & Reinhold, 2010; Galtry & Callister, 2005).
>
> **What Do You Think?**
>
> What arguments would you make to support raising family-leave policies in the United States to the level of many European countries? What other examples of family support policies (e.g., health care) that fall short of what is needed for children's healthy development can you think of? Would you make the same arguments for these that you did for family leave?

and angry and the distress that such exposure causes may contribute to disorganized infant-caregiver attachment behavior (Belsky, 1996; Owen & Cox, 1997).

The Effects of Maternal Employment

As we noted earlier, in 2007 approximately 63 percent of mothers with children six years old or less and around 77 percent of mothers of school-aged children were in the work force (HHS, 2009). Length of maternity leave may influence the quality of mother-infant interactions. Roseanne Clark and her colleagues interviewed and videotaped employed mothers of four-month-old infants in their homes during feeding time. They found that shorter maternity leaves were associated with lower quality of mother-infant interactions. This was especially true for mothers who reported more depressive symptoms or who perceived their infants as having more difficult temperaments. These mothers expressed less positive effect, sensitivity and responsiveness in interactions with their infants compared to mothers who had longer leaves (Clark et al., 1997). Family-leave policies in the United States and Europe are discussed in the "Focusing On" feature.

WORKING WITH Rachelle Turner, Infant Day-Care Coordinator

Understanding Infant Social Development

Rachelle is the infant coordinator in a day-care center, where she has taught for the past four years. She began working as a day-care teacher during her college years and plans to eventually work as a therapist in a program serving young children and their families.

Rob: *What do you like most about working with infants?*

Rachelle: I find working with infants fascinating because so much is packed into the first year of life. It's amazing to see how rapid the changes are. Because you're with the children eight hours a day, five days a week, you can observe the very small changes in development that happen, even on a week-to-week basis.

Rob: *What differences in early infant temperament do you find?*

Rachelle: There are differences in napping patterns, for example. If, as an infant, a child needs you to rub his back or rock him gently to go to sleep, often he will want the same kind of thing as a three-year-old when he is going down for a nap on a cot. Or you might see him rocking himself to go to sleep. On the other hand, there's the child you can just put in his crib, and he'll just grab his blanket and go to sleep. When he's older, you can say, "OK, it's nap time," and he'll get on his cot and go to sleep. It often seems like children are their own person from day one.

Rob: *Do you have another example?*

Rachelle: Some infants aren't happy until they can crawl and go get what they want, while others seem perfectly content with just sitting up and having you plop toys in front of them. Infants can really differ in how active or passive they are in learning to crawl or walk and in their style of exploring their physical and social world. They also differ in their moods and in whether they are irritable or not.

Rob: *What about their social relationships?*

Rachelle: Their changing interactions with other children are interesting. A five-month-old infant will be attracted to another child, but will not, of course, play with the child. She'll pull the other infant's hair and touch its face and clothes. She'll want to explore it and see what it is, just like a doll. Toward the end of the first year, infants recognize their friends, and smile and laugh when they see them. They now want to go on the climber or play blocks together.

Rob: *So their social skills change during the first year from exploring each other as objects to interacting with each other as unique individuals. What changes do you see during the second year?*

Most infants of mothers who are employed either full or part time are securely attached, although full-time employed mothers are somewhat more likely than part-time employed and mothers who are not employed outside the home to have insecurely attached infants (Belsky, 1988b; Clarke-Stewart, 1989; L. Hoffman, 1989). However, these results must be viewed with caution because the effects of maternal employment on the infant or young child are rarely direct. They are almost always based on a variety of family factors, including SES and cultural differences, the mother's "morale," the father's attitude toward his wife's employment, the type of work and number of hours it demands, the husband-wife relationship, the father's role in the family, the availability and quality of nonmaternal care, and the mother's and father's feelings about separation from their child (Scan, 1998; Silverstein, 1991).

Cynthia Stifter and her colleagues compared mother-child interactions and attachment patterns in families in which mothers returned to full- or part-time employment outside the home before their infants were five months old with those in families in which mothers remained at home full time, and found that employment did not directly affect attachment. However, when employed mothers were experiencing high levels of separation anxiety because of the severe time constraints imposed by work schedules, they were more likely to have infants who developed anxious-avoidant attachments. Although they were equally sensitive and responsive to their infants as working mothers who were not anxious, highly anxious mothers were much more likely to be "out of synch" and overcontrolling when interacting with their infants (Stifter et al., 1993).

WORKING WITH Rachelle Turner, Infant Day-Care Coordinator

Understanding Infant Social Development *continued*

Rachelle: Once they can actually say the child's name, they'll call him to come play. Games like hide-and-seek, chasing each other, or knocking blocks over together. They interact because the child makes it fun. It's not the imagination that three-year-old friends have, but it's definitely play and excitement when they see each other. They'll run up to each other, and they'll hug and kiss and be affectionate, and they know the other child isn't a doll. And if one gets hurt, they'll say, "Oh, Anne has a boo-boo," because she's a person in their life.

Rob: *What have you observed about infants' ability to form attachment relationships with nonparental adult caregivers?*

Rachelle: If you are affectionate and responsive to an infant's unique habits and needs around feeding, changing and sleeping, and comforting and stimulation, she'll quickly come to know you and form an attachment to you. Particularly if a child is in day care full time, if an unfamiliar parent or delivery person comes into the center, or if a child is upset for some other reason, she will crawl or run to a caregiver or want to be held or to sit in your lap.

Rob: *How does it feel from the caregiver's perspective?*

Rachelle: Very strong feelings of attachment develop. Remember, unlike a typical household where laundry, cooking, and other tasks compete with childcare, we spend almost all of our time observing and interacting with the children. I get very attached. When children leave, it's very hard to have children coming in and out of your life. You think about them constantly.

Rob: *Are parents sometimes jealous of your relationship with their baby?*

Rachelle: Yes. A parent might give the child excessive gifts, or become critical of the teacher, or make a point of telling the teacher something she didn't know about the child. I try to reassure parents by asking them for information about their child and by being interested in changes they have observed rather than just focusing on changes I have noticed.

What Do You Think?
1. What qualities do you think make a good day-care teacher?
2. As a current or prospective parent, how comfortable would you feel putting your child in Rachelle's care? Why?
3. How closely do Rachelle's examples of temperamental differences and attachment fit your own understandings based on reading the chapter?

The Effects of Day Care and Multiple Caregivers

The growing number of dual-wage and single-parent families and changing views about child-rearing and family life have led to increased interest in nonmaternal childcare to supplement the care given within families. The effects of day care and other forms of nonmaternal care on attachment in infants and toddlers are difficult to evaluate for many of the same reasons cited in the discussion of maternal employment. The gender of the child, the child's temperament, the mother's (and father's) feelings about both day care and maternal employment, and the mother's reasons for working all play a role. Other factors include the type of childcare arrangement (day-care center, in-home day care, relative), the stability of the arrangement, the child's age of entry, the quality of day care, and the quality of the child-caregiver relationship (Belsky & Rovine, 1988; Scarr, 1998). See the interview with Rachelle Turner in the "Working With" feature for a look at social interactions in an infant day-care center.

While some infant care researchers have found evidence that one-year-olds who attend centers more than twenty hours per week tend to form less secure attachments to their parents (Belsky & Nezworski, 1988; Belsky & Rovine, 1988) and to fathers in particular (Quan et al., 2013), others have reported that negative attachment outcomes tend to be associated with little or part-time rather than full-time infant care. Babies in infant care centers show *more* social confidence than do infants reared at home (Anderson, 1989; Roggman et al., 1994). Moreover, children of mothers who work outside the home exhibit fewer internalizing behaviors, such as anxiety and depression, as well as higher levels of achievement overall (Lucas-Thompson, Goldbert, & Prause, 2010).

A large-scale study of more than one thousand infants and their mothers at ten different sites supports the finding that an infant's childcare experience alone is neither a risk nor a benefit for the infant-mother attachment relationship as measured by the Strange Situation. Childcare that is of poor quality or unstable may increase the developmental risks to an infant whose caregiving already lacks sensitivity and responsiveness, but high-quality childcare and preschool programs might serve to buffer the negative impacts of less-than-optimal home environments (Love et al., 2005) or of children without a secure maternal attachment (Buyse, Verschueren, & Doumen, 2009). Thus, the effects of childcare on attachment and the attachment relationship itself depend primarily on the nature of ongoing interactions between mother and child and on the family, neighborhood, and other contexts that either support or undermine the quality and reliability of the mother-infant relationship (Belsky, 1996; Cowan, 1997; NICHD, 1997; Owen & Cox, 1997; Posada & Kaloustian, 2010).

What about attachments to multiple caregivers? Though expectations based on infant-mother attachment relationships may help guide an infant in forming new attachments, infants and nonmaternal caregivers are capable of establishing unique and independent relationships based more on their reciprocal exchanges and individual qualities than on a "model" developed from mother-child interactions (Zimmerman & McDonald, 1995). The attachments infants form with their center caregivers, for example, appear to be no less secure than their attachments to their parents, and the two sets of attachments are relatively independent of each other. Thus, even an infant who exhibited an insecure pattern of attachment relationships with his or her family might still form secure attachments with other caregivers (Buyse, Verschueren, & Doumen, 2009; Goosens & van IJzendoorn, 1990).

There is also evidence that in a variety of other contexts, including extended families and communal child-rearing settings such as the Israeli kibbutz and the Efe people of Zaire, secure relationships with multiple professional and nonprofessional caregivers are not only possible but may even contribute to the child's well-being by either adding to a network of secure attachments or compensating for their absence (Sagi et al., 1997; Tronick et al., 1992). On the Israeli kibbutz, infants and toddlers are raised in same-age peer groups by community childcare providers. Among the Efe, infants and toddlers experience a pattern of multiple relationships—with mother, father, other adults, and children. In such cases, the extended family or community child-rearing network may be more predictive of attachment relationships than the mother-child relationship alone.

Long-Term and Intergenerational Effects of Attachment

The long-term and intergenerational effects of attachment have been of growing interest to developmental researchers. Attachment patterns in infancy are predictive of attachment in childhood, adolescence, and adulthood, and the attachment relationships parents experienced in their own childhoods are related to the attachment relationships they develop in romantic relationships (Simpson et al., 2007) and with their own children (Main, 1995; Mickelson et al., 1997; Pesonen et al., 2003; Trinke & Bartholomew, 1997; van IJzendoorn & Bakermans-Kranenburg, 1997).

The Adult Attachment Interview (AAI) has been used to evaluate the childhood attachment relationships adults had with their own parents and other caregivers (George et al., 1985). Based on their responses, adults are classified into four main attachment patterns that parallel the infant attachment patterns identified by the Strange Situation (SS). Marinus van IJzendoorn (1995) analyzed eighteen studies of how well parents' AAI attachment classifications predicted their own infants' attachment classifications in the Strange Situation. He found that in approximately 75 percent of the cases, the security of the parents own attachment classification predicted the security of the infants attachment.

In one longitudinal study, AAI classifications of expectant mothers and fathers predicted the attachment classifications of their infants at twelve and eighteen months in the SS. Mothers and fathers with a dismissing attachment pattern were more likely to

> **What Do You Think?**
>
> What advice would you give new parents about the roles of fathers, maternal employment, and infant day care in supporting secure attachment and optimal social/emotional development for their infants? What recommendations would you give to your elected representatives regarding infant and toddler day-care programs for families with working and nonworking mothers?

have an insecure-avoidant pattern of infant-parent attachment in the Strange Situation. An autonomous-secure pattern for both parents predicted secure infant-parent patterns of attachment. Mothers whose adult attachment patterns were classified as unresolved were likely to show a disorganized pattern of attachment to their infants in the SS (Steele et al., 1996). Attachment patterns appear to be transmitted across the lifespan as well. Diane Benoit and Kevin Parker (1994) studied the transmission of attachment across three generations: infants, mothers, and grandmothers. They found that mothers' AAI classifications during pregnancy predicted infants' SS classifications in approximately 68 percent of the cases and grandmothers' AAI classifications did so in 49 percent of the cases.

What accounts for the long-term, intergenerational transmission of attachment? One important factor is the caregiver's sensitivity in reliably and appropriately responding to the baby's signals (Barlow & Durand, 1995; Posada & Kaloustian, 2010). Another is living in families and communities that provide the economic, social, and emotional conditions that support and promote the working models and interactions that are the basis for secure attachment and adequate parent-child relationships. In fact, parents with a history of insecure attachment are more likely have children with a secure attachment when those parents obtain sufficient social support (Raby et al., 2015)

Toddlerhood and the Emergence of Autonomy

By the second year of life, infants who have experienced sufficient caregiver-infant synchrony and achieved relatively secure attachment relationships with their parents and other caregivers have developed a sense of *basic trust* (versus *mistrust*) about the world. According to Erik Erikson (1963), by resolving this crisis in the first stage of psychosocial development, an infant's trusting view of the world leads to the development of *hope,* the enduring belief that one's wishes are attainable (see Chapter 2's overview of the eight stages in Erikson's theory of psychosocial development across the lifespan).

Despite lingering anxieties about separations, the achievement of a basic sense of trust in their relationships with their caregivers enables toddlers to become increasingly interested in new people, places, and experiences. For example, an eighteen-month-old may no longer bother to smile at his mother while he plays near her, and he does not need to return to her for reassurance as often as he used to. Parents may welcome these changes as a move toward greater independence and at the same time experience a loss of intimacy for which they may not be quite ready. This shift is both inevitable and developmentally important. For one thing, an older infant can move about rather easily and therefore find much to explore without help from others. The newfound abilities to crawl, climb, and walk make her more interesting as a playmate for other children and thus less dependent on her parents for her social life. For another, her rapidly developing thinking and communication skills contribute to her increasing autonomy.

These competencies create new challenges for both toddlers and their families as a new developmental crisis emerges: the psychosocial crisis *of autonomy versus shame and doubt.* **Autonomy** refers to a child's capacity to be independent and self-directed in his activities and his ability to balance his own demands for self-control with demands for control from his parents and others. *Shame* involves both a loss of approval by people important to the child and a loss of self-respect due to a failure to meet one's own standards (Lewis, 1992). Toddlers must somehow practice making choices—an essential feature of autonomy—in ways that cause no serious harm to themselves or others.

autonomy An individual's ability to govern and regulate her or his own thoughts, feelings, and actions freely and responsibly while at the same time overcoming feelings of shame and doubt.

After their first birthday, infants begin to show increasing autonomy in their play and other activities, which sometimes leads them to unsafe situations. This autonomy is fostered by their improving motor skills and cognitive development.
Source: Michael Pettigrew/Shutterstock.com.

Parents must learn to support their child's efforts to be autonomous, but must do so without overestimating or underestimating the child's capabilities or the external dangers and internal fears she faces. If they are unable to provide such support and instead show their disapproval of failures by shaming their child, a pattern of self-blame and doubt may develop. In such a case, the child is more likely to be either painfully shy and unsure of herself or overly demanding, self-critical, and relatively unable to undertake new activities and experiences freely. Cross-cultural research demonstrates that maternal use of shaming is linked to higher levels of anxiety throughout childhood (Gershoff et al., 2010).

Parents also must help their infant master this crisis of autonomy by continually devising situations in which their relatively mature baby can play independently and without undue fear of interference—by putting the pots and pans within reach but hiding the knives, for instance. Children also need social as well as physical safety. Chewing on a sister's drawing or dumping the dirt out of the flowerpots may not have dangerous physical consequences, but it can have negative social effects. Thus, parents must help their infant learn how to avoid social perils by being selective about the child's activities.

Sources of Autonomy

Why should infants and toddlers voluntarily begin to exert self-control over their own behavior? Developmental psychologists have suggested several possible answers to this question based on the various theories outlined in Chapter 2. Each has some plausibility, although none is complete in itself.

Operant Conditioning

Operant conditioning stresses the importance of reinforcement for desirable behaviors. According to this view, adults will tend to reinforce a child for more grown-up behaviors, such as independent exploration ("What did you find?") and self-restraint ("I'm glad you didn't wet your pants"). Operant conditioning resembles identification in assuming parents can motivate children, but it also assumes their influence occurs in piecemeal ways; that is, the child acquires specific behaviors rather than whole personality patterns.

Observational Learning

According to the theory of *observational learning,* the key to acquiring autonomy and self-control lies in the child's inherent tendency to observe and imitate parents and other caregivers. If parents act gently with the child's baby sister, for example, the child will come to do so too (although his interpretation of *gently* may occasionally be influenced by feelings of sibling rivalry). Similarly, if a young child observes her mother taking pots and pans from the kitchen cabinet, it is a fair bet that she will attempt to do the same. In fact, much home "childproofing" is necessitated by a young child's skill at observational learning. The process of observational learning implies that autonomy and self-control are acquired in units, or behavioral chunks, that are bigger than those described by operant conditioning but smaller than those acquired in identification.

Social Referencing: A Common Denominator

All three explanations of the development of autonomy have something in common: they involve **social referencing**, the child's sensitivity to the feelings of his parents and other adults and his ability to use these emotional cues to guide his own emotional responses and actions (Baldwin & Moses, 1996; Bretherton, 1992; Pelaez et al., 2012; Witherington et al., 2010). For example, infants and toddlers exhibit social referencing when they visit a strange place. Should they be afraid of the new objects and people or not? How safe is it to be friendly and to explore? In the absence of past experiences of their own, they evaluate such situations based on their parents' responses: if their parents are relaxed and happy, they are likely to feel that way too; if their parents are made tense or anxious by the situation, the children probably will feel that way also. Even very young infants use their caregivers and even strangers to guide their responses, for example, approaching and

social referencing
The child's sensitive awareness of how parents and other adults are feeling and ability to use these emotional cues as a basis for guiding his or her own emotional responses and actions. Social referencing is important for the development of autonomy.

playing with unfamiliar toys if a nearby stranger is smiling and avoiding them if the person looks fearful (Klinnert et al., 1986; Walden & Kim, 2005; Witherington et al., 2010).

Development of Self

The sense of self that develops late in infancy shows up in everyday situations as well as in situations involving self-control. Its development appears to follow a sequence that begins with *physical self-recognition and self-awareness,* followed by *self-description and self-evaluation,* and then by *knowledge of standards and emotional response to wrongdoing* (Kochanska et al., 1995; Stipek et al., 1990).

Self-Recognition and Self-Awareness

One interesting series of studies explored this phenomenon in infants nine to twenty-four months old by testing their ability to recognize images of themselves in mirrors, on television, and in still photographs (Asendorpf et al., 1996; Lewis et al., 1985; Rochat, 2003). Because most of the infants could not verbally indicate whether or not they recognized themselves, the researchers secretly marked each infant's nose with a red mark. When placed in front of a mirror, infants from fifteen to twenty-four months of age touched their bodies or faces more frequently than they did before they were marked. Infants around fifteen to eighteen months also began to imitate their marked images by making faces, sticking out their tongues, or watching themselves disappear and reappear at the side of a mirror. These self-recognition behaviors never occurred in infants younger than fifteen months and increased from 75 percent at eighteen months to 100 percent at twenty-four months. When presented with videotaped images of themselves in which a stranger sneaked up on them, infants as young as nine months displayed self-recognition based on *contingent cues,* that is, connections between their own movements and the movements of the image they were viewing. By approximately fifteen months, infants were increasingly able to distinguish themselves from other infants by using *noncontingent cues* such as facial and other physical features (Lewis & Brooks-Gunn, 1979a; Lewis et al., 1985). Many children do not refer to the child on the video as "me" reliably until they are nearly four years old (Rochat, 2003).

Self-Description, Self-Evaluation, and Emotional Response to Wrongdoing

Between nineteen and thirty months of age, children develop the cognitive competence and vocabulary to describe and represent themselves in terms of physical characteristics such as size (*little, big*), type of hair *(curly, red),* and eye color. By the end of their second year, most children show an increasing appreciation of the standards and expectations of others regarding their behavior toward both people and things. For example, a broken toy can trouble a child even if she did not break it; she may show it to an adult and verbally express concern and a need for help ("Broken!" or "Daddy fix?"). A crack in the kitchen linoleum may now receive close scrutiny, even though several months earlier, it went unnoticed, and several months later, it may go unnoticed again. Language that implies *knowledge of standards*—evaluative vocabulary such as *bad, good, dirty, nice*—appears as well (Bretherton, 1995). Such knowledge combines with other behaviors to suggest that the child is beginning to sense an identity for himself. There is also reason to believe that verbal and nonverbal reactions of toddlers to flawed objects are associated with the early development of a sense of morality. When faced with situations in which they believe they have been responsible for a "mishap" such as breaking a toy, toddlers' responses include acceptance of responsibility, apologies, a focus on reparations (repairing the wrong), and distress (Kochanska et al., 1995).

By age two, children show satisfaction in *initiating challenging activities* or behaviors for themselves, and they often smile at the results. A child builds a tower of blocks higher than usual and smiles broadly the moment she completes it. Another makes a strange noise—say, a cat meowing—and then smiles with pride. In each case, the child confronts a task that is somewhat difficult by her current standards, but attempts it anyway. Her behavior suggests an awareness of what competent performance amounts to and of her own ability to succeed. This knowledge reflects part of her sense of self and contributes to its further development.

Development of Competence and Self-Esteem

From the beginning of infancy through the end of toddlerhood, children achieve a growing sense of basic trust, autonomy, competence, and ultimately self-esteem. In fact, these developments go hand in hand. Autonomy, as we discussed earlier, is made possible by a child's secure and basically trustworthy relationships with his primary caregivers. **Competence**—skill and capability—develops as a result of the child's natural curiosity and desire to explore the world and the pleasure he experiences in successfully mastering and controlling that world (White, 1993). Much like the infants need for proximity and attachment to caregivers, his motivation to explore and master the world is thought to be relatively autonomous and independent of basic physiological needs for food, water, sleep, and freedom from pain.

Based on many years of observational study, Burton White (1993) suggests that a socially competent toddler is likely to display capabilities in the following areas:

1. Getting and holding the attention of adults in socially acceptable ways
2. Using adults as resources after first determining that a task is too difficult
3. Expressing affection and mild annoyance to adults
4. Leading and following peers
5. Expressing affection and mild annoyance to peers
6. Competing with peers
7. Showing pride in personal accomplishments
8. Engaging in role play or make-believe activities

What everyday rules for behavior guide parents' efforts to socialize their toddlers and preschool-age children? To answer this question, Heidi Gralinski and Claire Kopp (1993) observed and interviewed mothers and their children in these age groups. They found that for fifteen-month-olds, mothers' rules and requests centered on ensuring the children's safety and, to a lesser extent, protecting the families' possessions from harm; respecting basic social niceties ("Don't bite"; "No kicking"); and learning to delay getting what they wanted (versus getting it immediately). As children's ages and cognitive sophistication increased, the numbers and kinds of prohibitions and requests expanded from the original focus on child protection and interpersonal issues to family routines, self-care, and other concerns regarding the child's independence. By the time children were three, a new quality of rule emerged: "Do not scream in a restaurant, run around naked in front of company, kick your sister, take the tablet when someone is using it, fight with children in school, or pick your nose."

Not surprisingly, a toddler's social competence is influenced by the nature of the parent-toddler relationship. Even though they do not spend more time interacting with their children than mothers of less competent children, mothers of highly competent children support and encourage their toddlers' curiosity and desire to explore the world around them by providing a rich variety of interesting toys and experiences that are both safe and appropriate to the children's level of competence. They also play with their toddlers in ways that are responsive to the children's interests and needs and use language their toddlers can clearly understand.

Observations of mothers and their two-year-olds found that toddlers' capacity for both compliance with parental directions and self-assertion was associated with *authoritative parenting* relationships (see Chapter 7) consisting of a combination of control and guidance and an appropriate sharing of power with warmth, sensitivity, responsiveness, and child-centered family management techniques (Farrant et al., 2012). High levels of defiance and parent-toddler conflict were most likely to be associated with more authoritarian, power-assertive control strategies. In situations where the toddler had said "no" to the mother, maternal negative control was most likely to elicit defiance (Crockenberg & Litman, 1990; White, 1993).

Mothers of competent toddlers are also more likely to encourage their children to accomplish the tasks they had initiated themselves by actively guiding them and praising

competence An individual's increased skill and capability in successfully exploring, mastering, and controlling the world around them.

> **What Do You Think?**
>
> How do you think seeing your toddler develop competence and self-esteem would affect your feelings and self-evaluation as a parent and caregiver? How might these feelings affect your child in turn?

them for achievements rather than actually performing the tasks for them (White, 1993). As you might expect, this approach requires considerable patience, the ability to tolerate the child's frustration when things do not work out the first few times, and a firm belief in the child's need and potential to be an autonomous and competent person. Perhaps the most important quality of these mothers is their ability to interact sensitively and appropriately with their children and to experience pleasure and delight in these interactions (at least most of the time). The same quality appears to be most important in the development of secure attachment relationships and continues to be important throughout childhood.

Toddlers who grow up in supportive environments are likely to be better adjusted in their development than children whose environments are less supportive. A natural outcome of such parenting is the early emergence of a strong sense of **self-esteem**: a child's feeling that she is an important, competent, powerful, and worthwhile person whose efforts to be autonomous and take initiative are respected and valued by those around her (Erikson, 1963; Harter, 1983; Robins & Trzesniewski, 2005). The development of self-esteem during infancy and toddlerhood is closely tied to the achievement of a positive ratio of autonomy versus shame and doubt and initiative versus guilt during the developmental crises that, according to Erikson, occur during this period (Erikson, 1963). Young children generally have very high self-esteem, likely due to the encouragement they receive when learning new tasks (Robins & Trzesniewski, 2005) As we will see, the childhood experiences that follow infancy continue to make major contributions to this important aspect of identity.

self-esteem An individual's belief that he or she is an important, competent, powerful, and worthwhile person who is valued and appreciated.

Looking Back/Looking Forward

Let us now look at how the lifespan themes outlined in Chapter 1 apply to our discussion of infancy. We will focus on attachment, which plays a central role in infancy and influences development throughout the life cycle.

- **Continuity within change**—Attachment relationships begin in early infancy and are an important aspect of the parent-child relationships that are the foundation of psychosocial development. Although the ways in which parent-child attachment is expressed change as a child moves from infancy through childhood and adolescence, and into adulthood, there is considerable continuity within these changes as reflected in the finding that a child who is classified as being securely (or insecurely) attached in infancy and early childhood will very likely continue to display that pattern as an adolescent, as a parent, and as a grandparent. One important reason is that the internal mental working models of both parent and child that are thought to organize and guide early infant-caregiver interactions continue to do so even though the particular forms of the interactions undergo developmental change.

- **Lifelong growth**—The physical, cognitive, and psychosocial growth that occurs from infancy through adulthood affects how attachment is expressed in important ways. How secure (or insecure) attachment is displayed during adolescence, for example, is markedly different than the way it was displayed in early childhood or the ways in which it will be manifested in romantic relationships during adulthood. These changes are also a product of the striking growth in cognitive abilities achieved in adolescence and early adulthood. Thus, a youngster who attends college in Colorado maintains a psychological sense of attachment with his parents in Connecticut, even though most of their interactions are by e-mail, Facebook interactions, phone calls, Skype, holiday visits and, on rare occasions, "snail-mail."

- **Changing meanings and vantage points**—The meaning of attachment to children and their parents changes significantly as they move through the life cycle. The meaning of attachment for a mother and her preteen daughter, for example, will differ significantly from that experienced during the daughter's early childhood years, and will likely have changed for each of them when the pre-teen is a parent herself and her mother is both a parent of an adult child and a grandmother. Remember, however, that despite the changes in vantage points and meanings, it is also highly likely that all three generations—grandmother, mother, and child—will share the same attachment classification, reflecting the theme of continuity within change mentioned earlier.

- **Developmental diversity**—The lifespan theme of diversity is reflected in the development of attachment in two ways. The first and more obvious way is in the four attachment classifications that appear to describe the great majority of children and parents who have been studied. As we have seen in this chapter, a secure pattern of attachment for both infant and parent during the first two years is generally associated with much more positive long-term developmental outcomes than is a disorganized pattern for the child and parent. The second major source of developmental diversity in attachment relationships is the many factors in addition to a parent's sensitivity and responsiveness that affect the quality of attachment and of the overall parent-child relationship. One example is differences in the frequency with which the various attachment patterns are observed in different cultures and in different contexts within a particular culture.

Chapter Summary

- **What emotional capabilities does an infant have? How do differences in infants' temperament affect their social development?** Newborn infants have a natural tendency to actively participate in their social world. *Caregiver-infant synchrony* refers to the closely orchestrated social and emotional interactions between an infant and his or her caregiver and provides an important basis for the development of attachment relationships. The similarities in the type and quality of an infant's interactions with mother and father are much greater than the differences. The effects of nonmaternal care and maternal employment on infant and toddler development depend on the specific circumstances, but in general do not appear to be negative. When given the opportunity to do so, infants engage in active social interactions with their siblings and peers and often prefer them to their parents as playmates.

- **In what ways is a newborn infant capable of participating in the social world? How does caregiver-infant synchrony expand an infant's social capabilities?** Infants appear to be capable of a complex range of emotional responses and are quite sensitive to the feelings of their caregivers. They probably use cues similar to those adults use, such as variations in voice quality, smell, touch, facial expression, and body language. Even at birth, infants exhibit differences in temperament, patterns of physical and emotional responsiveness, and activity levels. These differences both influence and are influenced by the feelings and responses of their caregivers.

- **What experiences enable infants to develop secure emotional attachments with their caregivers? What are the consequences of different attachment patterns?** Attachment, the tendency of young infants and their caregivers to seek and maintain physical and emotional closeness with each other, is thought to provide an important basis for achieving secure and trusting relationships during early infancy. Attachment develops in a series of phases from indiscriminate sociability at birth to goal-coordinated partnerships at two years. The Strange Situation, in which the infant is confronted with the stress of being in an unfamiliar place, meeting a stranger, and being separated from his or her parent, has been used to study the development of attachment. Secure attachment is most likely to develop when the caregiver responds sensitively and appropriately to the infant and the infant can use the caregiver as a safe base for exploration. Insecurely attached infants tend to be less able than securely attached infants are to get help from parents and teachers when they need it or to accept it when it is offered. Infants are equally capable of forming secure attachments to their mothers and to their fathers, and to other caregivers as well, even though in the majority of families the mother is the primary caregiver. The effects of both maternal employment and day care on attachment depend largely on how the mother feels about herself and her role as a parent and how the situation helps or hinders her ability to care for and enjoy her baby. The quality of her experience and the quality and consistency of the day care are also important. Attachment patterns can be long-term, often affecting three generations of parents and their children.

- **Why is autonomy so central to development during toddlerhood? What parenting qualities contribute to its successful development?** Sources of the growing autonomy that characterizes the second year of infancy include identification, operant conditioning, observational learning, and social referencing. Toddlerhood also brings significant increases in self-knowledge and self-awareness. These changes are reflected in the toddler's increasing awareness of adult standards, distress at behaviors modeled by unknown adults, and pride in her or his accomplishments. Toddlers are strongly motivated to achieve greater competence through successfully mastering and controlling the physical and social worlds around them. Competence is fostered by parents who encourage their infant's curiosity by providing opportunities that are challenging, safe, and appropriate to the child's capabilities. Increased self-esteem in the infant is the natural outcome of supportive parenting.

Key Terms

anxious-avoidant attachment (p. 163)
anxious-resistant attachment (p. 163)
attachment (p. 160)
autonomy (p. 171)
caregiver-infant synchrony (p. 151)
competence (p. 174)
coparenting (p. 150)

disorganized-disoriented attachment (p. 163)
secure attachment (p. 162)
self-esteem (p. 175)
social referencing (p. 172)
Strange Situation (p. 162)
temperament (p. 158)
working models (p. 160)

PART 3

Early Childhood

Source: Samuel Borges Photography/Shutterstock.com.

Chapter 6
Physical and Cognitive Development in Early Childhood

Chapter 7
Psychosocial Development in Early Childhood

Although most of us remember relatively little from our preschool years, parents often believe those years are among the most gratifying for their children. Perhaps, this is because children become more equal participants in their families during this time than during infancy; yet, they have not begun the process of creating lives for themselves outside the family. Parents therefore have much to do during these years, and they may still believe they can shape or influence their children fully. Later, it will become harder to hold to this idea.

Preschoolers become more social during this period, partly because of the more complex motor skills they acquire—skills such as riding a tricycle or climbing a jungle gym—which can impress parents as well as friends. In addition, new cognitive skills allow preschool children to express themselves more precisely than they could as infants, as well as try out new social roles in play. Their world expands rapidly during these years—a process that is both exhausting and exhilarating for children, as well as for their parents.

Physical and Cognitive Development in Early Childhood

CHAPTER 6

Source: Gserban/Shutterstock.com.

Chapter Outline

PHYSICAL DEVELOPMENT
Influences on Normal Physical Development
The Connection Between Health and Poverty
Bladder Control
Motor Skill Development
The Impact of Children's Growth on Adults
COGNITIVE DEVELOPMENT
Thinking Among Preschoolers
Language Acquisition in the Preschool Years
Language Variations
Early Childhood Education
From Preschooler to Child

Focusing Questions

- What pathway does physical growth normally take during early childhood?
- How is poverty related to children's health?
- When do children achieve bladder control?
- What motor skills do children acquire during the preschool years?
- How does children's growth affect parents and other adults?
- What are the special features and strengths of preschoolers' thinking?
- How does the language of preschool children differ from that of older children?
- What social and cultural factors account for variations in preschoolers' language and speech?
- What constitutes good early childhood education?

"Kitty run!" says Zöe, age three. She is pointing to the neighborhood cat.
  "Yes," replies her father. "She's chasing a bird."
  Zöe nods and says, "Bird gone now. Bad kitty?" and looks to her father for confirmation.
  "It's OK this time," says her father. "The bird flew away soon enough."
  At this, Zöe walks off to find the cat, curious to learn what else it might do.

Two features of this incident are especially noteworthy: Zöe's language and her mobility. Little more than a year ago, neither could have occurred. As a preschooler, however, she is developing the ability to deal with her world in symbols, in this case through oral language. She is also developing new physical skills that serve her interests and abilities; for example, she can walk up to the cat simply to learn more about it.

In this chapter, we look in detail at physical and cognitive development during early childhood. Many of the examples will suggest relationships between the two domains, as well as their impact on the third domain of psychosocial development. Furthermore, as we will see in the chapters on development during adulthood, the physical and cognitive changes among preschoolers influence the development of the adults who care for them. The fact that preschoolers sleep less than they did as infants, for example, is the beginning of a lifelong trend that will affect both child and parents, creating new options for each. For the child, staying awake longer facilitates attending school; for parents, the child's attending school makes adult-focused activities, such as a job or a hobby, easier to arrange than before their children began school. Parents who are ready for the growth and changes in their preschoolers but do not feel pressured to hurry those changes will likely influence their children's development in many positive ways. The changes will also set the stage for even more indirect forms of parenting typical of later phases of childhood and adolescence, discussed in Chapters 8 and 10.

PHYSICAL DEVELOPMENT

Influences on Normal Physical Development

Physical growth during the preschool years is relatively easy to measure and gives a clear idea of how children normally develop during this period. Table 6.1 and Figure 6.1 show the two most familiar measurements of growth, standing height and weight. At age two, an average child in North America measures about thirty-three or thirty-four inches tall, or about two feet, ten inches. Three years later, at age five, he or she measures approximately forty-three inches, or about one-third more than before. The typical child weighs twenty-seven to twenty-eight pounds by age two but about forty-one pounds by age five. Meanwhile, other measurements change in less obvious ways. The child's head grows about one inch in circumference during these years, and body fat decreases as a proportion of total bodily tissue.

For a preschool child who is reasonably healthy and happy, physical growth is remarkably smooth and predictable, especially compared to many cognitive and social developments. Overall, physical growth contains no discrete stages, plateaus, or qualitative changes such as those Piaget proposed for cognitive development. At the same time, however, important differences develop among individual children and among groups of children. Often the

TABLE 6.1 Average Height and Weight During Early Childhood

	Girls		Boys	
Age (Years)	Height (inches)	Weight (pounds)	Height (inches)	Weight (pounds)
2	33.5	26.5	34.1	28.6
3	37.0	30.9	37.4	31.7
4	39.8	35.0	40.2	35.3
5	42.3	39.7	42.9	40.8

Source: Centers for Disease Control and Prevention (2000).

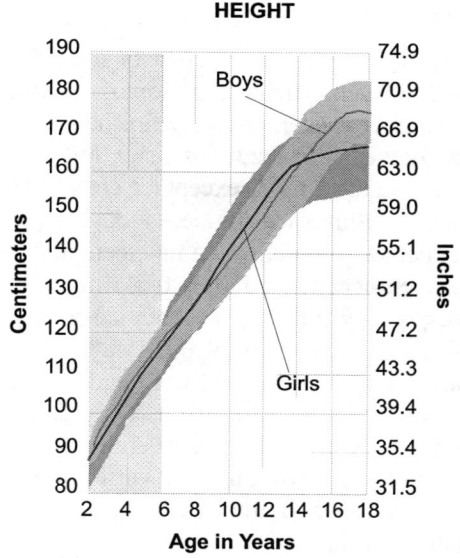
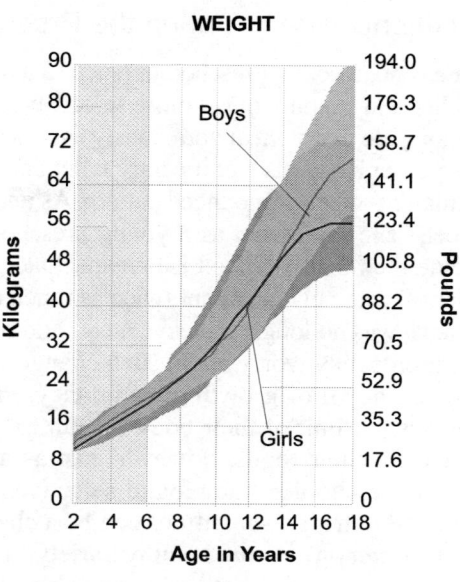

FIGURE 6.1
Growth in Height and Weight from Two to Eighteen Years

differences simply create interesting physical variety among children, but sometimes they do more than affect appearance. Being larger (or smaller) than usual, for example, can make a child stronger (or less strong) than others of the same age, and therefore more (or less) able to master certain sports or other physical activities. Size can also affect how parents and other adults respond to the child; larger children may seem older and be treated as such, whether or not they are psychologically ready. For both reasons, a child might gain (or lose) self-confidence, and even gain (or lose) popularity among peers.

The overall smoothness of growth means that childhood height and weight can predict adult height and weight to a significant extent, although not perfectly. A four-year-old who is above average in height tends to end up above average as an adult. Nevertheless, correlation between childhood height and adult height is imperfect because of individual differences in nutrition and health and, most of all, in the timing of puberty. In particular, children who experience puberty later than average tend to grow taller than children who experience it early (Sanfilippo et al., 1994; Yousefi et al., 2013)—a source of diversity that we will say more about in Chapter 10 in connection with adolescence and its impact.

Genetic Background

Most dimensions of growth are influenced substantially by heredity. Tall parents tend to have tall children, and short parents usually have short children. Weight shows similar patterns, although it can be influenced strongly by habits of exercise and diet.

Races and ethnic groups around the world also differ slightly in average growth patterns (Eveleth & Tanner, 1990), and general trends demonstrate that children born in countries with low to middle income are more likely to be low birth weight (5.5 pounds or less) and to exhibit slower growth throughout childhood (Adair et al., 2013). Children from Asian groups, such as Chinese and Japanese, tend to be shorter than European and North American children are. The latter, in turn, tend to be shorter than children from African societies are. Shape differs among these groups as well, although the differences do not always become obvious until adolescence. Asian children tend to develop short legs and arms relative to their torsos, and relatively broad hips. African children do just the opposite: they tend to develop relatively long limbs and narrow hips. Keep in mind, though, that these differences are only average tendencies. Racial and ethnic groups tend to overlap in size and shape more than they differ (that is what makes us all human!). From the point of view of parents, teachers, and other professionals, the most important physical differences among children are individual ones: there are large and small children in every racial and ethnic group, among both boys and girls, and in every community (Doherty, 1996). If you are responsible for children as individuals, recognizing their individual differences is likely to be your priority.

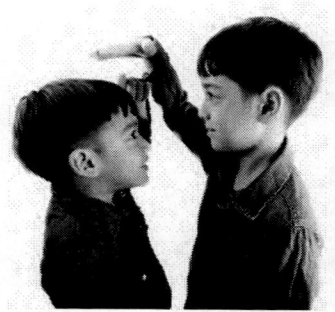

As a result of improvements in nutrition and health care, children in industrialized nations are often taller than in earlier times. But there are important variations among societies—even among industrialized ones—that apparently are influenced genetically.
Source: wckiw/Shutterstock.com.

Chapter 6 Physical and Cognitive Development in Early Childhood

Nutritional Needs During the Preschool Years

For a time, a young preschooler (such as a three-year-old) may eat less than he or she did as a toddler and become much more selective about foods as well. Michael, the son of one of the authors, ate every meal voraciously as a two-year-old; a year later, he rarely finished a meal, even though he was significantly taller and heavier by then. Elizabeth, his sister, followed a similar but more pronounced pattern. As a toddler, she ate most foods except ice cream ("Too sweet," she said!), but as a young preschooler, she sometimes hardly ate—though she did decide then that she liked ice cream. Later, their appetites returned. As a nineteen-year-old, Michael routinely ate about twice as much as other members of the family did. Elizabeth, at sixteen, was no longer a picky eater—and became especially enthusiastic about ice cream.

Parents may worry about such changes, but in fact, they are normal and result from the slowing down of growth after infancy. Preschool children simply do not need as many calories per unit of their body weight as they did immediately after birth. They do need variety in their foods, however, just as adults do, to ensure adequate overall nutrition. Given preschoolers' newfound selectiveness about eating, providing the variety needed for good nutrition sometimes can be a challenge to parents and other caregivers.

How can one ensure healthy variety in a preschool child's diet? Experts generally discourage coercion ("Eat your vegetables because I say so!") because it teaches children to associate undesired foods with unpleasant social experiences (Endres & Rockwell, 1993; Ventura & Worobey, 2013). They also discourage using sweet foods and drinks as a reward for eating undesired foods ("If you eat your vegetables, then you can have your ice cream") because it implicitly overvalues the sweets and undervalues the undesired food still further. For children who are particularly picky and who do not like to try new foods, sticker rewards for trying new foods have been successful (Corsini et al., 2013). In addition, providing many opportunities for children to try foods, even vegetables the children "don't like," in conjunction with nonfood reinforcement like a sticker increases liking for those vegetables (Fildes, van Jaarsveld, Wardle, & Cooke, 2014). The best strategy seems to be casual, repeated exposure to the food without insisting that the child eat it (Andrien, 1994). Getting children involved in age-appropriate food preparation, such as tearing and washing lettuce, cleaning and breaking apart cauliflower or broccoli, and weighing pasta, was linked to children eating more overall, including vegetables (van der Horst, Ferrage, & Rytz, 2014). Observations of children's eating habits confirm what parents often suspect as well: children's food preferences are influenced by the adult models around them. In the long term, preschoolers tend to like the same foods as their parents and other important adults. More generally, as we will see in the Chapter 12 discussion of physical development in early adulthood, they practice many of their parents' other health behaviors (such as exercise) as well.

The Connection Between Health and Poverty

In settings of middle and high socioeconomic status, preschool children as a group are among the healthiest human beings alive, though not as healthy as they will become in childhood, adolescence, and young adulthood. They experience comparatively few major illnesses as long as they get enough of the right things to eat and as long as their parents have reasonable access to modern medical care. As parents often note, preschoolers do experience frequent minor illnesses: various respiratory infections, ear infections, and stomach flus. These typically strike a young child several times per year, which is three or four times as often as for adults and about twice as often as for school-age children (Engels, 1993). For well-fed children whose families have access to medical care, however, these illnesses rarely prove serious or life threatening. Colds and flu do cause worry, as well as create challenges for working parents in arranging childcare.

But this optimistic picture of preschoolers' health may be misleading. Since 1997, when the Children's Health Insurance Program (CHIP), which provides low- or no-cost insurance to children whose families make too much to qualify for Medicaid but cannot afford insurance, passed, rates of uninsured children have decreased significantly. This

> **What Do You Think?**
>
> How do you suppose parents evaluate their child's height and weight? Explore this problem by asking two or three parents how satisfied they are with their child's height and weight. Do you think parents' feelings have any relationship to the actual size of their child?

trend has stabilized with the passage of the Affordable Care Act (ACA), so that currently, only 7 percent of children lack health insurance coverage. However, most states that have not accepted the Medicaid expansion of the ACA have uninsured child rates of 10 percent or higher (Kenney et al., 2014). Young children from these families are substantially less healthy than are those from middle- and high-SES families. Low-SES preschoolers contract 25 to 50 percent more minor illnesses than do preschoolers as a whole, and they are more often malnourished and face food insecurity, meaning that they chronically lack the quantity and quality of food to thrive, as well as essential vitamins, iron, and protein (American Academy of Pediatrics, 1993; McCurdy, Gorman, Kisler, & Metallinos-Katsaras, 2012; Wilkinson, 1996). Children growing up at or near the poverty level are also substantially more likely to be overweight or obese (McCurdy et al., 2012).

Whether in North America or around the world, minor illnesses combined with malnourishment put children's health at risk for additional illnesses, both minor and major. Malnourishment also contributes to delays in social, language, and cognitive development, possibly because it leads to lack of energy and lack of interest in new experiences. In one study based in Kenya (Africa), even a temporary food shortage (due to a few months of local drought) impaired children's health and school performance two years later (McDonald et al., 1994).

How can we counteract these problems? In general, strategies can focus either on individuals and their particular communities or on systematic reorganization of the health care system and food security systems as a whole. Among individually oriented strategies, an important one is to educate children and families about health and nutrition. For example, pamphlets can be distributed in schools or medical clinics, and public health professionals can make presentations in classrooms, community clubs, or churches. However, these efforts work best when they are multifaceted, including education in combination with improving access to high-quality food and health care. The "Focusing On" feature proposes additional alternatives.

Educational activities can be effective if they build on the knowledge of health and nutrition low-SES parents and their children already have and avoid assuming the public is completely ignorant about these matters. Good programs also improve individuals' self-efficacy about engaging in health-promoting behaviors, and as noted earlier, work best when public policy (like changes to the health care system or expanding programs such as the Supplemental Nutrition Assistance Program) makes engaging in health-promoting behaviors easier. In this sort of situation, it is helpful to organize intervention programs aimed at providing parents and children with the knowledge they need. However, such programs must respect the culture and economic situations of the families, which usually influence food preferences in major ways. Put simply, certain foods acquire symbolic meanings (such as turkey for American Thanksgiving), regardless of their precise nutritional value. Other foods may never be tried, no matter how worthwhile they are nutritionally, because they cost too much or seem too strange or foreign to a particular family or cultural group.

Bladder Control

Sometime during the preschool years, to parents' great relief, most children acquire control of their bladder. The process includes many false starts and accidents. Most commonly, daytime control comes before nighttime control, generally beginning between the ages of

Focusing On...

Reforming Children's Health Care

In all societies, the health care system provides less help to poor families than to well-off ones. Low-SES mothers receive less medical attention during pregnancy, causing health problems in themselves or their fetuses to be overlooked, and are more likely to give birth to a low birth-weight infant (Krans & Davis, 2014). Infants of low-income mothers are less likely to receive checkups from a doctor and less likely to be seen by a doctor if they get sick (Bury, 1997; Wilkinson, 1996). However, children who have access to Medicaid and CHIP, described next, are much more likely to get checkups and to see health professionals early in an illness (Rudowitz, Artiga, & Arguello, 2014).

Why does access to health care depend so heavily on personal income? In the United States, medical services for the poor are paid through Medicaid, a federally sponsored insurance program created in the 1960s. It pays for some basic health services, such as taking a child with an ear ache to a general practitioner, but it reimburses the doctor only up to a certain point. Doctors who charge more price themselves out of the market for low-SES families, which have significantly fewer doctors and clinics to choose from but children who experience more illnesses than do children from higher-SES families (Fitzgerald et al., 1994). In 1997, the Children's Health Insurance Program (CHIP) was created, which assists states in providing insurance to children whose families cannot afford insurance but make too much money for Medicaid eligibility. As of 2013, over eight million children in the United States were enrolled in CHIP (Medicaid, 2014).

Though there have been significant strides in improving access to health care for children and adults alike, many children still lack access to health care. In some states, uninsured rates for children are over 15 percent, due in part to lack of parents' awareness of eligibility (Rudowitz, Artiga, & Arguello, 2014).

How can society and concerned individuals reduce these economically based inequalities in health care? Numerous reforms have been proposed centering on one of three ideas: community involvement, prevention, and reorganization of services. Reforms that focus on community involvement seek to reduce the psychological and geographical distance between medical staff and the people they serve. Some hospitals and cities have established small community health clinics in areas of greatest need (the inner city). They hire medical staff who establish rapport with the parents and children who seek help, recruit local community members to serve on their governing and advisory boards, and charge low fees based on families' ability to pay.

Reforms that focus on primary prevention seek to keep disease from striking in the first place. These actions often deal with relatively healthy children (who have not gotten sick yet) and the conditions that make illness likely rather than illness itself. Lead poisoning is a good example: community health experts often cite lead as one of the most hazardous health threats to preschool children (Tesman & Hills, 1994). Lead accumulates in the body and eventually damages the nervous system and can cause death. People pick it up accidentally from many sources, but the most prominent culprit is the interior wall paint used in about 75 percent of all homes and apartments built before 1980. Because there is no cure for lead poisoning, prevention strategies have dominated the response of the health care profession: educating parents to the dangers, pressing for legislation outlawing lead-based paints (and lead-based gasoline), removing leaded paint in some homes, and checking/remediating local water systems when tap water tests high for lead content.

Reforms that focus on reorganization generally involve more self-conscious planning of medical services. Immunization and health-screening programs based in schools, for example, allow programs to reach a higher percentage of children than programs in community health clinics (Behrman, 1993; Behr-man & Stacey, 1997; Jacob et al., 2016). "Front-line" professionals often can improve access dramatically without compromising quality of care: most childhood illnesses, for example, can be treated effectively by a nurse as long as the nurse knows when a particular illness deserves referral to the doctor and appropriate specialized services are indeed available.

What Do You Think?

1. Look back on your own elementary school hearing or eye tests from the point of view of the teachers and nurses. Can you see any limitations to "mass screening," as well as advantages to it?

2. Is there a case to be made for *limiting* health care to the poor? What would it be? And what might be the long-term implications of limiting health care?

> **What Do You Think?**
>
> Suppose you are a teacher or caregiver at a childcare center, and one of your children often seems hungry throughout the day. How could you tell whether the child is undernourished or simply has a big appetite? Compare your strategies for answering this question with those of a classmate.

two and three (Bloom, Seeley, Ritchey, & McGuire, 1993) and becoming reliable for most children by the age of four (Jansson, Hanson, Sillén, & Hellström, 2005), although individual children vary widely and somewhat unpredictably. Typically, too, daytime control of the bladder occurs at very nearly the same time. Some pediatricians believe this fact implies that children decide when they wish to begin exercising control, perhaps to begin feeling more grown up. In the early stages of toilet training, therefore, reminders and parent-led visits to the toilet may make little difference to most toddlers. Nonetheless, they may help in the long term as a form of behavioral conditioning: a child comes to associate seeing and sitting on the toilet with the relief of emptying a full bladder, as well as with the praise parents confer on the child for successes.

Nighttime bladder control often takes much longer to achieve than daytime control. About one-half of all three-year-olds still wet their beds at least some of the time, and as many as one in five six-year-olds do the same (American Psychiatric Association, 1994). The timing of nighttime control depends on several factors, such as how deeply children sleep and how large their bladders are. It also depends on anxiety level; worried children tend to wet their beds more often than relaxed children do. Unfortunately, parents sometimes contribute to young children's anxieties by becoming overly frustrated about changing wet sheets night after night.

Achieving bladder control reflects the large advances children make during the preschool years in controlling their bodies in general. It also reflects parents' accumulated efforts to encourage physical self-control for their children. The combined result is that children of this age can begin focusing on what they actually want to do with their bodies.

Motor Skill Development

As young children grow, they become more skilled at performing basic physical actions. Often a two-year-old can walk only with considerable effort; hence the term *toddler*. But a five-year-old can walk comfortably in a variety of ways: forward and backward, quickly and slowly, skipping and galloping. A five-year-old also can do other vigorous things that were impossible a few years earlier. Running, jumping, and climbing all occur with increasing smoothness and variety. Children can carry out certain actions that require accuracy, such as balancing on one foot, catching a ball reliably, or drawing a picture.

In this section, we examine in more detail how children reach milestones such as these. Because family conditions vary a great deal, we will make certain assumptions. In particular, we will assume children have no significant fears of being active—that they have a reasonably (but not excessively) daring attitude toward trying out new motor skills, they are in good health, and their physical growth has evolved more or less optimally. These assumptions do not hold for all children or families, as we note later in this section, but they make a good starting point for understanding motor development.

In the long run, successful bladder control depends on both physical growth and the child's own motivation. Forcing children prematurely to control themselves may produce results, but only in the immediate future.
Source: Maurizio Milanesio/Shutterstock.com.

Fundamental Motor Skills

Healthy preschool children obviously have moved well beyond the confines of reflex action, which constituted the first motor skills of infancy. From ages two to about five, they experiment with the simple voluntary actions that adults use extensively for their normal activities, such as walking, running, and jumping (Kalverboer et al., 1993). For older children, these actions usually are the means to other ends. For very young children, they lie very much in the foreground and frequently are goals in themselves. Table 6.2 summarizes some of these activities.

> **What Do You Think?**
>
> Imagine how you would talk to a parent who was concerned about the child's bed-wetting at night. What would you say? If you or your instructor can arrange it, try acting out a meeting to discuss bed-wetting between a concerned parent and a childcare center worker or director.

Walking and Running

From a child's point of view, walking may seem absurd at first: it requires purposely losing balance, then regaining balance rapidly enough to keep from falling (Rose & Gamble, 1993). As older infants, children still must pay attention to these facts, even after a full year or so of practice. Each step is an effort in itself. Children watch each foot in turn as it launches (or lurches) forward; they may pause after each step before attempting the next. By their second or third birthday, however, their steps become more regular and their feet get closer together (Adolph et al., 2012). Stride, the distance between feet in a typical step, remains considerably shorter than that of a typical adult. This makes short distances easy to walk but long distances hard to navigate for a few more years.

Jumping

At first, a jump is more like a fast stretch: the child reaches for the sky rapidly, but her feet fail to leave the ground. Sometime around her second birthday, one foot, or even both feet, may finally leave the ground. Such early successes may be delayed, however, because the child may thrust her arms backward to help herself take off, as though trying to push herself off the floor. Later, perhaps around age three, she shifts to a more efficient arm movement—reaching forward and upward as she jumps—which creates a useful upward momentum.

Success in these actions depends partly on the type of jump the child is attempting. Jumping down a step is easier than jumping across a flat distance, and a flat or broad jump is easier than a jump up a step. By age five or so, most children can broad-jump across a few feet, although variations among individuals are substantial.

TABLE 6.2 Milestones in Preschool Motor Development

Approximate Age	Gross Motor Skill	Fine Motor Skill
2.5–3.5 years	Walks well; runs in straight line; jumps in air with both feet	Copies a circle; scribbles; can use eating utensils; stacks a few small blocks
3.5–4.5 years	Has a walking stride 80 percent that of adult; runs at one-third adult speed; throws and catches large ball, but is stiff-armed	Buttons with large buttons; copies simple shapes; makes simple representational drawings
4.5–5.5 years	Balances on one foot; runs far without falling; can "swim" in water for short distance	Uses scissors; draws people; copies simple letters and numbers; builds complex structures with blocks

Note: The ages given above are approximate, and skills vary with the life experiences available to individual children and with the situations in which the skills are displayed.

Source: Kalverboer et al. (1993).

Throwing and Catching

For infants and toddlers, first throws may consist of simply waving an object, releasing it suddenly, and watching it take off. Once intentional throwing begins, however, children actually adopt more stereotyped methods initially, using a general forward lurch, regardless of the ball's size or weight. As skill develops, children vary their movements according to the size of the ball. Catching proceeds through analogous phases, from stereotyped, passive extension of arms to flexible movement of hands in a last-minute response to the oncoming ball.

Fine Motor Coordination: The Case of Drawing Skills

Not all motor activities of young children involve the strength, agility, and balance of their whole bodies. Many require the coordination of small movements but not strength. Tying shoelaces calls for such **fine motor coordination**; so do washing hands, buttoning and zipping clothing, eating with a spoon, and turning a doorknob.

fine motor coordination Ability to carry out smoothly small movements that involve precise timing but not strength.

One especially widespread fine motor skill among young children is drawing. In North American culture, at least, virtually every young child tries using pens or pencils at some time and often tries other artistic media as well. The scribbles or drawings that result probably serve a number of purposes. At times, they may be used mainly for sensory exploration; a child may want to get the feel of paintbrushes or felt-tip pens. At other times, drawings may express thoughts or feelings; a child may suggest this possibility by commenting, "It's a horse, and it's angry." Children's drawings also probably reflect their knowledge of the world, even though they may not yet have the fine motor skills they need to convey their knowledge fully. In other words, children's drawings reveal not only fine motor coordination but also their self-concepts, emotional and social attitudes, and cognitive development.

Drawing shows two overlapping phases of development during early childhood. From about two and a half to four years of age, children focus on developing nonrepresentational skills, such as scribbling and purposeful drawing of simple shapes and designs. Sometime around age four, they begin attempting to represent objects (Coles, 1992). Yet, although representational drawings usually follow nonrepresentational ones, the two types stimulate each other simultaneously. Children often describe their early scribbles as though they referred to real things, and their practice at portraying real objects helps them to further develop their nonrepresentational skills (Coates & Coates, 2006).

Prerepresentational Drawing

Around the end of infancy, children begin to scribble. A two-year-old experiments with whatever pen, crayon, or pencil is available, almost regardless of its color or type, behaving like an infant and like a child. As with an infant, efforts focus primarily on the activity

Skills that require fine motor coordination—like creating this drawing—develop through identifiable steps or stages. At first, children tend to make random marks or scribbles; later, they coordinate these into patterns; still later, they coordinate patterns into representations of objects that become increasingly recognizable by parents and teachers.
Source: borisow/Shutterstock.com.

Chapter 6 Physical and Cognitive Development in Early Childhood

itself: on the motions and sensations of handling a pen or pencil. But like an older child, the two-year-old often cares about the outcome of these activities: "That's a Mommy," he says of his drawing, whether it looks much like one or not. Contrary to a popular view of children's art, even very young children are concerned not only with the process of drawing but with the product as well (Broughton et al., 1996).

A child's interest in the results of her drawing shows up in the patterns she imposes on even her earliest scribbles. Sometimes, she fills up particular parts of the page quite intentionally—the whole left side, say, or the complete middle third. And she often emphasizes particular categories of strokes: lots of straight diagonals or many counterclockwise loops. Different children select different types of motions for emphasis, so the motions are less like universal stages than like elements of a personal style.

Representational Drawing

While preschool children improve their scribbling skills, they also develop an interest in representing people, objects, and events in their drawings. This interest often far precedes their ability to do so. A three-year-old may assign meanings to scribbles or blobs in his drawing; one blob may be "Mama," and another may be "our house." Events may happen to these blobs, too: Mama may be "going to the store" or "looking for me." During the early childhood years, and for a long time thereafter, the child's visual representations are limited by comparatively rudimentary fine motor skills. Apparently, children know more, visually speaking, than their hands can portray with pens or brushes. Only as children reach school age do their drawings of people become relatively realistic.

What happens to drawing skills beyond the preschool years depends on a child's experiences and on the encouragement (or lack thereof) received from others. Drawings in later years become even more realistic—more "photographic" or draftsmanlike in style. But not all children stay with art in the long term, due to the combined influence of competing academic interests, the priorities of friends, or even dislike of a teacher. We will discuss these types of influence again in Chapter 9 in connection with social and motivational changes during middle childhood.

Gender Differences in Physical Development

As is true during infancy, preschool boys and girls develop at almost exactly the same average rates. This applies to practically any motor skill of which young children are capable, and it applies to both gross and fine motor skills. Any nursery classroom, therefore, is likely to contain children of both sexes who can run very well and children of both sexes who can paint well or tie their shoelaces without help. This is especially true among younger preschool children (age three or four).

By the time children begin kindergarten (usually at age five), slight gender differences in physical development and motor skills appear, with boys tending to be (slightly) bigger, stronger, and faster (Kalverboer et al., 1993) and with better ball skills, while girls demonstrate better manual dexterity (Junaid & Fellowes, 2006). Yet these differences are noticeable only as averages and only by basing the averages on very large numbers of children. Despite the slight differences, therefore, more than 95 percent of children are more skillful and bigger than some members of *both* sexes, and less skillful and smaller than certain others of both sexes.

By the time children start school, a few children in any community are bigger, stronger, and faster than *any* other children, and most of them are boys. Furthermore, these few individuals may get much more than their share of attention because of their superior physical skills. This contributes to the (mistaken) impression that boys are larger and more skillful than girls *in general*. In this way (among many others) are stereotypes born.

The differences in motor skills might be more accurately called *gender* differences than *sex* differences because they probably derive partly from the social roles boys and girls begin learning early in the preschool years. Part of the role differences includes how preschool children spend their time. Preschool boys do spend more time than girls in active and rough-and-tumble play, and girls spend more time doing quiet activities such as drawing or playing with stuffed animals. Children of both sexes, furthermore, reinforce or support one another more for engaging in gender-typed activities, behavioral shaping that is often less flexible for boys than for girls (Davies, 1991; Kite, Deaux, & Haines, 2008). These differences may create the twin impressions that boys are less capable of fine motor skills and that girls are physically weaker, or at least are less inclined toward gross motor activity.

Variations in Motor Skill Development

Although the preceding sections may have implied that young children acquire motor skills at highly similar rates, in reality they show considerable variability in both fundamental and fine motor skill development. At age three, some children already can walk fast and catch a ball skillfully, but others are still having trouble with both tasks. At age five, some children can use scissors skillfully to cut out shapes for kindergarten art projects, but others still find scissors difficult or even mystifying. Whatever the motor skill, individual children will vary at it.

Like other human differences, these probably result from variations in experience, motivation, and biological endowment. Because of family background or preschool educational experiences, some children may be encouraged more than usual toward active play. Not surprisingly, they develop the skills for active play—like running, jumping, or throwing—sooner than children who experience less encouragement for active play. Weight also plays a role. Children who are overweight or obese lag behind their normal-weight peers in gross motor skills—a gap that grows over time (D'Hondt et al., 2013). Research has demonstrated that children with parents who engage in more physical activity, particularly if that activity is with their children, are more active, skilled, and healthy (Hinkley et al., 2008; Loprinzi & Trost, 2010; Spurrier et al., 2008).

Experience also plays a large role in drawing or other fine-motor activities. Some children receive more encouragement and opportunity than others. Early successes breed satisfaction with the emerging skills and encourage the development of motivation to refine the initial skills further. Before long, as we saw earlier in the case of gender differences in motor skill development, small initial differences in opportunity and skill become larger differences in skill and motivation.

Biological and genetic background probably also plays a role in motor skill development, although for most children it is hard to sort out how strong these influences are. The most obvious evidence for biological influence—as well as for the questionability of its importance—is the experiences of children with physical disabilities. A child born with cerebral palsy (a disorder of the nervous system that impairs motor coordination) may not

On the average, boys and girls develop motor skills at almost the same rate during the preschool years. But marked differences emerge among individuals within each sex, even at this age.
Source: Andresr/Shutterstock.com.

Chapter 6 Physical and Cognitive Development in Early Childhood

> **What Do You Think?**
>
> Suppose you are a childcare center worker, and one of your four-year-olds seems to be especially clumsy at throwing and catching a ball. Should you do something about this, and if so, what should you do? Consult with a classmate for a second opinion. Would you feel the same way if the child seemed clumsy or "uninspired" at drawing?

learn to walk, jump, throw, or draw at the same times or to the same extent as a child who never experiences this condition. Yet contrary to common stereotypes of children with disabilities, the motor development of a child with cerebral palsy is *not* determined solely by the disability; it is also determined by the child's opportunities and encouragement to learn new motor skills. The final motor achievements of children with this disability will show diversity just as will the achievements of nonhandicapped peers, and some of the diversity will be the result of education, not biology (Smith, 1998).

The Impact of Children's Growth on Adults

Even though physical growth unfolds largely independently of other forms of development in infancy, growth interacts indirectly in a number of ways with a child's social relationships. A child's physical appearance and particular motor skills can affect how adults and older children respond to the child. A family's attitudes, as well as their economic and social circumstances, can affect opportunities for children to acquire physical skills, and constrain opportunities as well.

Effects of Appearance

From birth—and despite the biases from their own parents—children vary in how attractive their faces seem to adults and other children. As a rule, some individuals look younger than others of the same age. In general, having a young-looking face depends on having large features and a large forehead; that is, facial features should be wide-set and located relatively low on the front of the skull. Even slight changes in these proportions—just a fraction of an inch—can make an adult seem many years older or younger, an infant seem six months older or younger, or a preschooler seem one or two years older or younger.

In general, younger-looking children are also rated as more attractive than older-looking children by both adults and peers, and adults tend to expect more mature behaviors from older-looking children (Parsons, Young, Kumari, Stein, & Kringelbach, 2011). This coincidence of stereotypes—of youthfulness and attractiveness—may contribute to differences in how parents and other adults respond to preschoolers as individuals. Parents and other caregivers need to be made aware of these possibilities, even if differences in response stem partly from innate human reactions to infantile (or babylike) appearance.

Effects of Motor Skills

Consider the changes in size that preschool children experience. A two-year-old often is still small enough to be handled. When necessary, parents can pick up and move a child from one place to another, physically removing the child from danger, and carrying the child (at least partway) if a distance is too far. By age five, a child often has outgrown these physical interactions, not only figuratively but literally. Parents or other adults may still lift and cuddle the child sometimes in play or in an emergency, but they probably are beginning to avoid doing so on a regular basis. To a significant extent, the child may now simply be too bulky and tall. More and more rarely can parents save the child from danger by picking the child up or by speeding the child along a long hallway by carrying the child piggyback. Parents must somehow get children to do these things for themselves.

Usually, of course, parents succeed at this task. By age five, a child can think and talk about her own actions much more than before, and these improvements help guide her own actions. The handling that used to be literal now becomes mostly figurative. Now *handling* means negotiating and discussing with the child rather than lifting her up or carting her around.

Improvements in motor skills also change the agenda for a child's daily activities. A two-year-old may spend a good part of his day experimenting with fundamental skills: walking from one room to another, tearing toilet paper to shreds, or taking pots and pans out of a cupboard. These activities often are embedded in an active social and cognitive life: the child may smile (or frown) at his parents while he works and may "talk" about what he is doing as well. But the motor aspects of his activities absorb a significant part of his attention throughout the day. The child may return repeatedly to a staircase, for instance, as though compelled to get the hang of climbing it; no reward needs to lie at the top step except the satisfaction of a job well done.

A two-year-old's parents therefore must spend a lot of time ensuring that the child comes to no physical harm during motor explorations. They must make sure the child does not fall down the stairs, tumble into the toilet bowl, or discover a sharp knife among the pots. Their role as safety experts can dominate their contacts with the child, particularly if the child is active. Table 6.3 lists common accidents, remedies, and preventions.

By the end of early childhood, minute-to-minute physical surveillance recedes in importance, even though, of course, a concern about safety remains. Rules about dangers make their appearance ("Don't climb on that fence; it's rickety"), along with the hope that a five-year-old can remember and follow the rules at least some of the time. The shift toward rules also results from increasing confidence in the child's motor skills. Now parents are apt to believe their child can go up and down stairs without stumbling very often—and they are usually right.

During the preschool period, many parents discover a special need for patience in their dealings with their children. Simple actions such as tying shoelaces or putting on socks may take longer than before, simply because children now insist on doing many of these things themselves. For similar reasons, walking to the store may now take longer; a three- or four-year-old may prefer to push the stroller rather than ride in it, thus slowing everyone down. And preschoolers may have their own agenda on a walk, such as noticing little rocks on the sidewalk or airplanes in the sky, which differ from parents' goals. On good days, these behaviors offer some of the joys of raising children, but on bad days, they often irritate even the most patient of parents.

The new motor skills that preschoolers develop bring new risks and create new safety concerns for parents and other caregivers. What hazards may be waiting for this boy? And how should adults deal with them?
Source: Viacheslav Nikolaenko/Shutterstock.com.

Chapter 6 Physical and Cognitive Development in Early Childhood

TABLE 6.3 Common Accidents, Remedies, and Preventions Among Preschoolers

Accidents	What to Do	How to Prevent
Drowning	Unless you are trained in water safety, extend a stick or other device. Use heart massage and mouth-to-mouth breathing when and as long as needed.	Teach children to swim as early in life as possible. Supervise children's swim sessions closely. Have children stay in shallow water.
Choking on small objects	If a child is still breathing, do not attempt to remove object; see a doctor instead. If breathing stops, firmly strike child twice on small of back. If this does not help, grab child from behind, put your fist just under his or her ribs, and pull upward sharply several times.	Do not allow children to put small objects in their mouths. Teach them to eat slowly, taking small bites. Forbid vigorous play with objects or food in mouth.
Cuts with serious bleeding	Raise cut above level of heart; apply pressure with cloth or bandage. If necessary, apply pressure to main arteries of limbs.	Remove sharp objects from play areas. Insist on shoes wherever ground or floor may contain sharp objects. Supervise children's use of knives.
Fractures	Keep injured limb immobile; see a doctor.	Discourage climbing and exploring in dangerous places, such as trees and construction sites. Allow bicycles only in safe areas.
Burns	Pour cold water over burned area; keep it clean; then cover with *sterile* bandage. See a doctor if burn is extensive.	Keep matches out of reach of children. Keep children well away from fires and hot stoves.
Poisons	On skin or eye, flush with plenty of water. If in stomach, phone poison control center doctor for instructions. Induce vomiting only for selected substances.	Keep dangerous substances out of reach of children. Throw away poisons when no longer needed. Keep syrup of ipecac in home to induce vomiting, but use *only* if advised by doctor.
Animal bites	Clean and cover with bandage; see a doctor.	Train children when and how to approach family pets. Teach them caution in approaching unfamiliar animals.
Insect bites	Remove stinger, if possible. Cover with paste of bicarbonate of soda (for bees) or a few drops of vinegar (for wasps and hornets).	Encourage children to recognize and avoid insects that sting, as well as their nests. Encourage children to remain calm in the presence of stinging insects.
Poisonous plants (e.g., poison ivy)	Remove affected clothing. Wash affected skin with strong alkali soap as soon as possible.	Teach children to recognize toxic plants. Avoid areas where poisonous plants grow.

Source: Adapted from O'Keefe (1998).

Effects of Differences in Families

A child's growth has a different impact on adults depending on the priorities of parents and on the circumstances of the family and community to which the child belongs. What seems like a risky behavior to one parent (e.g., climbing up on a large boulder) may seem like constructive skill building to another, with consequent differences in encouragement or prohibitions for the child. What seems like a healthy amount of weight for a child to one parent may seem skinny (or plump) to another, with consequent differences in parents' unconscious appraisals of the child's attractiveness.

But settings and circumstances matter as well. In families with many children and few adults, child minding may become the responsibility of older siblings as much as (or more than) of adults. In extended families—those with nonparental relatives living at home or nearby—child minding may become partly the responsibility of other adult relatives. If parents work (or if a single parent works), relatives or other "caregivers for hire" take on much of the responsibility. All of these circumstances alter the settings in

> **What Do You Think?**
>
> How did your own parents' work schedules, the number of children in your family, and family finances influence the joy or irritation they experienced? Did the *number* of parents raising you (one or more than one) make a difference?

which preschoolers grow and the relationships that become prominent during early childhood. Some settings may provide the child with safer places for physical exploration than do other settings, resulting in fewer worries about safety expressed by caregivers. Some families may include so many children that differences in a particular child's physical appearance make little difference simply because caregivers are distributing their attention widely among many children or activities. Individual parents may or may not be aware that alternatives to their particular childcare arrangements exist, and because they often have not participated in the alternatives, they may find them hard to appreciate. But the range of childcare arrangements is very real, as is the range of opportunities they offer to young children (Cannella, 1997).

COGNITIVE DEVELOPMENT

In addition to their physical changes, preschool children develop new abilities to represent objects and experiences. They begin to notice, for example, that their particular way of viewing the objects across a room differs from the perspective of a family member already sitting on the other side. They begin to distinguish between appearances and reality; that is, when you cover a doll with a costume, it still is "really" the same doll. And they become able to communicate new understandings such as these to others. The changes are in thinking, or *cognition,* and are called *cognitive development.*

Thinking Among Preschoolers

Much of the research on cognitive development owes its intellectual roots to the observations and theorizing of Jean Piaget. During the 1960s and 1970s, considerable effort went toward testing his ideas about cognitive development. Overall, the research led first to modifications of, and in some cases, challenges to, Piaget's major proposals, such as the existence of comprehensive cognitive stages that unfold in a predictable order or the idea that thinking is really an individual activity rather than a social one. To put these later findings in proper context, however, we must first keep in mind Piaget's key ideas about the changes young children experience during the preschool years.

Piaget's Preoperational Stage

At about age two, according to Piaget, children enter a new stage in their cognitive development (Piaget, 1963; Wadsworth, 1996). Infancy has left them with several important accomplishments, such as the belief that objects have a permanent existence and the capacity to set and follow simple goals, such as emptying all the clothes from every drawer in the house. Infancy has also left them with the knowledge that all of their senses register the same world; now a child knows that hearing his mother in the next room means that he will probably see her soon and that seeing her probably also means he will hear from her.

The **preoperational stage**, roughly ages two through seven, extends and transforms these skills. During this stage, children become increasingly proficient at using *symbols*—words or actions that stand for other things. During this period, they also extend their belief in object permanence to include *identities,* or constancies, of many types: a candle remains the same even as it grows shorter from burning, and a plant growing on the windowsill remains the same plant, even though its growth changes its appearance from day to day.

preoperational stage
In Piaget's theory, the stage of cognition characterized by increasing use of symbolic thinking but not yet by logical groupings of concepts.

The play of preschoolers often relies on their growing abilities to represent objects and events symbolically. A cardboard box becomes a car, and the porch becomes a racetrack.
Source: Orange-studio/Shutterstock.com.

Preoperational children also sense many *functional relationships,* or variations in their environments that normally occur together. Preschool children usually know that the hungrier they are, the more they will want to eat; the bigger they are, the stronger they tend to be; and the faster they walk, the sooner they will arrive somewhere. Of course, they still do not know the precise functions or relationships in these examples—exactly how *much* faster they will arrive if they walk a particular distance more quickly—but they do know that a relationship exists.

These are all cognitive strengths of preschool children, and they mark cognitive advances over infancy. But as the *pre-* in the term *preoperational* implies, Piaget's original theorizing actually focused on the limitations of young children's thinking relative to that of school-age children. The term *operations* referred to mental actions that allow a child to reason about events he or she experiences. Piaget's observations suggested that from age two to seven, children often confuse their own points of view with those of other people, cannot classify objects and events logically, and often are misled by single features of their experiences. As later sections of this chapter point out, however, more recent research has substantially qualified this perspective; in essence, it has found that children often are more cognitively astute than Piaget realized. Their specific cognitive skills are all based on a key ability that Piaget *did* recognize: the ability to represent experiences symbolically.

Symbolic Thought

As we just noted, *symbols* are words, objects, or behaviors that stand for something else. They take this role not because of their intrinsic properties but because of the intentions of the people who use them. A drinking straw is just a hollow tube and does not become a symbol until a preschooler places it in the middle of a mound of sand and declares it to be a birthday candle. Likewise, the sound /bahks/ lacks symbolic meaning unless we all agree that it refers to a hollow object with corners: *box.*

Probably the most significant cognitive achievement of the preoperational period is the emergence and elaboration of **symbolic thought**, the ability to think by making one object or action stand for another. Throughout their day, two-year-olds use language symbolically, such as when they say "Milk!" to procure a white, drinkable substance from the refrigerator. They also use symbolic thought in make-believe play by pretending to be people or creatures other than themselves. By about age four, children's symbolic play often combines complex actions (getting down on all fours), objects (using a table napkin for a saddle), language (shouting "Neigh!"), and coordination with others (getting a friend to be a rider).

symbolic thought Mentally using one thing to represent something else.

Symbolic thinking helps preschool children organize and process what they know (Carlson & Beck, 2009; Goldman, 1998; Nelson, 1996). Objects and experiences can be recalled more easily if they have names and compared more easily if the child has concepts that can describe their features. Symbols also help children communicate what they know to others, even in situations quite different from the experience itself. Having gone to the store, they can convey this experience to others either in words ("I went shopping") or through pretend play ("Let's play school, and I'll be the teacher."). By its nature, communication fosters social relationships among children, but it also fosters cognitive development by allowing individual children to learn from the experiences of others. More precisely, communication allows individuals to learn from the symbolic representations of others' experiences.

Egocentrism in Preschool Children

Egocentrism refers to the tendency of a person to confuse his or her own point of view and that of another person. The term does not necessarily imply selfishness at the expense of others, but a centering on the self in thinking. Young children often show egocentrism in this sense, but not always. Piaget illustrated their egocentrism by showing children a table on which models of three mountains had been constructed and asking them how a doll would see the three mountains if it sat at various positions around the table. Three-year-olds (the ones in Piaget's preoperational stage) commonly believed the doll saw the layout no differently than they did (Piaget & Inhelder, 1967).

egocentrism Inability to distinguish between one's own point of view and that of another person.

On the other hand, when the task concerns more familiar materials and settings, even preschool children adopt others' spatial perspectives (Steiner, 1987). For example, instead of using Piaget's three-mountain model, suppose we use a "police officer" doll that is searching for a "child" doll and place them among miniature barriers that sometimes obscure the dolls' "view" of each other and sometimes do not. When these procedures are followed, four-year-olds have relatively little difficulty knowing when the two dolls can "see" each other and when the barriers truly are "in the way."

In oral communication, preschoolers also show distinct but incomplete egocentrism. A variety of studies have documented that preschoolers often explain tasks rather poorly to others, even though their language and understanding are otherwise skillful enough to explain them better (Nelson, 1996). Copying a simple diagram according to instructions from a preschooler can prove next to impossible, no matter how sensitive the listener is. On the other hand, preschool children do show awareness of the needs of a listener. They explain a drawing more clearly, for example, to a listener who is blindfolded, apparently because the blindfold emphasizes the listener's need for more complete information.

In these studies, young children show both similarity to and difference from the adults they will become. All of us, young or old, show egocentrism at times; indeed, our own thinking is often the only framework on which we can base our actions and conversations with others, at least initially. As we mature, though, we learn more about others' thoughts, views, and feelings, as well as more about how to express ourselves more precisely. In these ways, we (hopefully!) differ from four-year-olds.

Other Aspects of Children's Conceptual Development

Along with their symbolic skills, preschool children develop specific cognitive skills. They become able to classify objects, and by the end of the early childhood period, some can even attend to changes in objects involving more than one feature at a time. They move beyond rote counting to a meaningful understanding of the concept of *number*. They also acquire an intuitive sense of the differences among fundamentally different types of concepts, such as the difference between a living dog and a toy robot made to act like a dog.

Classification Skills

Classification refers to the placement of objects in groups or categories according to some specific standards or criteria. Young preschool children, even those just three years old, can reliably classify objects that differ in just one dimension, or feature,

classification Grouping of objects according to standards or criteria.

Chapter 6 Physical and Cognitive Development in Early Childhood

especially if that dimension presents fairly obvious contrasts. Given a collection of pennies and nickels, a preschooler usually can sort them by color, which is their most obvious dimension of difference. Given a boxful of silverware, a young child might sort the items by type: knives, forks, and spoons. Or she might group dishes by how they are used in real life, putting each cup with one saucer rather than separating all the cups from all the saucers. These simple groupings represent cognitive advances over infancy.

Reversibility and Conservation

reversibility Ability to return mentally to earlier steps in a problem.

Some classification problems require **reversibility** in thinking, or the ability to undo a problem mentally and go back to its beginning. If you accidentally drop a pile of papers on the floor, you may be annoyed, but you know that in principle the papers are all there: you believe (correctly) that the papers that have scattered can be "unscattered" if you pick them up and sort them into their correct order again. Reversibility, it turns out, contributes to a major cognitive achievement of middle childhood: **conservation**, or the ability to perceive that certain properties of an object remain the same or constant despite changes in the object's appearance. On average, children do not achieve conservation until about age six.

conservation A belief that certain properties (such as quantity) remain constant, despite changes in perceived features, such as dimensions, position, and shape.

To understand reversibility and conservation, consider the task shown in Figure 6.2. First, you show a preschool child two tall glasses with exactly the same amount of water in each. Then the child watches you pour the water from one of the glasses into a third, wide glass. Naturally, the water line in the wide glass will be lower than it was in the tall one. Finally, you ask the child, "Is there more water in the wide glass than in the [remaining] tall glass, or less, or just as much?"

Children less than five years old typically say that the tall glass has either less or more water than the wide glass, but not that the two glasses are the same. According to Piaget, this happens because the child forgets the identity of the water levels seen only a moment earlier; in this sense, the child is a nonreversible thinker and cannot imagine pouring the water back again to prove the glasses' equality. Instead, the child is limited to current appearances. More often than not, a big difference in appearance leads a child to say that the amount of water changes as a result of its being poured. In Piagetian terms, the child fails to conserve, or to believe in the constancy of the amount of liquid, despite its visible changes (Inhelder & Piaget, 1958). Not until the early school years do conservation and reversibility become firmly established.

FIGURE 6.2
Conservation of Liquid Quantity

Does a child believe that liquid quantity remains constant (is "conserved"), despite changes in its shape? The method illustrated here, or some variation of it, is often used to answer this question.

In the meantime, tasks that require conservation are affected significantly by how they are presented or described to the child. When given a series of conservation tasks, for example, a child tends to alternate conserving with nonconserving responses (Elbers et al., 1991). Why? Perhaps repeating the question makes some children believe that the experimenter wants them to change their response; after all, why else would she repeat

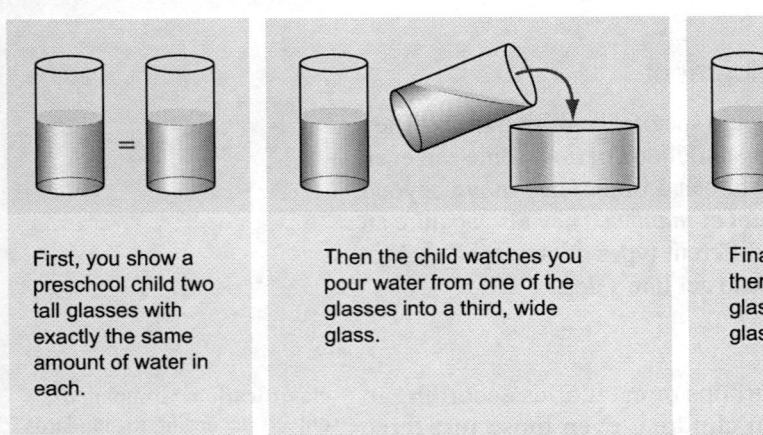
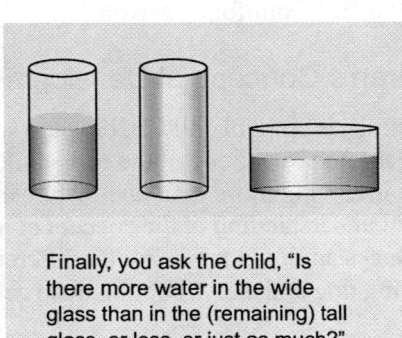

First, you show a preschool child two tall glasses with exactly the same amount of water in each.

Then the child watches you pour water from one of the glasses into a third, wide glass.

Finally, you ask the child, "Is there more water in the wide glass than in the (remaining) tall glass, or less, or just as much?"

A child who lacks reversibility (is nonconserving) in thinking about liquids says either, "The tall glass has more," or "The wide glass has more." The child is fooled by its appearance.

Part 3 Early Childhood

herself? Because most children begin the conservation task by agreeing that the glasses hold equal amounts of water, obliging children may feel compelled to give nonconserving responses against their own better judgment. It seems, therefore, that children may take Piagetian tasks as social events, as well as cognitive ones.

The Concept of Number

Like many parents, Piaget correctly noted that children do not fully grasp how the conventional number system works during the first few years of life (Piaget, 1952). Preschoolers may, of course, count, such as when a three-year-old says, "One, two, three, blast off!" before tossing a ball high into the air. But such counting, Piaget argued, lacks understanding; it essentially is a rote activity, though children as young as two or three understand the *magnitude* of numbers, which is demonstrated when a child asks for "more" or "a lot more" when a parent is doling out a treat (Ginsburg, Cannon, Eisenband, & Pappas, 2008). To fully understand the concept of number, a child must comprehend three ideas. The first is that a one-to-one correspondence exists between items in a set and number names. The second is *cardinality*, the idea that the total number of a set corresponds to the last number named when the items are counted. And the third is *ordinality*, the concept that numbers always occur in a particular order (the second item to be counted is always called the "second," for example).

Research stimulated by these ideas about number generally has concluded that Piaget underestimated preschoolers' knowledge of number. Many four-year-olds, and even some three-year-olds, can reliably say the numbers in sequence, at least up to some modest limit such as *five* or *six*. They also know that different sets of items should be counted with the same sequence of numbers, that each item should be counted only once, and that any set can be counted in more than one order. For this and other reasons, some psychologists have argued that children may have an innate conception of number, or at least that they can learn underlying notions of number from appropriate experiences during infancy (Case, 1998; Ginsburg et al., 2008; Kirschner, 1997).

Cognition as Social Activity

Variations in cognitive performance occur partly because young children depend on the social context or circumstances to develop new thinking skills. In spite of our stereotypes of thinking as a solitary, independent activity, children learn not only from interacting with objects and the physical environment but also from interacting with adults or others with more experience. Psychologists who study this sort of thinking often call it **situated cognition** and call their perspective **social constructivism** (Kirschner & Whitson, 1997; Rogoff et al., 1993). A parent who is cooking dinner, for example, may invite a four-year-old to help with preparations, during which the child observes and works on a number of cognitive tasks: measuring amounts for ingredients, sequencing the steps in the preparations, attending to the time needed for each task. Interactions about the tasks being pursued in common form a context, or **activity setting**, for learning (Lave, 1997). In an activity setting, the older or less experienced individuals provide problems and activities, as well as tasks that allow a younger, less experienced person to become a legitimate—though perhaps marginal or peripheral—participant in the situation. When cooking, for example, the parent determines the menu and in other ways sets the agenda for the activity: "We will make X instead of Y tonight." The parent also provides tasks for the apprentice-cook (in this case, the child) to do. The tasks ensure that the child belongs or participates successfully, although they also provide only a marginal role for the child at first, in keeping with his or her immaturity and lack of experience with the challenges of cooking.

Viewed this way, thinking seems far less solitary than Piaget pictured it, and far more social. Children figure things out not by manipulating objects and observing the results of the manipulations but by interacting (in activity settings) with a community of people, including parents, teachers, and peers. In doing so, the young, inexperienced preschooler is able to work on problems or tasks that might prove too difficult to attempt alone; yet the support and guidance of others allow considerable success! The interactions that

situated cognition Thinking that occurs jointly with others and is embedded in a particular context or activity setting.

social constructivism A theory that views learning as resulting from active dialogue and interaction between an individual and his or her community.

activity settings Group situations in which a shared focus of attention and shared goals facilitates an individual's learning from others in the group.

zone of proximal development According to Vygotsky, the level of difficulty at which problems are too hard for children to solve alone but not too hard when given support from adults or more competent peers.

allow the child to succeed are sometimes called the **zone of proximal development** (or **ZPD**). The concept of the ZPD originated with the Russian psychologist Lev Vygotsky (Newman & Holzman, 1993; Vygotsky, 1978) and has created a lot of interest among developmental psychologists because it suggests ways in which knowledge and thinking skills may originate and evolve. Consider this conversation between a six-year-old girl and her grandfather, while the two sort some scrap lumber piled behind the grandfather's hardware business:

Grandfather: We have to put the spruce here and the pine over there.

Girl: Spruce here? (Tosses one piece, but to the wrong pile)

Grandfather: No, there. (Moves her piece to the correct pile)

Girl: What's this? (Notices letter S scribbled in pencil on a piece)

Grandfather: That's for *spruce*. Put it with the spruce.

Girl: (Pondering the letter S). Spruce. OK. (Tosses piece correctly) So this is pine? (Looks at a piece with a *P* written on it)

Grandfather: Yep. Put it over there. (The two continue sorting for a while. Girl examines each piece for letters. Eventually she finds one with no letter written on it.)

Girl: Someone should write the name on this one. (Notices a knothole in the piece) I think it's pine.

Grandfather: You're right about that. Here's a pencil. (Tosses her a pencil)

Girl: (Writes *P* on the piece of scrap pine.) Know what? I can write *pine*! (Smiles) I bet I can write *spruce*, too.

Grandfather: (Looks at the letter *P* she has written.) Yeah, says *pine* all right. You might say it says *pine*.

In this example, the grandfather (and his pile of scrap wood) provided an activity setting in which the girl learned about differences between two woods, spruce and pine, as well as a way to represent the differences with letters. Without his presence and comments, considered *scaffolding* by Vygotsky, she might not have succeeded as well in this task. On the other hand, the grandfather did not simply "teach" the girl how to sort wood or to read the letters *S* and *P*, as a teacher might conventionally do in a classroom. Instead, he provided a task needed in his world (sorting the scrap wood is part of his business) and a way to involve the girl in the task. The interactions create a zone of proximal development for the girl. When she makes a mistake, the grandfather either simply corrects it matter-of-factly (such as when she tosses a piece in the wrong pile) or revises his own goals temporarily to fit hers (such as when she claims, mistakenly, that she has spelled the whole word *pine* using only its first letter). At the beginning of the task, the girl needs more assistance, or scaffolding. However, as the girl comes to understand and, eventually, become an expert at the task, she needs less scaffolding, or assistance.

As you might suppose, the nature of the ZPD depends on the experiences and circumstances of the child. Parents with "bookish" interests, for example, and the resources and time to provide book-related activity settings will more often provide ZPDs that encourage bookish and school-oriented skills in their children. Those with an outgoing, social disposition will provide ZPDs that encourage interpersonal interest and sensitivity in their children. Yet, reproduction of parents' priorities is not inevitable. Much also depends on how a child interprets an activity setting. An opportunity to learn to play the piano, for example, can be experienced as either attractive or boring, or as either an invitation or burdensome drudgery. What is provided is not necessarily what the child takes up or appropriates (Cobb et al., 1997; Guralnick, 2008).

Much cognitive change occurs because of the mutual development of meaning that happens in the "zone of proximal development," where two people focus on a common activity. In this case, the mother stimulates her daughter to learn about cooking, and the daughter stimulates the mother to learn about the daughter's growing knowledge and abilities.
Source: Simone van den Berg/Shutterstock.com.

Neostructuralist Theories of Cognitive Development

As the studies described so far suggest, preschoolers show considerable new strengths in using symbolic thought. They can take others' perspectives to some extent, develop a usable theory of how the human mind works, and distinguish between appearances and reality at least some of the time. Many of Piaget's classic observations on Swiss children have proven true: preschool children do have trouble focusing on two dimensions of an object at once and therefore have difficulty with conservation tasks throughout most of the preschool period. Other Piagetian observations have underestimated children's ability and stimulated research that has led to new ways of thinking about children's capacities. For example, unlike Piaget's claims, preschool children have a partial understanding of number.

Research has complicated our picture of children's cognitive development. Many psychologists have sought to keep Piaget's commitment to stagelike progressions in development and at the same time revise the content or details of those progressions (Case, 1998). Instead of proposing comprehensive, "grand" stages of thinking, as Piaget did, they argue that stages may be much more focused in content. Research based on this premise has, in fact, identified stages of spatial representation, of shapes, of mathematical ability, of patterns, and of interpersonal awareness, among others (Case, 1992; Ginsburg et al., 2008). Each of these skills seems to develop through predictable stages, but do so independently of the other domains. As individuals, children therefore show unique patterns and timing of development across many areas of thinking and skills (Wozniak & Fischer, 1993).

This newer view of cognitive stages is sometimes called **neostructuralist theory**, or *neo-Piagetian theory* because of its roots in the ideas of Piaget. As a result of focusing attention on more specific cognitive achievements, it has also paid more attention to *how*, or by what processes, children acquire new cognitive skills. One neostructuralist line of research explored the process of learning to draw by noting how it consists of the successive coordination of simpler skills (Dennis, 1992). Natalia begins her second year of life able to visually track objects as well as reach for objects. With practice, by the time she reaches age three, Natalia has learned to coordinate these two schemes into a single cognitive skill that enables scribbling. As she continues to practice with this newly consolidated scheme, she begins coordinating it with other, more advanced schemes, such as *comparing* scribbles with the orientation and edges of the paper. When tracking edges of a paper and tracking scribbles eventually become coordinated, Natalia can finally begin controlling lines and curves. Now the stage is set for her first representational drawings, such as stick-figure people.

neostructuralist theory Relates to recent theories of cognition that emphasize the structure or organization of thinking.

From the neostructuralist perspective, then, cognitive development during early childhood is not all of one piece when it unfolds but has many components—many forms of thinking, as well as perceptual and language developments. As a result, it is important to understand each piece separately from the others and to combine them to get a well-rounded picture of young children. Therefore, in the next section we look at another major piece of the puzzle of children's thinking: language acquisition.

Language Acquisition in the Preschool Years

For most children, language expands rapidly after infancy. They learn words, form ever-longer sentences, and engage in more-complex dialogue. Fairly early in the preschool years, most children have mastered the basic sounds, or *phonology*, that make their first language meaningful and distinctive. They have also made a good beginning at acquiring a vocabulary of single words. We described both of these achievements in Chapter 4 in connection with infants' cognitive development. Now, during early childhood, children's most striking achievements involve *syntax*, or the way the child organizes utterances, and *pragmatics*, or knowledge about how to adjust utterances to the needs and expectations of different situations and speakers. As it turns out, these twin achievements show both diversity and uniformity across children, and therefore, they raise important questions about language acquisition and how parents and other caregivers can influence it. In this section, we look at these questions, beginning with preschoolers' achievements in the area of syntax.

> **What Do You Think?**
>
> What do you think parents of young children *believe* about preschoolers' cognitive abilities? What if you asked parents (1) how much their *children* know when *parents* are happy or upset and (2) would their children think that a clay ball was the same "amount" if it were squashed into a pancake shape? Would parents' expectations about these questions coincide with the research described in this section? If possible, interview a real-life parent or two to test your prediction.

The Nature of Syntax

syntax Rules for ordering and relating the elements of a language.

The **syntax** of a language is a group of rules for ordering and relating its elements. Linguists call the elements of language *morphemes. Morphemes* are the smallest meaningful units of language; they include words as well as a number of prefixes and suffixes that carry meaning (the /s/ in *houses* or the /re/ in *redo*) and verb-tense modifiers (the /ing/ in *going*).

Syntactic rules operate on morphemes in several ways. Sometimes, they mark important relationships between large classes or groups of words. Consider these two pairs of sentences:

1a. Roberto helped Barbara.   1b. Barbara helped Roberto.

2a. Frank helps Ruije.   2b. Frank helped Ruije.

These sentences differ in meaning because of syntactic rules. In the first pair, a rule about the order, or sequence, of words tells us who is giving the help and who is receiving it: the name preceding the verb is the agent (the helper), and the name following the verb is the recipient (the "helpee"). In the second pair, the morphemes /es/ and /ed/ tell something about when the event occurred; adding /es/ to the end of the word signifies that it is happening now, but adding /ed/ means it happened in the past. These rules, and many similar ones, are understood and used by all competent speakers of the language. Unlike textbook authors, however, the speakers may never state them and may be only barely aware of them.

Unfortunately, for a child learning to talk, some syntactic rules have only a small range of application, and still others have irregular exceptions. Most words, for example, signal pluralization (the existence of more than one) by having an /s/ or /es/ added at the end; *book* means one volume, and *books* means more than one. But a few words use other methods to signal the plural. *Foot* means one, and *feet,* not *foots,* means more than one; *child* means one and *children* more than one; and *deer* can mean either one animal or several.

Thus, in acquiring syntax, a young child confronts a mixed system of rules. Some apply widely and regularly, and others apply narrowly and exceptionally. Added to these complexities is the fact that the child often hears utterances that are grammatically incomplete or even incorrect. Somehow, he or she must sort these out from the grammatically acceptable utterances while at the same time trying to sort out the various syntactic rules and the contexts for using them.

Beyond First Words: Semantic and Syntactic Relations

Before age two, children begin linking words when they speak. Initially the words seem to be connected by their *semantic relations,* or the meanings intended for them, rather than by *syntactic relations,* the relations among grammatical classes of words such as nouns, verbs, and adjectives. This is particularly true when the child is still speaking primarily in two-word utterances (sometimes called *duos*). As the mean length of a child's utterances increases to three words and more, syntactic relations become much more noticeable.

Duos and Telegraphic Speech

These ideas were documented in a classic set of three case studies of early language acquisition by Roger Brown (1973). When the children Brown observed were still speaking primarily in two-word utterances, their utterances were organized around eight possible semantic relationships; these are listed in Table 6.4, along with examples. The meanings of the utterances were determined by the intended relationships among the words, and the intentions of the preschool speakers often were discernible only by observing the context in which the utterances were made. "Mommy sandwich" could mean "the type of sandwich Mommy usually eats," or "Mommy is eating the sandwich," or "Mommy, give me a sandwich," all depending on the conversational context.

The reason for the ambiguity is that two-word utterances leave out indicators of syntactic relationships. One syntactic indicator is word order: due to word order, "the boy chased the girl" means something different than "the girl chased the boy." Children who still speak in duos do not use word order randomly, but they do tend to be less predictable about it than more linguistically mature children, whose utterances can be several words long. Another indicator of syntactic relationships is inflections, prepositions, and conjunctions. An older child will add *'s* to indicate possession (as in "Mommy's sandwich") and use words such as *in* and *on* to indicate location (as in "jump on the stair"). Leaving these indicators out makes the speech sound stilted and ambiguous; therefore, it is also called **holographic speech** or *telegraphic speech*—presumably because it sounds like a telegram. Telegraphic speech is characteristic of children's first efforts to combine words (around eighteen months to two years), but it can persist well after children begin using longer, more syntactic utterances some of the time.

holographic speech When a single word is used to communicate a thought, such as when a child says "up" instead of "pick me up."

Regularities and Overgeneralizations

After highly individual beginnings, certain aspects of syntax develop in universal and predictable patterns. English-speaking children have a tendency to know more nouns than verbs, a bias that is not as marked among children learning languages such as Korean or Mandarin. In many Asian languages, verbs end sentences, likely making them "stick out" to the children (Hoff, 2008). The present progressive form *-ing* occurs quite early in most children's language, the regular plural morphemes *-s* and *-es* somewhat later, and articles such as *the* and *a* still later (Hoff, 2008; Marcus et al., 1992).

At a slightly older age, most English-speaking children begin using auxiliary verbs to form questions, but they do so without inverting word order, as adults normally do. At first, a child will say, "Why you are cooking?" and only later "Why are you cooking?" This suggests that language acquisition involves more than just copying adult language;

TABLE 6.4 Semantic Relations in Two-Word Utterances

A child's earliest utterances are organized not according to adultlike grammar but according to particular semantic or meaning-oriented relationships such as those listed in this table. Often the intended, underlying relationships are ambiguous and can be discerned only by an attentive, observant adult at the time of the utterance.

Relationship	Example
Agent + action	Baby cry
Action + object	Eat cookie
Agent + object	Bobby cookie
Action + locative (location)	Jump stair
Object + locative	Teddy bed
Possessor + possessed	Mommy sandwich
Attribute + object	Big dog
Demonstrative + object	There Daddy

after all, adults rarely model incorrect forms. To a certain extent, children's language seems to compromise between the new forms children hear and the old forms they already can produce easily.

Sometimes, in fact, early syntax becomes *too* regular, and children make **overgeneralizations**. Around age three, preschool children often make errors, such as always adding *–ed* to indicate past tense, even when it is not appropriate as in the sentence: "I runned faster than Maddie." The child uses the wrong but more regular form as opposed to the correct but irregular forms of an earlier age. Usually by early school age, they shift back again, although not necessarily because anyone teaches or forces them to do so. Apparently, their overgeneralizations represent efforts to try out new rules of syntax that they have finally noticed.

overgeneralizations When children use common rules of speaking in all situations, even when inappropriate, such as adding *–s* to indicate a plural form such as, "Do you see all the deers?"

The Predisposition to Infer Grammar

As these examples suggest, and as research confirms (Marcus et al., 1992), young children seem to infer grammatical relationships, rather than simply copy others' speech. The tendency was first documented about sixty years ago in a research study by Hilda Berko (1958), but it is still used in many current tests of children's language development (Brindle, 2015; McDaniel et al., 1996). Instead of asking children about real words, the experimenter in Berko's classic study showed them pictures of imaginary creatures and actions that had nonsense words as names. With one picture, a child was told, "Here is a wug." Then he was shown two pictures and told, "Here are two of them. Here are two_____." Most children, even those as young as two and a half, completed the sentences with the grammatically correct word, *wugs*. Because they could not possibly have heard the term before, they must have applied a general rule for forming plurals, one that did not depend on copying any language experiences specifically but came from inferring the underlying structure of many experiences taken together. The rule most likely operated unconsciously because these children were very young indeed.

The Limits of Learning Rules

Preschoolers' skill at acquiring syntactic rules, however, obscures a seemingly contradictory fact about the acquisition of syntax: much syntax must be learned by rote. As we have pointed out, most children use irregular forms (such as *foot/feet*) correctly before they shift to incorrect but more regular forms. The most reasonable explanation for the change is that they pick up the very first sentence forms simply by copying, word for word, the sentences they hear spoken. Presumably, they copy many regular forms by rote, too, but the very regularity of these forms hides the haphazard, unthinking way in which children acquire them.

Although children eventually rely on rule-governed syntax, they probably still learn a lot of language by rote. Many expressions in a language are *idiomatic,* meaning they bear no logical relation to normal meanings or syntax. The sentence "How do you do?", for example, usually is not a literal inquiry as to how a person performs a certain action; and the sentence "How goes it?", meaning "How is it going?", does not even follow the usual rules of grammar. Because words and phrases such as these violate the rules of syntax and meaning, children must learn them one at a time.

Mechanisms of Language Acquisition

Exactly how do children learn to speak? For most children, several factors may operate at once. In general, current evidence can best be summarized as follows: language seems to grow through the interaction of an active, thinking child with certain key people and linguistic experiences. The preceding sections describe in part this active, thinking child; the upcoming sections describe some possible key interaction experiences.

Reinforcement

A commonsense view, one based essentially on behaviorist principles, is that children learn to speak through reinforcement. According to this idea, a child's caregivers reinforce vocal noises whenever they approximate a genuine word or utterance, and this reinforcement causes the child to vocalize in increasingly correct (or at least adultlike) ways (Skinner, 1957). In the course of babbling, an infant may happen to say "Ma-ma-ma-ma," to which his proud parent smiles and replies cheerfully, "How nice! You said 'Mama'!" The praise reinforces the behavior, so the infant says "Ma-ma-ma-ma" more often after that. After many such experiences, parents begin to reinforce only closer approximations to *mama*, leading finally to a true version of this word. The process would be an example of *shaping*, discussed in Chapter 2 in connection with behavioral/learning theory.

Among preschool children, the same process could occur if parents reinforced correct grammatical forms and ignored or criticized errors or relatively immature utterances. Parents might respond more positively to the sentence "I have three feet" than to the sentence "I have two foots." According to the principles of reinforcement (see Chapter 2), the child would tend not only to use the correct version more often but also to generalize the correct elements of this sentence to other, similar utterances.

Analysis of conversations between parents and children confirms this possibility, at least in indirect form and for the early stages of language acquisition. One study compared parents' responses to simple but grammatical sentences made by their two- and three-year-old children to their responses to ungrammatical utterances (Penner, 1987). Parents did not correct their children's grammar directly, but they were more likely to elaborate on the child's topic if the utterance was a grammatical one.

Imitation and Practice

In some sense, children obviously must imitate their native language to acquire it. This is an idea borrowed from the social learning variety of behaviorism. In daily life, though, the process of imitation is subtle and often indirect. Children do not imitate everything they hear, but most copy certain selected utterances, often immediately after hearing them. Sometimes the utterances chosen for imitation involve familiar sentence forms that contain new, untried terms, and sometimes they contain familiar terms cast into new, untried forms. The imitated terms and forms return later in the child's spontaneous speech. At first, these utterances resemble the rote learning mentioned earlier, and they seem to help the child by emphasizing or calling attention to new morphemes and syntax.

Imitation may also help children acquire language by initiating playful practice with new expressions. The child in essence plays around with the new forms she learns and in doing so consolidates her recently acquired knowledge, just as she does in other forms of play, such as those discussed in Chapter 7. Because quite a bit of language play remains unobserved by adults, its extent is hard to judge, but a lot obviously does go on even in children as young as two years (Messer, 1994). Children ages eighteen to thirty months

Much learning happens through imitation and practice. These boys see both reading and social skills demonstrated by their grandmother and then practice the same skills themselves.
Source: rSnapshotPhotos/Shutterstock.com.

who had older siblings diagnosed with autism demonstrated delays in communication, language, gesturing, and social skills, suggesting that such imitation may be maladaptive as well (Toth, Dawson, Meltzoff, Greenson, & Fein, 2007).

Innate Predisposition to Acquire Language: LAD

The ease and speed children show in acquiring language have caused some linguists and psychologists to conclude that children have an innate predisposition, or built-in tendency, to learn language (Chomsky, 1994). For convenience, the innate tendency is sometimes called the *language acquisition device,* or *LAD.* According to this viewpoint, LAD functions as a kind of inborn road map to language. It guides the child to choose appropriate syntactic categories as he tries to figure out the comparatively confusing examples of real speech that he ordinarily hears. It helps him find his way through the mazelike structure of language with relatively few major errors instead of having to explore and construct his own language map, as the Piagetian viewpoint implies.

The most persuasive reason for postulating the LAD is the *poverty of content* in the speech to which most infants and preschoolers are exposed. According to this argument, the language children encounter is too incomplete and full of everyday grammatical errors (too "impoverished") to serve as a satisfactory guide in learning the grammatical structure of the language (Baker, 1995). Parents sometimes speak in incomplete sentences, sometimes make grammatical errors, and sometimes do not speak at all when speaking might prove helpful to a child learning the language.

However, children who hear a wider variety of words have larger vocabularies that grow more quickly than children who hear fewer, more simple vocabularies (Hoff, 2008). But even in spite of any poverty of content children seem remarkably resilient in acquiring language. Children isolated from language through parental neglect, for example, have learned some language later in life, but their language usually is limited in amount and complexity. In a less tragic example, identical twins often create a private language that they speak only with each other. In many cases, their private language seems to delay normal language development, though the delay rarely causes serious lasting damage to their development (Mogford, 1993).

A final piece of evidence that a LAD exists is that preschool children do not simply copy their parents' language directly, yet they seem to figure out and use many of its basic syntactic relationships remarkably well. Berko's "wug" experiment discussed earlier illustrates this ability dramatically. In forming plurals they have never heard spoken before, children seem to demonstrate a grammatical skill that is more innate than learned.

The Limits of LAD

Although this evidence suggests that children have a built-in ability to acquire language, it does not show that experience plays no role at all. The evidence from twins and neglected children emphasizes just the opposite: that certain experiences with language may be crucial, especially early in life. Ordinarily, almost every preschooler encounters these experiences. They may consist of hearing others talk and of being invited to respond to others verbally. But the fact that they happen to everyone does not mean that children do not learn from them; it means only that what children learn is universal.

Furthermore, experiences affect the version of language children acquire, even when they supposedly grow up in the same language community. As pointed out earlier, children vary in the vocabulary they learn and in the grammar they use; even by age three or four, children often do not define grammatical categories as abstractly as adults do or necessarily in the same way other children do. Most preschoolers eventually revise their grammatical categories to coincide with conventional adult grammar, thus obscuring their individuality. But as we will see in Chapter 8, large differences persist in older children's styles of communicating, even after they have mastered the basic structure of language.

All things considered, the fairest conclusion we can draw is a moderate one: that children are both predisposed to acquire language and in need of particular experiences with it. Skill with language is neither given at birth nor divorced entirely from other cognitive development. A special talent for language may be given to all normal children, however, and many crucial experiences for developing that talent may happen to occur rather frequently among infants as they grow up.

Parent-Child Interactions

Certain kinds of verbal interactions apparently help children acquire language sooner and better. Parents can help by speaking in relatively short sentences to their preschoolers and using more concrete nouns than pronouns, though this also depends on whether the task or topic at hand calls for concrete or abstract ideas (Hoff-Ginsberg, 1997). For children under the age of eighteen months, parents can make sure that they respond to children's speech with information that relates to what the child is doing or experiencing (Hoff, 2008). In the following pair of comments, the first helps a child learn language more than the second does:

Parent 1: Take your shoes off. Then put your shoes in the closet. Then come kiss Mama goodnight.

Parent 2: After you take off your shoes and put them in the closet, come kiss me goodnight.

As we noted in Chapter 4, the simplified style of the first set of comments is one aspect of a version of language called **infant-directed speech**, or sometimes "motherese." Another aspect of this version is the use of a high-pitched voice. Infant-directed speech is used intuitively by adults with young children and even by older children with younger children (Messer, 1994).

infant-directed speech The style or register of speech used by adults and older children when talking with a one- or two-year-old infant.

One of the most helpful kinds of verbal interactions is *recasting* a child's utterances: repeating or reflecting back what the child says, but in slightly altered form. For instance:

Child: More milk.

Parent: You want more milk, do you?

Recasting helps because it highlights slight differences among ways of expressing an idea. In doing so, it may make the child more aware of how she expresses her idea—its form or organization—as well as call attention to the idea itself.

Most of the techniques for stimulating language development provide young preschoolers with a framework of language that simultaneously invites them to try new, unfamiliar language forms and simplifies and clarifies other aspects of language. Some psychologists call this framework *scaffolding* (Bruner, 1996; Reeder, 1996): like real scaffolds used in building construction, parents' language scaffolds provide a temporary structure within which young children can build their own language structures. As such, it functions much like Vygotsky's zone of proximal development mentioned earlier: helpful scaffolding changes and grows in response to the child's continuing development, always building a bit beyond the child's current independent abilities but never very far beyond.

These and similar findings have been translated into curricula for education of young children, particularly for those learning English as a second or third language (Proctor, Dalton, & Grisham, 2007) and even of infants (Spodek & Saracho, 1993). Fortunately, the most useful methods of interaction often are those that parents and teachers use intuitively anyway; training for them therefore really consists of emphasizing and refining their use.

Language Variations

Not surprisingly, parents vary in how they talk to their children, and these differences may influence the version of language children acquire as they grow up. It is unclear, however, how language variations affect other aspects of children's development, such as thinking ability. Let's consider three other sources of language variation: gender, socioeconomic status (SES), and hearing ability.

Chapter 6 Physical and Cognitive Development in Early Childhood

> **What Do You Think?**
>
> Suppose that you were asked to speak to a parent group, and a parent complained about her four-year-old's use of poor grammar. What advice could you give to this parent? Rehearse your comments with a classmate to determine how appropriate they are.

Gender Differences in Language

Within any one community, girls learn nearly the same syntax boys do, but they acquire very different pragmatics, or discourse patterns. Overall, the differences reflect society's gender stereotypes. For example, girls phrase requests indirectly more often than boys do; girls more often say, "Could you give that to me?" instead of "Give me that." Also, they more frequently expand on comments made by others, rather than initiating their own. These differences appear especially in mixed-gender groups and are noticeable not only among adults but also among children as soon as they are old enough to engage in conversation (Coates, 1993; Coates, 2015).

The sexes reinforce their language differences with certain nonverbal gestures and mannerisms. Girls and women tend to maintain more eye contact than boys and men do; they blink their eyelids at more irregular intervals and tend to nod their heads as they listen (Arliss, 1991). Boys and men use eye contact less in ordinary conversation, blink at regular intervals, and rarely nod their heads when listening.

Gender differences in discourse patterns may contribute to gender segregation: members of each gender may feel that members of the other gender do not really understand them, that they do not "speak the same language." Boys and girls therefore begin drifting apart during the preschool years, almost as soon as they begin using language (Ramsey, 1995), possibly due in part to acquiring language. The emerging segregation, in turn, reinforces gender differences in language patterns (Fagot, 1994). Boys reinforce one another for their assertive discourse style, and girls and their (mostly female) teachers reinforce one another for their "considerate" style. In the end, then, cognitive development supports social development, and social development supports cognitive development.

Socioeconomic Differences in Language

Most research has found low-SES children to be less skilled in using formal, school-like language than middle- or high-SES children (Heath et al., 1991). Research also shows that low-SES children are up to a year behind their higher-SES peers by the age of four, due in part to the infrequency with which they hear adults with large vocabularies speak (Hoff, 2008). In practice, this means low-SES children perform less well in verbal test situations, but outside of those situations, their language differences are less clear-cut. These facts have created controversy about the importance of socioeconomic differences in language development.

What is the significance of socioeconomic differences in tests of language development? Some psychologists point out that most tests of language skills favor middle-SES versions of English in both vocabulary and style of *discourse,* or conversational patterns (Gopaul-McNicol & Thomas-Presswood, 1998; Miramontes et al., 1997), and that several popular verbal intelligence scales confound actual verbal ability with socioeconomic status (Chapman, Fiscella, Duberstein, Kawachi, & Muennig, 2014). This bias is due to the content selected for individual test questions and to the ways tests are normally conducted. A question on one of these tests might ask children to describe a dishwasher, but few low-SES families own this appliance. Other questions might draw on experiences that only middle-SES children usually enjoy, such as trips on airplanes or visits to museums.

Perhaps most important, middle-SES families use styles of discourse that include many "test" questions or questions to which parents already know the answers. At the dinner table, parents may ask their preschooler, "What letter does your name begin with?" even though they already know the answer and their child knows that they know. Exchanges such as these probably prepare young children for similar exchanges on genuine tests by making testing situations seem more natural and homelike.

In contrast, low-SES children more often lack prior experience with "test" question exchanges. They can give relatively elaborate answers to true questions such as "What did you do yesterday morning?" when the adult really does not know the answer. But they tend to fall silent when they suspect the adult already can answer the question (for example, "What are the names of the days of the week?"). Their silence is unfortunate because rhetorical, or "test," questions become especially common when preschoolers enter school and because active participation in questioning and answering helps preschoolers' learning substantially.

Language of Deaf and Hearing-Impaired Children

Children with hearing impairments often do not develop oral language skills as fully as other children do, but they are quite capable of acquiring a language of gestures called **American Sign Language (ASL)**. In fact, language development in ASL children provides much of the reason for considering ASL a true language, one as useful for communication as any verbal language, such as English.

How can this be so? Signing consists of subtle gestures of the fingers and hands made near the face. In general, each gesture functions like a morpheme. For example, holding the fingers together gently (which signers call a "tapered O") can mean either *home* or *flower*, depending on whether it is placed near the cheek or under the nose. Other sign-morphemes affect the syntax of expressions: gestural equivalents of *-ing* and *-ed*. Individual signs are linked according to syntactic rules, just as in English. After some practice, signers can "speak" (or gesture) as quickly and effortlessly as people who use English can.

What happens to infants and young children with hearing impairments who grow up learning ASL from their parents as their first language? Studies show they experience the same steps in signing development that speaking children do in language development. At about the age when infants babble, signing children begin "babbling" with their hands, making gestures that strongly resemble genuine ASL signs but that signers recognize as gestural "nonsense" (Marschark, 1993). As with verbal babbling, signing infants apparently engage in gestural babbles playfully when waking up in the morning or going to sleep at night.

When signing infants reach ages two and three, they experience a phase of one-word signing similar to the holophrases often observed among speaking children. They also experience two-word, telegraphic signing. As with speech, their signs at this point often omit important syntactic gestures and do not follow the usual conventions of word order

American Sign Language (ASL) System of nonverbal gesturing that is used by many people who are deaf or hearing impaired and that functions as a language.

Sign language has the qualities of oral language, including grammar, subtlety, and expressiveness. This mother and child are communicating about the child's day at school. Unfortunately, in hearing communities (such as classrooms), it can be hard to appreciate the capacities of sign language.
Source: adriaticfoto/Shutterstock.com.

WORKING WITH   Carolyn Eaton, Preschool Teacher

Introducing Sign Language to Young Children

Carolyn Eaton teaches in a nursery school that serves only children who are deaf or who have moderate or severe hearing impairment. Everyone in the school communicates in American Sign Language (ASL): teachers, the children themselves, and (as much as possible) the parents. When they start the program, the children and parents often know very little ASL.

Kelvin: *How do they acquire this new language? Carolyn talked about some of the ways.*

Carolyn: In a lot of ways, the program really looks like any other nursery program, though maybe one with a lot of language emphasis. We always have a theme for the week. That's how we organize the vocabulary, the signs.

Kelvin: *Can you give an example of a theme?*

Carolyn: Last week's theme was "The Three Little Pigs." I told the story in ASL and read a picture book—one of the children had to hold it because I needed two hands to sign with. I emphasized key signs, like the ones for pig and three and the signs for brick, and straw, and house. I invited the children to make those signs with me when I came to them in the story.

Kelvin: *Do you do other things related to the week's theme?*

Carolyn: We'd have other conversations—in ASL, of course—about pigs and animals. And about trusting strangers, for that matter—that's in that story too! We might act out the story at some point, with signs instead of words. It depends partly on the vocabulary and fluency of the children.

Kelvin: *Is it harder to understand preschoolers' signing than adults'?*

Carolyn: It varies with the child, just like oral language. Most three- and four-year-olds tend to use less complex sign vocabulary and simpler expressions than adults. I found it hard at first to simplify my signing appropriately, the way you simplify oral language for young hearing children. There's a signing equivalent of "motherese" that you have to learn, or you won't be understood.

Kelvin: *I noticed a parent today in the class signing to the kids. Does that happen a lot?*

Carolyn: We have a parent volunteer just about every day. Because not all parents can volunteer, we have the kids take home a page each day that describes what's going on in the class and shows drawings of the signs we're currently emphasizing. We encourage the parents to learn them and use them at home. We also run two signing

---

(or, in this case, signing order) (Bellugi et al., 1993; Goldin-Meadow, 2008). Signing vocabulary increases rapidly during the early preschool period, in amounts comparable to the increases speaking children experience. Even the kinds of words acquired parallel those speaking children acquire; signing preschoolers tend to learn signs for dynamic, moving objects first, as is true for speaking children. The "Working With" interview with preschool teacher Carolyn Eaton describes some of these developments.

Still another reason to consider ASL a true language comes from observations of hearing preschoolers whose parents purposely used both English and ASL during the period when the children normally acquired language (Prinz & Prinz, 1979). During their preschool years, these children became thoroughly bilingual, using ASL and English interchangeably. Especially significant, however, were their patterns of language development, which essentially paralleled those shown by conventionally bilingual children. A clear example concerned vocabulary. Like verbal bilinguals, these children first acquired a single vocabulary that intermingled elements from both ASL and English but included few direct translations. If children understood and used the sign for "tree," they would be unlikely to understand and use the spoken word *tree*. The children eventually acquired translations and thus finally possessed duplicate vocabularies. But acquiring duplicate terms took several years, just as it does with verbally bilingual children.

Language Deficits or Language Differences?

Although we have presented gender differences, socioeconomic differences, and American Sign Language as variations on language development that are equally worthy, society

> **WORKING WITH** Carolyn Eaton, Preschool Teacher
>
> **Introducing Sign Language to Young Children** *continued*
>
> classes for the families of the preschoolers to help them communicate with their signing child.
>
> **Kelvin:** *Is it hard for them to learn?*
>
> **Carolyn:** Like everything else, people vary a lot. Some start learning immediately as soon as they learn that their child will always be deaf, and they're fluent by the time the child is a toddler. Others still haven't learned by the time the child is in grade school.
>
> Personally, I think it has a lot to do with how accepting the parents are of the child's hearing impairment. If they're still grieving over the child's loss, they make less progress at ASL.
>
> **Kelvin:** *Your program does seem language oriented—ASL oriented, that is.*
>
> **Carolyn:** It really is, though we also deal with all the other stuff that happens to children—friendships among peers, for example. Did you see that argument between two kids that was going on just as you were arriving today?
>
> **Kelvin:** *It looked fierce, judging by the children's faces. What was it about?*
>
> **Carolyn:** Well, Billy wrecked a roadway that two other kids had made in the sand table. They were upset, signed Billy to get lost, and that got Billy upset. That's when I stepped in.
>
> **Kelvin:** *I noticed how intently you were looking at Billy when you gave him a "talking to."*
>
> **Carolyn:** I sure was—but in all ASL conversations, not just scoldings, you have to look to see the signs. You get good at reading people's moods that way too, especially if you learn signing as early as these children did.
>
> **What Do You Think?**
>
> 1. Judging by Carolyn's comments, how does the acquisition of ASL resemble the acquisition of oral language? How does it differ?
> 2. Among speech-language pathologists and deaf people generally, there has been heated debate about whether to emphasize ASL experiences, even if they sometimes segregate children from the hearing community, or to emphasize oral language experiences, even if hearing-impaired children have trouble acquiring them. How might you decide between these alternatives? Compare your thoughts on this issue with one or two classmates' thoughts.

as a whole does not always agree with this assessment. In certain situations, each variation tends to be considered unsatisfactory, and the speaker (or, for ASL, the signer) may be considered deficient in linguistic or cognitive ability. The discourse patterns associated with females are often considered less satisfactory for learning and discussing mathematics, for example, than the discourse patterns associated with males (Walkerdine, 1997). In school, therefore, some girls are more likely to be judged less competent in math than they really are. Students with a language background other than English, whether it is Spanish, ASL, or something else, are at risk for being considered "unintelligent" simply because they cannot communicate fluently in the particular land of language—middle-class oral and written English—that historically has dominated schooling at all levels. Language biases pose a challenge for anyone who works with children professionally (Gopaul-McNicol & Thomas-Presswood, 1998). However, as we will see in Chapter 8, where we look further at bilingualism and its effects, there are ways to overcome language biases and to honor the diversity and talents of all children.

Early Childhood Education

Developing cognitive skills influence an important experience for many preschool children: early childhood education. Programs for three- and four-year-olds take many forms. Look at these experiences:

- Juan goes to *family day care* for three full days each week. His care occurs in his caregiver's home, with only four other children.

> **What Do You Think?**
>
> How do you think early childhood teachers should respond to language variety in preschoolers? Should they encourage it, discourage it, or simply accept it? This is an important issue in education and would make for a lively debate in class!

- Denzel goes to a *childcare center* full time, five days a week. The center consists of two rooms modified from a church basement. About twenty children attend the center and are cared for by four adults.
- Cary goes to a part-time *nursery school* four mornings per week. There are twelve children and two adults.

Early Education and Cognitive Theories of Development

As with the diversity of these childcare arrangements, there is diversity in the developmental perspectives guiding the arrangements. Some programs draw heavily on Piaget's ideas about cognitive development, especially the notion that children construct knowledge by interacting with the environment actively (Marlowe, 1998). They provide sensorimotor activities, such as sand and water play, as a basis for fostering preoperational activities such as make-believe play. Other programs organize cognitive activities around structured materials, which teachers guide children to use in particular ways. Nurseries and centers inspired by Maria Montessori (Cuffaro, 1991; Montessori, 1964; Lillard, 2012) may give children sets of cylinders graded by size and designed to fit snugly into a set of size-graded holes in a board. A child experiments with the cylinders and holes to discover the best way to fit them.

Still other early education programs borrow from Vygotsky's views of cognition as originating in social and cultural activities. These programs emphasize cooperative problem-solving activities and *emergent literacy,* a way of introducing reading and writing by situating it in everyday, valued experiences (Morrow, 1996). For example, instead of teaching children to recognize letters or familiar words at a special time each day, the early childhood teacher might simply provide a classroom rich in print materials and encourage children to come to him with words or letters that they themselves want to learn.

Effectiveness of Early Childhood Education

Evaluations of early childhood programs suggest that a wide range of approaches, including those just mentioned, are about equally effective in promoting overall cognitive growth, although the choice of curriculum does seem to influence *the pattern* of skills children acquire (Lillard, 2012; Schweinhart et al., 1993).

Three factors seem to underlie successful early childhood programs, whatever their format and curriculum. First, the staff members of successful programs regard themselves as competent observers of children's educational needs and as being capable of making important decisions in tailoring a curriculum to particular children. Second, the vast majority of successful programs and teachers view an early childhood curriculum as an integrated whole, rather than as consisting of independent subject areas or skills. Singing a song, for example, is not just "music"; it also fosters language development, motor skills (if the children dance along), arithmetic (through counting and rhythm), and social studies (if the words are about people and life in the community).

Third, successful early childhood programs involve parents, either directly as volunteers in the classroom or indirectly as advisers on governing boards, in certain school activities, or in additional services that support families. The federally sponsored program of early education called *Head Start,* for example, owes much of its effectiveness to parent involvement (Ames, 1997; Love, Banks Tarullo, Raikes, & Chazan-Cohen, 2008). To get federal funding, local centers are required to create parent advisory boards to guide policy and practice at the centers. They are also encouraged to provide other family support services, such as parent support groups and dental screening for children.

Cultural Diversity and Best Practice in Early Education

A careful look at successful programs for young children raises an important question: are there "best" ways to support children's learning despite the cultural and individual diversity among children? A major professional association for early childhood education, the National Association for the Education of Young Children (NAEYC), argues that there are and has described its recommendations in detail in an influential book called *Developmentally Appropriate Practice: Birth to Age Eight* (Bredekamp & Copple, 1997; Copple & Bredekamp, 2009; Gestwicki, 1995). **Developmentally appropriate practices** are ways of assisting children's learning that are consistent with children's developmental needs and abilities. Table 6.5 lists a few of the practices recommended by the NAEYC as they relate to the preschool years.

developmentally appropriate practice Methods and goals of teaching considered optimal for young children, given current knowledge of child development.

The NAEYC recommendations seem reasonable in many ways. Who can object, for example, to providing children with choices for their preschool play or to supporting their dialogues and initiatives with comments from the teacher or caregiver? Yet cross-cultural comparisons of early childhood programs complicate the picture somewhat by revealing that some practices in early education in North America are really culture bound rather than universally beneficial to children.

In Japan, for example, early childhood programs are more likely to value large-group activities (such as singing or putting on a skit) in the belief that such activities develop commitment to the child's community—in this case, the community of the classroom (Kotloff, 1993). The time given to large-group activities, however, probably would seem excessive to some preschool educators in North America, where the development of individual initiative is more highly valued.

In Italy, early childhood programs emphasize involvement of parents much more heavily than do most North American programs (Edwards & Kutaka, 2015). They also place children in permanent groups from their entrance at age three until they leave the program for public school at age six. Over recent decades, societal changes, such as higher divorce rates,

TABLE 6.5 Developmentally Appropriate Practices with Preschoolers

Principle	Examples
Caregivers provide ample space for active play.	Program has access to outdoor space or gymnasium with climbing apparatus, tricycles, etc.
Caregivers allow children choices in activities.	Classroom has several learning centers: dramatic play (dress-up), block building, books and reading area, art area, etc.
Caregivers provide long periods of uninterrupted time.	Group transitions (e.g., from indoor to outdoor activities) are kept to a minimum. Activities tend to begin and end individually.
Activities and materials are relevant to children's experiences.	Books are gender fair and culture fair. Relevant cultural holidays are noted and celebrated through appropriate activities in class.
Caregivers ensure that the environment is safe and free of hazards.	Climbing apparatus has soft mats underneath (if indoors) or soft sand (if outdoors). Furniture is sturdy. Sharp objects (knives, scissors) are supervised carefully when used.

Source: Adapted from Bredekamp & Copple (1997).

> ### A Multicultural View
>
> #### Parents' Beliefs about Intelligence: A Cross-Cultural Perspective
>
> In our society, parents mean particular things when they refer to children's *intelligence:* they are usually talking about a child's verbal skills and reasoning abilities, especially as they occur in school or school-like tasks. This view of intelligence is so deeply grounded in our culture that an entire psychological field has developed to measure it, complete with standardized "intelligence" tests and experts to help teachers and parents interpret the tests.
>
> But not all societies think of intelligence in this way. The Kipsigis in East Africa frame the idea of intelligence rather differently, placing it more explicitly in its social context (Harkrtess & Super, 1992). They speak of a child being *ng'om,* meaning not only verbally skilled and sociable but also responsible to others. A child who is *ng'om* is quick to learn household tasks, for example, but also reliable about doing them without being reminded. The Kipsigis recognize, in principle, that a child can have verbal skill in the abstract. In practice, however, they regard such an isolated or abstract skill as a unique ability that requires a special term to describe it: *ng'om en sukul,* or "smart in school." Furthermore, *ng'om* is a quality shown only by preschoolers; neither an infant nor an adult can be *ng'om* because she or he is not expected to be responsible to others in the same way preschoolers are.
>
> Such a socially embedded notion of intelligence differs radically from the usual North American idea. In our society, parents are likely to distinguish clearly between a child's sense of responsibility to others and his or her intelligence (Goodnow, 1996). They may consider the former desirable but not an intrinsic part of intelligence as such. When interviewed about the qualities shown by preschoolers, parents of preschoolers tend to name relatively "cognitive" features: an intelligent child is inquisitive, curious, imaginative, self-reliant, and able to play independently (Harkness & Super, 1992). These features of intelligence take individual autonomy for granted rather than social harmony: being intelligent is something you do by or on behalf of yourself, not with or on behalf of others.
>
> These cultural differences begin to make sense if we consider the settings in which Kipsigis and North American parents and preschoolers live. A Kipsigis preschooler typically is part of an extended family. There are likely to be children of all ages close at hand, related to one another in largely complex ways; older children typically care for younger children from an early age; and children's chores are likely to take on "real" economic importance as children get older. Such a setting seems sure to reward children for showing responsibility to others.
>
> In our own society, a preschooler is likely to live with a small family; relatively few or even no immediate relatives may be close at hand; parents expect that school will figure prominently in the preschooler's future; and parents themselves are likely to be working for a living. This sort of setting favors children who can "teach themselves" to a certain extent, that is, play with and learn from materials on their own. It also favors children who orient themselves toward school-like activities—toward number and memory games, for example, and books and letters. An "intelligent" child is one who can do these things, which have much less to do with responsibility to others than is the case for a Kipsigis child. Cultural differences such as these can pose problems for many preschoolers in our own society when they finally enter school. Historically, modern schooling has encouraged the culturally conventional definitions of intelligence as individual activity and those of cognitive activity as separate from the daily needs of the community. Students generally "do their own work" and focus on tasks (such as a set of math problems) that are created specifically for school settings.
>
> When these assumptions do not fit the cultural expectations of particular children or their families, however, teachers are challenged to modify them. Teachers must then find other ways for children to "be intelligent"—ways that involve greater responsibility to others, for example, and greater concern for the real needs of the child's community (Gopaul-McNicol & Thomas-Presswood, 1998). Though it takes effort, there are ways to accomplish these changes in teaching philosophy; some of these changes are discussed in Chapter 8 in connection with bilingualism and the influence of school in the middle years.

increasing numbers of women working outside the home, and economic difficulties, have challenged the early childhood care systems, but Italian culture persists in supporting these programs (Edwards & Kutaka, 2015).

These comparisons suggest that the best practices in early education may need to take account of cultural differences and values regarding children's development (Mallory & New, 1994). For programs in ethnically diverse societies such as the United States, this means more than including songs and brief mentions of the holidays

> **What Do You Think?**
>
> Is early childhood education a "social" or a "cognitive" activity? Decide what you think about this question. Then, if you can, talk about it with one or two experienced teachers of young children. How does your opinion compare to theirs?

of various cultural groups. The central values and attitudes of cultural groups served by a particular center or nursery school must find their way into the daily activities of the program. Particular centers, therefore, will experience cultural diversity in different ways.

As the "A Multicultural View" feature shows, in these culturally diverse programs, cognition, or thinking, itself can take on diverse meanings. Educators who work with young children therefore need to do more than understand preschool cognition: they also need to explore how it might be understood and used by particular children and communities with specific social relationships and values. The next chapter turns to these important topics.

From Preschooler to Child

The physical and cognitive changes we have talked about in this chapter create new relationships with parents and other caregivers, who in turn stimulate further changes. Preschoolers' new motor skills may stimulate adults to encourage various talents actively and with more focus than before. Once catching and throwing make their appearance, playing ball becomes a possibility; once scribbling stabilizes, skillful and interesting drawing seems just around the corner. And so parents and other interested adults encourage children toward these new skills, among others. Sometimes, the teaching and learning seem easier now, too, because adults no longer have to monitor a child's every move and can concentrate increasingly on the goals of movements. Just a few years before, "one false step" might have meant a child would literally fall. But now, this term has become only a metaphor for mistakes in general, not for physical mishaps specifically.

The cognitive developments of early childhood are equally influential on relationships. New cognitive abilities create new individuality in children. In spite of differences in temperament among infants, it is not they but preschoolers who have more identifiable personalities. By age four or five, conversations become possible; moods can be expressed not only through gestures and body language but also through words; and a child's lasting interests become more obvious to those who know the child. All of these changes create new meanings for the idea of parenting. Attending to physical needs begins to recede in importance (though not completely), and attending to psychological needs comes more to the fore. As parents shift their relationship to accommodate these changes, they are more likely to remember their own childhoods once again, and with renewed vividness. The memories can be good, bad, traumatic, or mixed; but whatever they are like, they force reassessment of parents' *own* personal histories and identities, and their relationships with their *own* parents, the preschooler's grandparents. We saw aspects of these changes in Chapter 5's discussion of attachment formation, and we will explore them further. We come to them first in Chapter 8, which describes where preschoolers' new physical growth and cognitive skills lead them during middle childhood. We come to them again in Chapter 13, which discusses the impact of parenting on parents in more detail. First, though, we must complete the portrait of young children by discussing the development of their social relationships and their emotional growth in the next chapter.

Chapter 6 Physical and Cognitive Development in Early Childhood

Chapter Summary

- **What pathway does physical growth normally take during early childhood?** Between the ages of two and five, growth slows down and children take on more adultlike bodily proportions. Usually growth is rather smooth during the preschool period, though genetic, social, and nutritional differences can affect growth to some extent. Children's appetites often are smaller in the preschool years than in infancy, and children become more selective about what they eat.

- **How is poverty related to children's health?** The general health of a child is associated with the economic resources of the child's family, with higher-SES preschoolers tending to be healthier than lower-SES preschoolers. A number of possible causes for the association exist, including greater access to health care among well-off families.

- **When do children achieve bladder control?** Children tend to achieve daytime bladder control early in the preschool period. Nighttime bladder control tends to come later in the period.

- **What motor skills do children acquire during the preschool years?** Preschoolers acquire and refine many fundamental motor skills, including walking, jumping, throwing, and catching. Fine motor skills such as drawing also emerge during this period, progressing from prerepresentational to representational drawings. Children vary in motor skill development because of both their biological endowment and their experiences.

- **How does children's growth affect parents and other adults?** Preschoolers' changing facial features, size, and motor skills influence parents' responses and methods of childrearing to some extent. Because of differences in circumstances, families respond uniquely to differences in children's growth.

- **What are the special features and strengths of preschoolers' thinking?** Several explanations of preschoolers' thinking exist. According to Piaget, preschoolers' thinking is preoperational, or characterized by emerging skills with symbolic representation. Preoperational thinking is also characterized by egocentrism, the assumption that your own point of view is shared by others, and by rudimentary skill with classification, reversibility, conservation, and number. A more recent but prominent explanation for preschoolers' cognitive development is social constructivism, the idea that thinking develops through shared, interactive activities. When activity settings are shared with more skilled or knowledgeable others, a zone of proximal development occurs that allows and encourages a child to learn and perform beyond what he or she could do alone. A third recent explanation is offered by neostructuralist theories of cognitive development, which use Piaget's belief in stages but focus on changes in relatively specific cognitive skills.

- **How does the language of preschool children differ from that of older children?** During the preschool years, children make major strides in acquiring the syntax, or grammar, of their native language. Young children's first word combinations are related by semantics and omit syntactic relationships. When syntax does appear, it is sometimes marked by errors of overgeneralization. Infants and preschoolers are reinforced, though only indirectly, for using correct syntax in their early utterances. Children probably acquire some syntax through imitation and practice of language models. The ease of language acquisition despite the poverty of the content of speech that children hear may mean that children possess an innate language acquisition device, or LAD. Parents assist children's language acquisition by recasting the children's utterances, providing expansions or scaffolding that support children's speech, and using a special style of talk called *infant-directed speech*.

- **What social and cultural factors account for variations in preschoolers' language and speech?** Language varies between girls and boys in ways that support gender stereotypes. It also varies according to socioeconomic class in ways that prepare middle-SES children better than low-SES children for school settings. The variations raise issues about when and whether particular children's language is deficient or merely different from the norm.

- **What constitutes good early childhood education?** Early childhood education programs take a variety of forms, many of which have been influenced by theories of cognitive development. Three factors characterize successful programs: a staff oriented toward observing the children, an integrated view of the curriculum, and significant involvement of parents in the program. Cultural diversity challenges early childhood educators to identify teaching practices that are not only developmentally appropriate but also culturally appropriate.

Key Terms

activity settings (p. 199)
American Sign Language (ASL) (p. 209)
classification (p. 197)
conservation (p. 198)
developmentally appropriate practice (p. 213)
egocentrism (p. 197)
fine motor coordination (p. 189)
holographic speech (p. 203)
infant-directed speech (p. 207)
neostructuralist theory (p. 201)
overgeneralizations (p. 204)
preoperational stage (p. 195)
reversibility (p. 198)
situated cognition (p. 199)
social constructivism (p. 199)
symbolic thought (p. 196)
syntax (p. 202)
zone of proximal development (ZPD) (p. 200)

Psychosocial Development in Early Childhood

CHAPTER 7

Source: bikeriderlondon/Shutterstock.com.

Chapter Outline

Relationships with Family
Relationships in an Expanding Social World
Play in Early Childhood
Gender Development
Child Abuse and Maltreatment
Looking Back/Looking Forward

Focusing Questions

- How do different styles of parenting influence preschoolers' relationships with peers?
- How do preschoolers handle conflicts with peers?
- Why is play so important in preschoolers' development, and how does play change as they approach school age?
- How does a child's understanding of gender differences change during the preschool years? What factors influence a child's flexibility about gender-role stereotypes?
- What factors appear to contribute to child abuse and neglect? What are the consequences of maltreatment, and how might child maltreatment be prevented?

When Selena was two, she would crouch down on the floor with her rear end sticking out in imitation of the prominent haunches of Tigger, the family cat. From time to time, she made a noise sort of like a cat's meow. Keeping her head low, she looked around carefully for acknowledgment from her parents. Occasionally she walked like a cat, although her walk looked more like a rabbit's hopping. Tigger himself was not impressed by all of this.

Selena's skills as a performer and her active awareness of her audience illustrate an important milestone during the early childhood years: the development of psychological and social skills. During early childhood, many activities and events that occupy a child's waking hours involve social interaction with other people. These others include parents, grandparents, and siblings, as well as friends and acquaintances in the neighborhood and community. Many of these interactions also involve play. The nature of our play and its role in our lives changes with age and experience, but the capacity to engage in playful activity and the social skills that make this possible continue to develop throughout our lives. The social skills and unique personality a preschool child develops are largely a result of social interactions within and outside his or her family.

In this chapter, we explore the process through which preschoolers develop the capacity to relate to others in empathic and prosocial ways and to successfully deal with conflict and aggression. As with play, psychosocial development is a lifelong process. We will examine the conditions that foster or undermine such development and their consequences for lifespan development. We will also explore an aspect of early childhood development with profound and lifelong impact: the development of gender. Finally, we will discuss the serious problem of child maltreatment, including its causes, long-term consequences, treatment, and prevention.

Relationships with Family

Are your earliest memories of yourself alone, or do they include other people? Chances are that it's the latter, for young children spend a good deal of their time relating to others. In this section, we discuss children's relationships with their parents and siblings—relationships that in many ways set the stage for social interactions beyond the family sphere.

Relationships with Parents

During the preschool years, the attachment relationships between children and their parents and other caregivers discussed in Chapter 5 continue to play a central role in children's social and emotional development. However, young children's expanding ability to initiate verbal and physical activity and their exploding powers of imagination can at times be a challenge to their parents. These changes require parents to support their preschoolers' efforts to take on the world while also appreciating young children's limitations and need for restraints that ensure their physical and emotional safety and protect their self-esteem. Preschoolers often test the limits their parents impose and are frequently inconsistent in their ability to understand and conform to parental wishes. At times they express their strong desire to control their environment by refusing to eat certain foods or wear certain clothing, or by insisting on playing the same game or having the same story read to them over and over again.

Understanding the need for family rules poses a challenge to preschoolers, but making those rules also creates a challenge for parents, at least those living in the individualistic culture of North America. In this society, unlike most others, parents are expected to devise their own standards for rearing children, largely independently of other families' standards or expectations—a kind of "private enterprise" system of child-rearing. For instance, it is up to parents as individuals to decide how much anger their child should be allowed to express, how early and well she should learn manners, or how much candy she can eat. Parents' independence in deciding on these standards increases their power to shape their child's behavior in the short run. But it also increases their dilemma over which standards to choose because they observe that other parents often make choices different from their own (Piotrowski, 1997). These factors may help explain why community members are often reluctant to say something to someone else's child who misbehaves or to offer advice or assistance to a parent who might find it useful. And as we will see in Chapter 12, the lack of clear standards for good parenting is precisely the kind of ambiguous role that creates stress during early adulthood.

Enforcing family rules may be less of a problem in cultures and societies that encourage less individualism and stronger, more prolonged interdependence among kin, community, or both. In Chinese American and Japanese American families, for example, grandparents and other relatives retain considerable prestige and influence in child-rearing matters, even

All parents discipline their children sometimes. Their methods make a difference. Being respectful of a child's thoughts and feelings and calling attention to the consequences of misbehaving is more effective than spanking, at least in the long run.
Source: Iakov Filimonov/Shutterstock.com.

after a couple has married and given birth to children (Chao, 1994; Huang & Ying, 1989; Nagata, Cheng, & Tsai-Chae, 2010). Even as preschoolers, children are taught ways to show respect for their elders, such as caution in asking questions and readiness to obey orders. In such a situation, parents lose some decision-making authority to grandparents, in-laws, or "the community." But parents also gain family and community backing for their position: it is not just an adult or two, Mom and Dad, who decide whether talking in a loud voice is rude but an extended array of relatives and friends (Skolnick & Skolnick, 1989). And for individuals who expect to have the support of extended family and friends, not having that social support can be quite difficult (Leidy, Guerra, & Toro, 2012). The "Focusing On" feature discusses extended family members' participation in child-rearing.

In general, parent-child relationships during early childhood that are warm, respectful, empathic, and mutually responsive generally work best for children and their families. This is revealed both by how children and their parents interact and by the perceptions they have about each other. When mothers shared a mutually responsive orientation with their young children, children developed a secure attachment and better internalized maternal rules and values, and mothers relied less often on power to influence their children (Heikamp, Trommsdorff, Druey, Hübner, & von Suchodoletz, 2013; Kochanska, 1997). Preschoolers who have more positive mental representations of the mothering they receive, as revealed in the stories they make up about a mother and her child, have fewer behavior problems and less psychological distress than children whose mental representations are more negative (Oppenheim et al., 1997; Stocker, 1994). In the section that follows, we discuss the main patterns of parental authority observed among North American families and their developmental impact.

Patterns of Parental Authority

One of the most important aspects of a parent-child relationship is the parent's style of authority. Observations of North American families of preschoolers suggest that child-rearing styles can be classified into four groups: *authoritative, authoritarian, permissive,* and *indifferent* (Darling & Steinberg, 1993; Grusec et al., 1997; Lamb et al., 1992; Maccoby & Martin, 1983; Sorkhabi & Mandara, 2013). In most families, however, none of these styles exists in a "pure" form and parenting styles can change as children grow older and as other family changes occur.

Authoritative Parenting

Authoritative parents exert a high degree of control, demand a lot of their children, and monitor their children's behavior, but also are responsive, child centered, and respectful of their children's thoughts, feelings, and participation in decision making. For example,

authoritative parenting A style of child-rearing characterized by a high degree of control, clarity of communication, maturity demands, and nurturance.

Focusing On...

Extended Family Supports for Child-Rearing

In American society in particular, parents are held, and hold themselves, responsible for the physical care of their children. Whether parents are rich or poor, Caucasian or African American, divorced or married, society expects them to provide food for their children, as well as clothing and a place to sleep. In reality, many families share these responsibilities with relatives, friends, and professionals of various kinds. In a typical week, a child may spend significant time not only with his biological parents but also with a grandparent, a neighbor, and (depending on the child's age) a teacher or day-care center worker. The mixture of responsibility depends partly on the local circumstances of the particular family. It also reflects cultural and economic differences. Mexican American families, for example, value the participation of grandparents and other relatives in child-rearing. Many nonwhite families report the participation in family life of *fictive kin*—neighbors or friends who develop a relationship with the family that closely resembles that of a blood relative (Leidy et al., 2012; Ramirez, 1989, 1998). Though fictive kin are more common among ethnic and racial minorities, they are also an important part of the white experience, as we will see in Chapter 17.

These additional adults supplement what parents provide, often literally by providing alternative persons to cook meals and arrange other daily routines and by bolstering the psychological goals and emotional supports provided by the biological parents. A study of African American families confirmed this conclusion by investigating the emotional climate in two- and three-generational families (Tolson & Wilson, 1990). Interviews with all members of the families, including the children, found that three-generational families (those with a resident grandparent) saw themselves as organized more informally and spontaneously than two-generational (two-parent) families, which in turn saw themselves as organized more informally and spontaneously than one-parent families. In other words, the greater the number of parents (including a grandparent), the *fewer* the rules for children to follow and the *more* flexible the daily scheduling of activities, even though larger families had to coordinate the activities of more individuals. While this trend may seem contradictory, the family members themselves suggested the reason when interviewed: more adults in the house meant individual parents had more backup support in carrying out their functions as parents and therefore needed to rely on preset procedures less heavily.

The benefits of backup support are psychological as well as physical. Children who report higher levels of kinship support also note that they are more likely to feel connected with their teachers and schools and to value hard work (Pallock & Lamborn, 2006). The interviews described earlier also found that African American families with more than one parent placed significantly greater emphasis on moral and ethical issues and on determining how best to deal with both individual members and people outside the family (Tolson & Wilson, 1990; Wilson et al., 1995). To achieve this benefit, however, it did not matter whether the second "parent" was a father; it occurred just as frequently when a mother and a grandmother were the resident parents. Other research, in fact, suggests that it may not even matter whether the additional parents live at home, as long as they participate actively in the life of the family. In another interview study, successful minority single parents reported developing and depending on networks of family and personal relationships (Lindblad-Goldberg, 1989). What mattered was not the form or pattern of the networks but their existence and importance in helping the parent carry out the roles of child-rearing.

What Do You Think?
What types of extended family supports did you experience during your childhood and adolescence? In what ways did you find them beneficial, and in what ways were they not?

---

although it may be easier for a parent to respond to a child's request for help in building something or getting dressed by doing it for the child, an authoritative parent is likely to provide only the amount of help that will enable that child to accomplish the task independently. Such parents tend to be democratic and rational in their decision making and to respond to their children with warmth and empathy.

When it comes to discipline, authoritative parents assume that their preschoolers should be treated with respect, even when they have misbehaved severely. They believe that discipline should be a positive learning experience, focused on helping children to understand what the rules are. They try to determine why children break the rules, and they expect age-appropriate responsibility for children's misbehavior. They want children to internalize parental standards and to develop competence so that children can make better decisions about how to behave in the future. For example, when faced with a preschooler whose water-play at the sink has resulted in a flood, an authoritative parent is likely to ask the child how it happened, what he was thinking, and what he remembered about the rules about using the sink for water-play. The parent's response would focus on helping the child understand why the parent was upset (the flood could damage the floor and downstairs ceiling and be costly to repair), helping him assume age-appropriate responsibility for his actions (perhaps by having him help mop up the floor), and having him explain how such "catastrophes" could be avoided in the future. The consequences would also be designed to increase the child's understanding of the misbehavior (for example, requiring him to help clean up the mess and not allowing water-play privileges for the rest of the week).

Preschoolers of authoritative parents tend to be self-reliant, self-controlled, and able to get along well with their adult caregivers and peers (Hart et al., 1992; Hoeve et al., 2009; Kuczynski & Kochanska, 1995). For example, Leon Kuczynski and Grazyna Kochanska (1995) found that children who experienced authoritative child-rearing as toddlers were more responsive to parental guidance and had fewer behavior problems at age five. In particular, the demands of these authoritative mothers emphasized competence, prosocial behavior, and positive actions ("Ask him to share"; "Pour the milk carefully"; "Put away your toys") rather than demands to inhibit behavior ("Don't hit"; "Don't spill the milk"; "Don't leave a mess").

Authoritative parenting is also associated with high self-esteem, internalized moral standards, psychosocial maturity, autonomy, and academic success. In addition, it appears to foster relationships with peers and family that display the same qualities of warmth and respect for others during middle childhood, adolescence, and beyond (Baumrind, 1991a, 1991b; Darling & Steinberg, 1993; Hoeve et al., 2009; Pettit et al., 1997). We will look at the relationship between authoritative parenting and prosocial behavior later in this chapter.

Authoritarian Parenting

Like authoritative parents, **authoritarian** parents are demanding of their children and exert high control over them. However, they tend to be less warm and responsive than authoritative parents, and more arbitrary and undemocratic in decision making. They frequently impose their rules or views on their children based on their own greater power and authority, with little sensitivity to their children's thoughts and feelings. They rarely explain the purpose behind the rules, making it less likely that children will internalize those guidelines. Parent-child relationships that depend on arbitrary, "power-assertive" control and that ignore children's feelings and need for independence often have a negative effect on children. Children of authoritarian parents tend to be relatively distrustful of others, unhappy with themselves, and to have lower self-esteem. They also tend to have poorer peer relations, poorer school adjustment, less life satisfaction, and lower school achievement than do children with authoritative parents (Hart et al., 1990; Lamb et al., 1992; Milevsky, Schlecter, Netter, & Keehn, 2006). We discuss the impact of authoritarian parenting on older children in Chapters 9 (middle childhood) and 11 (adolescence).

The disciplinary techniques authoritarian parents use differ from those of authoritative parents, in part because they do not see the development of responsibility in young children as a collaborative process and place less emphasis on mutual respect. When faced with misbehavior, they are more likely to focus on the arbitrary assertion of parental power and authority than on understanding the child's thoughts and feelings about the misbehavior or on helping the child understand and take responsibility for it. In the extreme, the combination of rigid and arbitrary power assertion and insensitivity to a child's thoughts and feelings can increase the likelihood of child maltreatment, which we discuss a little later in the chapter. By modeling disrespectful and insensitive behavior, such parenting can elicit and reinforce similar behavior in children and lead to escalating cycles of negative reinforcement and coercion (Patterson, 1982).

Authoritarian parenting is more frequent in large families, in minority families, and in working-class families (Greenberger et al., 1994), and fathers are more likely to be

authoritarian parenting A style of child-rearing characterized by a high degree of control and demands on children's maturity and a low degree of clarity of communication and nurturance.

authoritarian than mothers. Parenting styles and beliefs about how children should be raised differ across societies and cultures (Bornstein et al., 1998; Rudy & Grusec, 2006; Stevenson-Hinde, 1998). For example, authoritarian parenting is more common in cultures in which family relations are hierarchically structured based on age, family role, and gender. Ruth Chao (1994) has questioned the validity of Western European concepts of authoritative and authoritarian parenting for Chinese families. Chinese child-rearing is based on Confucian principles that require children to show loyalty to and respect for their elders and require elders to responsibly train, discipline, and otherwise "govern" young children. High degrees of parental authority and control are viewed as positive and essential aspects of the *chiao shun,* or "training," needed to set a standard of acceptable family and community conduct. Chao suggests that cultural differences such as these may explain why authoritarian parenting, which is associated with poor school achievement among European American children, is linked to high levels of school achievement among Chinese children. Authoritarian parenting is more common among mothers in collectivistic societies than individualistic societies, and authoritarian parents in collectivistic cultures were not as likely as authoritarian parents in individualistic cultures to view their children negatively (Rudy & Grusec, 2006). Central to such cultural differences are differences in values and assumptions about what kind of people parents want their children to be and what kinds of parenting and other developmental influences will best help them get there. It is also important to consider the context in which families live. In poor neighborhoods with high rates of violence and risky behavior, the use of punitive authoritarian parenting does not seem to have the same negative outcomes among African American boys as with other demographic groups, perhaps demonstrating a better "match" for these boys (Roche, Ensminger, & Cherlin, 2007).

Permissive Parenting

Permissive parents appear to show two patterns. **Permissive** parents are warm, sensitive, caring, and generally responsive to their children's thoughts and feelings. However, they exert low levels of control and make relatively few demands, permitting their children to make almost all of their own decisions. Also, while they clearly communicate their warmth, love, and caring, their communication tends to be less clear in situations requiring them to set limits on their children's behavior.

Permissive parents rarely assert their disciplinary control directly. They tend to rely on their children to learn and conform to what is expected and to internalize parental values on their own, based on observing their parents and reacting to their parents' expressions of upset and satisfaction regarding their children's behavior. Therefore, children with permissive parents tend to lack self-reliance and self-control and to have lower self-esteem and slightly higher rates of depression as they enter their adolescent years (Milevsky et al., 2007). This is also true of children with indifferent parents, described next, who seem to be emotionally detached and not to care what their children do (Loeb et al., 1980). Permissive and indifferent parenting might be particularly problematic when children are raised in more dangerous, high-risk neighborhoods (Roche et al., 2007). However, cross-cultural research linked both authoritative and permissive parenting with positive outcomes, such as high self-esteem, low numbers of problem behaviors, and personal competence among Spanish families (Garcia & Gracia, 2009).

Indifferent Parenting

Indifferent parents are detached and emotionally uninvolved. They are inconsistent in setting and maintaining age-appropriate standards and expectations for their children and in fulfilling their parental responsibilities (Lamb et al., 1992; Maccoby & Martin, 1983). Discipline by indifferent parents tends to be inconsistent, erratic, and out of step with the developmental needs of their children.

Children with indifferent parents may turn to peers or others for help in setting limits and learning morality, which puts them at increased risk of peer pressure. These children tend to have various degrees of developmental difficulties, including a low ability to

permissive parenting A style of parenting in which parents make relatively few demands on their children but clearly communicate their warmth and interest and provide considerable care and nurturance.

indifferent parenting A style of parenting in which parents' permissiveness reflects an avoidance of child-rearing responsibilities, sometimes with detrimental results.

tolerate frustration and control their impulsive and aggressive behavior. They also tend to have difficulty in making life choices and setting long-term goals. These factors likely play a role in the higher rates of delinquency found among these children (Hoeve et al., 2009). Additionally, they experience the highest rates of depression and the lowest rates of self-esteem and life satisfaction, compared to children reared with any of the other three parenting styles (Milevsky et al., 2007). At the extreme, indifferent parents may neglect their children's physical and emotional needs in ways that place them at risk for serious developmental and emotional problems. Child neglect and abuse are discussed later in this chapter.

Table 7.1 summarizes the main patterns of parental authority. While most parents are fairly consistent in their parenting styles, under certain circumstances, they may exhibit other styles. For example, a parent with an authoritative style may respond, on occasion, to an overtired child in an impatient and authoritarian manner after explaining to her for the tenth time why it is time to go to bed.

Changes Over Time

Patterns of child-rearing tend to change over time. Authoritarian parents, for instance, often ease up and shift to a more permissive or authoritative style as their children grow older. Changes in the family situation, such as the birth of another child, also can make a difference. The experience gained from rearing their first child frequently enables parents to be more comfortable and flexible in rearing the children who follow. Help from older children in caring for younger siblings can also reduce the stresses of parenting. On the other hand, additional children increase the family's overall childcare and economic burdens, so more relaxed parenting is not always the outcome. As we will see when we look at psychosocial development in adulthood in Chapters 13 and 15, other changes within a family, such as separation, divorce, and remarriage, as well as changes in employment, standard of living, and health, also may influence child-rearing. Families that are under stress tend to be more rigid, arbitrary, and authoritarian in rearing their children than families that are not.

Although parenting styles influence early childhood development, it should not be assumed that they alone determine a child's developmental course. First, these styles reflect average patterns and do not describe the unique pattern of interactions and experiences that characterizes the relationship between any particular parent and child. The quality and developmental impact of a particular parent-child relationship will be influenced by the unique qualities of the parent, the child, and their interactions and experiences in the relationship. Second, although parents are certainly important, other individuals both within and outside of the family may contribute in vital ways to psychosocial development during early childhood.

Relationships with Siblings

Brothers and sisters are major participants in the social activities of many preschoolers. Though adjustment to the birth of a sibling often leads to increased behavior problems in older siblings, these increases tend to be temporary (Baydar et al., 1997). Studies have shown that most young children are very interested in babies and speak to their

TABLE 7.1 Patterns of Parental Authority

Parenting Style	Control	Responsiveness
Authoritative	High	High
Authoritarian	High	Low
Permissive	Low	High
Indifferent	Low	Low

baby brothers and sisters in ways very similar to those of adult caregivers. Preschoolers also listen carefully to conversations between their parents and older brothers and sisters, as reflected in their efforts to join in family conversations. Their awareness of caregiving interactions between their parents and younger siblings helps them to respond to their younger siblings' distress with appropriate caregiving behaviors (Dunn & Shatz, 1989; Garner et al., 1994) and to initiate prosocial, helping behaviors (Howe, Ross, & Recchia, 2011).

Older siblings show similar behavior when they simplify their language while explaining a task to a younger sibling (Hoff-Ginsberg & Krueger, 1991). Among bilingual families, children who communicate with their siblings using the second language tend to be more proficient in that language (Duursma et al., 2007). Siblings also provide important role models for their preschool brothers and sisters, helping them learn social skills and parental expectations. Both the friendly and aggressive interactions of siblings contribute to the development of preschoolers' understandings of the feelings, intentions, and needs of people other than themselves (Brown & Dunn, 1992; Dunn, 1985; Howe et al., 2011).

Influences on Sibling Relationships

Sibling relationships do not occur in a vacuum. For example, they are influenced by the quality of the relationships their parents have with their children and with each other. Negative behaviors of both older and younger siblings, such as aggression (East, 2009), were linked to negative aspects of the mother-child relationship and, for older siblings, to negative aspects of the parents' marital relationship (Erel et al., 1998). When parents have good relationships with their children, siblings are more likely to get along (East, 2009). The quality of young children's social relationships with siblings is also predictive of the quality of their relationships with friends, not only in early childhood but in middle childhood, adolescence, and adulthood as well (Bank et al., 1996; East, 2009; Volling et al., 1997). In a seven-year longitudinal study of the relationships between thirty-nine sibling pairs from mixed-SES families, Judy Dunn, Cheryl Slomkowski, and Lynn Beardsall (1994) followed the children from preschool through middle childhood and early adolescence. Sibling pairs included older male—younger female, older female—younger male, boy-boy and girl-girl dyads. The average ages of the sibling pairs were three years and six and a half years at the beginning of the study and ten years and thirteen and a half years when the study was completed. Sibling pairs were studied at four points in time: when the younger sibling was three years old, six years old, eight years old, and ten years old.

Sibling relationships are important to social development. The warm and relaxed relationship between this preschooler and his school-age brother is likely to contribute positively to the quality of their other social relationships.
Source: Blend Images/Shutterstock.com.

> **What Do You Think?**
>
> What style of parental authority best describes what you experienced as a child? Did it change during middle childhood and adolescence? If you now have children or expect to in the future, which pattern of parenting do (will) you use? Why?

Dunn and her colleagues found considerable continuity in siblings' positive feelings and behaviors (affection, warmth, intimacy, cooperation) and negative feelings and behaviors (competition, jealousy, fighting) toward one another from early childhood and through early adolescence. Their detailed interviews with the children and their mothers revealed that the majority of children provided support for each other when faced with such problems as difficulties with other children at school, maternal illness, or accidents and illnesses that they themselves had suffered. Good relationships among siblings also helped protect children who were experiencing the stress of parental conflict (Waite, Shanahan, Calkins, Keane, & O'Brien, 2011). Finally, both siblings and their mothers attributed negative changes in sibling relationships to new friendships the children formed outside the family during middle childhood.

Given the social opportunities that siblings offer, one might expect children growing up with brothers and sisters to develop social skills earlier and more rapidly, and perhaps to end up with better skills than children who lack siblings. But having siblings can have its down side as well. For instance, caring for a younger sibling is likely to enhance the younger child's social competence, but being burdened with the younger child's care may also limit the older child's opportunities to spend time with peers. How siblings will affect a particular child's social development is likely to depend on the degree to which parents recognize and respond appropriately to the social needs of all of their children. Siblings continue to play an important role in childhood and adolescence, and as we will see, while they become less important in early adulthood (see Chapter 13), they regain importance in middle adulthood (Chapter 15) and late adulthood (Chapter 17).

Only Children

Of course, not every child has a sibling. What impact does growing up as an "only child" have on development? Two widely held but conflicting views exist regarding this question. One view suggests that being an only child is a negative experience because it deprives only children of the advantages of having siblings and "spoils" them because they are the sole focus of their parents' attention. The second view sees only childhood as an advantage, allowing parents to be more responsive and attentive than they would be if they had to share their time and resources with other children (Rosenberg & Hyde, 1993). Research suggests that only children perform as well or somewhat better on various measures—including self-esteem, achievement motivation, and academic success—than those from two-child families who must share their parents with siblings, and that the greatest problem only children and their families face may be the prejudicial views about them (Eckstein et al., 2010; Falbo, 1992; Falbo 2012; Laybourn, 1990). There is some evidence that only children have slightly less social contact with family members as they grow up, but these differences between only children and those with siblings are quite small (Trent & Spitze, 2011).

Relationships in an Expanding Social World

As we have just seen, parents and siblings have a profound and long-lasting impact on the child's developing social skills. In early childhood, the child's social world expands and changes, providing new opportunities for testing out these skills, and new challenges as well. Children learn from many sources that they can influence their social relationships through their own helpful or aggressive behavior, as we now explore.

Empathy and Prosocial Behavior

empathy A sensitive awareness of the thoughts and feelings of another person.

Empathy, the ability to experience vicariously the emotions of another person, is thought to play an important role in the successful development of friendships and other close emotional relationships (Eisenberg et al., 1989). *Prosocial behavior* refers to positive social actions that benefit others, such as sharing, helping, and cooperating. Some prosocial behaviors are *altruistic,* meaning they are voluntarily aimed at helping others with no expectation of rewards for oneself. The development of both empathy and prosocial behavior is related to sound parent-child relationships and secure attachment during infancy and toddlerhood, which we discussed in Chapter 5.

Preschool children will respond helpfully to another person's distress in a variety of situations. For example, mothers' observational reports of the prosocial behavior of their four- and seven-year-olds at home indicate that spontaneous helping occurred in both age groups more frequently than did sharing and giving, affection and praise, or reassuring and protecting (Grusec, 1991). Young children are able to empathize in other settings as well. One study of children at a day-care center playground found that more than 90 percent of the time, a crying child generated concerned and mostly helpful responses from the other children (Sawin, 1979). About half of the children who were near the distressed child looked as though they would cry themselves. Almost 20 percent of the nearby children tried to console the child directly (and their actions did, in fact, help reduce the crying); other children sought out an adult on the playground; still others threatened revenge on the child who caused the upset. Children as young as fourteen months will reliably help another person retrieve an object that they cannot reach, and as they get older, children engage in more complex prosocial tasks (Hamann, Warneken, & Tomasello, 2012; Warneken & Tomasello, 2007).

Development of Prosocial Behavior

Prosocial behavior, or helpfulness, is well established by the time a child reaches the preschool years. An early, classic study found that all of the following helping behaviors occurred with significant frequency among four-year-olds (Murphy, 1937): assisting another child, comforting another child, protecting another child, warning another child of danger, giving things to another child, and inquiring of a child in trouble. Today, we find these behaviors not only among preschool children but even among children younger than two (Eisenberg & Mussen, 1989; Radke-Yarrow & Zahn-Waxler, 1987; Warneken & Tomasello, 2007).

Between the ages of two and six, children give increasingly complex reasons for helping and are more strongly influenced by nonaltruistic as well as altruistic motives and concerns (Eisenberg et al., 1989; Yarrow & Waxler, 1978). An older child may justify

These two children are concerned about the unhappy toddler. Important gains in children's capacity for empathy and emotional support develop during the preschool years.
Source: Ermolaev Alexander/Shutterstock.com.

helpfulness in terms of gaining approval from peers in general, rather than in terms of concern for the well-being of the child in distress. Or a child may justify withholding help because of fear of disapproval from adults—for example, if the child has been instructed to let the day-care or nursery school teachers handle children in trouble.

Sources of Prosocial Behavior

Potential sources of individual differences in prosocial responses include age, gender, temperament, childcare experience, social competence with peers, and friendship status (Farver & Branstetter, 1994). Prosocial behaviors increase with age due to gains in cognitive functioning, social skills, and moral reasoning and to more socialization experiences that enhance prosocial responsiveness (Eisenberg & Mussen, 1989; Warneken & Tomasello, 2007). No consistent gender differences in prosocial responses have been found, although some studies have found girls to be more prosocial than boys.

There is some evidence that differences in temperament affect children's prosocial behavior. Young children who display high levels of prosocial behavior tend to be active, outgoing, and emotionally expressive. This pattern is similar to the temperamentally *easy child,* whose high levels of adaptiveness, positive mood, and approachfulness (tendency to approach) may help him initiate and sustain more peer interaction than *difficult* or *slow-to-warm-up children,* who are more likely to avoid peer contact (Buss & Plomin, 1984; Farver & Branstetter, 1994; Kim & Jang, 2010).

Early exposure to prosocial experiences with peers, parents, and other important individuals may be the best predictor of later prosocial behavior. Jo Ann Farver and Wendy Branstetter (1994) studied prosocial behavior among preschoolers ages three to four and a half in three childcare programs. They found that the type and quality of peer contact children experienced more than the length of time children spent in their prior or current preschool programs influenced their prosocial tendencies. Early peer relationships are most likely to foster prosocial responsiveness when teachers, parents, and other adults create an environment that supports it and provides models for children to observe and imitate.

Prosocial competence among preschoolers may also depend on how often parents initiate informal play activities. Gary Ladd and Craig Hart (1992) found that children whose parents frequently arranged for them to play with peers and actively involved them in arranging play activities displayed higher levels of prosocial behavior. Children who more frequently initiated informal peer contacts were better liked by their classmates.

Overall differences in parenting styles also appear to influence preschoolers' prosocial behavior. Children whose parents are authoritative in their disciplinary styles engage in more prosocial, empathic, and compassionate behavior and less antisocial behavior in day-care, playground, and school settings later in life (Carlo et al., 2007) than do children whose parents have authoritarian discipline styles (Hart et al., 1992; Main & George, 1985; Zahn-Waxler et al., 1979). There is also evidence that fostering sympathy among children increases their prosocial behaviors (Carlo, McGinley, Hayes, Batenhorst, & Wilkinson, 2007; Carlo, Mestre, Samper, Tur, & Armenta, 2011).

Cross-cultural studies have provided some additional insights into the significance of parental support and encouragement (Carlo et al., 2011; Trommsdorff, Friedlmeier, & Mayer, 2007). In mainly rural societies where mothers worked in the fields and children assumed major childcare and household responsibilities, children had more opportunities to experience prosocial roles and to behave prosocially. Firstborn children, who had the most helping experience, tended to be more prosocial than lastborn or only children. Children raised in close-knit, communal Israeli kibbutz communities, which place high value on cooperation and prosocial behavior, exhibited higher levels of cooperation and prosocial behavior than did children from rural or big-city areas (Eisenberg et al., 1990; Whiting & Edwards, 1988).

What practical steps can parents and teachers take to increase altruism and prosocial behavior in the children they care for? Two techniques that have proven successful in increasing such behavior among preschoolers are (1) verbal approval and encouragement for being empathic, sympathetic, respectful, and helpful to others and (2) arranging regular play opportunities that support and encourage sharing, cooperation, and helping.

Conflict and Aggression

So far, our discussion of social relationships has focused on the ability of preschoolers to get along reasonably well with one another. However, preschoolers also get very angry and express their feelings in aggressive ways: grabbing one another's toys, pushing, hitting, scratching, and calling names. What types of interpersonal conflicts make preschoolers angry, and how do they cope with their angry feelings? Richard Fabes and Nancy Eisenberg (1992) observed the causes of anger and reactions to provocations among preschool children between ages 3 and 6½ while the children were at play. Conflict over possessions was the most common cause of anger, and physical assault was the second most frequent cause. In most types of anger conflicts, the majority of children responded by expressing angry feelings (particularly boys) or by actively attempting to defend themselves in nonaggressive ways (particularly girls). Active resistance was most likely in conflicts over material things such as toys and least likely in conflicts involving compliance with teachers and other adults. In contrast, venting of angry feelings was least likely in material conflicts and most likely in compliance conflicts with adults, suggesting that the particular coping strategy chosen depends, in part, on how controllable the child sees the situation to be. Children's use of aggressive revenge (hitting or threatening) and tattling was most frequent when their anger was caused by physical assault.

Aggression refers to actions that are intended to harm another person or an object. Aggressive actions frequently are divided into two types. **Overt aggression** harms others through physical damage or the threat of physical damage such as pushing, hitting, kicking, or threatening to "beat up" a peer. In contrast, **relational aggression** harms others through damage or threat of damage to their peer relationships, for example, by threatening to withdraw friendship to get one's way or by using social exclusion or rumor spreading as a form of retaliation. Children tend to express their aggression in ways that are most likely to interfere with or damage the social goals of their target and in ways that are socially acceptable for their gender. Consequently, boys are more likely to use overt, physical forms of aggression that hinder the dominance goals of boys, whereas girls are more likely to use more verbal, relational forms of aggression that effectively hinder the social intimacy goals that are more typical of girls' peer relationships (Card, Stucky, Sawalani, & Little, 2008; Crick et al., 1997). Although the harmful effects of overt aggression have long been obvious, recent studies indicate that relationally aggressive behaviors are also highly aversive and damaging to both victims and aggressors. The majority of children view these behaviors as mean, hostile acts that cause harm and are often carried out in anger, and children who are frequently the target of relationally aggressive acts experience more psychological distress, such as depression and anxiety, than do their

aggression A bold, assertive action that is intended to hurt another person or to procure an object.

overt aggression Actions that harm others through physical damage or the threat of such damage, such as pushing, hitting, kicking, or threatening to "beat up" a peer.

relational aggression Actions that harm others through damage or threat of damage to their peer relationships.

Hostile aggression among preschoolers is frequently associated with frustrations at being unable to solve a conflict over wants and desires, as well as with angry and jealous feelings that may result when they cannot get what they want.
Source: SpeedKingz/Shutterstock.com.

228 **Part 3** Early Childhood

nontargeted peers (Card et al., 2008). Relationally aggressive boys and girls have poorer social and emotional adjustment and report higher levels of loneliness, depression, and negative self-perceptions than do their nonrelationally aggressive peers. Children who frequently engage in relational aggression are also far more likely to experience peer rejection, currently and in the future (Card et al., 2008; Crick, 1996; Crick & Grotpeter, 1995; Grotpeter & Crick, 1996).

When expressed in acceptable ways, aggression may be not only tolerable but even desirable. Aggressive actions allow a child to communicate and fulfill legitimate needs, such as when he takes back a toy that is rightfully his or stands up for his integrity against unfair insults. Often, however, hostile motivations complicate matters and create additional distress. The anger and rage children sometimes experience can be quite upsetting to them as well as to their parents and others. For example, a mother who observes her four-year-old attack a playmate, perhaps biting her or pulling her hair, is likely to be upset for multiple reasons, including her own child's unhappiness, the pain and distress of the other child, her belief that biting is "dirty fighting," and concerns about how all of this reflects on her as a parent.

Temperamental Differences in Aggression

Temperamental differences that are present at birth may make aggressive behavior and parent-child conflict more likely during early childhood. For example, babies who are low in their ability to regulate their physical and emotional states and high in emotional intensity may be especially prone to overt expressions of anger, frustration, and aggressive behavior, whereas those with a high ability to regulate these states are more likely to cope more constructively with their anger and frustration. Children who have difficulty regulating emotions are particularly prone to be aggressive when reacting to some type of perceived offense, such as someone bumping into them (Vitaro, Barker, Boivin, Brendgen, & Tremblay, 2006).

Consistent with this view, Nancy Eisenberg and her colleagues found that babies with especially "difficult" temperaments at six months of age experienced significantly more conflict with their mothers at age three than did babies with less difficult temperaments (Eisenberg & Fabes, 1992; Eisenberg et al., 1994; Rothbart, 2007). As three-year-olds, these children were more likely to be uncooperative, ignore their parents' disciplinary efforts, and respond in insulting and unpleasant ways. Their frustrated parents used a wide variety of methods to attempt to control them, including forbidding certain activities, threatening punishment, and using physical restraint. Thus, the ongoing interactions between these difficult children and their parents seemed likely to be escalating a cycle of aggression (Eisenberg et al., 1994). Of course, many active or difficult babies do not become aggressive three-year-olds, perhaps because the expression of temperament is largely a product of child-caregiver interactions. For example, when parents engage in authoritarian-type parenting, their children were more likely to be reactively aggressive, as described earlier, and proactively aggressive, such as intimidating others to get what they want (Vitaro et al., 2006).

A fifteen-year longitudinal study conducted by Avshalom Caspi and his colleagues found a relationship between early childhood temperament, including emotional instability, restlessness, impulsiveness, negativism, and teacher and parent reports of problems with aggression in middle childhood and adolescence (Caspi et al., 1995). Temperamental and family characteristics at age three have also been found to predict convictions for violent criminal activities at age eighteen (DeLisi & Vaughn, 2014; Henry et al., 1996).

Child-Rearing Styles and Aggression

As in the case of prosocial behavior discussed earlier, styles of child-rearing and the overall quality of the parent-child relationship are likely to significantly influence children's use of aggression in coping with interpersonal anger. There is some evidence that both indifferent and extremely authoritarian parenting styles are likely to be associated with higher levels of aggression and lower levels of prosocial behavior (DeKlyen et al., 1998; Herrenkohl et al., 1997; Hoeve et al., 2009). Longitudinal research by Kenneth Dodge and his colleagues found that children who experienced family violence, harsh, punitive (and potentially abusive) parenting styles, and parental rejection or hostility in their preschool years were much more likely to be both aggressive and victims of bullying in middle childhood than peers who received more supportive parenting (Deater-Deckhard et al., 1996; Schwartz et al., 1997; Vitaro et al., 2006).

All of the following child-rearing characteristics have been found to contribute to aggressiveness in preschoolers, especially when they are part of an ongoing pattern (Hart et al., 1990; Martin, 1975; Vitaro et al., 2006):

1. Lack of acceptance of the child, dislike of the child, and criticism of the child for being the sort of person she or he currently is or is becoming

2. Excessive permissiveness, particularly if it includes indifference to the child's true needs for reasonable but consistent limits and emotional support

3. Discipline that does not respect the child's ability and need to understand the reasons for the punishment and its meaning to the parent

4. Inconsistent discipline, which fails to provide the child with a reasonable and predictable basis for learning to regulate his or her behavior

5. A "spare the rod and spoil the child" belief that *too little* physical discipline would be harmful, which often results in impulsive and overly harsh use of discipline

6. Unclear rules and expectations for the child, particularly those regarding interactions with other family members

Children whose parents are able to accept their hostile-aggressive impulses and actions and respectfully guide their efforts to discover nonhostile methods for resolving conflicts and asserting their needs are most likely to learn to manage their aggression. The child-rearing orientation of such parents closely corresponds to the authoritative parenting style, which is strongly associated with the development of prosocial behavior.

Peer Influences on Aggression

Peers can also contribute to aggression by acting in ways that provoke aggressive retaliation. A child surrounded by provocative peers is likely to acquire a similar style herself and, in doing so, stimulate further aggressive behavior in her peers.

Some preschool children are continually involved in conflicts. They constantly either lose battles and arguments or lose potential friends by depending too much on hostile, aggressive actions to get what they need. Kenneth Dodge and his colleagues (Dodge & Coie, 1987; Schwartz et al., 1997) believe that a combination of low peer status and lack of social competence in the preschool period may contribute to a child's tendency to behave aggressively. When entering a new group, for example, aggressive children have difficulty in accurately processing and evaluating information about what is expected and in generating appropriate responses when faced with threats or provocation. Such children may have a biased pattern of thinking that leads them to overestimate the harmful intentions of their peers and to respond aggressively in situations that do not warrant it. The labeling of others' behavior that may actually be neutral and innocuous as aggression is called **hostile attribution bias**. Children are more likely to engage in hostile attribution bias and to react aggressively with those perceived as enemies (Peets, Hodges, Kikas, & Salmivalli, 2007). The aggressive, hostile behavior of an unpopular preschooler may also be his way of externalizing anger and distress he is experiencing due to similar problems at home.

Media Influences on Aggression

As many concerned parents realize, television, films, video games, and other media exert a strong influence on children, and much of that influence centers on physical violence. Researchers estimate that three-to-four-year-olds watch two or more hours of television each day and that viewing TV violence increases children's aggressive behavior, at least in the

hostile attribution bias
The tendency to view others' behavior as aggressive, even when those behaviors are innocuous, which often leads to a hostile, reactive response.

short run. Numerous studies indicate that watching violence *disinhibits,* or releases, violent behavior in children who are already prone to anger and aggression, and also sets up scripts that guide behavior (Bushman & Huesmann, 2006; Clarke & Kutz-Costes, 1997; Huston et al., 1989). Viewing violent media may also increase the likelihood that a child engages in hostile attribution bias, which subsequently increases aggression (Gentile, Coyne, & Walsh, 2011). Longitudinal studies have linked the amount of TV violence viewed between the ages of two and five to antisocial behavior five years later for boys, even when accounting for preexisting behavioral problems and parenting factors such as education, depression, and responsiveness (Christakis & Zimmerman, 2007). Media are so pervasive in many preschoolers' lives that we consider their impact separately in the next section.

Responding to Aggressive Behavior

Children who have difficulty controlling their aggression experience considerable problems. Often they become aggressive at inappropriate times and in self-defeating ways, getting into fights with children and adults who are stronger than they are. Peers and parents alike find it difficult not to attribute malicious motives to children who seem out of control and appear unresponsive to generally agreed-on standards of behavior (Kutner, 1989). Children who are overly aggressive can stimulate strong feelings of inadequacy, guilt, anger, and loss of control in their parents, leading to an increased risk that parents will respond in angry, punitive, ways.

Spanking and Other Forms of Punishment

In general, preschoolers conform to parental expectations, especially if those expectations are communicated in a clear, understandable way that conveys warmth and respect for the child. Even when a child resists, patient explanation and responsiveness to his feelings and perceptions generally resolve the problem. In instances when a preschooler "loses it" and throws a tantrum or refuses to comply with a parent's reasonable and necessary demands, firm but respectful physical restraint and guidance may also be needed until the child has regained self-control. In dangerous situations requiring immediate action, such as when a child runs into the street or is about to touch something hot, parents may use strong reprimands or spanking to stop the risky behavior and prevent it from happening again. However, using spanking as a punishment is not only ineffective, it can teach children to fear their parents and that physical violence is an appropriate means to control others.

Some parents rely on spanking and punishment as a regular part of their child-rearing discipline. James Comer and Alvin Poussaint (1992), two prominent child psychiatrists, point out that children who were spanked by thoughtful, loving parents rarely have problems as a result of the spanking. Nevertheless, Comer and Poussaint caution that punishment is not the best way to provide discipline, especially in cases where parents are having difficulty with their preschoolers. A better alternative is to physically remove the child from the dangerous situation and to talk about why the parent is upset, why the child's behavior is unacceptable, and expectations of how to behave in the future.

What problems are associated with spanking and punishment in general? Although verbal or physical punishment can suppress misbehavior in the short run, it is not an effective or desirable long-run strategy, particularly if it is harsh or frequent. One obvious problem is that preschoolers are very likely to imitate the behavior of the adult models who punish them (Bandura, 1991; Emery, 1989; Taylor, Manganello, Lee, & Rice, 2010). Using aggressive behavior such as verbal threats or spanking to reduce a child's unacceptable behavior is likely to increase the very behavior it seeks to control. A child who is hit by an angry parent learns to act on his own anger in similar ways, which is surely not the lesson his parents intend. Even moderate use of spanking appears to contribute to child aggression. One large-scale study conducted by Robert Larzelere (1986) using a nationally representative sample of parents with at least one child age three to seventeen living at home found that the use of physical punishment was positively associated with child aggression. In situations where spanking was frequent and reasons were rarely provided, the association between spanking and child aggression dramatically increased. Excessive reliance on spanking and other forms of punishment is strongly linked to child maltreatment, a topic we discuss later in this chapter.

A second problem with spanking and other forms of punishment is that a child quickly learns to fear and avoid the punishing adult, thus reducing opportunities for adult supervision and constructive adult-child interactions. Third, because punishment quickly suppresses the child's undesirable behavior in the short run, it serves to reinforce adult reliance on punishment and reduce the likelihood of exploring other ways to respond to the child's unacceptable behavior. Fourth, to the extent that punishment reduces the guilt a child feels for misbehaving, it reinforces the child's reliance on external (parental) control rather than internal, self-control of his behavior (Comer & Poussaint, 1992).

Helping Aggressive Children and Their Parents

Several principles have emerged from work with aggressive children and their families aimed at helping them learn more constructive ways of interacting. The most successful approaches frequently involve working with the entire family. The first step is to carefully observe the child's interactions with peers and adults to discover consistent patterns in what triggers the aggression and how each family member may unintentionally reinforce the patterns of problem behavior (Kutner, 1989; Patterson et al., 1989).

Structure, predictability, and consistency of routine are important for all preschoolers, especially for children who have difficulty controlling their aggressive behavior. For such children, aggressive outbursts are most likely to occur in unstructured and ambiguous situations. Such circumstances aggravate their tendency to distort information about potential harm and to perceive themselves as being at risk. Thus, neutral behavior, such as the approach of another child, is misinterpreted as an aggressive act (Dodge et al., 1994; Peets et al., 2007).

Once the patterns of aggression are discovered, parents can learn to recognize the early signs and intervene by either changing the situation or removing their preschooler before things escalate. The most successful methods involve reinforcement of positive behaviors through warmth, affection, and parental approval; reasoning with children and talking to them calmly about the situation (Sheehan & Watson, 2008); assertiveness training to help children meet their needs for attention in less self-destructive ways; and increasing predictability and consistency in children's everyday lives (Kutner, 1989; Patterson, 1989).

Another successful approach to modifying destructive family processes and problems with childhood aggression uses social learning theory methods such as coaching, modeling, and reinforcing alternative patterns of parent-child interaction. After carefully observing the parent-child interaction, the therapist describes and then demonstrates alternative ways to deal with the child's hostile, aggressive, or disobedient behaviors. As parents gain more confidence in their competence, they become more effective parents; as children learn to resolve conflicts in more appropriate ways, their problematic behavior decreases (Patterson, 1982, 1985).

The Effects of Media on Preschoolers' Development

As influential as parents and family are in the lives of preschoolers, media have become another potent force in teaching preschoolers about the wider world. More than 99 percent of American homes have at least one television set (Siebens, 2013). Eighty-four percent of homes have a computer, and 75 percent of households have Internet access (File & Ryan, 2014). When all media consumption is combined, the average American consumes about 15.5 hours of media per day (Short, 2015). Most children are exposed to media on television and computers from the time they are born, and American children spend as much or more time, on average, watching TV than in any other waking activity, including play (Calvert, 2008; Condry, 1993). Differences in family circumstances significantly affect young children's TV viewing. Living in neighborhoods that parents thought of as unsafe was linked to increased media use, and children whose parents engage in limit setting consumed less media than those with parents who did not set limits (Lee, Bartolic, & Vandewater, 2009).

As Figure 7.1 shows, a typical three-year-old is in front of a TV set approximately two hours per day. Viewing time increases during the preschool years and peaks at about 2.5 hours per day (Ofcom, 2014; Vandewater, 2007). Boys and girls appear to watch equal

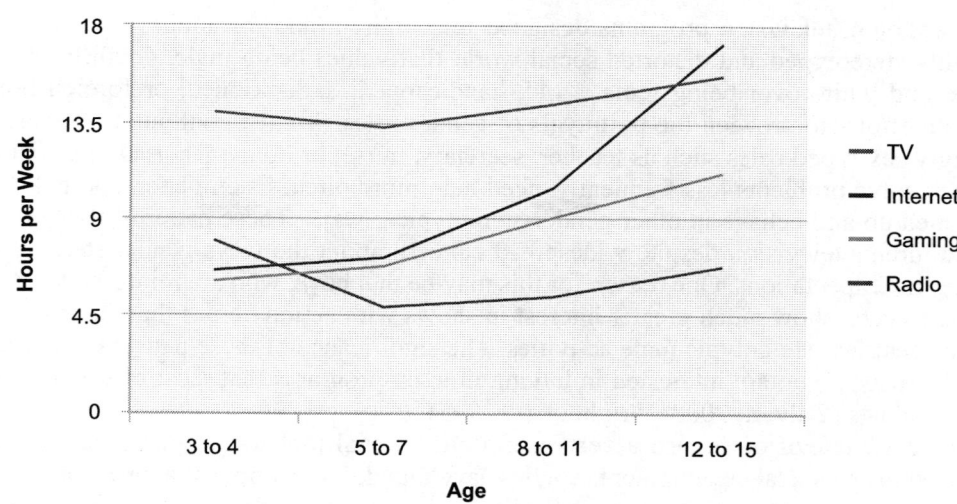

FIGURE 7.1
Media Use Among Children

Hours of media consumption per week for children of different ages.
Source: Ofcom, 2014.

amounts of television. The same basic developmental pattern has been found in a number of European countries, Canada, and Australia, and the amount of time using any kind of media other than print has increased significantly since 1999, mostly due to increased time using multiple types of media at one time (Rideout, Foehr, & Roberts, 2010).

Not surprisingly, the types of programs children prefer to watch also change with age. Until they are age three or four, children prefer programs such as "Bubble Guppies," "Sesame Street," and "Caillou," which are designed for children and feature language, characters, and events at a level children can readily understand. Children ages three to five tend to watch more cartoons, and children ages five to seven increasingly watch comedies, action shows, and special-interest programs that are more cognitively demanding and aimed at general audiences (Huston et al., 1990).

What Do Kids See on TV?

Television viewing has been found to influence children's social development in a number of areas, including aggression, prosocial behavior, consumer behavior, executive functioning, eating behaviors, and gender stereotypes (Anderson & Anderson, 2010; Christakis & Zimmerman, 2007; Coyne, Linder, Rasmussen, Nelson, & Collier, 2014; Huston & Wright, 1996; Lillard & Peterson, 2011). The relationships between viewing aggression on TV and children's aggressive behavior are notable.

Preschoolers have a special problem in coping with violence on TV: their lack of skill in figuring out the motives of characters portrayed and the subtleties of plots. A heinous murder on television may look the same to a preschooler as one committed in self-defense or to protect innocent people. Also, some of the most violent TV programs are those produced for children; Saturday morning cartoons, which are now available any time on cartoon-based channels and streaming content services like Netflix, average more than twenty violent acts per hour (Gerbner et al., 1986; Kirsh, 2006). Programs such as "Spider Man," "Iron Man," "Teen Titans," and "Adventure Time" and many films that young children view also contain substantial amounts of violent content. Violent video and computer games pose similar problems for young children and their parents (Adachi & Willoughby, 2011; Emes, 1997). Adult supervision and help in understanding television programs therefore are especially important for very young children. Unfortunately, one of television's main attractions for some parents is that it makes adult supervision unnecessary by keeping children passively occupied.

Recent widespread concern about children's exposure to television violence has led to a new U.S. communications law stipulating that all new TV sets be equipped with a "violence chip," or V-chip. The V-chip "reads" TV programming and allows parents to tune out shows that they consider too violent for their children based on a rating system. Though technologies exist to control children's media consumption and limit exposure to violent programming, most parents do not actually use them (Calvert, 2008).

In addition, television programs designed for children (and for adults) often convey a highly stereotyped and distorted social world that values being male, youthful, handsome, and white over being female, old, handicapped, dark-skinned, or foreign born. Despite efforts to broaden the portrayals of gender roles, women continue to be cast in strongly sex-typed roles such as teacher, secretary, nurse, or homemaker. On television, women solve problems less frequently, need help more often, listen better, and talk less than men do and behave in other gender-stereotypical ways. These patterns also prevail for children's television despite widespread concern about the ways gender stereotypes limit girls' expectations. One reason for this may be that boys, who are reinforced largely by their peers, show much greater interest in shows with action heroes than in programs that present less stereotypic male activities. The significance of these patterns is not lost on advertisers, who are interested in buying time on programs that most effectively sell their products (Calvert, 2008; Wright et al., 1995).

However, television is also a very useful educational tool for supporting children's intellectual and social development. Studies have found, for example, that programs modeling cooperative, prosocial behavior are likely to increase children's prosocial behavior and that children who are exposed to nongender and nonracially stereotyped programs are more likely than other children to behave in less stereotypic ways (Calvert, 2008; Liebert & Sprafkin, 1988).

How Do Parents Affect Viewing Patterns?

The types of programs TV networks and streaming services provide and the choices parents make about what their children view strongly affect young children's viewing patterns (Calvert, 2008; Huston et al., 1992). Families vary considerably in their attitudes toward television and the amount and type of guidance they provide for their children. While nearly 40 percent of the parents of preschoolers sometimes use TV to keep their children occupied, between 40 and 60 percent state that they regularly limit the number of hours their children can watch, and 50 to 60 percent have consistent rules regarding which types or which specific programs their children are allowed to view (Calvert, 2008; Comstock, 1991; Gentile, Nathanson, Rasmussen, Reimer, & Walsh, 2012). It is important to note that when surveying children and their parents, parents' estimates of these monitoring behaviors are significantly higher than their children's estimates of the same monitoring behaviors (Gentile et al., 2012).

Current recommendations for media use during early childhood are that children age two and under should not watch TV or use other types of entertainment, and that after age two, media should be limited, that parents should use media along with their children, and that families should set up times and places that are "screen-free" to encourage physical activity, reading, and traditional game playing (American Academy of Pediatrics, 2016; Connell, Lauricella, & Wartella, 2015). Though increasing numbers of children have televisions in their bedrooms (33 percent of children age six or under have their own television—Vandewater et al., 2007), the amount of time that parents spend watching television is the strongest predictor of child viewing time, even when accounting for bedroom TV access (Bleakley, Jordan, & Hennessy, 2013). When considering other types of media, co-use rates shift. Parents are most likely to use books and TV along with their children, but much less likely to use computers or video games along with their children, even though this type of media sharing has been linked to more prosocial behaviors, higher levels of cohesiveness within a family, higher child self-efficacy, and more use of educational websites (Connell, Lauricella, & Wartella, 2015).

Play in Early Childhood

In our society and many others, play dominates the preschool years. What are the play activities of a preschooler like, and what important contributions does play make to a child's development? Before we tackle these questions, we must first agree on what we mean by *play*.

> **What Do You Think?**
>
> When you were a child, how did your family deal with the issues of prosocial behavior, aggression, and television? If you become a parent (or are now a parent), what might you change and what might you keep the same? Why?

The Nature of Play

One useful approach to defining *play* focuses on the attitudes and dispositions of children themselves (Saracho & Spodek, 1998). First, play is *intrinsically* (rather than *extrinsically*) motivated. Children engage in play mainly because it is enjoyable and reinforcing for its own sake rather than because it is useful in achieving external goals.

Second, play is *process* oriented rather than *product* oriented. At the local playground, for instance, children may care very little about the goal of using the slide, to get from top to bottom, but likely care a lot about their style of sliding—whether they go head first or feet first, or how fast they go.

Third, play is *creative* and *nonliteral*. Although it resembles real-life activities, it differs from them in that it is not bound by reality. For example, a child who is "play fighting" looks different than one who really is fighting, and a child playing Mommy typically acts differently than one who is actually caring for a baby brother or sister. The features that reveal an activity as play rather than the real thing vary with the particular type of play and the situation; a play fight may include smiles and laughter, and a make-believe mother may be exaggeratedly bossy. Whatever the signs, they communicate the message that "this behavior is *not* what it first may appear to be." Even so, it is common for a preschooler to become so caught up in a round of dramatic play that he forgets for a moment that it is not real and becomes truly frightened when his make-believe mother tells him he has been bad and must sit in the corner.

Fourth, play tends to be governed by *implicit rules*—that is, rules that can be discovered by observing the activity, rather than rules that are formally stated and that exist independently of the activity. For example, although no rule book exists for playing house, children implicitly understand that there can be two parents and that these actors must live up to certain expectations. If one player deviates too widely from the expected role, the other children are likely to correct her for it ("Hey, babies don't drive cars; only big people do that!").

Fifth, play is *spontaneous* and *self-initiated,* meaning it is engaged in only under a child's own free will and is not evoked or controlled by others. Finally, play is *free from major emotional distress*. Play does not normally occur when a child is in a state of fear, uncertainty, or other kind of significant stress. It might be interesting to think about play in your own childhood, adolescence, and adulthood and see to what degree it has involved these six qualities.

Theories of Play

There are four main theoretical approaches to play: psychoanalytic, learning, ethological, and cognitive. Although each theory emphasizes a somewhat different aspect of play, all hold that play activities make a major contribution to the development of important social and emotional skills and understandings during the preschool years. Moreover, play during early childhood has important implications for the development and refinement of social information processing, empathy, emotional regulation, conflict management, perspective taking, and skilled social interaction over the lifespan (Creasey et al., 1998; Power, 2011).

Psychoanalytic Theory

Psychoanalytic theories emphasize the social and emotional importance of play in early childhood. Play gives a child an opportunity to *gain mastery* over problems by rearranging objects and social situations in ways that allow her to imagine she is in control. Following an especially painful and upsetting experience, such as being suddenly separated from a parent who is hospitalized for a serious illness, a child may display *repetition compulsion,* repeating the experience over and over in symbolic play with dolls or other toys to gain greater control, or resolution, of the distress.

Play also allows a child to use fantasy to *gain satisfaction for wishes and desires* that are not possible to fulfill in reality due to limitations in the child's abilities and life situation. Play also provides an opportunity for *catharsis,* the release of upsetting feelings that cannot be expressed otherwise. Finally, play allows children to *gain increased power* over the environment by rearranging it to suit their own needs and abilities (Lewis, 1993). These facets of play are particularly useful in helping young children in therapeutic sessions (James & Countryman, 2012; Kool & Lawver, 2010).

Learning Theory

Learning theorists view play as a major means by which children progressively learn adult skills and social roles. A child learns in three ways: through her own experience of being praised or encouraged for her own actions (direct reinforcement), through observations of adults and other children being reinforced for their activities (vicarious reinforcement), and through the experience of setting a goal and achieving it (cognitive or self-reinforcement).

For example, what might a three-year-old who is playing with wooden blocks be learning about the adult world? For one thing, building with blocks gives the child an opportunity to learn about the nature and design of physical structures and space. The child also learns about how hard blocks are, how high they can be piled, and how many small ones equal a larger one. He might also learn about his own capabilities and limitations as a builder: how high he can reach, how many blocks he can carry at once, and so forth. Playing with blocks also exposes the child to adult expectations and practices, such as when and where blocks can be used, picked up, and stored and how to share blocks, take turns, and cooperate with others.

Ethological Theory

physical activity play Vigorous physical activity that occurs in a playful context, has a basis in human evolution, and serves several adaptive developmental functions.

Theorists such as A. D. Pellegrini and Peter Smith (1998) believe that children's **physical activity play**—vigorous physical activity that occur in a playful context—has a basis in human evolution and serves several adaptive developmental functions. Examples include running, climbing, chasing, and play fighting. Physical activity play begins in early infancy, peaks during childhood, declines during adolescence, and all but disappears by adulthood. It appears to take three forms. The first is *rhythmic stereotypies.* These repetitive movements, such as body rocking and foot kicking displayed by

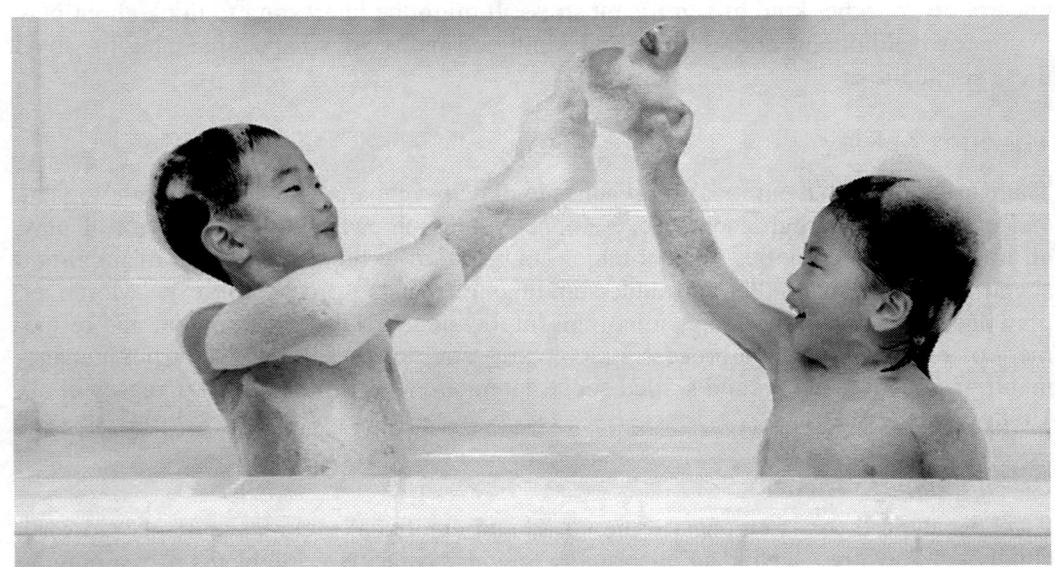

In early childhood, the process of doing things often matters more than the outcome. Even taking a bath can seem like play.
Source: Blend Images/Shutterstock.com.

infants and the repetitive play interactions between parents and older infants, such as bouncing the baby on one's knee or tossing and catching the infant, are thought to help infants improve their sensorimotor skills. A second form of physical activity play, *exercise play*, emerges at the end of the first year. Exercise play includes chasing, jumping, pushing and pulling, lifting, and climbing. It appears to peak in the preschool and early primary grades, and is thought to contribute to the development of physical strength, endurance, and coordination. The third form, *rough-and-tumble play*, includes vigorous behaviors such as wrestling, grappling, kicking, tumbling, and chasing in a playfully aggressive way. Rough-and-tumble play increases through the preschool years and peaks at around eight to ten years, just prior to early adolescence. It is thought to provide a way for children to assess their own physical strength compared to the strength of others, establish dominance status in peer groups, assist in emotion-regulation development, and gain skill at recognizing and responding appropriately to the emotional states of others (Power, 2011). Fathers are more likely than mothers to engage in rough-and-tumble play with their children, which can lead to higher rates of aggression later in childhood if those fathers do not take a dominant role in that play (Flanders, Leo, Paquette, Pihl, & Séguin, 2009).

Cognitive Theory

Cognitive theorists, discussed in Chapter 2, have identified four major kinds of play that they believe develop sequentially in parallel with the major stages of cognitive development (Piaget, 1962; Smilansky, 1968). Table 7.2 describes the different types of cognitive play.

Cognitive Levels of Play: Developmental Trends

Functional Play

Functional play, which involves simple, repeated movements such as splashing water or digging in a sandbox, is most common during the sensorimotor period. Because it requires no symbolic activity, functional play makes up more than one-half of the play activity of older infants and toddlers. By the time a child reaches kindergarten or first grade, however, functional play has decreased to less than one-quarter of his total play time. This shift occurs partly because some of the physical activities typical of functional play become incorporated into more symbolic forms of play (Hetherington et al., 1979; Sponseller & Jaworski, 1979).

functional play A cognitive level of play that involves simple, repeated movements and a focus on one's own body.

TABLE 7.2 Types of Cognitive Play

Type	Description and Examples
Functional play	Simple, repetitive movements—sometimes, with objects or own body
	Example: Shoveling sand, pushing a toy
Constructive play	Manipulation of physical objects to build or construct something
	Example: Building with blocks
Pretend play	Substituting make-believe, imaginary, and dramatic situations for real ones
	Example: Playing house or Superman
Games with rules	Play that is more formal and governed by fixed rules
	Example: Jumping rope, hide-and-seek

Constructive Play

Constructive play involves manipulation of physical objects, such as using blocks to build something. This form of play is evident in older infants and preschoolers, although it is not always clear where functional play ends and constructive play begins. For example, a child who at first appears to be building a mountain out of sand may forget about her goal and end up just shoveling the sand for the fun of it. As the child grows older, however, the constructive elements of play become quite clear. Not only does she build a mountain; she builds it in a certain shape and adds a road leading to it and perhaps a car or two to make the trip.

Constructive play, such as block building, is probably the most common form of play in early childhood.
Source: Ami Parikh/Shutterstock.com.

constructive play A type of play that involves manipulation of physical objects to build or construct something.

pretend play Play that substitutes imaginary situations for real ones. Also called *fantasy* or *dramatic play*.

Pretend Play

Pretend play (also called *fantasy* or *dramatic play*) substitutes imaginary situations for real ones, such as in playing house or Superman, and dominates the preoperational period. Pretend play occurs even among toddlers and probably begins as soon as a child can symbolize, or mentally represent, objects. Family roles (including mother, father, brother, sister, baby, and even family pet) and *character roles* based on fictionalized heroes, such as Batman, Disney princesses, Iron Man, and Kung Fu Panda, are most likely to be dramatized by preschool children. Pretend play grows in frequency and complexity during the preschool years and eventually decreases again later in childhood, when social pressures to act more "grown up" reduce it in public settings (Dunn, 1985; Howes & Matheson, 1992; Kavanaugh & Engel, 1998; Russ & Dillon, 2011). The complexity, flexibility, and elaborateness of preschoolers' fantasy play also appear to be positively related to the quality of their family relationships, to the support and the nurturance preschoolers receive from their parents, and to the specific reinforcement parents give them for such play (Howe et al., 1998; Ladd & Hart, 1992). Though children have less unstructured time for play than they did in the past, they display just as much emotional expression and more imagination in their play (Russ & Dillon, 2011).

Pretend play is a good example of how new forms of experience are assimilated into existing schemes of cognitive understanding. In addition to allowing the child to practice and expand schemes already acquired, such play contributes to the consolidation and expansion of cognitive skills during early childhood (Piaget, 1962; Vygotsky, 1967). Early pretend play, when suitably nurtured by family members and other individuals or settings in which a child participates, plays an important role in the development of fantasy and make-believe in middle childhood and of daydreaming and overt pretend play in adulthood (Power, 2011; Singer, 1995).

Games with Rules

games with rules A cognitive level of play involving relatively formal activities with fixed rules.

Games with rules, such as Simon Says and hide-and-seek, first appear during the concrete operational period, when children are five or six years old, and peak in frequency toward the end of elementary school (Rubin & Krasnor, 1980). Piaget (1964), in fact, did his original studies of moral development by interviewing and observing children playing rule-based games. The rules for many such games apparently develop out of the more flexible, "made-up" rules of pretend play. Instead of continuing to negotiate roles and behaviors as they go along, young children gradually learn to agree on them beforehand and to stand by their agreements throughout a play episode. Due to their greater formality, games with rules can become traditions handed down from one sibling to another, from older to younger playmates, and from generation to generation. Hopscotch, for example, has been around in some form for many generations.

Other Influences on Play and Friendship

The composition of a particular child's play is likely to be influenced by the range of play opportunities caregivers provide and the types of play they encourage. For example, a parent or caregiver who insists that the child always be learning something or trying something

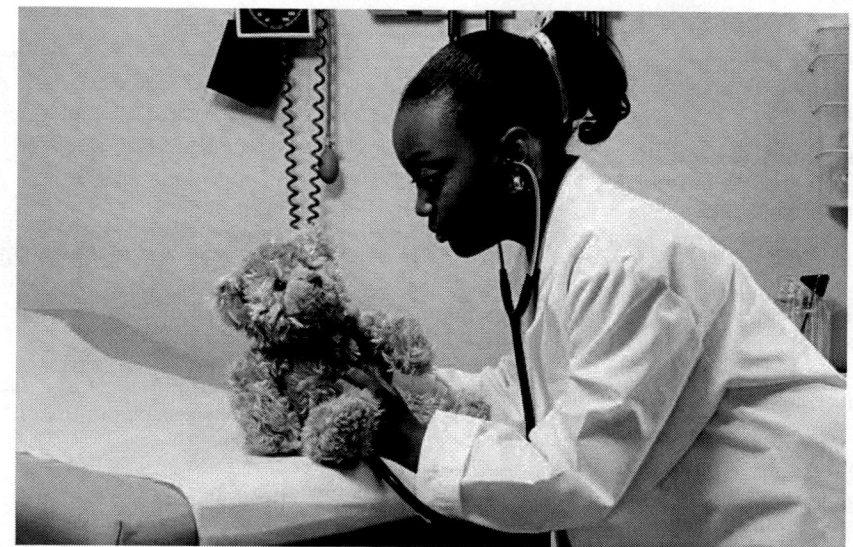

In dramatic play, children take on pretend roles, like the "doctor" and "patient" here. Realistic props such as the white coat and stethoscope in the photograph encourage dramatic play, although they are not always necessary.
Source: XiXinXing/Shutterstock.com.

new may make play a stressful rather than a rewarding experience for the child. Outside the home, children who attend childcare centers with qualified staffs, developmentally appropriate programs, and safe, well-designed, and well-equipped play areas have been found to develop more complex forms of pretend play at earlier ages, to engage in much less unoccupied and solitary play, to have less screen time, and to interact more positively with adults than children in less adequate centers (Howes & Matheson, 1992; Susa & Benedict, 1994; Tandon, Zhou, Lozano, & Christakis, 2011; Trawick-Smith & Dziurgot, 2011). Some centers help teach pretend play to children with autism spectrum disorder to help them glean the benefits of pretend play with their peers, such as language development (Barton & Pavilanis, 2012).

Having adequate time for play is also important. Large amounts of television viewing can reduce the amount of time available for play, and watching programs with high levels of violence has been associated with decreased levels of fantasy play (Tandon et al., 2011; van-der-Voort & Valkenburg, 1994).

Although play is a universal activity and occurs in all cultures, its frequency, forms, and functions also vary with cultural and socioeconomic contexts (Farver & Shin, 1997; Milteer et al., 2012; Roopnarine et al., 1994). For example, in countries such as Kenya, India, Ecuador, and Brazil, where many children spend a large part of the day doing household chores and assisting their families in getting food or money, time and opportunity for play are far more limited than for children in Mexico, the Philippines, or the United States (Campos et al., 1994; Hoffnung, 1992; Whiting & Whiting, 1975).

Even when free time, space, and toys are limited, however, most children find a way to play. They use common household objects such as pots, pans, and furniture, as well as outdoor items such as trees, sticks, rocks, sand, empty cans, and discarded equipment, as props for their make-believe and sociodramatic play. However, the range and developmental appropriateness of play activities under such circumstances are likely to be more restricted than in the case of children who play in more supportive settings. Table 7.3 summarizes age-appropriate recommendations for preschool play materials for children growing up in the United States.

Social Levels of Play

Play also varies according to how social it is—that is, how much and in what ways children involve others in their play activities. Mildred Parten studied social participation among children ages two to five and proposed that children's play develops in six stages, or levels, of sociability (Parten, 1932). Although subsequent researchers have questioned whether Parten's

TABLE 7.3 General Characteristics and Appropriate Play Materials for the Preschool Child

Age	General Characteristics	Appropriate Play Materials
2	Uses language effectively. Large-muscle skills developing, but limited in the use of small muscle skills. Energetic, vigorous, and enthusiastic, with a strong need to demonstrate independence and self-control.	Large-muscle play materials: Swing sets, outdoor blocks, toys to ride on, pull toys, push toys. Sensory play materials: Clay, finger paints, materials for water play, blocks, books, dolls and stuffed animals.
3	Expanded fantasy life, with unrealistic fears. Fascination with adult roles. Still stubborn, negative, but better able to adapt to peers than at age two. Early signs of product orientation in play.	Props for imaginative play (e.g., old clothes). Miniature life toys. Puzzles, simple board games, art materials that allow for a sense of accomplishment (e.g., paintbrushes, easels, marker pens, crayons).
4	Secure, self-confident. Need for adult attention and approval—showing off, clowning around, taking risks. More planful than threes, but products often accidental. Sophisticated small-muscle control allows for cutting, pasting, sewing, imaginative block building with smaller blocks.	Vehicles (e.g., tricycles, Big Wheels). Materials for painting, coloring, drawing, woodworking, sewing, stringing beads. Books with themes that extend well beyond the child's real world.
5	Early signs of logical thinking. Stable, predictable, reliable. Less self-centered than at four. Relaxed, friendly, willing to share and cooperate with peers. Realistic, practical, responsible.	Cut-and-paste and artistic activities with models to work from. Simple card games (e.g., Go Fish), table games (e.g., Bingo), and board games (e.g., Chutes and Ladders), in which there are few rules and the outcomes are based more on chance than on strategy. Elaborate props for dramatic play.

Source: Hughes (1991), p. 70.

categories actually form a developmental sequence, her distinctions continue to be useful to people who study young children. Table 7.4 describes the six types of play Parten identified.

How Play Changes with Age

As we saw in the Chapter 5 discussion of psychosocial development during infancy, even very young infants actively interact with the objects and people in their environment, and by twelve months of age, their play interactions with peers become more frequent, particularly those that involve toys. Access to peers through play groups or day care and parental support tend to increase the likelihood of peer play.

Mildred Parten (1932) found that parallel play accounted for almost half of early childhood play activity, whereas solitary play occupied about one-fourth, associative play one-fifth, and cooperative and unoccupied play less than one-tenth of the total. Parallel and solitary play appeared to decline throughout the preschool years, whereas associative play and cooperative play, which involve greater social participation, increased with age.

As preschoolers get older, play involving coordinated interactions increases. These interactions include imitation; complementary exchanges in which playmates take different roles, such as driver or passenger in pretend play; and more complex combinations of imitation and complementary exchanges (Eckerman et al., 1989; Power, 2011). Preschool children's highest level of peer social play also increases with age, progressing through a sequence of parallel play, simple social play, complementary and reciprocal play, cooperative social pretend play, and finally complex social pretend play. Children who spend more of their play time in complex forms of play appear to have

TABLE 7.4 Parten's Social Levels of Play

Type	Description and Examples
Unoccupied play	The child wanders about, watching whatever is of momentary interest, but does not become involved in any activity.
Solitary play	The child plays alone with different toys or other objects and with no direct or indirect awareness of or involvement with other children, even if nearby.
Onlooker play	The child watches others play without actually entering into the activities; is clearly involved with what is happening and usually is within speaking distance of the participants.
Parallel play	Two or more children play with the same toys in a similar way, in close proximity, and with an awareness of each other's presence; they do not share toys, talk, or interact except in very minimal ways.
Associative play	Children engage in a common activity and talk about it with each other, but they do not assign tasks or roles to particular individuals and are not very clear about their goals.
Cooperative play	Children consciously form groups to make something, attain a goal, or dramatize a situation; one or two members organize and direct the activity, with children assuming different roles and responsibilities.

Source: Parten (1932).

greater overall social competence with their peers. The nature and number of available playmates are also important (Benenson et al., 1997; Howes & Matheson, 1992; Power, 2011). See the "Working With" interview with Javier Hernandez for a discussion of play and friendship during early childhood.

Play and Friendship in Early Childhood

Preschool children are simultaneously pulled in two directions. On the one hand, they seek the security and intimacy that come from playing continually with a familiar friend; on the other, they want to participate in the variety of activities that many different children make possible.

The Evolution of Friendship

John Gottman and Jennifer Parkhurst (1980) made extensive home observations of preschoolers between ages three and six as the children played with friends and new acquaintances. They found that play between younger children and their friends included frequent and extensive fantasy role playing, whereas older children's friendships focused more on the actual activities they were doing than on make-believe roles. Younger children communicated more clearly with their friends than did older children and were more responsive to their friends' requests for information or explanation. They also worked harder to create a "climate of agreement" by avoiding disagreements. They did this by immediately discussing the reasons for a disagreement or explaining them away and by using positive social comparisons with their friends to create a sense of common ground and solidarity. Older children were better able to tolerate differences and disagreements and had less need to use positive social comparisons to manage conflict in their friendships.

Due to the "management" problems just noted and the emphasis on overt, concrete, shared activities—such as whether to build a sand castle, how to draw a dog, how to cook a pretend dinner—early friendships tend to be somewhat unstable and may change on a

> **WORKING WITH** Javier Hernandez, Preschool Program Coordinator
>
> **Play and Friendships Among Preschoolers**
>
> Javier Hernandez coordinates a privately run preschool program that serves a middle- and working-class community. A parent himself, he has a degree in early childhood education and has worked in preschool and day-care programs for almost six years. Javier was interviewed during nap time in the day-care center office and talked about ways in which children's playing styles evolve over time.
>
> **Rob:** *Your program serves a pretty wide age range. Do you see the kids' play change as they grow older?*
>
> **Javier:** Yes, I do. Most of the two-year-olds' play involves sharing toys and turn taking—"it's my turn, it's your turn." They might share building blocks or share crayons when they draw. They can follow simple directions, like for circle time at the beginning and end of the day and for various other activities.
>
> **Rob:** *How do three-year-olds play differently?*
>
> **Javier:** Between three and three and a half, you see an amazing increase in dramatic and fantasy play. The games become more complex and are rarely what they appear to be. The two-year-olds see the climber, as just a climber, but the three-year-olds see it as a car, a spaceship, a house, or anything else they decide. The kids all make up different names and are deeply into imaginative role playing. They're always trying to involve you in their fantasy play.
>
> **Rob:** *What about rules?*
>
> **Javier:** They're very interested in rules—setting them and following them. They'll tell each other, "Oh, we can't do that now" or "We can't go that way" or "That's not the way we do it," or "You have to sit down." They're really into structure and delight in pointing out the right and wrong way to do things. There's a lot of tattling; I'll frequently overhear "You're going to get in trouble if you do that" or "You can't walk up the slide."
>
> **Rob:** *This is quite different behavior than the two-year-olds.*
>
> **Javier:** Yes. The two-year-olds are more apt to hit or push another kid, who will cry until the teacher comes over. With three-year-olds, the one who gets hit or pushed cries, but goes and then tells the teacher, "He hit me" and watches to see what you're going to do about it.
>
> **Rob:** *So this also reflects the superior verbal and cognitive abilities of three-year-olds?*
>
> **Javier:** Yes. The two-year-olds do a lot of copycatting. What one wants, the other one wants, and they want everything to be the same. Their attention spans are much shorter, and they change their minds quickly. They often forget

weekly or even daily basis. A preschool child will drop a friend relatively easily and later make up to her just as easily. Sometimes she will even exchange goods for friendship: "If you give me a piece of candy, I'll be your best friend!"

Preschoolers are also capable of sustaining relationships with playmates that last for a year or more (Howes, 1988; Howes et al., 1998; Poulin & Chan, 2010). These preferences are an important step in forming more lasting friendships later in childhood, as well as a basis for learning to get along with others. By age three to four, friendships become more involved and durable. Certain pairs of children develop a liking for each other and purposely try to spend time together. In fact, approximately 80 percent of three-to-four-year-olds spend a substantial amount of time with at least one special "associate," or playmate. Children in nursery school spend at least 30 percent of their time with one other peer. Typically, the pairings develop in situations that encourage physical proximity, such as the children's neighborhood play group, day-care center, or preschool classroom. Pairs of preschool friends exhibit greater reciprocity and interdependence with each other in their parallel play, requesting, and following/imitating activities than they do with mere acquaintances (Goldstein et al., 1989; Power, 2011).

About 75 percent of nursery school children are involved in reciprocated friendships, as reflected in time spent in one another's company, nursery school teachers' reports, and interviews with their mothers. This number increases through adolescence, with 80 to 90 percent of teenagers reporting having mutual friends and several "close" or

> **WORKING WITH** Javier Hernandez, Preschool Program Coordinator
>
> **Play and Friendships Among Preschoolers** *continued*
>
> what they want, and you can never be sure just what they're after.
>
> **Rob:** *And the three-year-olds?*
>
> **Javier:** They have much longer attention spans. They'll get so involved in a story that they won't move a muscle. And you have to point out and explain every detail of every picture in the book.
>
> **Rob:** *You have to satisfy their desire to fully understand exactly what is going on?*
>
> **Javier:** Exactly. Two-year-olds will keep on saying *why* just for the sake of it. Three- and four-year-olds really want a solid answer and are generally satisfied once they hear one they like. They're really listening to what you're saying, whereas the two-year-olds are mainly practicing their verbal skills.
>
> **Rob:** *What about friendships and prosocial behavior among preschoolers?*
>
> **Javier:** If one two-year-old is aggressive toward another and you say, "That wasn't very nice, you hurt his feelings and I think you need to say you are sorry," she may go over to the child and say, "sorry," but five minutes later might do the same thing again. Three-and four-year-olds tend to be more aware of other children's feelings and of their own. They base their friendships on who is nice to them and are better able to appreciate how it feels to be hurt. If you say, "Well, would you like it if she did that to you?" they are likely to say, "No, I wouldn't like it."
>
> **Rob:** *Are they better able to take care of each other?*
>
> **Javier:** Yes. We have two children who started in the infant room and went all the way up to kindergarten together. By the last few months they were here, if Larry said anything to Jenelle that she was sensitive about, she would just fall apart because "He's my best friend." She would get very sad and look to us to help them make up and mend their friendship. Then Larry would apologize, and they would hug. Older preschoolers seem to know a lot about each other's personalities. They know what to expect of each other and are very aware of what other children are doing.
>
> **What Do You Think?**
>
> 1. In what ways do Javier's examples of preschool play and peer interactions demonstrate the interplay of cognitive and social development?
> 2. In what ways do Javier's descriptions of preschool friendships parallel the discussion of preschool friendship and its management in the chapter?

"good" friends. Friendship networks are small among preschool children, consisting of one or two best friends. School-age children, in contrast, average three to five best friends, a figure than remains fairly constant during adolescence and early adulthood (Hartup & Stevens , 1997; Poulin & Chan, 2010).

These children are involved in parallel play. They are probably aware of each other's presence, but they are using separate toys and are preoccupied primarily with their own activities.
Source: otnaydur/Shutterstock.com.

Chapter 7 Psychosocial Development in Early Childhood

The development of social competence and the ability to understand others' emotions and mental states during early childhood depend in part on the frequency with which playmates, parents, and other children initiate informal play activities. During the preschool years, children begin to initiate their own peer contacts and receive play invitations from peers, a trend that increases through the early childhood years (Bhavnagri & Parke, 1991; Maguire & Dunn, 1997; Power, 2011).

Conceptions of Friendship

Young children form internal representations of peer and friendship relations in much the same way they form internal representations of adult caregivers and attachments, a working model for friendships they will utilize into adulthood (Howes, 1996; Welch & Houser, 2010). In the minds of younger preschoolers, a friend is someone who does certain things with you; a friend is someone (anyone, in fact) whom you like to play with, share toys with, or talk with a lot, rather than someone with whom they share a compassionate relationship (Ahn, 2011; Field et al., 1994). "A friend," as one preschooler put it, "lets you hold his doll or truck or something."

As children near school age, more permanent, personal qualities enter into their conceptions (Howes, 1996). Now the crucial features of a friend are more often dispositional, that is, related to how the friend is likely to behave in the future. A friend is still very much "someone you like," but she is also someone whom you trust, whom you can depend on, and who likes and admires you. To be friends in this sense, two children must know each other's likes and preferences better than before, and they must also be increasingly aware of thoughts and feelings that the friend may keep hidden. Nevertheless, each child is still likely to focus primarily on his own needs to the exclusion of his friend's. As one child said, "A friend is someone who does what you want"; and as another said, "A friend doesn't get you in trouble." Neither of these children understands that sometimes he or she should return these favors; later, during the school years, they will likely think of this.

Making and keeping friends requires good social skills and is an important indication of good social adjustment. Kindergarten children who already have maintained earlier established friendships with children who now attend the same school have more positive attitudes toward school than children without such friendships. Having friends predicts increases in self-esteem among preadolescents, and adolescents who have good friends are less likely to experience psychosocial disturbances during school transitions than those without good friends (Hartup & Stevens, 1997; Poulin & Chan, 2010). In fact, when children experienced a stressful event—for example, being excluded from an activity—those children with friends had less of a stress response than those without friends (Peters, Riksen-Walraven, Cillessen, & de Weerth, 2011). Finally, a twelve-year longitudinal study found that having friends during preadolescence predicted successful social adaptation in early adulthood, including positive attitudes toward family members and general feelings of self-esteem (Bagwell et al., 1996). As we will discover in the chapters that follow, having friends, the identities of one's friends, and the quality of the friendships one has play an important developmental role throughout the life course (Hartup & Stevens, 1997; Poulin & Chan, 2010).

Now that we have concluded our discussion of play in early childhood, we turn to discussing gender development, which profoundly affects almost all other developmental changes in early childhood and in the years that follow.

Gender Development

Gender influences important aspects of social development in early childhood. As used here, the term **gender** refers to learned or socially constructed categories (feminine and masculine) in contrast to *sex,* which refers to biological categories (male and female). Most children go through at least three steps in gender development (Shepherd-Look, 1982). First, they develop beliefs about *gender identity,* that is, which sex *they* are. Second, they develop *gender preferences,* attitudes about which sex they wish to be; gender

gender The thoughts, feelings, and behaviors associated with being male or female by one's culture.

> **What Do You Think?**
>
> Many political leaders (and a significant number of parents who have voted for them) have criticized spending money on preschool programs in which children spend their time "playing" rather than learning important preschool skills. How would you respond to such critics regarding the importance of play for preschool children?

preference does not always coincide with gender identity. Third, they acquire *gender constancy*, a belief that the sex of a person is biologically determined, permanent, and unchanging no matter what else about the person changes. All three aspects of gender contribute to a child's general knowledge of **gender-role stereotypes** (also called *sex roles*), the very powerful (but not necessarily welcome or accurate), culturally sanctioned messages regarding which gender-related behaviors are and are not acceptable. Different cultures have different stereotypes and therefore send different messages to parents and children.

gender-role stereotypes The culturally "appropriate" patterns of gender-related behaviors expected by society. Also called *sex roles*.

Learning Gender Schema

From age two onward, preschoolers use gender-role stereotypes to guide their behaviors. Children's gender preferences and knowledge of stereotypes regarding toys and activities increase significantly with age: whereas twenty-four-month-olds typically do not show consistent gender preferences in toys and activities, thirty-month-olds consistently prefer "same-gender" to "opposite-gender" objects and activities. Gender-role stereotypes about personal qualities develop more slowly. Only by age five or so do children begin to know which gender is "supposed" to be aggressive, loud, and strong and which is "supposed" to be gentle, quiet, and weak. Knowledge of gender stereotypes regarding personal qualities continues to develop throughout childhood and adolescence (Bailey & Zucker, 1995; Halim & Ruble, 2010; Huston & Alvarez, 1990).

Most children acquire *gender identity*, the ability to label themselves correctly as boys or girls, between ages two and three and are able to correctly label other children and adults as well. Some children develop gender identity early, before age twenty-eight months, and others not until later. Early identifiers exhibit significantly more gender-stereotyped play, such as car play for boys and doll play for girls, than later identifiers do (Fagot & Leinbach, 1989; Fagot et al., 1992; Halim & Ruble, 2010).

Gender constancy, the understanding that one's sex is permanent and will never change, first appears by age four or five. A young preschool child may say she can switch gender just by wanting to or say that even though she is a girl now, she was a boy as an infant or may grow up to become a man as an adult. And a two-year-old may have only a hazy notion of what defines gender, believing perhaps that certain hairstyles, clothing, and toys make the crucial difference. Most children, however, achieve a reliable sense of gender constancy between ages seven and nine (Bem, 1989; Emmerich & Sheppard, 1982; Halim & Ruble, 2010).

A *gender schema* is a pattern of beliefs and stereotypes about gender that children use to organize information about gender-related characteristics, experiences, and expectations. A child's gender schema is thought to develop through a series of stages. First, a child learns through social experiences what kinds of things are directly associated with each sex, such as "boys play with cars" and "girls play with dolls." Next, around ages four to six, the child moves to the second stage and begins to develop more indirect and complex associations for information relevant to his or her own sex but not for the opposite sex. For example, a child who knows that boys like trucks and boys like cars should now be able to infer that someone who likes trucks will also like cars. Finally, by age eight or so, the child moves to the third stage, where he has also learned the associations relevant to the opposite sex and has mastered the gender concepts of masculinity and femininity that link information within and among various content areas. Thus, a child will know the pattern of interests that are stereotypically associated with being masculine (cars, action toys, football) or feminine (dolls, "dress-up," princesses) (Bem, 1987; Halim & Ruble, 2010; Martin et al., 1990; Ruble, 1988).

Though not pertinent in this chapter, the previous terms regarding gender are independent of the discussion of sexual orientation—whether an individual is homosexual, heterosexual, or bisexual. We will discuss sexual orientation in Chapter 11.

Influences on Gender Development

If gender development is largely a process of learning socially constructed definitions of "boy" and "girl," we would expect the child's social circle of parents and peers to influence that process. In the following section, we explore how this occurs.

Parents

Many theorists hold parents responsible for the development of gender differences, either blaming or congratulating them depending on the theorist's point of view. When asked about their child-rearing philosophies, parents tend to express belief in gender equality, but their actions often differ from their statements (Fagot, 1982). Observations of parents playing with their preschool children reveal that parents support their children for gender-stereotyped activities more than for cross-gender activities. Boys get praised more for playing with blocks than for playing with dolls, and parents generally support physical activity in boys more than in girls. Boys who engage in cross-gender behaviors are viewed more negatively than girls who engage in cross-gender behaviors (Sandnabba & Ahlberg, 1999), and parents who reinforce children for playing with same gender and punish cross-gender play have children who seem to develop gender schemas earlier (Halim & Ruble, 2010). As children approach school age, parents begin assigning household chores according to gender: girls more often fold the laundry, and boys more often take out the trash. Parents are also more likely to reward sons for being assertive, independent, active, and emotionally unexpressive and to reward daughters for being accommodating, dependent, more passive, and emotionally expressive (Fagot & Hagan, 1991; Halim & Ruble, 2010; Lytton & Romney, 1991).

The socialization of females appears to emphasize interpersonal relatedness and emotional expressivity, whereas socialization of males emphasizes autonomy and agency. These orientations have been associated with sex-typed differences in the way parents talk to and interact with their children. In emphasizing causes and consequences of emotions with boys, mothers might orient them toward seeing emotions as problems to be solved and controlled rather than experienced and understood. Mothers' conversations with girls focus on the emotional states themselves, perhaps encouraging girls to focus directly on their own feelings and reactions and orienting them toward an interpersonal approach involving emotional sensitivity, and parents are more likely to talk to their daughters about physical appearance than their sons (Cervantes & Callanan, 1998; Halim & Ruble, 2010; Leaper et al., 1998).

Peers

In some ways, peers may shape gender differences more strongly than parents do. Early in the preschool years, even before age three, children prefer to play in same-sex groups and respond differently to partners of the opposite sex than to those of the same sex (Maccoby, 1990; Martin & Ruble, 2010; Power, 2011). In play situations, girls tend to withdraw from a boy partner more often than from a girl partner, and boys heed prohibitions made by another boy more often than they do those that come from a girl. Even when preschoolers are not playing actively, they watch peers of the same sex more often than they do peers of the opposite sex.

Children of this age also respond to a reinforcement more reliably if it comes from a child of their own sex. If a boy compliments another boy's block building, the second boy is much more likely to continue building than he is if a girl compliments it. Conversely, if a boy criticizes the building, the other boy is more likely to stop than if a girl criticizes it. Parallel patterns occur for girls, who tend to persist in whatever other girls compliment or praise and stop whatever they criticize or ignore. For both sexes, teachers' reinforcements have less influence

The ease with which these children adopt both stereotyped and nonstereotyped roles in playing "tea party" illustrates the flexible qualities associated with androgyny.
Source: Monkey Business Images/Shutterstock.com.

than peers' in determining children's persistence at activities (Fagot, 1982). What makes these patterns important is that children tend to reinforce play activities that are considered appropriate for their own sex. Children who deviate from expected gender-stereotyped activities, such as boys playing with dolls, often find themselves largely ignored and unpopular, even after they return to expected activities (Martin & Ruble, 2010; Lamb & Roopnarine, 1979). As we saw earlier, the content of many children's TV shows—and the toys they promote—also sends powerful messages about gender stereotypes (Coyne et al., 2014). Thus, peer pressures to practice conventional gender roles are both strong and continuous, and they occur even if teachers and other adults try to minimize gender-typed play.

Androgyny

How we choose to define *gender* also can affect our understanding of what it means to be male or female. On the one hand, definitions that tend to exaggerate positive gender differences run the risk of perpetuating gender-role stereotyping and inequality; on the other hand, definitions that minimize real differences may be used to deny boys and girls the physical, cognitive, and social developmental opportunities appropriate to their different gender-related needs. One positive consequence of focusing on differences associated with gender is that doing so increases our awareness and appreciation of feminine (and masculine) qualities. A positive consequence of efforts to minimize gender differences is to help equalize treatment under the law and access to equal opportunity for males and females (Hare-Mustin & Marecek, 1988).

Androgyny refers to a situation in which gender roles are flexible, allowing all individuals, male and female, to behave in ways that freely integrate behaviors traditionally thought to belong exclusively to one or the other sex. Many people think of "masculine" and "feminine" as opposite ends of a single scale. Rather, "masculinity" and "femininity" are separate scales, and androgyny is a state of being high in both. In this view, both girls and boys can be assertive *and* yielding, independent *and* dependent, instrumental (task oriented) *and* expressive (feelings oriented). Sandra Bem (1981, 1987) and others (e.g., Lamke, 1982a, 1982b) have found that adolescent and young adult males and females use both masculine and feminine characteristics to describe their own personalities. Bem believes androgynous individuals are less concerned about which activities are appropriate or inappropriate and therefore are more flexible in their responses to various situations. For example, we find that girls who are less strict in their gender

androgyny A tendency to integrate both masculine and feminine behaviors into the personality.

> **What Do You Think?**
>
> A hockey coach's five-year-old son enjoys playing with dolls with his female peers. Because of this, his dad has encouraged him to play with GI Joe dolls and play football more often because he is worried that his son may become homosexual. What gender influence is this hockey coach having on his son's gender development? What advice would you give this parent based on your reading of this chapter?

roles are also less likely to experience stereotypically feminine psychological disorders, such as eating disorders (McHale, Corneal, Crouter, & Birch, 2001).

What are the implications of androgyny? Because the notion of androgyny challenges certain fundamental beliefs that individuals have about gender, it holds the potential to reduce gender-role stereotyping and its detrimental developmental effects in early childhood and beyond (Stake, 1997). Because society holds stricter sex-role expectations for males, androgyny might be more beneficial for women than it is for men.

Child Abuse and Maltreatment

Child abuse and maltreatment by parents and other caregivers is a serious social problem, with approximately 2.1 million new cases reported each year, nearly 20 percent of which are substantiated (U.S. Department of Health and Human Services, 2015). A significant number of these cases involve infants, toddlers, and preschool-aged children, who are particularly vulnerable because of their immaturity and dependence. In 2013, children less than one year of age had the highest victimization rate (U.S. Department of Health and Human Services, 2015). Maltreatment may consist of physical, sexual, or emotional *abuse,* or of physical or emotional *neglect,* and nearly 80 percent of the cases of maltreatment in 2013 were due to neglect (Finkelhor, 1995; Wolock, 1998; U.S. Department of Health and Human Services, 2015). Parents—in particular, mothers—are the most likely perpetrators of abuse.

Causes

The causes of physical child abuse and neglect are best understood within the developmental-ecological contexts within which they occur. These include parent and child characteristics, parenting and parent-child interactions, and the broader context of family, community, and culture.

Parent and Child Characteristics

One explanation for maltreatment is that the aggressive and antisocial behavior involved in abuse was previously learned by the parent during her or his own childhood, through modeling and direct reinforcement. The risk of maltreatment is much higher when parenting is extremely authoritarian (overly harsh and lacking in empathy) or when it is indifferent and neglectful of a child's needs. This explanation, however, fails to explain why two-thirds of parents who were abused themselves do not abuse their own children.

A second, more promising explanation of the causes of abuse is based on the idea of *internal working models,* the mental representations that organize and guide a parent's experiences, relationship, and interactions with the child (Bowlby 1988; Farrangy et al., 1991; Stern, 1985b). The internal working models of an abusive parent are based on past experiences with the child, the parent's own childhood experiences, and the beliefs and expectations held by his or her own abusive parents. These models are often characterized by a distorted, unbalanced view of the child (overly negative or overly positive) and are associated with pervasive failures in parental empathy, parent-infant synchrony, and attachment (Belsky, 1993; Ferholt, 1991; Main & Goldwyn, 1989; Wolock, 1998).

Mothers who were abused as children are much less likely to abuse their own children if they experienced one nonabusive, supportive, and close relationship while growing up (Jaffee et al., 2013). It may be that these close relationships help reduce the trauma of having been abused because research has demonstrated that victims of child abuse who continue to experience trauma from that abuse as an adult are more likely to become abusers themselves (Milner et al., 2010). These mothers are also likely to display greater self-awareness regarding their own abuse, be involved in a more satisfying social relationship, and have more extensive social supports than mothers who do abuse (Belsky, 1993; Caliso & Milner, 1992).

Personality characteristics that significantly compromise a parent's ability to provide good parenting may also increase the risk of abuse, particularly if they interfere with getting social and emotional support from others. Difficulty with impulse control, emotional instability, high levels of depression, anxiety, or hostility, and abuse of alcohol or drugs can all impair a parent's capacity to respond to a child in empathic and responsible ways.

Parenting and Parent-Child Interactions

Parenting and parent-child interactions also play a role. Abusive parents are more likely than nonabusive parents to rely on physical punishment and negative control strategies such as hitting, grabbing, and pushing, or threats and disapproval, rather than on reasoning to guide or discipline their children. They are also less likely to adjust their disciplinary techniques appropriately to different kinds of misbehavior (Belsky, 1993; Herrenkohl et al., 1997). During an abusive episode, the overtly aggressive behavior (physical punishment) on which an abusive parent relies is transformed into an act of interpersonal violence. A parent with a strong predisposition toward anxiety, depression, and hostility may become so irritated with the child that she or he loses control and physical or verbal punishment escalates into abuse.

Family, Community, and Cultural Factors

Poverty, unemployment, marital conflict, social isolation, and family dysfunction can increase the risk of abuse; so can shorter-term stressors, such as emotional distress, economic or legal problems, or the birth of a new baby (Belsky, 1988b; Cicchetti & Olson, 1990; Garbarino, 1992b). Economic conditions, child and family social welfare policies, and cultural values and expectations regarding the care and protection of children can indirectly contribute to the risk of abuse and neglect (Black & Krishnakumar, 1998). In fact, the home and family environment is the single most important factor in determining whether a child is likely to be abused or not (Jaffee et al., 2004). For example, societies that condone the use of violence against women (who are the primary caregivers of children) are likely to have higher rates of child abuse than societies that treat women with respect. The role of differing cultural values and expectations regarding child maltreatment is discussed in the "A Multicultural View" feature.

Consequences

Neglected infants, toddlers, and preschoolers often are deprived of sufficient food, clothing, shelter, sanitation, and medical care, which may interfere with their physical, intellectual, social, and emotional development and place them at risk for serious illness or even death (Egeland, 1988; U.S. Department of Health and Human Services, 2015). Abused or neglected preschoolers often develop emotional problems that include insecure attachment relationships, lack of empathy, and emotional detachment. They are also more likely to exhibit behavioral problems, such as aggressiveness and withdrawal, toward peers than other children are (Cicchetti & Olson, 1990; Dodge et al., 1990; Klimes-Dougan & Kistner, 1990; Pianta et al., 1989; Sousa et al., 2011). Physical abuse in early childhood is linked to aggressive and violent behaviors in adolescents

A Multicultural View

The Cultural Context of Child Abuse and Neglect

Can the ideas one culture holds about child abuse and neglect be validly applied to others? According to Jill Korbin, who has extensively studied child abuse and neglect in many different cultural and societal contexts, culturally appropriate definitions of child abuse and neglect require an awareness of both the viewpoint of an "insider" to a particular culture, termed the *emic* perspective, and the viewpoint of an "outsider" to that culture, or the *etic* perspective (Korbin, 1991, 1987, 1981). Such definitions must include three dimensions: (1) cultural differences in child-rearing practices, (2) treatment of children that deviates from cultural norms, and (3) societal abuse and neglect.

Cultural differences in child-rearing include practices considered acceptable in the culture in which they occur but abusive or neglectful by outsiders. For example, most middle-class American parents believe it is developmentally important for young children to sleep separately from their parents, but traditional Japanese and Hawaiian-Polynesian cultures, which highly value interdependence among family members, view isolating children at night as potentially dangerous to healthy child development. Another example concerns a woman in London who cut the faces of her two young sons with a razor blade and rubbed charcoal into the cuts. She was arrested for child abuse, but officials soon learned that she and her children belonged to an East African tribal group that traditionally practiced facial scarification. When viewed from within her culture, her actions were an attempt to protect her children's cultural identity, for without such markings they would be unable to participate as adults in the culture of their birth (Korbin, 1987).

Many cultures have practiced such initiation rites as a normal part of child-rearing before and during adolescence. Where, for example, is the line drawn between male circumcision during adolescence and circumcision at birth? How would a European or an American convince traditional people in highland New Guinea that circumcision is more painful for an adolescent than for an infant? How would traditional highland New Guinea people convince Europeans or Americans that (1) circumcision has no meaning for an infant, who cannot understand its deep cultural significance, and (2) infancy is a time when the child should be spared all discomfort? How is the line drawn between facial scarification and orthodontia (braces), both of which cause pain and discomfort but are intended to enhance the child's attractiveness?

Idiosyncratic child abuse and neglect involves treatment of children that deviates from established standards of acceptable treatment within a particular culture. Although they may differ, all societies have such standards. For example, in one Polynesian culture known for its indulgence of children, a child can be pinched lightly on the mouth for misbehavior, but more severe punishments are prohibited. When one man left a scratch on the lip of his grandchild, he was severely criticized by his cultural group. By their *emic* standards, his behavior was abusive, although from the *etic* perspective of American parents, it is unlikely that such behavior would be of great concern.

Societal abuse and neglect refers to harm caused to children by societal conditions, such as poverty and inadequate housing, health care, and nutrition, all of which either contribute significantly to abuse or neglect or are considered abusive or neglectful in themselves. For example, the widespread famine in Ethiopia and Somalia and the inadequate nutrition in India and Chile have had devastating effects on the physical, cognitive, and socioemotional development of millions of children. In many countries, physical, sexual, and emotional exploitation and abuse of children are very common. Even in affluent countries such as our own, social policy regarding aid to parents with dependent children, early childhood health care and nutrition, childcare, and employment can significantly harm (or help) the development of young children. Where does responsibility lie, and what should be done about this?

It seems likely that neither a single, universal standard nor a completely relativistic, "anything goes" standard for determining abuse and neglect is acceptable. The challenge, then, is to develop an approach that incorporates developmental values and standards for "good enough" care and treatment of children that should be universal and values standards that afford more room for cultural and societal diversity.

and adults, including violence toward nonfamily members, children, dating partners, and spouses; higher rates of mental-health problems; higher rates of risky sexual behavior; and higher rates of drug abuse (Kendall-Tackett et al., 1993; Malinosky-Rummell & Hansen, 1993; Norman et al., 2012). Victims of child abuse have lower earning potential as adults and lower educational attainment (Currie & Widom, 2010). Abuse and neglect have also been lined to higher risk of serious chronic health problems, such as diabetes, lung disease, and malnutrition, as an adult (Widom, Czaja, Bentley, & Johnson, 2012).

The most common symptoms reported for preschoolers who have been sexually abused include nightmares, posttraumatic stress disorder (see Chapter 12's discussion of physical development in early adulthood), depression and emotional withdrawal, regressive and immature behavior, anxiety disorders, and problems with aggression and inappropriate sexual behavior (Hornor, 2010; Kendall-Tackett et al., 1993). The developmental stage at which sexual abuse occurs is particularly significant in determining longer-term outcomes. For example, incest (sexual abuse by a parent or other family member) disrupts the development of social functioning and self-esteem and increases risk for personality disorders, eating disorders, and substance abuse during adolescence and early adulthood (Finkelhor, 1995; Spaccarelli, 1994), as we will see in Chapters 10 and 12.

Treatment and Prevention

Dealing with child maltreatment involves working directly with the abused infant, toddler, or preschooler, the parents, and the family after abuse (or the threat of abuse) has been discovered. One goal is to protect the child from further mistreatment and help her recover from the physical and psychological consequences. Another is to assist the abusing parent(s) in establishing a parent-child relationship and family environment that adequately ensures the preschooler's safety and supports his developmental needs.

Intensive professional help, including family counseling and psychotherapy, often can help parents and child understand the causes, consequences, and personal meanings of their destructive feelings and behaviors so they will be able to live together in less destructive ways. A key aspect of treatment is to help parents improve their parenting skills. Self-help groups such as Parents Anonymous, parent aides who assist abusive and neglectful families in their homes, crisis nurseries, foster care or respite care for the abused child, and short-term residential treatment for family members or the entire family unit are among the treatment alternatives that have met with some success (Willis et al., 1992; Wolfe et al., 1997). Unfortunately, those who would benefit from these programs and services often lack availability and access to them (Burns et al., 2004).

Early intervention programs that target "high-risk" families, including those headed by low-SES mothers and teenage mothers, have focused on helping parents improve their parenting skills, the family climate, and their ability to better cope with the stressful life events and conditions. Programs that teach parents how to evaluate why problems occur and then make those problems less likely to occur in the future have reduced the rate of abuse among high-risk families (Bugental et al., 2010). Programs that include early and extended contact between parents and their newborn infants to improve the early parent-child relationship, parent education about child development and everyday childcare problems, and home visitors and parent aides who assist parents with young children tend to be effective. They also offer training and support in home safety, money management, job finding, health maintenance and nutrition, leisure time counseling, and help in developing stronger social support networks (Rosenberg & Reppucci, 1985; Willis et al., 1992).

Other prevention efforts attempt to reduce or eliminate the causes of abuse by changing more general conditions that affect *all* children and families. These *social policy* efforts include education for parenthood programs, elimination of corporal punishment, the development of a bill of rights for children, and various social policy supports for parents and their children, including more and better jobs, funding for preschools and day-care centers, affordable health care, and so forth.

> **What Do You Think?**
>
> If you were a preschool teacher, what behaviors in a child might lead you to suspect child maltreatment? What help is available to parents who may be at risk for abusing or neglecting their children?

Looking Back/Looking Forward

Let us explore how the lifespan themes outlined in Chapter 1 apply to early childhood. Our focus here will be on friendship and its developmental importance throughout the life cycle.

- **Continuity within change**—Friendships emerge in toddlerhood and early childhood and continue to play an important developmental role throughout middle childhood, adolescence, and adulthood. An individual's capacity to make friends, the types of friends one chooses, and the quality of one's friendships over the lifespan show considerable continuity, and having (or not having) enough good friends is predictive of better (or worse) adjustment and developmental well-being at every age. Some of this continuity may be due to temperamental characteristics, such as shyness or outgoingness, as well as to relationships and developmental opportunities within and outside the family that stay fairly constant. On the other hand, changes in one's family, school, and neighborhood environments and the major physical and cognitive changes that occur through middle childhood, adolescence, and adulthood facilitate significant changes in opportunities to make friends, whom one chooses as friends, and the nature of one's friendships. For example, moving to a new school or spending a month at summer camp creates new possibilities for friendship experiences, the friends one chooses, and the quality of one's friendships. The physical, cognitive, and psychosocial changes that occur from early childhood through adolescence and adulthood also expand and alter the nature and meaning of friendship.

- **Lifelong growth**—The ability to establish and maintain friendships, sophistication in thinking about qualities of friendship, and the breadth and complexity of friendship activities grow as physical, cognitive, and psychosocial skills expand. Although preschoolers do participate in initiating and maintaining new friendships, they still largely depend on adults to arrange opportunities to be with the peers with whom friendships eventually develop. These capacities undergo major growth as an individual progresses through middle childhood, adolescence, and young adulthood, growth that for many continues throughout middle and later adulthood, when increases in wisdom and good judgment based on past experience replace gains in physical and cognitive skills and capacities as the main source of growth.

- **Changing meanings and vantage points**—How one thinks about friendship and the role and meaning of friendship in one's life changes as one moves through the life cycle. Whereas a preschooler may think of friendship largely in terms of a partner with whom to share enjoyable play activities, older children, adolescents, and adults attribute progressively deeper meanings to their friendships, which include intimacy, trust, and mutual understanding. Similarly, as individuals move through the life cycle, they become increasingly reliant on the friendships they establish outside of their immediate families for intimacy and social and material support.

- **Developmental diversity**—The diversity of friendships is a product of differences in the opportunities and expectations associated with gender, culture, SES, and family background, as well as individual differences in personality, life experiences, and personal choices. In European American culture, for example, friendships among females tend to place greater emphasis on relationship and emotional intimacy, whereas friendships among men tend to emphasize shared activities. However, differences in relationships with parents and siblings during early and middle childhood, in school and neighborhood settings during middle childhood and adolescence, or in work and family settings during early and middle adulthood can all contribute to developmental diversity in the friendships of a given individual.

Chapter Summary

- **How do different styles of parenting influence preschoolers' relationships with peers?** In early childhood, a child's relationships with parents and other family members are a central source of psychosocial development. Parenting styles differ in their demands for maturity, need for control, and responsiveness to their children's feelings and needs. Such differences are associated with differences in parent-child relationships and developmental outcomes. Authoritative parents display high levels of control, demands for maturity, and responsiveness to their children's feelings and needs. Their children tend to show greater self-reliance, self-control, and achievement. Authoritarian parents display high levels of control and maturity demands but low levels of responsiveness to their children's feelings and needs. Their children tend to be more distrustful and unhappy with themselves, and show lower school achievement than children of authoritative parents. Permissive parents display high levels of responsiveness but very low levels of control and maturity demands. Their children tend to lack self-reliance and self-control. Indifferent parents are detached, uninvolved, and inconsistent. They display low levels of control, maturity demands, and responsiveness. Their children tend to lack self-reliance and self-control and may be at risk for more severe social and emotional problems. Parents often use mixtures of parenting styles, and the preferred parenting style may change as children grow older.

  Both siblings and friends also make an important contribution to social development during the preschool years. The quality of children's social relationships with their siblings is predictive of the quality of their relationships with their friends. Ultimately, however, it is the parent's responsibility to help children establish and maintain positive social relationships.

- **How do preschoolers handle conflicts with peers?** As children grow older, the support and judgments of parents and other adults contribute increasingly to children's feelings of empathy and prosocial activities. Preschoolers commonly exhibit both overt and relational aggression to assert their needs and resolve conflicts. As they grow older, verbal methods replace physical ones and overall aggression declines. Children who cannot control their aggression can be helped to do so with methods such as assertiveness training and social learning theory strategies. Parents can learn to spot the triggers of their children's aggression and respond effectively. Television viewing and video and computer game playing significantly influence preschoolers' social development in such areas as aggression, prosocial behavior, and gender stereotyping.

- **Why is play so important in preschoolers' development, and how does play change as they approach school age?** Play for its own sake is the major waking activity of preschoolers. Psychoanalytic theory emphasizes the mastery and wish fulfillment functions of play, whereas learning theory stresses the acquisition of social skills through imitation and observation. Ethological theory emphasizes the evolutionary roots and adaptive developmental functions of physical play. Cognitive theory emphasizes that play develops in a sequence that generally parallels the major stages of cognitive development. It includes functional play, constructive play, pretend play, and play involving games with rules. Mildred Parten has identified six social levels of play: unoccupied, solitary, onlooker, parallel, associative, and cooperative play. The type of setting is important to the development of social play. Whereas early friendships are unstable and depend on specific shared play activities, friendships along older preschoolers involve expectations about future behavior. Preschoolers' friendships become more durable and involve a greater degree of shared activity with age. As they near school age, the more permanent and personal qualities of friendship become increasingly important.

- **How does a child's understanding of gender differences change during the preschool years? What factors influence a child's flexibility about gender-role stereotypes?** During early childhood, children acquire an understanding of gender-typed behaviors and gender identity. A sense of gender constancy—the belief that being male or female is biologically determined and permanent—typically is not achieved until ages seven to nine. Because the development of stereotypes about personal qualities appears to depend on the ability to think abstractly, children do not gain a clear and stable concept of gender until the school years. Influences on gender development include differential expectations and treatment of boys and girls by parents, peers, and the media. A more flexible approach to gender roles enables children to adopt more androgynous behaviors and attitudes.

- **What factors appear to contribute to child abuse and neglect? What are the consequences of maltreatment, and how might child maltreatment be prevented?** More than two million cases of child abuse are reported annually. Types of abuse include physical, psychological, and sexual. Neglect can be physical or emotional. Causes of maltreatment occur at the levels of the individual parent, the family, the community, and the culture. Consequences of abuse and neglect include a range of developmental, adjustment, and emotional problems. Responses to abuse and neglect frequently focus on treating the victims and their families. Prevention efforts include early intervention programs targeting "high-risk" families and attempts to change more general conditions that affect all children and families.

Key Terms

aggression (p. 228)
androgyny (p. 247)
authoritarian parenting (p. 221)
authoritative parenting (p. 219)
constructive play (p. 238)
empathy (p. 226)
functional play (p. 237)
games with rules (p. 238)
gender (p. 244)
gender-role stereotypes (p. 245)
hostile attribution bias (p. 230)
indifferent parenting (p. 222)
overt aggression (p. 228)
permissive parenting (p. 222)
physical activity play (p. 236)
pretend play (p. 238)
relational aggression (p. 228)

Middle Childhood

PART 4

Source: iofoto/Shutterstock.

Chapter 8
Physical and Cognitive Development in Middle Childhood

Chapter 9
Psychosocial Development in Middle Childhood

Because growth slows after the preschool years, children in middle childhood have more time and energy to develop skills of all sorts, from riding a skateboard to making friends. An accumulation of language practice and symbolic, make-believe play pay off: school-age children can think more logically than ever before, at least if they choose to and usually only when thinking relates to concrete matters. These new competencies, combined with children's experience of attending school, make peers more important than ever before.

Adults often remember middle childhood as the best years of their youth, though it is not clear that children themselves would agree with this assessment. For high-SES families, the world now likely seems secure, children's health is excellent, and children's skills and abilities improve steadily and visibly year by year. For families with fewer resources, though, the middle childhood years can be just as challenging as the periods before and after.

Physical and Cognitive Development in Middle Childhood

CHAPTER 8

Source: Rawpixel.com/Shutterstock.

Chapter Outline

PHYSICAL DEVELOPMENT

Trends and Variations in Height and Weight

Motor Development and Athletics in Middle Childhood

Health and Illness in Middle Childhood

COGNITIVE DEVELOPMENT

Piaget's Theory: Concrete Operational Skills

Information-Processing Skills

Language Development in Middle Childhood

Defining and Measuring Intelligence

Information-Processing Approaches to Intelligence

School Influences

The Changing Child: Physical, Cognitive, and Social

Focusing Questions

- What trends in height and weight occur among school-age children?
- What improvements in motor skills do children usually experience during the school years, and how do these improvements affect children's involvement in athletic activity?
- What kinds of illnesses occur among schoolchildren? How does children's socioeconomic status affect their health?
- What new cognitive skills do children acquire during the middle childhood? What are the psychological and practical effects of these new skills?
- How does memory change during middle childhood? How do these changes affect thinking and learning?
- What new changes in language emerge during middle childhood?
- What is general intelligence, and how can it be measured?
- How does school affect children's cognitive development?

Carmen and Mercedes were sisters. When Carmen was six and Mercedes nine, they both decided they wanted to buy skates. The problem was to find the money. They sold lemonade at the curbside: "DRINX, 25 SENTS" said a sign made by Carmen. In three days they had sold ten drinks. "That's $2.50," noted Mercedes. "Not nearly enough." Carmen puzzled over how long it would take them to earn enough; she thought maybe about a year, but she wasn't sure.

After a few more days—and increasing discouragement—their mother brought home one pair of used skates. "It's to share," she said, "because it's all I can afford. And besides, the two of you are nearly the same size!" This arrangement was not ideal. At first the girls did try to take turns with the skates, but trouble soon developed. Carmen had a way of taking rather long turns, and tended not only to use the skates herself but to share them with her friends. When it was Mercedes' turn, Mercedes took the skates to school to use at practices with the recently formed skating team. Soon Mercedes became the student-manager for the team, and spent a lot of her practice time arranging tournaments and other activities rather than actually skating herself. Eventually differences emerged between the sisters. Carmen became more skilled at actually skating, but Mercedes came to know more about the sport itself and could say more about it when asked. Carmen complained about sharing the skates because Mercedes "didn't really use them" at school. Mercedes complained that Carmen was selfish and unfair, and "ought to learn to share better," but eventually she gave up her turns altogether, despite continued encouragement from her mother.

The events between Carmen and Mercedes hint at features of development that we will discuss in this chapter and the next. One feature is the diversity of children's development: children grow and change at different rates, just as Carmen and Mercedes in terms of both their skating skills and their knowledge of skating. Children can also show profound differences in the meaning they give to the "same" activity, differences that result from diversity in the ways the domains of development work together in the lives of individuals. For one child (such as Carmen), success at a physical skill can be a source of self-esteem and peer approval. For another (such as Mercedes), success provides a stimulus for cognitive growth: it becomes something about which to talk and think, and perhaps to win friends as an indirect result. For still another person (their mother), success at skating becomes a challenge in providing for others fairly rather than gaining personal recognition.

These features of middle childhood are variations on two of our lifespan development themes: developmental diversity and changing meanings and vantage points, which have come up throughout this book and we will revisit in this chapter as well. As Carmen's and Mercedes' experiences also show, developments in all three domains—physical, cognitive, and psychosocial—occur simultaneously and influence one another intimately. We explore them separately only for convenience of discussion.

PHYSICAL DEVELOPMENT

In general, children's physical growth slows during middle childhood (ages six to twelve) even more than it does during early childhood. Specific physical skills are easier to teach than they used to be because children now find them easier to learn. For a school-age child, instruction and practice in baseball make a more obvious difference in skill development than they did when she was still a preschooler. This means the child can now acquire physical and athletic skills that may give a lifetime of satisfaction. But children *can* get hurt during physical activity, and athletic games can emphasize competition that is unrealistic or discouraging.

Children are relatively healthy during the school years, but they do sometimes have accidents or get sick. A few children also develop problems that have ambiguous physical causes; such children may show excessive motor activity even in quiet situations or difficulties in learning specific academic skills. Such problems may originate from subtle differences in how the nervous system operates in these children, although this is far from certain.

In the sections that follow, we review these ideas in more detail. We begin by looking at normal trends and variations in overall growth during middle childhood. Then we examine specific motor skill and athletic development and their psychological effects on children. Finally, we discuss health in the school years, with special reference to children who are overly active and on normative sleep and common sleep disorders among children.

Trends and Variations in Height and Weight

As Figure 8.1 shows, children grow steadily during middle childhood, from about forty-six inches and forty-five pounds at age six to almost sixty inches and eight pounds at age twelve (Center for Disease Control, 2000; Engels, 1993). At the same time, variations among children are often significant. For example, that the average height of eight-year-old girls varies from forty-five inches in South Korea to almost fifty-one inches in Russia. And at any age within any one society, individual variations are even more dramatic. The shortest and tallest six-year-olds in North America differ by only two or three inches, but the shortest and tallest twelve-year-olds differ by more than one foot. The changes are a source of both pride and dismay to individual children.

Toward the end of elementary school, girls tend to become significantly taller than boys of the same age. The difference results partly from girls' earlier puberty and partly from the timing of the growth spurt associated with puberty for each sex. For boys, a spurt in height tends to *follow* the other physical changes of adolescence, such as the growth of pubic hair and the deepening of the voice. For girls, a spurt in height usually *precedes* the growth of breasts and pubic hair. We look again at these and other physical changes of puberty in Chapter 10. For some children, the gap in timing creates problems with self-esteem and relating to the opposite sex. As we will see, though, the impact is far from uniform. Boys react differently than girls, as do their families and communities, and some young adolescents mind very little if they look young for their age—or old.

A more lasting problem than early or late puberty is **obesity**, a condition of being significantly overweight. Medically, obesity is defined by the ratio of a person's height and weight, a statistic called the *body mass index,* or BMI. The nature of the BMI is discussed further in Chapter 12, in connection with young adulthood. For now, though, it is enough to note that individuals with an excessive BMI tend to be about 30 to 50 percent overweight compared to their peers of the same height and age (St. Jean, 1997). By this definition, a child who is obese and is fifty-four inches tall will weigh more than eighty-five pounds instead of the normal sixty-five pounds. In our society, about one-third of children are overweight and 18 percent of children are obese (Centers for Disease Control and Prevention, 2015). The condition can be especially difficult for girls because current cultural norms emphasize physical thinness for females and fashion models in the media typically are thin to a degree that would be considered medically underweight and unhealthy for most girls and women. Most people (including most medical professionals) assume that the problems associated with obesity are caused by excess weight as such, and therefore assume a primary goal for obese people is to lose weight (Dalton, 1997). A

obesity The state of being extremely overweight, specifically to a body mass index of 30 or over.

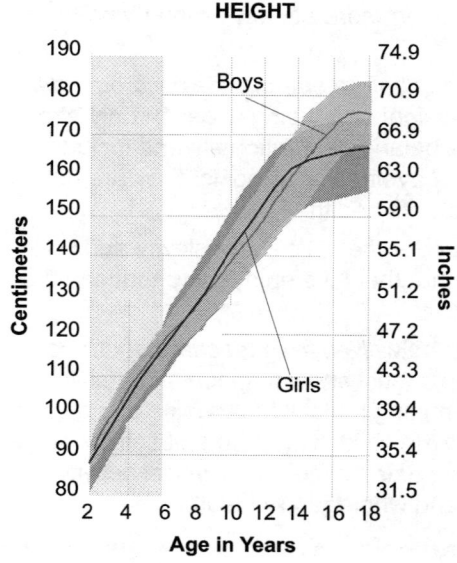
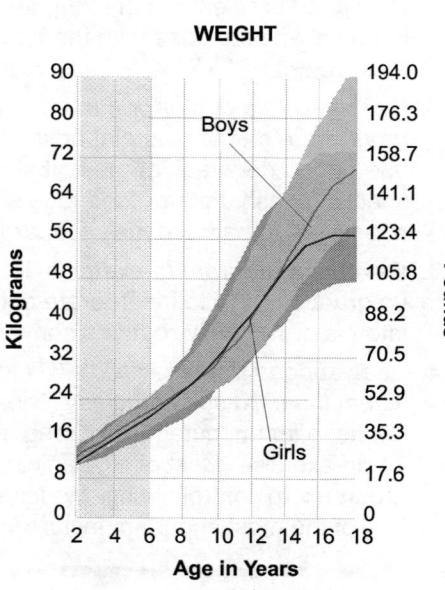

FIGURE 8.1

Growth in Height and Weight from Two to Eighteen Years

During the early school years, children continue to grow at a smooth rate, though more slowly than in early childhood and infancy. By the middle and later parts of this period, however, weight and height begin to accelerate as children move into puberty. The growth spurts usually begin sooner for weight than for height and sooner for girls than for boys.

Chapter 8 Physical and Cognitive Development in Middle Childhood

Late in childhood, girls often grow taller and faster than boys of the same age. The disparity can create awkward moments for members of both sexes, though many children do not seem to be concerned about it at all. When these children become older adolescents or young adults, they may not even remember that a disparity occurred.

Source: Franck Boston/Shutterstock.

careful look at medical research about obesity and weight control, however, suggests that the link between weight and health is not so simple (Gaesser, 1996). Sometimes excess weight may be the result rather than the cause of an ailment (as in the case of diabetes). Other times it may be the result not of eating too much but of insufficient physical activity. Inactivity, in turn, may be caused not by "laziness" buy by social prejudices. An overweight person may feel self-conscious about exercising in public due to our society's bias against the "wrong" type of body, yet also be unmotivated to exercise in private, where no social support is available. Moreover, issues like not having access to affordable, nutritious, less-processed food (Swinburn et al., 2011), parents not having cooking skills or the time to cook (Davis et al., 2011; Fulkerson et al., 2011), increasing portion sizes (Fisher, Liu, Birch, & Rolls, 2007; Wanink, Painter, & North, 2005), and even insufficient sleep (Chen, Beydoun, & Wang, 2008; Cappuciio et al., 2008) all contribute to the explosion of obesity rates in the past few decades. These attitudes and factors are essentially social problems, not personal ones; and as the "A Multicultural View" feature (see page 261) indicates, the attitudes are *not* shared by all societies.

Unfortunately, for either a child or an adult, losing weight permanently is difficult to do. For a child, dieting or exercise must have the full support of parents and siblings, because these people have such substantial influence on meal preparation and on a child's daily activities (Ebbeling, Pawlak, & Ludwig, 2002; Pittman & Kaufman, 1994). Yet family members may find support is difficult to sustain over the long periods of time most weight control programs require. The collective willpower may simply be lacking, especially because overweight children tend to have siblings and parents who are overweight themselves. Table 8.1 lists some additional guidelines for addressing weight issues in children.

Motor Development and Athletics in Middle Childhood

Fundamental motor skills continue to improve during the school years and gradually become specialized in response to each child's particular interests, physical aptitudes, life experiences, and the expectations of others. Unlike a preschooler, older children are no longer content simply to run, jump, and throw things; now they put these skills to use in

TABLE 8.1 Guidelines for Responding to a Child's Weight Problem

1. *Make sure the child really needs to lose weight.* Weighing only a little (10 percent) more than average poses no medical risk and may cause a child few social problems in the long term. If a child is teased for his or her weight, learning ways to cope with the teasing may be more effective than trying to lose weight.

2. *Consult with a doctor or a trained nutritionist before starting the child on a diet program.* A diet should aim at stabilizing weight or causing a loss of only about one pound per week at most. It should be balanced nutritionally and include snacks. Crash diets or food fads should be avoided at all costs; they are not effective and can seriously jeopardize a child's health.

3. *Develop a program of exercise appropriate for the child.* Start slowly and build up gradually. Try to incorporate activities that the child enjoys and that can fit into his or her daily routines conveniently.

4. *Seek support from the child's whole family, as well as from teachers or others whom the child sees regularly.* These people must show respect for the child's efforts, offer encouragement, and avoid tempting the child to break a diet or give up on exercise. Most of all, participate *with* the child in programs of activity or programs to control eating. Modeling appropriate eating and physical activity is one of the most important factors in child and whole-family health.

A Multicultural View

Dieting in Cross-Cultural Perspective

In our society, self-administered dieting and exercise has become a major industry. Countless books have been published to help individuals lose weight and gain muscle, and many of them are intended for children. A quick search of Amazon.com produces thousands of hits for children's diet books. Attaining a culturally valued bodily "look" can become a major personal project, one that for many children begins in middle to late childhood and continues well into adulthood.

At the heart of North Americans' preoccupation with body image is not only a concern with nutrition and health but also a commitment to crucial cultural values. One of these values is *individualism,* a belief that people are fundamentally autonomous and responsible for themselves. From this notion comes the belief that your body indeed belongs to you and that you personally are responsible for how it looks. How it compares to social ideals of physical beauty therefore indicates your success as a member of society as well as your ongoing commitment to participation in society. A lean, thin body (supposedly) shows self-discipline and restraint, two socially admired qualities, because it implies that you have been eating and exercising responsibly. To achieve these things, numerous individuals embark on exercise and diet programs for varying periods of time. Girls and women are especially likely to do so because they are almost certain to be judged by their physical appearance repeatedly, even during childhood, and children who perceive themselves as being overweight are more likely to "diet" by means of skipping meals, reducing food intake, or exercising at a younger age (Balantekin, Savage, Marini, & Birch, 2014; Chung, Perrin, & Skinner, 2103). Children are at particular risk for early dieting if their parents encourage them to diet or lose weight (Balantekin et al., 2014), which is linked to higher risk of adult obesity and with risky dieting, such as fasting, using laxatives, or using diet pills (Enriquez, Duncan, & Schur, 2013).

Yet a preoccupation with diet and exercise is not universal. The Fiji islanders in the South Pacific, for example, seemed generally indifferent to the size or weight as recently as the mid-1990s (Becker, 1994). Fijians had definite ideals about physical appearance: a person should have sturdy calf muscles, for example, and generally look "well fed" (a bit plump by our standards), and Fijians would frequently comment on one another's physical looks constantly and directly: everyday greetings often included teasing about whether a person looks fatter (or thinner) than in the past.

The paradox of personal indifference combined with public frankness was accounted for by the Fijians' fundamental orientation to their *community* rather than to themselves as individuals. What was important to an individual Fijian was not personal achievement or standing out from the average but showing a nurturing and caring attitude toward friends, family, and children. A primary vehicle for attaining these goals was food: serving food was and is a major way to show interest and attention to others' needs, both physical and emotional. According to custom, Fijians open their windows and doors during mealtimes so that the event becomes more truly public, and anyone passing by is cordially (and sincerely) invited in to share the food. Extra food is routinely prepared for each meal to allow for this possibility, because it is considered a social disgrace to be unable to share food generously with whoever happens to come by.

The Fiji islanders, therefore, considered dieting to be self-centered and irresponsible because it prevented a person from either giving or receiving nurturance from the community. In a sense, a person's body "belongs" to the community rather than to the individual. Secret eating was a serious social mistake, as was secret noneating (dieting). Parents observed their children carefully for changes in appetite, as well as for changes in weight (either up or down) that might imply fluctuations in appetite not because they wanted their children to achieve a certain size but because they wanted them to participate fully in both the giving and receiving of community care, and an important way of participating is through food.

However, between the 1990s and 2010, Fiji experienced great economic development, leading to more exposure to Western values, ideals, and media (Gerbasi et al., 2014). This influx of Western influence changed both perception of the ideal body and peer attitudes toward ideal body types, which led to a significant increase in the number of girls dieting and engaging in disordered eating (Becker, 2004; Gerbasi et al., 2014).

In pre-1990s Fiji, it was not the cultivation of a certain body image that conferred prestige, as was and is true in North American society. Instead, it was the cultivation of social relationships, particularly those that made nurturance possible. Which orientation toward body image and food do you think is preferable? The focus on caregiving spared most Fijian children from worries about their physical appearance, as well as from discouragement caused by unsuccessful dieting or exercise programs to improve physical looks (Gerbasi et al., 2014; Sault, 1994). But a negative effect also is possible: the focus on community can create problems for children who *must* limit their eating for health reasons, such as diabetes or intestinal flu. In a strongly communal society, these situations can prove especially worrisome to both child and family because they require deliberately limiting participation in a central social practice: the daily abundant sharing of food.

> **What Do You Think?**
>
> Is concern about height and weight really a gender issue? Why or why not? Check your perceptions by polling ten male and ten female acquaintances (it's easier if you collaborate in doing this task) about whether they think they weigh more than, less than, or close to the ideal. Then ask them how they think members of the opposite sex would answer the same question, on average.

complex, active play. Sometimes this consists of informal, child-organized games, such as hide-and-seek, in which children use motor skills. At other times, active play involves formal sports such as gymnastics, swimming, or hockey.

During the school years, children develop the ability to play games with rules. Some of these games are informal, such as after-school hopscotch, and some are formal and adult sponsored, such as Little League softball. In any case, traditional team sports now begin to have meaning for children because they can understand and abide by a game's rules. At the same time, children's improvements in coordination and timing enhance their performance in all kinds of sports, whether individual or group.

What lasting physical and psychological effects do early athletics have on children? This question has not been studied as thoroughly for children as it has for adolescents and adults, but a few tentative answers are possible. On balance, athletic activity probably helps children much more than it hurts them. However, it does carry a few significant risks. Table 8.2 summarizes the benefits and the risks.

Physical Effects of Early Athletics

The most obvious risks in athletics are sports-related injuries: bruises of various kinds and severity, damage to muscles (sprains), concussions, and broken or dislocated bones (Backx, 1996; Caine, Maffulli, & Caine, 2008). Do such injuries actually pose a problem for child development? Some researchers express concern about the frequency of athletic injuries, especially in childhood. The injuries usually receive only short-term medical attention: once bones or muscles appear to be healed, they are promptly ignored, and the athlete is encouraged to return to play. Given the special stresses of athletic activity, this short-run approach may allow minor but long-term disabilities to develop (Caine et al., 2008; Smith, 1996).

Other researchers point out that most children who are injured during sports have relatively minor injuries, and the benefits of participation therefore considerably outweigh the risks. They cite the physical benefits of athletics. For example, children involved in

In addition to obvious physical benefits, athletics can also encourage achievement motivation, discipline, and a sense of self-esteem. Critics worry, though, that some sport activities may also cause injuries and destructive competition.
Source: Fotokostic/Shutterstock.

262 Part 4 Middle Childhood

TABLE 8.2 Physical and Psychological Effects of Childhood Athletics

	Physical Effects	Psychological Effects
Positive Effects	Better physical fitness Improved motor coordination	Training in achievement motivation (e.g., bettering previous running times) Support for teamwork (e.g., basketball)
Negative Effects	Sports-related injuries, such as knee injuries (football), back problems (gymnastics), shoulder pain (baseball), concussions (football, rugby)	Competition engendering more concern with winning than with performance as such Excessive pressure from adults to practice, perform well, and win

regular athletics may develop better physical endurance than nonathletic children; this means their hearts and large muscles may function more efficiently (Rowland, 1993), and more fit children are less likely to get injured (Caine et al., 2008). As a result, they may be better able to undertake ordinary daily activities with less effort.

Psychological Effects of Early Athletics

The immense popularity of early athletics probably stems at least in part from the psychological benefits attributed to participation. Participation in athletics has been linked to having fewer mental health problems during adolescence (Steiner et al., 2000). Sports, it is hoped, develop achievement motivation, teamwork, and a tolerance for or even enjoyment of competition. How well do early athletics in fact realize these goals?

Training in Achievement Motivation

Most sports provide standards against which children can assess their performances. Goals can be scored, distances measured, and times clocked. Children's performances can then be compared with the youngsters' own previous scores, with those of their peers, or with those of top-scoring individuals or teams.

Whether this information really encourages higher athletic achievement depends on how a child uses it. Kindergarten children tend to remember their sports history poorly. Therefore, they approach each performance as a unique event. For example, Dalia may find each swim meet enjoyable in its own right, but she thinks little about bettering a past performance or correcting previous mistakes. During the school years, however, comparing oneself to standards becomes a prominent concern (Weiss, 1993). This concern does motivate some children to better their performances, but it also undermines motivation for children who believe athletic standards are arbitrary, externally imposed, or unreasonably difficult to meet.

Teamwork and Competition

Many sports promote teamwork, that is, cooperation with a select group of individuals. This goal certainly is a positive one, but it comes only if a child's team wins. What happens to losers? Among schoolchildren, even the most gracious loser shows significant stress. Research has found that losers become less sociable, refuse to talk about the game, and miss game practices more often than winners do (Petlichkoff, 1996). Losing teams also show a marked tendency to pinpoint blame by scapegoating individual members or events during a sporting season. If one "big play" seemingly lost a crucial basketball game, the players may dwell on that event more than it deserves, and they may stew about one or two players who seemed most responsible for that play. These negative effects of losing are exacerbated and likely, in part, caused by parent behavior. When parents model

> **What Do You Think?**
>
> Do childhood athletics by nature foster a competitive spirit among players? Or does competitiveness develop from stimulation by coaches and parents? This issue can spark a lively in-class discussion, especially if you can include a person who has been successful at competitive athletics as well as someone who has not!

bad sportsmanship—yelling at coaches, referees, their own children, or other children—children also engage in negative behaviors, but when coaches and spectators display positive behaviors like encouragement, the players will model those positive behaviors (Arthur-Banning, Wells, Baker, & Hegreness, 2009).

For some children, the path away from being a loser consists of training harder to win. For substantial numbers of others, however, it consists of learning not to take a sport too seriously—to treat it as "just a game" played for social and fitness reasons rather than for competitive success. Unfortunately the historical association of athletics with competition, glory, and "manliness" (for boys) can make this transition difficult for certain sports in some communities (Messner & Sabo, 1994). When a truly recreational approach to sports proves impossible, some children may adopt new interests and activities (such as watching television) that have fewer health benefits than sports do.

Health and Illness in Middle Childhood

Whether they are physically active or not, children usually are relatively healthy in the school years in the sense that they experience illnesses or accidents with serious medical consequences only rarely. School-age children also have colds and minor viral illnesses less often than preschool children and infants do. But illnesses and accidents can still disrupt the lives of individual children, which partly accounts for why medical professionals and parents may disagree about whether or not schoolchildren are "really" healthy in general.

mortality The proportion of persons who die at a given age; the rate of death.

One sign of good health is very low **mortality**, or the proportion of persons dying at a given age. In recent years, only about three or four children in every ten thousand die between ages six and thirteen, compared to twice this number among preschoolers and four times this figure among adolescents (U.S. Department of Commerce, 1998). The low rate of mortality is part of a historical trend extending back over the past century in which death rates have declined for all age groups, but especially for children.

On the average, schoolchildren get sick only about one-half as often as preschoolers do, though still about twice as often as do their parents. From parents' point of view, therefore, illnesses probably still seem rather frequent; nearly one-quarter of the parents in one survey reported that during the preceding two weeks their children were "too sick to carry on as normal" (Coiro, 1994), meaning the children stayed home from school for at least one day. As parents often point out, a sick child has a substantial impact on the work and leisure schedules of the rest of the family, especially parents. This is particularly true for families living at or near the poverty line, discussed later.

Most common childhood diseases are *acute illnesses,* meaning they have a definite beginning, middle, and end. Most childhood acute illnesses, such as colds, gastrointestinal flu, chicken pox, and measles, develop from *viruses,* complex protein molecules that come alive only when they infect a host tissue (such as a child's nose). Despite popular belief, no drugs can combat viral infections. (This is not the case with bacteria that invade the body; they can be effectively fought off with antibiotic drugs.) Instead, viral illnesses must run their course, and the child's natural immunities must work the real cure.

By the school years, about 5 to 10 percent of children develop *chronic illnesses,* or conditions that persist for many months without significant improvement. In the United States and other developed countries, the most common chronic conditions occur in the lungs and affect breathing (United Nations International Children's Emergency Fund, 1998). Some children develop *asthma*, or persistent congestion in the lungs; others develop chronic coughs or allergies. Other chronic complaints concern specific sensory organs. About one child in one hundred, for example, experiences problems in hearing or seeing. These and other chronic health problems become more frequent with age; among older adults they become commonplace, as we will see in Chapter 16's discussion of physical development in late adulthood.

Social Influences on Illness

The seriousness of illnesses varies according to children's social and socioeconomic status, but not the frequency. In general, parents in higher-SES families report that their school-age children get sick just about as often as those from lower-SES families, but higher-SES parents report keeping their children at home for shorter periods of time (Fitzgerald et al., 1994). Moreover, families near or below the poverty line are less likely to note that their children are in very good or excellent health (about 75 percent), compared to families with incomes of $75,000 or more reporting very good or excellent health (90 percent) (CDC, 2014).

What accounts for the difference? Low-SES families probably lack money for doctors' visits, access to special child care when a child is sick, and permission to take time off from work to tend to a sick child. Therefore, to merit staying home from school or visiting a doctor, a child must have a relatively major illness, such as a seriously high fever or severe diarrhea. The result of these circumstances shows up in the longer average stay at home when illness finally receives special attention.

Race and sex appear to matter too. African American families report *fewer* illnesses per child than do white families of similar SES, and all families of both races report *more* illnesses for girls than for boys of the same age (CDC, 2014; Johnson, 1995). In fact, school-age girls appear to get sick almost as often as preschool children of both sexes do; boys, however, get sick less frequently as they get older. Each of these differences probably reflects cultural influences. Medical care and an "on-call," stay-at-home parent may be less available to African American children than to white children, for example, necessitating that they continue to attend school even with minor illnesses. Furthermore, gender expectations may encourage girls to seek care for minor ailments and encourage boys to ignore such ailments, trends that continue into adulthood. In these ways, "illness" is not simply an objective reality but a perception by the child—or, more precisely, a perception combined with a response by the community.

Attention Deficit Hyperactivity Disorder

A small number of school-age children, especially boys, seem to be extremely active and have considerable trouble concentrating on any one activity for long (American Psychiatric Association, 2013). Their problem is called **hyperactivity**, or **attention deficit/hyperactivity disorder (ADHD)**. A second-grade teacher described one student with ADHD like this:

> Joey was friendly when you greeted him; "Hi!" he would say brightly, and smile. But he would never settle down. First he dumped the class's main supply of pencils out on a table; he sort of lunged at one of the pencils, but before he began writing, he left the table, looking for something new. During a reading lesson, I asked Joey to read silently until I finished helping another child; but Joey found this hard to do. He glanced in my direction; tapped a neighboring child on the shoulder; giggled; and kept scanning the room for "more." A child happened to drop a book; Joey laughed at this harder than the others, and jumped up quickly to pick the book up. He was probably trying to help, but in doing so he knocked his own papers all over the floor. Instead of picking up the papers, he only picked up his pencil, and headed off to sharpen it. And the morning was still only half over!

Note that *most* children show excessive activity—behavior such as Joey's—*some* of the time. Only a few children really exhibit extremely high activity levels consistently enough to warrant professional attention, and there is evidence that ADHD is overdiagnosed, particularly

hyperactivity Excessive levels of activity and an inability to concentrate for normal periods of time.

attention deficit/hyperactivity disorder (ADHD) Excessive levels of activity and an inability to concentrate for normal periods of time.

Chapter 8 Physical and Cognitive Development in Middle Childhood

among boys (Bruchmüller, Margraf, & Schneider, 2012). In fact, other problems, such as insufficient or disturbed sleep, have symptoms similar to ADHD among children (Chervin et al., 1997).

Current guidelines require a minimum of six symptoms (a partial list follows) be present for a minimum of six months and in at least two domains (school, home, social) before the age of twelve, and the symptoms must interfere with daily functioning and not be explained by other disorders to be diagnosed as ADHD (American Psychiatric Association, 2013; CDC, 2016):

- Has trouble maintaining attention on tasks, work, or play
- Makes careless mistakes
- Does not follow through on tasks
- Is easily distracted or forgetful
- Has difficulty organizing activities
- Loses things
- Is fidgety or squirms
- Talks excessively and interrupts
- Acts as if "driven by a motor"
- Cannot stay in seat or moves about when inappropriate

Because no one is sure what makes some children overactive, and because ADHD usually persists throughout an individual's childhood and beyond, no single strategy for treating or dealing with the condition exists (Rutter, 1995). However, a group of strategies, usually involving stimulant medications in conjunction with other therapies, have proven helpful for the majority of children with this problem.

To reduce immediate symptoms, the most effective treatment is a stimulant medication. Some commonly used and effective stimulants have been *Ritalin* and *Focalin* (also called *methylphenidate*), *Adderall* (also called *mixed-salts amphetamine*), and *Strattera* (also called *atomoxetine*) which, paradoxically, quiet the child's behavior by "waking up" the central nervous system, that is, making it more alert (Heal, Smith, & Findling, 2011). When used properly, these medications have few short-term or long-term negative side effects; contrary to popular belief, they do not blunt growth, make the child lethargic, depressed, drowsy, or lacking in spontaneity (Barbaresi et al., 2006; Cherkes-Julkowski et al., 1997; Spencer et al., 2006). Instead, these medications make the child less bossy, argumentative, and noisy and better able to focus on tasks. In fact, long-term use of the stimulant medications used to treat ADHD might actually normalize activity in certain parts of the brain responsible for attention (Hart, Radua, Nakao, Mataix-Cols, & Rubia, 2013).

In addition to medication, behavior modification often helps to alter some of the most undesirable or counterproductive behaviors of an ADHD child. As the term implies, **behavior modification** is a psychotherapeutic technique that identifies specific behaviors that need changing, as well as straightforward techniques for eliminating or reducing them (Kazdin, 1994). In classrooms, several behavioral techniques are commonly used either alone or in conjunction, such as reviewing classroom rules regularly and having children earn points for following the rules or receiving a "time-out" for breaking rules (Fabiano et al., 2007). Praise, stickers, and special privileges also might be earned for following rules, and daily "report cards" of behaviors are often sent home to parents. Sometimes high-status peers are used to model or demonstrate appropriate behaviors. The active child simply watches a classmate complete an assignment slowly instead of at lightning speed; then the child tries to copy the same slow style in doing the assignment himself. The teacher, of course, reinforces (usually with praise) the modulated behavior when it occurs. One study found that medications, behavior modification, and the combination of the two positively impacted children's classroom

behavior modification
Techniques based on the principles of learning theory that can be used by parents, teachers, therapists, and other professionals to help children, adolescents, and adults reduce or eliminate undesirable behaviors and learn desirable ones.

> **What Do You Think?**
>
> Some experts argue that children with ADHD are not so much "disturbed" as "disturbing." What do you suppose they mean by this comment? Speculate about ways that home and school could be made less "disturbing" for a hyperactive child. Offer your ideas to a teacher or some other person who has experience with children's behavior problems. What does this person think?

behavior, and that low-intensity behavior modification in combination with low-dose stimulants had the same effect as high dosages of stimulants (Fabiano et al., 2007).

One key quality of behavior modification is its consistency and predictability, and parents and teachers can help significantly by striving to provide these qualities in the child's everyday environment. At home this means meals, play times, and bedtimes should come at about the same times every day and follow roughly the same pattern. At school, lessons should have a regular, predictable format. In either setting, rules of acceptable and unacceptable behavior should be clear, simple, and relatively consistent. All of these strategies help the ADHD child by temporarily reducing the demands on her attention-directing capacities and allowing these abilities to develop at her own pace.

When these strategies are followed, between 25 and 50 percent of all children eventually outgrow the problem, although they often report continuing to feel restless and distractible as adults (Fischer & Barkley, 2007; Karam et al., 2015; Weiss & Hechtman, 1993). The remaining children show some greater risk as adults for antisocial behaviors, such as failure to pay parking tickets, some inattention and impulsivity (Karam et al., 2015), and more fidgety behavior than those never diagnosed with ADHD (Halperin et al., 2008).

Sleep

As noted previously, some children with sleep disorders, which limit or disrupt sleep, seem as though they suffer from ADHD (Chervin et al., 1997). During middle childhood, children should be awake and alert during the day, sleep between nine and eleven hours each night, and rarely nap, a shift that occurs when children begin formal schooling (National Sleep Foundation, 2015). As with other areas of wellness during middle childhood, most children during this period of life get adequate, good-quality sleep, though it is important for parents to maintain a relaxing bedtime routine in a dark, cool, quiet room with a regular bedtime and wake-time for children. Prepubescent children are often lark-like—that is, their natural preference is to go to sleep early and wake early in the morning—a trend that, as we will see, changes with puberty. As with earlier childhood, refusal to go to sleep is a common problem during middle childhood as is difficulty going to sleep due to anxiety (Meltzer & Mindell, 2006). Practicing good sleep hygiene (noted previously) may help with these problems. If a child is sleepy or distracted during the day or does not wake up feeling refreshed, it is best to discuss the specific problems with a pediatrician, as these issues may be indicative of a serious sleep disorder, such as obstructive sleep apnea or an anxiety disorder.

COGNITIVE DEVELOPMENT

The ADHD example described previously is a good illustration of how a particular human change or condition can affect all domains of development simultaneously: it is partly physical (due to differences in the brain and brain functioning) as well as social (expectations about what is normative and what is expected), but influences the child's ability to think, as well as his feelings and relationships with others. It is also a relatively unusual condition, the kind we called *nonnormative* in Chapter 1. Therefore, it does not directly represent the most common or even universal changes in thinking or social life in middle childhood, the ones we have been calling *normative*. In this section, we describe the normative changes with respect to children's cognition (or thinking). As you will see, though, understanding the "usual" changes in thinking is not straightforward. Even when a cognitive development occurs widely in the school years, it usually varies in timing, intensity, and context. This caution applies to all four of the topics that follow: the development of concrete operational thinking, of information-processing skills, of language, and of general intelligence. In each of these areas there are "typical" developments in middle childhood, but also diversity.

Piaget's Theory: Concrete Operational Skills

As we discussed in Chapter 2, Jean Piaget developed a comprehensive theory of cognitive development from birth through adolescence. During middle childhood, according to this theory, children become skilled at **concrete operations**, mental activities focused on real, tangible objects and events. Concrete operations have three interrelated qualities, none of which is reliably present among preschool children: decentration, sensitivity to transformations, and reversibility (Piaget, 1965; Wadsworth, 1996). *Decentration* means attending to more than one feature of a problem at a time. For example, in estimating the number of pennies spread out on a table, a school-age child probably will take into account not only how large the array is but also how far apart individual pennies seem to be. *Sensitivity to transformations* means having different perceptions of the same object and combining them in logical ways. For example, when judging whether two clay balls have the same volume after one ball is squeezed into a pancake, a school-age child concentrates on the actual process of change in appearance—the transformation—rather than on how the clay looks either beforehand or afterwards. *Reversibility* of thought means understanding that certain logical operations (for example, addition) can be reversed by others (subtraction). All in all, the concrete operational child constructs a view of the world that emphasizes quantitative relationships for the first time. Now many facts seem logically necessary that earlier appeared arbitrary or even incomprehensible. In judging whether the amount of clay stays the same after being squashed flat, the child now reasons that the amount *must* be the same if nothing was added or taken away when the clay was squashed.

Concrete operations cause important transformations in the cognitive skills children develop in the preoperational period. In classifying objects, children can group things in more than one way at a time by about age seven. They know that a person can be *both* a parent and a teacher at the same time, for example, rather than just one or the other. They also understand that some classifications are inclusive of others, for example, that a particular animal can be both a dog and a pet. As a result, they usually can answer correctly a question such as "Are there more boys in your class or more children?" Preschool children, in contrast, often fail to answer such a question correctly unless it is further simplified or clarified.

Conservation in Middle Childhood

Some cognitive skills make their first real appearance during middle childhood. Probably the best known of these skills is **conservation**, a realization that certain properties of an object necessarily remain constant despite changes in the object's appearance. An example of conservation of quantity is the one described in Chapter 6 in which two tall, narrow glasses contain exactly the same amount of water. If you empty one glass into a wide, low tray, you create a substantial perceptual change in the water; it looks quite different than before and quite different than the water in the remaining tall glass, as Figure 8.2 shows. Will a child know that the wide tray has the same amount of water the tall glass does? If he does, he conserves, meaning he shows a belief in the water's underlying constancy despite a perceptual change.

Piaget (1965) found that after about age seven, most children did indeed conserve quantity in the water glass experiment. In fact, he found that by a year or two later, children conserved on a lot of other tasks as well, including the ones illustrated in Figure 8.2. Each task depicted requires believing in some form of invariance despite perceptual change. The clay balls, like the water glasses, require believing that mass remains constant; the bent wires and the pencils, that distance or length remains constant; and the coins, that number remains constant.

concrete operations Logical thinking about concrete or tangible objects and processes; especially characteristic of middle childhood.

conservation A belief that certain properties (such as quantity) remain constant despite changes in perceived features such as dimensions, position, and shape.

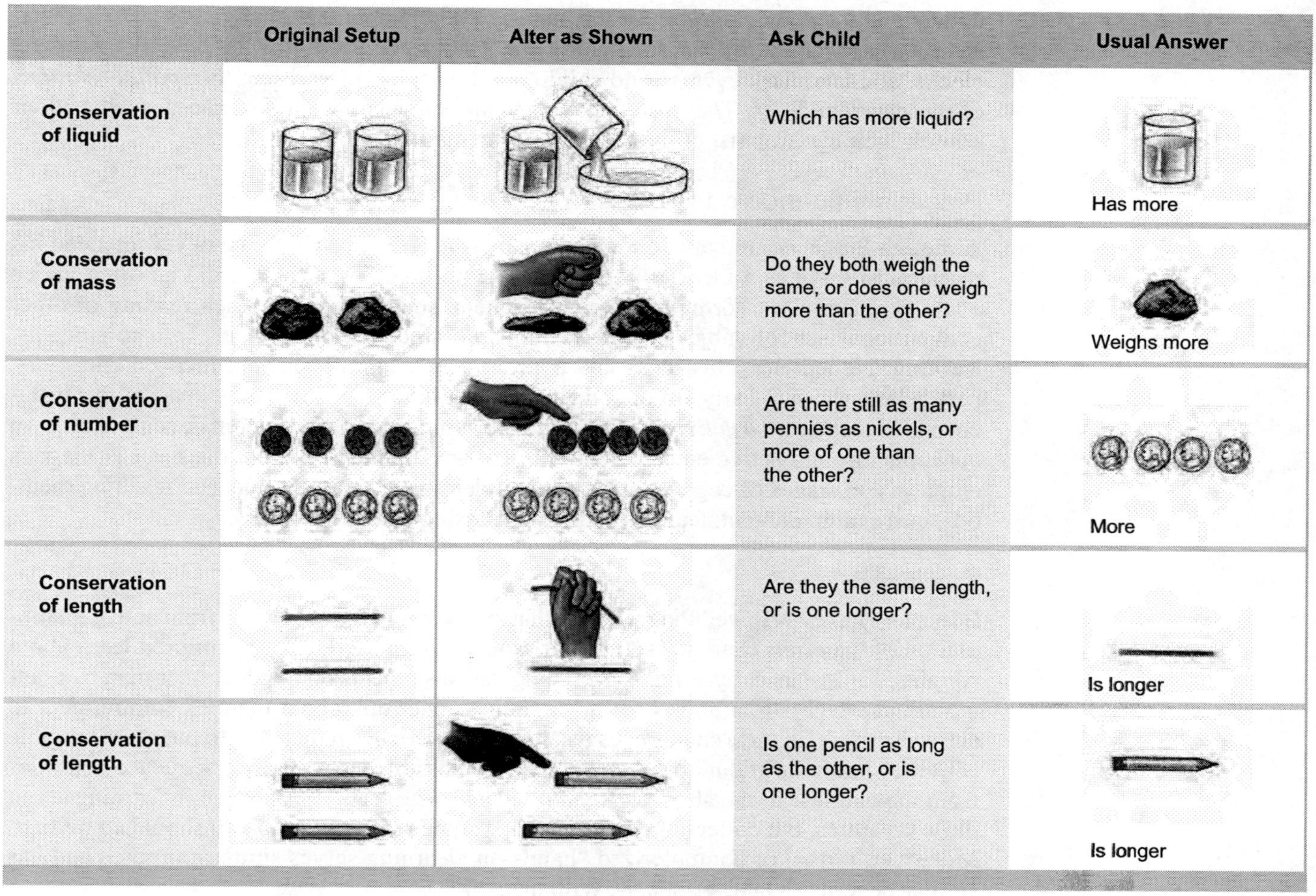

	Original Setup	Alter as Shown	Ask Child	Usual Answer
Conservation of liquid			Which has more liquid?	Has more
Conservation of mass			Do they both weigh the same, or does one weigh more than the other?	Weighs more
Conservation of number			Are there still as many pennies as nickels, or more of one than the other?	More
Conservation of length			Are they the same length, or is one longer?	Is longer
Conservation of length			Is one pencil as long as the other, or is one longer?	Is longer

FIGURE 8.2
Conservation Experiments

As Piaget demonstrated, conservation (or the perception of invariance) emerges on a wide scale in middle childhood. In some cases, the child realizes that amounts of liquid or of solid mass remains constant; in other cases, he or she realizes that length or number remains constant. Early in middle childhood, however, the child often holds one of these beliefs without necessarily holding another, or holds one belief only on some occasions and not on others.

Conservation Training

Specialists agree that children do not begin life conserving but instead acquire this skill somehow. How do they do it? Piaget argued that biological maturation and countless experiences with physical objects that show conservation properties enable children to mentally construct conservation. These experiences are numerous and diverse, and although they can be taught explicitly, Piaget believed they have a fuller, more general influence on development if allowed to emerge naturally.

But many psychologists have tried to teach conservation anyway. In recent studies, investigators tried to prevent children from being distracted by coaching them to talk about what was happening ("Nothing is being added or taken away") or to compare the important dimensions closely ("Watch the height *and* the width"). Such efforts do produce greater conserving in a large number of children, though not in all (Wadsworth, 1996). Conservation has even been taught successfully to children with developmental delays and intellectual disabilities. (Hendler & Weisberg, 1992).

However, trained children often do not maintain conservation concepts the same way "natural" conservers tend to do; they are more likely to give up their belief when even slightly challenged. "Natural" conservers are more steadfast in their commitment to conservation (although even they can be led to give it up if an experimenter shows strong skepticism about it). All in all, it seems that conservation may not develop during childhood as inevitably as Piaget first believed.

The same can be said about other forms of logical thinking that emerge during middle childhood (Piaget, 1983). Piaget noted, for example, that children become able to *seriate*, or arrange objects in sequence according to some dimension such as length or size. They understand *temporal relations,* or the nature of time, better than they did as preschoolers; an eight-year-old knows that time unfolds in a single, constant flow marked by calendars, clocks, and landmark events. And children at this age can represent the *spatial relations* of their surroundings. They can make maps and models of familiar places, such as their homes, their classrooms, or the local shopping mall.

Piaget's Influence on Education

Although Piaget commented on educational issues (Piaget, 1970), he never intended his research to serve as a theory of education. At no time, in particular, did he offer advice about problems that normally concern teachers, such as how to teach reading or other conventional school subjects, how to motivate students, or how to evaluate students' learning. Nonetheless, his ideas and approach have significantly influenced educators, particularly those in early childhood education (Elkind, 1994a). At the heart of this influence is Piaget's *constructivist philosophy:* the assumption that children develop their own concepts through active engagement with the environment. Also at the heart is Piaget's emphasis on stages of cognition. These two ideas have jointly influenced teaching methods, curriculum content, and methods for assessing student progress.

Teaching Methods

Educators have borrowed Piaget's idea that true knowledge originates from active manipulation of materials (Samuelsson & Carlsson, 2008; Seifert, 1993). Children learn about weights, for instance, by actually weighing various objects on a scale rather than by reading about weights in a book or hearing their teacher talk about them. A commitment to active learning, in turn, encourages teachers and curriculum planners to put more tangible activities into educational programs wherever possible, as well as to sequence activities from the tangible to the abstract. Reading about insects still has a place in learning about those creatures, but collecting (and handling) some real bugs probably should come first. Moreover, virtual or computerized "hands-on" learning serves similar purposes and has similar benefits (Klahr, Triona, & Williams, 2007).

Curriculum Content

Piagetian theory has influenced specific curriculum content by providing many particular ideas about what cognitive competencies to expect from children of particular ages or levels of development (Kamii, 1994; Waite-Stupiansky, 1997). The conservation skills described earlier imply that elementary school children should develop a greater ability to solve problems no matter *how* the problems are presented. Compared to preschoolers,

Piaget's idea that thinking begins with manipulation and activity has been interpreted to support many elementary education programs that emphasize active learning. Here, a child discovers the properties of conservation of mass by shaping bowls from clay.
Source: file404/Shutterstock.

> **What Do You Think?**
>
> Given Piaget's ideas about how thinking develops in middle childhood, what would be a good way to evaluate students' academic work in elementary school? Work with a classmate or two to devise an evaluation plan for a favorite grade level and subject. Then see how your plan compares to plans devised by classmates and (if possible) to those composed by an experienced teacher.

older children should be less distracted by seemingly small changes in drawings in their books or seemingly insignificant changes in how a teacher phrases assignments. In Piagetian terms, the children have become more "decentered."

Likewise, acquisition of concrete operations should help school-age children in a number of other ways. For instance, many academic tasks require multiple classification, which preschoolers often do not understand reliably. A written assignment may ask children to "list all the machines you can think of that begin with *c*." This task requires classifying objects in two ways at once: first, by whether or not something is in fact a machine, and second, by whether or not it begins with the letter *c*.

Piaget's cognitive theory has guided many curriculum planners and teachers to select and evaluate academic tasks such as these. The theory itself does not, of course, lead to accurate selections for all children, because not all children move through Piagetian stages at the same rate. In addition, most children are capable of abstract thinking to a certain extent, even if they are not as skilled as adolescents or adults are (Keating, 2011; Metz, 1995). Despite these limitations, though, Piagetian theory gives us valuable guidance about how children gradually adapt and reorganize their thinking as they grow older.

Assessment of Students' Progress

Throughout his work, Piaget emphasized the importance of children's actual thought processes and what those processes actually allow children to accomplish. This approach is evident in Piaget's heavy use of partially structured interviews and problem-solving tasks. Many educators believe such dialogues and tasks offer a much better way to assess students' progress than do traditional classroom tests and assignments, which tend to emphasize knowledge that is rote and taken out of context (Hill & Ruptic, 1994; Ruiz-Primo, 2011). Recent revisions to Piaget's approach, sometimes called "neo-Piagetian" theory, have made the approach even more attractive to educators by focusing more closely on *how* children learn and proposing cognitive stages that are more specific, and therefore more accurate, than Piaget's original proposals (Case & Edelstein, 1994).

Information-Processing Skills

A major alternative to Piaget's way of understanding the cognitive changes of middle childhood is in terms *of information-processing theory* (described in Chapter 2), which focuses on how children organize and remember information. By school age, children's short-term memories already are well developed—though not perfectly, as we indicate shortly. Their long-term memories, however, have significant limitations at the beginning of this period. For most children the limitations diminish as they get older, but for a few information processing remains a problem serious enough to interfere with school performance throughout elementary school and beyond. As with the development of concrete operational thinking, then, children simultaneously show both common trends and individual diversity in developing this form of thinking.

Memory Capacity

According to popular wisdom, children remember better as they get older. But how true and universal is this idea really? In everyday life, children obviously do not perform as well as adults do on some tasks, such as remembering to put away their clothes at the end of the day.

But in other ways they seem to perform equally well; for example, they will remember their grandparents when they see them again after months or even years of absence.

Working Memory

Some of these differences in memory may depend on which parts of the information-processing model the children happen to be using. Some tasks rely primarily on *working memory,* a feature of thinking that holds information only for a short period, perhaps up to twenty seconds, and allows mental manipulation of that information (see Chapter 2). On tasks that emphasize working recognition memory, school-age children perform less well than adults do. This tendency can be demonstrated by showing individuals a set of digits briefly and then immediately asking them whether the set included a particular digit (Cowan, 1997). Under these conditions, recognition of a test digit improved steadily, with eight-year-olds remembering only about three digits and adults remembering about seven. Not surprisingly, too, the time it took a participant to recognize a test digit *did* depend on how many digits were shown in the original set, regardless of the person's age. Showing six digits made the task take longer than showing just three, no doubt because the person evaluated the test digit against a larger number of alternatives.

recognition memory Retrieval of information by comparing an external stimulus or cue with preexisting experiences or knowledge.

recall memory Retrieval of information by using relatively few external cues.

This study assessed a variation of **recognition memory**, in which a person merely compares an external stimulus or cue with preexisting experiences or knowledge. Recognition memory is involved when children look at snapshots of a holiday celebration months in the past: their faces light up, and they may describe aspects of the celebration they had apparently forgotten. **Recall memory**, in contrast, involves remembering information in the absence of external cues, such as when trying to remember a friend's telephone number without looking it up. In research, recall is often studied by providing a list of numbers and asking participants to provide that list in the order it was provided or in backward order. Children also get better at recall tasks such as this over the course of childhood and adolescence (Conklin, Luciana, Hooper, & Yarger, 2007). Recall generally is more difficult than recognition, but it shows the same developmental trend recognition does: school-age children can recall better than preschoolers, but not as well as adults. Figure 8.3 illustrates this trend.

selective attention The ability to maintain focus on one thing even in the presence of distractions.

Another factor that plays a role in working memory is that of attention. To succeed at any of the tasks noted earlier, one must actually pay attention to what is being presented even if there is some distraction. Our ability to focus on a single thing and ignore any other stimuli, much like you are doing now by focusing on this sentence even though there is ambient noise in the room, is known as **selective attention**. Over the course of childhood and adolescence, selective attention improves in part because we get better at inhibiting responses as the frontal cortex of the brain matures (Booth et al., 2003). Thus, ten-year-old Da'Sean is much better at focusing on his prealgebra homework than when he was seven even though his sister is watching cartoons in the same room.

Long-Term Memory

Long-term memory (LTM) is the feature of thinking that holds information for very long periods, perhaps even indefinitely. It is not clear how much long-term memory changes during childhood, or even whether it changes at all, because LTM relies increasingly on complex strategies of information storage and retrieval. Younger children may remember less because they have experienced fewer memorable events or because they use fewer methods of deliberately remembering information and experiences.

To understand how LTM changes during childhood, consider how children and adults recall short stories they have heard (Wolf, 1993). By age six, children already understand the basic narrative structure of stories—that such stories contain characters, situations, and plots with a beginning, a middle, and an end. Not surprisingly, therefore, children show many similarities to adults in recalling stories. Like adults, they recall important features of a story ("Goldilocks was not supposed to enter the bears' house") and ignore or forget trivial details ("Goldilocks was wearing brown shoes"). They also recall the essences of sentences rather than their exact wording.

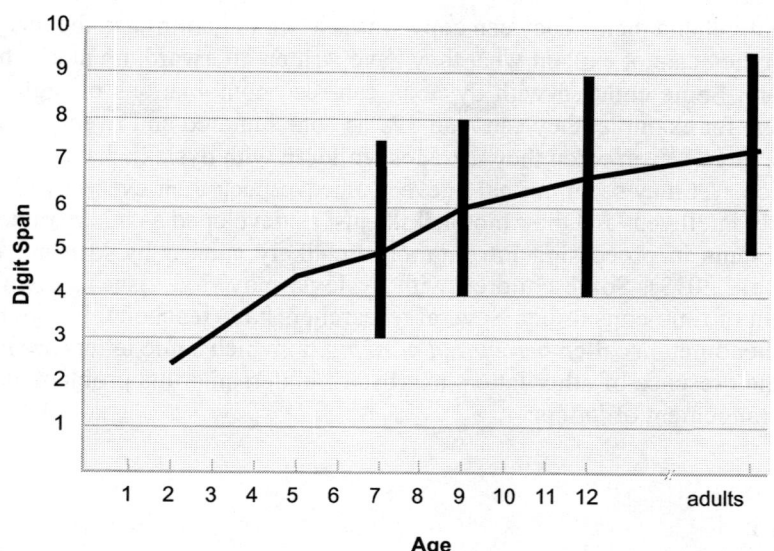

FIGURE 8.3
Developmental Changes in Recall Memory

In the study represented here, children were asked to recall a series of digits shortly after hearing them. The points on the graph represent the average number of digits subjects were able to recall, and the bars represent the ranges of typical performance at each age. Recall of digits improves during middle childhood and almost reaches adult levels by age twelve, though not quite.

But compared to adults, the recollections of school-age children include fewer inferences based on the sentences they actually hear (McNamara et al., 1991). As children get older, they begin to "read between the lines" more frequently, at least when recalling stories, and making inferences about characters' goals within a story may improve recall for a story (Lynch & van den Broek, 2007). This tendency lends color and detail to their retellings as they get older, although they sometimes risk misstating the facts of a story.

Implications for Elementary Education

The structure, or "architecture," of memory may affect how children can learn during the school years. A younger student who can remember only three bits of information needs to have information organized in smaller chunks than an older student who can remember six bits at a time. The younger child may have trouble remembering a phone number long enough to dial it, for example, unless the teacher can offer some learning strategies for doing this task. More significant for learning, research shows that elementary school students' ability to solve arithmetic problems is correlated with the extent of their working memories; in one study, "larger" working memory meant greater accuracy in solving problems (Swanson et al., 1993). Children's limitations in terms of long-term memory, on the other hand, pose a different challenge: school-age children *can* remember ideas and facts for long periods, but their teachers may need to help them see connections among the stories, ideas, and other material they learn in school.

Difficulties with Information Processing: Learning Disabilities

However, improvements in information processing do not occur uniformly for all children. During middle childhood, between 5 and 12 percent of children are diagnosed with neurodevelopmental disorders, or specific learning disabilities, disorders in basic information processing that interfere with understanding or using language, either written or spoken (Geary, 2004; Lerner, 1993; Olulade, Napoliello, & Eden, 2013). Usually a **learning disability** causes poor academic achievement, although low achievement is not in and of itself evidence of a learning disability. Learning disabilities have no obvious physical cause, as blindness or hearing impairment do, and do not result from a general slowness of thinking, as intellectual disability does.

Learning disabilities take many forms. One of the more common forms is called *dyslexia,* literally an inability to read. The diversity of symptoms among children with dyslexia reflects the diversity among learning disabilities in general. For some children, dyslexia consists of "word blindness": they can read letters singly (such as *c, a,* or *t*) but not in combinations that make words, such as *cat.* In other forms of dyslexia, children can read words

learning disability Difficulty in learning a specific academic skill such as reading or arithmetic.

Chapter 8 Physical and Cognitive Development in Middle Childhood

but fail to comprehend them. They can copy words accurately or transcribe them from oral dictation, but they cannot explain what they have written afterward, no matter how simple the vocabulary. Some children with dyslexia can read combinations of digits that make large numbers; for example, they can read *123* as "one hundred and twenty-three" but not as "one, two, three," even when they try. Most children with dyslexia have these problems in combination. Yet they seem normal in every other respect; their everyday conversations seem perfectly intelligent and their motor skills just as developed as other children's.

Such problems in processing information are likely caused by learning disabilities (Olulade, et al., 2013). Some children with dyslexia may find visual recognition especially difficult or time-consuming. Several researchers have reached this conclusion after studying a phenomenon called *perceptual masking,* in which some letters are hard to read because of the presence of other letters nearby. To understand this problem, consider the following arrangement of letters:

```
w e k
q w e k l
a q w e k l m
s a q w e k l m n
d s a q w e k l m n p
g f d s a q w e k l m n p y b
c v g f d s a q w e k l m n p y b h t
```

If you look at the *e* in the top line, you probably will still be able to see the letters *w* and *k* clearly using your peripheral vision (the corner of your eye). If you look at the *e* in a line farther down, you can still see the end letters relatively clearly, but the middle letters become almost impossible to pick out clearly. Trying to notice the middle letters does help you to perceive them, but when you make this effort, the end letters become hard to discern. Perceiving one set of features in this display masks others—hence the term *perceptual masking*. Without a lot of practice, few people, adults or children, can see very many letters at once.

Some (though not all) children with dyslexia show especially strong perceptual masking (Snowling & Stackhouse, 1996). Compared to same-aged normal readers, they must stare at words for rather long periods, consciously shifting attention from one subset of letters to another in a way similar to the staring required to "see" the letters displayed on this page, similar to "normal" readers who are younger. Once they figure out the letters in a word, however, they can connect meanings with them fairly quickly and accurately.

The gap in speed between perceiving and associating may account for many errors made by children with dyslexia. A ten-year-old may look at the word *conceal* and say something like "concol," or look at *alternate* and say "alfoonite." In making these mistakes, children may literally be reading what they see and guessing about the rest. Unfortunately, they may see fewer letters than normal same-aged readers usually discern.

Causes of Learning Disabilities

What causes some children to have a learning disability such as dyslexia? The symptoms sometimes resemble what happens to individuals who suffer injuries to their brains (Rourke & Del Dotto, 1994). For this reason, some professionals have suggested that many learning disabilities, including dyslexia, may reflect undetected minimal brain damage that occurred during the birth process or even before birth which discourages some parents and professionals from helping children with learning disabilities on the grounds (probably mistaken) that organically based problems are beyond control. However, relatively high rates of learning disabilities among children with a close family member, such as a parent or twin, with learning disabilities suggest some kind of genetic basis (Geary, 2004). Current thought suggests that a combination of genetics and environment likely plays a causal role in the development of learning disabilities (Peterson & Pennington, 2012).

A more helpful explanation for learning disabilities focuses on cognitive functions rather than on brain anatomy. In this view, disabilities may result from subtle differences in how the mind of a child normally organizes, focuses on, and processes information. To see what this idea means, consider what children must do to read an ordinary page of print. First, they must perceive the letters and words as visual patterns. Then they must combine those patterns into larger strings that constitute phrases and sentences resulting in phonological coding, which can be thought of as "words in their head." Finally, they must connect those strings with meanings to form ideas. While all of these steps are going on, they must also scan ahead to recognize the upcoming visual patterns on the page. If any of these steps fails to occur or occurs in the wrong sequence or at the wrong speed, a child may appear to have dyslexia. Current research suggests that difficulty in visual recognition might be caused by dyslexia rather than being a cause of dyslexia, suggesting that the breakdown occurs with the phonological coding (Olulade et al., 2013; Peterson & Pennington, 2012).

Helping Children with Specific Learning Disabilities

Because learning disabilities become a problem primarily in school settings, school professionals have taken increasing responsibility in recent years for helping children who develop these problems. Most commonly, help consists of careful diagnosis of which steps of thinking cause difficulty for a child, followed by individual educational plans to strengthen those particular steps (Alexander & Slinger-Constant, 2004; Lyon, 1993). For instance, children with problems in perceptual masking can be given exercises in which they purposely work to improve this skill. Often such special work can be done in a regular class during a normal school day, but at least some of it requires individual tutoring so that the professional can monitor and give precise assistance to the child's thinking as it actually occurs. Depending on the child's needs and the school's circumstances, regular classroom teachers, parents, or trained special educators can act as tutors as well as additional sources of encouragement and support for the child. The Working With interview with Terry Wharton discusses issues of special education in more detail.

Children with learning disabilities usually are old enough to have feelings and opinions about their problems. Eventually, in fact, a major problem in some learning disabilities may become *self-consciousness* about failing to learn, in addition to any cognitive or perceptual problems as such. A child who cannot read well usually becomes painfully aware of this fact sooner or later and worries about what teachers, parents, and peers may think of her as a result. Parents can help with this problem by being optimistic about the child's eventual capacity to learn academic skills, in spite of current difficulties, and being supportive rather

There are numerous ways of helping children with learning disabilities; no single way is guaranteed to be always effective. This teacher, for example, is helping a girl with her reading by using a computer that provides extra assistance and responds to her particular learning needs.
Source: Rob Marmion/Shutterstock.

WORKING WITH Terry Wharton, Special Education Teacher

Giving Children a Second Chance to Learn

Terry Wharton has a wide range of experience in classroom teaching and special education. He currently teaches a class of second to fourth graders who have shown significant behavioral and emotional problems in regular classrooms. There are only eight students in his class, all of them boys, and two teacher assistants—definitely not the typical teacher-to-student ratio. Terry spoke about the philosophy guiding his program and about how he and his assistants reconcile it with conventional academic expectations for the primary grades.

Terry: We emphasize making the class nonpunitive and nonaversive. For these kids, school has been a disaster socially—lots of fights with classmates, conflicts with teachers and other adults. We have to provide successes and confidence to counteract the downward spiral of their self-esteem.

Kelvin: *How do you do that without leading to further fights and conflicts? Eight of these kids in one room could be explosive!*

Terry: Well, we do have to plan activities carefully and guide their choices more than usual. At the start of the year, the children only come for half a day, and I plan a series of activities they are sure to enjoy and to be able to do, like setting up a personal datebook or calendar to use later in the year. By the end of that first day, they really feel successful.

Kelvin: *Given your students, how much is it like ordinary school?*

Terry: Oh lots, actually! Academics is a priority. We have a "news" time where everyone relates some interesting personal experience. Then I read to them for a few minutes. Then they write in journals, either about the story or about something else that concerns them.

Kelvin: *Do the kids like the journals?*

Terry: I must admit, at first they resisted. They seemed very self-conscious about their writing skills and about revealing their thoughts and feelings. But lately it's been amazing; you should read them! Their growth with the journals is impressive. They talk about the story, or about their fears and hopes for their family.

Kelvin: *What about math?*

Terry: They don't seem as uncomfortable about math as they do about writing and reading; I'm not sure why. We work on basic arithmetic skills using some of the latest manipulatives.

Kelvin: *Manipulatives?*

Terry: Like sets of unit blocks that you can combine to illustrate addition problems. They seem to like that. But you know what surprised me the most? Workbooks! When I taught a regular primary-grade class, I tried to avoid those because I felt they were too structured, but these students love them; they even ask to do them! I think it gives them a feeling of clear progress and a sense of control over their own efforts. They can see clearly that they are getting work done.

Kelvin: *So your program is indeed academic? You do work on cognitive skills?*

Terry: Absolutely. The cognitive skills develop only because we're also supporting these students socially, though. The two go hand in hand. I think that's true for all children, but working with these kids with behavior problems has really brought that idea home to me.

Kelvin: *Where else do you see academic and social connections?*

Terry: With the parents, certainly. We make a big effort to involve the parents in our program. Several times a year we have "family celebrations," lunches where the child's whole family is invited. The parents have responded enthusiastically. Some parents work as volunteers in the school. They've been a real help, and even if they are not in the same classroom, it's reassuring to be in the same building as their child.

Kelvin: *These sound like good ideas for all classrooms and parents. Do you agree?*

Terry: Yes, I do. But they're especially valuable for these particular parents because they've had so many bad experiences with schools, either because of their child's problems or when they were students themselves. It builds their confidence as parents.

What Do You Think?

1. Do you think Terry would define the word *cognitive* the same way this chapter does?
2. Terry did not comment on the fact that his class is all boys. Do you think gender is important to consider in teaching a class like this? Why or why not?
3. Terry mentions that his students enjoy workbooks for mathematics, even though he personally does not consider them a good idea initially. How do you feel about this issue? What do you suppose Piaget or an information-processing theorist would say about using workbooks?

Part 4 Middle Childhood

> **What Do You Think?**
>
> Think about the methods you yourself have used to remember new information. What are they, and how are they consistent with the discussion in this chapter about how memory develops during middle childhood? Compare your own memory strategies with those of classmates. How are they similar? How are they different?

than critical of the child's efforts to do so. Teachers can help in these same ways, and in addition can encourage a positive, supportive climate in the child's classroom and school. In fact, children and adolescents with high levels of determination and self-efficacy, which can be fostered by parents and teachers, do better in school and are more likely to go on to college than those with low levels of these qualities (Field, Sarver, & Shaw, 2003).

Another major problem among children diagnosed with learning disabilities is the social stigma associated with the diagnosis. This stigma may serve as a self-fulfilling prophesy, leading some to feel hopeless about their abilities. The label of having a learning disability also puts many children at increased risk for bullying (Mishna, 2003). The social impact of school is so important, in fact, that we discuss it again later in this chapter. First, though, let us look at another major cognitive change of middle childhood: the development of language. As we will see, this development also has both cognitive and social effects.

Language Development in Middle Childhood

As we saw in Chapters 4 and 6, language development is a gradual process, one that continues to unfold during middle childhood. Vocabulary keeps growing, of course, and the ways children use words and sentences become more subtle and complex and more like adults' (Anglin, 1993). Contrary to the impressions young school-age children sometimes give, though, they have not necessarily mastered syntax. They often are confused by a number of common sentence forms until well into the elementary school years. To six-year-olds, for example, the sentence *The baby is not easy to see* means "The baby cannot see very well"; the sentence *I don't think it will rain tomorrow* is likely to mean "I know for a fact that it won't rain."

Mistakes like these may hardly be noticeable to parents and teachers if a child otherwise has normal language ability and has been acquiring only one language since birth. A school-age child can make himself understood for most everyday purposes and can express basic feelings. What is primarily still missing at this age is an extended vocabulary and skill in the more subtle or specialized uses of language—needs that therefore become the focus of many elementary school programs. The fact that language is actually changing or "developing" during middle childhood, in fact, may seem obvious only if a child is acquiring *two* languages during this period. In that case, the basic issues of language acquisition all come to the fore: problems in phonology (the sounds of a new language), lexicon (vocabulary), syntax (grammar), and pragmatics (language use). Next, we investigate the cognitive and social effects of bilingualism.

Bilingualism and Its Effects

Although most monolinguals may not realize it, a majority of children around the world are able to speak two languages and therefore are bilingual (Romaine, 1995). Bilingualism is common in the United States even though most American households primarily use English at home; somewhere between 60 million and 65 million individuals regularly use a language other than English (U.S. Bureau of the Census, 2015a). This represents about 26 percent of the population, but the proportion is actually much higher in some cities and regions such as Los Angeles where more than 50 percent of the population speaks a language other than English at home (U.S. Bureau of the Census, 2015a).

Does bilingualism benefit children's cognitive development? Research suggests that it does, but primarily when children acquire both languages equally well and when both

Fully bilingual children have cognitive advantages over monolinguals, but only as long as both languages and their related cultures are treated with respect by teachers and society. These Latino children are well on their way to becoming bilingual. What attitudes will they encounter about their language and heritage?
Source: wkstock/Shutterstock.

languages are treated with respect by teachers and other representatives of the community (Bialystok & Hakuta, 1994). Language specialists call such children **balanced bilinguals**.

balanced bilingual A person who is equally fluent in two languages rather than more fluent in one language than in the other.

Cognitive Effects of Bilingualism

For one thing, balanced bilingual children show greater cognitive flexibility—skill at detecting multiple meanings of words and alternative orientations of objects—than monolingual children do. Bilingual children can substitute arbitrary words for normally occurring words relatively easily without changing any other features of the sentence. If asked to substitute *spaghetti* for *I* in the sentence "I am cold," bilingual children more often produce the exact substitution, "Spaghetti am cold," and resist the temptation to correct the grammar ("Spaghetti is cold") as monolinguals more often do. Such flexibility shows **metalinguistic awareness**, the knowledge that language, and in this case individual words, can be an object of thought. Metalinguistic awareness develops because bilingual experiences often challenge children to think consciously about what to say and how to say it (Jimenez et al., 1995). A question such as "What if a dog were called a cat?" therefore poses fewer conceptual problems for bilinguals. So do follow-up questions such as "Would this 'cat' meow?" or "Would it purr?" Those who are bilingual are also better at aspects of cognitive control. That is, when speaking, they must inhibit one language to speak in another language, demonstrating superior executive control compared to monolingual individuals (Costa, Hernández, & Sebastián-Gallés, 2008).

metalinguistic awareness The ability to attend to language as an object of thought rather than attending only to the content or ideas of a language.

However, all of these cognitive advantages apply primarily to balanced bilingual children, those with equal skill in both languages. What about the unbalanced bilinguals, those with more skill in one language than in the other? Does knowledge of a second language help, even if it is limited? Some research suggests that even those children without balanced language skill demonstrate improved attentional performance on tasks (Yang, Yang, & Lust, 2011). Though many cognitive benefits have been associated with bilingualism, overall impact may be more mixed largely because of the interplay of social attitudes surrounding language differences in society (Pease-Alvarez, 1993; Yang et al., 2011).

Social Effects of Bilingualism

When children acquire two languages, one language usually has more prestige than the other. In the United States, the "best," or most important, language almost always is English. Its prestige results not only from its widespread use but also from its association

> **What Do You Think?**
>
> Think about a language you wish you could speak fluently. Why would you like to be able to use this language? In forming your opinion, what assumptions are you making about the culture or people who use this language?

success and power: all the important people in American society, it seems, speak English fluently. These circumstances create negative attitudes or stereotypes about people who speak other languages and challenge educators to overcome social prejudices at the same time they facilitate learning new grammar, vocabulary, and usage (Soto, 1997). Negative stereotypes also apply to those who can speak English but do so with a "foreign" accent (Gluszek & Dovidio, 2010).

The influence of language on attitudes can be documented through experiments using the *matched guise technique*. In this procedure, perfectly balanced and fluent bilinguals tape record standard messages in each of their two languages, and the messages are interspersed among other tape-recorded messages to disguise the identities of the bilingual speakers. Then listeners evaluate the competence and social attractiveness of each speaker. Time after time, two consistent trends occur in studies of this type. First, speakers of English are rated more highly than speakers of other languages. Second, listeners from non-English-speaking cultural groups rate the English speakers more highly than they do speakers of their own language. The prestige of English, in other words, comes from sources in addition to English speakers themselves.

Negative attitudes toward non-English languages reduce children's school performance by making them less willing to use their primary, or first, language in public and reducing their self-confidence about linguistic skills in general. Fortunately, however, educational programs exist that can counteract these effects by treating children's first language as an educational resource rather than a liability. Overall, research favors *additive bilingual education*, programs that develop language skills in *both*, of a child's languages rather than attempting to replace a first language with English (Hernandez, 1997). As a practical matter, such programs usually are conducted partly in each language, depending on children's current language skills, but they do not confine either language to isolated "lessons" lasting only short periods each day. The challenge is a double one: to foster new language skills while promoting respect for a child's original language and culture. In countries where language is less strongly associated with economic or social status (for example, Canada, where about 25 percent of the population speaks French as a first language), bilingual education often does not include this double agenda (Johnson & Swain, 1997). Therefore, successful bilingual programs more often emphasize simple immersion in a second language and tend to ignore a child's first language without negative educational effects.

Defining and Measuring Intelligence

All of the cognitive changes discussed so far—concrete operational thinking, memory development, and language—constitute aspects of **intelligence**, a term that refers to adaptability or a general ability to learn from experience. Often *intelligence* also refers to the ability to reason abstractly especially by using language, as well as an ability to integrate old and new knowledge. In recent years, some psychologists have broadened the term *intelligence* to refer to social skills, talents of various kinds (such as a talent for music), or bodily skills. The traditional orientation toward reasoning and problem solving, however, still dominates discussions of intelligence, and partly as a result many standardized tests have been developed to measure these forms of intelligence.

intelligence A general ability to learn from experience; also refers to ability to reason abstractly.

The multitude of definitions of intelligence can create confusion for parents and professionals who have responsibility for helping children to develop their fullest potentials. Some of the complexity can be sorted out by noting that views of intelligence can be organized around three major theoretical approaches. The oldest and therefore best

Chapter 8 Physical and Cognitive Development in Middle Childhood

psychometric approach to intelligence A view of intelligence based on identifying individual differences in ability through standardized test scores.

developed view is the **psychometric approach**, which is based on standardized, quantitative measurement of abilities and achievement. More recently, researchers oriented toward *information processing* and toward *sociocultural* issues also have developed theories of intelligence, although these approaches have not been tied to standardized testing to any significant extent.

Psychometric Approaches to Intelligence

Psychometric definitions of intelligence have developed out of *standardized tests,* all of which share three important features. First, they always contain clearly stated questions that have relatively specific answers. The questions usually draw on logical reasoning and verbal skills, which schools typically require. Second, standardized tests always include clear, standard procedures for administration and scoring. Often they provide a script for the person giving the test, as well as specific printed guidelines about when and how to credit particular answers. Third, such tests present information about how large groups of comparable individuals perform to allow evaluation of the performances of particular groups or individuals (Aiken, 1996).

Kinds of Standardized Tests

Standardized tests serve many purposes, but for convenience we can classify them into two major groups: achievement tests and aptitude, or ability, tests. **Achievement tests** measure individuals' existing skills or knowledge; they try to assess current attainment in a particular realm of human behavior. Children often encounter such tests in the form of scholastic achievement tests, such as tests of reading achievement or arithmetic achievement. By nature, such tests usually draw heavily on the typical curriculum content of the subject area being tested.

Aptitude tests measure ability or try to estimate future performance in some realm of behavior. A test of scholastic aptitude, for instance, tries to estimate a child's potential for success in school. Because of their goal, aptitude tests contain a broader range of questions than achievement tests do. A scholastic aptitude test probably would include questions from several major school subjects and draw on basic academic skills such as reading and mathematical reasoning.

In practice, aptitude and achievement tests are less distinct than these definitions make them sound. Often achievement tests are very effective predictors of future performance; children's current skills in arithmetic, for instance, predict their future mathematical performance about as well as any aptitude test can do. Also, aptitude tests can successfully predict future progress only by sampling skills and knowledge children have already attained. Nonetheless, the distinction remains useful for those who develop and use tests. In general, measuring aptitude means looking to the future, whereas measuring achievement means assessing the past.

Once norms have been calculated, standardized tests, and especially achievement tests, can serve two purposes. On the one hand, they can help educators know how well particular schools or classrooms are functioning in general. For example, all classrooms using a particular curriculum can be compared with classrooms using another curriculum, or all classrooms in one school can be compared with all classrooms in the city or even with a national cross-section.

On the other hand, standardized tests sometimes can aid individual children. The most common approach involves screening students who need special educational help. If teachers find that a certain student is learning the curriculum very slowly, they may ask a school psychologist to test the child's general scholastic ability in the hope of diagnosing or clarifying his or her learning problems. Although the results of such a test cannot stand alone, they often contribute to the complex process of assessing the learning needs of a particular child. Standardized tests can also help to identify students with superior abilities in specific areas; the Focusing On feature looks at educational issues pertaining to these gifted students.

As you may suspect, standardized tests serve neither of these purposes perfectly. Factors other than ability, such as a child's health or motivation to succeed, affect performance. So do physical disabilities, such as visual impairment. More indirectly, cultural and language

achievement test A test designed to evaluate a person's current state of knowledge.

aptitude test A measurement of ability that estimates future performance in some realm of behavior.

differences among children affect performance on standardized tests. These additional influences deserve special discussion because they affect all children throughout society.

Biases of Intelligence and General Ability Tests

Although they attempt to measure general qualities, tests of ability and intelligence contain various biases. For example, many intelligence tests rely heavily on language in all of its forms— listening, speaking, and reading. Many also emphasize problems that have specific answers and that play down divergent or creative thinking. Also, although they do not focus on speed, intelligence tests tend to favor children who answer fairly rapidly and take little time to mull over their solutions.

Because schools also emphasize all of these features, intelligence tests measure academic ability better than they do any other skill. Some psychologists, in fact, have suggested calling them measures of *academic intelligence,* or school ability, to make this limitation clear (Anastasi & Urbina, 1997).

The biggest problem with intelligence tests, however, comes from their cultural assumptions, which have originated entirely from white, middle-SES experiences in Western Europe and North America. The tests show their assumptions or biases in at least two ways. First, individual questions often demand knowledge that children can gain only by thorough immersion in white, middle-SES society. One question might ask children to describe the purpose of a garden hose, thereby assuming previous contact with a garden in their backyards. Another question might ask children to define the word *drama* or *concerto,* thereby assuming the sort of education that provides this information.

Even when tests avoid this type of bias, they suffer from other, more subtle cultural assumptions. Some ethnic groups and cultures do not value conversations that emphasize abstract or general propositions, as is common in classrooms or intellectual discussions; using this style may seem rude or at least boring (Heath, 1993). Children from these groups therefore cannot be expected to take tests that rely heavily on this form of dialogue. Also, in some cultural groups contact with strange adults is extremely rare, so children from such groups may find sitting alone in a room with an unfamiliar test administrator rather perplexing or even frightening. For such children, any questions the administrator asks may seem much less important than figuring out this adult's real motives.

Information-Processing Approaches to Intelligence

Some psychologists have responded to the limitations of psychometric views by developing other definitions and theories of intelligence. One way or another, all of the newer approaches broaden the nature and sources of intelligence. From these perspectives, more children seem to qualify as "intelligent" than is the case when children are assessed psychometrically.

The Triarchic Theory of Intelligence

An approach that draws explicitly on principles of information-processing theory is the **triarchic theory of intelligence** proposed by Robert Sternberg (Sternberg, 1994, 1997, 2006). This theory broadens the psychometric approach by incorporating recent ideas from research on *how* thinking occurs. To do this, Sternberg proposed three realms of cognition or, in his words, "subtheories" (hence the name *triarchic),* each of which contributes to general intelligence.

The triarchic theory of intelligence, developed by Robert Sternberg, identifies three different realms of thinking: componential, experiential, and contextual. Philosophically, the theory is rooted in information-processing theory.

The first realm of intelligence concerns the *components* of thinking. These resemble the basic elements of the information-processing model described in Chapter 2. Components include skills at coding, representing, and combining information, as well as higher-order skills such as planning and evaluating one's own success in solving a problem or performing a cognitive task.

triarchic theory of intelligence A view of intelligence as consisting of three components: (1) adaptability, (2) information-processing skills, and (3) the ability to deal with novelty.

Focusing On . . .

Gifted Students: Victims or Elite?

For years some educators have worried that *gifted students* (those capable of high performance in some or all academic areas, social leadership, or the performing arts) (see Table 8.3) become bored with the normal curriculum, isolated from their peers socially, and sometimes unproductive in school and career (Ross, 1993). Their "problem" was too much talent, but gifted students were believed to be potential victims of conventional schooling in the way students with learning or physical disabilities are and, similarly, often face the stigma of labeling (Berline, 2009).

In response to these concerns, some schools have created programs of gifted education. Typically these include a "pull-out" program: for an hour or two each week, students designated as gifted work in a separate classroom on activities designed to meet their needs or more commonly in high schools a school-within-a-school model that provides a special curriculum to students (Matthews & Kitchen, 2007). Often students work independently on projects of their own choosing, such as learning about local butterflies, designing a computer program, or creating a portfolio of paintings. Sometimes they are also linked with community experts (called *mentors*) who help them develop these interests. Regular classroom teachers are encouraged to recognize their interests and abilities by-allowing time to pursue the projects and periodically grouping gifted children together for tasks related to the regular curriculum (Gallagher & Gallagher, 1994).

This portrait of gifted education is attractive but highly controversial. A number of educators, parents, and political leaders argue that gifted education creates an overprivileged group of students (Margolin, 1994). In the pull-out programs, students receive much more time and attention from teachers than in a typical classroom and enjoy more freedom in using their time. Ironically, it is argued, the curriculum for gifted students is much *less* rigorous than that for regular students; gifted children do not necessarily read more books, write more essays, or learn more

TABLE 8.3 Some Characteristics of Gifted Students Renzudlli (1994)

Characteristic	Examples
Well-above-average ability	Can think abstractly; skilled at verbal and numerical reasoning; adapts well to novel situations; rapid and accurate memory
Task commitment	Shows high level of interest, enthusiasm, perseverance, and self-confidence; sets high standards for success
Creativity	Shows original thoughts; open to new experiences and information; curious, speculative, sensitive to detail and to aesthetic characteristics of ideas and things

---

The second realm of intelligence concerns how individuals cope with their *experiences*. How effectively do they respond to novelty in solving new problems? For example, a person may follow a dinner recipe accurately when it is written in imperial measurements (ounces, teaspoons) but fail miserably when the same recipe is presented in metric units (milliliters, grams). How quickly can that person adjust to the new form of the task and solve it as automatically as was possible with the old form?

The third realm of intelligence concerns the *context* of thinking. People show this form of intelligence to the extent to which they can adapt to, alter, or select environments relevant to and supportive of their abilities (Sternberg & Wagner, 1994). In taking a university course, for example, a student may try diligently to complete the course assignments as given, in essence adapting himself to the environment of the course. If this strategy does not work satisfactorily, the student may complain about the assignments to the professor in an effort to alter them. If the altered assignments do not work for him, the student may drop the course and select another. All of these behaviors show contextual intelligence (though not necessarily of a kind that may please professors!).

Table 8.4 summarizes the three realms of thinking, or cognition. These realms describe the processes of intelligence in more detail than classic psychometric approaches to intelligence have done. They also suggest an explanation for why

> **Focusing On...**
>
> ### Gifted Students: Victims or Elite? *continued*
>
> mathematics than others do. There has been a call to improve the curriculum of gifted programs by incorporating more critical thinking, problem solving, social studies, and foreign languages (VanTassel-Baska, 2006).
>
> Furthermore, the gifted programs tend to treat students as if they were broadly talented in all areas, even though research and professional teachers' experiences suggest that almost all students have selected talents—math but not English, for example, or music but not athletics (Gardner, 1997). This makes gifted programs more compatible with the preexisting strengths of high-SES families and white, English-speaking families, which may constitute a subtle form of racism. In fact, African American students are significantly less likely to be part of gifted programs and are disproportionally placed in special education programs that provide unequal education (Blanchett, 2006; Darlin-Hammond, 1997).
>
> Gifted education responded to these criticisms by making entrance into gifted programs more flexible: relying less on standardized test scores and more on students' own interest in volunteering for the program. Another is to arrange more activities for gifted students in the regular classroom and fewer in pull-out situations (Maker, 1993). A third is to redefine gifted education as *enrichment*: activities that tie conventional curriculum goals (reading, arithmetic) to students' own prior interests and talents. All students may be invited to pull-out activities, and activities focus on particular areas of the normal curriculum.
>
> Integrating gifted and regular education in these ways is more equitable but does not eliminate the basic educational controversy underlying gifted education: fostering excellence and fostering equality of education. Some researchers argue, for example, that having highly talented students work with less talented ones may accentuate rather than reduce elitism. Differences between higher and lower performers become obvious to all students, day in and day out, and create tensions within the classroom that can be reduced when the gifted program is integrated into classrooms and schools (Berlin, 2009; Gallagher, 1993). Students may still prefer classmates with similar levels of academic motivation, both to work with and to be friends with; so informal social segregation may develop even in a room that is officially integrated. Enrichment activities also are harder to schedule if they invite volunteers and focus on specific school subjects; they cannot overlap with regular class times because some students are ahead and motivated in the enrichment subject but may need extra help in the "regular" subject that they miss. That leaves lunch periods and before and after school for enrichment periods, times that teachers may need for class preparations and "refueling." Despite problems, many excellent enrichment programs exist in schools and have succeeded reasonably well in creating flexible yet challenging learning opportunities.
>
> **What Do You Think?**
> Some educators argue that the idea of a "bored gifted student" is a contradiction in terms. Why do you think they believe this? What do *you* think of this possibility?

individuals sometimes seem intelligent in different ways: perhaps one person has an advantage at internal processing of information, another adjusts to new experiences especially well, and a third has a knack for adapting, altering, or selecting appropriate environments in which to work. Given these possibilities, it would not be surprising

TABLE 8.4 The Triarchic Theory of Intelligence

Realm of Intelligence	Examples
Componential	Coding and representing information; planning and executing solutions to problems
Experiential	Skill with novel problems and familiar problems in novel settings; skill at solving problems automatically as they become familiar
Contextual	Deliberate adaptation, alteration, and selection of learning environments to facilitate problem solving

if psychometric tests favored certain children and cultural groups more than others, because the environments of some families and cultures foster the learning of testlike behaviors more than others do.

Gardner's Theory of Multiple Intelligences

Like Sternberg, Howard Gardner (1993a) has proposed that general ability consists of several elements or factors. However, Gardner has defined these factors in ways that reflect the influence of culture and society even more explicitly than the triarchic theory does. He argues that not one but **multiple intelligences** exist and take the following forms (Davis, Christodoulou, Seider, & Gardner, 2011):

multiple intelligences According to Howard Gardner's theory of intelligence, alternative forms of intelligence or adaptability to the environment.

- *Language skill* A child with this talent speaks comfortably and fluently and learns new words and expressions easily. She also memorizes verbal materials, such as poems, much more easily than other children do.
- *Musical skill* This child not only plays one or more musical instruments but also sings and discerns subtle musical effects. Usually musical talent also includes a good sense of timing, or rhythm.
- *Logical skill* A child with this skill organizes objects and concepts well. Using a microcomputer, for example, comes easily, as does mathematics.
- *Spatial skill* This child literally can find his way around. He knows the streets of the neighborhood better than most children his age do; if he lives in the country, he can find his way across large stretches of terrain without getting lost.
- *Kinesthetic, or body balance, skill* This child is sensitive to the internal sensations created by body movement. As a result, she finds dancing, gymnastics, and other activities requiring balance easy to learn.
- *Interpersonal skill* A child with interpersonal skill shows excellent understanding of others' feelings, thoughts, and motives.
- *Intrapersonal skill* A child with intrapersonal skill has a good understanding of his own. For children with either interpersonal, intrapersonal, or both of these skills, handling social encounters comes relatively easily.
- *Naturalist* This child has the ability to identify and categorize different things in the natural world such as plants and animals.

This boy's skill playing the piano, keeping time, and playing accompaniment for himself demonstrates an important part of intelligence: musical ability.
Source: Arvind Balaraman/Shutterstock.

Gardner argues that these intelligences are distinct, for several reasons. First, some of them can be physically located within the brain. Certain language functions occur within particular, identifiable parts of the brain, as do kinesthetic or balance functions. Second, the intelligences sometimes occur in pure form; some individuals with intellectual disabilities play a musical instrument extremely well, even though their language ability may be limited and they cannot reason abstractly. Third, each intelligence involves particular, core skills that clearly set it off from the others. Being musical requires a good sense of pitch, but this skill contributes little to the other intelligences.

Like Sternberg's ideas, the theory of multiple intelligences implies criticisms of psychometric definitions of intelligence and of the standardized intelligence testing associated with psychometric definitions. Strictly speaking, however, the notion of multiple intelligences may really criticize the *use* of conventional tests beyond their intended purposes.

Sociocultural Approaches to Intelligence

Sociocultural definitions of intelligence give even more importance than information-processing theories do to the social setting. In the **sociocultural perspective**, intelligence is not actually "in" individual persons but instead resides in the interactions and activities that occur *among* individuals (Wertsch et al., 1995). In this view, it is not the individual who adapts to, learns, and modifies knowledge but the person and his or her environment in combination. For example, a child may make many mistakes on a test of arithmetic computation but be able to locate the most economical items at the local candy store almost infallibly, even if the items come in odd sizes (1⅞ versus 2¼ ounces) or odd prices (34 cents versus 49 cents) (Chaiklin & Lave, 1993). That is because the knowledge needed for comparison shopping is contained not only in the shopper's mind but also in the overall structure of shopping in the candy store's environment. With practice, a child learns how to sort out pricing clues that depend very little on the computational procedures learned in grade school. Some of the clues involve rough estimations, such as when the prices of two items differ widely but their sizes differ only a little. Others involve nonarithmetic knowledge, such as recommendations from other shoppers or memories of where the store kept the bargains on previous visits. The intelligence needed for comparison shopping thus is only partly "in" the child; the rest is more accurately said to be distributed among the store shelves, the conversations with other shoppers, and the history of events at the store.

A key concept in understanding the sociocultural view of intelligence is the *zone of proximal development (ZPD),* originated by the Russian psychologist Lev Vygotsky and discussed in Chapter 6 (Vygotsky, 1978, 1997). The ZPD refers to the level of problem solving at which a child cannot solve a problem alone but can do so when assisted by an adult or a more competent peer. For example, a six-year-old may find the telephone directory too difficult to use alone but may be quite able to look up a phone number when given a bit of help from a parent. Implicit in the ZPD is the idea of shared knowledge, or shared cognition. Knowledge of how to use the phone directory exists at first in the interaction or relationship between two people—parent and child—and only gradually becomes located fully within the developing child. Likewise, knowledge of academic skills such as reading and mathematics also begins in the interactions between adults and children and only later becomes internalized by individual children. In fact, as the internalization progresses, children tend to perform better on tests of reasoning and language and therefore seem more "intelligent" in the psychometric sense.

Note that in emphasizing the social context of intellectual development, the sociocultural approach turns the issue of cultural bias on psychometric tests into an outcome to be expected and explored rather than a problem to be overcome or minimized. This changes the key question about intelligence from one about individuals to one about groups and communities. Instead of asking why some individuals seem more intelligent than others, the sociocultural view points out that some social *settings* may nurture and encourage individuals who show extra measures of talent, skill, and knowledge more than individuals

sociocultural perspective on intelligence A view of intelligence that emphasizes the social and cultural influences on ability rather than the influence of inherent or learned individual differences.

Good balance, as shown by this girl, is not a prominent goal of the academic curriculum, but it may be an expression of a fundamental form of human intelligence: kinesthetic ability.
Source: Nataliya Turpitko/ Shutterstock.

Even though building a model boat may be too difficult for these children to do alone, they are able to successfully turn some scrap wood into a seaworthy vessel when assisted by a more experienced adult. Change in performance because of such assistance is part of what Vygotsky meant by the zone of proximal development.
Source: Brendan Delany/ Shutterstock.

from other settings. In this sense, some families, classrooms, and workplaces may be more "intelligent" than others. The differences are well known by all psychologists interested in intelligence, including those who do not approach the topic from a sociocultural perspective. What is unique about the sociocultural perspective is the priority it gives to the impact of the community on individuals' cognitive development (Salomon & Perkins, 1998).

School Influences

Next to the family, school probably is the single most important influence during middle childhood. Each year children spend about eleven hundred hours at school and often many additional hours in school-related activities. Experiences at school give children opportunities to develop cognitive skills, language, and various talents and abilities. School also provides an arena for social development: for developing a self-image and self-esteem, cultivating peer relationships, and learning to deal with the diversity and conflicts that are an inevitable part of most people's lives. In the next chapter we look at social developments like these more fully, not only as they unfold in school but also in the lives of children more broadly. First, though, we will look at how school affects children's learning and therefore their cognitive development as well. Schools—and classrooms in particular—affect learning in three main ways: through fostering particular patterns of discourse, through the social biases of students and teachers, and through assessment (or evaluation) of student's learning. These factors also influence students' social development, but for now we will focus on how they affect learning and cognition.

Participation Structures and Classroom Discourse

discourse Extended verbal interaction.

participation structures Regular patterns of discourse or interaction in classrooms with unstated rules about how, when, and to whom to speak.

Classrooms provide particular patterns and styles of **discourse**, or language interaction, that influence how, when, and with whom children can speak (Gee & Green, 1998). Recurring patterns of classroom interaction are sometimes call **participation structures** and probably seem familiar if you have attended school for many years. They correspond roughly to common teaching strategies, except that participation structures include not only the teacher's behavior but students/ as well. Table 8.5 lists several of the most common participation structures.

As you may have noted from your own experience as a student, however, participation structures do not always work as intended, nor do they usually have the same effect on

> **What Do You Think?**
>
> Should standardized tests of ability be used in schools? If so, when and with whom, and for what purpose? Consult with several classmates about this issue. Then, if possible, compare the opinions of several professionals, such as a special education teacher and an occupational therapist. How do you think their work affects their opinions?

TABLE 8.5 Common Participation Structures in Classrooms

Structure	Teacher's Behavior	Students' Behavior	Assumptions
Lecture	Talk; tell ideas; answer questions	Listen; take notes; ask questions	Students think about what teacher says; do not daydream
Discussion	Set topic or broad question	Say something relevant; take others' comments into account	Know something about the topic before beginning class
Group work	Set general task; select group members	Work out details of solution to task	Do a fair share of the work; cooperate; compromise as needed

all students. One reason is that students bring to a classroom different expectations about discourse language and about work relationships: what seems like an invitation to work on a group project to one student may seem like an invitation to relax to another, in spite of a teacher's explicit efforts to focus students on work per se. This can be a problem if the discourse a student experienced at home has differed significantly in style from the discourse typically used at school.

Another reason is that teachers' discourse is always heavily laced with **control talk**, patterns of speech that collectively remind students that the teacher has power over their behavior and verbal comments. Even during "indirect" participation structures such as discussion or group work, teachers regularly do all of the following, among other things, to remind students of the teacher's influence:

- *Designate speakers* by calling on one student rather than another
- *Declare when a comment is valuable or irrelevant* by saying, for example, "That's a good idea" or "How can you relate [your comment] to what we were just talking about?"
- *Changing the topic or activity* by saying "Now let's do X [instead of Y]."

Hopefully teachers' control talk empowers rather than silences students by providing fair opportunities for individual children to express ideas, ask questions, and engage in higher-order thinking (O'Connor & Michaels, 1996; Orland-Barak & Yinon, 2007). There is a constant danger, however, that teachers' talk will empower only certain students at the expense of others. The inequity can occur when certain students get called on more than others or the ideas of certain students are declared to be irrelevant or inappropriate more often than the ideas of other students. One way to combat control talk and bias is to have teachers critically evaluate their own performance in the classroom (Orland-Barak & Yinon, 2007). As we note in the next section, such inequities sometimes do occur in practice as a result of social biases on the part of both teachers and other students. But they are not inevitable.

control talk A style or register of speech used by teachers to indicate their power over activities, discussion, and behavior of students.

Social Biases That Affect Learning

Observations of classroom teaching show that both teachers and other students sometimes respond differently to a student on the basis of gender, race, or ethnic background in ways that parallel gender, racial, and ethnic biases in society at large. On the average, for example, teachers are more likely to speak to boys from a physical distance, such as from across the room, and to speak to girls at close range, such as at arm's length (Delamont, 1996; Wilkinson & Marrett, 1985). During discussions and question-and-answer sessions, furthermore, teachers tend to call on boys 10 to 30 percent more often than on girls, depending on the subject and grade level (Measor & Sykes, 1992). Both behaviors create an impression in the minds of students that boys are somehow more important than girls—more worthy of public notice. However, other studies have demonstrated that children, particularly boys, perceive that teachers treat boys more harshly than girls (Myhill & Jones, 2006).

Classmates too show biases like these. During group work, for example, teammates sometimes reproduce society's gender and racial biases: speaking and listening to boys more than to girls, for example, and to white children more than to nonwhite children (Cohen, 1994). However, when similar bias was investigated examining not just race but proportion of African American and Caucasian children in a classroom, an interesting pattern appeared: When the number of African American children in a classroom increased, measures of bias decreased (Jackson, Barth, Powell, & Lochman, 2006).

This suggests that as we saw in Chapter 7's discussion of gender development, children tend to reinforce one another for gender-appropriate behavior—including being assertive if, and only if, you are a boy and cooperative (or nonassertive) if, and only if, you are a girl (Maccoby 1995). But the biases are not inevitable. Some teachers and classmates do not express them at all, and educational interventions have successfully trained teachers and even classmates to include all students equitably, regardless of gender, race, or ethnic background (Cohen & Latan, 1997; Denson, 2009; Leaper, 1994).

The Impact of Assessment

assessment The diagnosis of an individual's strengths, needs, and qualities.

For most children, school becomes a primary setting for **assessment**, teachers' diagnosis and evaluation of students' strengths, weaknesses, and progress at learning. Assessment has a profound impact on students' perceptions of themselves and of one another (Wigfield et al., 1998), either positive, negative, or both at once. The nature of the influence depends on the structure of goals the child experiences. Most schools and teachers use some combination of individualized, competitive, and cooperative goals, and educational research has found that each has distinct effects both on students' learning and on their social relationships.

Individualized Goals

With individualized goals, each student is judged on his or her own performance, regardless of the performance of others. In principle, therefore, every student could achieve top evaluations, failing evaluations, or any mixture in between. Sometimes this kind of assessment is called "grading on an absolute standard," because performance of each individual is compared to a standard rather than to other students. It is common in the teaching of relatively structured subjects, such as elementary arithmetic, where standards can be defined clearly. Research on individualized goal structures generally has found that this arrangement heightens students' attention to mastering content and skills, and makes them relatively indifferent to judging their overall abilities or those of other students (Johnson & Johnson, 1994). Unfortunately individualized goals also make students less interested in what they can teach one another and less appreciative of (because less focused on) one another's diverse knowledge and skills. Individualized goals also do not lend themselves equally well to all content or topics; performing in a school play or on a sports team, for example, depends as much on good coordination among individuals as it does on skills possessed by individuals themselves.

Competitive Goals

With competitive goals, students are assessed in comparison to one another, and some individuals therefore are judged to be better than others; there are "winners" and "losers." Competitive goals are common in school sports competitions (only one person or team can take first place), but also in many nonathletic tournaments and contests of all kinds (e.g., a schoolwide spelling bee). They are also implied, though not stated, when teachers post marks or scores in rank order for students' inspection. Competitive goals make students concerned with how they expect to perform relative to others, regardless of how well they perform in any absolute sense. Competitive goals also tend to make students think of their own abilities as fixed entities ("You either have it or you don't") rather than as the result of effort and hard work on their own part. For both these reasons, competitive goals can interfere with sustained motivation to learn, and eventually therefore reduce engagement with activities that develop thinking skills such as those described earlier in this chapter. They can also reduce the self-esteem of "losers" as well as lower the status of losers among peers. Every year, for example, about 35 percent of children drop out of competitive athletics, and the most common reason is a feeling of discouragement about losing (Gould & Eklund, 1996; Petlichkoff, 1996; Salguero, Gonzalez-Boto, Tuero, & Marquez, 2003).

Cooperative Goals

With cooperative goals, individuals share in rewards or punishments, and a group's overall performance is the key to success. Cooperative goals are commonly used, for example, for major group projects or presentations in elementary school (e.g., a term project about "castles and dragons"). They focus attention on helping other group members and on attending to and being accepting of diversity among fellow students, and away from judging differences along some single scale of performance. They also promote a belief that learning or knowledge is intrinsically a shared or group phenomenon rather than something that exists only inside the heads of individuals (Salomon & Perkins, 1998).

Cooperative goals have become increasingly common in elementary schools partly because research strongly suggests that they benefit students' learning, motivation, and social relationships more than either individualistic or competitive goals, particularly in

Educational research has found important benefits when students have cooperative, rather than competitive goals. Individuals learn from each other, both slower and faster students feel more motivated, and students become more tolerant of the differences among them.
Source: Monkey Business Images/Shutterstock.

Chapter 8 Physical and Cognitive Development in Middle Childhood

> **What Do You Think?**
>
> What participation structures worked best for you in elementary school? Is there a single answer to this question either for you or for others? If you were a teacher, which structure would you try to emphasize, and why?

classrooms that are multicultural or otherwise diverse (Slavin, 1996). But cooperative learning does have problems. If cooperative groups of students are not supervised enough, they can reproduce the gender and racial biases of the larger society, as described earlier in this section. This problem can be alleviated if the teacher chooses tasks that truly need diverse talents for completion (e.g., a project that needs an artist, a good writer, and a good oral presenter) and highlights this fact to students. Another problem is that some individuals in a cooperative work group may "overspecialize," that is, focus only on their own tasks and ignore helping and learning from others. Other individuals can "free load," meaning they can take advantage of others' hard work without contributing their own fair share of effort. Teachers report that students get off-topic and socialize during work time and that preparation for these types of activities can be cumbersome (Gillies & Boyle, 2010). Some of these problems can be alleviated by combining individualized and cooperative assessments; some part of students' final grade depends on their own efforts, and another part on the group's combined performance as well as monitoring students' time management.

The Changing Child: Physical, Cognitive, and Social

Among the examples of development discussed in this chapter, one quality surfaces repeatedly: neither physical nor cognitive development occurs in isolation from a child's social experiences. Even a child's height and weight influence acceptance by peers and personal self-esteem. Thinking skills such as conservation or long-term memory are influenced not only by a child's own efforts to make sense of her world but also by learning experiences often provided by others. And language turns out to be more than an automatic acquisition of grammatical rules; it also involves learning how a child's community prefers to communicate. Evidently a child's social surroundings—the people around him, both young and old—make quite a difference in development during these years. In the next chapter, we look at these surroundings in more detail.

Chapter Summary

- **What trends in height and weight occur among school-age children?** Although growth slows during middle childhood, children still develop significant differences in height and weight by the end of this period. Toward the end of the elementary school years, girls tend to grow taller than boys, and the difference can create embarrassment for some children. Weight can become a significant issue for some children in the school years because of both fears of social rejection and (in extreme cases) risks of medical problems.
- **What improvements in motor skills do children usually experience during the school years, and how do they affect children's involvement in athletic activity?** Motor skill development during middle childhood emphasizes coordination and timing rather than strength and fundamental skill. Athletics during middle childhood involve physical risks, as well as experience in achievement motivation, teamwork, and competition—with both good and bad effects.
- **What kinds of illnesses occur among schoolchildren? How does children's socioeconomic status affect their health?** Overall, schoolchildren are among the healthiest people in society, as shown by their low mortality. Compared to preschoolers, school-age children catch fewer minor acute illnesses, but a small percentage do suffer from significant chronic medical problems. Family SES and parents' beliefs about illness affect how much children actually stay at home as a result of getting sick. Attention deficit hyperactivity disorder (ADHD) affects a small percentage of school-age children and may result from a combination of genetic, physical, and social causes. Treatment of ADHD sometimes includes medications and behavior modification techniques.

- **What new cognitive skills do children acquire during the middle childhood? What are the psychological and practical effects of these new skills?** School-age children develop concrete operational thinking, that is, reasoning focused on real, tangible objects. A very important new skill is conservation, the belief that certain properties, such as size or length, remain constant in spite of perceptual changes. Efforts to train children in conservation have had moderate success, although when applied in a variety of circumstances, training does not persist as strongly as naturally developed conservation. Concrete operational children also acquire new skills in seriation, temporal relations, and spatial relations. Piaget's ideas about cognitive development have influenced educators' styles of teaching and the content of early childhood curricula.
- **How does memory change during middle childhood? How do these changes affect thinking and learning?** Both short-term and long-term memory improve with age, partly as a result of other cognitive developments such as growing skills in using learning strategies. Improvements in logical reasoning sometimes assist the development of long-term memory, as does increasing richness or familiarity of knowledge as schoolchildren grow older. Learning disabilities can be understood in part as the result of problems in information processing. Providing learning assistance that focuses on specific aspects of information processing can sometimes benefit students.
- **What new changes in language emerge during middle childhood?** Although school-age children already are quite skillful with language, they continue to have difficulties with certain subtle features of syntax. Bilingual children develop certain cognitive advantages over monolingual children, at least if their bilingualism is relatively balanced; the advantages include cognitive flexibility and metalinguistic awareness. Often, however, bilingual individuals must cope with prejudices against their native language and the culture of that language.
- **What is general intelligence, and how can it be measured?** Intelligence is a general ability to learn from or adapt to experience. Traditionally, intelligence has been studied from the perspective of psychometric testing, but newer perspectives based on information-processing theory and on sociocultural principles have challenged this perspective. A view of intelligence based on information-processing theory is the triarchic theory of Robert Sternberg, which divides intelligence into components, experiences, and the context of thinking. Howard Gardner's theory of multiple intelligences identifies six distinct cognitive capacities: language skill, musical skill, logical skill, spatial skill, kinesthetic skill, and interpersonal/ intrapersonal skills. The sociocultural view of intelligence regards thinking as being distributed among individuals who interact and communicate, and it locates cognitive development in the zone of proximal development.
- **How does school affect children's cognitive development?** School provides experience in particular patterns of language interaction called participation structures. The teacher's language is marked by large amounts of control talk, comments or other linguistic markers that remind students of the power difference between students and teachers. Classroom interaction is also marked by a gender bias in which teachers and students both favor boys' comments over girls'. School is also a primary arena of assessment for children, as well as a setting that provides experience with individual, competitive, and cooperative goals.

Key Terms

achievement test (p. 280)
aptitude test (p. 280)
assessment (p. 288)
attention deficit/hyperactivity disorder (ADHD) (p. 265)
balanced bilingual (p. 278)
behavior modification (p. 266)
concrete operations (p. 268)
conservation (p. 268)

control talk (p. 287)
discourse (p. 286)
hyperactivity (p. 265)
intelligence (p. 279)
learning disability (p. 273)
metalinguistic awareness (p. 278)
mortality (p. 264)
multiple intelligences (p. 284)
obesity (p. 259)

participation structures (p. 286)
psychometric approach to intelligence (p. 280)
recall memory (p. 272)
recognition memory (p. 272)
selective attention (p. 272)
sociocultural perspective on intelligence (p. 285)
triarchic theory of intelligence (p. 281)

Psychosocial Development in Middle Childhood

CHAPTER 9

Source: bikeriderlondon/Shutterstock.

Chapter Outline

Psychosocial Challenges of Middle Childhood
The Sense of Self
The Age of Industry and Achievement
Family Relationships
Peer Relationships
Death, Loss, and Grieving During the School Years
Looking Back/Looking Forward

Focusing Questions

- What major psychosocial challenges do children face during middle childhood?
- What important changes occur in a child's sense of self during middle childhood?
- What is *achievement motivation,* and what forms does it take?
- How have changes in the nature of the family, such as increases in the proportion of single parent and dual-wage-earner families, affected children's psychosocial development?
- How do peers contribute to development during middle childhood?
- How do children deal with death, loss, and grieving during the school years?

Nickie is nine years old and in second grade. Between practicing soccer, baseball, and basketball and playing with his friends, playing video games, or watching TV with his older brother Alex, doing his homework, walking the dog, and carving a model race car for his Cub Scout den with his father, he is always on the go. Until recently, if asked about his popularity or how he was doing at school or sports, Nickie would answer with a noncommittal "OK" or "I don't know." Lately, however, he has begun to talk more about himself: who he is and how well he is (or is not) doing as a ballplayer, a friend, a student, a brother, and a son.

Middle childhood, approximately ages six through twelve, is a time when the developmental changes of early childhood are rapidly consolidated and children ready themselves for adolescence and the movement to full adulthood. By the time they start school, most children have learned something about human nature and are beginning to learn the psychological and social skills needed to successfully deal with an increasingly complex world. Children's increasing involvements outside the family and their growing capacity for independence and self-direction contribute to changes in their relationships with parents and other family members.

Middle childhood also brings about an increased focus on peer relationships, and school offers the primary arena for contacts with **peers**, children of about the same age and development level who share common attitudes and interests. Peers offer certain benefits, such as freedom from the watchful eyes of parents and teachers. But they also demand loyalty and conformity. "Be nice to everyone except Rachel" may be a rule in one circle of friends; "Homework is for geeks" may be a rule in another. School-age children must learn to coordinate these expectations with those of parents, who sometimes disagree with peers.

To meet all of these demands simultaneously, children must learn to regulate their behavior from within. Somehow they must find ways to control their expressions of aggression, impatience, grief, and other strong impulses and emotions. Doing so becomes easier as they develop concepts of themselves as individuals, knowledge of their own needs and values, and a sense of how these needs and values compare with those of other people. In this chapter, we will explore how the changes that occur during middle childhood build on the achievements of early childhood and provide the groundwork for the major changes that accompany adolescence, which will soon follow.

peers Individuals who are of approximately the same age and developmental level and share common attitudes and interests.

Psychosocial Challenges of Middle Childhood

During the school years, children's psychosocial development includes five major challenges: the challenge of knowing who you are, the challenge to achieve, the challenge of family relationships, the challenge of peers, and the challenge of school. We summarize the nature of those challenges and then discuss the first four in greater detail in the sections that follow (see Chapter 8 for school influences).

The Challenge of Knowing Who You Are

Throughout middle childhood, children develop a deeper understanding of the kinds of people they are and what makes them unique. They also acquire a more fully developed sense of self as a framework for organizing and understanding their experiences. These notions do not yet constitute a final, stable identity, such as that develops during adolescence and adulthood and continues to form throughout life, but they do lay the groundwork for later development. During middle childhood, a child at least can ask, "Am I a popular sort of person?" or "Am I a good athlete?" The answers may still be rather simplistic, but they are beginning to take on meaning nonetheless.

The Challenge to Achieve

Some psychologists consider the major crisis of this age period to be the development of competence, self-confidence, and willingness to achieve to the best of one's ability. Of course, children care about their competence even in infancy. But during middle childhood, this motive is complicated by children's growing awareness of others opinions about their efforts.

The Challenge of Family Relationships

We discuss several important aspects of family life in this chapter, including recent changes in family roles and family membership due to changing employment patterns and divorce rates. These changes in the traditional family structure have raised the questions of who is responsible for doing what within a family and what constitutes a family in the first place. Furthermore, all too often school-age children must share the challenge of holding the family together. While family relationships remain an important part of schoolchildren's lives, peers become increasingly important.

The Challenge of Peers

The fourth major challenge of middle childhood is relationships with other children, or peers. As we point out later in this chapter, peers serve even more important purposes for schoolchildren than they do for preschoolers, and most school-age children choose to spend a great deal of their time in peer-related activities.

The Challenge of School

During middle childhood, school is second only to the family in influence on children's social and emotional development. Observing and interacting with a large number of diverse children and adults other than their parents give children an opportunity to learn new social skills, values, and beliefs and to develop a fuller sense of identity. As we saw in Chapter 8, participation structures, gender and racial bias, and assessment goals can all influence cognitive development, as well as the child's sense of self.

The Sense of Self

Throughout infancy, childhood, and adolescence, children actively construct a **sense of self**, a structured way of thinking about themselves that helps them to organize and understand who they are based on the views of others, on their own experiences, and on cultural categories such as gender and race. This structure rapidly evolves during middle childhood and becomes increasingly organized and complex. In fact, although a sense of self often is called a *self-concept,* it functions more as a theory that organizes a pattern of related ideas than as a single concept. A child actively constructs and continually revises his or her sense of self based on increasing age and experience (Damon & Hart, 1992), and throughout life we form and shift our identity as a means to maintain self-esteem, find meaning in our lives, and obtain feelings of belongingness (Vignoles, Regalia, Manzi, Golledge, & Scabini, 2006).

sense of self A structured way in which individuals think about themselves that helps them to organize and understand who they are based on the views of others, their own experiences, and cultural categories such as gender and race.

For example, at age six, Mina loved playing with dolls and also loved holding and caring for babies. She noticed that her parents and others commented on this preference, so nurturance became part of Mina's idea of herself: "I'm someone who likes babies," she sometimes thought. But later experiences modified this idea. Toward the end of elementary school, Mina discovered that she often preferred playing softball to playing house. Somehow, at age ten or eleven, she had to incorporate this reality into her sense of self: "I'm a good ballplayer," she realized. By the start of adolescence, she still was not sure how to reconcile these two concepts of herself: her interest in child care and her interest in sports. Someday she may succeed in doing so, but not at age twelve.

To a large extent, a child's notion of self grows out of social experiences with other selves or, put more plainly, out of contacts with other children and adults. Learning what it means to be female in their cultural context, for example, occurs as girls meet other individuals who also are female. Learning what it means to be happy occurs as children see other people express happiness. As personal and individual as a sense of self is, then, it reflects generalizations about others, and it cannot develop without considerable social contact (Lewis & Brooks-Gunn, 1979b).

The Development of Self in Childhood

How do children acquire a sense of self? Once children recognize themselves in a mirror, at about eighteen months of age, the next step involves basic social labels or categories. By the end of the second year of life, most children can correctly label their gender ("I'm a boy" or "I'm a girl"), their age ("I'm two"), and their species ("I'm a person"). Labels such as these pave the way for later, more complete knowledge of self.

During middle childhood, children develop preliminary notions of their personal qualities and psychological identity. What do you suppose this girl's sense of herself might be?
Source: Zurijeta/Shutterstock.

self-constancy The belief that one's identity remains permanently fixed; established sometime after age six.

At first, however, most such labels lack permanence. At age two or three, a boy may claim he can become a girl under certain circumstances—"when I grow up" or "if I grow my hair long" (Marcus & Overton, 1978). Or a very young child may say she can become a different individual "if I change my name" (Guardo & Bohan, 1971). **Self-constancy**, a belief that identity remains permanently fixed, does not become firm until the early school years, sometime after age six. At this time, a child becomes convinced he will stay the same person indefinitely into the future, will remain human in all circumstances, and will keep his gender forever. Beliefs such as these are what a sense of self means.

Younger children, up to age five or six, tend to define themselves in terms of observable features and behaviors such as hairstyles or how fast they can run (Rosenberg, 1979). Around age eight, some children form a more stable sense of self by including psychological traits in their self-descriptions. At first, the traits are feelings and qualities that have no apparent reference to other human beings: "I am brave," says the child, or "I am cheerful." By implication these traits describe her as an entire personality and in all possible situations, with little recognition of people's usual variations in moods. At first, too, the child describes the traits in bold, global terms that ignore the possibility that opposing feelings or qualities sometimes exist within the same person. The child may vacillate in describing her own qualities without realizing it. Sometimes she will say, "I am dumb," meaning *completely* dumb, and other times she will say, "I am smart," meaning *completely* smart (Harter, 1977). Neither statement suggests the child recognizes that both descriptions contain an element of truth.

By the end of middle childhood, fuller integration of contradictory traits occurs. Around age ten or twelve, children begin to recognize that they can feel more than one way about any particular situation or person; they can both like and hate their teachers or enjoy and dislike school more or less at the same time (Selman, 1980). With this recognition comes the ability to use trait labels in less global ways and to express qualities in particular situations. When an older child says, "I am smart," he no longer means "I am always smart in every possible way and in every activity." Now he more likely means "I am smart in a number of significant situations, but not in all." During middle childhood, children become increasingly able to interrelate the different categories of traits and develop more patterned and integrated self-descriptions (Damon & Hart, 1988; Fischer et al., 1990). They develop a more coherent sense of self, as demonstrated in their ability to write long, interlinked stories of their lives, a skill with which younger children struggle (Bohn & Bernsten, 2008).

These changes contribute to the development of a more flexible sense of self, in which the same individual can be characterized in a variety of ways depending on the circumstances.

> **What Do You Think?**
>
> What do you remember about changes in your sense of self during your school years? What conflicting traits do you recall, and how did you integrate them?

The situation-bound qualities school-age children express usually describe them more accurately than the global traits and observable features on which younger children rely. But a school-age child's consciousness of inner traits still lacks the subtlety and flexibility found in adolescents and adults, who recognize that the stability of self involves multiple dimensions and ongoing change.

However, significant cultural differences exist in how the concept of self is constructed, and the idea of self probably is not a discrete psychological entity in all cultures (Hoare, 1994). In Asian countries such as India, Japan, and Nepal, for example, three distinct senses of self appear to exist simultaneously even in adulthood: a family self, in which one's sense of self is defined almost exclusively in relationship to one's family; a spiritual self, which is defined and organized in terms of religious beliefs; and an individualized self, which is closer to the European-American sense of self just described (Roland, 1988).

Processes in Constructing a Self

To a large degree, the process of developing an identity and a sense of self during middle childhood reflects a growing awareness of relationships with other people (Damon & Hart, 1988). Children construct their identities by distinguishing their thoughts and feelings from those expressed by others. When children of various ages are asked how they would feel if their parents expressed certain emotions, such as sadness, anger, or happiness, preschoolers are likely to say they would feel the same emotions: they would be angry if their parents were angry, sad if they were sad, and so on. Older children, however, are more likely to name complementary rather than identical emotions; if their parents felt angry, for example, they would feel fearful (Harter & Barnes, 1983).

Additional evidence comes from studies of how children gradually acquire a fuller understanding of shame and pride. By the early school years (age six or seven), children begin to explicitly mention an external audience in defining these two terms (Seidner et al., 1988). For example, one seven-year-olds definition was "My teacher was proud

School-age children often devote themselves to the long, slow mastery of complicated skills, such as learning to play the violin.
Source: wavebreakmedia/Shutterstock.

when I earned 100 percent on the test"; another's was "My mother was ashamed when I lost my temper at the neighbor." Such attention to others implies awareness that others sometimes observe the child's self and suggests that school-age children distinguish between their own emotions and those of others—something they must do to develop a mature sense of self. Additionally, the shame and guilt children perceive from the adults around them impact their own experience of shame and guilt throughout childhood and adolescence (Rosemary, Arbeau, Lall, & De Jaeger, 2010; Walter & Burnaford, 2006).

A child's emerging sense of self during middle childhood is part of a broader process of personality development. In the following section, we briefly discuss how two major developmental theorists, Sigmund Freud and Erik Erikson, view this process.

The Age of Industry and Achievement

When viewed as part of the overall lifespan, the years from six to twelve seem especially important to the achievement of competence. Children spend countless hours in school acquiring skills in reading, writing, and mathematics. Many of these hours also contribute to learning the unofficial curriculum of school: how to get along with teachers and with other children. Outside of school, children often devote themselves to the long, slow mastery of particular skills. One child may spend years learning to play baseball; another may devote the same amount of time to learning how to care for a zoo of pet hamsters, dogs, and birds.

Latency and the Crisis of Industry

Psychodynamic theories such as those proposed by Freud and Erikson explain such behavior in terms of the emotional relationships that precede it in early childhood. Preschool children feel envy, awe, and competitiveness with respect to their parents. At first, these feelings have a magical quality: children simply want to be like their parents. Inevitably they are disappointed to learn that merely wanting such things does not make them come true.

In this regard, Freud emphasized the emotional hardship of preschoolers' disappointment and their consequent repression of their magical wishes regarding their parents (Freud, 1983). A five-year-old, he argued, cannot continue indefinitely to wish for intimacy with his opposite-sex parent and for success in competition with his same-sex parent. These feelings (which Freud termed the *Oedipus* and *Electra conflicts*) disrupt life if they persist too long. The child eventually represses the feelings, meaning he pushes them completely out of awareness. As it happens, this repression occurs at about the time most children begin school—around age six or seven—and continues until adolescence. Freud called this the **latency** period, meaning a child's earlier unresolved feelings have gone underground and are waiting to resurface in the future (at the beginning of adolescence). During this period, the schoolchild focuses on building competencies and skills as a defense—an unconscious, self-protective behavior—against his earlier romantic feelings toward his parent. Developing talents, whether in sports, art, academics, or whatever, also helps to keep the child's mind off his earlier disappointment, which lingers on unconsciously.

Erikson went beyond Freud's ideas to stress not only the defensive, negative functions of skill building but its positive functions as well (Erikson, 1963, 1968). According to Erikson, children try consciously to become more like their parents and more like adults in general. Becoming competent helps children reach this goal in two ways. First, it helps them through *identification,* a process by which they experience themselves as being like their parents and thus capable of becoming genuine adults; second, it helps them to gain similar recognition from others.

Erikson called this process the crisis of **industry versus inferiority**, meaning children of this age concern themselves with their capacity for *industry,* or the ability to do good, productive work. Children who convince themselves and others of this capacity develop relatively confident, positive concepts of themselves. Those who do not tend to suffer from feelings of poor self-esteem and *inferiority,* a sense of inadequacy or general lack of competence. According to Erikson, most children end up with a mixture of self-confidence and fear of inferiority, but self-confidence predominates in most cases (we hope). (See Chapter 2.)

---

latency According to Freud, the stage of development between the phallic and genital stages. Sexual feelings and activities are on hold as the child struggles to resolve the oedipal conflict.

industry versus inferiority Erikson's fourth crisis, during which children concern themselves with their capacity to do good work and thereby develop confident, positive self-concepts or else face feelings of inferiority.

In addition, the crisis of industry versus inferiority gives healthy school-age children a more or less permanent motivation to achieve particular, definable standards of excellence. Children's continuing sense that they can achieve and that their industry will pay off is shaped by their earlier successes and failures in school. No longer are children happy just to draw pictures, for example; now they want to draw *well*. With persistence and support, children often do reach higher standards of excellence in many activities than they did as preschoolers, and most of the time they are happy about doing so.

Partly because of the connection between industry and increasing competence, psychologists have devoted a lot of attention to the development of achievement motivation among school-age children. In the next section, we look at some of this work.

Achievement Motivation

Achievement motivation is the tendency to show initiative and persistence in attaining certain goals and increasing competence by successfully meeting standards of excellence. What matters most is the approach to a task rather than the importance of the task itself. An individual can reveal achievement motivation as either a student or a college professor, for example, and as either an amateur chess player or a world-class chess grand master. As long as the individual strives toward a standard of excellence that is reasonable, he or she possesses achievement motivation. Usually, too, this motivation leads to increased competence compared to one's previous level.

achievement motivation Behavior that enhances competence or enhances judgments of competence.

Differences in Achievement Motivation

There appear to be two distinct kinds of achievement motivation. The first, **learning orientation**, relies on *intrinsic motivation*, that is, motivation that comes from within the learner and relates directly to the task and its accomplishment. A learning orientation leads children to concentrate on learning as an end in itself; they will practice jumping rope just to see whether they can do it. The second type of motivation, **performance orientation**, involves *extrinsic motivation*, meaning motivation comes not from the learner but from other individuals who see and evaluate her. In this instance, the person the child is trying to please or satisfy is not herself but others (Dweck & Leggett, 1988; Elliot & Dweck, 2013; Erdley et al., 1997; Ginsburg & Bronstein, 1993; Hayenga & Corpus, 2010).

learning orientation Achievement motivation that comes from the learner and the task.

performance orientation Achievement motivation stimulated by other individuals who may see and evaluate the learner rather than by the intrinsic nature of the task itself.

Motivational orientations play an important role in children's development. For example, higher levels of intrinsic motivation have been associated with an internal sense of control, feelings of enjoyment, and various mastery-related characteristics such as curiosity, creativity, exploration, persistence in completing tasks, and a preference for taking on challenges. They are also linked to higher academic performance and learning, feelings of academic competence, and perceptions of what contributes to academic success or failure (Cain & Dweck, 1995; Ginsburg & Bronstein, 1993; Hayenga & Corpus, 2010; Masten & Coatsworth, 1998; Vansteenkiste, Lens, & Deci, 2006).

Achievement Motivation in Middle Childhood

During middle childhood, children become more performance oriented than they were at earlier ages. At the beginning of this period, children express considerable optimism about their abilities. Kindergartners tend to rank themselves at the top of their class in scholastic ability, even though they rank other children relatively accurately (Stipek & Hoffman, 1980). This implies a learning orientation; for young children, achievement is something they do without either the involvement or the evaluations of others (Frieze et al., 1981).

During the next several years, however, children begin to believe that having an ability depends partly on whether other people give them credit for having it. This belief lies at the core of the performance orientation. It does not replace a learning orientation; rather, it takes a place alongside it. Now being "smart" means partly that a child's teachers, parents, and friends *say* she is smart and partly that she possesses certain skills in reading, mathematics, and the like regardless of what others say (Feld et al., 1979).

Chapter 9 Psychosocial Development in Middle Childhood

Successful achievement becomes more complicated in middle childhood. Consider swimming. Late in infancy and during the preschool years, a child may be motivated to learn to swim simply by being given chances to experiment in the water. During the school years, however, that child may ask herself or himself what other people, especially parents and friends, will think about learning to swim. Most people will value swimming to some extent, of course. But even very respectable progress in swimming may not look like much of an achievement if the child's family and friends hold very high athletic standards or place little value on athletics in the first place.

As we saw in Chapter 8, academic achievement is one of the principal types of achievement children focus on during middle childhood. Also, because schools tend to group children homogeneously by age and ability, children of similar age and ability form the principal peer group for many developing children. The main exception to this pattern is siblings, who often are an important peer system influence as well. We will take a closer look at sibling influences later in this chapter.

Environmental factors also can influence motivational orientation. Environments that provide optimal challenge, offer feedback that promotes competence, and support children's autonomous and independent behaviors are likely to facilitate the development of intrinsic motivation, whereas environments that strongly emphasize extrinsic rewards, deadlines, and adult control tend to undermine intrinsic motivation and foster an extrinsic motivational orientation (Deci & Ryan, 1987; Masten & Coatsworth, 1998; Reynolds & Temple, 1998; Vansteenkiste et al., 2006).

Cultural background also can influence children's achievement orientations. For example, Chinese and Japanese mothers believe more strongly than American mothers do that academic success depends on one's own efforts rather than on factors beyond one's control, such as inborn ability or external conditions. This intrinsically motivated, achievement-oriented view is likely shared by their children and may help account for the higher academic achievement of Asian students over American students (Jose & Bellamy, 2011; Stevenson & Lee, 1990). The Multicultural View feature discusses ethnic differences in parental expectations for academic achievement.

As children grow older, they shift toward a performance orientation and become more similar to adults in their achievement motivation. This in part reflects the increasing importance of peers and children's changing perceptions of social comparisons (Pomerantz et al., 1995). At this stage, children take others' opinions more and more seriously and often seek out those opinions on a variety of matters.

Family factors are also important. Several studies have examined how parental monitoring of homework, parental reactions to grades, and general family style influenced achievement motivation orientation among children. When parents heavily supervised homework (by helping, checking, reminding, or insisting), reacted to grades with punishment, criticism, uninvolvement, or extrinsic rewards, and displayed overcontrolling (authoritarian) or undercontrolling (permissive) styles of parenting, children were more likely to have extrinsic (performance) motivational orientations and lower academic performance. On the other hand, children whose parents responded to grades with encouragement and were supportive of their children's autonomy (authoritative parenting style) were more likely to have intrinsic motivational orientation and higher academic performance (Ginsburg & Brostein, 1995; Gonzalez & Wolters, 2006). This academic benefit of authoritarian parenting persists throughout a child's education, including college (Turner, Chandler, & Heffer, 2009). Paradoxically, Asian parents are more likely to utilize authoritarian parenting with their children without the negative impact noted previously (Kordi & Baharudin, 2010). As we will see in the section that follows, the opinions of family members are quite important in this regard.

Family Relationships

Families continue to influence children's development strongly during middle childhood, although, as we will soon see, the influence of peers grows dramatically in this period as well. However, parental influence differs from that of peers due both to parents' greater

> **What Do You Think?**
>
> Survey several classmates about their current learning orientations and the extent to which those orientations grew out of middle childhood experiences. What advantages and disadvantages do you see in each of these orientations?

experience and psychological maturity and to the greater material resources and power they possess. In this section, we discuss how the particular circumstances and characteristics of families affect family relationships and psychosocial development during middle childhood.

The Quality of Parenting and Family Life During Middle Childhood

During middle childhood, as children gradually learn more about their parents' attitudes and motivations and the reasons for family rules, they become better able to control their own behavior. This change has a major impact on the quality of relations between school-age children and their parents. Parents find themselves monitoring the moment-to-moment behavior of their children less closely than in earlier years. They need not always watch carefully as their child pours a glass of milk, and they do not always have to remind him to use the toilet before getting in the car. Parenting style affects the ways in which such monitoring is expressed, and as discussed in the Focusing On feature, also affects the quality of parent-child interactions.

Nevertheless, parents do continue to monitor children's efforts to take care of themselves, but in more indirect ways. Instead of simply arranging for a child's friend to visit, parents increasingly use comments such as "If you want to have Lin sleep over next week, you'd better call by tomorrow." Instead of helping their child put on each item of clothing in the morning, they will more likely confine themselves to some simple reminder ("It's time to get dressed") on the assumption that the child can take care of the details of dressing.

The Changing Nature of Modern Families

The stereotypical family—a father who works, a mother who cares for the family full time—shows little similarity to families of today. In 1955, 60 percent of families in North America fit this popular stereotype. By 2012, only 20 percent of North American families conformed to this model, and unlike the stereotype of a well-educated, affluent woman staying at home to care for her child or children, nearly half of stay-at-home mothers have a high school diploma or less, with 34 percent living in poverty (Cohn, Livingston, & Wang, 2014). Additionally, fathers make up 16 percent of all stay-at-home parents, a number that has been steadily increasing over the last three decades (Livingston, 2014).

Today an increasing number of mothers work outside the home. Eighty percent of married women and 91 percent of single women with children under eighteen are employed (see Figure 9.1). This is more than double the rates in 1960 and a trend that is expected to remain relatively stable, with most fluctuations being due to economic changes over time (Cohn, Livingston, & Wang, 2014).

Divorce also has become much more common, as Figure 9.2 shows. Between 1950 and 2015, the U.S. divorce rate quadrupled, with about 10 percent of those age fifteen and up reporting that they are currently divorced (U.S. Bureau of the Census, 2015b). Approximately 70 percent of first marriages will last at least ten years, with that number dropping to about 55 percent after twenty years (Copen, Daniels, Vespa, & Mosher, 2012). Approximately 27 percent of children younger than eighteen live in single-parent households, 86 percent with their mothers and 14 percent with their fathers (U.S. Bureau of the Census, 2015c). Because approximately two-thirds of divorced parents remarry, most children of divorce will live in a *reconstituted family* consisting of parent, stepparent, siblings, and stepsiblings.

A Multicultural View

Parental Expectations and Academic Achievement

Differences in academic achievement among African American, Latino, and Caucasian children appear early during the elementary school years and continue throughout elementary, junior, and senior high school. One study found that at second grade, about 5 percent of white children and more than 15 percent of African American and Latino children were performing below grade level in mathematics, and by sixth grade 20 percent of white children, more than 40 percent of Latino children, and 50 percent of African American children were performing below grade level (Norman, 1988).

One popular explanation is that lower achievement of minority children is due to low levels of achievement motivation resulting from poverty, family disruption, inadequate academic support, low parental education, and low parental expectations for children's academic success (De Civita, Pagani, Vitaro, & Tremblay, 2004; Häkkinen, Kirjavainen & Uusitalo, 2003; Lee & Bowen, 2006). This view has been challenged by a large-scale study of African American, Latino, and white urban elementary school children and their mothers (Stevenson et al., 1990). In one study, Harold Stevenson and his colleagues examined the role parents played in their children's education and parents' and children's beliefs about children's current school performance and their educational future. Mothers and teachers were also asked how the children's performances might be improved.

What did the researchers find? First, when only families from similar economic and educational backgrounds were compared, the achievement levels of the African American and Latino children were *not* substantially lower than those of the white children. Second, beliefs about the children's educational achievement held by both the Latino and African American children and their mothers were very similar to those typically associated with higher rather than lower levels of achievement.

When the entire sample was examined, the following findings emerged. All mothers agreed that parents should work closely with their children on schoolwork. African American mothers expressed the

Active encouragement and support from parents plays an important role in fostering academic achievement during middle childhood.
Source: zulufoto/Shutterstock.

FIGURE 9.1
Percentage of Working Mothers, 1967–2012

The long-term trends for working mothers with children age 18 and under.
Source: Cohn, Livingston, & Wang (2014).

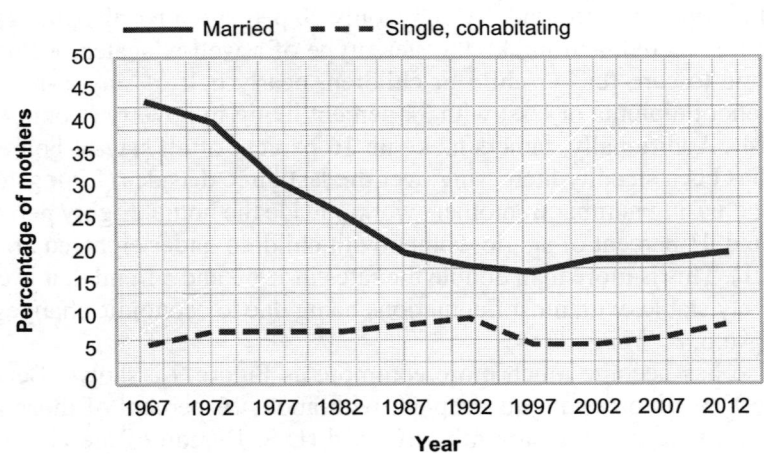

Divorce and Its Effects on Children

Most parents who divorce must make major adjustments in their lives, and these adjustments often affect their children deeply. First, many divorcing parents face sudden economic pressures. Some find themselves financially responsible for two households, that of

A Multicultural View

Parental Expectations and Academic Achievement *continued*

greatest interest in helping their children, followed by Latino and then white mothers. Latino mothers were less confident about their knowledge of English and of the American school system, but were still eager to help their children with schoolwork, stressed the importance of school, and had high regard for their children's intellectual abilities and academic achievement. They also shared with the African American mothers (and their children's teachers) a strong belief in the importance of homework and competency examinations, and the potential value of a longer school day. They held high expectations for their children's futures, though not as high as those of the African American and white mothers.

Most of the African American mothers were familiar with what teachers expected of their children. They reported spending more time teaching their children academic skills than the other parents and evaluated their children's skills, abilities, and academic achievement in reading and math very highly. Their children rated their own performances very highly as well and believed they were working hard. Surprisingly, though, African American students' evaluations of their school performances were unrelated to their actual levels of achievement in reading and math, which suggests they had not received or internalized realistic feedback about their academic performances from either their parents, their teachers, or both (Alexander & Entwisle, 1988; Bock & Moore, 1986).

These findings challenge the view that the below expected performances of African American and Latino elementary school children are due to low levels of achievement motivation, parental expectations, or parental support, though there is evidence that particularly among poorer children lower academic achievement may be due to lower maternal educational expectations for their children (De Civita et al., 2004; Häkkinen et al., 2003). What else, then, accounts for the decreasing academic achievement of minority elementary school children and increasing rates of academic failure and dropping out in junior and senior high school? One possibility is that teachers and staff may have lower academic expectations for minorities, who are overrepresented in the low academic tracks compared with other student groups, leaving these students with both inadequate preparation and unrealistic expectations about the academic demands of junior and senior high school (Reed, 1988). Additionally, less parental involvement among African American and Latino parents, perhaps due to schedule constraints, lower educational attainment, or subtle racism has been linked to lower achievement (Lee & Bowen, 2006). As these children approach adolescence, the schools they attend and the families in which they live fail to adequately meet their emerging needs for intellectual challenge and academic support, for adult supervision and independence, and for relationships with teachers and parents that enable them to believe a relationship exists between their academic efforts and the rewards available to them in American society (De Civita et al., 2004; Eccles, 1993; Lee & Bowen, 2006; Stevenson et al., 1990).

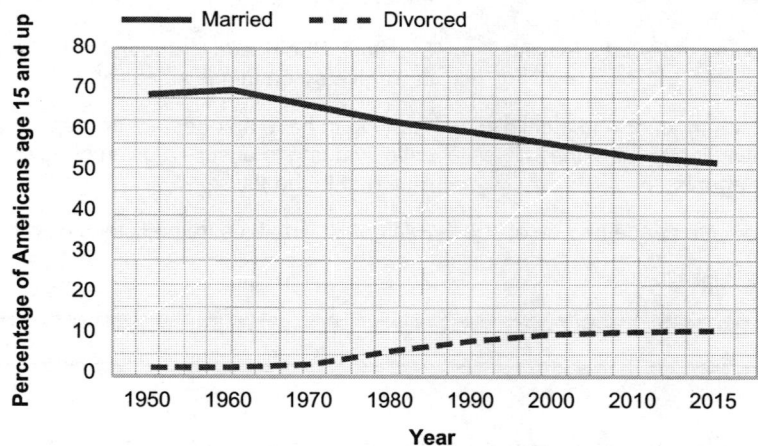

FIGURE 9.2
Percentage of U.S. Citizens Reporting That They Are Currently Married or Divorced Each Year

This chart outlines the percentage of people in the United States age fifteen and up reporting each year that they are either married or divorced. Though approximately 45 percent of all first marriages end in divorce within twenty years, only about 10 percent of the population reports that they are currently divorced.
Source: U.S. Bureau of the Census (2015b).

their former spouse and children and that of the new spouse and children. Many divorced mothers must take on new or additional employment to meet their household responsibilities, and even so their standard of living frequently declines (Dewilde & Uunk, 2008; Hetherington et al., 1989). For many of these women, a reduction of economic resources often is accompanied by dependence on welfare; poorer-quality housing, neighborhoods,

Focusing On...

The Quality of Parenting and Family Life During Middle Childhood

As in the early childhood years that precede and the adolescent years that follow, the quality of the parent-child relationship and overall family life play an important developmental role in middle childhood. A seven-year longitudinal study conducted by Gregory Pettit, John Bates, and Kenneth Dodge (1997) found that supportive, authoritative-style parenting involving high levels of mother-to-child warmth, active teaching of social skills, positive interest and involvement in their children's peer relationships, and use of discipline based on reasoning rather than power assertion observed when children were five years old predicted higher levels of adjustment at age 12.

High levels of supportive parenting also helped reduce the negative developmental effects of low SES, family stress, and single parenthood. Studies of school-age African American children living in both two-parent and single-parent families have demonstrated that children's academic and psychosocial competence was positively related to harmonious family interactions, emotional caregiving and support, low levels of overt conflict between parents (in two-parent households), family involvement with children's school activities, parental optimism and religious involvement, and adequacy of family financial resources (Bean, Barber, & Crane, 2006; Brody & Flor, 1997, 1998; Brody et al., 1994). For single-parent, mother-headed households, *no-nonsense* parenting, which included high levels of physical and emotional control and displays of warmth and affection, helped to protect children from dangerous neighborhood surroundings and involvement in antisocial activity and promoted the development of self-regulation. This type of parenting falls between the

TABLE 9.1 Immediacy and Focus of Parental Concerns and Parenting Goals

Focus of Parental Concern	Immediacy of Parental Concern	
	Short Term	*Long Term*
Focus on relationship	Wanting to reach fair and equitable resolutions to an interaction; wanting to promote everyone's happiness.	Wanting to build or maintain love, trust, and close family connections.
	Example: I want us to be able to enjoy doing this together.	*Example:* I hope she realizes that I'll always be here to help her through hard times.
Focus on child	Wanting to understand the child's point of view in a given situation; wanting to promote the child's happiness.	Wanting to teach the child values, social rules or important lessons for the child's future benefit.
	Example: I want to find out what's making him so upset.	*Example:* She needs to understand that she can't give up on things so easily.
Focus on parent	Wanting to control, change, or end a child's current behavior; wanting to meet the parent's wishes or agenda.	Wanting to have an obedient or respectful child; wanting to ensure a given behavior isn't repeated in the future.
	Example: I need to have peace and quiet.	*Example:* I'll make sure he listens next time.

Source: Adapted from Hastings & Grusec (1998), p. 470.

schools, and child care; and the need to move to a neighborhood they can afford, which often leads to loss of social support for the child from familiar friends, neighbors, and teachers. In contrast, both noncustodial and custodial fathers are more likely to maintain or improve their standard of living following divorce.

Divorce involves many psychological pressures as well. The parent who takes primary custody of the children must learn to manage a household alone, which is a major physical and psychological burden. Some parents may feel deeply isolated from relatives or

Focusing On...

The Quality of Parenting and Family Life During Middle Childhood *continued*

authoritative and authoritarian parent styles, employing a higher level of control than authoritative parenting style and greater warmth and nurturance than authoritarian parenting style (Brody & Flor, 1998), and it seems that higher levels of psychological control might not carry the same risk for depression and anxiety when displayed by African American parents as compared to European American parents (Bean et al., 2006).

The goals that parents hope to achieve also play an important role in determining how they interact with their children, especially when faced with parent-child disagreements. Paul Hastings and Joan Grusec (1998) studied a sample of 78 fathers and 110 mothers to explore how their parenting goals influenced interactions during disagreements with their young children. Parenting goals reflected three main areas of parental concern: *relationship-centered* goals, focused on maintaining and improving the parent-child relationship; *child-centered* goals, focused on concern with understanding the child's viewpoint and promoting the child's happiness and well being; and *parent-centered* goals focused on controlling or changing the child to meet the parent's wishes or agenda. The interventions parents reported using also depended on whether their focus was on the short-term or long-term consequences. Table 9.1 shows descriptions and examples of these three parenting goals, both short-term and long-term.

Hastings and Grusec found that women were more likely than men to focus on relationship-centered goals. Short-term, parent-centered goals were more likely when parent-child disagreements occurred in public situations (e.g., while grocery shopping, visiting friends, playing in the park). Long-term, child- and relationship-centered goals were associated with higher levels of parental empathy. Parent-centered goals were associated with power assertion, child-centered goals with reasoning, and relationship-centered goals with warm, negotiating, and cooperative parenting behavior. Parents who focused on solving parent-child disagreements that fulfilled their own needs (parent-centered goals) were most likely to be punitive and controlling and least likely to resolve conflicts by talking with their children, working out a compromise, or being warm and accepting. When parents' concerns were centered on children's needs, however, open communication and providing explanations were the strategies most preferred, and coercion, punishment, and negative criticism were avoided. Strong power assertion was even less likely when parents were highly invested in promoting the quality of family relationship. Instead, negotiation, compromise, shared control, and affection were the strategies of choice.

Parenting goals were related not only to what the child had done but to the parents' judgments about their child's motivations and to parents' feelings about the situation. Parents who were focused on parent-centered, long-term goals were more likely to believe that their children's misbehaviors were deliberate, to experience annoyance, upset, and concern, and to have decreased sympathy for their child's wishes compared to parents who focused on child-centered, short-term goals. Although changes occur in parental goals and in the context of parent-child disagreements as children move through adolescence and adulthood, parenting goals continue to play an important role in how parents and their children interact with and experience each other.

What Do You Think?

1. What is your view of the "no-nonsense" parenting described earlier? How successfully do you think it joins the advantages of authoritative and authoritarian parenting styles? Why do you think psychological control is related to higher rates of depression and anxiety among European American children but not African American children?

2. Thinking back to conflicts with your parents in your own middle childhood, what long-term and short-term goals best describe the parenting you experienced?

Two dimensions on which parenting goals may vary are the immediacy of a parent's concern (short term versus long term) and the focus of concern (parent, child, or relationship). This table presents the six types of parenting goals that result when two dimensions are combined and examples of the goals a parent might have when dealing with a child's tantrum during the shared activity.

---

friends to whom they used to feel close. If relatives do live nearby, divorcing parents often must rely on them for the first time, simply to procure help with child care and household work. Even before actual separation and divorce, many such families go through long periods of distress, tension, and discord. For most, these pressures continue to create stress for two or three years following separation (Coley, 1998; Hetherington et al, 1998). However, when there is a great deal of strife in a marriage, many adults feel happier after a divorce, particularly if they were the one to initiate it, and children fare better when their parents do not experience psychological distress following a divorce (Amato, 2010). Divorce is especially hard for children during the school years. Having outgrown the self-centeredness of the preschool years, school-age children increasingly identify with and rely on their parents as role models to help them establish their own sense of who they are and how they should behave. At a time when children are just learning to be independent from home life, divorce threatens the safe base they have come to rely on to help make increasing independence possible. The adjustment to divorce is easier for some children than for others, and the process is more difficult for children whose parents use less effective parenting styles following divorce, whose parents argue and do not make an attempt to get along following a divorce, if a parent is suffering from mental health problems, or when children lose contact with one of their parents (Amato, 2010). Though previous research has found differential impact of divorce for boys versus girls, more recent research has not demonstrated sex differences among children whose parents divorce (Amato, 2010; Amato & Dorius, 2010). However, the loyalty conflicts frequently created by parents who are competing for their children's allegiance can make children fearful that they will lose one of their parents in the process.

Moreover, couples who divorce are more likely to demonstrate maladaptive behaviors when they argue, such as criticizing one another, displaying contempt, being defensive, and stonewalling one another (Fowler & Dillow, 2011; Gottman & Levenson, 2000). These types of behavior, which may present as hostility or becoming distant, are related to higher rates of anxiety and antisocial behaviors among children (Katz & Gottman, 1993). It may be that preexisting factors that increase risk for divorce also increase risk for problem behaviors among the children living in these homes.

Perhaps the most important factor in reducing the negative effects of divorce during the school years is parents' efforts to reduce their own conflicts and cooperate in providing the best parenting possible for their children. Also important is the appropriate use of professional help to successfully work out postdivorce arrangements, resolve emotional conflicts more effectively, and develop the skills needed to sustain strong and supportive parent-child relationships (Amato, 2010; Amato et al., 1995; Stolberg & Walsh, 1988). Close relationships with authoritative parents who are warm and supportive, but still provide firm, consistent control and supervision, particularly in the period immediately following divorce, are associated with positive adjustment in children and adolescents (Hetherington et al., 1998; Simons & Johnson, 1996). Table 9.2 presents suggestions for parenting during or following divorce.

Custody Arrangements

The parent with physical custody of the children (usually the mother) finds herself dealing not only with her children but also with major new roles and likely the financial stress of being a single parent.

Parents without physical custody of the children (usually fathers) do not face these daily hassles, but they do report feeling rootless, dissatisfied, and unjustly cut off from their children. Seeing his children every other week or on school vacations may prevent a father from knowing them intimately and being part of their everyday lives, and lead him to become increasingly reliant on special events (such as going to Disney World) when contacts do occur. Noncustodial parents may also believe their financial and emotional support for their children goes unappreciated. As a result, some fathers decrease contact with their children.

For noncustodial fathers and mothers alike, both the quantity and quality of parent-child relationships differ compared to parents who have custody. Noncustodial mothers are, on the average, less competent than custodial mothers in controlling and monitoring their children's behavior, although they are more effective at this than noncustodial fathers. Noncustodial mothers are also more interested in and better informed about their children's activities, more supportive, sensitive, and responsive to their children's needs, and better able to communicate with their children than noncustodial fathers are (Hetherington et al., 1998). Compared to noncustodial mothers, the postdivorce parenting of fathers is less predictable. Some fathers who were previously attached to and involved

TABLE 9.2 Suggestions for Divorcing Parents with School-Age Children

1. Don't pretend that the divorce is "good," and don't expect your child to appreciate your reasons for the divorce.
2. Avoid assigning blame for the divorce or criticizing the other party in your child's presence.
3. Reassure your child that she or he did not cause the divorce and will continue to be loved and cared for by both parents.
4. Don't put your child on the spot by involving him or her in divorce-related decisions.
5. Keep your child informed about divorce-related events and decisions in a timely and frank manner.
6. Avoid making changes in your child's normal routines as much as possible.
7. Allow your child full freedom to express his or her feelings both to you and to other trusted adults.

Here are some suggestions for helping children handle parental dating and remarriage:

1. Wait until you know your new romantic interest fairly well before arranging for your friend and your child to spend time together.
2. Allow your child to get used to this person gradually, at the child's own pace.
3. Keep your child informed about your relationship, but don't force your child to make decisions about it.
4. Involve your child in plans regarding living arrangements, marriage, and other important changes in an appropriate manner.
5. Seek agreement with your new partner or spouse on childrearing philosophy and practices.

Source: Adapted from Philadelphia Child Guidance Center (1994), pp. 85–90.

with their children find their new role too limited and painful and drift away from their children, whereas others become more involved with their children. The quality of the noncustodial father's relationship with his children and the circumstances in which contacts with them occur are much more important than frequency of visits. When noncustodial fathers remain actively involved in their children's activities and emotional lives, positive developmental outcomes are supported. Even limited contact with noncustodial fathers can enhance children's adjustment when it occurs under supportive, low-conflict conditions (Clarke-Stewart & Hayward, 1996; Simons & Beaman, 1996). In recent years we have seen a trend among fathers being quite involved in their children's lives, which is linked to fewer behavioral problems and better psychological and academic outcomes for their children (Amato & Dorius, 2010).

Sometimes parents are able to *establish joint custody,* a legal arrangement in which parental rights and responsibilities continue to be shared in a relatively equal manner. The mechanics of the arrangement vary with the child's age and the family's circumstances. The children may live with each parent during alternate weeks, parts of weeks, or even parts of the year. Or, when the children are older, one or more children may live with one parent and the rest with the other parent. Joint custody tends to promote greater contact with both parents after divorce, facilitate fathers' involvement, and make mothers' parenting responsibilities less burdensome. Its success, however, depends on parents' willingness and ability to rearrange their lives and maintain the levels of mutual respect and cooperation required to make this arrangement work (Arditti, 1992). The cooperation and negotiation necessary for joint custody might be easier for families who obtain divorce education and/or have someone to help mediate points of contention (Amato, 2010).

Remarriage and Blended Families

Most divorced parents remarry within a few years, creating blended families consisting of the remarried parents and their children. The most common type of **blended family** results when a mother marries a man who does not have custody of his children by a previous marriage, but families with stepmothers occur as well. In both situations, the stepparent and stepchildren must somehow acknowledge the previous attachments they bring to the new family. Children may need to recognize and accept the fact that their new stepparent has other children, about whom he or she cares a great deal, living somewhere else. Also, the new stepparent must accept the fact that the stepchildren have another, "real" father or mother somewhere and strong attachments to that parent.

blended family A family created from a combination of stepchildren, stepparents, and stepsiblings.

Younger children are able to eventually form an attachment with a competent stepparent who utilizes authoritative parenting (Hetherington et al., 1999). This is particularly true when children maintain a good relationship with their biological father and stepfather (King, 2006). (Stepfathers who establish parent-child relationships based on warmth, friendly involvement, and mutual respect rather than on assertion of parental authority are more likely to be accepted by both boys and girls, although daughters, especially those approaching adolescence, appear to have a more intense and sustained negative reaction to their mothers' remarriage and more difficulty accepting and interacting with their new stepfathers (Hetherington et al., 1998; Vuchinich et al., 1991).

Stepmothers generally are more emotionally involved and take a more active role in discipline than stepfathers do, but gaining acceptance from the stepchildren is not easy for them either (Hetherington et al., 1998). In one study of parent-child relationships in stepmother families, John Santrock and Karen Sitterle (1987) found that despite their active involvement in parental and childrearing activities and ongoing efforts to establish good relationships with their stepchildren, stepmothers tended to be viewed as somewhat detached, unsupportive, and uninvolved, a feeling the stepmothers themselves shared. One explanation for these negative views is that the stepmother may be a target for her stepchildren's displaced anger, hurt, and disappointment toward their noncustodial mother. It might also be the case that stepmothers and children compete for the fathers' attention (Pasley & Moorefield, 2004). Child attachment and closeness to their biological father are related to lower rates of depression, anxiety, and externalizing problems among children living with a biological father and a stepmother, with no impact, positive or negative, for the relationship with a stepmother (King, 2007). However, other studies have demonstrated that children feel closer to their stepmothers than their fathers (Berg, 2003). Though research sometimes conflicts on the exact impact of stepparents, the overall story is that children fare best when they have good relationships with biological parents and stepparents who utilize authoritative parenting.

Because divorce is a social reality that affects development throughout the lifespan, we return to this issue when we discuss psychosocial development in adolescence (Chapter 11) and early adulthood (Chapter 13). In the next section, we look at the developmental effects of work on families during the school years.

The Effects of Work on Families

Regardless of family structure, work affects family life profoundly, although not always in simple or straightforward ways. Jobs determine daily schedules, of course, which in turn affect how much time parents have for their children. Job schedules also influence which parent or child does particular household chores. Men and women who have more flexible work schedules and autonomy within their work tend to negotiate work/life balance more easily (Grzywacz & Butler, 2005; Hegewisch & Gornick, 2011). Moreover, in countries with policies supporting families, including time off to care for sick children and affordable childcare, women, in particular, are more likely to work and have better jobs than those in countries without such generous policies (Gupta, Smith, & Verner, 2008; Hegewisch & Gornick, 2011). However, it is important to note that such policies may limit women's career advancement (Gupta, Smith, & Verner, 2008; Hegewisch & Gornick, 2011).

Work affects parents' self-esteem and thus their happiness as human beings and as parents. People with jobs that they find challenging and rewarding report they tend to experience a positive spillover effect that makes their family lives easier and more rewarding (Grzywacz & Butler, 2005). However, it is also true that people might experience a negative spillover effect when they work jobs that are stressful and cause conflict at home (Cinamon, Weisel, & Tzuk, 2007). Jobs also contribute to SES and therefore affect many aspects of family life (Greenberger et al., 1994; Kohn et al., 1986). All of these effects are magnified by the fact that an increasing number of families are headed by two working parents or by a single parent who works.

Effects of Maternal Employment

Despite the once popular view that mothers should stay at home to care for their children, research suggests that maternal employment as such usually does children no developmental harm (Gottfried et al., 1994; Hoffman, 1984a, 1984b), and it might actually improve the woman's home life and interactions with her children and spouse (Greenhaus & Powell, 2006; Grzywacz & Butler, 2005; Patel, Govender, Paruk, & Ramgoon, 2006). What does matter is whether a woman chooses to work or not to work and the family and systems-based support that is given—or not—to families (Hegewisch & Gornick, 2011). Mothers who can make this choice and who live in relatively supportive families apparently suffer no setbacks in their relations with their children. Mothers who feel forced either to work or not to work are less fortunate; they report more stressful relations with their children.

However, maternal employment often does influence children's development in some ways. For example, families with working mothers divide housework and child care more evenly than do families without employed mothers (Hoffman, 1983). In dual-worker families, fathers do some household chores relatively more often and spend more time alone with their children. Even so, parents tend to take on gender-stereotypic tasks with working mothers still doing the majority of housework and child care equaling thirty-four hours per week compared to husbands doing about twenty hours of housework per week (Bartley, Blanton, & Gilliard, 2005). This can lead to discord and feelings of inequality within the home, particularly when either parent is doing the majority of stereotypically female work, such as cooking and cleaning (Bartley et al., 2005). Additionally, in families with working mothers, children often are expected to help with household chores and caring for younger brothers and sisters.

The blend of housework and breadwinning seems to create less stereotyped attitudes in the children of working mothers regarding the "proper" roles of mothers and fathers.

In most families with two working parents, all family members share household responsibilities.
Source: J2R/Shutterstock.

Both sons and daughters witness nurturant behavior in their fathers and occupational competence in their mothers. Especially as they approach adolescence, children are likely to support women's employment in general, and daughters usually expect to work outside the home when they get older. Studies of school-age children of employed women indicate they are as well or better adjusted and hold less rigid views of gender roles than do children of women who do not work outside the home (Hoffman, 1984a, 1984b, 1989; Kawaguchi & Miyazaki, 2009; Moorehouse, 1991).

Many working mothers compensate for possible negative effects of their employment through more frequent shared activities or "quality time" with their children. A high level of shared mother-child activities serves as a buffer against the long hours and other disruptive demands of full-time jobs. Children are likely to match or exceed their peers in school achievement and adjustment when shared mother-child activities are more frequent (Gottfried et al., 1994; Moorehouse, 1991).

Effects of Parental Unemployment

When a parent loses a job, significant economic, social, and psychological disruption for children and their families can result. Loss of income can require parents and their children to make major sacrifices in their lifestyles. In many cases, the search for a new job or for affordable housing may cause a family to uproot itself, forcing children and parents to leave their friends and social support network behind. Leaving their existing school and neighborhood peers and gaining acceptance in a new neighborhood and school is particularly difficult during middle childhood (Cooksey et al., 1997; Liem & Liem, 1988; Price, 1992). Parental job loss also has a negative impact on child academics, specifically when a father becomes unemployed (Rege, Telle, & Votruba, 2011).

Children who experience family economic hardship are vulnerable to a broad range of difficulties, including problems with peer relations, academic performance, and psychological adjustment. The impact of such hardships is significantly influenced by how severe they are, how long they last, and how well parents can mobilize their material and psychological resources to deal with adversity while continuing to provide good parenting for their children (Bolger et al., 1995; Yoshikawa, Aber, & Beardslee, 2012).

After-School Care

One common challenge working parents face is finding after-school supervision for their children. In cases where after-school programs do not exist and siblings, friends, and other relatives are not available, older (and sometimes younger) elementary school-age children are left at home by themselves. Many parents in this situation carefully work out after-school procedures, including strict limits on what a self-care child may do and a checkup phone call from work to ensure that everything is okay; others leave their children to their own resources.

Comparisons of formal after-school programs with three other arrangements (mother care, informal adult supervision, and self-care) for a sample of low-SES third-graders from nine urban schools showed that attending after-school programs was associated with better grades and conduct in school as well as with better peer relations and emotional adjustment (Posner & Vandell, 1994). Children who attended such programs were exposed to more learning opportunities, spent more time in enrichment lessons (such as music and dance), and spent less time watching TV and in unstructured neighborhood activities than children in other forms of care. They also demonstrate better social competence and have more motivation in school when they attend engaging after-school programs (Mahoney, Parente, & Lord, 2007).

Formal after-school programs may be less important for children who live in communities that provide safe and constructive after-school opportunities. Nevertheless, even for these children, close parental monitoring of their after-school plans and activities and authoritative parenting (respectful acceptance and firm control) tend to promote good academic performance and social adjustment as well as keep them out of trouble. Lower levels of such parental involvement and stressful, unsupportive family circumstances are associated with poorer academic and social adjustment and more problem behaviors

(Bean, Barber & Crane, 2006; Galambos & Maggs, 1991; Roelofs et al., 2006; Steinberg, 1986; Vandell & Ramanan, 1991).

Other Sources of Social Support

Most school-age children establish sources of social support other than parents, including siblings and other adults. When interviewed about people, places, and activities that they found satisfying and helpful in conducting their lives, children revealed a large number of social supports from pets and make-believe friends to family members, peers, and sponsored activities such as church or the local library (Bryant, 1985).

Sibling Support

Perhaps most noteworthy is the high frequency with which siblings (as well as peers) were named as sources of support. During middle childhood, brothers and sisters provide one another with companionship, friendship, social support, and mentoring. Because of their greater maturity, older children frequently serve as role models and mentors to younger siblings, helping to transmit customs and family expectations and providing challenges that (hopefully) lead the younger children to new learning (Azmitia & Hesser, 1993; Howe, Ross, & Recchia, 2011). When siblings have caring, trusting relationships with one another, they have better relationships with their peers, and among girls, there are fewer symptoms of depression (Kim, McHale, Crouter, & Osgood, 2007). As we will see in later chapters, siblings continue to serve as an important source of social support through adolescence and adulthood as well.

Many studies have examined how siblings transmit knowledge by teaching one sibling a new task and then having that child teach their siblings. When older siblings are put into the "teacher" role, they tend to use scaffolding (discussed in Chapter 8), especially when their sibling is significantly younger (Howe et al., 2011). Much younger siblings are also less likely to ask questions of their older sibling. In more structured "teaching" situations, older siblings provided more explanations and positive feedback and gave learners more control over the task than did older peers; young children more often prompted their older siblings' explanations, pressured them into giving them more control over tasks, and performed at higher levels than when taught by their peers (Azmitia & Hesser, 1993). When younger siblings are assigned the "teacher" role, they tended to focus on learner-centered strategies, collaborating with their older siblings to teach the new task (Howe et al., 2011). During unstructured learning tasks, younger siblings tended to observe, imitate, and consult

During the school years, grandparents and other adults and other children within and outside the immediate and extended family provide invaluable sources of social support for children.
Source: Monkey Business Images/Shutterstock.

> **What Do You Think?**
>
> What are your views about the impact of maternal employment on child development? In what ways do your views reflect your own experiences as a child?

with their older siblings, who in turn were more likely to spontaneously provide them with guidance than were older peers (Azmitia & Hesser, 1993).

It is not surprising that older brothers and sisters tend to develop relationships with younger siblings that combine dominance and nurturance, the two major elements of mentoring relationships. However, as children moved toward the end of middle childhood, relationships between siblings became less domineering and more egalitarian, and reported levels of intensity and conflict also decreased (Buhrmeister & Furman, 1990).

Siblings tend to be less domineering and more nurturant in families in which children feel secure and parents get along well together (Brody et al., 1992; Dunn et al., 1994). Gene Brody and his colleagues (1992) found that school-age siblings whose fathers treat them with equality and impartiality during problem-solving discussions, whose families are generally harmonious even when discussing problems, and whose parents perceive family relationships to be close are less likely to experience sibling conflict than children in families that function less effectively. However, when there is conflict between parents and children, there is also likely to be conflict between siblings (Pike, Coldwell, & Dunn, 2005), and sibling conflict has been linked to higher rates of depression symptoms (Kim et al., 2007).

Beyond Siblings

As noted previously, many children report seeking out adults other than their parents, especially grandparents, with whom to talk and confide. Family pets and sometimes even neighbors' pets also served as confidants. Children also reported using hobbies to unwind and feel better about themselves (although some of the hobbies, such as collecting stamps or playing a musical instrument, were relatively nonsocial). Other children reported having special hideaways where they went to be alone for awhile. Many children sought out peers for activities when they needed an emotional lift or felt confused; but this was not the case on every occasion, and not all of the children did so (Bryant, 1985, 1994).

In general, as children move through middle childhood, their sources of support increasingly broaden. This makes them better able to manage particular stresses, whether inside or outside their families. At all ages during the elementary school years, children seemed happiest when they reported the widest range of social supports and when that range emphasized informal rather than formal supports.

As the preceding discussions imply, family members offer significant support in middle childhood. So do peers, as we explore in the next section.

Peer Relationships

The peer group is second only to the family as a context within which developmental changes occur (Hartup, 1989). Throughout childhood, some of children's most important relationships involve peers. As early as age two, children enjoy playing with or next to one another, and by age three or four they often prefer the company of peers, even when adults are available. Time spent with peers increases steadily during middle childhood. By the late elementary school years, about one-half of children's social interactions are with peers (Ellis et al., 1981). Peer relationships acquire a special intensity during late childhood and the transition to adolescence that typically occurs between fifth and seventh grades. During this period, children have increased unsupervised contact with peers and begin to place greater importance on peers' approval, views, and advice. At the same time, they spend less time with their parents and display greater emotional distance and psychological independence from them (B. Brown, 1990; Grundy, Gondoli, & Salafia, 2010; Larson et al., 1996).

What Theorists Say About Peer Relationships

Piaget

According to Jean Piaget, one important function of peers is to help school-age children overcome their *egocentrism,* or their tendency to assume everyone views the world in the same way they do (Piaget, 1963). Playing together, children inevitably run into conflicts over toys and priorities, arguing over who should use a new set of felt pens or what and where they should draw. In settling such disagreements, children gradually come to understand and value different points of view, a capacity that is central to living successfully in a pluralistic, democratic society.

Sullivan

The most comprehensive theory about peers was proposed by Harry Stack Sullivan. Like Piaget, Sullivan argued that relationships with peers have fundamentally different qualities than those with adults (Sullivan, 1953; Youniss, 1980). In particular, peers foster skills in compromise, cooperation, and competition. But unlike Piaget, Sullivan emphasized the value of peers in promoting emotional health. Peers create a life for children outside their families, and in doing so they help correct the emotional biases families inevitably give their children, biases that Sullivan called emotional *warps.* For instance, an eight-year-old with shy, reserved parents may learn from peers that not all people are shy and reserved. Or a ten-year-old whose parents care little about competitive athletics may discover from peers that athletic competition matters quite a lot to some people.

According to Sullivan, this form of learning occurs during the **juvenile period**, which begins around age five and continues until nine or ten. In this period, children show increasing interest in playmates of similar age and status. As they near the end of the elementary school years, they supposedly focus this interest on just a few select friends of the same gender, whom Sullivan called *chums.* These relationships provide children with models for later intimate relationships.

juvenile period Proposed by Sullivan, a period between ages five and ten when children show increasing interest in developing intense friendships or "chum relationships" with peers of the same gender.

The Functions of Friends

Children's relationships with peers consist of multiple levels of interpersonal experiences. At one level, a child interacts with a group of peers in the classroom or neighborhood and occupies a social position among those peers. This level, which is referred to as *social status, group acceptance,* or *popularity,* is group oriented and reflects social acceptance or popularity of the individual from the peer group's perspective. Another level of peer relationship involves *friendship,* a subjectively defined, voluntary, and reciprocal relationship between two individuals. Peer popularity and friendship are distinct but interrelated, and success or failure in one does not necessarily dictate success or failure in the other (Bukowski & Hoza, 1989; George & Hartman, 1996; Rodkin, Ryan, Jamison, & Wilson, 2013).

During the early school years, friendships provide an arena for "activity and opportunity": children base friendships on shared interests and activities, exchanges of possessions, and concrete supportive behaviors. By second or third grade, children become better able to live with differing perspectives within their friendships and feel less pressure to choose between one or the other, which, in part, contributes to more stable friendships as children move toward adolescence (Hartup, 1997; Hartup & Stevens, 1997; Poulin & Chan, 2010; Rawlins, 1992; Selman, 1981).

As children move into later childhood and preadolescence, *equality* and *reciprocity* become key elements of friendship interactions. Exchanging favors and sharing activities continue to matter as children get older, but by the time they enter fifth and sixth grades they place greater emphasis on psychological qualities such as intimacy, trust, mutual support, and loyalty. This is particularly true for girls. Friendship begins to involve a concept of a relationship based on a reciprocity between equals, each with distinct but compatible personalities. Sharing between friends shifts from an unreflective, *symmetrical reciprocity* based on "tit-for-tat" to a *cooperative reciprocity* based on mutual and deliberate sharing of assistance and resources that are intended to serve as tokens of friendship. Actually doing the same things or sharing the same objects becomes correspondingly less important. (Hartup & Stevens, 1997; Keller & Wood, 1989; Pasterski, Golombok, & Hines, 2011; Rawlins, 1992).

By fifth or sixth grade, children can even adopt an independent, or third-party perspective, comparing their own points of view with those of their friends (Berndt, 1988; Choudhury, Blakemore, & Charman, 2006; Furman & Bierman, 1984; Selman, 1980). As one eleven-year-old put it about a good friend, "He thinks that I don't study enough, and that he studies just about the right amount for schoolwork. But you know what *I* think? I think that I'm just trying to keep schoolwork from bothering me too much, and that *he* works too hard. I wonder what the teachers think." Judging by statements such as this, friendship at this stage appears to be an intimate collaboration between two people who are mutually committed to building the relationship, which has acquired an importance beyond the particular needs of either friend.

In a review of literature on friendships and their developmental significance, Willard Hartup (1997) argues that the developmental implications of friendships cannot be specified without distinguishing among *having friends,* the *identity of one's friends,* and *friendship quality.* Friends provide one another with cognitive, emotional, and social *scaffolding* that differs from what nonfriends provide and that having friends supports favorable developmental outcomes across *normative transitions,* predictable changes that almost all children experience, such as entering school, starting middle school, and puberty (Denham et al., 2011; Hartup, 1997). However, predicting developmental outcomes also requires knowledge of the attitudes and behavioral characteristics of children's friends as well as the qualitative features of those relationships. Cognitive and social scaffolding are similar to Vygotsky's zone of proximal development, and normative transitions are similar to the *normative crisis model* of adult development, both of which we discussed in Chapter 2.

The Functions of Other Peers

Like friendships, peer activities appear to serve several important functions. First, they provide a context for sociability, enhancement of relationships, social status, and a sense of belonging. Second, they promote concern for achievements and a reliable and integrated sense of who one is. Finally, they provide opportunities for instruction and learning (Rodkin, et al., 2013; Rubin, Fredstrom, Bowker, 2008; Zarbatany et al., 1990).

Children's reliance on peers versus parents for help appears to increase with age. According to fourth-graders, friends provide support less frequently than do mothers and fathers, the most frequent providers. Seventh-graders, however believe same-sex friends and parents are equally supportive, whereas tenth-graders view same-sex friends as the most frequent source of support even though parents remain important throughout childhood and adolescence (De Goede, Branje, Delsing & Meeus, 2009; Furman & Buhrmester, 1992). Although the functions of children's peer relationships show considerable similarity to those with adults, several features are unique to peer relationships. Attachments with parents and other adults or older children are "vertical and complementary," meaning they involve individuals who have greater knowledge, competence, and social power. Peer relationships, in contrast, are "horizontal and symmetrical" in that they involve individuals of approximately equal knowledge, competence, and social power (Hartup, 1989). They are by nature voluntary and reciprocal relationships among comparative equals. This means that a child must act in a way that explicitly supports the relationship—be friendly, that is—if he expects the relationship to survive. Children apparently understand these differences intuitively, because they typically attribute an obedience orientation to relationships between adults and children but attribute play and recreation orientations to relationships among children (Berndt, 1988; Youniss, 1980).

Influences on Peer Group Membership

Most of children's peer interactions occur in groups. In defining a peer group, elementary school children emphasize the importance of shared activities such as walking to school, talking on the telephone, listening to music, playing games, and just hanging out; however, sharing attitudes becomes most important as children approach adolescence (O'Brien & Bierman, 1988; Pasterski et al., 2011; Zarbatany et al., 1990). Living in the same neighborhood, attending the same school, and participating in the same community organizations all contribute to the likelihood that peer groups will form.

Children's peer groups are not simply random assortments of individuals but are influenced by many factors. Three of the most important factors are age, gender, and racial or ethnic background.

Age

Children play mostly with others of approximately the same age and, when asked, say they prefer to be friends with their agemates. But contrary to a common impression, schoolchildren may spend anywhere from one-quarter to one-half of their time with companions who are more than two years older or younger and say they prefer to seek help and comfort from older children (Ellis et al., 1981; French, 1984). School imposes an upper limit on these cross-age contacts, however, because classrooms usually group children according to age, and there is relatively little research examining benefits and drawbacks to mixed-age peer groups (Poulin & Chan, 2010; Rubin et al., 2008).

Groups with mixed ages have certain special qualities. Older children show more nurturant behavior, such as tying the shoelaces of a younger child or buttoning the child's sweater. Younger children show greater dependence by asking for help with schoolwork or agreeing to older peers' preferences for play activities, and it is likely that older children help scaffold skills for the younger children (Poulin & Chan, 2010; Rubin et al., 2008; Vygotsky, 1978). However, mixed-age groups also tend to be less "sociable" than same-age groups; they chat or have friendly conversations less often, for example. Same-age groups encourage the opposites of all of these qualities: children give and receive less practical help, show more friendliness to one another, and get into conflicts more often (Brody et al., 1983; Furman & Buhrmester, 1992).

Gender

Although mixed-gender play occurs during the elementary school years, first-graders generally name children of their own gender as best friends. Observations of younger schoolchildren during free play show that during cooperative play periods, they interact about four times as often with children of their own gender as they do with those of the opposite gender (Golombok & Fivush, 1994; Maccoby & Jacklin, 1987; Pasterski et al., 2011). This ratio actually increases as children approach adolescence; by third grade most peer groups contain only one gender, and by fifth grade virtually all do. As children move into middle school and adolescence, however, the trend reverses (Poulin & Chan, 2011; Shrum et al., 1988).

How do we interpret this tendency toward gender-based separation during middle childhood? Eleanor Maccoby argues that gender differences emerge primarily in social situations and vary with the gender composition of the dyads (two-person relationships) and groups involved, and that children spontaneously choose same-gender playmates even in situations where they are not under pressure from adults to do so because they find same-gender play partners more compatible (Maccoby, 1990; Pasterski et al., 2011). During the later preschool years, two factors seem to be important. First, the rough-and-tumble style and emphasis on competition and dominance that is characteristic of boys appear to be unappealing to most girls, who in general prefer play that is more cooperative and less aggressive (Pasterski et al., 2011). Second, girls discover that their growing reliance on polite suggestion to influence others is increasingly ineffective with boys and therefore avoid choosing boys as playmates (Maccoby, 1990).

Further support for the idea that playmate selection may be more heavily influenced by sharing gender-based play activities than by merely being of the same gender comes from a laboratory study of playmate choice among six-to-eight-year-olds conducted by Gerianne Alexander and Melissa Hines. When given the choice of selecting a playmate based on gender versus preferred style of play, style of play appeared to be more important for both boys and girls. Boys chose female playmates who had masculine play styles (including toys, rough-and-tumble play, and activity level), whereas girls chose male playmates with more feminine play styles (Alexander & Hines, 1994).

Over time, children find same-gender play partners more compatible and segregate themselves into same-gender groups. As children enter adolescence, childhood patterns carry into cross-gender interactions in which girls' styles may put them at a disadvantage. Though patterns of mutual influence may be more symmetrical in intimate, young adult male-female couples, these gender-related differences in style are still present and subsequently manifest themselves in the roles and relationships of parenthood (Maccoby, 1990). However, because girls tend to have smaller friend groups with higher levels of disclosure and intimacy, boys, too, might be at a disadvantage when they begin having other-sex friendships or romantic partnerships if they lack these skills (Pasterski et al., 2011; Poulin & Chen, 2010). We look at the impact of these differences on parenthood in Chapter 13's coverage of psychosocial development in early adulthood.

Despite the pervasiveness of gender segregation in peer relationships, a small but stable subgroup of children maintain cross-gender relations beyond the age when such relationships are the norm. Donna Kovacs, Jeffrey Parker, and Lois Hoffman (1996) studied cross-sex friendships among more than seven hundred third- and fourth-grade boys and girls from diverse SES backgrounds. They found that 14 percent of the children had one or more reciprocal opposite-sex friendships. Children with primarily opposite-sex friendships had poorer social skills than other children with friends, but held fewer stereotypes about gender roles than other children and were better adjusted than children with no friends. Children involved in opposite-sex friendships that were secondary to their same-sex friendships were as well adjusted as children with only same-sex friendships. African American children, who comprised about one-third of the children studied, were more likely than European American children to have opposite-sex friends. African American children from single-parent homes had more opposite-sex friends than those from two-parent homes, perhaps because they were likely to live in extended, multigenerational family settings in which they interacted with many female family members and few adult males.

Adult norms and expectations regarding gender stereotyping also can have an impact. Children growing up in families that downplay gender typing in their child-rearing values and practices are less stereotyped in their activities, interests, and gender-typed beliefs. However, gender flexibility in children's play behavior or friendship preferences is more likely to be evident in situations where it is supported, or at least not actively discouraged, by parents, teachers, and other adults (Halim & Ruble, 2010; Hoffman, 1989; Maccoby, 1990; Moorehouse, 1991; Weisner & Wilson-Mitchell, 1990).

Even when parents work hard to encourage friendships that are not gender stereotyped, peers often exert considerable pressure toward conformity with same-gender friendship patterns. On his ninth birthday, Alex, a fourth-grader, solved this problem by having an all-boy "public" birthday party and later having a special "private" one with his lifelong best friend, Katie. For interesting firsthand observations of the role of gender in peer group play, see the interview with Lisa Truong.

Racial and Ethnic Background

Patterns of segregation and preferences based on racial and ethnic differences are a fact of life in much of our society (Havekes, Bader, & Krysan, 2016; Quintana, 2011; Shrum et al., 1988). Racial and ethnic awareness are especially important during middle childhood, because children of this age are in the process of committing themselves to society and to the values and standards of the majority culture. They are also developing their own self-concepts.

Racial segregation and preference often reflect certain types of prejudice. *Prejudice* is a positive or negative attitude toward an individual based solely on the person's membership in a particular group. Prejudices are frequently based on *stereotypes,* patterns of rigid, overly simplified, and generally inaccurate ideas about the characteristics of another group of people. Stereotypes often involve negative ideas associated with race, ethnic or cultural background, religion, SES, age, gender, and sexual orientation. Although prejudices based on stereotypes do not necessarily determine a person's overt behavior, they often do. Frequently prejudice is associated with *discrimination*—actions toward members of the targeted group, such as exclusion or mistreatment, that reflect prejudicial attitudes toward that group.

A school or neighborhood setting that is ethnically diverse may foster peer interactions and friendships among schoolchildren from different ethnic groups. The playground of their school provides an excellent place for these girls to "hang out" and take selfies.
Source: Mat Hayward/Shutterstock.

Studies that asked children to name their friends have found that children are more likely to name peers of their own race, particularly if that race is the majority one. This trend begins in the preschool years and increases throughout middle childhood until children reach high school (Asher et al., 1982; Poulin & Chan, 2010; Rubin et al., 2008; Shrum et al., 1988). The degree to which family, neighborhood, and school settings are supportive (or unsupportive) of cross-race friendships is also likely to influence a child's peer preferences. Among children and adolescents, social contact both inside and outside of school may influence intergroup attitudes. Maureen Hallinan, Roy Teixeira, and Richard Williams studied black-white interracial friendships among fourth- through seventh-graders in integrated classrooms. They found that the more African American students a classroom contained, the more likely European American students were to choose a black peer as a best friend. One study found that for African American students to be "liked" on average, as much or more than European American students in a class, the class needed to be at least 66 percent African American (Jackson, Barth, Powell, & Lochman, 2006). However, having a higher proportion of white students in a classroom did not increase the likelihood of a black student choosing a white friend, nor does having a low proportion of white children reduce how much they are "liked" on average (Hallinan & Teixeira, 1987; Hallinan & Williams, 1989; Jackson et al., 2006). Similar findings were found in studies examining Latino children. Latino children had higher ratings of liking in classrooms that were at least half Latino and where there was bilingual instruction (Tropp & Prenovost, 2008). Yet though cross-race friendships are more likely to develop in integrated schools, they are difficult to maintain outside of school unless the children live in interracial neighborhoods or participate in team sports or other integrated activities (DuBois & Hirsch, 1990; Howes & Wu, 1990).

Can racial and ethnic prejudice be reduced? Middle to late childhood seems to be an age period in which people display high levels of prejudice and are more susceptible to programs designed to reduce prejudice (Raabe & Beelmann, 2011). Elementary school programs that emphasize multicultural competence and awareness by integrating multicultural activities in both academic and extracurricular activities and actively involve children's families and other community members in school activities can successfully foster friendship and peer acceptance among students from different racial, ethnic, and cultural backgrounds (Bojko, 1995; Raabe & Beelmann, 2011). *Magnet schools* that use specialized programs in science, language, or the arts to attract students from school districts representing a variety of ethnic and cultural backgrounds have also successfully increased diversity on a long-term basis, though their implementation often requires several school districts to work together, which can be difficult and cumbersome (Ayscue & Orfield, 2016; Rossell, 1988).

Cooperative learning experiences that allow mixed groups of children to work as a team to achieve common academic goals also have had some success in fostering cross-race acceptance and enhancing children's self-esteem. In one program based on this "jigsaw" technique, children from different racial and ethnic backgrounds were assigned to different parts of a single project. They quickly learned to work together to complete the task and developed more positive feelings about both themselves and one another (Johnson et al., 1984; Slavin, 1996). Other programs have successfully reduced prejudice and stereotyping while increasing liking long term by having children from different ethnic backgrounds spend several sessions playing games, exploring their similarities and differences, and practicing perspective taking and empathy skills (Berger, Benatov, Abu-Raiya, & Tadmor, 2016).

Popularity and Rejection

When peers are asked to evaluate one another's popularity, or likability, by "nominating" whom they like most or would choose to play with, children generally are classified as "popular" or as occupying one of three unpopular statuses: "rejected," "controversial," or "neglected." Popular children receive many positive and very few negative votes from their peers; rejected children receive many negative and few positive peer nominations; controversial children receive many positive and negative peer nominations; and neglected children receive few positive or negative nominations (Coie et al., 1982).

The Popular Child

Easily noticed characteristics, such as having the "right" hairstyle or the "right" body build, being athletic, or having an attractive-sounding name, are quite important to acceptance and popularity in the early grades. As children get older, they increasingly choose their friends on the basis of personal qualities such as honesty, empathy, kindness, trust, humor, and creativity (Furman & Bierman, 1983; Hymel, Closson, Caravita, & Villancourt, 2011; Poulin & Chan, 2010; Reaves & Roberts, 1983).

Some popular children are well liked, are able to easily initiate and maintain social interactions, and understand social situations. They possess a high degree of interpersonal skills and tend to behave in ways that are prosocial, cooperative, and in tune with group norms (Hymel et al., 2011; Masten & Coatsworth, 1998). These children have **sociometric popularity**, which is based on being well liked by peers due to having good social skills (Hymel et al., 2011).

Some children are popular based on status and prestige—a type of popularity known as **perceived popularity**. They excel in athletics, wear stylish clothing and special material possessions, such as an expensive pair of athletic shoes, and influence status with peers (Dodge, 1986; Hartup, 1983; Hymel et al., 2011). These children might actually not be well liked among their peers, but still maintain social status (Hymel et al., 2011). In fact, children who try to build their social status might actually be aggressive and still see increases in their perceived popularity (Neal, 2009; Rodkin et al., 2013).

Some of the assets just noted, such as peer competence and athletic ability, remain valuable to children as they move into adolescence, and others (such as the athletic shoes) may not. But during childhood, such advantages create prestige for individual children within particular peer groups and also make membership in the "best," or highest-status, groups possible. Because of the importance of peer relationships during the school years, the interpersonal competencies associated with peer acceptance and popularity are likely to have a positive impact not only on a child's current adjustment but also on her or his longer-term psychological well-being (Bukowski et al., 1996; Hymel et al., 2011; Masten & Coatsworth, 1998).

The Unpopular Child

Peers describe unpopular children, particularly those classified as "rejected," as unpleasant, disruptive, selfish, and having few positive characteristics. Such children are likely to exhibit socially inappropriate aggression, overactivity, inattention or immaturity, and,

---

sociometric popularity
A type of popularity based on social status and prestige.

perceived popularity
A type of popularity based on how well liked someone is.

Unpopular children may behave aggressively or selfishly without realizing it. Ironically, because they tend to be excluded from groups, they find few chances to learn new ways of relating.
Source: karnavalfoto/Shutterstock.

not surprisingly, behavioral and academic problems in school (Bier-man et al., 1993; Cillessen & Bellmore, 2011). Because they lack the social skills needed to successfully join and participate in peer groups, they are blamed by peers for their own deviance and are often actively disliked and excluded from activities (Cillessen & Bellmore, 2011; Coie et al., 1991; Masten & Coatsworth, 1998).

Some children are considered unpopular because they are shy, which is often due to social anxiety or being overly self-conscious (Buss, 1986). Very withdrawn children carry many of the burdens of lacking a friendship network, such as rejection and being victimized, as well as increased symptoms of anxiety and depression and academic problems (Rubin, Coplan, & Bowker, 2009).

Thomas George and Donald Hartman (1996) studied the friendship networks of popular, average, and unpopular fifth- and sixth-graders. They found that all children reported having at least one *unilateral friend,* a person whom they consider to be a friend but who does not feel the same way about them. Unpopular children were less likely than popular children to have at least one *reciprocal friend,* someone who shares their view that a mutual friendship exists. The unilateral friendship networks of unpopular children contained more younger school-age friends and fewer same-age friends than the friendship networks of popular children. Moreover, in unilateral friendships, there is a pattern of one child being disliked (this child usually does not have good social skills) and one child who dislikes but remains "friends" (this child usually has good social skills) (Olsen et al, 2012). The reciprocal friendship networks of unpopular children were smaller, more evenly distributed within and outside of the classroom, and contained fewer average and popular friends of the opposite sex than those of popular children.

In a twelve-year longitudinal study that followed fifth-graders to young adulthood, Catherine Bagwell, Andrew Newcomb, and William Bukowski (1998) found that peer-rejected children were at risk for later difficulties. Children who were rejected by their peers and had no good friend at age ten had lower levels of aspiration, participated in fewer organizations and activities, had a less active social life and experienced more psychological problems, including depression and anxiety in adolescence and early adulthood, compared to children who were not rejected and who had a friend.

Aggression

Among both boys and girls, the highest levels of aggression are displayed by children who are classified as unpopular-rejected. However, girls and boys appear to differ in the form their aggressive behavior most typically takes. Boys are more likely to attack peers through *overt aggression* (such as hitting, pushing, or verbally threatening to hurt others), whereas girls are more likely to display *relational aggression* involving harming others through purposeful manipulation and damage of their peer relationships (Card, Stucky, Sawalani, & Little, 2008; Crick & Grotpeter, 1995; Crick, 1997).

Jennifer Grotpeter and Nicki Crick (1996) conducted a study to discover whether the social problems that relationally aggressive and overtly aggressive children typically experience in peer group situations also occur in their one-to-one friendships. Children who were relationally aggressive in their peer group did exhibit high levels of relational aggression, intimacy, exclusivity, and jealousy within their friendships. In contrast, children who were overtly aggressive with their peers exhibited low levels of intimacy but greatly valued companionship and spending time with their friends, and placed great importance on having friends who joined them in using aggression to harm children outside the friendship. Thus, children who are not themselves aggressive but develop friendships with overtly aggressive peers may nevertheless be pulled into aggressive encounters against other children. Children who possess high levels of emotional expressiveness, emotional insight, and empathy are better able to manage their own anger in social interactions and to display higher levels of empathy and prosocial behavior with friends than children who lack such qualities (Roberts & Strayer, 1996).

Family, culture, and neighborhood contexts also are important when understanding aggressive behavior. In families where parents are hostile, coercive, disrespectful, or engage in corporal punishment, children are much more likely to be more aggressive and less socially competent with their peers (Coyne, Nelson, & Underwood, 2011; MacKinnon-Lewis et al., 1994, 1997). In a large-scale study of second- through fifth-graders, Janis Kupersmidt and her colleagues found that living in middle-SES neighborhoods had a strong protective effect on aggressive behavior and peer rejection, particularly among African American children from low-SES, single-parent families who lived in such neighborhoods (Kupersmidt et al., 1995). Similar patterns of disadvantaged boys utilizing increasing rates of physical aggression have been found in another large-scale longitudinal study conducted in Canada (Côté et al., 2006).

For children living in war zones or in other dangerous environments such as communities where gang and drug activity and the wounding and killing of friends and relatives are everyday occurrences, the developmental toll on children and their parents is immense (Wandersman & Nation, 1998). Youngsters who are exposed to ongoing violence suffer from chronic emotional distress, learning problems, sleep disturbances, and preoccupation with their own safety and the safety of those they depend on and care about. They are also more likely to have problems with aggression, impulse control, and conflict resolution in both school and nonschool settings. Children may cope with chronic danger by adopting a world view that may be dysfunctional in any "normal" situations in which they are expected to participate. For example, although being hyperaggressive may help ensure survival in a dangerous neighborhood, it is likely to be dysfunctional and stimulate peer and teacher rejection if used to cope with disappointments and disputes in most school situations (Garbarino & Kostelny, 1996; Kozol, 1995; Marsella, 1998; Masten & Coatsworth, 1998; McCloyd, 1998; Sagi-Schwartz, 2008). In addition, some adaptations to chronic danger, such as emotional withdrawal, may cause problems for the next generation when those individuals themselves become parents.

The same links between danger and trauma observed in children may operate directly among parents. Parental adaptations to dangerous environments may produce childrearing strategies that interfere with normal development. A parent who forbids her child to play on the floor to keep him away from the poison put there to kill rats that infest the apartment may deprive her child of opportunities for exploratory play. A parent who forbids his child to play outside for fear of shooting incidents may limit the child's opportunities for athletic and social interaction with other children and adults outside the immediate family (Garbarino et al., 1991).

How successfully such children cope with their circumstances also depends on the support and guidance they get from family members and school personnel, social services, and the community at large. Considerable success in reducing aggression and fostering prosocial behavior has been reported for school-based intervention programs designed to teach older elementary and junior high school children assertiveness and interpersonal cognitive problem-solving skills as well as home-based programs focused on training parents how to avoid behaviors that increase child aggression (Coyne et al., 2011; Hudley & Graham, 1993; O'Donnell et al., 1995; Shure & Spivak, 1988). Despite such efforts, however, it is unlikely that these problems will be resolved without social and economic changes that significantly reduce or eliminate the dangerous conditions under which many children and their families currently live.

Aggression Over the Life Course

Based on their recent review of studies of the development of aggression over the life course, Rolf Loeber and Magda Stouthamer-Loeber (1998) propose three developmental types of violent individuals: (1) a life-course type, (2) a limited-duration type, and (3) a late-onset type. Individuals with a life-course type of aggression display aggressiveness in childhood and become increasingly aggressive as they move through adolescence and into adulthood (Pakiz et al., 1997). This group accounts for the largest proportion of violent adults. Individuals who display a limited-duration pattern of aggression outgrow aggression either during the preschool-elementary school period or in late adolescence-early adulthood. Finally, a small minority of individuals display a late-onset pattern of aggression, showing no signs of aggression earlier in their lives and first displaying violent behavior during adulthood.

Gender differences in aggression, as expressed by frustration and rage, are not found in infancy, but do emerge in the preschool period, when boys are more likely than girls to display both overt (physical) aggression and relational (emotional) aggression. During the school years, girls display significantly more relational aggression, whereas boys exhibit substantially more overt aggression, including, in the extreme, group and gang fighting, aggravated assault, sexual violence, and homicide (Loeber & Stouthamer-Loeber, 1998).

Conformity to Peers

Because peer groups involve social equals, they give children unique opportunities to develop their own beliefs without having parents or older siblings dominate or dismiss them. But in doing so, peer groups also present challenges. Acceptance and support by groups matter intensely to children, who are still learning what kind of people they are and acquiring the skills they need to interact with others. As a result, peer groups often influence their members very strongly indeed: they demand conformity to group expectations in return for continued acceptance and prestige.

Pressures to conform sometimes lead children to violate personal values or needs or those of parents and other adult authorities. One child might feel pressured into paying dues she cannot afford, joining fights she does not want to participate in, or shunning children who do not belong to her own group. Another might feel pressured to wear clothes that his parents consider outrageous or to perform poorly at school. In return for these behaviors and attitudes, the children remain in good standing with their peers. Despite these differences, however, there tends to be high agreement between children, their peer group, and parents on important issues such as moral and ethical standards, standards of appropriate behavior, schooling, and future goals (Damon, 1988; Fine, 1982; Knafo & Schwartz, 2003).

Peer groups can exert positive pressures as well. For example, they can encourage athletic and academic achievement and create commitments to fairness and reciprocity, at least within an immediate circle of peers: "When someone buys a candy bar at the drugstore, she shares it with the rest of us. Then we do the same thing the next time if *we* get something nice." Peer conformity can also support "good" behavior such as avoiding smoking, drinking, or other drugs or abstaining from risky sexual activity. Whether the pressures are positive or negative, however, peer groups offer a key setting for acquiring social skills, evaluating and managing personal relationships, and handling competition and cooperation.

A study of the natural, self-selected peer groups of fourth- and fifth-graders conducted by Thomas Kindermann (1993) found that children tend to associate with peers who share similar norms regarding involvement in school. Children who were academically oriented and highly engaged in school tended to affiliate with classmates who had similar motivational orientations; the same was true for children who were disengaged from school and lacked academic motivation. Although their memberships changed somewhat during the year, peer groups remained quite stable in terms of their norms regarding academic orientation.

School Influences on Peer Relations

According to Erik Erikson, school is one of the main arenas in which children resolve the crisis of industry versus inferiority. Interactions with teachers and other children provide important opportunities to develop cognitive and social skills, gain knowledge about the world, and cultivate peer relationships that are central to the development of self-concept during middle childhood.

School Culture

Each school has its own culture, which includes the values, beliefs, traditions, and customary ways of thinking and behaving that make it unique and distinguish it from other schools and institutions. One school may especially value its innovative academic programs and the high achievement levels of its students, another the degree of student involvement in school-sponsored activities, and a third the active involvement of parents in providing special resources. The closer the fit between the school culture and the values and expectations of the children (and families) it serves, the more likely will the school's developmental impact be positive. Students both learn and function better in classrooms in which the instructional approach, pattern and rhythm of verbal interaction and student participation, and strategies for motivating students are in tune with their family and cultural expectations and when teachers utilize strategies similar to authoritative parenting (Vygotsky, 1997; Walker, 2008; Wigfield et al., 1998).

Clearly, teachers strongly influence a school's culture—and its children. In fact, with the exception of their parents, most elementary school children spend more time with their teachers than with any other adults. Teachers therefore play a very significant role in the lives of school-age children. Observational studies of daily classroom life reveal that the elementary school teacher engages in as many as one thousand interpersonal exchanges with pupils each day (Cazden, 1988). As we saw in Chapter 8, teachers' styles of classroom management vary considerably. However, all effective teachers establish learning environments that are calm, predictable, and engaging and provide smooth transitions from one activity to the next. They also stay on top of the classroom situation by keeping in tune with their students, in both their communication of academic content and their responses to the constantly changing social and emotional needs of thirty or more children (Linney & Seidman, 1989). In other words, they create an environment with clear rules and expectations, effective controls, open communication, high nurturance, and respectful relationships that encourage students to participate as fully as possible in school and classroom life. Not surprisingly, effective teacher-student relationships tend to be authoritative in that their qualities parallel those of the authoritative parenting style discussed in Chapter 7 (Walker, 2008).

The Student's Experience

What do students experience in the classroom? According to Philip Jackson, particularly in traditional, teacher-centered classrooms, students spend a great deal of time waiting for the teacher or other students, delaying fulfillment of their needs until given permission to do so by the teacher, and contending with distractions and social disruption. Students must wait to ask a question, wait to get permission to leave their seats, wait to have a question answered, wait for the next assignment, or wait to use the computer (Jackson, 1986).

Although these observations are cause for concern, many classrooms are conscientiously organized to minimize such difficulties and provide a learning environment that is academically stimulating and supportive of children's developmental needs. Though

> **What Do You Think?**
>
> Children's growing exposure to peer group influences during middle childhood is a source of concern for both parents and teachers. What advice might you give to parents and teachers regarding the best ways to deal with this challenge?

the teaching styles may vary, the experiences of the great majority of students in well-run classrooms are largely positive. Students in such classrooms feel like respected members of their classroom and school communities. They are eager to learn and are active participants in classroom activities, both academic and nonacademic. Effective school environments also provide children with opportunities to freely interact with and form developmentally beneficial relationships both with peers and with children of different ages, developmental levels, and backgrounds. The Working With interview with fourth-grade teacher Lisa Truong (page 324) is a good example of how a teacher uses her authoritative relationships with her students and her awareness of school and classroom culture to reduce gender-role stereotyping in peer group activities.

Death, Loss, and Grieving During the School Years

While for obvious reasons interest in death and dying has been greatest for those interested in the adult years (see Chapters 15, 17, and 18), experiences with death have a developmental impact throughout the lifespan. For example, approximately 1.5 million children in the United States live in single-parent families because the other parent has died (Owens, 2008). One study of death, loss, and grieving among middle school children found that 41 percent had been personally involved with death within the previous year; death of a grandparent or great-grandparent was most frequently mentioned (Glass, 1991). However, deaths of parents, siblings, other relatives, family friends, other children, and pets were also noted. Though the loss of a parent may be the most difficult for children, the death of a sibling due to an illness such as sudden infant death syndrome (SIDS), AIDS, cystic fibrosis, or cancer, or to accidents or suicide, also can have a profound effect on children at various ages (Birenbaum et al., 1991; Davies, 1995; Dyregorov & Dyregrov, 2005; Fangos & Nickerson, 1991; Packman, Horsley, Davies, & Kramer, 2006; Powell, 1991).

Approximately 1.5 million children in the United States live in single-parent families because the other parent has died, and experiences with death have developmental impact throughout the lifespan.
Source: Twin Design/Shutterstock.

Chapter 9 Psychosocial Development in Middle Childhood

WORKING WITH Lisa Truong, Fourth-Grade Teacher

Reducing Gender Role Stereotyping in Play

Lisa Truong is a fourth-grade teacher at a "follow-through" elementary school that serves students from citywide head-start preschool and kindergarten programs as well as children from the local neighborhood. Her classroom is a well-organized, friendly, cheerful place filled with children's drawings and other projects. Lisa provides richly detailed observations of gender differences in peer group and play activities among fourth-graders.

Rob: *How would you describe peer relations among fourth-graders?*

Lisa: Often children's academic ability sets the tone and pace for their friendships. Children who do well academically tend to be friends with other kids who are bright.

Rob: *Why do you think this is so?*

Lisa: In part because of parent pressure. Parents are interested in their children having good friends. Another reason may be that much of the teaching here occurs in small skill groups. These group children with the same academic needs together. They also focus on group dynamics, teaching the children to work with other people. When we go outside for recess, the children do tend to stay in those same groups.

Rob: *What other factors seem to influence peer groups?*

Lisa: Boy-girl differences are very important. As much as I've tried to encourage girls to play football or soccer and boys to do things like four-square and jump-rope, it really does break down by gender as to how they play outside. Girls tend to play jump-rope, and boys tend to play soccer on the field—it's almost automatic. Girls also tend to go to the swings and slide much more than the boys.

Rob: *Why do you think this happens?*

Lisa: At this age, girls are getting more social and interactive. Often I see girls walking slowly and talking. Even their jump-rope is more consistently interactive and coordinated—with turn taking and things like that—than the boys' play. You should see the girls play foursquare! It involves a lot of verbal interaction and social coordination.

Rob: *How so?*

Lisa: Four people stand in a 10-foot-by-10-foot square drawn in chalk and divided into four smaller squares. The person in the fourth square is in control of whatever the category will be. So, for example, that person will say "Colors" and then bounce the ball into any of the other players' squares. They will have to name a color and catch the ball, or they're out.

Rob: *There's a rhythm to it?*

Lisa: You have to keep the rhythm, and you can't name the same color twice— or animal, country, movie star, or whatever the category is.

The Process of Grieving for a Childhood Loss

Loss or bereavement refers to being separated from someone to whom one was emotionally attached; *grieving* refers to the complex emotional, cognitive, and perceptual reactions and experiences that accompany the loss (Mullan et al., 1995). John Baker and his colleagues propose that for bereaved children the grieving process includes three phases, each involving certain psychological tasks (Baker et al., 1992).

Early-phase tasks include understanding the fact that someone has died, the implications of the death, and protecting oneself and one's family from both physical harm and the full emotional impact of the loss. Children need information at an age-appropriate level about death in general and about the nature of the particular death. Euphemistic explanations (e.g., "Mother has gone to sleep") should be avoided because they tend to interfere with children's need to understand what really happened. Bereaved children listen intently and watch others' reactions, ask questions, and reenact elements of the events in their play; if there are gaps in their understanding, they tend to fill in the missing pieces with fantasy. Children also need to feel they are safe and in a secure environment. Because of fears that they too will die or that their families will disintegrate, children and their families may engage in a variety of self-protective mechanisms such as denial, distortion, emotional numbing, and even physical isolation from people.

> **WORKING WITH** Lisa Truong, Fourth-Grade Teacher
>
> ### Reducing Gender Role Stereotyping in Play *continued*
>
> The categories get more complex as the year goes on. The kids almost always start the year with colors, and by the end of the year it will be something much more specific, like Spice Girls songs or names of rock stars. This group of girls also made up a great hand-clapping game about music groups; the way they thought it through and the rules they made up were fascinating.
>
> **Rob:** *What are the boys doing?*
>
> **Lisa:** They're playing soccer and kick-ball, building forts, or skateboards, if they can. Or they'll collect things and investigate the environment. At the beginning of the year, we studied insects and their natural habitats in science. Once the boys got outside, they tried to find every single little bug they could, and they would come in and show it.
>
> **Rob:** *It seems fourth-grade boys are less interested in make-up games than girls.*
>
> **Lisa:** Yes, that's true. Boys tend to play games that emphasize physical rather than social interaction and where they follow rules that are already made up for them.
>
> **Rob:** *How permanent are these peer group patterns?*
>
> **Lisa:** They seem long-lasting. The group I described was made up of five girls who are very, very close. They're all good students, and all happen to be white. I've been trying to encourage them to be less of a clique and interact with other people more.
>
> **Rob:** *How else might teachers encourage greater interaction?*
>
> **Lisa:** Our school is committed to helping children interact in a way that doesn't break down along sex role or racial lines. I talk to them about it very upfront, and I say I think there should be more interaction between boys and girls and blacks and whites. When we have social studies activities, the rule is that groups will be mixed. The children understand this and help make it work.
>
> ### What Do You Think?
>
> 1. Lisa's observations of her students illustrate how closely play and social development are interrelated. What examples in the interview demonstrate this?
> 2. How has Lisa attempted to reduce gender-role stereotyping in her fourth-graders' peer group and play activities? Based on this chapter, what additional things might she consider trying?
> 3. Discuss how Lisa's observations demonstrate the interaction of physical, cognitive, and social domains in her fourth-graders' development. How are the three domains reflected in gender differences in peer groups and play activities?

Middle-phase tasks of grieving include accepting and emotionally acknowledging the reality of the loss, exploring and reevaluating one's relationship to the person who died, and bearing the intense psychological pain involved. *Late-phase tasks* require that the child consolidate a new sense of personal identity that includes both the experience of the loss and identifications with the deceased person; safely develop new emotional relationships without excessive fear of loss or guilt; construct his or her own inner representation of the deceased, based on past and current experiences, thoughts, and feelings, that enable the child to maintain an ongoing emotional connection (attachment) with the deceased; wholeheartedly resume the age-appropriate developmental tasks and activities that were interrupted by the loss; and successfully cope with the painful memories associated with the loss that are likely to resurface at points of developmental transition or on specific anniversaries, such as the date of the person's death.

Just as the adopted child faces the question "How could they give me up?" and the child of divorce the question "Why did my father (or mother) leave me?", the child who has lost a parent to death must deal with how and why the parent died and what the parent's presence may have been like had it continued over time. Children's efforts to remain connected to the deceased parent include locating the deceased (for example, "in heaven"), experiencing the deceased (such as believing the parent is watching them), reaching out to the deceased (visiting the cemetery and "speaking" to the person), having waking memories of the deceased, and cherishing physical objects linked to the deceased (Silverman et al., 1992).

Children's Understanding of Death

Between ages five and seven, when the transition from preoperational to concrete operational modes of thinking occurs (see Chapter 8), most children come to understand that death is an irreversible, nonfunctional, and universal state: that once a living thing dies, it cannot be made alive again; that all life-defining functions cease at death; and that all living things eventually die. In contrast, younger children think death is reversible under some circumstances, attribute various life-defining functions to dead things, and think that certain individuals (often including themselves) will not die (Slaughter, 2005; Speece & Brent, 1984).

Developmental Impact

The developmental impact of death experienced during childhood depends on a number of factors, including the significance of the person to the child, the nature of the death and the conditions surrounding it, the child's strengths and vulnerabilities at the time of the loss, the amount of support available to the child to successfully grieve the loss, the amount of material and psychological disruption in the child's family as a result of the loss, and the quality of the child's relationships with other survivors. When children understand the biological basis of death, they have less fear and anxiety about death (Slaughter & Griffiths, 2007). Studies of college students and older adults who experienced the death of a parent during childhood have found that being able to talk freely with the surviving parent about the circumstances of the death, express sorrow about the death, or ask questions about the deceased parent helped to protect them from the onslaught of depression in adulthood. Greater involvement in activities such as attending funeral-related events, keeping mementos of the dead parent, openly expressing anger about the death to someone else, hearing stories about the deceased parent, seeing pictures in the home of the dead parent, and visiting the grave decreased the risk of subsequent depression (Saler & Skolnick, 1992).

Helping Children with Bereavement

The work of Kelly Lohnes and Neil Kalter (1994) is an excellent example of preventive intervention with groups of parentally bereaved elementary school-age children. Groups of five to seven children met for twelve weeks of one-hour sessions designed to achieve the following: (1) normalize children's reactions to and experiences of the death of a parent, (2) clarify confusing and frightening death-related issues, (3) provide a safe place for children to experience and rework emotionally painful aspects of the death and the stresses of living in a single-parent household, (4) help children develop coping strategies for particularly troubling feelings and family and peer dynamics, (5) help children maintain an emotional connection (attachment) to the deceased parent, and (6) share the children's concerns about parental death and its aftermath with surviving parents (and stepparents) through newsletters.

Group activities included bereavement stories, drawings, role playing, and discussion to help children express and understand their feelings and experiences related to loss and bereavement. Some of the thoughts, feelings, and experiences of these children, which in other contexts might have raised concerns about severe disturbance, were in fact common for parentally bereaved children who were otherwise developmentally normal. For example, children typically reported hallucinations of their dead parent, believed the parent would return, and wished to be "dead" to be reunited with their parent. If ignored or misunderstood by adults, such fantasies, distortions, and symptoms may contribute to psychological disorder. Knowledge that such behaviors are normal for such children, however, can enable mental health professionals, surviving parents, school personnel, pediatricians, and other concerned individuals to more effectively

> **What Do You Think?**
>
> Based on your own experiences with death during your middle childhood, how well does the description of the mourning process fit with what you remember? How are the challenges of dealing with loss due to death similar to the challenges of dealing with the losses due to divorce discussed earlier in this chapter?

help these children mourn their loss and minimize negative developmental effects such as health problems, decline in school performance, and emotional problems (Lohnes & Kalter, 1994).

A similar program, the Family Bereavement Program (FBP), has been associated with reduced risk for problematic grief—having intrusive negative thoughts about a loved one's death or having impaired ability to function normally. This program focuses on improving the relationship between the child and caregiver by helping the parent (cognitive behavioral techniques are taught to caregivers to help with their own bereavement), the child (providing coping techniques and more realistic perceptions of their experiences, providing opportunities to discuss feelings), and the relationship between the two (teaching positive parenting skills, communication skills, and strategies to reduce child stress) (Ayers et al., 2013). In a study comparing those who went through the FBP to a control group, the FBP group showed significantly fewer markers of problematic grief up to six years later (Sandler et al., 2010).

Looking Back/Looking Forward

In a variety of ways, middle childhood is the time when a child becomes a person in a more adult sense than ever before. Although relationships with peers, teachers, and others outside the family play an increasingly important role, the family and the relationships it provides are still central to a child's development. Let us now briefly review how the changing contributions of family to development illustrate our four lifespan development themes.

- **Continuity Within Change**—In many ways, the family of middle childhood is a continuation of the family a child experienced during early childhood and infancy. For the majority of children, the cast of characters is much the same, although additional siblings may have been added, and the basic relationships, assumptions, and expectations that constitute the family's culture are still recognizable. The parent-child relationships of middle childhood are fairly continuous with those of early childhood, and are predictive of adolescence and early adulthood. On the other hand, significant changes in the family and its developmental role also come about. In middle childhood, families must change to adapt to the expanding worlds of school, neighborhood, and peers in their children's lives. The micro-management that characterized the toddler and preschool years gives way to more arm's-length oversight and more active collaboration between parent and child in maintaining and monitoring activities. For some families, relocation, divorce, or remarriage may alter established patterns that significantly influence developmental trajectories in the short and longer run.

- **Lifelong Growth**—The developmental changes and growth experienced by the individuals who constitute a family contribute to and are influenced by developmental changes in the family unit itself. The physical, cognitive, and psychosocial growth that school-age children experience is not independent of the developmental changes taking place in the young and later middle-aged adults who are their parents and in younger and/or older siblings. The family and its culture, values, and material and emotional support will continue to be a presence through preadolescence, adolescence, early adulthood, and beyond.

- **Changing Meanings and Vantage Points**—Talk with a kindergartner, a third-grader, and a fifth-grader about their families and the changing meanings that come with their changing vantage points will most likely be obvious. By fifth grade, the self-knowledge, intellectual and physical mastery, and skills at forming and maintaining relationships with peers and adults contribute to more complex and sophisticated views of family. The greatly expanded knowledge of one's own family and of the families of friends and neighbors that accompanies middle childhood and early adolescence allows children to more fully assess and understand their parents, siblings, aunts, uncles, and cousins in new ways. The profound physical, cognitive, and psychosocial changes that occur in adolescence contribute to identity consolidation and to an accelerated process of separation and individuation that significantly alters relationships between a teenager and his or her family and the meaning of *family* to each member. This process continues during early adulthood, when most individuals leave home and eventually create new families, developments that lead once again to altered vantage points and changing meanings, During the adult years that follow, the developmental meanings of *family* and the vantage points from which it is viewed continue to change as we parent our own children, our aging parents, and our grandchildren.

- **Developmental Diversity**—Although we can discern many similarities in families and their developmental functions, families are quite diverse, varying with SES, religious and cultural traditions, and—most important—the unique personalities and developmental trajectories of the members that comprise them. Families differ in the challenges and adversities they face; the kind of work family members do; how they work together; and how they resolve disputes, celebrate joys, cope with misfortune, raise children, view the world, and so on. Thus, a family that has recently emigrated in search of better opportunities will likely face the challenges and adversities of newcomers with few economic resources, limited social support, and the need to learn a new language, cultural skills, and traditions while maintaining the integrity of their own. They may also experience discrimination if their culture is one that faces prejudice or if they have arrived at a time when newcomers in general are viewed as threatening. The many different cultural groups that have immigrated to this country have contributed greatly to the diversity of families and the developmental opportunities they provide.

  Another important source of developmental diversity lies in the uniqueness of each family. Because no two family members can have exactly the same vantage point or experience their family in exactly the same way, considerable diversity exists in the relationships between children and their families and in how a given family affects a given child. The richness and variety of developmental opportunities a particular family provides for a particular school-age child will depend in part on where that family and immediate and extended family members are in their own individual and collective developmental trajectories.

Chapter Summary

- **What major psychosocial challenges do children face during middle childhood?** During the school years, children face challenges concerning the development of an identity or a sense of self, achievement, family relationships, peer relationships, and school.
- **What important changes occur in a child's sense of self during middle childhood?** During middle childhood, children develop a sense of self, acquire a belief in self-constancy and in relatively permanent psychological traits, and learn to distinguish their thoughts and feelings from those of others.

- **What is *achievement motivation*, and what forms does it take?** According to some psychodynamic theorists, schoolchildren repress their earlier romantic attachments to their parents and focus instead on developing a sense of industry and achievement. During middle childhood, children shift their achievement orientation from an exclusive focus on learning, or a task orientation, to a performance orientation that includes others' responses to their achievements.

- **How have changes in the nature of the family, such as increases in the proportion of single-parent and dual-wage-earner families, affected children's psychosocial development?** Most mothers now work at least part time, and their employment generally seems to have no negative effects on their children. Nevertheless, maternal employment influences the division of household labor and children's attitudes about gender roles. When parents are unemployed, both they and their families experience significant stress. Providing good after-school supervision is a challenge for working parents. For children in unsupportive environments, formal after-school programs offer considerable benefits. Schoolchildren often find emotional support from adults other than parents, as well as from siblings, friends, pets, and hobbies.

  Divorce has become more common in North American families and usually creates stress for all family members, although girls and boys react differently to divorce. Blended families, which result from remarriage, pose considerable challenges; however, younger children form attachments with stepparents more easily than adolescents do.

- **How do peers contribute to development during middle childhood?** Piaget believes that peers help children to overcome their egocentrism by challenging them to deal with perspectives other than their own. According to Sullivan, peers help children to develop democratic ways of interacting and also offer the first opportunities to form close or intimate relationships with others outside the family. Early in the school years, a friend is someone with whom a child shares activities and toys, but later in this period, a friend becomes someone whom the child can count on and with whom she or he can share intimacies.

  In general, peers seem to serve unique functions by creating voluntary relationships of equality among children. Groups of peers vary in membership and behavior in terms of age, gender, and racial or ethnic group. Peer groups tend to segregate themselves by both gender and race. Popular children possess a number of socially desirable qualities, including well-developed social skills and confidence in themselves, Unpopular children exhibit less desirable qualities, such as aggression, selfishness, and bossiness. Peers exert pressure to conform on individual children, and this pressure can have either positive or negative effects. Children are influenced by their school's culture. This influence is more likely to be positive if the school's culture and the child's familial culture are compatible. The environment a teacher creates and his or her expectations of students shape children's school experiences and can contribute to greater student learning and positive peer involvement.

- **How do children deal with death, loss, and grieving during the school years?** Between ages five and seven, most children come to understand that death is an irreversible, nonfunctional, and universal state: that once a living thing dies, it cannot be made alive again; that all life-defining functions cease at death; and that all living things eventually die. Prevention groups help parentally bereaved children normalize their reactions to and experiences of the death, clarify confusing and frightening death-related issues, safely deal with emotionally painful aspects of the death and stresses of living in a single-parent household, cope with troubling feelings and family and peer dynamics, maintain an emotional connection (attachment) to the deceased parent, and help make surviving parents (and grandparents) aware of their children's concerns.

Key Terms

achievement motivation (p. 299)
blended family (p. 308)
industry versus inferiority (p. 298)
juvenile period (p. 313)

latency (p. 298)
learning orientation (p. 299)
peers (p. 294)
perceived popularity (p. 318)

performance orientation (p. 299)
self-constancy (p. 296)
sense of self (p. 295)
sociometric popularity (p. 318)

Adolescence

PART 5

Source: Syda Productions/Shutterstock.com.

Chapter 10
Physical and Cognitive Development in Adolescence

Chapter 11
Psychosocial Development in Adolescence

The adolescent years are a time of change, challenge, conflict, and confusion for everyone. We must come to terms with changes in our bodies as they suddenly grow taller and mature sexually. We must learn to negotiate the conflicts that arise when establishing a more equitable relationship with parents. And we are faced with the natural challenges that follow when thinking about leaving home someday, even if not immediately. Achieving independence becomes a driving issue during this developmental period, though one that will take years to resolve.

How difficult these challenges turn out to be depends on a variety of circumstances. For some teens, the timing of puberty can make adolescence especially hard—or easy. For others, newly forming abilities to think about life's larger issues can make life seem suddenly confusing, though at the same time full of exciting future possibilities. For many young people, dating or even just talking to the opposite sex becomes both intriguing and frustrating as they overcome childhood habits of relating only to members of their own sex. Despite these unique experiences and the myths about the troubling teen years, for most individuals, on average, adolescence is no more or less stressful than other periods of development across the lifespan.

Physical and Cognitive Development in Adolescence

CHAPTER 10

Source: PressMaster/Shutterstock.com.

Chapter Outline

PHYSICAL DEVELOPMENT
Growth in Height and Weight
Puberty
Health in Adolescence
COGNITIVE DEVELOPMENT
Beyond Concrete Operational Thinking
Moral Development: Beliefs about Justice and Care
Information-Processing Features of Adolescent Thought
The Influence of School

Focusing Questions

- What is meant by *adolescence,* and what changes in society contributed to its gaining recognition as a developmental stage?
- What changes in height, weight, and appearance can be expected during adolescence, and how do they differ for girls and boys?
- What are the effects of early, "on-time," and late development during puberty, and how do the effects differ for girls and boys?
- What major health problems do adolescents face, and in what ways are adolescents more at risk than other age groups?
- What has recent research in neuroscience discovered about brain development during adolescence?
- To what extent are adolescents capable of abstract reasoning?
- How does cognitive development affect adolescents' knowledge and beliefs about their identities and about morality?
- How do adolescents show improved information processing in everyday activities?
- What cognitive and social effects do school and work have on adolescent development?

Dillon is fourteen. Beginning last summer, he has started looking and acting different than before. He has grown nearly two inches in the last six months, a fact that his mother comments on with pride, but also with a note of dismay when his clothing no longer fits. Sometimes, Dillon would prefer that no one notice the changes. Just a year or two ago, he appeared well coordinated and athletic in school sports. Now he feels clumsy, trips over himself, and bumps into things. Even his "normal" voice has abandoned him. Sometimes it has that familiar sound; then suddenly, it will have the deep resonance of his father's voice. Worst of all for Dillion is when, unexpectedly and at the most embarrassing moments, his voice cracks and breaks into awkward high-pitched expressions.

Yet physically, Dillon feels very optimistic. So far, he has experienced no major illnesses, accidents, or violence; in fact, he secretly feels invulnerable to these mishaps, as if they could happen only to others, not to him. Feeling physically invulnerable allows him to be careless about his body in small but significant ways. He sometimes eats more "junk food" than he should, fails to brush his teeth, or goes a few days without enough sleep. Sometimes, especially when his parents aren't aware of it, he performs reckless stunts on his bike or considers joining his friends in their casual experimentation with smoking or drinking. At times, he consciously rides in a car without wearing a seat belt, not realizing that driving is statistically the most dangerous current activity in his life. Eventually, he may pay a price for these behaviors, but for now, he has other things on his mind.

adolescence The stage of development between childhood and adulthood, around ages ten to twenty-two.

Dillon is experiencing one version of **adolescence**, the period of development from about age twelve to age twenty that leads from childhood to emerging adulthood. As you might imagine, Dillon's is not the only possible experience of adolescence; in this chapter and the next, we will catch glimpses of other, very different experiences, as well as look at key programs of research meant to describe adolescence in general terms. As we will see, adolescence is a paradoxical time when young girls and boys sometimes resemble children, while at other times, they resemble young women and men. For any teenager, the particular mix of qualities and behaviors depends on the teenager's age and on the unique roles and responsibilities that he or she encounters along the way.

Compared to adolescent roles and responsibilities in many traditional cultures around the world, those in modern industrial societies are relatively unpredictable, and young people often feel ill prepared to meet them as a result. Most male teenage Australian aborigines, for example, go on a yearlong walkabout through the desert, carrying only a few simple weapons for protection; their chances of survival, however, are high due in large part to much of their childhood being spent developing the skills that will help them meet the challenges in this rite of passage. Most adolescent girls in the hunting-and-gathering society of the Inuit of Alaska and northern Canada have a good idea of what it takes to be an adult woman: they have already witnessed and perhaps assisted in the bearing of and caring for children, as well as gathering and preparing food. But because of technology, urbanization, and other social changes, teenagers in many developed countries often have little idea of what kind of work they will do as adults, what kind of family they will live in, or even where they will live.

In fact, some psychologists have proposed that adolescence be defined primarily as a time of transitions (Blakemore & Mills, 2014). Friendships for teenagers, for example, share qualities with friendships in childhood (friends are not yet a primary source of advice and support on the most important questions of life), but also some qualities with friendships in adulthood (friends *are* a source of support about many matters, such as clothing styles and assessments of mutual acquaintances). Thinking skills are in some ways childlike (the limits of thinking and reasoning are not yet noticed) and in other ways adultlike (much thinking can now be abstract). Physically, adolescents can sometimes look like children and sometimes like adults, and sometimes like a cross between the two; for confirmation, simply attend a social event at any junior high school.

Because viewing adolescence as a transition highlights the place of this period in the human lifespan as a whole, we will often use it to frame the discussion in this chapter. But sometimes we will also use two other widely held views of adolescence. One, as described by G. Stanley Hall, sees adolescence as a time of "storm and stress," a period when major physical, intellectual, and emotional changes create tremendous distress and crisis within the individual and conflict between the person and society. As you may recall, Sigmund Freud believed development is full of conflict, especially in adolescence. Erik Erikson and others have suggested that a lack of stable and predictable role expectations due to rapid changes in society may make the transition from childhood to adulthood more difficult (Erikson, 1963, 1968; Elkind, 1994).

Current research, however, suggests that adolescence is not intrinsically a time of severe "storm and stress" in personality development or in relationships with parents. Most adolescents in the United States adapt to the changes in themselves quite well and adjust to the changing demands and expectations of parents and society in a relatively smooth and peaceful way (Arnett, 1999). The same appears to be generally true in a number of other cultures, both Western and non-Western, where the majority of teenagers have been found to have positive self-images and good emotional adjustment (Hurrelmann, 1994; Seiffge-Krenke et al., 2012).

Though adolescence is not an unusually problematic period for most youngsters, in the United States and Great Britain the onset of adolescence is associated with more frequent negative feelings among many adolescents and increased rates of behavioral and psychological problems for some (Brooks-Gunn & Warren, 1989; Hamburg, 1994; Larson & Ham, 1993; Oldehinkel, Verhulst, & Ormel, 2011). In certain ethnic groups, for example, between 15 and 20 percent of adolescents in the United States drop out of school before completing high school; adolescents have the highest arrest rate of any age group; and a large number of adolescents use alcohol and drugs on a regular basis (Eccles et al., 1993; Johnston et al., 2012). How negative or positive the changes associated with adolescence are likely to be will depend on the degree of fit between adolescents' developing needs and the opportunities offered them by their social environments, school and home being two of the most important. Furthermore, the increased stress some adolescents experience may be due not simply to the external environment but also to developmental changes in adolescents' subjective construction of their environments (Larson & Ham, 1993).

We discuss these and other social aspects of adolescence in detail in this chapter and the next. First, though, let's look more closely at the physical changes of adolescence and their effects on development.

PHYSICAL DEVELOPMENT

Growth in Height and Weight

Although nearly everyone—including Dillon at the start of this chapter—experiences a rapid **growth spurt** during adolescence, there is much irregularity in the pattern and pace of growth, and significant variability in its timing. The change in height is particularly striking, as Figure 10.1 shows. The maximum rate of growth occurs around age eleven or twelve for girls and about two years later for boys. In those years, many girls grow three inches in a single year, and many boys grow more than four inches, ultimately achieving average heights of approximately sixty-four inches for females and sixty-nine inches for males (Merenstein et al., 1997). The reason for males' greater average height is that boys start their growth spurt two years later than girls do and thus undergo two additional years of childhood growing. The average girl is around fifty-four or fifty-five inches tall when she begins her growth spurt, whereas the average boy is fifty-nine or sixty inches tall when he begins his. Because both boys and girls add around nine or ten inches during adolescence and grow relatively little afterward, women end up being shorter than men on average.

Weight also increases during adolescence, as a result of both overall growth and the adolescent growth spurt in particular. But weight is more strongly influenced than height by diet, exercise, and general lifestyle, and therefore changes in weight are less predictable from past size and growth patterns. What *is* relatively predictable, however, is the impact of diet, exercise, and lifestyle on a young person's future: more calories and less exercise contribute to heavier weight as an adult. Unfortunately, teenagers' social habits

growth spurt A rapid change in height and weight that occurs in puberty and is preceded and followed by years of comparatively little increase.

> **What Do You Think?**
>
> In what ways has the "discovery" of adolescence as a developmental stage been helpful for teenagers and their families? In what ways has it been a problem? How would you describe your personal experience with adolescence?

often contribute to the problem because "junk food" and sedentary activities (like playing video games or surfing social media) are both inexpensive and easily available, not to mention socially preferred, or "in."

These changes in weight tend to affect girls more than boys because of society's gender-role expectations. In general, girls are expected to look slender, while at the same time a bit curvaceous. Yet girls, not boys, are the ones who experience the greatest gains in body fat as a part of the adolescent growth spurt. During this period, total body fat for boys declines from an average of 18 or 19 percent to 11 percent of body weight, whereas for girls it increases from about 21 percent to around 26 or 27 percent (Sinclair, 1990). The average weight gain during the growth spurt is about thirty-eight pounds for girls and forty-two pounds for boys. These pounds are distributed differently among individuals, of course, but in general, girls end up with more fat tissue than boys at the end of adolescence, a sex difference that continues into adulthood.

Whether male or female, most teenagers (and adults!) do not end up with the height, weight, or other physical characteristics that match either society's ideals or their own. Teenage boys may worry about not looking muscular or tall enough. But because of social pressures to "look good," girls will worry even more: at some time or other, most may feel they are too heavy, and many may worry about being too tall as well. The "Focusing On" feature later in the chapter describes how such concerns contribute to eating disorders in some young athletes; later in this chapter, we will discuss how chronic worries about physical appearance affect many adolescent girls and adult women.

FIGURE 10.1
Physical Development During Adolescence

Puberty involves a number of specific changes in both boys and girls, as this graph shows. One of the most obvious changes—the "growth spurt" or rate of increase in height—occurs significantly sooner in girls than in boys. But as with trends in final adult stature, many individual exceptions exist.

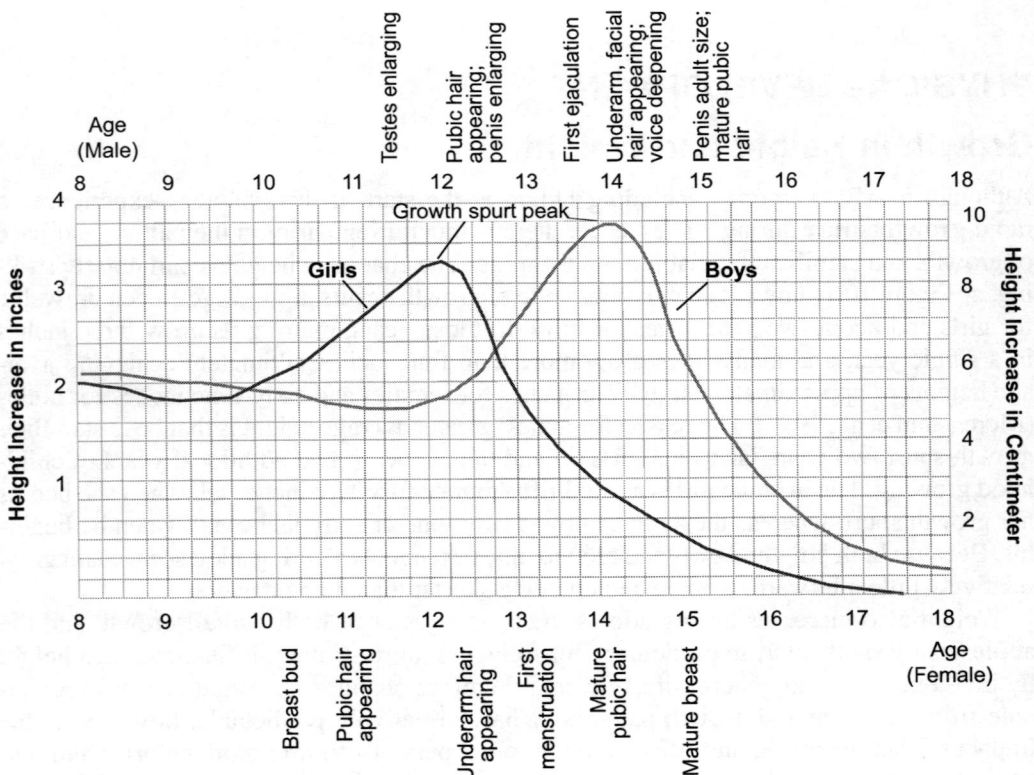

> **What Do You Think?**
>
> What pattern (timing, rate) did changes in your own height and weight follow during adolescence? What do you remember thinking and feeling about those changes?

Puberty

Puberty is a set of physical changes that marks the completion of sexual development, or reproductive maturity. The changes that contribute directly to making sexual reproduction possible are called **primary sex characteristics**. Other changes, which are simply correlated or associated with the primary changes, are called **secondary sex characteristics**.

puberty The period of early adolescence characterized by the development of full physical and sexual maturity.

primary sex characteristics Characteristics that make sexual reproduction possible. For females, consist of the vagina, uterus, fallopian tubes, and ovaries; for males, consist of the penis, scrotum, testes, prostate gland, and seminal vesicles.

The Development of Primary Sex Characteristics

For boys, the most basic sign of sexual maturation is rapid growth of the penis and scrotum (the sack of skin underneath the penis that contains the testicles), which begins at around age twelve and continues for about five years for the penis and seven years for the scrotum (Kagan, 1998). During this time, the penis typically doubles or triples in length, prompting the almost inevitable locker room comparisons as boys become increasingly aware of the physical changes in themselves and their friends. Although penis size has almost nothing to do with eventual success at overall sexual functioning, for adolescent boys it sometimes seems to be an all-important sign of their new status as men (Malina, 1990; Merenstein et al., 1997).

secondary sex characteristics Sex characteristics other than the sex organs, such as extra layers of fat and pubic hair.

During adolescence, enough live sperm are produced in the testes to make reproduction a real possibility for the first time. Sometime around age twelve, boys are likely to experience their first ejaculation of *semen,* a sticky fluid produced by the prostate gland, which is located near the penis just inside the body cavity. Semen carries the sperm to the penis and provides it with a medium in which to live after ejaculation. Most boys have their first ejaculation during masturbation; as *nocturnal emissions,* or "wet dreams," during sleep; or, less frequently, as emissions that occur spontaneously upon waking. Most males report experiencing nocturnal emissions about one or two years before puberty and the accompanying dreams are frequently, but not always, erotic in nature. The sexual changes just discussed and the unexpected erections and uncomfortable sexual fantasies and sensations that boys sometimes experience are common sources of embarrassment. Less frequently, they are a source of more serious discomfort and conflict.

For girls, the appearance of the first menstrual period, called **menarche**, signals sexual maturity. In most societies, menarche also symbolizes the shift from girlhood to womanhood, and typically occurs after the peak of the girls' growth spurt. Even though the girls may be experiencing their first periods, it does not necessarily mean that they are fertile. From the occurrence of the girls' first periods, their menstrual cycles may take between twelve and eighteen months to achieve regularity in terms of predictable timing and consistency with respect to the release of ova from the ovaries (Christensen et al., 2010). Menarche occurs rather late in a girl's sexual maturation and is preceded by a number of other changes, including enlargement of the breasts, the appearance of pubic hair, and broadening of the hips and shoulders. As the growth spurt peaks, the uterus, vagina, labia, and clitoris continue to develop, as do the ovaries.

menarche The first menstrual period.

The Development of Secondary Sex Characteristics

Both boys and girls experience a number of physical changes that create secondary sex characteristics, notably in their breasts, body hair, and voices. These changes do not directly contribute to their physical ability to reproduce, but they do make the two sexes look more adultlike and more stereotypically masculine or feminine.

Breasts

Girls first develop breast "buds," or slightly raised nipples, at the beginning of puberty. During the following several years, the nipples grow darker, the areolas (the pigmented areas surrounding the nipples) increase in size, and the breasts continue to grow until they reach their full size. Given the attention our culture devotes to breasts, it is not surprising that breast development is a potential source of concern for many adolescent girls. Breasts that are "too big," "too small," different sizes, or the "wrong" shape may cause embarrassment, lower self-esteem, and depressive symptoms (Yuan, 2012), and in many cases, girls experience outright harassment due to these physical developments.

Boys, too, undergo a small amount of breast development, and their areolas become larger and darker much as they do in girls. A few boys experience enough tissue growth to cause them some embarrassment, but these "breasts" usually return to typical male size in a year or two.

Body Hair

When their genital development is relatively advanced, both boys and girls acquire more body hair, although boys generally grow more of it than girls do. The first growth is simply a fine fuzz around the genitals called *pubic hair*, which then darkens and becomes coarser. At the same time, underarm or *axillary hair* begins to appear which eventually becomes dark and coarse as well (Archibald, Graber, & Brooks-Gunn, 2006).

Voice

In both sexes, the voice deepens near the end of puberty and becomes richer in overtones so that it sounds less like a flute or whistle and more like a violin or clarinet. These changes make the adolescent's voice sound more truly adult, but the fluctuations in voice qualities that some adolescents experience can be a cause of considerable (although usually temporary) embarrassment.

Hormonal Changes: Physical and Social Consequences

For both boys and girls, the onset of puberty brings increases in the levels of all sex hormones in the blood, but the pattern by which it does so differs for each sex. **Testosterone** (also called *male sex hormone*), a particular type of androgen, and **estrogen** (*or female sex hormone*) are two of the most important sex hormones. Although both hormones are present in males and females, the high concentration of testosterone in boys stimulates the growth of the penis and related male reproductive organs, and the high concentration of estrogen in girls stimulates the growth of the ovaries and vagina. Androgens are thought to influence the strength of the sex drive in both sexes.

Hormones affect more than just sexual characteristics. For example, they are responsible for the typical differences between girls' and boys' overall body builds. In general, the sex that has shorter bones and more rounded curves (female) also has higher estrogen levels, and the sex that has longer bones and larger muscles (male) also has higher levels of testosterone (Cheek, 1974; Tanner, 1990).

Testosterone stimulates muscle and bone growth in both sexes. Throughout most of childhood, boys and girls are about equally muscular. Prior to adolescence boys and girls have roughly the same number and sizes of muscle fibers, and they can exert about the same amount of strength with their muscles. Although individual children vary around the averages, as groups, the two sexes differ very little until the onset of puberty (Malina, 1990; Lundgren et al., 2011).

Puberty changes this gender equality to some extent. On average, boys become more muscular than the average girl does, even though postpubescent girls are more muscular than their childhood selves. From early childhood to adolescence, boys experience close to a fourteenfold increase in the size of the largest muscles in their bodies (for example, in their thighs), but girls experience only a ten-fold increase (Froberg & Lammert, 1996; Malina, 1990). Because these changes are only averages, it is not unusual for many adolescent girls in middle school and high school to actually be stronger than some of their male classmates.

Individual differences in physical development result in part from differences in life experiences that either promote or interfere with muscular growth. And some of the differences in experiences are linked to society's gender-role expectations. Teenage boys more often receive encouragement or feel pressure to participate in sports and to take on jobs and responsibilities that involve physical work (Coakley, 1996). The higher level of activity and physical exertion leads to greater bone and muscle mass as boys mature and

---

testosterone A sex hormone, sometimes called the *male sex hormone* because its high concentration in boys stimulates growth of the penis and related male reproductive organs.

estrogen A sex hormone, sometimes called the *female sex hormone* because its high concentration in girls stimulates the growth of the ovaries and vagina during puberty.

become adults. In the decades since the passage of Title IX—an act that eliminated sex discrimination in publicly funded educational and co-curricular activities—young girls have also received greater encouragement and support for being physically active and for participating in organized sports, resulting in stronger muscle development than had been seen in prior generations of adolescent girls. The emphasis on muscle development for girls as a whole is less intense than what is felt by their male peers.

In spite of these social effects, many of the physical differences between the sexes result from genetically programmed development. Genetically triggered changes in estrogen levels during adolescence, for example, lead to increases in the fat deposited under the skin, as well as to final maturation of b ones. The higher concentration of estrogen in girls, combined with the higher concentration of testosterone in boys mentioned earlier, means that girls end up with more fat tissue than boys do as a proportion of their body weight, and boys end up with more muscle tissue than girls do. Hence, the tendency toward conventional sex differences in physical appearance: boys look more muscular and girls have more curves (Kagan, 1998)—though only as average trends.

Psychological Effects of Physical Growth in Adolescence

Given how rapid the physical changes of puberty are, it is not surprising that adolescents often are preoccupied—and dissatisfied—with how they look. When dissatisfaction occurs, it is most noticeable early in the adolescent years, but it is also common during the later teen years and well into adulthood (Blashill & Wilhelm, 2013; Connolly et al., 1996; Fox, 1997; Yuan, 2012). It would seem, then, that a milestone as important as puberty should affect individuals deeply, perhaps leading to long-term effects that last even into adulthood. Psychologists therefore have searched for predictable psychological effects of physical growth, both short term and long term; however, the results of this research have not been fully conclusive.

Timing of Puberty

Research exploring the social-emotional consequences related to when an adolescent begins and ends puberty accelerated in the 1980s. A series of longitudinal studies explored the impact of the timing of puberty on individuals' well-being (Livson & Peskin, 1981a, 1981b; Tobin-Richards et al., 1983). The studies tried to answer some very important questions: Was it better to experience puberty earlier than usual, or later, or "on time"? And did these timings have a different effect depending on whether you were a boy or a girl?—Teenage participants were followed for several years, and eventually even for several decades—they were especially helpful in determining the effects of timing. This research suggested intriguing trends in the effects of timing and gender, as summarized in Table 10.1. The trends themselves, however, also masked important individual differences in responses to puberty, which more recent research has highlighted.

Even among adolescents who are the same age, differences in physical maturity are common and can contribute to social advantages, challenges, or anxieties. And while there is great variability in the timing of puberty, there is an increased interest in physical appearance experienced by most adolescents, as revealed through the recent trend—explosion?—in taking, sending, and posting "selfies."
Source: Edyta Powlowska/Shutterstock.com.

TABLE 10.1 Trends in Adolescents' Reactions to the Onset of Puberty

For adolescents who begin puberty early, initial reactions among males tend to be positive and later reactions are negative, while the reverse is true for females. Late-maturing males first react negatively and later react positively. Late-maturing females first react positively, and later reactions are mixed. These trends, however, conceal variability among individuals.

Time of Onset	Time of Reaction	Typical Reactions of Males	Typical Reactions of Females
Early maturation	Initial/short term	Positive	Negative
	Later/long term	Mixed	Positive
Late maturation	Initial/short term	Negative	Positive
	Later/long term	Positive	Mixed

What did the original longitudinal research find? First, it suggested that *early-maturing boys* seemed to experience initial advantages as teenagers. They enjoyed a head start on muscle growth compared to their peers, a change that apparently stimulated peers, teachers, and others to treat them like adults sooner. The boys responded positively to this treatment and, through a sort of self-fulfilling prophecy, actually became more confident and mature in their behavior. By the same token, though, they were more conforming to adult standards than usual for adolescents and less open to the minor risk-taking characteristic of adolescents as a whole (Lightfoot, 1997). These differences continued into early adulthood: a decade after puberty, early-maturing men were still more responsible and self-controlled, but also more rigid in relating to peers. Most important, though, was a lowering of their self-esteem; as later-maturing boys caught up with them physically, the early-maturing boys received less attention and respect from others, and experienced a loss of self-esteem.

Late-maturing boys, on the other hand, face some very specific and paradoxical outcomes. Many still resembled children as late as age sixteen, and unfortunately, tended to be judged as children as a result. Teachers and parents rated these individuals as impulsive, immature, and lacking self-confidence. Their ratings may have been partly stereotypical based on how the boys looked, but also partly based on accurate observations. The late-maturing boys generally participated less in key social activities, such as sports and sports-focused social activities, and therefore had fewer opportunities to learn social skills in the same way as their early maturing peers. The good news, however, was that these boys tended to feel less pressure to become socially or sexually active. Perhaps as a result, they felt better about themselves as young adults than did the early maturers.

What about girls? *Early-maturing girls* did not experience early timing as an advantage as boys did. Their earlier physical development put them out of step with gender-role expectations for girls of the same age. Because they now looked older and more sexually mature, parents and teachers worried about their behavior, especially because they often received attention from older students at their school. In addition, because they were relatively short when they acquired normal female fat tissue and "curves," they tended to look plumper than average. Both changes tended to create stress for early-maturing girls. Yet the effect did not last into adulthood: at age thirty, the early maturers reported feeling *more* poised and self-directed than usual, perhaps *because* of experiencing and surviving social disapproval as teenagers.

Late-maturing girls experienced a complementary trend. As teenagers, they were rated by parents and teachers as more attractive and as better social leaders. In fact, the girls actually did become school leaders more often than usual. By age thirty, though, they reported feeling *less* poised than early maturers, and less sure of where their lives were heading.

> **What Do You Think?**
>
> Talk with one or two classmates about how the timing of their own maturation affected their adolescence. Did it fit any of the patterns described here? Or were they one of the people who created the variability also described here? On balance, what implications do you see for teachers and parents, given that puberty creates both pattern and diversity at the same time?

Nonnormative Effects of Puberty

Although the trends regarding the timing of puberty are intriguing, they also mask variability in teenagers' experiences. Newer research about the psychological impact of puberty has highlighted this fact, and has been more cautious in generalizing about both the short- and long-term effects of timing. In reviewing studies about this question, the psychologist Sucheta Connolly and her colleagues concluded that puberty has little lasting impact on adolescents, immediately or during emerging adulthood (Connolly et al., 1996). In the short term, physical changes are co-occurring with stresses in the family. As a result, parents and the young adolescent are conflicted about how to respond to the changes—as a welcome transition or as a source of ongoing worry. Yet, in the long run, during later adolescence or early adulthood, family relationships return to a quality characteristic of the prepubescent family dynamic, good or bad. Other social and emotional effects, such as changes in self-esteem or in peer relationships, are much more variable than similar, both in the short term and in the long term. As older adolescents move into adulthood, furthermore, the effects of puberty become even more obscure and harder to generalize about. For example, in a longitudinal study based on interviews of women from college age through midlife, the psychologist Ruthellen Josselson found that self-esteem and attitudes about self commonly changed markedly—either for good or for ill—regardless of what they were initially (Josselson, 1996).

Health in Adolescence

During adolescence, health concerns for both teens and their parents represent a "good news/bad news" paradox. In some ways, adolescents are among the healthiest of all people. They tend to have fewer colds and ear infections than young children or adults do (Fry, 1974). Compared to adults, they suffer fewer of the illnesses and physical damage associated with prolonged exposure to physical and emotional stress and with aging.

Nevertheless, there are a few select experiences that occur during adolescence where the health risks are greater than those for younger children and adults. Compared to either age group, teens are much more likely to be injured in motor vehicle accidents, misuse alcohol and other substances, experience unwanted pregnancy, as well as problems associated with inadequacies in their diet and health and mental health care (Balk & Corr, 1996).

These statistical realities have a number of effects. During adolescence, teenagers assume a sense of personal invulnerability. As a result, they often dismiss or discount risky behaviors in themselves or in the situations in which they find themselves. In a similar fashion, their view of death or potential disability is one of a distant phenomenon, not something that can happen to them. This contributes to a sense of insulation from danger, a manner of thinking that we will discuss in detail later in this chapter. Ironically, many teens then consider the possibility of an accident, drug abuse, or pregnancy as less risky than they really are. As adolescents grow into adulthood, furthermore, they discover that these same risk factors have created diversity among young adults: those young adults who have experienced them face very different lives than those who have not.

Causes of Death Among Adolescents

Although adolescents are less affected by some of the health problems that lead to death in younger children and adults, the death rate during adolescence is one of the highest

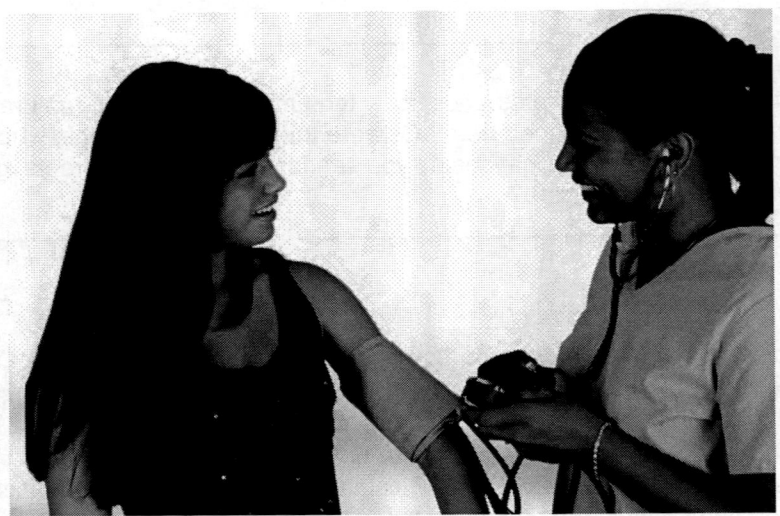

School-based health care programs that are responsive to the special needs and vulnerabilities of adolescents can make an important contribution to helping teenagers to take responsibility for their own health care. As teenagers get older, it may be less and less realistic to rely on parents to ensure that they get the medical attention that they need.
Source: Rob Marmion/Shutterstock.com.

for all age groups. Both the risky environments in which many teenagers live and the risk-taking behavior associated with adolescence undoubtedly contribute to this statistic (Lightfoot, 1996; Nappe & Nappe, 1996). Most causes of death among adolescents are preventable. The leading causes are motor vehicle accidents (more than fifteen thousand per year), homicide and other forms of intentional violence (more than six thousand per year), and self-inflicted harm or suicide (more than five thousand yearly) (Balk & Corr, 1996). More recently, the overall percentage of teen deaths has dropped to below 1 percent of all deaths that occur in the United States each year, to an average of 16,375 deaths per year from 1996 to 2006 (Minino, 2010). Nevertheless, the top-five causes remain constant, with unintentional accidents causing 48 percent of all deaths, over 70 percent of which are traffic accidents, followed by homicide (13 percent) and suicide (11 percent), and then deaths due to physical causes like cancer (6 percent) and heart disease (3 percent) (Minino, 2010).

Race, gender, and social-economic status (SES) also play a significant role in mortality rates for teens. For all adolescents, regardless of gender, non-Hispanic black teenagers are 37 percent more likely to die during adolescence than their Hispanic and non-Hispanic white peers (Minino, 2010). The mortality rate for males, however, a consistently greater for males at all ages than it is for adolescent females, significantly so as teenagers transition into emerging adulthood.

Male mortality rates are in large measure due to certain lifestyle choices and/or conditions in their communities that make them significantly more at risk than their female peers. Middle-SES males are likely to believe that risk taking and experimentation with cars and motorcycles, alcohol consumption, and drug use are signs of masculinity. Males from low-SES families and those from minority groups fare even worse. They are at still greater risk for accidental death and homicide because of dangers inherent in their inner-city environments. Survival in these neighborhoods often lead to the use and sale of drugs, participation in gangs, and exposure to various forms of physical violence, including the use of lethal weapons (Takanishi, 1993). The figures for young black men are alarmingly high due to disproportionately high rate of death by homicide in this group. A non-Hispanic black teen is two times more likely to die by a homicide than a Hispanic male, and fifteen times more likely than a non-Hispanic white male (Minino, 2010).

Health-Compromising Behaviors

Although adolescents are not prone to the infectious diseases of childhood, they often adopt habits that are damaging to their health. Poor diet, lack of sleep, use of alcohol or drugs, and unsafe sexual practices can all lead to a number of serious diseases. Infectious mononucleosis, hepatitis, and a variety of *sexually transmitted infections (STIs)* constitute major health risks during adolescence.

Sexually Transmitted Infections

Teenagers and young adults under twenty-five account for more than 50 percent of the 20 million STI cases reported annually. It is estimated that 25 percent of adolescents will become infected with an STI before graduating from high school (CDC—Division of STD Prevention, 2013; Moore et al., 1996). Adolescent females have the highest rates of gonorrhea, cytomegalovirus, chlamydia, and pelvic inflammatory disease of any age group. STIs can cause pelvic inflammatory disease, which places young women at risk for subsequent development of ectopic pregnancy and infertility (Shafer & Moscicki, 1991).

Risk factors for STIs include the increased acceptability of early sexual activity throughout our culture and inadequate use of contraceptives. The acceptability of early sexual activity in the United States is apparent when fifteen-year-old American adolescents are compared to their counterparts in other developed countries (including France, England, Russia, Canada, and Israel): The percentage of fifteen-year-olds in the United States who are sexually active is far higher (41 percent) than any of the other countries (whose rates range from 14 percent in Israel to 33 percent in Russia) (Nic Gabhainn et al., 2009). Another specific, significant risk factor is the age of first sexual intercourse. Later initiation of sexual intercourse is correlated with lower rates of STIs among adolescents (Kaestle et al., 2005). Early adolescents often lack the cognitive maturity to plan ahead, accurately appraise their risks, and make effective decisions—especially in emotionally charged situations. These characteristics result in inconsistent or ineffective contraceptive practices (Nelson & Neinstein, 2008). Additional data from the cross-cultural study of fifteen-year-olds just mentioned also revealed that rates of condom use among those same fifteen-year-olds was lowest among the American adolescents; just 68 percent of sexually active American fifteen-year-olds reported using a condom during their last intercourse, compared with 84 percent of the teen respondents from France (Nic Gabhainn et al., 2009).

The most common form of contraception used by adolescents in the United States is condoms; condoms are the contraceptive method of choice for approximately two-thirds of sexually active adolescents (American Academy of Pediatrics, 2007). While the pill may be more effective in reducing the chances for an unwanted pregnancy, condoms provide significant protection against STIs and HIV, whereas the pill provides none. However, as noted earlier, adolescents frequently do not make use of any form of contraception, putting them at risk for STIs and pregnancy. Inadequate health and sex education at home and in the schools must be held accountable. Comprehensive sex education, ideally provided *before* adolescents begin having sex, provides information about sex, data on effectiveness and how to use different forms of contraception, and how to talk about and refuse unwanted sexual activity. There is no evidence that comprehensive sex education encourages adolescents to engage in sex, a worry for many parents and educators (Kirby & Laris, 2009). Moreover, comprehensive sex education increases use of contraception, reduces unwanted pregnancies, and may delay adolescents' initiation of sex (Kohler, Manhart, & Lafferty, 2008; Stanger-Hall & Hall, 2011; Tortolero et al., 2010). Abstinence-only sex education, which is still quite common in many school districts, has been found to be ineffective: it does not delay initiation of sex, it actually decreases the likelihood that an adolescent will have safe sex, and it has been linked to higher rates of teen pregnancy (Stanger-Hall & Hall, 2011).

Drug Use

High rates of experimentation with drugs, alcohol, and tobacco are typical of adolescents. Since 1975, thousands of high school seniors across the United States have completed annual surveys about their drug use as part of a large, ongoing research program at the University of Michigan called "Monitoring the Future." (Eighth- and tenth-graders were included in this national survey starting in 1991.) These data have revealed several interesting trends in drug use over the past several decades, as depicted in Figure 10.2:

- Overall, rates of drug use among high school seniors has declined for almost all types of drugs;
- Alcohol—by far—remains the most frequently used drug;
- Rates of marijuana use have fluctuated over the years as a direct result of changing perceptions of its harm—as public concern about the harmful effects of marijuana use decrease, marijuana use increases;
- Unlike the trends for all other drugs in the survey, rates of marijuana use among high school seniors are currently rising (Johnston et al., 2014).

Drug use continues to be a problem for youth and young adults, and by extension, society at large. As shown in Figure 10.3, despite exposure to D.A.R.E. ("Drug Abuse Resistance Education") or other drug and alcohol education programs, as adolescents mature, they become increasingly likely to use alcohol and other drugs. Despite what appear to be disappointing results regarding educators' attempts to reduce the risks to adolescents that are posed by the use of drugs and alcohol, the overall decline in drug use and significant decreases in the use of specific drugs should offer some sense of optimism. When societal attitudes toward specific drugs change, so too do use of those drugs among adolescents. For example, the consumption of synthetic marijuana and the use of bath salts, both sold over-the-counter, showed steep drops in the 2013 Monitoring the Future survey data after news stories and drug resistance curricula highlighted the risks posed by their use (Johnston et al., 2014). Significant declines for use of synthetic marijuana and bath salts were seen at all three grade levels: down 3.5 percent for seniors, 1.3 percent for tenth-graders, and 0.4 percent among eighth-graders (Johnston et al., 2014). Rates for bath salts have shown a similar decline, even though their usage rates are low to begin with. Johnston (2014) and his team found that more teens are accurately perceiving the serious risks with synthetic drugs and are more disapproving of the drugs and even of their peers who use these substances.

Marijuana use seems to ebb and flow with the times for teens. But recent legislation to legalize marijuana in two states and to make medical marijuana available in twenty-one

FIGURE 10.2
Trends in Drug Use Among American High School Seniors

According to an annual survey, rates of drug use among high school seniors in the United States have been declining since the 1990s. However, marijuana use appears to be increasing among today's high school seniors.
Source: Johnston et al., 2014.

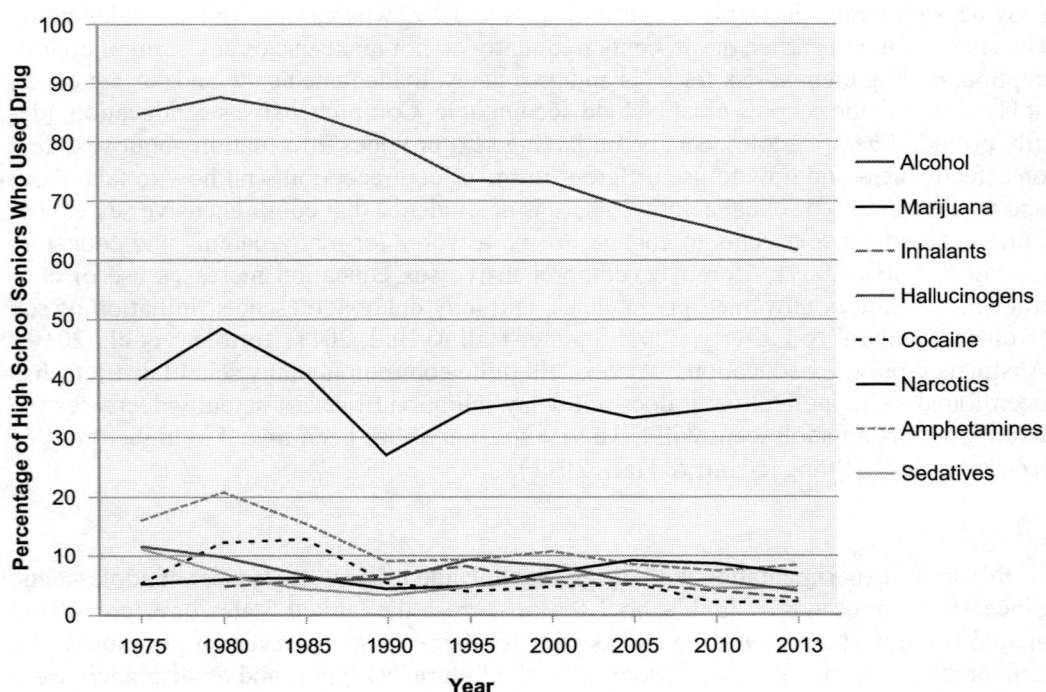

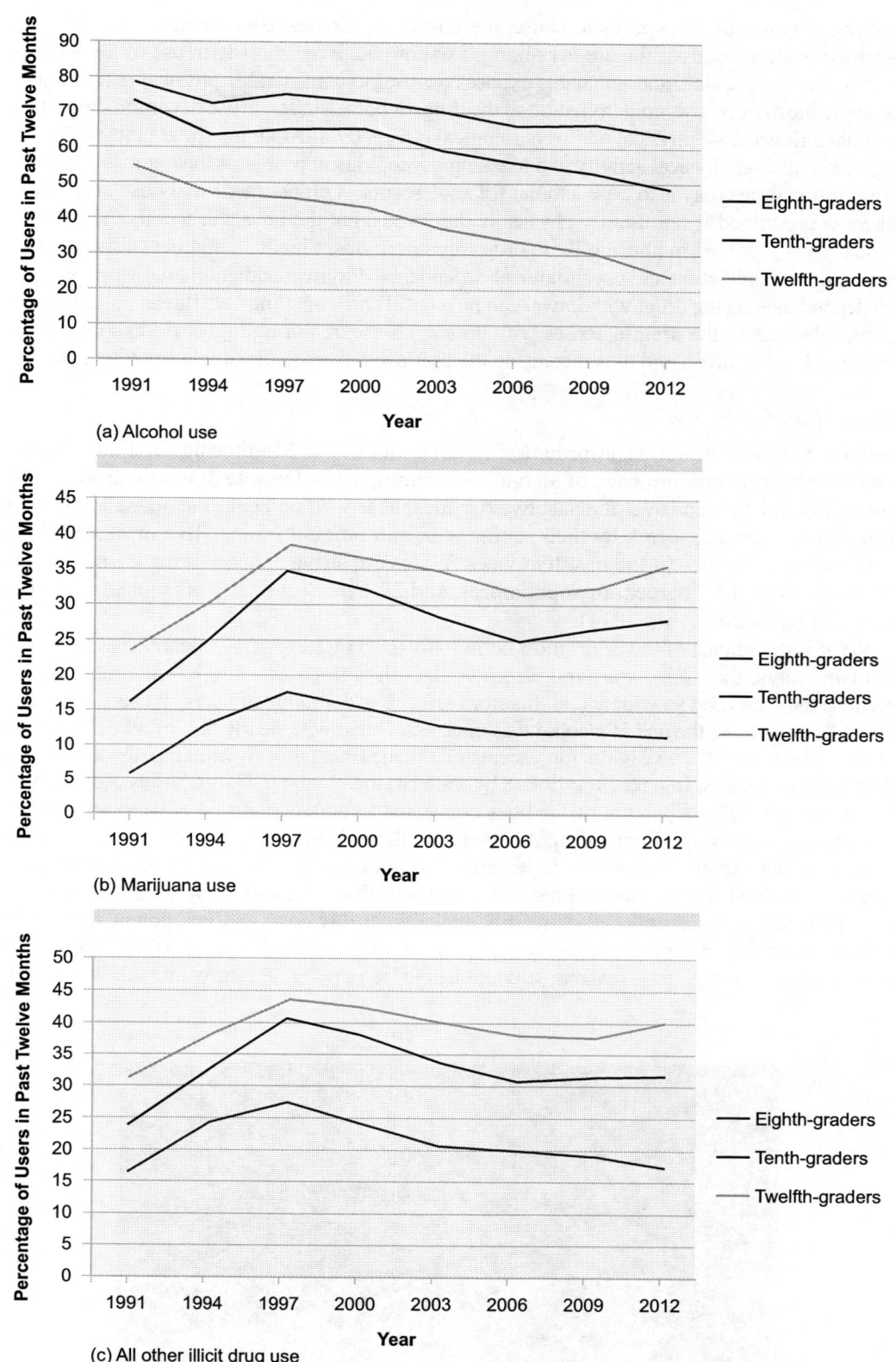

FIGURE 10.3
Rates of Selected Drug Use Among Eighth-, Tenth-, and Twelfth-Graders in the United States

Each of these graphs reveals a similar pattern of drug use among students in the eighth, tenth, and twelfth grades: the percentage of users increases as the grade level increases. Rates of (a) alcohol consumption, (b) marijuana use, and (c) the use of all other illicit drugs are highest among high school seniors, who report having greater access to drugs and alcohol and the financial resources to be able to buy them.
Source: Johnston et al., 2014.

other states has had a significant effect on the perceived risk and level of disapproval associated with using this substance. Legal marijuana appears to have reduced the perceived risks of using the drug and lowered one's disapproval of its use, while conversely increasing the availability of the drug to teens. In fact, Johnston et al. (2014) noted that just over a third of teens reported that in states where marijuana was legal, their source for the drug was a person who had a prescription for medical marijuana.

Chapter 10 Physical and Cognitive Development in Adolescence

When the use of drugs turns to abuse, the effects on personal development are extremely destructive, particularly if the use is prolonged or chronic. Even short-term use of illicit drugs such as heroin, cocaine, and inhalants exposes the user to considerable physical risk of injury or death due to overdose, contamination of the drug, or both. Moderate use of certain drugs may also have destructive physical and psychological effects by disrupting normal patterns of eating, sleeping, and physical activity and masking psychological problems that require attention. Prescription drugs may also pose a threat for adolescents. A proper medicinal dose of the drug taken as prescribed is not usually physically dangerous, but the physical, social, and psychological risks involved in abusing these drugs are enormous. Finally, a number of these drugs cause physical addiction and psychological dependence. Physical addiction involves a biological dependence on the drug; withdrawal can be painful and sometimes life threatening. In most cases, tolerance to the drug increases with prolonged use, requiring higher doses to maintain the same level of effect and thus increasing the user's exposure to the drug's negative effects.

Alcohol and Tobacco

Perhaps the most troubling information to come out of the Monitoring the Future study was the continued prominence of alcohol use among teens. Despite dramatic drops in the use of alcohol by teens over the past two decades, nearly 70 percent of teens will have had at least one alcoholic drink by their senior year, and binge-drinking (five or more drinks in a row, at least once in the past two weeks) rates are still a concern with 5.1 percent of eighth-graders, 13.7 percent of sophomores, and 22.1 percent of seniors engaging in this behavior (Johnston et al., 2014).

What is the impact of the drugs most commonly used by teenagers—alcohol and tobacco? In many ways, their effects are more serious than the effects of more exotic drugs simply because they are used so widely and therefore affect a wider range of users, abusers, and non-users. For example, the use of alcohol was once associated with nearly half of all deaths from motor vehicle crashes involving adolescents (Tillman, 1992). It now accounts for less than a third of these deaths. In a recent estimate by the FBI, the National Traffic Safety Administration, and the CDC, 68 percent of fatalities connected to underage drinking were for reasons other than motor vehicle accidents. Alcohol was directly implicated in 30 percent of teen homicides, 14 percent of suicides, 9 percent of alcohol poisonings, and 15 percent by other means (Copeland, 2013). Because alcohol is heavily advertised and socially valued as a sign of adulthood and independence, is readily available at low cost, and is a potent short-term reducer of anxiety, it continues to be very popular among adolescents, even as the lifetime use rates decline. For the same reasons, it continues to be popular among young adults as well.

Cigarette smoking makes some teenagers feel more grown up and more sociable and accepted by their friends. As a result, many teenagers smoke cigarettes in spite of the health risks.
Source: Elena Rostunova/Shutterstock.com.

We will discuss problems of substance abuse among adults in detail when we look at physical development in early adulthood in Chapter 12.

The use of tobacco products were at one time widely advertised as a sign of adulthood. Early adolescents were particularly susceptible to this "ready-made" symbol of maturity. Beginning in the 1970s, warning labels were required on every pack of cigarettes, and ads for cigarettes were banned from television and radio. Anti-smoking campaigns replaced the pro-smoking ads that permeated the airways. As a consequence, the use of smoking tobacco (in the past 30 days) has declined, especially over the past two decades. After peaking in the mid-1990s, use of cigarettes has fallen by 79 percent for eighth-graders and 70 percent for tenth-graders, and a less dramatic but significant drop of over 50 percent for high school seniors (Johnston, et. al., 2014). The rates for lifetime use, having smoked a cigarette at any time through high school, has also declined to 15, 26, and 38 percent, respectively, for eighth-, tenth-, and twelfth-graders in the same Monitoring The Future Study.

Three factors have contributed to these dramatic declines in the use of cigarettes. First, fewer and fewer young adolescents are even experimenting with smoking. Second, the strong anti-smoking campaigns have been successful in heightening the perceived risks inherent in smoking, and finally, teens are increasingly more likely to view smoking in a disapproving manner today than at any time in the past (Johnston et. al, 2014). For more adolescents, the idea of smoking appears to no longer be "cool," and eight out ten eighth-graders responded on the MTF Study for 2013 that they would rather date someone who did not smoke! Peer pressure appears to be having a positive effect on teens turning away from smoking. The results were not as dramatic for the use of smokeless tobacco. Additionally, between 4 and 14 percent of adolescents report having used e-cigarettes, which is an emerging concern, especially as many perceive e-cigarettes as less harmful than traditional cigarettes—a belief not necessarily backed by scientific evidence (Hildick-Smith et al., 2015; Raloff, 2015; Russell & Ludwig, 2015).

Patterns of both drinking and smoking are strongly influenced by the lifestyles of family members and peers and by the environments in which they live. Among family members, minimal, moderate, and heavy levels of drinking, smoking, and drug use, including legally prescribed medications, are strongly associated with very similar patterns of use among adolescents. Peer pressure is also thought to significantly influence which drugs a teenager uses, in what circumstances, and how much and how often, although some findings indicate that its contribution may be overestimated (O'Connell, Boat, & Warner, 2009; Bauman & Ennett, 1994).

Because most initial experiences with cigarettes, alcohol, and illicit drugs occur during the early teenage years, prevention efforts are now being directed at this age group. These efforts have focused on reducing exposure to drugs, altering the social environment, and changing the attitudes and behaviors of the drug user (or potential user). In general, however, drug prevention programs have not proven very effective. Those that show promise are peer programs and school-based prevention efforts involving life skills training designed to increase knowledge and build confidence and overall social competence in areas such as risk assessment, decision making, self-directed behavior change, capacity to cope with anxiety, and conflict resolution (Hamburg, 1997; Lynch & Bonnie, 1994). Another area showing promise are recent studies looking at parenting practices that encourage greater self-disclosure between parents and teens and increased levels of parental warmth. Improved communication within the family has a positive effect on delaying substance use by adolescents and in improving outcomes for adolescents already involved in substance abuse treatment (Bertrand et al., 2013).

Sleep

When Caia's parents go to bed at 10:00 p.m. each weekday, she goes into her room and finishes her homework for the day. She knows she should go to sleep because she has to be up at 6:00 a.m. to get ready for school, but she first wants to see the pictures that her friends have posted on Instagram and if anyone has favored any of her tweets. Before she knows it, it is 12:00 a.m., so Caia turns off the lights, but she's not very tired. She lays in bed for nearly forty-five minutes before she finally dozes off to sleep.

The average adolescent needs between 9 and 9.5 hours of sleep per night to feel well rested and function during the daytime hours (Mercer, Merrit, & Cowell, 1998). As you might suspect, most adolescents do not obtain nearly that much sleep—the average American teenager gets 7 to 7.5 hours of sleep per night (Mercer et al., 1998). So why such a wide discrepancy in the amount of sleep adolescents *need* and what they *get*?

Our sleep drive works like a gas tank - at night we fill up our sleep reserves, and we use those sleep reserves during the day. Part of the job of our circadian rhythm is to keep us awake at the end of the day when our sleep reserves are running low and to keep us asleep at night to completely fill up those reserves. During childhood, these two processes - sleep drive and circadian rhythm - work so that children feel sleepy relatively early in the evening. There is a curious change in the circadian rhythm that coincides with the beginning of puberty such that melatonin onset shifts to a later time, as does sleep onset (Carskadon, 1990; Carskadon, Acebo, & Jenni, 2004; Carskadon et al., 1998). Therefore, a child like Caia who, before puberty, was tired at 8:00 and would fall asleep at 8:30, now does not feel sleepy until much later in the night. In fact, if Caia went to bed when her parents did, she would likely just lay in bed for hours unable to fall asleep. To compound the problem of this biological shift, Caia is also exposing herself to light when looking at her computer and cell phone late in the evening which, as we have already learned, further delays melatonin release and subsequent sleep time (Burke et al., 2015; Chang et al., 2015; Orzech et al., 2016).

Changes in adolescent sleep are especially problematic because, though onset of sleep has a biological shift toward a later time, adolescents must still wake up early for school, which effectively truncates adolescents' sleep (Carskadon, 1990; Wolfson & Carskadon, 1998). Sleep deprived adolescents do not perform as well as well-rested peers in school, have a more difficult time paying attention, and are more likely to get into car accidents (Carskadon, 1990; Danner & Phillips, 2008). When adolescents do not obtain enough sleep, they are more likely to engage in a host of risky behaviors such as smoking, not getting enough exercise, using drugs and alcohol, as well as reporting sadness, hopelessness, and thoughts about suicide (McNight-Eily et al., 2011).

To combat this very serious, widespread problem, some school districts have changed their school start times to allow adolescents to obtain more sleep. Not surprisingly, students in these districts got more sleep, reported feeling more awake and alert in class, were absent and late less often, reported better mental and physical health, were more motivated in school, and had fewer car accidents (Boergers, Gable, & Owens, 2014; Danner & Phillips, 2008; Owens, Belon, & Moss, 2010; Wahistrom, 2002).

Nutritional Problems

Consider these two students:

- Miguel, age sixteen, leaves school at 4:00. On his way home, he stops by a convenience store with his friends and buys himself a large soft drink (300 calories) and a bag of French fries (400 calories). As a result, he is not hungry when dinner is served at 6:00; in fact, he doesn't finish his dinner. By the next morning, he is hungry again because he has not eaten for more than fourteen hours. He is too rushed to have breakfast, but on his way to school, he buys a candy bar at the same convenience store he visited yesterday.

- Susan, also age sixteen, leaves school at 4:00. On her way home, she stops by a convenience store with her friends, where they buy themselves various snacks. Susan buys herself nothing, though, because she believes she is slightly overweight. Later, for the same reason, she eats almost none of her dinner, causing mild worry for her parents. Still later, she sneaks out of the house without telling anyone, goes to the convenience store, and buys herself several candy bars, which she consumes on the spot. She feels sick, but doesn't throw up—this time.

Miguel and Susan are not unusual in their eating habits. Of all age groups in society, adolescents have some of the most unsatisfactory nutritional behaviors (Barness, 1993). Many of their eating habits—a tendency to skip meals, to snack (especially on "junk" foods), to consume fast foods, and (especially for girls) to diet—place them at dietary risk. Inadequate nutrition can interfere with a teenager's ability to concentrate at school or work, and it can interfere with activities with peers. The negative effects may not seem serious to many teenagers because their youth gives them comparative resilience to bounce back after a period of poor nutrition, preventing them from feeling ill as a consequence. In the short term, furthermore, many (but not all) teenagers neither gain weight from eating too many calories nor lose it from too much dieting. Yet poor nutritional habits definitely contribute to serious health problems in adulthood if they persist on a long-term basis.

Like dependence on drugs, dependence on "empty calories" and the obesity that sometimes results are problems that affect a significant portion of the teenage population. Adolescents and young adults who are overweight suffer increased health risks, including hypertension, respiratory disease, orthopedic disorders, and diabetes. In a bi-annual survey of American high school students, an estimated 13 percent of today's teenagers are considered obese, while another 15 percent were identified as overweight (Center for Disease Control, 2012). Major causes of obesity include a biologically inherited tendency to be overweight, childhood diet, family attitudes and habits regarding food, and lack of exercise (Mela & Roberts, 1998). Parental concerns about weight, especially with daughters, are strong indicators for young girls to begin internalizing about their weight and perhaps inhibiting their ability to self-regulate their eating patterns (Nickerson & Nagle, 2005).

Obesity is particularly difficult for adolescents who already are struggling to develop a comfortable and realistic view of their changing bodies. It can significantly impair teenagers' sense of themselves as physically attractive people and their overall identity development. In some cases, obesity can severely limit social opportunities due to both exclusion by peers and self-isolation. Because overweight adolescents do not conform to the social ideal of thinness, they also suffer from discrimination that limits their access to education, employment, marriage, housing, and health care (DeJong, 1993; Gortmaker et al., 1993; Puhl & King, 2013).

An obsession with excessive thinness is also a problem, especially for girls. Despite a growing appreciation of physical strength and fitness in women, thanks in part to women like Serena Williams and Abby Wambach, a lean body is still the dominant cultural standard for feminine beauty. Many adolescent girls try to lose weight to achieve a degree of slenderness that may not be possible for them. Eaton's study (CDC, 2012) of youth risk behaviors revealed the pervasiveness of a teen's concern with weight. Almost a third (29.2 percent) of all high school students described themselves as overweight, with 35 percent of females using this description, compared to 24 percent of their male peers. In addition, students reported going to significant lengths to either lose weight or simply not gain weight. Almost half (46 percent) of high school students reported wanting to lose weight, including 12.2 percent who fasted for twenty-four hours; 5.1 percent who took diet pills, powders, or liquids; and 4.3 percent who used laxatives or vomited within the past thirty days prior to the survey (CDC, 2012). These risky behaviors, paired with inadequate knowledge about dietary requirements and poor eating habits, often lead to inadequate nutrition for many teenage girls and serious eating disorders for a vulnerable few.

Eating Disorders

In its extreme form, the quest for thinness can become an eating disorder. **Anorexia nervosa**, **bulimia nervosa**, and **binge eating disorder** are three types of eating disorders that include extreme emotions, beliefs and attitudes, and behaviors regarding food and weight issues (Swanson, Crow, LeGrange, Swendsen, & Merikanagas, 2011). Recent prevalence rates have remained steady nationwide, affecting 0.3 percent of teens diagnosed with anorexia, 0.9 percent who are bulimic, and 1.6 percent with binge eating disorders (Swanson, et al., 2011). Also, it is estimated that about 20 percent of adolescent girls (2.5 million) exhibit less extreme bulimic behaviors and an additional 20 percent engage in less extreme but still unhealthy dieting behaviors (Graber et al., 1996).

The *Diagnostic and Statistical Manual of Mental Disorders* (American Psychological Association, 2013) made some changes to the definition and criteria for eating disorders in the *DSM-5*. The major symptom of anorexia is extreme weight loss, or in adolescents, failure to maintain normal weight gain for age and gender through self-starvation that is tied to an obsessive fear of becoming fat. Anorexic youngsters experience severe disturbances in three areas of psychological functioning. The first is in persistent energy intake restriction, resulting in significant weight loss, or an unhealthy lack of weight gain for teens and children. A girl (call

anorexia nervosa A physical and psychological disturbance that causes a person to refuse to eat sufficient food and to develop an increasingly unrealistic view of his or her body; most individuals with anorexia are teenage girls.

bulimia nervosa A disorder in which a person, usually a teenage girl, eats huge amounts of food and then vomits it to avoid gaining weight.

binge eating disorder A disorder in which a person feels out of control of his or her eating and consumes much more than most people would eat in a short period of time, sometimes even when he or she is not hungry.

her Jill) is five feet, six inches tall and weighs eighty-seven pounds. Jill looks like a walking skeleton. Her weight is twenty-seven pounds less than what is expected for her, using the measure of 85 percent of expected weight for age. Jill's current weight is consistent with anorexia. But when she views herself in a mirror, she sees someone who is too fat and needs to continue dieting, the second disturbance of functioning. Her distorted perceptions activate behaviors that interfere with weight gain and lead to the third disturbance, a dangerous and unrealistic view of her own body image. Jill does not recognize the danger in her severe weight loss, believing that her thinness is what defines her (APA, 2013). A common physiological side effect of anorexia is amenorrhea, the cessation of menstruation in women. This is no longer considered a criterion in the new *DSM-5* diagnosis for anorexia nervosa.

Bulimia is a related eating disorder that frequently involves a recurrent "binge-purge" syndrome in which as many as 4,800 calories are eaten at a time, mostly in the form of sweets and other "forbidden" and fattening food, and then immediately purged by forced vomiting, laxatives, excessive exercise, and/or other cathartics. About half of all people suffering from anorexia also have bulimic eating patterns (Fairburn & Wilson, 1993). Women at greatest risk for bulimia are those who have most deeply accepted and internalized the social and cultural norms that equate fat with the bad and ugly, and thinness with the good and beautiful (Hesse-Biber, 1996).

Binge eating disorder (BED) is a new addition to specific types of eating disorders identified in the *DSM-5*. This separate disorder was included to address the risky eating patterns of large numbers of adolescents and college-age samples whose loss-of-control eating or recurring episodes of binge eating are becoming more common (APA, 2013). Like the other eating disorders, BED is more prevalent among adolescent girls than among their male peers, where roughly 10 percent of those seeking treatment for eating disorders are male. One commonality with all eating disorders, regardless of gender, is the high degree of comorbidity with other psychological conditions like anxiety disorders, depression, bi-polar disorders, and stressors within the family (APA, 2013; Rieck, Jackson, Martin, Petrie, & Greenleaf, 2013).

Anorexia, bulimia, and binge eating are frequently associated with various influences from family members, friends, and the media. For adolescent females and males, their body image and self-esteem are closely aligned with messages they receive from parents, peers, and images in the media, where thinness (for girls) and upper body strength (for boys) is highly valued (Ata, Ludden, & Lally, 2007).

Successful treatment of anorexia generally requires a multiple focus and an effective team of physicians, therapists, and family members. First, it must deal with the medical concerns and risks associated with severe weight loss, and then it must be supported by family counseling with the adolescent and her parents. Second, antidepressant medications have proven helpful in reducing the depression and risk of suicide that are present in many cases, and may require a psychiatric consult or monitoring of medications by the family practice physician. Family therapy has also proven effective for treating teens with anorexia nervosa, while intensive cognitive behavior therapy (CBT) is recommended for bulimia nervosa and binge eating disorders (Hay, 2013). The treatment must address the underlying family problems and the self-defeating interactions among family members that are invariably related to anorexia. Finally, individual therapy with the anorexic adolescent must focus on helping her to uncover her own abilities and resources for independent thinking, judging, and feeling. It must help her, or him, to achieve autonomy and self-directed identity by helping the adolescent become aware of, express, and act on his or her own impulses, feelings, and needs. The "Focusing On" feature looks at how these issues and solutions express themselves in the lives of competitive athletes.

Adolescent Brain Development

The recent emergence of interest among neuroscientists in the developing adolescent brain is providing new ways of understanding both the cognitive and social-emotional changes that have an impact on how teens function. In the not too distant past, it was assumed that brain development reached maturity by midadolescence. The significant gains in adolescent

> **Focusing On...**
>
> ### Female Athletes and Eating Disorders
>
> Statistics show that athletic activities requiring a lean physical body predispose serious, competitive female participants to eating disorders. In figure skating, gymnastics, and ballet, more than half of competitive females report some form of pathological dieting, and as many as 25 percent are dangerously underweight or undernourished (Graber et al., 1996; Zerbe, 1993). This figure is more than double that for other women athletes (e.g., softball or basketball) and many times higher than for women in general. Eating disorders among skaters, gymnasts, and ballet dancers usually take the form of either *anorexia nervosa* or *bulimia*.
>
> Several factors contribute to the prevalence of eating disorders among women in the "lean" sports. Competitive skating and ballet require much practice and pencil-like proportions to make turns and lifts, setting the stage for excessive exercise and a compulsion to prove one's worth through competitions. Most winners of Olympic competitions in these sports are teenagers, and the females are five to ten years younger than their male counterparts (Ryan, 1995). Youth makes them likely to be slender, both because some have not yet fully experienced puberty and because exercising so intensely tends to delay the onset of puberty. Their immaturity makes them less likely to question the intense exercise needed to succeed at skating or gymnastics.
>
> These young females may seem not obviously troubled because their activities support society's gender-role expectations. Both their talent and appearance are what the public often wants to see: a childlike body combined with a cooperative spirit, one that performs on demand and does not mind being looked at intently or even erotically (Guttmann, 1996; Hesse-Biber, 1996). Under these conditions, it becomes easy to hide an eating disorder. The public at large is eager *not* to hear about the downside to its image of perfection. And coaches, parents, and the girl herself find it easier to interpret symptoms as normal signs of stress or as normal self-discipline associated with training. At the beginning of a girl's sports career, in fact, they may be right: self-disciplined practice only later deteriorates into an addiction to public acclaim.
>
> The experience of these athletes suggests ways to prevent and treat girls with eating disorders. For example, both girls and their families need to understand the pervasiveness of gender-role expectations and social conventions that value thinness, docility, and youth for females (Hesse-Biber, 1996). This goal usually takes two strategies. One is to control and simplify a girl's environment to eliminate behaviors and stimuli that contribute to weight loss—by counseling family members about appropriate behavior or arranging for the girl or woman to live away from her family for a time. Unsolicited compliments on thinness should be reduced. So should criticisms for *not* eating, which can be interpreted as personal attacks and contribute to feeling helpless. The second strategy is to encourage a sense of autonomy and self-direction so that the girl feels less at the mercy of others' expectations and admiring (and sometimes envious) gazes. Accomplishing this goal usually requires counseling or therapy for the girl herself (Zerbe, 1993). To the extent that a girl can understand the link between an action as personal as eating and broad social issues about gender equity and about respect for the young, she can begin to see that eating problems are widespread and that her growing insights about her experiences, if shared appropriately, can sometimes help others with similar experiences.
>
> **What Do You Think?**
>
> 1. Not everyone with an eating disorder is a young female. How would the experiences of others with this problem differ from those presented here?
> 2. If you knew someone who you suspected had an eating disorder, how might you deal with it? Compare your answer with that of a classmate.
> 3. When boys participate in sports that fit traditional male gender stereotypes for looks and behavior, what risks are they exposed to that may be analogous to the experience of some girls with eating disorders?

problem-solving abilities—described in the next section—and the relative absence of further obvious cognitive changes during adulthood led to the belief that the brain achieved full physiological maturity during the teen years. Research conducted at the National Institute of Mental Health (Giedd, 2004), the Institute for Cognitive Neuroscience in London (Blakemore, 2012), and elsewhere has demonstrated that the human brain continues to develop, with some exuberance, during adolescence and into emerging adulthood.

Research using fMRI (functional magnetic resonance imaging) technology has revealed that during adolescence the human brain experiences a period of rapid growth that continues into early adulthood (Luna et al., 2013). An increase in the production of gray matter is

Chapter 10 Physical and Cognitive Development in Adolescence

> **What Do You Think?**
>
> Why do you think adolescents are at such high risk for injury, death, and health problems? What recommendations for preventing such serious outcomes might you make to a group of high school students and their parents?

also accompanied by increases in myelination, resulting in faster and more efficient neural pathways. Also contributing to the efficiency in neural processing is a resurgence of synaptic pruning (see the coverage of brain development during infancy in Chapter 4), a process that "weeds out" unused neural connections and allows more space for new pathways to form for information processing and storage (Giedd, 2004). It is now understood that brain development during adolescence occurs in a process guided by two principles. One is the "use it or lose it principle" seen in increased synaptic pruning, and the second is a "back-to-front" maturing process that is reexperienced during the teenage years (Gogtay et al., 2004).

"Use It or Lose It"

The process of pruning eliminates redundant or rarely used synapses and neurons, producing a brain that not only processes information more efficiently, but also a brain that is more specialized and differentiated than the brains of children (Casey et al., 2008). Abilities and knowledge acquired during childhood but not practiced or accessed during adolescence may be lost during adolescence as the synapses and neurons in inactive neural pathways are pruned. This is not to say that specific memories from one's past, knowledge acquired years ago, or actions that have not been performed in a long time (when was the last time you folded a paper airplane or a paper fortune teller?) will be lost forever as a result of pruning. Accessing the memories or knowledge may take longer or require some mental reconstruction, or you may have to relearn some skills that have gotten "rusty" over the years. There are some serious implications to the "use it or lose it" principle, however. During the rapid period of brain development occurring during adolescence, how the adolescents choose to stimulate their brains will significantly shape the physiological development of their brains (Casey et al., 2008). The adolescent who sits at a computer and spends hours playing video games online every day will likely have a brain that develops in different ways than the adolescent who spends hours after school with basketball teammates, volunteers in the community every month, and works for the family business on weekends.

"Back to Front"

This second principle suggests that the prefrontal cortex, home to much of the executive functioning of the brain, matures later during adolescence than regions further back in the brain, like the limbic system (Gogtay et al., 2004). The limbic system is associated with the processing of emotions and attaching meanings to memories, whereas the executive functions of the prefrontal cortex are used for logical reasoning, impulse control, and planning. Because the limbic system is maturing faster than the prefrontal cortex in teens, their impulses may be driving their development in ways that impact their social functioning (Blakemore, 2012) and risk-taking behaviors (Winters & Arria, 2011) that we will examine more closely in Chapter 11. Also, as a result of their limbic system maturing earlier than their prefrontal cortex, the decision making and behavior of adolescents are more likely than that of children or adults to be highly influenced by affective information and emotional cues. Specifically, when adolescents are in situations where they are trying to control their behavior, emotions will likely win out over logic (Casey et al., 2008). This physiological "back-to-front" maturational sequence helps to explain why sex education and drug awareness programs so often fail to impact the actual behavior of many adolescents. As Laurence Steinberg (2004) eloquently observed:

> It is easier to put on a hypothetical condom during an act of hypothetical sex than it is to put on a real one when one is in the throes of passion. It is easier to just say no to a hypothetical beer than it is to a cold frosty one on a summer night. (p. 53)

> **What Do You Think?**
>
> Try to remember a situation during your early adolescence where you acted in a way that, looking back, causes you to ask, "What was I thinking?!" Why do you think you acted that way? Could your behavior be, in part, explained by the "back-to-front" principle? What roles did emotion or logic play in your decision-making at the time?

The changes in the adolescent brain described earlier may also shed insights on the underlying causes for increasing sophistication in the reasoning abilities of adolescents. The proliferation of neuronal synapses and the process of myelination, complemented by the pruning process, enable adolescents to confront the many challenges of adolescence—numerous changes in family and peer relationships, expectations to assume increased responsibility inside and outside of the home, greater challenges being presented in their schoolwork, and growing pressure to clarify what kind of an adult they want to become in the future, just to name a few. We'll take a look into the mind of the adolescent next.

COGNITIVE DEVELOPMENT

Teenagers' growing cognitive competencies broaden the horizons of their world substantially. For example, the question "What if the United States went to war again when I'm older?" is more meaningful to an adolescent than to a child, even though both are equally inexperienced with the realities of war. So is the question "What if I had been born really poor or fabulously rich?" Adolescents can imagine what these situations might be like even though they have not experienced them in a concrete way. In general, thinking about the possible creates a new skill for speculating about important events and guessing about daily experiences (Keating & Sasse, 1996). It also stimulates adolescents to daydream or fantasize about their actions and feelings. And it helps them to make more astute inferences about human motivations ("Perhaps she did that because . . .") and to critique their own and others' actions.

Psychologists have explained and interpreted these new talents from two major points of view. The first is the *cognitive developmental viewpoint,* often associated with the work of Piaget. The second is the more recent approach of *information-processing theory,* which analyzes human thinking as a complex storage, retrieval, and organizing system for information, much like a computer. Both theories have been discussed elsewhere in this book (see especially Chapter 2); here we focus on how they relate to adolescence in particular.

Beyond Concrete Operational Thinking

During adolescence, many teenagers go beyond the *concrete operational thought* described in Chapters 6 and 8 and begin developing a more abstract way of thinking called **formal operational thought**. Piaget (1983) saw this new operational thinking emerging around age eleven in many though not all adolescents. This new form of thinking frees individuals from reasoning only about the here-and-now, and allows them to be more fully logical and systematic in analyzing ideas. When using formal operational thought, individuals show some combination of three skills: they can imagine the possible rather than being limited to the real, they use scientific reasoning, and they combine ideas skillfully. Although these skills represent cognitive advances over the concrete thinking of childhood, it is important to note that they are not necessarily the "final," most mature forms of cognitive development. Later research indicates that there is a wide range of variance with how, when, and how often adolescents and young adults use formal operation thinking (Keating, 2004; Kuhn, 2008). Some teenagers and young adults never develop formal operational thought at all, and as we will see in later discussions of adult thinking (Chapters 12, 14, and 16), other kinds of thinking develop later in life that might best be called "wisdom." Before we get to those chapters, though, let us look in more detail at the main features of formal operational drought.

formal operational thought Thinking based on previously acquired concrete mental operations and involving hypothetical reasoning and attention to the structure or form of ideas.

Many teenagers become able to solve problems scientifically. But like these students in a chemistry laboratory class—and like most adults—they still need ample concrete experiences to support their abstract thinking. It is also common for them to have trouble using scientific thought outside a structured school situation.
Source: Miles Studio/Shutterstock.com.

Possibilities Versus Realities

Formal thought involves attention to possibilities rather than merely to actual realities. A parent discovers this when presenting a problem to be solved by her two children, ages nine and fifteen. When asked how to get the cable television signal working again, the nine-year-old said call the cable company, while the fifteen-year-old offered three possible fixes (like checking the cable hook-up, rebooting the system, checking the input device on the TV) that could be tried before calling cable company help line. All offerings were possible solutions; the difference was that the younger child, using concrete operational thought, saw one option, while the teenager, using formal operational thought, imagined multiple solutions and their outcomes when reasoning through the problem. Even though the teenager is not a "cable repair-person," she is knowledgeable about electronics from personal experience, and more importantly, understands that there is more than one solution to any problem. In fact, this young adolescent is approaching the problem more scientifically than her younger brother, utilizing the second new skill developed at this stage.

Scientific Reasoning

Formal thought also involves scientific reasoning, the same kind psychologists use in designing many of their studies of human development. This quality reveals itself when adolescent students must solve some problem systematically. Piaget called this newly developed ability *hypothetical-deductive reasoning*, thinking that involves forming a hypothesis, testing possible solutions, and making judgments about the outcomes (Inhelder & Piaget, 1958). For example, how do youngsters in an art class figure out methods for mixing basic colors of paint to produce various intermediate shades and other colors? Those capable of formal operations in effect design an experiment to test all the available combinations of colors. They form hypotheses, or hunches, about how certain colors affect each other when mixed. Then they try out their hypotheses by mixing each basic color with every other basic color, being careful to try every possibility. By carefully observing the results of this procedure, they can draw logical conclusions about how to mix colors. This procedure in effect uses the scientific method.

The major difference with using this skill compared to a concrete operational child is the systematic way the older teen works toward a solution. A younger child would play around with the paint, mixing colors as well, but doing so in a more random and haphazard manner, most likely taking little formal notice of the results of her random actions. A precocious ten-year-old, familiar with painting, may solve the problem, but it is more likely this solution is a blend of experience and memory, rather than hypothetical-deductive reasoning. Even very bright kids in middle childhood do not use combinatorial thinking with the skill and persistence of a teen who is capable of formal operational thought.

Logical Combination of Ideas

The third feature of formal operational thought involves combining ideas logically. Unlike less cognitively mature children, formal thinkers can hold several ideas in mind at once and combine or integrate them in logical ways. When asked to explain why some students perform better in school than others do, concrete operational thinkers are likely to latch on to one reason or another: "Some kids are smarter" or "Some kids work harder." In contrast, formal operational thinkers often give combinations of reasons, as this first-year college student did:

> Well, I think it depends. Sometimes it pays just to be smart. But it also helps to work hard—except when the teacher doesn't notice. Some kids do better too because they have taken courses before in the same area. Your first class in literature is likely to be harder than your fifth class in that subject.

As this example shows, the ability to combine ideas sometimes makes formal operational thinkers qualify their opinions more than preformal operational thinkers do. The world is no longer black and white. It has many more shades of gray for the adolescent than it does for a concrete operational thinker.

Cognitive Development Beyond Formal Thought

Piaget and other psychologists have identified formal, or abstract, thought as a major achievement of the adolescent years. But for most human beings, it may not be the final or highest cognitive achievement. One clue to this possibility comes from adolescents themselves: some teenagers overuse logical thinking when they first achieve facility with it (Leadbetter, 1991). They may believe all problems, including ambiguous ones such as achieving world peace, can be solved by the proper application of rational principles and careful reasoning. Teenagers may fail to notice that some problems by nature resist the application of general logic and may inherently have multiple, partial solutions. Later, as adults, they will take a more ad hoc, pragmatic approach to most problem solving (Sinnott, 1998). Additionally, the use of formal operational skills may not prove helpful when applied to problems or situations that are more emotional than logical or rational.

Consider Ana, a twelfth-grader who recently has begun a sexual relationship with her boyfriend. Ana gets along well with her parents, and respects their values. She knows they will worry and feel hurt if they learn of her sexual intimacy. She further believes that, generally, friends and family should have no secrets. By continuing her sexual activities, she seems to be violating this principle. On the other hand, she and her boyfriend regard their behavior as a personal and private matter, and she worries that telling her parents would violate this privacy, which she also considers her right. Telling her parents might also create a lot of bad feelings among Ana, her boyfriend, and her parents. In this case, her principles do not seem to point her toward a good solution: Ana believes that no matter what she does, somebody will get hurt, some ethical principle will be violated, or both.

Ana's situation suggests the importance of nonrational choices or judgments in solving real-life problems. Like Ana, many people may wish to be reasonable; that is, they may wish to rely on formal logic and may even believe they use it a lot. But in practice, most people use formal logic consistently only when solving academic problems posed by teachers, especially when the problems are deliberately scientific in nature (Bartsch, 1993). Less systematic reasoning serves as well or better for solving daily problems.

For older adolescents, the cognitive challenge consists of converting formal reasoning from a goal in itself to a *tool* used for broader purposes and tailored to the problems at hand (Myers, 1993). Ana cannot reach a sound decision about informing her parents of her sexual activities if she focuses on formal principles about truthfulness and privacy to the exclusion of more personal facts, which in this case include her knowledge of her boyfriend's and her own parents' probable responses and feelings. Taking these circumstances into account leads to the "best," or most mature, solution, but it may not lead to a solution that is fully logical in Piaget's sense. As adolescents grow into young adults, this sort of postformal thought becomes more common, as we will see in Chapter 12 when we discuss cognitive development in early adulthood.

> **WORKING WITH** Jerry Acton, Math and Science Teacher
>
> ### Blending the Social and Emotional with the Cognitive
>
> Jerry Acton teaches math, chemistry, and physics in high school. I wanted to interview him to learn more about how students think about these traditionally "cognitive" subjects. What I learned, though, was that success in these subjects depended heavily on social and emotional factors—on students' attitudes and motivations, and not just on their thinking abilities as such. The blending of the domains of development was especially evident in Jerry's tenth-grade math class, the one we spent most time discussing.
>
> **Kelvin:** *I've heard a lot of generalizations about math—stereotypes about learning it, so to speak. I've heard that math is inherently abstract, for example, and that it's very sequentially organized, and that you have to be willing to work independently if you want to do well in math. What do you think about these ideas? Do they explain why some students do better in math than others? Tell me about your own classes.*
>
> **Jerry:** For my classes, I would say that *maturity* makes the biggest difference. Maybe it's because these are tenth-graders—people who have just arrived at senior high school and are still getting used to it. The more successful students in math classes are the ones who are the most mature.
>
> **Kelvin:** *What do you mean by "mature"?*
>
> **Jerry:** I mean the ones who are prepared to come to class to work, to listen, to ask questions, and to do work in class, as opposed to coming to class because it is a convenient place to socialize with friends. The mature ones already seem to see value and usefulness to math, without my having to persuade them of that idea.
>
> **Kelvin:** *That makes it sound like there's not much need for you as the teacher—like students either choose to work or they don't, and there's not much you can do about it. Surely that's not what you mean?*
>
> **Jerry:** Oh no, there's still lots to do! One thing I do to motivate the less self-motivated students is give them a structured environment: one where our tasks are predictable, where there's routine. With a good routine, they know what to expect and the tasks are organized into steps that they understand and can do. We always do mental math first, then review the day's homework, then start a new lesson, and so on. I find that variations from the format inevitably throw some students "off their stride," and less gets done.
>
> **Kelvin:** *That reminds me of the sequencing idea. People sometimes say that you have to learn math concepts in a certain sequence or else you risk getting hopelessly lost in the long term. Is that true?*
>
> **Jerry:** Yes, in a sense it *is* true. But teachers can do things to keep students from getting lost as a result. In our new curriculum, for example, we use "spiral sequencing," where we revisit topics periodically and give daily review in between visits. If you're sick for a whole week, you don't miss out altogether on a particular math topic. And all the teachers in my school now use cumulative testing, which gives students incentives for consolidating

Implications of the Cognitive Developmental Viewpoint

As indicated earlier, formal operations begin developing early in adolescence and are fully formed by the end of the high school years (Piaget, 1983). All teenagers supposedly develop wide-ranging thinking abilities that have a formal, abstract nature and apply to many specific experiences and daily problems. In reality, however, the actual cognitive performances of adolescents fail to conform to this picture in several ways. First, a majority of adolescents (and even adults) use formal thinking inconsistently or even fail to use it at all (Lakoff, 1994). In explaining why a car is not working properly, for example, many adolescents and adults merely describe the car's symptoms: "The brakes are making a weird noise" or "It won't shift into third gear." An adolescent must have both an *experience base* and a *skill base* to mechanically resolve the problem using a structured and logical approach to the problem (Flavell et al., 1993). Yet, the inconsistency remains when this skilled teenage mechanic has difficulty applying the same logic and reason in his English classroom when trying to write a persuasive essay on gun control or on the soccer field when trying to devise strategies to neutralize an exceptionally skilled midfielder.

> **WORKING WITH** Jerry Acton, Math and Science Teacher
>
> ### Blending the Social and Emotional with the Cognitive *continued*
>
> what they know so that there are no "holes" in their math knowledge at the end of the course.
>
> **Kelvin:** *Still, by its nature, math must be pretty abstract, even in tenth grade.*
>
> **Jerry:** You're right about that. Especially in the course called "precalculus," which actually says in its advertising that it *is* abstract and is intended for students who already enjoy math. How do you offer concrete, hands-on activities related to factoring? What are the everyday uses for factoring? [*Smiles.*] Most students *do* learn better if you can make the material more down to earth and relate it to familiar activities.
>
> But I have found ways to move in that direction. This year we used graphing calculators, for example, which the students really enjoy. The calculators make it a lot easier to create graphs—much faster and less laborious. With the calculators, you can actually play around with graphing different functions instead of taking fifteen minutes just to draw one by hand. When we get tire computer lab set up properly, we'll be able to do even more.
>
> **Kelvin:** *Sounds like with the calculators, students could even work together. They could do problems and projects cooperatively.*
>
> **Jerry:** That's indeed the case. Students can do problems independently, for example, and then compare their results. We'll be able to do more joint work, in fact, when we get the computer lab set up.
>
> **Kelvin:** *I often think of math as being an especially "solitary" activity, not one that lends itself to working with others. Would you agree?*
>
> **Jerry:** I've found that there are ways for students in math to work together, like with the graphing calculators. Sometimes, in fact, I've actually had trouble with students cooperating *too* much; it seems like they're always wanting to consult with each other about how to do certain problems or about what the answers are. Then I wish they would function more independently of each other. A mix is best: cooperation combined and independence combined.
>
> ### What Do You Think?
>
> 1. Given Jerry Acton's comments, would you describe mathematical success as a "cognitive" skill, a "social" skill, or as some combination? Explain your reasoning.
> 2. Do you believe there is indeed truth in the stereotypes or expectations about mathematics that Kelvin expressed at the beginning of the interview? How would you qualify these ideas, taking into account both Jerry's comments and your own knowledge and beliefs?
> 3. Sometimes mathematics is traditionally thought of as a "boy's" subject more than a "girl's." Judging by Jerry's comments, do you think this is true for his class? Do you still think it could be true for mathematics students in general?

It seems, then, that formal operational thought does describe adolescents' thinking, but only partially or intermittently. Formal thought helps teenagers to argue with their parents more skillfully than they could as children, thereby contributing to the stereotype of teenagers as being relatively "rebellious." Formal thought also makes teenagers more skillful at cultivating friendships, potential dates, and social contacts; now they can imagine and anticipate the consequences of various friendly (and unfriendly) strategies. And formal thought means teenagers are more ready than children are to grapple with philosophical and abstract topics at school; literary analysis can now begin to make sense, for example, and so can at least some theoretical concepts in science. The "Working With" interview describes how these changes look from the point of view of one high school mathematics teacher, Jerry Acton.

Moral Development: Beliefs about Justice and Care

As adolescents move into adulthood and gradually develop formal thought, allowing them to reason with concepts of greater complexity and abstract thinking, they also develop a personal **morality**, or sensitivity to and knowledge of what is right and wrong. Moral thinking

morality Sensitivity to and knowledge about what is right and wrong.

> **What Do You Think?**
>
> Outside of school- or job-related tasks, most people actually use formal operational thinking rather little in their everyday lives. How much do *you* actually use it? Think of a situation other than school (shopping, visiting a friend, cooking) in which you need to use abstract thinking to function effectively. What does your answer imply about the place of formal thought in adolescents' overall development?

develops in two ways: in the form of increasingly logical and abstract principles related to fairness and justice and in the form of increasingly sophisticated ways of caring about the welfare of friends, family, and self (Noam & Wren, 1993). Each of these trends is somewhat related to gender: boys tend to emphasize ethical thinking about justice rather abstractly, and girls typically emphasize an ethics of care. But the gender difference is not large; most individuals develop both kinds of ethical thinking to a significant extent. Lawrence Kohlberg (1963; Kohlberg et al., 1983) developed a major theory of moral development constructed around the issues of fairness and justice, while Carol Gilligan (1982) looked at the ethics of care as the basis for moral development in women. Both are stage theories in the cognitive developmental tradition, reminiscent of Piaget's approach to cognitive development.

Kohlberg's Six Stages of Moral Judgment

Lawrence Kohlberg proposed six stages of moral judgment that develop slowly across three levels, well into middle adulthood (Schrader, 1990; Kohlberg & Hersh, 1977). The stages were derived initially from interviews of boys aged ten, thirteen, and sixteen, but later research included adolescent females. The interviews were conducted in much the same style as Piaget's classic interviews about cognitive development: Children and adults of various ages responded individually to hypothetical stories that contained moral dilemmas. Kohlberg, like Piaget, believed that moral development occurred in a stage-like fashion and was based on an individual's level of cognitive development; over time, as cognitive abilities change, one's moral reasoning will also change.

Kohlberg identified three distinct levels of moral reasoning. Level 1 was *preconventional reasoning*, based on one's automatic acceptance of cultural rules of right and wrong, and the perception of the consequences (rewards or punishments) that may result from one's actions. Good behaviors are those that are rewarded, while a behavior is reasoned to be bad if punishment follows that action. Level 2 was defined as involving *conventional reasoning*. At this level, reasoning is less egocentric and embraces the expectations of others important to the individual, including family, school, and community. What is considered right is whatever conforms to the rules or values established by society at the macro level and the family at the micro level. Level 3 of moral development identified by Kohlberg was *postconventional reasoning*. Moral values, or what is right, are now considered independent of what an authority says is right. What is right is based on an individual's perception of universal moral principles apart from the group's rules or laws (Kohlberg & Hersh, 1977). Each of Kohlberg's three levels of moral development was subdivided into two stages, resulting in a model of moral reasoning that comprised six stages.

Table 10.2 summarizes the six proposed stages. The stages form a progression in two ways. First, earlier stages represent more egocentric thinking than later stages do. Second, earlier stages by their nature require more specific or concrete thinking than later stages do. For instance, in Stage 1 (called *heteronomous morality*, which focuses on punishment and obedience), a child makes no distinction between what he believes is right and what the world tells him is right; he simply accepts the perspectives of the authorities as his own, primarily to avoid punishment for doing wrong, or "being bad." By Stage 4 (social system orientation), when the child is an adolescent, he realizes that individuals vary in their points of view, but he still takes for granted the existing overall conventions of society as a whole. This stage is often referred to as the "law-and-order" stage because laws are needed to maintain the social order. He cannot yet imagine a society in which those conventions might be purposely modified, for example, by passing laws or agreeing on new rules. Only by Stage 5 (the stage of social contract) and Stage 6 (the stage of universal principles) can he do so fully. At Stage 5, one understands that laws and authority can be questioned and that changes can be made for increased fairness and justice for the greater good of society. Stage 6—a level that few individuals exhibit—describes a person who has developed an independent moral code based on universal ethical principles, which may justify violating established laws to honor these principles.

In the school years, children most commonly show ethical reasoning at Stage 2, the instrumental-relativist orientation, but some may begin showing Stage 3 or 4 reasoning toward the end of this period (Colby & Kohlberg, 1987). For the majority of youth and adults, Stage 3 (interpersonal-conformity orientation) and Stage 4 (social system orientation) characterize their most advanced moral thinking. In Stage 3, a person's chief concern is with the opinions of her peers: an action is morally right if her immediate circle of friends says it is right. Often, this way of thinking leads to helpful actions, such as taking turns and sharing possessions. But often it does not, such as when friends decide to shoplift from a store or bully a kid at school who is perceived as weaker and more vulnerable. The desire to be a "good boy" or "good girl" is often defined by what the peer group determines is the right thing to do.

In Stage 4, the person shifts from concern with peers to concern with the opinions of community or society in the abstract: now something is right if the institutions approve. This broader source of moral judgment spares Stage 4 children from the occasional tyranny of friends' opinions; now they may refuse to sneak a smoke or to experiment with alcohol or drugs just because their friends urge them to do so. This change makes teenagers less *opportunistic* than children and less inclined to judge based on immediate rewards or punishments they experience personally. Instead, they evaluate actions on the basis of principles of some sort. For the time being, the principles are rather conventional; they are borrowed either from ideas expressed by immediate peers and their parents, or from socially accepted rules and principles, whatever they may be. If friends agree that premarital sex is permissible, many teenagers are likely to adopt this idea as their own, at least as a general principle. But if friends or family believe premarital sex is morally wrong, teenagers may adopt this alternative belief as

TABLE 10.2 Kohlberg's Stages of Moral Judgment

Stage	Nature of Stage
Preconventional Level *(emphasis on avoiding punishments and getting awards)*	
Stage 1 Heteronomous morality; punishment and obedience orientation	Good is what follows externally imposed rules and rewards and is whatever avoids punishment
Stage 2 Instrumental-relativist orientation purpose; ethics of market exchange as it benefits the individual. "The 'I'll scratch your back, if you scratch my back" orientation.	Good is whatever is agreeable to the individual and to anyone who gives or receives favors; no long-term loyalty
Conventional Level *(emphasis on social rules)*	
Stage 3 Interpersonal conformity; ethics of peer opinion, the "good boy" or "good girl" orientation	Good is whatever brings approval from friends as a peer group
Stage 4 Social system orientation: conformity to social system; ethics of law and order	Good is whatever conforms to existing laws, customs, and authorities
Postconventional Level *(emphasis on moral principles)*	
Stage 5 Social contract, legalistic orientation; ethics of social contract and individual rights	Good is whatever conforms to existing procedures for settling disagreements in society; the actual outcome is neither good nor bad
Stage 6 Universal-ethical principles orientation. Ethics of self-chosen universal principles	Good is whatever is consistent with personal, general moral principles

a principle. (Note, however, that whether a teenager actually acts according to these principles is another matter. Moral action does not always follow from moral belief.)

A few young adults develop **postconventional moral judgment**, meaning that for the first time ethical reasoning goes beyond the judgments society conventionally makes about right and wrong. Adolescents' growing ability to use abstract formal thought stimulates this development, though it does not guarantee it. Unlike schoolchildren, they can evaluate ethical ideas that *might* be right or wrong given certain circumstances that can only be imagined.

postconventional moral judgment In Kohlberg's theory, an orientation to moral justice that develops beyond conventional rules and beliefs.

Issues in the Development of Moral Beliefs About Justice

As Figure 10.4 indicates, Kohlberg's six stages of moral judgment have held up well when tested on a wide variety of children, adolescents, and adults. The stages of moral thinking shown in Table 10.2 do seem to describe how moral judgment develops, at least when individuals focus on hypothetical dilemmas posed in stories. When presented with stories about risky but fictional sexual behaviors, adolescents of both sexes evaluated the actions of the stories' characters in line with Kohlberg's stages (Jadack et al., 1995).

Even so, Kohlberg's theory of moral judgment leaves a number of important questions unanswered. One is whether the theory really recognizes the impact of prior knowledge on beliefs; another is whether the theory distinguishes clearly enough between conventions and morality. One especially important question has to do with gender differences: does Kohlberg's theory really describe the moral development of girls as well as that of boys?

Issue 1: Form Versus Content of Moral Beliefs

Despite the theory's plausibility, a number of developmental psychologists have questioned important aspects of it. Can the form of ethical thinking really be separated from content to the degree Kohlberg proposes? Perhaps not. Some studies have found that when people reason about familiar situations, they tend to have more mature (that is, higher-stage) ethical responses (Lickona, 1991). For instance, children have a better sense of fairness about playing four-square on the playground than about whether to steal a drug for a spouse who is dying (one of Kohlberg's fictional dilemmas). In addition, young women think in more mature (more "developed") ways about ethical problems of special concern and familiarity to women, such as whether to engage in premarital sex or whether to have an abortion (Bollerud et al., 1990). To some extent, therefore, what someone thinks about affects the ethics she or he applies.

Issue 2: Conventions Versus Morality

According to some psychologists, some inconsistencies in moral beliefs may arise because the theory does not fully distinguish between social conventions and morality (Nucci & Turiel, 1993). **Social conventions** refer to the arbitrary customs and agreements about behavior that members of society use, such as table manners and forms of greeting and dressing. *Morality*, as we already pointed out, refers to the weightier matters of justice and right and wrong. By nature, social conventions inevitably generate widespread agreement throughout society, whereas morality does not necessarily do so. Yet Kohlberg's six-stage theory glosses over these differences by defining some of its stages in terms of social conventions and others in terms of morality. Stage 4 (social system orientation), for example, seems to refer to social conventions as well as to moral matters, but Stage 5 (social contract orientation) refers only to moral judgment. It is also important to keep in mind that Kohlberg's focus was not delineating between social conventions and morality per se, but in viewing the moral reasoning used in commenting on the actions of people facing the fictional moral dilemmas.

social conventions Arbitrary customs and agreements about behavior that members of a society use.

Issue 3: Gender Differences in Morality?

One especially important criticism of Kohlberg's theory of moral justice has to do with possible gender bias. Do Kohlberg's stages describe both genders equally well? And does his theory undervalue ethical attitudes that may develop more fully in girls and women than in boys and men? The best-known investigations of these questions have been pursued by one of Kohlberg's colleagues at Harvard, Carol Gilligan, and her associates.

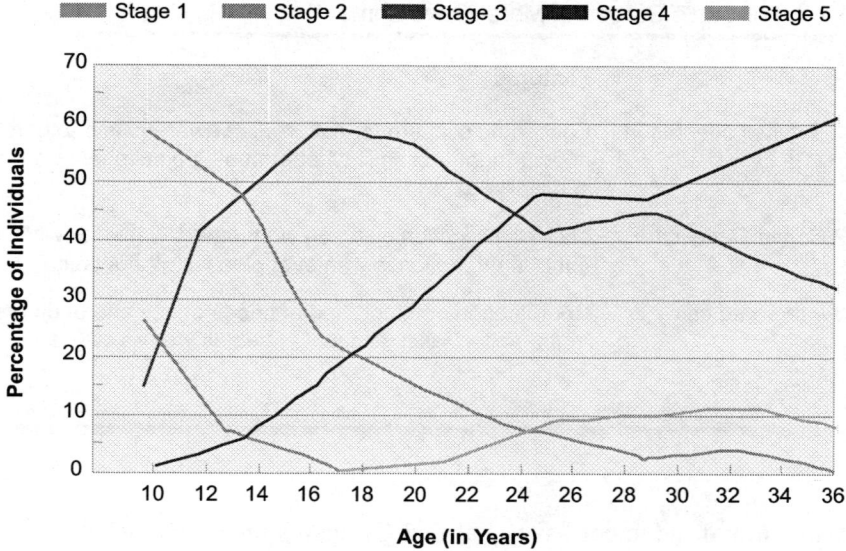

FIGURE 10.4
Longitudinal Development of Moral Reasoning

In a longitudinal follow-up study of Kohlberg's original sample, Colby and her colleagues showed that participants showed consistent upward advances in moral reasoning with age. The graph shows the extent to which participants gave responses characteristic of each of Kohlberg's six stages from age ten through adulthood. With development, responses associated with the preconventional level (Stages 1 and 2) declined, whereas responses associated with the conventional level (Stages 3 and 4) increased. Few young adults moved to the postconventional level (Stages 5 and 6) of moral reasoning.
Source: Adapted from Colby et al., 1983.

Gilligan's Ethics of Care

According to Gilligan and others, boys and girls tend to view moral problems differently (Taylor, Gilligan, & Sullivan, 1995; Gordon, Benner, & Noddings, 1996). As they grow up, boys learn to think more often in terms of general ethical principles that they can apply to specific moral situations. They might learn that deception is bad in principle and thus evaluate a specific instance of deception of a friend against this generalization. The principles boys learn also tend to emphasize independence, autonomy, and the rights of others. This orientation biases boys to ignore or minimize others' possible needs. Perhaps reasoning that if a friend is at home sick with a cold, it may seem better to leave him alone until he gets better, rather than check on how well he is recovering.

Girls tend to develop a different sort of morality as they grow up. Instead of seeing moral judgment as a set of abstract principles to apply to specific situations, girls tend to develop an ethics of care, a view that integrates principles with the contexts in which judgments must be made. A girl therefore may have learned that deception is usually bad, but she may also reason that deception is ethical in certain circumstances, such as when a friend needs reassurance about the quality of a term paper that is actually mediocre but took a lot of time and effort to write. Viewing ethics in context grows out of a general concern for the needs of others more than for one's independence. A friend who is depressed therefore deserves a visit or a phone call; leaving her alone seems more like neglect than like respect for her autonomy. Table 10.3 summarizes Gilligan's stages of moral development.

These differences are only tendencies, not dramatic or sharply drawn gender differences. But they are enough, argues Gilligan, to make Kohlberg's theory seem to underestimate the moral development of girls and women. Concern with context and with others' needs causes girls to score closer to the middling, conventional levels of moral judgment, where peers' opinions matter most. When asked if a child should inform authorities about a friend who often shoplifts small items from a local department store, a girl is likely to give priority to one part of the problem in particular: that of balancing each person's views and needs in the particular situation. Doing so means wondering, among other things, whether informing will alienate peers not only from the shoplifter but also from the informer. On the other hand, it also means wondering whether keeping silent will make her risk losing the trust and respect of important adults, such as parents and teachers. It also means considering the amount of emotional pain that will befall the shoplifting friend at the hands of either angry parents or the police. Taking all of these considerations into account can make the final decision seem hesitant, tentative, and apparently lacking in principle, whichever way the decision goes.

Chapter 10 Physical and Cognitive Development in Adolescence

TABLE 10.3 Gilligan's Stages of Moral Development

Stage	Features
Stage 1 *Survival orientation*	Egocentric concern for self, lack of awareness of others' needs; "right" action is what promotes emotional or physical survival
Stage 2 *Conventional care*	Lack of distinction between what others want and what is right; "right" action is whatever pleases others best
Stage 3 *Integrated care*	Coordination or integration of needs of self and of others; "right" action takes account of self as well as others

Source: Gilligan (1982).

Reviews of moral judgment have qualified Gilligan's ideas somewhat but have also lent them support. When faced with hypothetical dilemmas, females show as much capacity as males to reason in terms of abstract ethical principles (Gilligan & Wiggins, 1987). When faced with real-life dilemmas, however, girls make different choices (Taylor et al., 1995). For example, adolescent girls who personally confront the decision of whether to engage in premarital intercourse often show more concern than do boys for the context in which they make their decisions and for the impact of their decisions on relationships with others. Gilligan's claims of gender bias in Kohlberg's stages have also proven to be unfounded; studies have shown females exhibiting higher levels of ethical reasoning than males using Kohlberg's stages (White, 1999). What appears consistent across both theories is that justice-oriented moral reasoning and needs/care-oriented moral reasoning takes time—years, in fact—to develop.

The Ethics of Care During Adolescence

As with the morality of justice, young people develop an ethics of care during adolescence, but like ethical justice, it remains somewhat conventional during the teenage years. During the school years, children develop significant concern about others' needs and welfare and begin viewing actions as good if the actions take others' needs and welfare into account (Larrabee, 1993). However, egocentrism persists in that teenagers often fail to distinguish between actions that merely *please* others and actions that are "right" in a deeper, ethical sense. For example, if parents will be pleased if their adolescent enrolls in complex science and mathematics courses in high school, doing so may seem "right" to the youngster, even if he has little interest or aptitude in those areas.

As with the ethics of justice, a few individuals move beyond conventional pleasing of others toward *integrated care,* in which the young person realizes that pleasing everyone is not always possible but it is important to balance everyone's needs, including her own (Larrabee, 1993). Deciding whether or not to take a part-time job, for example, now becomes a matter of reconciling the impact of the job on family, friends, and self. Some individuals may gain (the teenager herself may earn more money and make new friends), but others may lose (parents and friends may see less of her). The gains and losses must be balanced, rather than viewed completely as gains.

Overall, then, the moralities of justice and care begin taking into account a broader array of both interpersonal circumstances and general principles than was true during the school years. Teenagers more often refer to principles in evaluating actions, although they still do not always act on their principles. Often they also regard pleasing others as ethically good or right, even though they are learning to deal with the impossibility of pleasing everyone perfectly. Like many other cognitive developments, these changes result from adolescents' growing capacities to reason abstractly.

The Development of Social Cognition

Most developmental psychologists agree that the new cognitive skills of adolescents have important effects on their **social cognition**, or their knowledge and beliefs about interpersonal and social matters. Moral beliefs are one example of social cognition; in this section we look at three others: egocentrism and its expression as beliefs in an imaginary audience and a personal fable.

social cognition Knowledge and beliefs about interpersonal and social matters.

Adolescent Egocentrism

When adolescents first begin to reason abstractly, they often become overly impressed with this skill; it seems to them that anything can be solved "if only people would be reasonable" (that is, logical). This attitude can make teenagers idealistic and keep them from appreciating the practical limits of logic (Bowers, 1995). They may wonder why no one has ever "realized" that world war might be abolished simply by explaining to all the world powers the obvious dangers of war. Or they may wonder why their parents have not noticed the many "errors" they have made in raising children.

The development of formal thought also leads to a new kind of confusion between an adolescent's own thoughts and those of others. This confusion of viewpoints amounts to a form of egocentrism. Unlike the egocentrism of preschoolers, which is based on concrete problems, **adolescent egocentrism** concerns more abstract thoughts and problems.

adolescent egocentrism The tendency of adolescents to perceive the world (and themselves) from their own perspective.

The Imaginary Audience

Adolescent egocentrism sometimes shows itself in teenagers' preoccupation with the reactions of others. Thirteen-year-olds often fail to differentiate between how they feel about themselves and how others feel about them. Instead, they act as though they are performing for an **imaginary audience**, one that is as concerned with their appearance and behavior as they themselves are (Elkind, 1985).

Teenagers also reveal concern with an imaginary audience through *strategic interactions* with their peers, encounters that aim to either reveal or conceal personal information indirectly. The almost universal use of the Internet and social media by adolescents today serves as a means of interacting with real people who make up an imaginary audience. Teens use Facebook, Instagram, and Twitter posts to solicit "likes" or "followers" that create the perception of popularity to the individual and to others. In day-to-day encounters with peers, the imaginary audience can make life miserable for a self-conscious teen. Can you recall going to school the day after you got your hair cut, or the day a pimple appeared on your nose or forehead? If you were like most teenagers, you were certain that everyone would notice and that they would tease and make fun of you. Throughout the day, you likely focused on wanting to go home or hide in the restroom.

imaginary audience A characteristic of young adolescents in which they act as though they are performing for an audience and believe that others are as concerned with their appearance and behavior as they themselves are.

Adolescent egocentrism is often expressed as a preoccupation with how others respond and as a belief in personal invulnerability. This girl (left photo) may be spending a lot of time choosing clothes because she is concerned about what others will think of how she looks. The boy (right photo) may be willing to risk a broken limb in skateboarding because he does not really believe that he can be injured.
Sources: (left) dean bertoncelj/Shutterstock.com; *(right)* bikeriderlondon/Shutterstock.com.

We all have experienced embarrassing moments. It is just that, during adolescence, they seem so much worse due to the natural changes inherent with the age, but also due to the existence of the imaginary audience. Alberts, Elkind, and Ginsburg (2007) acknowledge that the imaginary audience does not disappear after adolescence—adults are also egocentric. It is just that during the teenage years, it is harder to differentiate between our own perspective and the view that others have of us and of their own world.

The Personal Fable

personal fable Adolescents' belief that their own lives embody a special story that is heroic and completely unique.

As a result of their egocentrism, teenagers often believe in a **personal fable**, the notion that their own lives embody a special story that is heroic and completely unique. For example, one high school student may be convinced that no love affair has ever reached the romantic heights of his involvement with a classmate. Another may believe she is destined for great fame and fortune by virtue of (what she considers to be) her unparalleled combination of charm and academic talent.

In experiencing these feelings and ideas, adolescents fail to realize how other individuals feel about them as well (Alberts et al., 2007). Early in adolescence, they still have only limited empathy, or the ability to understand reliably the abstract thoughts and feelings of others and compare those thoughts and feelings with their own. In fact, much of adolescence consists of developing these social skills. So does most of adulthood, for that matter; we never really finish learning how to understand others or comparing our own experiences with those of others. But adolescence is the time when most people begin learning to consider other viewpoints in relation to their own and developing complex ideas about moral, political, and religious questions, among others, in response.

However, not all teenagers seem equally egocentric, and even those who do show this quality only when compared to adults, not to younger children. Investigations of adolescents' belief in an imaginary audience show that teenagers are just as likely to develop greater empathy or interpersonal sensitivity during this developmental period as they are to develop greater self-centeredness (Lapsley, 1991). Accurate awareness of others' opinions about oneself apparently develops alongside, and sometimes even instead of, self-conscious preoccupation with others' opinions. The relative balance between these two developments depends, among other things, on the quality of relationships between parents and the adolescent: closer and more supportive relationships lead to greater realism and less self-consciousness.

Information-Processing Features of Adolescent Thought

As we saw in Chapter 2, information-processing theory sees human cognition as a complex storage and retrieval system, governed largely by an "executive" control system that transfers information between working and long-term memory and organizes information for more efficient and meaningful handling and retrieval. When cognition is viewed this way, development consists largely of overcoming the bottlenecks in processing information, especially those caused by the limited capacities of the executive and short-term memory. As children mature into adolescents, they develop strategies for taking in, organizing, and remembering larger amounts of information more quickly and with less effort. The most important of these strategies are included in Figure 10.5 and explained more fully next.

Improved Capacity to Process Information

Typically, an adolescent can deal with, or process, more information than a child can (Gathercole et al., 2004). A first-grader may remember three or four random digits (3 9 5 1), but a teenager usually can remember six or seven. And when a first-grader asks an adult how to spell a word, he can hold only two or three letters in his mind at a time; the adult has to dole them out singly or in very small groups *(LO...CO...MO...TI...VE)*. A teenager, however, can more often encounter much longer groupings of letters and still reconstruct the word accurately.

> **What Do You Think?**
>
> Suppose you are starting your first job in a helping profession, such as nursing or teaching. How much would you want your work to be guided by an ethics of justice and how much by an ethics of care? Exchange your feelings about this question with a classmate or a friend.

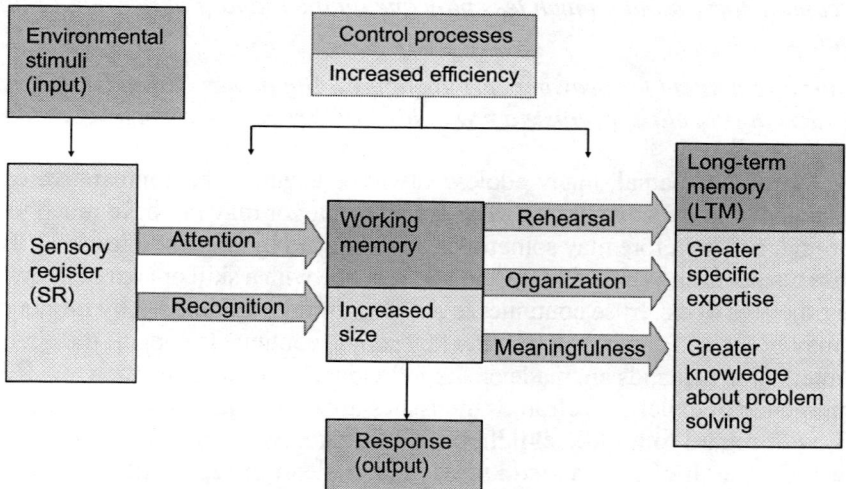

FIGURE 10.5

Developmental Changes in Information Processing

Although the basic nature of information processing remains the same from childhood to adolescence, important changes occur in several features, as the figure indicates. Working memory may increase in capacity, control processes become more efficient, and long-term memory contains more specific knowledge about problem solving, or "how to think."

Several developmental changes allow for this increase in processing capacity during adolescence. As mentioned earlier in this chapter, changes in the physiology of the brain contribute to more efficient processing of information. The streamlined neural networks that result from pruning and the myelination process are especially important changes when it comes to processing information in working memory. Because the capacity of working memory is limited with respect to quantity of information it can hold and length of time that it can be accessed, *speed of processing* is a significant determinant of how much information can be handled at one time and, therefore, the degree of complexity of the problems or situations that can be addressed at any given time (Demetriou et al., 2002).

Metacognition (awareness and regulation of one's own thought processes) also improves during adolescence, enabling teenagers to select increasingly more effective strategies for handling whatever cognitive challenges they face (Kuhn, 2009). For example, if an adolescent has an exam in one of his classes next week, he will choose a strategy that will help him best prepare for that exam based upon his knowledge about the exam structure (Will it be a multiple-choice or an essay exam?), the teacher (Does the teacher usually expect lots of details, or does the teacher focus on larger, key constructs?), his desired grade (How much time and effort will it take to get an "A" on this test?), and his current level of mastery of the content (Does the material make sense to some extent, or do I need to invest considerably more effort to comprehend the content?). And then, while studying, the adolescent's metacognitive abilities will allow him to assess his level of mastery and to change tactics if his approach to studying is not producing the desired results. Metacognition impacts processing capacity in that the adolescent does not allocate limited cognitive resources to information he already understands, and he can invoke strategies that will reduce the volume of information he needs to process at one time (e.g., mnemonics or other strategies for organizing or clustering information reduce the cognitive "load" posed by the information being processed).

Increases in *attention* also enhance information-processing capacity during adolescence. Compared to children, adolescents are able to stay on task longer, select more relevant information to the task at hand, and inhibit intrusive or distracting thoughts as they tackle challenging problems (Luna et al., 2013). Looking back at Figure 10.5, you can see

Chapter 10 Physical and Cognitive Development in Adolescence

how many elements of the model of information processing undergo significant changes during adolescence that result in their achievement of almost adult-like sophistication in their problem-solving abilities. What limits the information-processing capabilities of adolescents, when compared to adults, is their relative lack of expertise and experience.

Expertise in Specific Domains of Knowledge

- *Jerry can play the piano well, but his math skills are so-so.*
- *Marni cannot carry a tune, much less play one on the piano. But her math skills are excellent.*
- *Jamal has a real talent for drawing cartoon figures. But he has learned not to make or display drawings in class, because a few of his teachers regard them as "doodling."*

Like Jerry, Marni, and Jamal, many adolescents have begun to be comparative experts in specific domains of knowledge or skill. The domains may or may not have much to do with school learning, and therefore may sometimes go unnoticed by friends or teachers. Typically, the expertise results from years of interest in and practice with a skill or area of knowledge. In some cases, the area of expertise continues to develop during adulthood. Any further development that may occur will depend on whether key people continue to support the development and what alternative demands are made on the individual's time and attention.

The emergence of expertise reframes the issues about general intelligence discussed in Chapter 8, with regard to middle childhood. During adolescence, the issue is now about the nature and breadth of specialized knowledge. Instead of representing an all-purpose competence, **expertise** refers to the long, slow acquisition of specific knowledge, along with improvements in how the knowledge is organized. In the long term, highly developed expertise resembles what we often think of as a general "ability" (Sternberg, 1998). The difference between expertise and "ability" is a focus on completion versus ongoing development: *expertise* tends to refer to knowledge and skills that are still growing, whereas *ability* implies knowledge and skills that have already been formed.

A place where ability and expertise merge may be viewed in the area of problem solving. Experts in a chosen area of interest or ability, even in adolescence, show identifiable differences in how they solve problems, compared to their peers with less expertise. Teens who are considered effective problem solvers are better at (1) focusing their attention on what is important, (2) holding more information in both working and long-term memory by chunking information into procedural knowledge that is easily retrieved, (3) taking more time to analyze a problem initially, and (4) monitoring their own performance and progress (Woolfolk, 2013). Here we see that, even during adolescence, the executive functions in the prefrontal cortex of the brain can show the maturity to balance the influences of the limbic system, especially in areas where the teen is highly interested and personally motivated. Referring again to Figure 10.5, notice how much the components of "expertise" focus on the relationship between working memory and long-term memory. A fast and fluid relationship between these two memory stores, governed by enhanced executive functioning (i.e., "control processes"), is central to the thought processes of experts.

In areas outside of one's zone of expertise, an adolescent's performance may be no better than average. Studies of expertise in adulthood show the nature of this sort of competence especially clearly (Gregg & Leinhardt, 1995). A highly trained physicist knows many more concepts about physics than a beginner does, but not necessarily more about geography, English grammar, or other areas of knowledge. A mathematician knows countless formulas and solution methods, thanks to years of experience in learning them, but her talent is no guarantee that she can solve problems about business management, classroom teaching, or nursing. This is also true in athletics: an outstanding baseball player may not be as proficient in golf, or a talented figure skater may be no better at skiing than a person first taking up the sport. The sort of "earned" competence such individuals show becomes increasingly prominent in adulthood, as we will see in Chapter 14's discussion of cognition in middle adulthood.

---

expertise Specialized experience in specific domains of knowledge that enables efficient and effective performance and is not hampered by age.

> **What Do You Think?**
>
> Think of an activity or area of knowledge in which you consider yourself a relative expert. How much of your expertise has resulted from knowing a lot of specific facts about the area? How much has resulted from organizing your knowledge better than other people do? Compare your opinions with a classmate's or a friend's, especially if she or he is an expert in areas other than yours.

The Influence of School

In modern industrialized countries, school plays a formal role in developing certain forms of expertise, while at the same time introducing young people to new social relationships. From the point of view of adolescents, school is *both* a cognitive and social experience, and activities often serve both purposes at once. Participating in the school's chess club may improve your cognitive functioning and problem-solving abilities, but it may also facilitate making new friends. Listening attentively to a math teacher may help clarify some part of the math curriculum and result in a good grade, but it also may result in the teacher becoming your advocate due to your work ethic. Participating on a school sport team may enhance your athletic abilities, but it may also improve your self-discipline and group functioning skills. Unfortunately, the converse can occur: an activity may fail either to teach, to provide desirable social contact, or both. To clarify the connections between the cognitive and social effects of schooling, we look at each area separately in this section. As you will see, each area influences the other significantly, though not always in ways teachers and parents desire.

Cognitive Effects of Schooling

School influences adolescents' thinking through both a formal curriculum and an informal curriculum. The *formal curriculum* refers to a school's official program: the courses offered, the books required for reading, and the assignments expected for completion. The *informal curriculum* includes the unplanned activities and relationships that influence students' academic knowledge and motivation to learn—their relationships with teachers, for example, or the "gossip" and other tips related to schoolwork picked up from classmates. Both the formal and the informal curriculum are extremely diverse. One emphasizes the cognitive skills that may influence or impede success, while the other is based on how a student performs using noncognitive skills like optimism, resilience, and grit (Tough, 2012). What one student learns can be quite unlike what another learns because of differences in students' experiences in school as well as differences in their personal backgrounds.

In spite of the diversity that normally exists among teachers, students, and classroom experiences, most schools *seek* to develop students' broad ability at **critical thinking**, the ability to solve problems and to think reflectively and creatively about ideas and issues, usually for purposes of making decisions or taking actions (Keating & Sasse, 1996). Schools are also recognizing that critical-thinking skills can be encouraged when understanding how students use preferences for learning that Howard Gardner (1993b) identified as multiple intelligence or seem to excel in the noncognitive skills mentioned earlier. Whether they actually succeed is another question, which we will return to soon. First, though, let's look at what critical thinking involves and what, therefore, may be required to encourage it among students.

critical thinking Reflection or thinking about complex issues, usually to make decisions or take actions.

The Nature of Critical Thinking

Critical thinking is a broad, practical skill: it can help a person figure out why an unfamiliar appliance broke down, how to compose a term paper, how to resolve a conflict with a friend, how to decide what kind of career path to pursue, or how to evaluate the quality and the source of information provided. As these examples suggest, not all critical thinking occurs in school settings, and this fact poses a challenge to teachers and curriculum experts whose access to students generally is limited to classrooms and related environments.

What does critical thinking involve? Educators and psychologists have analyzed it in various ways, but usually point out the following elements (King & Kitchener, 1994):

1. *Basic operations of reasoning* To think critically, a person must be able to classify, generalize, deduce conclusions, and perform other logical steps mentally.

2. *Domain-specific knowledge* To deal with a problem, a person must know something about its topic or content. To evaluate a proposal for a new, fairer tax system, a person must know something about the existing tax system. To resolve a personal conflict, a person has to know something about the person with whom he is having the conflict.

3. *Metacognitive knowledge* (knowledge about how human thinking works, including one's own) Effective critical thinking requires a person to monitor when she really understands an idea, know when she needs new information, and predict how easily she can gather and learn that information. In other words, she has to be able think about her own thinking!

4. *Values, beliefs, and dispositions* Thinking critically means valuing fairness and objectivity. It means having confidence that thinking does in fact lead to solutions. It also means having a persistent and reflective disposition when thinking.

Interestingly, research has found that students themselves understand these elements of critical thinking (Nichols et al., 1995). Furthermore, compared to grade-school children, adolescents regard critical thinking as a fairer and more appropriate purpose of schooling.

Programs to Foster Critical Thinking

Educators have devised a number of programs intended to foster the qualities needed for critical thinking (French & Rhodes, 1992), many of which serve adolescents. The programs differ in their particulars: they last for various lengths of time, emphasize different thinking skills, and draw on content from different areas of the standard school curriculum. Some programs are integrated into the curriculum, meaning they replace a traditional course in some subject area; others are taught separately and draw content from several areas at once.

But experts do agree on several general principles that enhance the quality of programs that teach critical thinking. First, critical thinking is best taught directly and explicitly. Critical thinking does not develop on its own by unconscious osmosis, so to speak (Keefe & Walberg, 1992). Watching the teacher or a classmate think critically does not guarantee that a student will become a better thinker. Neither does giving a student a lot of practice in simple mental operations, such as basic addition or simple logical puzzles.

Second, good programs for teaching thinking offer lots of practice at solving actual problems. Merely describing the elements of critical thinking (as this text is doing) does not turn students into skillful thinkers. To accommodate the need for practice, the most successful educational programs last at least a full academic year and sometimes also weave the thinking skills into other, related courses to extend the effects of the program still further.

Third, successful programs try to create an environment explicitly conducive to critical thinking. Typically, they expect teachers to model important critical-thinking skills themselves, such as thinking out loud while they explain a solution to a problem. The programs also expect teachers to convey confidence in students' ability to think while providing constructive, explicit criticism of ideas, whether their own or those of the students. For example, one technique is to invite individual students to temporarily act as teacher or constructive critic (Slavin, 1995). Teaching critical-thinking skills is not a passive enterprise. It requires active learning, timely feedback, and increasingly more challenging experiences to keep the students and teachers engaged.

No Child Left Behind Act

A fairly recent and controversial national reform effort to enhance the cognitive impact of schooling on children and adolescents likely had an impact on your school experiences if you are a traditional-aged college student. In 2002, the U.S. Congress passed the *No Child*

Left Behind Act (NCLB). This act was designed to improve school performance overall and to increase the level of academic proficiency in high school graduates. The law specified detailed educational benchmarks for many grades and mandated standardized testing to assess the learning of every child (however, many children, school districts, and even entire states have been exempted from these standards). The law has faced much criticism on several fronts. Mandating that students pass tests simply forces teachers to "teach to the tests" (Koretz, 2008); anxiety levels in students are greatly increased (Samuels, 2005); some students—especially those in low-income districts or those with learning disabilities—are greatly disadvantaged under the structure of the standardized tests (Yeh, 2008).

The long-term impact of the No Child Left Behind Act is still not clear, and the debate about its merits continues, yet educators and the public support the increases in funding that the law brought to many districts, the attempt to gather objective measures of school and student success, the emphasis on teacher training, the adoption of more effective pedagogies, and the heightened national interest in improving K–12 education in the United States (Sunderman, 2008). In December 2015, NCLB was replaced with the Every Student Succeeds Act (ESSA), which maintains the funding increases of NCLB while providing more local control over educations systems and reducing some of the testing burden placed on schools and educators by NCLB (U.S. Department of Education, 2015).

Whatever differences may exist in programs designed to improve the educational experiences of adolescents, programs that teach critical thinking develop greater expertise in academic disciplines draw on the spirit, if not the literal, research findings, of several strands of cognitive theory concerning the adolescent years. One strand is Piagetian, with its concern for how logic and reasoning gradually develop. Another is information-processing theory, with its focus on specific ways of organizing ideas and coordinating new ideas with preexisting ones. A third strand is the concern with the social and cultural context of cognitive development in adolescence: how people and settings affect a young person's thinking. As the "A Multicultural View" feature indicates, cultural differences and misunderstandings can complicate teachers' efforts to encourage critical-thinking skills and content mastery in the classroom. Social influences are so important, in fact, that we discuss them more fully in the next section.

Social Effects of Schooling

For early adolescents, the period following graduation from elementary school can be one of increased social and emotional stress: their new school is usually larger, teachers are more numerous, new friendships must be formed, and students must adjust to being the youngest, least knowledgeable members of the school community. In the United States, schools have tried to address these concerns with transitions and school buildings that are more developmentally appropriate. The older model of a K–6 elementary school, followed by junior high school for grades 7–9, and ending with a grades 10–12 high school, while still used in some areas, is no longer the norm. Research in the 1990s on the junior high school model indicated a need for change. Some of the studies found that in the course of their first year of junior high, students report less positive attitudes about school, poorer achievement, and lower levels of participation in extracurricular activities (Eccles et al., 1996; Finders, 1997; Otis et al., 2005). New students (especially girls) report feeling less positive about themselves (Benner & Graham, 2009), and instances of both bullying and being bullied—often with sexual overtones—are widespread (Lee et al., 1996). A new structural model—including less disruptive school transitions—needed to be instituted, one that was both developmentally sound and safe for young adolescents.

A major response to these stresses has been to create **middle schools**, which are deliberately organized to take students' developmental needs into account. Middle schools typically span fifth through eighth grades. They share features both of elementary schools, such as smaller size and fewer class changes per day, and of high school, such as specialization in class subjects. A primary feature of middle schools is the assignment of students to a "home-base" or homeroom class that students visit every day and where the teacher acts as an adviser to help them to navigate the new challenges of postelementary education (Galassi et al., 1997).

middle school School designed to meet the needs of young adolescents, and usually spanning approximately fifth- through eighth-grade and enrolling students of about age ten through thirteen.

> ### A Multicultural View
>
> #### Cross-Cultural Misunderstandings in the Classroom
>
> Consider these classroom situations and their impact:
>
> - Student 1 is quiet when his teacher speaks to him, but he generally looks down at the floor or away from her when she speaks. Even when the teacher encourages him to express his own ideas, Student 1 pauses and looks away for what feels like an eternity to the teacher.
>
> - Student 2 writes an essay for a social studies class entitled "Jobs in the Global Economy." To the teacher, the essay seems to meander all over the place and does not state its theme until the final paragraph. "It's as if you were telling me what you were thinking," the teacher wrote on the essay afterward, "instead of stating and then justifying a position."
>
> - Student 3 rarely answers questions completely when the teacher calls on her in class; she just mumbles an answer or remains silent. But when collaborating with a small group on a project or an activity, she is lively, talkative, and focused on the task.
>
> There are many possible reasons for these situations. One common explanation is *cross-cultural miscommunication,* culturally based differences in how individuals interpret comments and behaviors. Observations of conversations show that cultures vary in communication styles and that children acquire the styles in the course of learning their native language (Scollon & Scollon, 1994).
>
> Cultural communication styles can vary in the following ways, among others:
>
> 1. *Timing:* speakers expect different lengths of pauses between conversational turns, from many seconds to only a fraction of a second or even to a "negative" pause (overlapping comments).
>
> 2. *Deductiveness/inductiveness:* in some cultures, speakers are expected to state their point immediately (use a "topic sentence") and then justify their position; in others, speakers more often lead up to the main point indirectly, describing their thought processes along the way.
>
> 3. *Politeness indicators:* in some cultures, it is especially important to indicate respect for those in authority, chiefly by listening quietly, head bowed, averting the speaker's eyes, and expecting the authority (teacher) to determine the topic and length of a conversation.
>
> These cultural differences can pose problems whenever members of more than one culture come together to interact. For children and adolescents, therefore, cultural mismatch is especially likely in classrooms in large urban areas or large culturally diverse suburbs, particularly in contacts between teachers and students. If the teacher "speaks the culture" of white, mainstream English, she or he will tend to use and expect relatively short pauses between conversational turns in classroom discussions. The teacher will also tend to use and expect a deductive style of turn taking, with the topic stated immediately by whoever initiates a conversational exchange. And although the teacher may expect moderate indications of respect for his or her right to initiate topics of conversation, she or he may also expect students to initiate ideas and concerns of their own.
>
> When a student s culture supports other communication styles, the teacher can easily misinterpret the cultural underpinnings of the behavior and view student as either unintelligent, lacking in confidence, or deliberately resistant to learning (Lustig & Koester, 1993). Yet these sorts of mismatches are precisely what occur, and always to the disadvantage of the student. What the teacher sees and hears are pauses that are too long, eye contact that is poor, comments that stray from the topic, and silence in response to invitations to speak. What the student experiences, though, may be quite different: he or she may see and hear a teacher who is too talkative, stares at individuals too much, and seems insincere in issuing invitations to ask questions.
>
> But such misunderstandings can be overcome. Training in intercultural communication exists and is effective when focused on the key cultural misunderstandings of particular conversational partners. In the teaching profession, some of the most elaborate training occurs for teachers of English as a Second Language (Paulston, 1992), but programs are also developing in many business communities (Brislin & Yoshida, 1994; O'Hara-Devereaux & Johansen, 1994), where economic activity increasingly spans more than one country, language, and cultural community. The programs vary in detail, of course, but share a common assumption: that awkwardness between culturally different speakers is likely the result of legitimate differences in communication styles rather than of inferiority of one style or the other.

Studies of the impact of middle schools suggest that these changes can indeed help young adolescents adjust—but only if the teachers actually understand the students' developmental needs and adjust their ways of relating to students accordingly. In general, adjustment is more likely to succeed if teachers work together collegially supporting one another's efforts to innovate in classroom practices (Louis et al., 1996; Peterson et al., 1996).

Dropping Out of High School

Despite the efforts of schools and parents to help students make the transition to high school, some adolescents may not make the adjustment. Approximately 7 percent of all students drop out of high school (U.S. Department of Education (2014), although for several reasons the significance of this percentage is somewhat hard to interpret (Ianni & Orr, 1996). First, school jurisdictions vary in how they define "dropping out" (some leave students out of their records if they are more than eighteen). Second, some dropouts—possibly as many as a third—return to complete school in any one year; they might better be called temporary school leavers rather than permanent dropouts. Third, students drop out for a variety of reasons, ranging from general alienation from schooling, to family crises, to difficulties in fitting in with peers and teachers. Some of the reasons are more serious and long lasting than others and contribute to variations in students' tendency to return to school to complete a diploma.

Although the dropout rate is not evenly distributed among schools and communities, the significance of concentrations of dropouts is surprisingly ambiguous. A few large, inner-city high schools have high dropout rates, for example; as many as 50 percent of each entering ninth-grade class may not graduate. Dropping out is more frequent among nonwhite students (8 to 13 percent) than among white students (4 percent); yet this trend obscures the fact that half of all dropouts are white. Furthermore, dropping out is more frequent among low-income families than among middle- and high-income families; yet this trend can distract attention from the fact that nationwide, half of all dropouts are from middle-income families. These somewhat paradoxical statistics suggest an especially important point for teachers and other people who work with youth professionally: that although social categories (race, SES, urban residence) *correlate* with dropping out, they do not *cause* it. (See Chapter 1 for a discussion of the difference between correlation and causation.) Most adolescents *do* graduate from high school, even in urban communities, as do most youth who are nonwhite or poor.

Educational research therefore has looked for factors contributing to **resilience** in youth, to the factors that allow individual adolescents to cope with and overcome difficult circumstances. In general, the studies point to the importance of adults seeing and responding to the potential of individual teenagers, whether the adults be parents, school personnel, members of the community, or some combination of the three (Altenbaugh, 1995; Caterall, 1998). This is supported by research showing that adolescents, particularly those at risk for dropping out, who are engaged in extracurricular pursuits are less likely to drop out (Mahoney & Cairns, 1997; Wang & Fredricks, 2014). The research also suggests that teenagers do not necessarily get discouraged, nor necessarily drop out, because they become aware of belonging to social categories that have high dropout rates.

resilience Ability to withstand and even profit from stressful experiences.

A supportive relationship between a teacher and student—like the one pictured here—is especially important to the academic success of the student. These students are more likely to achieve greater academic proficiency and are less likely to drop out because of this caring relationship. Of course, it is also helpful if the school district is well funded, as this one appears to be, equipped with current technology and the training to use it effectively in the classroom.
Source: Goodluz/Shutterstock.com.

One study of urban African American youth found that those with the most conscious, articulate knowledge of racial discrimination were precisely the individuals most likely to *stay* in school and perform well (O'Connor, 1997)!

Even though the existence of dropouts implies that high schools may be limiting the potential of some students, it is important to recognize that many high schools are quite successful at providing both academic and social opportunities to which many students might not have access otherwise. Many educational observers and researchers have identified the qualities that lead to school effectiveness and success (Gallagher, 1996; Sizer, 1996; Slavin, 1998). For one thing, both teachers and students must be able to work in their own ways, even when those ways may be unconventional. Only by doing so can they honor the developmental diversity in most high school communities. For another, schools need to focus the attention of everyone—teachers, students, and parents—on their primary purpose: to promote learning. Given the diversity among students, teachers, and communities, it can be challenging to reconcile this second purpose with the first. Yet most high schools manage to do so, even if not perfectly.

Employment

School is not the only arena in which adolescents test their growing cognitive skills. Many also join the work force, either in addition to or in place of attending school. The majority of teenagers report participating in "formal" paid work outside the home, and many others engage in "informal" paid work such as babysitting and yardwork within their own homes (Mortimer & Finch, 1996). Informal work is likely to be a first paid job. Because it is fairly continuous with the chores and responsibilities of childhood, it provides a more gradual transition to the demands of adult work. Formal adult work typically takes place in commercial or other organizational settings. It represents a greater departure from childhood work and involves more relationships with adults, closer supervision, and more systematic monitoring of job performance.

The types of jobs frequently reported by teenagers include supermarket, restaurant, or retail store worker; office worker; and semiskilled worker. Most of these jobs are on the margins of the economy, and as such tend to offer low wages and little future as a career. For teenagers from economically well-off families, these facts may be just as well, because they create little temptation to pursue the job to the exclusion of schoolwork. For a large percentage of teenagers from low-SES families, the dead-end quality of first jobs poses a serious problem: these young people often depend on employment to pay their daily living expenses as well as those of their families (Newman, 1996).

Ideally, work during adolescence serves three important functions. First, it facilitates the transition from school to work. Second, it provides structure for involvement in family- and school-related activities. Finally, it provides an arena outside of home and school for gaining social experience and the material rewards needed to have an independent life with peers. How work influences adolescent mental health and adjustment depends on the type and level of workplace stress, the relevance of job-related skills to future careers, and the compatibility between the demands and experiences of work and school (Bell et al., 1996).

The intensity of formal work as measured by the number of hours worked per month is also important. Students who work more than ten hours per week do more poorly academically, report more psychological problems (depression, anxiety fatigue, sleeping difficulty), and physical problems (headaches, stomachaches, colds) than other students. They are also more likely to use drugs, smoke cigarettes, and engage in delinquent activities, regardless of ethnicity, SES, or age. In contrast, working fewer than ten hours per week generally appears to have no negative effects (Mortimer et al., 1994). It is also possible, of course, that students with intensive work involvements had more preexisting problems.

For teenagers whose families can afford it, working more than a moderate number of hours per week may be developmentally unwise because it interferes with aca-

> **What Do You Think?**
>
> Some educators argue that you cannot teach thinking skills in *general*, because a person always thinks about something in *particular*. Why do you think they take this position? This issue makes for a useful debate in class, especially if you adopt the position contrary to the one you truly embrace!

demic activities, exposes them to negative environments and role models, and limits the amount of monitoring and supervision they receive from parents, teachers, and other positive role models. Moreover, becoming accustomed to having a paycheck that may be used entirely for leisure pursuits might be a financial hindrance when these adolescents become adults and the majority of their income goes to food, rent, insurance, and the like (Bachman, 1983). Many students, particularly those receiving appropriate levels of adult monitoring and support, make sensible decisions about the role of work in their lives, adjusting their choice of work and number of hours to meet their other important academic and social needs. This adjustment continues to be made throughout life, as we will see in later chapters on adulthood.

Chapter Summary

- **What is meant by *adolescence*, and what changes in society contributed to its gaining recognition as a developmental stage?** Adolescence, which begins around age ten and lasts until about age twenty-two, is a developmental transition between childhood and adulthood. Some theories of adolescence emphasize the "storm and stress" of the period, whereas others portray it as a continuation of developmental trends begun in childhood.

- **What changes in height, weight, and appearance can be expected during adolescence, and how do they differ for girls and boys?** Adolescents experience significant increases in height and weight, but variations in the timing of the "growth spurt" among teenagers are even more striking. On average, boys start their growth spurt later than girls. Individual variations create worries about personal appearance for some adolescents.

- **What are the effects of early, "on-time," and late development during puberty, and how do the effects differ for girls and boys?** In addition to increases in height and weight, a larger pattern of changes occurs called *puberty*, which leads to full physical and sexual maturity. Primary sexual maturation among boys includes rapid growth of the penis and scrotum and production of fertile semen; among girls, it is marked by menarche, or the beginning of menstrual cycles. Maturation of secondary sex characteristics includes enlargement and development of the breasts, growth of body hair, deepening of the voice, and increased production of sex-related hormones.

    Although girls and boys are equally muscular prior to adolescence, during puberty boys experience significantly greater increases in muscle tissue than girls do. Girls experience a somewhat greater increase in body fat than boys do. The physical sex differences of puberty are accentuated by differences in life experiences related to gender-role expectations. For boys, the effects of early maturation tend to be positive in the short run but negative in the long run. Late maturation tends to have the reverse effects. For girls, early maturation tends to be more stressful in the short term but positive in the long term. Late maturers tend to experience immediate benefits during adolescence and no serious long-term negative effects. The timing of puberty affects only average response to puberty; individuals with identical timing vary widely in their responses, depending on their circumstances.

- **What major health problems do adolescents face, and in what ways are adolescents more at risk than other age groups?** Adolescent patterns of illness and health care are influenced by individual and family attitudes and resources. Adolescents are a high-risk group for injury and death due to risky lifestyles and their myth of invulnerability. Major health-compromising behaviors of adolescence include exposure to sexually transmitted diseases; alcohol, tobacco, and drug abuse; inadequate diet; insufficient sleep; and eating disorders.

- **What has recent research in neuroscience discovered about brain development during adolescence?** The brains of adolescents experience a period of rapid development, including the formation of new synapses, myelination, and the pruning of excess or unused neural pathways. Consistent with the "use it or lose it" principle, these changes have long-term implications for the cognitive functioning of the adolescent. Also, different parts of the brain mature at different points during adolescence, resulting in the increased influence of emotion over logic when it comes to adolescent decision making.

- **To what extent are adolescents capable of abstract reasoning?** During adolescence, some teenagers (though not all) develop formal operational thought, or the ability to reason about ideas regardless of their content. Formal thought is characterized by an ability to think about possibilities, by scientific reasoning, and by an ability to combine ideas logically. Research on adult thinking suggests that formal operations are not the final point of cognitive development, or necessarily a step toward mature thinking.

- **How does cognitive development affect adolescents' knowledge and beliefs about their identities and about morality?** Adolescents develop two forms of morality—one oriented toward justice and one oriented toward caring for self and others. Lawrence Kohlberg proposed six stages in the development of moral judgments oriented toward justice. A number of issues regarding Kohlberg's theory have yet to be resolved, including the significance of the content (versus the form) of moral beliefs, differences between conventions and morality, and the possibility of gender differences in moral development. Carol Gilligan proposed forms of moral development oriented toward interpersonal caring; on average, these forms may be slightly more characteristic of females than males, though many exceptions exist. Despite their improved cognitive skills, adolescents still sometimes show egocentrism by believing in an "imaginary audience" and in a "personal fable," or biography of their lives.

- **How do adolescents show improved information processing in everyday activities?** During adolescence, information-processing skills continue to improve. Teenagers acquire greater expertise in particular areas of knowledge or skill, a trend that continues into adulthood.

- **What cognitive and social effects do school and work have on adolescent development?** School has significant effects on adolescents' lives, both cognitively and socially. Cognitively, school encourages the development of critical thinking, the ability to reflect about complex issues to make decisions or take actions. Educational programs to foster critical thinking usually do so explicitly, offer practice in solving problems, and create an environment conducive to critical thinking. Socially, school can be stressful for youngsters, especially early in adolescence. Many teenagers drop out of high school each year, though their reasons vary; the majority, however, complete school with a reasonable degree of success. Many students work part time while attending school, and the experience has diverse effects, depending on the particular job and circumstances of the student.

Key Terms

adolescence (p. 334)
adolescent egocentrism (p. 363)
anorexia nervosa (p. 349)
binge eating disorder (p. 349)
bulimia nervosa (p. 349)
critical thinking (p. 367)
estrogen (p. 338)
expertise (p. 366)
formal operational thought (p. 353)

growth spurt (p. 335)
imaginary audience (p. 363)
menarche (p. 337)
middle school (p. 369)
morality (p. 357)
personal fable (p. 364)
postconventional moral judgment (p. 360)
primary sex characteristics (p. 337)

puberty (p. 337)
resilience (p. 371)
secondary sex characteristics (p. 337)
social cognition (p. 363)
social conventions (p. 360)
testosterone (p. 338)

Psychosocial Development in Adolescence

CHAPTER 11

Source: melis/Shutterstock.com.

Chapter Outline

Theories of Identity Development

Family Relationships During Adolescence

Social Relationships During Adolescence

Sexuality During Adolescence

Special Problems of Adolescence

Looking Back/Looking Forward

Focusing Questions

- What conflicts do adolescents typically experience in their search for identity? What factors support or hinder successful identity development?
- What special challenges does adolescence pose for parents? How do differences in parenting style affect parent-teenager relationships?
- In what ways do adolescent friendships and peer groups play a constructive role, and how are concerns about their negative influence justified?
- What changes in sexual activities and attitudes occur among teenagers? How are they related to other aspects of adolescent development?
- Why are adolescents at risk for problems such as pregnancy, depression, and delinquency?

As we have discovered, adolescence is a time of dramatic physical and cognitive changes. Although the rate at which these changes occur varies greatly, by the end of this period, most adolescents look like adults and are physically and intellectually capable of most adult activities. But as important as these changes are, the changes that occur in the social-emotional domain may be even more significant. Perhaps the most important change is the progress adolescents make in achieving a full-fledged and integrated psychological identity that is mature, adult, unique, and separate from those of parents, friends, and other important childhood figures. A stable identity gives teenagers a more integrated sense of who they really are, what they believe in, and their realistic limitations and capabilities. Zoe, who has just begun her senior year of high school, put it this way:

> It's not just that I'm all grown up now—physically, I mean. It's that I have grown up inside, too. I feel different, more like a grownup than a child. Although there are still many things I'm unsure of, I finally have a much clearer sense of who I am and what is important to me and what I believe in. And this may sound strange, but the sense of independence and separateness that I now feel means I can often be close to my parents and friends without losing a sense of who I am and my confidence in my ability to succeed at achieving the things I really want. In a way, it feels like I'm at the end of a long journey and ready to start off on a new one.

As Zoe's thoughts reveal, she has embraced an enhanced capacity for psychological autonomy, intimacy, and relatedness to her parents, family, and friends, and she has made significant strides in achievement and self-esteem. All are very important accomplishments of adolescence (Allen et al., 1994).

In this chapter, we initially look at the process of adolescent identity development, as well as the related processes by which adolescents develop a healthy sense of autonomy, achievement, intimacy, and sexuality. We explore several important aspects of the teenager's changing social world, including relationships with parents and peers, the development of friendships, and the impact of school and work. We also look at adolescent sexuality and how it is influenced by current social trends and personal beliefs. Finally, we explore the special problems adolescents face today and some strategies for preventing them.

Theories of Identity Development

Parents often are surprised at how much care and reflection an eighteen- or nineteen-year-old has given to who he is and how strong his sense of personal direction can be. Just a few short years ago, this same child was irritable and uncertain at home and with his peers. A clear path forward was uncharted and navigated with frustrating fits and starts. Now, this emerging adult reveals a sense of purpose, welcomes opportunities for demonstrating his maturing skills, and transitions from someone who was only interested in the moment to someone with an eye on attainable goals and aspirations in the near future. How is this possible? What are the contributing factors that lead to the development of a strong sense of personal identity? Several theorists have explored this process.

Ruthellen Josselson: Individuation and Identity Development

individuation The process by which an adolescent develops a unique and separate personal identity. Consists of four subphases: differentiation, practice and experimentation, rapprochement, and consolidation.

Individuation is the process by which an adolescent develops a unique personal identity or sense of self, one distinct and separate from all others. Ruthellen Josselson (1980) has proposed that the individuation process consists of four separate but overlapping subphases: differentiation, practice and experimentation, rapprochement, and consolidation of self.

During the *differentiation* subphase early in adolescence, the teenager recognizes that she is psychologically different from her parents. The dual discovery that she is no longer an extension of her parents and that they are not as wise, powerful, and all-knowing as she thought earlier sometimes leads her to often question and reject her parents' values and advice, even if they are reasonable.

In the *practice and experimentation* subphase, the fourteen- or fifteen-year-old may believe he knows it all and can do no wrong. He may deny any need for caution or advice and actively challenge his parents at every opportunity. A sense of youthful invincibility clouds his judgment. He now turns to like-minded friends, who provide the support and approval he previously sought from adults. In a discussion of plans to go to a multiband rock concert with his friends, for example, Alonzo will completely dismiss his parents' concerns about the risks and dangers in attending. Instead, he will convincingly plead to his parents (and himself) that his friends, who went to last year's concert, have assured him that it was perfectly safe. After all, they know what they are talking about!

During the *rapprochement* subphase, teens begin to make a healthy course correction. Toward the middle of adolescence, a teenager has achieved enough separateness from her parents that she is now able to *conditionally* reaccept their authority. Often, she will alternate between experimentation and rapprochement—on some occasions, challenging her parents, and at other times, being conciliatory and cooperative. Maria is a good case in point. Having just turned fifteen, she goes to great lengths to accept responsibility around the house, but often becomes highly indignant and argumentative when her parents still insist on a curfew and on knowing where she is going and who she is going with when she leaves the house in the evening.

It is during the final *consolidation-of-self* subphase, which lasts through adolescence and into early adulthood, that an individual develops a sense of personal identity. This milestone development provides the basis for understanding self and others, and for maintaining a sense of autonomy, independence, and individuality. Shannon, a high school junior who will soon be applying to colleges, is a good example. Viewed by herself and her family as somewhat disorganized and lacking maturity and a clear life direction, Shannon in fact surprised them during the college application process. On her own initiative, Shannon met with the school counselor and accessed college websites to take virtual tours of the schools she was interested in for starters. She then created her own "self-evaluation plan," in which she listed the academic and social qualities she wanted in a school, along with her personal strengths and weaknesses as a student. Added to her plan were the cost, location, admission criteria, and application deadlines for the top seven schools she thought would be a good fit for her. Shannon then invited her parents into the decision-making process by viewing the schools online and planning college visits with them. Her parents were amazed by the initiative and industriousness Shannon displayed in the search process. But they were also very proud of her maturity and independence in taking on this important task.

The process of individuation continues throughout the teenage years and into early adulthood. As we will see shortly, Josselson's ideas about individuation dovetail with Erikson's theory, which holds that the major task of adolescence is to resolve the crisis of identity successfully.

For these adolescent girls, it is likely that their willingness to engage in what has traditionally been a male sport reflects a strong sense of individual identity and self-direction, as well as changing cultural expectations regarding female participation in sports.
Source: Shawn Pecor/Shutterstock.com.

Erik Erikson: The Crisis of Identity Versus Role Confusion

According to Erik Erikson (see Chapter 2), the key developmental challenge of adolescence is to resolve the crisis of **identity versus role confusion** (Erikson, 1963). In forming an identity, an adolescent selectively accepts or rejects the many different aspects of herself that she acquired as a child and forms a more coherent and integrated sense of unique identity (Damon & Hart, 1988; Harter, 1989; Harter & Monsour, 1992). During middle childhood, she may have formed separate views of herself based on her school success or athletic abilities, and most significantly, on how her friends viewed her. In adolescence, however, she mulls over the significance of all of these impressions taken together and integrates them into a single identity encompassing all of her strengths and weaknesses and an awareness of what this all means. An adolescent's increasing capacity for abstract thought and self-understanding (see Chapter 10) plays a central role in this process.

identity versus role confusion The fifth of Erikson's psychosocial crises, in which one must integrate one's many childhood skills and beliefs and gain recognition for them from society.

As adolescents experiment with different roles in their search to create a coherent sense of identity, many experience a sense of *false self*—that is, a sense that one is acting in ways that do not reflect one's true self as a person, or the "real me." Each of the many different role-related selves that adolescents experience, such as self with parents, self with friends, self as a classmate, and self with a girlfriend or boyfriend, contains qualities that seem to contradict one another. For example, an adolescent may be outgoing with friends but shy with a romantic partner, or cheerful with friends and depressed with parents (Harter et al., 1996).

Susan Harter and her colleagues (Harter et al., 1996) asked middle school and high school students to describe their true and their false selves. Descriptions of their true selves included "the real me inside," "my true feelings," "what I really think and feel," and "behaving the way I want to behave and not how someone else wants me to be." False selves were described as "being phony," "putting on an act," "expressing things you don't really believe or feel," or "changing yourself to be something that someone else wants you to be." False-self beliefs and behaviors could have both a positive role in identity formation and a negative one. The path taken by a teen is often influenced by parental support and one's perception

Chapter 11 Psychosocial Development in Adolescence 377

of exploring their false self. Adolescents who reported high levels of positive support from parents and peers engaged in fewer false-self behaviors than those who experienced lower levels and poorer quality of support. Teens who engaged in false-self behavior as a healthy way to experiment with new roles reported more positive feelings about themselves, higher self-worth, greater hopefulness about the future, and more knowledge of their true selves than teens who engaged in false-self behavior to please, impress, or win the approval of parents and peers or because they were experiencing depression or other problems.

Psychosocial Moratorium

psychosocial moratorium According to Erikson, the latency period that precedes puberty and provides a temporary suspension of psychosexual development.

According to Erikson (1968), adolescence provides a **psychosocial moratorium**, a period during which the youth is free to suspend or delay taking on adult commitments and to explore new social roles. The goal of role experimentation is to find a place, or niche, that is clearly defined and yet seems uniquely made for him. The adolescent may devote this time to study, work, travel, or even rebellious and/or delinquent behaviors, depending on prevailing social, cultural, and economic conditions, as well as on his individual capacities and needs.

The type of psychosocial moratorium an adolescent encounters (or whether she encounters one at all) will largely depend on the opportunities for identity exploration provided by her family, culture, society, and the global pathways available in a changing world (Jensen & Arnett, 2012). For example, children growing up under conditions of poverty and deprivation, gender inequality, or during periods of war and social upheaval are likely to experience more limited and less supportive moratorium opportunities than are children living under more optimal circumstances.

Identity Diffusion

identity diffusion A failure to achieve a relatively coherent, integrated, and stable identity.

Identity diffusion is one of the four identity statuses researched by Marcia (1966) that we will explore in detail. However, in a broader context, identity diffusion is the failure to achieve a relatively coherent, integrated, and stable identity, and it may take a number of forms. The first is *avoidance of closeness* with others. A second form—*diffusion of time perspective*—involves the belief that one is out of sync with others, fearing that important opportunities may be lost forever. Time diffusion is sometimes followed by feelings of depression and despair over the length of time it takes for a comfortable sense of identity to finally be achieved. The third form—*diffusion of industry*—may involve an inability to concentrate on school- or work-related tasks or an excessive preoccupation with a single activity that interferes with accomplishing other things. A final and more extreme form of identity diffusion is the choice of a negative identity. A **negative identity** involves the rejection of positive roles and valued opportunities made available by one's family or community resources, and the acceptance of socially undesirable roles, leading to delinquent and/or antisocial behaviors that we will discuss later in the chapter.

negative identity A form of identity diffusion involving rejection of the roles preferred by one's family or community in favor of socially undesirable roles.

The Relationship Between Identity and Intimacy

According to Erikson, successful resolution of the crisis of identity versus role confusion prepares the adolescent for the crisis of intimacy versus isolation, which occurs in early adulthood. A clear and coherent sense of identity provides a basis for achieving intimacy in friendships and love relationships and for tolerating the fear of losing one's sense of self when intimacy becomes very intense and of experiencing loneliness and isolation if a relationship ends. However, as we will see in Chapter 13's discussion of psychosocial development in early adulthood, the establishment of an intimate relationship with a partner frequently occurs prior to, or simultaneously with, the resolution of identity issues. The lifelong challenges of successfully forming and maintaining intimate long-term relationships with friends, co-workers, lovers, marriage partners, and eventually our own children all require that we develop an increasingly reliable sense of who we are and where we are going.

Identity Status

Guided by Erikson's ideas, researchers such as James Marcia (1966, 1980) and Jane Kroger (2007; Kroger et al., 2010) have empirically studied identity development during adolescence. Marcia interviewed students ages eighteen to twenty-two about their occupational choices and religious and political beliefs and values, all central aspects of identity (Marcia, 1980, 1993; Marcia et al., 1993). He classified students into four categories of **identity status**, based on varying combinations of (1) *exploration* (whether or not they had gone through an "identity crisis" as described by Erikson) and (2) *commitment* (the degree to which they were now committed to an occupational choice and to a set of personal, religious, and political values and beliefs). Table 11.1 describes these categories.

Marcia's findings were as follows:

identity status Marcia's four categories of identity development: identity achievement, identity diffusion, moratorium, and foreclosure.

1. *Identity-achieved* individuals have experienced and successfully resolved a period of crisis by either reevaluating past choices and beliefs and accepting those of value or by adopting new beliefs based on their own terms and exploration, not solely those of their parents or another authority figure.

2. *Identity-diffused* individuals may or may not have experienced a crisis but are defined by the absence of exploration and commitment regarding their values and beliefs. These individuals lack a meaningful sense of direction in general and display little concern about personal identity formation (Dunkle & Anthis, 2001).

3. *Moratorium* individuals are presently *in* crisis, actively struggling to make commitments based on their own beliefs and goals. They remain preoccupied with exploring, and hopefully achieving, successful compromises among their parents' wishes, the demands of society, and their own capabilities.

4. *Foreclosed* individuals have "prematurely" committed themselves to important aspects of identity without having experienced any significant exploration through conflict or crisis. Consequently, the commitments formed are mostly through identification with their parents' beliefs and goals, or the influence of another external authority.

Most adolescents seem to progress toward a status of identity achieved. For both males and females, identity achievement is rarest among early adolescents and most frequent among older high school students, college students, and young adults. During junior and senior high school, identity diffusion and identity foreclosure are the most common identity statuses. Although diffused and foreclosed statuses significantly decrease during the later high school and college years, only about one-third of college juniors and seniors and one-quarter of adults studied have been found to be identity achieved (Archer & Waterman, 1988; Meilman, 1979).

Dunkle and Anthis (2001) conducted a short-term longitudinal study testing the relationship of identity exploration and commitment to the creation of possible selves. As young adolescents begin to imagine possible selves, both ideal and feared, identity exploration

TABLE 11.1 Crisis and Commitment in Marcia's Theory of Identity Status

According to James Marcia, adolescents can be classified into four categories of identity status based on the presence or absence of an identity crisis or exploration and whether or not they are committed to an occupational choice and a set of religious values and beliefs.

Identity Status	Crisis (Exploration)	Commitment
Achieved	Present	Present
Diffused	Present/absent	Absent
Moratorium	In process	In process
Foreclosed	Absent	Present

Source: Marcia (1980).

was more active as the number of possible selves generated grew. The researchers also discovered that as teens entered later adolescence and established more consistent possible selves, the commitment to setting and working toward these goals also increased. By exploring many possible selves in early adolescence, young teens begin to prune and shape the real self they present to the world as they transition from later adolescence into emerging adulthood.

Differences in social class, culture, and ethnicity may also affect identity development, depending on the context specific to an individual's life circumstances. Just as adolescents growing up during the Depression were much less likely to have the opportunity to experience a moratorium, minority youths living in poverty today are also likely to be much more limited in opportunities for identity status exploration than middle-class suburban teens attending college. Youngsters who live in poor neighborhoods where gangs, drugs, and violence are common and rates of school dropout and unemployment are high, and who lack positive adult and peer role models, are more likely to encounter difficulties in forming positive identities than adolescents growing up in a more supportive environment (Bat-Chava et al., 1997; McCloyd, 1998).

The proportion of individuals at each identity status appears to vary with the specific identity area involved. Identity achievement was the most frequent status in the area of *religious beliefs;* identity achievement and moratorium were the most frequent statuses where *vocational choice* was concerned; identity foreclosure was the most common status in the area of *gender-role preferences;* and identity diffusion was the most frequent status in the area of *political philosophies* (Archer, 1982; Krager, 1995; Marcia et al., 1993; Waterman, 1982, 1985). For example, when Jean Phinney and her colleagues conducted in-depth interviews with Asian American, Hispanic, and white American-born male and female high school students to assess stage of ethnic identity development, they found no significant differences based on either ethnic group or gender in the percentages of youngsters who were in the diffusion/foreclosure stage, moratorium stage, or achievement stage of ethnic identity development (Phinney et al., 1997). Groups did differ, however, in which issues were of most concern in resolving their identity crises. Nearly one-third of all adolescents in the United States are from non-European American backgrounds, and they, in turn, are from a variety of life circumstances (see Figure 11.1).

Few differences between males and females have been found on measures of identity. Both genders are equally represented among the four identity statuses and seem to develop in similar ways. Although early studies suggested that the identity statuses might have different psychological meanings and consequences for males and females, more recent research indicates that the meanings and implications appear to be quite similar for both genders (Archer & Waterman, 1988; Gilligan, 1987; Marcia, 1993).

FIGURE 11.1
Ethnic Minority Youth in the United States

Adolescents with African origins make up the largest percentage of ethnic minority youth in the United States, followed by adolescents from Hispanic, Asian Pacific, and Native American/Alaskan Native backgrounds.

Source: Adapted from Harrison et al. (1990), p. 350.

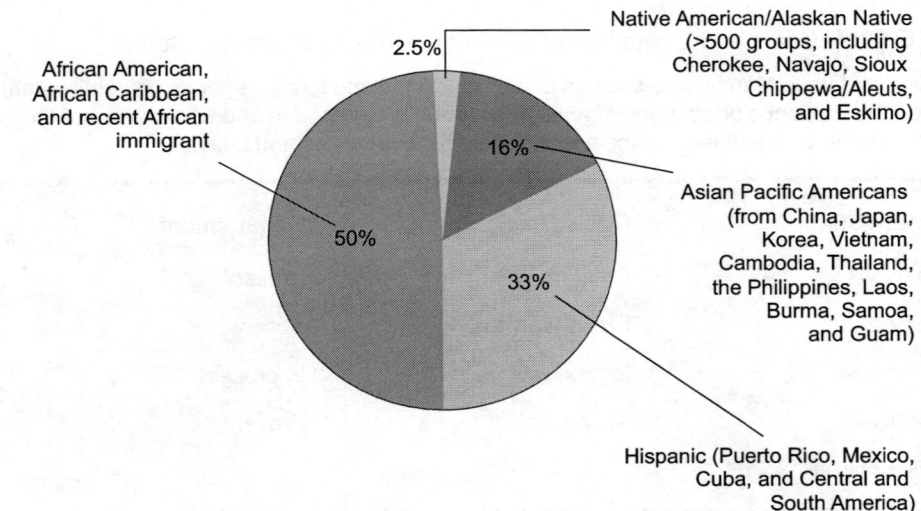

> **What Do You Think?**
>
> To what degree have you experienced the developmental crisis of identity versus role confusion proposed by Erikson? Which of Marcia's four identity statuses best describes you at this point in your development?

Although making progress in mastering Erikson's crisis of identity versus role confusion is a central task of adolescence, the process of developing an identity continues throughout the entire lifespan, as we will discover in Chapters 15 and 17. Identities continue to be formed as the young adult establishes a sense of intimacy in her relationships, rather than experience social isolation in her life. Similarly, in Erikson's final two stages, a stable identity allows a man in middle and late adulthood to successfully achieve a sense of generativity and ego integrity.

Family Relationships During Adolescence

The search for identity and the achievement of a mature psychological sense of autonomy and relatedness affect all of an adolescent's relationships. Ties with parents must make room for an increasing interest in peers and a new commitment to the life among comparative equals that peers provide. A young teenager's efforts to become more physically and emotionally independent from his parents and closer to his friends may be stressful, but more often than not, the problems and conflicts of this period are relatively minor. Full-blown upheavals and more serious problems of adolescence are most likely to occur in families and communities in which a poor fit exists between the developmental needs of adolescents and the opportunities and supports that are available (Eccles et al., 1993; Offer & Schonert-Reichl, 1992). We first explore relationships within the family, and then look at social relationships in the wider world.

Relationships with Parents

Even though the majority of teens get along well with their parents on a daily basis, parent-teenager relationships are likely to feel slightly "unstable" or "out of joint" some of the time. This is in part a result of the increasingly stressful pace of modern family life and the different ways adolescents and their parents choose to spend their time. Both adolescents and their parents tend to agree that differences in the activities, expectations, and interests of each family member make it difficult for them to find times to do things together and find activities that are of mutual interest (Larson & Richards, 1994).

The disconnectedness that parents and teenagers sometimes feel may also reflect teenagers' sensitivity to the discrepancies between their own and their parents' views of how their families function—whether individuals really get along with one another, for example, and who really makes decisions around the house (Carlson et al., 1991). Parents may think they listen to their teenager's opinions about what household chores she should do, but she herself may regard the "listening" as shallow or meaningless because parents evidently decide who does what chores anyway. When discrepancies such as these come into the open, conflicts usually arise ("You always say X, but you really mean Y!"). That is the bad news. The good news is that the conflicts frequently serve as catalysts for further growth in teenagers' social maturity and to reconcile gaps between parents and their nearly grown children (Holmbeck & O'Donnell, 1991; Robin et al., 1990). An important task of adolescence is to achieve adequate psychological separation, or independence, from one's parents, complimenting a parental goal of parent-adolescent relationships evolving to a more egalitarian and horizontal dimension by the later teenage years (Collins & Steinberg, 2006; Van Doon et al., 2011).

Achieving psychological separation from one's parents entails four important accomplishments: *functional independence*—the ability to manage one's own personal and practical affairs with minimal help from one's parents; *attitudinal independence*—a view of oneself as unique and separate from one's parents and having a personal set of values and beliefs; *emotional independence*—freedom from being overly dependent on parents for approval, intimacy, and emotional support; and *conflictual independence*—freedom from excessive anxiety, guilt, resentment, anger, or responsibility toward one's parents (Moore, 1984, 1987; Sullivan & Sullivan, 1980). From the perspectives of adolescents themselves, the most significant indicators of successful separation from parents are gaining economic independence, living on their own, graduating from school, and being free to make their own life choices without being overly concerned about what their parents may think (Moore, 1987). These indicators may continue to need more time to fully develop before feeling fully independent. This further exploration occurs during emerging adulthood, a new period of development that Jeffery Arnett (2004) described as the winding road from the late teens through the mid-twenties.

The lifespan perspective reminds us that the process of separating from parents to achieve emotional independence during adolescence continues during early adulthood. As we will see in Chapter 13, during early adulthood the safe-base function parents continue to provide for adolescents generally shifts to a significant other, a spouse, or a friend (Hazen & Shaver, 1990). With the development of intimacy within a relationship, and the decision to start a family, the emerging adult now enters the stage of young adulthood envisioned by Erikson (1963), but starting much later in the lives of those in the millennial generation (Arnett, 2004; Arnett, 2012; Arnett, Ramos, & Jensen, 2001).

Although the majority of college students expect to live briefly with their parents after graduation, in our culture leaving home is still a powerful metaphor for achieving psychological separation, and differences in how parents and adolescents understand and react to this experience are common. Many of the everyday conflicts between adolescents and their parents over chores, curfews, school, and social activities reflect different perspectives about the approaching separation. Adolescents' tendency to view themselves as increasingly emancipated from their parents' conventional perspectives and control may create conflict between a parent's need to maintain the usual family norms while allowing the child increasing independence (Smetana, 1995). We will examine the varying dynamics behind parent-adolescent conflicts, but first, let's explore the changes that occur in the amount of time, the interests, and the activities that teenagers share with their family from early through later adolescence.

In studies by Reed Larson and his colleagues, fifth- through twelfth-graders from white working- and middle-class backgrounds carried electronic beepers and provided reports on their experiences when contacted at random times over the course of a week (Larson, 1997; Larson et al., 1996). Figure 11.2 shows the amount of time adolescents spent with family decreased from 35 percent of waking hours in fifth grade to just 14 percent in twelfth grade.

Although leaving home is often accompanied by mixed feelings, the overall quality of adolescent-parent relationships often improves after teenagers have left.
Source: XiXinXing/Shutterstock.com.

By the end of senior high school, these teenagers were spending significantly less time in leisure and daily maintenance activities with family, and this decline was greatest for time spent with the entire family and time spent with siblings. Despite these changes, however, the connection between these adolescents and their parents remained stable over time, as reflected in the amount of time they spent talking with and being alone with their parents. In many cases, stable parent-teen relationships encourage more time for exploration—first in the home and then outside the home. Early adolescents replaced family time with time spent alone at home, whereas for older adolescents, access to friends, having a car, having a job, and receiving permission from parents to stay out later all affected time spent away from home. Table 11.2 presents the changes in percentage of different activities with family by grade.

These changes, even in healthy families, often lead to conflicts between the teen seeking more independence and the parents who want to hold on a little longer to the child they miss and the adolescent they encounter. The changes and conflicts often stimulate unresolved feelings in parents. As one parent put it, "Sometimes I'm not sure which is more upsetting to me, my teenage daughter's pain and confusion about who she is or similar feelings that are stirred up from my own difficult adolescence." Whether designed to protect their child, or to remain in control, arguments will erupt between parents and adolescents. As many psychologists and parents alike have discovered, arguments during the teenage years are a "ubiquitous phenomenon" during this developmental stage (Montemayor, 1983; Robin et al., 1990; Robin & Foster, 1989). Higher levels of parent-adolescent conflict are more likely to occur in families experiencing divorce, economic hardship, or other serious stressors, including mental health disorders (Flanagan, 1990; Hetherington et al., 1998; McLoyd, 1990; Robin & Foster, 1989; Smetana et al., 1991). Keep in mind, too, that high overall levels of adolescent-parent conflict are frequently a continuation of a pattern that existed during middle childhood.

Where adolescents and parents do differ is in the emphasis, or strength, of those attitudes and values. Most disagreements between teens and parents are about relatively mundane matters affecting the teenager's current social life and behavior, such as styles of dress, hair length, choices of friends, dating, curfews, telephone use, participation in household chores and family activities, and choice of music. For preferences such as these, teenagers agree more with their peers than with their parents, thus leading to arguments about differing points of view and who should decide the outcome. Resolving these conflicts has been the focus of a good deal of research. As teens move from early to later adolescence, they seek more of an equal say in their daily activities, and parents are not opposed to join them in this. In a perfect world, the ideal transition from vertical, asymmetrical parent-child relationships to ones that are more

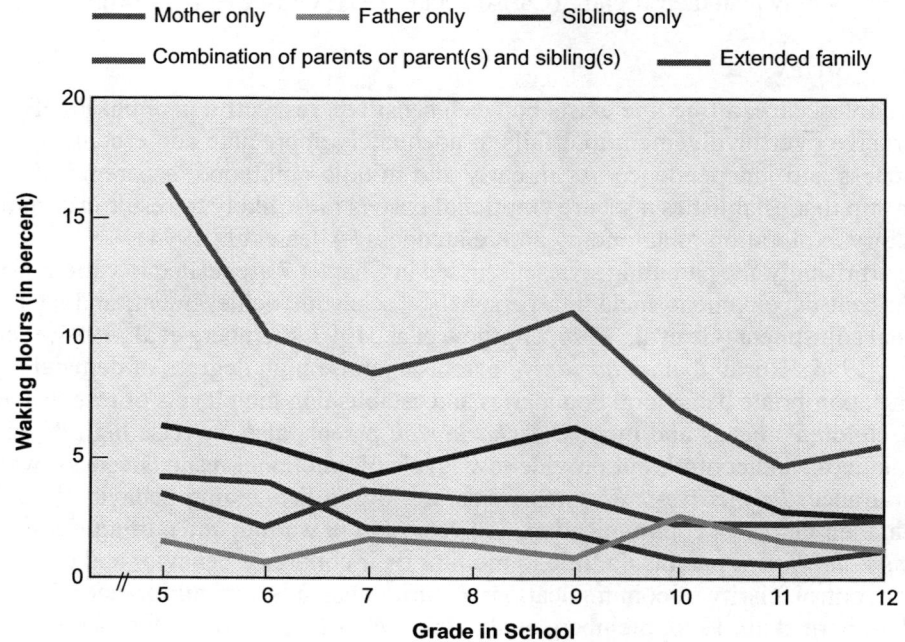

FIGURE 11.2
Age Differences in Time Spent by Adolescents with Family Members

Between fifth and twelfth grades, the amount of time spent with various family members decreases. The greater decrease is in time spent with the entire family.
Source: Adapted from Larson et al. (1996) p. 748.

TABLE 11.2 Percentage of ESM Reports in Different Activities with Family, by Grade Level

All activities with family decrease with increasing grade level, except talking and transportation.

Activity	5	6	7	8	9	10	11	12
Homework	3.1	1.4	1.5	2.2	1.7	0.9	0.3	0.4
Chores	1.5	1.8	1.7	1.4	2.0	1.2	0.9	1.1
Eating	3.9	2.6	1.8	2.6	2.2	1.6	1.4	1.8
Transportation	1.5	1.5	0.9	1.1	1.6	1.4	0.9	0.8
Personal maintenance	3.5	2.1	1.7	2.0	2.1	1.6	1.1	1.7
Watching TV	9.9	7.6	6.0	6.7	6.9	4.5	2.9	3.4
Active leisure	5.4	3.4	3.5	2.0	2.4	1.2	0.5	1.2
Talking	2.3	3.1	2.8	2.7	3.0	2.2	2.1	2.3
Idling	2.1	1.3	1.3	0.8	1.6	1.1	0.5	0.4
Totals	33.2	24.8	21.2	21.5	23.5	15.7	10.6	13.1

Note: ESM = Experience sampling method.
Source: Larson et al. (1996).

horizontal and even (Collins & Steinberg, 2006; VanDoon et al., 2011) would happen without conflict. Yet, in reality, this change takes place by successfully navigating and negotiating the minefields of parent-adolescent conflict. Despite the many changes taking place, the majority of adolescents and parents continue to get along rather well together. They also tend to share similar attitudes and values about important issues and decisions, such as ideas of right and wrong, what makes a marriage good, and the long-run value of education. (Collins, 1991; Larson, 1997; Larson & Richards, 1994). More importantly, despite the increasing time that teens spend with peers and the increasing influence of peers, when it comes to the basic attitudes and values that guide long-term life choices, adolescents have consistently rated their parents' advice more highly than their friends' (Carlson et al., 1991; Grusec et al., 1996).

Parenting Styles

During adolescence, a fine line exists between sensitive, respectful parental involvement and intrusive over involvement that fails to adequately appreciate adolescents' need for separateness and independence. As in early and middle childhood, a parent-adolescent relationship that establishes a secure emotional base is most likely to result in a mutually satisfactory exploration of autonomy and relatedness (Allen et al., 1994).

Not surprisingly, the parenting styles discussed in Chapter 7 are related to various aspects of adolescent development, including personality, academic achievement, and social and emotional adjustment (Ge et al., 1996; Glasgow et al., 1997; Steinberg et al., 1994; Weiss & Schwarz, 1996). Recall that *authoritative* parents exercise high degrees of demandingness in setting appropriate behavioral boundaries and establishing high levels of responsiveness to their children's needs and moods. *Authoritarian* parents also exercise high degrees of demandingness and control, but provide low levels of emotional responsiveness, warmth, and nurturance. *Permissive-indulgent* parents are low in demanding behavioral controls, mixed in their clarity of communication, and very high in warmth and nurturance, whereas *permissive-indifferent* parents do little to monitor their children's behavior and exhibit low levels of control, clarity of communication, maturity demands, and nurturance (Baumrind, 1991; Lamborn et al., 1996; Steinberg et al., 1994). Adolescents whose families display an authoritative parenting style have been found to experience better relationships at home and better performance and social adjustment at school (Smetana, 1995; Steinberg et al., 1992). Adolescents with permissive-indifferent (neglectful) parents experience the lowest level of adjustment. Parenting styles were found to have significant effects on a wide range of adolescent behaviors. For example, in a one-year longitudinal study of 2,300 fourteen- to eighteen-year-olds from different ethnic and SES backgrounds, Laurence Steinberg and his colleagues discovered that differences in parenting styles were related to differences in psychosocial development, school achievement, internalized distress, and behavior problems (Steinberg et al., 1994).

These developmental differences continued or increased over time. Generally, teenagers raised in authoritative homes maintained or improved in all areas. Adolescents from authoritarian homes maintained good adjustments in all areas except internalized distress, which increased during the year studied. Adolescents from permissive-indulgent homes were psychosocially well adjusted in interactions with peers and family, but showed declines in school adjustment and increases in school misconduct over the year. Finally, teens raised in permissive-indifferent homes showed the poorest adjustment in all areas at the beginning of the year, with sharp drops in work and school adjustment and increases in delinquency and drug and alcohol abuse one year later.

Parenting style and the quality of the parent-child relationship can exert influence far beyond the boundaries of the family. Contact among parents in a community and between adolescents and nonfamilial adults can benefit (or harm) children by creating and supporting shared community expectations regarding adolescent behavior (Coleman, 1988). For example, adolescents whose friends described their parents as authoritative earned higher grades in school, spent more time on homework, felt more academically competent, and reported lower levels of delinquency and substance abuse (Fletcher et al., 1995).

How children perceive their relationships with their parents may also influence their relationships with peers, particularly during early adolescence (Fuligni & Eccles, 1993). Early adolescents strongly desire relationships with parents that are less restrictive and provide increased opportunities to participate in decisions that affect their own lives. Children who fail to perceive these opportunities may lose hope that their parents will ever acknowledge that they are maturing and deserve to be treated more like adults. These teenagers may sacrifice developmentally important experiences with adults for the sake of peer relationships that appear to offer greater opportunity for respect and support. They are less likely to seek advice from their parents and more likely to consult with friends about important issues. In some cases, they may orient toward peers so strongly that they are willing to forgo their parents' rules, their schoolwork, and even their own talents to ensure peer acceptance (Fuligni & Eccles, 1993).

Craig Mason and his colleagues found that the style of parental control that African American mothers employed depended on who their children's peers were (Craig et al., 1996). For teenagers whose peers engaged in a relatively low level of problem behaviors—such as gang activity, drug use, stealing, truancy, and fighting, with or without a weapon—the optimal level of parental control required to influence their problem behaviors was relatively low, and remained relatively low, even if parents increased or decreased their control. But for adolescents who associated with peers involved in higher levels of problem behavior, the optimal level of parental control was higher, and deviations from this level led to significant increases in their own problem behavior.

In summary, parents and adolescents get along best when decision making is consistent and collaborative, decisions are perceived as being fair and reasonable rather than arbitrary, and the developmental needs and sensitivities of all family members, both parents and children, are respected. Self-reliance and self-control and the successful academic and social achievement associated with authoritative parenting during childhood are also fostered by these qualities during adolescence (Baumrind, 1989, 1991a; Hart et al., 1990). An authoritative style of parenting continues to be positively associated with the quality of parent-child relationships throughout the lifespan. This is true of the relationships *sandwich generation* parents have with their adult children and aging parents in middle adulthood and of the relationships grandparents have with their grandchildren and their grandchildren's parents during late adulthood (see Chapters 15 and 17).

The closeness of this mother, daughter, and grandmother illustrates that good parenting styles affect the quality of relationships throughout the lifespan.
Source: Blend Images/Shutterstock.com.

SES The socioeconomic status of an individual or family that is determined by level of education, income, and type of work, as well as by lifestyle and social values. Also called *social class*.

SES and Ethnic Differences in Families

As noted earlier, the type of family in which they grow up significantly influences adolescents. One useful way to describe families is by **SES** (*socioeconomic status,* or *social class*), which is determined by parents' levels of education, incomes, and type of work, as well as by their lifestyles and cultural values. Studies of families in the United States, Great Britain, and Italy have found that differences between the values, child-rearing practices, and expectations of middle-class parents and those of working- and lower-class parents closely parallel differences in the amount of autonomy, independence, and satisfaction enjoyed in their day-to-day work experiences (Greenberger et al., 1994; Kohn et al., 1986).

These studies found that adolescents in middle-class families were encouraged to be independent and to regulate or control their own behavior rather than rely on the rewards or punishments of others to determine how they would act. The parents' child-rearing styles tended to be democratic or authoritative rather than authoritarian. Working-class parents were much more authoritarian than middle-class parents in their child-rearing patterns and were less likely to support their children's attempts to be independent and participate in family decision making until their children were ready to leave home.

Recent research supports these findings (Greenberger et al., 1994; Glasgow et al., 1997; Steinberg et al., 1994). For example, Laurence Steinberg and his colleagues found similar relationships among parenting styles and SES in a sample often thousand ninth through twelfth-grade students from different ethnic backgrounds and family structures (biological parents or other parenting arrangement). Authoritative parenting (based on student reports) generally was more common in middle-class than in working-class families, although ethnic differences and differences in family structure were also important. Table 11.3 gives the percentages of authoritative families for each level of SES and ethnic group. In addition, for all ethnic groups and family types, adolescents from authoritative families had better school grades, were more self-reliant, and exhibited less delinquent behavior than those from nonauthoritative families (Steinberg et al., 1991).

There is, however, some reason for caution in drawing conclusions. For one thing, it is unlikely that the categories the researchers used to classify family structure, SES, culture, and parenting style adequately capture the range of relationships and contexts that are at work. For another, these categories do not adequately take into account changes in family structure and parenting style and differences in parenting styles when more than one parent is involved. (In thinking about your own adolescence, how accurately is the parenting

TABLE 11.3 Percentages of Families with Authoritative Parenting Styles in Different SES Levels, Ethnic Groups, and Parenting Situations

SES differences: Middle-class parents were more likely to be authoritative than working-class parents in all ethnic groups, with the exception of white biological parents.

Ethnic differences: The highest percentage of authoritative parenting occurred for whites, followed by African Americans, Hispanics, and Asians.

Differences in family structure: In both working-class and middle-class Hispanic and Asian families and for working-class white and African American families, authoritative parenting occurred more frequently with biological parents than with other parenting arrangements. For both middle-class white and African American families, however, authoritative parenting was less frequent with biological parents than with other parenting arrangements.

| | Working-Class Family Structure || Middle-Class Family Structure ||
Ethnic Group	Biological Parents	Other*	Biological Parents	Other
White	17.2	11.5	15.0	17.6
African American	13.4	12.2	14.0	16.0
Hispanic	10.7	9.8	15.8	12.9
Asian	7.5	6.1	15.6	10.8

*Includes single-parent households, stepfamilies, and other family arrangements.
Source: Adapted from Steinberg et al. (1991), Table 1, p. 25.

style in your family, including the family structure, cultural, SES, and community contexts in which you were raised, captured by the categories just mentioned?)

The Role of Ethnicity and Community in Family Decision Making

Susie Lamborn, Sanford Dornbusch, and Laurence Steinberg (1996) conducted a two-year longitudinal study of the relationship among ethnicity, community context, and styles of family decision making and adolescent adjustment among European American, Hispanic American, African American, and Asian American high school students. Three types of family decision making were studied: *unilateral teen* (decisions made by the teenager alone), *unilateral parent* (decisions made by the parent alone), *and joint parent-teen* (decisions made jointly be parent and teenager). For all four ethnic groups, unilateral teen decisions were associated with poorer adolescent adjustment one year later, whereas joint parent-teen decision making was associated with improved adjustment. Teens whose parents allowed them a great deal of decision-making autonomy over a wide range of issues reported higher rates of deviant behavior, lower academic competence, and poorer psychosocial functioning, whereas those whose parents engaged in joint decision making with them reported higher academic competence and more positive psychosocial functioning.

Community context interacted with ethnic background in three distinct patterns of influence. For Hispanic Americans living in ethnically mixed neighborhoods, the impact of joint decision making on adjustment was more positive and the impact of unilateral teen decision making more negative. Among African American youth, however, the negative impact of unilateral teen decision making was greater for those living in predominantly white communities, compared to those in ethnically mixed communities. Finally, for European and Asian Americans, living in an ethnically mixed versus an all-white or Asian American neighborhood did not appear to affect the impact of type of decision making on adolescent adjustment (Lamborn et al., 1996). The "A Multicultural View" feature describes adaptive strategies that families of minority youths use to cope with the challenges they often face.

A Multicultural View

Differing Cultural Views of Delinquency

Cultures differ widely in how they judge the appropriateness of adolescents' delinquent behavior and how they respond when it occurs. Jeffrey Arnett (1992) suggests that this is largely due to important forces outside of the microsystem of family and peer group that strongly influence adolescent socialization. As we saw in Chapter 1's discussion of ecological systems of development, mesosystem, exosystem, and macrosystem influences include the school community, legal system, cultural beliefs, and the media. In Arnett's view, some cultures value independence and free self-expression more highly than they value conformity. These *broad socialization* cultures have no commonly accepted belief systems by which to judge right and wrong behavior. Such cultures tolerate a wide range of deviations from cultural expectations without severe upset or punishment. In contrast, *narrow socialization* cultures subscribe to ideologies that strictly set forth what constitutes right and wrong behavior. Such cultures value conformity and adherence to standards of the community over individual autonomy, and are more likely to severely punish deviations from community standards or norms. This helps explain why behaviors considered delinquent in one society are tolerated in others.

A study by Jeffrey Arnett and Lene Jensen (1997) which compared socialization and risk behavior among middle class adolescents in Denmark and the United States lends support to this view. Overall, socialization was narrower among the Danish youth, who had more household obligations, greater community stability, and more adults beyond their immediate families involved in their socialization. Rates of risk-taking and delinquent behavior were higher for American teens, who were raised in a more broadly socialized culture. American teens had higher rates of high-speed and drunk driving and of minor criminal behavior such as shoplifting and vandalism, whereas Danish youth had higher rates of riding a bicycle or moped while intoxicated. Danish adolescents also had higher rates of sexual intercourse than American adolescents, but because Americans were less likely to use contraception, overall rates of unprotected sex (without contraception) were almost identical.

Another good example of cultural difference with regard to delinquent behavior is the use of alcohol. While adolescent drinking of alcoholic beverages is a cause of great concern in the United States, in Jamaica, adolescent drinking is not a sign of delinquent behavior and there are few legal restrictions against it (Smith & Blinn Pike, 1994). In European countries, attitudes about teenage drinking and the amount of weekly drinking that occurs vary widely. Adolescents in Greece and Italy, for example, drink almost twice as much alcohol per week than teenagers in Ireland, and adolescents in Spain are able to consume considerably more alcohol per week than are adolescents in the United States before they are categorized as "drinkers" (Recio Adrados, 1995; van Reek et al., 1994). Studies of juvenile delinquency in England, France, Germany, Japan, South Africa, and the United States also find that differences in cultural tradition and national character play an important role in how delinquency is defined, how prevalent it is, and how it is treated (Corley & Smitherman, 1994; McCall, 1995).

Whether or not adolescent social behavior is viewed as deviant is also affected by the status of the particular adolescent subculture within the majority culture and by how adolescents view that culture. For example, Mexican American teenagers may decide to join a gang as a way

Divorce, Remarriage, and Single Parenthood

Over the past half century, divorce has become a common event in American domestic experience. Almost half of all first marriages in the United States end in divorce, with about one million children experiencing their parents' divorce each year (CDC, 2009). Divorce affects children of every race, religion, ethnic background, and socioeconomic level. Adolescents feel the impact of a change in family structure, whether that change occurs in their childhood or during their teenage years. In addition, one-third of American children will experience the remarriage of a parent because roughly one-half of divorced adults will remarry within four years of their first divorce (Hetherington, 2005). Creating new family structures from intact, single-parent, blended family, and stepfamily configurations, each with their own set of challenges, tests adolescents who are in the process of establishing their own separate identity (Hetherington, 2005; Kleinsorge and Covitz, 2012). Adjusting to a parent's divorce is truly a transactional process, especially for adolescents. A number of factors influence whether the outcomes associated with parental divorce are positive, negative, or a combination of the two. (For a more detailed statistical picture, see Table 15.5 in Chapter 15).

> **A Multicultural View**
>
> **Differing Cultural Views of Delinquency** *continued*
>
> of retaining their own culture of origin and rejecting the majority values found in American public schools (Calabrese & Noboa, 1995). A large-scale international survey of youth-related offenses among fourteen- to twenty-one-year-old boys and girls from thirteen countries found that youth from low educational and low-SES circumstances reported more violent and property-related-offenses than did those from more mainstream social and economic circumstances, but that drug offenses and more minor youth-related offenses were equally distributed across all SES backgrounds (McQuoid, 1996).
>
> Most of the research discussed earlier focuses on Western industrialized countries. To what extent is adolescent antisocial behavior an expected occurrence in nonindustrial societies? To answer this question, cultural anthropologists Alice Schlegel and Herbert Barry (1991) analyzed cross-cultural differences regarding such expectations in a sample of 186 nonindustrial societies from around the world. The antisocial behaviors studied included hostile speech, fighting, crimes against persons, theft, sexual misbehavior, destruction of property, and drunkenness or misuse of other drugs. Direct information about antisocial behavior among adolescent boys was available for fifty-four societies, twenty-four of which expected antisocial behavior to occur and thirty of which did not. Similar information was available for adolescent girls in thirty-four societies, six of which expected it to be present and twenty-eight of which did not. In general, antisocial behavior was less likely in societies in which adolescent boys spent a significant amount of time with adults, and was more likely in societies in which adolescents spent much of their time in organized peer groups, particularly when peer activities were highly competitive.
>
> Schlegel and Barry also found that some societal organizations appear to promote adolescent misbehavior, either because the conditions that contribute to it are not recognized or because preventing such conditions would be too costly or disrupt other arrangements. For example, when it is economically advantageous to have groups of adolescent boys working apart from adults and adult supervision, risk of aggressive and other antisocial activities is likely to increase. They cite the case of the African Masai, who live in the highlands of Kenya and Tanzania. Masai adolescent boys are responsible for herding cattle and are sometimes suspected of stealing cattle to add to their own herds. Among Abkhaz adolescent boys, who live in the Georgian Republic (formerly part of the Soviet Union) and spend much of their time with peers, theft is a central feature of economic and political life and boys are trained to steal. However, if this thievery is turned against community members and even other peers, it is then punished. Antisocial behavior, while publicly deplored, may also be tolerated or even condoned if it serves individual family interests, such as fighting with an enemy's child or stealing from a disliked or envied neighbor.
>
> Antisocial behavior, particularly among adolescent boys, is more likely in cultures that define adolescence as a new stage that involves a sharp break from childhood and includes a rapid transition to adult character, the development of new roles in the family and in the community, and increased opportunities to own property and to choose a spouse. Adolescent antisocial behaviors are also more likely when such behavior is prevalent among adult men.

Based on their extensive review of the literature on the impact of divorce and remarriage on children and adolescents, Mavis Hetherington and her colleagues proposed a transactional model similar to the ecological model used by Uri Bronfenbrenner (see Chapter 1) to understand how the many complex factors work together to influence children's adjustment (Hetherington et al., 1998). Figure 11.3 diagrams how these factors interact. The main factors to consider include (1) the individual characteristics of the parents, including their personality, education, and psychological problems; (2) the nature of the marital transition (marriage and remarriage); (3) stressful life experiences and economic changes associated with divorce (and remarriage); (4) the composition of the family following divorce or remarriage; (5) the types and amount of social support available to family members; (6) the amount of parental distress; (7) the family process, including the nature and quality of the relationships among family members; (8) the individual characteristics of the children, including age, gender, temperament, and intelligence, as well as strengths and vulnerabilities; and (9) the adjustment of the child or adolescent. This "transactional model" helps us to understand the risks associated with divorce and remarriage to the adjustment of children, adolescents, and adults. Chapter 9 includes additional discussion of the impact of divorce on school-age children.

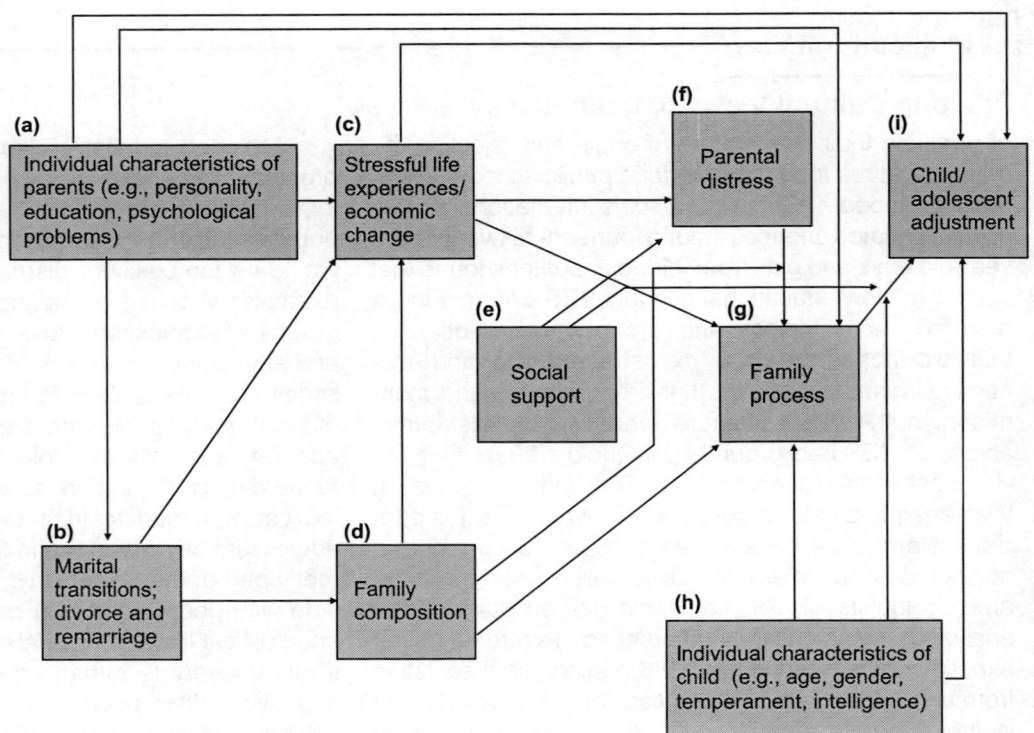

FIGURE 11.3
A Transactional Model of the Predictors of Children's Adjustment Following Divorce and Remarriage

The arrows connecting the boxes indicate their influence on one another in together contributing to children's and teens' adjustment to marital transitions.

Source: Hetherington et al. (1998).

Marital Conflict

Marital conflict is a well-known source of distress for both parents and children, and particularly for adolescents, whose struggles to separate from their families to establish an independent and autonomous identity often involve an increased need for a safe "home base" from which to separate and a heightened awareness of hostility and conflict between their parents (Harold & Conger, 1997; Hetherington et al., 1998). Some conflict is normal in marriages; in fact, children learn the strategies and skills needed to deal with conflict in their own lives by observing their parents' successful strategies for coping with marital discord. However, in families where levels of conflict and disagreement are too high because parents are unable to resolve them, children and adolescents are negatively affected (Cummings & Cummings, 1988). Recent research has shown both behavioral adjustment problems as well as a physiologic reaction in children living in a family where the parents are experiencing a high degree of conflict (Kleinsorge and Covitz, 2012; Nunes-Costa et al., 2009). Life in high-stress families can produce higher levels of cortisol in the brain, increasing anxiety, sleep disturbances, weight management, and greater irritability for both children and adolescents (Nunes-Costa et al., 2009). A majority of divorces involve a failure of parents to successfully resolve their conflicts, a problem that often intensifies during the process of separation and divorce, and may persist even after the marriage has ended, when the need to share parenting responsibilities may continue.

The Impact of Divorce and Remarriage

Between one-quarter and one-third of adolescents in divorced and remarried families become disengaged from their families, minimizing the time they spend at home and avoiding interactions, activities, and communication with family members. When this disengagement is associated with lack of adult support and supervision and with involvement with a delinquent peer group, antisocial behavior and school problems are more likely. However, if the adolescent has a relationship with a caring adult outside the home, such as the parent of a friend, a teacher, a neighbor, or a coach, disengagement may be a positive solution to a disrupted family situation (Hetherington et al., 1998).

Children in divorced families tend to "grow up" faster due in part to early assignment of responsibilities, more autonomy in making decisions, and less adult supervision. Whether this is a positive or negative developmental consequence depends on whether or not the demands are within the adolescent's capabilities. If adolescents perceive themselves as being unfairly burdened with responsibilities that interfere with their other activities, resentment, rebellion, and noncompliance may result (Hetherington et al., 1998).

Adolescents who grow up in troubled families that remain together but have high levels of unresolved marital conflict and hostility are likely to experience negative developmental consequences as well. For families in which destructive and unresolved conflicts between parents cannot be resolved, divorce may provide the best solution and result in improved developmental outcomes for the teenagers and other children involved (Harold & Conger, 1997; Hetherington et al., 1998).

Lifespan Effects

The effects of divorce and remarriage are experienced throughout the lifespan. Compared to children from two-parent, nondivorced families, children, adolescents, and adults from divorced and remarried families are at increased risk for developing difficulties in adjustment, including academic problems, psychological disorders, lower self-esteem, and problems in their relationships with parents, siblings, and peers. The normative developmental tasks of adolescence and early adulthood—developing intimate relationships and autonomy—are especially hard. In addition to experiencing some of the same behavior problems found in childhood, adolescents are more likely to drop out of school, be unemployed, become sexually active at an earlier age, have children out of wedlock, associate with antisocial peers, and be involved in delinquent activities and substance abuse. Both male and female adolescents whose parents have divorced are more likely to become teenage parents, and single parenthood most adversely affects the lives of adolescents who experience declining SES and who drop out of school (Conger & Chao, 1996; Demo & Acock, 1996; Hetherington et al., 1998; Simons & Chao, 1996; Whitbeck et al., 1996).

Adult children of divorced and remarried families have more adjustment problems, less satisfaction with their lives, lower socioeconomic achievement, higher marital instability, and more problems in their marital interactions than adults from families that remained intact (Hetherington et al., 1998). Many young adults who are children of divorce have witnessed their separated, divorced, or widowed mothers become **displaced homemakers** due to loss of their conventional roles of wife and mother and lack of preparation for employment and single parenthood. They tend to hold more negative views of marriage as a result (see Chapter 13). Many divorced fathers lack the *kinkeeping skills* needed to keep in touch with their children and other family members, such as phoning, sending birthday cards, or visiting, skills that traditionally have been in the province of women. A detailed discussion of the important role of separation, divorce, and remarriage during middle adulthood appears in Chapter 15. Finally, as we will see in Chapter 17, married people of all ages have the lowest risk of suicide and widowed or divorced people have the highest, particularly in late adulthood.

displaced homemaker
A woman who committed herself to the conventional roles of wife and mother, lost these roles due to separation, divorce, or widowhood, and was unprepared for employment and single parenthood.

Social Relationships During Adolescence

We already touched on the interplay among peer group, ethnic and community context, parenting styles, and family decision making, and their impact on development. Now we will consider the direct influence of friends, peers, and work on adolescent development in more detail.

Friendship

Friends matter a lot during adolescence. Peer relationships temporarily supplant the parent's role as the source of greatest influence for the adolescent. As teens become more mobile, and spend more time away from home, they seek the company of others who look, think, feel, and act like themselves. Friends offer reassurance, understanding and advice, and emotional and social support in stressful situations. The opportunity to share

> **What Do You Think?**
>
> Think about your own separation and individuation with regard to your parents. How similar were your concerns to those described in the text?

inner feelings of disappointment as well as happiness with close friends enables the adolescent to better deal with her emotional ups and downs. Furthermore, a capacity to form close, intimate friendships during adolescence is related to overall social and emotional adjustment and competence (Buhrmester, 1990; Reid et al., 1989).

Especially during early and middle adolescence, friendships help teens to become more independent of parents and other authority figures and to resist the seemingly arbitrary demands of family living. Friends provide one another with cognitive and social scaffolding that differs from what acquaintances provide. Having good friends supports positive developmental outcomes during periods of developmental change (Hartup, 1996). Friends also promote independence simply by providing knowledge of a world beyond the family. Teenagers learn that not every young person is required to be home by the same hour every night, that some parents expect their children to do more household chores than other parents do, and that other families hold different religious or political views. The processes of sharing feelings and beliefs and exploring new ideas and opinions with friends play an important role in helping adolescents define their sense of self (Rawlins, 1992).

Qualities of Adolescent Friendships

Friends strongly influence adolescent development by virtue of their positive and negative characteristics, attitudes, values, and behaviors and through the quality of the friendship. A friendship based on mutual respect and trust, intimacy, and prosocial behavior is likely to help the adolescent cope with stressful situations in the family and in school. Friendships that lack these qualities are likely to be less helpful or even destructive (Dusek, 1991; Hartup, 1996).

During the teenage years, the basis of what makes a close friendship changes. When asked to define close friendships and how they are initiated, maintained, and ended, adolescents report that *mutual understanding* and *intimacy* are most important, whereas school-age children emphasize shared activities. Unlike cooperation between younger children, adolescent mutuality depends on the understanding that other people share some of one's own abilities, interests, and inner experiences and on an appreciation of each person's uniqueness. In fact, early adolescents share a fascination with the particular interests, life histories, and personalities of their friends; young teenagers want to understand friends as unique individuals and be understood by them in the same way. The ability of adolescents to recognize the advantages of complementary relationships—relationships in which two people with different strengths and abilities cooperate for mutual benefit—makes possible friendships that involve greater commitment, permanence, and loyalty. Intimacy in adolescent friendships includes self-revelation, confidence (in keeping secrets), and a sense of exclusivity (Damon, 1983; Youniss, 1980).

The quality of friendships during early adolescence appears to have long-term effects on development. Catherine Bagwell, Andrew Newcomb, and William Bukowski (1998) conducted a twelve-year longitudinal study of thirty young adults who had a stable, reciprocal best friend or "chum" in fifth grade and thirty young adults who had been without a chum. Adults who had close friends as early adolescents experienced better adjustment in school and family relationships and had less difficulty with authority figures than those who did not. Adults who had been rejected by peers in their early adolescence did more poorly in school, had greater difficulty with authorities, had lower levels of aspiration, and participated in fewer organizations and social activities in later adolescence and early adulthood. Finally, lower levels of peer rejection during early adolescence predicted more successful overall life adjustment and feelings of self-worth in adulthood.

Gender and Friendships

How do friendships between girls and boys differ? Friendships formed by boys generally involve lower levels of emotional intimacy than those of girls, who are better able to express feelings and more comfortable with giving emotional support to one another. During the junior high and early high school years, girls appear to develop greater intimacy with the opposite sex than boys do. They also tend to have one or two close friends, whereas adolescent boys often have many friends with whom they are less intimate. Adolescent boys may be more likely to equate intense intimacy exclusively with heterosexual friendships, whereas girls at this age can be comfortably close with both male and female friends.

To better understand developmental changes in the patterns and gender differences in the activities, thoughts, and feelings associated with friendship during adolescence, Maryse Richards and her colleagues had 218 adolescents in fifth through eighth grade carry electronic pagers for one week and complete self-report forms in response to signals received at random times during their waking hours (Richards et al., 1998). When paged, the teens responded to questions about with whom they were talking, about whom they were thinking, and what their subjective experiences were, including body image, mood, motivation, self-esteem, and excitement, at the moment they were contacted. These same adolescents underwent the same procedure four years later, when they were in grades nine through twelve.

The researchers found that both the amount of time adolescents spent with and thought about same-sex friends and the positive feelings they experienced did not decline across adolescence and into high school. Compared to fifth- and sixth-graders, adolescents in high school spent more time with opposite-sex friends and more time thinking about them. Fifth- and sixth-grade girls spent approximately an hour a week in the presence of a boy and less than two hours thinking about an individual of the opposite sex, while fifth- and sixth-grade boys spent less than an hour in the presence of a girl and less than an hour thinking about girls. By eleventh and twelfth grades, however, girls were spending almost ten hours a week with a male companion, whereas boys were spending approximately five hours a week with a female companion.

Compared to boys, girls' opposite-sex companionship and frequency of thoughts about boys had increased dramatically from eighth to twelfth grade. The oldest girls spent roughly eight hours each week thinking about a boy, while the oldest boys spent approximately five to six hours per week thinking about a girl. During early adolescence, seventh- and eighth-graders spent more time thinking about the opposite sex (four to six hours) than actually being with the opposite sex (thirty to eighty minutes). By eleventh and twelfth grades, this trend had shifted, and more time was spent in the actual presence of the other sex. In general, girls spent more time interacting with and thinking about boys and girls, whereas boys, when not with their peers, spent very little time thinking about either.

According to Richards and her colleagues, it is developmentally normative for pre- and young adolescents to be more romantically involved in fantasy than in reality. The adolescents in their study reported that time spent with opposite-sex peers was more exciting and that they felt more attractive and important, enjoyed more positive feelings, and felt much more "in love" than when they were with same-sex peers. However, when alone and thinking about the opposite sex, subjective experiences were less positive. Older adolescents felt especially negative and unmotivated, perhaps because they missed the company of their girlfriend or boyfriend. We take a closer look at these and related issues later in this chapter.

Interethnic Friendships

Friendships between adolescents from different ethnic groups tend to be relatively rare. One national study of students enrolled in more than one thousand public and private high schools in the United States found that fewer than 3.5 percent of the eighteen thousand friendships identified by students involved friendships between African American and white teens (Hallinan & Williams, 1989). As we saw in Chapter 9's discussion of psychosocial development in middle childhood, however, the social contexts in which potential friendship interactions occur seem to make an important difference. In one study of school and neighborhood friendship patterns among African American and white students attending integrated junior high

Sharing interests with friends is important to teenagers, as it is to children. At the same time, though, less tangible qualities, such as loyalty, mutual respect, and intimacy, become increasingly important in friends, especially among older adolescents.
Source: oliveromg/Shutterstock.com.

schools, most students reported having a close other-race school friend, but only about one-quarter saw such a friend frequently outside school. (Giordano et al., 1993).

Living in a neighborhood with children from other ethnic groups appears to increase the likelihood of having close other-race friends outside of school. Having a higher proportion of neighborhood friends attending one's school also affects other-race friendship. Living in a racially mixed neighborhood may help to create more positive attitudes toward members of other ethnic groups and provide a meeting ground on which cross-race friendships can develop outside of school. The informal peer activities that occur in neighborhood settings are more likely to promote close friendships across groups than the more formal, teacher-directed activities in school. Interethnic friendships are strongly influenced by the attitudes adolescents hold about their own and other ethnic groups (DuBois & Hirsch, 1993; Giordano et al., 1993; Phinney et al., 1997).

Peer Groups

Peer groups play an even greater role in the everyday lives of adolescents than they do for younger children. They also tend to be more structured and organized, frequently include individuals from a relatively wide age range, and are much less likely to be all male or all female. Peer groups are an important component of an adolescent's *social convoy,* the network of social relationships that follow a person over his or her lifetime, changing in structure but providing continuity in the exchange of support, as we will see in Chapter 17 on psychosocial development in late adulthood. Who is included in this social convoy of support is determined by the adolescent's emotional attachment to the person and by the person's role in the adolescent's life (Levitt et al., 1993). Peers provide a teenager with critical information about who he is, how he should act, what he is like, and so forth. They offer him an environment for making social comparisons between his own actions, attitudes, and feelings and those of others. These are important ingredients in an adolescent's development of self-concept and identity (Connolly et al., 1987). Most important, peer groups provide a support base outside of the family from which the teenager can more freely try on the different identity roles that ultimately will contribute to her adult personality: popular, brain, normal, druggie, outcast, partyer, punk, grind, clown, banger, nerd, lover, and so forth (B. Brown et al., 1993; Stone & Brown, 1998; Durbin et al., 1993).

Peer groups can also exert powerful pressures to conform. Especially when the family fails to serve as a constructive corrective force, such pressures may contribute to a prolonged period of identity diffusion or to premature identity foreclosure, for example, as a teenage parent, drug addict, or gang member (Dishion et al., 1988; Patterson & Dishion, 1985). Conformity to peer pressure can be particularly disruptive during early adolescence. Frank Vitaro and his colleagues examined how the characteristics of their friends affected delinquency among eleven- and twelve-year-old boys who were judged by their teachers to be either highly disruptive, moderately disruptive, moderately conforming, or highly conforming (Vitaro et al., 1997). They found that only moderately disruptive boys appeared to be negatively influenced by hostile-aggressive friends and exhibited more delinquent behavior at age thirteen. Highly disruptive boys were the most delinquent at age thirteen, regardless of their friends' characteristics, and boys who were judged to be moderately or highly conforming appeared to be unaffected by their friends' characteristics. We will explore the contribution of peers to negative developmental outcomes more fully when we discuss juvenile delinquency later in this chapter.

Peer Group Structure

Adolescent peer groups generally are of two types—the clique and the crowd. The **clique** is a small, close-knit group of two or more members (with an average of six members) who are intimately involved in a number of shared purposes and activities and exclude those who are not. The **crowd** is a larger, less cohesive group of between fifteen and thirty members (with an average of twenty members) and generally consists of from two to four cliques.

Clique membership allows teenagers to have a few select friends they know well and who share important interests and activities, whereas membership in a crowd provides contact with a much broader group of peers on a more casual basis. The small size and intimacy of a clique make it like a family in which the adolescent can feel comfortable and secure. The major clique activity seems to be talking, and cliques generally meet during the school week. Advantages of clique membership include security, a feeling of importance, and acquisition of socially acceptable behaviors (such as academic, social, or athletic competence) that are part of conforming to the clique's norms. However, conformity can also suppress individuality and may promote "in-group" snobbishness, intolerance, and other negative values and behaviors. Involvement with a clique of antisocial peers is associated with various adolescent adjustment problems, including substance abuse, school dropout, delinquency, and gang membership, although which is cause and which is effect is uncertain (Dishion et al., 1988; Patterson & Dishion, 1985).

Crowds usually gather at parties and other organized social functions, which typically take place on weekends. They tend to include both males and females, thereby providing opportunities for mixed-sex interactions and promoting transition from same-sex to mixed-sex cliques. Crowd membership also provides opportunities to interact with individuals from a broad range of backgrounds and experiences, but can also promote snobbishness and can pose real or imagined threats to parental and teacher authority. Cliques and crowd affiliations were often limited by geography, at least until teens became more mobile after receiving their driver's license. Access to new peer groups and crowds is now available worldwide with adolescent use of the Internet and the new technological advances in social media.

clique A small, close-knit peer group of two or more members (average of six members) who are intimately involved in a number of shared purposes and activities and exclude those who are not.

crowd A large, loosely knit peer group of between fifteen and thirty members (average of twenty members) that generally consists of from two to four cliques.

Social Media and Peer Influence: Teens and Social Media

Adolescents born between the early 1980s and 2000 are collectively known as the Millennials, or Generation Y. Following on the heels of the preceding generations identified as the Baby Boomers (born between 1946 and 1964) and Generation X (born between 1965 and 1982). This generation has grown up in an ever-expanding world of technological advances and the rise of the global community. Nowhere is this more evident than in the Millennials' involvement in and interactions with social media.

Teens in the second decade of the twenty-first century are as connected to the Internet for social development as earlier generations were to the schoolyard or their community neighborhood. In fact, most adolescents spend as much time, if not more, in their "virtual neighborhoods" as they do interacting with peers in the hallways of their schools or the streets of their hometown. The use of social media and accessing social media sites on the Web is, according to O'Keeffe and Clark-Pearson (2011), one of the most common activities engaged in by children and teens today. In a recent survey conducted by the Pew Research Center (Madden et al., 2013), 95 percent of teens reported that they use the Internet. Every day, and multiple times each week, young teens and transitional teens go online to share "what's happening" with others in their school, in neighboring towns, and across the globe. They do so on sites like Facebook, Snapchat, and Instagram. Half of all teens use Facebook, followed closely by the 39 and 38 percent who use Snapchat and Instagram, respectively, while a quarter of all adolescents use Twitter to follow and inform their friends about their daily activities (Madden et al., 2013). Roughly 75 percent of all teenagers have cell phones and use them primarily for texting and instant messaging, and also for access to social media sites with the more advanced phones (O'Keeffe & Clark-Pearson, 2011). The same Pew Center survey found that 40 percent of teens now have smart phones, a 15 percent jump in just the last year of survey data. Smart phones allow teens to connect at all times to their virtual neighborhood via tweets, posts, and instant updates on important events in their busy lives.

When "hanging out" on these social media sites, many adolescents wrestle with a classic adolescent paradox. In striving for identity formation, all teens crave the dual constructs of privacy from their parents and greater personal and social independence (Erikson, 1968; Dunkle & Anthis, 2001; Jensen & Arnett, 2012). In their virtual neighborhoods, where their online reputations are formed, many teens are vulnerable to sharing too much private information, especially to strangers. Madden et al. (2013) found that while on various social media sites, 92 percent of teens use their real names and post pictures of themselves and their friends and family. In addition, 85 percent will share their actual birthdays online, 53 percent will post their e-mail addresses, 25 percent will include "selfie" videos of various activities, while 20 percent of all teens will give out their cell phone numbers. In keeping with the advances in technology, roughly 16 percent of all teens will activate the location app on their social media sites, so anyone who is following them knows exactly where they are at that moment. The privacy paradox emerges when the latest survey data indicate that only 60 percent of all adolescents using social media set their profiles to private! What may be private to mothers and fathers, who do not access their teens' websites, is common knowledge to friends, acquaintances, and total strangers.

The other half of the paradoxical problem with teens and social media is in their desire for independence in establishing their own separate identity. The identity they form online may not be congruent with their persona in the "real" world of day-to-day interactions with people at home and at school. Opportunities or pressure to participate in cyberbullying or being coerced to engage in innocent flirting that may evolve into hard-core sexting are often hard to resist (Patchin & Hinduja, 2006). In much the same way as face-to-face peer pressure is difficult to resist for the developing adolescent, giving in to "virtual" social pressures can define an adolescent's online reputation in ways that can be hurtful and damaging (Geddes, 2014; Hinduja & Patchin, 2007).

By nature, adolescents struggle with the self-regulation of their behaviors and emotions, and thus are very susceptible to peer pressure as they navigate through their vast social media networks. But not all peer pressure is negative. Proper use of social media often benefits adolescents by enhancing their technological skills, developing their communication skills, and providing opportunities for social connections with peers who share similar interests (O'Keeffe & Clark-Pearson, 2011). For teens who are socially awkward in face-to-face interactions, social media allow them to engage in conversations that may reinforce their social confidence. Like any new phenomenon that gains enormous popularity with adolescents, more research is needed to assess both the benefits and the cost of social media for teens, their parents, and the community.

Parental Influence

Parents of adolescents frequently are concerned that their children will be excessively influenced by peer pressure and that peer influence will replace their own guidance. Laurence Steinberg and Anne Levine (1990) suggest that parents can help their adolescents with their friendships and relationships with peers in a number of ways. Table 11.4 lists

TABLE 11.4 Guidelines for Parents Concerning Their Adolescents' Friends

Helping Adolescents to Deal with Peer Pressure
- Build self-esteem by helping your adolescent discover her or his strengths and special talents.
- Encourage independence and decision making within the family.
- Talk about situations in which people have to choose among competing pressures and demands.
- Encourage your adolescent to anticipate difficult situations and plan ahead.
- Encourage your adolescent to form alliances with peers who share his or her values and your family's values.
- Know your adolescent's friends.
- Don't jump to hasty conclusions based on peers' appearance, dress, language, or interests.
- Allow time for peer activities.
- Remain close to your adolescent.

When to Be Concerned
- If your adolescent has no friends at all
- If your adolescent is secretive about her or his social life
- If your adolescent suddenly loses all interest in friends
- If all of your adolescent's friends are much older than him or her

Source: Adapted from Steinberg & Levine (1990), pp. 183–187.

these guidelines. The "Focusing On" feature discusses recent research findings on parental influence.

Adolescents in the World of Work

Adolescents balance many roles: son or daughter, friend, peer, student. Many also add "employee" to the mix. As we saw in Chapter 10, work has an impact on cognitive development and on identity formation as well. Participation in work within and outside the family provides a major base for the development of competence and sense of identity and self, especially during adolescence. Working with others can produce a broad range of benefits, from sound work habits to the development of helpfulness toward others, responsibility for the welfare of others, a sense of agency or personal efficacy, and an appreciation of the needs and feelings of others (Grusec et al., 1996).

For both male and female adolescents, participation in household work and the consequences of such involvement depend on the helper's motivations, the meaning of the work activity, and the social context in which it occurs. In a two-year longitudinal study of one thousand ninth-graders and their parents, Kathleen Call, Jeylan Mortimer, and Michael Shanahan (1995) found that adolescents from large families with fewer financial resources and mothers who were employed responded to the needs of their families by taking on more household responsibilities than adolescents from smaller families with more resources. Girls who were more competent to begin with chose work that allowed them to be helpful to others, and the opportunity to be helpful to others at work strengthened their sense of competency. Doing household chores increased a sense of competency for African American and Hispanic American boys, but decreased such feelings for European American boys, perhaps because the former group saw helping out as being

Focusing On...

Can Parents Influence Their Adolescent's Choice of Peer Group?

It has long been accepted that parental influence declines sharply during adolescence due to the increasing counterinfluence of peer groups over which parents have little control. However, recent large-scale studies of high school students challenge this view.

Bradford Brown and his colleagues studied parenting practices and peer affiliation in a sample of more than 3,700 high school students drawn from a variety of socioeconomic, ethnic, and family backgrounds (e.g., first-time two-parent, divorced, remarried) and types of communities (urban, suburban, rural) (Brown et al., 1993; Brown & Huang, 1996). To determine peer group affiliation, school administrators identified a set of boys and girls in each grade and within each ethnic group who represented a cross-section of the student body. Researchers interviewed students in small groups composed of individuals of the same sex, grade level, and ethnic background. Each group listed the school's major crowds and identified two boys and two girls in the same grade who were the leaders or most prominent members of each crowd.

Identified leaders then individually placed each student in the same grade level in one of the crowds that had been named. In addition, all students in the sample were surveyed about family characteristics, parenting practices, and adolescent behaviors related to academics, drug use, and self-reliance.

Brown and his colleagues found that levels of authoritative parenting (as reflected by parental monitoring, encouragement of achievement, and support for joint decision making) were significantly associated with teenagers' levels of academic achievement, drug use, and self-reliance. These factors, in turn, were closely related to the type of crowd an adolescent belonged to (popular, jock, brain, normal, druggie, and outcast).

The authors concluded that parents can indirectly influence the behaviors by which teenagers become associated with a particular crowd and that peer group norms serve to reinforce behaviors and predispositions that parenting strategies and/or family background characteristics influence. Although parenting practices and family background cannot *determine* a teenager's crowd affiliation, their influence should be taken seriously.

How might this parental influence work? Anne Fletcher and her colleagues (Fletcher et al., 1995) asked students about parenting practices in their families and about their academic achievement, psychosocial competence, behavior problems, and personal distress. Each student's friends independently evaluated the degree to which authoritative parenting was present in the peer network, as indicated by parental acceptance and involvement, behavioral supervision and strictness, and granting of psychological autonomy.

What did they find? Adolescents whose friends described their parents as authoritative earned higher grades in school, spent more time on homework, had more positive perceptions of their academic competence, and reported lower levels of delinquency and substance abuse. Fletcher and her colleagues suggest that authoritative parenting is associated with adolescent competence; competent, well-adjusted adolescents with authoritative parents select (and are selected by) peers similar in competence and background; and within-peer-group experiences maintain and strengthen a higher level of adjustment. Less competent adolescents with nonauthoritative parents are more likely to select peers who are similar to themselves, thus maintaining and amplifying their limitations. Adolescent delinquent activities may be unlikely due to the higher level of shared social control provided by a network of authoritative parents.

What Do You Think?

What role did your parents play in your peer relationships? What role did the parents of your friends play? If you were the parent of a teenager, how would you help your child make wise choices about peers?

This small, close-knit clique of high school students hangs out at this table during lunch period on a fairly regular basis to relax, talk, and play cards.
Source: Lucky Business/Shutterstock.com.

---

important to their families' functioning, whereas the latter saw them as burdensome and lacking in value.

Family dynamics also affected the relationship between helping with household work and feelings of competency and concern for others. For girls living in families where the father-daughter relationship was not supportive and the mother's manner of assigning

> **What Do You Think?**
>
> In what ways are your own experiences similar to the text's description of friendship, peer groups, and work during adolescence? In what ways do they differ?

household tasks diminished the girl's sense of autonomy and independence, participating in household chores undermined rather than enhanced feelings of competency (Call et al., 1995). Teenagers who were expected to do household work that benefited members of the family and expected to do it on a routine or self-regulated basis were more likely to show spontaneous concern for the welfare of others. Work that focused on what is one's "own," such as cleaning one's own room, or was based on frequent requests for assistance (i.e., nagging) was not associated with increased concern for others (Grusec et al., 1996).

How work outside the family influences adolescent development depends on how well it fits the developmental needs of the individual and his or her family, including the type and level of workplace stress, the relevance of job-related skills to future careers, and the compatibility between the demands and experiences of work and those of school. Further discussion of the relationship between work and school activities appears in Chapter 10.

Sexuality During Adolescence

The popular idea that adolescence is a highly sexual period of life is accurate, but for reasons beyond the physical. Sexual identity and sexual activity are not solely focused on sexual intercourse and the risks of pregnancy. During adolescence, the expression of sexual urges interacts closely with the need to establish a secure sexual identity that is reasonably free from anxiety, shame, or despair—an identity that is capable of fulfilling the need for healthy, intimate relationships with others (Zimmer-Gembeck & Helfand, 2008).

Sexual Experience

Trends in adolescent sexual activity in the United States peaked in the 1980s and 1990s, showing earlier initiation of intercourse, increased premarital intercourse, a greater number of partners, and ineffective and inconsistent use of contraceptives. Recent studies have attempted to add clarity to the prevailing data that the median age of first intercourse was 15.5 years for girls and 14.75 years for boys (Guttmacher Institute, 2013; CDC-YRBS, 2012). The national Youth Risk Behavior Survey reviewed the trends in adolescent sexual behaviors from 1991 to 2011. The trends in prevalence data showed a steady decrease from a high in 1991 of 54.1 percent of teens reporting they had had sexual intercourse, to a low of 45.6 percent a decade later in 2001. Over the next ten years, the prevalence rates remained statistically unchanged (CDC-YRBS, 2012). Table 11.5 lists the trends from 1991 to 2011. A fact sheet by the Guttmacher Institute (2013) broke this down further by age. Fewer than 2 percent of twelve-year-olds have had sex by their twelfth birthday, but within the next three years, by age fifteen, the figure rises to 16 percent, reaching close to half of all teens (48 percent) by age seventeen, and 61 and 71 percent by ages eighteen and nineteen, respectively (Guttmacher Institute, 2013).

These trends, as alarming as they were to parents, were about the same in the United States as in Western European nations (Coley & Chase-Lansdale, 1998; Seidman & Rieder, 1994). A close review of this most recent data from the Center for Disease Control's (CDC) biennial Youth Risk Behavior Surveillance survey (2012) is important in other ways. While showing a slight decline in adolescent sexual behaviors from previous decades, one area that has remained constant is the timing of a teen's first sexual activity and its impact on later development. In a sequential longitudinal study of the timing of first intercourse and psychosocial adjustment, Raymond Bingham and Lisa Crockett (1996) surveyed seventh-, eighth-, and ninth-grade adolescents annually through their graduation from twelfth grade. They found that for both boys and girls, earlier timing of first sexual intercourse was associated with longitudinal patterns of

TABLE 11.5 Rates of Adolescent Sexual Activity by Gender, Ethnic Group, and Grade

Gender	Ethnic Group			Grade				Total
	White	African American	Hispanic	9	10	11	12	
Male	44.0%	66.9%	53.0%	37.8%	44.5%	54.5%	62.6%	49.2%
Female	44.5	53.6	43.9	27.8	43.0	51.9	63.6	45.6
Total	44.3	60.0	48.6	32.9	43.8	53.2	63.1	47.4

Note: Percentages are of high school students who report ever having sexual intercourse.
Source: Centers for Disease Control (2012).

greater difficulty with the transition to adolescence and with poorer psychosocial adjustment. Similarly, Armour and Haynie's (2007) longitudinal study also found that an early debut of sexual experience increased the risks of engaging in delinquent behaviors within the following year for both genders. Later developmental difficulties were found to last well beyond that first year and were more disruptive if teens were sexually active much earlier than members of their peers (Armour & Haynie, 2007).

Longitudinal patterns of development differed for early (before the median age), middle (after the median age), and late (still virgins) initiators of intercourse. Adolescents who had first sexual intercourse early demonstrated the poorest psychosocial adjustment in ninth grade, and the same negative pattern persisted through twelfth grade. Adolescents who postponed first sexual intercourse the longest (were still virgins) had the most positive ninth-grade adjustment and the most positive developmental trajectory through twelfth grade. They reported more positive psychosocial development, more positive family relationships, more frequent church attendance, greater commitment to education, and lower involvement with problem behaviors than those who initiated intercourse earlier. These longitudinal outcomes were not associated with the timing of first intercourse; rather, they appeared to be a continuation of enduring developmental paths based on childhood differences in temperament, personality, and family and life circumstances that were already well established before ninth grade (Bingham & Crockett, 1996; Dorius et al., 1993).

Sexual Attitudes and Behaviors

In 1992 Robert Michael, John Gagnon, and Edward Laumann conducted the National Health and Social Life Survey (NHSLS). They interviewed more than three thousand U.S. residents ages eighteen to fifty-nine about their sex lives, histories, and attitudes (Gagnon et al., 1994; Michael et al., 1994). (See Chapter 13 for a review of what they found.) They report that people's attitudes about sex fell into three broad categories: traditional, relational, or recreational. *Traditional* people said that "their religious beliefs always guide their sexual behavior." *Relational* people said that "sex should be part of a loving relationship." *Recreational* people said that "sex need not have anything to do with love." Not surprisingly, older married people had more traditional views of sex, whereas younger unmarried people held more recreational views.

Table 11.5 presents sexual activity rates by gender, ethnic group, and grade based on data collected by the U.S. Centers for Disease Control (2012). As the table indicates, rates of intercourse increase from ninth through twelfth grade for both males and females, with a higher percentage of males reporting intercourse at each grade level and overall. African American high school students report the highest overall rate of sexual intercourse (60.0 percent), followed by Hispanic teens (48.6 percent) and white teens (44.3 percent). For each ethnic group, in past surveys, a higher percentage of males than females reported having had sexual intercourse. The exception was this latest YRBS survey (CDC, 2012), which showed white males and white females with almost identical percentages for the category of ever having had sexual intercourse.

By and large, girls tend to be more conservative than boys in their sexual attitudes, values, and actions, whereas boys tend to be more sexually active and to have more sexual encounters. This may be due to the fact that although boys' and girls' interest in sex is driven, in part, by testosterone, girls tend to be influenced more by environment and social expectations than are boys (Crockett, Raffaelli, & Moilanen, 2006; James et al., 2012). Girls are more likely to emphasize intimacy and love as a necessary part of sexual activity and less likely to engage in sex merely as a physically pleasurable activity (Leigh, 1989; White & DeBlassie, 1992; Zimmer-Gembeck & Helfand, 2008).

Dating

Since the beginning of this century, dating has tended to begin earlier, thus increasing the time span over which teenage dating takes place. Currently many adolescent girls begin dating at age twelve and boys at age thirteen, with almost one-half of boys and more than one-half of girls reporting dating at least once a week and approximately one-third dating two or three times per week. Only 10 percent of male and female seniors report never having dated (Savin-Williams & Berndt, 1990).

Dating is a major avenue for exploring sexual activity in both consensual (Zani, 1993) and nonconsensual (Small & Kerns, 1993) experiences. Because dating is occurring at younger ages and can also lead to violence and victimization, where and how young people learn about dating can be an important asset to establishing healthy boundaries in relationships. Regarding sources of information on dating and relationships, young girls tend to use a wider range of sources than their male peers. Not only do girls seek out friends, parents, and traditional and social media, as well as sexual education teachers in school, but they also trust these sources of information more than young boys (Wood et al., 2002). Boys, according to Wood et al. (2002), tend to explore fewer sources of information and appear to trust and value what they learn from the girls they date.

In recent years, with the advent of social media, dating has taken on a different aura than what was considered traditional dating just a few years ago. Group dating has become more common, which is less formal than one-to-one dating, and terms like "hooking-up" are often used synonymously with having a date. Cell phones and Internet access have led to an increase in teen cyberdating, making teens more vulnerable to cyberbullying and incidents of dating violence. Teen dating violence has become more frequent, leading to efforts to educate and protect young women and men as they embark on more intimate relationships. Whether dating in a group, or in a special dyad, there has been a growing awareness that dating situations may lead to sexual activity that is coerced. In a nationally representative survey, 42 percent of rape victims were first raped before age eighteen, and 30 percent of female rape victims were first raped between the ages of eleven and seventeen (Black et al., 2011). Among those who had first experienced rape, physical violence, or stalking from an intimate partner, over 22 percent of females and 15 percent of males also report this occurring in adolescence, between the ages of eleven and seventeen (Breiding, Chen, & Black, 2014). Teen dating violence also mirrors incidents of stalking, coercion, and intimidation that occur in emerging adult and adult relationships, often leading to serious, and at times tragic, outcomes for the developing adolescent (Zweig et al., 2013).

When there is a confluence of sexual intimacy, social media, and adolescent disinhibition, a perfect storm of tragic proportions is a very real potential outcome. The suicidal death of Jessica Logan is such an occurrence. Jessica, a high school senior in Ohio, sent nude pictures of herself to her boyfriend, at his urging. When they broke up, the pictures appeared on social media sites of Jessica's classmates, and the cyberbullying went viral at her school. Jessica even appeared on a local TV station in her hometown to share her story in hopes that no one else would have to go through what she had to endure. After that show, and after her graduation, having attended a friend's funeral, Jessica returned home and hung herself. Jessica's story made national news, and in 2012, the state of Ohio passed the Jessica Logan Act to help schools enforce cyberbullying in their school districts.

Sexual Orientations

Our discussion so far has centered on issues related to heterosexual orientation. But as in the population at large, not all adolescents are heterosexual. Reliable statistics on sexual orientation are difficult to obtain. Kaufman (2008) reports on a large-scale Canadian study in which 1.5 percent of adolescent males and 3 percent of females identified themselves as either bisexual, mostly homosexual, or 100 percent homosexual. In one large-scale study in the United States of thirty-eight thousand adolescents in grades seven through twelve, 88.2 percent described themselves as predominantly heterosexual (exclusively interested in the other sex), 1.1 percent as predominantly homosexual (exclusively interested in the same sex) or bisexual (interested in members of both sexes), and 10.7 percent as uncertain about their sexual orientation (Remafedi et al., 1992, 2007). Other studies have found that between 3 and 6 percent of teenagers report that they are lesbian or gay (Patterson, 1995).

Due largely to the political and educational efforts of the "equal rights" and "gay rights" movements, public acceptance of gay, lesbian, and bisexual orientations has increased significantly during the past several decades. This acceptance acknowledges the right of individuals to freely practice their own sexual orientations and lifestyles and to receive protection from discrimination. However, other researchers have found that **homophobia** (dislike and fear of homosexuals) remains strong among adolescents (Stokes, 1985; Williams & Jacoby, 1989). Negative attitudes toward gay, lesbian, bisexual, and transgendered individuals put LGBT youth at risk for greater mistreatment and victimization than other students. Violence against students in the LGBT community can include bullying and cyberbullying, harassment, and physical assault. In one large study of middle school and high school students, 80 percent of the students had been harassed verbally at school, while 40 percent were physically harassed, and one in five had been physically assaulted, all because of their sexual orientation (Kosciw et al., 2009). Unsurprisingly, in this same study, roughly 60 percent of the LGBT youth indicated they did not feel safe at school.

Because of persisting widespread homophobia, gay, lesbian, and bisexual adolescents are likely to experience feelings of attraction for members of the same sex for several years before actually *coming out,* or publicly acknowledging their sexual orientation (Patterson, 1995). A study by Ritch Savin-Williams (1995) found that for gay males initiation of sexual behavior with same-sex partners was closely associated with biological changes of puberty (early maturers initiated same-sex encounters earlier than did late maturers), whereas sexual behavior with opposite-sex partners began according to a youngster's age and level of social and emotional development.

Current understanding of the development of sexual-minority orientations is that the trajectory of development—same-sex interest, recognizing one's sexual orientation, and dating—is quite different for different individuals, depending on where they live, ethnicity, gender, socioeconomic status, etc. (Diamond & Savin-Williams, 2006). Though cross-gender behavior in childhood appears to be strongly associated with sexual-minority orientations in adolescence and adulthood for both males and females, a substantial proportion of gay and lesbian adults report no or few cross-gender behaviors in childhood (Bailey & Zucker, 1995; Golombok & Tasker, 1996; Green, 1987). In a unique longitudinal study, Susan Golombok and Fiona Tasker (1996) compared the sexual orientations of twenty-five adults who had been raised as children by lesbian mothers with a group of twenty-one adults who had been raised by heterosexual single mothers. Although children from lesbian families were more likely to explore same-sex relationships, all but two children raised by lesbian mothers (and all children raised by heterosexual mothers) identified themselves as heterosexual in adulthood, a difference that was not statistically significant.

A number of researchers are also exploring the contributions of biological and genetic predispositions to the development of sexual-minority orientations (Balter, 2015; Byne, 1994; Diamond & Savin-Williams, 2006; LeVay & Hamer, 1994; Patterson, 1995). One approach has sought to discover physical differences between the brains of male and female animals and humans; the second has explored the role of genes by using family and twin adoption studies to analyze the frequencies with which homosexuality occurs in families

homophobia Fear, dread, hostility, or prejudice directed toward gay and lesbian persons and the resulting mistreatment and discrimination.

> **What Do You Think?**
>
> When you were an adolescent, what were your attitudes toward premarital sex, dating, and sexual orientations? In what ways, if any, have your attitudes changed since then?

and by directly examining DNA. There is evidence that activity among certain genes, without differences in DNA, is linked to homosexuality among men (Balter, 2015), and there have also been links to prenatal development in that men with more older brothers are more likely to identify as gay (Ashley, 2013). However, as with most aspects of development, who we become is due to an interplay of nature and nurture that is different for each of us, and sexual orientation is likely due to a complex interaction between environment and genetics (Diamond & Savin-Williams, 2006).

The challenging task of achieving a secure sexual identity is considerably more difficult for nonheterosexual adolescents, who have the added burdens of grappling with their difference and the anxieties and dangers involved. Homosexual and bisexual teenagers frequently experience rejection by their families, peer groups, schools, places of worship, and other community institutions—the very groups adolescents depend on for support. The verbal abuse, the AIDS-related stigmatization, the threat of physical attack, and other forms of victimization they encounter put them at greater risk for mental health problems. However, strong support from family, friends, school and community, and antidiscrimination legislation and education about nonheterosexuality can all serve as buffers against these negative outcomes by creating an environment that allows these adolescents to successfully master the challenges of identity formation (Diamond & Savin-Williams, 2006; Hershberger & D'Augelli, 1995). Chapter 13 discusses lesbian and gay lifestyles in early adulthood.

Sex and Everyday Life

Although sexuality plays an important role in adolescents' feelings, fantasies, and social relationships, it does not necessarily dominate their lives. As noted earlier, changes in sexuality during adolescence involve not only physical maturation and the development of new social skills; they also play a major role in the development of intimacy and personal identity. Reasons for engaging in sexual activity or for not having sex during adolescence vary, based on social, emotional, and moral attitudes and beliefs of the teenager. For those who abstain from having sex, religious reasons tend to predominate for males and females, followed by the desire to not get pregnant or to get someone pregnant, followed by not having found the right person yet (Martinez, Copen, & Abma, 2011). Keep in mind, however, that the nature and role of sexual activity in the lives of adolescents vary considerably depending on culture, SES, and overall life circumstances (Seidman & Rieder, 1994).

Sometimes, identity development is complicated by sexual issues. It can also be affected by social problems specific to teenagers, as we will see in the next section.

Special Problems of Adolescence

In Chapter 10, we looked at the special physical and health risks adolescents face as a group. Their lack of experience, their need to experiment with new and sometimes risky social roles, and the lack of educational and economic opportunities and social support they frequently encounter can place adolescents at high risk for developing certain psychosocial problems. In this section, we discuss three special problems of adolescence: teenage pregnancy and parenthood, adolescent depression and suicide, and juvenile delinquency.

Adolescent Pregnancy and Parenthood

Despite the declining rates in teen pregnancy over the past decades, nearly one million adolescent girls get pregnant each year. In the United States, nearly four out of every ten teen girls will get pregnant at least once before they turn twenty, according to the National Campaign to Prevent Teen Pregnancy (Kirby, 2007). In 1990, 1,040,000 adolescents under age twenty became pregnant, and approximately 530,000 (51 percent) of them gave birth (Alan Guttmacher Institute, 1994). By the end of the decade, the teen pregnancy rate declined by almost 20 percent, from 117 pregnancies per 1,000 women ages fifteen to nineteen, to 94 per 1,000 (Guttmacher Institute, 2002). Birth rates for nineteen-year-olds were double those for fifteen- to seventeen-year-olds, and rates for those under fifteen years were extremely low. In 1995, birth rates for white fifteen- to nineteen-year-olds were 39.3 per 1,000, compared to 106.7 per 1,000 for Hispanics and 99.3 per 1,000 for African Americans (Ventura et al., 1997). Like pregnancy rates, teen birth rates have also declined to their lowest rates ever recorded: 39.1 births per 1,000 women ages fifteen to nineteen—a decline of 37 percent since the all-time highs were recorded in 1991 (Ventura & Hamilton, 2011). However, it is important to note that current teen pregnancy rates in the United States are still significantly higher than in any other industrialized nation (Sedgh et al., 2015).

Causes of Teen Pregnancy

Causes of teen pregnancy include individual, family, neighborhood, and societal characteristics, suggesting that a contextual or ecological approach similar to that used in our discussion of the impact of divorce earlier in this chapter will be useful here. Female adolescents who live in communities with high rates of poverty and who themselves are raised in poverty by single parents with low levels of education are at higher risk of becoming pregnant. In fact, in 1988, 60 percent of adolescent mothers lived in poverty at the time of their babies' birth (Alan Guttmacher Institute, 1994; Coley & Chase-Lansdale, 1998). The majority of teen pregnancies are thought to involve experiences of poverty and perceptions of limited life opportunities and choices. Life experiences associated with poverty, such as alienation at school, being surrounded by role models of unmarried parenthood and unemployment, and lack of educational opportunities and stable career prospects, tend to lower the perceived costs of early motherhood (Coley & Chase-Lansdale, 1998). In addition, the loss of most low-skill, high-paying manufacturing jobs due to changes in the U.S. economy has increased unemployment and poverty in our inner cities and strikingly changed the context and course of development during the teenage years and the early twenties. Although median ages of completing school, marriage, and childbearing have significantly increased for middle-class adolescents, lower-SES populations have not adapted to these changes by delaying starting their families. Adolescent childbearing, which in the past occurred mostly in the context of marriage with an employed husband, is now occurring among unmarried teenagers with few prospects for economic security (Coley & Chase-Lansdale, 1998; Rosenheim & Testa, 1992; Wilson, 1996).

Decisions About Contraception

Although American teenagers do not exhibit different patterns of sexual activity than adolescents in many industrial countries, they use contraception less consistently and effectively. In 1990 the rate of teenage births in the United States was almost twice that of Great Britain, the country with the next highest rate; more than four times greater than those of Sweden and Spain; seven times greater than those of Denmark and the Netherlands; and fifteen times greater than that of Japan (Coley & Chase-Lansdale, 1998). Recent data show very little change in the United States compared to other developed countries. According to data from the United Nations Statistical Division (2008), the adolescent birth rate in Canada was one-third the rate in the United States (fourteen versus thirty-nine births per one thousand fifteen- to nineteen-year olds). The rates per one thousand teen women in Germany and Italy were ten and seven, respectively—less than 25 percent the U.S. rate.

The great majority of teenage pregnancies are the result of inadequate or no contraception. Despite the steady decline in teen pregnancy over the past twenty years, many teenagers remain startlingly uninformed about the basics of reproduction or feel emboldened by their own personal fable, believing they are "immune" to pregnancy or at least at very low risk. Roughly 20 to 25 percent of all teenagers do not use contraceptives the first time they have sex, and many—

particularly, younger adolescents—delay using contraception for a year or more after the first intercourse (Coley & Chase-Lansdale, 1998; Martinez, Copen, & Abma, 2011).

Although birth control pills are popular, they are not reliable during the first month of use. Only foam and condoms or a diaphragm and contraceptive jelly are really effective for first intercourse. But adolescents do not like to use these contraceptives because they imply a preparedness for sex, are expensive or unavailable when needed, can be messy, reduce pleasure, and increase anxiety due to inexperience in their use. Irregular use of contraception is associated with lack of knowledge about contraceptives, low SES, poor communication with parents, having teenage friends who became parents, low educational achievement and aspirations, high levels of anxiety, low self-esteem, and feelings of fatalism, powerlessness, and alienation (Coley & Chase-Lansdale, 1998). Because lack of knowledge and lack of planning are major barriers in adolescent use of contraception, other more long-acting forms of birth-control, such as implants and intrauterine devices (IUDs), might be most beneficial for many teens and have been linked to lower birth rates and lower abortion rates (Peipert et al., 2012). In fact, after the passage of the Affordable Care Act, which made contraception free to those with insurance, several states recorded lower teen pregnancy rates and lower abortion rates (Rickettes, Klinger, & Schwalberg, 2014). In the "Working With" interview, Janet Whallen, a nurse practitioner, discusses her experiences with pregnant teens.

Parent-Teen Communication About Sexual Behavior

The helplessness that many parents feel about influencing their teens' sexual behavior may in part reflect a failure to communicate effectively about such matters. This is illustrated in a recent study by James Jaccard and his colleagues of African American adolescents ages fourteen to seventeen, which found little agreement between the mothers' perceptions and reports of their teenagers' sexual behavior and the teenagers self-reports (Jaccard et al., 1998). Adolescent perceptions and reports were more predictive of actual sexual behavior than maternal reports. Mothers significantly underestimated the sexual activity of their teens, and teens tended to underestimate their mothers' level of disapproval of their sexual activity. While 58 percent of the teens in the study had engaged in sexual intercourse, only 34 percent of the mothers thought that was the case. This was particularly true for older mothers who were satisfied with their parent-teen relationship but did not talk with their teens about sex and strongly disapproved of premarital sex. Teens were more likely to underestimate their mothers' opposition to premarital sex if the mothers were not religious, if the teens' friends viewed it favorably, if they reported little communication about sex with their mothers, and if they were male.

Parent-teen communication is a complex process, especially when adolescent sexual behavior is the topic. It takes good communication, which allows both parties to share their needs and expectations and to negotiate differences, for parents to successfully influence their teens. Efforts to improve parent-teen communication must address five important aspects: (1) the *extent* of the communication, as indicated by the frequency and depth; (2) the *style* or manner in which the information is communicated; (3) the *content* of the communication; (4) the *timing* of the communication; and (5) the *general family environment* in which the communication takes place, as reflected in the overall quality of the parent-teen relationship (Jaccard et al., 1998).

Consequences of Teenage Parenthood

Many teenage mothers may see having a baby as a way to prematurely crystallize their identities because motherhood and marriage promise to establish them in a secure adult role and help them to escape role confusion. Such fantasies generally are not realized, however. Teenage mothers are less likely to finish high school, find a stable paying job, enter secure marriages, or achieve equal job status or income in their lifetimes. They are also more likely to get pregnant again within two years (Richio, Phipps, & Raker, 2010; Rigsby et al., 1998). Teenage fathers are less negatively affected, largely because they generally do not assume responsibility for raising their children (Coley & Chase-Lansdale, 1998; Furstenberg et al., 1989).

WORKING WITH Janet Whallen, Nurse Practitioner

Helping Pregnant Teenagers

Janet Whallen was interviewed in her office, which is located in a neighborhood health care center serving disadvantaged Hispanic and African American individuals and families. Janet's warm, low-key style made it easy to see why teenagers would find her easy to talk with. Our interview focused on the experiences of pregnant teens.

Rob: *What special problems do pregnant teenagers face?*

Janet: Most of the sexual relationships these teenagers are involved in are fairly short-lived. A young woman or man might have three or four partners in a year. When a young woman becomes pregnant, the chances that she'll still be with the same boyfriend when she delivers nine months later are fairly slim.

Rob: *Nine months would be a long relationship?*

Janet: For someone who is only fourteen or fifteen, it is. Very few of these girls have the baby's father with them in any way, shape, or form at the time of delivery.

Rob: *Why is this so?*

Janet: Sometimes, the guy gets scared or loses interest because the girl is starting to get fat. Or the girl or guy was already losing interest even before the pregnancy occurred. Whatever the reason, I think shorter relationships are fairly typical of early adolescent behavior.

Rob: *In what other ways are the experiences of pregnant teenagers typical of adolescents in general?*

Janet: They have very little sense of the implications of the decisions they make. They make most choices based on short-term consequences, and those choices are tightly connected to peer approval. There are also lots of rebellion issues against important adults, whether parents or teachers.

Rob: *How does this rebelliousness affect pregnancy?*

Janet: Teenagers are very sensitive about many things, from small issues to big ones: being told to eat certain things or to wear certain clothes—you know, "you're going to look fat if you wear that"—about smoking or not smoking, getting home on time after school or staying out late on Friday night, about how their parent will feel about their being sexually active or getting pregnant. I have to be very careful to give advice in a way that they don't find threatening.

Rob: *Sounds like typical adolescent behavior.*

Janet: I have kids who will come in for an appointment with four or five giggling teenage friends, who'll sit outside the office and heckle and laugh. They'll all be talking about who is going out with whom, who passed notes to whom in class, who cut class for what reasons, where they bought their clothes. You would never know you were in the middle of an inner-city clinic for pregnant teenagers.

Rob: *Are these pregnant teenagers in danger of losing connection with their peer culture?*

Teenage mothers are more likely than older women to experience complications such as anemia and toxemia during pregnancy, as well as prolonged labor. Their babies are more likely to be premature, have low birth weight, and have neurological defects, and are also more likely to die during their first year. For some children of teenage mothers, delays in cognitive development begin to emerge during the preschool years and continue into the school years. Many children show behavioral problems, including aggression and lack of impulse control. In adolescence, they have higher rates of grade failure, delinquency, incarceration (for males), and early sexual activity and pregnancy than their peers born to older mothers (Coley & Chase-Lansdale, 1998). As Rebekah Coley and Lindsey Chase-Lansdale point out, however, both teenage mothers and their children display a wide range of diversity in their development and functioning, due in large part to the resources available to the mother and child (Pittard, Laditka, & Laditka, 2008). Although children of teenage mothers are at risk of becoming teenage parents, it is estimated that only between one-quarter and one-third of the daughters and one-tenth of the sons of teen parents become teen parents themselves. These researchers also note that the lower SES experienced by the majority of teen parents appear to be more important predictors of children's and adolescents' functioning than is maternal age at birth.

> **WORKING WITH** Janet Whallen, Nurse Practitioner
>
> **Helping Pregnant Teenagers** *continued*
>
> **Janet:** Not as much as you might think. Unlike in middle-class communities, where teenagers are expected to complete high school and go to college, there is relatively little stigma attached to becoming pregnant during high school—although there may be a little bit more if pregnancy occurs in junior high.
>
> **Rob:** *Why do teenagers become pregnant in the first place?*
>
> **Janet:** I wish I knew the answer to that one! Failure to use effective birth control is, of course, the immediate factor. And some teenagers want to have a little baby to care for and be close to and to feel important and needed, or they see pregnancy as a way to gain adult status. Another reason is that sex is a big deal and getting pregnant isn't.
>
> **Rob:** *What do you mean?*
>
> **Janet:** Many of these kids become sexually active at age twelve or thirteen, and some even before they start having their periods. Most of them have little extra money, so they don't go shopping, or buy CDs, or collect this or that. A lot of them are involved in Pentecostal or Baptist churches, so they don't do drugs and they don't drink. But they do sex.
>
> **Rob:** *It's an enjoyable activity, and it's inexpensive.*
>
> **Janet:** Well . . . intimacy is involved too, but for many young teens, sex is mainly a way to have immediate fun. Getting pregnant simply happens, with little thought about its deeper social, emotional, or philosophical significance.
>
> **Rob:** *What social supports are available to these youngsters?*
>
> **Janet:** Family or extended family members often will babysit and share other childcare responsibilities. Sometimes the boyfriend's family will also become involved, even when he's out of the picture. Many teen moms are back to being teenagers fairly soon after having their babies. Some graduate from high school and get a job, and a few go on to college. A significant number do not finish school. Unfortunately, we are finding that an increasing number get pregnant again soon after the first baby.
>
> **What Do You Think?**
>
> 1. If Janet Whallen were working with pregnant teens in the community in which you spent your adolescence, in what ways might her observations be different? In what ways might they be the same? Why?
> 2. What are your views about the causes of teenage pregnancy?
> 3. What strategies might you recommend for preventing teen pregnancy among low-SES, inner-city youth?

Involvement of Grandmothers

An understanding of teenage parenthood truly requires a lifespan perspective. As we will see in Chapter 13, the transition to parenthood is a challenging one, even for married young adults who are well educated and enjoy economically and socially supportive circumstances. For single teenage mothers, the transition often is much more difficult. Many teenage mothers end up living with their own mothers. The quality of child-rearing practices for teenage parents living in three-generation families appears to be positively related to the quality of their relationships with their own mothers (the baby's grandmother). Adolescent mothers whose own mothers provided authoritative parenting, helped them care for their new babies, and modeled appropriate parenting behaviors in a way that respected their daughters' autonomy became better parents themselves than teen mothers without such support. However, although living in the same household as their mothers resulted in positive mother-grandmother relationships for younger teen mothers, mother-grandmother relationships were better for older teenage mothers when the adolescent daughter and her mother lived in separate households (Apfel & Switz, 1991; Chase-Lansdale et al., 1994; Wakschlag et al., 1996).

Chapter 11 Psychosocial Development in Adolescence

Prevention and Support Programs

Programs to prevent teen pregnancy must be responsive to adolescents' developmental needs and life contexts. As noted in Chapter 10, comprehensive sex education is most effective at getting adolescents to delay initiation of intercourse and to use contraception. For teens who are at high risk because of their life circumstances, programs that include comprehensive, developmentally oriented services—medical care and contraceptive services, social services, family and educational support, and school-linked parenting education— appear to be maximize efficacy. One such program conducted at Johns Hopkins University was successful in delaying the age at which sexual activity was initiated, increased contraceptive use, reduced the frequency of sexual relations, and reduced the pregnancy rate by 30 percent, while comparison school rates increased by 58 percent (Hardy & Zabin, 1991).

Effective support programs for pregnant teenagers and teenage parents generally focus on providing pre- and postnatal health care, economic support, childcare and parenting support, education, and job training. The Prenatal/Early Infancy Project (Olds, 1988) still stands as a model for assisting teenage parents and their children and for reducing the likelihood of unplanned pregnancies in the future. It clearly demonstrates close connections between issues in adolescent development and themes associated with prenatal development, infancy, and early childhood development. It also highlights the interconnectedness of the three main developmental domains of physical, cognitive, and psychosocial development discussed in Chapter 1.

This five-year longitudinal study focused on single, first-time-pregnant adolescents from low-SES circumstances. The program (1) provided prenatal parent education; (2) helped to involve family members and friends in the pregnancy, birth, early care of the child, and support of the mother; and (3) helped to link family members with formal health and human services. Prenatal and pediatric care was available through a local team of private obstetricians and pediatricians. A central feature of the program was an ongoing caregiving relationship with an experienced nurse who made regular home visits during and for two years following the pregnancy. During the pregnancy, the nurse provided parenting education focused on helping the pregnant teen improve her diet and monitor her weight gain, identify signs of pregnancy complication, adopt a healthy lifestyle (e.g., eliminate use of cigarettes), prepare for labor and delivery, prepare for the early care of the newborn, make appropriate use of the health care system, and make plans regarding subsequent pregnancies, returning to school, and finding employment. After the baby was born, the nurse provided home-based infancy education designed to improve the young mother's understanding of her infant's temperament and to promote the infant's physical, cognitive, and psychosocial development.

To evaluate the long-term impact of the program, the teen mothers and their children were followed from early pregnancy until their children were four years old. Adolescent mothers who received postnatal nurse home care made better use of formal health and social services, experienced greater informal social support, improved their diets more, and reduced the number of cigarettes smoked compared to a similar group of women who had not received such nursing care. High-risk teen mothers benefited the most. For very young teenagers, there was a 335-gram improvement in their babies' birth weight and for women who smoked, a 75 percent reduction in preterm delivery. Among poor, unmarried, high-risk teens who received postnatal nurse home care, there was a 75 percent reduction in reported cases of child abuse and neglect (from 19 to 4 percent). These at-risk mothers found their children easier to care for, used less punishment and restriction and a greater number of growth-promoting playthings, needed to use the emergency room fewer times for their babies' health care, and, during the children's second year, used the emergency room 56 percent fewer times for children's accidents than did similar mothers who did not receive nurse home care (Olds, 1988).

Teenage Depression and Suicide

Depressive disorders involve disturbances of emotion that affect individuals' entire mental lives. Two key subtypes of depressive disorder exist: major depressive disorder (MDD), which involves a single episode or recurrent episodes of depression, and dysthymia, which involves chronic depressive symptoms. Individuals with either type of depressive disorder experience a pervasive mood disturbance that involves feelings of sadness and loss of interest or pleasure in most activities; feelings of fear, anger, self-criticism, and hopelessness; and disturbances in sleep, appetite, ability to concentrate, sexual interest, and energy level. Depression is frequently accompanied by other problems such as anxiety, social withdrawal, disruptive disorder, and substance abuse (Cicchetti & Toth, 1998; American Psychiatric Association, 2013; Peterson et al., 1993).

It is estimated that at any point in time, between 0.4 and 2.5 percent of children and from 0.4 and 8.3 percent of adolescents suffer from MDD, and between 15 and 20 percent of adolescents suffer from MDD over their lifetimes. Approximately 0.6 to 1.7 percent of children and 1.6 to 8.0 percent of adolescents suffer from dysthymia at any point in time. Depression during childhood and adolescence are nonnormative experiences that interfere with children's development. The average length of an episode of MDD in children and adolescents is from seven to nine months. Approximately 90 percent of MDD episodes end within two years following their onset, and the remaining 10 percent last longer. MDD frequently recurs in children and adolescents. Dysthymia episodes last much longer than MDD episodes, with the average length being four years. Because the development of dysthymia often leads to a recurrent depressive disorder, early diagnosis and treatment are important. There is some evidence that a significant increase in the prevalence of depression during early to middle adolescence occurs among both males and females and that rates are higher for girls, who may be more likely to deal with their upsets by internalizing them rather than externalizing them in a more aggressive manner (Cicchetti & Toth, 1998).

Causes of Depression in Adolescence

Dante Cicchetti and Sheree Toth (1998) suggest that the causes of depression are best understood from an ecological systems perspective similar to that of Uri Bronfenbrenner (see Chapter 1). In this view, the development of depression is related to the multiple, dynamic interactions among environmental forces, caregiver characteristics, and the characteristics of the developing child and adolescent. At each ecological level of influence, certain risk and preventive factors may influence the development of depressive problems. At the individual level, some infants may be born with a biological vulnerability to depression due to genetic or nongenetic factors. Family influences include the unique family circumstances, both biological and psychosocial, in which the child and adolescent develops. Although genetic factors account for some within-family depression, genetics alone cannot fully explain the development of depression. For one thing, many depressed children display rapid recovery when hospitalized, even without additional interventions. For another, a number of family characteristics have been associated with the development and maintenance of depression, including parental depression, anxiety, substance abuse, and maltreatment. Family transitions, low SES, and acute and chronic negative life events involving significant losses through parental death, divorce, or separation or involving child maltreatment have been associated with the occurrence of depression during childhood and adolescence (Bronfenbrenner, 1989; Cicchetti & Toth, 1998; Downey & Coyne, 1990).

Children and adolescents who live in a family in which one or more parents are depressed, have other serious emotional problems, or experience a serious and pervasive disturbance in the parent-child relationship, including physical or emotional abuse, are at much greater risk for depression as well as other forms of psychopathology. In addition, the environments provided by the schools and neighborhoods in which a child grows up can play an important role in the development of depression. Neighborhoods that are unsafe and unsupportive may create levels of stress that are developmentally disruptive, particularly during early and middle adolescence. Especially during the early adolescent transition to middle school, school environments that respond inappropriately to adolescents' academic and psychosocial needs can alienate them from academic activities and from prosocial activities with peers, and contribute to school failure, antisocial behavior, drug abuse, and depression (Cicchetti & Toth, 1998; Downey & Coyne, 1990; Garbarino, 1992b; Eccles, 1993; Jacobvitz & Bush, 1996). Depression is often a factor in adolescent suicide.

Suicide in Adolescence

Among adolescents and young adults, suicide is the third leading cause of death among individuals ages fifteen to twenty-four (CDC, 2005). Between 6 and 13 percent of adolescents have reported attempting suicide at least once in their lives, and the ratio of attempted to successful suicides is estimated to be as high as fifty to one (Garland & Zigler, 1993; Meehan et al., 1992; Rubenstein et al., 1998; CDC-MMWR, 2012). Suicide attempts are estimated to be three to nine times more common among girls, but boys succeed three times as often, in part because they use more effective methods, such as knives and guns (Holden, 1986).

More adolescents seriously consider suicide (15.8 percent) and make a suicide plan (12.8 percent) than actually take the step to attempt suicide (7.8 percent), according to the most recent data on youth risk behaviors by the Center for Disease control (2012). Native Americans maintain the highest prevalence rates for attempted suicides, compared to other racial/ethnic groups, with African Americans reporting the lowest rates for all age groups (CDC, 2005; Prinstein, 2008). When considering prevalence rates among youth in grades nine through twelve, however, black teens show a higher incidence of attempting suicide (8.3 percent) than white or Hispanic teens, even though both black males and females are less likely to consider suicide attempts or make a suicide plan (CDC-MMWR, 2012). Nonfatal suicide attempts are also a major concern for adolescents, given that this form of self-injurious behavior occurs much more frequently, There are twenty-five incidents of nonfatal self-harm for every single completed suicide, according to recent estimates (Evans et al., 2005; Prinstein, 2008).

For teens, the reasons for attempting suicide or self-injury are complex and occur within a context of various psychological disorders but may also present in the absence of any prevailing psychopathology. Students who are depressed or suffer other mental or physical disabilities are at risk for suicide ideation and attempts, but the desire to self-harm may also stem from unresolved family conflicts, social rejection, sexual orientation issues, or an impulsive act occurring at a moment of deep despair or impaired functioning (Bradley, 2002; Duncan & Hatzenbuehler, 2014; Institute of Medicine, 2002; Prinstein, 2008). Whatever the individual reason, suicide attempts almost always represent cries for help with the personal turmoil and feelings of intense loneliness, isolation, and hopelessness that depressed or troubled youngsters experience (Rubenstein et al., 1998). Although most teenagers who are not depressed still experience moments of unhappiness, and most who are depressed do not attempt suicide, signs of unhappiness and depression should not be dismissed, particularly if they persist. Also, because a large percentage of those who attempt suicide have threatened or attempted it before, such threats should be taken very seriously. Adolescent egocentrism, the exaggerated feeling that one's uniqueness makes it impossible for anyone else to truly understand one's problems, may intensify a teenager's feelings of loneliness and isolation and contribute to a tendency not to seek help and to reject help that is available.

Attempts to prevent suicide include early detection and intervention in family and personal crises, school-based education about depression and suicide risk factors, training in problem solving and coping skills, crisis counseling, and emergency hot lines. Treatment for teens who attempt suicide generally involves therapy with both the adolescent and his or her family (Garland & Zigler, 1993; Rubenstein et al., 1989).

Juvenile Delinquency

juvenile delinquency A pattern of destructive or antisocial activities and lawbreaking offenses committed by adolescents.

Juvenile delinquency refers to a pattern of destructive or antisocial activities and lawbreaking offenses committed by adolescents. In 2012, more than half a million juveniles were arrested in the United States for less serious *status offenses*, or offenses that are illegal based on age, such as joy riding, drinking alcohol, or running away (Federal Bureau of Investigation, 2013). For more serious crimes, such as larceny or theft, robbery, or forcible rape, arrests for violent offenses by juveniles decreased by approximately 40 percent between 2006 and 2012 (Federal Bureau of Investigation,

2013). Arrests and imprisonment for status offenses may serve as an introduction to the criminal world for some adolescents, especially those who already feel very weak ties to the rest of the majority society.

There is some evidence that the main route to chronic delinquency follows a predictable developmental sequence of experiences. The first step involves ineffective parenting and problematic family interaction processes, both of which frequently contribute to childhood conduct disorders. In the second step, the conduct-disordered behaviors lead to academic failure and peer rejection. During later childhood and early adolescence, continuing failure at school and peer rejection lead to a third step: increased risk for depressed mood and involvement in a deviant peer group. Children who follow this developmental sequence are assumed to be at high risk for engaging in chronic delinquent behavior (Patterson et al., 1989).

Factors associated with delinquency include a caregiver-child relationship characterized by hostility, lack of affection, underinvolvement, and lack of supervision; overly harsh and authoritarian methods of discipline; a high degree of family conflict and disorganization; a parent with a personality disturbance and a delinquent history of her or his own; impoverished living conditions; lack of attachment to any prosocial institution such as school, job, or religious organization; lack of positive adult role models; and exposure to neighborhood environments in which violence, crime, and delinquent behavior are prevalent (Dishion et al., 1995; Romig et al., 1989; Sarafino & Armstrong, 1986). As discussed in the "A Multicultural View" feature, these factors vary from culture to culture, as do the delinquent behaviors in which teens engage.

Longitudinal studies of delinquency and antisocial behavior have found that aggression during the preschool period is predictive only of serious forms of antisocial behavior in adolescence and adulthood. For these children, who are mostly boys, the onset of minor aggression (annoying others and bullying) tends to precede the onset of physical fighting (including gang fighting), which in turn precedes the onset of more extreme violence (aggravated assault, robbery, and rape). The majority of violent male adults exhibited a life course pattern initially characterized by both aggressive behavior and symptoms of attention deficit hyperactivity disorder (ADHD) during their preschool years, followed by more serious forms of conduct disorder and antisocial behavior during adolescence and adulthood. A second, limited-duration pattern is shown by individuals who outgrow aggression either during the preschool-elementary school age period or in late adolescence-early adulthood. A third, late-onset pattern accounts for individuals who become violent during adulthood but do not have a history of aggression earlier in their lives (Loeber & Stouthamer-Loeber, 1998).

Gangs

Many delinquent youngsters belong to gangs. A gang is a relatively permanent group of individuals with a clearly identified leadership and organizational structure and clear role expectations for its members. Gangs identify with or claim control over "territory" in the community and engage in violence and other forms of illegal activities, such as fighting, vandalism, theft, and drug dealing, on an individual or group basis. A gang is likely to have a group name, an initiation rite, nicknames for members, and gang symbols such as colors, tattoos, hand signs, or jewelry (Miller, 1990; Winfree et al., 1994).

The incidence of gang-related homicides, drive-by shootings, home invasions, and related violent and illegal activities in schools and communities is an ongoing national concern (Pryor & McGarell, 1993; Takata & Zevitz, 1990). Typically gangs are formed by individuals from low-SES and racial or ethnic minority and immigrant backgrounds. Traditionally gang members have mainly been adolescent males, but the growth of gangs in prisons and increased gang involvement in the drug trade have expanded the age range to include children as young as nine as well as adults, and also increased female involvement to some degree (Goldstein & Soriano, 1994; Lasley, 1992).

Gangs are thought to provide alternative economic opportunities and social supports for disadvantaged and alienated youths who face high levels of uncertainty, instability, and danger in their families and neighborhoods. For such adolescents, gang membership offers a surrogate "family," a sense of identity and belonging, and status, power, and protection, as well as the material benefits of criminal activity (Curry & Spergel, 1988; Knox, 1991).

A gang typically reinforces its members for associating exclusively with other members, conforming to pro-gang attitudes and behaviors, and rejecting the values of parents, teachers, and mainstream peers (Winfree et al., 1994). Many of the individual, family, and social factors associated with gang membership, gang activity, and its prevention are similar to those linked to juvenile delinquency.

Reducing and Preventing Delinquency

Most adolescents, of course, do not become delinquents or join gangs. Adolescents who are at risk for delinquency sometimes can be helped by programs that make available the support and opportunities that will allow successful experimentation with other roles and identities. These include community houses, YMCAs, police athletic leagues, summer camps, crisis drop-in centers, and telephone hot lines, as well as outpatient and residential treatment programs to assist more disturbed teenagers and their families. Unfortunately, such interventions have been found to produce mostly short-term effects and lose their impact unless continued on a long-term basis (Patterson et al., 1989).

Intensive early childhood intervention programs for at-risk preschool children and their families have achieved significant success in reducing delinquency and related problems later in life (Zigler et al., 1992). The High/Scope Perry Preschool Program, for example, provided a high-quality preschool, weekly home visits by teachers, and extensive parent involvement for three- and four-year-olds from low-SES families. Long-term longitudinal follow-up studies of these children at age nineteen and again at age twenty-seven found significantly lower rates of school dropout, illiteracy, unemployment, welfare dependence, and arrest for delinquent or criminal behavior than for a comparable group of children who did not participate in the program. They reveal how early childhood intervention can help generate and support ongoing family processes that foster positive development into the adulthood years (Hamburg, 1994; Luster & McAdoo, 1996; Schweinhart & Weikart, 1992).

Looking Back/Looking Forward

We have reached the end of our discussion of adolescence. How do the developmental issues of adolescence reflect the four lifespan themes discussed in Chapter 1? Changing relationships with parents are an important aspect of adolescent development. Let's look at the four lifespan themes with this issue in mind.

- **Continuity within change**—The theme of continuity and change is very much in evidence during adolescence. Though the attachment relationships with parents that have developed during childhood continue to grow and develop, the separation from parents and the emergence of a more integrated and adult identity and sense of self strongly indicate that adolescence is indeed a transition to adulthood that heavily involves change. And though the striking changes in physical and cognitive capabilities that emerge in adolescence most certainly affect the quality of parent-teen relationships, lifelong consistencies in temperament, cognitive style, and beliefs about parenting ensure a certain degree of continuity as well. The various styles of parenting that we first discussed in Chapter 5 continue to be associated with better or worse developmental outcomes during the teen years, and there is good reason to believe that an authoritative parenting style will continue to benefit midlife parents as their children become young adults and their parents age. Patterns of parenting and the nature of a particular parent-child relationship can also change in response to the changing experiences, needs, and expectations of both parent and child. For example, family changes such as the birth of additional children, divorce, and remarriage may have a significant impact on children, parents, and their relationships.

> **What Do You Think?**
>
> What advice might you give to concerned parents regarding how they can protect their children from teenage pregnancy and delinquency? What advice might you give to the governor of your state regarding programs to prevent these problems?

- **Lifelong growth**—The quality of parent-teen relationships significantly reflects a process of lifelong growth in physical, cognitive, moral, and psychosocial complexity, competence, and maturity rooted in the earlier developmental experiences of both adolescents and their parents. Effective parenting during infancy and childhood reflects parents' growing ability to respectfully and appropriately respond to their children's unique temperament and attachment needs, and to provide parental caregiving with the appropriate amount of control, clarity of communication, demand for maturity, and nurturance for their children at each period of development. Likewise, the capacity of children to participate in a relationship with their parents grows with age and experience, continuing through adolescence into early adulthood, when many adolescents will become parents themselves, and into middle adulthood, when they may provide care for their own parents as well.

- **Changing meanings and changing vantage points**—The meaning of the parent-child relationship undergoes significant changes as children and their parents move through the developmental life cycle. During infancy and toddlerhood, the child's experience of herself is largely tied to her attachments to and dependence on her caregivers, who in turn experience strong attachment to the child and an intense sense of responsibility for all aspects of her well-being. Meanings of their relationship and vantage points of both child and parent undergo major developmental changes as the physical, cognitive, and psychosocial capabilities of the child unfold and as the parents, who are experiencing their own developmental changes of adulthood, respond to and are responded to by their developing child. As a first- or second-grader, a child may see his parent(s) as all-knowledgeable and all-powerful. He has limited capability to understand the dynamics of the parent-child relationship, and expects his parent(s) to meet all of his needs and solve all of his problems. By the time he is in fifth or sixth grade, the child's capabilities, needs, and expectations will have changed significantly, as will his understanding of the parent-child relationship and his own contributions to it. As we will see, changes in meaning and vantage points will continue to occur during adolescence and the early, middle, and late adult years.

- **Developmental diversity**—Parents the world over share the goal of caring for their children in a way that fosters their physical, cognitive, and psychosocial development and well-being. However, the ways in which parents from different societies, cultures, and ethnic groups and from different cultural, ethnic, racial, religious, gender, and SES backgrounds and circumstances within a particular society or culture actually raise their children show great diversity. This diversity is influenced by the beliefs, values, expectations, and life circumstances of parents, their children, and others around them, all of which may change over time. Relationships between teenagers and their parents today differ significantly from those of their parents' or grandparents' generation. The information revolution we are now experiencing may further influence the diversity of parent-child relationships in ways we can only imagine. And while all parent-child relationships have much in common, even within a given set of life circumstances, each follows a diverse developmental course because every individual family and the parents and children within it experience and interact with one another and the world around them in ways that are unique.

Chapter Summary

- **What conflicts do adolescents typically experience in their search for identity? What factors support or hinder successful identity development?** The process of individuation, or becoming a separate and independent person, appears to follow a predictable pattern: differentiation, practice, and experimentation; rapprochement; and consolidation of self. A key task of adolescence is successful resolution of the psychosocial crisis of identity versus role confusion. Erik Erikson calls the period of experimentation and uncertainty that precedes the achievement of a stable adult identity the *psychosocial moratorium*. Identity formation involves selectively keeping and integrating certain aspects of one's earlier childhood identity and discarding others. Successful resolution of the identity conflicts typical of adolescence depends in part on having adequate opportunities to experiment with different identities and roles. Differences in life circumstances due to social class, culture, and historical period may increase or decrease such opportunities. James Marcia has identified four identity statuses among older adolescents: identity achievement, identity diffusion, moratorium, and foreclosure. Though ethnic groups do not appear to differ in the percentages of youngsters who are in each stage, groups may differ in which issues are of most concern in resolving their identity crises.

- **What special challenges does adolescence pose for parents? How do differences in parenting style affect parent-teenager relationships?** Although not conflict free, relationships between adolescents and their parents are for the most part mutually rewarding. Teenagers appear to feel most positive about authoritative parenting styles and more negative about parents who are authoritarian. Authoritative, authoritarian, permissive-indulgent, and permissive-indifferent parenting styles are related to various aspects of adolescent development, including personality, academic achievement, social and emotional adjustment, delinquency, and substance abuse. Although adolescents and their parents may differ on some details of everyday life, they generally agree on the more important questions involving basic values. Approaching parent-adolescent conflicts in ways that are mutually respectful and that are performed with an understanding of active listening skills reduces complications brought about through these natural conflicts. Social class differences influence the educational and career expectations parents have for their adolescent children and adolescents have for themselves, and ethnicity, community context, and styles of family decision making also may influence adolescent adjustment. Finally, in recent years, an increasing number of adolescents have encountered the stresses of growing up in a family that has experienced marital conflict, divorce, remarriage, or single parenthood.

- **In what ways do adolescent friendships and peer groups play a constructive role, and how are concerns about their negative influence justified?** During adolescence, friendships become increasingly stable, intimate, and mutual. They also become the primary source of influence in a teen's life. Both small, cohesive cliques and larger, less intimate crowds appear to be important aspects of peer group participation. Teenagers participate in peer groups to please parents and teachers, gain peer acceptance and popularity, and conform. The meteoric rise in the use of social media, (cell phones and the Internet) has altered adolescents' social world and their communication skills. Parents and teens are traveling this new road together. Adolescents need a supportive hand in helping them navigate their "virtual neighborhood" in the same way parents guided them through the trials and tribulations of their real neighborhood in the past.

    Participation in work within and outside the family provides a major base for the development of competence and sense of identity and self during adolescence. Participation in household work and its consequences depend on the helper's motivations, the meaning of the work activity, and the social context in which it occurs. How work outside the family affects adolescent development depends upon how well it fits the developmental needs of the individual and his or her family.

- **What changes in sexual activities and attitudes occur among teenagers? How are they related to other aspects of adolescent development?** Adolescents' sexual needs are closely tied to their need to establish a secure identity and to achieve both intimacy and independence. Girls and boys differ in their reasons for their first experience of sexual intercourse and in their attitudes toward sexual activities. In the United States, dating is the major pathway to adolescent sexual activity. Unfortunately, sexual aggression and date rape continue to be serious problems, with long-term consequences for both the victims of teen dating violence and also for those who do the intimidation, harassment, or physical assaults. Acceptance of youngsters with nonheterosexual orientations has increased significantly in the first decades of the twenty-first century. Yet, the prejudice and discrimination that persist can make accepting their true identity more difficult for gay, lesbian, and bisexual adolescents as they transition into the emerging adulthood years of college or the world of work.

- **Why are adolescents at risk for problems such as pregnancy, depression, and delinquency?** Although a great deal is known about the causes, pregnancy and parenthood continue to be a major problem faced by a growing number of adolescents. The majority of teen pregnancies involve experiences of poverty and perceptions of limited life opportunities and choices. American teenagers do not exhibit different patterns of sexual activity than adolescents in many industrial countries, but they use contraception less consistently and effectively. Effective parent-teen communication is essential if parents are to positively influence their teens' sexual behavior, as is comprehensive sex education. Two other problems common during adolescence are depression and juvenile delinquency. Causes of depression include environmental influences, family and caregiver characteristics, and the characteristics of the developing child and adolescent. Longitudinal studies have found that aggression during early childhood is predictive of more serious forms of delinquent behavior in adolescence and adulthood.

Key Terms

clique (p. 395)
crowd (p. 396)
displaced homemaker (p. 391)
homophobia (p. 402)

identity diffusion (p. 378)
identity status (p. 379)
identity versus role confusion (p. 377)
individuation (p. 376)

juvenile delinquency (p. 410)
negative identity (p. 378)
psychosocial moratorium (p. 378)
SES (p. 386)

PART 6

Early Adulthood

Chapter 12
Physical and Cognitive Development in Early Adulthood

Chapter 13
Psychosocial Development in Early Adulthood

Source: KreativKolors/Shutterstock.

While we are children, and especially as adolescents, we often look forward to adulthood as a time when we will be "all grown up" and have fewer problems with which to cope. Certainly we expect to be in charge of our own lives; no longer will parents and teachers tell us what we can and cannot do. Therefore, as young adults, it comes as a shock to many of us that although we are fully grown in size and reproductive capacity, we do not feel as grown up as we expected. Additionally, many of us will begin adulthood with a period of emerging adulthood—a time when we are much more independent from our parents as we move away from home but also a time when we still rely on our family of origin for emotional and financial support. Going through a period of emerging adulthood is becoming much more common as more of us attend colleges and universities after high school, as we will discuss later in this section (Arnett, 2000).

Development continues throughout emerging and early adulthood, roughly from twenty to forty years of age, as physical and cognitive skills expand and psychosocial concerns change to include independent households, self-supporting work, intimate partnerships, and parenthood. These are complex roles and responsibilities that call on all we have learned thus far, as well as push us to new learning.

In Part Six, we explore the issues of emerging and early adulthood. Just as in childhood and adolescence, in adulthood physical, cognitive, and psychosocial aspects of development are intertwined. The psychosocial choice to become a parent, for example, raises concerns about fertility; involves the physical and psychological demands of pregnancy, postpartum, and childrearing; and causes changes in work, marriage, and other family relationships. Likewise, experience at earlier stages of development influence choices and problems during early adulthood, which in turn affect middle and late adulthood. Although we focus separately on the physical, cognitive, and psychosocial domains in early adulthood, keep in mind that our lives are continuous and the domains are inseparable.

Physical and Cognitive Development in Early Adulthood

CHAPTER

Source: Lightwavemedia/Shutterstock.

Chapter Outline

PHYSICAL DEVELOPMENT
Physical Functioning
Health in Early Adulthood
Stress
Sexuality and Reproduction
Adult Choices
COGNITIVE DEVELOPMENT
Postformal Thought
Development of Contextual Thinking
Adult Moral Reasoning
College
Work
Growth and Change

Focusing Questions

- Why is early adulthood typically a time of physical well-being?
- How do adopting health-promoting behaviors and avoiding health-compromising behaviors contribute to the quality and longevity of adult life?
- What is stress, and what is its relation to illness?
- In what ways are women and men similar in their sexual responses? In what ways do they differ? What treatments are available for infertility?
- In what ways does adult thought differ from adolescent thought?
- Why are gender and context important to adult moral development?
- How does attending college contribute to cognitive development?
- What is the transition to work like for emerging adults, and how are they affected by gender, race, sexual orientation, gender identity, and SES??

Lilly, age thirty-five, is the mother of two-month-old Devon. When she and Jamal married, she was thirty-three and he was twenty-nine, and both wanted a baby soon. Once they bought a little house and got settled, they stopped using contraception. Much to their dismay, it took almost a year for Lilly to get pregnant, and a couple of months later she miscarried. Her doctor advised her to wait two months before trying to conceive again. A few months later, Lilly got pregnant again. During this pregnancy, Lilly was more health conscious than usual. She exercised daily and tried to follow a nutritious diet. Her job as a bartender, however, exposed her to considerable secondhand smoke. Because of that she stopped working six weeks before the baby was due, even though she felt fine.

Now that Devon is two months old, Lilly has returned to work three days a week. She has arranged her hours so that on two of those days, Jamal cares for Devon; on the third day, she drops Devon off at her mother's. The combination of infant care, employment, and postpartum adjustment are physically and emotionally demanding. Trying to do all she would like as a mother, wife, daughter, and employee creates stress and leaves her little time or energy for herself. She might choose not to work for a while longer, but her family needs her income and she does not want to lose her job.

Early adulthood, generally the years between twenty and forty, is a period of assuming adult roles, earning a living, and taking on the responsibilities of a household. These changes usually occur sometime in the twenties, but there is considerable variability. The main tasks of early adulthood are establishing oneself in work and forming intimate connections with another person, usually leading to marriage and family. While in their twenties, Lilly and Jamal each still lived in their parents' homes; they worked, but were not fully independent. Like many of their peers, as postadolescents they entered *youth* as a stage of life before proceeding to early adulthood. Youth is a distinctive period of growth devoted to figuring out who you are and who you want to be (Miller & Winston, 1990). Young people who find jobs and start families right after high school enter the conventional adult world sooner than those who take time to explore alternative paths before settling down. Being adult, then, depends on behaving in adult ways rather than on reaching eighteen, or twenty-one, or any other "magic" age.

In this chapter, we focus on physical and cognitive aspects of early adulthood. First we look at physical functioning and issues of health, stress, sexuality, and infertility. Later we look at cognitive aspects of early adulthood, including the contributions of college and work to cognitive development. In the next chapter, we focus on psychosocial development during early adulthood.

PHYSICAL DEVELOPMENT

Physical Functioning

Young adults are at the peak of their physical abilities. The heart, lungs, and other body organs have reached maturity and are at their strongest by the mid-twenties. In fact, researchers use early adulthood as the baseline against which to measure declines in functioning during middle and late adulthood. Although signs of normal aging do appear between ages twenty and forty, any decline in physical functioning is likely to be so gradual that it goes unnoticed. In this section, we consider three aspects of physical functioning: growth in height and weight, strength, and age-related changes in body systems during early adulthood. We then look at how genetic makeup, diet, exercise, and stress affect these changes.

Growth in Height and Weight

Recent generations of adults have been getting taller and heavier, as well as maturing earlier, than previous ones. We see this in our own families when we grow taller than our aunts, uncles, parents, and grandparents. These generational changes in height, weight, and maturation constitute a secular trend. As we saw in Chapter 6's discussion of physical development in early childhood, a variety of factors have contributed to this trend, including better nutrition, healthier environmental conditions, and interbreeding of genetically dissimilar individuals, which produces hybrid vigor.

Though many people reach their full height during adolescence, virtually all reach it by their mid-twenties. Skeletal development is completed in the twenties as the process of ossification changes the cartilage to bone. Although women tend to reach their maximum height and go through the ossification process earlier than men do, considerable variability in cessation of growth occurs for both women and men (Spirduso, 1995). Both sexes

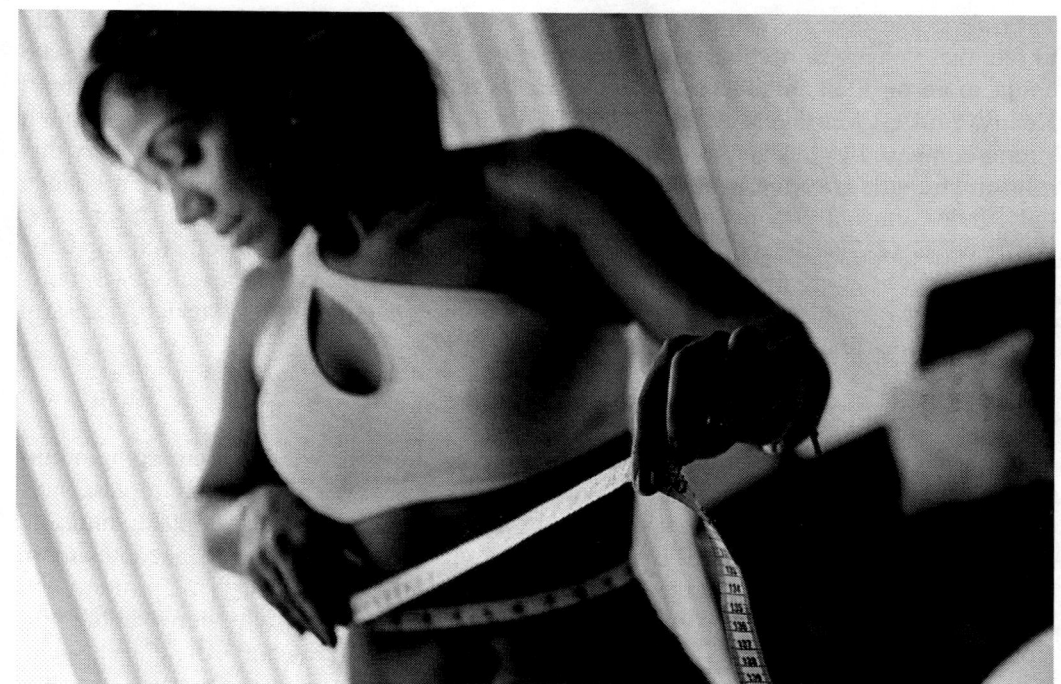

Both women and men experience weight increases during early adulthood as their bodies continue to develop and high activity levels of adolescence give way to more sedentary routines. Because contemporary American society emphasizes being slim as an essential element of female attractiveness, women are particularly attuned to weight and weight control.
Source: Diego Cervo/Shutterstock.

achieve maximum bone mass by age thirty. The combination of exercise and good nutrition while bone mass is developing produces a reservoir of bone and calcium that can alleviate the bone loss associated with aging in later stages of adulthood (Recker et al., 1992).

Both women and men experience weight increases during early adulthood as their bodies continue to fill out. Women's breasts and hips and men's shoulders and upper arms generally increase in size. For most people, the high activity level of adolescence gives way to a more sedentary routine; if they do not adjust their diets, they gain weight. As we saw in our discussion of adolescence, normal body changes during puberty result in a higher proportion of body fat in females than in males. A recent study of multiethnic young adults in their early twenties demonstrated average body fat percentage of 20 percent for men and 28 percent for women, with Asian males having the lowest body fat among males and Hispanic males having the highest and Caucasian women having the lowest body fat among females and Hispanic females having the highest (Carpenter et al., 2013). Body fat content increases and muscle content slowly decreases over the course of adulthood (Guo, Zeller, Chumlea, & Siervogel, 1999; Spirduso, 1995). Most researchers believe the larger amounts of fat in women of normal weight are related to sex-specific reproductive functions.

In addition to the physiological differences that account for the different proportions of body fat in women and men, social factors contribute to adult patterns of weight gain. Contemporary American society puts heavy emphasis on physical attractiveness, and being slim is an essential element of this, particularly for females. Models and movie stars are thinner than ever, at a time in human history when women's bodies are larger than ever before. As a result, females are very attuned to weight and weight control, long before they reach adulthood (Clay, Vignoles, & Dittmar, 2005; Grabe, Ward, & Hyde, 2008). During early adulthood, women continue to be more concerned about their weight than men are.

Strength

Strength continues to increase after full height is reached. The muscular system gains in strength throughout the twenties and peaks in the early thirties. The middle and late twenties are the prime time for doing hard physical labor or playing strenuous sports. Lilly's husband Jamal, for example, typically runs four miles after his eight-hour shift of heavy factory work and still faces the evening full of energy. After the peak comes a slow but steady decline in strength—so slow that it has little impact on most people until age forty or fifty.

The muscular system gains strength throughout the twenties and peaks in the early thirties. This makes the middle and late twenties prime time for doing strenuous activities such as rock climbing, as this young couple is doing.
Source: CandyBox Images/Shutterstock.

Chapter 12 Physical and Cognitive Development in Early Adulthood

organ reserve The extra capacity the lungs, heart, and other organs have to respond to particularly intense or prolonged effort or unusually stressful events. Primary aging affects organ reserve so that most people first notice decline under stressful conditions.

Professional dancers, athletes, and others with physically demanding jobs are likely to feel these changes more acutely. They are likely to feel older sooner than people who count more on their intellectual or social skills for their self-esteem (Ilmarinen, 2002; Kenny, Yardley, Martineau, & Jay, 2008). Individuals who are strong are likely to remain strong compared to their cohort, but younger adults will have the edge in activities that rely on strength after the peak in the thirties. Most young adults will notice a change only under unusual circumstances, such as chopping wood on a camping trip or moving heavy boxes, because under ordinary circumstances we do not use our full capacity. The declines of aging primarily affect our **organ reserve**, the extra capacity each body organ has for responding to particularly intense or prolonged effort or unusually stressful events, such as running for a bus (Fries & Crapo, 1981).

Brain Development

Though our bodies develop an adult appearance by the time we reach emerging adulthood, our brains our still changing in some fascinating ways. Throughout adolescence, our prefrontal cortex, which is responsible for planning ahead, impulse control, intuition, and evaluating risk and reward, is pruned based on our experiences and becomes more myelinated (Bechara, 2005; Casey et al., 2005; Galvan et al., 2006). This pruning and myelination allow for activity within the prefrontal cortex and activity between the prefrontal cortex and other areas of the brain to occur more quickly and efficiently (Spear, 2010). This process of development in the prefrontal cortex is not complete until we enter our mid-twenties (Casey et al., 2005; Paus, 2009; Taber-Thomas & Perez-Edgar, 2016). As we move through emerging adulthood and young adulthood, this process of brain maturation is impacting our experiences: when invited to go to a party the night before an exam, the evaluation of risk and reward occurs more quickly for a twenty-eight-year-old compared to a nineteen-year-old. Prefrontal cortex development is also being impacted by our experiences: drug and alcohol use peak during emerging adulthood, which may forever change the functioning of this area (Bechara, 2005; Taber-Thomas, & Perez-Edgar, 2016). We will discuss drug and alcohol use during emerging and young adulthood later in this chapter.

Age-Related Changes

Appearance changes relatively little during early adulthood, although by the late twenties some people may get a few creases in the face or a few gray hairs, the first visible signs of aging. These signs of aging reflect changes in skin elasticity and a reduction in the number of pigment-producing cells (Warren et al., 1991).

Age-related changes occur in all body systems: cardiovascular, respiratory, nervous, and sensory. In our twenties our body systems are at peak performance, after which gradual decline begins, proceeding at different rates for different systems.

Cardiovascular Changes

The cardiovascular system undergoes a steady decline in functioning throughout the adult years. The function of this system is to pump blood through the body in an efficient and continuous manner to provide the cells with nutrients and oxygen and rid them of waste products, both when the body is at rest and during exertion. In healthy individuals free of cardiac disease, the major age-related cardiovascular change is a gradual decrease in maximum heart rate; resting and submaximal heart rate are relatively unchanged (Spirduso, 1995). The maximum rate at which the heart can beat during heavy exertion decreases about five to ten beats each decade following peak capacity in the twenties (Shephard, 1987).

Respiratory Changes

The respiratory system enriches the blood with oxygen and rids it of carbon dioxide by exchanging air from outside the body with air inside. Because pollutants are so pervasive, it is hard for researchers to distinguish between normal aging of the lungs and respiratory system and aging due to damage caused by environmental factors such as smoking and air pollution. Sam, who smokes a pack of cigarettes a day, often finds himself out of breath while playing basketball with his friends, even though he is in his twenties and they are in their thirties. Gradual decreases in respiratory efficiency start at about age twenty-five and noticeable decreases by age forty.

Sensory System Changes

Peak central nervous system functioning characterizes early adulthood. Although age-related changes in the central nervous system begin during this period, they are very gradual. As Figure 12.1 shows, nerve conduction speed, the time it takes to transmit impulses, decreases less during early adulthood than other physiological functions do, although most decreases are small.

The senses vary in the degree of age-related changes during early adulthood. Visual acuity increases until the twenties or thirties and remains relatively constant to age forty or fifty (Pitts, 1982). From about age thirty, the eyes become progressively more farsighted as the lenses thicken and flatten, but most people usually do not notice changes in vision until middle adulthood, when they may need reading glasses for the first time (Whitbourne, 1985). Hearing peaks at age twenty, followed by a gradual loss, usually too small to be noticed by young adults. Taste and smell sensitivity remain constant during early adulthood, whereas sensitivity to touch continues to increase until age forty-five.

What do these physiological changes mean for most young adults? Typically, not much. This is the period of life when physical functioning is most stable; growth is virtually complete, and decline is only beginning and is largely unseen. While in the early adult years, people feel young and strong; the slight physical changes usually do not concern them. As we will see next, however, these feelings of strength may make young adults less sensitive to their health habits than they should be.

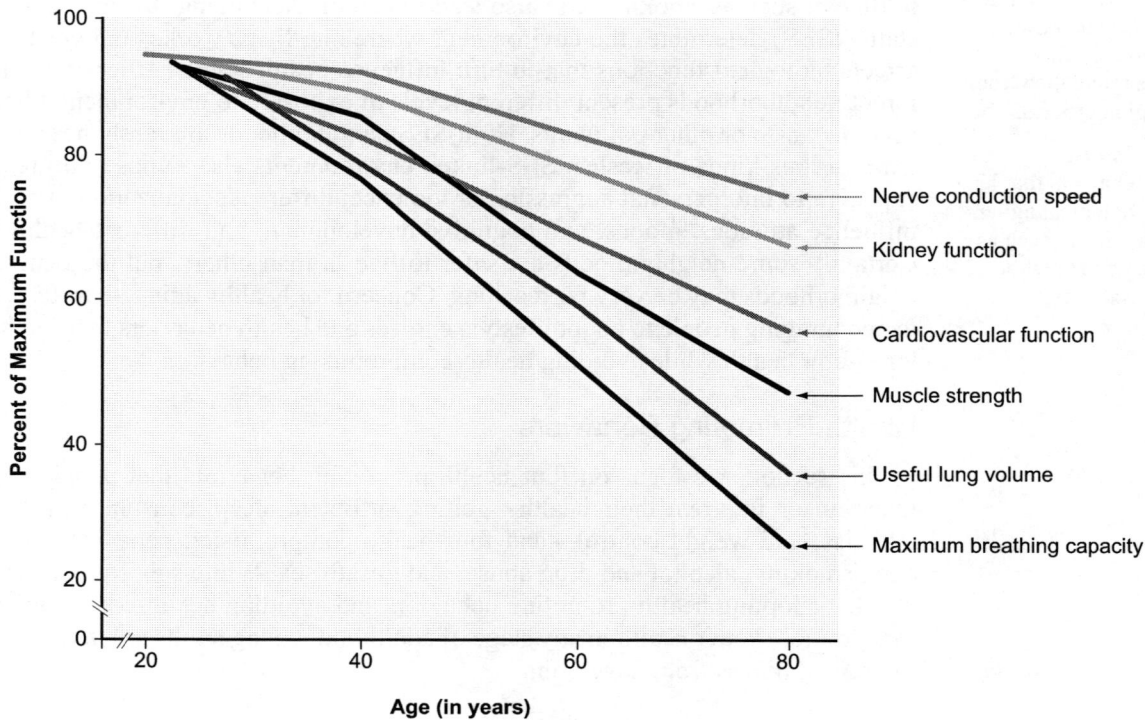

FIGURE 12.1 Average Declines in Major Biological Systems

Age-related changes occur in all bodily systems. The rate of decline differs for each system, with nerve conduction speed showing the slowest decline and maximum breathing capacity the fastest decline. Decline in all systems is minimal during early adulthood.
Source: Rybash et al. (1995).

Chapter 12 Physical and Cognitive Development in Early Adulthood

> **What Do You Think?**
>
> Are concerns about weight common among your friends? Are they more frequent among your female friends than your male friends? How can you explain any differences?

Health in Early Adulthood

Young adults are generally healthy. Even if disease is present, the person is likely to feel fine because the disease is likely to be in the early stages, unsymptomatic and undiagnosed. For example, adolescents and young adults have sex with more different partners than do people in any other age group, do not reliably use condoms, and are likely to have sex while drinking, lowing their inhibitions, which puts them at higher risk for contracting the human immunodeficiency virus (HIV) (Centers for Disease Control and Prevention, 2016b). The period between contracting the virus and developing full-blown AIDS may be as long as eight or nine years, however, so infected young adults often feel fine. In fact, the Centers for Disease Control and Prevention (CDC) estimate that 44 percent of young adults between the ages of eighteen and twenty-four have HIV and do not know it (CDC, 2016b). Similarly, young adults with poor health habits such as smoking or tanning are not yet likely to suffer from the negative effects, although the damage is already going on in their bodies. A body system, such as the respiratory system in the case of a smoker, need not be working at its best for the person to still feel fine. Because of this, most young adults feel healthy and vigorous, regardless of genetic makeup, environmental factors, socioeconomic factors, and health behaviors.

Many of the losses in functioning people suffer as they age may result not from the normal aging process but from **pathological aging** caused by illness, abnormality, genetic factors, or exposure to unhealthy environments. **Health-compromising behaviors** that lead to illness, such as smoking, can also lead to pathological aging. Because socioeconomic status (SES) determines the environment where one lives, works, and goes to school, it affects biological functions that in turn influence health status (Adler et al., 1994). Different neighborhoods present different levels of exposure to environmental hazards such as toxic waste or other pollutants. High-SES neighborhoods are rarely near factories that emit various kinds of wastes. SES-linked environments also impose different levels of exposure to interpersonal aggression or violence; different socialization experiences that influence attitudes, moods, and cognitive development; and different health behaviors. Certainly some neighborhoods are safer to live in than others, but the benefits of such neighborhoods may be very far reaching. Concern for healthy aging, therefore, has turned to encouraging people to adopt lifestyle choices and health behaviors that set the stage for long-term health while avoiding health-compromising behaviors.

pathological aging Losses in functioning people suffer as they age that result from illness, abnormality, genetic factors, or exposure to unhealthy environments rather than from the normal aging process.

health-compromising behaviors Behaviors that lead to illness, pathological aging, and premature death, such as smoking, drug and alcohol abuse, and unsafe sex.

Health-Promoting Behaviors

In this section, we focus on four health-promoting behaviors that people engage in to maintain or improve their health—getting sufficient sleep, consuming a healthy diet, exercise, and weight control—and four health-compromising behaviors—eating disorders, smoking, alcohol and drug abuse, and unsafe sex. While subsequent chapters point out that adopting health-promoting behaviors and avoiding health-compromising behaviors promote better health in any stage of adulthood, young adults are in the best situation to prevent illness from developing.

Sleep

Most young adults need between seven and nine hours of sleep each night to be fully rested and functional the next day (National Sleep Foundation, 2015). However, between 21 and 37 percent of young adults and college students report that they get fewer than seven hours of sleep per night (Centers for Disease Control and Prevention, 2015c; Steptoe, Peacey, &

Wardle, 2006). Our culture suggests that if we want to be successful in work or school while having a viable family and social life, something must be sacrificed, and that something is usually sleep. We believe we can get by on less sleep or counteract sleepiness with caffeine or by sleeping longer on the weekends. However, the function sleep plays in so many critical operations such as our immune system, memory consolidation, metabolic system, and cardiovascular system means that there is no replacement for sleep, and the *function* of sleep lost today cannot be made up for tomorrow even if the minutes can (Besedovsky, Lange, & Born, 2012; Gottlieb et al., 2006; Schmid et al., 2008; Stickgold, 2005).

Insufficient sleep or poor quality sleep has been linked to poorer physical health overall, including diabetes, cancer, hypertension, and diabetes (Centers for Disease Control and Prevention, 2015c; Gottlieb et al., 2006; Steptoe et al., 2006), increased susceptibility to the common cold (Cohen et al., 2009), worse mental health (Orzech, Salafsky, & Hamilton, 2011), and worse academic performance (Gilbert & Weaver, 2010; Orzech et al, 2011). Later, we discuss the importance of diet and exercise, which are also impacted by sleep. People who do not get enough sleep are more likely to overeat, make poorer choices about what they eat, and disrupt metabolism in a way that makes them more hungry than someone who is well rested (Brondel et al., 2010; Hogenkamp et al., 2013; Schmid et al., 2008). Table 12.1 outlines several tips to make sure you are getting sufficient good quality sleep.

Diet

What we eat also affects our health. Diet plays a major role in the development of cardiovascular disease and cancer. About 35 to 40 percent of cancers are believed to be diet related (Alexander & LaRosa, 1994; Divisi et al., 2006); for instance, alcohol, high saturated fat, high red meat, low fiber, low antioxidant intake is associated with the development of colon, rectal, gastric, and breast cancers (Conner, 2016; Gonzalez & Riboli, 2010). In addition, high calorie intake is associated with obesity, high salt intake with hypertension and cardiovascular disease, and high fat and cholesterol intake with atherosclerosis (hardening and narrowing of the larger arteries due to the formation of plaques that reduce the flow of blood) and coronary heart disease (Taylor, 1998). All of these negative health effects are under the control of the person making food choices.

A healthy diet is low in cholesterol, fats, calories, red meats, sugar, and additives and high in fiber, fruits, and vegetables. Fats should contribute fewer than 30 percent of one's daily calorie intake, protein no more than 12 percent, complex carbohydrates about 60 per-

TABLE 12.1 Tips for Better Sleep

- Go to bed and wake up at the same time every day—even on the weekends.
- Have a relaxing routine before bed, preferably with low light.
- Do not use your cell phone, tablet, or other light-emitting devices in bed or in the time leading up to your bedtime.
- Avoid naps after about 3 p.m.
- Have a relaxing sleep area that is dark, quiet, and cool with a comfortable and supportive mattress and pillows. Use of ear plugs, white noise machines, black out curtains, and eye masks are helpful if you do not have control over your sleeping area.
- Use your bed only for sleep and sex.
- Avoid alcohol, caffeine, cigarettes, and heavy meals in the evening.
- If you are having trouble falling asleep, get out of bed and do something relaxing in low light until you feel tired.

Source: National Sleep Foundation, n.d.

The USDA recommends that we eat a diet high in fruits, vegetables, whole grains, and lean proteins. This meal—consisting of plenty of colorful fruits and vegetables, which make up half the meal; quinoa, a whole grain; and tofu, a lean protein—does a good job of following the USDA guidelines for a healthy diet.
Source: Brent Hofacker/ Shutterstock.

cent, and refined sugar around 10 percent or less (Russell, 1992). The U.S. Department of Agriculture (USDA) recommends portion control and that fruits, vegetables, and grains make up the bulk of what we eat, while limiting simple carbohydrates, added sugars, and saturated fats. The National Cancer Institute recommends five servings (each roughly one-half cup) of fruits and vegetables a day as a cancer prevention measure. Unfortunately, this is not the typical American diet. Many adults learned poor eating habits when they were children and adolescents and need to modify their diets to make them healthy. Additionally, our environments impact diet. One study found that people with low incomes who live near more fast-food restaurants are more likely to eat fast food on a regular basis, though living near a grocery store was not related to higher consumption of fruits and vegetables (Boone-Heinonen et al., 2011). Though this may seem counterintuitive, other studies have shown that it is not just the availability of healthier options, but also the cost thereof—it is more expensive to eat fruits, vegetables, whole grains, and lean meat than less healthy options (Jetter & Cassady, 2006). Because of our environments and learned behaviors, lifelong dietary change is hard to induce, even when an individual is at high risk for coronary heart disease (Taylor, 1998). Attitudes have an important effect on diet; people who feel able to change, have a high level of health consciousness, have an interest in exploring new foods, and are highly aware of the link between eating habits and illness are better able to establish good dietary habits (Hollis et al., 1986). As we will see next, people can amplify the positive effects of a good diet by exercising.

Exercise

Physical activity is associated with maintaining physical health (Spirduso, 1995; Telama et al., 2005; Vita et al., 1998), cognitive health (Cotman, Berchtold, & Christie, 2007), and mental health (Bartholomew, Morrison, & Ciccolo, 2005; Stathopoulou et al., 2006). The positive effects of regular aerobic exercise are well documented and far reaching. Aerobic exercise such as jogging, bicycling, and swimming is high-intensity, long-duration, and high-endurance activity. It is recommended that a healthy individual exercise at 70 to 85 percent of maximum heart rate nonstop for at least twenty to thirty minutes three times a week or at a moderate level for at least thirty minutes five or more times per week (Garber et al., 2011). Moderate exercise will increase fitness and decrease the risk of early death for less fit individuals (Alexander & LaRosa, 1994).

The primary benefit of exercise is to the cardiovascular system. Regular aerobic exercise counteracts the age-related decreases in cardiovascular functioning we discussed earlier. People who exercise maintain higher levels of cardiac functioning and

Though the primary benefit of regular aerobic exercise is to the cardiovascular system, its positive impact on health and well-being are far reaching. This couple incorporates jogging into their routine by taking their baby along.
Source: Halfpoint/Shutterstock.

blood flow than those who do not. The heart can more efficiently supply blood to the other tissues of the body, and the respiratory, muscular, and nervous systems all benefit as well. The benefits do not stop there, however; exercise improves endurance, helps to optimize body weight, builds or maintains muscle tone and strength, and increases flexibility. It reduces or controls hypertension and improves cholesterol levels. Exercise also improves mood and self-esteem and reduces stress (Bartholomew et al., 2005; Cotman et al., 2007; Plante & Rodin, 1990; Stathopoulou et al., 2006). People who exercise tend to engage in fewer health-compromising behaviors, including smoking, alcohol consumption, and poor diet (Leon, 1983; Leon & Fox, 1981). Weight gain is one of the key age-related changes that people try to counteract with exercise.

Weight Control

Obesity, the excessive accumulation of energy in the form of body fat, is a major health problem. Normal body weight is determined by a person's body mass index (BMI), which is based on the person's height-to-weight ratio. Table 12.2 presents the National Heart, Lung, and Blood Institute (1998) BMI chart. The federal guidelines consider a person with a BMI of 25 to 29.9 as overweight and a person with a BMI of 30 or more as obese. The lines between normal weight and overweight, and between overweight and obese, are not clear-cut, however. BMI does not account for bone structure, body fat versus muscle, cultural norms, or level of fitness, age, or sex, which means that it can and does misclassify people (Rothman, 2008). Asians, for example, generally are smaller and thinner, and therefore may be overweight at a lower BMI. On the other hand, very muscular people may be categorized as overweight by the guidelines, yet be fit because of their high muscle-to-fat ratio. Obesity increases the risk for high blood pressure, adult-onset diabetes, coronary heart disease, stroke, gallbladder disease, osteoarthritis, respiratory problems, and certain cancers (National Heart, Lung, and Blood Institute, 1998). Because of its connection with these chronic diseases, obesity is associated with early *mortality* (death). As we saw in Chapter 10's discussion of physical development in adolescence, it is also associated with a poor self-image.

According to the 2016 Centers for Disease Control and Prevention report, nearly 71 percent of the U.S. population is overweight or obese, and almost 38 percent of the

TABLE 12.2 Body Mass Index Chart

Body Mass Index

Height (inches)	19	20	21	22	23	24	25	26	27	28	29	30	31	32	33	34	35	36	37	38	39	40
	Body Weight (pounds)																					
58	91	96	100	105	110	115	119	124	129	134	138	143	148	153	158	162	167	172	177	181	186	191
59	94	99	104	109	114	119	124	128	133	138	143	148	153	158	163	168	173	178	183	188	193	198
60	97	102	107	112	118	123	128	133	138	143	148	153	158	163	168	174	179	184	189	194	199	204
61	100	106	111	116	122	127	132	137	143	148	153	158	164	169	174	180	185	190	195	201	206	211
62	104	109	115	120	126	131	136	142	147	153	158	164	169	175	180	186	191	196	202	207	213	218
63	107	113	118	124	130	135	141	146	152	158	163	169	175	180	186	191	197	203	208	214	220	225
64	110	116	122	128	134	140	145	151	157	163	169	174	180	186	192	197	204	209	215	221	227	232
65	114	120	126	132	138	144	150	156	162	168	174	180	186	192	198	204	210	216	222	228	234	240
66	118	124	130	136	142	148	155	161	167	173	179	186	192	198	204	210	216	223	229	235	241	247
67	121	127	134	140	146	153	159	166	172	178	185	191	198	204	211	217	223	230	236	242	249	255
68	125	131	138	144	151	158	164	171	177	184	190	197	203	210	216	223	230	236	243	249	256	262
69	128	135	142	149	155	162	169	176	182	189	196	203	209	216	223	230	236	243	250	257	263	270
70	132	139	146	153	160	167	174	181	188	195	202	209	216	222	229	236	243	250	257	264	271	278
71	136	143	150	157	165	172	179	186	193	200	208	215	222	229	236	243	250	257	265	272	279	286
72	140	147	154	162	169	177	184	191	199	206	213	221	228	235	242	250	258	265	272	279	287	294
73	144	151	159	166	174	182	189	197	204	212	219	227	235	242	250	257	265	272	280	288	295	302
74	148	155	163	171	179	186	194	202	210	218	225	233	241	249	256	264	272	280	287	295	303	311
75	152	160	168	176	184	192	200	208	216	224	232	240	248	256	264	272	279	287	295	303	311	319
76	156	164	172	180	189	197	205	213	221	230	238	246	254	263	271	279	287	295	304	312	320	328

To use this chart, first find your height in the left-hand column; then move your eye along that row until you find your weight. Next move your eye up that column from your weight to the top row, where you will find your BMI. Normal range for BMI is between 25 and 29.

Source: National Lung and Heart Institute (1998).

---

population is obese (2016e). Despite changes toward healthier diets, the percentage of overweight adults has been growing since 1960, particularly among economically disadvantaged groups.

Several factors are known to increase the risk of obesity. First, overweight parents are more likely to have overweight children. This is because both the tendency toward obesity is partially genetic and eating patterns are learned, encouraged, and innate. Children who became obese were found to have had distinctively vigorous feeding styles very early in life (Agras et al., 1987). When feeding, they sucked more rapidly, more intensely, and longer and took shorter breaks between sucking than other infants did, meaning they consumed more calories and gained more weight. Overweight parents are likely to have overweight children, and obese mothers have a tendency to be more concerned about their infants becoming overweight or obese but exert less control over feedings (Burdette, Whitaker, Hall, & Daniels, 2006). Childhood patterns of eating and exercise contribute to obesity in childhood and adulthood. Children who overeat, those with low daytime activity, and those who spend more than two hours per day watching television are more likely to become obese (Hills, King, & Armstrong, 2007; Mendoza, Zimmerman, & Christakis, 2007; Rey-Lopez, Vincente-Rodríguez, Biosca, & Moreno, 2008). About 80 percent of people who were overweight as children are overweight as adults (Taylor, 1998). SES is another significant factor in the incidence of obesity. In lower income countries, higher SES is related to higher rates of obesity (Dinsa, Goryakin, Fumagalli, & Suhrcke, 2012). However, in the United States, the story is more complex. Since the 1970s, there was a pattern of obesity being related to low SES—a relation that has been weakening since the turn of the century, primarily due to the skyrocketing rates of overweight and obesity in the United States during that time (Wang & Zhang, 2006). African American children of all SES categories were at high risk for being overweight with high SES African American girls being at particular risk for being overweight (Wang & Zhang, 2006). High SES Caucasian American girls were less likely than their low SES counterparts to be overweight, with no correlation being found for Caucasian American boys or for any Hispanic children (Wang & Zhang, 2006). Again, while these results might seem promising, they are most likely due to the fact that children of all SES groups and all ethnic groups have moved into the overweight and obese categories over time, and these children are likely to grow into overweight and obese adults.

The best strategies for weight loss include an increase in exercise and a switch to a healthy diet such as the one discussed earlier. Exercise burns calories by increasing one's basal metabolic rate, which controls the automatic activities of the body, such as breathing and heartbeat, and regulates body temperature. Long-term changes like these, rather than fasting, following a fad diet, or taking diet pills, will promote gradual weight loss without leaving the dieter hungry. It is also important to be realistic about one's body type and not strive to be unrealistically thin.

Health-Compromising Behaviors

Many young adults who incorporate a good diet, exercise, and weight control into their daily lives still engage in behaviors that put them at increased health risk. Eating disorders, smoking, alcohol and drug abuse, and unsafe sex—all prevalent among adolescents, as we saw in Chapter 10—persist among some young adults as lingering adolescent egocentrism enables them to maintain the personal fable of invincibility.

Eating Disorders

Though eating disorders typically begin between ages fourteen and twenty (as you may remember from Chapter 10), they frequently continue into early adulthood. Individuals at highest risk are young women between ages eighteen and twenty-five. Because contemporary young women typically diet, it is important that diagnoses of eating disorders be based on clinically significant symptoms and not simply on dieting or weight concern. Symptoms of eating disorders include restrictive dieting and harmful weight control behaviors, such as induced vomiting, excessive exercise, and use of laxatives, as well as overeating.

Recent research indicates that eating disturbance occurs across a wide spectrum of the population; no race, ethnic, or SES group is more at risk than any other. Individuals at most risk for eating disorders are athletes, obese individuals, individuals who were once overweight, and adults who were sexually abused as children (Striegel-Moore, 1997). Studies comparing white and African American women show that patterns of eating problems differ for various American subcultures (Wilfley et al., 1996). Whereas anorexia is most frequent among highly educated, affluent white women, binge eating is more common among African American and Latina women (Alegria et al., 2007; Striegel-Moore & Bulik, 2007; Striegel-Moore & Smolak, 1996).

Cognitive behavioral treatment and interpersonal therapy, sometimes in conjunction with antidepressants, is an effective treatment for bulimia nervosa and binge-eating disorders (Williams, Goodie, & Motsinger, 2008). However, anorexia nervosa is often difficult to treat due to patients refusing treatment and high relapse rates (Guarda, 2008; Williams et al., 2008). Cognitive behavioral treatment can be effective to treat anorexia nervosa, as can therapy focused on changing ideas of acceptability of behaviors, self-esteem, and working on interpersonal relationships (Zipfel et al., 2014). Use of family therapy seems to be helpful in avoiding relapse (Courturier, Kimber, &Szatmari, 2013). Nevertheless, some of the medical complications of eating disorders may be irreversible even with successful treatment.

Smoking and Tobacco Use

Between 2011 and 2015, the number of high school students who reported smoking in the last thirty days decreased from nearly 16 percent to about 9 percent, and in 2014, nearly 17 percent of young adults reported that they were smokers (Centers for Disease Control and Prevention, 2016d, 2016g). Though these statistics seem quite promising, it is important to note that many youths are utilizing alternatives like smokeless tobacco (6 percent of high school students) and electronic cigarettes, or e-cigarettes (16 percent of high school students) (Centers for Disease Control and Prevention, 2016g). The use of e-cigarettes is particularly concerning because many people perceive them as being relatively harmless. Though rates of carcinogens and toxins in e-cigarettes are less than in traditional cigarettes, they are still more dangerous than not smoking at all (Goniewicz et al., 2014).

It is also important to note that there are marked differences in who smokes: people living at or near the poverty line and with less education are more likely to smoke than those who are middle- or high-SES (Centers for Disease Control and Prevention, 2016d). There are also high rates of smoking among Native Americans (29.2 percent) and multiracial individuals (27.9 percent) compared to European Americans (18.2 percent) and African Americans (17.5 percent). Hispanic Americans (11.2 percent) and Asian Americans (9.5 percent) reported the lowest rates of smoking (Centers for Disease Control and Prevention, 2016d).

Jacqueline Royce and her associates (1993) analyzed racial/ethnic differences in smoking patterns and attitudes. They interviewed about 1,200 smokers and 1,200 nonsmokers, 22.5 percent of whom were African Americans. African Americans started smoking significantly later than white respondents at all levels of education. African Americans of both genders smoked fewer cigarettes than whites on average, yet some indicators suggested they were more nicotine dependent. First, they more often smoked menthol cigarettes (which are higher in tars and nicotine). Second, they were more likely to be "wake-up" smokers (which is a measure of nicotine dependence). Third, they had more difficulty quitting. Royce and her colleagues also found that significantly more African Americans had made at least one serious attempt to quit in the preceding year; of the total sample interviewed, African American women made up the highest proportion of those who had tried to quit and white men the lowest. More than 65 percent of the sample wanted to quit smoking; more African American than white smokers wanted to quit "a lot." Royce and her associates point out the many life factors, such as stress and targeted advertising campaigns by tobacco companies, that may contribute to the difficulty African Americans have in quitting even with their higher motivation to quit.

Smoking is responsible for more preventable illnesses and deaths than any other single health-compromising behavior. If the current rates of smoking among adolescents and young adults continue, 5.6 million of these individuals will die early due to an illness caused by their smoking (Centers for Disease Control and Prevention, 2016g). Smoking is associated with cancer of the lung, larynx, oral cavity, and esophagus; it is also a major risk factor for other cancers throughout the body. Smoking is also related to cardiovascular *morbidity* (illness) and mortality. Smoking increases the risk of emphysema, chronic bronchitis, peptic ulcers, cirrhosis of the liver, and respiratory disorders and aggravates the symptoms of allergies, diabetes, and hypertension. In women, smoking increases the risk of osteoporosis and lowers the age of menopause (Taylor, 1998).

Smoking does not only pose health risks to smokers. *Passive smoking,* or the breathing in of secondhand smoke from other people's cigarettes, increases the health risks to nonsmokers who are subjected to air contaminated by smokers. Children and spouses of smokers are at particular risk for respiratory infections, asthma, cancer, and heart disease (Greenberg et al., 1984; Hirayama, 1981; Öberg et al., 2011). Even dogs owned by smokers had a 50 percent greater risk for lung and nasal cancer than dogs owned by nonsmokers (Reif, 1992; Reif, Bruns, & Lower, 1998).

Although the negative health consequences of smoking are clear, smoking-related illnesses take years to develop, which enables young, healthy people to deny or ignore the threat to their health. As we saw in Chapter 10, adolescents are more likely to smoke if their parents, older siblings, best friends, or peers smoke. People who suffer from multiple addictions report that smoking is harder to stop than taking drugs or drinking alcohol (Kozlowski et al., 1989). Media campaigns have been effective in providing knowledge about the health risks caused by smoking, establishing an antismoking attitude in the general public, encouraging adults to remain nonsmokers, and encouraging smokers to quit. Media campaigns used in conjunction with laws increasing the price of tobacco and limiting where people can smoke are effective in getting people to utilize smoking cessation programs (Centers for Disease Control, 2011c). Increasing the price of tobacco products by increasing the tax on these products has been particularly effective in reducing the number of adolescents and young adults who start smoking (van Hasselt et al., 2015). Additionally, laws and rules restricting smoking in restaurants, in public buildings, on college campuses, and within a certain perimeter of buildings like hospitals reduces opportunity and amount people can smoke; they also protect all of us from passive smoke.

Alcohol and Drug Abuse

Adolescents and young adults between ages twelve and twenty-five are particularly vulnerable to chemical dependency (Dupont, 1988). In Chapter 10 we focus on the destructive effects of drugs; here we concentrate on the effects of heavy drinking.

Moderate alcohol consumption, defined as up to two drinks a day for men and one drink a day for women, can affect health in many ways. Alcohol consumption increases the risk of some cancers and cirrhosis of the liver, and the calories in alcoholic beverages can contribute to obesity. Yet light to moderate alcohol consumption may improve longevity by

Heavy drinking and smoking are promoted by certain social settings young adults frequent, such as this house party. The illnesses related to these health-compromising behaviors take years to develop, enabling young and healthy people to deny or ignore the threat to their health.

Source: oneinchpunch/ Shutterstock.

decreasing coronary heart disease, which is the leading cause of death for both women and men (Kushi et al., 1995; Roerecke & Rehm, 2012). Alcohol abuse, however, sharply reduces longevity (Criqui & Ringel, 1994). People with higher SES consume alcohol more frequently, but in moderate amounts, which promotes better health (Adler et al., 1994). Alcohol abuse, not alcohol use, is a health-compromising behavior.

Even one or two drinks a day may be too much for many people, however. As discussed in Chapter 3 on genetics, prenatal development, and birth, women who are trying to get pregnant, are pregnant, or are breast feeding should not consume any alcohol because there are no "safe" levels for the fetus and the infant. Heavier drinking greatly increases the risk of fetal alcohol syndrome in the infant. Even for nonpregnant women, the physiological costs of heavy drinking (more than two drinks a day) may be more severe than for men. Research indicates that women get more intoxicated than men do from the same amount of alcohol (Frezza et al, 1990). This is because they have more fatty tissue, which retains alcohol, and less body water, which dilutes it, than men do and a less active stomach enzyme to break down the alcohol before it reaches the bloodstream.

Alcohol abuse can damage nearly every organ and function of the body. It is responsible for or associated with more than one hundred thousand deaths per year. Alcohol-related accidents are the leading cause of death in young adult men (McGinnis et al., 1992). For young adults ages twenty-five to thirty-four, unintentional injury is the leading cause of death followed by suicide, homicide, cancer, and heart disease, in that order (Centers for Disease Control and Prevention, 2010). Alcohol abuse increases risks for liver, larynx, esophagus, stomach, colon, breast, and skin cancers and for cirrhosis of the liver, and is also associated with hypertension, or high blood pressure. Drinking also causes temporary and permanent cognitive impairments. A drunk driver, for example, may have blurred vision, poor perception of speed, and slowed reaction times.

Problem drinking and alcoholism are two behavior patterns that can result from heavy drinking. Alcoholism is characterized by the inability to control one's drinking, a high tolerance for alcohol, and withdrawal symptoms when drinking is stopped. Problem drinking does not produce those symptoms, but like alcoholism it creates social and medical problems. Problem drinkers and alcoholics are likely to consume large amounts of alcohol at times, often resulting in a loss of memory and violent outbursts. They often have family- and job-related problems. Sometimes, however, alcoholism and problem drinking are hard to recognize because many afflicted individuals drink privately and quietly.

Several factors have been found to increase the risk of problem drinking. Drinking and heavy drinking are more common among younger adults than older adults (National Institute on Alcohol Abuse and Alcoholism, 1997; Barnes et al., 1992). About 60 percent of college students are drinkers, about 38 percent are binge drinkers (consumption of five drinks in a row for a man and four drinks in a row for a woman), and about 12 percent are heavy drinkers (eight drinks or more per week for a woman and fifteen drinks or more per week for a man (National Institute on Alcohol Abuse and Alcoholism, 2016). Young adult males have the highest rate of alcohol misuse of any age group (Barnes et al., 1992; National Institute on Alcohol Abuse and Alcoholism, 2006). Among those aged eighteen to twenty-two, college students are more likely to drink, drink more heavily, and are more likely to binge drink than their same-aged peers not attending college (National Institute on Alcohol Abuse and Alcoholism, 2016). Grace Barnes and her colleagues (1992) found that drinking at an early age and growing up with a father who was a heavy drinker were strong predictors of both later heavier drinking and alcohol-related problems, especially for males. They also found that living in a college dorm contributed to alcohol misuse.

Unsafe Sex

In addition to posing direct health risks, drug and alcohol use facilitates the health-compromising behavior of unplanned and often unsafe sex as well as increases the risk that one will sexually assault or be sexually assaulted by someone else (National Institute on Alcohol Abuse and Alcoholism, 2016). People who ordinarily would not engage in risky sexual activities may be less inhibited about doing so when under the influence of these substances (Desiderato & Crawford, 1995; Leigh & Stall, 1993; Townshend et al., 2014).

> **WORKING WITH** Daniel Longram, Case Manager

Helping Families Cope with AIDS

Daniel Longram is a case manager at AIDS Project New Haven (APNH), a nonprofit community organization that works to improve the quality of life of area residents who are affected by HIV-associated illnesses.

Michele: *What is APNH?*

Daniel: APNH was started by six gay men in their living room. It's modeled after a program in New York City called Gay Men's Health Crisis. As the spread of AIDS has changed, APNH has evolved to include a multicultural approach in helping HIV+ people and their families.

Michele: *What do you do?*

Daniel: I'm a full-time case manager. Overall I would describe myself as a broker of services, but I do all sorts of jobs. I run errands, I coordinate volunteer services, I console overwhelmed caregivers. My caseload includes Hispanic, African American, and heterosexual people as well as gay men. To work in this field, you need to be bilingual.

Michele: *So do you mainly counsel individuals?*

Daniel: No, most of my caseload is made up of families. Sometimes the husband is HIV+, and I provide him with physical support while the wife gets emotional support from support groups at APNH. Other times the husband, wife, and/or some of the children are HIV+ and the whole family needs a combination of physical and emotional support through APNH.

Michele: *What aspects of your job do you find difficult?*

Daniel: In this line of work, it's important to be nonjudgmental and to go with the flow, and that can be tough. I had one case where my client was an Hispanic woman who was HIV+. She was a mother of four children and had her mother living with her. Over a nine-month period I helped her make hospital visits, provided groceries, and did the majority of her communicating for her because she couldn't speak. Her mother was giving her traditional Puerto Rican folk medicines during that time, which worried me. I felt uneasy about those herbal remedies. But I'm glad I kept my mind open, because nine months after I started visiting her, she started to speak.

Michele: *What other services does APNH provide?*

Daniel: We have the Caring Cuisine program, community outreach, support groups, a hot line, and the buddy program. The Caring Cuisine program provides isolated homebound clients with daily meals that meet their specific nutritional needs. The buddy system is also set up to reach isolated clients who need a supportive friendship. The support groups and the hot line are targeted to reach not only the AIDS community but also the general public that are affected by AIDS. The community outreach program is targeted to educate the general public, both young and old. This is done in a variety of ways, ranging from high school and college talks to discussing risky behavior with people who are prostitutes.

What Do You Think?

1. How are changes in the populations at risk for AIDS reflected in Daniel's caseload and in the concerns of APNH?
2. The discussion of STDs in the chapter emphasizes prevention. How does Daniel's description of the work of APNH reflect a concern for this issue?

Sex without a barrier to protect against potentially infected blood, semen, or vaginal fluids constitutes unsafe sex and creates risk for STIs and HIV infection. As we saw in Chapter 10, adolescents and young adults are at greater risk than other age groups because they have more sexual partners. As of 2010, HIV/AIDS was the sixth leading cause of death in the United States among people ages twenty-five to thirty-four (Centers for Disease Control and Prevention, 2010). New HIV/AIDS cases reported to the Centers for Disease Control and Prevention declined 19 percent from 2005 to 2014, perhaps as a result of public health campaigns promoting safe sex. For sexually active people condoms provide the best protection from infection, although vaginal spermicides also reduce the risk of catching STIs. The best way to deal with STIs is to avoid getting them in the first place. Many women and some men have no symptoms, so they do not know to seek treatment. Furthermore, some diseases, such as HIV and genital herpes, have no cures at this time. Although new drug combination therapy treatments provide some hope in managing HIV, they do not cure it.

> **What Do You Think?**
>
> Discuss with your classmates your levels of health consciousness. In which health behaviors and which health-compromising behaviors do you regularly engage? What changes could you make to reduce your long-term health risks?

HIV/AIDS is the most feared sexually transmitted disease because it is fatal, but other STDs—such as pelvic inflammatory disease—also present serious complications. STDs may cause low-grade inflammations in both men and women that lead to infertility (Morell, 1995), discussed later in this chapter. Young adults often do not consider the consequences of unsafe sex, forget about them when under the influence of alcohol or drugs, or protect themselves from HIV/AIDS but not other STDs. Andrew and Kathy provide an example of this last behavior. When they first became intimate, they always used a condom because Andrew was open about his many previous sexual partners. After each tested negative for HIV twice over a six-month period, they stopped using condoms. Because genital herpes is not always active, they did not worry about the fact that Kathy had it. Now Andrew is also infected with herpes.

Risk for HIV has been greatest for gay and bisexual men especially African American and Hispanic/Latino gay and bisexual men, intravenous drug users, and minority populations, but the number of women affected is growing (Centers for Disease Control and Prevention, 2016c). David Longram, an AIDS case worker, talks about these issues in the "Working With" interview on page 433. Women make up 19 percent of HIV diagnoses, and African American and Hispanic women make up 44 and 23 percent of female AIDS cases, respectively, even though they are only 12 and 17 percent of the population (Centers for Disease Control and Prevention, 2016c). However, rates of infection are decreasing among African American women with a 42 percent reduction in diagnoses between 2005 and 2014 (Centers for Disease Control and Prevention, 2016c). Socioeconomic factors and stigma play a role in race differences. There are similar rates of needle sharing, risky sex, and number of partners when comparing racial and ethnic groups (Earnshaw, Bogart, Dovidio, & Williams, 2013). Differences in HIV/AIDS rates are more likely due to living in areas with high concentrations of HIV, being involved in the criminal justice system, and perceiving a stigma about condom use or one's sexual orientation (Earnshaw et al., 2013). Moreover, African Americans and Hispanic Americans tend to be screened later in the disease progression compared to European Americans, making treatment more difficult, and are more likely to delay or discontinue treatment due to cost, availability, or language barriers (Earnshaw et al., 2013).

Fear of STDs causes stress for sexually active adults of all ages, but particularly for young adults who are delaying marriage and consequently are likely to have multiple partners. Other life changes make early adulthood a stressful period as well, as we will see next.

Stress

stress The arousal of the mind and body in response to demands made on them by unsettling conditions or experiences (stressors).

Stress, the arousal of the mind and body in response to demands made on them by unsettling conditions or experiences (stressors), is not unique to the early adult period. However, early adulthood is a time of life when the demands of establishing a career and starting a family are likely to bring new types of stress. Unfortunately, many young adults ignore or deny stress as they do other health-related issues and rely on health-compromising behaviors to make them feel better. Tobacco, alcohol, and drugs are used to reduce tension and anxiety and to improve mood; yet they are not very effective ways to cope with stress. Learning to identify and cope with stress at this stage of life can provide lifelong benefits.

Stress can be *eustress* (positive stress), such as when you are chosen to give a speech, or *distress* (negative stress), such as when your car will not start and you need to get to an exam or a job interview. What serves as a stressor for one person may not be a stressor for another person or for the same person at another time. Important to the definition of stress is the person's appraisal of whether his or her personal resources are sufficient to meet the demands of the situation. Studies have consistently found that the level of stress is associated with a wide range of health problems.

Stress affects all the systems of the body. Hans Selye (1985) identified a pattern of physical response to stress that he called the **general adaptation syndrome**. This pattern has three stages: alarm, resistance, and exhaustion as shown in Figure 12.2. Confrontation with a stressor sets the stress response in motion. During the alarm stage, the body becomes mobilized to meet the threat. The sympathetic nervous system (which helps to control the heart) and the adrenal glands increase the production of hormones that bring on typical stress responses; rapid heart rate, dilated pupils, shallow and quick breathing, and higher blood pressure all result from increased blood supply to heart, brain, liver, and peripheral muscles. During the resistance stage, the body mobilizes to cope with the stressor. The adrenal glands produce hormones that attempt to keep the stressor as localized as possible while still enabling the body to overcome it. If the energy of the system is depleted before the body has overcome the stressor, the exhaustion stage is reached and illness results. The syndrome appears to be irreversible and accumulates to constitute the signs of aging. Wear and tear on the system brought about by repeated or prolonged stressors depletes the body's resources and lays the groundwork for disease.

general adaptation syndrome The pattern of physical response to stress identified by Hans Seyle, which has three stages: alarm, resistance, and exhaustion. Confrontation with a stressor sets the stress response in motion. The syndrome appears to be irreversible and accumulates to constitute the signs of aging.

Stress and Health

There is ample evidence that stress causes illness—but how? The answer is not simple. Stress can have a direct effect by increasing wear and tear on the physiological system and producing physiological changes that lead to illness. Tight shoulders, trembling hands, and fatigue are all signs of stress that, if untreated, can lead to conditions such as headaches, psoriasis, ulcers, skin rashes, colitis, gastritis, chronic lower back pain, vertigo (dizzy spells), high blood pressure, and even heart attack (Schafer, 1987). When we experience stress, our bodies release hormones that help us deal with acute, short-term stressors. However, most of our stressors are long acting—paying bills, relationship difficulties, traffic, exams. Our bodies respond similarly to acute and prolonged stressors, and when we are exposed to stress hormones over long periods of time, they can reduce our ability to fight off illness, damage memory centers in our brains, and overwork our cardiovascular systems. Stress also indirectly influences our health by changing our behaviors, which can make us more susceptible to disease and illness. When we are overly stressed, our sleep suffers, we tend to eat more and more poorly, we are more likely to use alcohol or drugs to self-medicate, and all of these things further damage our health and well-being (Âkerstedt, 2006; Leeies, Pagura, Sareen, & Bolton, 2010; Torres & Nowson, 2007).

The Experience of Stress

Psychological factors significantly contribute to a person's experience of stress; the meaning a person attaches to an event determines the degree of stress. Richard Lazarus (1993) identified a two-step process, which he calls *primary* and *secondary appraisal*, that people go through when faced with a stressor. During *primary appraisal,* the person determines if the stressor is positive, neutral, or negative. If it is a negative stressor, the individual assesses

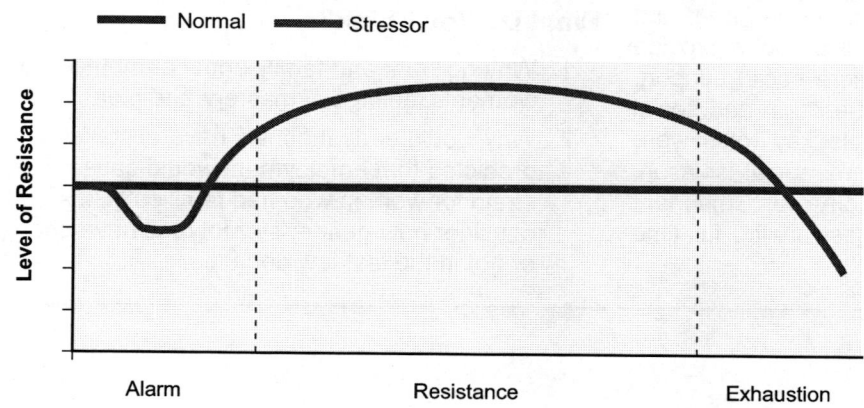

FIGURE 12.2
General Adaptation Syndrome

Hans Selye's research showed that physical reactions to stressors include an initial alarm reaction, followed by resistance and then exhaustion. During the alarm reaction, the body's resistance temporarily drops below normal as it absorbs a stressor's initial impact. Resistance increases, then levels off in the resistance stage, but ultimately declines if the exhaustion stage is reached.

Source: Adapted from Selye (1974).

Chapter 12 Physical and Cognitive Development in Early Adulthood

Focusing On...

How Does Stress Relate to Women's Employment?

Without considering the positive role employment can have and the fact that men have always been workers as well as husbands and fathers, the mental health field predicted serious negative health effects in the 1940s when women began their rapid influx into the labor force. Psychologists and sociologists predicted that working women would suffer "role strain" from the multiple roles of worker, wife, and mother.

This prediction was based on two faulty assumptions concerning stress. First, the assumption that employment simply adds one more complex and demanding role to a woman's life ignores the reality that homemaking is work and homemakers' lives often already include many demanding roles. The role of daughter, for example, can be a complicated one that creates role strain in a homemaker's life.

The second faulty assumption is that people have a limited amount of energy, so the more activities one has, the less energy one has available for any one of them. This ignores the fact that a different role can call on different resources and give different satisfactions and therefore can create more energy than it depletes. Going for a run after work, for example, often refreshes rather than depletes energy. Likewise, the workplace can feel refreshing after a weekend of doing laundry, cleaning house, and entertaining guests. Role strain is a function not only of how many roles but of what roles and in what combinations.

Nonetheless, for years multiple roles for women were viewed negatively. Only as researchers have examined the lives of women have we been able to ascertain the actual effects of multiple roles. Phyllis Moen, and her colleagues (1989) interviewed mothers in the 1950s and recontacted them thirty years later. They found that multiple roles predicted a longer, not a shorter, life. In an early review of the literature, Lois Verbrugge (1982) found that having several key roles was associated with good health for women; having too many roles may tax health, but having few or no roles may impair it.

Employment, marriage, and parenthood are all related to good health for women (Verbrugge, 1989b). Two of these roles combined are better than one, and all three are better than any two. Multiple roles provide more privileges, more resources, more social support, and more avenues for attaining self-esteem and social involvement. Women without multiple key roles were found to be more subject to boredom, social isolation, and stress. Employment is the single most important factor. Employed women had the best health; full-time homemakers had the worst health.

Grace Baruch, Rosalind Barnett, and Caryl Rivers (1983) assessed the ways major areas of life contribute to a woman's sense of well-being. Based on a survey of three hundred women, they found two major components of well-being: *mastery,* which includes self-esteem, sense of control, and low levels of depression and anxiety, *and pleasure,* which includes satisfaction, happiness, and optimism. The women who scored highest on all the indices of well-being were married women with both children and high-prestige jobs. This is the group role strain theorists would have predicted to be the most harried and overloaded, but in fact they were the happiest and healthiest and scored highest in mastery and pleasure.

The women who scored lowest on mastery were those with the fewest roles: married, childless, full-time homemakers. Their self-esteem was very closely tied to their husbands' lives; if anything went wrong, they had no individual resources. They were under-loaded in terms of roles but, more important, they felt they had little control over their lives.

Mothers who are married and employed clearly have strains in their lives. Often working mothers put in a "second shift" in which they carry a heavier load of child-rearing and household work than their male spouses, spending an hour more each day on these tasks than their partners and up to four times as much time doing tasks such as laundry (Bureau of Labor Statistics, 2015). Married, employed mothers have the rewards and resources associated with each of their roles particularly when household chores are shared more equally. If something goes wrong at the office, the successes of home can renew the spirit and give perspective to the office problem. If something goes wrong at home, such as a fight with a spouse or teenager, a day at the office can provide self-esteem and civility and perhaps give perspective on the problems of home. In fact, evidence suggests that employment serves as a buffer for women, protecting them from the worst effects of difficulties experienced in other parts of their lives.

What Do You Think?

1. Why do work and family both contribute to a woman's feelings of mastery and pleasure?
2. Why would early theorists have mistakenly predicted that employment would cause role strain for women who had families? Be sure to consider how gender stereotypes have changed or not in the last few decades.

its potential for harm, threat, or challenge. *Harm* refers to the present damage. If a police officer pulls you over and gives you a ticket for speeding, the harm might include the cost of the fine, the embarrassment in telling your parents or spouse, and the distress of being late for work. *Threat* refers to future damage, in this case the increase in automobile insurance premiums, the difficulties that might arise from the additional points on your license, and the history of being late for work. *Challenge* involves the potential to overcome and benefit from the event. In this case, the challenge lies in learning not to speed or getting up earlier so there is less need to speed. *Secondary appraisal* refers to the person's assessment of whether he or she has sufficient coping resources to meet the harm, threat, and challenge of the negative stressor. The experience of stress involves the balance between primary and secondary appraisal. High stress arises when harm and threat are high and coping ability is low.

People tend to perceive negative, uncontrollable, ambiguous, or overwhelming events as more stressful than positive, controllable, clear-cut, or manageable ones. Planning a wedding requires time and energy that often taxes the resources of a busy family, but it is a positive event and unlikely to be reported as stressful. Planning a funeral, on the other hand, typically is less work but is experienced as far more stressful. When faced with a negative event, feeling that it can be predicted, changed, or stopped reduces the person's experience of stress. Being able to predict and control allows the individual to adjust to the stressful event and reduces the physiological reactions to stress (Bandura et al., 1988).

Ambiguous events increase stress because the person does not know how to react to them. Unlike with a clear-cut stressor, an individual must devote resources to figuring out the ambiguous stressor rather than being able to confront it directly and effectively. For Lilly and Jamal, the couple described at the beginning of this chapter, new parenthood is an ambiguous event. Although Devon's arrival was long desired and a positive event, his infant needs appear uncontrollable, ambiguous, and overwhelming to young adults who have never before been responsible for a child. Similarly, occupational stress often results from role ambiguity, or not knowing what the expectations are for job performance. Young adults face this kind of stress as they leave school and begin their careers. Longitudinal data from the Framingham Heart Study, one of the longest-running health studies in the country indicate that high job demands, in combination with lack of clarity of expectations and feedback from supervisors, lead to an increased risk of coronary heart disease (LaCroix & Haynes, 1987). Those who work long hours over long periods of time, especially women, are more likely to develop cardiovascular disease, various types of cancer, and diabetes (Dembe & Yao, 2016). People who are "overloaded"—who have more responsibilities than they can meet in the available time—are subject to more stress. On the other hand, having too few or no roles is also associated with poor health, as discussed in the "Focusing On" feature.

Societal Stress

Societal stress is also related to illness. War and natural disasters, as well as geographical mobility that disrupts social ties, produce psychological distress. The term **posttraumatic stress disorder (PTSD)** describes the physical and psychological symptoms of a person who has been the victim of a highly stressful event, such as an assault, war, or earthquake, that last long after the event is over (Herman, 1992; Leor et al., 1996; Steinglass & Gerrity, 1990). Typical PTSD reactions include feelings of numbness, reliving aspects of the trauma, sleeping problems, difficulty in concentrating, and strong reactions to other stressful events. Women are more susceptible than men to PTSD following a traumatic event, perhaps because of overall higher risk for psychological disorders or due to differences in the way that DNA is activated in the presence of stress, (Breslau, 2009; Uddin, Sipahi, Li, & Koenen, 2013). Lower SES exposes individuals to more stress and associated health problems (Adler et al., 1994). Individuals with lower SES and less power are more likely to encounter negative events that create stress, such as the loss of a job, and to have fewer resources to cope with stressful events, such as savings to live on until they find a new job or friends who can give them temporary employment, and thus experience even greater stress.

posttraumatic stress disorder (PTSD) The physical and psychological symptoms of a person who has been the victim of a highly stressful event, such as violent war, rape, or earthquake, that last long after the event is over. Typical reactions include feeling numb, reliving aspects of the trauma, having sleeping problems, finding it difficult to concentrate, and reacting strongly to other stressful events.

> **What Do You Think?**
>
> What stressors can you identify in your life? What mechanisms do you use to cope with them? Which of these mechanisms are good ways of coping with stress? Which are not?

Rape

Of the many traumatic events that affect civilians, including robbery, other physical assault, the death of a close friend, or natural disaster, rape is the most likely to result in PSTD. Even many years after the rape, psychological evaluation indicates that victims are significantly more likely than nonvictims to suffer from major depression, eating disorders, alcohol abuse, and drug abuse (Koss et al., 1994). Victims also report headaches, gastrointestinal disorders, and gynecological problems. Because adolescents and young adults between twelve and thirty-four years of age are at highest risk, rape constitutes a major long-term health concern for young adult women. In the United States, women under age thirty-five fear rape more than they fear murder and limit their activities, such as by not going out alone at night, to prevent it (Rozee, 1996). In this way, rape functions to control women and contributes to their feeling of powerlessness. It is also important to remember that between 10 and 13 percent of all sexual assault victims are male, though they are significantly less likely to report their assault and the perpetrators are rarely punished (Chapleau, Oswald, & Russell, 2008; U. S. Department of Justice, 2013).

Rape is categorized as stranger rape or acquaintance rape. Though most people believe **stranger rape**, a surprise attack by someone the victim does not know, is more common, about 78 percent of cases are **acquaintance rape**, where the attacker is a friend, family member, or romantic partner (U. S. Department of Justice, 2013). The psychological impact of acquaintance rape can be far worse than those of stranger rape, because the victim feels betrayed by someone she trusted and may doubt her ability to judge men wisely. Additionally, victims of sexual assault often feel doubly victimized because they are often blamed for their rape: they were wearing something revealing, they were consuming alcohol, they were sexually promiscuous, and so they are, in part, responsible for the crime (Grubb & Turner, 2012; Suarez & Gadalla, 2010). This narrative is not only false but also further damaging to the victims of rape.

Rape can cause stress related to issues of sexual intimacy; sexual intimacy is itself a source of stress for young adults. As our discussion of STDs and HIV indicated, sexual activity can pose high risks for those who are in the process of establishing intimacy and not yet in steady relationships. Sexual functioning is the one area of physical development of which most young adults are very much aware. We turn to this subject next.

stranger rape Sexual assault by someone the victim does not know.

acquaintance rape Sexual assault in which the attacker is a friend, family member, or romantic partner of the victim.

Sexuality and Reproduction

Early adulthood is a time of sexual and reproductive maturity. Although many of today's adolescents are sexually active (as discussed in Chapter 11), adult status brings a greater demand for sexual intimacy. Sexuality is one of the most important aspects of adult relationships. In this section we look at the physiology of the human sexual response, a survey of contemporary sexual behavior, and common sexual problems. We then explore issues of reproduction, including infertility and reproductive technologies.

The Sexual Response Cycle

William Masters and Virginia Johnson (1966) watched and measured women's and men's physiological responses in more than ten thousand episodes of sexual activity and made several important discoveries. First, they found that while sexual excitement can come from many different sources, such as touch, smell, or fantasy, healthy individuals go through the same physiological process. Second, male and female sexual responses are much more similar than different. Masters and Johnson describe four physiological stages

Feelings or thoughts that awaken sexual interest constitute the desire stage that begins the sexual response cycle. Desire can be awakened in nonromantic settings, such as while out on a walk.
Source: Dzmitry Kliapitski/Shutterstock.

in the human sexual response cycle: excitement, plateau, orgasm, and resolution. Other researchers have suggested the desire stage as an initial stage that precedes the other four (Kaplan, 1979; Zilbergeld & Ellison, 1980).

Feelings or thoughts that awaken sexual interest and desire begin the sexual cycle. In the *desire stage,* both physiology and emotion contribute to sexual arousal. Desire, which is mainly an emotional state, leads to excitement. In the *excitement stage,* both women and men experience the first signs of physiological arousal called *vasocongestion,* when increased blood flow to the surface of the skin causes swelling of the pelvic region, a more rapid heartbeat, and erection. The excitement phase can be rapid or it can be slow. Whether ardent and passionate or slow and gentle, the physiological process of building arousal remains the same. When the changes of the excitement stage reach a high state of arousal and then level off, the *plateau stage* has been reached.

Young men often reach plateau very quickly, but as they approach forty they may find that sexual responsiveness is slower. They need more time and more direct stimulation to get fully erect. Women too vary in the time needed for arousal; variations occur among women and at different times for the same woman. Because orgasm is the shortest part of the sexual response cycle, the slowing with age has the benefit of lengthening the pleasure and providing women with more opportunity for orgasm (Brecher, 1984).

Orgasm, the involuntary, rhythmic contractions in the muscles of the pelvis, releases the buildup of muscular tension and vasocongestion. A man typically has only one orgasm, whereas a woman may have no orgasm, only one orgasm, or multiple orgasms. Whether single or multiple, orgasms for women typically result from direct clitoral stimulation, either oral or manual, rather than from the indirect stimulation provided by sexual intercourse alone.

After orgasm, the body returns to its nonaroused state. During this *resolution stage,* men have a refractory period during which orgasm is impossible. The refractory period varies from thirty minutes to several hours. It is shorter for younger men and longer for older men.

Sexual Attitudes and Behaviors

Sex involves psychosocial and cognitive aspects in addition to physical ones. Whereas Masters and Johnson studied the physiology of the sexual response, other investigators have focused on sexual attitudes and behaviors.

In 2009 the National Survey of Sexual Health and Behaviors (NSSHB) was conducted in which 5,865 U.S. residents ages fourteen to ninety-four were surveyed about their sex behaviors over the previous month, the previous year, and over the course of their lifetime (Herbenick et al., 2010). Responses for previous year sex behaviors can be found in Table 12.3. As you can see, people engage in a wide variety of sexual behaviors, and there seems to be some marked age differences in those behaviors. Many sex behaviors, such as vaginal intercourse, giving or receiving oral sex, and anal sex seem to peak during emerging adulthood and early adulthood. However, the NSSHB is a cross-sectional survey, which means that this peak might be part of development or a cohort effect. Similar results were found for individuals between 2010 and 2012 in the National Surveys of Sexual Attitudes and Lifestyles (NATSAL), a longitudinal study of individuals in Great Britain who were surveyed at three times: 1990–1991, 1999–2001, and 2010–2012 (Mercer et al., 2013). Findings from NATSAL demonstrated some changes in sex behaviors over time. Over the course of the study, young adults reported less frequent vaginal intercourse and engaged in oral and anal sex more, suggesting that they are incorporating more variety into their sex lives (Mercer et al., 2013).

NATSAL also surveyed attitudes toward sexual behaviors. Over the course of the study, all age groups generally agreed in monogamy within a marriage, and participants reported more negative attitudes toward both men having one-night stands and toward people having extramarital affairs (Mercer et al., 2013). Additionally, NATSAL findings demonstrated that between the early 1990s and 2012, people have become much more accepting of same-sex relationships, and younger age groups tended to be more accepting than older age groups (Mercer, et al., 2013). We will discuss LGBT issues later in this chapter and in more detail in Chapter 13.

Common Sexual Dysfunctions

Sexuality, as we have seen, includes physical, psychosocial, and cognitive aspects. It depends on healthy body functioning, on feelings and attitudes conducive to arousal, and on thinking ahead about protection from disease and unwanted pregnancy. As with any behavior that depends on integration of all of these domains, problems with sexual performance are not uncommon. A **sexual dysfunction** is an inability to function adequately in or enjoy sexual activities. Most couples have some sexual problems at some time in their relationship, but these are usually of a temporary nature (MacNeil & Byers, 1997; Mercer et al., 2003).

sexual dysfunction
An inability, often temporary, to function adequately in or enjoy sexual activities.

TABLE 12.3 Selected Sexual Behaviors in Previous Year by Gender and Age

	Men					Women				
Age	14–17	18–24	25–39	40–59	60 +	14–17	18–24	25–39	40–59	60 +
Masturbation	69%	81.7%	81.9%	74.1%	53.8%	42.6%	62.2%	67.2%	59.9%	39.7%
Received oral sex from a female	21.4%	58.2%	77.4%	55.3%	28.4%	2.9%	6.2%	3.8%	1.6%	1.1%
Received oral sex from a male	1.7%	6.1%	5.2%	7.1%	2.5%	16.8%	64.2%	65.3%	43.3%	16.3%
Gave oral sex to a female	13.1%	52.8%	71.1%	50.8%	29.3%	4.4%	5.6%	3.3%	1.7%	1.2%
Gave oral sex to a male	1.7%	5.5%	4.9%	7.4%	2.8%	17.1%	66.4%	67.6%	44.5%	15.1%
Vaginal intercourse	19.6%	58.1%	85.5%	65.8%	48.2%	20.2%	71.0%	80.0%	60.9%	31.9%
Anal sex	5.3%	12.9%	28.9%	20.8%	7.6%	4.2%	20.7%	21.4%	8.7%	2.5%

Source: Herbenick et al., 2010.

Low Sexual Desire

Low sexual desire is a common complaint of both women and men. It can stem from a variety of physical causes. Androgen (the sex hormone associated with sex drive) deficiencies, either those caused naturally or those caused by medications for nonsexual ailments, can lower sex drive in both sexes, as can a wide range of medical conditions. Although biological causes are important to consider, the majority of cases of low sexual desire are due to psychological factors. Preoccupation with problems of work or children, fear of sexual intimacy, anger or hostility toward one's partner, low self-esteem, or negative attitudes about sex are all examples of psychological causes of low sexual desire.

Female Orgasmic Problems

If a woman has never experienced an orgasm, she is considered to have *primary orgasmic dysfunction*. Although the causes of this problem are little known, they are usually psychological rather than physiological. Learning from an early age that one's body is "dirty" or that masturbation and sex are "bad" can contribute to guilt about sexual feelings and sometimes lead to dysfunction of the orgasmic response. A religious upbringing that is extremely negative about sex can have an adverse impact on a woman's orgasmic functioning (Kelly et al., 1990). Sexual responsiveness requires shedding inhibitions, which is relatively difficult if the inhibitions are strong and deeply ingrained. Additionally, women who are concerned about their sexual functioning, particularly worrying about taking too long to become aroused and if they will orgasm, are more likely to have trouble with sexual functioning (Sanders, Graham, & Milhausen, 2008). Part of successful treatment for primary orgasmic dysfunction entails therapy designed to defuse negative attitudes about sex.

More frequently women are orgasmic, but they fail to have orgasms without direct clitoral stimulation. Manual or oral stimulation is more likely than intercourse alone to lead to orgasm. Inability to experience orgasm during intercourse is not considered a sexual dysfunction, but it does make many women (and their partners) unhappy and therefore is sometimes seen as a problem.

Male Ejaculatory and Erectile Problems

The most common male sexual dysfunction, *premature ejaculation*, exists when a man reaches orgasm with minimal sexual stimulation before, during, or right after sexual penetration. The causes typically are psychological rather than physiological. Using a condom sometimes can help, because it reduces penile sensitivity. Fortunately, counseling helps many men learn to delay ejaculation.

Most men are unable to get or keep an erection at some point due to illness, fatigue, stress, or heavy alcohol consumption. This condition is considered an *erectile dysfunction* when a man is generally unable to get or keep a firm enough erection to have intercourse. Between 5 and 20 percent of men experience erectile dysfunction, and it is very prevalent among men with cardiovascular problems (Hatzimouratidis et al., 2010). For those who experience chronic erectile dysfunction, physical examinations and laboratory tests are used to examine possible cause and then treatments including lifestyle changes, education, psychosocial therapy, and pharmacological therapies such as Viagra (sildenafil) or Cialis (tadalafil) (Hatzimouratidis et al., 2010). One added benefit of such drugs is that the availability and advertising of them reduced the taboo surrounding erectile dysfunctions, which frequently cause feelings of shame, helplessness, anxiety, and depression (Berger, 1998).

Both causes and treatments of erectile problems vary widely. Physical causes such as alcohol or drug abuse, diabetes, vascular disease, side effects from medications for medical problems (notably high blood pressure), or severe chronic illnesses play a role in about half the cases; psychosocial factors contribute to the other half. Depression is a common psychological cause. Upsetting life events, such as losing a job or failing in a business venture, may threaten a man's self-confidence and lead to erectile difficulties. As we saw with female primary orgasmic dysfunction, an upbringing that stresses strong negative attitudes about sex may cause erectile dysfunction in men. Current difficulties in a relationship may set off the problem. Physically based erectile dysfunctions sometimes respond to medication or surgery. In many cases, couples are treated together in sex therapy.

Infertility

So far we have discussed sexuality for the pleasures it can bring on its own terms, but, as we all know, sex is very much connected to developing intimacy, a key aspect of psychosocial development in early adulthood that we discuss in Chapter 13. Establishment of intimacy during early adulthood frequently leads to the decision to start a family, yet a significant minority of couples, such as Lilly and Jamal at the beginning of this chapter, have trouble conceiving a child. **Infertility** refers to a couple's inability to conceive a pregnancy after one year of sexual relations without contraception. In a nationally representative survey of women ages fifteen to forty-four, 6 percent reported being unable to conceive a pregnancy after one year of trying, and over 7 million report having an infertility consultation at some time in their adult lives (Centers for Disease Control and Prevention, 2015b). Many couples who face infertility eventually do conceive, but success rates among those getting medical assistance in conception vary with age with 40 percent of those thirty-four and younger eventually conceiving to a success rate of about 2 percent among women age forty-four and up (Centers for Disease Control and Prevention–Division of Reproductive Health, 2016f). However, due in part to medical advances and better understanding of when medical intervention might be necessary, rates of infertility in the United States have decreased since the early 1980s even though more women are waiting longer to have children (Chandra, Copen, & Stephen, 2013).

Although women are likely to seek treatment for infertility before men do, the problem can be due to the woman, the man, the combined infertility of the couple, or to undetermined causes. Often multiple causes contribute to infertility.

infertility A couple's inability to conceive a pregnancy after one year of sexual relations without contraception.

Female Infertility

The two major causes of female infertility are failure to ovulate and blockage of the fallopian tubes, though uterine problems such as fibroids may also inhibit pregnancy. Ovulatory problems may be treated with drugs that induce ovulation. Blocked fallopian tubes may be due to scarring after a pelvic infection associated with an STD such as gonorrhea or chlamydia or by endometriosis (a condition in which the tissue lining the uterine cavity grows outside of the uterus into other pelvic or abdominal organs). Treatment for blocked fallopian tubes usually entails corrective surgery. The pregnancy rate after surgery varies greatly, depending on the location of the blockage (Davajan & Israel, 1991). Intra-uterine insemination of sperm into the uterus (also known as artificial insemination) and assisted reproductive technologies such as in vitro fertilization, when the sperm and egg are combined in a laboratory and then placed in the uterus, are two methods of managing female infertility (Centers for Disease Control and Prevention-Division of Reproductive Health, 2016f).

Male Infertility

Male infertility may be due to a low sperm count, low sperm mobility, poor semen quality (a high percentage of abnormal or immature sperm), or blockage of the ducts of the reproductive tract. Less attention has been paid to developing treatments for male infertility than for female infertility, and the treatments have been studied less thoroughly; thus, their usefulness is less well documented. Hormonal treatments can improve testicular functioning, while reproductive tract infections often respond to antibiotics. Surgery can repair varicose veins in the scrotum and correct blockage of ducts of the reproductive tract. Most male infertility cases are managed with intra-uterine insemination or in vitro fertilization (Centers for Disease Control and Prevention–Division of Reproductive Health, 2016f).

Psychological Reactions to Infertility

Infertility becomes apparent only over a period of time. When a couple has been trying to conceive month after month and nothing happens, what are the psychological reactions? Christine Dunkel-Schetter and Marci Lobel (1991) describe five common emotional responses to infertility. Most frequently, people respond with grief and depression. Feelings of sadness, mourning, and disappointment at being unable to have a child predominate. Anger, another very common response to infertility, may be directed inward, but may also be directed at the spouse or others who have children. Guilt, the next most common emotional response, may be linked to prior sexual behavior, delaying child-bearing, or any other previous "transgression."

When people receive an infertility diagnosis, they respond initially with shock or denial. Anxiety often accompanies treatment for infertility, in part because the treatment is stressful and in part because the outcome is uncertain. These emotional effects have an impact on the person's general functioning. A feeling of loss of control may result because the person's life goal of having a child cannot be met, and also because treatment for infertility directs a couple's sexual relationship and invades their privacy (Cousineau & Domar, 2007). Self-esteem may be threatened. Some people develop negative body images, others believe their potency is threatened, and still others question their gender identity. All of these psychological effects have an impact on the marriage and other relationships.

Reproductive Technologies

Given that infertility is so common and its effects on couples who experience it are so emotionally trying, it is not surprising that many treatments for infertility have been developed. As we saw in Chapter 3, couples may try artificial insemination, in which doctors inject the male partner's (or a donor's) sperm at the mouth of the cervix; in vitro fertilization (IVF), in which doctors combine egg and sperm outside the body and reintroduce fertilized eggs into the uterus; or intrafallopian tube transfers, in which gametes or zygotes are placed in the fallopian tube rather than the uterus. These treatments are not without drawbacks; they tend to be expensive and carry some health risks. And they are not always successful. A single round of IVF can cost anywhere from $12,000 to $15,000, making it unaffordable for many infertile couples especially if they do not have insurance that covers fertility treatment. Having a college education and having a household income of $100,000 or more per year are both predictors of whether a couple will go through more than one round of fertility treatment (Smith et al., 2011). The drugs used to stimulate the ovaries to produce multiple eggs have been linked to uterine cancer, melanoma, non-Hodgkin lymphoma, and slightly higher risk for breast cancer (Calderon-Margalit et al., 2008). The cost and the health risks push for limiting the number of infertility treatment procedures an individual undergoes. Couples must decide how much time, money, and emotional energy to put into reproductive technologies (Corman, 1995).

Successful infertility treatment often brings new stresses because of the increased likelihood of multiple births like this couple with twins. Families with larger multiple births like triplets, quadruplets, and quintuplets require more care than can reasonably be provided by a couple that also must make a living and perhaps care for other children.
Source: anekoho/Shutterstock.

Chapter 12 Physical and Cognitive Development in Early Adulthood

> **What Do You Think?**
>
> Consider ways to convince adolescents (who think they are never going to die) to give up risky sexual behavior. Do you think that explaining the connection to infertility would be likely to have an impact?

Women who do conceive with these treatments have a higher likelihood of multiple births. Largely because of the increase of fertility-enhancing treatments, the frequency of twins has nearly doubled, and triplet or higher-ordered births have increased more than 600 percent since the early 1970s (Kulkarni et al., 2013). However, this number has been decreasing since the late 1990s as fertility specialists have decreased the number of implanted embryos in an attempt to reduce the rate of multiple births, which are more dangerous to the mother and the children (Kulkarni et al., 2013). Twins and "supertwins," groupings of three or more babies, are at greater risk for long-term disability and early death. They also require more care than can reasonably be provided by a couple that also must make a living and perhaps care for other children, which is why education classes, social support, and various supportive services are recommended for these families (Jackson, 1996; Leonard & Denton, 2006). Successful infertility treatment therefore often brings new stresses as well as the joys of a larger family.

Adult Choices

Early adulthood is a time of major life decisions. Although we vary greatly in how rapidly and in what order we assume the tasks that will make us independent from our parents and connect us in intimate relations with peers, we typically face these challenges in our twenties and thirties. When Lilly and Jamal were still living at home at about age thirty, their mothers worried that their children would never marry and move out. Three years later, Lilly and Jamal delighted their parents with their new marriage, new home, and new baby. The early adult years, which extend through our thirties, provide time for trying different paths and finding ones that suit us. They also set some limits for the years to come. We establish attitudes and habits that will affect our physical well-being for the rest of our lives. We also make decisions about sexuality and childbearing. These choices have major implications for our cognitive and psychosocial development, for what we will think about and what roles we will play, for which struggles we will face and what regrets might later haunt us.

We now turn our attention to cognitive development in early adulthood. In addition to being of theoretical interest, adult cognition has implications for many aspects of people's lives. We begin by considering the development of postformal thought after adolescence, of contextual thinking, and of adult moral reasoning. Then we look at the effects of college on intellectual functioning. Finally, we consider issues of work, occupation, and career during early adulthood.

COGNITIVE DEVELOPMENT

Cognition concerns how and why people know rather than what and how much they know. Though there is little doubt that adults continue to accumulate new information throughout their lives, disagreement abounds about when cognitive functions are fully developed and if and when cognitive loss begins. Jean Piaget's strong influence on cognitive developmental theory has led to the belief that cognitive development reaches its final stage during adolescence with the emergence of formal operations. Some cognitive theorists accept his idea that the structures of mature thinking are in place by the time we reach adulthood; others believe this view is too limited. This is the first issue we will explore as we focus on cognitive development in young adults.

Postformal Thought

Formal operational thought is the final Piagetian stage of cognitive development. A person progresses through the *sensorimotor stage,* based on direct experience, as an infant; through the *preoperational stage,* based on language and symbols; through *concrete operations,* based on concrete problem solving; to *formal operations.* According to Piaget, as we saw in Chapter 10's discussion of cognitive development in adolescence, formal operational thought emerges between ages eleven and sixteen. It enables the adolescent to think abstractly in addition to thinking about the properties of concrete objects. Formal thought involves the ability to generate possibilities, use scientific reasoning, combine ideas logically, and think critically. A high school senior, for example, uses formal operational thought when she systematically compares the advantages and disadvantages of the three colleges that have accepted her. For Piaget, formal thought does not involve specific behavior; rather, it represents a generalized orientation toward problem solving (Blackburn & Papalia, 1992). Formal operations emphasize logical-mathematical thought structures, the solving of problems by using rational principles, logic, and careful reasoning.

Because formal operational thought is Piaget's final stage, it has been taken to represent his conceptualization of mature cognition and has occupied a central place in the study of adult cognition. Researchers using Piagetian methods and assumptions have focused on the development and use of formal operational thought in late adolescence and adulthood. Chapter 10 points out limits of the applicability of Piagetian theory to the study of adolescent cognitive development. Not all adolescents achieve formal thought, and those who do achieve it do not use it in all situations. In addition, emotions influence thought. Our high school senior may generate a logical conclusion that she should attend the local university (it is the cheapest, has the best reputation, and offers the program that interests her), yet feel it is the wrong choice for her.

Critiques of Formal Operations as the Final Stage of Cognitive Development

John Rybash, William Hoyer, and Paul Roodin (1986) have criticized the theory of formal operations. They acknowledge that emergence of formal thought is a significant achievement, but see it as an unsatisfactory description of adult thought. This is because formal operational thinking emphasizes finding the one right answer to a problem regardless of the specific nature of the problem, overemphasizes abstraction, and underemphasizes the ambiguities of real life. When you consider the complex, open-ended problems that mature adults encounter every day, the inapplicability of formal operations to adult thought becomes clearer. Whereas choosing the best car to buy in your price range may be possible using formal operational comparisons and contrasts, deciding whether or not to have a child, as Lilly did, is not. Lilly's decision depended on the circumstances of her life (Did she have emotional support? Could she afford a child? Was she healthy? Would there be someone to care for the baby when she works? Would waiting increase the chances of infertility?) and not on abstract possibilities. As Robert Sternberg (1992, p. 393) points out, "Solving a problem is less important than solving an important problem," and important problems often do not fit the laboratory model.

These limitations to Piaget's conception of formal operational thought have led cognitive psychologists to construct other formulations for mature thought. Dierdre Kramer (1989) found three basic characteristics these models of **postformal thought** have in common. First, postformal thinkers understand that knowledge is *relative and nonabsolute.* They realize that knowledge always has a subjective component that necessarily makes it incomplete, and that in the world there is no black and white, but rather only shades of gray (Sinnott, 1989, 2003). Second, postformal thinkers *accept contradiction* as a basic aspect of reality. For example, physicists must recognize that light can be both a wave and a particle. Similarly an intense personal relationship can call forth simultaneously the contradictory emotions of love and hate. Third, postformal thinkers can *synthesize contradictions* into coherent wholes. Instead of choosing among alternatives, they construct a framework that integrates the contradictions.

postformal thought A level of thought that may develop after formal operations and is characterized by relative and nonabsolute thinking that accepts and synthesizes contradiction.

When planning a dinner for guests who include both vegetarians and meat-and-potato lovers, for example, a choice of Mexican or Indian fare can include a coherent array of meat and nonmeat dishes that suits all. As we examine some of the formulations of postformal thought, these features will be apparent.

Because many adults move beyond the absolute nature of formal operational thought as they face the ambiguities of real life, several theorists have proposed a fifth stage of adult postformal thought. These fifth-stage formulations emphasize the pragmatic, relative, and changing nature of adult knowledge. In their work on cognitive development through adulthood, Patricia King and Karen Kitchener (1994, 2004, 2016) examine how people understand knowledge. Their model of reflective judgment has seven distinct stages that fall into three separate levels of understanding. For brevity, we will investigate the three levels of reflective judgment. In the first level, *prereflective thinking*, individuals believe that knowledge is absolute and that there is a correct answer to everything. Prereflective thinkers rely on perceived authority figures to know and share those absolute truths. During the second level, *quasireflective thinking*, individuals begin to understand that knowledge is abstract and constructed. Quasireflective thinkers understand that different people can have different opinions on topics and both be correct—knowledge is not absolute because our source of information may be incorrect and all information we "know" is based on our interpretation of that information. In the third level of reflective judgment, *reflective thinking*, individuals gather evidence of information and evaluate the sources and quality of that evidence. Reflective thinkers continually reevaluate the information they "know" and, if warranted, use new information to change previous assumptions. Both longitudinal and cross-sectional studies evaluating this model have shown that individuals tend to advance from prereflective to quasireflective thinking during their time in college (King & Kitchener, 2016). True reflective thinking is not very common, and when it is demonstrated, it is usually among individuals who are advanced in doctoral studies (King & Kitchener, 2016).

Gisela Labouvie-Vief (1985) sees the clash between logic and reality as the impetus for development of a more pragmatic type of adult cognition. Labouvie-Vief and Julie Hakim-Larson (1989) propose two modes of thought, one abstract and one emotional. The *formal mode* is distanced and objective; the *internalized mode* is intuitive, subjective, and imaginative. Formal operations represent the development of the first mode, but mature thought requires the balanced use of both ways of knowing. Labouvie-Vief (1992) stresses that the mature thinker must reconnect reason with emotional and social reality, making decisions within the context of commitments to careers, relationships, and children. A less mature thinker, for example, would take an individualistic approach to a work problem, do it singlehandedly at the cost of work overload and some blunders, with hope for career advancement. A more mature thinker would admit his or her limitations and rely on a team of experts and advisers. In Labouvie-Vief's theory *intrasystemic thought*, which is the last phase of formal operations, is the precursor to mature cognition, which she calls *intersystemic thought*. Intersystemic thought enables thinkers to understand multiple intellectual perspectives and to see the truth as part of a changing reality. Her final stage is *autonomous thought*. Autonomous thinkers see the role of their perspectives and values in the construction of their personal truths.

Taken in combination, these different ideas reflect the emergence of a new view of adult thought. The multiplicity of postformal models indicates recognition that Piaget "failed to represent adequately the thought and emotions of mature people" (Blackburn & Papalia, 1992, p. 141). Although the theoretical formulations we have discussed vary, most emphasize the increasingly pragmatic, relative, and changing nature of adult knowledge. Current thinking emphasizes that adult intellectual performance cannot be separated from its social and cultural context.

Development of Contextual Thinking

While the researchers discussed so far have used experiments to try to discover the stages of adult thinking, other psychologists have used other approaches. K. Warner Schaie (1994) measured intellectual development in the same individuals over many years (see Chapter 14). Based on twenty years of longitudinal research, Schaie (1977/1978) proposes three

> **What Do You Think?**
>
> Have you noticed ways in which your thinking has changed since you have been in college? Do they fit the chapter's description of postformal thought?

or four stages of adult thought that represent different goals of knowledge corresponding to changing adult patterns of commitment.

Schaie's Stages of Adult Thinking

Schaie's stage theory of lifespan intellectual development builds on Piaget's stages. Schaie believes cognitive abilities develop as Piaget described, but become more goal directed during adulthood. His stages highlight a clear relationship between psychosocial and cognitive development; external context, such as the demands of work and family, rather than internal organizing structure defines each stage. Thus, whereas Piaget's stages describe how an individual acquires new information, Schaie's stages go a step further: considering how adults use knowledge differently throughout adulthood.

Childhood and adolescence, according to Schaie, constitute the **acquisitive stage** and encompass all four of Piaget's stages, as shown in Figure 12.3. During the acquisitive stage, the person builds basic skills and abilities, from walking and talking to abstract reasoning about future possibilities.

Young adults are in the **achieving stage**. They direct their intelligence toward specific goals rather than following every inclination as might an adolescent who has not yet formulated clear personal choices. Young adults must consider both the contexts

acquisitive stage Schaie's term for all four of Piaget's stages, during which the child or adolescent builds basic skills and abilities that precede Schaie's stages of adult thinking.

achieving stage Schaie's first stage of adult thinking during which young adults direct their intelligence toward specific goals rather than following every inclination as might adolescents who have not yet formulated clear personal choices.

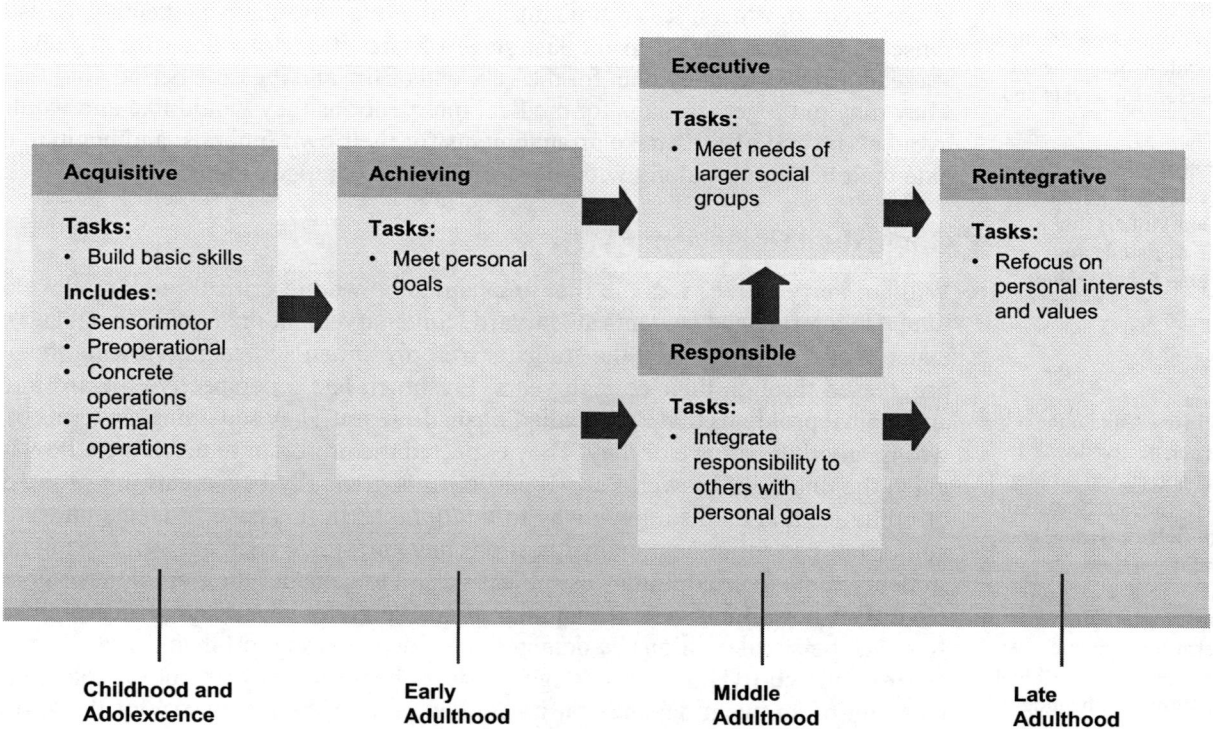

FIGURE 12.3 Schaie's Stages of Adult Thinking

Schaie focused on how adults use their knowledge at different periods of adulthood, in contrast to Piaget, who focused on how children and adolescents acquire knowledge. Young adults are typically in Schaie's achieving stage; they direct their intelligence toward specific personal goals.

Source: Adapted from Schaie (1977/1978).

and the consequences of their decisions when solving real problems associated with planning careers and establishing families. The decision about whether to take a job, for example, must balance consideration of short-term factors, such as salary and commuting distance, with longer-term factors, such as retirement benefits and promotion opportunities. The decision about when to have a baby must balance the desire for parenthood, the ability to support a child, and the willingness to rearrange other commitments to care for an infant.

In middle adulthood, people enter the **responsible stage**. Whereas in the achieving stage people strive to meet personal goals, in the responsible stage they also consider their responsibilities to others—mates, children, aging parents, and community—when making decisions. A middle-aged lawyer, for example, cannot just leave a well-paying job that she dislikes to begin a private practice that will take time to develop when her family depends on the steady income. A promotion may have to be rejected if it requires the family to relocate.

Some middle-aged people have powerful positions that bring broader and more complex responsibilities. For them, middle adulthood also brings the **executive stage**. This calls for a new type of cognition—applying postformal thinking about systems to practical problems—as they work to understand and meet the needs of competing groups in a large organization, such as a business or community organization, that affects many people beyond themselves and their families. A college president, for example, must make decisions about community relations that concern not only members of the college but local residents and perhaps an entire city economy and social structure as well. Not all middle-aged individuals have an opportunity to use their cognitive skills to meet this kind of challenge, which is why Schaie talks of three or four adult stages.

Late adulthood is the **reintegrative stage**, when people have fewer long-range plans to make and fewer responsibilities to job and family. This enables them to focus again on their personal interests and values. Older adults are more likely to focus selectively on the issues that have meaning for their own personal lives rather than on abstract questions or the needs of others. It is a time during which they use their intellectual skills to make sense of their own lives. In the last stage of late life, adults enter the **legacy-creating stage**, during which they plan for the very end of life and the time period after their death. They may put together plans for medical interventions they would like and would like to avoid at the end of life, make arrangements for their own funerals, and begin to disseminate their belongings along with the stories that accompany them.

Contextual Relativism

William Perry (1970) was the first to examine how adult critical thinking develops over time. He interviewed students at Harvard University about their educational and personal experiences, starting when the students were freshmen and reinterviewing them as they progressed through their college years. Freshmen had a perspective toward intellectual and ethical problems that Perry called **basic dualism**. They saw things in terms of right or wrong, good or bad, we or they. They expected the professor to teach them how to distinguish the one right answer. Perry's participants gradually became aware of the diversity of opinions, and dualism gave way to *multiplicity*. In this case, students understand that authorities can differ, that many questions have no single right answer. During this stage, students come to see opinions as subjective and to consider their opinions as good as any other. But not all answers are equally good. Perry found that as professors challenged students' personal opinions by demanding evidence to support them, students moved into **contextual relativism**. In this stage, students begin to see that truth is relative, that the meaning of an event depends on its context and on the framework of the knower who is trying to understand the event. Abortion, for example, has different meaning from a "pro-choice" perspective than from a "pro-life" one. Understanding the importance of perspective pushes students to make a commitment to a particular intellectual and/or ethical point of view. As they make a personal commitment to a world view, they transcend subjectivity and the limits of formal operations.

---

responsible stage Schaie's second stage of adult thinking during which middle adults also consider their responsibility to others—mates, children, aging parents, and community—when making decisions.

executive stage Schaie's stage of adult thinking that applies to some middle adults who have powerful positions that bring broader and more complex responsibilities and require a new type of cognition, applying postformal thinking about systems to practical problems, as they work to understand and meet the needs of competing groups in a large organization that affects many people beyond self and family.

reintegrative stage Schaie's stage of adult thinking during which late adults focus again on their personal interests and values.

legacy-creating stage Shaie's final stage of adult thinking in which individuals make end-of-life decisions and arrangements for after their death.

basic dualism William Perry's term for a perspective toward intellectual and ethical problems from which students view truth in terms of right or wrong, good or bad, and we or they.

contextual relativism William Perry's term for a perspective toward intellectual and ethical problems from which students begin to see that truth is relative and that the meaning of an event depends on its context and on the framework of the knower who is trying to understand the event.

College interactions with professors and other students foster the development of contextual relativism, a postformal mode of thinking that enables the person to embrace abstract ideals and to develop an ethical point of view.
Source: Monkey Business Images/Shutterstock.

Limitations of Perry's Work

Perry's (1970) sample of Harvard University students, however, did not represent all adults or even all college students. Harvard University represents only the most prestigious of colleges, and most of the students Perry used to establish his scheme of intellectual and ethical development were males of traditional college age along with some women attending Radcliffe College.

Broadening Perry's Approach

Nevertheless, Perry's work has had a great deal of influence on subsequent researchers, who have broadened the picture to include women, less prestigious institutions, and a range of adult ages.

In one such study, Mary Belenky, Blythe Clinchy, Nancy Goldberger, and Jill Tarule (1986) interviewed 135 women from six academic institutions ranging from an inner-city high school to a prestigious women's college, as well as several family agencies, or "invisible colleges," that assist clients with questions about parenting. They believed that relationships to authority matter in how we know. Given the diversity of participants, they found some women (none of whom were in college) who experienced *silent knowing.* These women felt "passive, reactive, and dependent, they see authorities as being all-powerful, if not overpowering" (p. 27). Among college freshmen, they found women who were concrete and dualistic in their thinking, as Perry's dualistic thinkers were. Belenky and her associates call this quality *received knowing,* because the women were receiving the truth from others.

The next development among the women was *subjective knowing.* Subjective knowing is like Perry's multiplicity in many ways, but subjectivist women seem to be less concerned than men with persuading others. Their predominant learning mode is one of inward listening and watching. Some women move from subjective knowing to *procedural knowing,* which is based on abstract reasoning (formal operations) and represents a shift from subjective opinions to reasoned arguments. Making this transition requires interacting with authorities who teach how to reason; the women who reached this stage were attending college or had graduated from college.

When women integrate subjective and objective knowing, they move to *constructed knowing.* This stage corresponds to Perry's contextual relativism. Women at this stage see that all knowledge is constructed, that truth is a matter of context and that frame of reference matters. At the most advanced ways of knowing, problem finding and other ways of critical thinking that are beyond formal thought become prominent.

Chapter 12 Physical and Cognitive Development in Early Adulthood

A Multicultural View

Moral Orientation in the United States and China

A basic criticism of Lawrence Kohlberg's stage theory of moral development is that it is based on data gathered from a culturally homogeneous and all-male sample. The problem of gender has received a lot of attention thanks to the work of Carol Gilligan and her colleagues, as discussed previously. But what about moral orientations in different cultures and subcultures? A meta analysis of moral development across cultures demonstrated a general trend toward postconventional morality as individuals move into emerging adulthood, particularly if receiving a college education (Padilla-Walker, 2016). However, the way this morality is demonstrated within the structure of Kohlberg's dilemmas might be misleading. John Snarey (1985) criticized Kohlberg's theory for being too bound to Western culture, especially at the postconventional level of reasoning. While Kohlberg's guidelines for scoring include examples of reasoning from a broad range of viewpoints at lower levels of reasoning, the guidelines and examples for scoring the fifth and sixth stages of moral reasoning are particularly culture bound. An answer to the Heinz dilemma that places the right to life over the right to property, for example, earns a stage 5 designation. However, a response such as "Everyone has the obligation to relieve human misery and suffering, if possible... I do think you have certain obligations to your wife and your friends or relatives that are just deeper" earns only a stage 4 designation because of the contextual consideration. This makes it difficult for people of other cultures to be considered to have reached the postconventional level of moral development or for someone in this culture who has developed a *contextual relativism* in Perry's sense (Murphy & Gilligan, 1980). Rosemary Mennuti and Don Creamer (1991) call for a sensitivity to the variations in moral perspectives in other cultures and within a culture.

The Chinese culture, for example, has been oriented toward collectivism and conciliation rather than justice and autonomy. Because of this, Valerie Stander and Larry Jensen (1993) expected that, compared to Americans, Chinese people might exhibit more of an orientation toward care than toward justice. They studied men and women undergraduates in the United States and China using two groups of Americans—Mormons and non-Mormons attending Brigham Young University—and one group of Chinese students from Beijing Normal University. The Chinese students all reported no religion. The non-Mormon Americans were predominantly Christians of various faiths.

The World View Questionnaire was designed by Jensen et al. (1991) to differentiate between caring and justice orientations; one adjective in each pair represents each orientation. Stander and Jensen (1993) gave the World View Questionnaire to American Mormons, American non-Mormons, and Chinese students reporting no religion. The Chinese respondents chose the fewest caring adjectives and the Mormons the most, indicating cultural differences in moral orientation based on both nationality and religion.

To assess moral orientation, the investigators asked each participant to fill out the World View Questionnaire. Each of the forty items consisted of a pair of adjectives, one representing each orientation, from which the participant was to choose. Sample items appear in Table 12.4. The Chinese students' form was printed in Chinese, the Americans' in English.

Stander and Jensen found differences in scores on the questionnaires based on culture. Unlike their prediction, the Chinese students chose the smallest number of caring adjectives, the Mormons chose the

---

You may have noticed that while the men in Perry's study all seemed to develop contextual relativism, only some of the women in Belenky et al.'s study reached procedural or constructed knowing. Why? Belenky and her associates interviewed women from a wide spectrum of institutions, whereas Perry interviewed only Harvard men. The differences in findings may be due to gender, or to one group being homogeneous and privileged and the other being diverse, or to a combination of both factors. In this regard, it is significant that the women who did progress to higher levels of thinking were those with college experience.

Whether called *contextual relativism* or *constructed knowing*, the development of a postformal mode of thinking enables the person to embrace abstract ideals and develop an ethical point of view. As we will see, these developments allow young adults to transcend conventional levels of moral reasoning.

Adult Moral Reasoning

As we saw in Chapter 10's discussion of cognitive development in adolescence, moral development depends on cognitive structures. Lawrence Kohlberg, building on Piaget's

A Multicultural View

Moral Orientation in the United States and China *continued*

most caring adjectives, and the non-Mormon Americans fell in between. The two American groups were more like each other than either was to the Chinese group. This clearly indicated cultural differences based on both nationality and religion.

Why did the cultural differences not confirm the prediction that the Chinese students would be more caring? It may be that the Chinese viewpoint of collectivism represents a different form of caring than that measured by the World View Questionnaire. Appropriate cross-cultural measurement may require more than just a language translation of a questionnaire. It may also be that Chinese culture is changing or is misunderstood. More recent studies have utilized different means of investigating moral development, including more culturally attuned dilemmas or simply by asking direct questions regarding moral development, and have found that people from varying cultural backgrounds tend to value life, honesty, and laws even if their responses to moral dilemmas differ (Gibbs, Basinger, Grime, & Snarey, 2007).

TABLE 12.4 Selected Items from World View Questionnaire

Circle the contrasting adjective you think is more important to you personally.

1.	Logic	Intuition
2.	Compromise	Power
3.	Consistency	Forgiveness
4.	Organized	Creative
5.	Those we love	Self
6.	Justice	Mercy
7.	Principles	People
8.	Getting along with others	Achievement
9.	Sense of right	Sensitivity to others
10.	Educating the mind	Educating the heart
11.	Competitive ability	Cooperative ability
12.	Loyalty	Leadership

Source: Adapted from Stander & Jensen (1993).

---

cognitive stages, developed stages of moral judgment. At the *preconventional level*, punishment and reward guide individual morality; at the *conventional level*, social rules guide it; and at the *postconventional level*, moral principles guide it. Just as Piaget's stages focus exclusively on logical skills and ignore social or emotional context, Kohlberg's stages focus on the abstract ethic of justice (or rules) and ignore the social or emotional context of moral decision making. Carol Gilligan and her associates have criticized Kohlberg's one-sided view of morality. Empathy, they argue, is a primary motivator for moral judgment and ethical behavior. They provide their own three-stage model of moral development. At the *survival orientation* stage, the person focuses on caring for the self to ensure survival. At the *conventional care* stage, she or he focuses on responsibility to others. At the *integrated care* stage, she or he coordinates the needs of self and of others, seeing all as being equal and, thus, moving toward a guiding principle of nonviolence.

How do the justice and care perspectives compare when directed toward the same issue? The public abortion debate serves as an example (Gilligan & Attanucci, 1988). When approached from the perspective of justice, the claims of the fetus and the pregnant woman are placed in opposition. Is the fetus a person? Should its claims take precedence

> **What Do You Think?**
>
> With your classmates, consider ways in which your college may be less hospitable to female than male students. How might this discrepancy affect male and female students' ways of knowing?

over the pregnant woman's? From the perspective of care, on the other hand, the connection between the fetus and the pregnant woman is central and the moral question becomes whether it is responsible or irresponsible to extend or end this connection. Which is caring and which is careless? We saw in Chapter 10 that adolescents develop more ethical beliefs about both care and justice, though few develop postconventional moral judgment or integrated care.

Context and Moral Orientation

Research investigating adult moral development has assessed orientation (justice or care) and level of moral reasoning as a function of gender, age, experience, and the content or situation of the moral problem. Much of the work has been done with college students. Mary Rothbart, Dean Hanley, and Marc Albert (1986) found that the content of the dilemma, or situational factors, had a strong influence on moral orientation. They interviewed undergraduate men and women about three different moral dilemmas: Kohlberg's classic Heinz dilemma (Should Heinz steal medicine from a druggist who is charging an outrageous price in order to save his wife's life?), a dilemma concerning physical intimacy, and a dilemma from their own lives. Responses were coded according to their justice or care orientation. The investigators found that all respondents used both care and justice orientations in the course of the interview, and only 4 percent used one orientation on any one dilemma exclusively. Whereas the Heinz dilemma more often called forth a justice orientation and the physical intimacy dilemma a care orientation, the "own life" dilemma was equally divided for both genders. Similarly, Fumagalli and colleagues (2010) looked at different types of moral judgments and gender differences. Some moral judgments in this study were impersonal, such as being on a runaway train coming to a fork in the track with five men on the left side of the fork and one on the right and having to choose which side of the track to take. Other moral judgments were personal, requiring the participant to actively hurt someone to save others, such as killing one person to harvest organs and save five other people who would otherwise die. Fumagalli and colleagues found no gender differences in the impersonal tasks, but found that in the personal tasks, men were more likely to choose the option that saved more lives and women less likely to do so, supporting Gilligan's ideas about nonviolence (2010). However, Nancy Yacker and Sharon Weinberg (1990) studied male and female law and social work students and found social work students were more likely to use care and law students justice, regardless of gender. It may be that people with different orientations choose careers in different fields, regardless of gender.

Kathleen Galotti (1989) asked male and female undergraduates to write responses to the question "When faced with a moral dilemma, what issues or concerns influence your decision?" The responses were coded according to one or more of thirteen themes. "Feminine" themes included *what others would think and/or feel, effects on others, situation specifics, effect on self, gut feeling/intuition,* and *personal guilt.* "Masculine" themes included *greater societal good, legal issues, general principles, reasoning systematically, religious teachings, personal code of ethics,* and *rights of others.* The people who coded the responses did not know whether men or women had written them. Galotti found that the essays of men and those of women were not distinguishable. There was no difference in the proportion of women and men who gave postconventional responses. Likewise, no differences were found in theme usage for twelve of the thirteen themes (men were more likely to use the theme *reasoning systematically).* Overall, usage of themes identified as feminine was double or triple the usage of themes identified as masculine.

> **What Do You Think?**
>
> Think of a moral dilemma that you expect would call forth similar orientations from male and female students. Think of one that would not. Try your choices out on some friends or classmates. What aspects of each dilemma seem to be important?

The growth of faith, according to James Fowler, is a universal progression through stages of spiritual development that is not necessarily religious in orientation. Its growth depends on the development of cognitive structures.

Development of Faith

Faith or spirituality is another aspect of moral development that depends on cognitive growth. Humans need to construct a reason for living. As young adults become able to understand different ethical perspectives and develop their own ethical points of view, they also become capable of finding their own spiritual meaning, or faith. The growth of faith, according to James Fowler (1991), is a universal developmental process that can occur within or outside a specifically religious context. Table 12.5 presents the stages of Fowler's faith-knowing system. As you can see, Fowler's stages develop from self-centered and one-sided to more complex, other-centered, and multisided levels of understanding, similar to Kohlberg's or Gilligan's stages of moral development and to Perry's or Belenky's stages of critical thinking.

Adolescents frequently argue with their parents about church or synagogue attendance, and participation in formal religious activities decreases during emerging adulthood (Stoppa & Lefkowitz, 2010). Even as formal religious behaviors decrease,

TABLE 12.5 Fowler's Faith-Knowing System

Stage	Age	Center of Power	Process	Value
0: Undifferentiated Faith	Birth–2 years	Symbiotic relationship with parent	Egocentric perceptions	Own needs
1: Intuitive-Projective Faith	2–6 years	Caregiving adult	Magical thought	Appeasement
2: Mythical-Literal Faith	6–12 years	Cultural and religious rules and traditions	Rituals and rules	Order, rituals, fairness
3: Synthetic-Conventional Faith	12 and beyond	Peers, cultural or religious leader	Symbols provide meaning	Approval
4: Individuative-Reflective Faith	Early adulthood and beyond	Self	Construct own symbols	Own meaning
5: Conjunctive Faith	Midlife and beyond	Truth	Verities expressed through symbols, awe	Openness to others, humility
6: Universalizing Faith	Midlife and beyond	The Ultimate God	Relationship expressed through life lived	Love, others' need

Source: Fowler (1991).

Chapter 12 Physical and Cognitive Development in Early Adulthood

Informal discussions in the dorms or around campus, such as these students are having, are one reason living on campus provides an intellectual advantage. But the largest advantage is that young adults who attend college grow more in intellectual skills compared to those who do not attend college.
Source: William Perugini/Shutterstock.

emerging adults report stability in their religious beliefs, suggesting that emerging adults are adopting their own ways of expressing their religiosity, a facet of individuative-reflective faith (Stoppa & Lefkowitz, 2010). There is also evidence that as young adults begin finding prospective mates, deciding whether to marry in a religious ceremony, and whether to give their children a religious education they shift toward engaging in more formalized religious behaviors such as regular church attendance (Hoge, Johnson, & Luidens, 1993). Whether they do return to their families' religious beliefs and practices or find new ways to organize their spiritual lives, emerging adults and young adults call on their developing cognitive skills to do this. As we will more fully discuss in Chapter 17, spirituality continues to grow and influence quality of life throughout adulthood.

College

More individuals are attending college than ever before, due in part to more women attending college, changes in expectations for workforces, and more people going to community colleges (Fry, 2009). The number of adults completing four or more years of college in the United States is comparable to other industrialized nations, as Figure 12.4 shows. However, these figures do not tell the whole story. Only 60 percent of people who begin a bachelor's degree actually complete that degree within six years (U.S. Department of Education, 2016a).

Public and private colleges and universities offer two- and four-year programs that address a diverse range of student needs. Junior and community colleges offer vocational training or the first two years of coursework at the college level. Colleges offer four-year programs leading to a bachelor's degree, as well as professional and graduate programs. Though parent level of education plays the largest role in predicting whether a student will attend college, family income is strongly associated with the type of institution a student attends (Davis-Kean, 2005; U.S. Department of Education, 1993). Students from low-income families are more likely to attend public two-year colleges than any other type; students from high-income families are more likely to enroll in four-year, Ph.D.–granting universities, and the cost of education was the most frequently cited reason people provided for choosing a two-year institution rather than a four-year school (College Board/National Journal, 2014). Moreover, students also utilize distance-learning, or online classes, more than ever. About 27 percent of college students report taking at least

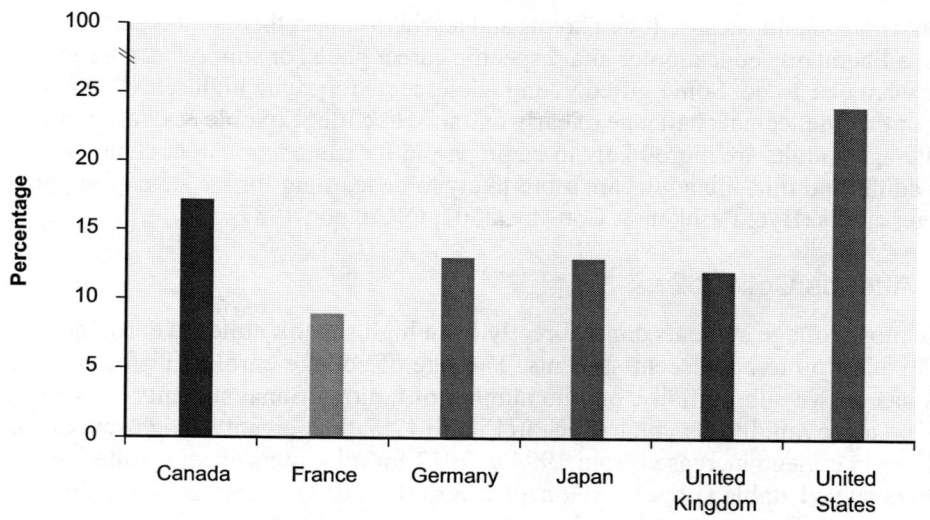

FIGURE 12.4
College Graduates in Large Industrialized Countries, 2014

In 2014, nearly 44 percent of all adults aged twenty-five to sixty-four in the United States had completed a bachelor's degree or some other advanced degree—a number comparable to other large, industrialized nations.
Source: OECD, 2015.

one course online, and about 13 percent completed their entire postsecondary education online (U. S. Department of Education, 2016b).

Does the kind of school you attend matter? Most studies have shown that the benefits of college can be realized at any type of school. Pascarella and Terenzini (1991) found that although there were differences in cognitive growth as a function of the kind of education, the largest difference was the fact that emerging adults who attended college grew in intellectual skills compared to those who did not attend college. Living on campus does seem to provide an intellectual advantage; dormitory residents make significantly larger freshman-year gains in critical thinking than do commuting students (Terenzini et al., 1996). Another factor that leads to cognitive growth is the amount of contact between students and faculty, especially informal interaction (Lamport, 1993; Terenzini et al., 1996). It should also be noted that people who attend a community college are less likely to complete a bachelor's degree than people who attend a four-year college or university (Alfonso, 2006). Among those taking online courses, learning and engagement are generally good but tend to be best in hybrid courses that combine in-person and online learning in the same course (Chen, Lambert, & Guidry, 2010; Jaggars & Bailey, 2010). Additionally, many of the studies that have examined the efficacy of online education have had included mostly well-prepared college students, meaning that these findings should be cautiously applied to the lower SES, under-prepared students who are most likely to use online courses (Jaggars & Bailey, 2010).

The college experience cultivates intellectual development, not only teaching large amounts of information but also fostering a progression in ways of thinking (Belenky et al., 1986; Montgomery & Côté, 2003; Perry, 1970). Darrin Lehman and Richard Nisbett (1990) studied 165 undergraduates majoring in the natural sciences, humanities, and social sciences and found they showed improvements in reasoning from the first through fourth years in college. Ernest Pascarella and Patrick Terenzini (1991) found that traditional- and nontraditional-age seniors performed better than freshmen in abstract reasoning and critical thinking; they were also more intellectually flexible and better able to develop abstract frameworks. It appears that all measures of adult cognition increase with level of education, as does maintenance of cognitive performance as people age (Ganguli et al., 2010; Labouvie-Vief, 1985; Reese & Rodeheaver, 1985). Susan Heidrich and Nancy Denney (1994) examined the effects of age, gender, education, and intellectual abilities on problem-solving performances of eighteen- to eighty-one-year-olds. They found that level of problem solving was positively related to higher levels of education and not to age.

Students go to college for a variety of reasons. Most people attend college, at least in part, to help them have a rewarding career and to increase earning potential (Phinney, Dennis, & Osorio, 2006). Minority students and students from lower SES households also note that they attend college to help their family, to prove their self-worth (Phinney et al., 2006). Younger students may attend because their parents and teachers expect them to, because they wish to obtain a liberal arts education or attain specific career goals, or simply because they do not know what else to do. Some gifted young adolescents forgo the high school experience in favor of the intellectual challenge of early entrance to college (Noble & Drummond, 1992). Middle-aged adults are more likely to be preparing for careers or career changes, and both older adults and mid-life adults are more likely to be learning for the sake of learning than younger adults (Bye, Pushkar, & Conway, 2007; O'Connor, 1987).

Who Attends College?

While most college students come directly from high school, colleges enroll adults of all ages in addition to adolescent students. The rate of college enrollment for younger students has grown substantially, but the number of nontraditional students has been growing even more rapidly. As you can see in Figure 12.5, the percent of high school students enrolling in college increased from 1994 to 2012 for all groups except white men, whose numbers stayed stable (Lopez & Gonzalez-Barrera, 2014). These demographic changes in college enrollment are due, in part, to changes in the demographics of the United States. However, though the race gap in college attendance seems to be shrinking, it is important to remember that minority groups are more likely to attend two-year colleges and are less likely to graduate from a four-year institution in six years than white students (U. S. Department of Education, 2016a, 2016b).

Women and Racial/Ethnic Minorities

Women are more likely than men to attend college. In 2012, 71 percent of female high school graduates were in college, compared to 61 percent of male graduates. Women are also more likely than men to complete college within six years of starting (Lopez & Gonzaelz-Barrera, 2014; U.S. Department of Education, 2016a). Why is there such a gender difference? Young men note that they dislike school more than young women, and young women tend to have better academic records than young men (Jacob, 2002). Additionally, young men from families

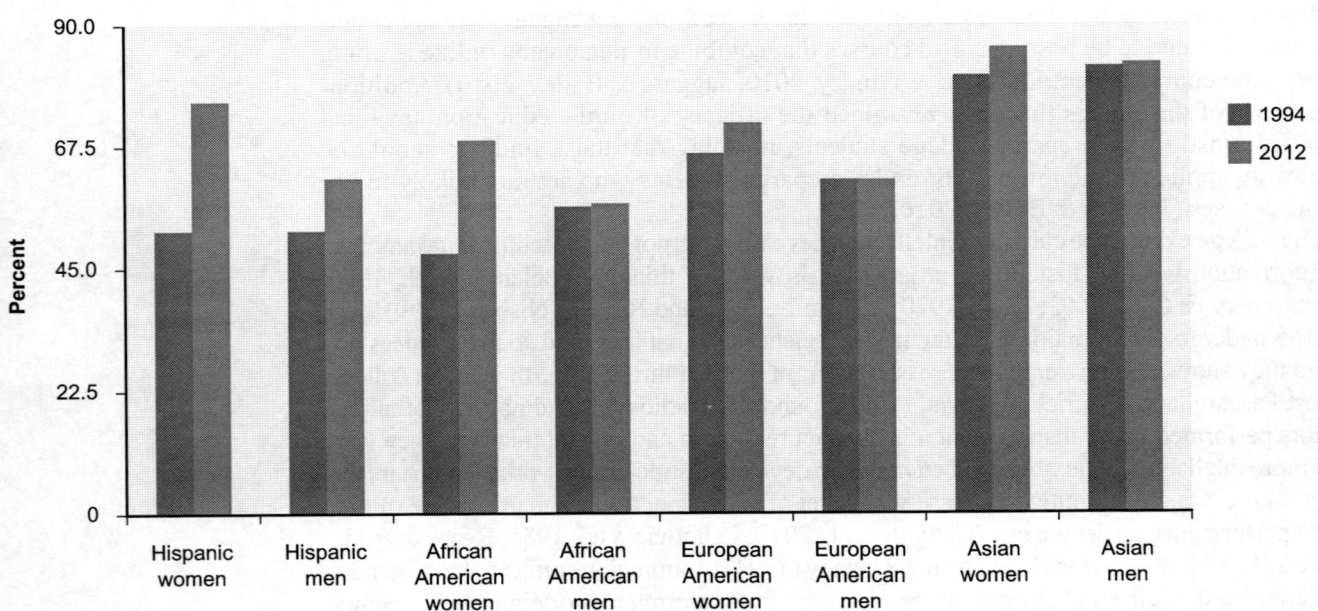

FIGURE 12.5 Percentage of Recent High School Graduates Enrolled in College by Gender and Race/Ethnicity in 1994 and 2012

Over the last few decades, the college population has become more racially and ethnically diverse. Much of the gains in diversity are due to more Hispanic and African American women attending college.

Source: Lopez & Gonzalez-Barrera, 2014.

> **What Do You Think?**
>
> Think about the ways that your college tries to encourage students to feel connected to the campus community. What are they doing well? What kinds of things do you think they could implement to make students feel more engaged?

with lower levels of education are less likely to attend college, and men who live in regions where there are construction and manufacturing jobs, typically held by men, are more likely to opt out of college to begin making money immediately (Buchmann & DiPrete, 2007; Jacob, 2002). Among women, particularly those from families with lower levels of education, there has been an increase in college attendance and completion, and it seems that as our economy and society have changed, women have more of a social and financial incentive to complete college (Buchmann & DiPrete, 2007).

More minority students are attending college more than ever. What about the college experience for minority students? African American and Hispanic American students are less likely than European American students to complete their bachelor's degree within six years (Museus & Quaye, 2009; U.S. Department of Education, 2016a). Minority students often report feeling disconnected on college campuses—that the campus does not support or understand their cultural differences, that minority groups tend to segregate, and that the faculty and staff are mostly European Americans who do not fully understand their culture (Museus & Quaye, 2009; Walton & Cohen, 2007). Students at predominantly African American campuses reported greater satisfaction because the social support systems assisted students in their social, cultural, emotional, intellectual, and spiritual development, and fewer incidents of misunderstanding or hostility enabled students to adjust better on these campuses (Hughes, 1987). Minority students also benefit from having a diverse faculty and staff on campus representing different races and ethnicities and value academic achievement and success (Museus & Quaye, 2009). Researchers point out that colleges and universities must help minority students to develop academically, socially, and personally, or they will become increasingly segregated (Cheatham & Berg-Cross, 1992; Gosman et al., 1983; Ponterotto, 1990; Wright, 1987). Walton and Cohen (2011) developed a simple intervention in which first-year college students read an account of an older student who felt lonely and homesick as a freshman but nurtured close friendships over the course of college. The first-year students then wrote a speech about how their experience thus far in college was like that of the account that they read. This intervention resulted in higher GPAs, higher ratings of well-being, and better ratings of overall health among African American students (Walton & Cohen, 2011).

College is one of the major events of early adulthood. For many people, it is the first step in the transition from adolescence to independence. The next step is establishing a career; for those who do not go to college, work is often the path to independence.

Work

Work is a major social role of adult life; it forms a critical part of one's identity. One of the first questions we ask when we meet someone new is "What do you do?" Except for the few who are very rich, adults need to work to support themselves and their families.

Experience with work generally starts long before an individual reaches adulthood. Many children set up lemonade stands or do chores for relatives or neighbors to earn spending money. Teenagers often baby-sit, mow lawns, walk dogs, or get part-time jobs. Work starts early in life and develops and changes throughout the life cycle. During early adulthood, individuals typically establish an occupation or a career. *Occupation* refers to all forms of work, whereas *career* usually refers to professional occupations such as doctor, teacher, lawyer, or engineer. In addition to providing economic rewards, one's occupation helps to define one's self, gives structure to one's life, establishes a context for relating to other people, organizes one's time, and gives meaning to one's life.

Transition to Work

The transition from school to employment is a major milestone of emerging adulthood. Though some make that transition right out of high school, as noted in the previous section, most young people spend some time in higher education. This is due, in part, to increasing demands of jobs to be not just educated, but to be flexible thinkers with some technical skills to succeed in the increasingly global job market (Karoly, 2009). Dietrich and Salmela-Aro (2016) have developed a model to examine the transition into the workforce in which we first examine possible careers and adjust our career goals based on how attainable those careers are and our evaluation of if a career would be a good "fit" for us. Once we have decided upon and prepared for that career, we disengage from our education and begin engaging with work that we, ideally, find enjoyable and fulfilling. Our success in this transition is dependent on finding employment, the support of friends and family, developing social ties at work as well as factors such as our race/ethnicity, social status, and gender, which we will explore later (Dietrich & Salmela-Aro, 2016; Marshall & Butler, 2016).

As noted in the Dietrich and Salmela-Aro model, transition to work includes self-exploration to discover one's interests, talents, and preferences (2016; Greenhaus, 1988). It includes training, such as college or vocational school, apprenticeship, or on-the-job skill development. It should also include learning about the actual work one does on the job. Many academic programs now include internships to give students the opportunity to learn about jobs that interest them, as well as to learn skills necessary for the jobs. This on-the-job experience can help reduce *reality shock*, the disappointment felt when the actual experience of being on a new job fails to meet the unrealistic, often idealistic expectations. Reality shock is common (Reilly et al., 1981). It occurs when a new teacher realizes that being a teacher includes lunchroom duty, parent conferences, and many other practical tasks that do not involve planning curriculum and working with students, or when a new reporter discovers that not all stories she will cover are exciting or even interesting.

One's early career involves gaining competence on the job as well as developing a balance between fitting into the organization and learning about other options and directions for one's career (Deitrich & Salmela-Aro, 2016; Greenhaus, 1988). Because of the increasing incidence of career changes, career and occupational counselors need to encourage people just beginning their first jobs to think about career change options (Keller, 1985). The early career stage also involves developing a balance between work and nonwork commitments. Given the challenges of establishing this balance, it is not surprising that older people tend to be more satisfied with their jobs than younger people are. As we will see in Chapter 14, there are many reasons for this difference.

Other factors play a role in career development as well. Sometimes a person cannot achieve personal goals because of an inhospitable or discriminatory work environment, as we will see next.

Gender, Race, Sexual Orientation, Gender Identity, and SES in the Workplace

If we look around us, it is easy to see that women and minorities are not equally represented in all occupations. Gender, race, sexual orientation, gender identity, and socioeconomic status (SES) affect which jobs people attain. Sociologists define **discrimination** as the valuation in the labor market of personal characteristics of a worker that are not related to productivity. Discrimination can be based on differences in prework experiences, such as educational background, health, and marital status, or on prejudice on the part of employers, coworkers, or customers (Thornborrow & Sheldon, 1995). An employer that requires a high school diploma even though one is not necessary for doing the job is practicing discrimination, as is a patient who will see only a male doctor. Women, racial/ethnic minorities, sexual minorities, and individuals from lower socioeconomic backgrounds experience differential treatment before they enter the labor force and continue to face it once they are employed. These factors account for their overall lower incomes and status in the labor market.

discrimination In terms of the labor market, the valuation of personal characteristics of a worker that are not related to productivity, such as educational background, health, and marital status, or based on prejudice on the part of employers, coworkers, employees, or customers.

In addition to gaining competence on the job, during her early career, this woman must learn about other work options and develop a balance between work and nonwork involvements.
Source: PhotoSky/Shutterstock.

How do women fare in the world of work? In 2015, women made up 43 percent of the full-time labor force and 57 percent of all women (70 percent of working mothers) were in the labor force (U.S. Department of Labor, 2015). The median annual earnings of women working full time were 79 percent of men's (U.S. Department of Labor, 2014). African American women earn 61 percent of what European American men earn, and Latina women earn just 54 percent of white men's earnings (U.S. Department of Labor, 2014). All of these statistics represent significant gains for women over the twentieth century. However, women still face serious discrimination in hiring and evaluation and are less likely than men to be promoted to upper-level managerial positions, and when they do reach leadership positions, it is often in companies that have a diverse group making decisions about the company and hiring (Cook & Glass, 2014; *Good for Business,* 1995).

Though there is the perception that racial discrimination in the workforce is no longer a problem, racial and ethnic minorities face disparities in pay and employment (Pager & Shepherd, 2008; U.S. Department of Labor, 2014). Applicants to jobs with African-American-sounding names like Lakisha or Jamal were less likely to be called back for an interview than applicants with European-American-sounding names like Emily or Greg in a field experiment (Bertrand & Mullainathan, 2004). In a study of African American, Latino, and European American workers, 37 percent of African American and Latino participants reported high levels of racial discrimination compared to only 10 percent of European American workers (Krieger et al., 2006). A breakdown of workplace discrimination can be found in Figures 12.6 and 12.7.

Discrimination in the workplace is not limited to racial and ethnic minorities and women. Gay, lesbian, and bisexual (LGB) individuals regularly face discrimination with 15 to 43 percent reporting that they had experienced some kind of discrimination (Badgett, Lau, Sears, & Ho, 2007). Among the most common types of discrimination regularly experienced by LGB workers include being fired, being denied a promotion, being paid unequally, or, the most common, being verbally or physically abused (Badgett et al., 2007). Additionally, transgendered individuals experience alarmingly high rates of discrimination, with between 20 and 57 percent reporting similar types of discrimination to LGB individuals (Badgett et al., 2007). Perhaps most concerning about the discrimination faced by LGB and transgendered individuals is that in most states it is completely legal. As of 2016, twenty-eight states had no laws protecting citizens from discrimination based on sexual orientation or gender identity, three states prohibited discrimination based on sexual orientation, and nineteen states had protections from discrimination for both sexual orientation and gender identity (American Civil Liberties Union, n.d.).

FIGURES 12.6 AND 12.7 Workplace Discrimination in Hiring and at Work

African American and Latino men and women experience discrimination in hiring and at work at a higher rate than European American men and women. African American men are most likely to report experiencing more frequent discrimination both at work and in hiring practices. Figure 12.7 also shows that both African American and European American women are likely to experience discrimination in the workplace.

Source: Krieger et al., 2006

FIGURE 12.6

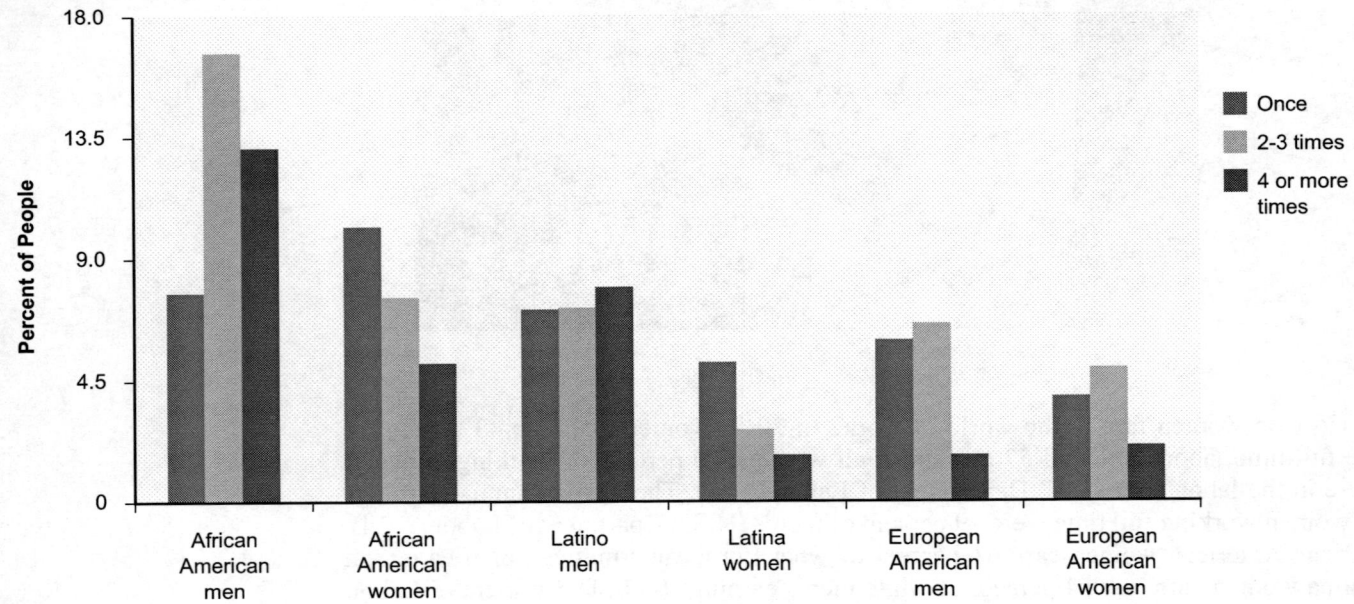

FIGURE 12.7

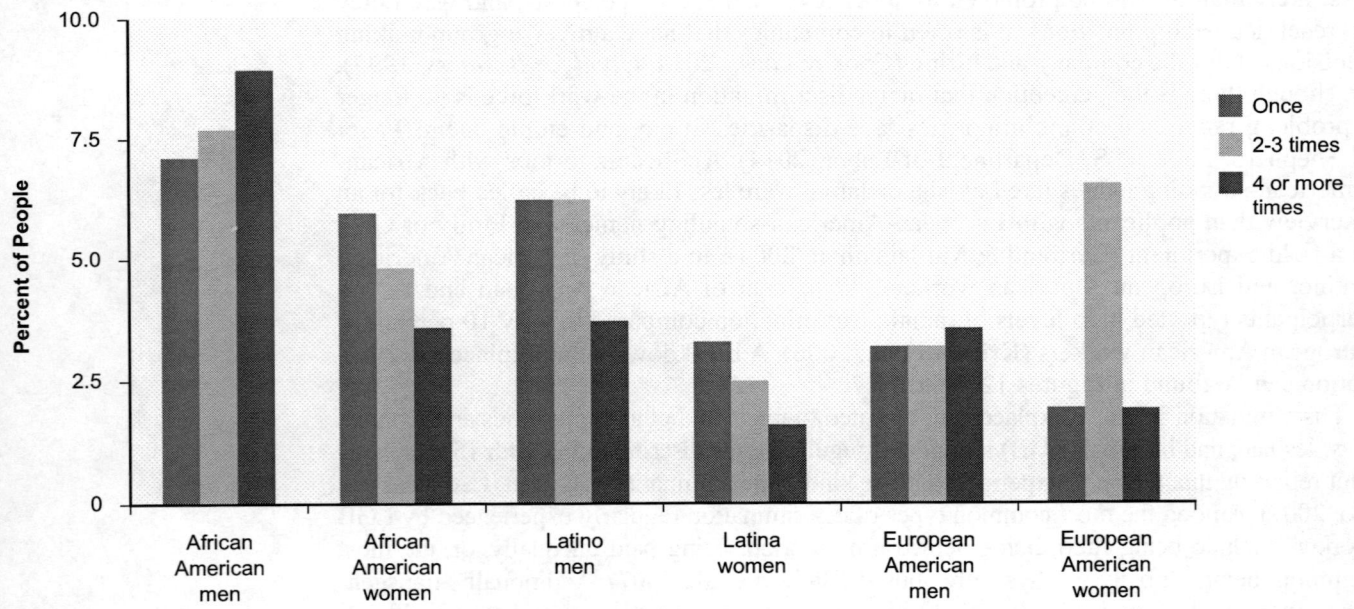

Occupational Segregation

occupational segregation
The reality that most jobs in the United States are held by females (e.g., typists) or males (e.g., architects) and few are truly integrated.

Most jobs today are held by either men or women; few are truly integrated. This situation is called **occupational segregation**. In 2009, for example, more than 95 percent of electricians were male and more than 95 percent of dental hygienists were female (Hegewisch, Liepmann, Hayes, & Hartmann, 2010). Whereas over the past fifty years women have been entering traditionally male occupations, men have not been entering traditionally female occupations. Women have been able to make much greater inroads into male-dominated professions than into male-dominated blue-collar jobs. In 2009, for example, fewer than 5 percent of carpenters were women. Occupations that depend on education have been more receptive to women than have occupations that require physical strength and skill (Lips, 1993). As we saw in the last section, women today are more likely to attend college than men are. Having a degree gives them proof of their qualifications for professions, but does not help them enter jobs that require on-the-job training. In a study of more than fifteen hundred individuals, Patricia Gurin (1981) found that white and African American women had tried job training or job changes less often and had acquired additional schooling more often than white or African American men. The largest gains for women have been in the higher-paying executive, administrative, and managerial positions (Thornborrow & Sheldon, 1995). However, when an occupation is made of predominantly female workers, the wages tend to be lower for those jobs, and this relation is particularly true for jobs that require a professional degree such as law or medicine (Hegewisch et al., 2010).

Sexual Harassment

Another factor that limits women at work is sexual harassment. Although **sexual harassment** typically is defined as unwelcome sexual behavior in the workplace, it is best understood as a subtype of aggression directed toward women by men with whom they are often acquainted or intimate and that limits the victim's ability to function effectively on her job (White & Kowalski, 1998). Harassment can include physical or verbal abuse or unwelcome sexual advances. It can also include a *hostile work environment* in which coworkers refuse to work cooperatively with the victim, interfere with the victim's work, make sexually explicit comments to the victim, or display suggestive images. Because men almost always have more power than women in the workplace, they are almost always the ones who harass. That does not mean that women are the only targets of sexual harassment: in 2011, 16.3 percent of sexual harassment claims were made by men (U.S. Equal Employment Opportunity Commission, n.d).

Harassment has many important characteristics in common with rape and spouse abuse. All include violence or threat of violence. All are situations in which the less powerful are victimized by the more powerful and left feeling more powerless as a result. All are kinds of violence that are trivialized. Victims are accused of "asking for it," or "making it up," or "making a big deal about nothing." All three types of violence are exaggerations of traditional gender roles that encourage men to be dominant and aggressive and women to be submissive and yielding. And in all three there is a tendency to "blame the victim" for the violence she or he has suffered.

Differences Between Jobs

Economists divide jobs into two categories, which they call the primary and secondary sectors. The *primary sector* includes high-wage jobs that provide good benefits, job security, and advancement opportunities. It includes professional jobs that require training and certification as well as some manufacturing jobs that offer relatively high wages and job security. The *secondary sector* includes low-wage jobs with few benefits and little advancement opportunity. The white-collar jobs in this sector include sales and clerical; the blue-collar jobs include private household, laborer, and most service jobs. It is very hard to move between sectors, because no career ladders connect the two types of jobs. Pat, for example, started as a departmental secretary and worked her way up to become the dean's secretary. When a new dean was hired, she did the work of an administrative assistant, because she knew the system better than he did. When it was time to hire an assistant dean, however, Pat was not considered because she was a secretary, not a managerial employee. Pat left the secretarial position and returned to college, which will enable her to get a job in the primary sector.

How do ethnic and racial minorities fare in terms of the job sectors? Teresa Amott (1998) reports, "For decades, the majority of women of all racial-ethnic groups, along

sexual harassment
Unwelcome behavior that limits the victim's ability to function effectively on the job. Although men are occasionally victims, it is best understood as a subtype of aggression directed by men toward women with whom they are often acquainted or intimate.

> **What Do You Think?**
>
> Has occupational segregation had any influence on the jobs you have had so far and/or the occupation you would like to enter? If so, how has it influenced your life? Has it affected what you think you can do?

with most men of color, were found in the secondary sector" (p. 239). This means they tend to have less desirable jobs and less job security than white men do. In 2016 the unemployment rate for whites was 4.2 percent, whereas for African Americans it was 8.3 percent and for Hispanics 5.6 percent (U.S. Department of Labor, 2016). Minority men earned less than white men, and women in each category earned less than the men in that category. Various factors contribute to the income differentials, including prejudice against minority workers, different access to education, and internalized negative self-images as an effect of racial/ethnic discrimination.

Growth and Change

As we have seen, early adulthood is a time of cognitive growth in response to higher education and the increasingly complex responsibilities that typically accompany this period. Emerging and young adults change as they meet the challenges of finding an occupation, establishing new friendships and families, and maintaining relationships with the families that raised them. As our discussions of physical and cognitive development indicate, the social context has a major impact on all aspects of development. In the next chapter, we direct our attention to psychosocial development in early adulthood.

Chapter Summary

- **Why is early adulthood typically a time of physical well-being?** Young adults are at the peak of their physical functioning. They reach their full height, their body systems are fully mature, and they are unlikely to exhibit many noticeable signs of aging. Age-related changes begin in many body systems during early adulthood, but the declines are gradual. The cardiovascular and respiratory systems show the most noticeable changes by age forty.
- **How do adopting health behaviors and avoiding health-compromising behaviors contribute to the quality and longevity of adult life?** Young adults generally feel healthy. Although diseases may be present, they are likely to be in early stages, undiagnosed, and unsymptomatic. Many of the losses in functioning suffered by aging adults are due to pathological aging resulting from unhealthy environmental conditions and health-compromising behaviors rather than to normal aging. Young adults can set the stage for healthy aging by eating a healthful diet, doing regular aerobic exercise, controlling their weight safely, and avoiding smoking, alcohol and drug abuse, and unsafe sex.
- **What is stress, and what is its relation to illness?** Stress is arousal of the mind and body in response to demands made on them by stressors. The general adaptation syndrome, a pattern of physical response to stress, accumulates to lay the groundwork for disease. Stress has psychological dimensions as well. Negative, uncontrollable, ambiguous, or overwhelming events are perceived as more stressful than positive, controllable, clear-cut, or manageable events.
  Stress contributes to illness in multiple ways. It can have a direct physical effect that wears down the physiological system. It can affect people with personalities that predispose them to stress. It can also contribute to illness by negatively influencing health behaviors.
- **In what ways are women and men similar in their sexual responses? In what ways do they differ? What treatments are available for infertility?** The sexual response cycle has five stages—desire, excitement, plateau, orgasm, and resolution—and is very similar for men and women. People's beliefs about sexual

morality are part of a broader social outlook that affects sexual practices in some ways but not others. Sexual dysfunctions are not uncommon; both men and women often complain of low sexual desire. For women, orgasmic problems are a frequent complaint. For men, ejaculatory problems and erectile dysfunctions are common problems.

Infertility, inability to conceive a pregnancy after one year of sexual relations without contraception, affects a substantial minority of couples at some time in their reproductive lives and often leads to psychological reactions of grief, anger, and guilt. Surgical and drug treatments are used for both male and female infertility, depending on the causes. When they fail, reproductive technologies may be used, but they are expensive and carry some health risks.

- **In what ways does adult thought differ from adolescent thought?** Cognitive theorists have proposed a fifth postformal stage of adult thought characterized as relative and nonabsolute, accepting contradiction, and synthesizing contradiction. Schaie's stage theory of intellectual development includes three or four stages that go beyond Piaget's formal operations and reflect the goal-directed and contextual nature of adult thinking. Examination of the development of critical thinking has led to an understanding that mature thought depends on the context of the event and the framework of the knower.

- **Why are gender and context important to adult moral development?** Studies of adult moral reasoning indicate that the context, or situation, of the problem may be more important than gender in influencing whether a justice or care orientation is used. As young adults become able to understand different ethical perspectives, they also become capable of finding their own spiritual meaning, or faith.

- **How does attending college contribute to cognitive development?** The college experience fosters intellectual development. Although different types of schools provide different benefits, the biggest difference in cognitive growth is found between adults who attend college and those who do not.

Today's college student body is diverse in terms of age, gender, and race/ethnicity. Older students often go to college for different reasons than younger students. More women than men go to college. Racial/ethnic minorities face an inhospitable climate on predominantly white college campuses and need more social support services than are currently provided.

- **What is the transition to work like for emerging adults, and how are they affected by gender, race, sexual orientation, gender identity, and SES?** Work is a critical part of adult life that helps to define the self, give structure to life, and provide means of support. Work starts early and continues throughout life, but with different emphases or stages. Gender, race, sexual orientation, gender identity, and SES affect which jobs people are likely to attain. Discrimination and occupational segregation channel white men into the primary sector of the economy and African American men, as well as all women, into the secondary sector. Sexual harassment, a subtype of aggression directed by men toward women, also limits women in the workplace.

Key Terms

achieving stage (p. 447)
acquaintance rape (p. 438)
acquisitive stage (p. 447)
basic dualism (p. 448)
contextual relativism (p. 448)
discrimination (p. 458)
executive stage (p. 448)
general adaptation syndrome (p. 434)

health-compromising behaviors (p. 424)
infertility (p. 442)
legacy-creating stage (p. 448)
occupational segregation (p. 460)
organ reserve (p. 422)
pathological aging (p. 424)
postformal thought (p. 445)

posttraumatic stress disorder (PTSD) (p. 437)
reintegrative stage (p. 448)
responsible stage (p. 448)
sexual dysfunction (p. 440)
sexual harassment (p. 461)
stranger rape (p. 438)
stress (p. 434)

Psychosocial Development in Early Adulthood

CHAPTER 13

Source: bikeriderlondon/Shutterstock.

Chapter Outline

Theories of Adult Development
Intimate Relationships
Marriage, Divorce, Remarriage, and Singlehood
Parenthood
Looking Back/Looking Forward

Focusing Questions

- According to key lifespan theories, how does development in emerging adulthood and early adulthood differ from development in childhood and adolescence?
- What are the various forms intimacy can take in early adulthood?
- In what ways have marriage and divorce changed in the last few decades?
- What are the lifestyle choices for young adults who choose to not marry?
- What is the impact of parenthood on couples, single parents, and remarried parents?

Dai is twenty-six. He has been living with his girlfriend, Marta, who is twenty-five, for six months. They met in college. Dai had been working for a year as a part-time tutor at the Writing Resource Center when, at the beginning of their junior year, Marta joined the staff. Each was already involved in a romantic relationship, but Marta and Dai became friends. They found they had a lot in common: both came from the same area of Connecticut, and they knew a few of the same people. They would chat at the Writing Resource Center and sometimes go out for coffee.

During their senior year, the nature of their relationship changed. Both had ended their romantic relationships over the summer, and they began to spend more and more time together. By second semester, Dai and Marta were a couple in a healthy, emotionally supportive sexual relationship. That was four years ago.

After graduation, Dai got a job as a reporter for a newspaper in Connecticut; Marta entered law school in Massachusetts. Dai worked four long days, Monday through Thursday. After work on Thursday, he would drive to Boston and stay with Marta until Monday morning, then drive back to work. Marta studied much of the time Dai was with her, but they liked being together and he used some of the time to look for a job in the Boston area. Before Marta completed her first year of law school, Dai found a job in the area and moved to a town outside of Boston. Although he would have liked to live with Marta, she had a lease and a commitment to roommates, and he felt he needed experience living on his own. They liked being closer, but each was very busy, so they still saw each other mostly on weekends and one night during the week. By the time Marta graduated from law school, Dai had a new job as assistant editor for a magazine, and they were ready and eager to look for a place to live together.

As you can see, Dai and Marta have faced the developmental tasks that are paramount in early adulthood. They have simultaneously begun the key tasks of establishing an intimate relationship, embarking on careers, and establishing independence from their parents. Much more still lies ahead. Marta has yet to find a full-time position as an attorney. Dai is balancing the benefits of on-the-job advancement and getting a graduate degree. Both will have to decide about marriage in the next few years, and both say they want children while they are still young. These challenges are easy to anticipate, but they will face many others.

Theories of Adult Development

Contrary to what many believe, reaching early adulthood is not the end of development, but it does mark a significant change. Physical maturation plays a key role in child and adolescent development and paves the way for new challenges at similar ages. As we saw in Chapter 12, physical changes in early adulthood have little effect on behavior. This continues to be true in middle adulthood for most individuals and in late adulthood for many. Biology has much less to do with adult development than do cultural, social, and personal factors, which serve as the impetus for lifelong growth. As adults face new challenges, they develop new behaviors, cognitive skills, and ways of interacting. They take on new roles, which set the stage for new demands.

Though there are similarities in the challenges of adulthood, individuals can follow many different paths. Most individuals living in industrialized nations who go to college enter a period of emerging adulthood during which they are no longer adolescents but not quite adults (Arnett, 2000, 2016). During emerging adulthood, people become more independent from families of origin but have not taken on many roles that we see as being part of adulthood, such as marrying and becoming a parent. Adulthood is marked by much greater developmental diversity than childhood or adolescence, and this diversity increases with age. People may marry early, late, or never. They may become parents early, late, or never. These are just two examples of variability, and each represents a very different set of social roles and responsibilities adults will face at similar ages. Whether or not adults marry, they will still have similar needs to establish intimacy with other people. Whether or not they become parents, they will still have similar needs to pass on what they know and care about to the next generation.

Given the diversity of developmental paths during adulthood, theorists have had a difficult time devising a neat stage model of adult development. Theories of adult development focus on common elements in diverse experiences, paying particular attention to the two basic psychosocial needs of mentally healthy adulthood first articulated by Freud: to love and to work. These theories suggest the various changes most people can expect more than they describe a specific developmental pattern. The theories fall into two broad categories: timing of events theories and normative crisis theories. *Timing of events theories* focus on the importance of the developmental context to adult psychosocial development. They would predict that Dai will marry Marta in the next few years because he has internalized his family's expectations about when to marry and because his friends are marrying. In contrast, *normative crisis theories* focus on the importance of

The social clock tells if we are "on time" in following the age-appropriate timetable of our social group. These two "on time" mothers provide social support for each other in their transitions to parenthood. Social support from friends makes adjustment to significant life events easier.
Source: Monkey Business Images/Shutterstock.

stirrings within the individual, or inner crises. Because they highlight impulses within the individual, crisis theories are also considered to be psychodynamic theories, as Erikson's theory is (see Chapter 2). Crisis theories would predict that Dai will marry Marta in the next few years because of his inner needs for intimacy and emotional support now that he has separated from his parents. For Dai and Marta to marry, of course, Marta will have to feel similar social expectations or inner needs, depending on the theory.

Despite the differing premises underlying these theories, most tend to overlook differences due to gender, race/ethnicity, or socioeconomic status (SES) and to be based on white, middle-class, male experiences. They tend to focus on one developmental domain rather than trying to map all of adult functioning. Most theorists look at adulthood in its entirety, or at the entire lifespan, rather than focusing only on early, middle, or late adulthood. Thus, we will revisit many of the theories presented here in subsequent chapters.

Timing of Events: Social Clocks

Joe entered law school when he was thirty-two years old, married, and the father of two young children. Twelve years later, he feels he is behind in his career as an attorney because of his "off-time" schooling. What is the origin of his sense of what is appropriate at a given time? For one thing, comparisons with others in his social group. His agemates are already established in their legal careers and have entered what Schaie calls the *responsible stage,* as we saw in Chapter 12. In contrast, Joe's former classmates are in Schaie's *achieving stage.* Joe finds himself alone; his level of career development places him in the achieving stage, while his family's maturity places him in the responsible stage. As a result, Joe feels "off time."

One way to understand the consistencies among disparate lives is to recognize that social expectations create an internalized **social clock** that tells us whether we are "on time" in following the age-appropriate social timetable (Neugarten, 1968). Cultural groups tend to develop a shared sense of when men and women "should" leave their parents' home, become sexually active, marry, or have children (see Table 13.1). These social norms dictate when certain life transitions should occur, and people strive to time their major life events to match societal expectations. Social support from friends who are "on time" in going through a significant life event, such as parenthood, makes that experience easier for individuals within the group. The social life of the new parents changes in ways similar to their friends'. As a group, they can share resources and advice. Being "off time" does not necessarily have negative outcomes, but it often creates discomfort. In Chapter 15, Psychosocial Development in Middle Adulthood, we will see how family

social clock Bernice Neugarten's timing of events approach to understanding the consistencies among disparate lives. Cultural groups tend to develop a shared sense of when certain life transitions, such as marriage or retirement, should occur, and people strive to time their major life events to match societal expectations.

TABLE 13.1 Racial and Ethnic Differences in Role-Timing Desires

	Hispanic American	African American	European American	Asian American
Best age for intercourse	19.30	19.16	20.29	21.74
Best age for first birth	21.88	23.04	23.55	24.39
Desired age at marriage	22.10	24.48	23.17	24.02
Desired age at first birth	23.26	24.35	24.70	26.38

life cycle, another timing of events theory, emphasizes similarities within family stages that depend on the children's ages.

When Patricia East (1998) asked 574 girls, average age 12.9 years, questions about "'best" and "desired" timing of intercourse, marriage, and parenthood, she found significant differences between racial and ethnic groups. Notice, for example, that African American girls chose the earliest age for intercourse and the latest age for desired marriage, whereas Hispanic girls chose the earliest marriage and first-birth ages.

Since the 1960s, American society has become less rigid in its expectations of when significant life events should occur (Elzinga & Liefbroer, 2007; Neugarten & Neugarten, 1987). Although the social clock still ticks, the range of acceptable ages for graduating from school, marrying, or starting a family is wider. Taking time off before completing college or graduate school has become common. As global economies have changed, many people have extended their educations by attending college, graduate, and professional school, which, in turn, has shifted the expected timing of many life events to later in young adulthood (Syed, 2016). One study examining the timing of life events during the period thought of as emerging adulthood (age eighteen to twenty-nine) in nineteen different countries showed that overall, the order in which people complete tasks like getting married and having children has remained stable over time, but the timing of these events has changed (Elzinga & Liefbroer, 2007). Women take longer today than in previous generations to get married and have children because they are spending their emerging adulthood getting an education and starting a career (Kokko, Pulkkinen, & Mesiäinen, 2009). And women in the United States tend to show more variability than women in other nations in the order they experience these milestones (Elzinga & Liefbroer, 2007). Returning to school is acceptable at any age. Nonetheless, in everyday conversation people often refer to themselves as having been "early to marry" or "late to start a family," which indicates that although there may be more latitude, people still know when "on time" is. Age-graded roles have lessened in importance, but they have not disappeared. They have also changed. Jen's mother had Jen, her fourth child, at the exact age Jen is now; Jen and her wife have just begun thinking about having children. Both Jen and her mother are "on time" for their cohort, because expectations for women have changed considerably in a generation.

Though all developmental theories strive to describe and explain consistencies in development, timing of events theories are better able than normative crisis theories to explain developmental diversity among groups, or cohorts. Dissimilarities in marriage or retirement patterns in other times or within other cultures result from different shared expectations. Crisis theories, on the other hand, emphasize the internal normative crises adults experience and tend to underrepresent diversity.

Crisis Theory: George Vaillant and the Grant Study

Life abounds with events that require a constant series of adaptations. How men adapt determines their levels of physical health, mental health, and life satisfaction. These are the basic premises of George Vaillant's many years of work on the Grant Study, a longitudinal study of college men to follow the course of their development and see what led them to function effectively in work, play, and love (Vaillant, 1977; Vaillant & Vaillant, 1990). In 1937 a homogeneous sample of 204 white men who were attending Harvard were selected to participate because they seemed healthy. Vaillant notes that "the absence of women in the Grant Study was an unforgivable omission, an omission that will require another study to correct" (Vaillant, 1977, p. 13). Participants went through tests, physical examinations, and interviews while in college and completed detailed questionnaires and had physical examinations at regular intervals after graduation.

The Grant Study led Vaillant to three basic conclusions about adult development (Vaillant, 1977). First, growth and development are a lifelong process. The men in the study clearly showed evidence of intellectual and moral development throughout adulthood. Second, isolated events, unexpected or traumatic as they might be, rarely mold individual lives; rather, sustained relationships with other people are what shape lives. Vaillant found that the loss of a parent, for example, was less devastating in the long run than the continued relationship with a disturbed parent. Third, the **adaptive mechanisms**, or coping styles, that people use to adjust to life events determine their level of mental health. Vaillant categorized four types of adaptive mechanisms. *Mature mechanisms* include sublimation, the redirecting of anxiety and unacceptable impulses toward acceptable goals, and altruism. *Immature mechanisms* include *hypochondriasis,* or the development of ailments without physical bases, and fantasy. *Psychotic mechanisms* include distortions of reality, such as hearing voices. *Neurotic mechanisms* include irrational fears and repression (Vaillant, 1977). Across adulthood, the participants in his study were more likely to use mature mechanisms: adolescents (ages twelve to nineteen) were twice as likely to use immature mechanisms as mature ones, young men (twenty to thirty-five) were twice as likely to use mature mechanisms as immature ones, and midlife men (thirty-six to fifty) were four times as likely to use mature mechanisms as immature ones (Vaillant, 1977).

adaptive mechanisms George Vaillant's term for the coping styles that people use to adapt to life events and that determine their levels of mental health. Vaillant categorized four types: mature mechanisms, immature mechanisms, psychotic mechanisms, and neurotic mechanisms.

Love and Work in the Grant Study

Like Schaie and Greenhaus (see Chapter 12), Vaillant (1977) sees work as the focus of development between the twenties and forties, a period he calls **career consolidation**. During career consolidation the men tended to work hard, devote themselves to career advancement, and sacrifice play. As Table 13.2 shows, Vaillant sees the Grant Study as confirming Erikson's adult life patterns. Recall from Chapter 2 that Erikson saw the normative crisis of early adulthood to be intimacy versus isolation and that of middle adulthood to be generativity versus stagnation. Vaillant describes a similar progression of development: career consolidation fits between Erikson's stages of intimacy and generativity. Adolescence is the stage of forging identity by separating from parents. The twenties is a period for developing

career consolidation A stage George Vaillant identified as fitting between Erikson's stages of intimacy and generativity and occurring in one's thirties. The men Vaillant studied tended to work hard, devote themselves to career advancement, and sacrifice play.

TABLE 13.2 Adolescent and Adult Stages of Normative Crisis Theories Compared

	Grant/Vaillant	Levinson	Erikson
Adolescence	Forging identity Separating from parents (12–19)	Era of preadulthood Early adult transition (17–22) establishing independence	Identity versus role confusion
Emerging and early adulthood	Development of intimacy (20s) Career consolidation (30s)	Era of early adulthood	Intimacy versus isolation
Middle adulthood	Generativity 40s and 50s	Era of middle adulthood	Generativity versus stagnation
Late adulthood		Era of late adulthood	Ego integrity versus despair

intimacy. Young adult men replace adolescent friendships with mature ones and seek out a spouse. The thirties is a period for career consolidation.

Normative crisis theorists take a psychodynamic view of development. They see each developmental period as focused around an internally motivated crisis, such as the need for intimacy to overcome isolation in early adulthood, when adults turn to their parents less frequently. Normative crisis theories were developed in studies of middle-class males and tend to underrepresent the diversity of adult experience.

Career Consolidation for Women

How might the findings of the Grant Study apply to women, who did not participate in the study? For women in the same cohort as the men in the Grant Study, not very well. Few of those women went to college, and fewer developed careers. During early adulthood, most women in this cohort devoted their energies to raising families while their husbands focused on the development of their careers. What about contemporary women? Indeed, many go to college and develop careers. Nonetheless, women are less likely than men to separate the stages of forging identity, developing intimacy, career consolidation, and generativity (Jordan et al., 1991). It is likely that the progression of stages Vaillant describes would be less ordered in a contemporary sample of both genders.

Crisis Theory: Daniel Levinson's Seasons of Adult Lives

Daniel Levinson, at age forty-six, wanted to study the transition into middle age so he could better understand his own experience. His initial formulation of developmental stages in early and middle adulthood also comes from the study of men, although he later studied women. Levinson (1978) studied forty men between ages thirty-five and forty-five, a smaller and older group of participants than in the Grant Study. To ensure some diversity in levels of education, SES, and race/ethnicity, Levinson included four occupational subgroups: hourly workers in industry, business executives, university biologists, and novelists. In contrast to the Grant Study's longitudinal method, Levinson (1986) used what he calls the *biographical method* to learn about these men's lives. The **biographical method** entails reconstructing the life course by interviewing the person and using a variety of other sources, such as visiting the person's home and place of work and, in the case of Levinson's novelists, reading the novels and reviews. Each man was interviewed and given a series of tests. There was also a follow-up interview two years later.

biographical method Daniel Levinson's method for reconstructing the life course by interviewing the person and using a variety of other sources, such as visiting the person's workplace and home.

Based on the "biographies" of the forty participants, Levinson (1978) identified three eras, or "seasons," in the male adult life, as shown in Figure 13.1: the era of early adulthood, the era of middle adulthood, and the era of late adulthood. During each of these eras a man builds a life structure, which is the underlying pattern for his life at a given time. Significant relationships form primary components of the man's life structure, usually work and marriage/family. Dai's life, for example, includes significant relationships with his career and with Marta. As a man outgrows these structures, he moves into a transition during which he builds a new life structure for the new era. For instance, Joe has moved into a transition as he reappraises his current position in the law firm and readies himself to strike out on his own. Change goes on within each era, and then a transition is needed for the shift from one to the next. Although the content of life structures varies greatly from individual to individual, "the life structure develops through a relatively orderly sequence of age-linked periods during the adult years" (Levinson, 1986, p. 7).

Do Women Have the Same "Seasons"?

Daniel Levinson (1978) excluded women from his initial study because he believed they might well follow a different course of development. Between 1980 and 1982, he conducted a parallel study of forty-five women: fifteen homemakers, fifteen businesswomen, and fifteen academics (Levinson, 1996). His goal was to create a stage theory of adult development that took both genders into account.

Levinson found that women progress similarly to men in some respects and differently in others. First, women go through the same sequences of eras that men do, and at the

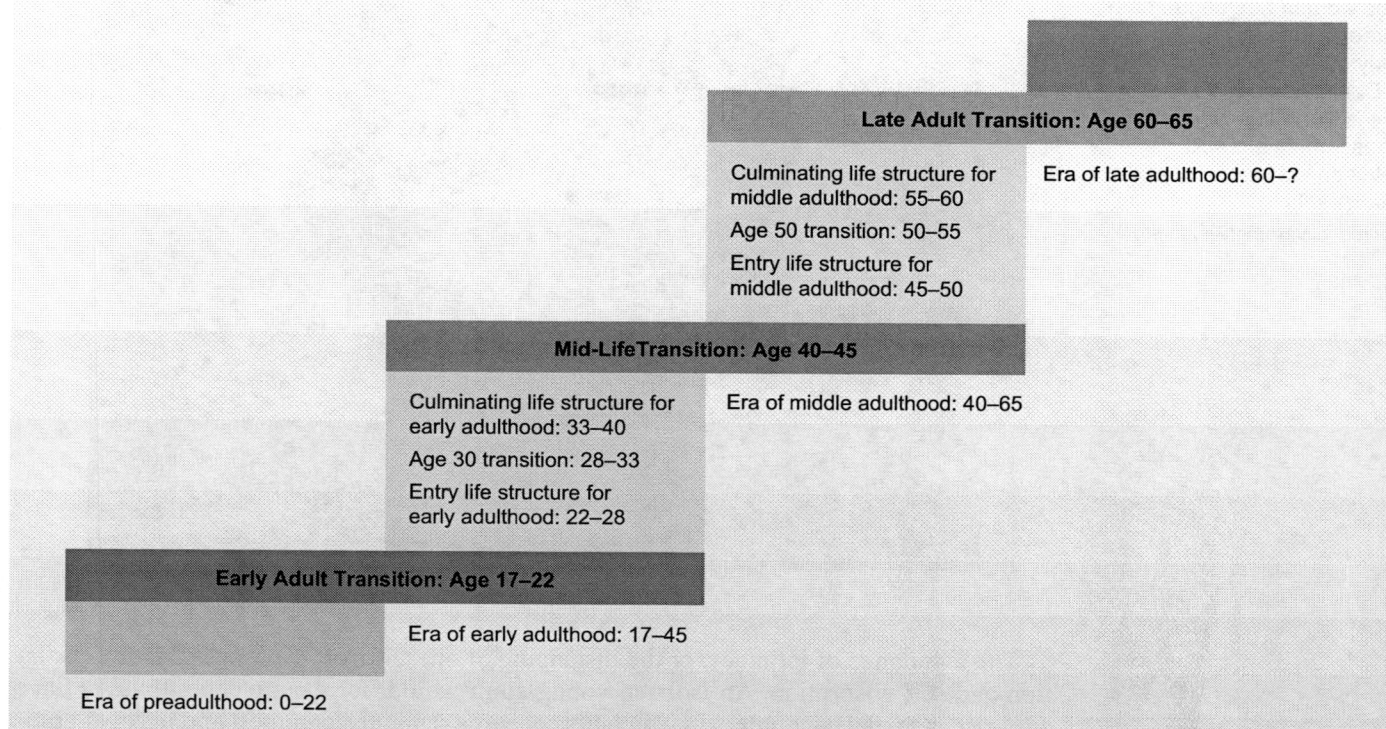

FIGURE 13.1 Levinson's Developmental Periods in the Eras of Early and Middle Adulthood

Each era, or season, is preceded by a transition that applies to both the earlier era and the coming era. Each era has three parts: the entry life structure, the transition, and the culminating life structure.
Source: Levinson (1986).

same ages (see Figure 13.1). Second, wide variations occur between and within the genders in the ways they traverse each period. Third, *gender splitting,* the sharp distinction between what is considered feminine and what is masculine, creates gender differences in the concrete life course. For example, Levinson found that although men could help with chores and participate in family events, they found it difficult to involve themselves in the intricacies of the domestic world.

Crisis Theory: Erik Erikson's Intimacy Versus Isolation

As we saw in Chapter 2, **intimacy versus isolation**, the crisis of early adulthood, follows and builds on Erikson's earlier stages of ego development. Trust versus mistrust, autonomy versus shame and doubt, initiative versus guilt, and industry versus inferiority precede the adolescent crisis of identity versus role confusion, in which the task is to develop a unique and integrated sense of self. During emerging adulthood, identity versus role confusion is still an issue. Emerging adults are learning about themselves, figuring out career plans, deciding the kind of person they might want to marry. We saw this with Dai and Marta as they became friends while in relationships with other people, and eventually decided that they preferred one another as potential partners. Essentially, emerging adulthood is an extended moratorium during Erikson's identity versus role confusion stage. During the intimacy versus isolation crisis, the young adult must develop the ability to establish close, committed relationships with peers and the ability to tolerate the threat of fusion and loss of identity that intense intimacy raises. As Dai and Marta have become closer, for example, Dai has begun to use the term *we* when he talks of plans and desires. This sharply contrasts with the strong *I* perspective he had as an adolescent. For Erikson, the development of identity is the necessary basis for establishing intimacy because true intimacy necessitates sacrifice and compromise, which require that you know who you are and what you want.

intimacy versus isolation The sixth of Erikson's psychosocial crises, in which young adults must be able to develop intimate relationships with others while dealing with the fear of loss of identity that such intimacy entails.

This woman has begun both career and family during her early adult years. According to Daniel Levinson's theory, she is like many women whose goals are split between achievement and relationships.
Source: oliveromg/Shutterstock.

The avoidance of intimacy, or the distancing of oneself from closeness, leads to isolation and self-absorption. An isolated young adult would, for example, continue to have adolescent sexual encounters in which his concerns remained conquest and his own gratification rather than reciprocally satisfying sex. Intimacy often includes sexuality, but not always. We can have intimate relationships with friends as well as romantic partners, and we can have sex with people with whom we are not emotionally close. Identity formation remains an issue in early adulthood, even as intimacy becomes a focus. As young adults face new life events and engage in new relationships, they redefine their sense of identity and alter their relationships.

Intimate Relationships

The need for intimacy, or attachment, begins at birth and continues throughout life. The first attachment, as you may remember from Chapter 5's discussion of psychosocial development in the first two years, is between the infant and the caregiver and changes as the child develops. Although attachment is a lifespan developmental process, developmental stages influence the nature of social relationships (Antonucci, 1990). We saw in Chapter 11 that during adolescence, friendships become important sources of loyalty and intimacy as relationships with parents became more strained. Nonetheless, adolescents continue to depend on parents for security when the going gets rough.

During early adulthood, attachment to friends and lovers increases while attachment to family decreases. Establishing independence requires gaining emotional independence from parents as well as setting up a separate residence. The safe-base function parents continue to provide for adolescents shifts during early adulthood to a significant other, a spouse, or a friend (Hazen & Shaver, 1990). This process of moving from a family with your parents to eventually become independent and have your own family is known as **recentering** (Tanner, 2006, 2016). Recentering is a three-stage process that starts during adolescence when we live with our family-of-origin but are legally adults and begin to act more independently (stage 1). During stage 2, which occurs during emerging adulthood, we move out, gain more independence, and gain skills and resources, but are still reliant on our family for some resources, such as a college student who relies on parents for financial support. Finally, as young adults, we become independent of our original family and begin careers and families of our own, or family-of-creation, while maintaining ties to our family-of-origin (Tanner, 2006, 2016). When Dai had a problem with his taxes, Marta was the first to hear about it and provide advice and emotional support. Only when he had calmed down and wanted additional expertise did Dai consult his mother who is

recentering A three-stage process in which individuals transition from being embedded in one's family of origin, become more independent, and eventually become completely independent of the family of origin and create a family of one's own.

> **What Do You Think?**
>
> Think of a life decision you are considering or have recently made. Construct a timing of events explanation and a normative crisis explanation. Which one better fits your vision?

knowledgeable about tax matters. He does not share many of his personal issues with his parents these days and discusses others with them only in retrospect putting Dai firmly in stage 3 of his recentering process.

Though Marta and Dai progressed through these stages at normative times, nearly half of emerging adults are delayed in meeting milestones like moving out of their parents' house (Seiffge-Krenke, 2016). One major reason for delaying such independence is finances: the job market is very competitive and entry-level positions do not pay well. A second reason is that emerging adults are relying on their parents for emotional support (Lanz & Tagliabue, 2007). A longitudinal study of emerging adults showed that those who lived independently tended to come from homes where parents gradually reduced their parental support and were more likely to have romantic relationships than those emerging adults living with their parents (Seiffge-Krenke, 2010). It seems that having parents who slowly decrease their support challenge their children to become independent and form securely attached relationships with friends and romantic partners (Seiffge-Krenke, 2016).

While parents and siblings continue to be important in young adults' lives, they are not as important as they were during the earlier life stages. We will see in Chapters 15 and 17 how secure attachment in early years results in continuing relationships with parents and siblings that contribute to health and happiness during middle and late adulthood. The developmental tasks of establishing an occupation, an independent household, and an intimate relationship push young adults to relinquish the primacy of their attachment to their parents and turn to peers for security.

Friendship

Friendship is one form of personal relationship that, while important throughout adult life, is particularly significant during emerging and early adulthood. As people transition from emerging adulthood to young adulthood, they relinquish dependence on their families and rely more on friends and romantic partners for intimacy and support (Markiewicz, Lawford,

During early adulthood, attachment to friends increases while attachment to family decreases. These young men prefer to engage in activities like basketball or go to a hockey game when they spend time with one another, which is typical of male friends. All close friendships include some shared activities and some sharing of confidences.
Source: XiXinXing/Shutterstock.

Doyle, & Haggart, 2006; Pulakos, 1989). Young adults felt closer to their friends than to their siblings, and they discussed most topics more frequently and engaged in most joint activities more often with friends (Pulakos, 1989). Mary Levitt, Ruth Weber, and Nathalie Guacci (1993) found that compared to their mothers or grandmothers, young adult women included fewer family members and more friends in their social networks and received more support from friends. In fact, many emerging and young adults have relationships with their friends that are very much like family relationships, and these individuals who act as de facto family are known as **fictive kin** (Muraco, 2006).

Adult friendship takes many different forms, which makes it hard to define. However, most researchers agree that the essential elements are its voluntary nature and its ability to provide at least some of the following: enjoyment, ego support, validation, stimulation, security, affection, intimacy, trust, acceptance, and companionship (Barry, Madsen, & DeGrace, 2016; O'Conner, 1992). High levels of practical support are not necessary characteristics of friendship (LaGaipa, 1990).

> **fictive kin** Constructed relationships, such as foster child or godparent, that by merging voluntary and obligatory relations take on the significance of blood kin.

Benefits of Friendship

Research consistently shows a positive relationship between friendship and individual well-being, especially mental health (Johnson, 1996). Friends bolster positive feelings by sharing activities, feelings, and ideas. They also serve as buffers against stress by providing intimacy and comfort during hard times such as the breakup of a romantic relationship, the failure to get a job, the death of a loved one, or a health crisis (Umberson, Crosnoe, & Reczek, 2010). Marta, for example, relies on Dai's encouragement as she sends out resumes and waits for interviews. His belief in her abilities, stories about his job searches, and computer assistance provide emotional and practical support.

Social relationships with friends have also been shown to encourage health-promoting behaviors such as healthy patterns of eating, exercising, and avoiding abuse of alcohol (House et al., 1988; Rakowski et al., 1988; Umberson, 1987; Umberson et al., 2010). A running buddy helps to keep you running, while a friend from a twelve-step program such as Alcoholics Anonymous (AA) helps you to face the challenges of quitting drinking. Friends encourage each other to seek medical attention when symptoms occur and encourage behaviors that reduce acute conditions, such as following special diets (Anson, 1989; Antonucci et al., 1989).

Gender Differences in Friendship

Although friendships answer basic human needs for intimacy and support, men and women tend to have different styles of friendships. When Dai and his male friends get together, they typically watch basketball or football on TV, play basketball, or talk about work or sports. When Marta sees her female friends, they talk about the issues in their lives: Marta discusses her job search, her relationship with Dai, a fight she had with her sister, what to wear to an interview. In friendships, men tend to define intimacy in terms of proximity and shared activities and interest, whereas women tend to define it in terms of emotional sharing of confidences (Barry et al., 2016). William Rawlins (1992) found that even when men and women talked with their friends about the same topics, women tended to do so in deeper and more self-revealing ways. The only areas of personal experience in which women appear to confide less than men do is their strengths, victories, and achievements (Cancian, 1986).

Both men and women experience intimacy within their friendships and share information with their friends equally, but men also tend to experience and display intimacy by engaging in activities (Radmacher & Azmitia, 2006). Feminine friendships involve providing and receiving emotional support, sharing problems, and being emotionally vulnerable; they are less likely to share activities (Cancian, 1986; Radmacher & Azmitia, 2006).

More typically, psychologists have focused on the advantages of the feminine style and highlighted it as the epitome of friendship (O'Connor, 1992). It provides emotional support for concerns and problems and helps to prevent loneliness. Almost all studies show that women have more close friends than men do and, at all stages of life, are more likely to have a friend in whom they confide. However, while intimacy of this kind has great benefits, it is not without costs. For instance, Kathryn Ratcliff and Janet Bogdan (1988) found that intimate friendships frequently were not helpful when a married woman lost her job because her friends believed she should not be working in the first place. The feminine style of friendship also imposes considerable costs in time and energy because it requires that a woman be available for friends in need.

As you read this section, you may well be thinking that your friendship style does not follow the gender stereotypes described. Several studies indicate more commonalities in men's and women's friendships than has previously been thought. Women and men both indicated meeting most often just to talk, less often to work on a task, and least often to deal with a relationship issue pertinent to the friendship (Duck & Wright, 1993). When asked about their friendships, men and women responded in stereotypical ways, but when the same relationships were looked at closely, men shared more feelings and women shared fewer feelings than they said (Walker, 1994). Paul Wright (1988) cautions against "dichotomous thinking" because "Virtually all close friendships involve shared interests and activities, various kinds of intimacy including self-disclosures and the sharing of confidences, emotional support, small talk, shop-talk and exchanges of tangible favors . . . . Rather we should think in terms of what qualities or characteristics are more typical on average of the friendships of women than of men and vice-versa" (p. 370). Both women and men find friendship deeply significant (Rawlins, 1992).

Single adults have more cross-gender friendships than any other group. Contact at work and school provides opportunities for men and women to become friends. Although cross-gender friendships are not considered inappropriate, especially for unmarried people, others often perceive them as unconscious or deceptive precursors to romantic involvement (West et al., 1996). Women have similar types of relationships with women and men friends that differ from their relationships with their partners. In contrast, men experience more self-disclosure, intimacy, and emotional involvement with women than with men and distinguish less closely between women friends and partners. As a result, men are more likely than women to consider cross-gender friends as potential romantic partners.

Friendships are particularly important to lesbian, gay, and bisexual (LGB) emerging and young adults who often feel alienated from their communities and families due to homophobia, which we will discuss later in this chapter (Barry et al., 2016). Gay and lesbian emerging adults report higher rates of depression and low self-esteem than heterosexual emerging adults, which might be buffered by having close relationships (Spencer & Patrick, 2009). In fact, many LGB young adults will form a fictive kin that serve many of the same purposes of close family ties (Muraco, 2006). There are some differences in with whom gay and lesbian adults have friendships: gay men have fewer but closer friendships with men than heterosexual men, and lesbian women have fewer female friends than heterosexual women (Diamond & Dubé, 2002).

Love

Intimacy is also an important ingredient of love. Although friendship is important, most young adults expect to find love in the form of a mate who will be a romantic partner and a friend and with whom life will be shared. Contemporary young adults are marrying later than did their earlier cohorts, so they typically have more experience with love relationships and more sexual partners before they marry (Michael et al., 1994; Shulman & Connolly, 2016). Nonetheless, each relationship is likely to be monogamous, resulting in a pattern of **serial monogamy**, or a series of committed, intimate relationships. Love differs from friendship, differs from person to person, and even differs within the same person. Like the person, love develops and changes over time.

serial monogamy A series of committed, intimate, sexually exclusive relationships with one person at a time.

The Triangle of Love

Robert Sternberg (1987) developed a triangular theory of love to explain the similarities and differences among love relationships. According to Sternberg, love has three essential components: intimacy, passion, and decision/commitment. *Intimacy* refers to feelings in a

> **WORKING WITH** Marilyn Kline, Suicide Hot Line Worker
>
> ### Helping Individuals Through Crises
>
> Marilyn Kline is a twenty-six-year-old college senior majoring in human services. With more life experience than the traditional-age college student, she is very sensitive to the problems young adults face. When we spoke, she was a paid worker at Helpline, a telephone counseling service that helps young adults who don't have friends to turn to for emotional support.
>
> **Michele:** *What is Helpline's purpose?*
>
> **Marilyn:** I think it serves several purposes. Mainly we give callers emotional support, pass on information about available services, and give referrals. Just today I got a call from a person who was really drunk; he felt awful and wanted to know where to go for help. After talking to him for awhile, I referred him to an AA meeting.
>
> **Michele:** *How do you know what to do in a situation like that?*
>
> **Marilyn:** You need to be able to listen responsibly, to be genuine and nonjudgmental. You can be trained to listen, but I think it helps to be a good listener to begin with.
>
> **Michele:** *What was the listening training like?*
>
> **Marilyn:** It was pretty extensive—five hours a week for eight weeks. We focused on active listening skills. We worked in small groups and did a lot of role plays. It felt like group therapy! The role playing helps you understand who you are and what issues you're dealing with, and that helps you help callers.
>
> **Michele:** *Who goes through the training?*
>
> **Marilyn:** Everyone who takes calls does. Most workers are volunteers who commit to working at least four hours a week for a year, but most people stay longer.
>
> **Michele:** *Who tends to call hot lines like yours?*
>
> **Marilyn:** Even though we're listed as a suicide prevention service, we get most calls from people who are having trouble handling their feelings. Maybe they're in an abusive situation, spousal or child, and don't know where else to turn. People who have recurring suicide thoughts and attempt to follow through will call. They're in crisis, and you help them get through it—to make a safety contact.
>
> **Michele:** *Do your callers tend to be younger or older?*
>
> **Marilyn:** Well, there's a range: I talk mostly to people between ages twenty and fifty. I know that two of my regular callers are college students.
>
> **Michele:** *Does that wide range match what you learned about suicide in your training?*
>
> **Marilyn:** Not really. Older white men have the highest suicide rates. Adolescent boys and young adult white males have the next highest rate. Then come elderly women and, last, adolescent girls.
>
> **Michele:** *You say that older adults have the highest suicide rates but most of your callers are young adults. Can you explain that?*

relationship that promote closeness, bondedness, and connectedness. Sternberg's definition of intimacy includes self-disclosing communication with the loved one, desiring to promote the welfare of the loved one, experiencing happiness with the loved one, holding the loved one in high regard, being able to count on the loved one in times of need, having mutual understanding with the loved one, sharing oneself and one's possessions with the loved one, receiving emotional support from the loved one, giving emotional support to the loved one, and valuing the loved one. His research indicates that not all of these elements are necessary at any one time to experience intimacy; the number varies for different situations and different people, as we will see in the upcoming discussion of gender differences in love. *Passion* refers to the expression of desires and needs for self-esteem, nurturance, affiliation, dominance, submission, and sexual fulfillment. Once again, the relative strengths of these needs vary among situations, individuals, and types of loving relationship. *Decision/commitment* includes both short-term and long-term commitment. *Short-term* refers to a commitment to love and *long-term* to a commitment to maintain that love. Marriage, according to Sternberg, represents the legalization of the commitment to maintain the relationship.

The three components of love have different properties and vary in different kinds of love relationships. Intimacy and commitment are relatively stable in close relationships,

> **WORKING WITH** Marilyn Kline, Suicide Hot Line Worker
>
> **Helping Individuals Through Crises** *continued*
>
> **Marilyn:** Young adults are more willing to ask for help outside the family than this generation of elders. Also, most callers at Helpline are young adults because they have problems with their families and have not established friendships they can turn to.
>
> **Michele:** *What's a typical call like?*
>
> **Marilyn:** A twenty-six-year-old woman is upset at her mother. She has two children, both under four, and is on welfare. Her husband is in jail. Her brother stays with her to help, but he drinks heavily and often abuses her. She's angry at her mother for her not being there when she was growing up and for not helping her now. She needs help.
>
> **Michele:** *What would you do for her?*
>
> **Marilyn:** Validate her feelings and offer emotional support. For callers like this, we're their support system, we're their friends, we're their family. We hear from them repeatedly.
>
> **Michele:** *How many calls would you expect on a typical shift?*
>
> **Marilyn:** Weekends are really busy. On my Saturday nights, I usually get about fifty calls. Of those, forty calls are for emotional support. One or two might be crisis calls, someone who's taken pills or has a loaded gun. We call a mobile crisis team at the associated clinic if the crisis warrants it. The rest of the callers need information and referrals.
>
> **Michele:** *Why do you think people need Helpline?*
>
> **Marilyn:** I think they need the communication we offer. Many of our regular callers just want to chat. They say hello and tell you what they did during the day. They don't have skills to talk about things with their friends. They have people around them, but they just don't feel comfortable talking about these issues with them. I think they appreciate that we're unconditional. They know there's a nice person on the other end of the phone who is willing to listen.
>
> **Michele:** *Do you find your work rewarding?*
>
> **Marilyn:** I really like to help people, and being on a hot line is the epitome of that. I don't honestly know why I love it so much, but I sure do. I love going there. I love being there for people. Sometimes the crisis team will call back to say that they got there and took the caller to the hospital. You know that what you did saved them.
>
> ### What Do You Think?
>
> 1. Many Helpline callers are looking for emotional support and companionship. To whom do young adults more typically turn? Why are emerging and young adulthood stages of life when people may lack secure personal relationships?
> 2. In what ways do the things Marilyn learned during training resemble skills that we all need to be good friends and romantic partners?

whereas passion is unstable and likely to fluctuate. In short-term romantic involvements, passion tends to play a large part, intimacy may play only a moderate part, and commitment plays no part at all. In long-term close relationships, intimacy and commitment play large parts while passion typically plays a moderate part. Passion tends to be most intense at early stages of a relationship and to be intermittent after that.

Different combinations of these three components characterize different types of love (see Figure 13.2). Sternberg describes seven possibilities (although liking is not actually a form of love):

1. *Liking:* Intimacy without passion or commitment. This describes many friendships. A relationship can be frustrating if one of the friends feels passion as well as intimacy and the other does not. Friendship can have some of the other elements as well as intimacy, but in that case it is more than liking.

2. *Infatuation:* Passion without intimacy or commitment. "Love at first sight" falls into this category, as does an infatuation with an unrealistic partner. Infatuation can be long-lasting, but only if it is unrequited.

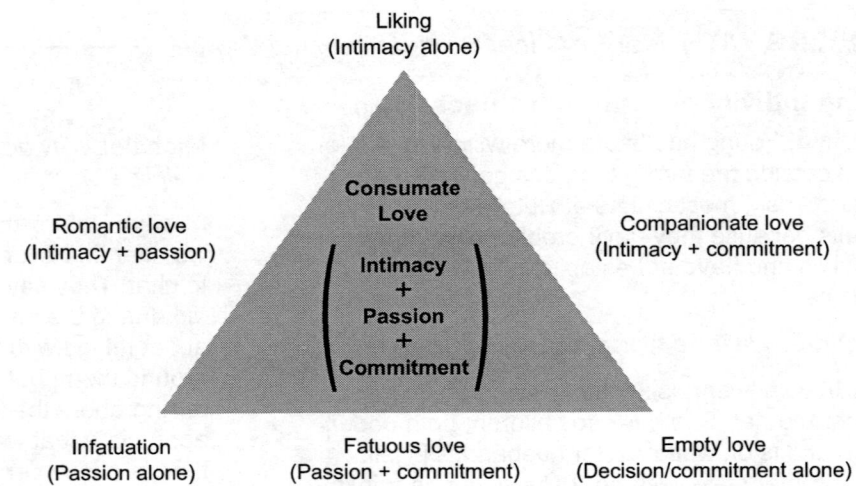

FIGURE 13.2
The Kinds of Loving as Different Combinations of Sternberg's Three Components of Love

The three components of love—intimacy, passion, and commitment—have different properties and vary in different love relationships. Consummate love consists of all three components in equal measure.
Source: Sternberg (1988).

3. *Empty love:* Commitment without intimacy or passion. This is a long-term relationship that has lost the intimacy and passion it once had. The people stay married because of their commitment to love each other rather than because of their feelings of love. Sternberg also points out that an arranged marriage may start out as empty love, but intimacy and/or passion may develop.

4. *Romantic love:* Intimacy and passion without commitment. This is the addition of physical attraction to liking.

5. *Companionate love:* Intimacy and commitment without passion. It is a long-term relationship in which the physical attraction has waned.

6. *Fatuous love:* Passion and commitment without intimacy. This is a "whirlwind" romance, often associated with Hollywood or with quick commitment on the rebound. Such a relationship is not likely to last.

7. *Consummate love:* Intimacy, passion, and commitment. This is what most of us are searching for: a balance of all the essential components in equal measure. It is hard to attain and, once you have it, takes work to maintain.

Sternberg's triangular theory of relationships is dynamic. Intimacy, passion, and commitment each change over time, and as a result the nature of relationships changes over time. Romantic love is difficult to maintain for a long period because passion is likely to wax and wane. This helps to explain why young adults who are not ready for long-term commitment often find themselves in a series of intimate relationships. Relationships take work, and work takes commitment. As Sternberg puts it, "Relationships are constructions that decay over time if they are not maintained and even improved. A relationship cannot take care of itself, any more than a building can. Rather, we must take responsibility for making our relationships the best they can be, and constantly work to understand, build, and rebuild them" (1987, p. 83). Table 13.3 shows the different types of love over the adult years.

Gender Differences in Love

Enduring love is a combination of instrumental qualities such as shared activities and expressive qualities such as shared feelings. We care for and assist our loved ones, and we express physical and emotional closeness to our loved ones. Women report significantly higher confidence in expressing liking, love, and affection to men than men do for women (Blier & Blier-Wilson, 1989). Consistent with the gender differences we saw in friendship, men and women seem to place different values on the instrumental and expressive aspects of love. Men consider practical help, shared physical activities, spending time together, and sex more important. Women place more emphasis on expressive qualities such as emotional involvement and verbal self-disclosure (Cancian, 1986). In line with this, one study had heterosexual couples

TABLE 13.3 Different Types of Love over the Adult Years

Adolescence	Early Adulthood	Middle Adulthood	Late Adulthood
Short-Lived			
Infatuation	Infatuation	Romantic love	Romantic love
	Romantic love	Fatuous love	
	Fatuous love		
Long-Lasting			
	Companionate love	Empty love	Empty love
	Consummate love	Companionate love	Companionate love
		Consummate love	Consummate love

talk about their first date while researchers recorded their behaviors and found that women engaged in more affiliation behaviors, such as smiling and leaning toward their partner, which is in line with companionate love, and men engaged in more sexual cues, such as touching or licking one's lips, which is line with more romantic love (Gonzaga et al., 2006). Most of us would probably choose a relationship that integrates both the masculine and feminine styles of loving, but women are much more likely to complain that their male partners lack verbal expressiveness, whereas men often do not understand this complaint because they express their feelings by doing so many things for their spouse (Tannen, 1990).

While adolescents often fall in love, they typically do so with unrealistic partners or with people they have only seen. During early adulthood, while most adults are experiencing short-lasting types of love, those who committed early may be moving into companionate and consummate relationships. All kinds of love are common during middle adulthood, when some make commitments for the first time, others are finding new love after divorce, and still others are in long-term relationships. During late adulthood romances still bloom, but many couples are in long-term relationships that have become empty, companionate, or consummate.

Though there are some gender differences in love, men and women think about it in similar ways. When eighty-three Hispanic American college students were asked, "What qualities and characteristics are important in a love relationship to you personally?" the top ten categories among women and men largely overlapped (Castañeda, 1993). Although the order differs, eight categories appear on both men and women's lists: trust, mutual respect, communication/sharing, honesty, friendship, shared values/attitudes, understanding, and compassion (Castañeda, 1993). The fact that men and women look for very similar qualities in a love relationship helps to explain why most succeed in finding partners.

Mate Selection

Emerging and early adulthood is a time when people look for partners, or mates. How do they find them? Many cultural myths lead us to believe that "opposites attract" or that we "will meet a stranger across a crowded room." These myths do not hold up to the scrutiny of scientific study. Similarities are what bring people together into romantic or sexual relationships (Murstein, 1988). Dai and Marta are a good example. They met on the same job on the same university campus and found they came from the same area and knew some of the same people. It seems that when potential partners first meet, they are attracted to one another based on how similar they think they are and physical attractiveness (Holmes & Johnson, 2009; Luo & Zhang, 2009; Tidwell, Eastwick, & Finkel, 2013). In the long term, partners who are complementary to one another in attachment style and personality remain together (Figueredo, Sefcek & Jones, 2006; Holmes & Johnson, 2009).

> **What Do You Think?**
>
> How have your intimate relationships changed from when you were an adolescent? In what ways, if any, have they become more important to you than family relationships?

Some people meet their partners in very conventional ways. They are introduced by people they know well, or they introduce themselves in familiar places where people come together because of their similarities. Throughout most of the 1900s, parents and friends, attending the same school or church, or living in the same community were the most common way people met their spouses (Rosenfeld & Thomas, 2012). However, since the rise of computers and the Internet, many more people are meeting their spouses online (Rosenfeld & Thomas, 2012). About 22 percent of heterosexual couples marrying today met online, and 60 percent of same-sex couples met online (Rosenfeld & Thomas, 2012). Some benefits of using online matchmaking services is that they provide access to a lot of information about many potential partners one might not otherwise meet (Finkel et al., 2012). Nonetheless, there are drawbacks of meeting online through dating services. Online profiles provide a limited view of potential partners and may lead to objectification of potential mates (Finkel et al., 2012). Moreover, there is no independent empirical evidence that the algorithms that dating sites use to match users actually work especially when evaluating the long-term feasibility of a relationship (Finkel et al., 2012).

As noted previously, online dating services might be particularly useful to emerging and young adults who identify as gay, lesbian, or bisexual (Rosenfeld & Thomas, 2012). This is due to several reasons. First, the proportion of the population who identifies as being lesbian, gay, or bisexual (LGB) is less than 4 percent, with emerging and young adults much more likely to identify as LGB with 6.4 percent identifying as LGB (Gates & Newport, 2012). Second, **homophobia**, which refers to fear, dread, hostility, or prejudice directed toward lesbian, gay, bisexual, and transgender (LGBT) people and the resulting mistreatment and discrimination, discourages many from the LGBT community from making their sexual identities public. Ethnic minority gay men and lesbians face the multiple stresses of coping with the gay and lesbian community's racism, the dominant culture's homophobia, and the homophobia of their own ethnic group (Greene, 1994). Because the ethnic community provides a protective buffer against racism, "coming out" may have greater costs for ethnic minorities. Even so, about 40 percent of Americans have a family member or friend who identifies as LGB, and as of May 2016, 61 percent of Americans support same-sex marriage (Morin, 2013; Gallup, 2016). Same-sex marriage has been legal in many European countries for some time now, and as of June 2015, same-sex marriage became legal in the United States. In most ways, marriages between gay, lesbian, bisexual, and heterosexual couples are very similar. Any differences will be discussed in the sections on marriage, divorce, and cohabitation later.

homophobia Fear, dread, hostility, or prejudice directed toward gay, lesbian, and bisexual persons and the resulting mistreatment and discrimination.

Marriage, Divorce, Remarriage, and Singlehood

Historically, almost everybody would experience their first marriage by the age of thirty. However, in 2010, only 53 percent of people aged twenty-five to thirty-four were married, and projections show that as of 2030, when those same people will be aged forty-five to fifty-four, a full 25 percent of those same people will still have never been married (Wang & Parker, 2014). Even so, marriage is an important part of young adulthood for many people. As we will discuss later in the chapter, marriage is not the only lifestyle choice of young adults, but it is the most frequent choice. Marriage is the socially sanctioned union of two people that, to some extent, symbolizes being an adult. It represents the establishment of a new household and the beginning of a new family, even though households and families do not necessarily begin with marriage. It is also the institution to which we look for love, companionship, and emotional gratification, and is the context for ego development (Bird & Melville, 1994). Because expectations for marriage are so multifaceted, societal change so prevalent, and people so varied, marriage itself is quite diverse.

Equal Partnerships

When asked about their ideal marriage, most people described an **equal-partner relationship** in which negotiating about shared concerns and responsibilities is the norm (DeStefano & Colasonto, 1990; Scanzoni, 1989). Everything (who works, who cooks, who pays the bills) is open for renegotiation except the principle that everything is negotiable. Instead of a preset assignment of roles and responsibilities, both partners expect change as they and their relationship grow and develop. This enables each partner to cultivate his or her capacity to function effectively both at home and at work. Equal partners would, for example, renegotiate household tasks if one of them faced a new job opportunity that required a longer commute. This form reflects the contemporary belief that each partner should be able to count on the loved one in times of need and to promote the welfare of the loved one, as we saw in Sternberg's theory of love.

Endorsing equal partnership as the ideal is not the same thing as having an equal-partnership marriage. Among heterosexual married couples, women put in about seventeen hours per week on housework while their husbands do about fourteen hours of housework (National Science Foundation, n.d.). The gap in housework time gets larger when couples have children. One study found that after the birth of a child, fathers put in an additional forty minutes of work each day, whereas mother's daily housework load increased two hours per day (Yavorsky, Kamp Dush, & Schoppe-Sullivan, 2015). We see here a pattern of women having what Arlie Hochschild (1989) has labeled the *second shift:* they work the first shift at their jobs and the second shift in the family. If sharing roles is the measure of equal partnership, very few marriages reach the ideal. While husbands of employed wives now help more at home, few men share the conventional female role of caring for home and family. Men who hold more traditional attitudes about gender roles spend less time on housework than men who hold less traditional attitudes, and in heterosexual marriages in which men have higher levels of education or in which men and women make similar amounts of money, they share household duties (Chesters, 2012). Among same-sex couples, household chores tend to be divided by preference rather than stereotypical gender roles, and it was far more likely in same-sex households for partners to share responsibility for activities such as laundry, household repairs, and childcare (Matos, 2015).

equal-partner relationship A couple relationship based on the principle of negotiating about shared concerns and responsibilities. Instead of a preset assignment of roles and responsibilities, everything (who works, who cooks, who pays the bills) is open for renegotiation except the principle that everything is negotiable.

Marital Satisfaction

What factors lead to different levels of satisfaction with marriage? Couples in more equal partnerships express the highest levels of marital satisfaction and psychological well-being. After reviewing many studies using many different measures, Steil (1995) concludes that "across these diverse measures the general pattern of findings seem to support equality as a desirable basis for marriage" (p. 154). Inequitable relationships cause distress in the form of a diminished sense of self-worth and negative judgments about the relationship (Keith & Schafer, 1991). Wives have fewer depressive symptoms when husbands help than when they do not (Steil, 1995). Couples that are satisfied with their division of household labor report greater marital happiness and lower marital conflict and aggression (Oshio, Nozaki, & Kobayashi, 2013; Stutzer & Frey, 2006; Suitor, 1991). In a comparison of LGB individuals who were either single, dating, in a relationship, or married, respondents who were legally able to get married demonstrated lower rates of stress and depression (Riggle, Rotosky, & Riggle, 2010). Moreover, a study examining patterns of interaction among heterosexual and homosexual couples, the initiator of arguments in gay and lesbian couples tended to utilize more positive emotions such as affection and humor in those discussions, and homosexual couples exhibited less tension, showed less domineering behaviors, and were less belligerent than heterosexual couples (Gottman et al., 2003). Lawrence Kurdek (1994) found that gay male couples do not differ from heterosexual men in their levels of relationship satisfaction (although gay men are more expressive than heterosexual husbands) and that lesbians do not differ from heterosexual

A Multicultural View

Cross-Cultural Similarities in Spouse Abuse

Young adults seek love and support from intimate partners, yet high levels of physical aggression against one's marriage or cohabiting partner are evident in almost all societies (World Health Organization, 2005). Although men and women report similar rates of being victims and perpetrators of intimate partner violence, common couple violence and female-against-male violence represent less severe cases of spouse abuse than male-against-female violence (Barber, 2008; Johnson, 1995). Even when both partners are violent, the experience and effects of violence are more physically damaging, more frightening, and more undermining of well-being for women than for men (Cantos et al., 1994; Ehrensaft, Moffitt, & Caspi, 2006; Ratner, 1998; Umberson et al., 1998).

In a cross-cultural study of women in both rural areas and cities of eleven different countries, the World Health Organization (WHO) found that the most common form of intimate partner violence (IPV) reported was being slapped by one's partner, with reports ranging from 9 percent in Japan to 52 percent in Peru (2005). In fact, Japanese women reported the lowest rate of physical or sexual violence (15 percent) while rural areas of underdeveloped countries such as Bangladesh (62 percent), Peru (69 percent), the United Republic of Tanzania (56 percent), and Ethiopia (71 percent) reported the highest rates of IPV (WHO, 2005). In the United States, the reported rate of IPV for the previous year is 2.1 percent for males and 2.3 percent for females, but lifetime rates of IPV including physical and sexual violence, are 35 percent for heterosexual women, 43.8 percent for lesbian women, 29 percent for heterosexual men, and 26 percent for gay men (Breiding et al., 2014; Walters, Chen, & Breiding, 2013). Particularly high rates of spousal abuse have been found among Hispanic and African American families in the United States (Capaldi, Knoble, Shortt, & Kim, 2012; Cazenave & Straus, 1990; Straus & Smith, 1990). What factors contribute to violence within the very relationships to which we turn to meet our most intimate needs?

Certain demographic, contextual, and structural characteristics of the perpetrators and victims of IPV seem to influence their levels of domestic violence. Factors that cause economic frustration, stress, and strain, which often include occupation, educational level, and income, increase the likelihood of partner abuse. All measures of high SES—educational level, occupational level, and income—as well as living in cohesive neighborhoods with low levels of violence are related to lower rates of IPV (Capaldi et al., 2012; Straus et al., 1980). Individuals who have witnessed or have been the object of aggression especially as children are more likely to be aggressive themselves (Capaldi et al., 2012; Umberson et al., 1998). Alcohol and drug usage is positively related to spouse abuse, and alcohol abuse among perpetrators and their partners seems to be a causal factor in cases of intimate partner violence (Capaldi et al., 2012; Julian & McKenry, 1993; Kantor & Straus, 1990; Stewart et al., 2006, 2008).

Two types of theories have been used to explain why, IPV occurs at all levels of SES, it appears more common and more severe among those with lower SES. The first theoretical approach focuses on structural factors associated with having fewer resources. When people lack status or money to control their lives, according to this theory, they use violence to gain a sense of control over at least one element of their environment, their mate (Umberson et al., 1998). Those with fewer resources generally experience higher levels of frustration and stress because they have fewer financial, emotional, and social supports to help them cope, and high stress and low self-esteem are risk factors for IPV (Capaldi et al., 2012). Individuals resort to violence to regain self-esteem when stress is high and resources are low.

The second theoretical approach focuses on cultural factors. According to this theory, people who grow up in cultural environments that expose them to more physical aggression and condone it, learn to be violent themselves (Stets, 1990). People who, as children, were physically punished engage in IPV and child abuse significantly more than those who were not (Capaldi et al., 2012; Straus & Smith, 1990). The culture of violence is very much affected by the socioeconomic forces that create high population density and high rates of unemployment, poverty, and crime in the inner cities (Capaldi et al., 2012; Zinn, 1989). In a dangerous environment, children and adults witness violence with some frequency and are more likely to see it as a necessary means of protection for themselves and their families. Parents see the risks of their children's misbehavior as potentially life threatening, and so are perhaps more likely to use physical punishment in this situation. Exposure to physical punishment adds to the experience of violence in the children's lives. The long-term effects of violence in daily life seem to be increased use of aggression within the family, because spouse abuse and child abuse are often linked (McKay, 1994).

Spouses in equal partnerships express the highest levels of marital satisfaction and psychological well-being.
Source: Iakov Filimonov/Shutterstock.

wives in their levels of relationship satisfaction. Lesbians and gay men report high levels of sexual satisfaction with their partners (Peplau & Cochran, 1990). William Masters, Virginia Johnson, and Robert Kolodny (1992) report that homosexual couples share more information about their sexuality and have better communication than heterosexual couples do.

What about comparisons between married and unmarried people? Married people in the United States generally fare better than unmarried people in terms of mortality, morbidity, mental health, and more general measures of psychological well-being (Friedman et al., 1995; Koball et al., 2010; Lee et al., 1991). While it is true that happier and healthier people are more likely to be selected as marriage partners, researchers agree that being married provides strong and important benefits (Stack & Eshleman, 1998; Stutzer & Frey, 2006). Formerly married people (divorced and widowed) have the lowest levels of well-being of all types, never-married people have intermediate levels, and married people have the highest levels though it seems that the happiness of married people is dependent on the quality of the marriage (Frech & Williams, 2007). Men seem to benefit more from marriage than women do (Ross et al., 1990).

Is the marriage-happiness relationship consistent across nations? To answer this question, Steven Stack and Ross Eshleman (1998) compared national surveys from Australia, Belgium, Britain, Canada, Denmark, France, Germany, Iceland, Ireland, Italy, Japan, Netherlands, Northern Ireland, Norway, Spain, Sweden, and the United States. Using measures of happiness, marital status, health status, and economic well-being, they found that married people had the highest level of happiness in all seventeen nations compared. Cohabiting individuals had substantially lower levels of happiness than marrieds but higher levels than singles. Though people from different nations had different levels of happiness, marital status had more impact on happiness than did nationality. Married individuals also reported higher financial satisfaction and better health than single ones. In contrast, cohabiting was not positively related to either financial satisfaction or health. Thus, across nations, marriage promotes happiness both directly and by increasing health and financial status.

Does happiness increase for both women and men in marriage? While both genders gain by pooling resources in marriage, women improve more financially (Ross et al., 1990). A longitudinal study of African American and European American couples demonstrated that married European American men reported the highest level of happiness, and African American women reported the lowest level (Corra, Carter, Carter, & Knox, 2009). However, between 1973 and 2006 that gap has decreased with African American wives showing a significant increase in their levels of happiness (Corra et al., 2009). While marriage helps both men's and women's health by encouraging health-promoting behaviors and discouraging health-compromising ones, men improve their health lifestyles more than women do and gain more emotional support (Joung et al., 1997; Ross et al., 1990). Married women and men reported greater happiness than cohabiting women and men, who reported greater happiness than singles of both genders. For both men and women, living in nations with a higher level of divorce was associated with higher levels of happiness, likely because those in unhappy marriages could end them (Stack & Eshleman, 1998).

Though in general married people are happier and healthier than never-married people, differences in personal happiness between the two groups have decreased in recent years. In fact, a comparison of married men and never-married men demonstrated no difference in self-reported health (Liu & Umberson, 2008). Over time, self-reported health has also decreased for those who are separated, divorced, or widowed (Liu & Umberson, 2008).

Divorce

Marriage is expected to meet such a wide array of social, emotional, personal, and sexual needs that it is little wonder many people find their actual marriages disappointing. About 44 percent of first marriages and between 43 and 46 percent of all marriages end in divorce (Amato, 2010; U.S. Department of Labor, 2013). Though 1.6 percent of heterosexual marriages end each year, a slightly lower number (1.1 percent) of same-sex couples who were legally married were divorced each year (Badgett & Mallory, 2014). In states where civil unions, but not marriage, were legal during that same time period, 1.85 percent of those civil unions or domestic partnerships ended, suggesting that the legality and formality of marriage makes all relationships, and particularly same-sex relationships, more stable (Badgett & Mallory, 2014).

Most divorces occur during midlife, and as Figure 13.3 shows, the age at which people divorce has been rising since the 1970s. Justin Lavner and Thomas Bradbury (2010) conducted a four-year longitudinal study of 464 newlywed spouses that demonstrated five patterns of changes in marital satisfaction over time. Three of the patterns of marital satisfaction were generally positive and demonstrated low rates of divorce (3 to 14 percent) after four years of marriage and divorce (3 to 14 percent after four years and 9 to 26 percent after ten years). The three positive patterns were those with high and stable satisfaction over time, moderately high satisfaction with minimal decline over time, and moderate satisfaction with minimal decline over time. However, two patterns of marital satisfaction—those with low marital satisfaction at the beginning of the marriage and those with a very rapid decline in satisfaction after marriage—were significantly more likely to get a divorce after four years (25 to 54 percent) and after ten years (40 to 60 percent; Lavner & Bradbury, 2010). So, it seems that not all marriages experience a significant drop in marital satisfaction after the honeymoon period, and those that do are more likely to end in divorce.

FIGURE 13.3
Median Age at Divorce, 1970 to 2010

The age at which people divorce has been rising steadily since the mid-1970s, but most divorces still occur during early adulthood.
Source: Office for National Statistics (2012).

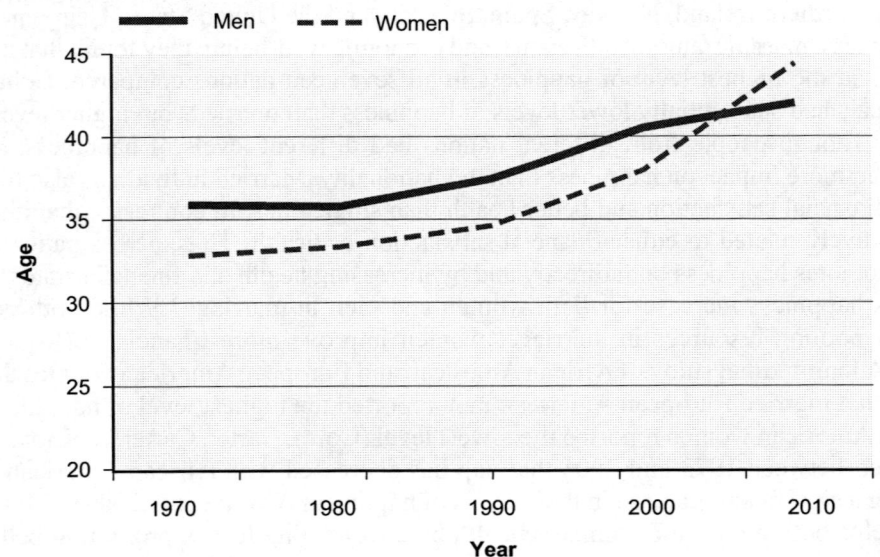

Many factors play a role in what marriages last and what marriages end in divorce. Some variables are routinely linked with higher risk for divorce, such as getting married during the teen years, being poor, not having a college education, and being unemployed (Amato, 2010; U. S. Bureau of Labor Statistics, 2013). As noted earlier, marital satisfaction, or lack thereof, is also linked with divorce. John Gottman (1994), one of the foremost researchers in marriage and divorce, conducted a longitudinal study in which newlywed couples were asked to have videotaped discussions about a source of contention in their marriage. The interactions, including facial expressions and physiological measures, were coded for a variety of emotion and behaviors. The couples were then followed up over time to determine whether they were still married. Gottman found four factors that reliably predict divorce, which he calls the Four Horsemen of the Apocalypse: criticism, defensiveness, contempt (the strongest predictor of divorce), and stonewalling, described in Table 13.4. Surprisingly, anger does not predict divorce (Gottman, Coan, Carrere, & Swanson, 1998). Moreover, Amato and Hohmann-Mariott (2007) found that couples who divorced were likely to either be uncommitted to the relationship or to experience a great deal of conflict within the marriage.

We discuss the impact of divorce on young children in Chapter 9, but what are the long-term effects of divorce on adult children? Because divorced families differ on so many dimensions, such as SES, age of children when the divorce occurs, and whether relationships with both parents continue, this question is difficult to answer. A long-term study that compared about twelve thousand twenty-three-year-old children of divorce with about ten thousand from intact marriages reported that most children of divorce showed no serious negative consequences at age eleven or twenty-three (Cherlin et al., 1995). Young adults whose LGB parents' relationships ended reported amicable separations, but because their parents' relationships occurred and ended before same-sex marriage was legal, that lack of legal recognition of the child's relationship and nonbiological parent caused stress (Goldberg & Allen, 2013). During adolescence, however, children of divorce showed a pattern of leaving home early, early sexual activity and cohabiting, and nonmarital childbearing. By young adulthood, though, children of divorce were no different from the others in their willingness to marry or have a child, though they are at higher risk of their own marriages ending in divorce (Amato, 2010; Cherlin et al., 1995).

Remarriage

The end of a particular marriage does not generally mean the end of a desire for a good marriage. Americans remarry at almost the same rate at which they marry (Ruth, 1995). Rates of remarriage are about 40 percent overall and are dependent on age, with previously married young adults between the ages of eighteen and twenty-four reporting a remarriage rate

TABLE 13.4 Gottman's Four Horsemen of the Apocalypse

Horseman	Antidote
Criticism—Verbally attacking one's partner	Complain about a situation and do not assign blame.
Defensiveness—Deflecting blame to protect one's self from attack	Accept responsibility for your own actions.
Contempt—Disregard and displays that your partner is inferior (may be name calling or behaviors like eye-rolling)	Show your partner that you respect and appreciate him or her.
Stonewalling—Withdrawing from an interaction	Let your partner know you need a temporary break and practice soothing yourself with something calming and distracting.

Source: Lisitsa, 2013.

Americans remarry at almost the rate at which they marry. Remarriage contributes to the changing nature of families. Because this bride and groom each have a child, their marriage forms a blended family.

Source: In The Light Photography/Shutterstock.

of 29 percent, whereas those aged fifty-five to sixty-four had a remarriage rate of 67 percent (Livingston, Parker, & Rohal, 2014). Men are more likely to remarry than women, and European Americans are the most likely race/ethnicity to remarry (Livingston et al., 2014). About half of these remarriages will end in divorce, and many of these divorcees will remarry again, with about 8 percent of newlyweds in 2013 entering a third or higher order marriage (Livingston et al., 2014). The pattern in marriage, as in cohabitation, is to move from one exclusive relationship to another, that is, engage in serial monogamy.

People who have divorced and remarried several times report less happiness and more frequent depression than people who have divorced once; the latter, in turn, report more frequent depression than those who have never divorced (Kurdek, 1991). Remarried people report as much satisfaction with their marriages as do people in first marriages when they have higher levels of education, but lower levels of satisfaction with their second marriage if they have lower levels of education (Mirecki, Chou, Elliott, & Schneider, 2013).

Joshua Gold, Donald Bubenzer, and John West (1993) found that the types of relationships marriage partners had with ex-spouses were related to the quality of their current marriages. Questionnaires were completed by sixty-nine male spouses (ages twenty-five to sixty-four) and fifty-eight female spouses (ages twenty-two to sixty-two). The questionnaires measured the degree of emotional attachment and interpersonal conflict between ex-spouses as well as the level of current marital intimacy. Among both men and women, the more attached they were to the ex-spouse, the less intimate they were with the current spouse. There was also a significant negative relationship between conflict with the ex-spouse and marital intimacy for both men and women. Relationships with ex-spouses that were low in conflict and low in emotional attachment to the ex-spouse had the best outcome for the new marriage.

Although the majority of Americans spend most of their adult lives in marriages, many spend significant portions as singles and some never marry. Singlehood can be the result of delaying marriage, a lack of opportunity to marry, divorce, widowhood, or a choice to remain single. Although parents, religious leaders, and politicians still exhort marriage as the ideal state against which other lifestyles are judged, today's unmarried people have a variety of lifestyle choices that carry less stigma than in earlier times (Byrne & Carr, 2005; Ganong et al., 1990).

Singlehood

Many contemporary Americans remain single throughout early adulthood. Raúl, for example, always expected to marry. During his early adult years he lived with and planned to marry a series of three women, but each relationship failed for a different reason. At age forty, he had all but given up. He bought a house for himself and prepared to be happily single. Three years later his wife and infant daughter live with him in that house, but Raúl represents a large proportion of his cohort who spent many adult years single. Of his two brothers, Jimmy spent many years as a single, but is now engaged to be married to his fiancé, Eric. Barry, the remaining brother, married at age twenty-four, divorced at age thirty, and spent six years as a single before he remarried. Their cousin Carmen will be forty-three on her next birthday and remains single. She has devoted herself to her acting career, a career she does not consider to be compatible with family life. As these examples show, singles are not a homogeneous group.

As of 2012, about 20 percent of all adults have never been married, a number that has steadily increased since the 1960s, and only about half of singles have a desire to ever get married (Wang & Parker, 2014). The reasons for this increase in singlehood among those who desire marriage are multifaceted: some are waiting until later in life to get married, and some are waiting until they have financial stability to get married, which takes longer in economically difficult times (Wang & Parker, 2014). Yet others simply have no desire for marriage. Half of Americans polled about the importance of marriage and children stated that society is better off if people have priorities other than getting married and starting a family (Wang & Parker, 2014).

Cohabitation

As noted previously, Figure 13.4 shows, contemporary young adults are marrying later than earlier cohorts did. However, they are forming sexual partnerships at about the same rate and same age at which older cohorts married. As in the case of Dai and Marta, the first union is now more likely to be **cohabitation**, or living together.. The majority of young adults now cohabit before marriage (Copen, Daniels, & Mosher, 2013; Horwitz & White, 1998).

Copen and colleagues (2013) examined the patterns of heterosexual cohabitation among more than 12 thousand American women and found that nearly 50 percent of women reported cohabitating with their partner at some point either as an alternative to marriage or as a "trial" for marriage compared to only 34 percent of women reporting cohabitation in 1995. Rates of cohabitation increased among all races and ethnicities between 1995 and 2010 except among Asian American women, and women with higher levels of education were less likely than those with a high school diploma to cohabitate (Copen et al., 2013). A similar pattern appears to exist in countries such as Australia, the United Kingdom, and Canada, where cohabitation is also prevalent (OCED, 2013). Many younger, never-married participants view living together as a temporary arrangement

cohabitation Unrelated adults living together in a sexual partnership.

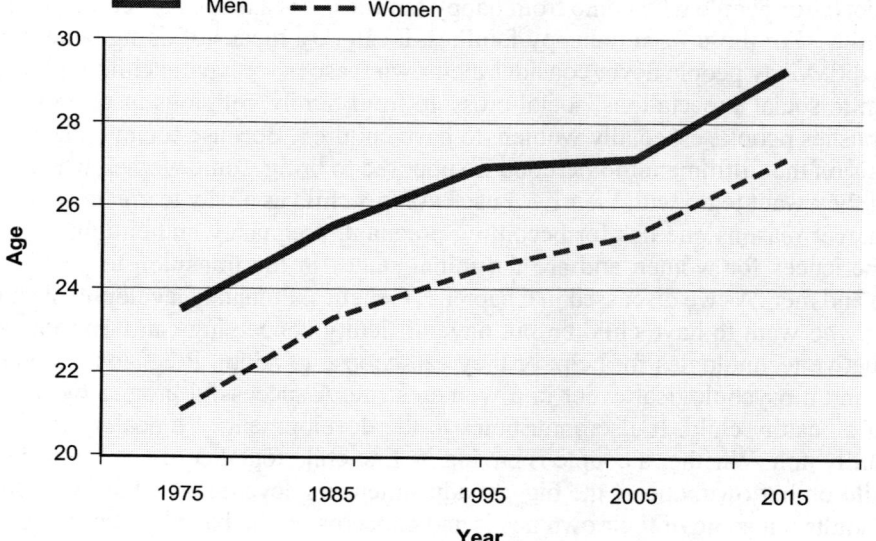

FIGURE 13.4
Median Age at First Marriage, 1975 to 2015

Since 1975, young adults have been marrying later than earlier cohorts. They are forming sexual partnerships at about the same age earlier cohorts did, but these unions are more likely to be cohabitation.
Source: U.S. Bureau of the Census (2015a).

prior to marriage. They live together when they have just finished their education or just started working and do not feel financially or emotionally prepared to take the more serious step of marriage. In contrast, young adults in countries such as Italy, Poland, the Slovak Republic, and Turkey are less likely to experiment with cohabiting and more likely to remain in their parents' home until marriage than young adults in any other Western country, whereas many northern European countries such as Sweden have higher rates of cohabitation than the United States (Kroeger & Smock, 2014; OCED, 2013; Rossi, 1997).

Heterosexual cohabitation in preparation for marriage typically does not last long. Within a few years, most relationships have either broken up or the couple has married. There are many social pressures to marry, and most adults do want to marry eventually. And, as we discussed earlier in this chapter, for those who remain not ready for marriage, the changes in intimacy and passion that are to be expected in a relationship over time mitigate against a continuing romance.

Does living together first improve the quality of a marriage? For older cohorts, the evidence was mixed showing that couples who had cohabited before marriage reported more problems, were at higher risk for divorce, and had less commitment to the institution of marriage than couples who had not lived together first (Booth & Johnson, 1988; Thomson & Colella, 1992). However, more recent research has demonstrated that those couples who cohabitated and who married in the 1990s or later do not face those negative consequences: they are no more or less likely than noncohabitates to have an unstable marriage (Kroeger & Smock, 2014). These historical changes are likely due to shifts in attitudes toward marriage and cohabitation.

These findings suggest that lasting intimate partnerships do not depend on marriage. Forming an intimate relationship helps the young adult to establish independence from parents. It also raises the issue of starting a family of one's own. Not so long ago, the word *family* brought to mind a breadwinner husband and a homemaker wife with at least two children. We have already seen that this image no longer reflects the typical marriage; today most wives and mothers are employed. Many families are headed by same-sex parents. We have also seen that many people now live together before or in place of marriage and that some people remain single. Just as there is no one way to establish an intimate relationship, so too are decisions about parenthood characterized more by variety than by any one pattern, as we will see next.

Parenthood

People who want children express many different reasons for their desire. Some really like children and want an opportunity to be involved with their care. Some women strongly desire the experience of pregnancy and childbirth. Many young adults see parenthood as a way to demonstrate their adult status because parenting is an acknowledged adult role in our society. For people who come from happy families, it is a means of recreating their earlier families. For those from unhappy families, it can be a means of doing better than their parents did. Many people never consider their own reasons for having children but do so to conform to social expectations; social pressure from family, religious institutions, and the media pushes people, especially women, to have children. Because society places so much emphasis on the fulfillment motherhood is supposed to bring, some women who are unsure of what they want to do with their lives use having a child as a way to create an identity.

Whatever reasons one has for becoming pregnant, pregnancy and childbirth are major life experiences for women and are the initial stages in the transition to parenthood for women and men. As we discussed in Chapter 3, Genetics, Prenatal Development, and Birth, couples who want to have children but have difficulty conceiving can turn to an array of reproductive technologies for help, or they can choose to adopt. Pregnancy is both a biological and a psychological event in a woman's life. A successful pregnancy leads to the birth of a healthy child. It also contributes to the development of a healthy mother and a new family unit. Whether a couple is having its first child together or a woman is having a first child on her own, one of the biggest adjustments is developing a family in which the young adults put some of their own needs and concerns on the back burner and take on the

> **What Do You Think?**
>
> What type of marriage did your parents have when you were growing up? If you are (or were) married, what type of marriage do (did) you have? What type of marriage would you like to have? Why?

responsibilities of caring for the next generation. This is an enormous change in the lives of the new parents (and, as you will remember from Chapter 11's discussion of problems of adolescence, an important reason teenage parenthood has such negative effects).

Transition to Parenthood

People prepare less for the parenting role than for the other important new roles of early adulthood, employment and marriage (Rossi, 1982). Emerging and young adults train for employment in school, in volunteer positions, in internships, or on the job. The experiences of dating, courtship, engagement, and cohabitation all help the young adult to prepare for marriage and other forms of intimate relationships. But many young adults have no experience with children before they become parents. They frequently find themselves expecting a child as a result of recreational sex rather than active reproductive choice. Furthermore, schools and other social institutions do not teach the skills necessary for adequate parenting, such as empathy, interpersonal competence, and caring for a child. Unlike the young adult's other new roles, parenthood hits full force with the birth of the baby and allows no time off. No other transition is so abrupt and complete. This is one reason waiting until the late twenties or early thirties can be advantageous (Daniels & Weingarten, 1982). Between 2000 and 2014, the average age at which women had their first child increased from 24.9 years to 26.3 years (Mathews & Hamilton, 2016). By this age, the parents typically have established their identities, have separated from their parents, have developed nurturing marriages, and are prepared to share the work of caring for a child.

Nonetheless, the impact of infant care responsibilities after the birth of the first child puts strain on the marital relationship. Several studies have found that women reported doing more housework and child care than they expected, and men reported doing less than they expected, though men's time spent doing housework stayed stable from pre- to postpartum (Baxter, Hewitt, & Haynes, 2008; Hackel & Ruble, 1992). The satisfaction and intimacy in relationships declines, and the conflict increases from pregnancy to postpartum (Hackel

Many young adults have no experience with children before they become parents and find themselves unprepared for the abrupt and demanding transition to parenthood. Although they experience some difficulty adjusting, most find parenting rewarding.
Source: Monkey Business Images/Shutterstock.

& Ruble, 1992; Lawrence et al., 2008). The discrepancy between the shared division of labor the couples expected and the more conventional one they experienced appeared to be the cause of the discontent. When the husbands' contributions to the division of labor were greater than expected, the wives felt more positive. Though fathers report spending more time with their children and on housework than in the past, they still do not spend as much time as mothers spend (Bond et al., 1998).

New fathers feel the strain as well as mothers, but mothers feel it more fully because they are expected to take primary responsibility for infant care and encouraged to believe they will feel fulfilled by motherhood. Fulfillment, however, comes not from the experience of a biological event but from development of and dedication to values, interests, and competencies over time (M. Hoffnung, 1995). The gap between many a new mother's expectations of fulfillment and the realities of exhaustion and distraction is often enormous. After being the center of attention during labor and delivery, many new mothers soon find themselves very much alone at home. This aloneness may be heightened by the fact that the new father needs to increase his work hours to meet the new financial responsibilities of the family. The birth of a first child therefore is the event that is most likely to cause the greatest psychological disruption in American middle-class women, especially if the birth is not followed by full-time involvement outside the home (M. Hoffnung, 1992).

Adapting to New Roles

In a longitudinal study of the adult-to-parent transition at the birth of the first child, Nicolina Fedele and her colleagues (1988) followed thirty working- to upper-middle-class couples in heterosexual marriages from early pregnancy to five years after the birth. They found that expecting the birth of the first child aroused anxieties in men about their capacity to provide. Women tended to become completely immersed in the world of mother and infant and greatly reduce their involvement with their husbands and the rest of the world. Fedele and associates measured *affiliation* (need for relatedness to others) and *autonomy* (need for separateness from others) in the parents-to-be early in the pregnancy and found these needs were related to parental adaptation in the postpartum period. Women who expressed high need for affiliation experienced less postpartum depression two months after the baby's birth, but their sense of well-being declined by the time the child reached the first birthday. Women with higher autonomy scores felt a greater sense of well-being at two months and at one year after the baby's birth. Men's affiliation scores during pregnancy had no relation to their well-being in the postpartum period, but the more autonomous their wives were, the greater was the men's well-being one year postpartum.

The researchers found that fathers in families in which the mother was more autonomous were more skillful parents. They conclude that "in families, things are often not what they seem. A mother who is completely devoted to her firstborn infant, who is always warm and empathetic, who never seems to miss a cue from the baby is satisfying to observe but is probably a mixed blessing for her family. It is probably mixed for her infant because, on the one hand, it provides the empathetic bond that allows the baby to thrive, but on the other hand, it may cement that bond in a way that will make it much harder for the baby to develop an early important attachment to his or her father" (p. 108). In families like this, therefore, the father has little room for involvement with the child, thus depriving the father of the growth-producing experience of active parenting, depriving the child of early attachment to the father, and depriving the mother of an empathetic partner. However, newer research demonstrates that when fathers have high levels of marital satisfaction before the birth of a child, the more time he will spend interacting with that child, allowing him to develop a secure attachment with the child as well (Lee & Doherty, 2007).

In most two-parent households, both parents work outside the home. Employment has multiple benefits for mothers, but it is not without costs (see Chapter 12's "Focusing On" feature on page 436). The most pressing problem for working mothers is lack of time: there are more tasks to be done than hours in the day. Surprisingly, married mothers today actually spend about two hours more per week and single mothers about four hours more per week caring for their children than women did in the 1960s, when far fewer women were employed outside the home (Bianchi, Robinson, & Milkie, 2006). Although many people think fathers today are more involved with their children than fathers in the past, contemporary evidence indicates that women still carry much more of the responsibility for children than fathers (LaRossa, 1992). This may be due in part to the fact that, especially with the birth of a first child, different sex parents become more traditional in their gender roles (Katz-Wise, Priess, & Hyde, 2010). This leaves working mothers with the heavy demands of doing two jobs, which often begin very soon after the birth of her child due to the lack of paid maternity leave in the United States, as we discussed in Chapter 3. Despite the practical problems, however, continuing maternal employment is strongly associated with paternal skillfulness at parenting and with maternal adjustment to motherhood.

Martial Satisfaction among New Parents

Almost all studies that measure marital satisfaction before and after the birth of the first child have found that marital satisfaction declines (Hackel & Ruble, 1992; Lawrence et al., 2008). Jay Belsky and Michael Rovine (1990) found that couples who were least satisfied with their marriages before the birth were most likely to report decline in satisfaction after, because problems that existed before were likely to have been magnified by the additional stresses brought on by the birth. Babies do not appear to create severe marital distress where none existed before, nor do they bring couples with distressed marriages closer together. Rather, the early postpartum months bring on a period of disorganization and change. The leading conflict in these first months of parenthood is division of labor in the family. Couples may regain their sense of equilibrium in marriage by successfully negotiating how they will divide the new family responsibilities. Husbands' participation in child and home care seems to be positively related to marital satisfaction after the birth. One longitudinal study found that the more the men shared in doing family tasks, the more satisfied the wives were at six and eighteen months postpartum and the husbands at eighteen months postpartum (Cowan & Cowan, 1988).

Though many couples experience a difficult transition to parenthood, they also find it rewarding. Children affect parents in ways that lead to personal growth, enable reworking of childhood conflicts, build flexibility and empathy, and provide intimate, loving human connections. They also give a lot of pleasure. In follow-up interviews of new parents when their children were eighteen months old, Philip Cowan and Carolyn Cowan (1988) found that almost every man and woman spoke of the delight they felt from knowing their child and watching the child develop. They reported feeling pride for and closeness to their spouses, more adult with their own parents, and a renewed sense of purpose at work.

As you read about the young, married adult's transition to parenthood, you may have wondered how single parents cope with this critical change. As you can imagine, single parents face very different issues than their married counterparts.

Same-sex couples have levels of satisfaction similar to those of heterosexual couples who are matched in age and other relevant characteristics. They face the same pressures that cohabiting and married couples face, plus the additional ones that result from the negative attitudes toward and treatment of homosexuals.
Source: CREATISTA/Shutterstock.

Single Parenthood

One important change in family life has been the dramatic increase in single-parent families. Thirty-four percent of children live in single-parent households, and 41 percent of children are born outside of a marriage (Livingston, 2014b). The rise in the number of single parents is due to increasing numbers of divorces and delayed marriages and the shifting social values we have been considering. Because poverty is so prevalent among single-mother families, and because most single parents are mothers, it is hard to separate the effects of single parenting from the effects of poverty (Edmondson et al., 1993). Women generally face discrimination in employment, as we discussed in Chapter 12, and single mothers often face increased discrimination because employers fear they may be unreliable due to their sole responsibility for their children. These factors contribute to female heads of household earning less than their male counterparts. For women who were full-time homemakers, the transition to becoming both provider and parent is a difficult one that typically includes a dramatic decrease in income. In addition to facing financial pressure, single parents often feel socially isolated, as we discussed in Chapter 9's discussion of family relationships. The demands of work and parenting may leave little time for their social and sexual needs.

The problems of single parenting are particularly acute for African American families. More than 70 percent of African American children are born outside of marriage including children born to cohabitating parents (Martin et al., 2012). This is due in part to changes in the status of African American males, such as high unemployment, mortality, and incarceration rates, ("It's Not Working," 1986). However, extended families and kin can help buffer the difficulties of being a single African American mother by helping with child care and providing social support, which, in turn, has a positive impact on mothers' parenting (Murry et al., 2001).

Extended families provide many single parents with support systems. Roland Wagner (1993) found that Latina mothers, despite being younger, less educated, and having more children, encountered fewer problems than white single mothers during their first year of single parenthood. Because members of the young mother's extended family tended to live close together, they offered a better family support network. In contrast, white single mothers, who often did not live near their extended families, were more likely to be upset or depressed. However, many single parents build wider support networks composed of nonfamily members to help combat their isolation (Donati, 1995).

Although research shows that single parents and their families suffer from more externally imposed stress than other parents—financial pressure, for example— many successfully raise happy and healthy children (Vosler & Proctor, 1991). Myrna Olson and Judith Haynes (1993) interviewed twenty-six single parents who were considered successful by qualified professionals. What contributed to their success? Olson and Haynes identified seven factors these parents had in common. First, they recognized and accepted the responsibilities and challenges of single parenthood. Second, they gave priority to the parental role; effective parenting requires time and energy. Third, they used consistent, nonpunitive discipline. Fourth, they emphasized open communication with their children. Fifth, they fostered individuality within a supportive family unit. Sixth, they recognized their need for self-nurturance. Last, they established and followed rituals and traditions, which contributes to the feeling of being a family.

As family structures have become more diverse, so has the group known as single parents. Most are women, but some are men. Some are heterosexual and some are not (see the "Focusing On" feature). Some have partners, some have family support networks, some have friendship networks, and some are isolated. The stereotypes that portray single mothers as the cause of poverty, alcohol and drug abuse, and other social problems are belied by the wide variety of causes, attitudes, and activities of single parents. A more constructive approach would be to develop community services, such as sick-child care, to ease the stress with which single parents must cope.

Stepparent/Blended Families

Remarriage frequently reconstitutes a single-parent family into a stepparent or a blended family, as we discussed in Chapter 9. Comparisons among single-parent, remarriage, and conventional families indicate that remarriage families show the highest number of within-family problems (Vosler & Proctor, 1991). Consider the complexity of the relationships in these families. The remarriage brings together not only two adults but children and ex-spouses as well. Stepparents need to establish good relationships with the stepchildren as well as respect the bonds the children have with their biological parents. Stepparents have to accommodate their partners' ex-spouses, who need to be in communication about visitation, disciplinary or school problems, and other important matters concerning their children. If the remarriage involves stepsiblings, differences in treatment of biological siblings and stepsiblings by the newly married parents usually arise. Family relationships are likely to be awkward for a time until the inconsistencies are ironed out.

Lawrence Ganong and Marilyn Coleman (1993b) studied the relationships among members of stepfamilies. They measured stepsibling, stepparent-child, and stepfamily relations in 105 stepfamilies consisting of adults and their seven-to-twenty-year-old children. Children's interactions with half-siblings and siblings were slightly more positive than those with stepsiblings (especially among cross-sex stepsibling pairs), although all relationships were relatively positive. Parental relationships with the children depended on whether the household was a stepfamily (one marriage partner with children from a previous relationship) or a blended family (both marriage partners with children from previous relationships). Parents in blended families felt closer to their biological children than did parents without stepchildren. They also believed that stepchildren negatively affected their relationship with their biological children. In blended families, parents more often disciplined only their biological children. In stepfamilies, the stepparent was more likely to be perceived as playing a parental role, which included disciplining the stepchildren. In general, adults in stepfamilies had more difficulty than children did in coping with stepsibling relationships.

Being a stepparent is an ambiguous role; one is neither a parent nor a nonparent. The problems are easier to resolve with younger children, who are likely to form special attachments to their stepparents. As we discussed in Chapter 11, adolescents often struggle with accepting stepparents as disciplinarians (Portrie & Hill, 2005). Men generally have an easier time being stepfathers than women do being stepmothers. Why? It may be that custodial fathers more often continue to have contact with the biological mother, which creates conflicts of loyalty. Or it may be that stepparenting relationships work best when the relationship is friendly but not intense, and men have less difficulty maintaining friendly distance than women do. Stepmothers tend to be more involved with their stepchildren than are stepfathers, but neither is as involved as the biological parent.

Child Free

About 20 percent of women never have a child, and the current birth rate of approximately 60 births per 1,000 women is the lowest it has ever been in the United States (Hamilton, Martin, & Osterman, 2016; Livingston & Cohn, 2010). Why has the birth rate been steadily declining over the last decade? There is less pressure to have children, women are waiting longer to have children in order to get an education and start a career, truncating her viable child-bearing years, and economic strain in conjunction with the constantly rising cost of raising a child impacts the number of children people want and have (Livington & Cohn, 2010). Though some of these women are unable to have children for a variety of reasons, more people than ever are child-free-by-choice. Between 3 and 5 percent of individuals report that their ideal number of children is zero (Hoffnung, 1995; Taylor et al., 2010). However, this figure underrepresents the number of voluntarily childless people, because some women and men who intend not to have children also choose not to marry.

In a study of college undergraduates' attitudes toward parenting, neither gender saw child-free-by-choice as a positive option. Women, however, thought having children would make both parents more satisfied with their lives, whereas men thought having children would make both less satisfied (Ross & Kahan, 1983). This may be because family and friends pressure both women and men to want children, yet women are encouraged to believe that children will provide them with fulfillment, whereas men are not.

People who choose not to have children pay a social price. Marsha Somers (1993) found that voluntarily child-free men and women perceived themselves as being viewed more

Focusing On...

The Effects of Growing Up with Same-Sex Parents

Many people assume that the best home environment for child development is the stereotypical white, middle-class, two-parent, breadwinner-father, homemaker-mother family. But as American families have become increasingly diverse, researchers have challenged this assumption and demonstrated that healthy development can occur in home environments that vary in race, ethnicity, SES, household composition, and maternal employment (Patterson, 1997). One area of parenting that has historically been and still is contentious to many people is that of same-sex parents.

Lesbian and gay families are diverse in themselves. Some children of gay and lesbian parents were born within the context of a heterosexual relationship between their biological parents. Later, when one or both parents "come out" as lesbian or gay, the parents may or may not divorce. The children may or may not reside with the gay or lesbian parent; the custodial parent may be single or in a relationship with a partner of the same or opposite sex. Other children of same-sex parents are conceived through donor insemination, and some same-sex couples adopt or become foster parents. It is clear that, though families with same-sex parents are often all grouped together, there is great diversity within families headed by gay and lesbian parents.

The principal conclusion of the body of research involving gay and lesbian divorced parents is that their children do not differ in significant ways from children of divorced heterosexual parents (Crowl, Ahn, & Baker, 2008; Flaks et al., 1995; Patterson, 1997, 2006; Perrin, Cohen, & Caren, 2013; Potter, 2012; Tasker & Golombok, 1997; Victor & Fish, 1995; Wainright & Patterson, 2006). They relate well to parents, peers, and other adults. Those with lesbian mothers are more likely to have contact with their fathers than children of divorced heterosexual mothers. Those with gay fathers are more likely to have authoritative fathers.

What are the effects of gay and lesbian parenting on the children when they reach adulthood? Fiona Tasker and Susan Golombok (1997) were the first to investigate this question with respect to lesbian mothers. In 1976 and 1977 they selected fifty-four single mothers, half of them lesbians and half heterosexual. None of the lesbians were mothers as a consequence of donor insemination or adoption. The researchers interviewed the mothers and their children. The children were also evaluated by a child psychiatrist and rated by their teachers. At the time of the initial interviews, the children were on average nine-and-a-half years old. Fourteen years later, in 1991, the researchers reinterviewed the children, who were now adults. Twenty-five children of lesbian mothers (seventeen women and eight men) and twenty-one children of heterosexual mothers (nine women and twelve men) took part in the follow-up.

Young adults who grew up in households headed by a lesbian mother were satisfied with family life and gave more positive accounts of their relationships with their mother's female partner than the comparison group did of their relationships with their mother's male partner. They also reported good relations with their nonresident fathers and were more likely than the comparison group to see their fathers. They were no more likely to have experienced peer stigma when they were adolescents, although if their father was not supportive of their mother's lesbian identity, they were more likely to remember being teased about it. SES appeared to have a stronger influence than family background on attitudes toward gay rights, with middle-class young adults being more accepting. Young adult children of lesbian mothers were no more likely than those of heterosexual mothers to identify themselves as gay or lesbian or to be attracted to someone of the same gender. But if they were attracted, they were more likely to pursue a sexual relationship. They were no more likely to have suffered from depression or to have sought mental health services than those with heterosexual mothers. There is also evidence that children living in homes with two mothers are less likely than their peers in any other family structure to be the victim of physical or sexual abuse at the hands of one's parent or caregiver (Gartrell, Bos, & Goldberg, 2011).

The consensus of the scientific community is that quality of parent-child relationships, not the sexual orientation of one's parents, matters when examining the impact of parenting (American Psychological Association, 2005; Patterson, 2006).

What Do You Think?

1. Given the few differences in growing up in a home with same-sex versus different parents, why do you think many states do not allow same-sex spouses to adopt?

A majority of child-free couples say they like children but are committed to being child free so they can pursue their marriage relationships, their work, and the other opportunities that life affords—such as traveling, as this couple is doing in Burano, Italy.
Source: ChiccoDodiFC/Shutterstock.

negatively by relatives and friends because of their parenting choice than did parents. Examples of the negative stereotypes include "selfish," "abnormal," and "immature." Relatives were perceived as being more negative than friends, and women perceived themselves as being evaluated more negatively than men by both relatives and friends (Kelly, 2009; Somers, 1993).

In couples who choose to forgo parenthood, the woman almost always makes the initial decision and remains more committed to the decision than the man does, though these women are often questioned about whether they are certain they will not change their mind (Kelly, 2009; Seccombe, 1991). The choice to be child free is more frequent among women who are college educated and career oriented. For example, Susan, now in her late forties, always knew she did not want children. She has two master's degrees and holds a vice-presidential position at a university. In addition to her demanding job, she leads several important civic organizations. She and Tom have been in a stable marriage since early adulthood. Tom says he would like to have been a parent, but he did not feel as strongly about the issue as Susan did.

Susan is an example of what Jean Veevers (1980) calls an **early articulator**, someone who knew from childhood that she or he did not want children. In her longitudinal study of fifty-two voluntarily childless marriages, Veevers found two types of child-free couples: early articulators and postponers. In about a third of Veevers' couples one partner, usually the woman, was an early articulator. Some early articulators knew they disliked children and were committed to a child-free lifestyle. The majority liked children but were committed to being child free so they could pursue their marriage relationship, their work, and the other opportunities life affords. **Postponers** were likely to be less definite about whether they would have children. First they delayed childbearing for a definite time, then for an indefinite time, then finally weighed the pros and cons and decided to remain child free. Veevers found the postponers were likely to see their decision as specific to the particular relationship they were in. If they had married someone else, their decision might have been different.

Women who complete their education, postpone marriage, and hold jobs outside their homes tend to have higher childlessness rates, which includes those who are child free by choice and those by chance (Ambry, 1992). Early articulators leave the path clear to develop their careers. Those who feel ambivalent usually decide not to become a parent because of the stress and worry associated with motherhood (Seccombe, 1991). In a comparison between childless adults in their twenties and those in their thirties, Mary-Joan Gerson, Linda Berman, and Ann Morris (1991) found that the younger respondents expressed a greater desire to become parents than the older ones. Though both groups saw the benefits of parenting, the older group was more attuned to the costs.

early articulator Jean Veevers' term for someone who knew from childhood that she did not want to have children.

postponer Jean Veevers' term for someone who was less definite about whether she would have children and made the decision to remain child-free after first delaying childbearing for a definite time and then for an indefinite time.

> **What Do You Think?**
>
> Do you have children or plan to have children? What would be the advantages and disadvantages to you of being a parent versus being child free?

Because children introduce a great deal of stress into a marriage, as we saw in our discussion of the transition to parenthood, we might expect child-free couples to be happier. Somers (1993) compared voluntarily child-free adults with parents. Both groups gave very similar reports of their marriages. There were no differences in the expression of affection or overall agreement between the two groups, but minimal differences existed in terms of satisfaction in life. The couples with no children showed a slightly higher degree of overall satisfaction and closeness. In comparisons of women who were childless by choice and women who were childless involuntarily, women who chose not to have children had higher levels of well-being and higher levels of control over their lives and environment (Jeffries & Konnert, 2002).

Looking Back/Looking Forward

How does our discussion of early adulthood exemplify the lifespan themes that we outlined in Chapter 1? Let us focus on the issue of establishing intimacy, which is critical to this stage of adulthood, according to Erikson and other theorists of adult development.

- **Continuity Within Change**—Intimacy is not new to the early adult period. It has its roots in the attachment to caregivers that begins in infancy and develops throughout childhood as relations with other family members, peers, and teachers become increasingly important. During adolescence, friendships and sexual relationships challenge the primacy of family relationships. But it is typically in emerging and early adulthood that the shift from emotional dependence on parents to emotional dependence on a significant other and/or friends takes place.

  Nor does the developmental task of establishing intimacy end in early adulthood. We will see in the chapters to come that relationships with significant others, children, siblings, parents, and friends remain important throughout the lifespan and continue to change and grow during middle and late adulthood as physical changes and new experiences alter how we think of ourselves and the social world around us.

- **Lifelong Growth**—Though physical growth, so apparent during childhood and adolescence, ends early in adulthood, cognitive and psychosocial growth continue. In early adulthood, we see growth in the way people think about problems. Instead of the categorical right or wrong that culminates in the development of formal thought in adolescence, young adults begin to give context and values more consideration as they work to develop intimacy with significant others who come from different families and have different needs. Likewise, the transition to parenthood calls on physical (especially for women), cognitive, and psychosocial growth.

  We will see in subsequent chapters that the challenges of family formation and maintenance continue to provide impetus for lifelong growth. As children become adolescents and adults, as marriages change from new romances to long-term relationships, and as parents age and die, these intimate relationships require continuing change and growth. And new intimacies continue to form: new friends and coworkers, new romances for some, and grandchildren and great-grandchildren for many.

- **Changing Meanings and Vantage Points**—As young adults leave their parents' families and begin to form households of their own, the meaning of family changes for both the children and the parents. The style of family life they took for granted as children is likely to be questioned in adolescence and even challenged as young adults attempt to balance the tasks of establishing work, love, and independence. In the coming chapters on middle adulthood, we will find that parents see the family from a new perspective as they relinquish caring for adult children and may begin caring for their aging parents and other relatives, and perhaps grandchildren too. Then late adulthood brings a new vantage point as relationships with siblings again become primary (as they are during childhood) for many as widowhood becomes more normative.

- **Developmental Diversity**—Social and cultural experiences vary so widely for young adults in different cultures, from different ethnic/racial backgrounds, and from different geographical regions that it is impossible to speak of a single pattern of establishing intimacy at this stage of life. Even if we limited our discussion to contemporary North American society, we would find differences due to SES, religion, ethnicity, race, sexual orientation, and gender, to name only a few. Some individuals form a significant sexual/emotional relationship in their teens and early twenties and shape their lives around it, while others have a series of relationships, and still others have few or no relationships until middle adulthood. Some focus on friendships rather than romantic attachments. In the United Sates, for example, cohabiting used to be a rebellious act. Now most young adults cohabit before marriage. In Italy, in contrast, cohabiting is infrequent and most young adults continue to live with their parents until they marry.

Even though developmental diversity is apparent throughout the lifespan, it increases as we move from the early to the later stages. As the long-term effects of earlier differences in advantages—both genetic and experiential—and choices accumulate, we see a broader range of diversity. Young adults may seek same-sex or different-sex partners, for example, whereas when they were children these differences would have been unlikely to surface. This difference in early adulthood will affect such lifelong choices as to whether to marry, have children, and maintain extended family connections.

One last reminder about diversity. Some of the issues that seem prominent in the lives of many young adults will not become prominent in the lives of others until middle adulthood. Raúl, as you might remember from our discussion of singles, was past forty when he married and started a family. He and his forty-year-old wife are confronting the tasks of forming a family in their middle years. Adult life follows many different patterns. When we discuss stages of adulthood, the boundaries are very fluid.

Chapter Summary

- **According to key lifespan theories, how does development in emerging adulthood and early adulthood differ from development in childhood and adolescence?** Physical maturation plays a key role in child and adolescent development, but in adult development cultural, social, and personal factors serve as the impetus for growth and change.

   According to timing of events theories, social clocks are internalized age expectations that govern when people marry, become parents, and retire. Although age grading has become less rigid in the past few decades, it has not disappeared.

   Normative crisis theories focus on internal or psychodynamic forces that are likely to be operating during a life stage. The Grant study indicates that development is a lifelong process, that sustained relationships have more of an effect on the shape life takes than do isolated events, and that the maturity or adaptive mechanisms determines level of mental health. Daniel Levinson considers early adulthood as one era in adult life during which they form mentor relationships, develop an occupation, and establish intimate relationships. Both the Grant Study and the research on which Levinson built his theory excluded women. Though Levinson has subsequently tried to place women within his theory, women's experiences differ from men's during the novice phase.

   During Erik Erikson's intimacy versus isolation stage, young adults who have established their identities develop close, committed relationships with peers. Relational theorists suggest that good interpersonal relationships can form the basis for identity, especially for women, who often develop more relational personalities than men.

- **What are the various forms intimacy can take in early adulthood?** Friendship is a form of intimacy of particular importance when young adults are establishing independence from parents. It is voluntary in nature, meets social and emotional needs, and contributes to individual well-being. Another form of intimacy most young adults expect to find is love. Contemporary young adults are delaying marriage and typically experience more love relationships and more sexual partners than earlier cohorts. Robert Sternberg's triangular theory of love highlights three essential components of lover intimacy, passion, and decision/commitment. Different combinations of these components produce different kinds of love relationships. Most people meet their mates in familiar places or are introduced by friends or family. This preselection leads to similarity in race/ethnicity, age, and educational level.

- **In what ways have marriage and divorce changed in the last few decades?** Most people say that the ideal marriage is an equal-partnership relationship, and those in more equal partnerships are happier. Marital equality, as measured by role sharing and decision-making power, leads to greater marital happiness and lower marital conflict. Those in same-sex marriages are more likely to negotiate roles. Marriage is associated with psychological well-being, although the differences in health and happiness between married and never-married people has decreased in recent years. Heterosexual and homosexual women and men all benefit from marriage.

  Divorce rates have stabilized in recent decades. Low SES, stress, and the ways that married couples interact are all linked to divorce. Couples who demonstrate the Four Horsemen of the Apocalypse (criticism, defensiveness, contempt, and stonewalling) have a much lower marital success rate than those who do not. Divorce often leads to remarriage; most divorced people remarry, and half of those who do divorce again. The result is a pattern of marriage called serial monogamy.

- **What are the lifestyle choices for young adults who choose to not marry?** Singlehood has become prevalent among young adults who are delaying marriage while they go to school and establish their occupations. Cohabitation is common among young adults who typically see it as a step in the courtship process and a way to test for compatibility before marriage. Couples that cohabitate before marriage are no more likely to divorce than those who do not.

- **What is the impact of parenthood on couples, single parents, and remarried parents?** Most people want to have children, although their reasons for doing so vary. The birth of the first child creates an enormous change in the lives of new parents as they are forced to put some of their own needs on the back burner and take on the responsibilities of caring for the next generation. Though fathers and mothers both feel the strain of the transition to parenthood, mothers feel it more fully because the primary responsibility for infant care usually falls on them. Employment of mothers is beneficial to the family, but it often leaves mothers doing two jobs.

  Single parenthood has increased due to high rates of divorce and out-of-wedlock births. Single-parent households are characteristically low-income families, so it is hard to separate the effects of single parenting from poverty. In spite of the financial and social pressures they face, many single parents are successful.

  Remarriage often leads to the creation of stepparent or blended families. These families have more within-family problems than other families because of the inherent complexity of the relationships.

  Couples who choose to be child free are likely to be college educated and career oriented. They do not seem to differ in life satisfaction from those who are parents.

Key Terms

adaptive mechanisms (p. 469)
biographical method (p. 470)
career consolidation (p. 469)
cohabitation (p. 487)
early articulator (p. 495)

equal-partner relationship (p. 481)
fictive kin (p. 474)
homophobia (p. 480)
intimacy versus isolation (p. 471)

postponer (p. 495)
recentering (p. 472)
serial monogamy (p. 475)
social clock (p. 467)

Middle Adulthood

PART 7

Chapter 14
Physical and Cognitive Development in Middle Adulthood

Chapter 15
Psychosocial Development in Middle Adulthood

Source: bikeriderlondon/Shutterstock.com.

Because the human lifespan has lengthened over the course of this century, middle adulthood begins later and lasts longer than it previously did. Middle adulthood, considered roughly the years from ages forty to sixty-five, is continuous with early adulthood at its beginning and with late adulthood at its close; no abrupt change occurs at either end. As we will see in Part 7, middle-aged adults resemble in many ways both younger and older adults, depending on the person and the life circumstances.

Middle adulthood is a stage characterized by change—gradual physical decline, occupational peaks, and new family relationships. The changes in physical functioning that began in early adulthood continue, leading to physical decline so gradual that it rarely impairs normal functioning. Society makes its maximum demands on middle-aged adults for social and civic responsibility; this is when men and women reach the peak of their influence on society. It is also the stage of life when individuals reconsider their priorities, their occupations, and their perspectives on mortality. And as children grow up and parents die, family relationships change as well. In Part 7, we examine physical, cognitive, and social development during middle adulthood.

Physical and Cognitive Development in Middle Adulthood

CHAPTER 14

Source: Pete Saloutos/Shutterstock.com.

Chapter Outline

PHYSICAL DEVELOPMENT
The Biology of Aging
Physical Functioning in Middle Adulthood
Health in Middle Adulthood
Reproductive Change and Sexuality
COGNITIVE DEVELOPMENT
Intelligence in Middle Adulthood
Practical Intelligence and Expertise
The Adult Learner
Work in Middle Adulthood
Change and Growth

Focusing Questions

- What age-related changes in appearance and physical functioning are to be expected during middle adulthood?
- What factors put middle-aged adults at risk for pathological aging or illness?
- How do the male and female reproductive systems change during middle adulthood, and how do these changes affect functioning, feelings, and sexuality?
- Does intelligence decline with age?
- Why do middle-aged and older adults hold most of society's leadership positions?
- What motivates midlife adults to engage in learning projects, participate in adult education, or return to college?
- What issues of work become important during the mid- and late-career stages, and how do race, ethnicity, and gender affect these issues?

If you look at family photo albums, you might notice that when your great-grandparents were your grandparents' ages, they looked older. Women and men a generation or two ago were more likely to dress and wear their hair in styles that were "old" than are contemporary middle-aged people. As baby boomers (born 1946–1965) and Generation Xers (born 1965–1980) have reached middle adulthood (ages forty to sixty-five), they have brought with them the blue jeans, athletic footwear, and youthful styles they have always worn. They have also brought their expectations for healthier and more youthful middle age. As youths and young adults, baby boomers took part in civil rights, student rights, and anti–Vietnam War demonstrations. Generation Xers ushered in the rise of the technological age. Their generations embraced the issues of women's liberation and gay rights. Compared to previous generations, more have remained single, and more with partners have remained child-free. Those with children have smaller families, and more of their families have two working parents (Easterlin et al., 1993; U.S. Bureau of the Census, 2010). As the baby boomer and X generations have entered middle adulthood, all of these social factors have blurred the dividing line between early and middle adulthood.

By middle adulthood, birthdays take on new meaning and often are greeted with mixed feelings. Each additional candle reminds us that we are likely closer to the end of our lives than to the beginning. Contemporary birthday cards dwell on the theme that after age thirty (just thirty!), one is "over the hill." This is not the universal response, however. A study on perspectives of aging found that successful agers were likely to be focused on self-acceptance and growth (Reichstadt, Sengupta, Depp, Palinkas, & Jeste, 2010). One participant noted:

> Every time we do something new, it is a new adventure and you have to learn new skills and you have to be adventurous. So I have reinvented myself a dozen times and this is a new reinvention . . . and it suits fine.

In fact, those who see aging as a positive experience have been found to live more than seven years longer than their less-positive counterparts (Levy, Slade, Kunkel, & Kasl, 2002).

Try to keep this joy in mind as you read in this chapter about physical functioning and cognitive competence during middle adulthood.

PHYSICAL DEVELOPMENT

Middle adulthood, a period characterized by changes in appearance and functioning of the body, spans roughly ages forty to sixty-five. There is enormous variability, however, in when and how these changes show up. During midlife, Oprah Winfrey's television and magazine empire peaked, and Winfrey shows little signs of slowing as she approaches later life. At age forty-five, George Foreman defeated a twenty-six-year-old's bid for the heavyweight boxing championship. Expectations of middle age have become more diverse. Many people, especially those from privileged backgrounds, see it as a continuation of early adulthood; others, especially those who work at jobs that are physically wearing, see it as time to begin slowing their pace.

The Biology of Aging

Chronological age, the measure of life in the years since birth, is not a good indicator of level of functioning because individual differences are so great. In determining physical or psychological functioning, it is more useful to measure the distance from death than the distance from birth. This has been done in some longitudinal studies but is not practical in everyday life, where we usually know date of birth but rarely know when death will occur. By age fifty, almost all adults show enough bodily changes to mark them clearly as being physically in middle adulthood.

The timing of middle adulthood depends on life expectancy. **Life expectancy** refers to a statistical estimate of the probable number of years remaining in the life of an individual based on the likelihood that members of a particular birth cohort will die at various ages. Life expectancy changes for each cohort from year to year as some people die and some survive. As Table 14.1 shows, life expectancy increased dramatically from 1900 to 2009. As life expectancy has increased, so have the number of years in each stage of adulthood. In 1900, for example, when a white female was expected to live 48.7 years, early adulthood ended much earlier than it does today; old age began earlier as well, and the middle years were the decade of the thirties. In 2009, life expectancy for a white female was 81.2 years, old age began at 65 years old, and the middle years were the decades of the forties through the mid-sixties.

life expectancy A statistical estimate of the likely number of years remaining in the life of an individual based on the likelihood that members of a particular cohort will die at various ages. This number changes for each cohort from year to year as some die and some survive.

TABLE 14.1 Life Expectancies by Sex and Race, 1900–2009

Age	1900 White	1900 African American	1950 White	1950 African American	1970 White	1970 African American	1990 White	1990 African American	2009 White	2009 African American	2009 Hispanic
Male											
At birth	46.6	32.5	66.5	58.9	68.0	60.0	72.7	64.5	76.4	71.1	78.7
65	11.5	10.4	12.8	12.9	13.1	12.5	15.2	13.2	17.7	15.8	19.4
Female											
At birth	48.7	33.5	72.2	62.7	75.6	68.3	79.4	73.6	81.2	77.6	83.5
65	12.2	11.4	15.1	14.9	17.1	15.7	19.1	17.2	20.3	19.3	22.0

Sources: National Center for Health Statistics (1993), U.S. Department of Health and Human Services (2014).

Life expectancies have increased dramatically since 1900, changing the timing and duration of adult life stages. Middle adulthood (which comprised the thirties early in the twentieth century), is now ages forty to sixty.

To understand why the variability in aging is so great, it helps to distinguish between primary aging and secondary aging. **Primary aging** refers to normal age-related changes that everyone experiences, such as menopause in women and similar hormonal changes in men. While differences exist in when primary aging occurs, the experience is universal and falls within a normal age range. **Secondary aging** refers to pathological aging, or the effects of illness or disease on the body due to environmental exposure or health-compromising behaviors. Because of vast differences in genetic makeup, health behaviors, and life circumstances, secondary aging shows much more variability. Some individuals experience secondary aging in their twenties or thirties, whereas others do not until their seventies or eighties.

primary aging Normal age-related changes that everyone experiences.

secondary aging Pathological aging, or the effects of illness and disease on the body due to genetic predisposition, environmental exposure, misuse or disuse of the body, or health-compromising behaviors.

Physical Functioning in Middle Adulthood

Physical functioning reaches its peak during early adulthood, plateaus for a period of time that depends on the particular bodily system, then gradually declines after that. Most adults do not feel the impact of the decline before age fifty, and some do so much later than that. **Organ reserve**, the extra capacity of lungs, heart, and other organs to respond to particularly demanding situations, shows the first signs of decline, but with no effect on normal activities. Most people enjoy good health and active lives for most, if not all, of their middle years. They continue to do the activities they have been doing, as well as try new activities.

organ reserve The extra capacity that the lungs, heart, and other organs have to respond to particularly intense or prolonged effort or unusually stressful events. Primary aging affects organ reserve so that most people first notice decline under stressful situations.

Strength

Strength slowly but steadily declines after its peak in early adulthood—so slowly that few people notice the change until age forty or fifty. After that, we experience approximately 8 to 10 percent reduction in strength for each ensuing decade (Katzel & Steinbrenner, 2012). However, people differ greatly in the amount of strength lost. During a ten-year study, Douglas Kallman, Chris Plato, and Jordan Tobin (1990) found that 29 percent of the middle-aged participants and 15 percent of the older ones lost no strength. Through experience, people develop greater skill and learn to use their strength more wisely, expending maximum effort only at the exact moment it is required. Strategies such as this conserve energy and make the decline in strength barely noticeable to most people.

Chapter 14 Physical and Cognitive Development in Middle Adulthood

After its peak in early adulthood, strength slowly but steadily declines. By engaging in regular physical activity like biking, this man retards muscle atrophy and may actually gain in muscle strength.
Source: bikeriderlondon/Shutterstock.com.

External and Internal Age-Related Changes

In middle adulthood, the outward signs of aging become apparent. Changes in skin, hair color, and body build result from a combination of primary and secondary aging. The skin becomes less elastic with age, but exposure to sun and wind accelerates these changes, so the face and other exposed areas of the body suffer the most damage. Sun and wind exposure at young ages is particularly damaging, although the damage does not show up until middle adulthood. In a comparison of young (twenty-five to thirty-one years) and middle-aged (forty-five to fifty-one years) women who had low sun exposure (less than two hours per week) and high sun exposure (more than twelve hours a week) over the prior year, high exposure did not substantially affect the appearance of the young women's skin, but the middle-aged group had significantly more wrinkles and lower skin elasticity (Warren et al., 1991). Judges perceived the high-exposure middle-aged women to be older than the low-exposure ones. The impact of sun exposure and the speeding-up of skin aging have been replicated in studies using objective measures of skin damage and wrinkling (Kimlin & Guo, 2012).

Age-related changes in hair color and distribution of hair growth also affect appearance. Although hair tends to darken with age, this process is reversed when graying begins due to loss of pigment, which may occur as early as the twenties. Half of men and women over age fifty have at least 50 percent gray scalp hair (Ashburn, 1992). Additionally, hair on the scalp begins to thin for both men and women, and may begin to grow or thicken in unwanted areas, such as on women's chins (Whitbourne, 2001).

Aging also changes body build. People tend to gain weight through the mid- to late fifties as fatty tissue and muscle are redistributed throughout the body. When individuals begin to lose muscle, fat will replace muscle if they do not increase their exercise or decrease their calorie consumption. As we saw in the Chapter 12 discussion of physical development in early adulthood, women tend to add more body fat than men do. So-called "middle-age spread" is not inevitable, however; regular exercise and proper diet can prevent or correct the addition of excess fat. Ellen DeGeneres, though into her fifties, shows no sign of middle-age spread. Adults who stay active in sports or run marathons lose little muscle and gain little weight (Kavanaugh & Shephard, 1990; Pollock et al., 1987; Ryan, 2011). Even sedentary adults in their middle and later years can strengthen muscles and lose body fat by engaging in regular endurance-type exercise, such as walking, biking, or jogging (Spirduso, 1995).

Cardiovascular Changes

The cardiovascular system continues to undergo the changes begun during early adulthood. Research shows decreases in maximum oxygen consumption and the heart rate attained during maximum levels of exertion starting in early adulthood and proceeding by about

In the middle years, the outward signs of aging become apparent. The differences we can see in the faces of this mother and daughter stem from the combination of primary aging of muscle, fibrous tissue, and skin and secondary aging from years of exposure to sun and wind.
Source: Tom Wang/Shutterstock.com.

10 percent per decade throughout the adult years (Bouchard & Shephard, 1993). Decreasing capacity of the left ventricle of the heart to contract completely lessens the amount of blood pumped with each heartbeat (atherosclerosis). This change, along with increasing rigidity of the arterial walls (arteriosclerosis), causes the losses in cardiovascular functioning. During midlife, lifelong eating and exercise habits may also result in arterial plaque buildup, further reducing cardiovascular functioning (Katzel & Steinbrenner, 2012).

Continuous and regular exercise helps to counteract these changes. Ample evidence indicates that athletes who continue their sports into their middle and later years experience considerably smaller reductions in cardiovascular functioning, though they still see some age-related reductions (Katzel & Steinbrenner, 2012; Pollock et al., 1987). The relative risk of heart attack decreases as a function of the level of energy expended in moderate to vigorous exercise for men and women, independently of other risk factors such as smoking, diet, medical history, and personality type (O'Connor et al., 1995). Additionally, improvement in diet and exercise has been related to lower levels of low-density lipoproteins (LDL), which lead to arterial plaque buildup, and higher levels of high-density lipoproteins (HDL), which help remove LDLs from the bloodstream (American Heart Association, 2014; Katzel & Steinbrenner, 2012).

Respiratory System Changes

The changes in the respiratory system that began in early adulthood continue and progress with age. Primary aging includes changes in the breathing apparatus and tissues of the lungs that are not due to pathological aging (Christiansen & Grzybowski, 1993). The amount of oxygen in the blood after it has passed through the lungs decreases with age across adulthood. This is due to loss of elasticity in the lung tissue, structural changes in the alveoli (the sacs in the lungs where the exchange of oxygen and carbon dioxide takes place), and resistance to expansion of the chest wall during breathing. Getting regular exercise and avoiding environmental pollutants and tobacco smoke beginning in early adulthood can prevent some, but not all, of the age-related respiratory system changes.

Sensory System Changes

Middle adulthood is a time when people start complaining that their arms have become too short to hold a paper far enough away from their eyes to read it. By age fifty, most people require reading glasses or bifocals if they already wear glasses because they have been nearsighted. The lens of the eye continually grows new fibers without shedding the old ones, so the lens continues to thicken and gradually loses its capacity to accommodate. *Accommodation* is the process of changing the shape of the lens to focus on things that are close.

Hearing loss begins gradually in early adulthood and progresses until the eighties. The loss comes sooner and is greatest in the high-frequency range and is due to

> **What Do You Think?**
>
> Try to imagine the kinds of physical changes you will experience at midlife, or consider the changes you have already experienced. How will (do) these changes affect the kinds of activities you currently engage in? How might (do) you compensate for these changes?

several changes in the inner ear, including loss of receptor cells, atrophy of the nerve fibers, changes in the conducting fluid, and deficiency in the vibrating motion of the basilar membrane, which helps to transform sound vibrations into electrical signals. Men have poorer hearing in the high frequencies than women do, likely because they have been exposed to more environmental noise at their jobs, they have higher rates of firearm use, and they have been exposed to louder noise during leisure activities, such as listening to loud music (Lin, Thorpe, Gordon-Slant, & Ferrucci, 2011). Despite the measurable losses, however, most adults in this stage are able to function normally. They may turn up the volume on the television set or ask someone to speak up, but only a small percentage have a loss that qualifies as a hearing impairment.

Taste and smell sensitivity both decrease slowly during middle adulthood. In a three-year study of nineteen-to-ninety-five-year-olds, smell identification decreased gradually with age but did not show a large decline until individuals were in their seventies (Ship et al., 1996). This is due in part to a reduction in the number of olfactory receptors throughout life and to less specific responding of those neurons (Rawson, Gomez, Cowart, Kriete, Pribitkin, & Restrepo, 2012). Women consistently identified smell better than men did. Changes in taste are even smaller than changes in smell and are unlikely to have an impact during middle adulthood (Hooyman & Kiyak, 1993). Similarly, though there is some evidence that our sensitivity to touch is gradually decreasing and our sensitivity to pain is gradually increasing, these changes are not likely to be evident during middle adulthood.

Although some losses occur due to primary aging, regular body maintenance starting in early adulthood can keep bodily systems in optimal shape so that aging does not take a serious toll on physical functioning during middle adulthood. While some adjustments are necessary, such as wearing glasses or getting better seats at a concert, quality of life is not negatively affected. Nevertheless, secondary aging can accelerate overall aging by adding pathological changes to age-related ones. These changes make health an important concern in middle adulthood, as we will see next.

Health in Middle Adulthood

Middle-aged adults become more aware of health issues than they were when younger as they continue to enjoy active, healthy lives. Bernice Neugarten (1968) found that men paid increased attention to their health as they felt their bodies become less efficient and learned of male friends and colleagues their own age having heart attacks, whereas women were more concerned with their husbands' health than their own and worried about becoming widows. This change in "body monitoring," or continual, low-key concern about health and well-being, reflects the realities that some chronic diseases do become apparent in the forties and fifties as the effects of lifelong behaviors take their toll and that they are likely to affect men sooner than women. Men are much more often victims of premature death, as the "Focusing On" feature indicates. Both morbidity and mortality rates increase in middle adulthood. **Morbidity** refers to the number of cases of a disease; **mortality** refers to the number of deaths. Poor diet, lack of exercise, smoking, obesity, and alcohol abuse influence the cardiovascular and respiratory symptoms, as do environmental elements. The cumulative effects of stress on the body may produce signs of wear and tear by middle adulthood because, as we discussed in Chapter 12, physiological responses to psychosocial stress can lead to fatigue, hypertension, ulceration, impotence, decreased growth and repair, and decreased immune system response.

The lines between early, middle, and late adulthood are blurring as increasing numbers of Americans continue to be healthy and vigorous well into their later years.

morbidity The measure of health that refers to the number of cases of a disease in a given population.

mortality The proportion of people who die at a given age; the rate of death.

Most middle-aged adults are not much different in physical health than young adults, whereas some already suffer the chronic diseases that are more common in late adulthood. Even among older adults, fewer than ever are reporting limitation in activities due to health, especially those who avoid smoking, excess weight, and inactivity (Chakravarty, Hubert, Krisnan, Bruce, Lingala, & Fries, 2012; Vita et al., 1998). For this reason, although cardiovascular disease, hypertension, cancer, and arthritis are chronic diseases that do show up with some frequency in middle adulthood, we save our discussion of them for Chapter 16 because they are more representative of health in late adulthood.

Health and Health-Compromising Behaviors

Many of the factors that contribute to secondary aging are related to the health behaviors and health-compromising behaviors we considered in our discussion of early adulthood in Chapter 12. Because life is continuous, behaviors at younger ages lay the groundwork for health and well-being (or ill health and disability) in the years to come and for the next generation as well. One study found that a year after teaching parents (ages thirty to forty-five) how to improve their diets, both parents and children (ages four to twenty-one) had less fat in their diets and better eating habits (Kashani et al., 1991). Smoking has a negative health impact on the smoker and on his or her immediate family, especially young children.

The best demonstration so far that choosing health behaviors can prevent disabilities and functional limitations that have been strongly associated with old age comes from an ongoing longitudinal study tracking more than seventeen hundred women and men who graduated from the University of Pennsylvania in 1939 and 1940. Participants were considered to be at high, moderate, or low risk for poor health based on three health-compromising behaviors: cigarette smoking, excess weight, and inactivity. The level of disability found was directly related to the degree of risk based on these health-compromising behaviors. Those who chose not to smoke, who controlled their weight, and who exercised regularly (the low-risk group) were least likely to develop disabilities (Chakravarty et al., 2012; Vita et al., 1998).

Health-promoting behaviors positively affect health in multiple ways. For example, in addition to benefiting the cardiovascular and respiratory systems and helping to control weight, exercise enhances the ability to cope with psychosocial stressors (Edenfield & Blumenthal, 2011; King et al., 1993). Compared to nonexercisers, regular aerobic exercisers have lower levels of chronic stress, react less strongly to stressors, and recover more efficiently from stressors (Edenfield & Blumenthal, 2011; Spirduso, 1998). Coming from a family that exercises regularly, having a positive attitude toward physical activity, having social support for exercising, and believing people should be responsible for their health increase the likelihood that a person will get involved in an exercise program (Lachman & Agrigoroaei, 2010; Taylor, 1998). Practical barriers and social attitudes that discourage exercise among middle-aged and older women, however, make it especially unlikely that they will get exercise (Lee, 1992). Successful interventions focus on these factors. A study focused on low-income midlife women, a group particularly at risk for obesity, found significant increases in physical activity and weight loss among women who attended sessions that included group discussions of health and wellness and demonstrations of exercises (Samuel-Hodge et al., 2013).

An often-overlooked health-promoting behavior is obtaining sufficient or undisturbed sleep. Sleep disturbance due to sleep disorders such as obstructive sleep apnea, restless legs disorder, and periodic limb movement disorder have been linked to hypertension (Calhoun & Harding, 2010), as has insufficient sleep (six or fewer hours) and excessive sleep (nine hours or more) (Knutson et al., 2009). Moreover, insufficient and excessive sleep is related to overall mortality risk (Cappuccio, D'Elia, Strazzullo, & Miller, 2010). Beyond the physical benefits of sleep, studies suggest that sufficient sleep is associated with maintenance of cognitive functioning (Ferrie, Shipley, Akbaraly, Marmot, Kivimaki, & Singh-Manoux, 2011).

Focusing On...

The Gender Gap in Life Expectancy

Women have a longer life expectancy than men do. Although the gender gap narrows with increasing age, it never disappears. This reflects the fact that women are afflicted less often by the leading causes of death at all ages. The two leading causes, heart disease and cancer, are excellent examples.

Diseases of the heart, the number one cause of death, afflict men earlier and more often than they afflict women. Figure 14.1 shows death rates for heart disease by age and sex for 2000–2011. Among the age group 45 to 54 years, the rate for men was two and a half times the rate for women; among individuals 75- to 84-years and over, the rate for men was one and a half that for women.

The second leading killer is cancer. As Figure 14.2 shows, men and women have essentially the same death rate from cancer in the 20- to 49-year-old age group. In this case, the gap widens rather than narrows with age.

Although no one knows why the gender gap exists, biological and psychosocial factors are clearly involved. Female sex hormones seem to provide biological protection from some diseases (Markides, 1990). This is especially clear for diseases of the heart, where rates for women increase dramatically after menopause and can be positively affected by postmenopausal estrogen replacement. Psychosocial factors include men's greater tendency to engage in smoking and other health-compromising behaviors, take risks, and be exposed to occupational toxins and hazards. There is reason to believe that psychosocial factors have more to do with the gender gap in cancer deaths. The gender gap in life expectancy has narrowed since 1980, a fact that has been

FIGURE 14.1
Death Rates from Heart Disease by Sex and Age, 2008

Although the gender gap gets smaller with age, it never disappears. Both biological and psychosocial factors contribute to women's lower death rates from heart disease.
Source: National Heart, Lung, and Blood Institute (2012).

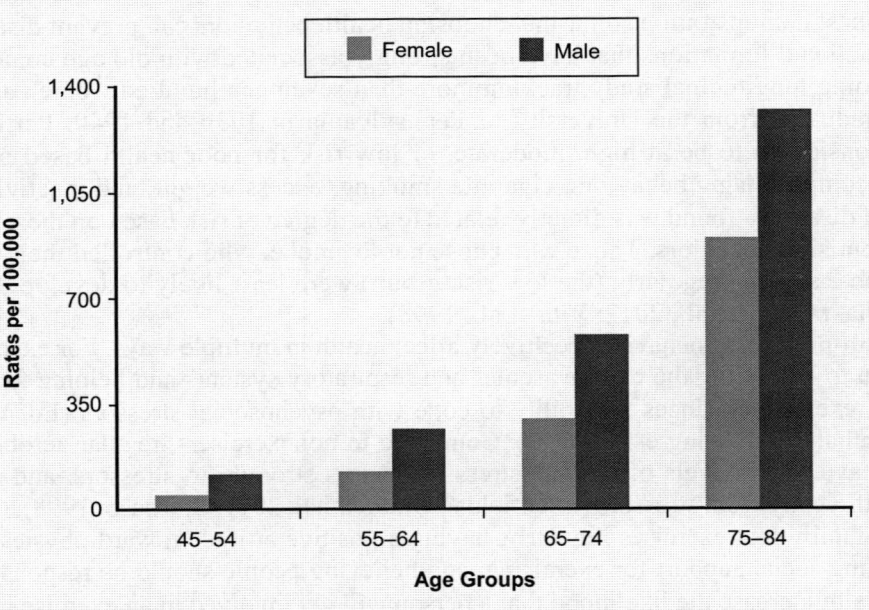

Health-compromising behaviors often are linked; individuals who smoke heavily are also likely to drink heavily, for example. Gary Friedman and his associates (1991) explored the relationship between alcohol drinking and cigarette smoking among middle-aged white and African American men and women. They found a strong association between drinking and smoking: the percentage of cigarette smokers increased as the amount of alcohol consumption increased. The number of cigarettes smoked per day was the best predictor of how much alcohol was consumed. Given the lower rates of smoking in recent years, smoking is a stronger predictor of drinking, rather than the opposite (Room, 2004).. Though some studies have linked moderate consumption of alcohol among women with better health during late life (Sun et al., 2011), heavy alcohol consumption increases risk of cardiovascular problems, including stroke (Reynolds et al., 2003). Health-compromising behaviors are also linked to cancers that become frequent in middle adulthood, such as breast and prostate cancer.

Focusing On...

The Gender Gap in Life Expectancy *continued*

attributed to the increase in smoking rates among women since World War II (Verbrugge, 1989a). Moreover, similar findings linking the shrinking gender gap and smoking have been found in Japan (Liu et al., 2013).

An additional behavioral difference that is likely playing a role in the gender gap in life expectancy is the utilization of health care. Women are more likely than men to use health care services, including preventive care services (Vaidya, Partha, & Karmakar, 2012). Additionally, men are more likely to engage in delay behaviors, meaning that when they do finally seek treatment, their prognosis is worse than if they had used health services earlier (Straub, 2014; Tannenbaum & Frank, 2011).

Women have longer life expectancies but suffer more from illnesses that are not life threatening, such as arthritis. Lois Verbrugge (1989b) reanalyzed several large-scale health studies and found that morbidity was influenced by social factors, such as less employment, more deeply felt stress and unhappiness, stronger feelings of vulnerability to illness, fewer formal time constraints, and less physically strenuous leisure activities. Women's biological advantage protects them from mortality, but their social disadvantage puts them at risk for morbidity.

What Do You Think?

List the changes men could make in their lifestyles to reduce the gender gap in death rates from these two diseases. Would these be positive or negative changes in other respects? Why or why not?

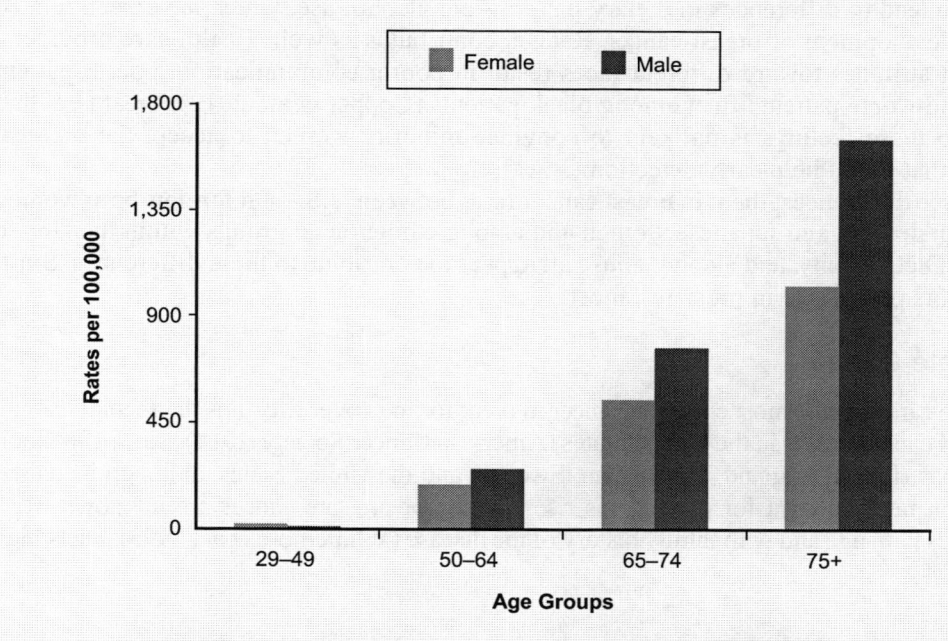

FIGURE 14.2
Death Rates from Cancer by Sex and Age, 2000–2011

In the case of cancer, the gender gap increases with age. There is reason to believe that psychosocial factors contribute more to the gender gap in cancer deaths because the gap has narrowed as more women have become smokers.
Source: National Cancer Institute (2011).

Breast Cancer

Breast cancer is frightening to women, young and old, because it is so prevalent in the United States. Breast cancer rates among foreign-born Chinese and Filipina women are substantially less than rates among Chinese and Filipina women born in North America, which points to lifestyle factors as likely causes (Lin Gomez et al., 2010). Although more women in the United States die of lung cancer than of breast cancer annually, more new cases of breast cancer than lung cancer are diagnosed each year. The widely published statistic that one out of eight women will develop this disease in her lifetime is both scary and misleading—scary because it indicates that breast cancer is bound to hit close to home and misleading because this figure is for women who live to be ninety-five years old. For women under age seventy, the incidence is one in fourteen. While breast cancer can occur at any age, incidence increases rapidly between ages thirty and fifty, then continues to rise, but more slowly, after fifty (Harris et al., 1992).

Death rates from breast cancer used to be higher for white women than for black women. As Figure 14.3 shows, while incidence rates of breast cancer have remained fairly stable over the last decade, with white women being slightly less likely to be diagnosed with breast cancer than black women, black women are substantially more likely to die from breast cancer than all other races and ethnicities (Center for Disease Control, 2013).

Socioeconomic, genetic, and cultural factors each contribute to this inequity. Early detection of breast cancer predicts a higher survival rate, and black women are less likely to be diagnosed at an early stage of the disease. Furthermore, minority women have less access to cancer prevention services, such as mammography, and use them less. After diagnosis, black women also receive less adjuvant therapies aimed at reducing relapse (van Ravesteyn et al., 2010). These are both likely related to socioeconomic factors because higher-income and better-educated women also use mammography more than do lower-SES women. With higher SES comes the greater likelihood of medical insurance and regular checkups rather than reliance on emergency medical care. Yet when Beth Jones and associates (1995) studied 145 black and 177 white women newly diagnosed with breast cancer, they found that mammography was better able to protect white women than black women from late-stage diagnosis. Genetic factors may affect how the cancer progresses (Shiao et al., 1995; van Ravesteyn et al., 2011).

Cultural factors can also contribute to differences in medical care by affecting attitudes toward seeking or following medical advice about breast cancer screening. Cultural values also lead to differences in dietary patterns and alcohol use, which have been related to the development of breast cancer. Racism contributes as well. Health care providers' implicit attitudes toward different races result in poorer communication, poorer patient care, and worse patient affect among black patients (Cooper et al., 2012). Treatment that leads to these feelings is unlikely to convince minority women to accept the medical advice that might help early detection.

We see differences, then, in breast cancer rates between U.S.- and foreign-born women of Asian descent and Japanese women and among ethnic/racial groups within the United States. Diet, obesity, and alcohol abuse all appear to contribute to these differences. Similar factors play a role in prostate cancer.

Prostate Cancer

Prostate cancer is the most common cancer in men; for men over fifty, it is the second leading cause of cancer deaths in the United States (American Cancer Society, 2014). Since 1968 incidence has risen in England, Italy, Japan, Sweden, and the United States, although increased detection rates account for part of this rise. Causes of prostate cancer are unknown. Risk increases with age and with family history of the disease (Whittemore et al., 1995). Diets high

FIGURE 14.3
Death Rates from Breast Cancer, White and African American Women, 2005–2011

Over the past four decades, death rates from breast cancer have been rising among black women while remaining stable among white women. Socioeconomic, genetic, and cultural factors all contribute to this inequity.
Source: Centers for Disease Control (2014a).

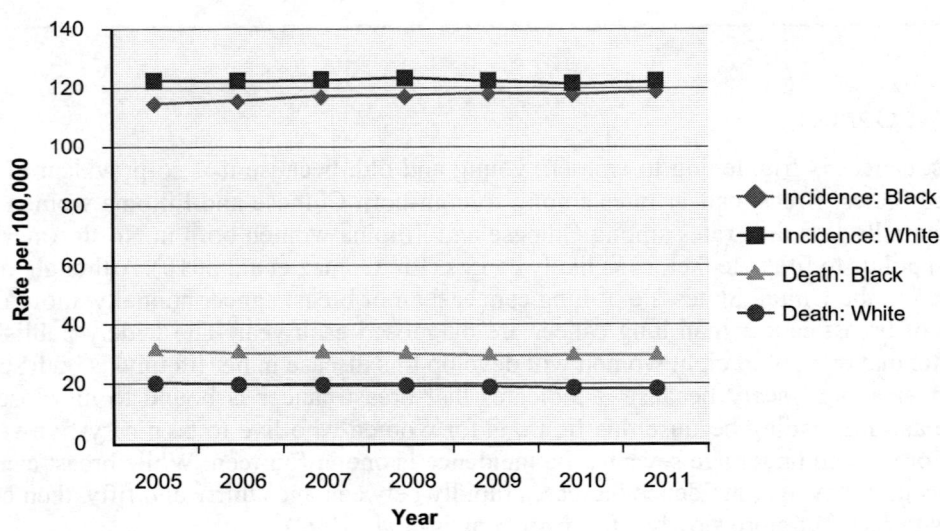

in red meats and dairy have been linked to increased risk for prostate cancer among Caucasian men (Wright et al., 2011). Marked differences in ethnic and racial trends have been observed both in the United States and internationally. Diagnosis rates for African American men are higher than those for white men, which in turn are higher than those for Hispanic men, Native American men, and Asian American men, respectively, although the reasons are not understood (American Cancer Society, 2014). As Figure 14.4 shows, African American men have both higher incidence and higher mortality rates from prostate cancer than do white men in the United States. This is most evident between ages fifty to seventy (Powell, 1994). As we saw with breast cancer, African Americans are diagnosed with prostate cancer at a more advanced stage, which partially accounts for their higher mortality rate. Additionally, African American men are provided with less aggressive treatment plans than Caucasian men when diagnosed with prostate cancer (Chornokur, Dalton, Borysova, & Kumar, 2011). When adjusting for age, black men, who receive less aggressive treatment, have mortality rates between two- and three-times higher than white men and had lower subsequent quality of life (Chornokur et al., 2011) Socioeconomic, environmental, dietary, and genetic factors may be involved in racial disparities in prostate cancer mortality rates as well (Morton, 1994; Wright et al., 2011).

Prostate cancer grows slowly and is unlikely to produce symptoms. It is usually discovered during surgery to relieve urinary problems, by a routine digital exam, or by a blood test called *PSA*. PSA measures blood levels of the prostate-specific antigen, a protein that may be elevated when cancer is present. Because "normal" PSA levels vary from man to man and can be elevated by other diseases, the blood test sometimes fails to detect cancer and sometimes falsely indicates prostate cancer. Because prostate cancer grows slowly, finding evidence of cancer cells in the blood early can lead to early treatment (Josefson, 1998). More recently, specialized MRIs also are being used to diagnose and evaluate prostate cancer (Verma et al., 2012). Even when detected, treatment recommendations vary from waiting until evidence of cancer progression appears to treating with radiation or radical prostatectomy (removal of the prostate) soon after detection. Treatment varies widely by geographic regions and by ethnicity of patient (Chornokur et al., 2011; Harlan et al., 1995).

Health and Inequality

As our discussions of breast and prostate cancer indicate, disadvantaged ethnic minorities, such as African Americans and most Hispanic American groups, experience greater health problems and earlier deaths than whites in the United States (Chornokur et al., 2011; Markides & Black, 1996; van Ravesteyn et al., 2010). Minority populations have less access to economic resources. They also have widely varying values, beliefs, and cultural practices that may have an impact on health. How can we understand the factors that contribute to the poorer health of racial/ethnic minorities?

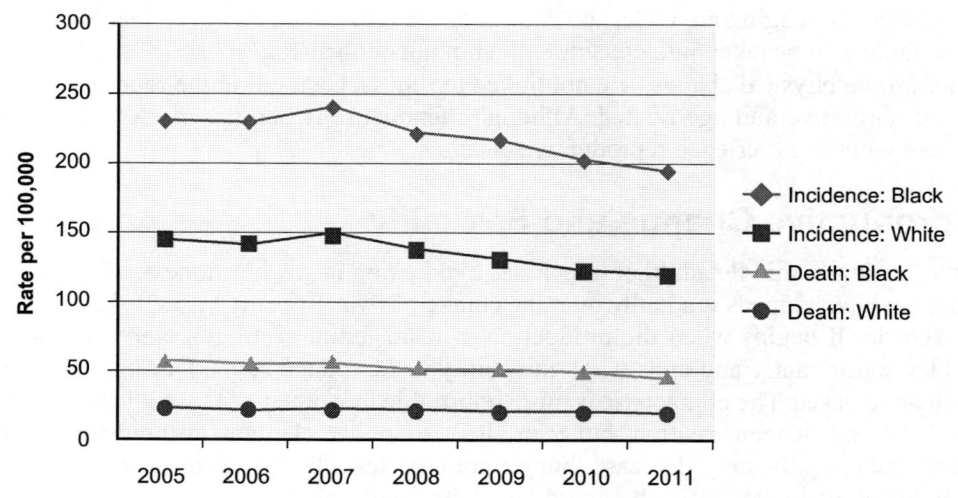

FIGURE 14.4

Age-Adjusted Prostate Cancer Incidence and Death Rates by Race, 2005–2011

African American men have both higher incidence of and higher mortality rates from prostate cancer than white men in the United States. Socioeconomic, genetic, and cultural factors all contribute to this difference.

Source: Centers for Disease Control (2014b).

In an effort to distinguish between health problems due to SES and those due to other racial/ethnic factors, Richard Cooper and his associates studied the black-white difference in hypertension in Cuba (Ordúñez-García et al., 1998). They wanted to know if biological factors were at work in addition to social factors. They chose Cuba for several reasons. First, Cubans trace their ethnic origins primarily to either Africa or Spain. Second, the life expectancy and ratio of physicians to the population are similar for Cuba and the United States. Third, the Cuban government has made significant progress in reducing differences in SES and status due to ethnic origins. Though inequalities still exist in Cuba, they are much less pronounced than in the United States. Would the investigators find substantially higher rates in hypertension among Cubans with African compared to Spanish heritage, similar to the higher rates of African Americans compared to European Americans in the United States?

Using a random sample of 1,633 adults from the city of Cienfuegos, the investigators measured blood pressure and asked questions about cigarette smoking, alcohol intake, physical exercise, and diet. They found that blacks of all ages were more likely to be smokers and to drink alcohol. Yet only the oldest black participants in the study had higher blood pressure than the white participants. Because these black older adults would have grown up before the current Cuban government made social and economic changes, the difference between hypertension rates in that segment of the sample and the rates of younger participants may have been due to inequality early in the older participants' lives. Overall, the researchers found that hypertension is more common in Cuba than in the United States (perhaps because Cuba is a poorer country than the United States, or perhaps due to cultural differences in health-compromising behaviors), but the magnitude of the racial/ethnic difference is smaller. In other words, a Cuban is at higher risk for hypertension than a U.S. resident on average, but an African Cuban is no more at risk than a Spanish Cuban, whereas an African American is more at risk than a European American. The implications of this study are that inequality rather than race/ethnicity is responsible for differentials in hypertension.

How does inequality create differences in health? It does so in physical, social, and psychological ways. First, inequality limits access to economic resources, which leads to more health-compromising behaviors among lower-SES compared to higher-SES groups (Ruzek, 1997). In the United States, low SES limits access to quality medical care and to educational resources that can teach health prevention. It also pushes people into more hazardous jobs and more dangerous neighborhoods (Loomis & Richardson, 1998). Second, the long-term challenges of financial strain, role overload, and unsafe working and living conditions create chronic stress (George, 1996). Third, low SES deprives people of self-esteem, a sense of control, and feelings of mastery, all of which are psychological resources that reduce stress and promote health. In fact, countries with standardized health care systems still see great SES disparities in health, suggesting that health-promoting behaviors, stress, and perceived control play substantial roles in health (Machenbach, 2012).

By middle adulthood, health concerns are more prevalent than in early adulthood, but behaviors in early adulthood and early middle adulthood can lead to healthy later years. Not all aspects of aging are under the control of the individual, however. Genetic factors, for example, can be taken into consideration but not controlled. As we will see in the next section, some physical changes are not linked to illness. Changes in the reproductive system are normative and age related. Although menopause is perhaps more familiar, both men and women experience reproductive changes.

Reproductive Change and Sexuality

Primary aging in middle adulthood includes a reduction in sex hormone production. This process, which happens gradually over the course of five to twenty years, is known as the **climacteric**. It begins when the production of testosterone, estrogen, and progesterone declines significantly and ends when the ability to reproduce stops. During the process, fertility decreases. The climacteric is more noticeable in women because it leads to menopause, the end of menstruation, but men also experience changes in their reproductive systems that significantly decrease, but do not end, fertility. What changes occur within the body? How do they affect how middle adults function and feel?

climacteric The gradual reduction in sex hormone production that is an aspect of primary aging during middle adulthood, leading to menopause among women and reproductive changes among men that decrease fertility.

> **What Do You Think?**
>
> What health-promoting behaviors could you adopt that would reduce your risk for secondary aging? What are some health-compromising behaviors that you might engage in less frequently?

Menopause

When a previously menstruating woman has gone an entire year without a menstrual period, she has reached **menopause**. The term *climacteric* more properly refers to the entire process that ends with menopause, but most people think and talk about the process as menopause—that is, if they talk of it at all. Until recently, menopause has been a little discussed and poorly understood topic. Doctors in the United States have considered menopause as an illness to be treated with hormones, tranquilizers, and surgery rather than as a natural process in women's bodies (Northrup, 1994). Research has demonstrated that women's attitudes toward menopause play a large role in their experiences. Attitudes toward menopause tend to shift from negative during early adulthood to neutral or positive as women move toward midlife (Ayers, Forshaw, & Hunter, 2010). Scientific research has failed to show that depression in midlife women is associated with menopause (Nicol-Smith, 1996). Despite the evidence, menopause is still stereotyped in the United States as causing moodiness, irritability, depression, and despair. In fact, women who view menopause in a negative light are more likely to experience worse symptoms and depression, though the direction of causality remains unclear (Ayers, Forshaw, & Hunter, 2010).

menopause The second stage of the female climacteric during which hormone production is reduced, the ovaries cease to produce eggs, and menstruation ceases.

Additionally, we find cultural differences in the experience of menopause. Margaret Lock found that Japanese women reported very few symptoms (especially in contrast to both American and Canadian women), including hot flashes, the most commonly reported symptom among the North American groups. Lock also found that Japanese doctors prescribe surgery and hormones infrequently (Lock, 1993). In fact, women from many Asian countries report fewer negative menopause symptoms (Reed et al., 2013). These differences in the experience of menopause may be due to diet (Adlercreutz et al., 1992), attitudes and expectations (Ayers, Forshaw, & Hunter, 2010), or possibly biological differences. Furthermore, as we will see in the next chapter, middle adulthood can be a difficult time for women, but more because of social factors than biological ones (Notman, 1990).

Physical Changes

Decreased ovarian functioning causes menopause. Because of age-related changes, the ovarian follicles, or egg-forming cells, are no longer able to react to the follicle-stimulating hormone (FSH), and estrogen production gradually decreases. When ovulation fails to occur, progesterone, which is secreted after the egg ruptures from the follicle, is not produced. The reduced levels of estrogen and progesterone give rise to the physiological changes of menopause.

Menopause is a gradual process and occurs in three stages. During *perimenopause,* the first stage, the ovaries gradually decrease hormone production. This decrease begins around age forty and continues until menstruation stops. A perimenopausal woman may notice a change in her menstrual cycle, with periods becoming more closely spaced, more widely spaced, or irregular. Her menstrual flow may change, becoming lighter or heavier. Decreased progesterone causes lighter flow, whereas an unusually high level of estrogen causes heavier flow. Some women experience no menstrual changes and simply stop menstruating. Inconsistent hormone production may cause erratic flow. As her body tries to adjust to the inconsistency, a woman may have more severe premenstrual symptoms, such as water retention and breast tenderness. Women tend to gain weight during perimenopause, but this can be reduced by restricting salt intake and exercising regularly.

Menopause itself is actually the second stage of the female climacteric. Hormone production declines further, the ovaries cease to produce eggs, and menstruation ceases. Because a woman may still ovulate sporadically after regular periods have stopped, she is said to have reached menopause when she has had no period for a year; at that point the woman is sterile, and pregnancy is no longer possible. The average age for menopause in the United States is 51.4 years (Ashburn, 1992; National Institute on Aging, 2013), a shift from an average of forty years in the last century (Mishell & Brenner, 1986). Age of menopause seems to be genetically determined; daughters and mothers tend to have similar timing. It is not related to number of pregnancies, breast-feeding experience, race, education, SES, age of onset of menstruation, or height or weight. It is related to health status; women who are malnourished or who smoke tend to have an earlier menopause (McKinlay et al., 1992).

During *postmenopause,* the third stage, hormonal levels stabilize and menopausal signs subside. A woman is not totally without estrogen during postmenopause because the ovaries continue to produce small amounts and the adrenal glands produce the precursors of estrogen, which are converted to estrogen by stored body fat. The estrogen level is far lower, however, than when the ovaries were producing large amounts.

Physical Signs

The most common sign of menopause in the United States is the *hot flash,* a sensation of internally generated heat beginning in the chest and moving to the face and the rest of the body (National Institutes of Health, 2008). Hot flashes are often accompanied by heavy perspiration and may be preceded or followed by a chill. They result from blood rushing to the surface of the skin when decreased estrogen causes vasomotor instability. Approximately 80 to 90 percent of Western women experience hot flashes, which most frequently occur at night (Hunter et al., 2012; Reed et al., 2013). Night sweats, as nighttime hot flashes are called, disrupt sleep and may bring on the insomnia that menopausal women sometimes experience. Some women have no or only occasional hot flashes, many have them once a day, and some have them more than once a day (Avis & Crawford, 2006). Obese women have fewer hot flashes because they have more estrogen converted from stored fat. While a majority of American women experience hot flashes and/or night sweats, only 10 percent experience severe symptoms (Gannon, 1985). Hot flashes are not common in all cultures, as noted earlier, and can be treated effectively with placebos, indicating that expectations play a part in causing them (Northrup, 1994), and more recently with soy supplements, indicating that diet is also playing a role in cultural variations (Kyoko et al., 2012). When they do occur, hot flashes typically last two or three years. They are sometimes referred to as *power surges* because they come at a time when women are relieved of their reproductive functions and, as we will see in the next chapter, likely to be gaining power at home and at work.

Vaginal changes are another common physical sign of menopause. Decreased lubrication, thinning of the vaginal lining, loss of elasticity, and foreshortening or narrowing of the vagina sometimes follow menopause (National Institutes of Health, 2008). These

This family's typical Japanese meal includes many soy products, such as tofu and miso, which are rich in phytoestrogens. This natural estrogen-rich diet contributes to the low incidence of hot flashes among Japanese women during menopause.
Source: kazoka/Shutterstock.com.

changes can lead to vaginal dryness, itching, painful intercourse, and greater susceptibility to infection. Some vaginal changes occur as early as premenopause, but more often, they occur during postmenopause and sometimes not until late adulthood.

Other less frequently reported signs include palpitations (rapid heartbeat), nervousness, dizziness, short-temperedness, mood swings, weight increase, and memory changes. However, the empirical evidence for these is limited, as it is unclear if these are due to menopause or are caused by other factors related to aging (National Institutes of Health, 2008).

Surgical Menopause

Thus far, we have been discussing natural menopause. Surgical menopause is the sudden onset of menopause due to removal of the ovaries or, in some cases, removal of the uterus. Surgical removal of the uterus, called **hysterectomy**, is performed with relative frequency in the United States, and the average age for the procedure is in one's mid-forties (Wu, Wechter, Geller, Nguyen, & Visco, 2007). At present rates, 37 percent of all women will have had a hysterectomy by the time they reach age sixty (Bachmann, 1990). In a cross-cultural comparison, Margaret Lock (1993) found that only 8.7 percent of Japanese women ages forty-five to fifty-five had had hysterectomies, in contrast to 28.1 percent of U.S. women. A hysterectomy is a risky procedure that is called for under certain circumstances, such as in the treatment of advanced cancers, but is performed for many often-questionable reasons, such as menstrual irregularities.

Whereas hysterectomy sometimes triggers menopause, **oophorectomy**, surgical removal of the ovaries, always does. Oophorectomy suddenly and drastically reduces estrogen production, bringing on surgical menopause. Lock (1993) found that only 3.4 percent of the Japanese women in her study had had bilateral (both sides) oophorectomy, in contrast to 16.2 percent of the U.S. women. The symptoms of surgical menopause are more numerous and severe than those of natural menopause because the body does not have a chance to adjust gradually to the changing hormonal levels. For this reason, studies of menopausal symptoms that have included women experiencing surgical menopause give an artificially negative picture of the natural process.

Hormone Replacement Therapy

Because the natural decrease in hormones brings on menopausal symptoms, one way to alleviate them is to replace the hormones. Replacement can be made by **estrogen replacement therapy (ERT)**, the taking of replacement estrogen, or by **hormone replacement therapy (HRT)**, the taking of a combination of estrogen and progestin (artificial progesterone). ERT has historically been recommended to reduce the symptoms of surgical menopause. For women who have not had a hysterectomy, ERT has been shown to increase the risk of endometrial cancer (cancer of the lining of the uterus) by 500 to 800 percent (Kaufert & McKinlay, 1985). There is evidence that the incidence of other kinds of cancer, particularly breast cancer and other gynecological cancers, increases with the replacement of estrogen, whether through ERT or HRT (Colditz et al., 1995: Schneider, Jick, & Meier, 2009). Although cancer can be treated if detected early, it is a serious risk factor associated with ERT and HRT.

Nevertheless, ERT and HRT have benefits beyond alleviating menopausal signs. In combination with exercise and diet, they can help to prevent **osteoporosis**, the degeneration of the bone that affects an estimated one in three postmenopausal women (Notelovitz, 1997). A class of drugs called bisphosphonates, such as Boniva, are now effectively used either alone or in conjunction with HRT among women who are at risk for osteoporosis (Boonen, 2007). Studies have also demonstrated a reduced risk of coronary heart disease with HRT (Grodstein et al., 1996), though scientists debate the magnitude of risk reduction overall and in relation to increased cancer risk (Alexandersen, Karsdal, & Christiansen, 2009). Additionally, studies measuring the impact of taking hormones have been done by following women who undergo ERT or HRT and those who do not, but the women are not randomly assigned to those who take or those who do not take the hormones. This means that women who take hormones are generally more affluent and healthier than those who do not and would have lower rates of disease anyway (Payer, 1992).

hysterectomy Surgical removal of the uterus.

oophorectomy The surgical removal of the ovaries; triggers surgical menopause.

estrogen replacement therapy (ERT) The administration of replacement estrogen to alleviate menopausal symptoms; sometimes recommended for women who have surgical menopause.

hormone replacement therapy (HRT) The administration of estrogen and progestin (artificial progesterone) to alleviate menopausal symptoms that is sometimes recommended for women who have not had a hysterectomy because ERT has been shown to increase the rate of endometrial cancer.

osteoporosis The degeneration of bone; affects about 33 percent of postmenopausal women and can be prevented by ERT or HRT in combination with weight-bearing exercise and a calcium-rich diet.

Chapter 14 Physical and Cognitive Development in Middle Adulthood

A woman's decision about hormone replacement requires weighing the risks and the benefits in conjunction with her family history and personal risk factors. Women with a history of breast cancer in the family are usually discouraged from taking replacement hormones, either ERT or HRT, whereas women with heart disease or osteoporosis in their backgrounds are usually encouraged to do so.

The Male Climacteric

The male climacteric is a gradual process that produces changes in the reproductive system and reduces fertility but, unlike menopause, does not lead to sterility. Men have been known to father children in their seventies and eighties. The male climacteric starts in the forties or fifties and continues over a longer period of time and at a much slower rate than the female climacteric does.

Physical Changes

Decreased testicular functioning characterizes the male climacteric. The testes decrease in size and firmness with age. Age-related changes cause the somniferous tubules in the testes to produce fewer viable sperm. The pituitary gland responds to the reduction in sperm production by increasing the secretion of FSH. Corresponding to the female case, the testes are not able to respond by producing more sperm. As a result, the number and vitality of sperm go down. Unlike women's eggs, which are fully formed during fetal development, the progenitor sex cells, which create men's sperm, continue to divide throughout a man's life. Older males' sperm are more likely to carry genetic defects because the older the man, the more cell divisions the sperm have made. Testosterone production very gradually decreases at the rate of about 1 percent per year, starting at the age of forty, a process known as andropause (Feldman et al., 2002), but most men see no noticeable functional change until age sixty (Kaufman & Vermeulen, 1997). Considerable individual differences exist, with excessive drinking and obesity being linked to accelerated loss; however, some older men continue to have testosterone levels as high as those of younger men (Feldman et al., 2002).

The most notable physical changes affect the prostate gland. The prostate gland contributes secretions that make up the largest volume of the semen during ejaculation. Glandular cells in the prostate begin to atrophy after age forty-five, leading to a gradual decrease in the volume of ejaculated fluid. By age sixty-five, the prostate gland may show other signs of deterioration, including development of benign hard masses, replacement of muscle fibers with connective tissue, and abnormal overgrowth of tissue. This overgrowth of tissue, or **hypertrophy**, produces pressure on the urethra that may restrict and eventually block urine flow. Whereas only 10 percent of men require surgery to improve urine flow, many others experience frequency of urination, waking at night to urinate, and some difficulty with bladder control (Christiansen & Grzybowski, 1993).

hypertrophy The overgrowth of tissue in the prostate gland, which is one of the physical changes of the male climacteric and sometimes leads to pressure on the urethra, which interferes with urine flow.

Physical Signs

Wu and colleagues (2010) conducted a study of more than three thousand men across midlife and late life in which the men were surveyed about a variety of symptoms and were also tested for testosterone levels (Wu et al., 2010). This research demonstrated that men with lower testosterone levels were more likely to report the following symptoms in each of three categories: sexual symptoms (erectile dysfunction, fewer sexual thoughts, and less frequent morning erections), physical symptoms (reduced ability to do vigorous activity, inability to bend and kneel, and inability to walk more than one kilometer), and psychological symptoms (low energy, sadness, and fatigue; Wu et al., 2010). Symptoms such as memory loss, mood swings, depression, and irritability, which had previously been linked to andropause, were not found in this study, though they are sometimes reported. As with women, these symptoms may be part myth and at least partly due to changes in life circumstances that occur in midlife.

Sexuality in Middle Adulthood

The changes in the reproductive systems of men and women have implications for sexual functioning in middle adulthood. Both men and women tend to become aroused more slowly, have less intense orgasms, and return to prearoused levels more quickly (Masters et al., 1994). Men have longer refractory periods. These changes occur over many years and sometimes go unnoticed until late adulthood. But focusing on the gradual physical changes does not give an adequate picture of sexuality in middle adulthood. This is often a period when women and men with partners have more time and energy for each other. Most individuals enjoy an active sex life throughout midlife, and those who remain in good health extend their sex lives into late life (Lindau & Gavrilova, 2010). Those in midlife also have less fear of pregnancy and better communication, which can increase sexual satisfaction (MacNeil & Byers, 1997). In addition, the slower pace of sex can invite more attention to what is pleasing to both partners. However, reduced risk of pregnancy contributes, in part, to the relatively low rate of condom use among adults in midlife and late life, increasing risk for sexually transmitted diseases (Schick et al., 2010).

Female Sexuality

Many women find that the hormonal changes of menopause affect their sexual responsiveness. All phases of the sexual response cycle (see Chapter 12) continue in middle adulthood, but with diminished speed and intensity. The most annoying change is the slower rate and reduced amounts of vaginal lubrication compared to those at younger ages, which can cause irritation or pain during intercourse. This can also be a problem if the woman feels out of touch with her level of arousal because her degree of vaginal lubrication has always served as an indicator of her sexual readiness. Vaginal dryness can usually be overcome by the use of saliva or water-based lubricants during lovemaking. Estrogen cream or other medications can be prescribed if surface lubricants do not help.

In lesbian couples, both women may be going through menopausal changes at the same time, so each partner's physical and psychological complaints may affect sexual interest and performance. In a study of forty-one middle-aged lesbians, Ellen Cole and Esther Rothblum (1991) found that 76 percent reported no sexual problems. The remaining women reported changes involving vaginal dryness, difficulty finding a partner, less interest in initiating sex, and taking longer to reach orgasm, changes no different than those heterosexual women report.

There is no evidence of decline in postmenopausal women's physical capacity for sex. Aging does not seem to affect the clitoris, which continues to enlarge with sexual arousal.

Menopause does not significantly affect sexual drive, which depends on androgens, not estrogen. Some women report more enjoyment from sex after menopause, when they no longer have to worry about becoming pregnant and when sex is likely to proceed at a slower pace.
Source: bikeriderlondon/Shutterstock.com.

The capacity for orgasm is unimpaired. Female sexual interest typically does not diminish, though hot flashes and disrupted sleep may reduce it temporarily. Menopause does not significantly affect sexual drive, which depends on androgens, not estrogen. In fact, some women report more enjoyment from sex after menopause, when they no longer have to worry about becoming pregnant.

Male Sexuality

The most noticeable change in sexuality for men is the fact that erections take longer to attain—minutes rather than seconds—and are not as hard as they were in younger years. This is due to changes in the vascular supply and spongy tissue beds running along the length of the penis. Men in their middle adult years often need more direct genital stimulation to become fully erect. These changes often upset even men in their thirties because they are used to the instantaneous erections of their youth and fear they are becoming impotent. Heterosexual women too are sometimes upset by these changes because they fear their partners are less interested in them or less interested in sex. Just as men have mistakenly taken speed of erection as a measure of their potency, women have taken it as a measure of their desirability. On the other hand, many women enjoy the slower pace of sex that middle age brings because it allows more time for their own arousal and enjoyment.

Aging men also experience changes in orgasm. Reduced semen production makes the need to ejaculate feel less intense. This, combined with reduced pumping action on the part of the prostate, leads to a reduction in the intensity of orgasm. In addition, the refractory period, the time between orgasm and the possibility of another erection, lengthens with age. These changes occur gradually and at different rates for different men. Things typically just take longer in the forties and fifties (Masters et al., 1994).

Although the physical changes of aging do affect sexuality, there are no physical reasons based on age alone that sex cannot be enjoyed throughout life. In fact, the age-related changes can actually bring some benefits. Slower can be better when it comes to sex. A man in his forties is likely to have more control over ejaculation than he did when he was younger. This gives both him and his partner more time to enjoy sex and reach orgasm. With continuing sexual activity, whether self-pleasuring or with a partner, the capacity for satisfying sexual relations can be preserved well beyond middle age.

In sexuality, as in other areas of adult experience, physical factors are not the overriding ones. How we feel about our bodies, how we feel about our partners, and how free we feel to explore what pleases us all contribute to our sexual satisfaction. Of greatest importance to sexual desire and interest is marital (or relationship) happiness (Northrup, 1994). We will see in the next chapter that adults in their middle years may be forming new sexual relationships or already enjoying long-term ones.

Physical changes are only one aspect of middle adulthood. Intellectual growth and expanded social roles bring many pleasures to this time of life. We now turn to the issues of cognitive development during middle adulthood. How does it change? What are the gains and what are the losses?

COGNITIVE DEVELOPMENT

James will turn fifty on his next birthday. During his early adulthood, he started graduate school and dropped out, married, started a family, held several jobs, returned to graduate school, divorced, and remarried. He earned his doctorate at age thirty-two and began the slow climb to a secure position in the academic world. At age forty-eight, he accepted an offer for a full professorship with an endowed chair at an elite university. More than ever before, his work now calls on him to view his field broadly, to comment on it for the academic and general public, and to train graduate students. James is an example of a successful man in his middle years. He has power in his field and is called on to exercise it nearly every day. He is at the height of what John Horn and Scott Hofer (1992) refer to as "the vital period of life," the time when adults are responsible for maintaining and enhancing the culture.

> **What Do You Think?**
>
> Why might adults in their middle years find sexuality to be more satisfying than young adults do? Would your reasons apply equally to women and men?

Intelligence in Middle Adulthood

The reality of power and influence during middle adulthood is often overlooked because youth and youthfulness are so much admired in contemporary America. Conflicting ideas from cognitive psychologists about when intellectual capacities peak and the speed of their decline contribute to contradictory popular images of middle adulthood as "the intellectual peak" or being "over the hill." For this reason, we start our discussion of cognitive development in middle adulthood with an examination of that controversy.

Does Intelligence Decline with Age?

Several problems confront us when we try to determine the course of cognitive competence or intelligence over the adult years. *Intelligence,* as we saw in the Chapter 8 discussion of cognitive development in middle childhood, refers to the general ability to learn from experience. This ability is not directly observable; it is a quality of a person that we infer from competent behaviors we consider characteristic of intelligent people, such as learning a new task quickly, solving a difficult problem, or performing well on a test. Competent behaviors, however, depend on more than intelligence alone. A person may do poorly on a test for reasons other than lack of ability to learn. Immediate factors such as illness or anxiety may negatively affect performance on a math test, for example, even though the individual knows the relevant concepts. Longer-range factors such as lack of training in math or inexperience with tests may also negatively affect performance, particularly when we test adults of different ages. Young adults who are still in school are likely to be more comfortable taking tests than older adults who have not been to school for decades or perhaps ever. Likewise, visual loss or arthritis may make filling in an answer sheet problematic for an older test taker. Timed tests may also cause lower performance by older adults due to slower response rather than lower intelligence. If we add to these problems the lack of agreement as to which and how many abilities the term *intelligence* refers to (see Chapter 8 for a full discussion of this issue), it is little wonder that different investigators have arrived at different answers to the question of how intelligence fares during the adult years.

Early Studies

Before the mid-1950s, developmental psychologists believed intellectual decline begins in the teenage years (Botwinick, 1977). This idea, you may remember from Chapter 12, is in keeping with the Piagetian notion that cognitive development reaches its highest level during adolescence. A study by Nancy Bayley (1955) demonstrated that this is not the case. Bayley found that intellectual growth continued until at least age thirty-six. It then seemed that early adulthood, not adolescence, is the peak of intellectual functioning. Research during the 1960s commonly found that young adults perform at a somewhat higher level than adults in their middle years, who in turn perform at a somewhat higher level than older adults (Willis, 1989). These differences were interpreted as reflecting age-related declines. "Early investigators had little doubt that increasing adult age brought about intellectual decline" (Botwinick, 1977, p. 583). Do these differences in performance actually reflect age-related decline, or can they be explained in other ways? To answer that question, we must examine the method used to conduct these early studies.

Cross-Sectional Versus Longitudinal Studies

A typical early study would compare the performance of separate groups of adults on a test of one or more abilities. This is called a *cross-sectional study* (see Chapter 1) because it compares groups of people of different ages at the same point in time. A cross-sectional study assumes the older groups all perform at the same level the twenty-year-olds did when they were twenty. If at their current ages they perform lower than the young adults, they are assumed to have declined because of their increased age. But when cross-sectional studies compare individuals of different ages, they also compare individuals of different cohorts. Cohort, or generational, differences include differences in educational level, medical care, nutritional resources, and experience with historical events such as war or economic depression.

Consider educational level. If, as in many families, you and your siblings attend college while your parents' generation went only to high school and your grandparents' generation went only to grade school, your respective opportunities for learning have been very different. Researchers have found higher correlations between intelligence test scores and educational level than between these scores and age (Botwinick, 1977). Cohort differences in educational level and other life experiences challenge the assumption that an older cohort performed as well as earlier cohorts even when they were the same age. Comparisons of different cohorts at the same ages indicate that this is rarely the case. Cohort differences in performance level exist and vary with the ability studied (Gerstorf, Ram, Hoppmann, Willis, & Schaie, 2011; Willis, 1989). The cross-sectional method may "create" age decline because it confounds cohort differences with age.

Using the longitudinal method to study changes in intelligence across adulthood minimizes negative age patterns. A *longitudinal study* (see Chapter 1) tests the same subjects periodically over an extended time period. Testing the same individuals at different ages controls for cohort differences. Figure 14.5 compares age gradients for the Verbal Meanings Test derived from cross-sectional and longitudinal studies. While the cross-sectional curve shows decline beginning around age forty, the longitudinal curve shows gain until around age sixty. The difference between these two curves is in part due to the control of cohort differences. A methodological problem may also contribute to the difference: longitudinal data may be biased in a positive direction because people who perform poorly are less likely to be available for retesting. Individuals who are less advantaged in terms of education, health, and SES are more likely to drop out of the study than are more advantaged individuals. If the older groups contain only the scores of the more able participants, the curve is biased in a positive direction. This bias in the experimental design is usually corrected for statistically (Schaie, 1994).

In contrast to findings from cross-sectional studies, findings from longitudinal research present a positive view of intellectual competence in middle adulthood. For many mental abilities, middle adulthood is a period of stability in intellectual functioning. Some abilities, such as verbal ability, peak in middle age. "Continued development in midlife is most evident for abilities that are extensively employed in tasks and responsibilities of daily living" (Willis, 1989).

Schaie's Sequential Studies

Confronted early in his career with the discrepancies between cross-sectional and longitudinal findings in the study of adult intellectual development, K. Warner Schaie began a longitudinal study of a cross-sectional sample that he had collected for his dissertation in 1956. (Early data from this study formed the basis for Schaie's stages of adult development, discussed in Chapter 12.) In 1963, he tracked down and retested as many of the sample of five hundred twenty-two to seventy-year-olds he had tested in 1956 as he could find and added a new cross-sectional sample of 997 twenty-two to seventy-year-olds. He retested and added new samples again in 1970, 1977, 1984, 1991, 1998, 2005, and 2012. This combination of cross-sectional and longitudinal characteristics produced a sequential study of adult intellectual development. Recall from Chapter 1 that a *sequential study* allows comparisons among cohorts at any one time and traces individuals' actual development over time.

In what is known as the ongoing Seattle Longitudinal Study (SLS), Schaie and his associates have assessed mental abilities of more than six thousand adults, some of whom have participated for as long as forty-nine years (Schaie, 1994). Schaie has recruited all

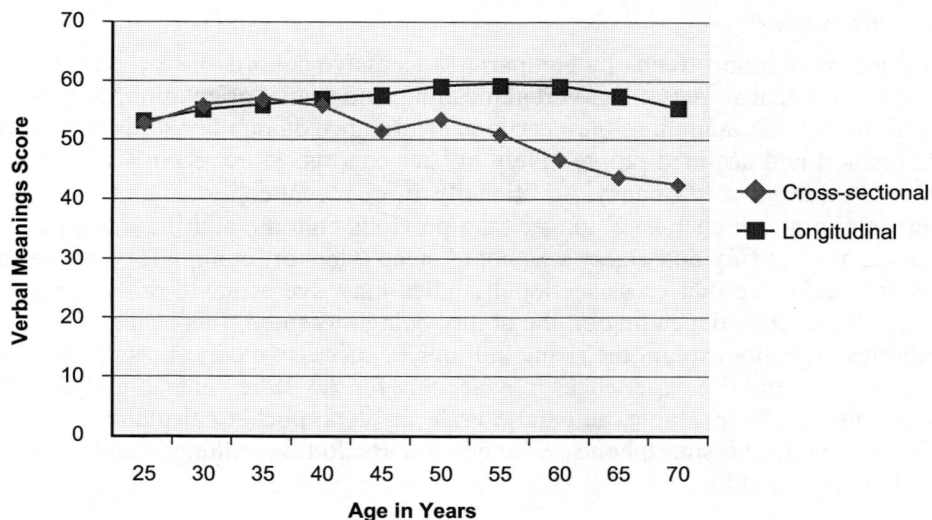

FIGURE 14.5

Comparable Cross-Sectional and Longitudinal Age Gradients for the Verbal Meanings Test

Cross-sectional studies show earlier and steeper declines than do longitudinal studies. Cohort differences contribute to the decline in cross-sectional studies.

Source: Schaie and Strother (1968).

participants from a health maintenance organization (HMO) in Seattle that serves a wide range of professionals, craftspeople, white-collar and blue-collar employees, and their families. In 2002, the grandchildren of participants began participating in the study, which will permit investigations of multiple generations of families (Schaie, 2014). While HMO membership underrepresents the lowest socioeconomic segment of the population, who likely have no health insurance, it adequately represents at least the upper 75 percent of the socioeconomic spectrum (Schaie, 1994).

The SLS used the same test battery throughout the study. The Primary Mental Abilities (PMA) battery includes subtests for verbal meaning (understanding what a word or a sentence means), spatial orientation (being able to use a map), inductive reasoning (finding the guiding rule to make a decision, such as reading a bus timetable), number skill (using numbers in simple arithmetic), and word fluency (being able to readily think of a word). Participants also periodically take a test of mental rigidity-flexibility; they have taken additional tests of mental abilities at later intervals. The test administrators also collected demographic data at each testing. During the first three intervals limited information was collected, but in subsequent intervals a more complete inventory asked about major work circumstances (with homemaking defined as a job), friends and social interactions, daily activities, travel experiences, physical environment, and lifelong educational pursuits. The researchers obtain health history records, collect blood samples, and get measures of health behaviors for participants as well.

Different Patterns for Different Abilities

The SLS data show no uniform pattern of age-related changes in adulthood across all intellectual abilities. Schaie and his colleagues combined their cross-sectional and longitudinal data to see the overall picture for each of the primary mental abilities. They combined data such that each age segment involves a longitudinal follow-up but successive segments are on different individuals. The resulting longitudinal curves show at least a modest gain for all abilities from early adulthood to early middle age. The abilities peak at different ages, change at different rates, and differ systematically for women and men. Women maintain stronger verbal meaning and inductive reasoning skills, whereas men do better in tests of spatial orientation and number skill.

Age-Related Changes

Schaie (1994, 2005) found that word fluency, which significantly declined by the early fifties, was the only primary ability that clearly decreased in middle adulthood. All abilities showed some decline by age sixty-seven, but these declines were modest until the eighties and even then were slow for more than half the participants. Remember, performance is not the same as cognitive ability; other factors may interfere with performance. According to Schaie (1994), "Much of the late life decline . . . must be attributed to slowing of processing and response speed" (p. 308).

Cohort Differences

The SLS assessed cohort trends by comparing successive cohorts observed at the same age. In tests of inductive reasoning, verbal meaning, and spatial orientation, cohorts born later performed better than those born earlier. Performance on number skills peaked with the 1924 cohort and declined progressively in later cohorts. More recently born cohorts also scored lower on word fluency. Additionally, more recent cohorts maintained cognitive functioning at a higher level longer than previous cohorts, and the rate of decline between the ages of fifty and eighty was not as steep (Gerstorf et al., 2011). These findings provide evidence that cross-sectional studies may overestimate or underestimate the age-related decline depending on the ability being measured. Increasing educational opportunities probably explain the rising abilities of successive cohorts, and changes in teaching methods and life experiences may account for the decrements in abilities. With the availability of, for example, automatic cash registers, pocket calculators, and most recently, computers and smartphones, younger cohorts do less arithmetic and so are less practiced in number skills.

Individual Differences in Age-Related Change

Individual performance on the PMA varied widely among SLS participants. Some individuals' intellectual performance changed significantly in midlife, while a few declined little even into the eighties. In addition to mapping the general pattern of age-related changes, the SLS looked at individual differences in life experiences that led to early loss for some individuals and maintenance of high levels for others. Schaie (1994) identified seven factors that reduce the risk of cognitive decline in old age, which are presented in Table 14.2. As you can see, advantageous genetic, personality, and environmental circumstances all contribute to the maintenance of cognitive abilities.

The SLS data provide a picture of age-related decline in intellectual abilities that is multifaceted and multidirectional. On average, decline begins gradually in the mid-sixties and accelerates in the late seventies. The onset and rate of decline differ for the various abilities and with gender. Number skills show the sharpest decline overall, although word fluency begins to decline the soonest. For men, the slowest decline is in spatial orientation; for women, it is in inductive reasoning. Environmental and personality factors in early and middle adulthood account for the large differences in how long individuals maintain their mental abilities. People who like learning new things and going new places and who adapt easily to change show less mental decline. We will see in the Chapter 16 discussion of cognitive development in late adulthood that some of the decline is reversible. Schaie and his associates are generally optimistic about maintenance of cognitive abilities into late adulthood. Other investigators, however, view this multifaceted and multidirectional picture negatively.

The seven factors that reduce the risk of cognitive decline in old age reflect advantageous genetic, personality, and environmental circumstances.

Fluid and Crystallized Intelligence

John Horn (1970) developed the theory of fluid and crystallized intelligence first proposed by Raymond Cattell (1963). Fluid and crystallized intelligence are two general types of abilities, both of which are influenced by hereditary and environmental factors. Both rely on memory, but on different types of memory. They show different patterns of age-related decline, which led Horn and his associates (Horn & Donaldson, 1976, 1977; Horn & Hofer, 1992) to take a much dimmer view of age-related changes in intellectual functioning than Schaie and his colleagues do.

Two Types of Intelligence

Crystallized intelligence refers to learned cognitive processes and primary abilities, such as vocabulary, general information, and word fluency, that remain relatively stable

---

crystallized intelligence The cognitive processes and primary abilities, such as vocabulary, general information, and word fluency, that are strongly shaped by formal education and increase or remain relatively stable with age.

TABLE 14.2 Factors That Maintain Good Cognitive Functioning in Later Life

1. *The absence of cardiovascular disease and other chronic diseases.* Behaviors that lead to early onset of disease probably reflect lifestyles that are unfavorable to maintaining cognitive functioning as well.
2. *Living in favorable circumstances.* Favorable circumstances, as would be likely for people with high SES, include above-average education, occupational pursuits high in complexity and low in routine, above-average income, and intact families.
3. *Substantial involvement in complex and intellectually stimulating activities.* Reading extensively, traveling, attending cultural events, belonging to clubs and professional associations, and pursuing continuing education are all activities of this type.
4. *Flexible personality style at midlife.* Being able to change plans, adjust to new circumstances, and cope with life's surprises demonstrate a flexible personality style.
5. *Being married to a spouse with high cognitive functioning.* When people of different cognitive levels marry, the lower-functioning spouse has been found to maintain or improve his or her level.
6. *High levels of performance speed.* Because the measurement of cognitive abilities depends somewhat upon perceptual and response speed, those who maintain high levels of perceptual processing speed because of genetics and/or health-promoting behavior have an advantage.
7. *Personal satisfaction with one's life accomplishments in midlife or early old age.*

Source: Adapted from Schaie (1994).

---

with increasing age. Institutional aspects of culture, such as formal education, shape crystallized intelligence. Researchers use vocabulary tests, simple analogies, remote associations, and social judgment tests to measure it. An example of a remote association test item used to measure crystallized intelligence is:

What one word is well associated with the words *bathtub, prizefighting,* and *wedding?*

Here is an example of a judgment item that is used to test crystallized intelligence:

You notice that a fire has just started in a crowded café. What should one do to prevent death and injury?

Fluid intelligence is the ability to process new information in novel situations. Fluid intelligence includes reasoning, which is central to almost any definition of intelligence. It concerns the processing of information that is less tied to education and depends more on neurological development than on transmission of formal knowledge about one's culture. Horn and Hofer (1992) report that high scores on measures of fluid intelligence can be obtained by people of relatively low education and SES, reflecting that it is acquired by personal experience that is not tied to formal education or acculturation and thus is relatively culture free. Tasks such as letter series, matrices, concept formation, common word analogies, and analysis synthesis are measures of fluid intelligence. An example of a letter series test item used to measure fluid intelligence presents the following letter series and asks which letter comes next:

A D G J M P

fluid intelligence
The cognitive processes and primary abilities, such as information processing, novel problem solving, and reasoning, that depend more on neurological development and less on formal education and that peak in early adulthood.

Another test item would entail flashing on a screen for a fraction of a second the following matrix:

```
Y O U A
R E A C
U T I E
```

The viewer is asked to remember as many letters as possible. If he or she can see the embedded words in the fraction of a second, remembering all twelve letters is easy.

These two types of memory change differently with age. Crystallized intelligence, or stored memory, improves or stabilizes with age; as you have probably noticed, older adults frequently are better informed than younger adults. In contrast, fluid intelligence peaks in late adolescence and declines rapidly as individuals go from early adulthood to old age. Whereas a great deal of variability exists in performance on measures of crystallized intelligence, with some older people showing loss while most are showing gain, there is little variability in the decline in fluid intelligence (Wang & Kaufman, 1993). Early in life, fluid intelligence and crystallized intelligence are indistinguishable because neurological growth during childhood and adolescence masks any damage to the central nervous system. In adulthood, however, the different patterns of these two kinds of intelligence become more noticeable as growth tapers off and damage accumulates (Horn, 1970). However, there is some evidence that fluid problem-solving skills in domains of expertise may not decline as we age, a process known as encapsulation (Hoyer & Rybash, 1994; Hoyer & Touron, 2003).

Negative Assessment

In their negative assessment of age-related changes in intellectual functioning, Horn and his colleagues (Horn & Donaldson, 1976; Horn & Hofer, 1992) focused on the vulnerability of fluid intelligence. They saw fluid intelligence as being the most salient indicator of intellectual capacities because it enables an individual to understand relations, comprehend implications, and draw inferences using inductive and deductive reasoning and is relatively independent of cultural and experiential influences. Earl Hunt (1993) agrees in the context of a changing work world. Whereas machines can handle routine problems, only people can deal with the "novel" problems that arise in any occupation. Hunt, like Horn, believes this ability depends on fluid intelligence. Horn and Scott Hofer posit that age-related declines in fluid intelligence result from accumulations of small losses of brain function. These losses are related to lifestyle factors that have harmful effects on the nervous system, such as drug or alcohol abuse, poor diet, or inactivity, health-compromising behaviors that we discussed in Chapter 12.

Conflicting Views

Horn's theory has been criticized on several grounds. First, because it is based on cross-sectional research, it confounds cohort differences with age differences (Labouvie-Vief, 1985). Gisela Labouvie-Vief points out that in times of rapid cultural and technological change, aged individuals seem deficient in comparison to younger adults rather than in comparison to their younger selves and that "these changes may not impact only on such 'crystallized' functions as information-related tests . . . but also on ones much closer to fluid functions (Reasoning, and, to a less extent, Space)" (Labouvie-Vief, 1985, p. 505). In other words, fluid intelligence is not totally unaffected by cultural and experiential influences. Also on methodological grounds, Jing-Jen Wang and Alan Kaufman (1993) point out that researchers disagree as to which scales are unequivocally crystallized or fluid.

As we discussed earlier, Schaie's sequential studies show gains in all but one of the primary mental abilities until the sixties. In response, Horn and Hofer (1992) criticize longitudinal research for painting a falsely positive picture, which they refer to as the "class reunion" effect: "If one were to estimate age changes in income from longitudinal samples of people returning for class reunions, one would be drawn to the conclusion

> **What Do You Think?**
>
> So, does intelligence decline with age? Set up a mock debate between Schaie and Horn/Hofer to examine this question.

that income increases with age. But this could mainly represent the fact that people who return for reunions have made money and want others to know this, but those who have not made money do not return for reunions" (p. 76).

Jack Botwinick (1977) sees the different patterns of age-related decline as being due to speed rather than to fluid-crystallized differences. Primarily because of changes in motor coordination, ability in tasks that involve speed, performance tests such as Digit Symbol and Picture Arrangement decline while ability in nonspeeded tasks does not. This assertion is supported by studies noting a strong correlation between processing speed and changes in fluid intelligence (Zimprich & Martin, 2002). James Birren (Birren et al., 1980) suggests that primary aging of the central nervous system and secondary aging due to disease and lack of physical fitness both affect processing speed. Other critics argue that fluid abilities are not a good measure of intelligence for older adults because in later life much of everyday cognitive performance depends less on fluid abilities than on contextual factors (Rybash et al., 1986). The conflict over whether intelligence declines during adulthood has not been resolved, nor have the methodological issues.

Thus far, we have been evaluating quantitative measures of adult intellectual functioning, using what we referred to in Chapter 8 as the psychometric approach to measuring intelligence. Do problem-solving measures of cognitive abilities show age-related changes? Do the kinds of problems to be solved matter? We explore these questions next.

Practical Intelligence and Expertise

Performance on traditional laboratory problem-solving tasks decreases during the adult years, whereas performance in the real world increases at least through middle age (Denney, 1989). In real life, many of us prefer to hire heart surgeons, attorneys, or investment advisers who are middle aged or older because we want experienced specialists to address our problems. As with James, whose work is in great demand in his middle years, we assume experience matters in real-world performance. How can we explain this multidirectional picture of adult performance?

Laboratory measures of problem solving were developed to measure intellectual development in children and young adults. Schaie (1977/1978) pointed out that these measures have limited value testing intellectual functioning in middle and late adulthood (see Chapter 12) because adults' abilities may qualitatively differ from children's. For this reason, investigators have turned to the study of real-world problem solving to better measure adult problem-solving abilities. Among studies that focus on real-world problem solving, Schaie (1990) distinguishes among practical intelligence, expertise, and wisdom. **Practical intelligence** involves the application of intellectual skills to everyday activities, whereas **expertise** and *wisdom* refer to behaviors that require intelligence as well as specialized experience in specific domains, as you may recall from the Chapter 10 discussion of cognitive development in adolescence. We will look at practical intelligence and expertise in this section; wisdom is discussed in Chapter 16.

Solving Real-World Problems

If we view intelligence as the mental abilities that enable individuals to adapt successfully to their environment, looking at practical problem solving may be a better assessment tool than performance on traditional abstract problem solving. Studies of practical problem solving use realistic stimuli, sometimes in a novel situation and sometimes in a realistic situation. For example, David Arenberg (1968), in a traditional concept-learning problem,

practical intelligence A form of real-world problem solving that involves applying intellectual skills to problems of everyday life and shows improved performance through midlife.

expertise Specialized experience in specific domains of knowledge that enables efficient and effective performance and increases with experience and age.

used food stimuli instead of abstract geometric figures so that the stimuli were familiar while the situation was novel. He told the participants that one of the foods was poisoned and they were to figure out which one. Participants were told whether they "lived" or "died" after each "meal" of three foods was presented. If they "lived," the poisoned food was not included in the three foods they had just "eaten"; if they "died," it was. From this information, they had to solve the problem. Studies of this type have found that both older and younger individuals perform better with the use of realistic stimuli, but, if anything, the younger adults outperform the older by even more (Denney, 1989).

Nancy Denney (1989) and her colleagues conducted a series of practical problem-solving experiments using realistic stimuli in realistic situations. They gave the participants real-life problems dealing with issues such as cooking, consumer issues, weather, crime, housing, and work and judged responses based on how many solutions were both safe and effective. Participants in these cross-sectional studies were men and women twenty to eighty years of age recruited from the community by calling individuals randomly selected from the census lists for Lawrence, Kansas. In the first study, Denney used problems such as the following:

> Let's say that one evening you go to the refrigerator to get something cold to drink. When you open the refrigerator, you notice that it is not cold inside, but rather is warm. What do you do?

Performance on the problems increased from age twenty to age fifty and then declined after that. Because the investigators were concerned that the initial set of problems may have been biased toward middle-aged individuals, they constructed problem sets that focused on issues young, middle-aged, and older adults would typically face.

In the two subsequent studies, Denney gave individuals between ages twenty and eighty three sets of problems, one geared to each adult stage. Here is an example of a young adult problem:

> Let's say that a young man who is living in an apartment building finds that the heater in his apartment is not working. He asks his landlord to send someone out to fix it, and the landlord agrees. But after a week of cold weather and several calls to the landlord, the heater is not fixed. What should the young man do?

An example of a middle-aged adult problem is the following:

> Let's say that a middle-aged woman is frying chicken in her home when, suddenly, a grease fire breaks out on top of the stove. Flames begin to shoot up. What should she do?

Here is an example of an older adult problem:

> Let's say that a sixty-year-old man who lives alone in a large city needs to go across town for a doctor's appointment. He cannot drive because he does not have a car and doesn't have relatives who live nearby who could drive him. What should he do?

In the first of these studies, performance on the young adult problems decreased with increasing age, while performance on the middle and late adult problems increased up to middle age and decreased after that. In the next study, the young and middle-aged groups performed best on the problems designed for them, but the older adult participants did not perform best on their problems. Even when older adults were recruited to help design problems that would give them an advantage, their performance peaked at fifty and declined after that.

Studies of practical intelligence do show that practical abilities increase with age, and most show an improvement in performance through middle age (Allaire, 2012; Cornelius, 1990). It is easy to construct problems that give either the young adult or the middle-aged adult an advantage. Although they have tried, researchers have been unable to develop a set of problems on which older individuals perform better than middle-aged or younger individuals (Denney, 1989, Thornton, Peterson, & Yeung, 2012). These findings are consistent with real-life experience, in which middle-aged adults typically are more knowledgeable than young adults. Many older adults are too, but that is harder to demonstrate in problem-solving studies.

Becoming an Expert

Adults in their sixties and seventies hold many of the most responsible and challenging leadership positions in society and are seldom perceived as being less cognitively competent than adults in their twenties, thirties, forties, and fifties. Yet, as we have seen, their performance on conventional psychometric and abstract problem-solving measures are lower than those of young adults and their performance on practical problem-solving measures are lower than those of both young and middle-aged adults. How can we resolve this paradox between competence in the real world and ability as measured in the laboratory?

Experience may be the answer. Experience is highly relevant to competence and much less relevant to abstract assessment of cognitive abilities. An expert has a lot of experience in a particular task or domain of knowledge, as we saw in Chapter 10. Years of cooking, playing chess, gardening, or any of the many activities adults do make them expert. Compared to novices, experts can accomplish their tasks with fewer steps and better results. Consider baking a pie. An expert combines the ingredients with less measuring than a novice would use because knowing what the pastry should look and feel like at each stage enables taking shortcuts. Similarly, expert physicians diagnose illnesses more efficiently than novices do because they recognize and interpret signs without having to go through the formal steps of asking and answering questions (Rybash et al., 1986). Well-rehearsed activities, such as tying your shoes, can be done automatically, although mastering those activities takes a lot of time.

Adults continue to accumulate knowledge, refining it with age and experience. Despite declining fluid abilities, they continue to function efficiently when given tasks that allow them to call on their expert knowledge (Hoyer & Rybash, 1994; Hoyer & Touron, 2003). Recent research in different domains of expertise has shown that expert performance is predominantly a result of acquired complex skills and physiological adaptations rather than innate abilities or capacities. For experts in any field, supervised practice typically starts at young ages and is maintained at high daily levels for more than a decade. The effects of extended deliberate practice are more far-reaching than is commonly believed (Ericsson & Charness, 1994). Experts can acquire skills that circumvent basic limits on working memory capacity and sequential processing. Deliberate practice can also lead to anatomical changes resulting from adaptations to intense physical activity. The study of expert performance in several different fields demonstrates that experts have domain-specific advantages.

Timothy Salthouse (1984) and Elizabeth Bosman (1993, 1994) compared typists who differed in age (young versus older adults) and skill level (novices versus experts). The typists were tested on three traditional laboratory tasks—simple reaction time, the fastest speed at which they could tap their fingers, and digit symbol substitution—and then tested on their actual typing speed. As you might predict from our discussion so far, the older typists performed less well than the younger typists on the three laboratory tasks, whereas the expert typists, both young and old, performed faster on the typing test than the novices. Salthouse and Bosman determined that the older expert typists compensated for age-related declines in speed by looking farther ahead in the printed text, which gave them more time to plan their next keystrokes. They did not use the same strategy in the other tasks, though it could have helped to improve their performance. Salthouse and Bosman conclude that the compensatory mechanism is domain specific.

Stephanie Dollinger and William Hoyer (1996) studied medical technologists who differed in age (young versus older adults) and skill level (novices versus experts). First, they tested their ability to identify abstract geometric figures flashing on a video screen. As you might expect, younger individuals performed better than older ones at this task. Then Dollinger and Hoyer showed participants pictures of complex microscopic slides of actual laboratory specimens. Each slide had some elements of clinically significant information and some of clinically insignificant information. The participants were shown a single piece of information and asked whether it had been on the slide. Experts in both age groups were equally fast and accurate at identifying whether clinically significant information had been on the slide and could do this even while performing another task simultaneously. Novices performed poorly at the microscopic identification task, especially when doing another task at the same time. Again, skill mattered more than age in the domain-specific task, whereas age was important in the general, abstract task.

Aging, then, appears to lead to poorer performance in nonpracticed tasks and slower acquisition of new skills, particularly those that depend on new types of knowledge. However, practice speeds up performance for both young and old. Evidence suggests that skilled older individuals (age sixty-five and older) who perform at levels similar to those of younger adults do so via some compensatory mechanism (Ericsson & Charness, 1997). They look farther ahead, as the expert typists did, or identify critical elements more quickly, as the lab technicians did. This explains how older skilled performers, doctors, attorneys, and so on continue to perform expertly and how older adults can perform competently in most real-world tasks.

The overall picture of intellectual functioning among middle-aged adults is very positive. Most functions do not decline before the mid-sixties, and frequently used skills typically are maintained well beyond that. Middle-aged adults continue to be competent in the areas in which they have developed skills and expert in the areas in which they have well-developed skills. But what about new learning? In the middle years adults often want to change jobs, take on new hobbies, and expand their horizons. Where do adults go to learn new things, and what kind of students do they make? In the next section, we look at the adult learner.

The Adult Learner

For most adults, learning projects are motivated by some fairly immediate problem, task, or decision that requires new skills or information. Adults have a variety of motivations for continued learning. Allen Tough (1981) found that most of the reasons people gave for efforts to learn fell into four broad categories: job or occupation, managing the home and family, hobby or leisure time activity, and puzzlement or curiosity. The most common reasons midlife adults enroll in educational programs are to improve their job skills or out of personal interest (National Center for Education Statistics [NCES], 2010). They turn to adult education programs, self-study, and colleges and universities for lifelong learning.

Adult Education

The last two decades have brought an explosion of adult education. *Adult education* refers to all non-full-time educational activities, such as part-time college attendance, classes or seminars given by employers, and classes taken for adult literacy purposes or for recreation and enjoyment. In 2005, 49 percent of adults ages forty to forty-nine, 47 percent ages fifty to fifty-four, 42 percent ages fifty-five to fifty-nine, 38 percent ages sixty to sixty-four, and 24 percent ages sixty-five and over had participated in adult education in the past twelve months (NCES, 2010). Women outnumbered men in all age groups, predominantly in the older groups. Adult education participants tend to be well educated, have high incomes, live in the suburbs rather than in cities or rural areas, and hold primary-sector jobs; blue-collar and farm workers, unemployed individuals, African Americans, and Hispanics are underrepresented (NCES, 2010; Schlossberg, 1984). In a study of nearly eight hundred adults age fifty-five and older, awareness of where educational activities were available was the best predictor of participation (Fisher, 1986). These figures describe participants in instructor- or institution-planned adult learning; many adults are involved in less formal lifelong learning, the rates of which hover around 72 percent throughout midlife (NCES, 2010).

In a broad study of adult learning that encompassed independent learning activities as well as organized instruction, Carol Aslanian and H. M. Brickell (1980) found that life changes, or transitions, often provide the impetus for adult learning. They define a *transition* as a "change in status . . . that makes learning necessary. The adult needs to become competent at something

> **What Do You Think?**
>
> What evidence do you see of increased performance through middle adulthood in people you know? Share your evidence with other members of the class. Do you see any patterns?

that he or she could not do before in order to succeed in the new status" (pp. 38–39). Often the transition is precipitated by what Aslanian and Brickell call a *trigger*, a specific life event that generates the decision to learn at that time, such as becoming widowed, losing a job, or having a health crisis. They identify seven life areas into which both transitions and triggers may be classified: career, family, health, religion, citizenship, art, and leisure. From their telephone interviews with about fifteen hundred adults over age twenty-five, they found that about half had engaged in some kind of adult learning in the previous year. Of the learners, 83 percent reported being motivated by a transition, 56 percent cited career transitions, 16 percent cited family transitions, and 13 percent cited leisure transitions.

Returning to College

While most adult education occurs outside of educational institutions, "when learning is measured in terms of effort or time invested, college easily emerges as the largest source for adult learning" (Peterson, 1981, p. 320). In recent years, adults have been returning to college in record numbers, with approximately 40 percent of college and university students being over the age of twenty-four (Wyatt, 2011).

Typically, adults return to college because they are dissatisfied with their lives and regard finishing their education as a way to improve themselves or to build skills within their career (Campbell et al., 1980). Rose is an example. After high school, she attended college for a year and earned twenty-five credits before dropping out and enrolling in secretarial school. Thirteen years later, Rose returned to college. She was now a married mother of three and wanted to become a lawyer. She took one course per semester until her youngest child was in nursery school, then increased to two and sometimes three courses. Friends helped her out with childcare. It took her nine years to complete her bachelor's degree as a continuing education student, at which point she entered law school as a full-time student. She will graduate from law school twelve years after returning to college, at age forty-two. Like Rose, most adults return with specific career goals in mind; see the "Working With" interview with Caroline Singer, dean of continuing education.

Adult education contributes to lifelong cognitive development (Glendenning, 1995). The cognitive gains in critical thinking that occur during college (discussed in Chapter 12) also benefit nontraditional/older students. In fact, obtaining a college education is an independent predictor of good fluid abilities during adulthood (Clouston et al., 2012). Karen Kitchener and Patricia King (1990) compared senior college students with two groups of students entering college for the first time—traditional first-year students and nontraditional first-year students. They found that the two groups of first-year students had similar critical thinking scores, while the scores of seniors were substantially higher. Growth in critical thinking seemed to be more closely related to the amount of postsecondary education than to increasing age. In a longitudinal study of returning students who completed a multicourse weekend program in the social sciences, the sixty-seven adults showed a statistically significant increase in critical thinking as measured before and after the program (Klassen, 1983/1984).

Career development is the most frequent reason for returning to college in middle adulthood. In the long term, a college degree leads to higher job status and income. Some professions, such as teaching, medicine, and accounting, require continuing education for continued certification (Willis & Dubin, 1990). It also influences how employees are regarded by their employers and by themselves (Pascarella & Terenzini, 1991). Because of the nature of work in middle adulthood, these aspects of returning to college often appeal to nontraditional-age individuals who did not finish college as young adults.

WORKING WITH Caroline Singer, Associate Dean of Continuing Education

Counseling Students Returning to College

Caroline Singer, associate dean of continuing education at a small, private New England college, began her career as a high school teacher. After earning her master's degree, she began teaching at a junior college. She continued graduate work, earned her Ph.D. in higher education, and became a professor at a four-year college. Caroline also advises continuing education students. Her own career is a good example of the many job changes that are often part of contemporary adult life.

Michele: *How did you get started working in continuing education?*

Caroline: I evolved into it. The program I taught in was being phased out of the college. When that happened, I gradually started to advise continuing education students. I saw a need, and I filled it. I found I was happiest working with nontraditional-age students.

Michele: *What are your continuing education students like?*

Caroline: Most start in their early to mid-thirties, others in their late twenties. Three out of four are women. Many are single parents. I am continually impressed by their extraordinary accomplishments. The single parents have support groups of friends or parents. If they don't, they stop coming. Most are working full time. A degree requires forty courses. If you take five per year, that takes eight years. Most of our students take five or six years for their bachelor's degree because they start out with some credits. They have so much else besides college going on in their lives that they rarely go straight through. Things intervene: they have a baby, their mother has an operation, they get sick. They are older, so they have different kinds of commitments; yet many excel in their academic work.

Michele: *You say your students work full time. What kinds of jobs do they have?*

Caroline: Secretaries, computer programmers, assistant managers, supervisors. Some have very high salaries, $45,000, but no college credentials. They often have unusually good jobs with less education than others around them. I hear, "I'm talking to Ph.D.'s and M.B.A.'s. I need to get my degree." Their companies often help pay their tuition. Now that women are able to take jobs where credentials count, they are returning to college.

Michele: *What motivates your continuing education students?*

Caroline: The students I see here are very focused. They want to improve their skills or get their degree so they can move up in their organization or into another company. Personal satisfaction motivates them too. They want to complete something they started. A high percentage, 85 to 90 percent, started college before and are returning. Very few come back just to expand their horizons.

Michele: *Are your male and female students motivated by different things?*

Caroline: I don't think so. I'm surprised by how few men there are, though. When they were nineteen, they didn't know what they wanted to do. Now they feel pressure to have a degree. Usually they are married or divorced. They say, "I never got this done; I need to get closure." Men in their mid-twenties don't stay in continuing education for very long. They get someone to finance them, or they get financial aid and they go full time.

Michele: *Do you find your work satisfying?*

Caroline: It's extraordinary work! I see these nontraditional students grow and change. One thing I've realized is that there is no typical continuing education student. They are a diverse group. They have some commonalties, but it's dangerous to generalize about nontraditional-age students. I often hear the same story: "I don't know how to get started." "I'm too old." "My brain cells are going." One totally competent-looking student, a personnel director for a nursing home, told me that the first day of class she sat in the parking lot for twenty minutes, afraid to come in. I've heard that again and again. They go from terrified to articulate; they become totally different people.

What Do You Think?

1. How do Caroline Singer's advisees reflect the profile of the adult learner discussed in the chapter?
2. What kinds of challenges might a nontraditional-age student face on campus?

Work in Middle Adulthood

As we discussed in Chapter 12, careers progress through a series of stages. Though young adults often believe the difficult parts of career development are figuring out the kinds of jobs for which they are suited, getting training, and finding employment, by middle adulthood other work concerns are often apparent. Midcareer, approximately age forty to fifty-five, is the time to reappraise early career decisions, reaffirm or modify goals, and make choices that enable continuing challenge and productivity. Late career, age fifty-five to retirement, entails remaining productive, maintaining self-esteem, and preparing for retirement by balancing nonwork and work involvements. During mid- and late-career stages, problems can arise from both success and lack of success.

Because of changes in the work world, "today's employee often experiences a dead-end job in a turbulent, financially constrained organization, which has just been restructured (or acquired or divested) and which cannot even promise that the present job will be there next year" (Hall & Rabinowitz, 1988, p. 67). Fear of job loss and **plateauing**, or reaching a point of constricted occupational opportunity, are serious concerns for midlife workers. Plateauing generally occurs in mid-career, when boredom may replace the feelings of activity, growth, and change that accompany earlier career stages. With a plateau, pay raises may level off, assignments may all feel the same, and an individual may experience a sense of stagnation.

plateauing Reaching a point of constricted occupational opportunity, usually during midcareer, resulting in boredom and feelings of stagnation.

Even for successful people at the executive/responsible stages of their careers, negative emotions and feelings of personal failure sometimes accompany the mid-to-late-career stages. From a review of research studies and anecdotal reports of successful managers, executives, and entrepreneurs, Abraham Korman (1988) concluded that no relationship exists between career success and personal life satisfaction among mid-to-late-career individuals. Successful individuals frequently complain that the stresses of their careers have damaged their relationships with their spouses and children. Korman attributes this age-related problem to emotions resulting from midlife crisis, a topic we focus on in the next chapter. Whether as a result of crisis or not, changes in the midlife adults perspective on life may result in a greater orientation toward the inner self and personal needs and a decreased interest in the incentives and promises offered by others, especially if earnings are already high. This may be accompanied by decreased interest in achievement, in looking toward future possibilities, and in having an impact on others through work activities. However, there is some evidence that serving as a mentor at work may buffer the negative effects of having reached a plateau (Lentz & Allen, 2009).

Mid-career issues are not the same for all working adults, however. **Burnout**, or disillusionment and psychological and physical exhaustion on the job, may result from a variety of causes. Workers whose jobs require heavy loads of caretaking for others are at particular risk for burnout (Sears, Urizar, & Evans, 2000). Discrimination based on race/ethnicity and gender, as well as different role expectations based on gender, often lead to different midlife work issues for white men, women, and minorities. Men are more likely than women in our society to have given up time with their families to pursue success in their occupations. Successful women are more likely to have maintained relationships during the course of their careers by juggling the roles of wife, mother, and extended family member (Crosby, 1991). Some successful women have delayed childbearing so that at midlife they are balancing careers and babies. These women may experience role strain as a result of their many commitments. On the other hand, women who did not delay childbearing and divided their attention between family and occupation while their children were young may feel free at midlife to devote more time and energy to their careers, whereas their husbands may feel regret for not having spent more time with their children when the children were still at home. At any rate, more women are employed outside the home, but the burden of housework still remains, meaning that many women pull a "second shift" at the end of the day, increasing risk for burnout (Chesters, 2012).

burnout Disillusionment and exhaustion on the job, often related to stress and caregiving, that may result in physical health problems. May be caused by multiple role commitments, discrimination based on race/ethnicity or gender, or other factors.

> **What Do You Think?**
>
> In what ways might increased access to online educational resources have an impact on midlife learning?

Age and Job Satisfaction

Research on work satisfaction has consistently shown that older people are more satisfied with their jobs than younger people. There are several possible explanations for this. First, older workers belong to a different cohort than younger workers, and that cohort may have learned to value work more highly. When your grandfather tells you he never missed a day of work from the day he turned sixteen, he is bragging about his work ethic. Second, as workers spend time on their jobs, they may accommodate so that they become happier with less. An older worker who encourages a younger worker to slow down and relax may be expressing this kind of accommodation. Third, older workers have better jobs than younger workers and therefore find them more satisfying. In most fields, middle-aged workers hold the upper-level positions. In a study of 1,102 economically active, salaried white males between ages sixteen and sixty-four, James Wright and Richard Hamilton (1978) found that a decisive choice among these hypotheses could not be made, but the bulk of the evidence favored the hypothesis that older workers have better jobs. Clifford Mottaz (1987) studied the relationship between age and overall work satisfaction, using data from 1,385 full-time workers in professional, managerial, clerical, and service occupational groups. He found some support for the second explanation, that age has an indirect positive effect on work satisfaction through its relationship to work rewards and values. Data suggested that in situations in which intrinsic rewards were generally not available, extrinsic rewards tended over time to become increasingly important sources of work satisfaction. This is supported by recent meta-analysis of research linking age and job satisfaction: as workers age, they have more intrinsic motivation to work (Kooij, DeLange, Jansen, Kanfer, & Dikkers, 2011). Gerald Zeitz (1990) found distinctly different age satisfaction curves among three employee groups: nonprofessionals, elite professionals, and ordinary professionals. He suggests a situational explanation of work satisfaction similar to the third explanation.

Racial and Ethnic Minorities

Because racial and ethnic minorities face discrimination in corporate America, they are more likely to plateau, or reach a *glass ceiling,* long before they reach their corporate dream. **Glass ceiling** refers to the invisible barriers that women and minorities confront as they approach the top of the corporate hierarchy. Glass ceiling barriers include social barriers, such as stereotyping and prejudice, that may be outside the direct control of business; internal structural barriers, such as lack of mentoring and different standards for performance evaluation, that are within the direct control of business; and government barriers, such as lack of consistent monitoring and law enforcement.

With the election of Barack Obama came the belief that we live in a postracial society in which racism is a nonentity. Historically, racism has been overt; however, as social norms have changed, racism has become less obvious and more difficult to measure. However, more than 30 percent of African Americans report missing out on jobs or promotions due to race (Schiller, 2004). This finding has been confirmed in experimental studies in which identical resumes with race-indicating names demonstrated that "white" names like Emily were contacted at a 50 percent higher rate than "black" names like Jamal (Bertrand & Mullainathan, 2004). The finding has also been confirmed with field studies in which equally qualified minorities are hired at a much lower rate than white candidates (Pager & Western, 2012). Beyond facing distinct disadvantages in obtaining a job, African Americans are often subject to discrimination on the job. In 2013, there were 33,068 charges of racial discrimination reported to the United States Equal Employment Opportunity Commission (EEOC, 2013).

glass ceiling The barriers that women and minorities confront as they approach the top of the corporate hierarchy, including social barriers, such as stereotyping and prejudice; internal structural barriers within the business, such as lack of mentoring and different standards for performance evaluations; and government barriers, such as lack of consistent monitoring and law enforcement.

Fernandez (1988) found that minorities and women face problems that do not affect white males. First, he found evidence of racial and gender stereotypes. The same assertive, self-confident, and ambitious behavior that would lead a white male to be considered a "go-getter" is interpreted differently when exhibited by an African American male or a woman, who would likely be considered too aggressive, arrogant, and wanting too much too fast. Second, he found that women and minorities held less power and authority. Third, he found they were systematically excluded from "powerful, political, informal groups" (Fernandez, 1988, p. 234). As the Glass Ceiling Commission report (1995) describes it, "Many middle- and upper-level white male managers view the inclusion of minorities and women in management as a direct threat to their own chances for advancement." As a result of these problems, minorities and women must meet higher performance standards than white men while they have fewer resources at their disposal, and white men create barriers to their progress. More recently, Cook and Glass found that when women and minorities were promoted to CEO positions in Fortune 500 companies, those companies tended to be companies that were not performing well (2014). Moreover, when those companies do not turn around, women and minorities tend to be replaced with white men, which the authors coined as the "savior effect" (Cook & Glass, 2014).

Gender

Men constitute 53 percent of workers ages forty-five to seventy-four (American Association of Retired Persons, 2014). As noted earlier, women are subject to a glass ceiling, meaning that they are unlikely to hold high-ranking, and subsequently, high-paying positions within organizations, which is due to a lack of upward mobility within companies and hiring practices (Fernandez & Campero, 2012). As women get older, the earnings gap between men and women that we discussed in Chapter 12 widens. Women reach their peak earnings at ages thirty-five to forty-five—ten years before men do. This is a result of the cumulative discriminatory forces we have discussed in relation to women's employment and the glass ceiling.

New family issues may put pressure on midlife women's employment as well. With more women in the labor force and increasing life expectancies, the number of working women who provide unpaid, informal caregiving for aging parents and other relatives has grown dramatically and will continue to grow (Stoller & Pugliesi, 1989). While some progress has been made in developing parental leaves (though these are often unpaid) and childcare programs to help parents balance the demands of family and employment, almost no attention has been given to the demands of family caregiving of aging and ailing relatives. Women acting as caregivers reduce formal work by three to ten hours and, subsequently, earn less than those not acting as caregivers (Van Houtven, Coe, & Skira, 2013). Employed caregivers report more missed meetings, losses in overtime pay, forgone promotions, and reduced job offers as a result of their conflicts between caregiving and work (Gibeau & Anastas, 1989).

Sexual Orientation and Identity

Lesbian, gay, bisexual, and transgender (LGBT) individuals face a particularly frustrating problem with employment discrimination—that it is completely legal in many states. Individuals who list LGBT organizations or clubs on their resume are less likely to be contacted for an interview than those not involved in such organizations (Tilcsik, 2011). Once in the workforce, LGBT individuals are likely to face discrimination. Twenty-one percent of gay and lesbian adults have experienced workplace discrimination (DeSilver, 2013). Though there are federal laws prohibiting racism and sexism, no such law exists to protect the LGBT population, and fewer than half of the states have laws protecting LGBT individuals from unfair hiring and firing practices or from workplace discrimination (American Civil Liberties Union, 2014).

Unemployment and Underemployment

Unemployed individuals lose much more than a regular paycheck when they lose their jobs. "They lose social contacts, a regular structure for the day, and a connection

> **What Do You Think?**
>
> Given your own race, ethnicity, and gender, what work-related issues might you expect to face in the years to come?

with goals and a sense of larger purpose" (Latack & Kaufman, 1988). People who are underemployed are generally overqualified for their current job due to education or experience or are engaged in part-time and/or low-paying work (Anderson & Winefield, 2011). Work is an important aspect of a person's identity, especially for managers and professionals, as we will discuss in Chapter 15. Being without their jobs leaves adults without part of themselves. Responses to job loss have been found to follow several stages (Latack & Kaufman, 1988). The initial reaction is likely to be shock, disbelief, and anger as the person copes with the news of being fired. After the initial shock, the first stage is likely to be relief and relaxation. The second stage includes efforts to become reemployed. If these efforts are not successful in a few months, the third stage, frustration at not finding work, sets in. The fourth stage is resignation to being out of work.

Unemployment and underemployment have been shown to have a negative impact on physical, mental, and social well-being (Anderson & Winefield, 2011). Job loss has been linked to increases in rates of suicide, diagnosed cases of mental illness, use of mental health services, alcohol abuse, lowered self-esteem, and severe depression (Mallinckrodt & Fretz, 1988). It may have particularly severe effects on older workers because workers age fifty-five and over who are laid off remain unemployed longer than their younger counterparts and are least likely to become reemployed (Quandagno & Hardy, 1996). Even for those in mid-to-late-career phases who do find new jobs, unemployment may result in permanent career damage because some will never be reemployed in satisfactory positions. An additional risk associated with unemployment and underemployment is loss of social contacts (Anderson & Winefield, 2011). Because they generally assume kinkeeping functions in the family, women are more likely than men to develop social supports outside of the workplace that can help to buffer the psychological distress associated with unemployment and underemployment. While multiple roles create stressors, such as when aging parents need caregiving at the same time that work is demanding, they also provide multiple avenues for support and self-esteem.

Change and Growth

As we have seen in this chapter, midlife is a time of new challenges, readjusting goals, learning new things, and adjusting to occupational changes. Looking at cognitive development, we see continued growth in many areas, particularly in practical intelligence and expertise. Looking at the issues of work, unemployment, and underemployment, we see that social forces have a great impact on the work experiences of middle-aged adults, as do earlier choices and opportunities. The economy determines whether people will face layoffs, low-paying positions, or job openings. As we saw in Chapter 12, socio-economic factors affect the educational and career opportunities an individual had in early adulthood. As a result, adults encounter no single midlife experience but a wide range of experiences. They also encounter changes in family and other social relationships, which take different forms in the lives of different individuals. In the next chapter, we examine these and other aspects of psychosocial development in middle adulthood.

Chapter Summary

- **What age-related changes in appearance and physical functioning are to be expected during middle adulthood?** Middle adulthood, roughly the period from ages forty to sixty, is characterized by changes in appearance and physical functioning. *Primary aging* refers to normal age-related changes that everyone experiences, such as the climacteric, while *secondary aging* refers to pathological aging. Because of differences in genetic makeup, health-compromising behaviors, and environmental exposure that lead to secondary aging, people age at different rates. Though strength peaks during early adulthood and then slowly and steadily declines, the loss is so minimal during middle adulthood that increased skill and experience often can compensate. Age-related changes in appearance become apparent during middle adulthood as skin loses its elasticity, hair thins and grays, and weight tends to increase. The cardiovascular and respiratory systems lose efficiency during middle adulthood because of changes in the left ventricle and the arterial walls. Regular exercise can considerably reduce (but not eliminate) these changes. Changes in vision and hearing become noticeable during the forties and fifties, while taste and touch change less.

- **What factors put middle-aged adults at risk for pathological aging and illness?** Health is more of a concern during middle adulthood than it was in early adulthood as individuals (particularly men) fall victim to premature death and chronic diseases. Health behaviors in early adulthood, such as regular aerobic exercise, a low-fat diet, weight control, and avoidance of cigarettes and heavy use of alcohol, can lead to healthy middle and later years. Rates of breast and prostate cancer increase during middle adulthood. Differences in SES, as well as genetic and cultural factors, can predict different outcomes for these diseases for racial/ethnic groups. Inequality creates differences in health via physical, social, and psychological mechanisms.

- **How do the male and female reproductive systems change during middle adulthood, and how do these changes affect functioning, feelings, and sexuality?** The *climacteric* refers to the gradual process of decline in reproductive capacity. In women, it is called *menopause* and ends with the cessation of the menstrual cycle and the ability to have children. For men, the climacteric reduces fertility but does not lead to sterility. The changes in the reproductive systems of men and women affect sexual functioning. All phases of the sexual response cycle continue, but with diminished speed and intensity. The capacity for satisfying sexual relations can continue well beyond middle age for healthy individuals.

- **Does intelligence decline with age?** How intelligence changes with age depends on the methods used to study this question. Cross-sectional studies show decline beginning around age forty, while longitudinal studies show gain until around age sixty and subsequent maintenance until late life. Schaie's sequential studies show at least modest gain for all abilities from early adulthood to early middle age. Abilities peak at different ages and change at different rates, and differ systematically for women and men. Schaie's studies show large differences in how long individuals maintain their mental abilities. People who like learning new things and going new places and who adapt easily to change show less mental decline. Fluid and crystallized intelligence show differential age-related decline. Crystallized intelligence improves with age, whereas fluid intelligence declines. Developmental psychologists disagree about how to interpret these changes.

- **Why do middle-aged and older adults hold most of society's leadership positions?** Real-world performance increases at least through middle age. Measures of practical intelligence show increased performance, although laboratory measures do not. Experience seems to explain the discrepancy. Experts rely on frequently used skills, which are well maintained with age.

- **What motivates midlife adults to engage in learning projects, participate in adult education, or return to college?** Studies indicate that 90 percent of all adults conduct at least one major learning effort each year. While most of these projects are self-planned, well-educated, high income, suburban adults are most likely to participate in formal adult education. Since 1980, record numbers of nontraditional-age students have been returning to college to improve themselves and to complete what they started but did not finish as young adults. They receive cognitive and career advantages similar to those of traditional-age students.

- **What issues of work become important during the mid-and late-career stages, and how do race, ethnicity, and gender affect these issues?** Mid- and late-career stages call for reappraisal of early career decisions and new choices that provide continuing challenge. Many factors, however, can lead to *plateauing*. Women and racial/ethnic minorities are more likely to plateau before reaching the top because of stereotyping and unequal treatment. In addition, family caregiving for aging parents and relatives puts pressure on midlife women's employment as life expectancies increase but care for older individuals is left to informal networks. Unemployment has particularly severe effects on older workers, who typically remain unemployed longer than their younger counterparts. Men may be more negatively affected than women because they have less social support.

Key Terms

- burnout (p. 531)
- climacteric (p. 512)
- crystallized intelligence (p. 522)
- estrogen replacement therapy (ERT) (p. 515)
- expertise (p. 525)
- fluid intelligence (p. 523)
- glass ceiling (p. 532)
- hormone replacement therapy (HRT) (p. 515)
- hypertrophy (p. 516)
- hysterectomy (p. 515)
- life expectancy (p. 502)
- menopause (p. 513)
- morbidity (p. 506)
- mortality (p. 506)
- oophorectomy (p. 515)
- organ reserve (p. 503)
- osteoporosis (p. 515)
- plateauing (p. 531)
- practical intelligence (p. 525)
- primary aging (p. 503)
- secondary aging (p. 503)

Psychosocial Development in Middle Adulthood

CHAPTER 15

Source: bikeriderlondon/Shutterstock.com.

Chapter Outline

A Multiplicity of Images of Middle Age
Crisis or No Crisis?
Marriage and Divorce
Family Relationships
Bereavement
Leisure
Preparing for Late Adulthood
Looking Back/Looking Forward

Focusing Questions

- How typical is "midlife crisis"?
- How are marriage and divorce different in middle adulthood than in earlier years?
- What are the important family relationships at midlife, and what changes can be expected in them?
- Why is the loss of a parent a significant event during middle adulthood?
- Is there continuity or change in leisure activities during this stage of life?
- How do wills and retirement planning help individuals to prepare for late adulthood?

Marcia is forty-eight. She has been a teacher for twenty-five years, married to José for twenty years, and a mother for seventeen years. These facts about her life make her sound middle-aged and established, which she is. She is also currently going through some very big life changes. Her older child, Adam, is now a teenager. He is a new driver, which worries his parents. He does not do what Marcia and José expect of him, especially in terms of school. He demands "the right to be a C student," while his well-educated parents want him to get into college and have choices about his future. Marcia's younger child, Felicia, is now thirteen and needs less supervision than when she was younger. These family changes have left Marcia with both more worries and more time to devote to her own career. She has recently taken on a contract to write a textbook. She finds this new commitment both exciting and challenging. She knows she must separate from her growing children while continuing to be a good parent to them. How to do that is not always clear.

Marcia is also confronting the aging of her parents. They are becoming frail, and she feels the need to cherish what time she has left with them. Their aging adds to her own sense of growing older. Her periods have become less regular, and she knows she will soon have to face the choice of whether or not to take hormone replacement therapy (HRT). In her desire to avoid HRT, Marcia has become health conscious. She is more careful than she used to be about what she eats. She exercises more regularly than ever before, walking at least three miles each day and going to a gym three days a week to lift weights. She also meditates.

As you can see, Marcia is involved in the tasks of middle adulthood. She is shifting her commitment to work as she adjusts to changes in her family relationships. She recently helped José bury and mourn for his mother. She has begun to anticipate an empty nest in the not so distant future. As Adam has become harder to live with, the idea of having him away at college has become something to which she looks forward. She knows her marriage will change when the kids leave home. As we will see, middle adulthood is a period of many changes and challenges.

A Multiplicity of Images of Middle Age

To many people, changes and challenges are not terms associated with middle age. The stereotype of midlife as a boring plateau is one shared by many young adults and some researchers (Chiriboga, 1989). Other researchers and many popular books present the opposite stereotype of midlife as a time of inevitable crisis. We have all heard stories of the seemingly stable husband/father hitting fifty, buying a sports car, and driving off with a woman young enough to be his daughter. Still others consider the early fifties to be the *prime of life* (Mitchell & Helson, 1990). How can such contrasting views continue to coexist? One answer is that middle-aged people are at least as different from one another as younger adults are. Some have routine lives, and some do not. Some have crises, and many do not. Middle adulthood has a multiplicity of images because no single experience represents this stage of life. Another answer is that midlife looks different depending on whether we consider social roles—which are very likely to change, as we saw in the case of Marcia—or personality traits, which research indicates are fairly stable after age thirty (Costa & McCrae, 1997).

What are people's conceptions about stability and change of personality in the adult years? Joachim Krueger and Jutta Heckhausen (1993) asked thirty young, thirty middle-aged, and thirty older adults in Germany to rate one hundred trait-descriptive adjectives along several dimensions, including desirability ("How desirable is it to have this trait?") and self-descriptiveness ("How well does the trait describe you?"). The respondents also rated whether each trait changed, and if so, how much and in which direction, for each of seven decades of the adult lifespan. All age groups judged desirable traits (such as energetic, good-natured, purposeful, realistic, intelligent) to increase in early adulthood (growth), followed by moderate decreases in old age (decline), and undesirable traits (such as discourageable, quarrelsome, irresponsible, nervous, blunt-witted) to moderately decrease in early adulthood (growth), then slightly increase in old age (decline). Based on self-descriptions, the overall personality was seen to be at its best during the decade of the sixties, when respondents judged they had the most positive traits and the fewest negative traits. Respondents of all ages were optimistic about development. They judged that more growth than decline occurs during the decades of adulthood. Older individuals considered personality to be quite stable and were more optimistic than their younger counterparts with regard to late-life development. As Figure 15.1 shows, views of development were related to age of the respondents. There were no differences for the young and the middle-aged groups, but for the sixties, the older group gave higher ratings for growth than did young or middle-aged respondents, a finding replicated among a French sample (Gruhn, Gilet, Studer, & Labouvie-Vief, 2011). Also, whereas the two younger groups expected decline in the seventies, the older respondents had balanced conceptions of growth and decline. Other research has demonstrated that when older participants weakly identified with the self-concept of an older person, they were more likely endorse feeling younger than their same-aged peers, and this was particularly strong when negative stereotypes were associated with aging (Weiss & Lang, 2012).

Perceptions of life periods vary by social class and by gender as well as by age. Upper-middle-class individuals usually describe middle age as the period of greatest productivity, whereas blue-collar individuals are more likely to describe it as a period of slowing down, physical weakening, or becoming a "has-been" (Neugarten, 1977). By age forty, blue-collar workers are likely to consider themselves middle-aged, whereas upper-middle-class men often do not consider themselves middle-aged until the early fifties (Turner, 1994). Lower-middle-class men fall somewhere between these two extremes. Women are more likely than men to perceive themselves as younger than their chronological ages, and this judgment becomes more pronounced as they get older (Rodeheaver & Stohs, 1991). Lower socioeconomic status is one of a series of factors that increase the likelihood of having a negative perception of aging, which is linked to subsequent difficulty in activities of daily living (Moser, Spagnoli, & Santos-Eggimann, 2011).

Crisis or No Crisis?

What do psychologists have to tell us about the experience of midlife? Again, we find a multiplicity of images. As we discussed in Chapter 2, Freud saw development as complete by the end of childhood, whereas Erikson extended Freud's stages beyond adolescence and throughout adulthood. Ravenna Helson addresses the idea of having normative and varied paths throughout adulthood. Carl Jung (1933), one of the earliest theorists to suggest that psychological development is lifelong, found middle age more interesting than any other stage of life because once one achieves an acceptable level of status according to societal expectations, one diverts "serious attention" from the demands of society to one's inner self.

Ravenna Helson takes a *normative perspective* of adult development, whereby the *social clock* regulates the age appropriateness of various endeavors of women and men, in part through feelings of anxiety or self-esteem that result from measuring how well one is doing for one's age (Helson et al., 1997). **Social clock projects** refer to age-related expectations about one's goals and activities. For example, a contemporary young woman might have a social clock project of marriage, motherhood, homemaking, and part-time

social clock projects
Age-related expectations about one's goals and activities, such as marriage, parenthood, or career development. Different historical periods and cultures vary in norms about the age at which various social clock projects should be accomplished, how different the projects assigned to men and women are, and how projects are combined over time.

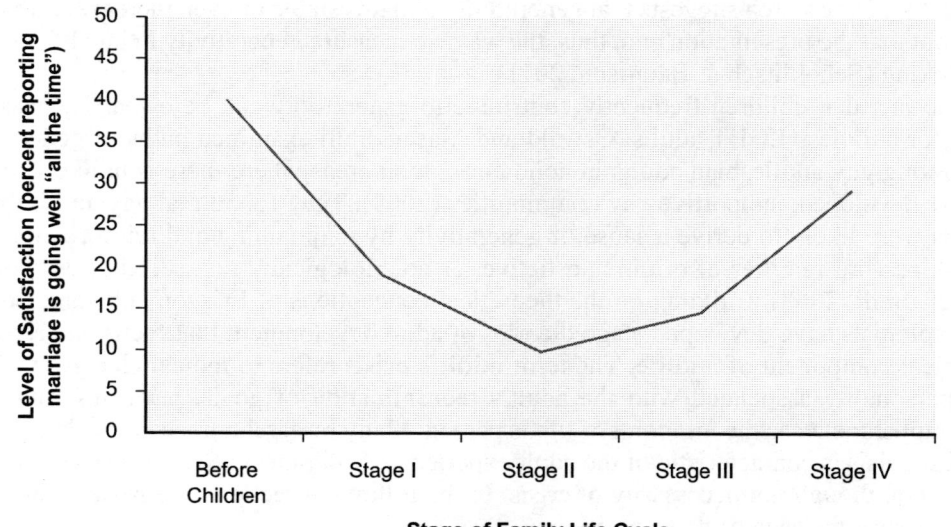

FIGURE 15.1
Level of Satisfaction at Stages of the Family Life Cycle

Marital satisfaction appears to follow a curvilinear path over the family life cycle, starting high, dropping sharply after the birth of the first child, reaching an all-time low when the children are adolescents, and increasing when the children leave home and the couple retires.

employment or a project of entering the traditionally male occupation of engineering and postponing family. Historical periods and cultures vary in the structure and strictness of norms about the age at which various social clock projects should be accomplished, how different the projects assigned to men and women are, and how projects are combined over time. As we discussed in Chapter 13, the age of expected marriage can be earlier or later at different times, among different ethnic groups, and for women and men. Though marriage itself is not a project, early marriage often is part of the "feminine social clock" that includes motherhood and homemaking as a project. Delayed marriage leaves time for the development of a "masculine occupations clock" that requires devotion to career as a project. Normative and non-normative life events both influence social clock projects. A **normative life event** is a life transition that occurs within a restricted time period, such as marriage, children leaving home, or retirement. A **non-normative life event** is one that occurs at any point in life, such as experiencing the height of the women's movement when in college, which today's midlife women report as having been a major influence in their lives (Duncan & Agronick, 1995).

Erikson's theory predicts a normative crisis as the midlife individual faces the task of **generativity versus stagnation**. Generativity requires expanding ego interests and developing a deep concern for the establishment and nurturance of the next generation. It involves creating a *personal legacy* that can serve as an enduring symbol of one's own existence. Stagnation results in life no longer feeling purposeful or having long-term meaning. According to Erikson, generativity appears to increase in importance and strength up through middle adulthood and then taper off somewhat in old age. It may be expressed through nurturing, teaching, mentoring, leading, and promoting the next generation. In the process of dealing with the crisis of generativity versus stagnation, an earlier conflict, such as intimacy versus isolation, may be reawakened and an earlier resolution reworked. Later in the chapter, we will see that middle-aged men who feel they have missed some of the intimacy of family life sometimes readjust their priorities from an emphasis on career toward an emphasis on family. For example, Ellen has been surprised by her father's caregiving devotion to his grandchildren because he was always working when she and her brothers were children.

Dan McAdams, Ed de St. Aubin, and Regina Logan (1993) measured differences in generativity among young (ages twenty-two to twenty-seven), midlife (ages thirty-seven to forty-two), and older (ages sixty-seven to seventy-two) adults. They found that midlife adults scored higher than young adults on generativity, but not higher than older adults. Both midlife and older adults expressed high generative commitments compared to young adults, as shown in Table 15.1, which presents examples of their answers to the open-ended question "I typically try to . . . ." This study supports Erikson's contention that generativity increases in middle adulthood, but not that it decreases during late adulthood. In fact, research suggests that generativity remains stable or even increases into late life, but that the presentation and, thus, the way we measure generativity in late life might be lacking (Schoklitsch & Baumann, 2011).

The fact that children frequently contribute to generativity can be of particular concern for childless LGBT adults. Oswald and Masciadrelli examined paths of generativity among gay and lesbian adults in nonmetropolitan areas where there is unlikely to be highly developed, supportive gay communities (2008). They found that gay and lesbian adults were likely to derive a sense of generativity by maintaining and reinforcing relationships with families of origin and fictive, or nonbiologically related, kin (Oswald & Masciadrelli, 2008). Building on the theoretical conceptions of Erikson and Jung, some psychologists have developed stage theories of adult development that focus on crisis as a typical component of midlife. The term **midlife crisis** refers to radical changes within the personality associated with the adult's reexamination of goals, priorities, and life accomplishments as the midpoint of life is passed. Many researchers see no evidence that midlife crisis is characteristic of the adult experience. Still others see midlife as a time of transition, though not necessarily of crisis. In the following sections, we review some of the evidence for each of these positions.

---

normative life event A life transition that occurs within a time period strong associated with chronological age, such as marriage, children, leaving home, or retirement.

non-normative life event A life transition that occurs in the lives of people but is not associated with a particular stage of life.

generativity versus stagnation The seventh of Erikson's psychosocial crises, usually reached during midlife, during which one must balance the feeling that life is personally satisfying and socially meaningful with feelings of purposelessness.

midlife crisis Radical change in personality associated with the reexamination of goals, priorities, and life accomplishment as the midpoint of life is passed. True midlife crises are relatively rare.

TABLE 15.1 Strivings of Young, Midlife, and Older Adults

When asked about their strivings, middle-aged and older adults expressed high generative commitments compared to young adults, perhaps because the tasks and circumstances young adults face do not encourage them to express generativity.

Age of Respondent	Completion of the Statement "I typically try to . . ."
26-year-old woman	"make my job more interesting than it really is" "be more open to others" "figure out what I want to do with my life" "be a good person" "enjoy life" "avoid uncomfortable situations" "keep up with current events" "be well liked" "make life more interesting and exciting" "make others believe I am completely confident and secure"
40-year-old woman	"be a positive role model for young people" "explain teenage experiences to my son and help him work through difficult situations" "provide for my mother to the best of my ability" "be helpful to those who are in need of help"
68-year-old woman	"counsel a daughter who has recently been let go from a job due to cutbacks" "help another daughter with her sick child" "help as a volunteer in a nonprofit organization" "assist a candidate running for election" "offer financial aid to someone close (friend or relative) if needed"

Source: Adapted from McAdams et al. (1993).

Normative Crisis Models: Midlife Crisis

Three studies support the crisis position: Robert Gould's (1978) study of five hundred adults, known as the UCLA study; George Vaillant's (1977) study of ninety-five men, known as the Harvard Grant study (see Chapter 13); and Daniel Levinson's (1978) study of forty men, done at Yale (see Chapter 13). Each of these studies provides evidence for regular stages of adult development that include a midlife crisis.

The UCLA Study

Roger Gould, a psychiatrist, noticed that many of his patients at the psychiatric clinic were seeking help with problems that appeared to be age related. To investigate this idea, Gould established a sample of five hundred individuals ages sixteen to fifty who were not patients. Gould used interview and questionnaire data gathered from these women and men to describe the major periods of adulthood. His methodology, it must be noted, was that of a clinician. His data are qualitative rather than quantitative, and his book is based on case material drawn from the study without any statistical analysis. This means the interpretation is distinctly subjective.

The Harvard Grant Study

George Vaillant's study of midlife is part of the ongoing longitudinal study of Harvard men we described in Chapter 13. The men were all selected as young adults at Harvard because they were considered healthy and well adjusted. At midlife, these privileged men expressed feelings of turmoil and a heightened awareness of aging (Vaillant & McArthur, 1972). Vaillant saw the pain of the forties as preparation for entering a new stage in which the values and career goals of the thirties are found to be too constraining and the interactions with adolescent children reawaken parts of the forgotten inner self. This heightened self-awareness leads to further growth and opens the way for achieving a sense of generativity. Major criticisms of Vaillant's theory are that it assumes that everyone has kids "on time" and that it was based on a small sample of well-educated, high-SES men.

The Era of Middle Adulthood

Levinson (1978) studied forty men between ages thirty-five and forty-five, a very narrow portion of midlife. Later in his career, Levinson (1996) studied the development of women, which we also discussed in Chapter 13, surveying only thirteen career women and eight homemakers who were between forty-two and forty-five years old, which constitutes a very small sample, especially when you consider that the homemakers and career women have followed diverse paths. Levinson posited that the mid-life transition, which begins between ages thirty-eight and forty-three, bridges early adulthood and middle adulthood. During this transition, the emphasis shifts from past to future, trying to compensate for past failures and resulting in drastic, such as divorce or occupation changes. However, as with other theories of midlife crisis, Levinson's theory is based on a small, nongeneralizable sample and is very heavily age-based and his findings have never been replicated.

No Crisis

Though discussion of a midlife crisis persists in popular media, the theories of a universal midlife crisis lack empirical support (Lachman, 2004). David Chiriboga (1989) points out that the evidence for midlife crisis derives from clinical impressions from people seeking help dealing with issues related to their stage of life or from nonrandomly selected samples of research participants studied by clinicians. He suggests that helping professionals are likely to overestimate the frequency of midlife crisis because they come into contact primarily with people seeking help. They may interpret evidence of "change" as evidence of "crisis." In contrast, when social and developmental psychologists randomly select middle-aged respondents drawn from the community, estimates of midlife crisis are only 2 to 5 percent. These researchers generally use checklists and rating scales rather than interviews. When people tell stories in interviews, they are more likely to dramatize their lives; in contrast, when they fill in scales, they rarely report a crisis (Haan, 1989). As further evidence of no crisis, Chiriboga (1989) reports that depression and other signs of stress and crisis do not increase during middle adulthood and that rates of suicide go down. Rather, midlife is simply another period of transition.

Personality Traits

Paul Costa and Robert McCrae (1997) argue that "roles clearly change with age, but roles are not personality and apparently do not have much influence on it" (p. 275). While life events cause changes in social roles, they do not cause changes in the psychology of the individual. Costa and McCrae criticize **normative crisis models** of adulthood because those models show little agreement as to which phenomena constitute the core of adult development. Instead of looking for stages or structures, Costa and McCrae (1997; Costa et al., 1994) focus on the trait as a dimension of psychological functioning. A **trait** is a relatively enduring disposition of an individual, a characteristic way of thinking, feeling, and acting. While thousands of different traits are used in natural language and in personality assessment, most traits can be categorized within five broad dimensions, as Table 15.2 shows.

Personality traits, according to Costa and McCrae (1997), contribute to the person's basic tendencies. Other factors, such as gender, intelligence, and left-handedness, also contribute, but they are not part of the personality. Basic tendencies must be distinguished from specific behaviors. A ninety-year-old who was the life of the party and danced on the tables in the Roaring Twenties is unlikely to do that today, but she is still likely to enjoy social gatherings and spirited conversation. Her specific behaviors have changed, but the basic tendency is still the same.

Stability of Traits

Hundreds of studies have been done to find out if personality traits change as people age. Most of these studies have been cross-sectional and show very little consistency (Costa & McCrae, 1997). Because cross-sectional studies confound cohort effects with age changes, as we saw in Chapter 14's discussion of cognitive development in middle adulthood, they are not able to provide answers to the question of stability or change in personality traits. In

---

normative crisis model Explanations that view developmental change in terms of a series of distinct periods or stages which are influenced by physical and cognitive performance.

trait A relatively enduring disposition of an individual; a characteristic way of thinking, feeling, and acting.

TABLE 15.2 The "Big Five" Dimensions of Personality

- **Neuroticism:** The tendency to experience negative emotions such as fear, anger, and sadness
- **Extroversion:** Sociability, but closely associated with the tendency to experience excitement, joy, and good spirits
- **Openness to experience:** Welcoming new experiences; imaginative and curious
- **Agreeableness:** Sympathy, trust, cooperativeness, and altruism
- **Conscientiousness:** Organization, scrupulousness, persistence, and achievement motivation

Source: Adapted from McCrae & John (1992).

a characteristic longitudinal study, Costa and his associates (Costa et al., 1986) gave brief scales to measure neuroticism, extroversion, and openness to experience to a national sample of ten thousand individuals ages thirty-five to eighty-four. Ten years later, they relocated and retested two-thirds of the initial sample. They found little effect of age on any of the three personality dimensions for men or women, African Americans or whites. More recent research has found modest increases in conscientiousness, agreeableness, and emotional stability and a slight decline in social vitality and openness to experience over the course of midlife and into late life (Roberts & Mroczek, 2008).

Normative Personality Change

Ravenna Helson takes a third position, which represents a timing of events approach (Helson, 1993; Helson & McCabe, 1994; Helson et al., 1997). In her longitudinal study of women who were in college in the late 1950s, she and her colleagues found considerable stability from early through middle adulthood, but they also found evidence for *normative personality change,* change in the same direction depending on the social expectations of their cohort. In their forties, the women increased in confidence and social assertiveness, which enabled them to reassess their social clock projects and find new direction. While this reassessment may create turmoil for some, turmoil is not universal. Rather than finding evidence for crisis or for no crisis, Helson found three types of change among women in midlife: normative change, change associated with different personality types, and change associated with roles.

The findings of change are not surprising, in that we know midlife is a time of numerous life changes. We saw in Chapter 14 that middle age is the time when men and women reach the peak of their influence on society. It is also the time when society makes its maximum demands on them for social and civic responsibility. At the same time, expectations of one's partner, friends, and family may also be changing. We turn now to normative and non-normative transitions in home and family life during middle adulthood.

Marriage and Divorce

During middle adulthood, marriages may just be starting, may be ending, or may be continuing. Although divorce rates are relatively high, between 50 and 60 percent of first marriages last 40 years (Kreider & Ellis, 2011). Because people typically marry for the first time and most often remarry as young adults, our focus in Chapter 13 was on the formation of new marriages. Middle-aged adults who newly marry or remarry face similar issues of marriage formation. In this section, we focus on continuing marriages, within which many couples in middle adulthood face the normative changes of their lives.

Long-Term Marriage

When Frances and Tom were in their fifties, they appeared to have little in common. Frances was a full-time homemaker; her youngest two children were still at home, navigating their adolescent years. Tom managed a small construction business. They both worked very

> **What Do You Think?**
>
> Consider a middle-aged adult you know well. Has that person experienced a midlife crisis or not? What is your evidence? What characteristics does the person have that may have contributed to the crisis or no-crisis experience?

hard; money was tight, and family time was stressful. Now in their seventies, Frances and Tom have only a dog and two cats living with them. Tom has retired, and they spend most of each day together, taking a long morning walk, going grocery shopping, or caring for their grandchildren. As older adults married for more than fifty years, they seem to enjoy each other's company in a way that was not apparent in their middle years. Each rarely complains about the other, and both are warm and supportive in their interactions with each other.

Laura Carstensen and her associates (1995) compared the emotional behavior of middle-aged and older adults in long-term marriage. They recruited participants on the basis of length of marriage (middle-aged couples had to be married for fifteen years, older couples for thirty-five years), age (the older spouse in middle-aged couples had to be forty to fifty years old, in older couples sixty to seventy years old), and marital satisfaction (both spouses relatively happy or both spouses relatively unhappy). Their sample included 156 couples: 86 percent white, 6 percent African American, 3 percent Hispanic, 3 percent Asian, and 2 percent with spouses of different races. Couples came to the laboratory and were recorded while they engaged in three conversational interactions: discussing events of the day, discussing an area of continuing disagreement in their marriage, and discussing a mutually agreed-on pleasant topic. A team of coders used a carefully constructed coding system to rate the interactions.

Older adult couples were coded as being more affectionate than middle-aged couples, while middle-aged couples were coded as displaying more interest, humor, anger, and disgust. Even when discussing conflict in their relationship, older couples still expressed higher levels of affection and lower levels of negative feelings toward their partners. In addition to these differences, there were similarities between older couples and findings from studies of younger couples. Regardless of age, positive emotions of humor, affection, and validation were more likely to emerge in happy marriages than in unhappy marriages even when discussing marital conflict. Also, wives showed more emotion and a greater range of emotions than husbands did, while husbands showed more defensiveness. Another factor that is consistently reported as a predictor of marriage satisfaction is sexual interactions. A longitudinal study of midlife couples demonstrated that sexual satisfaction subsequently increases reports of marriage quality and reduces divorce risk (Yeh et al., 2006). Other researchers have asked couples in long-term marriages to what

Husbands and wives in long-term marriages agree that being friends, liking one's spouse as a person, and laughing frequently together lead to long, stable, and satisfying marriage. This couple, spending a leisurely afternoon together, appears to have a relationship with all of these qualities.
Source: Monkey Business Images/Shutterstock.com.

factors they attribute their success (Lauer et al., 1995). Husbands and wives mention very similar qualities; Table 15.3 shows they agree on eight of the top ten factors.

The Family Life Cycle

To analyze the similar activities, joys, and problems people experience at different points in their married lives, some scholars have developed the concept of the **family life cycle**, a series of predictable stages through which families pass. You may recognize this as a timing of events model from our discussion in Chapter 13. Families are placed into stages based on the ages of the children and the age of the wife. Young families (stage I) have young children; the wife is less than forty-five years old, and at least one child is under six. Maturing families (stage II) have school-age children; at least one child is between six and eighteen years old. Middle-aged empty-nest families (stage III) have no children at home; the wife is age forty-five or older. Older families (stage IV) have no children at home; the wife is sixty years or older. Figure 15.1 shows that different stages of the family life cycle are associated with different levels of marital satisfaction. Stage analysis deemphasizes the irregularities in family life. It excludes families that are exceptions to the stages, for example, those without children, those who have their first child after age forty, those in which all of the children are over eighteen but some are still living at home, or those in which adult children have special problems, which are discussed in the "Focusing On" feature.

family life cycle A series of predictable changes that families experience based on the age of the children.

Marital Satisfaction and Family Stage

Pat Keith and Robert Schafer (1991) investigated well-being in households with different lifestyles (one- and two-job families, modern and traditional spouses) and in each of the four family stages just described, as well as in single-parent households containing at least one child less than nineteen years old. They found that gender-role attitudes correlated with many of the other factors measured: "Whether gender-role attitudes were modern or more traditional was linked to the household involvement of husbands and wives in most of the life stages. Thoughts about gender roles were especially salient in predicting the division of labor in younger families . . . traditional wives spent more

TABLE 15.3 Perceived Reasons for Successful Long-Term Marriages (top ten, listed in order of frequency of naming)

Husbands	Wives
Mate is best friend	Marriage a long-term commitment
Like mate as person	Like mate as person
Marriage a long-term commitment	Mate is best friend
Marriage a sacred institution	Laugh together frequently
Agree on aims and goals	Agree on aims and goals
Laugh together frequently	Marriage a sacred institution
Proud of mate's achievements	Agree on expression of affection
Mate more interesting now than when first married	Agree on philosophy of life
Engage in outside interests	Proud of mate's achievements
Agree on major decisions	Mate more interesting now than when first married

Source: Lauer et al. (1995).

Focusing On...

The Effects of Middle-Aged Adult Children's Problems on Older Parents

The family life cycle emphasizes predictable parental responsibilities when children are young and subsequent freedom from these responsibilities when children reach adulthood. By the time one's children are late-middle-aged, they are expected to begin caring for their parents. But what if adult offspring have problems? Studies of young children and young adult children have shown that their physical and mental disorders often lead to parental distress (Cook, 1988: Noh et al., 1989; Seltzer et al., 2001). Does this relationship between children's problems and parental distress continue into later life, when the children are middle-aged adults and the parents are elderly?

Karl Pillemer and Jill Suitor (1991) set out to investigate this question. They believed that because parents identify with their children and view their children's accomplishments and difficulties as indicators of their own success and failure, elderly parents would be affected by the problems of their adult offspring. Also, because mothers typically invest more of their time and energy in childrearing, elderly mothers were expected to be more distressed by their children's problems than would elderly fathers.

Pillemer and Suitor conducted a telephone survey of 1,421 noninstitutionalized elderly (ages sixty-five to one hundred) women (67 percent) and men (33 percent) in Canada, asking them about their relationships with their children. People with no living children were excluded. Up to two children were selected in each case: one child who lived with the respondent (if any did) and one child who lived independently. If there was more than one child in either category, the respondents were asked to select "the child with whom they had the hardest time getting along" (p. 588).

The interviews measured psychological distress and children's problems, along with several other variables. The psychological distress scale asked questions about how frequently in the preceding week the respondent felt a certain way (e.g., "You felt downhearted or blue"). The respondent could answer "very often," "fairly often," "once in a while," or "never." Children's problems were measured by asking the respondent whether the target child (or, if two, either child) had any of four problems: mental or emotional problems (3.5 percent of respondents reported these), serious problems with his or her physical health (14.2 percent), a drinking or alcohol problem (2.2 percent), or serious stress during the past year (21.3 percent). Twenty-six percent of the respondents reported that their child had at least one of these problems. One question assessed parent-child conflict: "How often does your child create tensions or arguments with you?" Another measured the amount of support received from the child: "How often does your child make you feel loved or cared for?" Another asked the extent to which the child depended on the parent for financial support. Respondents also answered questions about their health, marital status, and education, and whether they had a confidant.

Parents who reported that their child had at least one of the four problems received higher depression scores than parents who did not report a child with a problem, a finding replicated in similar studies (Seltzer et al., 2001). The strength of the relationship between children's problems and parents' psychological distress was the same for mothers and fathers and for parents living with their children and those living independently. Pillemer and Suitor thought the direct practical impact of the children's problems on the parents might explain the parents' depression: perhaps the problem children were more financially dependent, or they did not provide their parents with emotional support. However, they found no such relation existed. Conflict with children, on the other hand, was positively related to depression.

This study clearly shows that even when the children are themselves adults in their middle years, their problems affect the well-being of their parents. This is not because they cohabitate, need financial help, or fail to provide emotional support but because elderly parents continue to identify with their children and to conclude that if the child does not "turn out right," they are at fault (Strom & Strom, 1995). Earlier studies have shown this to be true at earlier stages of the parent-child relationship (Goldsteen & Ross, 1989; Umberson, 1989). Similarly, Pickett and colleagues (1997) found that parents' perception of their relationship with their child but not the child's disability status is associated with perceived caregiving burden, further supporting the findings of Pillemer. As with any timing of events theory, the family life cycle cannot account for the unpredictable problems that occur in families.

What Do You Think?

1. How could a timing of events model explain parental distress in late adulthood, long after the children have reached adulthood? How could a normative crisis model explain it?
2. Do you think timing of events theory or normative crisis theory better explains diversity in family problems? Why?

time on stereotypically feminine tasks and, correspondingly, nontraditional husbands did more housework" (p. 152). More stage I and II families aspired to equal partnerships (modern), while in stage III and IV families the wife was likely to be modern and the husband traditional. This may well be due to cohort differences because age and stage are not possible to separate in this cross-sectional study. However, in households where partners feel that household chores are divided equitably, both partners report higher levels of happiness (Frisco & Williams, 2003). Gender-role attitude correlated with employment of stage I and II wives; when husbands and wives were both traditional, the young wife was unlikely to be employed. By middle age, wives were employed, regardless of gender-role attitudes, because childcare needs no longer conflicted with employment. Recent research has found that mothers who were never married, divorced, or widowed report lower levels of happiness and higher levels of depression, even when accounting for socioeconomic status (Koropeckyj-Cox, Pienta, & Brown, 2007).

Dual-Earner Families

Keith and Schafer found that wives and husbands in dual-earner families responded differently to the strain of balancing the demands of home and work. Wives reported distress when their husbands experienced competing demands, while husbands reported distress when their wives spent large amounts of time at work. It is likely that these findings are related to the research examining the role of perceived equity of household responsibilities, noted earlier (Frisco & Williams, 2003). There is evidence that when men hold highly traditional expectations of gender roles and are married to women with more modern expectations, there is substantially more conflict and lower ratings of marital satisfaction (Minnotte et al., 2010).

Keith and Schafer also found that family life stage was highly correlated with strain for dual-earner families. More than one-third of the young families reflected high role strain between occupational and family demands for both partners, compared to fewer than 10 percent of the middle-aged and older couples. This is probably clue to the intensity of the demands of establishing new careers and parenting young children that we considered in our discussion of early adulthood.

Which Family Stages Are Happier?

Some studies indicate that middle-aged (stage III) and older (stage IV) marriages are happier than those in the earlier stages. Marital satisfaction appears to follow a curvilinear path over the family life cycle, starting high during the honeymoon, dropping sharply after the birth of the first child, reaching an all-time low when the children are adolescents, and increasing when the children leave home and the couple retires, as Figure 15.1 shows (Anderson et al., 1983; Levenson et al., 1993). As we saw in the discussion of transition to parenthood in Chapter 13, the presence of younger children at home creates demands that lower both marital interaction and marital happiness for husbands and wives (Zuo, 1992). This decline in marital satisfaction following the birth of a child is true for all types of couples but is buffered when the pregnancy was planned and when the couple had high levels of satisfaction pre-pregnancy (Lawrence, Rothman, Cobb, & Rothman, 2008). Women and men in long-term happy marriages report increasing satisfaction over time, with a dip during the child-rearing years (Lauer et al., 1995). On the other hand, Caroline Vaillant and George Vaillant (1993) analyzed data from men in the Harvard Grant study and their wives and found little support for the family life cycle curve. They suggest that the curve may be an artifact of cross-sectional methodology, but their sample was so small and so select that it alone is not a good test of the U-shaped curve of marital satisfaction. (See Chapter 13 for a description of the sample.) However, more recent longitudinal research conducted throughout midlife and into late life replicates some of the findings of the family life cycle curve. In particular, women's marital satisfaction increases throughout midlife and into late life, which is due, in part, to increased freedom that comes with children leaving the home (Gorchoff, John, & Helson, 2008). Robert Levenson, Laura Carstensen, and John Gottman (1993) found that children were rated as the largest source of marital conflict for middle-aged couples and only the fourth in importance for older couples. Additionally, wives' report of marital and personal satisfaction is highly predictive of their husbands' marital satisfaction over the course of midlife (Carr, Freedman, Cornman, & Schwarz, 2014; Faulkner, Davey, & Davey, 2005). Financial stress is one important factor that brings on decline in marital satisfaction, and that is missing in the privileged Harvard Grant sample (Norris & Tindale, 1994). Other sources of conflict that middle-aged couples rated significantly higher than older couples included money, religion, and recreation (Levenson, Carstensen, & Gottman (1993).

Same-Sex Marriage

Due to long-standing restrictions on same-sex marriage, there is a paucity of research in this area. However, the research that exists largely suggests that homosexual partnerships are very similar to heterosexual partnerships (Peplau & Fingerhut, 2007; Roisman, Clausell, Holland, Fortuna, & Elieff, 2008). Differences between heterosexual and homosexual relationships are few and oftentimes suggest that homosexual couples experience added benefits. Gay and lesbian couples, though often less stable than heterosexual couples due to restrictions on marriage, are more likely to split household work and are more likely to resolve disagreements in a beneficial manner (Kurdek, 2005). Gottman and colleagues (2003) conducted a study examining interactions between both married and partnered gay, lesbian, and heterosexual couples and found that same-sex couples engaged in more positive behaviors during their interactions than heterosexual couples. Moreover, during disagreements same-sex couples were more likely to start a discussion positively, influencing the other partner to respond positively whereas heterosexual couples initiated these discussions negatively (Gottman et al., 2003). The researchers attribute these findings, in part, to increased equity within same-sex partnerships. Additionally, the inability to marry when marriage is the desired outcome of a relationship causes undue stress and increased risk for psychological problems for both heterosexual and homosexual couples (Wight, LeBlanc, & Badgett, 2013).

Midlife Divorce

Although marital satisfaction tends to increase among long-term married couples, divorce does occur. Between 1990 and 2010, divorce rates among those age fifty and older doubled, with those who had been remarried divorcing at a rate more than twice that of those in their first marriage (Brown & Lin, 2012). Still, most divorces occur before middle adulthood: only 25 percent of recent separations and divorces occurred among women over age forty (Brown & Lin, 2012). During midlife, the rate of separation and divorce for African Americans is more than twice as high as for whites and nearly twice as high as midlife Hispanics (Brown & Lin, 2012). Divorce during middle adulthood has a significant impact on women, men, and their children.

For those who do not remarry, divorce represents entry into a lifetime single status, which has been linked to poorer physical health and increased risk for depression (Hughes & Waite, 2009). The younger a woman is when she divorces and the fewer children she has, the more likely she is to remarry. This reflects in part the decrease in the number of potential marriage partners. Remarriage is less common among African Americans and Hispanics than among whites. Men are more likely to remarry than women.

Wives

For women, separation and divorce usually lower the standard of living significantly. This is especially true while children still live in the home. Because 45 percent of mother-only families live in poverty, divorce has a substantial impact on the quality of life for children (Edmondson et al., 1993). Divorced women with children face greater risk for depression than women without children, and this impact is greater among women with young children (Williams & Dunne-Bryant, 2006). Even when women remarry, the majority of children living in single-parent families because of divorce will live out their childhood without ever entering a second family (Bumpass & Sweet, 1989). Among women without children, the impact of divorce does not demonstrate the same long-lasting negative consequences (Williams & Dunne-Bryant, 2006), particularly if the woman initiates divorce or knows divorce is inevitable (Sakraida, 2008).

> **What Do You Think?**
>
> Suppose you have a friend who has two teenagers and is having some problems in her marriage. If she obtained the help of a marriage counselor, what advice do you think this professional would be likely to give to your friend based on what you have learned about the family life cycle?

Husbands

For men, divorce or separation usually means they see their children far less often. Because custody of young children is more frequently awarded to mothers, fathers' interactions with their children often are disrupted due to physical separation. Teresa Cooney (1994) estimates that 13 to 51 percent of children of divorce have infrequent, if any, contact with their noncustodial parent. Alan Booth and Paul Amato (1994) found that divorce was most disruptive to father-child relations when it occurred early in the child's life, which has subsequently been linked to higher rates of depression among divorced fathers than married fathers (Williams & Dunne-Bryant, 2006). This has implications for the well-being of men after age fifty, when divorce has a pronounced negative effect on the frequency of fathers' contacts with their adult offspring and sharply reduces the probability that fathers consider their adult children as potential sources of support in times of need (Cooney & Uhlenberg, 1990). Moreover, children of divorce are less likely to provide assistance to frail fathers than mothers (Lin, 2008).

Young Adult Children

Both parental divorce and level of pre-divorce marital conflict during childhood affect offspring during the transition to adulthood. In high-marital-conflict families, children have higher levels of well-being as young adults if their parents divorced than if they stayed together. But in low-marital-conflict families, children have higher levels of well-being if their parents stayed together than if they divorced. Even in marriages that do not end in divorce, parental marital conflict is negatively associated with the well-being of offspring (Amato, 2010; Amato et al., 1995; Cooney & Kurz, 1996).

What happens if divorce does not occur until the parents are in their middle years and the children are already out of the house? Cooney (1994) studied the influence of recent parental divorce on contact and feelings between 485 young white adults (ages eighteen to twenty-three) and their parents, half of whom had experienced divorce in the past fifteen months. Because these children were already adults, Cooney could assess the changes in the relationship with each parent in the absence of court-imposed custody. Recent parental divorce was associated with reduced intimacy and contact between fathers and their children but not mothers. Approximately 15 percent of nonresident adult children of recent divorce saw their fathers less than once a month, which was virtually unheard of in intact families. "Less than 60 percent of children of divorce had weekly contacts with their absent fathers, compared to 80 percent of those in intact families" (p. 53).

Speculations as to the reasons for this lack of contact include lack of interest on the part of the father (Furstenberg & Cherlin, 1991), ongoing conflict with the ex-partner that could force the children to take sides, personal problems such as alcoholism, and geographic distance (Dudley, 1991), but it is hard to understand why some of these reasons would not affect mothers' contact as well. It seems likely that these fathers lack the kinkeeping skills that are necessary for continuing contact. *Kinkeeping skills* are those skills that keep the individual in touch with other family members, such as phoning, sending birthday cards, or visiting. These are skills that men can learn but traditionally have been the province of women. "Perhaps as the scope of men's responsibilities in the home widens, more fathers will have the opportunity to develop their relationship skills and form stronger, independent relations with their children and other kin" (Cooney, 1994, p. 54).

Parental divorce does not influence the amount of contact between young adults and their grandparents because adult children can and do independently facilitate contact. The chances that adult grandchildren from divorced families will initiate contact with grandparents are higher than those for grandchildren from intact families. Also, the likelihood that adult grandchildren of divorce will contact their paternal grandparents without their fathers' knowledge is higher than for grandchildren from intact families (Cooney & Smith, 1996). This provides evidence of continuing family interest on the part of the young adult.

Family Relationships

The concept of the family life cycle clearly indicates how closely intertwined marriage is with other family relationships. As we have seen, the ages of the children affect the marital relationship, and marital disruption affects parental relationships with children. Yet, married or not, adults in their middle years tend to have a rich array of family relationships. For adults, attachment is an emotional closeness that does not depend on physical immediacy. (See the Chapter 5 discussion of attachment formation in early life.) Adults who feel secure in their attachments approach work with confidence and report greater well-being than those who do not (Hazen & Shaver, 1990). Without necessarily being in constant contact, middle-aged adults maintain relationships with the younger generations of children and grandchildren, with the older generations of parents and grandparents, and with their own generation of siblings. Because their loved ones call on them when they are in crises, middle-aged adults have been called the **sandwich generation**, caught between the needs of adjacent generations. However, most midlife adults, though staying in touch with various generations, do not constitute a true "sandwich generation" because throughout midlife, they are unlikely to be simultaneously caring for parents and children (Grundy & Henretta, 2006). In fact, helping one generation decreases the likelihood that a midlife adult will provide assistance with the other (Grundy & Henretta, 2006). As we discuss the various relationships, it is necessary to keep in mind the diversity among middle-aged adults in terms of race/ethnicity, educational level, occupational attainment, gender, and health status to understand that not every midlife adult will have all of the relationships we consider and not every relationship will be experienced in the same way by different individuals. Disjunction and disruption sometimes occur in family relationships as well, as Joan Stone, a victim advocate, mentions in the "Working With" interview.

sandwich generation Middle-aged adult caught between the needs of adjacent generations: their children and their aging parents.

Delayed Parenthood

For many reasons, such as late marriage, the desire to establish financial and professional security, or fertility problems, some couples make the transition to parenthood in their late thirties and early forties, rather than in early adulthood. Risks of low infant birth weight and prematurity are twice as high for first births after age forty than for those between ages twenty and twenty-four, but they are still not high (Aldous & Edmonson, 1993; Joseph et al., 2005). Studies of marital satisfaction, parental stress, and family functioning of "delayed" parents compared to "on time" parents suggest that older parents may be better prepared and adapt more easily to parenthood (Garrison et al., 1997). Research is needed on the long-term implications of delayed parenthood, such as its impact on adolescent-parent relations.

Adolescent Children

Although the transition to parenthood puts a lot of strain on the marital relationship, as we discussed in Chapter 13, adolescent children have the most detrimental impact on marital satisfaction (Gecas & Seff, 1990). This is particularly true among parents who experience conflict regarding their adolescent children (Ciu & Donnelan, 2009). As children grow into adolescence, parents need to become less hierarchical and more flexible in their parenting style (Norris & Tindale, 1994). Adolescents need the opportunity to make their own decisions and make their own mistakes within the safe confines of parental supervision. As you may remember from Chapter 11, an authoritative style that combines high acceptance, supervision, and respect for adolescent autonomy promotes adolescent development. Adolescent adjustment in both biological families and stepfamilies is positively related to parental supervision, warmth, and interest and negatively related to conflict (Fine & Kurdek, 1992; Reuter & Conger, 1995). Parents of adolescents face continual challenges to their judgment, which often results in discomfort and conflict between the parents. Parents may revisit their own adolescent conflicts and want to prevent their children from making the same mistakes. Realizing their offspring are close to independence may spur midlife reassessment of self and goals that in itself is often disconcerting and may cause crises. Parents who have not lived alone with each other for years may worry about how they will get along without children. In addition, adolescents take up a lot of space and time. Unlike younger children, they do not have a bedtime that allows parents private time. Few parents can even stay up as late as their teenagers do due to circadian shifts in adolescent sleep and because parents generally must wake early to days filled with work and family responsibilities.

Young Adult Children

Relationships change as children move out to attend college or to begin their own adult lives, but this does not mean they have become fully independent. As you may remember from Chapter 11, entry into adulthood increases interaction and closeness between child and parents compared to adolescent levels (Rossi & Rossi, 1990). Parents are often pleasantly surprised to discover that the same child who, while living at home during high school, answered questions with monosyllables calls from college with lots to talk about. Parents continue to provide financial and emotional support for children in college and reside in what have been called "semiautonomous households" because the children return for holidays, summer vacations, and whenever they feel the need (Goldscheider & DaVanzo, 1986). Even when the young adult offspring have established households of their own, like Bill and Karen in Chapter 13, parents are likely to continue to give emotional and material support.

While emotional support is a two-way interaction between adult children and their parents, material support tends to be parent to child until parents are well into their seventies and the children are in their forties (Sechrist et al., 2012; Spitze & Logan, 1992). There is some evidence, however, that ethnicity and family income strongly influence the flow of money between generations. In a comparison of intergenerational financial support among whites, African Americans, and Hispanics, Yean-Ju Lee and Isik Aytac (1998) found that African American and Hispanic parents were less likely than white parents to give financial support to their adult children, largely because they had fewer resources to give.

The Empty Nest

Children moving out appears to be conducive to well-being in parents, especially mothers, and to improved marital satisfaction for the couple (Norris & Tindale, 1994). Having an "empty nest" typically results in time to spare and, when the children are out of college, money to spare as well. This provides midlife parents with opportunities for self-development, autonomy, and time to spend with one another (Gorhoff, John, & Helson, 2008). When the children leave home, mothers have the freedom to develop occupations or careers or to increase their commitment to those they have, and couples have the opportunity to do more things together, especially travel. One result is that, regardless of marriage type or gender-role attitudes, middle-aged wives tend to be employed (Keith & Schafer, 1991). Studies have focused on mothers rather than on fathers because mothers traditionally have been the more involved parents.

Mothers tend to benefit more than fathers, either because they have put off or limited independent activities to tend to family needs or have been doing a "second shift" (first shift at work, second shift at home), as we saw in the Chapter 13 discussion of parenting issues in early adulthood. Mothers in young dual-earner families experience the most intense role strain (Keith & Schafer, 1991). The empty nest is a source of freedom for women; they become more assertive, less depressed, and less strained (Cooper & Gutman, 1987; Norris & Tindale, 1994). This appears to be true regardless of ethnicity. In a study of 243 middle-aged, empty-nest Mexican American mothers, Linda Rogers and Kyriakos Markides (1989) found that the women enjoyed levels of well-being equal to

> ## WORKING WITH Joan Stone, Victim Advocate
>
> ### Helping Victims of Abusive Family Relationships
>
> Joan Stone graduated from college a year ago with a major in psychology and a minor in women's studies. Since then she has been working as a victim advocate for victims of domestic violence. She provides legal assistance and referrals for services and counseling.
>
> **Michele:** *What is a victim advocate?*
>
> **Joan:** Connecticut mandated the victim advocate position in response to a case in which a woman who had no adequate protection from domestic violence was disabled by her husband. The Domestic Violence Project, where I work, places victim advocates in the courts so we are readily available for those who need us. The Project provides victims with a safe place to live for up to ninety days, counseling, legal assistance, referrals for services, and other social supports. To qualify you have to be a victim of abuse by someone you are intimate with or are related to, such as a husband, a father of your children, or a child.
>
> **Michele:** *What training did you have?*
>
> **Joan:** I did a yearlong internship my senior year. I also earned a twenty-hour certificate of training before the internship.
>
> **Michele:** *What exactly do you do?*
>
> **Joan:** I help victims in both civil and criminal court. If a person is in an abusive relationship but can't get the abuser arrested, I help get a restraining order through civil action. The victim calls the twenty-four-hour hot line for our help, which takes an enormous amount of self-confidence to do. In contrast, when the abuser has been arrested, the case goes to criminal court. In criminal court, the victim can receive a protective order through the state-mandated law. In criminal cases, the victim advocate sees the victim in person or makes contact by phone or letter. Most victims cooperate, but some are unwilling.
>
> **Michele:** *How are cases assigned to you?*
>
> **Joan:** An arrest takes place. The defendant is arraigned the next day. Speedy results are mandated due to the severity of domestic violence. The only way the victim advocates can initiate contact with victims is if they go through the court process. On the first offense, the defendant is often referred to the family violence course, and if the defendant finishes the course, the charges are dropped. The victim can be referred to the domestic violence program and to counseling.
>
> **Michele:** *Can you give me some examples of your cases?*
>
> **Joan:** Some victims in criminal cases will say, "Yes, I want him out of the house," but a lot will drop charges. They will say, "It was a one-time thing," although if you look at the records, you see they have been to court before. Experienced victim advocates say it takes eight or nine arrests before the victims leave their relationships.
>
> I once worked with a woman in her late eighties whose son, in his mid-forties, was abusing her. She was rushed to the emergency room, she was beaten so badly. We called elderly services to help her. She needed her son to care for her but wanted him out. I worked with another elderly woman who lived with her three middle-aged unmarried children. They all abused each other. There was a cycle of violence in the family.
>
> **Michele:** *So far, you have spoken of women victims. What are they like?*

those of other ethnic groups. In their study, the women who were employed were, on average, five years younger and less likely to report depressive or physical symptoms than were the nonemployed mothers. This is consistent with findings from research with white middle-aged mothers (Barnett & Baruch, 1985).

Multigenerational Households

Parents tend to fare best emotionally when children physically move out but remain in close contact (Bookwala, 2012; White & Edwards, 1990). The parents can reorganize their time and interests but still maintain their parenting relationship. However, many young adults never leave home, or they return one or more times to the parental household, known as the boomerang phenomenon (White & Rogers, 1997). Individuals who reached early adulthood in the 2000s were more likely to reside with their parents than were those

WORKING WITH Joan Stone, Victim Advocate

Helping Victims of Abusive Family Relationships *continued*

Joan: Well, it depends. Those who come to the office are seeking counseling and support voluntarily, but when we meet clients in court, they are there because police officers directed them. That puts me in the position of working with people who don't want help. I have to let them make decisions themselves. For example, a woman in her late thirties was in court because her boyfriend, who had a drinking problem, had been beating her sixteen-year-old daughter. She was very upset and wanted him to stop. Even though the woman didn't ask for one, the court assigned a protective order. She was trying to protect her daughter and the defendant at the same time, although she certainly understood the problem. I talked to her for a long time and got her to let me talk to the daughter. The daughter said, "I really like this man, but when he drinks they get into a fight." The mother and daughter were hesitant, but with help and support, they made a decision to restrict him to visits, which was positive and productive for them.

Michele: *What segment of the population do victims come from?*

Joan: All types of people are victims of domestic violence: minority, lower-class white, and upper-class white. In fact, the person sitting next to you may be a victim of domestic violence. The other day I called a prominent woman in town because her husband was arrested for harassment. She was in her fifties; they were married over thirty years. It turns out he was a problem drinker, and she wanted him to get help. He was arraigned in court and assigned counseling. She got a partial protective order, which means he can continue to live at home but not harass her. This solution fit her needs, but it wouldn't work for everyone. Part of what I do as a victim advocate is help victims come up with the best solution given the specifics of their situation.

Michele: *Do you deal only with spousal abuse cases?*

Joan: No, we see a lot of victims abused by their children. I have seen middle-aged fathers abused by sons in high school or college. The child often has a drug or alcohol problem. The father may not like the friends his son is hanging out with or that the son's grades are going down. The father and son get into a fight that turns physical. The child may threaten, "I'm going to kill you." It's hard for parents to call the police. It is sad to see people abused like this.

Michele: *What do you like about your work?*

Joan: It's exciting. I learn how different people think. It's also frustrating. You can't tell people what to do. You don't want to be judgmental, but I have a hard time accepting what they want. If a victim wants her abuser back, she has a right even if she is in danger. The best thing is the gratification I get when the victim has a positive outcome and is *safe*!

What Do You Think?

1. What strains in family relationships are reflected in the types of domestic violence Joan describes?
2. Why might women with children be reluctant to leave their marriages or cohabiting relationships even though those relationships are abusive?
3. Notice the involvement of alcohol and drugs in several of the cases Joan mentions. How is this consistent with what you learned in Chapters 12 and 14?

---

who came of age in the 1980s or 1990s, probably because they remained single longer and because shifts in economics made living independently financially unfeasible (Glick & Lin, 1986; Sechrist et al., 2012). William Aquilino (1990) used an extensive collection of family life interviews to study African American, white, and Mexican American parents who had at least one child or stepchild over nineteen years of age. He found that middle-aged parents (age fifty-four or younger) were more likely to have an adult child living with them than were older parents (fifty-five or older); 28 percent reported adult coresident children. Children's marital status was the best predictor of coresidence: only parents with *unmarried* adult children were likely to have children coresiding. Parents whose youngest adult child was age nineteen to twenty-one were more likely to have children at home than parents with older children. Sons were more likely than daughters to live with their middle-aged parents. Married parents, particularly those still married to each other, were most likely to have adult children coresiding. There was little evidence for stronger preference for coresidency among minorities than among whites. Although more African American and Mexican American adult children lived with their parents, the racial differences were entirely accounted for by the children's marital status. Minority parents were more likely to have adult children living with them because they were more likely to have unmarried adult children. James Jackson, Toni Antonucci, and Rose Gibson (1990) report that all racial and ethnic minorities, especially Native Americans, are more likely than whites to live in multigenerational households. They suggest socioeconomic differences, cultural preferences, values, and feelings of filial devotion as reasons for maintenance of these multigenerational households.

Among coresiding families, conflict has been found to increase and parental satisfaction to decline if the children are financially dependent or unemployed and separated or divorced with accompanying grandchildren. Decreases in parental well-being and marital satisfaction may occur, particularly when there is conflict with the child or when the child is experiencing major life upheaval (Putney & Bengtson, 2001; Sechrist et al., 2012). Mothers may be at particular risk for reductions in well-being when adult children return to the home (Umberson, Pudrovska, & Reczek, 2010). Coresidence works best when the young adult children are older, employed, or in school (White & Rogers, 1997). Although coresident young adult offspring give and receive more support from their parents than do nonresident ones, they report lower levels of affection than nonresident adult children. This may be due to the day-to-day strains of sharing a household. The quality of affective ties between parents and their adolescent and young adult children has long-term consequences for the offspring's self-esteem. Robert Roberts and Vern Bengtson (1996) measured self-esteem and affective ties to parents in sixteen- to twenty-six-year-olds. They reevaluated the same individuals seventeen and twenty years later. Young people who reported stronger affective ties with their parents had higher self-esteem at all times of testing.

Grandparenting

Couples today typically become grandparents in their late forties and early fifties, which is young compared to couples in the early 1900s (Gee, 1991). This is likely to change in the future as more young adults delay starting families. Because contemporary grandparenting begins early and life expectancies are long, the role of grandparent is likely to last for three or four decades. As the "A Multicultural View" feature indicates, contact between the generations shows considerable diversity. Women, who tend both to be younger than men when their children are born and to live longer, have a particularly long period of grandparenthood. Frances was forty-six and Tom was fifty-one when their first grandchild was born. Still healthy and vigorous, they have already been grandparents for more than thirty years and step-great-grandparents for five years.

Timing affects how people experience the transition to grandparenting (Kaufman & Elder, 2003). Most Canadian women state that late middle age is the "right time" (Burton, 1996; Gee, 1991). Very early "off-time" grandparenthood can be very distressing. It is likely to be caused by a teenage pregnancy (which may in itself be upsetting) and provides less time for the grandparent-to-be to prepare for the new role (Norris & Tindale, 1994). While grandparenthood pushes a person to feel older, a negative feeling in our youth-oriented culture, many grandparents report that interacting with their grandchildren "keeps me young" (Newton & Stewart, 2012). Social class has a significant impact on timing of grandparenthood. Teenage childbearing is more common among working-class women and, after several generations, can result in a grandmother in her late twenties and a great-grandmother in her forties. Linda Burton (1996) found that many very young African American grandmothers rejected the role of grandmother and shifted the responsibilities to the great-grandmother, though other researchers have found very high levels of involvement among African American grandparents (Hayslip & Page, 2012). When grandparenting is on time, the transition typically is a positive experience for the older couple and one that is likely to reinforce the connections between the two older generations as both form attachments to the new generation (Hayslip & Page, 2012).

A Multicultural View

Diversity in Intergenerational Families

Contemporary Americans have fewer children and live longer and thus spend more years in intergenerational families than did earlier generations. Families have changed structurally, too. As couples have fewer children, young people have fewer aunts, uncles, and cousins. As family members live longer, young people are more likely to know their grandparents, great-grandparents, and even great-great-grandparents. "Individuals are now more likely to grow older in four- or even five-generation families, spend an unprecedented number of years in family roles such as grandparenthood, and be part of a more complex and varied web of intergenerational family ties" (Burton, 1992b; Goldscheider, 1997). These changes have produced the **beanpole family structure**, which has more generations but fewer people in each generation.

Declining birth rates and mortality rates have produced similar changes in family structure in most areas around the world (Bianchi, 2014). In India, for example, conditions that tend to discourage couples from having large families include the general scarcity of goods and services, limited opportunities for a good education and subsequent employment, and the dowry-dominated marriage market (Ramu, 1991). Social policy, such as the one-child policy in China, has also contributed to a decline in births and an increase in the beanpole family structure in Asia.

Intergenerational bonds show considerable diversity among contemporary families, reflecting gender, ethnic, and social class differences. Four social characteristics above and beyond individual circumstances and choices predict interaction among American family members (Bengtson et al., 1990). First, gender matters. Daughters tend to interact more frequently with their parents than do sons, and middle-aged daughters assume the responsibilities of kinkeepers (Brown & DeRycke, 2010; Fry, 1996). Second, marital status of both generations predicts contact. Widowhood brings more frequent contact with children, and unmarried children have more contact with parents (Connidis et al., 1996). Third, social class seems to have an impact. Working-class children have more contact with parents than do white-collar children, in part because they live closer to home. Fourth, ethnic or racial differences affect contact. Hispanics show the high levels of interaction, and African Americans tend to be more involved with grandchildren than whites (Hayslip & Page, 2012). In a comparison of African American, white, and Mexican American grandparents, Vern Bengtson (1985) found that Mexican American grandparents had many more grandchildren and reported higher levels of contact and more satisfaction from that contact. These social characteristics vary in other cultures. In China, for example, sons are preferred and daughters-in-law, rather than daughters, are expected to provide care (Ikels, 1993). In communal cultures, such as the !Kung, households are not separated and kinship and caregiving are continuous interactions with people with whom one has always lived rather than a matter of "contact" or "kinkeeping" (Draper & Keith, 1992).

As parents and grandparents live longer, relationships within the family last longer and need to be transformed dramatically as the needs of family members change over the life course. According to Frances Goldscheider (1997), relational changes in the direction of equality and away from hierarchy will facilitate these transformations. We know, for example, that authoritative parenting, in which the parent provides guidance but enables the child to make choices, is conducive to better parent-adolescent and parent-adult child relations. Likewise, equal partnership promotes well-being and flexibility in handling new circumstances. We can expect that while families remain diverse, they will also change to accommodate new realities of the twenty-first century.

Beanpole families, with many generations but few people in each generation, have become prevalent as people around the world have fewer children and live longer.
Source: Monkey Business Images/Shutterstock.com.

Grandparents as a Family Resource

Families generally view grandparents as a valuable resource, although the ways that resource is called on depends on the family's circumstances (Bengtson et al., 1990). Grandparents help by just being there, providing a sense of family continuity and family history. In times of crises in the lives of children, such as divorce, widowhood, teenage pregnancy, or prolonged unemployment, grandparents frequently provide substantial

beanpole family structure The contemporary family structure, which has more generations but fewer people in each generation because of increased longevity and a decreased birth rate.

assistance to their adult children and become more involved in the daily lives of their grandchildren. When the crises pass, the adult children are likely to resume fuller responsibility. For example, when Frances and Tom's younger daughter's marriage broke up, their granddaughter was only two months old. Lauren moved back into the parental home with baby Rachel. Frances became Rachel's caregiver while Lauren worked and found her emotional balance. Rachel was already in first grade by the time Lauren remarried and moved in with her new husband. By then the bonds between grandparents and grandchild were very strong. Frances and Tom have also provided financial assistance to a married adult son out of work, after-school and vacation care for grandchildren, and care for grandchildren too sick to attend school.

In most respects, grandmothers and grandfathers view their relationships with their grandchildren similarly, but some gender differences exist. Jeanne Thomas (1995) found that both expressed a similar sense of responsibility toward the grandchild, similar feelings of centrality of the relationship in their own lives, and similar feelings that the relationship permitted reinvolvement with their past, and placed similar value on sharing wisdom with the grandchild (Hayslip & Page, 2012; Thomas, 1995). Grandmothers reported greater satisfaction from these relationships than did grandfathers; grandfathers placed greater stress on generational extension of the family and indulging grandchildren than did grandmothers. Thomas interprets her results as being in keeping with the earlier experiences of men and women: grandmothers enjoy the continuity of family experiences, while grandfathers are concerned with continuing the family line. Grandfathers' indulgence of their grandchildren "may reflect male nurturance and expressivity of middle and later adulthood" (p. 191).

Grandparents as Surrogate Parents

In the Chapter 11 discussion of teen parents, we saw that grandmothers often care for their grandchildren and their daughters, when their daughters are single teenage mothers. When their children are unable to act as parents, grandparents are called on to become surrogate parents. In 2006, approximately 2.4 million children in the United States lived with grandparents without their parents present in the household (Statistical Abstract of the United States, 2006). Of those custodial grandparents, approximately 60 percent are white and 25 percent are black (Statistical Abstract of the United States, 2006). Factors that contribute to the larger number of grandparents serving as surrogate parents include declining mortality, demographic trends such as parental joblessness, economic problems, divorce, and family circumstances such as the drug addiction of young parents (Baker, Silverstein, & Putney, 2008).

The pain endured by middle-aged parents whose adult children have problems that prohibit them from parenting their own children is one of the difficulties of surrogate grandparenting. Studies of African American grandparents who were surrogate parents found that the role was associated with both challenges and rewards (Burton & DeVries, 1992; Crowther, Huang, & Allen, 2014). The grandparents had many other responsibilities: they were often caring for adult children who were drug addicted and/or elderly relatives, as well as the grandchildren. This left them no time for their personal needs. On the other hand, they reported enjoying the companionship, love, and opportunity to parent again, and saw being needed by their grandchildren as the reason for living. Burton (1992a) found that all of the African American grandparents who were surrogate parents reported one or more stressful outcomes, such as feeling "depressed and anxious" most of the time, smoking more than ever before, drinking heavily, or having heightened medical problems. Surrogate grandparents often become so unexpectedly, leading to undue social, physical, and financial burdens, and those grandparents who are at highest risk for facing negative consequences are frequently unlikely to receive support (Baker, Silverstein, & Putney, 2008).

Aging Parents

As middle-aged adults become grandparents, their own parents are likely to be reaching late adulthood. Middle-aged adults and their aging parents report high levels of regard, closeness, warmth, and satisfaction with their interactions (Atchley 1997; Rossi & Rossi,

1990; Sechrist et al., 2012). This seems to be especially true of African American and Hispanic families (Bengtson et al., 1990; Sechrist et al., 2012). Mothers and daughters are more likely to be close than any other family combination. In a study of the patterns of intergenerational contact among parents over sixty-five years old who were not in any particular need of help, Glenna Spitze and John Logan (1990) analyzed 8,516 sets of responses to a national health survey. They found that daughters telephoned and visited their parents more often than sons did. More highly educated aging parents had less contact with their children. Older and less healthy unmarried parents and married parents with more needs experienced more contact. Those who lived farthest from a child had less contact and fewer visits and telephone calls. Unmarried mothers were visited somewhat more often and called significantly more than married parents.

Still-healthy aging parents tend to provide the most financial and emotional support to their children (Bengtson et al., 1990). Parents seem to give to their children in one way or another as long as they are able. When adult children have stressful problems, older parents often assume responsibility by providing, for example, care for developmentally disabled adults, housing and financial assistance for divorcing adult children, and emotional support for middle-aged widowed children (Atchley, 1997; Sechrist et al., 2012). Donna Hoyert (1991) examined intergenerational household and financial aid flows between adult children and older parents and found that young-old parents (under age eighty) tended to give more aid, while old-old parents (over age eighty) tended to receive more aid. The aging parents who gave aid tended to be middle to upper income, white, and married. The adult children they aided tended to be young adults, particularly previously married daughters and sons and never-married daughters. Adult children tended to aid aging mothers who were older, low income, widowed, or divorced. In a review of race and ethnicity differences in the exchanges between adult children and their parents, Sechrist and colleagues (2012) noted that African American and Hispanic children are more likely to provide financial assistance to their parents than are Caucasian children, who, in turn, are more likely to be financially assisting their children than are African American or Hispanic midlife adults.

When aging parents become frail, middle-aged adult children are second only to spouses in providing care. Gender plays an important role in family caregiving; parental care falls primarily on a particular daughter as principal caregiver, if there is a daughter (Calasanti & Kiecolt, 2012; Cicirelli, 1992; Connidis et al., 1996). Daughters not only are more likely than sons to provide assistance but are also likely to provide a different type of assistance. Daughters are more likely than sons to help with household chores, such as food preparation and laundry, and personal care tasks that require daily "hands-on" assistance (Montgomery, 1992). Sons are more likely to perform home repair and maintenance tasks. When sons are primary caregivers, they are more likely to be managers of care rather than direct providers.

The relationships between this son and his mother reflect the closeness, warmth, and satisfaction characteristic of connections between middle-aged adults and their aging parents.
Source: Lighthunter/Shutterstock.com.

Never-married and widowed daughters, who are likely to have the fewest competing family roles, provide the largest proportions of care themselves, while married, remarried, and divorced or separated daughters have informal and paid helpers (Brody et al., 1994). Employed daughters provide as much shopping, transportation, household maintenance, emotional support, and service management as do nonworking daughters, but provide somewhat less personal care and help with cooking, with the reduction being offset by purchased services (Brody et al., 1987).

Joyce Warshow (1991) sees special problems for midlife lesbians with aging mothers. As she points out, the "unmarried" daughter historically has been considered the best candidate for caregiving. In fact, lesbian daughters are more likely to be called on to provide caregiving to parents than are heterosexual daughters (Calasanti & Kiecolt, 2012). While this may be an enormous burden for any single woman to integrate with her career and friendship network or intimate relationships, a lesbian daughter faces the additional issue of whether the parent accepts her lifestyle and her partner and whether the partner accepts the need for caregiving.

Raymond Coward and Jeffrey Dwyer (1990) interviewed 683 caregiving sons and daughters who were part of a large national survey. Participants were grouped according to the nature of their sibling group—single-gender, mixed-gender, and only children—to determine the effects of gender composition of sibling group on parental caregiving. Sons from all three sibling groups were less likely to provide parental care or to be the primary caregiver than daughters were. Sons from families with no available sisters who provided care, however, provided as many hours of care as did daughters from families where no brothers were available. Only in mixed-gender sibling groups did daughters provide significantly more hours of care than did sons. Because mixed-gender sibling groups are the most frequent, daughters were providing the majority of care.

Siblings

Sibling relationships are special because they are among age peers, meaning they are longer lasting, more egalitarian, more sociable, and more like friendships than are other family relationships (Bedford & Avioli, 2012; Connidis & Campbell, 1995). As children, siblings are in daily contact and share a sense of family belonging. As young adults, they tend to go their separate ways and contact is likely to be the most limited. During the period when young adults are establishing their own homes, siblings may not see one another very much, but they find communication easy when they do get together. Two-thirds report feeling close or very close to the sibling with whom they have the most contact (Cicirelli, 1995). During middle adulthood, when children are leaving home, siblings often increase contact and get closer as they face family crises of divorce, illness, or decline of a parent.

Ingrid Connidis (1992) studied how various life transitions changed ties among adult siblings. Sixty sibling pairs (120 respondents) were interviewed separately about marriage, children, divorce, widowhood, and other life events of both the respondent and any of his or her siblings. Respondents ranged in age from twenty years to over eighty. About 40 percent of the respondents reported that marriage, childbearing, maturing children, or their own widowhood had affected their relationships with their siblings. Greater emotional closeness was the most commonly noted effect reported for all transitions except the marriage of the respondent. Marriage led to improved relations but a decline in contact and a reduction in emotional closeness, which is likely due to siblings moving. Remarriage after a divorce or loss of a partner also decreases contact with siblings, possibly because the lack of a partner leads to increased reliance on siblings and because of the stress incorporating a new spouse into the sibling relationship (De Jong Gierveld & Peeters, 2003). Shifts in contact between siblings did not seem to reflect shifts in emotions. Divorce and widowhood led to closer, more supportive, and more active sibling ties. Duiaux and colleagues (2007) found that siblings become closer in the time leading up to widowhood and remain high for several years thereafter. Siblings often had dormant emotional ties, such as protectiveness and loyalty, that were mobilized by crises. Death

> **What Do You Think?**
>
> Given your gender, what benefits and costs might you expect (or have you experienced) in your relationships with your family during middle adulthood? How would those benefits and costs differ for a sibling of the other gender?

or poor health of parents or other family members typically drew siblings closer together and strengthened their ties with one another.

Helping aging parents is a new developmental task for middle-aged siblings. Based on clinical work with adult children, Mario Tonti (1988) outlined a series of stages they go through as they face this challenge, as shown in Table 15.4. Most adult children deny the parent's aging until some critical event, often a health crisis, forces a reappraisal. Increased communication about the parent's situation initially moves the siblings emotionally closer together. As the parent's needs increase to the point where the children need to provide more care, one sibling assumes the role of primary caregiver. As the parent becomes more frail, he or she may move in with the primary caregiver. Finally, when the parent's needs become more intense, the parent may be transferred to a long-term care facility.

Parental caregiving arrangements can be a source of conflict for middle-aged siblings. Sarah Matthews and Tena Rosner (1988) found that about half of the families they studied experienced such conflict, although much of the conflict stemmed from events of the past and had longer histories than did the caregiving responsibilities. Brothers and sisters often have a backlog of tensions that current issues can reawaken. The current source of conflict tended to center on the issue of whether or not a sibling had met her or his filial responsibilities. In fact, there is evidence that siblings very rarely explicitly negotiate the expectations of caregiving but, rather, individuals take responsibility for caregiving duties as the need arises (Connidis & Kemp, 2008). Elaine Brody (1990) found that 30 percent of principal caregivers, 40 percent of their sisters, and 6 percent of their brothers reported strain with siblings regarding parental care. Principal caregivers had difficulty with their siblings not doing their fair share, while other siblings were critical of the caregiver's performance. High levels of family conflict, not surprisingly, increase the stress and subsequent mental health

TABLE 15.4 Stages in Sibling Response to Parent's Aging

Based on clinical work with adult children, Tonti (1988) outlined a series of stages they go through as they face the challenge of helping their aging parents.

1.	Denial	Adult children deny the age-related changes in their parent and continue to count on the parent's assistance as they have all their lives.

Health or Other Crisis Forces Reappraisal

2.	Increased sibling communication	Siblings agree to monitor and/or provide assistance for parent.
3.	Primary caregiver emerges	One sibling assumes the role of primary caregiver.
4.	Coresidence with primary caregiver	The parent moves in with the primary caregiver.
5.	Long-term care	The parent needs such comprehensive care that a long-term facility is chosen and the parent is moved.

Source: Adapted from Tonti (1988).

problems of the caregiver (Kwak, Ingersoll-Dayton, & Kim, 2012). When the parent dies, siblings can be both a comfort and a source of unresolved old conflicts (Dane, 1989).

Bereavement

Parental death has become a normative feature of midlife; more than half of American women between ages forty and sixty will experience the death of one or both parents (Scharlach & Fuller-Thomson, 1994). No matter what our age, a parent's death involves many emotions because of the intensity and uniqueness of the parent-child relationship. The child in each of us may feel abandoned at the loss of a parent, our first deep attachment. The process of parental loss can be particularly difficult when death was unexpected and unnatural (Rotila & Saarela, 2011). **Bereavement**, the process of getting over another person's death, elicits feelings of being alone or unattached, memories of earlier losses, guilt over unresolved conflicts or imagined wrongs, and questions concerning our purpose in life. Roslyn was forty-three years old when her mother died. She was divorced and had two young children. Her mother had always been healthy and seemed very young at age sixty-nine, when she became ill and died within six months. This six months of warning enabled the mother to make provisions for her husband, children, and grandchildren, and allowed Roslyn to spend time with her mother, sharing feelings and providing mutual support. Nonetheless, when her mother died Roslyn felt orphaned. In her grief, she felt as sorry for herself being left without her mother as she did for her mother who had died.

bereavement The process of adapting to the loss of a significant relationship, usually because of the death of a loved one.

Mourning for One's Parents

According to Barbara Dane (1989), the mourning middle-aged sons and daughters undergo entails three tasks: stocktaking, reminiscence of harsh and meaningful memories, and internalization and passage. Each of these tasks focuses on a different aspect of the child's relationship to the deceased parent. Stocktaking involves exploration of changes caused by the parent's death. For Roslyn, that included the loss of her mother's kinkeeper function, which kept her in touch with the extended family. It included the loss of her mother's grandparenting role with her children. It also included an increased sense of responsibility for her aging father and a better financial situation due to a small inheritance from her mother.

The second task, reminiscence of harsh and meaningful memories, involves reviewing memories of events that were difficult and unfulfilling as well as those that were wonderful and positive. Roslyn's initial memories were all positive; she would dream of earlier times when she felt totally cared for and loved by her mother. Part of the grieving

In reaction to the death of a parent, middle-aged children feel more aware of the eventuality of their own deaths, which often leads to reevaluation and adjustment of personal priorities. It may also lead to reading the obituaries in a more personal way.
Source: vseb/Shutterstock.com.

process is to explore the ambivalent feelings about the deceased parent, which provides comfort and encourages growth. When a person clings only to the good memories, there is denial that every relationship involves some conflict (Weizman & Kamm, 1985). For adult children who have experienced a difficult relationship with their parent, angry, hostile, or resentful memories are the first ones they experience. Mourning occurs for the disappointments in the relationship as well as for the death. It is still necessary to find the good memories to be able to deal with the total relationship.

The third task of bereavement, internalization and passage, involves discussion about the present without denying the past. In this task, the adult children attain satisfaction with having known the deceased parent and see themselves as conveying the internalized values of that parent in their own middle-aged lives. Holding onto the values and ideals by which your parent lived provides nurturance. Remembering your parent's wisdom and errors in parenting can bring both laughter and tears and keep your parent nurturing you after he or she has died. Roslyn found herself seeing similarities with her mother in her appearance, her parenting style, her political commitments, and her devotion to her brothers and extended family. Acknowledging these similarities to herself and to her children made her feel that her mother was still with her symbolically.

Bereavement and Growth

Bereavement for a parent during middle age may promote personal growth. Parental death often provides an impetus to resolve midlife developmental tasks and promotes age-appropriate levels of maturity, responsibility, and generativity (Douglas, 1990/1991; Scharlach & Fredriksen, 1993). Based on interviews with eighty-three middle-aged adult children (ages thirty-five to sixty) who had lost a parent in the previous five years, Andrew Scharlach and Karen Fredriksen (1993) found that most respondents reported a greater sense of personal maturity. They spoke of "feeling more autonomous, more self-reliant, and more responsible for themselves and others. Respondents also reported increased awareness of the eventuality of their own deaths, often leading to a reevaluation of personal priorities, significant changes in career plans and personal relationships, and modifications in religious practices" (pp. 314–315). These changes are consistent with the midlife developmental theories of Gould, Grant, Levinson, and Helson that we examined earlier.

Joan Douglas (1990/1991) interviewed forty midlife adult children (ages thirty-five to fifty-five) who had lost a parent as adults. She also found that the parent's death was followed by a time of upheaval and, for most of the sample, a change in outlook on life. Issues of mortality, moving to the head of the line, loss and finality, and feeling alone and orphaned were common. "Some said they grew up, that the deaths had liberated them to become more independent and more themselves," and two-thirds "spoke of positive changes in other relationships" (p. 134). While there was loss, from the loss had come "new beginnings" (p. 134). The initial reactions to grief that precede these new beginnings can be emotionally and physically challenging.

Reactions to Grief

Initial grief reactions to parental death include a substantial increase in psychological distress (for example, difficulty sleeping) and a reduced sense of personal mastery (for example, finding it hard to keep up with normal activities). Unresolved grief reactions include depression, thoughts of suicide, and other psychiatric symptoms (Lawrence et al., 2006; Scharlach & Fuller-Thomson, 1994). In a study of initial and residual grief reactions in 220 adult children ages thirty-five to sixty, Andrew Scharlach (1991) found that primary factors contributing to both kinds of grief were the expectedness of the parent's death and the extent of filial autonomy. Expected deaths allow for preparatory grief and reduce the impact of the immediate loss. Adult children who have achieved mature relationships with their parents are less vulnerable when the parent dies than adult children who still look primarily to the parent for validation and support. Other factors that contributed to grief reactions were the respondent's age for initial reaction to the mother's death, with younger adults having more grief reaction. Overall, losing a mother is more detrimental than losing a father (Lawrence et al., 2006; Rostila & Saarela, 2011), and sons demonstrated higher risk of mortality following the death of a parent than daughters (Rostila & Saarela, 2011). Table 15.5 shows the resources middle-aged children considered helpful in coping with their parents' death.

Because society does not support adults' "overreacting" to the loss of a loved one, many adults deny the impact of the loss and express their feelings of pain through physical symptoms. Andrew Scharlach and Esme Fuller-Thomson (1994) found that 40 percent of their middle-aged respondents who had lost a parent one to two years earlier reported experiencing physical reactions, including poorer overall health, physical illness, and fatigue. Using survey data from a large national sample, Wesley Perkins and Lynne Harris (1990) compared subjective health, hospitalization, and satisfaction with health for young, middle-aged, and older adults who had versus those who had not experienced deaths of a spouse, a sibling or sibling-in-law, a child or child's spouse, or a parent within the last five years. Neither young adults nor older adults exhibited much evidence of a relationship between bereavement and current health. However, all three health measures indicated poorer health among midlife adults. When the middle-aged respondents' bereavement status and health reports were broken down by the four types of familial deaths, Perkins and Harris found that the negative effect came primarily from the loss of a sibling or a sibling-in-law and the loss of a spouse. In understanding these findings, it may be that younger adults are protected by their greater physical capacities, which buffer them against the strain of readjustment. Older adults, on the other hand, are likely to be better prepared for the death of other family members as they prepare for their own deaths and as their friends experience similar losses. Death is "on time" in late adulthood. Middle-aged adults may have a similar buffer concerning the death of a parent that is "on time," but they have neither of these protective mechanisms in the case of death of siblings and spouses, who are more likely to be members of their own generation. The deaths of spouses and siblings are most likely to affect their daily lives on the one hand and remind them of their own mortality on the other. We return to the topic of bereavement when we discuss dying and death in Chapter 18.

Leisure

We have seen that middle age is a time of many changes: physical changes, cognitive changes, occupational changes, changes in family relationships, changes in priorities, and changes in perspective on mortality. As a result of many of these changes, midlife adults often feel less constrained than they did in their early adulthood. Like Marcia, they find their children need them less, their parents are still relatively healthy, their work has plateaued,

TABLE 15.5 Resources Considered Helpful in Coping with Parent's Death

Scharlach and Fuller-Thomson (1994) found that having these resources was considered helpful in relieving the psychological distress that accompanies the initial grief reaction to a parent's death.

	Mother's Death ($n = 72$)	Father's Death ($n = 66$)
Friends	79%	75%
Peer whose parent had died	77	78
Family	76	66
Spouse or partner	73	69
Work	71	75
Religion	61	55

Source: Adapted from Scharlach & Fuller-Thomson (1994).

> **What Do You Think?**
>
> In addition to loss, bereavement brings impetus for growth. What developmental experiences have you had that combined loss with positive growth?

and they can make choices about what to do with their time. **Leisure**, according to John Neulinger (1981), is choosing whatever activities one enjoys and participating in them at one's own pace. Marcia, for example, took on a new writing project and increased her exercise activities. To many other individuals, these new activities sound like work rather than leisure, which illustrates a difficulty in defining *leisure*.

leisure Activities chosen freely and enjoyed at one's own pace.

The same activities have different meanings for different individuals. LeBron James plays basketball for a living, while Dai, whom you met in Chapter 13, plays basketball for recreation. Dai writes and edits for a living, while many individuals write prose or poetry for recreation. Although both LeBron James and Dai enjoy many aspects of their work, they are constrained to doing it on a schedule that others determine to get a paycheck. Leisure, then, is freedom from constraint. It includes activities chosen freely and done for intrinsic reward (enjoyment). In contrast, *a job* is activity that is highly constrained and done for extrinsic reward (pay). Obviously, some activities people do as work also give them pleasure. Ballplayers such as LeBron James usually love to play ball. Their work is not pure leisure (because of the constraints), but it is not pure job either (because of the enjoyment). People are most satisfied with their jobs when the jobs include larger aspects of leisure, namely discretion over time and intrinsically rewarding activities. People are least satisfied when the job is pure job (no discretion over time and all extrinsic reward) (Neulinger, 1981). Notice that none of these definitions is based on the amount of physical energy expended. Playing tennis works up a sweat and answering the phone is physically easy, but playing tennis is leisure if you choose to do it in your free time and answering the phone is job if you earn a living as a receptionist.

Do leisure activities change in middle adulthood? Cross-sectional studies provide some evidence that as people enter middle age, their view of leisure shifts (Kelly et al., 1987). They seek out new avenues for gratification and affirmation as their roles change. By shifting some of her focus from her family to her new writing project, for example, Marcia expects validation to come from this new activity. As people age, they tend to shift from activities requiring physical exertion and high-intensity involvement to more sedentary, moderate-intensity activities (Cutler & Hendricks, 1990; Iso et al., 1994). Young adults play more sports and do more running with friends, for example, whereas older adults play more golf and more cards. But Marcia has started to lift weights at age forty-seven, and Tom began running every morning only after retiring at age seventy. Perhaps today's health-conscious midlife and older adults will establish new trends for leisure, at least while they remain healthy. Once again, remember the key limitation to cross-sectional studies: because they have different individuals in each age group, they cannot separate cohort effects from age-related changes.

Longitudinal studies, on the other hand, provide some evidence of continuity in level and types of leisure activities over the life course. A pattern of frequent childhood leisure participation is associated with higher levels as an adult (Cutler & Hendricks, 1990). Though there seems to be continuity in leisure pursuits, when measured longitudinally, we do see reduced engagement in physical activity throughout adulthood (Shaw et al., 2010). These seemingly disparate findings might support the selection, optimization, and compensation theory (further discussed in Chapter 17), which suggests that throughout life, we compensate for age-related change so that we may remain active in areas of interest (Baltes & Baltes, 1990; Baltes & Rudolph, 2012). It may be that as we age, we enjoy the same leisure activities but become less physically active in them.

How do socioeconomic status (SES), race/ethnicity, and gender affect leisure activities? Higher SES is associated with greater leisure involvement (Lawton, 1985). Individuals in professional occupations engage in a greater variety of activities and participate more frequently in activities that require a certain expense of energy (Burrus-Bammel & Bammel,

1985). Higher income, higher educational level, and higher occupational attainment all provide more options for leisure. Racial and ethnic minorities have been relatively worse off than the general population on all of these dimensions of SES and therefore have had more limited leisure options. Additionally, individuals with lower SES are more likely to live in neighborhoods that are considered unsafe, impeding their ability to engage in leisure in their neighborhoods (Annear, Cushman, & Gidlow, 2009). In an examination of the relationship among race, leisure preferences, and class, Myron Floyd and his colleagues (1994) found similarities in leisure preferences between African Americans and whites who defined themselves as middle class, but leisure preferences diverged among those who defined themselves as poor or working class, especially women. Overall, Caucasian women are most likely to engage in physical activity during leisure time, followed by Hispanic and Asian American women, and African American women were least likely to engage in leisure-time exercise (Lee & Im, 2010). Leisure-time physical activity increased with level of formal education; the largest racial differences were found between those who had a high school diploma or less. These differences in leisure activities were likely the result of both differences in what people are taught to prefer and differences in financial resources. Little difference has been found in membership in voluntary organizations between whites and ethnic/racial minorities (Jackson et al., 1990).

Involvement in leisure activities seems to promote psychological well-being and, if leisure includes physical activity, also promote physical and cognitive health later in life (Kåreholt, Lennartsson, Gatz, & Parker, 2011). The number and types of activities appear to be less important than the degree of satisfaction derived from them. People who spend time doing what they wish have higher life satisfaction than those who desire to change their allocation and use of time (Seleen, 1982). Once adults establish an activity pattern, it tends to persist. Middle adulthood, when family and work are less demanding than in early adulthood, affords an opportunity to expand leisure pursuits. Positive attitudes toward leisure are associated with more positive attitudes toward retirement, consideration of early retirement, and more thought given to retirement (Cutler & Hendricks, 1990). Pursuing leisure activities that give satisfaction, then, is good preparation for some of the life changes associated with late adulthood.

Preparing for Late Adulthood

While many aspects of adulthood are continuous, aging changes activities and perspectives in several predictable ways. We have seen how the demands of childrearing decrease as parents launch their children into adulthood. We have seen how more leisure time results from that change in the family life cycle and from occupational changes in mid- and late-career stages (see Chapter 14). We have seen how the death of a parent enhances awareness of one's own mortality. With late adulthood come the additional changes of retirement and even less need on the part of adult children for assistance. Physical changes occur as well (a focus of the next chapter), and death approaches. Beginning preparation for these new challenges in middle adulthood is a good way to face them. Richard Schulz (1978) found that the more opportunities and time people have to prepare for stressful events such as death, the more they will feel in control, and the less they will feel helpless and anxious. Taking more responsibility for one's own life increases the middle-aged adult's sense of mortality, which leads to specific concrete behaviors such as drafting a will or making funeral arrangements (Scharlach & Fredriksen, 1993).

Wills and Advance Directives

A *will* is a legal document that can distribute property, appoint a guardian for children, provide for pets, provide for funeral and burial, and appoint an executor to oversee distribution of property. Although many people think one needs a will only if one has property, that is not necessarily so. Adults with personal wishes that run contrary to those of their blood families or with lifestyles that are unconventional can arrange for after-death choices, such as cremation rather than burial, and provide for nonkin loved ones. If you

> **What Do You Think?**
>
> Consider with several of your classmates the leisure activities you engage in. What are they? When did you begin them? Are you likely to pursue them as you get older? In what ways do you think they will change? Why?

are not married but cohabit, you will need a will to ensure that your property goes to your partner rather than to your blood kin, if that is what you desire. This is a special problem for lesbians and gay men who do not have the legal right to marry in most states and may have families that do not accept their partners' legitimacy (Ettelbrick, 1991). When gay and lesbian couples can legally marry, it reduces the fear that their wishes both for their property and for other end-of-life issues will not be respected (de Vries, Mason, Quam, & Acquaviva, 2009). Because wills serve many functions, people write wills at all stages of adulthood and revise them as life circumstances change.

An **advance directive** is a legal document specifying what medical care can be given in the event the person becomes unable to make or communicate his or her decisions. They allow an individual to arrange to die with dignity and to avoid expensive, invasive, and fruitless procedures. Most states have two types of advance directives. The **living will** notifies your physician of your wishes regarding the withdrawal of life-sustaining equipment even if the result is your death. A living will goes into effect only when you are unable to make or communicate your decision about your medical care *and* when you are in a terminal condition or permanently unconscious. A **durable power of attorney for health care** designates a person to make medical decisions on your behalf other than the withdrawal of life support systems. The designee could decide, for example, whether to change physicians, obtain a second opinion, reject surgery, or provide physical therapy. Once again, designating a person to make health care decisions may be especially important if your choices would differ from those of your blood family or if your closest relationship is one that is not legally recognized.

Middle age is the optimal time to make decisions about long-term care because, on the one hand, you are not facing the immediate crisis of an illness and, on the other hand, you are thinking about these issues as you and your friends assume responsibility for your aging parents. The living will requires that you understand the full impact of your decision. Middle-aged adults have the emotional and mental competence to consider and decide on these issues. Public opinion polls show that almost 90 percent of American adults would not want life support systems in place if there were no prospect of recovery, yet fewer than one in five have actually prepared any written advance directive (Moody, 1994b). Eric Diamond and his associates (1989) found that supportive counseling regarding planning for terminal illness and death was very helpful in enabling people to specify their wishes. The vast majority of people who have living wills prefer limited care (9 percent) and/or care-maximizing comfort (96 percent) at the end of life and that those wishes are by and large respected (Silveira, Kim, & Langa, 2010).

advance directive A legal document specifying what medical care can be given in the event the person becomes unable to make or communicate their decisions.

living will A legal document notifying one's physician of one's wishes regarding the withdrawal of life-sustaining equipment even if the result is death.

durable power of attorney for health care A legal document designating a person to make medical decisions on one's behalf other than the withdrawal of life support systems.

Retirement Planning

Another developmental task of midlife is planning both financially and psychologically for retirement, one of the normative life events of late adulthood. Midlife is traditionally a time of peak earning years and thus is a time to save a portion of income for the future. As we saw in our discussion of leisure, midlife is also a time for developing interests and activities that can continue after retirement. Individuals who prepare for retirement have a better idea of their retirement needs, more favorable attitudes toward retirement, higher morale, and fewer longings for their jobs once they retire (Teaff & Johnson, 1983; Topa et al., 2009). Research indicates that a highly work-committed professional may avoid retirement planning and have difficulties just before and just after retirement (Kilty & Behling, 1985; Richardson & Kilty, 1992).

> **What Do You Think?**
>
> Will your generation be better prepared for late adulthood than your parents' and grandparents' generations? If so, in what ways? If not, why not?

Looking Back/Looking Forward

Once again, it is time to return to the lifespan themes outlined in Chapter 1 and see how they apply to our discussion of middle adulthood. Work is a major concern of this stage of adulthood-work for pay and family work-and thus is our focus as we review the themes.

- **Continuity within change**—For most of us, work begins during middle childhood or early adolescence—when we learn to baby sit, mow lawns, or do other chores to earn spending money—and becomes an enduring aspect of our lives. During late adolescence, part-time and summer jobs become normative. In early adulthood, career development becomes a major developmental task as young men and women establish economic independence from their parents and set goals for their futures. During middle adulthood, reassessment of those early goals, occupational change, and shifting priorities of work and nonwork activities become paramount for many individuals. For women who as young adults adopted family roles as their primary work, middle adulthood typically is the time when they reconsider their priorities as their adolescent and young adult children leave the nest. Reassessment of occupations and roles often sends adults back to school in their middle years. It may also increase interest in nonwork activities as middle-aged adults look forward to retirement and more leisure time.

- **Lifelong growth**—Though the physical changes associated with middle adulthood do not affect the work of the many workers in industrial society who depend on their brains and on machines, they do alter the career path for individuals who depend on their youthful bodies, such as dancers, athletes, and some manual laborers. For many, middle adulthood is a time of expanded prestige and power in the work they have mastered. Cognitive styles may change so that expert skills get used in more cooperative, practical, and generative ways than during early adulthood, when individual effort was directed toward proving oneself. As successful workers feel increasingly comfortable with their accomplishments, they are likely to begin passing along their expertise to the generation that will replace them when they reduce their work hours or retire.

- **Changing meanings and vantage points**—Older workers generally are more satisfied with their jobs than younger ones are; they have better jobs and earn more money, both of which make work more satisfying. Even so, many middle-aged workers experience disillusionment: successful ones may feel bored, unchallenged, or burned out, and unsuccessful individuals may feel stagnant and unable to move ahead. In either case, workers may be unwilling to change jobs for fear of risking their security or benefits in the years close to retirement.

- **Developmental diversity**—When it comes to work, race/ethnicity and gender matter. Even today, both racial/ethnic minority and female workers are less likely to get jobs in the primary sector and are less likely to advance in those jobs if they do get them. Many factors contribute to these inequities.

As a result of the differences in treatment and circumstances experienced throughout childhood, adolescence, and early adulthood, some minorities and women are less well educated than their white male counterparts. Even when training is equal, differential hiring and promotion practices discriminate against them during early career stages, typically in early adulthood, and they earn less for the same work. In middle adulthood, the glass ceiling functions to stop the progress of the few who are making their way to the top.

Expectations about family roles contribute to differences in work and pay as well. While both women and men want families as well as work, women are called on to do more of the family work than are men. Although gender roles have become less restrictive and women now work in all fields, women still provide the bulk of child and family care. They are more likely to have split dreams of achievement and relationships, while men dream of achievement and expect the relationships to come along as well. As a result, women's work patterns are more varied than men's are.

This diversity, which we will look at further in the next two chapters on late adulthood, provide white men with more financial resources on which to retire, while women and racial/ethnic minorities often have more social resources in the form of kin and nonkin relationships. Because they have been employed less consistently and in less secure jobs, women and minorities may continue to work and not consider retirement at the same time white men begin to collect pensions. Because they have devoted time to maintaining relationships, women and minorities are more likely to have family and community connections, which help to sustain them in their later years. As always, these generalizations do not fit all individuals, all cultures, or all times. As work and family roles have become less gender stereotyped in early adulthood for recent cohorts, we can expect that when they reach middle adulthood, women will have more secure pensions and men will have more kin-keeping skills.

Chapter Summary

- **How typical is "midlife crisis"?** Contrasting stereotypes of middle age present it as a boring plateau and a time of inevitable crisis. Perceptions of this stage of life vary by social class, gender, and age. Psychologists also have differing views of midlife. Theorists such as Gould, Vaillant, and Levinson build on Erikson's model of midlife crisis; other researchers have found little evidence of crisis; and still others, such as Helson, see transition rather than crisis as the normative midlife experience. Personality theorists note that traits show stability after about age thirty.
  Gender and class are factors determining whether the transition of midlife will result in crisis. Men are more likely than women to experience a midlife crisis, especially upper-class men and well-educated, middle-class men.
- **How are marriage and divorce different in middle adulthood than in earlier years?** There is evidence that middle-aged and older marriages are happier than those in earlier stages of the family life cycle. Although divorce is less frequent than in early adulthood, it has significant impact on women, men, and children. For women, especially those with children at home, marital separation is associated with markedly lower economic well-being. For men, it is associated with less contact with children, even if the children are adults.
- **What are the important family relationships at midlife, and what changes can be expected in them?** Middle-aged adults assume responsibility for family relationships with older and younger generations, which has led to the label the *sandwich generation*. Gender, race/ethnicity, and SES have an impact on the various relationships.

Parenting adolescent children often has a large negative impact on the marital relationship. Parents and young adult children have increased interaction and closeness compared to adolescent levels. Emotional support is a two-way interaction, whereas material support generally is parent to child, depending on ethnicity and family income. Many young adults remain at home or return home; however, parental well-being is optimized when children physically move out but remain in close contact. Grandparents are called on to assist in many different ways depending on the family's SES, race/ethnicity, and circumstances. Grandparents help by just being there, help in regular caregiving, help in times of crisis, and help by becoming surrogate parents.

Middle-aged adults generally have warm and satisfying relations with their aging parents, especially in African American and Hispanic families. Daughters have more contact with their parents than do sons. Older, unmarried, and needy parents are visited and called more often. While aging parents are still healthy, they continue to give financial and emotional support if they are able. When they become frail, the parents tend to receive more support than they give. Daughters typically provide more care for aging parents than do sons.

Siblings often increase their contact during middle adulthood in response to children leaving or a family crisis, such as the illness of a parent.

- **Why is the loss of a parent a significant event during middle adulthood?** Parental death is a normative feature of midlife and involves many emotions because of the importance of this first deep attachment. In addition to grief, parental death often brings on growth-producing changes in levels of maturity, responsibility, and generativity.
- **Is there continuity or change in leisure activities during this stage of life?** There is evidence of both continuity and change in leisure activities during midlife, depending on whether the studies are cross sectional or longitudinal. Higher SES provides more options for leisure; race/ethnicity and gender are associated with different patterns of leisure activities.
- **How do wills and retirement planning help individuals to prepare for late adulthood?** Wills and advance directives enable individuals to take control of after-death choices as well as choices about medical care and life-sustaining equipment in case of terminal illness or lack of consciousness. Midlife is also a time to prepare for retirement by saving and developing nonwork interests.

Key Terms

advance directive (p. 565)
beanpole family structure (p. 555)
bereavement (p. 560)
durable power of attorney for health care (p. 565)
family life cycle (p. 545)

generativity versus stagnation (p. 540)
leisure (p. 563)
living will (p. 565)
midlife crisis (p. 540)
non-normative life event (p. 540)
normative crisis model (p. 542)

normative life event (p. 540)
sandwich generation (p. 550)
social clock projects (p. 539)
trait (p. 542)

PART 8

Late Adulthood

Chapter 16
Physical and Cognitive Development in Late Adulthood

Chapter 17
Psychosocial Development in Late Adulthood

Source: Diego Cervo/Shutterstock.com.

Late adulthood encompasses the years after age sixty-five. Because of the increasing longevity of our population, which we will discuss in Chapter 16, this designation has become too broad to meaningfully describe the wide variety of individuals it includes. K. Warner Schaie suggests that grouping all older adults together is like grouping all individuals "under twelve" together. As we know from the first nine chapters of this book, too much development occurs within the first twelve years of life to lump all individuals into one age category. For the same reason, Schaie encourages making a distinction among the young-old (those in their sixties and early seventies), the old-old (those in their late seventies and early eighties, and the very-old (those in their late eighties and beyond). It is important to keep in mind the great diversity among older individuals.

Although we tend to think of all older adults as frail, that stereotype only fits some of the very-old, and not even all of the individuals within that category. The young-old are often more like individuals in middle adulthood (and often would classify themselves as still being middle-aged), except that they are more likely to be retired than those in midlife. As we will see in Part 8, older adults are a diverse population that can be understood only within the context of their ethnicity, gender, level of education, income, occupational status, family status, and health status. "Many age differences that are reported in the literature, instead of being 'caused' by aging, are more likely to be attributable to differences in demographic characteristics and cohort-specific experiences than to adverse maturational changes" (Schaie, 1988).

Physical and Cognitive Development in Late Adulthood

CHAPTER 16

Source: Alex Brylov/Shutterstock.com.

Chapter Outline

PHYSICAL DEVELOPMENT
Longevity
Physical Functioning in Late Adulthood
Health Behaviors in Late Adulthood
Chronic Illnesses
COGNITIVE DEVELOPMENT
Wisdom and Cognitive Abilities
The Aging Brain
Mental Health and Aging
Work and Retirement

Focusing Questions

- What historical changes have occurred in the lifespan and in life expectancy, and what further changes can we anticipate?
- What factors affect changes in physical functioning during late adulthood?
- Do health-promoting behaviors change in importance once a person is old?
- What chronic illnesses become common in late adulthood, and how do they affect daily life?
- What age-related losses and gains in cognitive functioning occur in older adults?
- In what ways is the aging brain a good example of both the loss and the compensation that are evident during late adulthood?
- Does the incidence of depression increase in late adulthood, and can it be treated effectively?
- What factors influence how retirees adjust to their new life circumstances?

Grace, now in her early sixties, has had high blood pressure for twelve years. She walks vigorously at least three times a week, takes medication to control her blood pressure, and tries to limit her intake of salt and fat. She likes to eat and drink, however, so she struggles with the dietary changes. Her career in publishing keeps her happily busy most of the time, although she sometimes feels so stressed that she wonders if she should continue at her current pace. Her husband, Larry, recently retired at age sixty-five. Grace enjoys the intellectual challenge and sociability of her work and fears retirement may lead to mental stagnation and isolation. While Larry has many house and yard projects that occupy him, Grace has always been more outgoing than Larry. Continuing her current activities seems best for now, although she has begun to think about ways to be active after retirement.

Most older individuals continue to be productive contributors to their families and their communities long after retirement, and others never really retire. Betty White hosted *Saturday Night Live* at age eighty-eight and, subsequently, has experienced a resurgence in her career while staying active working with animal rights organizations. In his nineties, George Burns continued to delight audiences and make them laugh. Dame Maggie Smith, Dame Judi Dench, and Meryl Streep are examples of older women who continue to be productive and successful well into late adulthood. Pablo Picasso, Michelangelo, and many other public (and private) figures have continued to actively contribute to society in their late adulthood.

PHYSICAL DEVELOPMENT

Longevity

As we saw in our discussion of physical development in middle adulthood in Chapter 14, the average life expectancy in the United States has gone from forty-seven years in 1900 to seventy-eight years today. During the nineteenth and twentieth centuries, improvements in diet, sanitation, and medicine contributed to the increase in average life expectancy. Most of the increase has come from the eradication of diseases that caused high infant and child mortality; since World War II, some has come from the control of fatal diseases of adult life, such as influenza and pneumonia, and some from adopting health behaviors (Vita et al., 1998). This, in addition to the aging of the baby boomers, means that one in every eight people in the United States is an older adult—an increase of 18 percent since 2000 (U.S. Department of Health and Human Services [HHS], 2012).

In addition to getting older, as Figure 16.1 shows, the population of the United States has been getting more diverse during this century. Although never homogeneous, recent immigrants have added Latin American and Asian influences. In 2008, the older adult population was about 20 percent nonwhite. Minorities make up a larger proportion of the early adult population and a smaller proportion of the older adult population than do

FIGURE 16.1
Growth and Diversity of Population Ages Sixty-Five and Older

During the twentieth century, the population of the United States has been getting older and more diverse. This trend is projected to continue.

Source: Reproduced from a chart in Gerst-Emerson, K, & Burr, J. A. (2014). The demography of minority aging. In K. E. Whitfield & T. A. Baker (eds.), *Handbook of Minority Aging* (pp. 387–403). New York: Springer Publishing Company.

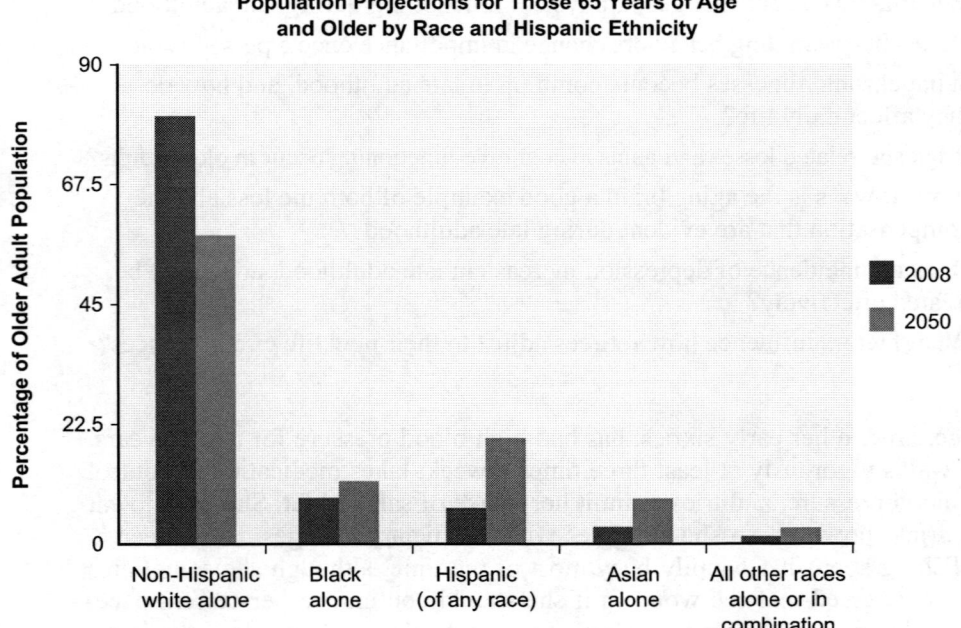

Part 8 Late Adulthood

whites because of higher fertility and mortality rates (Hooyman & Kiyak, 1993). For the foreseeable future, the proportion of minority older adults is expected to increase at a faster rate than whites because so many nonwhite children will be growing older and mortality rates are decreasing. The faulty stereotype of older people as white, middle-class, and part of traditional families will become even harder to maintain.

The growing number of older adults from a wider diversity of backgrounds has resulted in a wide range of economic and social conditions among older adults. Older adults as a group have made social and economic progress. Poverty levels have declined, and median income for people sixty-five and over has increased. Today, about 10 percent of older adults live in poverty, however, and that number nearly doubles when those living just above the poverty line are included (Reno & Veghte, 2011). But, as Table 16.1 shows, poverty and near-poverty still characterize subgroups of the older adult population—namely, unmarried women, minority older people, people living alone and in rural areas, and the very old (Reno & Veghte, 2011). *Poverty* refers to having less income than the official poverty level, the figure the government has established as necessary to provide a household with adequate goods and services. Married individuals as a group are less likely to be below the poverty level than are any of the other marital statuses. The most advantaged segment of the late adult population is employed married men in their early sixties. The least advantaged is minority widowed women over seventy-five years old who rely on social security for their incomes. Not surprisingly, socioeconomic status (SES), which we saw in our discussion of physical development in early adulthood in Chapter 12 as being strongly related to health, affects mortality and morbidity among older adults. In fact, in 1980, an individual with high SES could expect to outlive someone of low SES by 2.8 years; by 2000, that gap had reached 4.5 years, with no signs of diminishing or slowing (Singh & Siahpush, 2006).

Mortality

In the late 1960s, after two decades of stability, mortality rates began to fall steadily. Experts identify several contributing factors. First, improvements in medical care and drugs enable better management of cardiovascular disease and hypertension. Second, more people have access to medical care. Third, health behaviors have increased; reduced smoking and drinking, as well as improved diet and physical fitness, prolong life. Men, who started out with higher mortality rates have made larger gains than women, except at advanced ages of seventy-five and above and except for African American and other nonwhite men. Nevertheless, women continue to have longer life expectancies. These data reflect several important dimensions of health in late adulthood: gender, race, and lifestyle improvements.

TABLE 16.1 Percentage of Households Below the Poverty Level, 2012

Although older adults as a group have made economic progress, poverty is still characteristic of subgroups of the older adult population, especially minority older women, and the very old.

	Male		Female	
Race	65–74	75 and Over	65–74	75 and Over
African American	14.6	12.8	17.3	26.4
Hispanic	20.6	16.7	20.7	23.4
White	5.5	5.7	7.8	11.7
Asian	9.1	18.3	9.4	15.9

Source: U.S. Bureau of the Census (2013a).

Gender and Mortality

Table 16.2 shows that though their rates differ, women and men die from the same causes. Men have higher mortality from all the leading causes of death except diabetes mellitus. As we saw in the Chapter 14 discussion of physical development in middle adulthood, many more males die during middle adulthood as a result of cardiovascular and respiratory diseases. Males also die more frequently of chronic liver disease, accidents, suicide, and homicide, all of which are lifestyle related. In late adulthood, the gap between men and women's mortality rates narrows as the pace of death and disease for older women increases relative to middle-aged women. But men continue to die at higher rates from cancer, heart disease, kidney disease, and suicide. As both genders get older and frailer, the body becomes more vulnerable to *septicemia* (infection that has entered the bloodstream), pneumonia/influenza, and atherosclerosis (hardening of the arteries), and these rise as causes of death, whereas deaths that are closely related to lifestyle behaviors, such as smoking and drinking, go down because these conditions have already taken their toll at earlier ages.

Race and Mortality

Mortality rates differ among different races. In 2010, the life expectancy of a white newborn male was 76.4 years, 71.4 years for a black male, and 78.5 years for a Hispanic male. Life expectancy for a white female was 81.1 years, 77.7 years for a black female, and 83.8 years for a Hispanic female. By age sixty-five, the gap narrows: white men can expect only 1.9 more years than black men, whereas Hispanic men can expect to live three years longer than black men. White women can expect to live 1.2 more years than black women, whereas Hispanic women can expect to live 2.9 years longer than black women (National Center for Health Statistics, 2013). The gap shrinks because the less hardy people have already died. The "A Multicultural View" feature explores the *mortality crossover,* the age at which African Americans can expect to live longer than whites do.

Hispanics are the largest ethnic minority population in the United States and the fastest growing (U.S. Bureau of the Census, 2012c). Hispanic mortality is closer to whites' than to

TABLE 16.2 Rank Orders of Causes of Death by Sex

Although men have higher rates of mortality from most of the leading causes of death, women and men die from the same causes.

	Men 65+	Women 65+
1	Heart disease	Heart disease
2	Cancer	Cancer
3	Chronic obstructive pulmonary diseases	Cerebrovascular disease
4	Cerebrovascular disease	Chronic obstructive pulmonary diseases
5	Alzheimer's disease	Alzheimer's disease
6	Diabetes mellitus	Diabetes mellitus
7	Accidents	Influenza and pneumonia
8	Kidney disease	Kidney disease
9	Influenza and pneumonia	Accidents
10	Parkinson's disease	Septicemia

Source: Division of Vital Statistics, National Center for Health Statistics (Heron, 2013).

African Americans'. In some age groupings and by some definitions (for example, Spanish origin rather than Spanish surname), Hispanic life expectancies are higher than those for whites and are always higher than those for African Americans. That Hispanics have better overall health and lower mortality rates than might be expected, considering factors such as SES, is known as the Hispanic paradox (Franzini, Ribble, & Keddie, 2001). However, Hispanics also have higher mortality rates from infectious and parasitic diseases, influenza and pneumonia, and accidents and all violent deaths than whites (Markides & Black, 1996).

Life Expectancy

Though life expectancy has increased, the human lifespan has not changed. *Maximum life expectancy* refers to the maximum possible period of time a species could be expected to live if environmental hazards were eliminated. For humans, the maximum life expectancy is approximately 120 years. This expectancy is based on the laboratory work of Leonard Hayflick (1994), which demonstrated that normal human cells can reproduce by doubling a maximum of fifty times and that as they approach that limit they undergo changes that affect every aspect of their functioning, known as the Hayflick limit. The longest life for which there is verification is just over 122 years. Jeanne Calment, a French woman, celebrated her 122nd birthday on February 21, 1997, and died that August. She lived in her own apartment until age 110 and rode a bicycle until age 115. At 120 years of age, Jeanne was described in the French press as frail, blind, and almost totally deaf—all age-related changes that we will soon see are associated with very old late adulthood—but with her mental faculties still intact.

Increased life expectancy means that more individuals' lives are approaching the maximum lifespan in length. As Figure 16.2 shows, the number of centenarians (people one hundred years old or older) is a rapidly growing segment of the U.S. population. Nonetheless, without some unanticipated and extraordinary biological discoveries, the average lifespan is not expected to go beyond eighty-five years (Olshansky et al., 1990), and there is evidence that average expectancies might decrease in the future, due to increasing rates of obesity and complications thereof (Olshansky et al., 2005). An extension of the lifespan would require a change in the rate of primary aging, which depends on biological factors that scientists do not know how to control.

Theories of Aging

Throughout life, the cells of most of the body's tissue die and are replaced. Exceptions are muscle and nerve cells, which are formed at birth and may live as long as the body does. In day-to-day life, body tissue is damaged and repaired, and cancers begin to grow and are destroyed by the immune system. This maintenance function breaks down in humans sometime between ages fifty and one hundred. The breakdown of

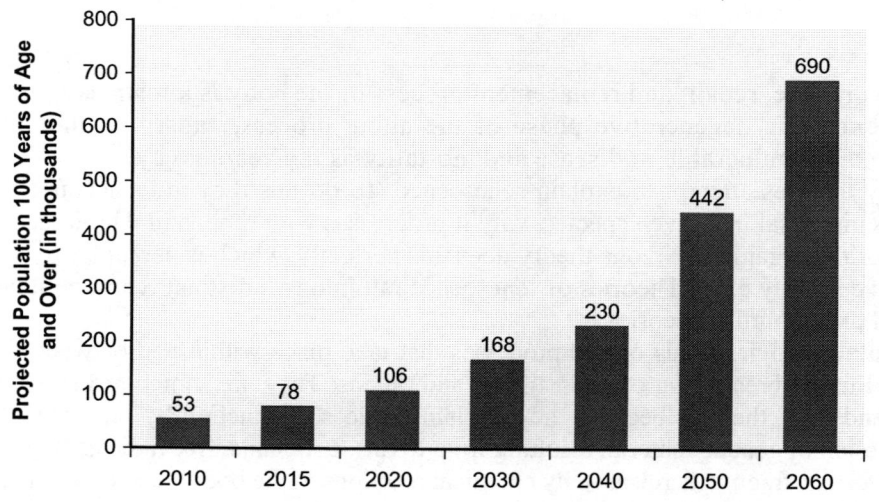

FIGURE 16.2
Hitting the Century Mark

The number of centenarians—people one hundred years or older—is growing faster than ever in the United States.
Source: U.S. Bureau of the Census (2012c).

A Multicultural View

The Mortality Crossover

Although over most of the lifespan African American and Native American populations are at higher risk for mortality and morbidity than whites, at advanced ages these minority populations are more robust. In contrast to any earlier age, if African Americans or Native Americans live to reach eighty-five, they can expect to outlive their white counterparts. Look back at Table 14.1 (page 503), and you will see the life expectancy by sex and race adjusted for birth and for age sixty-five. In 2010, a white male had a life expectancy of almost seventy-six at birth; if he was already sixty-five in that year, he could expect to live until almost eighty-three. This is because sixty-five-year-olds are beyond risk for infant mortality and other causes of early death. Life expectancies and mortality rates are adjusted to a specific age. At ages eighty-five and over, the probabilities of death rates for African Americans become lower than those of whites; this trend is called the *mortality crossover*. Not all minority populations are similarly affected. Hispanic mortality rates, which are closer to white than African American rates all along, do not reverse themselves in old age. Asian Americans have age-adjusted mortality rates that are consistently lower than those for the general population (Jackson et al., 1990; National Center for Health Statistics, 2013).

Although a couple of explanations for mortality crossover have been proposed, considerable evidence has accumulated for the selective survival thesis (Jackson et al., 1990; Markides & Black, 1996). According to this theory, high-mortality populations experience the deaths of a greater number of the least robust members before they reach old age. This leaves only very hardy individuals at very old ages. In comparison, low-mortality populations have more weak individuals reaching very old ages, and they are more vulnerable.

This leads to the question of why some populations have mortality crossovers and others do not.

Because members of the Navajo tribe have high mortality rates from external factors such as accidents and infectious disease, the hardy older adults who survive, like this woman, are likely to outlive their white counterparts.
Source: David P. Smith/Shutterstock.com.

We know, for example, that males have higher mortality rates than females in middle and early old age (see the "Focusing On" feature on the gender gap in life expectancy in Chapter 14). Why is there no gender mortality crossover? The answer seems to be that mortality crossover is a result of extreme environmental situations. Different environmental factors affect men and women, as do differences in biology. Over time, women have increased their rate of smoking and their

---

senescence The degenerative phase of the aging process that causes an individual to become more vulnerable to disease and mortality as time passes.

cellular theories Theories of aging that focus on the processes that take place within and between cells, leading to the breakdown of cells, tissue, and organs. Sometimes referred to as *wear and tear theories*.

the surveillance, repair, and replacement process of the body is known as *senescence*. **Senescence**, the degenerative phase of the aging process, causes an individual to become more vulnerable to disease and mortality as the years go by.

Many theories attempt to explain senescence. To do this they must account for why aging is universal in a given species, why it progresses with time, and why it leads to the failure of the organism. No one theory does this perfectly, which is perhaps why so many theories currently exist. Theories of senescence fall into two distinct types: cellular theories and programming theories.

Cellular theories focus on the processes that take place within and between the cells and lead to the breakdown of cells, tissue, and organs. They are sometimes referred to as "wear and tear" theories because they explain the loss of function by repeated errors of transmission of genetic material resulting from toxins, pollutants, free radicals (highly reactive molecular fragments released by chemical reactions in the body), and other factors that

> ### A Multicultural View
>
> **The Mortality Crossover** *continued*
>
> participation in hazardous occupations, narrowing the gender gap in life expectancy. But there is no crossover because women and men are not similarly genetically endowed. Although environmental factors have become more similar, the biological advantage of being female remains.
>
> The mortality crossover shows up among poor populations that experience high mortality in the childhood, adolescent, early adult, and middle adult years. Causes of death among these populations differ from those for more affluent populations. Poor populations tend to die from infectious diseases and accidents, or exogenous causes, whereas affluent populations typically die from cardiovascular disease and cancers, or endogenous causes (Kunitz & Levy, 1989). Additionally, lower-SES individuals disproportionately benefit from access to programs like Medicare late in life, helping to account for some of the crossover (Sautter et al., 2012).
>
> Individuals belonging to the Navajo Nation can serve as an example. Stephen Kunitz and Jerrold Levy (1989) found that heart disease, cancer, and hypertension were all much lower among Navajo than among non-Navajo older adults, yet many external factors have contributed to Navajo high mortality rates. Native American adolescents and young adults attempt suicide at higher rates than other ethnicities, and suicide is the second leading cause of death behind accidents for this age group (Shaughnessy, Doshi, & Everett Jones, 2004). Additionally, during 1988–1991, the age-adjusted motor vehicle-related death rates for Navajos were fivefold greater than for the total U.S. population (97.9 per 100,000 versus 19.5 per 100,000) and almost three times the rate for all New Mexico residents (35.2 per 100,000). Like other Native Americans and Alaskan Natives, Navajos are at increased risk for motor vehicle-related deaths and injuries, for at least three reasons. First, because many live in rural areas, their access to advanced emergency medical care may be limited when a crash occurs, and as a consequence, treatment for injuries may be delayed. Second, they may travel more on isolated two-lane highways and ride unprotected in the backs of open pickup trucks, placing them at higher risk for injury if a crash occurs. Third, this population is younger than the total U.S. population (median age twenty-three years versus thirty years); young people are at higher risk for injury because of risk-taking behaviors, such as drinking and driving and not wearing safety belts. In addition, because alcohol is not legally available in the Navajo Nation, those residents who drink may drive long distances while impaired (Safety-Belt Use, 1993).
>
> According to the selective survival thesis, exogenous factors such as these contribute to the high mortality rates of poor minority populations. Poverty and powerlessness create life circumstances that predispose people to the highest rates of social dysfunction, the highest rates of morbidity and mortality, the lowest access to health care, and little or no access to primary preventive programs (Braithwaite & Lythcott, 1989). Only the hardiest survive to be very old. Because these populations are initially similar to the general population with regard to genetic endowment for longevity, these hardy older adults are likely to live longer than the mix of survivors in the general population (Clark et al., 1993; Sautter et al., 2012).
>
> The racial inequality in social and economic resources leads to premature death and is responsible for the mortality crossover. When younger people die of illness that could have been prevented or treated if they were more privileged, the survivors are hardier and live longer (Markides & Black, 1996). A good sign of equality will be the disappearance of the mortality crossover.

affect cell reproduction. These stressors result from continuous use. As cells are replicated, some number of the new cells will contain genetic errors. The older the individual, the greater the number of cells that will have errors and the greater the number of cells that will have multiple errors. The increase in genetic errors causes inefficiency in the cell, leading to cell death and eventually to organism death.

Programming theories consider the maximum lifespan to be predetermined by the genes in each species. Leonard Hayflick (1994) demonstrated that human cells in the laboratory will replicate only to a certain point—about fifty replications—which constitutes the Hayflick Limit. After that, the genetic material runs out. Hayflick believes that death is programmed into complex organisms. Each species has its own characteristic lifespan that is preset by the number of possible cell replications. Other variations of programming theories posit other preprogrammed mechanisms. Daniel Rudman and his colleagues (1990) administered human growth hormone (HGH) to adult men ages sixty-one to eighty-one and reversed some of the

programming theories Theories of aging that consider the maximum lifespan to be predetermined by genes.

> **What Do You Think?**
>
> Why do you think people of different races have different mortality rates? What information would you need to be sure your reason was correct? What other possible reasons can you think of?

effects of aging. However, more recent research has suggested that small practical benefits of HGH are far outweighed by the associated health risks (Liu et al., 2007). The point of programming theories is that at birth, our eventual deaths are already built in; anything less than *ideal* environmental conditions may shorten it, but nothing can lengthen it.

The Telomere Hypothesis

Biologists who study aging at the level of cells and genes recently have extended reproduction of human cells beyond the Hayflick Limit in laboratory cultures (Johnson et al., 1998). They have discovered that the tip of each human cell contains a telomere gene that breaks off a little at each cell division until finally the cell can no longer divide. The telomere gene produces *telomerase*, an enzyme required for cell division. The telomere hypothesis of aging states that sufficient telomere loss on one or more chromosomes in normal somatic cells triggers cell senescence, whereas reactivation of the enzyme telomerase is necessary for cell immortalization (Harley, 1997). Normally, telomerase is produced in embryonic cells and cancer cells, but not in adult cells. Although it is not clear that telomere shortening is the fundamental cause of cellular aging, it is a very good marker for aging as it occurs. In twin studies, shorter telomeres, which would be an indication of cell aging, has been related to lower SES, smoking, obesity, and lack of exercise, all of which has been linked to accelerated aging (Cherkas et al., 2006, 2008). Additionally, women with chronically ill children who experience and perceive high levels of stress on a regular basis have shorter telomeres (equal to a decade of aging) than women with healthy children and low stress levels (Epel et al., 2004).

It is very likely that both cellular wear and tear and genetic preprogramming operate to produce senescence. Breakdown occurs in many different forms: the generating of free radicals; the instability of molecules; finite cell life; accumulated genetic and metabolic errors; and cross-linkage of collagen, the main supportive and connective tissue in the body. Wear-and-tear theories encourage consideration of how to reduce stressors to inhibit secondary aging and prolong life. Programming theories remind us that the gradual declines of primary aging are beyond our control.

Physical Functioning in Late Adulthood

Late adulthood is a time of loss in efficiency of body systems, but it is also a time of compensation. The most significant age-related changes are diminished pumping capacity of the heart, which we discussed in Chapter 14 because it begins early and continues throughout adulthood, and loss of neurons from the central nervous system. These are aspects *of primary aging*, normal age-related changes that everyone experiences, although they can be accelerated by *secondary aging*, the effects of illness or disease on the body. Though measures of cardiovascular functioning demonstrate a decline of about 1 percent per year (primary aging), many people experience a steeper decline due to physical inactivity (Katzel & Steinbrenner, 2012.) These changes have a negative impact on other body systems as well. But the aging process is not one of unmitigated and increasing loss. The body is an organism that repairs and restores itself as damage occurs. In some cases there is regeneration, in others compensation, and in still others growth due to the plasticity of the system. Although it is not possible for the body to prevent eventual death, it is possible for it to work to enhance life. In this section, we consider the age-related changes in late adulthood. We focus on changes due to primary aging, but, as we have pointed out before, it is often difficult to differentiate between the effects of primary and secondary aging.

Slowing with Age

Research examining motor responses, sensory processes, and certain aspects of intellectual functioning consistently shows that behavior slows with age (Spirduso, 1995). Older individuals can do what younger ones can, but it takes more time. The cause of the slowing is not fully understood, although animals of all species slow down as they age. There are many changes in neurons throughout the nervous system as we age: neurons have fewer dendrites and synapses, the myelin that coats axons changes, and damaged axons regenerate more slowly (Pannese, 2011). Health and physical fitness, however, are more closely related to performance than is age, and physical fitness and exercise are related to longer life, less disease and disability, and maintenance of cognitive abilities (Katzel & Steinbrenner, 2012). In fact, exercise-based interventions with sedentary older adults have been shown to improve physical (Magistro et al., 2013) and cognitive (Scherder et al., 2013) performance.

Although it is generally true that behavior slows with age, physical fitness serves to minimize age differences in speed.
Source: Tom Wang/Shutterstock.com.

Skin, Bone, and Muscle Changes

The most noticeable changes of late adulthood occur to the skin. Aging skin becomes more wrinkled, dry, sagging, and less regular in pigmentation, especially on the face, hands, and neck, which are exposed to the sun and wind. Very old skin is likely to bruise more easily, heal more slowly, and grow lesions. Several age-related changes cause wrinkling: thinning of the skin, changes in blood vessels that impede circulation to the skin's surface, loss of skeletal and muscle mass, and the loss of fat below the skin surface (Christiansen & Grzybowski, 1993). Age-related decrease of melanocytes, which give the skin its color, cause pigmentation changes. After age thirty, active melanocytes decrease 8 to 20 percent in each decade, causing the skin to become paler (Kligman et al., 1985). The remaining melanocytes may be irregularly distributed, leading to irregular pigment deposits—so-called "age spots." Light-skinned people are more affected by ultraviolet light than darker-skinned people and are likely to develop more pigmentation irregularities. As we saw in Chapter 14's discussion of physical development in middle adulthood, aging of the skin can best be prevented by avoiding sun exposure, especially during childhood.

In addition to changes in appearance of skin, the functioning of subcutaneous sweat glands also changes. As we age, our body produces less sweat in response to higher temperatures or physical assertion, which appears to be due to changes in sweat glands rather than to changes in the hypothalamus (Dufour & Candas, 2007; Smith, Alexander, & Kenney, 2013). As a result, older adults' bodies are not as adept at regulating body temperature, putting older adults at increased risk for heat stroke in hot climates or during heat waves. However, as with most aging, this change in sweat production was not as severe among older adults who regularly exercised (Best, Caillaud, & Thompson, 2012).

Another aspect of primary aging, demineralization, results in a lighter bone mass in older adults. The bone becomes more porous and brittle as the supporting bone matrix breaks down. This bone degeneration is called *osteoporosis,* which you may remember from Chapter 14. Osteoporosis has a two-phase pattern of bone loss. The first phase is gradual and occurs in both sexes throughout adulthood. Children and teenagers with low-calcium diets are at greater risk for osteoporosis as well as other health problems, when they reach adulthood (Kotchen & McCarron, 1998). Maintaining a calcium-rich diet, regularly engaging in weight-bearing exercise, not smoking, and maintaining a body weight on the high side of normal (a BMI of 24–25) can prevent this phase of osteoporosis (Wilsgaard et al., 2009). The second is rapid and occurs in postmenopausal women (Murray et al., 1996). Women experience far greater bone loss than men do; women lose about 30 percent of their bone mass, whereas men lose about 17 percent (Hayflick, 1994). Table 16.3 shows risk factors for osteoporosis. Clinical osteoporosis is not a separate disease of old age but an extreme form of primary aging. It puts older women—and in particular, older Native American, Asian, and Caucasian women—at risk for hip and bone fractures (Cauley, 2011; Murray et al., 1996). Regular weight-bearing exercise, estrogen replacement therapy, and calcium supplements, separately or together, have been shown to slow bone loss and reverse osteoporosis in postmenopausal women (Hayflick, 1994), though estrogen replacement has also been linked to increased risk for certain types of

TABLE 16.3 What Puts You at Risk for Osteoporosis: A Checklist

While some of the risk factors for osteoporosis, such as gender, body build, and family history, are beyond an individual's control, many are linked to health-compromising behaviors.

- **Increasing age.**
- **Being female.** By age sixty-five, the average man still has 91 percent of his bone mass, but the average woman has only about 74 percent.
- **Being chronically underweight** or having a slight frame.
- **Being Caucasian or Asian** (usually small-boned).
- **Having osteoporosis in the family.**
- **A poor diet,** low in vitamins and minerals, especially calcium.
- **Being sedentary** and lack of weight-bearing exercise.
- **Smoking.** In women, this lowers the estrogen content of the blood, thus weakening the bones. Smoking is particularly dangerous for women who have other risk factors for osteoporosis.
- **Heavy drinking.** It is not known why heavy drinking weakens the bones—perhaps because heavy drinkers often eat a poor diet.
- **Long-term use of certain medications.** Some people with asthma and rheumatoid arthritis take cortisone for long periods, which can diminish bone strength. So can long-term use of thyroid hormones, which are sometimes used to treat obesity, although most physicians do not recommend them for this purpose.

cancer (Lobo, 1995). Additionally, bone loss can be slowed by increasing intake of protein, magnesium, and vitamin D supplements (Whitbourne & Whitbourne, 2011).

With aging comes a progressive loss of muscle strength and speed. As we saw in Chapter 14, muscle mass starts its gradual decline in middle adulthood. Recent studies clearly indicate that much of the loss that previously has been attributed to primary aging in fact results from sedentary lifestyles that reduce muscle mass and increase obesity (Goldberg et al., 1996). Loss of muscle mass varies with the muscle and how much it is used; muscles used in daily activities are maintained, whereas those used infrequently decline. Loss of muscle fibers results from atrophy due to disuse or to damage and atrophy of the nerve fibers that carry impulses to the muscle. Older adults maintain strength if they have engaged in lifelong patterns of physical exercise and can overcome losses by taking up regular exercise training. Although atrophied muscles do not regenerate, exercise helps muscle fibers that have not yet atrophied to function more efficiently (Grimby, 1988).

Cardiovascular System Changes

The heart is a muscle, too, and like all muscles, it changes with age. Cardiovascular changes begin in early adulthood and continue throughout middle and later adulthood. With increasing age, the muscle cells of the heart contract at a slower rate and respond less well to the pacemaker cells that synchronize the contractions. Older hearts of sedentary individuals have fewer muscle fibers and more fat and connective tissue. They eject a lower volume of blood as the left ventricle becomes weaker and less expandable, and this decline is more marked among men (Goldspink et al., 2009). The atherosclerotic changes we discuss in Chapters 12 and 14 also contribute to the reduction of blood flow. As physician Sherwin Nuland (1994) describes it, "each cigarette, each pat of butter, each slice of meat, and each increment of hypertension make the coronary arteries stiffen their resistance to the flow of blood." Even a heart that is free of cardiovascular disease has reduced *maximum cardiac output,* the volume of blood pumped by the heart every minute under conditions of peak exertion, and *aerobic power,* the amount of oxygen carried by the blood every minute under conditions of peak exertion, although resting cardiac output does not decline (Lakatta, 1990). These changes can be kept to a minimum by regular aerobic exercise and good nutrition, as we discuss in Chapter 14. Even among sedentary older people, physical training has been shown to increase aerobic capacity and reduce fat composition, and in many conditioned older individuals, maximum oxygen consumption rate is equal to or better than those of younger sedentary individuals (Goldberg et al., 1996). Exercise also keeps the respiratory system healthier.

Respiratory System Changes

The respiratory system becomes less efficient as a function of age. Though many studies examining respiratory system change neglect to include the oldest-old in their samples, there is evidence that some respiratory decline is normative but that it only becomes noticeable when the system is stressed (Zeleznik, 2003). However, most of the decline in respiratory function is due to secondary aging: poor nutrition, smoking habits, exercise patterns, and sleep-related disorders. Because brain cell functioning relies on oxygen and nutrients, decreased efficiency of the heart and lungs increases risk of stroke or loss of brain functions. Normal daily functioning is unlikely to be impaired, but under conditions of stress, an older adult may have difficulty breathing or become fatigued. Cilia, the hair-like structures in the air passages, become fewer in number and less effective in removing foreign particles. Declining muscle strength makes coughing less efficient. These changes make older people more susceptible to chronic bronchitis, emphysema, and pneumonia. The rate of aging of the respiratory system varies from individual to individual and is strongly influenced by lifestyles factors, such as regular aerobic exercise, smoking, and exposure to air pollutants.

Sensory System Changes

Visual loss is part of the primary aging process. The percentage of older people with significant visual loss increases with age. Loss of accommodation, the ability to change the focus of the eye, is a nearly universal aspect of senescence. By age fifty, people need reading glasses to see things close up. Sensitivity to dim light also decreases steadily with advancing age. In addition to these age-related developments, two visual diseases affect older adults. *Cataract,* a clouding of the lens, is the most common correctable cause of blindness. Cataracts usually develop first around the periphery and impair vision when they spread to the central portion of the lens. Replacement of the lens through surgery is increasingly common and very effective (Nagy et al., 2009). *Glaucoma,* increased pressure in the eyeball, can also cause blindness. Glaucoma is caused by blockage of the Canal of Schlemm, which drains aqueous humor from the eye and returns it to the bloodstream. The aqueous humor continues to be produced, which builds up pressure in the eye. Topical drugs usually control glaucoma, but some types of glaucoma can be effectively treated with laser surgery (Rosenfeld, Shemesh, & Kurtz, 2012). Glaucoma is the leading cause of blindness among African Americans. Even when socioeconomic differences and access to health care are controlled, glaucoma is more prevalent and more difficult to treat in African Americans than in whites (Wilson, 1989).

Hearing loss is also a part of the primary aging process. *Presbycusis* is age-related hearing loss caused by changes in the conductive system in the outer and middle ear and loss of hair cells and nerves in the inner ear. It interferes with the ability to hear high-pitched sounds and consonants in normal speech. It is difficult to separate deafness due to presbycusis from deafness due to loud noise, damage from past infections, or other causes. The percentage of older Americans with significant hearing loss increases with age, and men have greater hearing loss than women, probably due to greater exposure to occupational and recreational noise. Noise is the largest contributor to hearing loss. Adolescents who attend rock concerts or listen to music at high volume, particularly using earbuds and headphones, put themselves at risk for hearing impairment later in life. Figure 16.3 shows speech intelligibility as a function of age. Hearing aids can compensate for hearing loss to some extent, but because they magnify background noise as well as speech, they are not helpful in all settings. There is also much less acceptance of hearing aids than of glasses, so a person may feel self-conscious or "old" wearing them.

FIGURE 16.3
Suprathreshold Measures Across Age for Three Major Sensory Systems

Visual acuity, odor identification, and speech intelligibility all show similar age-related changes.

Source: Doty et al. (1984).

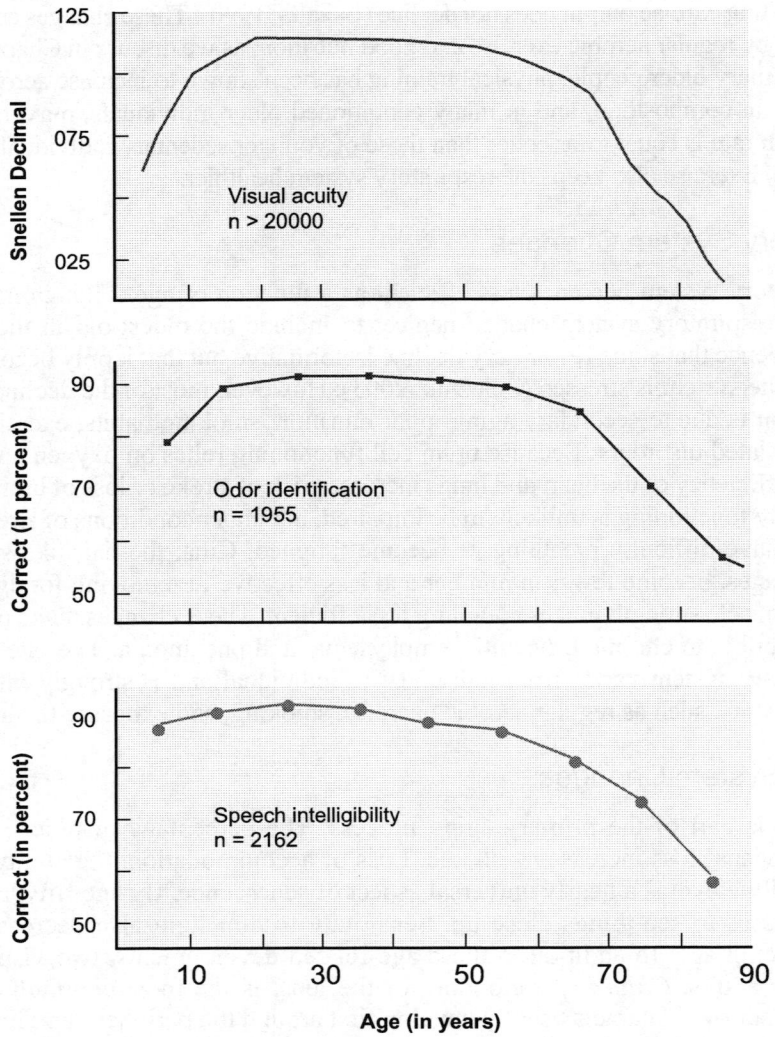

Primary aging affects both taste and smell, with age-related declines in smell being greater than those in taste (Bartoshuk & Weiffenbach, 1990). Taste buds continually regenerate and do not show reduction in numbers with age (Miller, 1988). While cross-sectional studies have shown that sensitivity to the four basic tastes (sweet, salty, sour, and bitter) decreases over the adult years, longitudinal studies have found much smaller age-related declines, rarely involving more than one of the four basic tastes (Hooyman & Kiyak, 1993). Ability to recognize a large number of foods goes down with age. These findings are based on cross-sectional studies, however, and are affected by tobacco smoking, use of dentures, and presence of dental diseases in the older cohorts. Because taste and smell work together in helping to identify foods, losses in smell may be responsible. Using a longitudinal design, Carolyn Tylanda and Bruce Baum (1988) found perception of taste intensity to be remarkably robust with age. The sweetness of sugar appears to be the most robust of all tastes (Bartoshuk & Weiffenbach, 1990).

Olfactory (smell) receptors regenerate continually too, but their numbers begin to decrease at about thirty years of age. Though self-reported olfactory problems remain stable over adulthood, decrements in the ability to distinguish between smells occur with age (Shu et al., 2009). As Figure 16.3 shows, ability to detect various types of odors peaks between ages twenty and fifty, decreases slightly over the fifties and sixties, and decreases markedly after seventy (Doty et al., 1984; Ship et al., 1996). At every age, females are better at identifying odors than males, and nonsmokers are better than smokers. Using a large, nationwide sample, Avery Gilbert and Charles Wysocki (1987) found that the ability to smell odors did not decline with age until respondents were in their seventies. However, the perceived intensity of an odor and the ability to identify it began to decline much earlier. Mercaptans, the odors added to natural gas,

> **What Do You Think?**
>
> Imagine that your eyesight is failing and you find it difficult to drive. How would you go shopping and get to the other places you usually go? What changes would you need to make in your lifestyle?

became harder to detect at about age fifty, whereas rose odor did not begin to decline until age seventy. It is important to note that marked sensory problems can be an indicator of underlying neurological problems, such as Alzheimer's disease or Parkinson's disease (Rawson, 2003). Thus far, we have been focusing on primary aging, age-related changes that all people in late adulthood experience to some degree. Older adults vary greatly in their levels of physical functioning. Many experience secondary aging caused by health-compromising behaviors, such as smoking, or environmental factors, such as pollution. Others continue to function as they did in middle age because of favorable genetic makeup and health behaviors.

Changes in Sexual Functioning

Few changes in sexual functioning occur in late adulthood. Although ageism includes the myth that old people are not interested in sex, as you will see in the Chapter 17 "Focusing On" feature (page 624), sex means much the same thing to older adults that it does to younger ones. There is no evidence that either men or women lose interest in or the ability to enjoy sex as they age. The best predictor of sexual interest in middle and late adulthood is frequency and enjoyment of sex at younger ages, and the best predictor of sexual activity is having a partner.

A recent large-scale survey of women and men age fifty-seven or older found that sex remains an important part of older Americans' lives and that interest in having a healthy sex life remains throughout late life. However, compared to midlife, those ages seventy-five to eighty-five reported that sex did become less important, a finding that was more marked among women than men. Additionally, with age, the prevalence and frequency of sex declined. Among those who are sexually active, most reported engaging in vaginal sex, with the prevalence of other sex acts declining with age, indicating possible cohort effects in sexual practices. The most common sexual problems reported were erectile problems for men and vaginal lubrication difficulties for women. Those who were not sexually active either lacked a partner, had a medical condition, or took a medication that prevented them or their partner from having sex (Waite et al., 2009). Among older men and women, sexual activity is associated with quality of life (Wiley et al., 1996). Aging couples who understand that both partners can be sexually satisfied without intercourse continue to have satisfying sexual relationships (Adams et al., 1996).

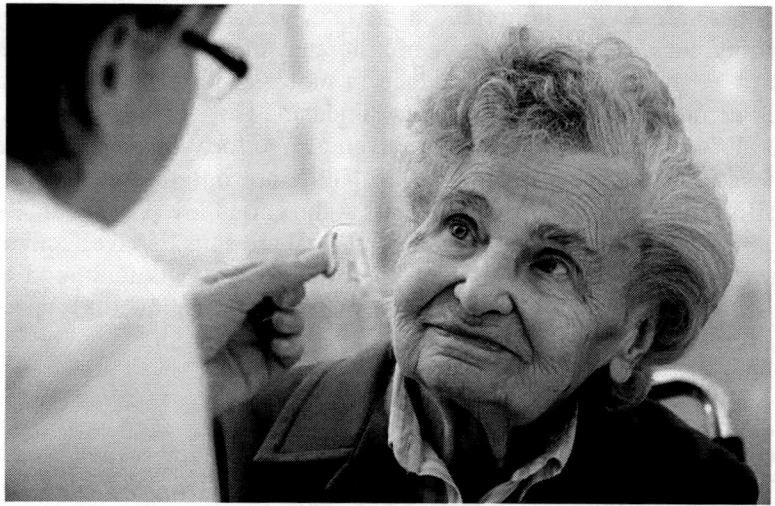

Hearing loss is part of the primary aging process. This woman is being fitted for a hearing aid to compensate for her loss. Though there is less acceptance of hearing aids than of glasses, smaller and less visible models increase an older adult's likelihood of using them.
Source: Alexander Raths/Shutterstock.com.

Chapter 16 Physical and Cognitive Development in Late Adulthood

Focusing On...

Older Adults Have Healthier Lifestyles Than Young and Middle-Aged Adults

Adopting a healthy lifestyle is the best strategy for decreasing illness and enhancing health throughout life, all adults are encouraged to avoid health-compromising behaviors and adopt health-promoting behaviors, but who actually follows that advice? Susan Walker, Kevin Volkan, Karen Sechrist, and Nola Pender (1988) set out to compare young, middle-aged, and older adults in their patterns of health-promoting behaviors. They recruited 167 young adults (ages eighteen to thirty-four), 188 middle-aged adults (ages thirty-five to fifty-four), and 97 older adults (ages fifty-five to eighty-eight) to fill out their Health-Promoting Lifestyle Profile. Participants rated forty-eight items on a 1 to 4 scale (1 = never, 2 = sometimes, 3 = often, 4 = routinely). Table 16.4 shows representative items for each of the six subscales of the profile.

Older adults had significantly higher total health-promoting scores and higher scores for the subscales health responsibility, nutrition, and stress management than young or middle-aged adults. There were no significant differences among age groups for self-actualization, exercise, and interpersonal support. For every age group, average scores for exercise were the lowest of all the subscales.

In addition to age, the researchers looked at educational level, gender, and income to see if these demographic factors were related to healthy lifestyles. Gender was found to be related to an overall health-promoting lifestyle and to the dimensions of health responsibility, exercise, nutrition, and interpersonal support. In all cases, women had significantly higher scores than men. Higher income was associated with health responsibility, and exercise, and more education was associated with nutrition, interpersonal support, and stress management. Marital status and employment status were both related to nutrition. Being married and not being employed were associated with higher health-promoting nutrition scores. In this sample, not being employed meant being a homemaker or being retired (only 2 percent of each age group was unemployed).

Because the Walker study was cross-sectional, it is impossible to explain why these differences were found. However, more current longitudinal research suggests that not all health behaviors improve over time and that changes are not reliable across socioeconomic status. Whitehall II is a longitudinal study of British civil servants (with a 19.5-year follow-up); GAZEL is a longitudinal study of French gas and electric workers (with a 16.5-year follow-up; Stringhini et al., 2011). Overall, both studies found a reduction in smoking and of physical activity over time, regardless of SES, though the high-SES groups were engaging in better health-promoting behaviors overall. Generally, rates of heavy drinking remained stable, except for high-SES Whitehall participants, who drank more at follow-up. Healthier diets were found at follow-up for all but high-SES Whitehall participants, who remained stable due to a floor effect: they were already eating quite healthy.

What do the findings from these studies tell us? In many cases, the older adults had healthier lifestyles, but why? Perhaps with maturity people become more health conscious and adopt healthier habits. Perhaps older adults have more time and resources to devote to health promotion than do younger adults. Other studies have also shown that desirable health practices increase with age (Bausell, 1986; Prohaska et al., 1985). Thomas Prohaska, Elaine Leventhal, Howard

Health Behaviors in Late Adulthood

Health and fitness are no less important in the later years than in early or middle adulthood; if anything, increased physical vulnerability may make them more important. Older adults seem to be aware of this and engage in more health-promoting behaviors than their younger counterparts, as this chapter's "Focusing On" feature suggests. In a study that followed 1,741 university alumni from average age forty-three years to average age seventy-five years, people with better health habits not only survived longer but also experienced disability later and for fewer years at the end of life (Liao et al., 2011; Vita et al., 1998). Table 16.5 presents seven health habits that are considered effective in improving health and prolonging life. Beginning these habits early in adulthood can provide cumulative benefits in later adult years, but they need to be continued. Of special concern during late adulthood are diet, exercise, and alcohol consumption.

Diet

Nutritional concerns increase during late adulthood because at the same time caloric needs decline, the need for many nutrients rises. Problems arise when older adults consume too

Focusing On...

Older Adults Have Healthier Lifestyles Than Young and Middle-Aged Adults *continued*

Leventhal, and Mary Keller (1985) found that older people considered themselves more vulnerable to disease and saw it as more serious for them. On the other hand, it may be that the older adults with less healthy habits had already died or become too sick to be part of this sample, which is supported by Liao and colleagues, who demonstrated that older adults who abstained from smoking, drank moderately, obtained sufficient sleep, and exercised regularly were less likely to suffer disability and subsequent death (Liao et al., 2011). Whatever the reason, these data do, however, contradict the negative stereotype of older people as unable or unlikely to care for themselves.

What Do You Think?

1. Think of a member of your family of the same gender as you in your grandparents' generation and your parents' generation. Rank yourself and each of these individuals according to the six subscales of the Lifestyle Profile. Who is highest, middle, and lowest in health promotion in each area?

2. Combine your results with those of classmates. Which generation scores highest, middle, and lowest? Does this result conform to the findings in the original study? What explanations can you suggest for the similarities and the differences?

TABLE 16.4 Sample Items for Each Subscale of the Health-Promoting Lifestyle Profile

Self-Actualization	Exercise	Interpersonal Support
Like myself	Exercise three times/week	Discuss concerns/problems
Look forward to future	Recreational activities	Enjoy touching and being touched
Know what is important	Check pulse rate	Time with close friends
Health Responsibility	**Nutrition**	**Stress Management**
Check cholesterol level	Eat three meals daily	Meditation/relaxation
Report symptoms to M.D.	Eat roughage/fiber	Express feelings
Observe body for changes	No preservatives	Aware of stress sources

Source: Adapted from Walker et al. (1987).

---

few vitamins and minerals or take medications that prevent them from getting the full benefits of the nutrients in the foods they eat. Under-nutrition can increase the risk of heart disease, cancer, osteoporosis, infectious illnesses, and acute brain syndromes. Obesity can contribute to a variety of health problems, such as troubled breathing, diabetes mellitus, gallstones, hypertension, atherosclerosis, and heart disease. Older adults have more varied caloric requirements than any other age group, but any given older individual needs fewer calories than in earlier years. Activity levels, gender, weight, height, genetic makeup, social environment, and SES all affect dietary needs. To control weight and meet nutritional requirements, it becomes more important in late adulthood to avoid eating empty calories and choose foods that are high in nutrients and fiber and low in fats and cholesterol.

A variety of physical, social, and emotional factors can contribute to nutritional deficits among older adults. Declining health or medications may make food uninviting. Dental problems, such as missing teeth or poorly fitting dentures, may make chewing difficult. Changes in taste and smell may make food less enjoyable. Reduced income from retirement or widowhood may make food less affordable. Loss of mobility because driving is no longer safe or walking is too difficult may make regular grocery shopping impossible. Social changes, such as the loss of a partner, may make meal preparation more problematic;

TABLE 16.5 Behaviors That Improve Adult Health and Longevity

Beginning health behaviors in early adulthood can provide cumulative benefits in later adult years, but they need to be continued. Health behaviors can improve health even if started during late adulthood.

- Sleeping an average of seven to eight hours nightly
- Eating breakfast almost every day
- Seldom, if ever, eating snacks
- Controlling weight
- Exercising regularly
- Limiting alcohol consumption
- Never having smoked cigarettes

Source: Adapted from Shoenbom & Danchik (1980).

cooking for one can challenge a person's dedication to variety and nutrition, and widowed men may find themselves alone and responsible for their own food preparation for the first time. Such difficulties often lead to skipping meals or eating snack foods and TV dinners rather than properly balanced meals.

Exercise

As people get older, their routine physical activity decreases (Lakatta, 1990; Stringhini et al., 2011). In Chapter 12, we discussed the challenge to young adults to lower their caloric intake as they experience a decrease in activity level from adolescence to adulthood. In late adulthood, retirement brings further decreases in physical activity, especially for men. Women have a greater variation of lifestyles. Older homemakers may continue to care for large homes, entertain extended family, and tend their grandchildren, which may require working as actively as they ever did. Although physical activity is less a part of the daily routine, exercise, along with good nutrition and adequate sleep, is considered

Loss of mobility because driving is no longer safe or walking is too difficult may make regular food shopping and preparation difficult or impossible during late adulthood. Meals on Wheels and meal delivery services help provide nutritious, ready-to-eat meals.
Source: Monkey Business Images/Shutterstock.com.

a significant health need for today's older adults. About half of what has generally been accepted as part of aging is now understood to be **hypokinesia**, a disease of disuse that causes degeneration and functional loss of muscle and bone tissue. In addition to preventing hypokinesia, regular exercise makes people feel better, reduces stress, facilitates weight loss, lowers blood pressure, controls depression, heightens resistance to disease, and improves the quality of life for older people (Goldberg et al., 1996; Stones & Kozma, 1996). It also increases longevity (Kushi et al., 1997; Liao et al., 2011).

During the past two decades, adults have been exercising more frequently—particularly, older adults. Data from Canada, Japan, England, and France indicate that people in their sixties have higher exercise rates than those in their forties and fifties. The number of "inactive" people is low at all ages, although the frequency doubles between the twenties and the sixties (Stones & Kozma, 1996).

Older people who continue to exercise do so because of established habits. Those who were involved in athletics early in life continue to participate in sports and exercise more than people without such experience (Harada, 1994), though the findings are reversed for children who were forced to exercise by parents (Schutzer & Graves, 2004). This helps to explain why older women exercise less than older men (Blair et al., 1989). Lois Verbrugge (1989a) sees the gender difference in late adulthood as a continuation of a pattern, established during adolescence, in which boys are more physically active than girls. However, this gender difference might be due to a cohort effect: women who are older adults today grew up in a time when exercising was not "ladylike" (Schutzer & Graves, 2004). Poor exercise habits acquired early in life and continued through middle age do not help women when they become older. For healthy adults, the recommendation on exercise by the American College of Sports Medicine is moderate training three to five times a week at 65 to 75 percent of maximal heart rate. A sedentary beginner should start out gradually. Though older adults will often begin exercising because of advice from medical professionals, those professionals frequently do not discuss exercise with their patients (Schutzer & Graves, 2004). Moreover, health professionals have tended to be overcautious in prescribing exercises for older adults that are sufficiently challenging to yield the full benefits of an exercise program (Frontera & Meredith, 1989). This is compounded by a self-fulfilling prophesy: many older adults perceive themselves as being too frail to engage in exercise, and not exercising does hinder their ability to engage in physical activity (McAuley et al., 2003; Schutzer & Graves, 2004).

hypokinesia A disease of disuse that causes degeneration and functional loss of muscle and bone tissue and can be prevented by regular exercise.

Sleep

Healthy adults obtain approximately ten minutes less sleep per night for each decade of life, and it takes longer to fall asleep once in bed as we age, which becomes more pronounced as we enter late life (Ohayon, Carskadon, & Guilleminault et al., 2004). Even so, the National Sleep Foundation recommends that older adults obtain about eight hours of sleep each night. One reason older adults get insufficient sleep is because the circadian rhythm advances, causing older adults to feel sleepy earlier in the evening and wake earlier in the morning. Many older adults overcome this sleepiness, staying up later. However, the signal to wake early in the morning remains, truncating the sleep period and resulting in sleepiness and fatigue (Ancoli-Israel, 2004), and putting older adults at an increased risk of falling (Ancoli-Israel, Ayalono, & Salzman, 2008). In a prospective study of community-dwelling older adults, those who felt tired most of the time were significantly more likely to have died ten years later than those who did not feel fatigued (Hardy & Studenski, 2008).

Another common sleep problem among older adults is sleep disordered breathing (SDB), the most common of which is sleep apnea—specifically, obstructive sleep apnea (OSA), in which the patient ceases to breathe during sleep due to some blockage in or collapse of the airway, which is called an apnea (Fetveit, 2009). OSA has been linked to many serious subsequent health problems, such as high blood pressure, obesity, heart disease, heart failure, diabetes, and stroke (Endeshaw, 2006; Endeshaw, Bloom, & Bliwise, 2008; Fetveit, 2009). OSA is becoming more common in the United States; it is unclear whether higher incidence is linked to increasing rates of obesity or simply to higher rates of diagnosis (Ancoli-Israel et al., 1991;

Barthlen, 2002; Fetveit, 2009). Obesity is one of the, if not the, major risk factor for developing OSA because large amounts of adipose tissue in the neck can cause the airway to collapse, leading to apneas. Moreover, older adults ages sixty-five to ninety have rates three times that for younger adults with OSA, even when considering mortality rates associated with subsequent health problems (Ancoli-Israel et al., 1991b; Fetveit, 2009). Loss of muscle tone also contributes to the development of OSA because respiratory muscle tone is necessary to keep the airway open to prevent apneas (Ancoli-Israel, 2005). Barthlen (2002) noted that the overall prevalence of OSA is 4 percent and that the prevalence among community-dwelling older adults is nearly 25 percent. OSA is most frequently treated with continuous positive airway pressure (CPAP) machines, which essentially push air into the airway via a mask, keeping the airway open and preventing collapse. CPAP machines are quite effective when used properly.

Alcohol Consumption

Although problem drinking and alcoholism constitute major health risks for adolescents and adults of all ages, light to moderate alcohol consumption, may actually promote a longer life (Gaziano et al., 2000; Kamsa-Ard et al., 2014; Kushi et al., 1995). One to two drinks per day may reduce risk for coronary heart disease. Heavy drinking, however, poses serious problems for older people.

During late adulthood, sensitivity to alcohol increases. For any given amount consumed, blood alcohol concentration is higher in an older individual than in a younger one, probably due to less dilution by body water volume, which decreases with age (Christiansen & Grzybowski. 1993). This might be of particular concern for older adults who maintain alcohol-consumption patterns from midlife: They may be unaware that a smaller amount of alcohol might have more of an effect, leading to the emergence of alcohol problems for the first time (Fiske, et al., 2012) Alcohol can block reaction time, impair coordination, and cloud mental abilities, especially memory. It may accelerate some of the cognitive changes associated with aging, as well as lead to damage in the gastrointestinal, cardiovascular, and central nervous systems.

Levels of alcohol consumption and the number of problem drinkers are lower in older age groups. However, it is unclear if changes in alcohol abuse over the lifespan are due to maturing or selective mortality (Fiske et al., 2012). Moos and colleagues (2009) followed a group of 719 alcohol-consuming adults over a twenty-year period and found that the amount of alcohol consumed over time decreased and that the number of people engaging in excessive drinking decreased. In a comparison of participants at the twenty-year follow-up with participants who left the study after the ten-year follow-up due to health problems or death, there were no significant differences in drinking behaviors at year ten, indicating that the decline in alcohol consumption over late life might not be due to the mortality effect (Moos et al., 2009).

Although alcohol consumption decreases in late adulthood, it remains a problem for some groups. Older alcoholics may be continuing a pattern established earlier in life or may be responding to stressful social changes in their lives such as loneliness, bereavement, or retirement. Older males are at greater risk for alcoholism than females. Scot Adams and Shirley Waskel (1993) found that among older alcoholic men, the onset of problem drinking was due less to stress than to the loss of a spouse, who may serve to regulate the man's drinking. Other risk factors include low income, low level of education, and a history of depression. Though some studies have suggested substantial benefits to the consumption of wine over other types of alcohol, other research has demonstrated that the link between wine consumption and lower mortality rates among older adults is largely accounted for by socioeconomic status, gender, and smoking (Holahan et al., 2012). Regular drinking is more common in retirement communities, where it is associated with social activity, than in the general population of senior citizens (Alexander & Duff, 1988). Stress, depression, pain, sleep problems, and lack of social support are all risk factors for late-life alcohol abuse (Fiske et al., 2012). Although stress has been associated with alcohol use, Neal Krause (1991) found that not all stressors led to an increase in alcohol use among older adults. Health problems were associated with a greater probability of older individuals

> **What Do You Think?**
>
> Assess your health-promoting behaviors. What improvements can you make now that would have a positive effect when you reach late adulthood?

abstaining from alcohol, while financial difficulties were associated with a lower probability of abstaining. Gender and race were also found to be significant factors; being a woman or being an African American increased the probability of abstaining. Being religious was also associated with a higher probability of abstinence.

Prescription Drugs

Increased sensitivity to drugs puts older individuals at high risk for adverse drug effects, especially if they take multiple drugs. In part because of the chronic illnesses discussed in the next section, older adults take one-third of the prescription drugs used. Sharon Willcox and her associates (1994) found that 23.5 percent of community-living adults age sixty-five and over had been prescribed one or more of twenty drugs that older people should avoid because of adverse side effects. Individuals most likely to receive hazardous prescriptions were women, people living in the South, those who rated their health as poor, and those on Medicaid. Improper medications may cause physical, cognitive, and social dysfunction, which sometimes leads to a misdiagnosis of neurocognitive disorder, as we will see later in this chapter. Moreover, it is expected that as the baby boomers age, late-life misuse and abuse of prescription medications is expected to double in the next ten years, which is a major public health concern (Briggs et al., 2011).

Late adulthood is characterized in far more negative terms than many individuals experience. Though losses in physical functioning occur during late adulthood, normal aging is not synonymous with loss. There are large differences in how different body systems age and in how different individuals age. Severe losses are the function of disease and disuse, not of normal aging, and do not affect everybody.

Chronic Illnesses

Chronic illness, a medical condition that cannot be cured but can only be managed, is a common feature of late adulthood. Most of us will eventually develop at least one chronic disease or disability that may ultimately cause our death. Chronic diseases are incremental and are characterized by progressive loss of organ reserve (the extra capacity to respond to stress). All chronic conditions have a clinical threshold, the point when the symptoms appear. The key to preventing chronic illness is to delay reaching the clinical threshold (Fries, 1996).

While chronic illness is associated with age, it is not special to late adulthood. For example, many children suffer from asthma, which is a chronic illness. At any given time, half of the population has some chronic condition that requires medical management (Taylor, 1998). Even if we focus only on chronic illnesses in adults, the lines between middle and late adulthood are blurring as increasing numbers of Americans continue to be healthy and vigorous well into their later years. While some middle-aged adults already suffer from chronic diseases, many young-old adults do not.

Because people may live with chronic diseases for many years, they often find all aspects of their lives affected (Saarelainen et al., 2010; Verbrugge & Patrick, 1995). At its most acute—for example, a person has a heart attack—a chronic disease disrupts all life activities, throwing the person into a state of physical, social, and psychological crisis. Once the crisis phase passes, people begin to develop a sense of how the chronic illness will alter their lives. They may need to make permanent changes in physical, vocational, and social activities and often need to learn to accept the role of patient. Denial, anxiety, and depression are common emotional reactions (Deeg et al., 1996). In fact, many older adults do not change their subjective ratings of their health even when they face a major health problem, which might be due, in part, to a change in the perception of what "good health" is (Galenkamp et al., 2012). However, increasing numbers of older adults living with chronic conditions are successfully utilizing online forums, blogs, and listservs to get information about their illness (Madden, 2010), as well as for companionship, reducing their perceived stress levels (Wright, 2000). We will see the implications of these psychological aspects of chronic disease when we discuss psychosocial development in the next chapter. Here we discuss the chronic diseases that become frequent in middle and late adulthood.

While chronic diseases become more frequent in late adulthood, they generally originate in earlier life stages and often have their onset earlier as well. In part, the great frequency of these illnesses is a result of people living longer. For many older adults, chronic diseases do not interfere with everyday activities. Faced with physical limitations, people have ingenious ways of adapting and compensating for losses. Nonetheless, late adulthood is a time when body decline is a part of life. While physical fitness accomplished through lifelong health behaviors can maintain most body systems at high levels of functioning, the levels are not as high as they were before because primary aging cannot be stopped.

Gender Differences

Lois Verbrugge's data indicate that the kinds of symptoms that bother men and women are very similar but are much more frequent in women. Women's chronic conditions tend to be nonfatal, such as arthritis, and men's tend to be fatal or precursors to fatal conditions, such as heart disease. Moreover, women are significantly more likely to use diagnostic services, primary care, and specialty care than men are (Bertakis et al., 2000). There is evidence that women also have an impact on their husbands' utilization of health care, specifically among Hispanic, Asian, and Native American men (Norcross, Ramirez, & Palinkas, 1996). As a result, men die at a faster rate, and women experience more frequent symptoms and health care. Because research and health services have focused on fatal conditions, the symptoms and disability associated with the nonfatal chronic conditions, which more often afflict women and men at older ages, have received less medical attention (Verbrugge & Patrick, 1995).

Cardiovascular Disease

Cardiovascular disease, any disease of the heart and blood vessels, is the major chronic illness in the United States. It is responsible for most illness and death among men during middle adulthood, usually after age forty-five. *Coronary heart disease (CHD)* refers to illnesses caused by atherosclerosis, the narrowing of the arteries that supply the heart. Atherosclerosis is the most common heart disorder in the United States (Go et al., 2014). Wastes in the form of fatty deposits (plaques) build up over the years, impeding blood flow. Narrowed or closed arteries wholly or partially block the flow of oxygen and nutrients to the heart. Atherosclerosis may progress evenly or may result in a sudden, catastrophic event. Temporary blockage may cause pain or tightness in the chest and radiating down the arms, called *angina pectoris*. The pain is due to insufficient oxygen and nutrients getting to the heart cells and is likely to occur when the body is under stress and the heart rate is elevated. Severe blockage may result in *myocardial infarction*, or heart attack. A heart attack damages heart cells beyond repair.

Risk Factors

CHD, the leading cause of death in the United States, is common among males and older people in general. Men are three times more likely than women to experience a major cardiovascular event before age sixty. At any level of risk factors, women have half the risk men of the same age do and tend to show signs of it ten years later than men (American Heart Association, 2010). Premenopausal women seem to be protected by their high levels of estrogen. This biological advantage is heavily influenced by environmental factors, as indicated by the finding that wives of men with CHD have twice the risks that wives of men who do not have it do (Strickland, 1988b). Furthermore, the biological advantage does not protect women from CHD indefinitely. As Figure 14.1 (page 508) shows, women's death rates from heart disease increase dramatically above age sixty-five, and heart disease is the leading cause of death among women, impacting 33 percent of women (Straub, 2012).

Risk factors for heart disease include family history, health-compromising behaviors, personality type, and stress. Offspring of parents who have had CHD are at greater risk. A diet high in fats and cholesterol, obesity, tobacco smoking, and low levels of physical activity are all risk factors a person can control, as we discussed in Chapter 12. A CHD-prone personality is characterized by strong feelings of hostility (Eysenck, 1990). Other risk factors include diabetes and high blood pressure.

Hypertension

Blood pressure, the pressure exerted when the left ventricle of the heart contracts, maintains equilibrium throughout the vascular system as it responds to the needs of the cells for oxygen during varying levels of physical exertion. Blood pressure varies greatly from individual to individual and according to activity. Hypertension, or high blood pressure, is determined by the systolic and diastolic blood pressure. *Systolic pressure* is the greatest amount of force developed during the contraction of the ventricles; *diastolic pressure* is the lowest pressure in the arteries when the heart is relaxed. Systolic pressure consistently over 140 and diastolic pressure consistently 90 or above constitute hypertension. Continuing high blood pressure can cause deterioration of the arterial walls and of the cell tissue. The small arteries become thicker and less elastic, causing arteriosclerosis. Arteriosclerosis puts a person at risk for heart attack, kidney damage, and *stroke,* which is a rupture or leak of a small artery in the brain.

Risk factors for hypertension include genetic predisposition, obesity, poor diet, and personality characteristics (Straub, 2012; Taylor, 1998). Males are at greater risk than females; African Americans are more at risk than whites; and older people are more at risk than younger people. Low-income African Americans are highest risk. They are more likely to have parents with a history of hypertension and to live in neighborhoods and work in jobs that cause chronic stress. Racism may also contribute to hypertension, as we saw in Chapter 14's discussion of health and inequality. Cheryl Armstead and her associates (1989) found that exposure to racist stimuli was associated with blood pressure increases among African American college students. Stress also seems to be a contributing factor. Treatment of hypertension often includes medication and adopting healthier behaviors.

Cancer

Cancer is actually a set of more than one hundred diseases characterized by uncontrolled cellular growth and reproduction due to a dysfunction of the DNA, the part of the cell that regulates these processes. Cancerous growths, called *malignant tumors,* can spread by invading other tissues and organs. This process of spreading is called *metastasis.* Once cancer has metastasized, local surgical removal usually becomes impossible.

Cancer is the second most frequent cause of death in the United States and the leading cause of mortality for adults ages forty-five to sixty-four (Heron, 2013). Half of all men and one-third of all women will be diagnosed with cancer at some point during their life (American Cancer Society, 2014). The leading cause of cancer deaths for both men and women is lung cancer, most likely caused by smoking (American Cancer Society, 2014). For men over age fifty, prostate cancer is the most common cancer (American Cancer Society, 2014). For women between ages thirty-five and fifty-five, breast cancer is second (Strickland, 1988b). As discussed in Chapter 14, these cancers are common enough in middle adulthood that regular breast self-examination (BSE) and professional breast and prostate examination are considered important health behaviors. BSE entails systematic palpation of each breast to detect alterations or lumps in the underlying tissue. Although regular mammograms and annual professional breast exams are recommended for women forty and older, 85 percent of lumps are still detected by women themselves. Professional digital rectal examination of the prostate is recommended as part of an annual physical for men starting at age fifty. Blood tests for all types of cancers are in development to better differentiate molecular subtypes of cancer, as well as to assist in cost-effective early detection (Hanash, Baik, & Kallioniemi, 2011). Because both are curable in their early stages, early detection of breast and prostate cancers saves lives.

Risk Factors

The causes of cancer are not fully understood, but some risk factors are known. Some cancers run in families; some are linked to gender, ethnicity, lifestyle, or marital status; and most are linked to diet. Overall, cancer rates among African Americans average 11 to 27 percent higher than among non-Hispanic whites (Garfinkel, 1991). Cancer-related mortality rates for African Americans are about 8 percent higher than for Caucasians (National Cancer Society, 2014). Hispanics appear to have lower rates of major cancers, especially cancers of the lung, breast, colon/rectum, prostate, and pancreas. However, Hispanics also have higher rates for cancers of the cervix, stomach, liver, and gall bladder (National Cancer Society, 2014). Among all racial and ethnic groups, Asian Americans and Pacific Islanders are the least likely to develop or die from cancer (American Cancer Society, 2014).

Charles Longino and his colleagues (1989) found that incidence of cancer was directly related to SES (the higher the SES, the higher the incidence of cancer). Yet lower-SES people with cancer have lower survival rates than wealthier people. The findings of this study have been replicated in international research, and they suggest that, all risk factors being equal, insufficient access to screening for early detection and treatment among lower-SES individuals decreases survival rates (Youlden et al., 2012). SES is directly related to health status, as discussed in Chapter 12. Lack of health insurance makes early detection of cancers less likely, but it is only one of many factors that put low-SES groups at higher risk for cancer and other chronic diseases. Low SES typically means greater exposure to *carcinogens* (cancer-causing substances) in workplaces and neighborhoods, higher rates of smoking, and greater exposure to chronic stress.

Stress

Research suggests that the onset of cancer is related to the experience of uncontrollable and chronic stressful life events, such as divorce or the death of a spouse. Chronic stress suppresses the immune system by inhibiting the action of certain lymphocytes whose job it is to identify and attack mutated cells (Glaser et al., 1986; Reiche, Nunes, & Morimoto, 2004). Stress also damages and interferes with DNA repair (Glaser et al., 1985; Maluf et al., 2013). Personality also has an influence on a person's likelihood of developing cancer. The cancer-prone personality is characterized by a tendency to suppress emotions such as anxiety and anger, difficulty in coping with stress, and the development of feelings of hopelessness, helplessness, and depression (Eysenck, 1996).

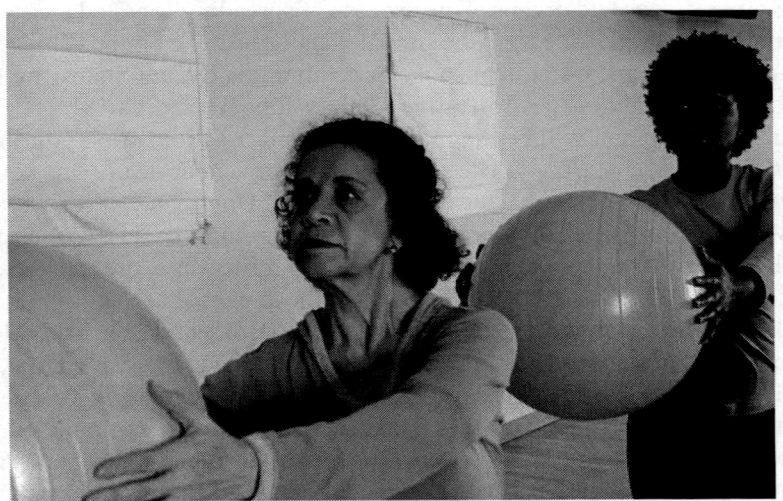

Half of women over age fifty suffer from rheumatoid arthritis. Regular, gentle stretching can prevent or reduce the disabling effects of this disease.
Source: bikeriderlondon/Shutterstock.com.

> **What Do You Think?**
>
> Imagine what your life would be like if you had severe arthritis or some other debilitating chronic disease. How would such a condition change your current lifestyle?

Arthritis

Joint discomfort is a common complaint among mid- and late-life adults. Two community-based studies in which participants kept daily diaries of symptoms provide a view of what symptoms pervade daily life in middle and late adulthood and how frequently they occur (Verbrugge, 1989a; Verbrugge & Patrick, 1995). Both older men and women most frequently report musculoskeletal symptoms, about half from disease (usually arthritis) and half from overexertion, strains, and sprains.

Arthritis, a set of more than eighty autoimmune diseases in which the body incorrectly identifies its own tissue as foreign matter and attacks it, is the second leading chronic disease in the United States. Arthritis attacks the joints and connective tissue and causes inflammation, pain, stiffness, and sometimes swelling of the joints. Although arthritis rarely leads to death, it can be crippling. *Osteoarthritis* is the most common type of arthritis, affecting mostly older people and some athletes. This degenerative joint disease wears down the cartilage through overuse, injury, or other causes. It most often affects weight-bearing joints: the hips, knees, and spine. Interestingly, runners experience lower levels of osteoarthritis in their knee joints than nonrunners, even among older adults. It is believed that, though the impact of running is greater than that of walking, the distance per step is also greater with running, resulting overall in less "wear and tear" on the knee (Miller et al., 2013). *Rheumatoid arthritis* affects the whole body, rather than specific, localized joints. The lining of the joint capsule becomes inflamed, producing enzymes that attack the cartilage, bone, and soft tissue. In severe cases, it destroys the joint. The exact cause of rheumatoid arthritis is unknown, but it is brought on by autoimmune processes. It is the most crippling form of arthritis and is most prevalent among people ages forty to sixty.

Rheumatoid arthritis afflicts three times more women than men. The onset usually occurs between ages twenty-five and forty-five; half of women over fifty suffer from it. Incidence is particularly high among women who have had an oophorectomy (surgical removal of the ovaries). Early diagnosis and treatment can prevent the disabling aspects of the disease. While it is not clear whether stress causes rheumatoid arthritis, it is known to exacerbate the disease.

Men and women suffer from similar chronic conditions, but because men die sooner, women tend to experience more sickness and disability.

COGNITIVE DEVELOPMENT

At age seventy-three, Sally occasionally can't find her keys or think of a name, and worries that she is losing her memory. Yet, she manages the household she shares with her husband and keeps track of her large extended family's many birthdays and anniversaries without mishap. She cooks and bakes from her vast mental store of recipes and shares news of everyone during calls and visits with her adult children and grandchildren.

As we saw in the Chapter 14 discussion of cognitive development in middle adulthood, patterns of age-related changes in cognitive abilities in adulthood differ widely. Both objective performance on memory tests and subjective appraisals of memory functioning are negatively associated with age (Smith, 1996). However, some aspects of memory, such as autobiographical memory and remembering procedures for tasks, do not decline with age (Whitbourne & Whitbourne, 2012). Performance on unfamiliar laboratory tasks shows greater age-related differences than performance on familiar real-life tasks (Willis, 1996). Older adults maintain domain-specific knowledge in areas of expertise. Schaie and his colleagues (1994) found that some individuals showed significant changes in intellectual performance in midlife, whereas a few showed little decline even into their eighties. Absence of chronic diseases, high SES, involvement in intellectually stimulating activities, a flexible personality style, marriage to a spouse with high cognitive functioning, and satisfaction with one's life accomplishments were all factors that reduced the risk of cognitive loss. But are there age-related gains? Do we become wiser with experience? This is the question to which we now turn.

Wisdom and Cognitive Abilities

wisdom Expert knowledge and good judgement about important but uncertain matters of life; a positive change associated with late life.

Wisdom, expert knowledge and good judgment about important but uncertain matters of life, is a positive change associated with late life. Jutta Heckhausen and associates (1989) asked groups of young, middle-aged, and old respondents about their views on the nature of adult development and aging. Respondents were given more than three hundred psychological attributes (such as aggressive, curious, excitable, intelligent, materialistic, proud) and asked which of these attributes they expected to change with age ("become more apparent, stronger, and/or more frequent") during the decades of adult life. They also were asked to indicate the degree of desirability of the expected change. Overall, respondents believed the attributes likely to change in early adulthood were more desirable than those expected to change in later adulthood. The two desirable attributes they expected to be more frequent and stronger in late adulthood were wisdom and dignity. Jutta Heckhausen and Joachim Krueger (1993) showed that participants expected to grow in wisdom in later adulthood, though, as we will note, true wisdom is rare and is not guaranteed by aging (Baltes & Smith, 2008).

During recent years, wisdom has become an area in which psychologists have made efforts to measure cognitive growth or potential for growth in late adulthood. Paul Baltes and Ursula Staudinger (1993, 1996) and their associates at the Berlin Max Planck Institute for Human Development and Education have been studying the losses and gains of the aging mind. They distinguish between *cognitive mechanics* (content free, such as processing speed and working memory) and *cognitive pragmatics* (knowledge rich, such as solving real-life problems) as two major intellectual categories, extending the distinction between fluid and crystallized intelligence presented in Chapter 14. They believe that in the fluid mechanics of the mind, biological conditions are most significant, and therefore decline with aging is likely. In the crystallized pragmatics of the mind, culture is most significant, and therefore progress may be possible in old age. Though related to intelligence, intelligence is not a strong predictor of the presence or absence of wisdom later in life (Baltes & Smith, 2008).

Cognitive Mechanics

cognitive mechanics Basic memory processes, such as sensory information input, visual and motor memory, and the processes of discrimination, categorization, and coordination that are likely to decline during late adulthood.

Cognitive mechanics refers to basic memory processes, which, as we saw in Chapter 14, are likely to decline in late adulthood. Baltes and Staudinger (1993) developed a memory technique that requires creative, quick, and accurate use of all of the cognitive mechanical operations (processes of sensory information input; visual and motor memory; the processes of discrimination, categorization, and coordination) to measure age-related changes in cognitive mechanics. They asked participants to remember a long list of words, such as thirty nouns (*car, plane, house, chair,* etc.) in the order of presentation. Most people can remember five to seven words if they do not use a memory technique, but can remember much longer strings of words when taught to create mental images that link the words to be remembered to a set series of mental locations. At recall, participants recreate the images, location by location, and decode the images into the original memory words. Table 16.6 shows this and other memory techniques. Baltes and Staudinger have found that when seventy-year-olds learn and practice memory techniques they do reasonably well, but they do not approach the performance of thirty-year-olds. "Even after about thirty-five sessions of training and assessment, most older adults do not reach the level that young adults display after a few training sessions. . . . this age-related decrement is robust and appears irreversible" (p. 76).

TABLE 16.6 Techniques for Maintaining or Improving Memory

People as old as seventy have been shown to benefit from memory techniques.

> **Use places.** Link a string of facts you must remember to familiar places. "Place" one fact at each location and "pick them up" when you need them by revisiting the locations in your mind.
>
> **Use rhymes.** Create your own rhymes, such as "*I* before *E*, except after *C*," to string together what you need to remember.
>
> **Rehearse new facts.** Repeat the name of the person who has just been introduced to you, and make a point of using the name several times as you speak to that person.
>
> **Chunk or regroup.** Turn directions to a new place into fewer items to remember by making up a sentence or story that includes each street you must turn on.
>
> **Make notes.** A shopping list or list of errands will be fixed in your mind if you write them down. If they are not, you have the list to consult.
>
> **Structure your life.** Put your keys on their special hook, your glasses on a particular shelf, and your checkbook in a particular drawer. You will then remember where they are.

Cognitive Pragmatics

Cognitive pragmatics refers to intellectual problems in which culture-based knowledge and skills are primary, such as reading and writing skills, language comprehension, professional skills, and knowledge about strategies to manage the peaks and valleys of life. Baltes and Staudinger (1993) consider wisdom to be one of the prototypes for growth in the pragmatics of intelligence in adulthood. To measure age-related changes in wisdom, they use verbal responses to various types of life dilemmas. An example of a dilemma they use is "A fifteen-year-old girl wants to get married right away. What should one/she do and consider?" Another example is "Imagine a good friend of yours calls you up and tells you that she can't go on anymore and has decided to commit suicide. What would one/you be thinking about? How would you deal with this situation?" Participants are asked to "think aloud" about the dilemmas. Table 16.7 shows the five wisdom-related criteria researchers use to evaluate the responses and how they are applied to the dilemma about the fifteen-year-old. In a comparison of young (average age thirty-two years) and older (average age seventy-one years) adults on wisdom-related dilemmas, the researchers found no differences in overall performance. Older adults showed higher levels of wisdom-related knowledge on tasks specific to their own age group than did young adults. A fairly large number of old adults were among the top scorers. Few responses among a well-educated group of participants were considered wise, however, so wisdom is not inevitable (Smith & Baltes, 1990).

Ursula Staudinger and her colleagues (1992) compared clinical psychologists, a professional specialty that involves a higher-than-average level of exposure to giving advice about the uncertain matters of life, and matched controls of various ages. The clinical psychologists did better than the controls, and at least as many old clinical psychologists as young ones were among the top scorers. When people nominated as wise were compared to clinical psychologists and two control groups of equally well-educated professionals, one young (average age twenty-nine) and one old (average age sixty-eight), both the group nominated as wise (average age sixty-four) and the group of clinical psychologists (average age sixty-six) performed equally well and better than the other groups (Bakes et al., 1995). Clearly, the research on wisdom, in which older participants are among those who do well, shows a very different age-related pattern than that of mechanics, in which none of the older participants are among the top scorers.

Historically, critics of the Berlin Institute researchers' optimism about gains in wisdom in late life point out that, as yet, no empirical evidence suggests that older adults *on the average* perform better on wisdom-related tasks than younger adults, that creativity is

cognitive pragmatics Intellectual problems in which culture-based knowledge and skills are primary, such as reading and writing skills, language comprehension, professional skills, and knowledge about strategies to manage the peaks and valleys of life, that may grow during late life.

TABLE 16.7 Use of the Wisdom-Related Criteria to Evaluate Discourse About Life Matters

This table illustrates how Baltes and Staudinger (1993) evaluated the wisdom of responses to the dilemma "A fifteen-year-old girl wants to get married right away. What should one/she do and consider?"

Criterion	Evidence
Factual knowledge	Who, when, where?
	Examples of possible different situations
	Multiple options (forms of love and marriage)
Procedural knowledge	Strategies of information search, decision making, and advice
	Timing of advice
	Monitoring of emotional reactions
	Cost-benefit analysis; scenarios
	Means-ends analysis
Lifespan contextualism	Age-graded contexts (e.g., issues of adolescence)
	Culturally graded contexts (e.g., change in norms)
	Idiosyncratic contexts across time and life domains (e.g., terminal illness)
	Interrelations, tensions, priorities of life domains
Relativism	Religious and personal preferences
	Current versus future values
	Historical period
	Cultural relativism
Uncertainty	No perfect solution
	Optimization of gain versus loss
	Future not fully predictable
	Backup solutions

Examples of Responses (abbreviated):

Low score	A fifteen-year-old girl wants to get married? No, no way. Marrying at age fifteen would be utterly wrong. One has to tell the girl that marriage is not possible, [After further probing] it would be irresponsible to support such an idea. No, this is just a crazy idea.
High score	Well, on the surface, this seems like an easy problem. On average, marriage for fifteen-year-old girls is not a good thing. I guess many girls might think about it when they fall in love for the first time. And, then, there are situations where the average case does not fit. Perhaps in this instance, special life circumstances are involved, such that the girl has a terminal illness. Or this girl may not be from this country. Perhaps she lives in another culture and historical period. Before I offer a final evaluation, I would need more information.

Source: Baltes & Staudinger (1993).

"the privilege of youth" (Simonton, 1990, p. 321), and that the measures used to test wisdom are lacking. The Wisdom Development Scale is an alternative instrument to measure wisdom by examining knowledge of oneself and others, judgment, knowledge, skills, and willingness to learn that has been validated with a large sample of adults (Brown & Greene, 2009). Regardless of the methods of measuring wisdom, there is now cross-cultural evidence that both wisdom and knowledge increase with age, but that not all who reach late life will develop wisdom (Baltes & Smith, 2008). However, it should be

Teaching about the function of different areas of the brain calls upon this man's store of knowledge, as well as his language and interpersonal skills, all of which are aspects of cognitive pragmatics that may increase in late life.
Source: A and N photography/Shutterstock.com.

noted that much of this research has been conducted among college students. The prevailing negative images still influence everyday life; measures and criteria used to evaluate performance are still youth oriented. The fact that any older adults perform at peak or near-peak levels demonstrates that high levels of functioning are possible and, with cultural change, may become normative. These researchers are not the only ones who are optimistic about the possible cognitive gains of later life.

Cognitive Plasticity and Training

Research showing that the environment has a significant impact on the structure and functioning of the brain has also led to optimism about cognitive functioning in late adulthood. Studies with animals have demonstrated plasticity of the neurons in the cerebral cortex. **Plasticity** refers to the ability of other neurons to take over the functions of neurons that have been damaged or lost. We will discuss changes in the brain more specifically in the next section. Here we look at research, first with animals and then with humans, demonstrating that aging brains can respond positively to enrichment in the environment and cognitive training.

plasticity The ability of other neutrons in the cerebral cortex to take over the functions of any neurons that are damaged or lost.

Animal Research

Marian Cleeves Diamond (1993) and her colleagues at the University of California at Berkeley have spent more than thirty years doing a series of experiments with rats that have given a new perspective on the brain, its functioning, and its aging. Their investigations have led to the understanding that environmental living conditions have an impact on the state of the cerebral cortex. In the enrichment condition, twelve rats live together in a large cage in which they have access to objects to explore. In the standard condition, three rats live together in a small cage with no objects to explore. In the impoverished condition, one rat lives alone in a small cage with no objects to explore. Diamond and her colleagues have shown that enrichment of the environment causes an increase in the growth of dendrites (the part of the nerve cell that connects with other nerve cells) and thickening of the cerebral cortex in the brains of rats, while impoverishment of the environment causes decreases in thickness of the cerebral cortex. Greater thickness of the cortex reflects more connections among nerve cells. First, the researchers found evidence of these cortical changes in young animals placed in enriched environments. Then they found measurable changes with prenatal enrichment. Later they looked at young, middle-aged, and old adult rats and found that at all ages environmental enrichment produced significantly thicker cortices, while environmental impoverishment produced diminished cortices (Diamond, 1988).

Let us look at an experiment done with very old rats. A particular breed of rat can live 904 days in the laboratory. (On average, rats have a life expectancy of two to three years.) At 766 days, after the rats had spent most of their lives in standard colony living conditions, Diamond (1988) and her research team separated them into enriched or standard conditions, with new living partners. After 138 days in these new living conditions (at 904 days old), the experiment was ended, and the rats' cerebral cortices were examined. The enriched rats had 10 percent thicker cortices than those in the standard condition, a difference as great as that seen among young rats. These old rats were in the enriched condition for 138 days rather than the thirty days typically used with the young rats. However, more recent research has demonstrated that providing an enriched environment to old rats for thirty days resulted in a higher density of synapses per neuron, compared to those rats housed individually or socially, and these changes persisted once rats were subsequently placed in individual, unenriched housing (Briones, Klintsova, & Greenough, 2004). Moreover, growth of capillaries resulting in increased blood volume and flow to the motor cortex of adult rats has been found in response to exercise programs, further suggesting that both experience and exercise improve the function of brain even into late life (Swain et al., 2003).

Obviously, it would be unethical to do similar studies with humans, but animal studies create optimism about the potential for aging human brains. Human studies have focused on whether older adults' cognitive performance can be improved through training, the nature of the training, and the training conditions under which improvement occurs. They demonstrate the ability of social and behavioral science to improve cognitive functioning in late adulthood (Cotmen & Neeper, 1996; Schaie, 1996).

Human Research

As we saw in Chapter 14, normative patterns of age-related changes in cognitive functioning begin in the early sixties, but great individual differences exist, with some individuals showing large changes in midlife and others showing only small changes in their eighties. K. Warner Schaie's (1994) sequential studies, you may remember, also indicate cohort differences in the course of cognitive functioning. Individual and cohort differences suggest that environmental factors influence the course of cognitive functioning in adulthood. Researchers have designed studies to test whether declines among older people can be remedied by training. They have focused on those abilities and processes that longitudinal studies have shown to exhibit earlier patterns of decline, such as abstract problem solving, fluid intelligence, formal operations, perceptual speed, and associative memory and memory span, to test the effects of cognitive interventions in late adulthood (Schaie, 1996).

How do researchers train older adults and test for improvement? Willis and Schaie (Schaie, 1994) did a longitudinal training study using the participants in the Seattle Longitudinal Study (SLS) (see Chapter 14). Sherry Willis developed training materials to provide five one-hour sessions of individual strategy training in inductive reasoning and spatial orientation, two fluid abilities that tend to decline early and to be considered resistant to training. Schaie and Willis used the longitudinal information from the SLS to identify individuals who had declined in one or both of these abilities in the previous fourteen years. They selected individuals who were sixty-five in 1983 and later those who were sixty-five in 1990. Each participant received training in one ability. Participants who had declined in only one ability got training for that ability; those who had declined in both abilities or neither ability were assigned to the training groups randomly. All participants received a pretest, then training, then a posttest. The inductive reasoning group served as a control for the spatial orientation group, and vice versa, because each person was in only one training group.

In the initial training study (1983–1984), about two-thirds of the experimental participants showed significant improvement and about 40 percent who had declined in the previous fourteen years returned to their predecline level. The 1990–1991 sample produced similar findings. Training was more effective for inductive reasoning than for spatial orientation. Men tended to benefit more from inductive reasoning training, while women benefited more from spatial orientation training. Training was somewhat more effective for those who had declined than those who had not. Participants who had been trained

> **What Do You Think?**
>
> Given the evidence that older people can benefit from plasticity and training, in what ways do you think ageism might contribute to decline in older adults? What life circumstances might emphasize respect for wisdom and help older adults to maintain cognitive abilities?

in the initial study still maintained a significant advantage over the controls seven years later. The improvements were not limited to laboratory tasks. Willis and her associates (1992) showed substantial correlations between the abilities that were trained and objective measures of performance on tasks of daily living.

These and similar studies show that intellectual decline is not necessarily irreversible and that intervention strategies may allow for longer maintenance of high levels of intellectual functioning in community-dwelling older persons (Schaie, 1996). Recent research has focused on both the maintenance and improvement of cognitive functioning. In a study of healthy older adults, participants wore a headband-like device containing EEG sensors, and changes in EEG readings were used to control a computer-based card game. The older adults who received this intervention reported enjoying the game, but moreover, they demonstrated improvements in immediate memory, delayed memory, attention, and visuospatial abilities (Lee et al., 2013). These findings highlight the considerable plasticity in older adults' cognitive performance. Such evidence of plasticity provides a very optimistic counterpoint to the irreversible cognitive decrements from which some older people suffer, which we will consider in the next section.

The Aging Brain

As with other bodily systems, age-related changes occur in the central nervous system. Brain weight and brain mass start to decrease gradually at age twenty, although in both cases the loss is moderated by health status. The decreases are very small by age fifty and accelerate after age sixty (Christiansen & Grzybowski, 1993). These cross-sectional differences in brain size may not be simply a function of age but may be due in part to the secular trend that has produced increased height and weight in succeeding generations. Without knowing for sure what the brain weight and mass of older adults were when they were young, we cannot be certain how much of their smaller brain size is due to age-related loss and how much is due to their brain size being smaller as young adults than that of the young adults to whom they are being compared.

Brain Changes

Cross-sectional studies show loss of nerve cells in some areas of the brain over the adult years, but most brain changes are not apparent until after age sixty. In the cerebral cortex, the neuronal loss seems to be greatest in the sensory and motor areas and smallest in the association areas. This may explain why we see a steady decrease in fluid intelligence, which is more closely tied to sensory input, over middle adulthood but an increase in crystallized intelligence, which, as discussed in Chapter 14, is the knowledge of specific information and the use of judgment.

Neuronal Loss and Growth

For many years, scientists believed that large numbers of human brain cells were lost during normal aging and did not regenerate. However, in the last two decades, research findings indicate that the loss was overstated and that regeneration of neurons is likely (Albert & Moss, 1996; Johnson & Finch, 1996). Peter Eriksson and his colleagues (1998) demonstrated that the human hippocampus is able to generate brain cells associated with memory throughout life. Even so, much of the cognitive loss seen as we age is attributable to loss of synapses and connections between neurons; neural loss is more typically seen among individuals with Alzheimer's disease and those with neurodegenerative conditions (Berlucchi, 2011).

Plasticity enables other neurons to take over the functions of neurons that have been lost. Some neurons have the inherent capacity to grow and repair their circuitries. They do this through axon sprouting, dendrite branching, and synaptogenesis. *Axon sprouting* and *dendrite branching* mean that when part of the input to a neuron or group of neurons is lost, the nerve fibers from undamaged neurons and dendrites sprout and form new connections to replace those lost. *Synaptogenesis* refers to the creation of new synapses to replace old ones that have been lost. While many studies have demonstrated the loss in number of neurons in the brain as it ages, others have shown that the density of synapses increases with age and with brain-stimulating activity (Cotmen & Neeper, 1996). Even in the face of neurological damage due to stroke, exercise and experience can improve neuronal function and connections (Overman & Carmichael, 2014). Sherwin Nuland (1994) has suggested that this plasticity may be the neurological source of wisdom that people are believed to accumulate with advancing age.

Other Changes

Other significant changes occur in the aging nervous system. As the cardiovascular system functions less efficiently, the blood flow to the brain is reduced. This contributes to the death of neurons, which cannot store oxygen and depend on the blood flow to keep them supplied. The neurons themselves develop *neurofibrillary tangles* within the cell body and dendrites. The brain develops *granulovascuolar degeneration,* empty spaces called *vacuoles* surrounding densely stained granules, and *plaques,* clusters of degenerating neurons. The brains of older individuals with senile neurocognitive disorder show these structural changes. It is not clear whether they occur in normal aging brains. Chemicals called *neurotransmitters* that regulate the nervous system also change, altering the patterns of communication among neurons.

Changes in the brain are the aspect of aging that people generally fear most. The word *senility,* which, like *senescence,* used to be a neutral term referring to old age, has become a negative term referring to mental and physical infirmity of old age (Covey, 1988). This usage implies that cognitive impairment is a normal consequence of aging and is another example of the historical changes in ageism that we discussed earlier in this chapter. In fact, most declines in mental functioning are related to changes in health and are not a function of age. Better cognitive functioning in old age is also associated with social factors such as more education, a professional occupation, and being active during retirement. There are, however, several brain disorders of age.

Organic brain syndromes are pathological states of the brain caused by physical damage of brain tissue. Physicians diagnose organic brain syndrome based on behaviors and not by examining the brain. Behaviors associated with organic brain syndrome include mood changes, irritability, fatigue, agitation, disorientation, and deficits of memory, learning, and judgment. Because any number of factors may cause these behaviors, there is ample room for misdiagnoses, which can be tragic because some syndromes are treatable, whereas others are not. Metabolic malfunctions such as diabetes, liver failure, or anemia and those due to medication effects, benign brain tumors, vitamin deficiencies, or alcoholism cause major or minor **neurocognitive disorders (NCDs)**. Although the symptoms often appear to be the same as those linked to irreversible brain damage, people with neurocognitive disorders are likely to have fluctuating periods of awareness when they are lucid. While these periods may be brief, they suggest that the damage is treatable and reversible. Physicians must attempt to rule out these potentially curable causes of neurocognitive disorder before diagnosing chronic brain syndrome (Prayson & Estes, 1994). Irreversible changes in the brain cause major neurocognitive disorders, including multi-infarct neurocognitive disorder, Alzheimer's disease, and senile neurocognitive disorder.

Vascular Neurocognitive Disorder

Vascular disease causes **vascular neurocognitive disorder**, the most common type of which is **multi-infarct neurocognitive disorder**. Vascular neurocognitive disorder accounts for 8 to 30 percent of neurocognitive disorder in adults (Alzheimer's Association, 2013; Fiske et al., 2012). Blockages in the blood vessels reduce or prevent blood flow to the brain, depriving it of oxygen and nutrients. This results in a series of tiny strokes, also known as infarcts, that may be so small that they go unnoticed at the time or may be accompanied by headaches or dizziness.

---

neurocognitive disorders (NCDs) A decline in cognitive abilities that begins with delirium and then gets progressively worse. NCD is a symptom of many health problems including, but not limited to, Alzheimer's disease, Parkinson's disease, Huntington's disease, traumatic brain injury, or vascular problems. NCDs are also sometimes referred to as types of neurocognitive disorders.

vascular neurocognitive disorder Neurocognitive disorder caused by a vascular disease.

multi-infarct neurocognitive disorder A chronic brain syndrome that results from blockages in the blood vessels that reduce or prevent blood flow to the brain, depriving it of oxygen and nutrients and causing a series of tiny strokes.

An attack of confusion or spotty memory may be the first sign of multi-infarct neurocognitive disorder. It is important to diagnose multi-infarct neurocognitive disorder because treating the hypertension and underlying vascular disease can slow the progress of the brain disease. Multi-infarct neurocognitive disorder is distinguished from other neurocognitive disorders by sudden rather than gradual onset and a step-like progression (Elias et al., 1990). Unlike with other chronic brain syndromes, individuals with multi-infarct neurocognitive disorder have periods when they are lucid and memories return. Risk factors for vascular neurocognitive disorders include hypertension, metabolic syndrome, diabetes mellitus, advanced age, being male, and smoking (Skoog, 1994; Solfrizzi et al., 2010).

Alzheimer's Disease

When a popular president of the United States begins to forget things, he has many people around him who provide him with notes, whisper cues from the sidelines, or fill in for him. All of these memory aids were in use at the end of Ronald Reagan's presidency. Only after he was out of office did the family announce that President Reagan was suffering from Alzheimer's disease.

Alzheimer's disease, a type of cortical neurocognitive disorder, affects more than 11 percent of individuals over sixty-five years of age (30 percent of those age eighty and over) and, including those patients under age sixty-five, around 5.2 million Americans (Alzheimer's Association, 2013; Zarit & Zarit, 2007). It accounts for 60 to 80 percent of all neurocognitive disorder (Alzheimer's Association, 2013). Alzheimer's disease is caused by degeneration of the brain cells in those portions of the cerebral cortex that are associated with memory, learning, and judgment. The progressive deterioration worsens the patient's neurocognitive disorder as it affects an increasing proportion of these cells. In addition to the loss of brain cells, the chemical neurotransmitter decreases, and lipofuscin granules (yellow-brown pigments that may interfere with cell activities), neurofibrillary tangles, and amyloid plaques increase. The hippocampus, a part of the temporal lobe associated with the storage of memories, degenerates. The presence of amyloid plaques and neurofibrillary tangles in the brain is the basis for the microscopic diagnosis of Alzheimer's disease, and neuroimaging technology allows presence of amyloid plaques to be confirmed in a noninvasive manner. Although these symptoms sometimes appear in the normal aging brain, they show up in large quantity in Alzheimer's patients.

Forgetfulness or confusion typically are the first signs of Alzheimer's. At this early stage of the disease, a person may get lost on the way home from work or forget what happened the previous evening. As the disease progresses, the confusion becomes intense and often includes belligerence. A husband, for example, may become violent with his wife for the first time after thirty-five years of marriage. Patients may no longer recognize their loved ones or may forget to dress before going outside. As the Alzheimer's progresses, symptoms include greater con-

Alzheimer's disease A chronic brain syndrome caused by degeneration of the brain cells in portions of the cerebral cortex that are associated with memory, learning, and judgement. Characterized by beta-amyloid plaques and tau protein tangles in the brain. Patients go through a series of stages beginning with loss of memory and ending with coma and death.

This husband shows pictures of their family to his wife, who has Alzheimer's disease. Caring for a spouse with Alzheimer's disease is a tremendous burden because as the disease progresses, the person may no longer recognize his or her spouse or other loved ones.
Source: michaeljung/Shutterstock.com.

Chapter 16 Physical and Cognitive Development in Late Adulthood

fusion and hyperactivity, often in the form of continual but aimless walking. Patients become increasingly less able to care for themselves and require more care and controlled environments to enable them to wander in safety. In the final stages, sleep increases, followed by coma and finally death. The course of the disease among those age sixty-five and older is usually four to eight years, but death can come as quickly as three years or as slowly as twenty years after its onset. Most people suffering from Alzheimer's disease will spend the majority of their diagnosis in the most severe stage (Alzheimer's Association, 2013).

Neither the causes of nor the cure for Alzheimer's disease are understood. Of all risk factors for Alzheimer's disease, genetic heritability appears to be the most prominent, with higher concordance rates (meaning that both twins either are or are not diagnosed with Alzheimer's among monozygotic twins than dizygotic twins; Fiske et al., 2012; Gatz et al., 2006). Rare early-onset forms of Alzheimer's tend to pass from generation to generation and have been most clearly linked with abnormalities in two of the three genes associated with Alzheimer's (Hardy, 1994; Nuland, 1994; Whitbourne & Whitbourne, 2011). Late-onset Alzheimer's has demonstrated common variations in APOE, a gene on chromosome 19 that produces a blood lipoprotein. Testing for APOE cannot predict if or when a person will get Alzheimer's because not everyone who suffers from Alzheimer's carries APOE, and some who have the gene show no signs of Alzheimer's, even in very old age (Alzheimer's Association, 2013; Sachs, 1995). Researchers can use APOE to identify people who are at greater biological risk for the disease to study progression of and treatments for the disease.

Other than genetic risk, research has identified several other environmental risk factors for the development of Alzheimer's disease. As with vascular neurocognitive disorder, hypertension and cardiovascular disease increase one's risk (Fiske et al., 2012). Obtaining regular exercise, staying socially active, avoiding traumatic brain injury, and maintaining a healthy diet full of vegetables and low in saturated fats have been linked to reduced risk for all types of neurocognitive disorder (Alzheimer's Association, 2013). It is also believed that education, intelligence, and engaging in stimulating tasks could buffer one's risk for neurocognitive disorder and Alzheimer's disease by increasing one's cognitive reserve (Alzheimer's Association, 2013; Fiske et al., 2012). That is, the increased neural connections that come with education and stimulating tasks might mean that even with neuron loss resulting from Alzheimer's disease, a brain with more baseline connections would be better able to compensate for that loss (Alzheimer's Association, 2013). Evidence for this has been found with twin studies in which when there is a discrepancy in the diagnosis of monozygotic twins, with the twin diagnosed with Alzheimer's disease having less education (Gatz et al., 2007).

As people have learned more about Alzheimer's, fear of the disease has grown. Older adults often experience *anticipatory neurocognitive disorder,* the concern that normal age-associated memory changes are signs of the onset of Alzheimer's disease. Stephen Cutler and Lynne Hodgson (1996) examined the link between memory appraisal and personal concerns about developing Alzheimer's among fifty adults ages forty to sixty, half with a living parent diagnosed with Alzheimer's and half a matched group with no family history of Alzheimer's. They found that changes in memory functioning created concern about developing Alzheimer's regardless of whether one had a family member with neurocognitive disorder; those with more memory loss had more anxiety. Among the adult children of Alzheimer's patients, concern about developing the disease was greater among women, among unmarried people, and among those who believed Alzheimer's is inheritable. Perhaps women have greater concern because as female adult children they are more likely to be caregivers, as we saw in Chapter 15. Cutler and Hodgson express concern that because anticipatory neurocognitive disorder may discourage people with remediable memory complaints from seeking help, it may represent a potential threat to well-being.

As of now, there is no way to prevent Alzheimer's disease. Alzheimer's patients are sometimes given drugs to lessen their agitation. Memory aids, such as making lists of things to do before leaving the house, sometimes can help patients in the early stages of Alzheimer's to maintain their functioning. Five drugs have been approved by the FDA to slow or lessen the symptoms of Alzheimer's disease, including to improve the cognitive abilities in those with mild symptoms (Alzheimer's Association, 2013; Fiske et al., 2012). Additionally, cognitive and behavioral treatments are also used to treat symptoms, such as wandering and sleep problems (Alzheimer's Association, 2013). However, at this time, the best one can

> **What Do You Think?**
>
> Imagine that one of the tests designed to identify risk for Alzheimer's indicates that a person is likely to develop the disease. Should the person be told? Debate this issue with one or more classmates.

do is provide loving care for the patients and support the families and friends who suffer the loss of their loved one while carrying the enormous burden of providing care. In the "Working With" interview, a caregiver in a long-term care facility discusses these issues.

Though people often exaggerate how frequently the neurocognitive disorders occur, the heartbreak for afflicted individuals and their families cannot be overstated. Though one in three people will die with neurocognitive disorder, mortality rates associated with neurocognitive disorder are much lower than those of cardiovascular disease and cancer (Alzheimer's Association, 2013). But these statistics do not lessen the burden of those families with a member who has neurocognitive disorder. Mild to moderate neurocognitive disorder requires special attention to care and safety on the part of caregivers. It also requires a sense of humor to deal with the pain of seeing once competent and capable partners, parents, and siblings act in forgetful and foolish ways. Severe neurocognitive disorder causes agony because in addition to exhibiting totally new patterns of behavior that require constant supervision, patients cease to recognize loved ones who provide care or make arrangements for care. The personal anguish of having your spouse or parent not recognize you or remember your shared history compounds the pain of watching the disease take its toll and the pressure of providing care. In addition, adult children worry about their chances of suffering the same fate.

Although we have come to associate neurocognitive disorder with old age, it is not inevitable. Most older adults are in good cognitive health. Changes in functioning should not simply be accepted as the inescapable effects of age. Some organic brain syndromes are treatable, as are many physical symptoms. Likewise, good health and good health behaviors can help to maintain brain functioning well into late adulthood, as we saw in our earlier discussion. In addition, because the physical, cognitive, and psychosocial domains interact, treatable psychological problems such as depression may contribute to the misdiagnosis of neurocognitive disorder. We turn to the mental health issues of aging next.

Mental Health and Aging

Depression and depressive symptoms are the most common psychiatric complaints of older adults (Gatz et al., 1996; Zarit & Zarit, 2007). However, rates of major depressive disorder (MDD) are lowest during late life, and those diagnosed with MDD are likely to have a history of depression (Fiske et al., 2012; Valvanne et al., 1996; Zarit & Zarit, 2007). Although its incidence is higher among older adults, its responsiveness to pharmacological and cognitive-behavioral treatments is the same as for younger adults (Farrell, 1997), though the symptoms may take longer to respond to treatment than for early-onset depression (Fiske et al., 2012). Symptoms associated with depression include appetite or weight loss; sleep disturbance; lethargy or agitation; loss of interest or pleasure in activities; feelings of worthlessness, guilt, or self-reproach; cognitive complaints; and thoughts of suicide or suicidal behavior. Because many symptoms of depression, such as sleep problems, memory complaints, or lack of sexual interest, are thought to be normal changes associated with aging or illness, they may go undiagnosed. Older patients tend to report physical symptoms, such as appetite loss, but deny affective symptoms, such as feeling worthless or suicidal ideation, which can mask the depression (Fiske et al., 2012; Rabins, 1992). In addition, the symptoms of depression in older people often mimic neurocognitive disorder, leading to misdiagnosis. As a result of underdiagnosing or misdiagnosing of depression among older adults, curable problems often are left untreated (LaRue et al., 1985).

Although we do not know how many older adults suffer from depression, clinicians generally agree that between 4 and 19 percent experience depression severe enough to require intervention (Anthony & Aboraya, 1992; Fiske et al., 2012). Rates as high as 20 to 44 percent have been reported among nursing home residents (Adler, 1992; Zarit

> ### WORKING WITH Mark John Isola, Therapeutic Recreation Director
>
> #### Helping Alzheimer's Patients and Their Families
>
> After first attending community college, Mark John Isola earned his bachelor's degree in gerontology. He was then hired as a therapeutic recreation director by the Alzheimer's Resource Center of Connecticut.
>
> **Michele:** *What is the Alzheimer's Resource Center?*
>
> **Mark John:** It's a long-term care facility for clients with neurocognitive disorders, primarily Alzheimer's. It provides care while preserving the dignity of the clients as much as possible. It's designed to be light, airy, and safe. The resident living areas are on an atrium, so there are no long halls. Clients can walk without interruption and not feel lost or frustrated by walls.
>
> **Michele:** *What does a therapeutic recreational director do?*
>
> **Mark John:** All long-term care facilities are required by state mandate to have therapeutic recreation directors or TRDs. The Resource Center has two full-time TRDs for 120 residents. Institutional life, no matter how good the institution, is very upsetting, so we try to alleviate that by developing therapeutic activities for the clients.
>
> **Michele:** *What kinds of activities?*
>
> **Mark John:** I run eight activities a day to help maintain and stimulate abilities. I gear them to three different levels: high-, moderate-, and low-functioning clients. I also design activities to provide social, task-oriented, and cognitive stimulation. Although word games and ball-playing activities are basic to therapeutic recreation programs, the real substance of the program includes art therapy, music therapy, sensory programs, arts and crafts activities, and live entertainment.
>
> We are very concerned with maintaining the dignity of our clients. We make sure our activities are age appropriate. If we want to hold a large-motor activity, for example, we don't blow bubbles and have the clients break them by waving their arms. Instead of stuffed animals, the Humane Society brings in real pets once a month.
>
> **Michele:** *How do your clients respond?*
>
> **Mark John:** It varies with the client. The activities keep clients involved. In most long-term care facilities, the TRDs try to cultivate a peer support group for each client. A support group of other clients and a TRD helps prevent disengagement and depression.
>
> **Michele:** *So do you mainly work with groups?*
>
> **Mark John:** No, I do a lot of one-on-one work, too. With neurocognitive disorder clients, the TRD becomes a caregiver working to balance out mood states and anticipate needs of the clients. I'm responsible for the thirty residents in one of our four units. I'm with them eight hours a day. I constantly help them make decisions or intervene in the things they're doing. Sometimes I help them to the bathroom or stop them from playing with dirty clothes in the hamper. Many have lost the ability to communicate, so I try to interpret from their behavior whether they are thirsty or hungry, or need personal attention.
>
> **Michele:** *What do you try to accomplish?*

& Zarit, 2007). Depression is more common in people over seventy-five (Gatz et al., 1996). Chronic health problems, functional impairment, and reactions to medications are factors leading to depression during late adulthood (Roberts et al., 1997; Zarit & Zarit, 2007). Among older people in institutions, deteriorating health and associated increases in depression have been found to be predictive of death (Parmelee et al., 1992).

Gender, race/ethnicity, and SES are associated with depression among older adults. Women are at more risk for depression, whereas men are more likely to be diagnosed with substance abuse or antisocial personality. For both men and women over age sixty-five, rates of these disorders are lower than for younger adults (Wykle & Musil, 1993).

Economic strain is associated with poor mental health, lower life satisfaction, and depressive symptoms (Wykle & Musil, 1993). Rates of depression among older African Americans are comparable to those for whites (Stanford & DuBois, 1992). Older Hispanics who have high illiteracy and poverty rates also have poor mental health. For instance, older Hispanic women who are widowed, have little education and low income, and

> **WORKING WITH** Mark John Isola, Therapeutic Recreation Director
>
> ### Helping Alzheimer's Patients and Their Families *continued*
>
> **Mark John:** With Alzheimer's, there is no rehabilitation. There is no time limit. I'm content when the client is content or in the best mood state he or she can be in. I ask myself: Why are people crying? Why are people tearing things off the wall? Why are they undressing themselves? It's not that I care if their briefs are off, but then they find themselves naked and feel embarrassed. I manage mood states to the best of my ability. If I see someone sobbing uncontrollably, I try music, I try touch, I try everything I know to help. Sometimes it works and sometimes I just have to walk away, but I go back two minutes later and try again.
>
> Keep her safe. Keep him safe. It's hard. The burnout rate is high, much higher than with other long-term care facilities. Working exclusively with this population is brutal. At the end of the day, you must let go of it and walk away. A blessing of the disease is that most of the clients achieve some level of contentment. It's harder on the families. I worry that many families keep Alzheimer's patients at home too long. It's often not functional in this day and age. If the adult child does not have the coping skills, it isn't necessarily better for the patient just to keep him in familiar surroundings. It's also a terrible burden on women.
>
> **Michele:** *Do you work with the families too?*
>
> **Mark John:** Often dealing with the family is more difficult than dealing with the actual client. A caregiver wife of that generation, who was a dependent spouse, is likely to be stressed and fearful. At age sixty, sixty-five, or seventy, she may be dealing for the first time with transportation, finances, and care-plan meetings. She misses her spouse and is going through anticipatory widowhood. She wants to be a caregiver, but can't any longer. Her husband may not even recognize her anymore, although there is often a sense of familiarity.
>
> **Michele:** *How do the clients' children take it?*
>
> **Mark John:** Adult children and spouses both find Alzheimer's frightening. Children can be more confused by seeing their parent change, but they see the light beyond. They have more life flexibility. Children are more likely to say, "We will do what is needed." Many wives see it as the end of the road. On the other hand, some spouses are as supportive of you and the staff as you are of them. You wonder in those cases who is helping whom.
>
> **Michele:** *Do you find your work gratifying?*
>
> **Mark John:** I like it. It's an opportunity to view the disease right up front. I feel I am helping people. I always knew I wanted a helping profession—I just wasn't sure what population. I think I have a talent for this. My coping skills are good; it doesn't drain me. I bring life and I bring balance to it. You need to have balance within yourself.
>
> #### What Do You Think?
> 1. Why is there no rehabilitation among Mark John's clients? How is this outcome for Alzheimer's similar to that for other ailments discussed in this chapter? How is it different?
> 2. How might a facility designed for Alzheimer's patients be better for the patient than at-home care provided by the family? How might it be better for the family?

are not English speaking are particularly vulnerable to depression (Stanford & DuBois, 1992). The interrelatedness of race and/or gender and SES, physical health, and negative life events may help to explain the apparent association between gender and race/ethnicity and mental health. Older women and minorities often are disadvantaged in terms of economic resources and, as we have seen, are more prone to depression.

Untreated depression increases the incidence of suicide among all age groups, especially older white males. Older adults are at a disproportionately higher risk for suicide: those age sixty-five and older have a 30 percent higher risk for suicide than those age sixty-four and under (National Institute of Mental Health, 2007). Men age sixty-five and older are more likely to commit suicide than any other age group; white men in this age group are more likely to do so than African American men (Kaplan et al., 1994). Kevin Early and Ronald Akers (1993) suggest that African Americans are protected by a belief that suicide is a "white thing" alien to African American culture. Suicide rates for females are much lower than for males and lower for African Americans than for whites.

> **What Do You Think?**
>
> What do you do when you feel depressed? Do you think that these same strategies would be effective if you were an older adult? Why or why not?

Effective treatments for older depression include pharmacotherapy (antidepressants) and psychotherapy. Few comparisons between treatments based on drugs versus psychotherapy have been conducted with populations over age sixty-five, so the relative merits or the two approaches are undocumented (Farrell, 1997). Combined pharmacotherapy and psychotherapy has been shown to be effective with older patients, as has short-term psychodynamic psychotherapy (Gorsuch, 1998; Little et al., 1998). Because most older adults who commit suicide are unlikely to seek mental health treatment but are very likely to have visited a primary care center in the month before death, it is imperative that all health care professionals provide screening for suicide risk (Fiske et al., 2012).

Exercise may reduce depression. While most studies of physical activity and depression have excluded older adults, Terry Camacho and associates (1991) used data from a longitudinal study of 8,023 adults, half of whom were over age forty. They took baseline measures of physical activity and depression in 1965, then again in 1974 and 1983. They wanted to know whether people who participated in physical activity were at a lower or higher risk for developing depression and whether a change in exercise pattern could predict depression. They found that men and women who reported low physical activity at the beginning of the study were at a much higher risk for developing depression ten or twenty years later than were those who reported high physical activity when the study began. Even when the researchers statistically controlled for physical health, SES, social supports, life events, and other health habits, this relationship between physical activity and depression persisted. Adults who began the study "inactive" and changed their pattern to "active" by 1974 had no greater risk of depression in 1983 than those who had been active continuously. On the other hand, those who had been active in 1965 and became inactive in 1974 had a 1½ times greater risk of suffering depression in 1983. For those who had been inactive continuously, risk of depression was highest. Statistical analysis revealed that the direct relationship was between physical health and depression. Moreover, a recent meta-analysis of randomized, controlled trials demonstrated that exercise is an effective way to decrease depressive symptomology among older adults (Bridle et al., 2012). Once again, we see how health-promoting behaviors adopted early in life can have long-term benefits.

Work and Retirement

While establishing a career or an occupation and achieving within it are the focus of early and middle adulthood, most Americans look forward to retirement in their later years. Although stereotypes often depict retirement as a time of depression and low life satisfaction, the reality turns out to be quite different. As with many areas of life, people who can control whether and when they retire can plan for and anticipate the change. This enables retirees to make a positive adjustment to retirement and contrasts sharply with the experience of involuntary retirement or losing a job that we discussed when we addressed cognitive development in middle adulthood in Chapter 14. The statistics on when people retire, however, are contradictory. The traditional retirement age is sixty-five; however, about 16 percent of people age sixty-five and older are still in the labor force, with the number of working sixty-five- to sixty-nine-year-olds being the largest and fastest-growing group over the last ten years (U.S. Census Bureau, 2013).

> **What Do You Think?**
>
> Discuss with classmates the retirement patterns of your older relatives and friends. In what ways have finances and health affected their retirement decisions? What other factors have influenced their choices?

Chapter Summary

- **What historical changes have occurred in the lifespan and in life expectancy, and what further changes can we anticipate?** Life expectancy in the United States has gone from forty-seven years in 1900 to seventy-eight years today, but the maximum lifespan for humans remains 120 years and is not expected to change. During the twentieth century, the U.S. population has been getting older, and the older adult population has been growing in diversity. Gender, race/ethnicity, and SES affect mortality rates.
  Cellular theories of aging attribute the breakdown of cells, organs, and the organism to "wear and tear" on the cells caused by stressors such as toxins, pollutants, and free radicals. Programming theories posit that the maximum lifespan is built into the genes of each species and is beyond human control.

- **What factors affect changes in physical functioning during late adulthood?** Late adulthood is a time of loss in efficiency of body systems, but it is also a time of compensation. As loss occurs, some systems experience regeneration and growth due to their plasticity. Slowing of behavior with age is a consistent finding in research examining motor response, sensory processes, and intellectual functioning. Health and fitness, however, are more related to performance than is age.
  Skin, bone, and muscle all show age-related changes. Protection from sun and other elements early in life can prevent some of the skin changes, and regular exercise can prevent some of the bone and muscle mass loss. Cardiovascular and respiratory system changes that begin in early adulthood continue into the later years. The rate of aging of these systems is strongly influenced by lifestyle factors such as diet, regular aerobic exercise, smoking, and exposure to air pollutants. Age-related loss occurs in all of the senses. Visual and hearing loss begin by age fifty; loss of smell shows a similar pattern; taste seems to have a smaller and later decline.
  Neither men nor women lose interest in or the ability to enjoy sex as they age, although their sexual behavior may be limited because they lack a partner or be modified because of men's changes in capacity for erections.

- **Do health-promoting behaviors change in importance once a person is old?** Health and fitness continue to be important in late adulthood. Nutritional concerns increase as caloric needs decline while the need for many nutrients rises. Regular aerobic exercise is needed to prevent hypokinesia and to maintain cardiovascular and respiratory fitness. Alcohol and drug sensitivity increase.

- **What chronic illnesses become common in late adulthood, and how do they affect daily life?** Chronic illness, a common feature of late adulthood, often begins during middle adulthood or earlier. Cardiovascular disease, the major chronic disease in the United States, is responsible for most illness and death among men during middle adulthood and men and women in late adulthood. Risk factors include family history, health-compromising behaviors, personality type, and stress. Hypertension can cause arteriosclerosis, which puts a person at risk for heart attack, kidney damage, and stroke. Risk factors include genetic predisposition, obesity, poor diet, personality characteristics, and stress. Cancer, the second most frequent cause of death in the United States, is a set of more than one hundred diseases characterized by uncontrolled cellular growth. Different cancers have different risk factors; all are linked to race, SES, and stress. Arthritis, the second leading chronic disease in the United States, consists of more than eighty diseases that attack the joint s and connective tissue. It afflicts three times more women than men and is exacerbated by stress.

- **What age-related losses and gains in cognitive functioning occur in older adults?** Wisdom is a positive cognitive change associated with later life. Research has shown that some older adults perform at near-peak levels on wisdom-related tasks. Research with both animals and humans shows that enrichment and training can lead to positive changes in older adults' brains and cognitive performance.

- **In what ways is the aging brain a good example of both the loss and the compensation that are evident during late adulthood?** Normal aging of the brain is associated with some neuronal loss as well as increased density of synapses and some regeneration of neurons. These changes may be the neurological source of memory loss on the one hand and the growth of wisdom on the other. Organic brain syndromes can be acute or chronic. Though the symptoms are similar, acute syndromes are treatable and reversible, whereas chronic syndromes are not reversible and often are fatal. Alzheimer's disease is the most frequent chronic organic brain syndrome.
- **Does the incidence of depression increase in late adulthood, and can it be treated effectively?** Depression is more common among older adults than among younger adults and, if untreated, can put them (especially white men) at risk for suicide. Low SES is associated with depression, which puts women and racial/ethnic minorities at greater risk because they are economically disadvantaged. Effective treatments include pharmacotherapy, psychotherapy, and a combination of the two.

Key Terms

Alzheimer's disease (p. 601)
cellular theories (p. 576)
cognitive mechanics (p. 594)
cognitive pragmatics (p. 595)
hypokinesia (p. 587)
multi-infarct neurocognitive disorder (p. 600)
neurocognitive disorders (NCDs) (p. 600)
plasticity (p. 597)
programming theories (p. 577)
senescence (p. 576)
vascular neurocognitive disorder (p. 600)
wisdom (p. 594)

Psychosocial Development in Late Adulthood

CHAPTER 17

Source: Diego Cervo/Shutterstock.com.

Chapter Outline

Aging and Ageism

Personality Development in Late Adulthood

Retirement

Marriage and Singlehood

Relationships with Family and Friends

Problems of Living: The Housing Continuum

Interests and Activities

Looking Back/Looking Forward

Focusing Questions

- What is ageism?
- What is successful aging, and what contributes to it?
- What factors influence how retirees adjust to their new life circumstances?
- How does marital status affect well-being in late adulthood?
- Which relationships are significant in late life, and in what ways?
- Why is choice in housing critical in old age?
- How do the interests and activities of late life show both continuity and change?

On his eighty-fifth birthday, John Kenneth Galbraith, renowned economist, retired economics professor, former economic adviser to government agencies, and U.S. ambassador, reflected on modern attitudes toward old people that he had experienced:

> In my youth, the sensitivity of the old was greatly respected. One did not emphasize physical and mental decline, inevitable and apparent though these are. Now, I find, they receive daily, even hourly, mention. *"Still* getting that exercise," I hear when I go out for a walk. *"Still* lecturing," I hear when I give a talk. *"Still* writing," many say when I publish a book or even a review. *"Still* interested in politics," I'm told when I show up at a meeting. *"Still* imbibing," when I have a drink. *"Still* that way" someone observes when my eyes are seen to light up on encountering a beautiful woman. . . ." (*Harvard Magazine,* 1994, 96[3], p. 108)

Aging and Ageism

ageism Stereotyping of and discrimination against people because of their age.

Robert Butler (1993) coined the term *ageism* in 1968 when middle-aged citizens protested the building of a high-rise "luxury" apartment building for the use of poor older adults. **Ageism**, according to Butler, "can be seen as systematic stereotyping of and discrimination against people because they are old, just as racism and sexism accomplish this with skin color and gender." From the very beginning, ageism has been linked to social policy that is seen as potentially discriminatory and unfair in an egalitarian society (Kimmel, 1988). Distributing social services on the basis of age rather than need denies the diversity among people of the same age and promotes discrimination and prejudice. Ageism reflects tension about the growing number of older Americans in the population and the cost of entitlement programs that benefit them, such as social security, Medicare, and Medicaid.

In our society, prejudicial attitudes toward older adults abound; more stereotypes exist about old age than about any other period of life. Stereotyped images of older adults can be positive or negative, but because they are based on general characterizations of "old people," rather than on actual appraisals of individuals, they reflect preconceived notions or prejudices. Negative stereotypes of older adults, which are more abundant than positive stereotypes, include physical traits such as *slow* and *feeble*, as well as personality traits such as *cranky* and *repetitive;* positive stereotypes include *sweet, cute, pleasant,* and *storytellers* (Shenk & Achenbaum, 1993). In fact, anxieties about our own aging contribute to negative attitudes toward the aging (Martens, Greenberg, Schimel, & Landau, 2004). Stereotypes ignore the diversity of older adult populations (Adamchak, 1993). When college students are asked to describe a particular older person, stereotypes break down, and the descriptions often are of healthy, active individuals who happen to be older. Unfortunately, it is easy to consider older individuals who defy the stereotypes as exceptions, while continuing to hold the stereotypes (Shenk & Achenbaum, 1993). Additionally, the stereotypes that older adults hold about themselves have an impact on the perception and the experience of aging through the self-fulfilling prophesy (Bennett & Gains, 2010). Older adults who perceived aging in a positive light were more likely to report better physical health, mental health, and life satisfaction than those who held negative attitude (Bryant et al., 2012).

Ageism abounds among professionals as well. Nicknames such as "vegetable" or "Gork" ("God only really knows" the basis of the person's symptoms) are part of medical students' everyday vocabulary. Few medical students choose geriatrics as a specialty, and few doctors devote as much energy to their older patients as they do to their young patients (Butler, 1993). Clinicians prescribe drug treatments to older depressed patients more often than they refer them to psychotherapists because they assume that older people are too "stuck in their ways" to be introspective (Pasupathi et al., 1995). This is in spite of the fact that older adults prefer nonpharmacological treatments, such as cognitive behavioral therapy (Mohlman, 2012). K. Warner Schaie (1988) describes similar problems of ageism among psychological researchers who assume lowered competence in older people and fail to use proper comparison groups in their research. Because older adults are a heterogeneous group, health status, education, occupational status, gender, and race must be specified and generalizations to other populations made cautiously. Lars Tornstam (1992) criticizes gerontological researchers for their tendency to approach their work from a "misery perspective" (older people as a problem), rather than from a "resource perspective" (older people as a resource). Tornstam points out the common assumption that the processes of industrialization and urbanization distanced older people and their children from each other; however, as we saw in Chapter 15, older adults have close contact with their midlife children.

Personality Development in Late Adulthood

successful aging The maintenance of psychological adjustment and well-being across the lifespan. Characterized by maintaining physical and cognitive function, avoiding disease and disability, and staying engaged with life.

Successful aging, from a psychological perspective, refers to the maintenance of psychological adjustment and well-being across the full lifespan. Rowe and Kahn (1987, 1997) proposed three components necessary for successful aging: freedom from disability and

> **What Do You Think?**
>
> Discuss with your classmates the stereotypes you hold about aging and old people. Where did these attitudes come from? In what ways could negative stereotypes be overcome?

disease, maintenance of cognitive and physical functioning, and maintenance of social engagement. Recent research indicates that the vast majority of older men and women who are not cognitively impaired show considerable psychological resilience in the face of stress (Costa & McCrae, 1997). Although older individuals are less satisfied than younger adults with their health, they are more satisfied with most other aspects of their lives. Happiness is not correlated with age but appears to be a stable outcome of personality traits (Costa et al., 1994). Personality traits are remarkably stable in adulthood, as we saw in Chapter 15's discussion of psychosocial development in middle adulthood. Old age brings many adaptational challenges, including death of loved ones, declining health, and often, economic hardship. Older adults call on the skills and styles they have honed over a lifetime to adapt to these new situations.

Continuity and Change in Late Life

George Vaillant and Caroline Vaillant (1990) reexamined the lives of the men in the Harvard Grant study (see Chapter 13) to determine predictors of physical health, mental health, and life satisfaction at age sixty-five. In 1990 the 173 remaining participants were examined by an internist to assess physical health, given a psychosocial adjustment scale to assess mental health, rated on life satisfaction, and asked to rate themselves on life satisfaction. Because this was a longitudinal study begun in 1940, the investigators already had many measures of adjustment and experiences from earlier stages of life.

What did they find? The authors identify five variables that contributed to late-life adjustment: First, long-lived ancestors predicted physical health only. Second, sustained family relationships predicted physical and mental health. Closeness to siblings was a powerful predictor of late-life adjustment. More than half of the men with a lifetime diagnosis of depression were only children or estranged from siblings, whereas only 7 percent of the men with the best psychosocial outcome had such a family history. Third, maturity of ego defenses assessed before age fifty contributed to psychosocial adjustment at age sixty-five (see Chapter 13). Fourth, absence of alcoholism and, fifth, absence of depressive disorder promoted health. The use of tranquilizers before age fifty (indicative of both depression and alcoholism) was the most significant predictor of both physical and mental ill health at age sixty-five. While childhood strengths were positively associated with health in late life and difficulty coping in early life negatively affected both mental and physical health in late life, many variables often thought to be associated with adjustment in early adulthood were not linked to late-life adjustment. These included childhood socioeconomic status (SES), orphanhood, and college scholastic aptitude. More recently, findings from this study have suggested that utilization of adaptive defense mechanisms during midlife help in building and maintaining social support, which is linked to good physical health during late life (Malone et al., 2013).

Limitations of the Grant Study

While the Harvard Grant study provides longitudinal data into late adulthood, it has several important limitations. First, it includes only men. Second, the sample, selected as successful young adults at Harvard, was very privileged. Consider, for example, Vaillant and Vaillant's finding that SES during childhood was not associated with late-life outcome. These men represented a narrow range of SES; all were from families that had enough food, shelter, and medical attention. We cannot tell from this study how other levels of SES would affect late-life outcomes. The same criticism applies to the restricted range

The Grant study found that closeness to siblings is a powerful predictor of late-life adjustment for men. Although women were not part of the study, sisters often are close friends and companions to their siblings during late life.
Source: Rob Marmion/Shutterstock.com.

of college scholastic aptitude: all of these men were successful enough to be admitted to Harvard. Third, sixty-five is only young-old age. What happens in the next twenty or more years? In summary, while the Harvard Grant study tells us a good deal about the aging of privileged men into young-old age, it does not answer questions about women, less privileged men, or people in old-old and very-old late adulthood.

The Berkeley Older Generation Study is a longitudinal study that includes women as well as men, has been going on for more than fifty-five years, and started out with a more representative sample than the Harvard Grant study. In 1928, about 420 young adult residents of Berkeley, California, were first interviewed. Every third child born in that city was selected for a child study, and these adults were their parents. Dorothy Field and Roger Millsap (1991) report on interview data collected from seventy-two survivors in 1969 (average age sixty-nine), when the respondents were young-old, and 1983 (average age 82.7 years), when forty-seven respondents were old-old (seventy-four to eighty-four years) and twenty-seven were very old (eighty-five to ninety-three years). The survivors—fifty-one women and twenty-one men—were educationally, intellectually, and financially advantaged (as survivors in longitudinal studies usually are because the less advantaged stop participating or die) and living in the community. All had been married at one time and had living children.

Stable Traits in Late Life

What does the Berkeley study tell us about stability and change in later life? Using statistical procedures to analyze ratings on twenty-one personality characteristics at each of the two interviews, Field and Millsap (1991) found five personality components that were stationary across the two time periods: intellect, agreeableness, satisfaction, energetic, and extraversion. If you look back at Table 15.2, you will see that four of these five components are similar to those identified by Paul Costa and Robert McCrae (1997), which we discussed in Chapter 15. *Intellect* represents cognitive functioning and open-mindedness. *Agreeableness* describes a person who is open-minded, cheerful, and accepting of his or her offspring and "things in general." *Satisfaction* describes a person with high self-esteem and life satisfaction. *Energetic* reflects activity and health and correlates highly with self-reports of health in the later years. *Extraversion* includes talkativeness, frankness, and emotionality. Field and Millsap found that four components—intellect, agreeableness, satisfaction, and extraversion—reflected enduring traits during the fourteen years between their two interviews. Notice that these are four of the traits that Costa and associates (1994) indicate are stable after age thirty. The trait that Field and Millsap add, *energetic,* showed low stability in their study, probably because it is linked to health and health declines for most individuals in old-old age. Change in measures of narcissism during adulthood among those from the Berkeley study was predictive of being maladjusted later in life (Cramer, 2011), and even though behaviors became more adaptive throughout adulthood, that pattern of behavior shifted during late-late life with adults in this study engaging in maladaptive behaviors (Diehl et al., 2014).

When they compared the old-old with the very-old, Field and Millsap found that the very-old were less energetic than the old-old and were declining on this trait more rapidly. The very-old showed some decline in intellect, but this was unchanged for the old-old. The most stable trait they found was satisfaction. While most of the respondents showed no change on this trait, 20 percent went up in satisfaction. More than a third of the respondents increased in agreeableness. The investigators saw evidence of Eriksonian generativity (see Chapter 15) in the respondents' interest, concern, and care for their offspring. Extraversion showed a decline for both genders. The Berkeley data indicate that longitudinal change was more likely to be age related than gender related. Only one trait, satisfaction, showed a gender difference at both points of measurement, with men having higher ratings than women. The data show relative stability in satisfaction and intellect well into very old age, an increase in agreeableness, and a decline in extraversion. Certainly, this is a far cry from the stereotype of cranky, conservative old people. In fact, Field and Millsap saw considerable evidence for the development of integrity.

Integrity Versus Despair

Eric Erikson's eighth stage of life, **integrity versus despair**, describes the developmental task of late adulthood (see Chapter 2). In the face of the loss of loved ones, declining health, and loss of meaningful work that can lead to *despair,* can the individual find *integrity,* or "acceptance of one's one and only life cycle and of the people who have become significant to it, as something that had to be" (Erikson, 1968, p. 139)? Successful resolution of the previous stage, *generativity versus stagnation,* shifts the aging adult's focus from personal concern for self and family to altruistic concern for guiding the next generation. This paves the way for finding enduring meaning for one's life, or integrity, in late adulthood. Only in late adulthood can "the fruit of the seven stages gradually ripen" (Erikson, 1968, p. 139). The progression of Erikson's adult stages moves the individual beyond adolescent identity to include a significant other in early adulthood (intimacy versus isolation), expands to the next generation during middle adulthood (generativity versus stagnation), and expands further to the sequence of the generations (integrity versus despair) so that the person becomes what survives after death, faith, love, care, and wisdom (Erikson, 1968). In fact, the development of integrity can be viewed as a slow refining of identity at the end of life in response to late-life issues (Newton & Stewart, 2012).

integrity versus despair The eighth and final crisis of development in Erikson's theory, during which older adults assess the value of their life's work and fight the loss of hope about life in general.

According to Erikson, wisdom, which we discussed in the previous chapter as a late-life cognitive development, is born of the conflict between integrity and despair. Dorothy Field and Roger Millsap (1991) found a normative, developmental increase in agreeableness that they interpret as evidence for ego integrity. Though not representing "the breadth and subtlety of Erikson's life stage," agreeableness described "a person who is coming to terms with life and accepting what it has been" (p. 306). They also note that the old-old increased in agreeableness, which Erikson would expect, while the very old, who he would expect to have attained this stage already, held steady. Erik Erikson, Joan Erikson, and Helen Kivnick (1986) interviewed participants in the Berkeley Older Generation Study and found convincing evidence for the stage of integrity versus despair. Eugene Thomas (1991) also found clear evidence for ego integrity in a study of Hindu religious renunciates in India. The older men he interviewed accepted their past as "something that had to be." Thomas, however, points out the culture-bound nature of Erikson's formulation. These Hindus did not accept their lives as their "one and only life cycle" because of their belief in previous and future reincarnations as well.

Theories of Successful Aging

What makes for successful aging? Psychologists and sociologists have been interested in what older people can do and what society can do to promote successful aging. Since the 1950s and 1960s, several theories have been advanced that try to describe or explain how people adapt to the changes characteristically associated with aging. As Table 17.1 indicates, *disengagement theory* and *activity theory* take opposing perspectives on the problem of adapting to the loss of roles or activities that occurs in late adulthood.

Chapter 17 Psychosocial Development in Late Adulthood

TABLE 17.1 Activity and Disengagement Theories Compared

Activity theory and disengagement theory take opposing perspectives on adapting to the loss of roles or activities that occurs in late adulthood.

Disengagement Theory	Activity Theory
Older people have increased preoccupation with the self and decreased investment in society.	Older people have the same psychosocial needs that middle-aged people do.
Decreased social interaction in old age comes from mutual withdrawal of both the individual and society.	Decreased social interaction in old age comes from withdrawal by society from the aging person.
Optimal aging occurs when the aging person establishes greater psychological distance from those around him or her.	Optimal aging occurs when the person stays active.
Decreased social interaction should be expected.	Substitute activities should be found for those who are lost (e.g., for work at retirement).

Disengagement Theory

disengagement theory
The theory of aging which views the reduction of older adults' social involvement to be a natural and mutual process between older adults and society.

Disengagement theory views the reduction in older adults' social involvement as the consequence of a mutual process between older adults and society. Proposed by Elaine Cumming and William Henry (1961), disengagement theory assumes aging individuals experience inevitable decline in abilities and, as a result, want to be released from societal expectations. As the older person retires and children leave home, his or her social circle begins to shrink. The individual anticipates, adjusts to, and participates in this shrinking. As people have fewer roles, their style of interaction changes from active to passive. Because they have become passive, they are less likely to be sought out for new roles.

Though disengagement occurs for some people, there is little evidence that it is normative. Reed Larson, Jiri Zuzanek, and Roger Mannell (1985) studied ninety-two retired adults who carried electronic pagers for one week. At randomly selected times throughout the week, a researcher would page the participants, and they would fill out a questionnaire about their companionship and internal states. From the 3,412 self-reports generated, the researchers found that half of the participants, waking hours were spent alone. Being alone, however, was not a negative or disengaged experience for most of them. When alone, they tended to do things that challenged them and demanded concentration. They reported feeling highly engaged, but in activities that were not interpersonal. In a sixteen-year longitudinal study of people who were over age fifty and living in the community when the study started, Robert Atchley (1998) found that functional limitation was responsible for all the cases in which dramatic decline in number and level of activities, or disengagement, occurred. Atchley found no cases of voluntary disengagement.

Activity Theory

activity theory The theory of aging that assumes that older adults who maintain social, physical and intellectual activity levels similar to those during middle adult year age more successfully than those who are less active.

As opposed to the disengagement theory, **activity theory** states that the maintenance of social, physical, and intellectual activity contributes to successful aging. This theory assumes that older people who are active will be more satisfied and better adjusted than those who are less active. When they articulated activity theory, Robert Havighurst, Bernice Neugarten, and Sheldon Tobin (1968) were presenting what has become both a dominant gerontological and commonsense perspective on aging. They proposed that unless constrained by poor health or disability, older people have the same psychological and social needs that middle-aged people do. Older people who are aging optimally stay active and resist shrinkage of their social world by maintaining activities or finding substitutes for the

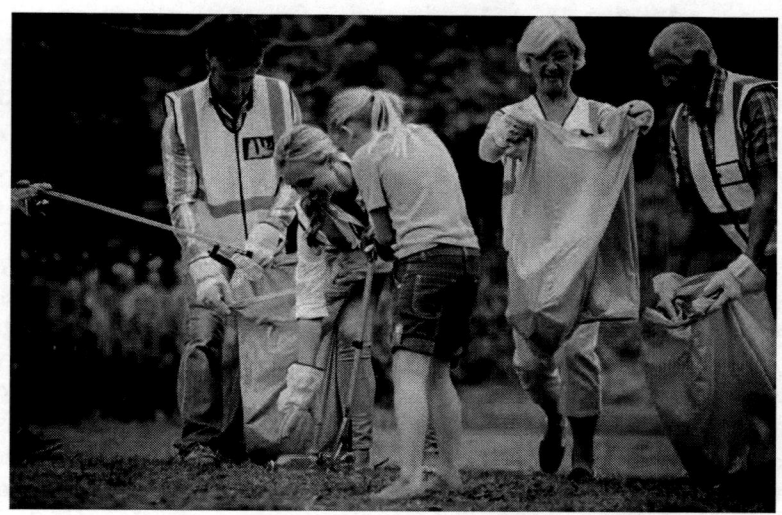

Activity theory states that older adults who are active will be more satisfied and better adjusted than those who are less active. This older couple, along with their family, is volunteering to clean up a roadside, indicating both maintenance of physical activity as well as social awareness. While they might not have the same activity levels as when they were younger, they still remain active.
Source: wavebreakmedia/Shutterstock.com.

ones they must give up. When disengagement occurs, it is because society withdraws from older adults, giving them gold watches and sending them home, rather than because older people seek this withdrawal.

As a test of activity theory, David Lee and Kyriakos Markides (1990) studied 508 older (age sixty or over) Mexican Americans and Anglos (whites) over an eight-year period to see if activity level would predict mortality. Participants were interviewed in 1976 and reinterviewed in 1980 and 1984. Activity level was assessed at each interview by means of a scale that asked questions such as "During the last two weeks, what was the farthest distance you traveled from your home (other than going to work)?"; "How often do you get together with friends or neighbors to play such things as bingo, cards, dominoes, etc.?" By the end of the study, 119 participants were confirmed to have died. The researchers found that activity level did not predict mortality or life satisfaction. Poorer self-rated health and advanced age did predict mortality. However, more recent research suggests that having quality social interactions is a better predictor of successful aging that simply engaging in activities (Litwin & Shiovitz-Ezra, 2006).

What the Theories Omit

Critics of both activity and disengagement theory point out that the theories place the burden of adjustment on aging individuals, independently of the circumstances in the world around them (Cutler & Hendricks, 1990; Marshall, 1996). One major reason older people change their activities is that they have reduced financial circumstances. Economizing to live within one's reduced retirement income often includes, for example, entertaining less often. As we saw in our discussion of leisure in Chapter 15, higher income, higher educational level, and higher occupational attainment all provide greater financial security and more options for leisure activities. In activity theory, we have the socially sanctioned value of productivity and keeping busy, prodding older people to "act middle aged." In disengagement theory, we have the acceptance of the stereotypes of passive, disengaged, decaying old people. Neither theory can account for the range of activity levels of successfully aging individuals; people have different levels of activity and life satisfaction based on their personalities and life experiences. Nor do these theories consider the role of social support in successful aging, which the research of Litwin and Shiovitz-Ezra (2006) suggests is important.

Selective Optimization with Compensation

A more comprehensive way to understand how older adults successfully age is to utilize a theory based in continuity theory—selective optimization with compensation (SOC) theory (Baltes & Baltes, 1990). This theory states that we select activities or domains that we prefer *or* choose based on the loss of alternatives. As we engage in the chosen activity

> **What Do You Think?**
>
> How have the ways people think of the older adults changed since disengagement theory was proposed in the early 1960s? Do you think this could influence how active today's older adults are? If so, in what ways?

or domain, we refine, or optimize, our skills, time, and resources, and finally, when we experience setbacks, loss of abilities, or loss of resources due to life changes, primary, or secondary aging, we overcome that loss by compensating (Freund & Baltes, 1998). In an examination of the measures of successful aging among older adults, it was found that those who utilized SOC were more likely to report that they were less lonely, less agitated, and more satisfied with aging (Freund & Baltes, 1998). In fact, there is evidence that many people choose careers in line with overarching life goals (selection and optimization) and that even after retirement, the work toward those goals continues, sometimes by utilizing bridge employment or by volunteering (compensation) similar to Neal, who is described in the next section (Baltes & Rudolph, 2012). Even if individuals' life goals are not tied to their career, the continuity of goals after retirement is important for life satisfaction (Baltes & Rudolph, 2012).

Retirement

What Is Retirement?

When Neal retired after twenty-five years on the police force, he didn't stop working. He began driving people to various places in their own cars and delivering packages. Because he knew so many people from his work on the force, his new business developed by word of mouth. He drives his regular customers to doctors' appointments, to the theater, and to and from airports. Often, he makes several trips in a day.

Continuous Work

Retirement often means departure from a *career job,* a job at which the individual has been employed at least thirty-five hours per week for ten or more years. Leaving a career job is a significant life event, but it does not necessarily mean leaving the labor force. In fact, the very definition of *retirement* may mean many things to different people: the cessation of work, reduced number of hours working, receiving pensions, or a career change (Wang, 2012). Shifting careers is known as bridge employment, and this continuous work, often in a different field, is often utilized for financial stability (Davis, 2003) or to contribute to feelings of generativity (Dendinger, Adams, & Jacobson, 2005). Retirement, then, may mean changed or reduced employment—not simply stopping work.

Discontinuous Work

Many adults, especially racial/ethnic minorities, never have held career jobs and thus never consider themselves retired. Only 5 percent of those who described themselves as retired in the AARP survey were African Americans. Rose Gibson (1993) found that many older African Americans did not define themselves as retired because they had discontinuous lifetime work patterns, thought of themselves as disabled, and felt economic need that pressed them to work from time to time. Perceptions of a discontinuous work life made the line between work and nonwork indistinct and created ambiguity of retirement status. Similar difficulties have been identified in defining retirement among Mexican Americans who often work, voluntarily or not, in part-time and seasonal jobs for much of their working lives. Because their lifetime work patterns have no clear line between work and nonwork, and because they lack access to private pensions, they do not define themselves as retired (Ralston, 1997; Saad-Lessler, Ghilarducci, & Richman, 2014). Additionally, due to lack of pensions and retirement funds, substantially larger portions of "retired" African American (19.3 percent) and Hispanic (19 percent) older adults fall below the poverty line than white older adults (7.4 percent; Saad-Lessler, Ghilarducci, & Richman, 2014).

In terms of retirement, women face problems similar to those of racial/ethnic minorities. Although women's labor force participation has increased dramatically in the last several decades, many older women have been homemakers for most, if not all, of their adult lives. Consider Tom and Frances, who you met in the last chapter. When Tom retired at age seventy, Frances continued her homemaking tasks. Although she had held a small number of jobs over the years, they had always been part time, short term, and secondary to homemaking for her family of ten. As Tom naps in his recliner during the afternoon, she often asks herself when *she* will get to retire. Even women who have had more labor force commitment than Frances are less likely than men to be covered by pension plans because they are more likely to have held part-time jobs or taken leaves to raise children or to care for aging parents (Carp, 1997; Hatch, 1995). Mexican American women are almost five times more likely than Mexican American men to describe themselves as retired, but they are one-third as likely to be considered retired when in terms of receiving retirement income (Zsembik & Singer, 1990). In fact, Hispanic women and African American men face similarly disjointed employment throughout adulthood, and subsequently, similar disadvantages during retirement (Flippen & Tienda, 2000). This gender disadvantage is likely to change as younger cohorts of women establish steady patterns of labor force participation in jobs that provide retirement benefits.

Retirement Patterns

We see, then, that retirement is not simply a *yes* or *no* status; nontraditional retirement patterns are common among older Americans. Even those who retire experience different phases as they adjust to their new status, as Table 17.2 shows. Retirement is best defined by both substantial withdrawal from the labor force and receipt of retirement benefits (Atchley, 1997). White men are most likely to meet both criteria. Race/ethnicity, gender, and occupational level all affect retirement possibilities and choices. Examination of retirement earnings indicates the long-term costs to African American and Hispanic workers who work "off the books" without social security benefits or who hit the glass ceiling. The racial earnings gap is greater in retirement than it was in employment, which is reflected in the poverty statistics in Table 16.1 (Hogan et al., 1997; Saad-Lessler, Ghilarducci, & Richman, 2014). Therefore, it may be beneficial to utilize a continuity perspective and to view retirement as a process consisting of a preretirement planning phase, which begins as omnibus but becomes more specific as retirement nears, and an adjustment period (possibly including bridge employment) as people transition to and through retirement (Wang, 2012). Throughout this process, health and pension status are important both to the planning, timing, and experience of retirement.

Physical and mental capabilities interact with the demands of the job to influence retirement decisions. Sam, for example, was a pipe fitter who counted the days until he reached retirement age and would no longer have to bend and lift. His brother, a pharmacist, had less physically demanding work, but his health was poor, so he reluctantly retired. The third brother, a teacher, suffered small strokes that gave him episodes of incoherence that made continuing his work impossible. If there had been a fourth brother with an intellectually but not physically demanding job and no physical or mental health problem, he likely would have delayed retirement. People with poor health or physically demanding work are more likely to leave the labor force, as are those with pension benefits. Those who are healthy and those without benefits are more likely to continue working. Self-employed individuals are more likely to simply reduce hours on their current jobs. Other individuals will likely have to change jobs and take lower-status jobs to reduce work hours.

How much individuals enjoy their work also influences retirement decisions. Workers with boring, repetitive jobs, such as assembly line and office work, are likely to choose retirement as early as they can afford it. In contrast, workers with interesting jobs that give them high satisfaction are less likely to retire early and more likely to continue to

TABLE 17.2 Atchley's Phases of Retirement

Based on studies of people facing retirement, Robert Atchley and his colleagues identified phases through which the retirement role is approached, taken on, and relinquished. Phases are not tied to particular chronological ages, and individuals do not go through all of the phases.

Preretirement: People gear themselves up for separation from their jobs.

Honeymoon: New retirees experience a euphoric period of doing the things they "never had time for" before.

Immediate retirement routine: People settle into new routines. Those whose off-the-job-lives were full prior to retirement often find new routines more easily than those who have focused exclusively on work.

Rest and relaxation: Instead of a honeymoon phase, many people go through an initial period of inactivity or "taking it easy" after working for a long period of time. After about three years, activity levels return to normal.

Disenchantment: After the honeymoon is over and a routine is established, a small number of people feel let down or even depressed. They may have had an unrealistic fantasy of retirement or may have encountered a disruption in their retirement plans due to the death of a spouse.

Reorientation: Those who are disenchanted usually go through a process of exploring realistic choices and choosing a retirement routine that is satisfying. Friends, family, and community groups often help people to reorient.

Retirement routine: Whether they first go through the honeymoon phase, rest and relaxation phase, or disenchantment phase, most people master the retirement role and settle into a satisfying routine.

Termination of retirement: While some people return to a job, for many retirement is overshadowed by illness and disability, which gradually leads to the loss of independence.

Source: Adapted from Atchley (1997).

---

work. Well-educated employees are less likely to retire early than those with a high school education or less (Hooyman & Kiyak, 1993). However, there is evidence that those who retire early often do so out of necessity rather than choice due to ill health, therefore possibly putting those with less education (and likely less retirement) at higher risk for worse overall well-being (Bender, 2012). Perhaps for these reasons, early retirement is more prevalent among African Americans and Mexican Americans with career jobs than among whites (Gibson & Burns, 1991). Three-quarters of employees would choose to retire gradually, but few jobs make this option possible (Jondrow et al., 1987), and ill health may also be a factor (Bender, 2012).

Well-Being in Retirement

Although retirement is a major life transition, 60 percent of retirees are relatively satisfied and adjust well to their new life circumstances (U.S. Senate Special Committee on Aging, 1990). Health and financial security seem to be the major determinants of life satisfaction after retirement. Poor health, low income, negative attitudes toward retirement, difficulty making transitions, and inability to confront job loss have been found to make retirement adjustment difficult. Early retirement has more negative effects than later retirement (Atchley, 1997; Bender, 2012; Wang, 2012). Retiring early often results from ill heath, dissatisfaction at work, or involuntary job loss, which probably accounts for its negative impact. Workers forced into early retirement due to downsizing adjust the most poorly (Isaksson, 1997). Occupational status also predicts retirement satisfaction, with lower-status workers having more health and financial difficulties, and therefore less satisfaction, than higher-level, white-collar workers. Higher-status occupations are likely to provide options for nonwork pursuits throughout life, including retirement. Harold, for example, recently retired at age seventy from his career as a college professor. He enjoyed his work and retired with a good pension. Because of his expertise, he is still sought after to lecture on trips and at special events, which provides opportunities for him and his wife to travel and enables him to continue to teach about the issues about which he has developed wisdom. In addition, Harold has research and writing projects that he never had enough time for when he was teaching. For those who, like Harold, have lifelong activities they can expand on during retirement, the transition is easier.

Retirement is just one of the role changes in late adulthood. Loved ones die and become ill; living situations must be adjusted to new physical, social, and economic circumstances. Physical and cognitive changes are a significant part of late adulthood as people adjust to and care for their aging bodies, but social changes are dramatic as well. Whether a person reduces his or her workforce participation gradually or abruptly, early or late, retirement leads to new options: leisure pursuits, community involvement, and adult education, to name a few.

Marriage and Singlehood

Older married people appear to be happier, be healthier, and live longer than widowed and divorced people of the same age (Blieszner & Roberto, 2012; Brubaker, 1985; Brubaker & Brubaker, 1995). Most older marriages have existed since early adulthood and, as we saw in Chapter 15, marital satisfaction generally increases among long-term married couples. Compared to middle-aged long-term marriages, old long-term marriages have reduced potential for conflict and greater potential for pleasure (Levenson et al., 1993; Orathinkal & Vansteenwegen, 2007; Ward, 1993). As older couples face retirement, relocation, and declining health, the marital relationship plays important support functions, especially for men. Marriage provides emotional intimacy, sexual intimacy, interdependence, and belonging. Men seem to depend emotionally on their spouses more exclusively than do women. While men and women are just as likely to consider their spouses to be companions, men are more likely to name their wives as confidants (Chappell, 1990; Gurung, Taylor, & Seeman, 2003). Married women are more likely to name a daughter or a friend as their confidants, either instead of or in addition to their spouses. Perhaps that is why while most older married people report satisfaction with marriage, men tend to report more satisfaction than women (Orathinkal & Vansteenwegen, 2007; Quirouette & Gold, 1995).

Both gender and race/ethnicity are related to marital status in later life. As Figure 17.1 shows, women over age sixty-five are much more likely to be widowed than men, especially in the oldest cohorts. Older African American women have the highest proportion of widows and are more likely to have never been married than other women (U.S. Census Bureau, 2012). African American women are more likely than white women to be divorced, with older Hispanic and Asian women reporting the lowest divorce rates (U.S. Census Bureau, 2012). White and Asian men are more likely to be married than Hispanic and African American men. Older widowed men are seven times more likely to remarry than widowed women (Longino et al., 1990). Divorced individuals are more likely to remarry than widowed people. Older women have fewer options for remarriage because they outlive men in their cohort and because older men tend to marry younger women. Widowed women may also find satisfaction in being single, especially if they have adequate financial resources, and may be reluctant to become caregivers to another aging husband.

Spouses as Caregivers

Declining health presents new challenges for older couples and brings changes to the couple relationship. Spouses serve as the first line of defense in coping with disease and disability. Spouses provide more hours of care and more personal care, and tolerate greater disability in their spouses for a longer period of time than do other caregivers (Stoller, 1992). Because caring for each other is a normative expectation of marriage, it is unlikely to stop until the caregiving spouse's deteriorating health prevents it. Caregiving spouses often report higher rates of depressive symptomology, more financial problems, and more physical burden

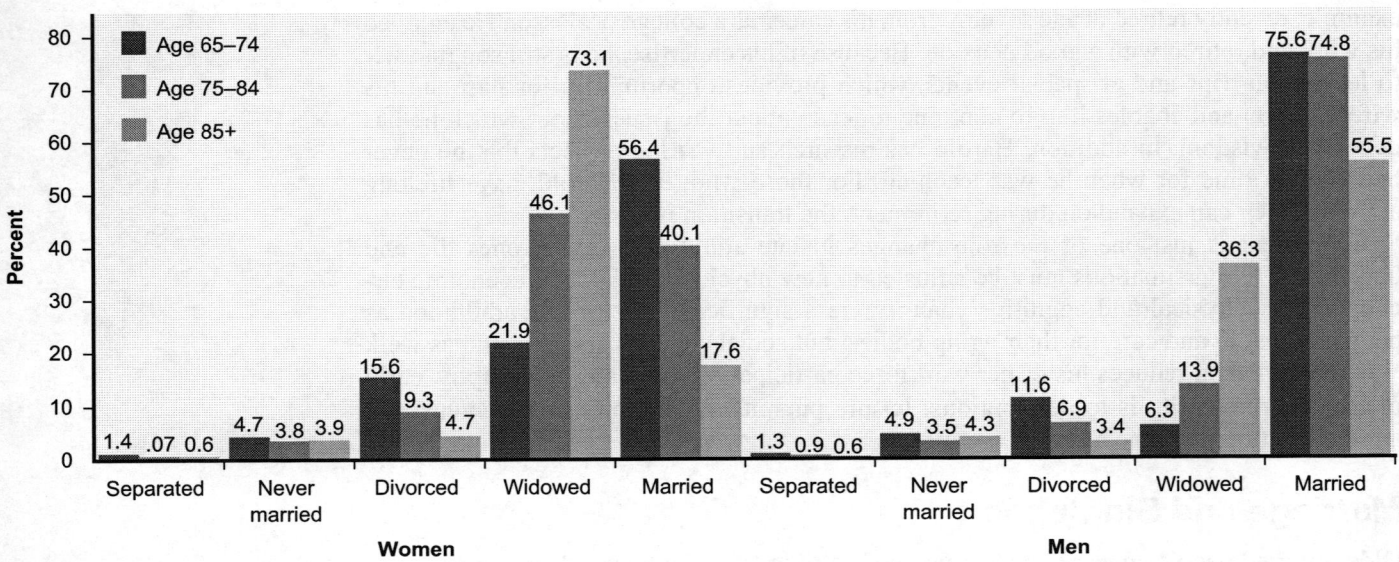

FIGURE 17.1
Marital Status of Older Adults by Age and Sex, United States, 2012

Women over age sixty-five are much more likely to be widowed than men, especially in the oldest cohorts.
Source: U.S. Bureau of the Census (2012).

than other common caregivers (Pinquart & Sorensen, 2011), which is of particular concern because high rates of burden and depression among caregivers is linked with decrements in quality of care provided (Smith et al., 2011). The rate of married older adults entering institutions such as nursing homes is about half that of never-married or previously married adults, even when the disability is extreme and the age very old (Stoller, 1992). Coping with disease and disability can increase closeness as the older partners express their love and gratitude by caring for each other (Ade-Ridder & Kaplan, 1993). The caregiving role is not limited to older spouses. Chronic illness and disability may strike in middle or even early adulthood, but it is more common in late life. Caregivers may receive satisfaction from working to maintain a high quality of life for their spouses, which seems to be dependent on the gender of the caregiver (women) and limited to caregiving tasks (Freedman, Cornman, & Carr, 2014). However, caregivers face burdens as well.

Psychosocial Aspects of Chronic Illness

As we discussed in Chapter 16, chronic illness generally begins with a crisis, such as a heart attack or a cancer diagnosis, and from that moment on the patient and his or her family face a changed future. Plans for daily living must be altered to include medical treatment and to revise exercise patterns, dietary practices, travel plans, and, perhaps, work and household chores. To adjust to chronic illness, patients must somehow integrate

Older married people are generally happier, healthier, and live longer than widowed and divorced people of the same age. Marriage provides emotional intimacy, sexual intimacy, interdependence, and belongingness as older couples face retirement, possible relocation, and declining health.
Source: WitthayaP/Shutterstock.com.

their illness into their lives. For example, a heart disease patient who continues to smoke or fails to exercise is a poor patient. Most patients cope with chronic illness in ways similar to how they cope with other stressful life events. Although most experience denial, anxiety, and depression as they adjust to the demands of the illness, many ultimately adopt active coping strategies, such as modifying health and lifestyle habits to reduce subsequent risk. In contrast to avoidant strategies, such as denial, active coping generally has been found to accompany good adjustment. In controlled studies, Ronald Grossarth-Maticek and Hans Eysenck (1996) have demonstrated that psychotherapy, behavioral therapy, group therapy, and self-instruction aimed at modifying vulnerable personality traits can effectively improve and prolong life for chronically ill individuals.

However, chronic illness can lead to interpersonal strains for patients and their families. Pity or social rejection may follow diagnosis, especially if negative stereotypes are associated with the illness, such as in the case of cancer (Rounds & Zevon, 1993). Cancer, Alzheimer's disease, and other chronic illnesses may cause fear and aversion in family and friends at the same time they call forth desire to provide social support. This ambivalence can lead to tense relationships and ineffective social support (Birditt & Wardjiman, 2012; Varni et al., 1992). Spouses, lovers, and other intimates may themselves be depressed by their loved one's condition (Stein et al., 1992).

Chronic illness also leads to positive outcomes. Patients report a greater ability to appreciate each day, to do things now rather than put them off, to put more effort into their relationships, to be more sensitive to others' feelings, and to be more compassionate (Taylor, 1998). They also report feeling stronger and more self-assured. People offset the negative impact of their chronic diseases by rearranging their priorities and extracting meaning and benefit from their experiences (Schaefer & Moos, 1992). It seems these benefits might be related to individuals' self-efficacy regarding their illness and the coping techniques being used, with problem-focused coping being most beneficial (Kristofferzon, Lindqvist, & Nilsson, 2010).

Problems of Caregiving Spouses

Spousal caregivers are subject to emotional, social, economic, and physical strain. Emotional stress results from concern for the spouse's physical and mental well-being, as well as from the need to establish new patterns of roles and responsibilities within the relationship. Not only is the caregiver likely to need to do more, but he or she is likely to get less. One of the most frequent problems of spousal caregivers is missing the way the spouse "used to be" (Chappell, 1990). Psychological reactions to many chronic illnesses, such as heart disease, stroke, and cancer, lead to decreased sexual activity (Taylor, 1998), and as noted in Chapter 16, chronic illness and worrying about a spouse's illness are two of the most common reasons older adults cease sexual activity (Waite et al., 2009). The disability of a spouse, especially if it entails cognitive impairment, removes emotional and social support and limits the personal freedom of the caregiver. Healthy spouses may restrict social activities to provide care and companionship or because they feel guilty enjoying themselves while their partners cannot. When Hassan became disabled, Minnah needed to assume all household and financial management. She also felt bound to the house to tend to his physical needs. When Minnah finally hired a nurse's aide to bathe him and watch him while she went for a walk or to the market, Hassan became upset and scared the helper away. As a result, Minnah left the house infrequently, only when responsibilities demanded it, and felt embarrassed to invite people in. Although financial strain was only a small part of Minnah's troubles, it often contributes to the caregiver's burden as the medical expenditures shrink the shared economic resources. The cost of nursing home care, which can lead to impoverishment, adds to the caregiver's desire to keep the spouse at home. These stresses may be greater for recently married older couples who do not have a lifetime of shared experiences to draw on.

Gender and Caregiving

Gender has a significant impact on the caregiving role. Because wives generally outlive husbands, more women than men provide spousal care. Husbands also appear to

Though spouses serve as the first line of defense in coping with disease and disability, having help from a child or other relative can relieve some of the caregiving spouse's strain.
Source: wavebreakmedia/Shutterstock.com.

derive less satisfaction from caregiving (Freedman, Cornman, & Carr, 2014) and to be less tolerant of caregiving burdens because a higher percentage of married women are institutionalized, compared to married men, and married women spend more days in nursing homes than married men do (Bengtson et al., 1996; Freedman, 1993; Stoller, 1992). Eleanor Stoller and Stephen Cutler (1992) found gender differences in husbands' and wives' responses to their spouses' need for help among frail older adults. Still, more than one-third of spousal caregivers in the United States are men (National Alliance for Caregiving, 2009). There is evidence that men and women experience spousal caregiving differently, which may reflect the traditional division of labor within marriages among the now old. The way a relationship is organized before the disease or disability strikes influences how the couple copes with it (Grand et al., 1995). The quality of the relationship before caregiving also seems to be more important for men than women. Relationship quality was not a factor in female caregivers' desire to institutionalize their loved one, though it was for men (Winter, Gitlin, & Dennis, 2011). A lifetime of traditional gender roles leads wives more than husbands to be responsive to the physical and emotional needs of their spouses. Baila Miller (1987) found that caregiving wives paid closer attention to interpersonal situations and focused on the changes in the marital relationship, whereas caregiving husbands emphasized structural activities. Wives, for example, would devise explanations for hiring a helper when they went out so that their impaired spouses would not feel demeaned by having a "baby sitter."

Susan Allen (1994) found that wives provided about twice the hours of care husbands provided. However, it does not seem that men and women utilize support differently (Pinquart & Sorensen, 2006). In terms of roles, the incapacity of a husband means a wife must assume his responsibilities, and vice versa. Because wives already do most of the household tasks, the change is greater for caregiving husbands than for caregiving wives. Illness is the factor that causes the traditional division of labor to change in older adult households (Brubaker & Kinsel, 1988). Caregiving husbands are more likely to experience decline in social contacts because wives generally are the kinkeepers. On the other hand, men are acknowledged more for their caregiving because it is less expected of them. Although some studies show that men experience less caregiving stress, more studies report no difference between the genders (Miller, 1990; Pinquart & Sorensen, 2006; Stoller, 1992).

The impact of race/ethnicity is hard to determine because most of the available research has focused on white couples. In a large-scale study of caregivers of the aged, African Americans of both genders perceived higher rewards from caregiving than did whites because of the greater comfort they found in religion and prayer (Picot et al., 1997). However, minority caregivers are more likely to be an adult child or other family member than for white caregivers (Gelman, Tompkins, & Ihara, 2014). In a study of older inner-city African Americans and whites, Colleen Johnson and Barbara Barer (1990) found that African Americans had more active support networks than did whites, and recent research has demonstrated that one important social network outside the family is their church (Gallant, Spitze, & Grove, 2010). Among Latino older adults, similar caregiving patterns emerge in which the primary support is the family, which is likely linked to the high prevalence of intergenerational families (Gallant et al., 2010; Gelman et al., 2014). However, it is likely that SES, extent of acculturation, length of time in this country, and circumstances in which the group or individuals arrived in this country are all factors that affect caregiving for minority older adults (Gelman et al., 2014; Lockery, 1991).

Widowhood

While illness of a spouse requires significant adjustment, the death of a spouse causes disruption to self-identity and relationships with others. The impact of widowhood depends on the age and social class of the widow. Older widows adjust better than younger widows. Becoming a widow late in life is "on time," whereas at younger ages, it puts a woman into minority status. Young widows are stigmatized and allowed to play the widow role for only a short time before they are considered single again (Lopata, 1973, 1984). However, for many people who have been widowed, life satisfaction may be impaired for a long period of time (Yap, Anusic, & Lucas, 2012). For most lower-SES women, widowhood means poverty, which results in lower social participation outside the home (Atchley, 1997), which may negatively impact subsequent well-being (Pinquart & Sorensen, 2000). Many studies have demonstrated that pre-widowhood social support is a predictor of well-being during widowhood; however, it seems that those with high life-satisfaction ratings before the loss of a spouse demonstrated significant decreases in life satisfaction during widowhood, regardless of social support (Anusic & Lucas, 2013).

Although far more women are widowed than men, in 2012, about 11 percent of males over age sixty-five were widowers (U.S. Census Bureau, 2012). Men often see their wives as part of themselves and rely more exclusively on them as confidants. This may be one reason why men report higher levels of depressive symptoms than women following the death of a spouse (Bennett, Smith, & Hughes, 2005). Because there are so many more older widows, women are likely to have friends with whom they can share activities, which can buffer the negative effects of widowhood (Subramanian, Elwert, & Christakis, 2008). A less established widowers' community is available for men to take part in. Widowers tend to be more cut off from families than do widows, although no apparent difference exists in the extent of older widows' and widowers' loneliness. Widows seem to expect more, get more, and want even more social interactions, whereas widowers expect little, get what they expect, and are satisfied (Atchley, 1997). Widowers generally have better financial resources than widows and greater opportunities for remarriage because there are more older women and because society is more accepting of marriages between older men and younger women than the reverse, for reasons presented in the "Focusing On" feature.

What effect does widowhood have on physical and mental health? Short-term problems and long-term recovery are common in both areas of health. Whereas the risks of negative health consequences are high immediately following the death of a spouse, the extended effects on health due to widowhood are minimal (Bradsher, 1997). In fact, mortality risk is substantially higher right after the death of a spouse and remains inflated up to ten years later, even after accounting for shared environment, a phenomenon known as the widowhood effect (Boyle, Feng, & Raab, 2011). Additionally, lower life satisfaction following widowhood can be long lasting—up to eight years among those who did not remarry (Lucas et al., 2003). Depressive symptoms associated with loneliness and grief are high during the first year of bereavement but return to pre-widowhood levels after that, although young-old widows (ages sixty-five to seventy-four) are particularly at risk of developing chronic depressive symptoms (Mendes de Leon et al., 1994). Widowhood does not increase risk of earlier mortality (McCrae & Costa, 1993).

However, widowhood has a significant impact on economic and social well-being. It is associated with a reduction in family income for both genders, but especially for women. The primary link between widowhood and depression among women is financial strain

Focusing On...

The Double Standard of Sexuality in Late Adulthood

Ageism makes being "older" difficult. We live in a youth-oriented culture. Youth is used as a metaphor for energy, mobility, appetite, and well-being. This makes us all aware of our age long before we approach old age. Men and women alike are made defensive about gaining years and losing the prestige of youth, but the glorifying of youth affects women much more harshly than it does men.

Women in our society are judged primarily on their physical attractiveness, whereas men are judged mainly on their accomplishments (Wilcox, 1997). Because the contemporary standard of female beauty is a slender and youthful one, as women age, they naturally move away from it; youthful appearance is something one outgrows, rather than develops, over the adult years. Accomplishments, in contrast, are achieved over time. As a man ages, he is more likely to be successful at work and gain money, power, and status. All of these things make him more attractive than he was before, despite his graying hair, wrinkles, and other signs of physical aging. Moreover, benefits such as wisdom among women are seen as not adding much to the perceived "women's intuition," whereas men's wisdom is perceived as valued (Saucier, 2004). The result is the *double standard of aging,* whereby getting older enhances a man's value but diminishes that of a woman. There are, of course, men who are not successful and distinguished, and many of them suffer profoundly in their middle and later years. All women, however, learn that they should hide their age by staying "thirty-nine" indefinitely and doing all they can to remain young looking. This is not a growth-producing or affirming process and puts women at a distinct disadvantage when looking for new sexual partners in their later years. Moreover, there is evidence that the beauty standards to which women are held negatively affects women's relationships with one another and, subsequently, their socioemotional well-being, particularly during late life (Gosselink et al., 2008).

Women are judged to be older than men of the same age. When asked to categorize photographs of men and women into adolescent, young, middle-aged, older adult, and aged adult, both men and women assigned the women to older age groups (Kogan, 1989). Wrinkles and gray hair, early signs of aging, are considered ugly on a woman. "Why doesn't she do something with herself?" people ask, meaning dye her hair, use cosmetics, or get a facelift. On men, however, wrinkles are considered "character" lines, and gray hair is considered distinguished.

Women are considered sexually unattractive at a much earlier age than men are. African American women are an exception. While young women can expect to attract men about their own age, middle-aged women have to settle for men who are considerably older. Older men, on the other hand, can date and marry women much younger than themselves. Films abound in which a young actress plays the romantic partner of an aging actor, and moviegoers find the pair quite believable. Imagine the age difference was reversed and the woman was twenty or so years older than the leading man. How would audiences react? In real life, older men often choose partners who are or look younger than themselves. We are used to this arrangement. We are not used to couples in which the woman is much older than the man, as was the case with Demi Moore and Ashton Kutcher, and research shows that people judge such marriages to be less likely to survive

(Umberson et al., 1992). For older adult widows, moving in with a family member provides a transition out of poverty (Dodge, 1995). For both recent widows and widowers, remarriage has been found to be one of the most important determinants of physical and economic well-being (Moorman, Booth, & Fingerman, 2006; Smith et al., 1991). In a longitudinal study designed to assess the effects of widowhood on health, ability to function, and well-being, Robert McCrae and Paul Costa (1988) found strong signs of psychological resilience from bereavement and the burdens of widowhood.

Dating and Remarriage

One type of resiliency is to form new intimate relationships in later life. Socially active older adults are more likely to meet people who are potential dating partners. Health, driving ability, organizational memberships, and contact with siblings are all positively associated with dating (Bulcroft & Bulcroft, 1991). Compared to younger daters, older ones are not experimenting with marital roles (because they have been married before) and place more emphasis on companionship. They date to select a marriage partner and

> **Focusing On...**
>
> **The Double Standard of Sexuality in Late Adulthood** *continued*
>
> (Cowan, 1984). Older men marrying younger women leaves older women (and older-looking women) with few available partners.
>
> Not only are older women seen as sexually unattractive; they are often thought of as not being sexual. Ageism includes the stereotype that old people are not interested in sex, that they are not sexual beings, and that sex is the province of the young, although half of older adults are sexually active and more would be if they had partners (Cutler, 1998). Because women are considered "old" sooner, they often fall subject to this prejudice when they are still in their middle years. Whereas people are likely to admire an old man's interest in sex, they see an old woman's sexual interest as being in bad taste. This is an extension of the sexual double standard, in operation during adolescence and early adulthood, that condones promiscuity in men but condemns it in women. Stereotypes and social expectations can affect how we think about our sexual feelings and make us feel guilty, ashamed, or inappropriate. Women more than men are subject to negative sanctions against sexual expression, and this situation worsens as they get older.
>
> While the double standard of sexuality is apparent in late adulthood, gender stereotypes are changing, and hopefully, these changes will diminish it. As women have moved into the public arena in full force, their accomplishments have been mounting and receiving more recognition. As women devote their time and energies to being competent, strong, and accomplished instead of just nice, pretty, and graceful, we can hope that female desirability and self-confidence will be based on more than physical attributes, just as men's are. Sara Wilcox (1997) found some evidence for this. She measured body satisfaction of women and men, ages twenty through eighty, and found that women who were *exercisers* (regularly exercised no fewer than three times a week for at least twenty continuous minutes) increased in body satisfaction with age, whereas women who were *nonexercisers* decreased in body satisfaction with age. Men did not change in body satisfaction, whether they were exercisers or nonexercisers. Change is occurring, but slowly. Mid- and late-life women continue to be underrepresented on television (Saucier, 2004), and media outlets often focus on physical features of aging among female political candidates, such as Hillary Clinton, rather than focusing on the content of messages (Carlin & Winfrey, 2009). As women allow their bodies to age more naturally, without hair dyes and facelifts, they will gain self-respect, and perhaps that will lead to new standards of attractiveness for older women. Many older women are indeed quite beautiful, but not in eighteen- or twenty-five-year-old ways.
>
> **What Do You Think?**
>
> 1. In what ways does the stereotype of sexuality in late adulthood contrast with the reality? (Look back at the section Changes in Sexual Functioning in Chapter 16 if you need to refresh your memory.)
> 2. Think of sexual stereotypes that people hold about adults your own age. Are they similar or different for men and women? Would you conclude that a *single* or a *double standard* of sexuality exists for your age group?

to maintain social activity. Older women report that dating increases their self-esteem because it makes them feel desirable. Older men report that dating gives them an avenue for self-disclosure. Both men and women expect the functions of dating relationships to include friend, confidant, lover, and, to a lesser extent, caregiver (McElhaney, 1992).

Marriage in later life is not uncommon, but it is likely to be remarriage. The major reasons for remarriage are companionship and economic resources. Older mate selection follows the same principle of similarity that we noted among younger adults (see the discussion of mate selection in Chapter 13), and this pattern of men seeking physical attractiveness and men seeking status stands even among older adults utilizing online dating sites (Alterovitz & Mendelsohn, 2009). Older adults choose mates who have similar backgrounds and interests; often they choose partners whom they have known for a long time. While older adults meet dating partners in public places or through friends, new spouses are more often known from the past (McElhaney, 1992). However, more recently, online dating has become a boon to older adults seeking a companion—between 3 and 6 percent of those in mid- or late-life had utilized online dating sites in 2005, which was before the advent of sites specifically developed for mid- and late-life adults (McWilliams & Barrett, 2014). Successful late-life remarriage is more likely when there has been a long prior friendship, when family and friends approve, when the pooled financial resources of the new couple are adequate, and when the marriage partners are personally adaptable (Brubaker, 1985). Some older couples choose to live together without remarriage. Charlie, for example, became a widower shortly after he retired at age sixty-five. Just as he and his wife were preparing to travel and enjoy their leisure years, she discovered she had cancer and died in less than a year. Ruth had lost her husband a few years earlier. The two couples had been close friends for many years. Now Charlie and Ruth are together, although they have chosen not to remarry. They travel together and are accepted by each other's children, but they like things the way they are. However, it is important to note that it is less likely that older cohabitating adults will provide caregiving to their partner, but if they do, that care is equivalent to that of a married caregiver (Noel-Miller, 2001).

Older Lesbians and Gay Men

While most older adults are married and living with a spouse, an estimated 10 percent are lesbian women and gay men (Quam & Whitford, 1992). Long-term relationships are much more frequent among gay men and lesbians than is commonly assumed, as we discussed in Chapter 13. Based on his own research as well as a review of the literature, Douglass Kimmel (1992) found that "when matched on age and background, lesbian, gay, and heterosexual couples do not differ on standard measures of relationship quality or satisfaction" (p. 38). Older lesbian and gay couples, like older heterosexual couples, tend to be more content in their relationships than their middle-aged counterparts (Berger, 1982). The one place differences have been found are in that gay and lesbian couples often negotiate and share household chores (Peoplau & Fingerhut, 2007).

Although until June 2015, same-sex marriage was only legal in seventeen states, many had ceremonies to celebrate their partnerships and, in several municipalities, received "marriage" benefits, such as health insurance and bereavement leave (Kimmel, 1992). While having partial recognition in these ways did provide a sense of stability to relationships and, in some circumstances, has been related to higher life and relationship satisfaction, particularly when there is an informal ceremony (Fingerhut & Maisel, 2010), research conducted more recently has demonstrated the benefits of formalized marriage. Many same-sex couples note that marriage makes the relationship more "real" both to those in the relationship and to the public

Long-term relationships are much more frequent among gay men and lesbians than is commonly assumed. Older lesbian and gay couples, like heterosexual couples, tend to be more content in their relationships than middle-aged couples.
Source: Belushi/Shutterstock.com.

(Lannutti, 2009), and many couples shift the way they dealt with investments (Fingerhut & Maisel, 2010). Additionally, the legal bonds of marriage serve to stabilize the relationship by increasing relationship capital and making it more difficult to dissolve the relationship (Fingerhut & Maisel, 2010). Among gay men, having a domestic partner or legally recognized same-sex spouse appears to buffer the negative impact of discrimination and aging on mental health, with married couples benefitting the most (Wight et al., 2012).

In a survey of eighty gay men and lesbians ages fifty to seventy-three, respondents' areas of concerns were primarily the same as those for most aging adults: loneliness, health, and income (Quam & Whitford, 1992). They had additional concerns about being rejected by adult children (58.7 percent reported having children) and grandchildren when they "came out" to their families. Older gay men and lesbians are a diverse population. Some are in a couple, and some are not. Some are "out of the closet," and some are not. Some have been out for years, and others are just coming out. Some have supportive connections with their families, and some do not. Some have children and grandchildren, and some have neither. Aging occurs within the context of these diverse life circumstances. In addition, older gay men and lesbians have lived most of their lives in a society that has been actively hostile and oppressive toward homosexuality. Discrimination and stigma have profoundly affected their aging experience (Fullmer, 1995).

Older gay and lesbian adults also report worries about discrimination in health care, employment, housing, and long-term care, which compounded their anxieties about aging. As a result, many gay, lesbian, bisexual, and transgender (LGBT) older adults have spent the majority of their lives hiding their identities (Butler, 2008). Though same-sex marriage is now legal nationwide, it is important to remember that, as of 2015, only twenty-two states had laws against discrimination based on sexual orientation. Additionally, it seems that fears about discrimination, particularly in the realm of health care, are not unfounded. Surveys of nurse assistants have demonstrated levels of homophobia that, though lower than historical levels, are still moderate and, thus, troubling (Dickey, 2012; Johnson et al., 2005). Moreover, the majority of nursing home social service directors and nurse assistants reported receiving no training in working with LGBT patients; nor had they received training in homophobia (Bell et al., 2010; Dickey, 2012). As a result, many LGBT older adults rely on fictive kin, or very close friends who act as a de facto family, for informal caregiving (Muraco & Fredriksen-Goldsen, 2011).

Support groups for older gay men and lesbians can address some of the special needs of this late-life population, which differ in some ways from those of other older adults and in some ways from those of younger gay men and lesbians (Slusher et al., 1996). Many older gay men and lesbians have been private about their sexual orientation and have not been part of the gay community. Some have no family supports because they never married, have no children, and may be unconnected to other members of their biological families. Support groups typically meet to socialize, share a meal, and discuss issues of concern. They also provide formal settings that can act as families to celebrate holidays and birthdays. Having a formalized social support or having an LGB social network has been shown to ameliorate the stress and loneliness often reported by LGB older adults (Kuyper & Fokkema, 2010).

Older gay men and lesbians have special concerns because, until recently, their partners have not been recognized by law. They need to know legal strategies for protecting property and wishes at death. They need options for home care that enable them to avoid homophobic nursing homes and retirement housing. They need help with fear of disclosing their gay identity, lack of freedom because of being "in the closet," and difficulty experiencing being gay as a "positive thing" (Slusher et al., 1996). Obviously, group organizers and leaders need to be sensitive to gay issues.

Ever-Single Older Adults

In 2012, only 5 percent of older adults in the United States had never married, as Figure 17.1 shows. Because ever-single adults have been on their own their entire lives, they have learned to cope with aloneness and to be autonomous and self-reliant, qualities that facilitate successful aging. The family life of ever-single older people revolves around

> **What Do You Think?**
>
> How would you advise a young-old person to prepare for later stages of adulthood? Would your advice differ for a person in a couple or for a single person? Would it differ for a man or a woman?

parents, siblings, nieces and nephews, and friends (Newton & Keith, 1997). Olga, for example, chose not to marry because she was blind, which she believed would prevent the marriage that was proposed from having enough privacy. She lived with her ever-single sister and mother for almost all of her adult life. By the time her mother died, two other sisters had become widows and moved back "home." She survived all three sisters and, in her seventies, moved in with a fourth sister and her husband. Although never married, she was never isolated and had many close family relationships.

Overall, those who are ever-single report less loneliness and strain than those who are either widowed or divorced, which is likely because those who never marry, in many cases, have chosen to never marry (Pudrovska, Schieman, & Carr, 2006). Robert Atchley (1997) found that social contact of ever-single women depended on SES. Middle-class ever-single older teachers had about the same level of social interaction married older teachers did, but ever-single older telephone operators had much lower social interaction than married telephone operators. However, those who are ever-single tend to have higher incomes and higher levels of educational attainment than their married or previously married counterparts, suggesting that they do not lack social contact (Pudrovska, Schieman, & Carr, 2006).

Relationships with Family and Friends

Relationships with family and friends are important at all stages of life. Social support has been shown to affect mental health, ability to cope with stressful events, health, and mortality from infancy to late life (Antonucci, 1997). It is a direct parallel to attachment, a concept we introduced in our discussion of infancy in Chapter 5. Secure relationships have lifelong importance; family and friend relationships among older adults emerge from the early social relationships between mothers and infants (Feeney & Noller, 1996; Hazen & Shaver, 1990; Troll, 1994). Primary attachments to parents persist throughout life. Bonds formed later to siblings, spouses, children, and grandchildren are also powerful.

The importance and structure of relationships with family and friends throughout life can be best understood using Laura Carstensen's socioemotional selectivity theory (SST), a continuity theory that states that, throughout life, we try to maximize benefits and minimize risks in our relationships (Carstensen, 1992). Across adulthood, interactions with acquaintances and friends decline in frequency, while interactions and emotional closeness increase with relatives and close friends, so that in late life, most of our social convoy, described next, consists of those who are close to us (Carstensen, 1992). As a result, the interactions we have become less negative and more positive (English & Carstensen, 2014).

social convoy The term used to describe the lifelong social network of family and friend relationships that develop over the life course and provide social support from infancy through late life.

The term **social convoy** is used to describe the dynamic concept of lifelong social networks. Figure 17.2 shows two examples of social convoys. The convoy model of social relations emphasizes, first, that some relations are more important than others; spouses, parents, and children are more important than other relatives, friends, and coworkers, which is in line with the SST theory described earlier. Second, relationships develop over time. The mother-infant relationship grows and develops as both child and mother grow and change, but stability and continuity exist in the relationship as well. Third, social relations are influenced by characteristics of the individual such as age, gender, ethnicity, marital status, and situational characteristics (for example, employment status). Toni Antonucci (1991) used data from a study of relationships among mature adults (age fifty or older) to provide evidence for the life course continuity of attachment and social support. Her data were both cross-sectional (ages fifty to ninety-eight) and longitudinal because she recontacted as many respondents as she could (404) four years later. She found that respondents had an easy time categorizing their social relations into three

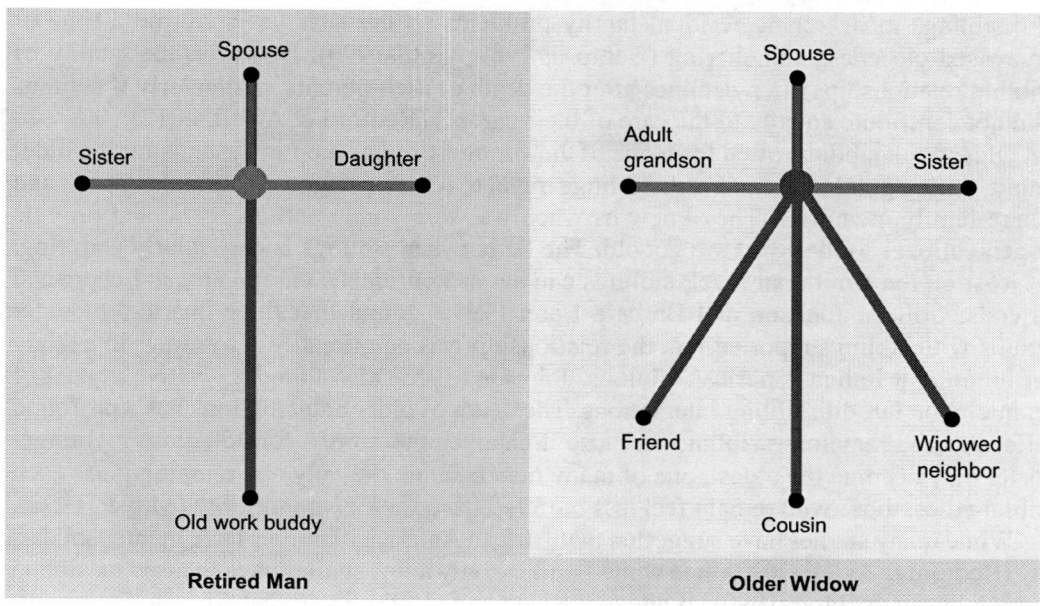

FIGURE 17.2
Examples of Social Convoys

As these two social convoys of an older adult man and woman show, members of convoys fall into three levels of closeness.

levels of closeness and that these categories stayed stable over the four-year interval. She found no gender differences in network composition—both men and women had more women in their network—and no age differences in the number of people who provided support. Older people were more likely to have network members who were older and had been in their network longer. They were less likely to live within an hour of the members of their network or to see them as often as younger people saw their network members. While no difference was found in how many people they received support from, they provided support for fewer network members than younger adults did. Antonucci also found that early social support had a positive influence on well-being, even in the presence of negative life events.

The most important relationships are with spouses, parents, and children, as we discussed earlier in this chapter and in Chapter 15 when we considered relationships during middle adulthood. For the young-old, the issues of aging parents and young adult children are the same as those for middle-aged adults facing the same family stage issues. Remember that the boundary between middle and late adulthood in not clear; family stage usually is more relevant than age. For the old-old and very old, the issues surrounding being cared for by middle-aged children become relevant. We looked at this from the perspective of middle-aged children in Chapter 15 and will address it again from the late-life parent's perspective when we consider the "problems of living" later in the chapter. Here, we focus on late-life relationships with siblings, grandchildren, great-grandchildren, friends, and fictive kin.

Siblings

When relatives outside of the inner circle of spouse, parents, and children are considered, the sibling relationship appears to be the strongest bond for those who have a surviving sibling (Johnson & Barer, 1990). After being very important in the child and adolescent years, relationships with siblings often go underground during early adulthood, when energy is devoted to establishing independent lives and families of one's own. As we discussed in Chapter 15, middle-aged siblings often focus on one another again for the first time when their aging parents need care. Siblings who may have had little involvement with one another find themselves in more frequent contact as they cooperate around arrangements for their parents' care. While tensions from earlier years are likely to affect families that come together in this way, most siblings work to keep their mutual rivalries and grudges from interfering with parental care, and many are able to get to know one another better and defuse petty issues from childhood (Moyer, 1992). This often enables the siblings to overcome residual family problems so the later years can be a time of increased closeness and sharing (Bedford, 1989; Gold 1990). However, the quality of sibling relationships often declines after the death of their parents, particularly if siblings did not contribute equally to the care of their parents (Bedford & Avioli, 2012).

Older adult siblings often form one of the strongest social support systems for the older adult, during good times and bad. Siblings travel together, provide emotional support, and share family memories. They knew us when we were young and energetic and provide a generational solidarity as we get old. The tie between siblings is particularly enduring, at least on the emotional level; siblings can act as confidants, caregivers, and cherished friends. Colleen Johnson and Barbara Barer (1990) found that three-quarters of older adults with siblings reported that the relationship was emotionally rewarding. In a study of immigrant Italian American siblings, Johnson (1985) also found a positive impact of ethnicity on late-life sibling interactions. The death of older adult siblings has a profound effect on the remaining siblings because it changes the family constellation: a younger sister may become the oldest, one of many may become the only one remaining. As each sibling dies, those who remain feel less buffered from their own mortality (Moyer, 1992).

While many studies have suggested that African American families have greater solidarity (Bedfore & Avioli, 2012) than white families, only a few studies have focused on sibling ties (Johnson & Barer, 1990). White and Riedmann (1992) found that African Americans, Mexican Americans, and whites were no different in the degree to which they viewed their siblings as a source of support, while Asian Americans had more faith in their sibling networks. In a comparison of suburban African American and white late-life sibling pairs, Deborah Gold (1990) found that African Americans tended to report more positive attitudes toward their siblings and to show greater interest in providing support for them than did whites. In analyzing the descriptions of eighty-nine white and sixty-four African American sibling pairs, Gold coded for mention of closeness, envy, resentment, instrumental support, emotional support, acceptance/approval, psychological involvement, and contact. Although an overwhelming majority of the sibling relationships were categorized as intimate, congenial, or loyal (95 percent African American and 78 percent white), a substantially greater percentage of the white relationships were categorized as apathetic or hostile (22 versus 4.5 percent). The concepts of envy and resentment were used far less frequently by African Americans than by whites to describe their sibling relations, but only among gender combinations that included men (male-male and male-female pairs). Similarly, more recent research has demonstrated that the most common reasons siblings stay in touch is out of obligation or for social support and liking (Myers, 2011).

In a large, national survey of adults with at least one full sibling who had left the parental home, Lynn White and Agnes Riedmann (1992) found that gender is also important to sibling relationships. This may well be because of the gender differences in kinkeeping skills that we discussed in Chapter 15. The presence of any living sister was associated with large increases in sibling contact, and this effect doubled for female respondents. Sister-sister ties were the strongest and brother-brother ties the weakest. Sisters are more likely to receive advice from siblings, and brothers are more likely to provide physical assistance to their siblings (Bedford & Avioli, 2012). In a survey of more than five hundred people over age fifty-five who had one or more siblings, Ingrid Connidis and Lori Campbell (1995) found that women and respondents with sisters, the ever-single, and the childless tended to have particularly active sibling ties. A majority of respondents said they would turn to their siblings for help if they needed. In fact, childless siblings, in general, provide both advice and assistance in child rearing well into their late life (Bedford & Avioli, 2012).

The importance of siblings in later life shows that the extended family rather than the nuclear family can serve as a source of social support. Siblings have a lifelong bond that can be rekindled or refined in late adulthood. Among inner-city African Americans, Johnson and Barer (1990) found that relationships with nieces and nephews often persisted after the deaths of their siblings. More distant relatives, such as cousins, may also become close friends. Only children, siblings who cannot reconcile their resentment or estrangement, and those whose siblings live very far away must look to other family members or friends as family.

Adult Grandchildren

Given the changing patterns of mortality that we saw in Chapter 16, more grandchildren know their grandparents not only as children but as adults, and more older people function as grandparents (and, in many cases, great-grandparents). Because grandparenthood usually begins in middle adulthood, we began our discussion in Chapter 15. Once again, the problems and pleasures of being a grandparent to young grandchildren do not differ for people who are already in late adulthood when they become grandparents. Stage of life is more important than age. In this section, we focus on the relationships of older grandparents and their adult grandchildren. Do grandchildren grow away from their grandparents as they grow up, or do they form more voluntary relationships with them? What characteristics of grandparent and grandchild lead to continuing association?

Continuing Connection

Research points to a continuation of the bond between grandparents and grandchildren that, as we saw in Chapter 15, begins early in the grandchildren's lives. Grandparents continue to interact with adult grandchildren, which can be a continued source of generativity (Hebblethwaite & Norris, 2011). Even when their parents divorce, adult grandchildren continue to see their grandparents on their own (Cooney & Smith, 1996). In fact, having a good relationship with a grandparent can ameliorate risk for depression among children living in a single-parent home (Ruiz & Silverstein, 2007). Karen Roberto and Johanna Stroes (1995) distributed questionnaires to 142 college students. Eighty-nine percent had living grandparents and 25 percent had both sets of grandparents still living. On average, the grandchildren interacted with their grandparents once a month or less. The researchers found that adult grandchildren, both grandsons and granddaughters, did more activities with their grandmothers than with their grandfathers, particularly participating in brief visits, attending family gatherings, talking over important issues, and helping with chores. Grandchildren reported being more influenced by their grandmothers than their grandfathers in religious beliefs, sexual beliefs, family ideals, educational beliefs, moral beliefs, and personal identity issues. There was no difference in the degree to which their grandmothers and grandfathers influenced their political beliefs and work ethics. Grandchildren rated their relationships with their grandmothers to be stronger than their relationships with their grandfathers. They believed their grandmothers understood them better, and vice versa; communication was better with their grandmothers; and they shared more similar life views with their grandmothers. No differences were found in grandchildren's appraisals of their relationships with maternal and paternal grandparents. The college students reported that enjoyment in being with their grandparents was a strong motivation for maintaining a relationship with them. In a separate study, when respondents were asked to identify the grandparent with whom they were emotionally closest, 75 percent mentioned a grandmother. This reflects the fact that many had only a grandmother living, in addition to a preference for the grandmother when the grandfather was also alive (Hodgson, 1995).

Although the degree of association between these adult children and their grandparents varied, overall it was "remarkably high." Contact was more frequent for younger than older grandchildren, for those living within an hour's drive than those living farther away, for those who felt emotionally close to their grandparent than those who did not, and for those who had frequent contact with their parents than those who had infrequent contact. Seventy percent of the grandchildren rated their relationship with their closer grandparent as "close" or "quite close." In addition to grandmothers being chosen as closer more frequently than grandfathers, maternal grandparents were chosen more frequently than paternal ones. Another important element was whether the grandchild had lived with the grandparent at some point in his or her life. If the grandparent had acted as a surrogate parent for the grandchild, the attachment was strong and permanent. While closeness often began early in life, many in the sample reported their relationships had become closer over time. As adults, the grandchildren appreciated their grandparents more and wanted their own children to know the grandparents as their great-grandparents. In addition, a personal crisis or increasing need on the part of the aging grandparent had brought them together.

Cultural Variation

Adult grandchildren assist their grandparents in a variety of ways that foster the grandparents' well-being (Piercy, 1998). Adult grandchildren are increasingly providing instrumental care to their grandparents (Blanton, 2013) and, subsequently, may face the unique challenge of also caring for their own parents and children, and frequently need additional assistance (Boquet et al., 2011). The degree to which this assistance is emotional or instrumental depends on the cultural attitudes of the particular ethnic group. Nieli Langer (1995) found that middle-class Jewish older adults had few expectations of material support from grandchildren. Their relationships with their adult grandchildren were based on reciprocity of meaningful emotional support. In contrast, the active role of grandparent in African American and Hispanic life is thought to be critical (Facio, 1997; Ralston, 1997; Yee, 1992). As we saw in Chapter 15, African American grandmothers take in grandchildren at a much higher rate than do white grandmothers, and thus develop strong emotional bonds with at least some of their grandchildren that continue when the grandchildren are adults. Among older inner-city African Americans, Johnson and Barer (1990) found that some had so many grandchildren that they could not keep track of them all; only grandchildren who were bound by ties of affection were counted. More than half of the respondents reported they had at least one grandchild who provided them with emotional support. While African American families often have a great many grandchildren, they are not the only families that do. Authors Robert and Michele Hoffnung were, respectively, the twelfth and fourteenth of their maternal grandmother's twenty grandchildren. While we saw this grandmother fairly often, it was usually in the company of many other aunts, uncles, and cousins. Although warm, there was nothing distinctive about our bond with her. We were part of an undifferentiated group of grandchildren.

Great-Grandchildren

Because we are living longer, it is more likely now than ever before that individuals will be alive to interact with their great-grandchildren. Similar to our experiences with our grandchildren, great-grandchildren provide a source of generativity to great-grandparents (Doka & Mertz, 1988). However, great-grandparents tend to be slightly less invested in their great-grandchildren than their grandchildren (Drew & Silverstein, 2004), perhaps due to the exponential increase in number of people from one generation to another or other life circumstances, even though the role both of grandparent and great-grandparent are linked with well-being of each generation. Overall, great-grandparents report that their role gives them a sense of longevity and that their contribution to their families will live beyond them (Doka & Mertz, 1988).

Friends

While interactions with family are crucial at times of crisis, studies show that interaction with friends is more important to everyday well-being in later life (Hatch & Bulcroft, 1992). Having friends is prevalent in middle age and later life; 85 to 93 percent of middle-aged and older people report they have close friends (Atchley, 1997). Individuals without close friends are more likely to be men, older, and working class. Of all types of support, friends most often provide emotional intimacy and companionship (Connidis & Davies, 1990). Larry Mullins and Mary Mushel (1992) found that among older persons, having friends was associated with not being lonely, whereas the presence or absence of spouse or children did not affect level of loneliness. Unlike family ties, which remain fairly consistent through old age, contact with friends can be subject to more variation. Health or economic problems, geographic distance, retirement, or change of neighborhood may make interaction difficult, and many late-life friendships end due to illness, moving, or death (Blieszner & Roberto, 2012). Minnah, for example, had many good friends in her neighborhood. When Hassan became ill, Minnah and Hassan sold their home and relocated to an apartment near a middle-aged niece and nephew. Minnah found it difficult to make new friends in her new neighborhood because she could not get out and would not invite people in due to Hassan's invalid behavior. She remained in phone contact with her old friends, but missed their companionship very much.

Does gender affect friendship in later life? The few consistent findings are that older women have more gender-homogeneous friendship networks than older men and are more likely to be involved in supportive relationships. Even in late life, women report that closeness, self-disclosure, and intimacy were the most important traits in a friendship, whereas the duration and frequency of contact in a relationship were more important factors for men (Blieszner & Roberto, 2012). Older men and women tend to have equally age-homogeneous friendship networks (Adams, 1997). However, the findings are generally inconsistent, with some studies showing no differences and others showing some. Believing that some of the inconsistency in previous findings was related to the importance of life circumstances, such as marital status and retirement status, Laurie Hatch and Kris Bulcroft (1992) used a longitudinal design to investigate gender differences in friendship contacts in ever-single, widowed, and divorced African American and white women and men. They found that widowed women had more frequent contacts with friends than did all other gender and marital groups. They also found declines in the frequency of contact with friends over time, with the declines greatest among formerly married men.

Fictive Kin

Often members of the social convoy become so important that the relationship between kin and friends becomes blurred. Parents' best friends often are treated like aunts and uncles while children are young and assume some of the attendant responsibilities. This family closeness can persist into adulthood. One mechanism for formalizing such relationships is through godparentage. Likewise, some relatives are so close in affection and interests that they become best friends. The merging of voluntary and obligatory relations sometimes produces **fictive kin**, or, as we referred to these relationships when discussing ever-single adults, *constructed relationships*. Among the Herero of Botswana, fictive kin relationships are common and provide flexibility in "family" caregiving for older adults (Keith et al., 1994). Fictive kin are particularly prevalent

fictive kin Constructed relationships, such as foster child, god-parent, or very close friendships, that merge voluntary and obligatory relations take on the significance of biologically related kin.

The emotional intimacy and companionship that these older friends provide each other is important to their everyday well-being. Men tend to have larger friendship networks with whom they engage frequently, whereas women place greater importance on friendship and engage in more intimate relationships.
Source: beeboys/Shutterstock.com.

in the African American kinship system, in which foster parents or foster children, for example, often are considered equivalent to relatives by blood or marriage (Chatters et al., 1994). As noted earlier in this chapter, gay and lesbian older adults are also highly reliant on fictive kin for social support and often caregiving as well (Muraco & Fredriksen-Goldsen, 2011). Sometimes fictive kin result from formal relationships; for example, a nanny may always hold the kinship title of *granny* in a child's life. Among older adults, a homemaking/companion may visit several times a week, share the same cultural background, and become an intimate companion thought of as a "daughter," "granddaughter," or "pal." Although fictive kin sometimes are accepted as though they were family members, they are not expected to fulfill the responsibilities of kin (Cicirelli, 1994). This is particularly significant to older adults as they consider their prospects for caregiving, as we saw in our discussion of ever-single adults.

Childlessness

Perhaps because of the ability of people to create fictive kin, as well as the importance of friends in late life, studies indicate that being without children does not have a negative impact on well-being in later life. Because none of the studies separate child free by choice, childless by circumstance, and childless due to death, *childless* refers here to all of these situations. However, rates of childlessness have doubled over the previous four decades, demonstrating the importance of understanding the impact of being childless in late life (Umberton, Pudrovska, & Reczek, 2010). In a study of confidant and companion networks, Ingrid Connidis and Lorraine Davies (1990) found that childless women tend to develop ties with friends as both companions and confidants to a greater extent than older adults who are parents. Unmarried childless women are very socially active, whereas childless men rely heavily on their wives for social support (Wenger et al., 2007), which explains why childless unmarried men experience high levels of depression and loneliness (Umberton et al., 2010). Siblings are a more primary component of their confidant network than for older parents, especially for a childless woman who is single or widowed. Childless men place greater emphasis on friends as companions as well, but turn to relatives for confidants. Among childless women, friends and siblings are especially important as confidants, while among childless men, siblings are less important in this role than other relatives. Living parents or children occupy the center stage in most adults' lives; when that inner circle is reduced, siblings become a more important part of adults' social support networks (White & Riedmann, 1992).

Internet and Social Media Use

Though the perception is that the Internet is used almost exclusively by the young, those in midlife and late life represent the most rapidly growing segment of the online population (Madden, 2010), with upward of 38 percent of those age sixty-five and older having an online presence (Maab, 2011). Though those in midlife and late life use the Internet primarily for email, news, and search engines, between 2009 and 2010, the number of those age sixty-five and older utilizing forms of social media like Facebook or LinkedIn doubled (Maab, 2011; Madden, 2010). Those in late life who use social media are more likely to rate highly on personality measures of openness to new experiences (Correa, Hinsley, & de Zuniga, 2010), and are likely to have joined a site at the encouragement of someone from their past trying to reconnect (Madden, 2010). Older adults who are highly engaged with their online community report lower levels of perceived stress (Wright, 2000). Considering both the exploding prevalence of social media use among older adults and the importance of social support during late life, additional research investigating the impact on social, psychological, and physical health outcomes is needed.

Problems of Living: The Housing Continuum

Aging in place—not moving to a nursing home—has become the ideal for both gerontologists and older people themselves. From the perspective of gerontologists, too many

> **What Do You Think?**
>
> Based on what you have read about relationships in late adulthood in this chapter, what family relationships do you imagine will be important to you in your old age? Why? In what ways does thinking about this issue make you want to change the way you relate to your kin? How do you think your use of social media might impact your well-being as you age? How might your use of technology make your late life different from older adults now?

older people enter nursing homes when they could and should have remained in their own households (Callahan, 1992). From the perspective of older adults, they prefer to grow older where they have been younger (Kinsella & Phillips, 2005). They feel comfortable and familiar with their surroundings and have developed informal support networks nearby. Older adults are likely to relinquish their own households only when they have limited economic resources and become frail or widowed. This is true for apartment dwellers as well as homeowners. Fully 95 percent of older people live in the community (outside of institutions), and only 13 percent live in households headed by relatives other than their spouses (Lipman, Lubell, & Salomon, 2012; Pynoos & Golant, 1996). Women are more likely than men to live with relatives other than their spouse or with nonrelatives, likely because they outlive their male spouses (Federal Interagency Forum on Aging-Related Statistics, 2012).

Economics plays a large part in the housing decisions of late adulthood, just as it does earlier in life. Eighty percent of all older persons live in their owner-occupied dwellings, 50 to 65 percent of which no longer have a mortgage (Lipman et al., 2012; U.S. Department of Health and Human Services, 2012). Even so, older adults are reported to spend between 30 percent (Federal Interagency Forum on Aging-Related Statistics, 2012) and 50 percent (Lipman et al., 2012) on housing expenditures, which is the most common housing problem. Older adults who own their homes can cash them in and buy entry into a home for the aged, provide housing for adult children, or continue to live on their own as independent couples or widows. Not surprisingly, large differences exist in the distribution of housing assets among older Americans. Women and racial/ethnic minorities have fewer assets. Homeownership rates are low among ever-single, separated, or divorced adults, among nonwhites and Hispanics, and among urban dwellers. African Americans, more than any other group, have been systematically limited as to choice of housing because of residential segregation. As older adults, they suffer from the multiple effects of low income, racial segregation, and ageism, which leave them with fewer housing choices (Skinner, 1992). Another option that homeowners are increasingly utilizing is the reverse mortgage, which permits homeowners to borrow against the equity in their home (Lipman et al., 2012). However, homeowners should be aware that being overly reliant on such funding could lead to loss of the house later in life (Lipman et al., 2012).

Although most adults prefer to continue living on their own, frailty brings the needs for housing modifications and special services. Stairs are likely to cause difficulty, for example, and shopping may become problematic. Limited finances may also push older adults to consider other housing alternatives. Older adults need a range of options, including independent living, semi-independent living, and group housing that provides long-term care. Table 17.3 lists housing types by the degree of independence they offer. As we discuss the various options, you will see that some facilities provide more than one level of independence and that similar housing types may provide older residents with different levels of control over their living conditions.

Most adults prefer to continue living independently for as long as they are able. Health and economics play a large part in the housing decisions of late life.

Source: Berna namoglu/Shutterstock.com.

Independent Living

Among older adults, renters tend to be older than homeowners, are more likely to be women, and are disproportionately Hispanic and African Americans. Renters are significantly more likely than homeowners to pay excessive housing costs, defined as more

Chapter 17 Psychosocial Development in Late Adulthood

TABLE 17.3 Levels of Housing by Degree of Independence

Notice that some types of housing, such as an independent household, provide the possibility of more than one degree of independence.

Type of Housing	Description	Examples
Independent Household:		
Fully independent	Household is self-contained and self-sufficient; residents do almost all of the cooking and household chores.	Private home, apartment, shared housing
Semi-independent	Household is self-contained but not self-sufficient; requires help with household chores.	Utilizes homemaker/companion, Meals on Wheels, adult foster care, or family caregiving
Group Housing:		
Congregate housing	Household may be self-contained but receives some communal services, typically meals.	Retirement community, assisted-living facility
Personal care home	Resident unit is neither self-contained nor self-sufficient.	Group home or adult care facility
Nursing home	Resident unit is neither self-contained nor self-sufficient; total care is provided, including personal and health care.	Skilled nursing facility

naturally occurring retirement community (NORC) A housing development that is not planned or designed for older people but attracts a majority of older residents because it provides a supportive social environment and access to services and facilities that can prolong independent living.

than 30 percent of before-tax income (Mutschler, 1992). Seventy-one percent of older adult renters spent more than 25 percent of their monthly income on housing expenses. Most renters live in apartments in buildings with more than five units (Lipman et al., 2012). This provides them with the advantage of neighbors close by, affording some security and some social support. Another advantage of renting is not being responsible for yard and building maintenance; the management may also provide, some routine inside maintenance, such as installing storm windows. On the other hand, renters may not be allowed to modify their homes to facilitate their functioning as they face increasing physical limitations.

Naturally occurring retirement communities (NORCs) are housing developments that are not planned or designed for older people but that attract a majority of residents age sixty or more. They provide a supportive social environment and access to services and facilities that can prolong independent living among older residents, and they are commonly used by middle-class older adults (Golant, 2011). They are unlike planned older adult housing in that they are not specifically designed for older adults, are age integrated, are often single buildings or small complexes of buildings, and go unnoticed as retirement communities (Hunt & Ross, 1990). NORCs are the most common form of alternative housing for older people in the United States; only 5 percent live in planned retirement communities, and 27 percent live in NORCs (AARP, 1990; Lipman et al., 2012). NORCs develop both by aging in place and by in-migration. These apartments are attractive to both younger and older people because of their location. Younger residents like being close to public transportation, work, and leisure activities, while older residents like being close to grocery stores, drugstores, banks, variety stores, department stores, post offices, doctors' offices, cleaners, libraries, churches and synagogues, and restaurants (Hunt & Ross, 1990). Safety of the neighborhood is of primary importance to both age groups. Older residents also value the proximity of friends and age peers. In fact, all of these characteristics are representative of NORCs that promote healthy aging (Masotti et al., 2006). Skinner (1992) points out that many older African American and other minority elders end up in inner-city neighborhoods that, although the buildings take on the identity of NORCs because of the density of the aging population, lack the services necessary to support the aging residents. Inner-city aging housing is likely to lack security and protection, convenience shopping, and transportation. This leaves older residents confined to their homes out of fear and frailty. These elders "are not only aging in place, they are stuck in place, prisoners in their own homes, without the ability to move to more appropriate housing" (p. 51). Safe neighborhoods, household modifications, and services and age peers available within walking distance facilitate independent living, but frailty or disability may render them insufficient.

Assisted Living

Assisted living, *or semi-independent living,* refers to some degree of help with daily living that enables older adults to age in place. Assisted living can include informal and formal supports. Informal supports are provided by relatives and friends; formal services include older adult housing, retirement communities, and community services. Informal supports, "the good efforts of their relatives and friends," enable at least three out of five marginally functioning elders to continue to reside in the community (Morris & Morris, 1992, p. 41). Retirement communities provide a range of options—from independent living to twenty-four-hour skilled nursing as the aging individual's needs change. Community services include senior centers, special transportation, Meals-on-Wheels, visiting nurses or health aides, homemaking companions, telephone reassurance, and adult day care. The wide variability in services is aimed to permit people to age in the same place, even if their health status should change. However, few facilities do this well, and the ones that do are often prohibitively expensive for many older adults (Whitbourne & Whitbourne, 2011). Services may be applicable to the needs of the elderly population in general or targeted to the specific needs of a subgroup of that population. The "Working With" interview, for instance, focuses on community services for Holocaust survivors.

assisted living Semi-independent living in which some degree of informal and formal help with daily living enables older adults to continue to live in the community.

Older adult or senior housing is federally subsidized and specially designed to meet the needs of old and disabled adults who are poor and have few other alternatives. Construction is barrier free so that walkers and wheelchairs can navigate easily and provides emergency alarm buttons and architectural features that can enhance functioning. There are common social areas, and residents usually have the opportunity to receive some supportive services, such as meals, transportation, homemaking, and nursing, depending on the facility. Despite the high visibility of older adult housing, however, only 3 to 5 percent of older Americans live in these projects (Kendig, 1990), and need is outpacing supply (Lipman et al., 2012).

Retirement communities are private, age-specific housing alternatives. Older people of means buy into nonprofit continuing care retirement communities before they are in need of care. The cost often amounts to a person or couple's life savings. The benefit is availability of a range of care options from congregate housing to long-term care for life as the individual's needs change. **Congregate housing** provides some communal services, at least a central kitchen and dining room. Amos and Barbara bought membership in a retirement community when both were seventy and in good health. Because they still needed to help their only daughter to manage her own life, they felt it was imperative to plan for their own caregiving. They sold their two homes and moved into an attractive, self-contained apartment in the retirement community. They made the choice to eat breakfasts and lunches in their own kitchen and dinners in the main dining room. If and when either needs more care, the community will provide increasing levels of assistance to long-term care. And if one of them needs institutionalization, this choice will enable them to continue to live together. Private retirement communities serve only a small percentage of older people, but recently have become more popular (Pynoos & Golent, 1996). Lower-SES older adults are more likely to rely on

congregate housing Housing that provides older adults with some communal services such as a central kitchen and dining room.

WORKING WITH Louise Staley, Community Worker

Helping Holocaust Survivors in Late Adulthood

As a caseworker for a private, nonprofit agency, Louise Staley makes home visits to community-living older Holocaust survivors. She assesses their needs, provides counseling, and helps them get the services necessary to age in place. Louise is in her late twenties, holds a bachelor's degree in gerontology, and had several years of social work experience before taking her current job.

Michele: *Who are your clients?*

Louise: They are all Holocaust survivors. The youngest are in their sixties; the oldest is 102. I would say 70 percent are women. All but two of the men are part of a couple in which I mostly work with the wife. My clients don't come to me; I go to them. A hospital or a friend calls the agency to refer the client. After my boss makes the initial call, I am assigned to the case. Then I call the client to introduce myself and set up the first visit.

Michele: *Do the clients pay the agency?*

Louise: No. The agency is funded by the United Jewish Federation, United Way, fund raisers, as well as donations from clients. The agency began in 1936 to help those escaping the Holocaust. When people would arrive in New York, the agency would help them find jobs, apartments, English-language lessons. The help was practical and didn't include a lot of counseling.

Michele: *Are your clients poor?*

Louise: No, the majority of my caseload is not poor, but agency-wide about 60 percent have money and 40 percent do not. Of my fifty cases, about five or six are poor. Before retirement they were homemakers, teachers, dressmakers, janitors, house cleaners. They may not have college education, but they have a decent amount of retirement money. The majority have pensions, some have inheritances, and all have savings. As Holocaust survivors, they are extremely good at saving. The negative part is that it is hard for them to spend when they need help. Even eight dollars an hour for a few hours of housekeeping help seems like a huge amount of money to them.

Hoarding is a big issue with this population because of their horrible experiences with scarcity. Two of my clients always used to meet me in the lobby; they refused to let me into their home. One finally let me in, and it was so cluttered I could barely walk. She saves everything.

Michele: *Are all of your clients Jewish?*

Louise: By birth, yes. Four have decided they are no longer Jewish, though they have not taken on another religion. All talk about how important being Jewish was to them before the Holocaust, but some are angry about their religion. Some are still very religious. Almost all are more trusting of Jews.

---

the community services discussed earlier as they age in place. Figure 17.3 shows that with increasing age, a greater proportion of older people who live alone use community services, and that use is more prevalent among the poor.

Long-Term Care

The term *long-term care* generally brings to mind nursing homes, which are stereotyped as the final destination of the very old. But **long-term care** is a much broader concept that refers to ongoing assistance to people with chronic illnesses and disabilities in a wide variety of settings. While some long-term care is *health care,* most of it is *personal care* and consists of help with everyday activities such as bathing, getting in and out of bed, using the toilet, grocery shopping, doing laundry and housework, and preparing meals. Most long-term care is provided by relatives and friends in the person's independent household. Only about 6 percent of older people live in institutions, including nursing homes, boarding homes, and psychiatric hospitals, although somewhere between 30 and 50 percent will spend a short time in a nursing home after an early discharge from the hospital (Atchley, 1997; Lipman et al., 2012; Whitbourne & Whitbourne, 2011).

Spouses, adult children, and other relatives are the major providers of personal care, as we have discussed, but paid help is also important. Robyn Stone, Gail Cafferata, and Judith Sangl (1987) found that the average caregiver spent four hours a day, seven days

long-term care Health care and personal care, such as bathing, shopping, and laundry, usually provided by friends and relatives but sometimes by nursing homes.

> **WORKING WITH** Louise Staley, Community Worker
>
> **Helping Holocaust Survivors in Late Adulthood** *continued*
>
> **Michele:** *Does it bother them that you aren't Jewish?*
>
> **Louise:** The first question they asked me is "Are you Jewish?" I tell them no, and then I work hard to win their trust. With two, I don't think I have succeeded yet. They let me come, but we haven't made significant progress. As Holocaust survivors, trust is a major issue, and many are understandably angry. This combination can be challenging to work with.
>
> **Michele:** *How is working with Holocaust survivors different from working with other older clients?*
>
> **Louise:** The circumstances of their lives are very different from the rest of the older adult population. They had a life-altering experience. They suffered major loss—something, someone, most likely a combination. Therefore, when they are looking toward their own death, they are also revisiting a death scenario they have been trying not to remember for fifty years. As a group, they dealt with their losses by denial—not thinking about them at all. This denial has been going on for fifty years. As clients they do not take well to counseling. Perhaps if they had had counseling when they first suffered their losses, it would have been different.
>
> To a Holocaust survivor, the idea of going to a place like a nursing home feels like being sent to the camp again. About twenty of my clients are camp survivors. Others had to leave their home and country and lost family members. The 102-year-old got out of Germany in her forties. She took a housekeeping job in England early enough to get her furniture out, too. But her family wouldn't budge, and she left them behind and feels guilty about that. She left everyone but one niece.
>
> **Michele:** *What services does your agency provide?*
>
> **Louise:** We try to help these survivors in a variety of ways. We identify services they need and help counsel them to accept them. During the winter we run what we call Kaffeehaus once a month, where they can come and socialize. We provide entertainment, coffee, tea, and Jewish cookies. We also have Passover seders and Hanukkah parties, so they will be able to celebrate Jewish holidays even if they are living alone.
>
> **What Do You Think?**
>
> 1. What role does religion play in the lives of these now older adult Holocaust survivors? In what ways is it positive? In what ways is it negative?
> 2. Why are formal caregiving services particularly important for this older adult population? Why is enabling them to age in place critical?

a week providing care for an aging relative. Many families combine informal caregiving with some formal services to enable the family to meet the heavy burden of providing personal care. Paid help seems to work best when it is supervised by family, because the people who need the care are vulnerable to abuse and exploitation by strangers. Late-life African Americans who experience functional declines are less likely to be institutionalized and more likely to rely on coresidence and informal caregiving than are whites (Gallant, Spitze, & Grove, 2010; Skinner, 1992). This is a joint result of the availability of social support systems in the African American community as well as poverty. Nursing homes are expensive, and those that participate in Medicaid often have long waiting lists. In addition, African American older parents value and expect more assistance from their children than do whites (Gallant, et al., 2010; Lee et al., 1998).

Adult day care, another formal service that can supplement family caregiving, can be especially helpful for people with Alzheimer's disease or other neurocognitive disorders, but care must be taken to ensure that *quality* care is provided (Zarit & Reamy, 2013). It is a community-based group program designed to meet the needs of adults with functional impairments. Within a safe, supervised environment, staff provide a comprehensive program of physical, social, cognitive, and functional activities to maximize remaining strengths and minimize deficits. Individuals participate on a planned basis, during specified hours, two to five days a week. This provides some relief and support to caregivers and enables them to continue car-

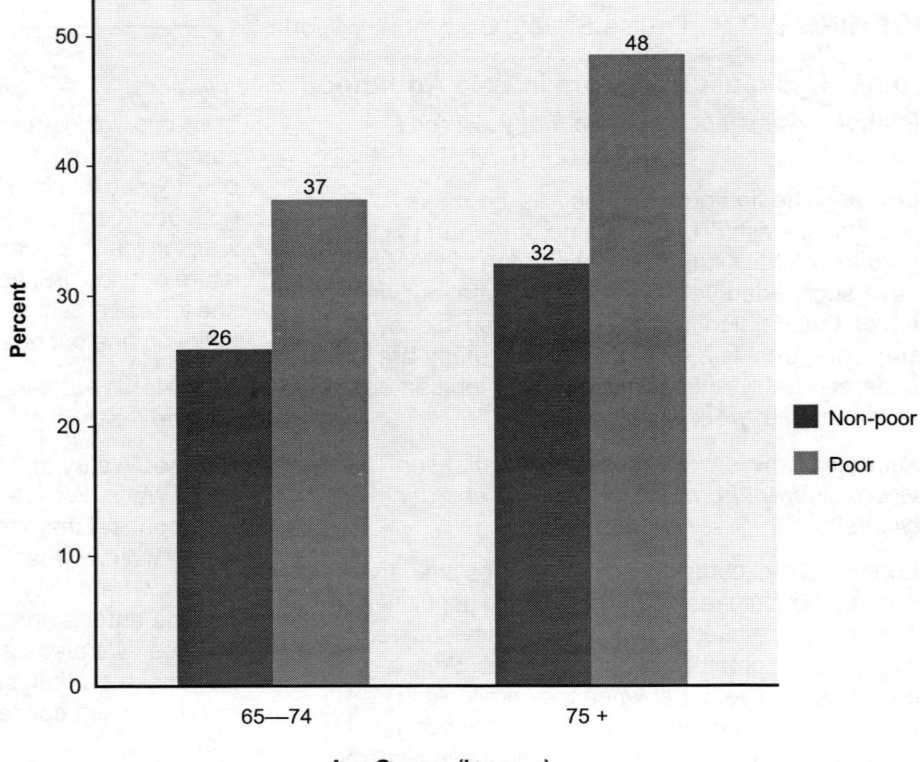

FIGURE 17.3
Proportion of People Age 65 and Older Who Live Alone and Use Community Services, by Age Group and Poverty Status, 1990

Older people who cannot afford private services are more likely to use community services.
Source: U.S. Senate Special Committee on Aging (1991).

ing for the impaired family member at home. Staff members also acquaint the caregivers with other community resources and provide them with emotional support (Engstrom et al., 1993).

Control over Living Conditions

It is not always possible for people to age in place. Their losses of function may be too great, or the dwelling may become inappropriate to their needs for safety and maneuverability. When they move, whether to the home of a family member or to group housing, the strong preference is for some space that they personally control. In a study of life satisfaction in a variety of older adult housing situations, Robert Vallerand, Brian O'Connor, and Marc Blais (1989) found that French-speaking Canadian residents of "high self-determination" nursing homes had levels of satisfaction comparable to those

The formal support of home health care enables this older couple to live semi-independently. Assisted living often includes informal help from family and friends, as well as formal services.
Source: Rob Marmion/Shutterstock.com.

of community-dwelling older adults and significantly higher than those of residents of "low self-determination" nursing homes. Table 17.4 presents the five criteria they used for self-determination. More recent research using the same model has demonstrated that when nursing home residents feel in control of their living conditions, they were much more likely to experience improvements in measures of depression, life satisfaction, and self-esteem over the following year (Philippe & Vallerand, 2008).

In a review of the literature, Judith Rodin (1986) found negative effects on the health of older people when personal control of their activities is restricted. For example, being forced to move has been associated with adverse health outcomes among older adults, such as more hospitalizations and nursing home admissions, greater incidence of stroke and angina pectoris, and poorer self-health assessment. When the older people were exposed to any control-enhancing experimental manipulation, such as choice of when or where to move or about aspects of their new living arrangements, little decline in health and psychological status was found.

Studies designed to encourage self-reliance among older adults in institutions such as convalescent and nursing homes showed that increasing responsibility among older adult residents led to increased alertness, more activity, and reports of feeling happier, in contrast to those who were encouraged to believe the staff would tend to their needs (Rodin, 1986). Enhanced control has also led to improvements in memory, satisfaction, and physical health in some studies. Rodin points out, however, that although "the strength of the relation between control and health increases with aging . . . there is more variability in perception and desire for control with advancing age, presumably because of the accumulation of different life experiences" (p. 1271). This means that most older people respond positively to the opportunities for control, but others prefer not to be responsible.

Choice, then, becomes one of the most important aspects of the housing continuum. It is wise for older people and their families to consider options and make housing choices in advance of health crises; yet a recent survey revealed that more than half of older people have done little or no planning for their future housing needs (AARP, 2012). This lack of planning is likely because 41 percent of mid- and late-life adults think they will maintain good health, 31 percent do not foresee any difficulty navigating their home during late life, and 35 percent believe that they will always be capable of driving (AARP, 2012). Looking into the possibilities for home remodeling or relocation to prolong independent living is best done in advance, as is learning about the opportunities for congregate housing in the geographic region most convenient to family and friends. As we have seen, Tom and Frances and Amos and Barbara made different choices at the same stage of life, but both couples chose before they experienced a crisis. Even when long-term care requires institutionalization, a nursing home should be chosen carefully, with an attempt to match the individual's need for control to the level of control available. While more than half of people over sixty-five will spend some time in a nursing home, it is not the

TABLE 17.4 Criteria for Self-Determination in Nursing Homes

Residents of "high self-determination" nursing homes had levels of satisfaction comparable to those of community-dwelling older adults and significantly higher than those of residents of "low self-determination" nursing homes.

1. How much choice do residents have regarding mealtimes?
2. To what extent is the nursing home staff responsible for residents' personal care?
3. How free are residents to decorate and arrange the furniture in their rooms?
4. Are the residents allowed to have or care for a pet?
5. To what degree does the staff encourage or discourage personal initiative?

Source: Based on Vallerand et al. (1989).

> **What Do You Think?**
>
> Consider one of your relatives who is in late adulthood. How suitable are his or her housing arrangements for aging in place? Consider the available housing alternatives. Role-play with a classmate how you might discuss the pros and cons of each alternative with your relative.

end of meaningful and enjoyable life. This becomes exquisitely clear in Tracy Kidder's (1993) description of the friendship and daily lives of two old men who met and became roommates in a nursing home. The nursing home Kidder studied has two levels of residency providing more or less control based on the resident's level of functioning. Despite increasing frailty, older adults continue to have interests that extend beyond their aging bodies. Even for individuals with neurocognitive disorders, a client-centered approach provides age-appropriate activities rather than treating them like children, promotes use of the cognitive abilities that remain intact, and encourages day-to-day decision making about clothing, food, and activities (Hofland, 1994; Zarit & Reamy, 2013). (See the "Working With" interview in Chapter 16 on page 604.)

Interests and Activities

We saw earlier in this chapter that many older adults continue to work, although most retire from their career jobs or reduce their hours if they are self-employed, especially after age seventy. How do they spend the hours freed from the constraints of employment? The answer depends to a large extent on the socioeconomic standing of the aging person. Those who have enjoyed high levels of education, occupational status, and income are likely to be in good health and to have resources that provide many options for activities, whereas those who have had low levels of education, occupation, and income likely have health limitations and fewer resources in their later years. Health acts as a threshold for leisure, and financial security plays a critical role in supporting various activities (Adams, Leibbrandt, & Moon, 2011; Cutler & Hendricks, 1990; Dorfman, 2013). Being in poor health and limiting social leisure pursuits is linked to low levels of subjective well-being (Simone & Haas, 2013). Poverty is a barrier to involvement in community activities, especially among people who formerly were middle class (Kelly, 1993). For low-income or ethnic/racial minority older adults who have never had secure regular employment, increased leisure may not be part of late adulthood because they need to continue earning.

Other factors influence the use of leisure time in late adulthood as well. Educational attainment and occupation influence the preference for activities. Although some individuals learn to dance or draw in late adulthood, there is evidence that developing **activity competence**, the skills and knowledge needed to take advantage of opportunities for activities, generally is established in earlier adult years. Those who are better educated therefore are better prepared to feel competent engaging in a variety of activities. Individuals with spouse, family, or friends tend to be more active in communal activities than those who are alone. Using an eight-year longitudinal method to study older adults (average age seventy-two at the start of the study), Frances Carp (1978/1979) found that type of living arrangement affected leisure activity patterns. People who moved to retirement communities or other congregate housing increased their activity levels, whereas those who remained in the community decreased their activity levels. Obviously self-selection was a factor: those who selected living situations with extensive activity programs must have desired such activities. As we saw in Chapter 15, gender affects choice of leisure activities: women are more likely to choose passive, social, and expressive activities, whereas men tend to choose active and less expressive activities and to join more organizations (Cutler & Hendricks, 1990). As a result of these many factors, the leisure pursuits of older people vary greatly.

activity competence The skills and knowledge necessary to take advantage of opportunities for leisure activities. Because it is generally established during earlier adult years, older adults who are better educated are more prepared to feel competent engaging in a variety of activities.

Past patterns of activity shape the way older adults use their time. When they retire, for example, most people continue to do the same activities they did before retirement, but at a different pace, in line with selection and optimization with compensation theory, discussed earlier in this chapter (Baltes & Baltes, 1990; Kelly, 1993). Activity patterns of middle age tend to persist into late adulthood, but gradually, as people become frail, the activity becomes constricted, which can have an impact on perceived well-being (Simone & Haas, 2013). In his nineties, Marcellus was tending a yard instead of a farm. Because of his interest in inventing things, he was able to continue tending the yard despite his frailty. Another old man might have eventually restricted his gardening even more—to tending flower boxes, for example. We discussed in Chapter 15 how older adults continue to work. Much of this chapter has indicated how their involvement with family continues. Here we examine older adults' involvement in community organizations, religion and spirituality, and the more solitary activity of contemplation.

Community Involvement

Community organizations include political parties, labor unions, veterans' groups, fraternal organizations, community service groups, professional organizations, religious institutions, parent-teacher organizations, neighborhood associations, and many other groups designed to achieve a purpose or pursue some shared interest. Midlife engagement in activities in which cognitive stimulation occurs has been linked to subsequent cognitive benefits up to twenty years later (Kareholt et al., 2011). People show considerable stability in their general levels of participation in community organizations from middle age until their sixties, when involvement gradually decreases (Cutler & Hendricks, 1990). Poor health, inadequate income, and problems with transportation all contribute to decreases in participation (Atchley, 1997). While membership in community organizations has been associated with well-being, it is impossible to separate the fact that members tend to have higher levels of health, income, and education—all of which are linked to well-being—than do nonmembers.

Volunteerism

Efforts have been made to involve older adults as volunteers to provide services for the community, enable older adults to pass on their knowledge to younger people, and provide the volunteers with meaningful activity (Chambré, 1993). The Foster Grandparent Program, Retired Senior Volunteer Program (RSVP), and Service Corps of Retired Executives (SCORE) are just three organizations formed especially for seniors. Volunteerism provides a continuing link with the community, as well as ways to substitute similar activities for the reduced work and family roles of later life (Chambré, 1993). Volunteerism is linked to higher quality of life, increased ratings of mental and physical health and well-being (McDonald et al., 2013), as well as with reduced mortality risk (Oun, Yeung, & Brown, 2013). According to the Administration on Aging, rates of volunteerism among older adults have been on the rise for the last several decades, and as of 2009, nearly 24 percent volunteer in some capacity. Looking only at formal organizations, however, greatly underestimates the amount of volunteering that older adults actually do because it does not include informal helping within the family and community.

If we broaden the definition of *volunteerism* to include providing informal service, almost all retired adults do volunteer work. In a study of retired Minnesota workers, Lucy Fischer, Daniel Mueller, and Philip Cooper (1991) found that nearly 60 percent of the older adults provided help for their families, most by caring for grandchildren. In fact, about 30 percent of preschool children with working mothers were cared for by their grandparents (U.S. Census Bureau, 2008). More than 40 percent provided help to their neighbors, usually in the form of transportation or visiting. In addition, 53 percent were doing organized volunteer work, mostly through their religious institutions. On average, these Minnesota adults were spending fourteen hours a month doing voluntary service. If we added caregiving to family members within the home, the percentages would likely be even higher. More recent research has demonstrated similar findings: women are likely to visit sick friends, help with housekeeping, and prepare meals for friends and neighbors, while men are likely to be running errands and driving friends and neighbors (Martinez et al., 2011). In a study of the help and support that older women provide to kin and friends, Sally Gallagher and Naomi Gerstel (1993) found that 96 percent of married women and 92 percent of widows had provided some type of help to at least one relative or friend in the previous month.

Older volunteers face some problems. First, talented older people sometimes find themselves assigned to menial work that is beneath their knowledge, experience, and dignity. This makes them feel undervalued. Second, volunteers are sometimes placed in positions without sufficient training. This puts them in the unfortunate position of feeling tested rather than feeling prepared and welcomed. Third, many older volunteers need additional income and would prefer paid part-time work. This has led the National Council of Senior Citizens to object to any program that recruits older people to do on a volunteer basis work for which younger people are paid. Fourth, people who are retired may be unwilling to commit to a rigid volunteer schedule that would limit their freedom to travel. Organizations need to find ways to encourage short-term contributions, such as to one-time events or recurring events. Fifth, transportation often is a problem for older volunteers. If it were provided, older adults who no longer feel comfortable driving would be able to volunteer their services.

Continuing Education

Another kind of community involvement is through Elderhostel programs. Begun in 1975, Elderhostel is a nationwide program in continuing higher education. It offers one-week summer programs that include a campus dorm room, cafeteria meals, college-level courses, and extracurricular activities at low cost. Participants are not expected to have prior knowledge of the subject matter and receive no grades. Elderhostel now has nearly two thousand educational sites in the United States, Canada, and 150 countries worldwide (Elderhostel, n.d.; Goggin, 1992). It has grown to include service programs, in which hostelers provide volunteer service to worthy causes around the world; performance programs, such as choral, instrumental, dance, and theater; and intergenerational programs that bring together hostelers and people under age twenty-five.

Michael Brady (1984) sampled 560 Elderhostel participants in twenty New England programs and found that the typical participant was sixty-eight years old, retired, married, and well educated. Only 12 percent had high school education or below, while 42 percent of the men and 24 percent of the women had graduate or professional degrees. More of the participants were women (67 percent) than men (33 percent), and more of the women (37 percent) than the men (9 percent) were widowed. Brady's participants completed two scales that measured their perceived academic benefit. Those persons with lower levels of education and lower annual incomes reported receiving more benefits from the Elderhostel programs than the more privileged participants. This may be because they were attending college for the first time and therefore derived more benefits from the noncognitive elements of college life, they actually learned more from the courses, or they were more willing to report having benefited. Huey Long and Dawn Zoller-Hodges (1995) found that Elderhostel programs had desirable personal and social outcomes for participants. The educational researchers assessed knowledge, attitudes, and behaviors following five Elderhostel programs. Participants grew in many ways, including cultural appreciation, self-appreciation, historical appreciation, social contact, travel, content learning, and general learning.

Lifelong learning takes place in many different settings. Many senior centers, community centers, and libraries offer topical or skill-based classes to older adults (Dorfman, 2013). Religious institutions often have classes to study their faith's literature as well (Merriam &

Houses of worship have been shown to be a very important institution for many older adults, and many note their religious faith as their most significant source of psychological support.
Source: bikeriderlondon/Shutterstock.com.

Kee, 2014). Additionally, many older adults take advantage of courses offered at local colleges and universities, all of which have been linked to maintenance of cognitive abilities, as well as well-being, for themselves and their communities (Merriam & Kee, 2014).

Religion and Spirituality

Churches or synagogues are the organizations to which older people most frequently belong. Membership in religious organizations is higher at older ages, especially after age seventy-five (Atchley, 1997; Hill, Burdette, & Idler, 2011). Church and synagogue attendance and membership in church-affiliated groups and fraternal organizations, as well as leadership positions in these organizations, all reflect greater involvement of people over age sixty-five than under (Koenig, 1995). As the "A Multicultural View" feature indicates, men often need more help than women to adjust to the loss of their spouses, and religious institutions provide support for widowers who are active members.

When attending formal services becomes too difficult as a result of declining health, disability, transportation problems, or relocation, many older adults compensate by increasing religious practices at home, such as reading the religious texts, listening to religious broadcasts, praying, or studying religion (Ainlay & Smith, 1984; Hill et al., 2011). Older people continue to feel an emotional attachment to the religious institution where they had been involved even when they have relocated and that institution is many miles away or when they are homebound and can no longer participate (Payne & McFadden, 1994). Involvement in religion has been linked to better mental health, physical health, and lower mortality risk (Hill et al., 2011). It seems that this relation between religious involvement and these benefits can be explained by the increased social support and the better health behaviors promoted by most religious institutions (Hill et al., 2011).

The Social Support of Religious Institutions

Religious institutions form an important source of social support among racial/ethnic minorities. For older Hispanics, the Catholic church has been shown to be the most important social institution in their communities, and their religious faith has been called their most significant source of psychological support (Gallant, Spitze, & Grove, 2010; Maldonado, 1995). Older African Americans look to their churches for both formal and informal support (Gallant et al., 2010; McFadden, 1996). Some African American churches create spiritual families and assign kin terms to their members, fostering

> ### A Multicultural View
>
> #### Men and Grief
>
> Grief is a natural and universal reaction to loss, but in the United States males and females express it differently. Although ethnicity and social class contribute to norms regarding the expression of grief, in our society gender has a large impact as well (Lister, 1991). In their study of 434 adult African Americans, Japanese Americans, Mexican Americans, and white Americans, Richard Kalish and David Reynolds (1981) found that men more often than women reported that they "never" thought of their own deaths, they would fight rather than accept their own deaths, they would try very hard to control their grief-related emotions in public, and grief should last three months or less. Men, especially Japanese American men, had attended more funerals than women in the prior year. Mexican American men were more accepting of crying than were other men.
>
> Men fare less well than women when their spouses die (Piazza & Charles, 2012). In a study of 350 widowed adults, Stephen Shuchter and Sidney Zisook (1993) found that compared to women, men showed less acceptance of the deaths of their spouses, became involved in romantic relationships sooner, expressed themselves less, and drank more, findings confirmed with meta-analyses (Stroebe, Schut, & Stroebe, 2007). Women felt a greater degree of helplessness and tended more to experience their dead spouses in a protective role. A greater proportion of women had an overall "good" or "excellent" adjustment to widowhood.
>
> While widows are at a somewhat higher risk for mortality than married women, widowers have an excessive mortality rate compared to married men and a rate typically higher than that of widows (M. S. Stroebe & Stroebe, 1993). In a study of older newly widowed men and women, Delores Gallagher-Thompson and her colleagues (1993) found that bereaved males faced a substantially higher risk of death, particularly within the first year of bereavement. Widowers also suffer greater health impairment compared to married men than widows compared to married women (W. Stroebe & Stroebe, 1993).
>
> Why do men adjust so relatively poorly after losing their spouses? Two explanations have been advanced. First, gender differences in adjustment, health, and mortality after widowhood have been attributed to the greater availability of social support to women than to men. Men are more likely to depend on their spouses for emotional support, nurturance, and connections to other social relationships with family and friends so that the loss of a partner results in a decrease of social supports for widowers but not for widows. Men have a difficult time assuming the kinkeeping and other social roles their wives have handled (Piazza & Charles, 2012). Camille Wortman and her colleagues (1993) found that widowhood was associated with significantly more strained relationships, particularly with children, for men but not for women. Loneliness and lack of social support are major problems in adapta-

the development of fictive kin. "Church mothers" are available as lay therapists and confidants to members of the church who have problems (Johnson & Barer, 1990).

Spirituality and Faith

Spiritual development appears to be age related but not age determined. Among members of more than five hundred Protestant congregations, individuals judged to have *mature faith* were likely to be older (Benson & Elkin, 1990). Mature faith is the final stage of James Fowler's (1991) faith-knowing system of growth and development of the spiritual domain (we discussed the development of faith in Chapter 12; see Table 12.5). The growth of faith, according to Fowler, is a universal process that is not necessarily religious in orientation; rather, it is an integral aspect of daily life that "serves to organize the totality of our lives and gives rise to our most comprehensive frames of meaning" (Fowler, 1986). Peter Benson and Carolyn Elkin (1990) conclude that "Maturity of faith is strongly linked to age, increasing with each successive decade, and is most likely to be found among those over 70" (p. 3).

Contemplation

Some of the activities that promote spiritual integration are solitary ones. Robert Butler (1975) has suggested that contemplation is a valuable use of time in late adulthood. Reminiscence and life review are two contemplative processes that are thought to serve special functions in late life. **Reminiscence** is the recall of past experiences and

reminiscence Recall of past experiences and events that occurs among people of all ages and promotes spiritual integration during late life.

> **A Multicultural View**
>
> **Men and Grief** *continued*
>
> tion to loss (Lopata, 1993). Widowed men who were active in church or synagogue were less depressed than those without this social connection, which reflects the importance of religious institutions in providing older adults with emotional as well as spiritual comfort. (Siegel & Kuykendall, 1990).
>
> Second, although men experience loss and grief, in American society their expression of grief is not always apparent. Bereaved individuals who are communicative with others about their thoughts and feelings are more likely to have a positive adjustment (Lund et al., 1993). Men are likely to report fewer symptoms and less affective distress than are women when their spouses die. Perhaps because of this, though widows have higher depression scores one year after the death of their spouses, widowers have higher depression scores two to four years later (Sanders, 1993). Women often respond more dramatically than men to the death of a child as well (Rubin, 1993).
>
> Although grief is expected of men following the death of a spouse or child, this is mediated by the cultural message that men should be stoic and controlled. Male socialization includes a sanction against the expression of feelings as well as an ideal of independent action (Lister, 1991). Taken together, these proscriptions on male behavior prepare men poorly for expressing grief. As a result, men tend to be instrumental, to "do something" after a death, rather than allow themselves to feel. Men tend to return to their usual activities sooner than women. Women are more likely to turn their feelings into social actions that do not deny the feelings, such as Mothers Against Drunk Driving and the movement to develop resources for AIDS babies and children. Men are also less likely to seek assistance, whereas women more often will turn to relatives, friends, or professionals for help with their grief. Men are much less interactional about their feelings and more likely to deny them or drown them in drink or drugs (Stroebe et al., 2007). However, it is important to note that different people grieve differently. Bonanno and colleagues described five separate patterns of grief in the 1.5 years following the loss of a spouse, demonstrating that there is no "right" way to grieve and that others should be mindful of this when interacting and possibly judging the bereaved (Bonanno et al., 2002).
>
> While individual men do express their grief and it is possible to imagine a culture in which men would be encouraged to do so, we have not found such a culture to describe. Perhaps some cultures exist and have not been studied, but the literature overwhelmingly indicates that men are encouraged to act and discouraged to express feelings. In anthropological studies of death rituals in diverse societies, "men say it is the women who feel the death most and it is they who do most of the crying and wailing" (Woodburn, 1982, p. 189), and "it is women who take on mourning for death" (Bloch, 1982, p. 215).

events, and occurs among people of all ages. Through it, individuals introspectively define themselves (Parker, 1995). Reminiscence has been associated with measures of life satisfaction and sense of well-being. Utilizing the Uses of Reminiscence scale shown in Table 17.5, Sharan Merriam (1993) compared African American and white men and women in their sixties, eighties, and one hundreds. She found no age differences in the uses of reminiscence among these three groups of older adults. She did find significant race and gender differences, though. African Americans more than whites used reminiscence to teach others about the past, lift their spirits, understand themselves better, tell of their accomplishments, combat loneliness, help them to accept changes in their lives, understand what life is all about, put their lives in order, and deal with knowing that life is finite. Men more than women used reminiscence to teach others about the past, tell of their accomplishments, make future plans, deal with a present problem, put their lives in order, cope with knowing that life is finite, and deal with unpleasant or troublesome memories. Those who reminisced more were less depressed and coped with health problems more effectively. Moreover, focused reminiscence on problem solving has been linked to decreased symptoms of anxiety, and focusing reminiscence away from bitterness can alleviate depressive symptoms among older adults (Korte et al., 2011).

Life review, according to Robert Butler (1975), is a universal inner experience of older people "characterized by the progressive return to consciousness of past experiences, in particular the resurgence of unresolved conflicts which can now be surveyed

life review A universal inner experience of older people that helps them evaluate their lives, resolve remaining conflicts, and make decisions about material and emotional legacies, according to Robert Butler. Life review promotes the resolution of Erikson's conflict of *integrity versus despair*.

TABLE 17.5 Uses of Reminiscence Scale

Reminiscence, the recall of past experiences and events, occurs among people of all ages and has been associated with measures of life satisfaction and sense of well-being.

People think about or talk about their past for many different reasons. Do you think about or talk about your past in order to:

	Never				Very Often
Relive a pleasant experience	1	2	3	4	5
Teach others about the past	1	2	3	4	5
Lift your spirits	1	2	3	4	5
Get relief from boredom	1	2	3	4	5
Entertain others	1	2	3	4	5
Understand yourself better	1	2	3	4	5
Cope with a loss	1	2	3	4	5
Tell of your accomplishments	1	2	3	4	5
Make future plans	1	2	3	4	5
Get over feeling lonesome	1	2	3	4	5
Help accept changes in your life	1	2	3	4	5
Understand what life is all about	1	2	3	4	5
Deal with a present problem	1	2	3	4	5
Put your life in order	1	2	3	4	5
Deal with knowing your life is finite	1	2	3	4	5
Help you to relax	1	2	3	4	5
Deal with unpleasant or troublesome memories	1	2	3	4	5

Source: Adapted from Merriam (1993).

and reintegrated" (p. 412). This evaluative process, an aspect of Erikson's developmental stage of integrity versus despair, enables old people to take stock of themselves and decide what they will do with the rest of their lives. It enables them to find new significance and meaning in their lives and to prepare for death. This preparation often includes decisions about the material and emotional legacies they wish to leave to others. Life review can lead to family reconciliation, which, as we saw in Chapter 15, may enable adult siblings to become friends as they arrange for care of aging parents. Life review may make the experience of social isolation one of pleasant solitude rather than loneliness.

Looking Back/Looking Forward

Let us look back once again to our lifespan themes presented in Chapter 1 and see how they apply to late adulthood. Because problems of living are most frequent among adults in their later years, we will use this topic as a focus as we revisit our themes.

> **What Do You Think?**
>
> For one week, keep a list of your daily contacts with people who are in late adulthood. You will probably have only limited contact if you are rarely off campus, but pair up with someone who commutes to broaden the possibilities. Where do you see older adults? What are they doing? What does your list reveal about their activities and interests? Do you recognize any ageist thoughts or behaviors you experienced?

- **Continuity within change**—Most people wish to age in place, preferring to continue living in their familiar homes and communities. A variety of factors, however, may make that difficult. Communities change and may no longer be safe. Functional disabilities, such as no longer being able to drive, may make the same community less desirable because it lacks adequate public transportation. An aging house may require too much work and money to keep up. The death of one's partner may make caring for a house alone too difficult or too expensive.

  Even before any of these changes occur, aging people sometimes look ahead to the prospect of frailty and needing care and decide to choose better locations for their later years. If they own a home that they can sell and have retirement funds, the options for housing located near adult children, in retirement communities, or in warmer climates may attract them. They exhibit continuity in wanting to extend as long as possible their years of independent living and satisfactory quality of life. They change by recognizing new circumstances and making new choices.

- **Lifelong growth**—Whether choosing to stay in place and modify the current residence, choosing a new one that better meets current needs, or moving to older adult housing or an adult child's home as the result of some unexpected change in fortune, older individuals and couples typically find opportunities for growth. Although not everyone adjusts easily, research amply demonstrates that older men and women are resilient in the fact of retirement, widowhood, and physical changes. If the new location enables more social participation, interaction with children and grandchildren, and access to libraries, museums, and elderhostels, it may well be cognitively stimulating and lead to the positive brain changes that come from environmental enrichment. Even quiet contemplation often produces growth in understanding, appreciation, and compassion.

- **Changing meanings and vantage points**—The social convoy of relationships established during infancy and maintained throughout the lifespan contributes to the quality of life in late adulthood. One motivation for aging in place is to stay close to friends and neighbors who have enriched daily life. But as friends age and die, the ties with adult children and grandchildren often take on new meanings. Aging parents move closer to the homes of their adult children and depend on them more for emotional and practical assistance. Both older parents and adult children must learn how to make this transition with mutual respect. We saw that parents who adopted an authoritative style and established patterns of listening to their children and to their children's opinions with caring concern and respect but without hierarchical pressure had better communication and relations with them when the children reached adolescence and early adulthood. The benefits of authoritative parenting continue well into late adulthood when the pattern of help flowing from parent to child needs to be reversed. The meaning of parenthood changes as parent and child reach different stages of development.

  Similar factors come into play between aging partners. A relationship started in early adulthood will need to undergo changes by the time it reaches late adulthood. As retirement changes daily life and as illness or disability alters what each partner can do, having a sharing, nonhierarchical relationship can make the transitions easier. It can also better prepare both partners for the possibility of widowhood, when the other will no longer be there to do gender-stereotyped tasks.

- **Developmental diversity**—Whether and when people become frail varies dramatically, which influences their ability to continue to live independently and age in place. Genetic makeup, social and economic circumstances, and lifelong health behaviors contribute to some people being active and spry in their very late adulthood while other people die or become disabled or disoriented much earlier. Late adulthood depends for its quality on all that has come before. Yet everyone lucky enough to live to be very old will face reduced sensory acuity and increasing frailty.

Gender matters in more pronounced ways during late adulthood than at other stages of adulthood. Women and men have different patterns of morbidity and mortality. In addition, currently older people had different work patterns, which have resulted in different economic circumstances in retirement. Most men have more pension provisions and more social security benefits because they have been the wage earners. Ever-single older women are more likely than married ones to have adequate pensions and social security because they have had work patterns most similar to men of their cohort. Because women live longer and have fewer economic resources, more women live to be very old and very poor. Housing choices are fewer for women without financial resources, and more of them end up in nursing homes. More women experience the death of their spouse and are alone when they look ahead and prepare for death, the final stage of life.

Chapter Summary

- **What is ageism?** Ageism is the stereotyping of and discrimination against people because they are aging or old, and is a part of contemporary American culture.
- **What is successful aging, and what contributes to it?** *Successful aging* refers to the maintenance of psychological adjustment and well-being across the full lifespan. It requires psychological resilience in the face of age-related stress. Longitudinal studies such as the Harvard Grant and Berkeley Older Generation studies show considerable evidence for continuity of psychological adjustment into late adulthood, as well as increased agreeableness and acceptance of the past as "something that had to be." These findings provide support for Erikson's eighth stage of life, integrity versus despair. Neither activity theory nor disengagement theory can account for successful aging. While remaining active has been associated with high life satisfaction, successfully aging individuals exhibit a range of activity levels based on their life experiences and personalities.
- **What factors influence how retirees adjust to their new life circumstances?** Retirement is not simply a work/stop-work decision; many individuals follow nontraditional retirement patterns. Health status and financial security affect satisfaction with retirement.
- **How does marital status affect well-being in late adulthood?** Older married people appear to be happier, be healthier, and live longer than widowed and divorced people of the same age. They rely on their spouses to provide care when coping with disease or frailty. Wives are spousal caregivers more often than husbands. They also tend to provide more hours of care, get less outside assistance, and experience considerable stress as a result. Widowhood causes a disruption to self-identity and relationships with others, but does not appear to have negative impacts on subsequent health, ability to function, or well-being.

Socially active unmarried older adults are more likely to meet potential dating partners. Successful remarriage is more likely when there has been a long prior friendship and the couple has social and financial resources. Older lesbian and gay couples have satisfactions in their relationships similar to those of heterosexual couples and concerns similar to those of most aging adults. They have additional concerns about discrimination in health care, housing, and long-term care because of their sexual preference. Ever-single adults learn to cope with aloneness and to be autonomous and self-reliant, qualities that facilitate successful aging. They develop a rich variety of supportive relationships.

- **Which relationships are significant in late life, and in what ways?** Starting in infancy, individuals develop social convoys of stable and continuous relationships that develop and change over time. The most important relationships are with spouses, parents, and children. Outside of this inner circle, siblings provide the strongest bond. They offer emotional support, share memories, and sometimes provide instrumental support as well. Adult grandchildren continue their bonds with their grandparents. They tend to be closer to grandmothers than to grandfathers and closer to grandparents they knew well as children.

Interaction with friends in later life is more important to well-being and more subject to variation than relationships with kin. Fictive kin are constructed relationships that blur the distinction between friends and family. They appear particularly important in the lives of ever-single adults and in the African American community. Childless older adults develop ties with friends and other relatives who provide them with a social network that sustains their well-being.

- **Why is choice in housing critical in old age?** Older adults generally prefer to age in place. This is generally easier for homeowners than renters, but in either case disease or frailty may require modification of the old home or a new housing alternative. *Independent living* refers to maintaining a household with little assistance. Older adults often choose naturally occurring retirement communities (NORCs), which provide a supportive social environment that can prolong independent living. Assisted living can occur in one's own home, in a retirement community, or in older adult housing. Informal services of relatives and friends, formal services, or a combination of both can provide assistance with activities of daily living that enable semi-independence. Long-term care can also be found in a variety of settings, such as a relative's home, a retirement community, or a nursing home. The level of self-determination in these settings is related to levels of satisfaction of the residents.

- **How do the interests and activities of late life show both continuity and change?** Though formal volunteering among the older is rather low, most older adults do volunteer when informal work is also considered. Membership in religious institutions is higher at older ages and declines more slowly than other community memberships. This is probably due to cohort effects, as well as to increased spirituality in late life. Reminiscence and life review are two contemplative activities that are associated with better adjustment among old adults.

Key Terms

activity competence (p. 642)
activity theory (p. 614)
ageism (p. 610)
assisted living (p. 637)
congregate housing (p. 637)

disengagement theory (p. 614)
fictive kin (p. 633)
integrity versus despair (p. 613)
life review (p. 647)
long-term care (p. 638)

naturally occurring retirement community (NORC) (p. 636)
reminiscence (p. 646)
social convoy (p. 628)
successful aging (p. 610)

Endings

PART 9

Chapter 18
Dying, Death, and Bereavement

Source: Photographee.eu/Shutterstock.

The final stage of life is death. Though most people die in late adulthood, at the end of a long life, this is not always the case. Because illness and death occur during all life stages, we have discussed aspects of death, loss, and bereavement while focusing on each stage of lifespan development. When death comes early in life, it is usually sudden and unexpected. During middle adulthood, chronic diseases make death more frequent. During late adulthood, death is expected.

Ways of coping with the death of a loved one also change over the lifespan. Children find it hard to grasp the finality of death and are less able to manage the loss of a significant person. Adults learn to cope with the loss of their parents and other loved ones and become increasingly aware of their own mortality. During late adulthood, grief and mourning become normative aspects of life. Concerns about care during terminal illness increase as well.

In Part Nine we explore death, loss, and bereavement with a focus on late adulthood. As you read this final section, keep in mind that life circumstances sometimes make these issues relevant at earlier stages too.

Dying, Death, and Bereavement

CHAPTER 18

Source: Alzbeta/Shutterstock.

Chapter Outline

Attitudes Toward Death
Facing One's Own Death
Caring for the Dying
Bereavement
Looking Back

Focusing Questions

- What are contemporary attitudes toward death, and how do they affect the treatment of the dying?
- Why are older adults likely to be more accepting of death than younger people?
- What choices are available for terminal care, and how do they differ?
- How does bereavement affect survivors, and what supports are available to help their recovery?

Betty entered the hospital on November 26, her seventieth birthday. She had been feeling very tired and finally decided to go for tests. The tests revealed widespread cancer; whether it had started in her colon or in her ovaries was unclear. The doctor surgically removed a large portion of her intestines and sent her home to enjoy what he said might be six good months. Betty returned to the home she shared with her husband Ricardo. A hospital bed was placed in the sunroom that for years had served as her home office. She had been an antique dealer and, although retired from her shop, until her hospitalization had continued to appraise and lecture on American antiques. Her office was filled with beautiful and familiar things. A round-the-clock nurse's aide tended to her personal care, and a licensed nurse visited daily to attend to her medications.

At home Betty was able to continue to be part of the family. From her bed she arranged for Christmas dinner. She and Ricardo had three adult children, one living in the same town, one an hour away, and the other a two-day drive away. They also had five grandchildren. At home the children were able to visit often, to help their father and talk to their mother about how much they would miss her. On January 14, Ricardo called the children to say that Mom was "really bad." The two children who lived close enough got there in time to spend the day with their mother. They left thinking Mom had pulled out, but that night she died in her sleep.

Betty's family arranged a day of viewing at a local funeral parlor. Friends and associates came to see her and then went to the family home to eat and pay condolences to Ricardo and the three adult children. After the viewing day, Betty was cremated and her ashes were scattered into the Pacific Ocean. Betty's daughter wrote an obituary and distributed it to all the papers in the towns where Betty had done business.

Because all humans die, Betty's death was in some ways a universal experience, but it was also particular to the contemporary American cultural tradition of which she and her family were a part. Specifically, Betty died in late adulthood of a degenerative disease. She received acute care in the hospital and terminal care in her home. She was prepared for viewing and was viewed at a professional funeral home, and then cremated. Compared to earlier times in the United States and to contemporary times in less developed countries, death is likely to be a late adult experience. Changing mortality rates mean most Americans will live past age seventy and die from **degenerative diseases**, such as cardiovascular disease and cancer, as we discussed in Chapter 16. This is in contrast to earlier times when **communicable diseases**, such as influenza, cholera, scarlet fever, measles, or smallpox, spread from person to person and killed large numbers of old and young people alike. Because degenerative diseases generally cause slower deaths than do communicable diseases, the dying process in twentieth-century America is more likely to be prolonged and painful. Although Betty died less than three months after she was officially diagnosed, her daughter believes Betty knew she was ill for some time but chose to be private about it.

Betty and her family made several choices. After Betty's surgery, they decided on home care rather than a nursing home. They decided on a viewing day rather than a funeral or memorial service after her death. They chose cremation rather than burial. While their choices are consistent with a recent trend toward swift and inexpensive disposal of the body, many different cultural and religious traditions lead to different choices as people try to find personally meaningful responses to death (Bryant, 2003; DeSpelder & Strickland, 1996). In this chapter we examine the various options available as we look at changing attitudes toward death, preparation for one's own death, caring for the dying, and bereavement.

degenerative diseases
Diseases that cause the slow, prolonged, and painful deaths typical of late adulthood, such as cardiovascular disease and cancer.

communicable diseases
Diseases that spread from person to person and formerly killed large numbers of old and young people alike, such as influenza, cholera, scarlet fever, measles, and smallpox.

Attitudes Toward Death

Social and technological changes in developed nations have made death less familiar in the twentieth century than ever before. While in 1900 more than half of reported deaths were among children age fourteen or younger, today fewer than 2 percent of deaths occur among this age group (U.S. Bureau of the Census, 1995, 2012). When infants died frequently, children commonly died of childhood diseases, and many women died giving birth, death was witnessed often by young and old alike. Today even an at-risk infant is kept in the hospital, where life-extending technologies increase its chances of survival. If the infant dies, it is in an institution away from siblings, parents, and other family. Seventy percent of contemporary deaths take place in hospitals, nursing homes, and other formal settings (Centers for Disease Control and Prevention, 2005). Death therefore has been removed from everyday life. Even when it is not, geographical mobility makes it likely that members of the extended family will not be present when their relatives die. The attitude conveyed by this separation is that death is or should be invisible. The cultural historian Philippe Ariès (1981) refers to this attitude toward death as *death denied*. Historically this is, according to Ariès, a totally new attitude toward death, one that makes death private rather than public, denies mourning, and includes funerary rites that erase signs of death. Coffins become caskets. Morticians beautify dead bodies so they look alive. Grief is expressed mostly in private, while community life goes on as if nothing had happened.

What is the impact of this attitude toward death? Most people feel uncomfortable around death. As we see in the Focusing On box on page 662, because of this discomfort we may send confusing messages about death to children, whose understanding of death already is vague. Not only are dying people usually placed in formal settings, but we are unlikely to visit them. We tell ourselves they would rather not be disturbed. We assign their care to specialists for whom contact with death has become routine and impersonal (Marshall & Levy, 1990). We leave the definition of *death* to medical science. As a result, the dying often experience a *social death* before their biological death, isolated in institutions away from family and friends and shunned by their medical caregivers as well (Kastenbaum, 1992b). Even in speaking we avoid the word *death*. People refer to it by euphemism; in polite conversation people *pass away,* are *called home,* or *go to heaven* rather than die. Caskets are likely to be closed so that people do not have to view death. If the casket is open, the deceased has been embalmed and made up to look alive. Children are likely to be kept away from funerals and burials, although they do best when they help to make the decision of whether to attend (Worden, 1996). Mourning rites and bereavement leave have become shorter in the United States and are shaped to the time constraints of the business world (Pratt, 1981). In fact, in the United States employers are not required to pay employees for time lost due to funerals or bereavement, nor is the loss of a loved one covered under the Family and Medical Leave Act, which provides up to twelve weeks of unpaid leave while protecting one's job for some extenuating life circumstances (U.S. Department of Labor, n.d.).

Partially in response to the lack of opportunities to learn about death and dying through direct observation, in the 1970s a movement to forge new meanings and patterns for handling dying and death emerged. The **death awareness movement** responded to the increasing number of very old people in American society, the prolongation of the dying process, the anxieties of the nuclear age, and the 1960s perspective that asserted the rights of the ignored and underprivileged, in this case the dying (DeSpelder & Strickland, 1996). Social issues of our time, such as abortion, AIDS, domestic and international terrorism, drug abuse, and alcoholism, also have pushed us to face death and dying (Doka, 2003; Feifel, 1990). The death awareness movement has led to the analysis of cultural messages about death. It has challenged the isolation of the dying and promoted the idea of *the good death,* in which the dying person is surrounded by family and friends with minimal technological interference. It has also led to the development of death education (Doka, 2003; Durlak & Riesenberg, 1991). As a result of the death awareness movement, most

death awareness movement A response to the increasing number of very old people in American society, the prolongation of the dying process, the anxieties of the nuclear age, the 1960s perspective that asserted the rights of the ignored and underprivileged (in this case the dying), and the AIDS epidemic. It has led to the analysis of cultural messages about death, increased sensitivity to the dying, and increased education about death.

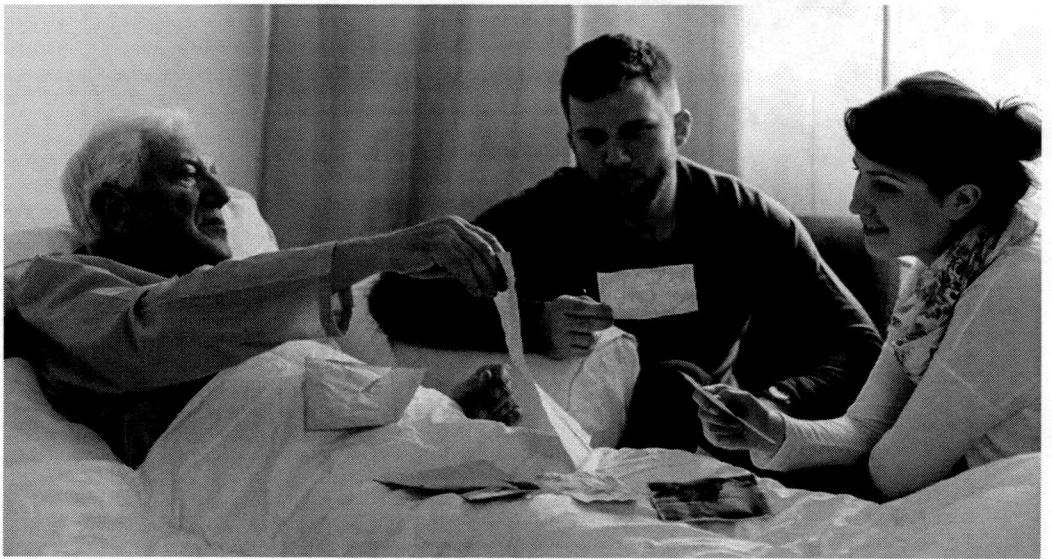

This man is dying a good death, surrounded by family and friends with minimal technological interference.
Source: Photographee.eu/ Shutterstock.

> **What Do You Think?**
>
> With several classmates, list as many euphemisms for *dying* that you can think of. Which ones were used in your families? What did they mean to you as a child when you heard them? What does the use of these euphemisms teach children about death?

colleges and universities and a few elementary and high schools now offer courses on death and dying; the topic permeates many books and chapters in textbooks such as the one you are now reading.

Facing One's Own Death

Death does not come only to the old, but it does come to older adults more frequently than children and younger adults. In 2007, 72 percent of deaths in the United States were among people age sixty-five and older (U.S. Bureau of the Census, 2012). There is evidence that as people age, recognition of their own mortality increases. Most people eighty-five or older expect to die within six years, whereas those ages sixty-five to seventy-four can expect to live fifteen to nineteen years (U.S. Bureau of the Census, 2012). Witnessing the death of peers, reaching the age of one's parent's death, and confronting health problems increase the salience of one's own mortality. Though these experiences are more typical of middle age, younger people are affected by these issues as well. Loss of a sibling during childhood forces a child to confront the fact that he or she also could die (Sood, Razdan, Weller, & Weller, 2006; Worden, 1996). The death of a twin can make even a very young survivor feel vulnerable, because the twin-twin relationship is so intimate and constant. Some African tribes believe the spirit of the dead twin must be preserved to ensure the wholeness of the surviving twin. In Nigeria, for example, surviving Yoruba twins wear a wooden image representing their dead twin around their neck or waist to give them company and to give the spirit of the dead twin a refuge. While this may sound unappealing to those of us unused to living with death, Western psychologists also find that it is best for the survivor that the loss and grief be recognized and that the deceased twin not be left unmentioned and unremembered (Bryan, 1995).

When an adolescent or a young adult dies, it is most likely a result of accident, homicide, or suicide. Such deaths typically are unexpected, traumatic or violent, shocking, and off time. All of these characteristics make the deaths difficult to accept, especially

This woman is visiting with a funeral director to preplan her funeral. As part of her planning, she is deciding details about her service and how she will be laid to rest. Choosing her casket, deciding on pallbearers, and designating a charity to receive donations in lieu of flowers help her feel less anxious about what will happen to her and her family after she dies.
Source: Phovoir/Shutterstock.

Part 9 Endings

if schools and parents respond by continuing life as usual rather than taking time out for bereavement (Corr et al., 1996; Vigilant & Williamson, 2003). Adults may give little thought to the effects of the deaths of young cultural icons, such as musicians Selena and Amy Winehouse, athletes Reggie Lewis and Sean Taylor, or actors Paul Walker, Heath Ledger, and Cory Monteith, on their teenage children, but adolescents respond with grief (Hayslip & Hansson, 2003). Consistent with their developmental stage, teenage grieving tends to come and go and may extend over a long period of time (Hogan & DeSantis, 1992). When adolescents experience the death of a peer, they frequently use social media as a means to deal with their grief—posting memories and sentiments, writing to the deceased, and providing coping strategies (Williams & Merten, 2009). Adolescents create online memorials, plan memorial events, and post messages on the deceased's and their own social media accounts regularly for at least the first year after the death as a means to cope with their loss (Williams & Merten, 2009). Starting in midlife, people begin to estimate the amount of time they have left to live, known as future time perspective. While not everyone makes such estimates, doing so was associated with planning for the future, having more favorable attitudes toward death, and helping individuals act to improve their generativity, discussed in Chapter 15 (Keith, 1982; Kooij & Van De Voorde, 2011). Perceptions of the amount of time left are affected by the ages at which one's parents died as well as by one's own age.

Death Acceptance

Studies show that people both accept and deny the reality of their dying; although we know that dying is universal, we find it hard to comprehend our own mortality (Wiseman, 1972). Young children see death as reversible or temporary, as we see in Focusing On: How Children Understand Death, but when faced with life-threatening illness they pay attention to what is happening in their lives and come to realize that they are dying (Beale, Baile, & Aaron, 2005; Corr et al., 1996). Adolescents tend to deny their own mortality as they cling to the personal fable of invincibility. When faced with a life-threatening illness, they continue to struggle for independence, need to control some aspect of their lives, and strive to maintain a sense of dignity and pride. Young adults often are very angry when faced with their own death because they are just beginning the tasks of building intimate relationships, establishing occupations, and raising children, and feel frustrated that their dreams will go unfulfilled. As we saw in Chapter 15, middle-aged adults' awareness of their own mortality increases as they bury and mourn for their parents. Late adulthood is associated with an increasing acceptance of death and increasing concern about the process of dying, preferring to die comfortably rather than extending one's life, with wishes to not die in pain, immobile, alone, and irreversibly confused (Marshall & Levy, 1990; Tobin et al., 1994; Wright et al., 2008). As we saw in our discussion of wills and advance directives in Chapter 15, that is one reason that thinking about end-of-life choices can reduce death anxiety.

End-of-Life Choices

Public opinion polls show that almost 90 percent of American adults would not want life support systems in place if there were no prospect of recovery, and 70 percent of older adults have actually prepared a written advance directive (Moody, 1994a; Teno et al., 2007). When advance directives are prepared and discussed with medical staff, individuals are much less likely to have unwanted aggressive treatment to extend their life, though many individuals and their families report inadequate treatment of pain and emotional support (Silveira, Kim, & Langa, 2010; Teno et al., 2007; Wright et al., 2008). Surveys also show that 68 percent of American adults approve of euthanasia and assisted suicide becoming legal options (Dugan, 2015). We see here a general openness to end-of-life choices but a personal reluctance to choose. This may be because people distinguish between whether they consider assisted suicide and euthanasia morally right and whether they would choose it for themselves (Cicirelli, 1997). Clive Seale and Julia Addington-Hall (1994) found that only 4 percent of people who died from cancer and other lingering illnesses had asked for euthanasia, a very small percentage compared to the percentage who would generally endorse having such an option. Though this may be due to laws forbidding euthanasia, countries in which euthanasia and physician-assisted suicide are not prosecuted, such as the Netherlands, still find relatively low rates of request—about 7 percent (Onwuteaka-Philipsen, Rurup, Pasman, & van der Heide, 2010).

In a study of end-of-life preferences, Victor Cicirelli (1997) gave interviews and questionnaires to 388 community-dwelling people ages sixty to one hundred. Table 18.1 presents the significant characteristics of some of the end-of-life scenarios used in the study. Participants were asked, "If you were in this condition, how would you feel about doing each of the following?" Seven options were then presented: to strive to maintain life, to refuse medical treatment or request its withdrawal, to allow someone close to decide what is best in the situation, to commit suicide, to ask the doctor (or someone else) for assistance in committing suicide, to ask the doctor (or someone else) to end one's life, or to ask the doctor (or someone else) to decide to terminate life.

Victor Cicirelli (1997) presented community-dwelling adults ages sixty to one hundred with a variety of end-of-life decision scenarios to assess attitudes toward different degrees of intervention in dying. Here is a sample decision situation as it was presented and a list of the characteristics of some of the other scenarios Cicirelli used in his study.

Cicirelli found that slightly more than half of the respondents favored a decision to strive to continue living even if they were to have a terminal illness or a nonterminal physical or mental condition that resulted in a continued low quality of life. Approximately

TABLE 18.1 End-of-Life Decision Scenarios

Sample End-of-Life Decision Situation

Mrs. Lee is an older-adult widow who has terminal bone cancer. She has had chemotherapy to try to cure the cancer, but it has not helped her, and the side effects from the chemotherapy itself have been difficult to deal with. She is slowly getting worse, and the pain is unbearable. Drugs for pain help some, but leave her in a stupor.

Characteristics of Selected End-of-Life Decision Scenarios

1. A widow has terminal bone cancer; chemotherapy has been unsuccessful, side effects are difficult, and the condition is worsening, with only partial relief of pain. (This is the situation presented in full earlier.)

2. A widower has regained consciousness after a stroke and coma, but requires a ventilator, is immobile, and cannot feed himself. His condition is unlikely to improve.

3. A person with an incurable disease has six months to live. While not experiencing pain now, later stages of the disease will involve suffering.

4. A person with a large, inoperable brain tumor has six months to a year to live. The ability to speak will soon be lost, followed by loss of mental functioning and coma.

5. A person with an incurable disease is unable to get relief from unbearable pain.

6. A person with immobility in arms and legs following a stroke or an accident has no chance of regaining mobility.

7. A person with an incurable illness is totally dependent on others for feeding, bathing, toileting, and the like.

8. A seriously ill person is being kept alive by machines and tube feeding; there is no hope for recovery.

9. A seriously ill person feels useless and believes that life no longer has any purpose.

10. A seriously ill person is anxious, upset, depressed, and in great despair, and feels unable to cope.

Source: Cicirelli (1997).

one-third of the respondents favored deferring any end-of-life decision to someone else, be it a family member, close friend, or physician. Those who favored maintaining life no matter what the circumstances tended to be African American, to have lower SES, and to be more religious. They also had less fear of the dying process but more fear of destruction of the body.

Cultures differ in how they think of and treat the corpse once death has occurred. Though embalming is popular among Christians in the United States because it delays the decomposition of the body, the Jewish tradition prohibits autopsy and embalming and requires quick burial. The Japanese tradition strongly prohibits tampering with the corpse.

Differences in Death Anxiety

Older people talk about death more than younger people do and seem to be less fearful of it (Kalish, 1985; Thorson & Powell, 1988). Conflicting evidence exists on gender differences. James Thorson and F. C. Powell (1988) found that women seem to be more accepting of death than are men. While they fear their own deaths, they see death as peaceful, whereas men view it as antagonistic. Women express more death anxiety than men do (Dattell & Neimeyer, 1990; Harding, Flannelly, Weaver, & Costa, 2005; Madnawat & Kachhawa, 2007). Death anxiety is also related to religiosity and whether one has found meaning in life: people with less death anxiety tend to have stronger religious conviction (Alvarado et al., 1995; Harding et al., 2005) and are more likely to report that they have life goals that give their life purpose (Routledge & Juhl, 2010). Richard Kalish (1985) found that people who were strongly religious and those who were affirmed atheists showed few death fears. Those with strong inner beliefs, whether in a traditional God or in a personal philosophy, seemed better able to contend with death. Those who were sporadically religious or uncertain about their religious beliefs showed the most death anxiety (Glass, 1990).

Factors That Reduce Death Anxiety

Why are older people less fearful of death even though they are closer to it? Several explanations have been proposed. First, older people deal frequently with the deaths of their friends and associates, especially if they live in age-segregated retirement communities or nursing homes. This helps to socialize them into acceptance of their own death. Death anxiety among those who work in the funeral industry is lower among those who have worked in the field the longest, particularly for those who had a lot of exposure to funerals, supporting the idea of socialized acceptance (Harrawood, White, & Benshoff, 2009). Second, if older individuals have lived past the time they expected to, they may view themselves as living on "borrowed time" (Kalish, 1985). Third, a painless death is viewed more favorably than slow mental or physical deterioration and becoming a burden to loved ones (Marshall, 1980). Fourth, as we discussed in Chapter 17, during Erikson's late adult developmental stage of ego integrity versus despair, the process of life review may enable the resolution of conflicts and relieve death anxiety. Robert Kastenbaum (1992a) found evidence of ego integration and life review among hospitalized geriatric patients, and other research has shown that those with high death anxiety had less sense of purpose in life, saw time as marching relentlessly on, felt harassed by time pressures, and saw less continuity in their lives than those with low death anxiety (Quinn & Reznikoff, 1985; Routledge & Juhl, 2010).

Impact of Off-Time Responsibilities

Unfinished business can interfere with the normative process of accepting death as one gets old. Young and middle-aged parents of dependent children typically feel concern about the impact of their death on their children. Lillian Rubin (1979) found that midlife women whose children were leaving home expressed relief from this concern. As one of them said, "It would be a tragedy, wouldn't it, to be a mother and to die before you thought your kids were ready?" (p. 29). Sheldon Tobin, Elise Fullmer, and Gregory Smith (1994) interviewed a sample of 235 mothers ages fifty-eight to ninety-six who were caring at home for an adult

Focusing On...

How Children Understand Death

In modern society, death has become rare in childhood and common in old age. This seemingly natural state of affairs actually is quite unusual; throughout history and around the world, the majority of deaths have occurred among infants and children. Today's reversal of this trend has had benefits, of course, but it may also leave children unprepared to understand and cope with death when they do experience it at close hand. Instead of seeming natural, inevitable, and universal, death may seem a rare and arbitrary event, a catastrophe that befalls only a few people. Such a view may create confusion about the nature and meaning of death.

Studies confirm that children who have not experienced the death of a loved one have only a hazy understanding of death, even well into middle childhood (Bonoti, Leondari, & Mastora, 2013). Early in this period, around age six, they describe death with analogies that are often reversible: "Death is when you go to sleep," said one six-year-old, as though death ended in waking up again. Often the analogies refer not to universal events but to special ones; "Death is going on a trip," for example, implying that not everyone will die because not everyone goes on trips (Webb, 1993). Perhaps for these reasons, young children do not seem to fear death as much as older children and adults do. They reveal concern and distress about the general idea of death, but unless they experience the death of a close relative (such as a parent or sibling) directly, their concerns tend to be comparatively limited. Not until around age ten do the large majority of children realize that death is irreversible, permanent, and universal. But even then their concern is rather abstract and emphasizes physical inevitability rather than psychological repercussions: "Dying is when your heart stops beating forever." In fact, as children get older, they are more likely to endorse beliefs that death IS reversible, likely due to increasingly abstract thinking about spirituality and religion (Bonoti et al., 2013).

All of these developments occur more rapidly and vividly, though, if a child has had a life-threatening illness (such as leukemia) or has lost a close relative, especially a parent (Bonoti et al., 2013; Worden, 1996). These children face challenges that develop their understanding of death very quickly. First, they must *understand* the death as realistically as possible: it indeed has occurred, cannot be ignored, and will never be undone. Unfortunately, younger children may have trouble understanding this reality because their general cognitive understanding is limited. They need to be told about the death repeatedly over time, in ways that are accurate and in language appropriate to their age. Second, children must have chances to *grieve* or mourn their loss and work through the feelings they still have about the person who died. The extent and nature of their grieving will depend on how emotionally attached they were to the deceased person, their overall cognitive maturity, and the support they receive for express-

---

child with developmental delays. Unlike most older mothers, although they had successfully launched other adult children, they still had a dependent offspring, which made it difficult for them to accept their own death. The mothers were given the Sentence Completion Test (SCT) stem *Death is . . .* and asked to complete the sentence. Responses were scored on a five-point scale. A score of 1 was assigned to completions reflecting fear or denial, such as "not being afraid if she were taken care of." A 2 was assigned to themes of loss, such as "losing everything." A 3 was assigned to themes that were neutral, such as "natural" or "inevitable." A 4 was assigned to themes of relief from pain or suffering, such as "knowing he will let me die in peace." And a score of 5 was given when there was a transcendental quality, such as "going to heaven." The responses to the SCT did not suggest a great fear of dying: 62 percent scored 3 (natural or inevitable); 20 percent scored 1 or 2 (indicating fear or loss); and 18 percent scored 4 or 5 (indicating death was a blessing).

However, when the mothers were further asked, "Has being a parent and caregiver of a mentally disabled son/daughter affected your feelings about your own death?", responses reflected internal conflict regarding death. Those who had said death was "natural" or "inevitable" also said things such as "I don't want to go before her"; "I hate the thought of leaving her; I wish I could live forever"; "I worry about him. He'll miss me"; and "I can't die." Tobin and his associates (1994) interpret these conflicting responses as indicating that "If they were not perpetual parents, death would be acceptable" (p. 192). Among their sample they found that death acceptance decreased with age and fears and losses increased, which is counter to normative aging. Only the handful of mothers who had

> **Focusing On...**
>
> ### How Children Understand Death *continued*
>
> ing their sadness. As one nine-year-old girl put it, "What bothered me most about my mother's death was that no one gave me a chance to talk about it; they were too busy with their own problems." Another child said, "My little brother didn't seem to react when my sister died [of meningitis], but I can't tell if it's because he wasn't very close to her emotionally, or because he was only four at the time, or because Mom and Dad kept telling him how 'strong' he was not to cry."
>
> Either despite or because of their cognitive limitations, children react strongly to the deaths of the most important people in their lives, usually their parents. Research shows that the effects can be quite long-lived (Hayslip & Hansson, 2003; Lichten, 2003; Silverman & Worden, 1993). Even ten years after losing a parent, bereaved children tend to be more submissive and introverted and less aggressive than other children, even including children who lose a parent through divorce. As you might expect, though, the extent and nature of a child's reactions depend heavily on the circumstances: losing a mother can be harder for a child than losing a father, on average, because the remaining parent—the father—more often has had less practice expressing his own grief and has fewer social relationships to offer emotional support. Furthermore, the reactions of the surviving parent and other relatives affect the child's ability to come to terms with the death. A parent depressed with his or her own grief has reduced ability to comfort a school-age child.
>
> What can professionals do to help children come to terms with death in general and a specific person's death in particular? The answer depends partly on the extent of their own involvement. Social workers and nurses who assist families during particular deaths can encourage children to talk about the death, say what they think and feel, and ask about what perplexes them or invite children to join support groups (Morgan & Roberts, 2010). Teachers and school counselors also can do this when a classmate has died. In addition, they can explore the issues and feelings about death in more general ways, such as by incorporating the topic into the overall school curriculum (Corr & Corr, 2003; U.S. Department of Health and Human Services, 1993).
>
> **What Do You Think?**
>
> 1. Given the difficulty a child may have understanding death, and given the functions of funerals in the grieving process, do you think it is wise to protect a child from attending his or her parent's funeral? Why or why not?
> 2. Remember (or look back and review) what you know of cognitive development in early and middle childhood. Based on that, explain why a child would have difficulty understanding that death is final, permanent, and unchangeable.

made future plans for their dependent offspring with which they were comfortable could talk positively about dying.

Unfinished business can come in forms other than a dependent adult child with a disability. An older person with dependent grandchildren or a disabled spouse may be less accepting of death than one who does not have those social responsibilities. The same may be true of older people still deeply involved in their careers, such as Supreme Court justices or artists still seeking to express the essence of their work, or even making sure one's finances and legal files are in order before death (Kehl, 2006; Tobin, 1991). The closure that comes with finishing up business is frequently noted as being an important part of having a "good death" (Kehl, 2006). There may also be cohort effects in death acceptance. The Baby Boomers have more education than their parents' cohort, a trend that has continued with Generation X, and there is evidence that among the better educated, more awareness of life's uncertain length exists at all ages (Marshall, 1980). On the other hand, in the absence of mandatory retirement, more older adults may continue active careers that interfere with death acceptance. We do not know how much of the documented differences in death acceptance have to do with age and how much with cohort effects. Although we know differences exist among ethnic and religious groups, little research has systematically measured them. We do know that more African American grandparents are raising their grandchildren, as we discussed in Chapter 15, which may have a negative impact on their death acceptance.

Late-life Suicide

It is important not to confuse age-related death acceptance with desire for death. As one hospitalized older woman said, "Death wants me—he'll have to find me at Bingo!" Among a sample of terminally ill late-middle-aged and late-life adults, Kastenbaum found that the desire and opportunity to affirm personal relationships through a process of leave taking helped to control anxiety and reduce impulses to end one's life through suicide, assisted suicide, or euthanasia (Kastenbaum, 1992a). Nonetheless, an association has been found between age and suicide; suicide rates are higher in later life: for the general population suicide rates are 12.7 out of 100,000, a number that increases to 15.3 for those age sixty-five and up and to 16.9 for those eighty-five and older (Koenig & Blazer, 1992; McIntosh & Drapeau, 2014). Moreover, though older adults attempt suicide less often than younger adults, those attempts are more likely to be fatal than when younger adults attempt suicide (American Association of Suicidology, 2014; Friedmann, & Kohn, 2008). Older adults commit 17 percent of the suicides but make up only 13 or 14 percent of the population (American Association of Suicidology, 2014). Longitudinal data, however, present a different picture of the age-suicide relationship. After World War II, the suicide rate was relatively stable despite an increasing older population; then it started to rise around 1986, even as rates among those in late life decreased (Conwell, Van Orden, & Caine, 2011). As the Baby Boomers move into late life, those rates appear to be increasing again (Conwell et al., 2011; Curtin, Warner, & Hedegaard, 2016). Harold Koenig and Dan Blazer (1992) point out that both period effects and cohort effects must be considered when looking at the impact of age on suicide rates. *Period effects* refer to the impact of a unique stressor on the suicide rates for a particular age group. Legalizing the use of handguns, for example, may increase the suicide rate among older adults because older men are more likely than younger men to use firearms. *Cohort effects* on suicide rates refer to stressors that affect members of a particular age group because of the generation into which they were born. Because of social security and Medicare, the current cohort of older adults has had fewer financial pressures and better health than other post-World War II cohorts, and that would predict lower suicide rates (Conwell & Thompson, 2008). These factors reduce opportunity or inclination to communicate with others during late adulthood and increase the risk of suicide.

Not all older adults are equally likely to attempt or commit suicide. Most of us know individuals who in late adulthood are full of zest for life. What factors put individuals at risk for suicide in later life? As Table 18.2 shows, the older adults who are at high risk are those with reduced opportunity or inclination to be engaged with others (American Association of Suicidology, 2014; Kastenbaum, 1992a). Living alone cuts down opportunities to share feelings, which is why married persons of all ages have the lowest risk of suicide and widowed or divorced people have the highest. Residing in a low-income,

TABLE 18.2 Risk Factors for Suicide in Late Adulthood

- Living alone and being socially isolated
- Experiencing financial difficulty
- Feeling depressed or useless
- Being alcohol or drug dependent
- Having a mental illness that reduces communication
- Suffering from chronic pain, illness, or incapacity
- Uncontrollable pain
- Being unable to express grief or suffering
- Losing significant relationships due to the death of loved ones
- Significant changes in one's social roles

transient urban area tends to cut down social contacts, whereas high-SES individuals seem to be buffered against the risk of suicide. Being depressed, dependent on alcohol, or mentally ill reduces communication and is likely to drive other people away and increase the suicide risk. A very large proportion of older men and women who commit suicide themselves do so because they suffer from depression, as we discussed in Chapter 16.

As Figure 18.1 shows, being male and white greatly increases the risk of suicide. Late-life white males take their own lives at a rate five times the national average (Nuland, 1994). Men show reluctance to seek help or to accept opportunities to express grief or suffering. Race is also a risk factor, although the reason is not fully understood. Suicide is less common in African American populations, likely because of tightly knit communities, particularly churches, that provide social support, stress management, and, particularly among older African Americans, high levels of respect for one's elders (Gibbs, 1997). The rate of suicide for white males age seventy-five or older is about four times that of African American males in this age group (Curtin et al., 2016). Anger, despair, and suicidality are more characteristic of the hospitalized older adults than of the independently living, which indicates that those who commit suicide are uncomfortable with life rather than looking forward to death (Kastenbaum, 1992a). It may be that when older adults are unable to adapt to health problems, loss of mobility, and other age-related difficulties, they feel as though they have less control over their lives, and this perceived lack of control increases risk for suicidality (Fiske & O'Riley, 2016). Also, poor health status, a precursor to hospitalization, is also a major risk factor. Because of this relationship between illness and suicide among those in late life, suicide among this group is probably seriously underestimated. Neglecting to take medication, refusing to undergo life-saving surgery or other treatments, or neglecting to seek medical care may lead to intentional deaths that get recorded as due to natural causes (Rodin et al., 1981).

Older suicides may be harder to predict, and therefore prevent, than younger suicides. In a study designed to assess what risk factors distinguish older from younger suicides, Susanne Carney and her associates (1994) compared early (sixteen to thirty years), middle (thirty-one to fifty-nine years), and older (sixty to eighty-eight years) adult suicides that had occurred during one year in San Diego County. Using extensive data-gathering techniques,

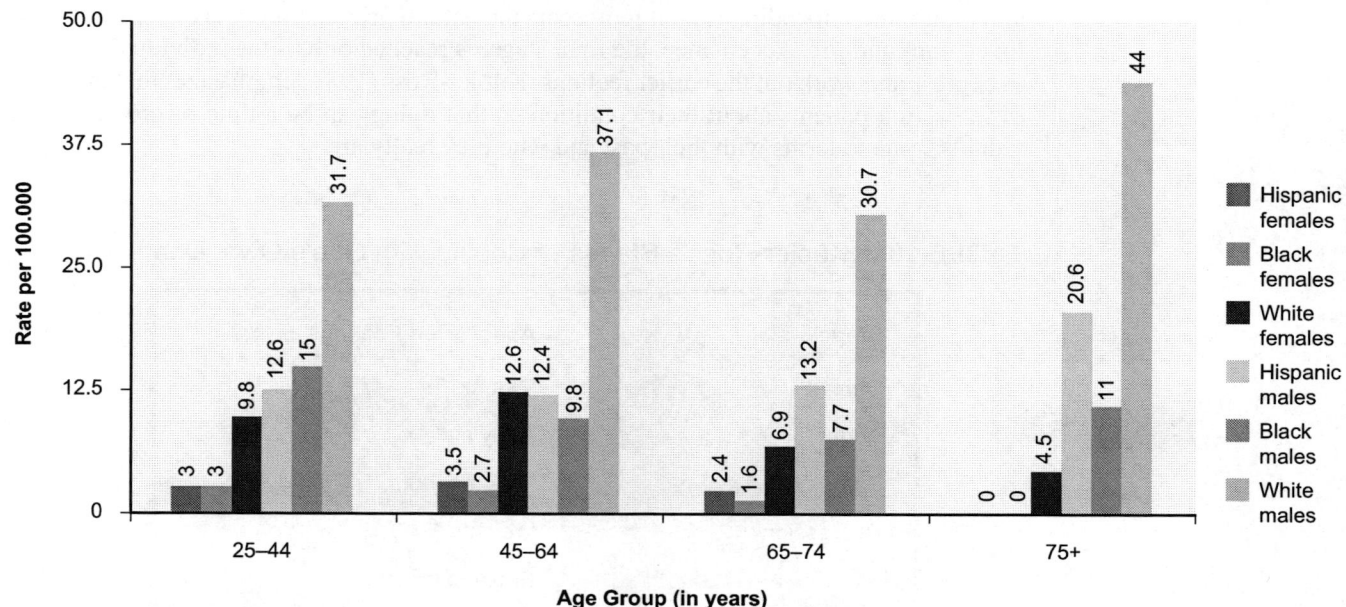

FIGURE 18.1 Suicide Rate by Age, Race, and Gender

Being white and male increases the risk of suicide across adulthood but markedly so above the age of 75.
*Fewer than twenty suicides were reported for the entire population of either Hispanic or black females over the age of seventy-five and so the rates were not reliable.
Source: Curtin, Warner, & Hedegaard, 2016.

they found that mental disorders played a major role in suicide at all ages, with depression the most common disorder. Interpersonal loss was a stressor associated with 43 percent of the older suicides, but it was also very common among the younger (64 percent) and middle-aged suicides (59 percent). While older people generally experienced the death of a spouse or long-term partner, young and middle-aged people tended to lose significant relationships because of fights or separations. Financial stressors were less frequent among the older group than the two younger groups. Health problems were more common in the older group of suicides. The older individuals were not more isolated socially, but were less likely to have talked of suicide or to have made a prior suicide attempt. The investigators conclude that the major risk factors of suicide differ little between older and younger people, but older adults seem to communicate warnings less frequently. Unfortunately, crisis prevention centers in the United States and Canada lack specific knowledge and training that could improve their effectiveness with elder suicide prevention (Adamek & Kaplan, 1996).

Suicide at any age appears sudden and unexpected to the people left behind. It also appears to have been chosen, although more frequently it is an escape or an inability to live with the human condition. These characteristics make suicide deaths hard for survivors to cope with, as they leave a complex combination of anger, sadness, and guilt (Corr et al., 1996). While family and peers may be more accepting of suicide in the face of poor health and deteriorating quality of life among older adults, suicide is still more difficult to accept than the unchosen, often protracted death that is the normal end to life.

The Dying Process

Our understanding of how people come to accept their own deaths has been greatly influenced by the work of Elisabeth Kübler-Ross. Working within a psychoanalytic framework, Kübler-Ross (1969) interviewed more than two hundred dying patients and proposed five distinct stages through which individuals pass. Table 18.3 shows these stages. Although the stages are distinct, they are not necessarily progressive and are likely to overlap. Denial, the refusal to believe the terminal diagnosis, is the initial response as the person defends against the news of impending death. Anger often is displaced onto the family or medical staff and is likely to be a hard stage for the caregivers to tolerate. Bargaining with a higher being often takes the form of asking for more time to do something good, such as being more religious or finishing a project. Depression is the stage in which the individual begins to acknowledge and mourn the impending loss. It represents the natural grieving process of separation from loved ones and life. Acceptance, the final stage, is reached only if the individual is allowed to express and work out the earlier feelings. Kübler-Ross (1981) emphasizes the importance of informing patients about their condition so that dying can be a time of growth as individuals come to terms with their past and who they really are.

TABLE 18.3 Kübler-Ross's Stages of Coping with One's Own Death

Stage	Associated Feelings
Denial	"Not me."
Anger	"Why me?"
Bargaining	"Yes me, but..."
Depression	"Yes me."
	Begin to mourn.
Acceptance	"My time is very close now, and it's all right."

Source: Kübler-Ross (1969).

Kübler-Ross's stages are not necessarily progressive and are likely to overlap. Because they are based on young and middle-aged adults dying of cancer, they do not represent the variability that exists in the course of dying.

Although Kübler-Ross's stage formulation has been widely accepted by clinicians who work with dying patients, it has also been amply challenged by research and theory (Corr, 1993; Marshall & Levy, 1990). The patients Kübler-Ross studied were young and middle-aged adults dying of cancer, which may account for the anger and bargaining she found. The age range of her sample makes generalizing to older adults problematic. As we have already discussed, older people generally are more accepting of death. Among people who were sixty years old on the average, Avery Wiseman (1972) found that acceptance of death without denial was possible. Kastenbaum (1992b) points out that the course of dying is much more variable than Kübler-Ross's stages imply. For example, cancer may go in and out of remission, which can cause alternation between acceptance and denial rather than a clear first and last stage. Besides variation due to age or type of death, a larger criticism is that Kübler-Ross focuses on the individual rather than the social relationships in which dying is embedded and one's cultural setting. Kathy Charmaz (1980) suggests that "the stages of dying . . . may indeed be a consequence of how illness and dying are socially handled in this society, rather than a psychological process of adjustment to death" (p. 155). In particular, because Kübler-Ross's dying patients were all in the hospital, "Denial may occur when the patients have not yet put together the cues [that they are dying], . . . anger when they learn that everyone else knew long before, depression when there is not much time and so much left unfinished, and acceptance when they realize that nothing more can be done" (Charmaz, 1980, p. 155). If our society did not deny death and isolate the dying, perhaps the experience of dying would be different. Although Eastern religions include a variety of traditions, they represent views of death and rebirth that place the experience of dying in a different perspective. Hindus seek a state of blissful union with a higher state of being-as-blissful consciousness. Buddhists consider "right livelihood" and the avoidance of nonvirtue as an avenue to correct understanding of the universe. By teaching that a meaningful life can be found by the individual detaching from self and finding unity with all, these beliefs contrast with Western views of dying. Despite the criticism of her work, Kübler-Ross has had a profound effect on making people more sympathetic to death and dying.

The Good Death

The good death is one that is appropriate to the dying person. This concept shows considerable cultural variation (see Table 18.4). Similar to Christian traditions, Muslims believe that death occurs when one's soul leaves one's physical body, and that on the Day of Resurrection, one will be judged by God to spend eternity in Paradise or Hell (Sultan, 2003). As with many religions, a "good death" for a Muslim man or woman is one surrounded by loved ones, and when possible, will include sitting up facing Mecca and professing one's faith (Sultan, 2003). For Buddhists and Hindus, who believe the last thought at the moment of death determines the character of the next incarnation, the good death is one in which the individual uses the *bardo,* or interval of suspension between death and rebirth, to awaken a more enlightened incarnation (DeSpelder & Strickland, 1996). As in many cultures, a "good death" for Hindus is thought to happen after a long, fulfilling life with little pain or loss of physical or mental abilities (Rambachan, 2003). In Indian culture, for instance, the final or *sannyasi* stage of Hindu life is initiated with a ritual that symbolizes death of the old self. The individual renounces his or her former life and directs his or her mind to the attainment of liberation. Family and acquaintances respect and admire the individual's renunciation of former status and power, which gives his or her life new meaning and purpose. They help the dying to focus on God by reciting prayers known as mantras. As part of the initiation rite, the individual conducts his own funeral ceremonies. One is not cremated at one's actual death because he or she has already experienced ritual death (Thomas, 1994).

When Robert Kastenbaum and Claude Normand (1990) asked American college students to picture their deathbed scene, the students generally described being alert, lucid,

the good death A death that is appropriate to the dying person. In the contemporary United States, it typically refers to a death in which the dying person is surrounded by family and friends with minimal technological interference.

TABLE 18.4 Ways in Which Culture Influences Death Concerns

> Like all other stages of life, death is influenced by culture, which
> - Affects the assessment of comfort needs of the dying and the kind of care provided.
> - Influences selection, perception, and evaluation of health care givers and their methods.
> - Shapes beliefs about causes of death.
> - Determines the disposition of the body and funeral and burial rituals.
> - Patterns grief responses and bereavement roles.
>
> *Source:* Adapted from Ross (1994).

and aware of their coming death as they died of old age, at home, with their friends and family gathered around them. Missing from their descriptions were institutional settings, medical interventions, pain, and long-term suffering that are the realities of modern life. One of the best ways to ensure that such needs and wishes of the dying are met is by using advance care planning. With advance care planning, individuals discuss their health and treatment options with medical professionals and loved ones, making their wishes known and naming a surrogate to follow through on the plan in the case that the dying person is incapacitated (Detering, Hancock, Reade, & Silvester, 2010). Ideally, advance care plans are decided upon while individuals are still capable of making such decisions for themselves. When trained advance care planning facilitators discussed end-of-life wishes with patients, family and surrogates, and medical staff, patients and their families felt more engaged in decisions and more satisfied with the medical staff (Detering et al., 2010). In cases when the patient died, the family reported they and the deceased believed that the death was a good death. They also experienced less anxiety, depression, and posttraumatic stress than a control group who did not receive advance care planning (Detering et al., 2010).

The death awareness movement has promoted conditions that can make the good death possible, such as honesty with the dying person, home and hospice settings that enable friends and family to remain close, and control of pain and technological interventions. The goal is to enable the dying individual to experience personal growth in this final stage of life. *Open awareness,* in which both the dying person and the loved ones know that the person is dying, has become more generally practiced since 1969, when *closed awareness,* in which the loved ones know but the dying person does not, was prevalent. Compared to people in closed awareness, people dying in open awareness are better able to plan the way in which they will die so that they and their loved ones are more satisfied with the degree of choice over the place of death. They are also less likely to die alone and are more likely to die in their own homes (Seale et al., 1997). Increasing the conditions for the good death can foster hope in the dying person, which can motivate attempts to control the disease and establish continuity between oneself and one's survivors.

Caring for the Dying

The way the dying are cared for influences the quality of their deaths. Often older adults facing a terminal illness are in need of both acute care and long-term care. Though not curative, surgery or other aggressive treatment may be able to slow the progress of the disease or make the dying person more comfortable. Pain control can also make a person more comfortable even though it does not cure the cause of the pain. Sometimes surgery reveals the terminal nature of the disease, as was the case for Betty in our opening vignette. A person therefore may need hospital or other acute care at some stages of the terminal illness and long-term care at others.

> **What Do You Think?**
>
> In what ways do you think death acceptance can help set the conditions for the good death? What evidence for this idea do you see in the vignette about Betty at the start of this chapter?

Terminal Care Alternatives

Contradiction is inherent in the fact that so many individuals die in hospitals. Hospitals are designed to prolong life, not to promote the good death. People like Betty go to the hospital to get sophisticated health care, not for personal comfort as they face death. Betty's decision to go home to die is one more families are now making in the wake of the death awareness movement. At home Betty was able to be with her family, eat her favorite foods, and enjoy her own familiar things. What would she have faced in the hospital? Routine care by impersonal caregivers. Medical intervention that would have been painful and costly but not curative. Not only would Betty's death have been more difficult for her; it would have been harder for her family. Being with Betty would have been limited by hospital rules concerning visiting hours and number of visitors, as well as the discomforts of a small, impersonal hospital room and dreary hallways. The family's focus might have been fighting the rules rather than engaging in grief work. **Grief work**, an initial phase of the bereavement process, entails anger, self-recrimination, depression, and taking care of unfinished business. Instead of the joy of having the family together for one last Christmas dinner, there would have been guilt had the rest of the family left Betty alone while they had Christmas dinner, or there may have been no annual family dinner at all as they hung around the hospital.

grief work An initial phase of the bereavement process that entails anger, self-recrimination, depression, and taking care of unfinished business.

Home Death

Home used to be where older adults died in the United States and continues to be where most people die in nonindustrialized countries. Caring for the dying was an integral part of American women's work until the early 1900s (Abel, 1991). Only when advances in medicine and nursing made it possible to delay death did dying move to hospitals. By the 1980s, most deaths were occurring outside of the home, a trend that more recently has begun to change (Flory et al., 2004; Teno et al., 2013).

Several recent developments have led to the reemergence of home death (Sankar, 1993; Teno et al., 2013). First, the death awareness movement has encouraged those in late life,

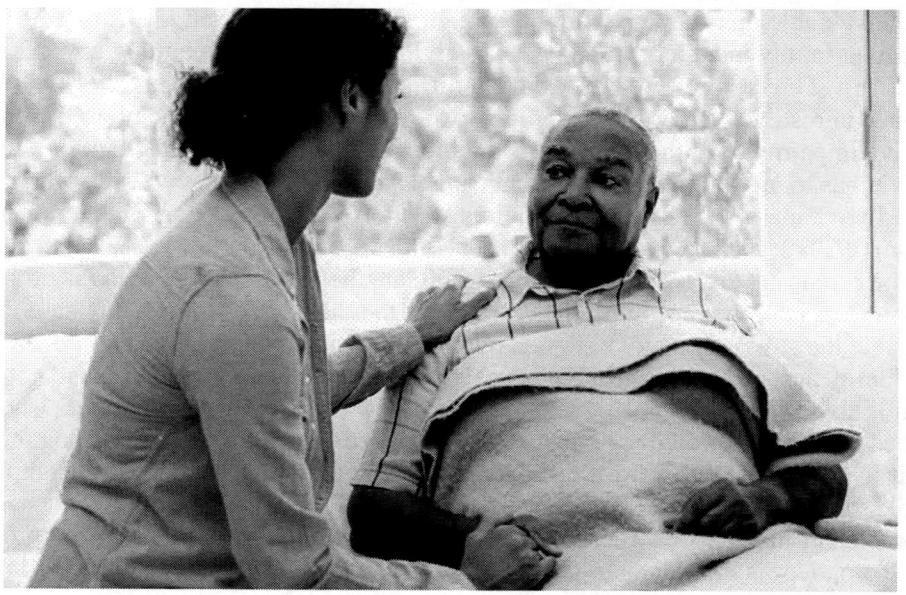

Home care provides familiarity, a sense of normalcy, and greater opportunities for sustaining relationships and allows for mutual caring of concerns and feelings. For a loved one, like this daughter, providing home care can be an emotionally challenging and rewarding experience.
Source: Monkey Business Images/Shutterstock.

hospice An interdisciplinary team and holistic approach to death by attending to the physical, emotional, spiritual, and aesthetic needs of patients and their families, primarily in their own homes but also at acute care facilities.

the terminally ill, and their families to control the conditions of their own deaths. Second, the hospice movement has promoted the expectation of the good death. **Hospice** takes an holistic approach to death by attending to the physical, emotional, spiritual, and aesthetic needs of patients and their families, predominantly in their own homes. The most important criterion for eligibility for hospice care is that the patient and family be choosing supportive care for the last six months of a terminal disease with the care focused on comfort rather than life-sustaining treatment delivered primarily in the home setting (Casarett, 2011; Gentile & Fello, 1990). Hospice is formally recognized by Medicare and private insurance companies, enabling many more people to utilize its services. Third, recognition of the limits of medical care has been growing. Heroic measures may prolong life, but they do not ensure quality of life. Care for pain and symptom relief may be preferable to invasive or aggressive medical treatment. Fourth, improvements in technology and pharmacology have made home-based care possible, particularly in the areas of pain control, oxygen therapy, intravenous treatments, nutritional supplements, and chemotherapy. Fifth, insurance companies have limited the duration of a hospital stay for which they will reimburse unless the patient is receiving active treatment. As a result of these diverse forces, people are increasingly choosing home death over hospital death.

While it is easy to see the benefits of home death, that choice has several difficult aspects for which many families are unprepared. On the positive side, home care provides familiarity, a sense of normalcy, and greater opportunities for sustaining relationships, and allows for mutual sharing of concerns and feelings (DeSpelder & Strickland, 1996). On the negative side, today's dying typically are much sicker than they used to be (Sankar, 1991). Medical advances have led to fewer deaths from secondary infections such as pneumonia and more from primary diseases such as cancer. One result is that by the time death comes, the patient is likely to be very weak and debilitated. Dying people are also likely to be older and frailer than they used to be. Home death, then, usually means having not a clear-headed and active patient but a very fragile patient for whom routine activities such as eating, eliminating, and bathing are major undertakings. Often it requires establishing the equivalent of an intensive care unit in the home. Many caregivers are not prepared for the level of care home death requires.

Another important change has occurred in the lives of women, who are most often the caregivers. Whereas fifty and more years ago few women worked outside the home, today most are employed. Because a high percentage of primary caregivers are employed and because of the physical and cognitive burden of caregiving, the risk for potential emotional well-being, mood, physical, and financial stress is considerable (Cantor, 1992; Ho et al., 2009; Pinquart & Sörensen, 2008). Home care requires that someone be on call around the clock. This is very difficult for many families to arrange. Hospice and other home care programs are designed to provide information and support services, which can be invaluable, but they may not be enough. In real (rather than ideal) families, conflict among family members may make caregiving under such demanding circumstances too difficult. The dying person may have a difficult time accepting death. The caregiver may have unresolved anger and bitterness toward the dying family member. In addition, cognitive impairment of the dying person may make home care too difficult because the caregiver has to interpret what the patient cannot say and also assess whether what is said is actually meant, a skill that often requires specialized training (Eggenberger, Heimerl, & Bennett, 2012; Sankar, 1993).

Home care is not always the best way to facilitate the good death. If dying is prolonged and disability is pronounced, moving the patient to a hospice or other acute care facility can enable the stressed caregiver to relax and be with the dying relative emotionally. Not every family has the emotional and physical resources to sustain home care, and not every patient is able to appreciate being at home. On the other hand, many caregivers who have provided home care through a home death experience found it a very rewarding moment in their lives, as well as the most difficult and challenging thing they have accomplished (Henriksson, Carlander, & Årestedt, 2015; Sankar, 1991).

Home care, then, is one alternative to hospital care. Home care is most appropriate when the patient is alert enough to relate to the caregiver and benefit from the familiar surroundings. Because it is predicated on close, caring relationships, it works best when honesty characterizes the terminal diagnosis. Secrecy or denial can make it difficult to continue to be close and prevent the dying and the bereaved from resolving the issues surrounding the death (Kalish, 1985).

Acute Care Facilities

What other options are available for patients besides hospital and home? Nursing homes are the institutions other than hospitals in which Americans most frequently die. Hospitals generally provide only short-term, aggressive care and then release the patient to nursing home or home care. Nursing homes have around-the-clock skilled nursing facilities, but provide less sophisticated care than do hospitals. They also tend to be impersonal in style and setting. Other innovative long-term care programs, such as On Lok Senior Health Services of San Francisco, enable older persons who are certified for nursing home care to remain in the community as long as possible (Der-McLeod & Hansen, 1992). On Lok combines primary medical, adult day health, and home care services complete with transportation. On Lok works with the patient and the family of culturally diverse elders; its participant population includes Chinese, Italian, Spanish, African American, German, Greek, Irish, Filipino, and Korean. The staff works with the family to supplement their care and relieve some of the caregiving stress, teaches new knowledge and management skills that increase the family's ability to cope with the difficulties of caregiving, and provides crisis intervention. The staff also works with the patients to establish what their health wishes are. This is an ongoing process that has enabled some older people—even among the Chinese and Italians, who have an unspoken tradition of not discussing matters of death or dying—to express their wishes concerning resuscitation (Der-McLeod & Hansen, 1992). The On Lok facility in San Francisco has served as a model for similar organizations in other locations including the Program of All-inclusive Care for Elderly People (PACE), which provides various services similar to those of On Lok throughout the United States with the goal of allowing older adults to remain in the community as long as possible (Kodner, 2006). PACE is covered by both Medicare and Medicaid, and those who utilize PACE use in-patient and out-patient services at a lower rate than those not benefitting from PACE (Kodner, 2006).

Hospice Service

While all hospices provide home care services, some also have centers that provide acute care. Whether at home or at a facility, hospice care is specifically designed to meet the needs of the dying patient and the bereaved family members. Hospices offer services that enable individuals to die with dignity and maintain a purposeful life to the end. The hospice philosophy is to provide **palliative care**, to manage the pain and other symptoms so that the dying individual can enjoy what remains of life. In addition to medical and nursing staff, trained volunteers and family members serve as caregivers, and there is a bereavement program for survivors. Hospice facilities are designed more like homes than hospitals. As the Working With interview on page 674 shows, hospice care encourages friends and family to be with their loved ones. The Connecticut Hospice was the first American hospice and is based on the model of St. Christopher's Hospice in Sydenham, England. The building, designed to handle fifty-three patients, provides natural lighting and garden views in every room, allowing even immobile patients to enjoy them. The commons has a glass ceiling so that daily performances and activities happen "outside" rain or shine. Doors are wide enough for beds to be wheeled to where the activities are. Flower beds are at wheelchair level so that patients can tend the flowers. Hospice pets come in regularly to visit. Arts and crafts keep patients involved in meaningful, goal-directed activities.

While there are some freestanding hospice facilities in the United States that offer both inpatient and home care programs, such as the one in Connecticut, many hospices are simply home care programs, and some hospice programs are set within traditional medical facilities. Most hospice care is provided at home. Even those patients who eventually move to an inpatient facility start with home care. Hospice provides social workers,

palliative care Management of pain and other symptoms of terminally ill patients that allows them to enjoy what remains of life.

nurses, and aides to assist families in caring for patients and help them with bereavement. Some hospices have arrangements with inpatient facilities, and some do not.

How do surviving spouses and family feel about hospice services? Spouses of people who had died of cancer in St. Christopher's Hospice were more likely to judge the institution as being "like a family" and less likely to want improvements than spouses of people who had died of cancer in a local hospital (Seale & Kelly, 1997a). Regret at not being present at the death was more common in the hospital group (Seale & Kelly, 1997b), but overall about 98 percent of those family members of those receiving hospice care say that they were very satisfied with the care and would recommend these services to others (Connor, Teno, Spence, & Smith, 2005).

Assisted Suicide

Given that many individuals face long, painful, debilitating terminal illnesses, some choose (or would like to choose) to end their lives while they are still rational rather than suffer and be a burden to their loved ones. As we have seen, older adults may welcome a timely death with dignity, the good death, over the pain and ravages of an incurable disease. This may be true as well for younger adults who face incurable and debilitating illnesses such as cancer. As physician and writer Sherwin Nuland (1994, p. 151) articulates it, "Taking one's own life is almost always the wrong thing to do. There are two circumstances, however, in which that may not be so. Those two are the unendurable infirmities of a crippling old age and the final devastations of terminal disease." Nuland emphasizes *unendurable, crippling, final,* and *terminal* because he sees them as the critical conditions for euthanasia. *Euthanasia* is the voluntary ending of life when illness makes it intolerable. In the Netherlands, a distinction is made between ordinary suicide and death under the circumstances of euthanasia. Euthanasia and physician-assisted suicide are legal in the Netherlands under very specific guidelines. The guidelines require that there be "severe suffering without the hope of relief; a financially and emotionally uncoerced, informed, and consistent choice by the patient; the absence of treatment options and second opinions from other professionals" (Cassel & Meier, 1990; Government of the Netherlands, n.d.). Additionally, the patient must be cognitively able to request such an act, and all such deaths are reviewed by a committee to ensure ethical, legal, and medical guidelines were followed (Government of the Netherlands, n.d.).

Contemporary debate in the United States has focused on the role of doctors in assisting the suicide of their patients and the role of family and friends in assisting the suicide of their loved ones. Euthanasia can be passive or active. **Passive euthanasia** refers to not doing something to prolong life, such as not utilizing life support equipment or not giving antibiotics, as you may remember from our discussion of advance directives in Chapter 15. **Active euthanasia** refers to taking steps to gently and painlessly end life, such as giving a fatal dose of painkilling medication. *Assisted suicide* refers to helping with active euthanasia. In 2016, assisting in suicide was illegal in all states but Oregon, Vermont, Washington, California, and Montana. Though most people condemn involuntary euthanasia, or killing someone "for his or her own good" but without the person's consent, opinions about voluntary euthanasia differ widely. Some, like Compassion & Choices and Death with Dignity, advocate legalizing assisted suicide and voluntary euthanasia so that patients have self-determination regarding the termination of their lives. Others fear this would encourage depressed older people to end their lives instead of changing the conditions that cause their depression (Moody, 1994b). A request for euthanasia may be a plea for help, a choice made in ignorance of other alternatives to alleviate pain, or a response to rejection from family or friends rather than a rational decision. This is why providing screening for those requesting assisted suicide is so important. In a review of literature examining depression and requests for assisted suicide, it was found that those who made a request for assisted suicide that was granted had lower depression rates than those who were denied, suggesting that screenings for comorbid conditions like depression by trained professionals is effective (Levene & Parker, 2011).

active euthanasia Taking steps to end life, such as giving a fatal dose of painkilling medication, when unendurable illness makes living intolerable.

passive euthanasia Not doing something to prolong life, such as not utilizing life-support equipment or not giving antibiotics, when unendurable illness makes living intolerable.

> **What Do You Think?**
>
> What is your position on assisted suicide? Should it be legal? If so, under what conditions? Do you have misgivings about your position? Why or why not?

The Right to Die

On April 15, 1975, twenty-one-year-old Karen Ann Quinlan was admitted to a New Jersey hospital in a comatose state. A mechanical respirator artificially sustained her vital processes, but she remained in a vegetative state, with no hope of recovery. Her parents requested that she be allowed to die with dignity, but the medical staff opposed their request. A court battle ensued, and Karen remained on the respirator until, in March 1976, the Supreme Court of New Jersey ruled in the parents' favor for continuing *ordinary care,* including feeding and cleaning, but discontinuing *extraordinary measures* to forestall death. Karen was then removed from the respirator and transferred to a nursing home. She died in June 1985, at age thirty-one, having become a focal point for the "right to die" movement (DeSpelder & Strickland, 1996).

Bereavement

Dying affects not only the person who dies but those with whom the person has close relationships. **Bereavement** is the experience of loss of a loved one through death. Nearly everyone experiences bereavement at some time in their lives, most of us long before reaching late adulthood. College students asked to recall their first experience with death indicated it was the death of a grandparent (42 percent), a pet (28 percent), another relative (15 percent), or an unrelated person (15 percent), and occurred at an average age of eight years old (Dickinson, 1992). The death of a significant person creates more difficulty for children than for adults because children are cognitively immature, have less ability to manipulate their environment to find new sources of love and nurturance, and may blame themselves for the death (Lichten, 2003). The death of a sibling, for example, may cause such extreme grief for the parents that they become emotionally unavailable to the surviving child, and the death of a spouse might have similar implications for the remaining adult's parenting. Adolescents tend to live in the present and deny death. Their feelings of grief may come out as anger: anger toward the loved one who died, anger toward a person who might have protected the loved one, or anger toward God (Worden, 1996). This anger often leads them to act out their grief in acts against society rather than mourning openly. As we saw in Chapter 15, in middle adulthood the death of a sibling, spouse, or partner is not uncommon, and the death of a parent is normative. During late adulthood, however, deaths of loved ones become more frequent. Bereavement has two important components: grief and mourning. **Grief** is the emotional response to one's loss. **Mourning** refers to the actions and manner of expressing grief, which reflect social and cultural prescriptions.

As the child grows, the quality of the parent-child relationship changes, and thus parents feel different types of loss if the child dies.

Grief

Grief results when people lose certain primary relationships, but not when they lose others. *Primary relationships* are close, face-to-face, emotionally important, and special to the particular relational partner. Robert Weiss (1993) distinguishes what he calls *relationships of attachment* from *relationships of community*. Relationships of attachment include spouses or partners, parents, children, and siblings during childhood. Grief, often in the form of severe and persisting distress, follows the death of any single relationship of attachment. Relationships of community include friends, work colleagues, and other family relationships. The death of one relationship of community, such as an adult sibling

---

bereavement The process of getting over the loss of a significant relationship, usually through death.

grief The emotional response to the loss of a relationship of attachment, such as a spouse, partner, parent, or child.

mourning The actions and manner of expressing grief that reflect social and cultural prescriptions.

WORKING WITH Susan Gardner, Social Worker

Helping the Dying and Bereaved

Susan Gardner is a social worker at The Connecticut Hospice, where she has worked for eight years. Before that she worked in medical social work, counseling patients with acute and chronic illnesses.

Michele: *What is Hospice?*

Susan: Hospice is a licensed acute care facility that provides highly skilled, not aggressive, intervention for advanced stages of life-threatening diseases. We provide home care and short-term care—two weeks, on average, although some patients are here three or four months. We have two groups of patients: those who have pain and symptoms and come for pain management and those who are at the end of the disease and come to die. The key is a need for highly specialized acute care.

Michele: *When do patients change from home care to residential care?*

Susan: When pain and symptoms get out of control. A patient may be afraid of getting addicted to strong medicine. Or the family may want a patient to stay alert. Or the patient may no longer be able to swallow pills and be scared of injections. Some patients can't let go because of the family's need to have them live. Others don't know how to read their own bodies. They can't describe what's happening verbally. Nurses and doctors can see changes and read body language. Sometimes home care patients come in for awhile. There was a home care patient who was in twice. He lived alone and didn't eat right. He began to dwindle. When he came here, he felt better. He ate better and got into pain control. Then he went back home.

Michele: *I didn't think you would accept a patient who lived alone.*

Susan: We try to identify a primary care person. Ideally the primary care person is someone who lives with the patient—usually a spouse, son, or daughter—who can notice if a change occurs. But it doesn't need to be a family member. In this man's case, it was a neighbor. The primary care person has to be a back-up for everything. We have aides and nurses, but sometimes they can't get out.

Michele: *Who are your patients?*

Susan: About 70 percent are over sixty-five. About two-thirds have children. About half have spouses. Sometimes a grandchild is the primary care person, sometimes a sibling. A patient with a big Italian family, four brothers and four sisters, was recently here. She was single and had two unmarried sisters. The three had lived together all their lives. The youngest was the caregiver. The other sister and the brothers were married. The married sister came every day. The brothers all came with their spouses. But the unmarried sisters were mutually dependent on each other, and the loss of one was devastating.

Michele: *I know you encourage family to be here with the patient. How do you facilitate that?*

Susan: Each unit has a family room. These include kitchen facilities so families can heat up or prepare the patient's favorite foods. We also have a dining room people can use. We have a couple of rooms with double beds for conjugal visits. Families often stay here when the patient is close to death. We set up cots next to the patient's bed. The rooms are big and have curtains for privacy.

We had a young woman in her early thirties. She had epileptic seizures since childhood and developed a brain tumor. Her parents lived in New York. They slept by her bed for 2½ months. It worked

---

living in a different household, is followed by distress and sadness but not persisting grief. Only the loss of an entire group or network of relationships of community produces grief (Weiss, 1993). Jimena, for example, expressed deep sadness after the death of each of her seven adult siblings, but her grief after the last died was immense. When the last sister died, she was likely grieving for them all. Loss of relationships of attachment triggers grief because we count on these relationships for security, as we discussed in Chapter 5. In relationships of attachment, another, similar relationship, such as a new spouse or another child, cannot substitute for the person who is lost, in contrast to relationships of community, which allow a new friend or colleague at work to be substituted.

Grief is a natural process that occurs after the loss of a loved one. Yet grief is a highly individualized process. "There are many and varied ways people grieve, . . . even one

> **WORKING WITH** Susan Gardner, Social Worker
>
> ### Helping the Dying and Bereaved *continued*
>
> very well. For awhile I feared they weren't dealing with her death, but they really needed to be with her. At the end, they were ready to give her up.
>
> **Michele:** *What do you do here as a social worker?*
>
> **Susan:** There are seven social workers. We start with home care and follow the family through. Each of us generally has fifteen to twenty families at different stages. We spend about two-thirds of our time with the family and a third with the patient. Bereavement is a monumental event in people's lives. Some do well and go on to have healthy lives; others suffer for long periods of time, especially older people. That's why Hospice got started. Bereavement has a big effect on emotional and physical wellness.
>
> **Michele:** *What factors make anticipatory grief more difficult?*
>
> **Susan:** Communication problems. It might be a close family, but if the members aren't honest and use euphemisms and denial, then it's difficult. Unclear communication tends to create conflict. People with a lot of unfinished business have a tough time. They are usually younger. Previous losses in life, such as the death of a parent when a person was very young, can cause problems now with one's own or spouse's death. Also, those who are unsure about seeking treatment have difficulty. For example, if the diagnosis is recent and the patient and family haven't accepted it, they may be actively seeking more treatment while the doctor is telling them there is no more treatment.
>
> **Michele:** *What is your commitment to the bereaved after the death?*
>
> **Susan:** They are followed by the bereavement department for thirteen months after the death. An assessment is made on every patient to identify the people at high risk. Normal follow-up includes support groups, letters four times a year, and an annual healing/grief day early in November. There are talks about how to cope, physical and emotional health, what to do if you are worried about yourself, and how to handle the holidays. Also, people make friends and follow up with each other. People at greater risk receive counseling by trained volunteers, counseling by social workers, and referrals for professional counseling.
>
> **Michele:** *How expensive is Hospice care?*
>
> **Susan:** Anybody can come regardless of ability to pay or insurance. We have had people without a penny. We get funds from Medicare, private insurance, and firm donations. We even have a small facility for people who don't have a home.
>
> **Michele:** *You obviously like your work. Why?*
>
> **Susan:** I like being a little bit helpful at a difficult time. Any social worker wants to be helpful—that's why we become social workers. Patients are very courageous. I find it very rewarding to work with families and help them grow to survive death and deal with grief. Also, there is a big spiritual component to Hospice care. The building has a nondenominational chapel at its center. Most people here are spiritual, not necessarily religious, and I like that. The older people feel they've had a good or meaningful life and are more ready to die.
>
> ### What Do You Think?
>
> 1. In what ways is Hospice care consistent with the concept of the good death?
> 2. How does Hospice address the special problems of bereavement presented in the chapter?

individual's grief varies from moment to moment" (M. S. Stroebe et al., 1993). All losses are not equivalent. For children, grieving for a sibling differs from grieving for a parent in that the surviving child feels more vulnerable because of the closeness in age (Worden, 1996). For adults, the loss of a child will be experienced differently at different stages of the family life cycle (DeVries et al., 1994). As Table 18.5 shows, the quality of the parent-child relationship changes as the child grows, and thus parents feel different types of loss. The loss of an infant is felt more strongly by the mother than the father, perhaps because the connection for the mother begins during pregnancy. Brian DeVries and associates (1994) found that while the child's age did not affect how much grief mothers experienced, fathers showed increasing intensity of grief with increasing age of the child at death. Additionally, other studies have shown that parental grief is also related to the

TABLE 18.5 The Perception of Loss for Bereaved Parents at Different Family Stages

	Infant	Young Child	Adult
Time	Dyssynchrony (infant is antithesis of death)	Futility (child on verge of productivity)	Dyssynchrony (old die before the young)
	Loss of potential	Loss as deprivation	Loss of long-lasting relationship (survival guilt)
Nature/quality	Loss as incompetence, failure, violation (guilt)	Loss as incompetence exacerbated by ambivalence (future expressions)	Loss of social heirs and continuity
Role deceased played	Loss of defining family feature (basis of parent role and adult identity)	Loss of family system/ organization	Loss as inability to procreate
			Loss of control and meaning
			Loss of beneficiary
Characteristics of the death	Loss as failure to protect (guilt) (congenital birth defects, SIDS)	Loss as failure to protect (guilt and stigma) (accidents, homicide, suicide)	Loss exacerbated by reduced involvement (disease: cancer, AIDS)
Social support system	Loss of young infant discounted or minimized (not yet a relationship)	Loss of social world (social withdrawal)	Loss discounted or minimized (forgotten grievers)
			Loss of confidant
			Loss as threatened health and independence

Source: DeVries et al. (1994).

number of children remaining in the family and the cause of death for the deceased child (Keesee, Currier, & Neimeyer, 2008; Wijngaards-de Meij et al., 2005). While the loss of an adult child typically causes the most pain because of the degree of relationship and interconnection, the parent who loses an adult child receives little social recognition; the child's spouse and children are the recipients of the condolences and comfort. People grieve in different ways. Although the grief process has three recognizable phases—(1) an initial period of shock, disbelief, and denial; (2) an intermediate intense mourning period of acute physical and emotional discomfort and social withdrawal; and (3) a culminating period of restitution (Shuchter & Zisook, 1993)—these phases at least partially overlap and do not reflect a unified experience.

In an attempt to understand people's conceptualizations of the normal bereavement reaction, Paul Burnett and his colleagues (1994) had seventy-seven workers in the field of bereavement fill out a scale designed to measure perceptions of bereavement phenomena. The scale was filled out twice, once for the first six weeks of acute bereavement and once for the longer bereavement extending beyond the first anniversary of loss. Although crying and distressing thoughts concerning the loss were perceived as common to acute bereavement and nostalgia was perceived as typical of longer-term bereavement, most common phenomena were seen as applying to both phases. These included sadness, yearning or pining for the lost person, a need to talk about the lost person, intrusive thoughts about the lost person, preoccupation with images/thoughts of the lost person, and distress at reminders of the lost person.

In many situations, there is a warning that a loved one is in the process of dying, such as when a terminal illness is diagnosed. Caregivers of neurocognitive disorder victims, for example, often experience a prolonged period during which they see their relative steadily lose dig-

Anticipatory grief during the caregiving period is common in cases of Alzheimer's disease, especially when the patient no longer recognizes the cargiving loved one.
Source: Photographee.eu/Shutterstock.

nity and quality of life as death approaches. In a study of caregivers of family members with Alzheimer's disease, intense sadness and grief during the caregiving period were common, especially when the family member no longer recognized the caregiver (Jones & Martinson, 1992). The grief one feels before the death occurs is referred to as **anticipatory grief**. Jennifer Klapper, Sidney Moss, Miriam Moss, and Robert Rubinstein (1994) found that 70 percent of their sample of adult married daughters who had lost their late-life mothers in the prior three to six months reported they had actually grieved for their mothers before the deaths. Anticipatory grief was more likely if the older parent had been ill for a long time and was not cognitively intact. In fact, levels of anticipatory grief are higher among those caring for individuals with worse cognitive impairment (Garand et al., 2012). Providing care to a family member during a prolonged and debilitating illness can result in grief before the death and relief from the distress of caregiving after the death (Waldrop, 2007). Jones and Martinson (1992) found that clear relief was more characteristic of the bereavement experiences of caregivers who felt comfortable with decisions made and care given during the illness, whereas relief mixed with guilt was more characteristic of caregivers who had ambivalent feelings about the care given and the feelings expressed. If, for example, they had expressed anger and frustration during the caregiving, they might have felt guilt later.

anticipatory grief The intense sadness and grief that one feels when a loved one is in the process of dying, such as when a terminal illness is diagnosed.

While anticipatory grieving sometimes begins the grief process, grief is a powerful emotion that is stimulated by the actual death. Funerals serve to support the reality and finality of death, an important step in the resolution of grief (Leming & Dickinson, 1994). Funerals also provide social support and human interaction for mourners, which facilitates sharing and diminishing of grief.

Funeral and Ritual Practices

Death constitutes a major rite of passage in the human experience for the deceased and for the mourners, one with which all societies have to cope. Funerals are ritual practices that aid in that coping. While anthropology suggests that funeral rituals were born of fear and designed to appease the dead, modern rituals focus on the expression of both grief and hope (Hayslip, Sewell, & Riddle, 2003; Irion, 1990/1991). Anthropologists and sociologists have found that funeral rituals have three functions (Corr et al., 1996). First, they organize for the appropriate disposal of the body. In contemporary American society, the choices for disposal of the body are burial, cremation, and donating the body for science (which requires prior arrangements).

Second, funerals contribute to the realization of the implications of the death. During a wake or a funeral survivors can view, touch, or kiss the dead body and make the death more real. When each of her parents died, looking at and touching their dead bodies felt necessary to author Michele Hoffnung, because it was so hard to comprehend their not being alive. The mental image of each parent in the coffin remains an important memory for her. In contrast, Ben remembers how difficult it was for him at age fourteen when, after his brother's death, the corpse was removed and cremated without an opportunity to see and say goodbye to it. After spending more than a week at the hospital bedside, Ben missed having a sense of closure. Funeral rituals serve to free people "to act out feelings of meanings that might not be expressible otherwise" (Irion, 1990/1991, p. 161). Kathryn remembers her Irish Catholic grandfather at the wake of his dead wife pouring whiskey into her mouth to "wake her up."

Third, funerals assist in social reintegration and meaningful ongoing life. Funerals and memorial services pull people together and show mourners they are not alone. People who do not regularly see one another share their memories and feelings, and sometimes become closer as a result. Funerals are significant ritual occasions, particularly for older adults, who are more likely to attend them, but also for bereaved children, to whom they provide support and comfort. As one teenage girl said about her mother's funeral, "Everyone gave me support. It made me feel better that all the people were there" (Worden, 1996, p. 22).

These ritual functions of funerals take different forms in different cultures. Cuaxomulco is a typical village of the Mexican highlands. When Don Indalecio, a political leader of the village, died in middle age of a burst appendix, his family and community responded with the patterned cultural response of that region (Grunloh, 1978). The early phase of the funeral focused the initial shock and anxiety of the loss of an important community member on the necessary tasks of food preparation. Being able to provide food demonstrates the family's vitality and the culture's ability to survive. Once the casket with Don Indalecio's body arrived, the large gathering of family and community members began wailing, shrieking, praying, and remembering. It was not until the third day of the funeral that a brass band from another village arrived, breakfast was served, and the casket was finally taken to the graveyard. The funeral procession stopped along the way at the schoolyard, where the teacher came out to honor Don Indalecio; the municipal hall, where the president honored him; and the church, where a mass was delivered. After the burial, the rosary was said every night for eight days, and then a cross was erected at the grave. The funeral provided an opportunity for people to come to terms with the death by gathering together and remembering, as well as for social reintegration as Don Indalecio's brothers reaffirmed the widow's ties to her husband's clan and assumed his community roles and responsibilities.

Funeral rituals also take different forms in different circumstances in the same culture. Funerals of public figures—especially those killed in the line of duty, such as Israeli Prime Minister Yitzhak Rabin or President John F. Kennedy—include ceremonies that help to ensure the continuity of leadership. Assassinations, like other off-time and sudden deaths, cause shock and grief but also fear. The public viewing of the casket, the gathering of public officials from many countries, the eulogies that exalt the significance of the life of the deceased, and the familiarity of the rituals all reassure the family and community that the culture will continue.

American funerals have been criticized because they have failed to serve these necessary functions and because commercial pressure has made them more elaborate. The use of embalming, cosmetics, and expensive linings for caskets seems to promote an image of life rather than death (Mitford, 1963). Closed caskets seem to deny death. In an effort not to upset the mourners, the casket often is not lowered or the grave refilled until after survivors have left the cemetery. This distances the mourners from the reality of the death. In addition, at a time when they are least able to resist because of their grief, the mourners are sometimes sold expensive products and services of dubious value, such as airtight caskets or big limousines. Some funeral directors may take advantage of guilt the bereaved feel for what they did not do while the deceased was living to sell expensive funeral amenities.

In response to these criticisms, there has been a countermovement toward simpler funerals and cremation rather than burial (Marshall & Levy, 1990). There has also been a rise in the number of people seeking out "green" or "natural" funerals that forgo embalming and use simple wooden caskets, if any at all, to reduce the environmental impact of one's death (Harris, 2007). Mortuary science colleges have added psychology, sociology, and ethics to their course requirements to better prepare their graduates to be sensitive practitioners (Ewing et al., 2010; Gose, 1995). Paul Irion (1990/1991) reports developments within most religious denominations of new rituals that take into account growing psychological knowledge of the grieving process and are more sensitive to the fact that those attending a funeral are likely to include members of several faiths and ethnic communities. Even when wakes, funerals, and memorial services do function to pull survivors together and help them to face the reality of the death, they do not go far enough in accomplishing these tasks. Mourning is a much longer process.

Mourning

Mourning is the social experience of grief. In all societies there are some things a person cannot do (restrictions) and some that must be done (obligations), although these things vary from one culture to the next. In a study of seventy-eight societies in Europe, America, Japan, Africa, and the Pacific Islands, Paul Rosenblatt, Patricia Walsh, and Douglas Jackson (1976) found striking similarities in grieving as well as wide differences in defining what is an appropriate expression of grief. Table 18.6 shows some ethnic differences in behaviors considered appropriate after the death of a spouse. Because the United States is culturally diverse, what is an "ethnically normal" expression of grief for one individual or family may be deviant for another. In families consisting of people from different cultures or in families that are assimilating and between cultures, the differences may cause discomfort and misunderstanding. For instance, in Japan and China white is the color of mourning, so imagine an immigrant's feelings when other mourners show up in black at their loved one's funeral.

In the culturally diverse United States, it is important to understand ethnic differences in what are considered appropriate behaviors after the death of a loved one, in this case a spouse.

White, Anglo-Saxon, Protestant social norms are such that displays of grief, such as crying, is acceptable only within the rigid confines of the funeral. Grief is something to be mastered, and mourners are expected to return to their normal routines quickly and not burden others with public displays of grief (Rosenblatt, 1993). Displays of grief are more socially acceptable from women than for men (Vera, 2003). The idea that grief should not be displayed and shared might dissuade those who need to seek grief counseling from getting the assistance they need. In fact, the recent death of a loved one is one of the largest risk factors for developing depression during late adulthood (Cole & Dendurkuri, 2003).

Additionally, there are few prescriptions for how to interact with one who is mourning. In a study that asked people how they would respond if they met someone who had lost a loved one through death since their last meeting, only 25 percent of the respondents said they would mention the death (Stephenson, 1985). Most reported they would not know what to say. The lack of rituals of mourning and rituals of interacting with mourners pushes people to deny their need to mourn. The status of the lost loved one is considered to warrant different levels of grief, which reflects a "widespread cultural sense of hierarchy in the permitted severity of grief: loss of a child (at any age) at the nadir, followed by loss of spouse, and finally the on-time loss of an elderly parent" (Klapper et al., 1994, p. 34). This too can push one toward denial of a need to mourn. Despite the grief an adult daughter may feel due to the death of her mother, she may believe she must control the expression of that grief because her mother was old and the death was on time. Off-time losses are expected to produce more expression of grief. The death of a child, a teenager, or a young adult is unexpected and tragic, whereas the death of an older person is expected and "merely" sad.

This denial of one's need to mourn and lack of customary mourning behavior contrast with the customs of Jews in the United States. Jewish law and custom give mourners a structure that encourages feeling their loss and thus healing. After the funeral, immediate mourners

TABLE 18.6 Behaviors Considered Appropriate After the Death of a Spouse

	African Americans	Japanese Americans	Mexican Americans	White Americans
To remarry				
Unimportant to wait	34%	14%	22%	26%
1 week–6 months	15	3	1	23
1 year	25	30	38	34
2 years or more	11	26	20	11
Other (including never/depends)	16	28	19	7
To stop wearing black				
Unimportant to wait	62	42	52	53
1 week–1 month	24	26	11	31
6 months	11	21	35	6
1 year or more	4	11	3	11
To return to place of employment				
Unimportant to wait	39	22	27	47
1 day–1 week	39	28	37	35
1 month or more	17	35	27	9
Other/depends	6	16	9	10
To start going out with other men/women				
Unimportant to wait	30	17	17	25
1 week–1 month	14	8	4	9
6 months–1 year	24	22	22	29
2 years or more	11	34	40	21
Other/depends	21	19	18	17

Source: Adapted from Kalish & Reynolds (1981).

(parents, spouse, and children) sit *shiva* for seven days, which is the intense period of formal mourning (Diamant & Cooper, 1991). Together in one home, they grieve, accept visitors, talk of their feelings, and share memories of the deceased. Shiva creates an emotionally protective setting for the mourners in which they are not expected to reciprocate what is done for them (Slochower, 1993). Friends and neighbors bring food, and mirrors are covered to discourage vanity; the mourners wear strips of black fabric as a visible symbol of being inwardly torn by grief, and sit on stools. Prayers continue to get said twice a day until, after eleven to twelve months, the family and friends return to the cemetery and the stone is placed on the grave. Only after the *unveiling* of the stone does the mourning period end. Remembering still continues. Every year on the eve of the day of the death, as well as on certain holidays, a special twenty-four-hour memorial candle is lit as an act of remembrance.

Hispanic Americans also believe it takes time to express one's feelings of grief. Funerals and wakes in the Los Angeles Mexican American community mark the coming together of large numbers of supportive people, family and friends, and the outpouring

These graves in a cemetery in Oaxaca, Mexico, have been decorated by the families of the dead in celebration of El Día de los Muertos (the Day of the Dead). This celebration encourages communication between the living and the dead. People clean and decorate the graves of deceased family members and offer food and gifts to their dead loved ones.
Source: Kobby Dagan/Shutterstock.

of emotions with little restraint (Kalish & Reynolds, 1981). Using an inventory of grief, Jo-Anne Grabowski and Thomas Frantz (1993) found significantly greater intensity of grief among Latinos than among Anglos. Latinos who were grieving a sudden death had significantly greater grief intensity than did Latinos grieving an expected death and Anglos grieving either kind of death. Mexican Americans consider the grieving process to involve the gathering together of a large support group of friends, family, and community members (Salcido, 1990). Among Puerto Ricans in New York City, the wake may continue for several days (Eisenbruch, 1984). This is also true of Dominicans. Puerto Ricans prefer lengthy formal mourning periods and strongly prohibit saying anything ill of the person who has died (Campos, 1990). Cultural traditions that facilitate the expression of grief can help survivors to mourn and thus to heal.

In Mexico, the dead are remembered once a year in a national fiesta, El Día de los Muertos (the Day of the Dead). The fiesta occurs on All Souls' Day, the Catholic Church's day for commemorating the dead, and encourages communion between the living and the dead. People eat bread and candy made in the shape of human bones. They clean and decorate the graves of deceased family members and offer food and gifts to their dead loved ones. This communal celebration pays respect to the dead and provides comfort for the living.

Many Asian Americans believe death allows for a continued relationship between the deceased and the survivors. In keeping with this belief, funerals and memorial services are considered very important events because showing respect for ancestors ensures that the ancestors will contribute to the well-being of the survivors (Kalish & Reynolds, 1981). Japanese Americans and Chinese Americans tend to hold traditional funerals at which people assume formal roles, bring gifts, and take extensive photographs. Because of the ongoing interaction between the living and the deceased, Asian Americans make frequent visits to grave sites, have very conservative mourning traditions, and are unlikely to remarry or even date after becoming widowed (Kalish & Reynolds, 1981).

Support Groups

Given that people have complex and varied feelings of grief and that cultural pressures compel one to get on with life, bereavement programs have developed to encourage survivors to feel normal about their grief reactions and to offer empathy (Schneidman, 1992; Vera, 2003). Although society rushes on, grief takes time and cannot be rushed. Support groups offer the opportunity for bereaved people to share their concerns and feelings with others going through similar experiences. Bereavement support groups take several forms. Some are self-help groups composed entirely of bereaved peers. Widow-to-Widow, WidowNet, and Healing Hearts, Healing Hands are programs that provide mutual aid and bereavement support and have served as models for many mutual help groups. Self-help groups are a low-cost, community-based alternative that can meet the social and psychological needs of a large segment of the bereaved population (Lieberman, 1993). Other support groups are organized by hospice and other palliative care programs and led by trained volunteers who assist bereaved family members. Still other groups are led by trained professional social workers or bereavement counselors. In addition to support groups, individual bereavement counseling has been shown to be effective, both as a preventative measure for people who are high risk and as a therapeutic intervention particularly because late-life bereaved are at increased risk for depression (Cole & Dendurkuri, 2003; Raphael et al., 1993).

Recovery

Grief involves a process of transition, a change in both the self and the family. "Severe grief, no matter how fully individuals emerge from it, should be expected to produce character change" (Weiss, 1993, p. 277). Survivors take on new roles and see themselves from a new perspective. In one study, preadolescent boys and adolescent boys and girls reported feeling they had matured as a result of the death of a parent two years earlier (Worden, 1996). As we discussed in Chapter 15, as a result of parental death, middle-aged adult children are likely to be more conscious of their own mortality, feel more responsible for themselves, and take on new kinkeeping responsibilities in the family. Likewise, as we discussed in Chapter 17, a bereaved spouse is likely to take on new roles and interact with the world in new ways. Grief therefore leads not simply to recovery but to change and transformation (Calhoun, Tedeschi, Cann, & Hanks, 2010; Klapper et al., 1994). Notice, for instance, how Susan Gardner talks about helping the bereaved "to grow to survive death" in the Working With interview on page 674.

What, then, is recovery if it is not a return to one's former self? Recovery is best understood as a return to previous levels of functioning. Indicators of recovery are the ability to find energy in everyday life, freedom from psychological pain and distress, the ability to feel pleasure when desirable events occur, hopefulness regarding the future, and the ability to function with reasonable adequacy as spouse, parent, and member of the community (Weiss, 1993). Not everyone goes through the same grieving process to reach recovery. In a series of studies of emotional reactions to significant

Grief can help survivors to mourn and thus to heal. Recovery, a return to previous levels of functioning, typically entails taking on new roles and interacting with the world in new ways. Here a widow mows her lawn.
Source: Aigars Reinholds/Shutterstock.

> **What Do You Think?**
>
> Consider the last wake, funeral, or memorial service you attended. In what ways did it meet the ritual functions that can help the mourners? (If you have not been to any, interview someone who has.)

loss, Camille Wortman, Roxane Silver, and Ronald Kessler (1993) found great variability in response. Intense distress or depression was not inevitable following a major loss, and the failure to experience such distress did not predict poor adaptation to loss. Among their sample of widows, for example, those with the best marriages were particularly distressed by the loss of a spouse, whereas those in unhappy marriages showed less depression after the loss. The data suggest that the meaning of the loss to the survivor and the survivor's coping resources have an impact on the grieving and recovery process. As with any other life experience, the social and cultural contexts affect the recovery process.

Looking Back

Even as life draws to an end, the lifespan themes first articulated in Chapter 1 are still evident. Let us focus on the concept of the good death as we review these themes for the last time.

- **Continuity Within Change**—The good death involves being surrounded by family and friends with whom the dying person has shared life. We see here the continued importance of the social convoy. Regardless of their age, dying people benefit from open awareness about their illness and open communication with their loved ones and caregivers. Even while physical changes lead to death, cognitive and psychosocial needs of the dying individual persist and exhibit continuity. The good death includes the control of pain (palliative care) so that physical discomfort does not overwhelm the other aspects of life in the final days.

- **Lifelong Growth**—Growth is still possible as dying individuals work to find resolution of discord they may have had with loved ones over the years. Most people have apologies to make, regrets to voice, forgiveness to bestow, or love to express. They also need time for introspection, reminiscing, and affirming their beliefs. These tasks require growth and change. Considerations about end-of-life decisions often take into account those who will live on. And those who survive experience growth and change as they return to normal levels of functioning with new strength and understanding after the period of bereavement.

- **Changing Meanings and Vantage Points**—The death of a loved one leaves friends and family with a gap in their lives. When the death is of a child or a young adult, the loss feels tragic. When the death is of an older adult, it feels sad but age appropriate. In either case, the survivors must deal with their grief, learn to live with their sorrow, and find ways to remember the deceased love one. For example, the experience of losing a parent means different things to a dependent child than to an independent adult. Although in both cases the loss is of a relationship of attachment, for the child who is still dependent on the parent the daily circumstances of life change dramatically, whereas for the adult child the changes are less profound. The loss of a sibling is also experienced differently at different times in the life cycle. For a child, the loss of a sibling is the loss of a relationship of attachment; for an adult, it is the loss of a relationship of community. While the loss of a spouse is always of a relationship of attachment, it is hardest when it occurs "off time," such as in early or middle adulthood, and less hard when it occurs "on time," in late adulthood.

- **Developmental Diversity**—How we think about death, how we bury and mourn our dead, and how we celebrate them in the years after death depend on the cultural practices of our time and place. While everyone in every culture must come to terms with death, some do so with denial and some with weeping and wailing—and there are many points in between these extremes. Just because death is universal does not mean that all people experience it in the same way.

  Even in the contemporary United States, many religious and cultural traditions influence mourning practices and burial/cremation rituals. While the body must be disposed of, this may be done publicly or privately. While people must grieve, this may be done publicly or privately. While people must remember, this may be done communally or individually. When we expand our consideration to other places and other times, the range of death practices becomes very varied indeed.

Chapter Summary

- **What are contemporary attitudes toward death, and how do they affect the treatment of the dying?** Social and technological changes in the twentieth century have led to a separation of death from everyday life and to an attitude that denies death. Recently the death awareness movement has promoted the idea of the good death and raised consciousness about issues of dying and bereavement that have influenced care of the dying and death education.
- **Why are older adults likely to be more accepting of death than younger people?** Aging is associated with increasing acceptance of death and heightened concern about the process of dying. Although most Americans approve of euthanasia and assisted suicide as legal options, most do not make those end-of-life choices. Unfinished business can interfere with normative death acceptance among older adults. Suicide rates are higher in later life, especially among white males and others who have reduced opportunity or inclination to communicate. Elisabeth Kübler-Ross has outlined five stages of reactions to dying. While these stages have been widely accepted by clinicians who work with dying patients, they have been challenged by theory and research.

  The good death is one that enables the dying individual to experience growth in this final stage of life. It emphasizes honesty, homelike settings, and control of pain.
- **What choices are available for terminal care, and how do they differ?** Nursing homes, hospices, and home care provide terminal care alternatives to hospital death. Home death provides familiarity and greater opportunities for sustaining relationships, and allows for mutual sharing of concerns and feelings. That choice also has many difficult aspects for which many families are unprepared. Controversy surrounds the issue of whether individuals suffering from a terminal disease should be allowed assistance in ending their lives. While the right to die movement argues in favor of physician-assisted voluntary euthanasia, opponents argue in favor of palliative care.
- **How does bereavement affect survivors, and what supports are available to help their recovery?** Grief is a highly variable experience. Although certain grief reactions are considered common, differences abound based on the nature of the relationship, the on-time or off-time nature of the loss, the amount of time allowed to anticipate the loss, and cultural expectations. Funerals and other ritual practices serve important functions for mourners, but the mourning process takes longer than the duration of these rituals. Although the white, Anglo-Saxon, Protestant expectation is that grief will be mastered and the individual will return to normal routines quickly, different ethnic cultural traditions within the United States express mourning differently. Bereavement support groups bring together people going through similar experiences to provide empathy and encourage survivors to feel normal about their grief reactions. Recovery entails growth and change as a survivor returns to previous levels of functioning while adjusting to a new set of life circumstances.

Key Terms

active euthanasia (p. 672)
anticipatory grief (p. 677)
bereavement (p. 673)
communicable diseases (p. 656)
death awareness movement (p. 657)

degenerative diseases (p. 656)
grief (p. 673)
grief work (p. 669)
hospice (p. 670)

mourning (p. 673)
palliative care (p. 671)
passive euthanasia (p. 672)
the good death (p. 667)

Glossary

A

accommodation According to Piaget, the process of modifying existing ideas or action-skills to fit new experiences.

achievement motivation Behavior that enhances competence or enhances judgments of competence.

achievement test A test designed to evaluate a person's current state of knowledge.

achieving stage Schaie's first stage of adult thinking during which young adults direct their intelligence toward specific goals rather than following every inclination as might adolescents who have not yet formulated clear personal choices.

acquaintance rape Sexual assault in which the attacker is a friend, family member, or romantic partner of the victim.

acquisitive stage Schaie's term for all four of Piaget's stages, during which the child or adolescent builds basic skills and abilities that precede Schaie's stages of adult thinking.

active euthanasia Taking steps to end life, such as giving a fatal dose of painkilling medication, when unendurable illness makes living intolerable.

activity competence The skills and knowledge necessary to take advantage of opportunities for leisure activities. Because it is generally established in earlier adult years, older adults who are better educated are more prepared to feel competent engaging in a variety of activities.

activity settings Group situations in which a shared focus of attention and shared goals facilitate an individual's learning from others in the group.

activity theory The theory of aging that assumes older people who maintain social, physical, and intellectual activity levels similar to those during their middle years age more successfully than those who are less active.

adaptation Piaget's term for the process by which development occurs; concepts are deepened or broadened by assimilation and stretched or modified by accommodation.

adaptive mechanisms George Vaillant's term for the coping styles that people use to adapt to life events and that determine their levels of mental health. Vaillant categorized four types: mature mechanisms, immature mechanisms, psychotic mechanisms, and neurotic mechanisms.

adolescence The stage of development between childhood and adulthood, around ages ten to twenty-two.

adolescent egocentrism The tendency of adolescents to perceive the world (and themselves) from their own perspective.

adoption study A research method for studying the relative contributions of heredity and environment in which genetically related children reared apart are compared with genetically unrelated children reared together.

advance directive A legal document specifying what medical care can be given in the event the person becomes unable to make or communicate his or her decisions.

ageism Stereotyping of and discrimination against people because they are old.

aggression A bold, assertive action that is intended to hurt another person or to procure an object.

allele One of several alternative forms of a gene.

Alzheimer's disease A chronic brain syndrome caused by degeneration of the brain cells in those portions of the cerebral cortex that are associated with memory, learning, and judgment. Patients go through a series of stages beginning with loss of memory and ending with coma and death.

American Sign Language (ASL) System of nonverbal gesturing that is used by many people who are deaf or hearing impaired and that functions as a language.

amniotic sac A tough, spongy bag filled with salty fluid that surrounds the embryo, protects it from sudden jolts, and helps to maintain a fairly stable temperature.

androgyny A tendency to integrate both masculine and feminine behaviors into the personality.

anorexia nervosa A physical and psychological disturbance that causes a person to refuse to eat sufficient food and to develop an increasingly unrealistic view of his or her body; most individuals with anorexia are teenage girls.

anticipatory grief The intense sadness and grief that one feels when a loved one is in the process of dying, such as when a terminal illness is diagnosed.

anxious-avoidant attachment An insecure bond between infant and caregiver in which the child rarely cries when separated from the caregiver and tends to avoid or ignore the caregiver when reunited.

anxious-resistant attachment An insecure bond between infant and caregiver in which the child shows signs of anxiety preceding separation, is intensely upset by separation, and seeks close contact when reunited while at the same time resisting the caregiver's efforts to comfort.

Apgar Scale A system of rating newborns' health immediately following birth based on heart rate, strength of breathing, muscle tone, color, and reflex irritability.

aptitude test A measurement of ability that estimates future performance in some realm of behavior.

assessment The diagnosis of an individual's strengths, needs, and qualities.

assimilation According to Piaget, a method by which a person responds to new experiences by using existing concepts to interpret new ideas and experiences.

assisted living Semi-independent living in which some degree of informal and formal help with daily living enables older adults to continue to live in the community.

assisted reproductive technology (ART) Any infertility treatment in which fertilization of the egg occurs outside the womb.

attachment An intimate and enduring emotional relationship between two people, such as infant and caregiver, characterized by reciprocal affection and a periodic desire to maintain physical closeness.

attention deficit/hyperactivity disorder (ADHD) See *hyperactivity*.

authoritarian parenting A style of childrearing characterized by a high degree of control and demands on children's maturity and a low degree of clarity of communication and nurturance.

authoritative parenting A style of childrearing characterized by a high degree of control, clarity of communication, maturity demands, and nurturance.

autonomy An individual's ability to govern and regulate her or his own thoughts, feelings, and actions freely and responsibly while at the same time overcoming feelings of shame and doubt.

autonomy versus shame and doubt The second of Erikson's psychosocial crises of children ages one to three during which they struggle to control their own thoughts, feelings, and actions.

B

babbling Infant vocalizations produced prior to acquiring language and without verbally meaningful intent.

balanced bilingual A person who is equally fluent in two languages rather than more fluent in one language than in the other.

basic dualism William Perry's term for a perspective toward intellectual and ethical problems from which students view truth in terms of right or wrong, good or bad, and we or they.

beanpole family structure The contemporary family structure, which has more generations but fewer people in each generation because of increased longevity and a decreased birth rate.

behavior modification Techniques based on the principles of learning theory that can be used by parents, teachers, therapists, and other professionals to help children, adolescents, and adults reduce or eliminate undesirable behaviors and learn desirable ones.

bereavement The process of getting over the loss of a significant relationship, usually through death.

binge eating disorder A disorder in which a person feels out of control of his or her eating and consumes much more than most people would eat in a short period of time, sometimes even when he or she is not hungry.

biographical method Daniel Levinson's method for reconstructing the life course by interviewing the person and using a variety of other sources, such as visiting the person's workplace and home.

blended family A family created from a combination of stepchildren, stepparents, and stepsiblings.

bulimia nervosa A disorder in which a person, usually a teenage girl, eats huge amounts of food and then vomits it to avoid gaining weight.

burnout Disillusionment and exhaustion on the job that may result from stress caused by multiple role commitments, discrimination based on race/ethnicity or gender, or other factors.

C

canalization The tendency of many developmental processes to unfold in highly predictable ways under a wide range of conditions.

career consolidation A stage George Vaillant identified as fitting between Erikson's stages of intimacy and generativity and occurring in one's thirties. The men Vaillant studied tended to work hard, devote themselves to career advancement, and sacrifice play.

caregiver-infant synchrony Patterns of closely coordinated social and emotional interaction between caregiver and infant.

case study A research study of a single individual or small group of individuals considered as a unit.

cellular theories Theories of aging that focus on the processes that take place within and between the cells, leading to the breakdown of cells, tissue, and organs. Sometimes referred to as *wear and tear theories*.

central nervous system The brain and nerve cells of the spinal cord.

cephalocaudal principle The tendency for organs, reflexes, and skills to develop sooner at the top (or head) of the body and later in areas farther down the body.

chromosome A threadlike, rod-shaped structure containing genetic information that is transmitted from parents to children; each human sperm or egg cell contains twenty-three chromosomes, and these determine a person's inherited characteristics.

circular reaction Piaget's term for an action often repeated, apparently because it is self-reinforcing.

classical conditioning According to Pavlov, learning in which a neutral stimulus gains the power to bring about a certain response by repeated association with another stimulus that already elicits the same response.

classification Grouping of objects according to standards or criteria.

climacteric The gradual reduction in sex hormone production that is an aspect of primary aging during middle adulthood, leading to menopause in women and to reproductive system changes in men that decrease fertility.

clique A small, closely knit peer group of two or more members (average of six members) who are intimately involved in a number of shared purposes and activities and exclude those who are not.

cognition All processes by which humans acquire knowledge; methods for thinking or gaming knowledge about the world.

cognitive development The area of human development concerned with cognition; involves all psychological processes by which individuals learn and think about their environment.

cognitive mechanics Basic memory processes, such as sensory information input, visual and motor memory, and the processes of discrimination, categorization, and coordination, that are likely to decline in late adulthood.

cognitive pragmatics Intellectual problems in which culture-based knowledge and skills are primary, such as reading and writing skills, language comprehension, professional skills, and knowledge about strategies to manage the peaks and valleys of life, that may grow in late adulthood.

cohabitation Unrelated adults living together in a sexual partnership.

cohort In developmental research, a group of subjects born at a particular time who therefore experience particular historical events or conditions.

communicable diseases Diseases that spread from person to person and formerly killed large numbers of old and young people alike, such as influenza, cholera, scarlet fever, measles, and smallpox.

competence An individual's increased skill and capability in successfully exploring, mastering, and controlling the world around them.

conception The moment at which the male's sperm cell penetrates the female's egg cell (ovum), forming a zygote.

concrete operations Logical thinking about concrete or tangible objects and processes; especially characteristic of middle childhood.

congregate housing Housing that provides elderly residents with some communal services, at least a central kitchen and dining room.

conservation A belief that certain properties (such as quantity) remain constant despite changes in perceived features such as dimensions, position, and shape.

constructive play A type of play that involves manipulation of physical objects to build or construct something.

contextual relativism William Perry's term for a perspective toward intellectual and ethical problems from which students begin to see that truth is relative and that the meaning of an event depends on its context and on the framework of the knower who is trying to understand the event.

control group In an experimental research study, the group of participants who experience conditions similar or identical to the experimental group, but without experiencing the experimental treatment.

control talk A style or register of speech used by teachers to indicate their power over activities, discussion, and behavior of students.

coparenting A parenting partnership in which child-rearing goals, strategies, and responsibilities are shared.

correlation An association between two variables in which changes in one variable tend to occur with changes in the other. The association does not necessarily imply a causal link between the variables.

critical period Any period during which development is particularly susceptible to an event or influence, either negative or positive.

critical thinking Reflection or thinking about complex issues, usually to make decisions or take actions.

cross-sectional study A study that compares individuals of different ages at the same point in time.

crowd A large, loosely knit peer group of between fifteen and thirty members (average of twenty members) that generally consists of from two to four cliques.

crystallized intelligence The cognitive processes and primary abilities, such as vocabulary, general information, and word fluency, that are strongly shaped by formal education and increase or remain relatively stable with age.

D

death awareness movement A response to the increasing number of very old people in American society, the prolongation of the dying process, the anxieties of the nuclear age, the 1960s perspective that asserted the rights of the ignored and underprivileged (in this case the dying), and the AIDS epidemic. It has led to the analysis of cultural messages about death, increased sensitivity to the dying, and increased education about death.

degenerative diseases Diseases that cause the slow, prolonged, and painful deaths typical of late adulthood, such as cardiovascular disease and cancer.

dependent variable A factor that is measured in an experiment and that *depends on,* or is controlled by, one or more independent variables.

development Long-term changes in a person's growth, feelings, patterns of thinking, social relationships, and motor skills.

developmentally appropriate practice Methods and goals of teaching considered optimal for young children given current knowledge of child development.

discourse Extended verbal interaction.

discrimination In terms of the labor market, the valuation of personal characteristics of a worker that are not related to productivity, such as educational background, health, and marital status, or based on prejudice on the part of employers, coworkers, employees, or customers.

disengagement theory The theory of aging that views the reduction of elderly people's social involvement to be a natural and mutual process between the elderly and society.

displaced homemaker A woman who committed herself to the conventional roles of wife and mother, lost these roles due to separation, divorce, or widowhood, and was unprepared for employment and single parenthood.

disorganized-disoriented attachment This pattern indicates the greatest degree of insecurity between infant and parent. When reunited with the parent, the infant exhibits confused and contradictory behavior, including unresponsiveness, turning away when held, frozen postures, and unexpected cries after being comforted.

domain A realm of psychological functioning.

dominant gene In any paired set of genes, the gene with greater influence in determining characteristics that are physically visible or manifest.

Down syndrome A congenital condition that causes mental retardation.

durable power of attorney for health care A legal document designating a person to make medical decisions on one's behalf other than the withdrawal of life support systems.

E

early articulator Jean Veevers's term for someone who knew from childhood that she did not want to have children.

ego According to Freud, the rational, realistic part of the personality; coordinates impulses from the id with demands imposed by the superego and by society.

egocentrism Inability to distinguish between one's own point of view and that of another person.

ego integrity versus despair Erikson's eighth and final psychosocial crisis, reached during late adulthood and old age, in which one looks back on one's life with dignity, optimism, and wisdom while facing the despair resulting from the negative aspects of old age.

embryonic stage The stage in prenatal development that lasts from week 2 through week 8.

empathy A sensitive awareness of the thoughts and feelings of another person.

equal-partner relationship A couple relationship based on the principle of negotiating about shared concerns and responsibilities. Instead of a preset assignment of roles and responsibilities, everything (who works, who cooks, who pays the bills) is open for renegotiation except the principle that everything is negotiable.

estrogen A sex hormone, sometimes called the *female sex hormone* because its high concentration in girls stimulates the growth of the ovaries and vagina during puberty.

estrogen replacement therapy (ERT) The taking of replacement estrogen to alleviate menopausal symptoms; often recommended for women who have surgical menopause.

executive stage Schaie's stage of adult thinking that applies to some middle adults who have powerful positions that bring broader and more complex responsibilities and require a new type of cognition, applying postformal thinking about systems to practical problems, as they work to understand and meet the needs of competing groups in a large organization that affects many people beyond self and family.

experimental group In an experimental research study, the group of participants who experience the experimental treatment while in other respects experiencing conditions similar or identical to those of the control group.

experimental study A study in which circumstances are arranged so that just one or two factors or influences vary at a time.

expertise Specialized experience in specific domains of knowledge that enables efficient and effective performance and is not hampered by age.

F

failure to thrive A condition in which an infant seems seriously delayed in physical growth and is noticeably apathetic in behavior.

family life cycle A series of predictable stages that families experience based on the age of the children.

fetal alcohol syndrome (FAS) A congenital condition exhibited by babies born to mothers who consumed too much alcohol during pregnancy. They do not arouse easily and tend to behave sluggishly in general; they also have distinctive facial characteristics.

fetal presentation Refers to the body part of the fetus that is closest to the mother's cervix; may be head first (cephalic), feet and rump first (breech), or shoulders first (transverse).

fetal stage The stage in prenatal development that lasts from the eighth week of pregnancy until birth.

fictive kin Constructed relationships, such as foster child or godparent, that by merging voluntary and obligatory relations take on the significance of blood kin.

fine motor coordination Ability to carry out smoothly small movements that involve precise timing but not strength.

fluid intelligence The cognitive processes and primary abilities, such as information processing and reasoning, that depend more on neurological development and less on formal education and peak in late adolescence, followed by rapid decline.

formal operational thought Thinking based on previously acquired concrete mental operations and involving hypothetical reasoning and attention to the structure or form of ideas.

functional play A cognitive level of play that involves simple, repeated movements and a focus on one's own body.

G

games with rules A cognitive level of play involving relatively formal activities with fixed rules.

gender The thoughts, feelings, and behaviors associated with being male or female by one's culture.

gender-role stereotypes The culturally "appropriate" patterns of gender-related behaviors expected by society. Also called *sex roles*.

gene A molecular structure, carried on chromosomes, containing genetic information; the basic unit of heredity.

general adaptation syndrome The pattern of physical response to stress identified by Hans Seyle, which has three stages: alarm, resistance, and exhaustion. Confrontation with a stressor sets the stress response in motion. The syndrome appears to be irreversible and accumulates to constitute the signs of aging.

generativity versus stagnation The seventh of Erikson's psychosocial crises, reached in middle adulthood, in which one must balance the feeling that one's life is personally satisfying and socially meaningful with feelings of purposelessness.

genetic imprinting A mode of inheritance in which genes are chemically marked so that the number of the chromosome pair contributed by either the father or the mother is activated, regardless of its genetic makeup.

genotype The set of genetic traits inherited by an individual. See also *phenotype*.

germinal stage The stage in prenatal development that occurs during the first two weeks of pregnancy; characterized by rapid cell division. Also called the *period of the ovum*.

glass ceiling The invisible barriers that women and minorities confront as they approach the top of the corporate hierarchy, including social barriers, such as stereotyping and prejudice; internal structural barriers within the business, such as lack of mentoring and different standards for performance evaluation; and government barriers, such as lack of consistent monitoring and law enforcement.

grief The emotional response to the loss of a relationship of attachment, such as a spouse, partner, parent, or child.

grief work An initial phase of the bereavement process that entails anger, self-recrimination, depression, and taking care of unfinished business.

growth spurt A rapid change in height and weight that occurs in puberty and is preceded and followed by years of comparatively little increase.

H

habituation The tendency to attend to novel stimuli and ignore familiar ones.

health-compromising behaviors Behaviors that lead to illness, pathological aging, and premature death, such as smoking, drug and alcohol abuse, and unsafe sex.

holographic speech A single word used to communicate a thought, such as when a child says "up" instead of "pick me up."

homophobia Fear, dread, hostility, or prejudice directed toward gay, lesbian, and bisexual persons and the resulting mistreatment and discrimination.

hormone replacement therapy (HRT) The taking of replacement estrogen in combination with progestin (artificial progesterone) to alleviate menopausal symptoms that is recommended for women who have not had a hysterectomy because ERT has been shown to increase the rate of endometrial cancer.

hospice An interdisciplinary team and holistic approach to death by attending to the physical, emotional, spiritual, and aesthetic needs of patients and their families, primarily in their own homes but also at acute care facilities.

hostile attribution bias The tendency to view others' behavior as aggressive, even when those behaviors are innocuous, which often leads to a hostile reactive response.

hyperactivity Excessive levels of activity and an inability to concentrate for normal periods of time. See *attention deficit hyperactivity disorder*.

hypertrophy The overgrowth of tissue in the prostate gland that is one of the physical changes of the male climacteric and sometimes leads to pressure on the urethra, which interferes with urine flow.

hypokinesia A disease of disuse that causes degeneration and functional loss of muscle and bone tissue and can be prevented by regular exercise.

hypothesis A precise prediction based on a scientific theory; often capable of being tested in a scientific research study.

I

id In Freud's theory, the part of an individual's personality that is present at birth, unconscious, impulsive, and unrealistic, and that attempts to satisfy a person's biological and emotional needs and desires by maximizing pleasure and avoiding pain.

identity diffusion A failure to achieve a relatively coherent, integrated, and stable identity.

identity status Marcia's four categories of identity development: identity achievement, identity diffusion, moratorium, and foreclosure.

identity versus role confusion The fifth of Erikson's psychosocial crises, in which one must integrate one's many childhood skills and beliefs and gain recognition for them from society.

imaginary audience A characteristic of young adolescents in which they act as though they are performing for an audience and believe that others are as concerned with their appearance and behavior as they themselves are.

independent variable A factor that an experimenter manipulates (varies) to determine its influence on the population being studied.

indifferent parenting A style of parenting in which parents' permissiveness reflects an avoidance of child-rearing responsibilities, sometimes with detrimental results; these parents are detached and emotionally uninvolved.

individuation The process by which an adolescent develops a unique and separate personal identity. Consists of four subphases: differentiation, practice and experimentation, rapprochement, and consolidation.

industry versus inferiority Erikson's fourth crisis, during which children concern themselves with their capacity to do good work and thereby develop confident, positive self-concepts or else face feelings of inferiority.

infant-directed speech The style or register of speech used by adults and older children when talking with a one- or two-year-old infant.

infant mortality rate The frequency with which infants die compared to the frequency with which they live.

infertility A couple's inability to conceive a pregnancy after one year of sexual relations without contraception.

information processing theory Explanations of cognition that focus on the precise, detailed features or steps of mental activities. These theories often use computers as models for human thinking.

informed consent An agreement to participate in a research study based on understanding the nature of the research, protection of human rights, and freedom to decline to participate at any time.

initiative versus guilt Erikson's third psychosocial crisis, during which a child's increasing ability to initiate verbal and physical activity and expanding imaginative powers lead to fantasies of large and sometimes frightening proportions.

intelligence A general ability to learn from experience; also refers to ability to reason abstractly.

intermodal perception The coordination and integration of multiple channels of sensory information.

interview A face-to-face, directed conversation used in a research study to gather in-depth information.

intimacy versus isolation The sixth of Erikson's psychosocial crises, in which young adults must be able to develop intimate relationships with others while dealing with the fear of loss of identity that such intimacy entails.

J

juvenile delinquency A pattern of destructive or antisocial activities and lawbreaking offenses committed by adolescents.

juvenile period Proposed by Sullivan, a period between ages five and ten when children show increasing interest in developing intense friendships or "chum relationships" with peers of the same gender.

L

latency According to Freud, the stage of development between the phallic and genital stages. Sexual feelings and activities are on hold as the child struggles to resolve the oedipal conflict.

learning disability Difficulty in learning a specific academic skill such as reading or arithmetic.

learning orientation Achievement motivation that comes from the learner and the task.

leisure Activities chosen freely and enjoyed at one's own pace.

life expectancy A statistical estimate of the probable number of years remaining in the life of an individual based on the likelihood that members of a particular birth cohort will die at various ages. It changes for each cohort from year to year as some die and some survive.

life review According to Robert Butler, a universal inner experience of older people that helps them evaluate their lives, resolve remaining conflicts, and make decisions about material and emotional legacies. Life review promotes the resolution of Erikson's conflict of *integrity versus despair*.

lifespan development The broad changes and continuities that constitute a person's identity and growth from birth to death.

living will A legal document notifying one's physician of one's wishes regarding the withdrawal of life-sustaining equipment even if the result is death.

longitudinal study A study of the same individuals over a relatively long period, often months or years.

long-term care Health care and personal care, such as bathing, shopping, and laundry, usually provided by friends and relatives but sometimes by nursing homes and boarding homes.

low birth weight A birth weight of less than 2,500 grams (about 5½ pounds).

M

menarche The first menstrual period.

menopause The second stage in the female climacteric during which hormone production is reduced, the ovaries cease to produce eggs, and menstruation ceases.

metacognition Knowledge and thinking about cognition, how learning and memory operate in everyday situations, and how one can improve cognitive performance.

metalinguistic awareness The ability to attend to language as an object of thought rather than attending only to the content or ideas of a language.

middle school School designed to meet the needs of young adolescents, and usually spanning approximately fifth- through eighth-grade and enrolling students of about age ten through thirteen.

midlife crisis Radical changes within the personality associated with the adult's reexamination of goals, priorities, and life accomplishments as the midpoint of life is passed.

midwife The person, usually a woman, who is the primary caregiver to a woman during pregnancy, childbirth, and the month or so following delivery.

morality Sensitivity to and knowledge about what is right and wrong.

morbidity The measure of health that refers to the number of cases of a disease in a given population.

mortality The proportion of persons who die at a given age; the rate of death.

motor skills Physical skills using the body or limbs, such as walking and drawing.

mourning The actions and manner of expressing grief that reflect social and cultural prescriptions.

multiinfarct neurocognitive disorder (NCD) A chronic brain syndrome that results from blockages in the blood vessels that reduce or prevent blood flow to the brain, depriving it of oxygen and nutrients and causing a series of tiny strokes.

multiple intelligences According to Howard Gardner's theory of intelligence, alternative forms of intelligence or adaptability to the environment.

myelination The process through which myelin, a fatty sheathing, covers the axon of some neurons.

N

naturalistic study A study in which behavior is observed in its natural setting.

naturally occurring retirement community (NORC) A housing development that is not planned or designed for older people but attracts a majority of elderly residents because it provides a supportive social environment and access to services and facilities that can prolong independent living.

negative identity A form of identity diffusion involving rejection of the roles preferred by one's family or community in favor of socially undesirable roles.

neonate A newborn infant.

neostructuralist Relates to recent theories of cognition that emphasize the structure or organization of thinking.

neurons Nerve cell bodies and their extensions or fibers.

neurocognitive disorder (NCD) A decline in cognitive abilities that begins with delirium and then gets progressively worse. NCD is a symptom of many health problems including, but not limited to, Alzheimer's disease, Parkinson's disease, Huntington's disease, traumatic brain injury, or vascular problems. NCDs are also sometimes referred to as types of dementia.

non-REM sleep The stages of sleep that vary from light sleep to very deep, restorative sleep. The deeper stages of non-REM sleep play a pivotal role in helping us feel rested, growing, repairing cells, and bolstering immune function.

nonnormative life event A life transition that occurs in the lives of people but is not associated with a particular stage of life.

normative crisis model Explanations that view developmental change in terms of a series of distinct periods or stages that are influenced by physical and cognitive maturation.

normative life event A life transition that occurs within a time period strongly associated with chronological age, such as marriage, children leaving home, or retirement.

norms Behaviors typical at certain ages and of certain groups; standards of normal development.

O

obesity The state of being extremely overweight, specifically to a body mass index of 30 or over.

object permanence According to Piaget, the belief that people and things continue to exist even when one cannot experience them directly; emerges around age two.

observational learning The tendency of a child to imitate or model behavior and attitudes of parents and other nurturant individuals.

occupational segregation The reality that most jobs in the United States are held by females (e.g., typists) or males (e.g., architects) and few are truly integrated.

oophorectomy The surgical removal of the ovaries that triggers surgical menopause.

operant conditioning According to Skinner, a process of learning in which a person or an animal increases the frequency of a behavior in response to repeated reinforcement of that behavior.

organ reserve The extra capacity the lungs, heart, and other organs have to respond to particularly intense or prolonged effort or unusually stressful events. Primary aging affects organ reserve so that most people first notice decline under stressful conditions.

osteoporosis The degeneration of bone; affects about one in three postmenopausal women and can be prevented by ERT or HRT in combination with weight-bearing exercise and a calcium-rich diet.

overnutrition Diet that contains too many calories and is therefore unbalanced.

overt aggression Actions that harm others through physical damage or the threat of such damage, such as pushing, hitting, kicking, or threatening to "beat up" a peer.

ovum The reproductive cell, or gamete, of the female; the egg cell.

P

palliative care Management of pain and other symptoms of terminally ill patients that allows them to enjoy what remains of life.

participation structures Regular patterns of discourse or interaction in classrooms with unstated rules about how, when, and to whom to speak.

passive euthanasia Not doing something to prolong life, such as not utilizing life-support equipment or not giving antibiotics, when unendurable illness makes living intolerable.

pathological aging Losses in functioning people suffer as they age that result from illness, abnormality, genetic factors, or exposure to unhealthy environments rather than from the normal aging process.

peers Individuals who are of approximately the same age and developmental level and share common attitudes and interests.

perceived popularity A type of popularity based on social status and prestige.

perception The neural activity of combining sensations into meaningful patterns.

performance orientation Achievement motivation stimulated by other individuals who may see and evaluate the learner rather than by the intrinsic nature of the task itself.

permissive parenting A style of parenting in which parents make relatively few demands on their children but clearly communicate their warmth and interest and provide considerable care and nurturance.

personal fable Adolescents' belief that their own lives embody a special story that is heroic and completely unique.

phenotype The set of traits an individual actually displays during development; reflects the evolving product of genotype and experience. See also *genotype*.

phonemes Sounds that combine with other sounds to form words.

physical activity play Vigorous physical activity that occurs in a playful context, has a basis in human evolution, and serves several adaptive developmental functions.

physical development The area of human development concerned primarily with physical changes such as growth, motor skill development, and basic aspects of perception.

placenta An organ that delivers oxygen and nutrients from the mother to the fetus and carries away the fetus's waste products, which the mother will excrete.

plasticity The ability of other neurons in the cerebral cortex to take over the functions of neurons that have been damaged or lost; the degree to which a developing structure or organ (like the brain) can be influenced by the environment.

plateauing Reaching a point of constricted occupational opportunity, usually in mid-career, resulting in boredom and feelings of stagnation.

postconventional moral judgment In Kohlberg's theory, an orientation to moral justice that develops beyond conventional rules and beliefs.

postformal cognitive development An adult stage of cognitive development that follows formal operations, the last of Piaget's four stages. Although different theorists use different terms, postformal thought is characterized by relative and nonabsolute thinking that accepts and synthesizes contradiction and helps adults deal with the ambiguities of real-life problems.

postformal thought A level of thought that may develop after formal operations and is characterized by relative and nonabsolute thinking that accepts and synthesizes contradiction.

postpone Jean Veevers's term for someone who was less definite about whether she would have children and made the decision to remain child-free after first delaying childbearing for a definite time and then for an indefinite time.

posttraumatic stress disorder (PTSD) The physical and psychological symptoms of a person who has been the victim of a highly stressful event, such as violent war, rape, or earthquake, that last long after the event is over. Typical reactions include feeling numb, reliving aspects of the trauma, having sleeping problems, finding it difficult to concentrate, and reacting strongly to other stressful events.

practical intelligence A form of real-world problem solving that involves applying intellectual skills to problems of everyday life and shows improved performance through middle age.

preoperational stage In Piaget's theory, the stage of cognition characterized by increasing use of symbolic thinking but not yet by logical groupings of concepts.

prepared childbirth A method of childbirth in which parents have rehearsed or simulated labor and delivery well before the actual delivery date.

pretend play Play that substitutes imaginary situations for real ones. Also called *fantasy* or *dramatic play*.

primary aging Normal age-related changes that everyone experiences, such as the climacteric.

primary sex characteristics Characteristics that make sexual reproduction possible. For females, consist of the vagina, uterus, fallopian tubes, and ovaries; for males, consist of the penis, scrotum, testes, prostate gland, and seminal vesicles.

problem finding Patricia Arlin's proposed postformal mode of thinking, which entails generating new questions about oneself, one's work, or one's surroundings, in contrast to the problem-solving nature of formal operational thought.

programming theories Theories of aging that consider the maximum lifespan to be predetermined by the genes in each species.

proximodistal principle Growth that exhibits a near-to-far pattern of development, from the center of the body outward.

psychometric approach to intelligence A view of intelligence based on identifying individual differences in ability through standardized test scores.

psychosocial development The area of human development concerned primarily with personality, social knowledge and skills, and emotions.

psychosocial moratorium According to Erikson, the latency period that precedes puberty and provides a temporary suspension of psychosexual development.

puberty The period of early adolescence characterized by the development of full physical and sexual maturity.

punishment According to Skinner, any stimulus that temporarily suppresses the response that it follows.

Q

quasi-experiments Experiments in which participants cannot be randomly assigned to the experimental and control groups; instead, members of pre-existing groups are selected for comparison (for example, males versus females, young adults versus older adults, or private school students versus public school students).

R

random sample In research studies, a group of individuals from a population chosen such that each member of the population has an equal chance of being selected.

range of reaction The range of possible phenotypes that an individual with a particular genotype might exhibit in response to the particular sequence of environmental influences he or she experiences.

recall memory Retrieval of information by using relatively few external cues.

recentering A three-stage process in which individuals transition from being embedded in one's family of origin, become more independent, and eventually become completely independent of the family of origin and create a family of one's own.

recessive gene In any paired set of genes, the gene that influences or determines physical characteristics only when no dominant gene is present.

recognition memory Retrieval of information by comparing an external stimulus or cue with pre-existing experiences or knowledge.

reflex An involuntary, automatic response to a stimulus. The very first movements or motions of an infant are reflexes.

reinforcement According to Skinner, any stimulus that increases the likelihood that a behavior will be repeated in similar circumstances.

reintegrative stage Schaie's last stage of adult thinking during which late adults focus again on their personal interests and values.

relational aggression Actions that harm others through damage or threat of damage to their peer relationships.

reminiscence Recall of past experiences and events that occurs among people of all ages and promotes spiritual integration in late adulthood.

REM sleep A stage of sleep in which one's body is paralyzed, but one's eyes and brain are very active. REM sleep is believed to be important for memory consolidation.

resilience Ability to withstand and even profit from stressful experiences.

responsible stage Schaie's second stage of adult thinking during which middle adults also consider their responsibility to others—mates, children, aging parents, and community—when making decisions.

reversibility Ability to return mentally to earlier steps in a problem.

S

sample A group that is studied for research purposes.

sandwich generation Middle-aged adults caught between the needs of adjacent generations, their children and their aging parents.

scheme According to Piaget, a behavior or thought that represents a group of ideas and events in a person's experience.

scientific methods General procedures of study involving (1) formulating research questions, (2) stating questions as a hypothesis, (3) testing the hypothesis, and (4) interpreting and publicizing the results.

secondary aging Pathological aging, or the effects of illness and disease on the body due to genetic predisposition, environmental exposure, or health-compromising behaviors.

secondary sex characteristics Sex characteristics other than the sex organs, such as extra layers of fat and pubic hair.

secure attachment A healthy bond between infant and caregiver. The child is happy when the caregiver is present, somewhat upset during the caregiver's absence, and easily comforted upon the caregiver's return.

selective attention The ability to maintain focus on one thing even in the presence of distractions.

self-constancy The belief that one's identity remains permanently fixed; established sometime after age six.

self-esteem An individual's belief that he or she is an important, competent, powerful, and worthwhile person who is valued and appreciated.

semantics The purposes and meanings of a language.

senescence The degenerative phase of the aging process that causes an individual to become more vulnerable to disease and mortality as the years go by.

sense of self A structured way in which individuals think about themselves that helps them to organize and understand who they are based on the views of others, their own experiences, and cultural categories such as gender and race.

sensorimotor intelligence According to Piaget, thinking that occurs by way of sensory perceptions and motor actions; characteristic of infants.

sequential study Research in which at least two cohorts are compared both with each other and at different times.

serial monogamy A series of committed, intimate, sexually exclusive relationships with one person at a time.

SES The socioeconomic status of an individual or family that is determined by level of education, income, and type of work, as well as by lifestyle and social values. Also called *social class*.

sex-linked recessive traits Recessive traits resulting from genes on the X chromosome.

sexual dysfunction An inability, often temporary, to function adequately in or enjoy sexual activities.

sexual harassment Unwelcome behavior that limits the victim's ability to function effectively on the job. Although men are occasionally victims, it is best understood as a subtype of aggression directed by men toward women with whom they are often acquainted or intimate.

sickle-cell disease A genetically transmitted condition in which a person's red blood cells intermittently acquire a curved, sickle shape. The condition sometimes can clog circulation in the small blood vessels.

SIDS Sudden infant death syndrome (or "crib death"), an unaccountable death of an infant in its sleep.

situated cognition Thinking that occurs jointly with others and is embedded in a particular context or activity setting.

social clock Bernice Neugarten's timing of events approach to understanding the consistencies among disparate lives. Cultural groups tend to develop a shared sense of when certain life transitions, such as marriage or retirement, should occur, and people strive to time their major life events to match societal expectations.

social clock projects Age-related expectations about one's goals and activities, such as marriage, motherhood, and homemaking, or career development. Different historical periods and cultures vary in norms about the age at which various social clock projects should be accomplished, how different the projects assigned to men and women are, and how projects are combined over time.

social cognition Knowledge and beliefs about interpersonal and social matters.

social constructivism A theory that views learning as resulting from active dialogue and interaction between an individual and his or her community.

social conventions Arbitrary customs and agreements about behavior that members of a society use.

social convoy The term used to describe the lifelong social network of family and friend relationships that develop over the life course and provide social support from infancy through old age.

social referencing The child's sensitive awareness of how parents and other adults are feeling and ability to use these emotional cues as a basis for guiding his or her own emotional responses and actions. Social referencing is important for the development of autonomy.

social trajectory The pathway or direction that development takes over an individual's life course, which is influenced by the school, work, family, and other important social settings in which he or she participates.

sociocultural perspective on intelligence A view of intelligence that emphasizes the social and cultural influences on ability rather than the influence of inherent or learned individual differences.

sociometric popularity A type of popularity based on how well liked someone is.

sperm Male gametes, or reproductive cells; produced in the testicles.

spirituality The human need to construct a sense of meaning in life that occurs within or outside of a specifically religious context.

stranger rape Sexual assault by someone the victim does not know.

Strange Situation (SS) A widely used method for studying attachment; confronts the infant with a series of controlled separations and reunions with a parent and a stranger.

stress The arousal of the mind and body in response to demands made on them by unsettling conditions or experiences (stressors).

stunting Being excessively short in stature—falling under the fifth percentile for height for one's age—caused by chronic undernourishment.

successful aging The maintenance of psychological adjustment and well-being across the full lifespan.

superego In Freud's theory, the part of personality that acts as an all-knowing, internalized parent. It has two parts: the conscience, which enforces moral and social conventions by punishing violations with guilt, and the ego-ideal, which provides an idealized, internal set of standards for regulating and evaluating one's thoughts, feelings, and actions.

survey A research study that samples specific knowledge or opinions of large numbers of individuals.

synaptic pruning The process through which unused synapses and neurons are eliminated.

synaptogenesis The forming of connections, or synapses, between neurons.

syntax Rules for ordering and relating the elements of a language.

T

temperament Individual differences in quality and intensity of emotional responding and self-regulation that are present at birth, are relatively stable and enduring over time and across situations, and are influenced by the interaction of heredity, maturation, and experience.

teratogen Any substance that can harm the developing embryo or fetus.

testosterone A sex hormone, sometimes called the *male sex hormone* because its high concentration in boys stimulates growth of the penis and related male reproductive organs.

the good death A death that is appropriate to the dying person. In the contemporary United States, it typically refers to a death in which the dying person is surrounded by family and friends with minimal technological interference.

timing of events model Explanations that view developmental change in terms of important life events such as marriage and parenthood that people are expected to complete according to a culturally determined time table.

transient exuberance The rapid but temporary increase in the rate of synaptogenesis and, hence, the number of synapses formed between neurons during infancy.

trait A relatively enduring disposition of an individual; a characteristic way of thinking, feeling, and acting.

triarchic theory of intelligence A view of intelligence as consisting of three components: (1) adaptability, (2) information-processing skills, and (3) the ability to deal with novelty.

trust versus mistrust In Erikson's theory, the psychosocial crisis of children from birth to one year involving whether they can rely on their parents to reliably meet their physical and emotional needs.

twin adoption study Research that compares twins reared apart with unrelated persons reared together.

twin study A research method for studying the relative contributions of heredity and environment in which the degree of similarity between genetically identical twins (developed from a single egg) is compared with the similarity between fraternal twins (developed from two eggs).

U

umbilical cord Three large blood vessels that connect the embryo to the placenta, one to provide nutrients and two to remove waste products.

V

validity The degree to which research findings measure or observe what is intended.

vascular neurocognitive disorder (NCD) NCD caused by a vascular disease.

visual cliff The classic laboratory setup of a ledge covered by a sheet of glass; used to test the acquisition of depth perception. Young babies crawling on the glass discriminate between the two sides of the "cliff."

W

wisdom Expert knowledge and good judgment about important but uncertain matters of life; a positive change associated with late life.

working models Internalized perceptions, feelings, and expectations regarding social and emotional relationships with significant caregivers based on experiences with those caregivers.

Z

zone of proximal development According to Vygotsky, the level of difficulty at which problems are too hard for children to solve alone but not too hard when given support from adults or more competent peers.

zygote The single new cell formed when a sperm cell attaches itself to the surface of an ovum (egg).

References

A

Abel, E. (1991). *Who cares for the elderly: Public policy and experiences of adult daughters.* Philadelphia: Temple University Press.

Abukabar, A., Holding, P., Vijver, F. J. R., Newton, C., & Baar, A. V. (2010). Children at risk for developmental delay can be recognized by stunting, being underweight, ill health, little maternal schooling or high gravity. *Journal of Child Psychology and Psychiatry, 51,* 652–659.

Adachi, P. J., & Willoughby, T. (2011). The effect of violent video games on aggression: Is it more than just the violence? *Aggression and Violent Behavior, 16*(1), 55–62.

Adair, L., Fall, C., Osmond, C., Stein, A., Martorell, R., Ramirez-Zea, … & Victoria, C. (2013). Associations of linear growth and relative weight gain during early life with adult health and human capital in countries of low and middle income: Findings from five birth cohort studies. *Lancet, 382,* 525–534.

Adamchak, D. J. (1993). Demographic aging in the industrialized world: A rising burden? *Generations, 17*(4), 6–9.

Adamek, M. E., & Kaplan, M. S. (1996). Managing elder suicide: A profile of American and Canadian crisis prevention centers. *Suicide & Life-Threatening Behavior, 26,* 122–131.

Adams, R. G. (1997). Friendship patterns among older women. In J. M. Coyle (Ed.), *Handbook on women and aging* (pp. 300–417). Westport, CT: Greenwood Press.

Adams, S. G., Jr., Dubbert, P. M., Chupurdia, K. M., Jones, A., Jr., Lofland, K. R., & Leermakers, E. (1996). Assessment of sexual beliefs and information in aging couples with sexual dysfunction. *Archives of Sexual Behavior, 25,* 249–260.

Adams, S. L., & Waskel, S. A. (1993). Late onset alcoholism: Stress or structure. *Journal of Psychology, 127*(3), 329–334.

Adams, W., Garry, P., Rhyne, R., Hunt, W., & Goodwin, J. (1990). Alcohol intake in the healthy elderly: Changes with age in a cross-sectional and longitudinal study. *Journal of the American Geriatrics Society, 38,* 211–216.

Ade-Ridder, L. (1990). Sexuality and marital quality among older married couples. In T. H. Brubaker (Ed.), *Family relationships in later life* (pp. 48–67) Newberry Park, Cal: Sage.

Ade-Ridder, L., & Kaplan, L. (1993, October). Marriage, spousal caregiving, and a husband's move to a nursing home. *Journal of Gerontological Nursing,* pp. 13–23.

Adler, T. (1992, February). For depressed elderly, drugs advised. *The APA Monitor,* pp. 16–17.

Adlercreutz, H., Hämäläinen, E., Gorbach, G., & Goldin, B. (1992). Dietary phyto-oestrogens and the menopause in Japan. *Lancet, 339,* 1233.

Adolph, K. E. (2008). Learning to move. *Current Directions in Psychological Science, 17,* 213–218.

Adolph, K. E., Cole, W. G., Komati, M., Garciaguirre, J. S., Badaly, D., Lingeman, J. M., … & Sotsky, R. B. (2012). How do you learn to walk? Thousands of steps and dozens of falls per day. *Psychological Science, 23*(11), 1387–1394.

Agras, W. S., Kraemer, H. C., Berkowitz, R. I., Korner, A. F., & Hammer, L. D. (1987). Does a vigorous feeding style influence early development? *Journal of Pediatrics, 110,* 799–804.

Ahn, J. (2011). "You're my friend today, but not tomorrow": Learning to be friends among young US middle-class children. *American Ethnologist, 38*(2), 294–306.

Aiken, L. (1996). *Assessment of intellectual functioning* (2nd ed.). New York, NY: Plenum Press.

Ainlay, S. C., & Smith, D. R. (1984). Aging and religious participation. *Journal of Gerontology, 39,* 357–564.

Ainsworth, M. (1973). The development of infant mother attachment. In B. M. Caldwell, & H. N. Ricciuti (Eds.), *Review of child development research: Vol. 3.* Chicago: University of Chicago Press.

Ainsworth, M. (1979). Infant-mother attachment. *American Psychologist, 34,* 932–937.

Ainsworth, M. S., & Bowlby, J. (1991). An etiological approach to personality development. *American Psychologist, 46,* 333–341.

Ainsworth, M., Blehar, M., Waters, E., & Wall, S. (1978). *Strange-situation behavior of one-year-olds. Its relation to mother-infant interaction in the first year and to qualitative differences in the infant-mother attachment relationship.* Hillsdale, NJ: Erlbaum.

Akande, A. (1994). What meaning and effects does fatherhood have in child development? *Early Child Development and Care, 101,* 51–58.

Åkerstedt, T. (2006). Psychosocial stress and impaired sleep. *Scandinavian Journal of Work, Environment & Health, 32*(6), 493–501.

Alan Guttmacher Institute. (1994). *Sex and America's teenagers.* New York, NY: Author.

Albert, M. S., & Moss, M. B. (1996). Neuropsychology of aging: Findings in humans and monkeys. In E. L. Schneider, & J. W. Rowe (Eds.), *Handbook of the biology of aging* (pp. 217–233) San Diego: Academic Press.

Alberts, A., Elkind, D., & Ginsberg, S. (2007). The personal fable and risk-taking in early adolescence. *Journal of Youth and Adolescence, 36,* 71–76.

Aldous, M. B., & Edmonson, M. B. (1993). Maternal age at first childbirth and risk of low birth weight and preterm delivery in Washington State. *Journal of the American Medical Association, 270,* 2574–2577.

Alegria, M., Woo, M., Cao, Z., Torres, M., Meng, X. L., & Striege-Moore, R. (2007). Prevalence and correlates of eating disorders in Latinos in the United States. *International Journal of Eating Disorders, 40*(S3), S15–S21.

Alexander, A. W., & Slinger-Constant, A. M. (2004). Current status of treatments for dyslexia: Critical review. *Journal of Child Neurology, 19*(10), 744–758.

Alexander, F., & Duff, R. W. (1988). Social interaction and alcohol use in retirement communities. *The Gerontologist, 28,* 632–636.

Alexander, G. M., & Hines, M. (1994). Gender labels and play styles: Their relative contribution to children's selection of playmates. *Child Development, 65,* 869–879.

Alexander, K. L., & Entwisle, D. R. (1988). Achievement in the first 2 years of school: Patterns and processes. *Monographs of the Society for Research in Child Development, 53*(2, Serial No. 218).

Alexander, L. L., & LaRosa, J. H. (1994). *New directions in women's health.* Boston: Jones and Bartlett.

Alexandersen, P., Karsdal, M. A., & Christiansen, C. (2009). Long-term prevention with hormone-replacement therapy after the menopause: Which women should be targeted? *Women's Health, 5,* 637–647. doi: 10.2217/whe.09.52

Alfonso, M. (2006). The impact of community college attendance on baccalaureate attainment. *Research in Higher Education, 47*(8), 873–903.

Allaire, J. C. (2012). Everyday cognition. In S. K. Whitbourne, & M. J. Sliwinski (Eds.), *The Wiley-Blackwell handbook of adulthood and aging* (pp. 190–207). Malden, MA: Blackwell Publishing.

Allen, J. P., Hauser, S. T., Bell, K. L., & O'Conner, T. G. (1994). Longitudinal assessment of autonomy and relatedness in adolescent-family interactions as predictors of adolescent ego development and self esteem. *Child Development, 65,* 179–194.

Allen, S. M. (1994). Gender differences in spousal caregiving and unmet need for care. *Journal of Gerontology, 49,* S187–195.

Altenbaugh, R. (1995). *Caring for kids: Critical studies of urban school leavers.* Washington, DC: Falmer Press.

Altman, L. K. (1998, June 30). U. N. plans to treat 30,000 HIV-infected pregnant women. *New York Times,* p. A–15.

Alvarado, K. A., Templer, D. I., Bresler, C., & Thomas-Dobson, S. (1995). The relationship of religious variables to death depression and death anxiety. *Journal of Clinical Psychology, 51,* 202–204.

Amato, P. R. (2010). Research on divorce: Continuing trends and new developments. *Journal of Marriage and Family, 72*(3), 650–666.

Amato, P. R., & Dorius, C. (2010). Fathers, children, and divorce. In M. E. Lamb (Ed.), *The role of the father in child development, 5,* 177–200.

Amato, P. R. , & Hohmann-Marriott, B. (2007). A comparison of high and low-distress marriages that end in divorce. *Journal of Marriage and Family, 69,* 621–638.

Amato, P. R., Loomis, L. S., & Booth, A. (1995). Parental divorce, marital conflict, and offspring well-being during early adulthood. *Social Forces, 73,* 895–915.

Ambry, M. K. (1992). Childless chances. *American Demographics, 14*(4), 55.

American Academy of Pediatrics. (1991). *Facts about children with AIDS.* Elk Grove Village, IL: Author.

American Academy of Pediatrics. (1993). *Pediatric nutrition handbook.* Elk Grove Village, IL: Author.

American Academy of Pediatrics. (2007). Contraception and adolescents. *Pediatrics, 120,* 1135–1148.

American Academy of Pediatrics. (2013a). *Apgar scores.* Retrieved from http://www.healthychildren.org/English/ages-stages/prenatal/delivery-beyond/pages/Apgar-Scores

American Academy of Pediatrics. (2013b). *A child care provider's guide to safe sleep.* Retrieved from http://www.healthychildren.org/English/family-life/work-play/Pages/A-Child-Care-Provider%27s-Guide-to-Safe-Sleep

American Academy of Pediatrics. (2015). *Fetal alcohol spectrum disorders.* Retrieved from http://pediatrics.aappublications.org/content/early/2015/10/13/peds.2015-3113

American Academy of Pediatrics. (2016). *Media and children.* Retrieved from https://www.aap.org/en-us/advocacy-and-policy/aap-health-initiatives/pages/media-and-children.aspx

American Academy of Pediatrics Task Force on Sudden Infant Death Syndrome (AAP Task Force on SIDS). (2011). SIDS and other sleep-related deaths: Expansion of recommendations for a safe infant sleeping environment. *Pediatrics, 128,* 1341–1367.

American Association of Retired Persons (AARP). (1990). *A profile of older Americans: 1990.* Washington, DC: Author.

American Association of Retired Persons (AARP). (1993). *America's changing workforce: Statistics in brief.* Washington, DC: Author.

American Association of Retired Persons. (AARP). (1990). *Understanding senior housing for the 1990s: An American Association of Retired Persons survey of consumer preferences, concerns and needs.* Washington, DC: Author.

American Association of Suicidology. (2014). Elderly suicide fact sheet based on 2012 data. Retrieved from http://www.suicidology.org/Portals/14/docs/Resources/FactSheets/Elderly2012.pdf

American Cancer Society. (1993). *Cancer facts and figures, 1993.* Atlanta: Author.

American Cancer Society. (2014). *Cancer facts and figures, 2014.* Atlanta: Author.

American Civil Liberties Union (ACLU). (2014). Employment non-discrimination act. Retrieved from https://www.aclu.org/hiv-aids_lgbt-rights/employment-non-discrimination-act

American Civil Liberties Union. (n.d.). Non-discrimination laws: State by state. Retrieved August 7, 2016 from https://www.aclu.org/map/non-discrimination-laws-state-state-information-map

American College of Nurse-Midwives (ACNM). (2012). *CNM/CM-attended birth statistics.* Retrieved from http://www.midwife.org/CNM/CM-attended-Birth-Statistics

American College of Obstetricians and Gynecologists (ACOG). (1995). *Planning for pregnancy, birth, and beyond* (2nd ed.). New York, NY: Penguin.

American College of Obstetricians and Gynecologists (ACOG). (2013). Weight gain during pregnancy: Committee opinion number 548. *Obstetrics & Gynecology, 121,* 210–212.

American Heart Association. (2014). *Good versus bad cholesterol.* Retrieved from http://www.heart.org/HEARTORG/Conditions/Cholesterol/AboutCholesterol/Good-vs-Bad-Cholesterol_UCM_305561_Article.jsp

American Institutes for Research. (2013). Parental leave that might pay for itself. Retrieved from http://www.air.org/resource/parental-leave-might-pay-itself

American Psychiatric Association. (2013). *Diagnostic and statistical manual of mental disorders* (5th ed.). Arlington, VA: American Psychiatric Publishing.

American Psychological Association. (1992). Ethical principles of psychologists and code of conduct *American Psychologist, 47*(12), 1060–1073.

American Psychological Association. (1996). *Body image, eating disorders, and obesity: Integrative guide for assessment and treatment.* Washington, DC: Author.

American Psychological Association. (2005). *Lesbian and gay parenting.* Washington, DC: Author. Retrieved from http://www.apa.org/pi/lgbt/resources/parenting-full.pdf

American Psychological Association. (2010). 2010 amendments to the 2002 "ethical principles of psychologists and code of conduct." *American Psychologist, 65,* 493.

Ames, L. (1997). *Women reformed, women empowered: Poor mothers and the endangered promise of Head Start.* Philadelphia: Temple University Press.

Ames, L. B. (1983). *Your one-year-old.* New York, NY: Dell.

Amott, T. (1998). Shortchanged: Restructuring women's work. In M. A. Anderson, & P. H. Collins (Eds.), *Race, class and gender* (3rd ed., pp. 238–247.). Belmont, CA: Wadsworth.

Anastasi, A., & Urbina, S. (1997). *Psychological testing* (7th ed.). Upper Saddle River, NJ: Prentice-Hall.

Ancoli-Israel, S. (2004). Sleep disorders in older adults: A primary care guide to assessing 4 common sleep problems in geriatric patients. *Geriatrics, 59,* 37–40.

Ancoli-Israel, S., Ayalon, L., & Salzman, C. (2008). Sleep in the elderly: Normal variations and common sleep problems. *Harvard Review of Psychiatry, 16,* 279–286.

Ancoli-Israel, S., Kripke, D. F., Klauber, M. R., Mason, W. J., Fell, R., & Kaplan, O. (1991). Sleep-disordered breathing in community-dwelling elderly. *Sleep, 14,* 486–495.

Anderson, A. M. (1996). The father-infant relationship: Becoming connected. *Journal of the Society of Pediatric Nurses, 1,* 83–92.

Anderson, B. (1989). Effects of public day care: A longitudinal study. *Child Development, 60,* 857–866.

Anderson, L. M., & Anderson, J. (2010). Barney and breakfast: Messages about food and eating in preschool television shows and how they may impact the development of eating behaviours in children. *Early Child Development and Care, 180*(10), 1323–1336.

Anderson, S. A., Russell, C. S., & Schumm, W. A. (1983). Perceived marital quality and family life-cycle categories: A further analysis. *Journal of Marriage and the Family, 45,* 127–139.

Anderson, S., & Winefield, A. H. (2011). The impact of underemployment on psychological health, physical health, and work attitudes. In D. C. Maynard, & D. C. Feldman (Eds.) *Underemployment: Psychological, Economic, and Social Challenges* (pp. 165–185). New York, NY: Springer.

Andrien, M. (1994). *Social communication in nutrition: A methodology for intervention.* Rome: Food and Agricultural Organization of the United Nations.

Angier, N. (1994, May 17). Genetic mutations tied to father in most cases. *New York Times,* p. C12.

Anglin, J. (1993). Vocabulary development: A morphological analysis. *Monographs of the Society for Research on Child Development, 58*(10, Serial No. 238). Chicago: University of Chicago Press.

Annear, M. J., Cushman, G., & Gidlow, B. (2009). Leisure time physical activity differences among older adults from diverse socioeconomic neighborhoods. *Health & Place, 15,* 482–490.

Anson, O. (1989). Marital status and women's health revisited: The importance of a proximate adult. *Journal of Marriage and the Family, 51,* 185–194.

Anthony, J. C., & Aboraya, A. (1992). The epidemiology of selected mental disorders in later life. In J. E. Birren, R. B. Sloane, & G. D. Cohen (Ed.), *Handbook of mental health and aging* (2nd ed., pp. 27–73). San Diego: Academic Press.

Antonucci, T. C. (1990). Social supports and relationships. In R. H. Binstock, & L. K. George (Eds.), *Handbook of aging and the social sciences* (3rd ed., pp. 205–226). San Diego: Academic Press.

Antonucci, T. C. (1991). Attachment, social support, and coping with negative life events in mature adulthood. In E. M. Cummings, A. L. Greene, & K. H. Karraker (Eds.), *Life-span developmental psychology: Vol. 11. Stress and coping across the life-span* (pp. 261–276). Hillsdale, NJ: Erlbaum.

Antonucci, T. C. (1997). A life-span view of women's social relations. In J. M. Coyle (Ed.), *Handbook on women and aging* (pp. 239–269). Westport, CT: Greenwood Press.

Antonucci, T. C., Jackson, J. S., & Gibson, R. (1989). Social relations, productive activities and coping with stress in late life. In M. A. P. Stephens, J. H. Crowther, S. E. Hobfoll, & D. L. Tennenbaum (Eds.), *Stress and coping in later life families.* Washington, DC: Hemisphere Publishers.

Apfel, N. H., & Seitz, V. (1991). Four models of adolescent mother-grandmother relationships in Black inner-city families, *Family Relations, 40,* 421–429.

Apgar, V. (1953). A proposal for a new method of evaluation in the newborn infant. *Current Research in Anesthesia and Analgesia, 32,* 260.

Aquilino, W. S. (1990). The likelihood of parent-adult child coresidence: Effects of family structure and parental characteristics. *Journal of Marriage and the Family, 52,* 405–419.

Aquilino, W. S., & Supple, K. R. (1991). Parent-child relations and parent's satisfaction with living arrangements when adult children live at home *Journal of Marriage and the Family, 53,* 13–27.

Archer, J. (1992). *Ethology and human development.* Lanham, MD: Harvester-Wheatsheaf.

Archer, S. L. (1982). The lower age boundaries of identity development. *Child Development, 53,* 1551–1556.

Archer, S. L., & Waterman, A. S. (1988). Psychological individualism: Gender differences or gender identity? *Human Development, 31,* 65–81.

Archibald, A. B., Graber, J. A., & Brooks-Gunn, J. (2006). Pubertal processes and physiological growth in adolescence. In G. R. Adams, & M. D. Berzonsky (Eds.), *Blackwell handbook of adolescence.* Malden, MA: Blackwell.

Archibald, J. (Ed.). (1995). *Phonological acquisition and phonological theory.* Hillsdale, NJ: Erlbaum.

Arditti, J. A. (1992). Differences between fathers with joint custody and noncustodial fathers. *American Journal of Orthopsychiatry, 62,* 186–195.

Arenberg, D. (1968). Concept problem solving in young and old adults. *Journal of Gerontology, 23,* 279–282.

Arend, R., Gove, F., & Sroufe, L. (1979). Continuity of individual adaptation from infancy to kindergarten: A predictive study of ego-resiliency and curiosity in preschoolers. *Child Development, 50,* 950–959.

Ariès, P. (1962). *Centuries of childhood: A social history of family life* (R. Baldick, trans.). New York, NY: Vintage.

Ariès, P. (1981). *The hour of our death.* (J. Lloyd, Trans.). Cambridge, MA: Harvard University Press.

Arlin, P. K. (1989). Problem solving and problem finding in young artists and young scientists. In. M. L. Commons, J. D. Sinnott, F. A. Richards, & C. Armon (Eds.), *Adult development: Vol. 1 Comparisons and applications of developmental models* (pp. 197–216). New York, NY: Praeger.

Arliss, L. (1991). *Gender communication.* Englewood Cliffs, NJ: Prentice-Hall.

Armour, S., & Haynie, D. (2007). Adolescent sexual debut and later delinquency. *Journal of Youth and Adolescence, 36*(2), 141–153.

Armstead, C. A., Lawler, K. A., Gordon, G., Cross, J., & Gibbons, J. (1989). Relationship of racial stressors to blood pressure responses and anger expression in black college students. *Health Psychology, 8,* 541–557.

Arnett, J. J. (1992). Reckless behavior in adolescence: A developmental *perspective. Developmental Review, 12,* 339–373.

Arnett, J. J. (1999). Adolescent storm and stress, reconsidered. *American Psychologist, 54,* 317–326.

Arnett, J. J. (2000). Emerging adulthood: A theory of development from the late teens through the twenties. *American Psychologist, 55*(5), 469–480.

Arnett, J. J. (2004). *Emerging adulthood: The widening road from the late teens through the twenties.* New York, NY: Oxford University Press.

Arnett, J. J. (2016). Introduction: Emerging adulthood theory and research: Where we are and where we should go. In J. J. Arnett (Ed.), *The Oxford handbook of emerging adulthood* (pp. 1–7). New York, NY: Oxford University Press.

Arnett, J. J., & Jensen, L. A. (1997). Socialization and risk behavior in two countries: Denmark and the United States, *Youth & Society, 26,* 1994, 3–22.

Arnett, J. J., Ramos, K. D., & Jensen, L. A. (2001). Ideological views in emerging adulthood: Balancing autonomy and community. *Journal of Adult Development, 8(2),* 69–80.

Arthur-Banning, S., Wells, M. S., Baker, B. L., & Hegreness, R. (2009). Parents behaving badly? The relationship between the sportsmanship behaviors of adults and athletes in youth basketball games. *Journal of Sport Behavior, 32*(1), 3–18.

Asendorpf, J. B., Warkentin, V., & Baudonniere, P. M. (1996). Self-awareness and other-awareness II: Mirror self-recognition, social contingency awareness, and synchronic imitation. *Developmental Psychology, 32,* 313–321.

Asber, S., Renshaw, P., & Hymel, S. (1982). Peer relations and the development of social skills. In S. Moore, & C. Cooper (Eds.), *The young child: Reviews of research: Vol. 3.* Washington, DC: National Association for the Education of Young Children.

Ashley, K. B. (2013). The science on sexual orientation: A review of the recent literature. *Journal of Gay & Lesbian Mental Health, 17*(2), 175–182.

Aslanian, C. B., & Brickell, H. M. (1980). *Americans in transition: Life changes as reasons for adult learning.* New York, NY: College Entrance Examination Board.

Ata, R. N., Ludden, A. B., & Lally, M. M. (2007). The effects of gender and family, friend, and media influences on eating behaviors and body image during adolescence. *Journal of Youth and Adolescence, 36(8),* 1024–1037.

Atchley, R. C. (1998). Activity adaptations to the development of functional limitations and results for subjective well-being in later adulthood: A qualitative analysis of longitudinal panel data over a 16-year period. *journal of Aging Studies, 12,* 19–38.

Aureli, T., & Presaghi, F. (2010). Developmental trajectories for mother-infant coregulation in the second year of life. *Infancy, 15,* 557–585.

Aviezer, O., van IJzendoom, M. H., Sagi, A., & Schuengel, C. (1994). "Children of the Dream" revisited: 70 years of collective early child care in Israeli kibbutzim. *Psychological Bulletin, 116,* 99–116.

Avioli, P. S. (1989). The social support functions of siblings in later life. *American Behavioral Scientist, 33*(1), 45–57.

Avis, N. E., & Crawford, S. (2006). Menopause: Recent research findings. In S. K. Whitbourne, & S. L. Willis (Eds.). *The baby boomers grow up: Contemporary perspectives on midlife* (pp. 75–109). Mahwah, NJ: Erlbaum.

Ayers, B., Forshaw, M., & Hunter, M. S. (2010). The impact of attitudes towards the menopause on women's symptom experience: A systematic review. *Maturitas, 65,* 28–36. doi: 10.1016/j.maturitas.2009.10.016

Ayers, T. S., Wolchik, S. A., Sandler, I. N., Twohey, J. L., Weyer, J. L., Padgett-Jones, S., ... & Kriege, G. (2013). The Family Bereavement Program: Description of a theory-based prevention program for parentally-bereaved children and adolescents. *Omega: Journal of Death and Dying, 68*(4), 293–314.

Ayscue, J. B., & Orfield, G. (2016). Perpetuating separate and unequal worlds of educational opportunity through district lines: School segregation by race and poverty. In *Race, Equity, and Education* (pp. 45–74). Springer International Publishing.

Azmitia, M., & Hesser, J. (1993). Why siblings are important agents of cognitive development: A comparison of siblings and peers. *Child Development, 64,* 430–444.

B

Bachmann, G. A. (1990). Hysterectomy: A critical review. *Journal of Reproductive Medicine, 35,* 862.

Bachman, J. G. (1983). Premature affluence: Do high school students earn too much. *Economic Outlook USA, 10*(3), 64–67.

Backx, F. (1996). Epidemiology of pediatric sports-related injuries. In O. Bar-Or (Ed.), *The child and adolescent athlete* (pp. 163–172). Oxford, UK: Blackwells.

Badgett, M. V. L., Lau, H., Sears, B., & Ho, D. (2007). Bias in the workplace: Consistent evidence of sexual orientation and gender identity discrimination. *The Williams Institute.*

Badgett, M. V. L., & Mallory, C. (2014, December). Patterns of relationship recognition for same-sex couples: Divorce and terminations. *The Williams Institute.* Retrieved from http://williamsinstitute.law.ucla.edu/wp-content/uploads/Badgett-Mallory-Divorce-Terminations-Dec-2014.pdf

Bagwell, C. L., Newcomb, A. F., & Bukowski, W. M. (1996). *Preadolescent friendships and peer rejection as predictors of adult adjustment.* Unpublished manuscript, University of Richmond, Department of Psychology, Richmond, VA.

Bagwell, C. L., Newcomb, A. F., & Bukowski, W. M. (1998). Preadolescent friendship and peer rejection as predictors of adult adjustment. *Child Development, 69,* 140–153.

Bailey, J. M., & Zucker, K. J. (1995). Childhood sex-typed behavior and sexual orientation: A conceptual analysis and quantitative review *Developmental Psychology, 31,* 43–55.

Baillargeon, R. (1991). Object permanence in infants: Further evidence. *Child Development. 62,* 1227–1246.

Baillargeon, R. (1993). The object concept revisited: New directions in the investigation of infants' physical knowledge. In C. Granrud (Ed.), *Visual perception and cognition in infants,* pp. 265–316. Hillsdale, NJ: Erlbaum.

Bain, L. (1993). *Parents' guide to childhood emergencies.* New York, NY: Delta.

Baird, P., & Sadovnick, A. D. (1987). Life expectancy in Down syndrome. *Journal of Pediatrics, 110,* 849–854.

Baker, C. (1995). *English syntax* (2nd ed.). Cambridge, MA: MIT press.

Baker, J. E., Sedney, M. A., & Gross, E. (1992). Psychological tasks for bereaved children. *American Journal of Orthopsychiatry, 62,* 105–116.

Baker, L. A., Silverstein, M., & Putney, N. M. (2008). Grandparents raising grandchildren in the United States: Changing family forms, stagnant social policies. *Journal of Social Policy, 7,* 53–69.

Balantekin, K. N., Savage, J. S., Marini, M. E., & Birch, L. L. (2014). Parental encouragement of dieting promotes daughters' early dieting. *Appetite, 80,* 190–196.

Baldwin, D. A., & Moses, L. J. (1996). The ontogeny of social information gathering. *Child Development, 67,* 1915–1939.

Balk, D., & Corr, C. A. (1996). Adolescents, developmental tasks, and encounters with death and bereavement. In C. A. Corr, & D. E. Balk (Eds.), *Handbook of adolescent death and bereavement* (pp. 3–24). New York, NY: Springer.

Balter, M. (2015). Can epigenetics explain homosexuality puzzle? *Science, 350*(6257), 148.

Baltes, P. B., & Baltes, M. M. (1990). Psychological perspectives on successful aging: The model of selective optimization with compensation. In P. B. Baltes, & M. M. Baltes (Eds.), *Successful aging: Perspectives from the behavioral sciences* (pp. 1–34). New York, NY: Cambridge University Press.

Baltes, P. B., & Ruldoph, C. W. (2012). The theory of selection, optimization, and compensation. In M. Wang (Ed.), *The Oxford handbook of retirement* (pp. 88–101). New York, NY: Oxford University Press.

Baltes, P. B., & Smith, J. (2008). The fascination of wisdom: Its nature, ontogeny, and function. *Perspectives on Psychological Science, 3,* 5–64.

Baltes, P. B., & Staudinger, U. M. (1993). The search for a psychology of wisdom. *Current Directions in Psychological Science,* 2(3), 75–80.

Baltes, P. B., & Staudinger, U. M. (Eds.). (1996). *Interactive minds: Lifespan perspectives on the social foundation of cognition.* New York, NY: Cambridge University Press.

Baltes, P. B., Staudinger, U. M., Maercker, A., & Smith, J. (1995). People nominated as wise: A comparative study of wisdom-related knowledge. *Psychology & Aging, 10,* 155–166.

Bamford, F., Bannister, R., Benjamin, C., Hillier, V., Ward, B., & Moore, W. (1990). Sleep in the first year of life. *Developmental Medicine and Child Neurology, 32,* 718–724.

Bandura, A. (1989). Social cognitive theory. In R. Vasta (Ed.), *Annals of Child Development. Theories of child development: Revised formulations and current issues.* Greenwich, CT: JAI Press.

Bandura, A. (1991). Social cognitive theory of moral thought and action. In W. Kurtines, & J. Gewirtz (Eds.), *Handbook of moral behavior and development: Vol. 1* (pp. 45–104). Hillsdale, NJ: Erlbaum.

Bandura, A., Cioffi, D., Taylor, C. B., & Brouillard, M. E. (1988). Perceived self-efficacy in coping with cognitive stressors and opioid activation. *Journal of Personality and Social Psychology, 55,* 479–488.

Bank, L., Patterson, G. R., & Reid, J. B. (1996). Negative sibling interaction patterns as predictors of later adjustment problems in adolescent and young adult males. In G. H. Brody et al. (Ed.), *Sibling relationships: Their causes and consequences* (pp. 197–229). Norwood, NJ: Ablex.

Barber, C. F. (2008). Domestic violence against men. *Nursing Standard, 22*(51), 35–39.

Barber, E., Lundsberg, L., Belanger, K., Pettker, C., Funai, E., & Illuzzi, J. (2011). Contributing indications to the rising cesarean delivery rate. *Journal of Obstetrics & Gynecology,* 118, 29–38.

Barbaresi, W. J., Katusic, S. K., Colligan, R. C., Weaver, A. L., Leibson, C. L., & Jacobsen, S. J. (2006). Long-term stimulant medication treatment of attention-deficit/hyperactivity disorder: Results from a population-based study. *Journal of Developmental & Behavioral Pediatrics, 27*(1), 1–10.

Barlow, D. H., & Durand, V. M. (1995). *Abnormal psychology: An integrative approach.* Pacific Grove, Cal: Brooks/Cole.

Barnes, G. M., Welte, J. W., & Dintcheff, B. (1992). Alcohol misuse among college students and other young adults: Findings from a general population study in New York State. *The International Journal of the Addictions, 27,* 917–934.

Barness, L. (Ed.). (1993). *Pediatric nutrition handbook* (3rd ed.). Elk Grove village, IL American Academy of pediatrics.

Barnett, R. C., & Baruch, G. K. (1985). Women's involvement in multiple roles and psychological distress. *Journal of Personality and Social Psychology, 49,* 135–145.

Barr, H. M., Streissguth, A. P., Darby, B. L., & Sampson, P. D. (1990). Prenatal exposure to alcohol, caffeine, tobacco, and aspirin: Effects on fine and gross motor performance in 4-year-old children. *Developmental Psychology, 26,* 339–348.

Barr, R. G. (1995). The enigma of infant crying: The emergence of defining dimensions. *Early Development and Parenting, 4,* 225–232.

Barrett, K. C. (2005). The origins of social emotions and self-regulation in toddlerhood: New evidence. *Cognition and Emotion, 19,* 953–979.

Barry, C. M., Madsen, S. D., & DeGrace, A. (2016). Growing up with a little help from their friends in emerging adulthood. In J. J. Arnett (Ed.), *The Oxford handbook of emerging adulthood* (pp. 215–229). New York, NY: Oxford University Press.

Barthlen, G. M. (2002). Sleep disorders: Obstructive sleep apnea syndrome, restless legs syndrome, and insomnia in geriatric patients. *Geriatrics, 57*, 34–39.

Bartholomew, J. B., Morrison, D., & Ciccolo, J. T. (2005). Effects of acute exercise on mood and well-being in patients with major depressive disorder. *Medicine and Science in Sports and Exercise, 37*(12), 2032–2037.

Bartick, M., & Reinhold, A. (2010). The burden of suboptimal breastfeeding in the United States: A pediatric cost analysis. *Pediatrics, 125*(5), e1048–e1056.

Barton, E. E., & Pavilanis, R. (2012). Teaching pretend play to young children with autism. *Young Exceptional Children, 15*(1), 5–17.

Bartoshuk, L. M., & Weiffenbach, J. M. (1990). Chemical senses and aging. In E. L. Schneider, & J. W. Rowe (Eds.), *Hand-book of the biology of aging* (3rd ed., pp. 429–443). San Diego: Academic Press.

Bartsch, K. (1993). Adolescents' theoretical thinking. In R. Lerner (Ed.), *Early adolescence: Perspectives on research, policy, and intervention*, pp. 143–159. Hillsdale, NJ: Erlbaum.

Baruch, G., Barnett, R., & Rivers, C. (1983). *Lifeprints: New patterns of love and work for today's woman*. New York, NY: McGraw Hill.

Basseches, M. (1984). *Dialectical thinking and adult development*. Norwood, NJ: Ablex.

Bat-Chava, Y., Allen, L., Aber, J. L., & Seidman, E. (1997, April). Racial and ethnic identity and the contexts of development. Paper presented at the annual meeting of the Society for Research in Child Development, Washington, DC.

Bauman, K. E., & Ennett, S. T. (1994). Peer influence on adolescent drug use. *American Psychologist, 49*, 820–822.

Baumrind, D. (1968). Authoritative vs. authoritarian parental control. *Adolescence, 3*, 255–272.

Baumrind, D. (1971). Current patterns of parental authority. *Developmental Psychology Monographs, 4* (No. 1, Pt. 2).

Baumrind, D. (1989). Raising competent children. In W. Damon (Ed.), *Child development today and tomorrow* (pp. 349–378). San Francisco: Jossey-Bass.

Baumrind, D. (1991). The influence of parenting style on adolescent competence and substance abuse. *Early Adolescence, 11*, 56–95.

Baumrind, D. (1991a). Effective parenting during the early adolescent transition. In P. Cowan, & M. Hetherington (Eds.), *Family transitions*. Hillsdale, NJ: Erlbaum.

Baumrind, D. (1991b). Parenting styles and adolescent development. In R. M. Lerner, A. C. Petersen, & J. Brooks-Gunn (Ed.), *The encyclopedia of adolescence*. New York, NY: Garland.

Bausell, R. B. (1986). Health-seeking behavior among the elderly. *The Gerontologist, 26*, 556–559.

Baxter, J., Hewitt, B., & Haynes, M. (2008). Life course transitions and housework: Marriage, parenthood, and time on housework. *Journal of Marriage and Family, 70*(2), 259–272.

Baydar, N., Hyle, P., & Brooks-Gunn, J. (1997). A longitudinal study of the effects of the birth of a sibling during preschool and early grade school years. *Journal of Marriage and the Family, 59*, 957–965.

Bayley, N. (1955). On the growth of intelligence. *American Psychologist, 10*, 805–823.

Beale, E. A., Baile, W. F., & Aaron, J. (2005). Silence is not golden: Communicating with children dying from cancer. *Journal of Clinical Oncology, 23*(15), 3629–3631.

Bean, R. A., Barber, B. K., & Crane, D. R. (2006). Parental support, behavioral control, and psychological control among African American youth: The relationships to academic grades, delinquency, and depression. *Journal of Family Issues, 27*(10), 1335–1355.

Bechara, A. (2005). Decision making, impulse control and loss of willpower to resist drugs: A neurocognitive perspective. *Nature Neuroscience, 8*, 1458–1463.

Becker, A. (1994). Nurturing and negligence: Working on others' bodies in Fiji. In T. Csordas (Ed.), *Embodiment and experience: The existential ground of culture and self* (pp. 100–115). New York, NY: Cambridge University Press.

Becker, A. E. (2004). Television, disordered eating, and young women in Fiji: Negotiating body image and identity during rapid social change. *Culture, Medicine and Psychiatry, 28*(4), 533–559.

Becker, G. (1996). *Accounting for tastes*. Cambridge, MA: Harvard University Press.

Bedford, V. (1989). Understanding the value of siblings in old age. *American Behavioral Scientist, 33*(1), 33–44.

Bedford, V. H., & Avioli, P. S. (2012). Sibling relationships from midlife to old age. In R. Blieszner, & V. H. Bedford (Eds.), *Handbook of families and aging* (pp. 125–152). Santa Barbara, CA: Praeger.

Behrens, K. Y., Hesse, E., & Main, M. (2007). Mothers' attachment status as determined by the Adult Attachment Interview predicts their 6-year-olds' reunion responses: A study conducted in Japan. *Developmental Psychology, 43*(6), 1553.

Behrman, J., & Stacey, N. (Eds.) (1997). *The social benefits of education*. Ann Arbor, Mich. University of Michigan Press.

Behrman, R. (Ed.) (1993). *The future of children: School-linked services*. Los Altos, CA: Center for the Future of Children. The David and Lucille Packard Foundation.

Belenky, M. F., Clinchy, B. M., Goldberger, N. R., & Tarule, J. M. (1986). *Women's ways of knowing: The development of self, voice, and mind*. New York, NY: Basic Books.

Bell, K., Allen, J., Hauser, S., & O'Connor, T. (1996). Family factors and young adult transitions: Educational attainment and occupational prestige. In J. Graber, J. Brooks-Gunn, & A. Petersen (Eds.), *Transitions through adolescence* (pp. 345–366). Mahwah, NJ: Erlbaum.

Bell, S. A., Bern-Klug, M., Kramer, K. W., & Saunders, J. B. (2010). Most nursing home social service directors lack training in working with lesbian, gay, and bisexual residents. *Social Work in Health Care, 49*(9), 814–831.

Bellugi, U., Van Hoek, K., Lillo-Martin, D., & O'Grady, L. (1993). The acquisition of syntax and space in young deaf signers. In D. Bishop, & K. Mogford (Eds.), *Language development in exceptional circumstances* (pp. 132–149). Hillsdale, NJ: Erlbaum.

Belsky, J., & Cassidy, J. (1994). Attachment and close relationships: An individual-difference perspective. *Psychological Inquiry, 5*, 27–30.

Belsky, J. (1988a). The "effects" of infant day care reconsidered. *Early Childhood Research Quarterly, 3*, 235–272.

Belsky, J. (1988b). Child maltreatment and the emergent family system. In K. Browne, C. Davies, & P. Strattan (Eds.), *Early prediction and prevention of child abuse* (pp. 291–302). New York, NY: Wiley.

Belsky, J. (1993). Etiology of child maltreatment: A developmental-ecological analysis. *Psychological Bulletin, 114*, 413–434.

Belsky, J. (1996). Parent, infant and social-contextual antecedents of father-son attachment security. *Developmental Psychology. 32*, 905–913.

Belsky, J., & Nezworski, T. (Eds.) (1988). *Clinical implications of attachment*. Hillsdale, NJ: Erlbaum.

Belsky, J., & Rovine, M. (1988). Nonmaternal care in the first year of life and the security of infant-parent attachment. *Child Development, 59*, 157–176.

Belsky, J., & Rovine, M. (1990). Patterns of marital change across the transition to parenthood: Pregnancy to three years postpartum. *Journal of Marriage and the Family, 52*, 5–19.

Belsky, J., & Cassidy, J. (1994). Attachment and close relationships: An individual-difference perspective. *Psychological Inquiry, 5*, 27–30.

Belsky, J., Crnic, K., & Gable, S. (1995). The determinants of coparenting in families with toddler boys: Spousal differences and daily hassles. *Child Development, 66*, 629–642.

Bem, S. L. (1981). Gender schema theory: A cognitive account of sex typing. *Psychological Review, 88*, 354–364.

Bem, S. L. (1987). Gender schema theory and its implications for child development: Raising gender-aschematic children in a gender-schematic society. In M. R. Walsh, et al. (Eds.), *The psychology of women: Ongoing debates* (pp. 226–245). New Haven, CT: Yale University Press.

Bem, S. L. (1989). Genital knowledge and gender constancy in preschool children *Child Development, 60*, 649–662.

Bender, K. A. (2012). An analysis of well-being in retirement: The role of pensions, health, and 'voluntariness' of retirement. *Journal of Socio-Economics, 41*, 424–433.

Benenson, J. F., Apostololeris, N. H., & Parnass, J. (1997). Age and sex differences in dyadic and group interaction. *Developmental Psychology, 33*, 538–543.

Bengtson, V. L. (1985). Diversity and symbols in grandparent roles. In V. L. Bengtson, & J. F. Robertson (Eds.), *Grandparent-hood* (pp. 51–57). Beverly Hills, CA: Sage.

Bengtson, V. L., Rosenthal, C., & Burton, L. (1990). Families and aging: Diversity and heterogeneity. In R. H. Binstock, & L. K. George (Eds.), *Handbook of aging and the social sciences* (3rd ed., pp. 263–287). San Diego: Academic Press.

Bengtson, V., Rosenthal, C., & Burton, L. (1996). Paradoxes of families and aging. In R. II. Binstock & L. K. George (Ed.), *Handbook of aging and the social sciences* (pp. 253–282). San Diego: Academic Press.

Benner, A. D., & Graham, S. (2009). The transition to high school as a developmental process among multiethnic urban youth. *Child Development, 80*, 356–376.

Bennett, K. M., Smith, P. T., & Hughes, G. M. (2005). Coping, depressive feelings and gender differences in late life widowhood. *Aging and Mental Health, 9*, 348–353.

Bennett, T., & Gains, J. (2010). Believing what you hear: The impact of aging stereotypes upon the old. *Educational Gerontology, 36*, 435–445.

Benoit, D., & Parker, K. C. H. (1994). Stability and transmission of attachment across three generations. *Child Development, 65*, 1444–1456.

Benson, P., & Elkin, C. (1990). *Effective Christian education: A national study of Protestant denominations*. Minneapolis: Search Institute.

Beresford, T. (1993). Abortion counseling. In B. K. Rothman (Ed.), *The encyclopedia of childbearing*. New York, NY: Henry Holt.

Berg, E. C. (2004). The effects of perceived closeness to custodial parents, stepparents and nonresident parents on adolescent self-esteem. *Journal of Divorce & Remarriage, 40*(1–2), 69–86.

Berger, A. (1998). The rise and fall of Viagra. *British Medical Journal, 317*, 824.

Berger, A. (2011). *Self-regulation: Brain, cognition and development*. Washington, DC: American Psychological Association.

Berger, R. M. (1982). *Gay and gray: The older homosexual man*, Chicago: University of Illinois Press.

Berger, R., Benatov, J., Abu-Raiya, H., & Tadmor, C. T. (2016). Reducing prejudice and promoting positive intergroup attitudes among elementary-school children in the context of the Israeli–Palestinian conflict. *Journal of School Psychology, 57*, 53–72. doi:10.1016/j.jsp.2016.04.003

Berko, J. (1958). The child's learning of English morphology, *Word, 14*, 150–177.

Berlin, J. E. (2009). It's all a matter of perspective: Student perceptions on the impact of being labeled gifted and talented. *Roeper Review, 31*(4), 217–223.

Berlucchi, G. (2011). Brain plasticity and cognitive neurorehabilitation. *Neuropsychological Rehabilitation, 21,* 560–578.

Berndt, T. J. (1988). The nature and significance of children's friendships. In R Vasta (Ed.), *Annals of child development: Vol. 5* (pp. 155–186). Greenwich, CT: JAI Press.

Bernhardt, J. S. (1990). Potential workplace hazards to reproductive health. *Journal of Obstetrical and Gynecological Nursing, 19,* 53–62.

Bertakis, K. D., Azari, R., Helms, L. J., Callahan, E. J., & Robbins, J. A. (2000). Gender differences in the utilization of health care services. *Journal of Family Practice, 49,* 147–152.

Bertrand, K., Richer, I., Brunelle, N., Beaudoin, I., Lemmieux, A., & Menard, J-M. (2013). Substance abuse treatment for adolescents: How are family factors related to substance use change. *Journal of Psychoactive Drugs, 45(1),* 28–38.

Bertrand, M., & Mullainathan, S. (2004). Are Emily and Greg more employable than Lakisha and Jamal? A field experiment on labor market discrimination. *American Economic Review, 94,* 991–1013.

Besedovsky, L., Lange, T., & Born, J. (2012). Sleep and immune function. *Pflügers Archiv-European Journal of Physiology, 463*(1), 121–137.

Best, S., Caillaud, C., & Thompson, M. (2012). The effect of ageing and fitness on thermoregulatory response to high-intensity exercise. *Scandinavian Journal of Medicine and Science in Sports, 22,* e29–e37.

Beveridge, D. (1993). Violence against pregnant women. In B. K. Rothman (Ed.), *The encyclopedia of childbearing.* New York, NY: Henry Holt.

Bhavnagri, N., & Parke, R. D. (1991). Parents as direct facilitators of children's peer relationships: Effects of age of child and sex of parent. *Journal of Social and Personal Relationships, 8,* 423–40.

Bialystok, E., & Hakuta, K. (1994). *The science and psychology of second language acquisition.* New York, NY: Basic Books.

Bianchi, S. M. (2014). A demographic perspective on family change. *Journal of Family Theory & Review, 6,* 35–44.

Bianchi, S. M., Robinson, J. P., & Milke, M. A. (2006). *The changing rhythms of American family life.* Russell Sage Foundation.

Bierman, K. L., Smoot, D. L., & Aumiller, K. (1993). Characteristics of aggressive-rejected, aggressive (nonrejected), and rejected (nonaggressive) boys. *Child Development, 64,* 139–151.

Bingham, C. R., & Crockett, L. J. (1996). Longitudinal adjustment patterns of boys and girls experiencing early, middle and late sexual intercourse. *Developmental Psychology, 32,* 647–658.

Bird, G., & Melville, K. (1994). *Families and intimate relationships.* New York, NY: McGraw-Hill.

Birditt, K. S., & Wardjiman, E. (2012). Intergenerational relationships and aging. In S. K. Whitbourne, & M. J. Sliwinski (Eds.), *The Wiley-Blackwell handbook of adulthood and aging* (pp. 399–415). Malden, MA: Blackwell Publishing.

Birenbaum, L. K., Robinson, M. A., Phillips, D., Stewart, B., et al. (1991). The response of children to the dying and death of a sibling. *Omega: Journal of Death and Dying, 20,* 213–228.

Biringen, Z. (1990). Direct observation of maternal sensitivity and dyadic interaction in the home: Relations to maternal thinking. *Developmental Psychology, 26,* 278–284.

Birren, J. E., Woods, A. M., & Williams, M. V. (1980). Behavioral slowing with age: Causes, organization, and consequences. In L. W. Poon (Ed.), *Aging in the 1980s: Psychological issues* (pp. 293–308). Washington, DC: American Psychological Association.

Black, M., & Krishnakumar, A. (1998). children in low-income, urban settings. *American Psychologist, 53,* 635–646.

Black, M. C., Basile, K. C., Breiding, M. J., Smith, S. G., Walters, M. L., Merrick, M. T., Chen, J., Stevens, M. R. (2011). *The national intimate partner and sexual violence survey (NISVS): 2010 summary report.* Atlanta, GA: National Center for Injury Prevention and Control, Centers for Disease Control and Prevention.

Black, M. M., Quigg, A. M., Hurley, K. M., & Pepper, M. R. (2011). Iron deficiency and iron-deficiency anemia in the first two years of life: Strategies to prevent loss of developmental potential. *Nutrition Reviews, 69,* S64–S70.

Blackburn, J. A., & Papalia, D. E. (1992). Adult cognition from a Piagetian perspective. In R. J Sternberg, & C. A. Berg (Eds.), *Intellectual development* (pp. 141–160). New York, NY: Cambridge University Press.

Blackman, J. A. (1990). *Medical aspects of developmental disabilities in children birth to three* (2nd ed.). Rockville, MD: Aspen Publishers, Inc.

Blair, S. N., Brill, P. A., & Kohl, H. W. (1989). Physical activity patterns in older individuals. In W. W. Spirdnso, & H. M. Eckert (Eds.), *The academy papers: Physical activity and aging* (pp. 120–139). Champaign, Ill: Human Kinetics.

Blakemore, S. J. (2012). Development of the social brain in adolescence. *Journal of the Royal Society of Medicine, 105,* 111–116.

Blanchett, W. J. (2006). Disproportionate representation of African American students in special education: Acknowledging the role of white privilege and racism. *Educational Researcher, 35*(6), 24–28.

Blanck, G. (1990). The man and his cause. In L. C. Moll (Ed.), *Vygotsky and education: Instructional implications and applications of sociohistorical psychology.* Cambridge, UK: Cambridge University Press.

Blashill, A. J., & Wilhelm, S. (2013). Body image distortions, weight, and depression in adolescent boys: Longitudinal trajectories into adulthood. *Psychology of Men & Masculinity.* Advance online publication. doi: 10.1037/a0034618

Bleakley, A., Jordan, A. B., & Hennessy, M. (2013). The relationship between parents' and children's television viewing. *Pediatrics, 132*(2), e364–e371.

Blier, M. J., & Blier-Wilson, L. A. (1989). Gender differences in self-rated emotional expressiveness. *Sex Roles, 21(3–4),* 287–295.

Blieszner, R., & Roberto, K. A. (2012). Partners and friends in adulthood. In S. K. Whitbourne & M. J. Sliwinski (Eds.), *The Wiley-Blackwell handbook of adulthood and aging* (pp. 381–398). Malden, MA: Blackwell Publishing.

Bloch, M. (1982). Death, women and power. In M. Bloch, & J. Parry (Eds.), *Death and the regeneration of life* (pp. 211–230). Cambridge, UK: Cambridge University Press.

Bloom, D. A., Seeley, W. W., Ritchey, M. L., & McGuire, E. J. (1993). Toilet habits and continence in children: An opportunity sampling in search of normal parameters. *Journal of Urology, 149*(5), 1087–1090.

Bloom, L. (1993). *The transition from infancy to language: Acquiring the power of expression.* New York, NY: Cambridge University Press.

Blumberg, M. L., & Lester, D. (1991). High school and college students' attitudes toward rape. *Adolescence, 26,* 727–729.

Bock, R. D., & Moore, E. G. J. (1986). *Advantage and disadvantage: A profile of American youth.* Hillsdale, NJ: Erlbaum.

Boergers, J., Gable, C. J., & Owens, J. A. (2014). Later school start time is associated with improved sleep and daytime functioning in adolescents. *Journal of Developmental & Behavioral Pediatrics, 35*(1), 11–17.

Bogdon, J. C. (1993). Childbirth practices in American history. In B. K. Rothman (Ed.), *The encyclopedia of childbearing.* New York, NY: Henry Holt, 1993.

Bohn, A., & Berntsen, D. (2008). Life story development in childhood: The development of life story abilities and the acquisition of cultural life scripts from late middle childhood to adolescence. *Developmental Psychology, 44*(4), 1135.

Bojko, M. (1995). The multi-cultural program at O'Brien Elementary School, Personal communication.

Bolger, K. E., Patterson, C. J., Thompson, W. W., & Kuper-smidt, J. B. (1995). Psychosocial adjustment among children experiencing persistent and intermittent family economic hardship; *Child Development, 66,* 1107–1129.

Bollerud, K., Christopherson, S., & Frank, E. (1990). Girls' sexual choices: Looking for what is right: The intersection of sexual and moral development. In C. Gilligan, N. Lyons, & T. Hanmer (Eds.), *Making connections: The relational worlds of adolescent girls at Emma Willard School* (pp. 274–285). Cambridge. MA: Harvard University Press.

Bonanno, G. A., Wortman, C. B., Lehman, D. R., Tweed, R. G., Haring, M., Sonnega, J., ... & Nesse, R. M. (2002) Resilience to loss and chronic grief: A prospective study from preloss to 18-months postloss. *Journal of Personality & Social Psychology, 83,* 1150–1164.

Bond, J. T., Galinsky, E., & Swanberg, J. E. (1998). *The 1997 national study of the changing workforce.* New York, NY: Families and Work Institute, Pub. #W98–01.

Bonoti, F., Leondari, A., & Mastora, A. (2013). Exploring children's understanding of death: Through drawings and the death concept questionnaire. *Death Studies, 37*(1), 47–60.

Bookwala, J. (2012). Marriage and other partnered relationships in middle and late adulthood. In R. Blieszner, & V. H. Bedford (Eds.), *Handbook of families and aging* (pp. 91–124). Santa Barbara, CA: Praeger.

Boone-Heinonen, J., Gordon-Larsen, P., Kiefe, C. I., Shikany, J. M., Lewis, C. E., & Popkin, B. M. (2011). Fast food restaurants and food stores: Longitudinal associations with diet in young to middle-aged adults: The CARDIA study. *Archives of Internal Medicine, 171*(13), 1162–1170.

Boonen, S. (2007). Bisphosphonate efficacy and clinical trials for postmenopausal osteoporosis: Similarities and differences. *Bone, 40,* S26-S31. doi: 10.1016/j.bone.2007.03.003

Booth, A., & Amato, P. R. (1994). Parental marital quality, parental divorce, and relations with parents. *Journal of Marriage and the Family, 56,* 21–34.

Booth, A., & Johnson, D. R. (1994). Declining health and marital quality. *Journal of Marriage and the Family, 56,* 218–223.

Booth, A., & Johnson, E. (1988). Premarital cohabitation and marital success. *Journal of Family Issues, 9,* 387–394.

Booth, D. A., Higgs, S., Schneider, J., & Klinkenberg, I. (2010). Learned liking versus inborn delight: Can sweetness give sensual pleasure or is it just motivating? *Psychological Science, 21,* 1656–1663.

Booth, J. R., Burman, D. D., Meyer, J. R., Lei, Z., Trommer, B. L., Davenport, N. D., ... & Mesulam, M. M. (2003). Neural development of selective attention and response inhibition. *Neuroimage, 20*(2), 737–751.

Boquet, J. R., Oliver, D. P., Wittenberg-Lyles, E., Doorenbos, A. Z., & Demiris, G. (2011). Taking care of a dying grandparent: Case studies of grandchildren in the hospice caregiver role. *American Journal of Hospice & Palliative Medicine, 28,* 564–568.

Borchardt, K., & Noble, M. (Ed.). (1997). *Sexually transmitted diseases: Epidemiology, pathology, diagnosis, and treatment.* Boca Raton, FL: CRC Press.

Bordo, S. (1993). *Unbearable weight: Feminism, Western culture, and the body.* Berkeley, CA: University of California Press.

Bornstein, M. H., Haynes, O. M., Azuma, H., Galperin, C., et al. (1998). A cross-national study of self-evaluations and attributions in parenting: Argentina, Belgium, France, Israel, Italy, Japan, & the United States. *Developmental Psychology, 34*, 662–676.

Bosman, E. A. (1993). Age-related differences in the motoric aspects of transcription typing skill. *Psychology & Aging, 8*(1), 87–102.

Bosman, E. A. (1994). Age and skill differences in typing related and unrelated reaction time tasks. *Aging and Cognition, 1*(4), 310–322.

Botwinick, J. (1977). Intellectual abilities. In J. E. Birren, & K. W. Schaie (Eds.), *Handbook of the psychology of aging* (pp. 580–605). New York, NY: Van Nostrand Reinhold.

Bouchard, C., & Shephard, R. J. (1993). Physical activity, fitness, and health: The model and key concepts. In C. Bouchard, R. J. Shephard, & T. Stephens (Eds.), *Physical activity, fitness, and health* (pp. 11–23). Champaign, IL: Human Kinetics.

Bowers, R. (1995). Early adolescent social and emotional development: A constructivist perspective. In M. Wavering (Ed.), *Educating young adolescents*, pp. 79–110. New York, NY: Garland.

Bowlby, J. (1969). *Attachment and loss: Vol. 1. Attachment.* New York, NY: Basic Books.

Bowlby, J. (1973). *Attachment and loss: Vol. 2. Separation, anxiety, and anger.* New York, NY: Basic Books.

Bowlby, J. (1979). *The making and breaking of affectional bonds.* London: Tavistock Publications.

Bowlby, J. (1980). *Attachment and loss: Vol. 3. Loss, sadness, and depression.* New York, NY: Basic Books.

Bowlby, J. (1988). *A secure base: Clinical applications of attachment theory.* London: Routledge.

Bowlby, J. (1988). Developmental psychology comes of age. *American Journal of Psychiatry, 145*, 1–10.

Boyd, M., & Pryor, E. T. (1989). The cluttered nest: The living arrangements of young Canadian adults. *Canadian Journal of Sociology, 14*, 461–477.

Boyle, P. J., Feng, Z., & Raab, G. M. (2011). Does widowhood increase mortality risk?: Testing for selection effects by comparing causes of spousal death. *Epidemiology, 22*, 1–5.

Bradley, M. (2002). *Yes your teen is crazy! Loving your kid without losing your mind.* Gig Harbor, WA: Harbor Press.

Bradsher, J. E. (1997). Older women and widowhood. In J. M. Coyle (Ed.), *Handbook on women and aging* (pp. 418–129). Westport, CT: Greenwood Press.

Brady, E. M. (1984). Demographic and educational correlates of self-reported learning among older students. *Educational Gerontology, 10*, 25–38.

Braithwaite, R. L., & Lythcott, N. (1989). Community empowerment as a strategy for health promotion for black and other minority populations. *Journal of the American Medical Association, 261*, 282–283.

Brazelton, T. B. (1976). Early mother-infant reciprocity. In V. G. Vaughn III, & T. B. Brazelton (Eds.), *The family: Can it be saved?* Chicago: Yearbook Medical Publishers.

Brazelton, T. B., and Nugent, J. (1997). *Neonatal behavioral assessment scale* (4th ed.), New York, NY: Cambridge University Press.

Brecber, E. (1984). *Love, sex, and aging.* Boston: Little, Brown.

Bredekamp, S., & Copple, C. (Eds.) (1997). *Developmentally appropriate practice in early childhood programs* (rev. ed.), Washington, DC; National Association for the Education of Young Children.

Breiding, M. J., Chen J., & Black, M.C. (2014). *Intimate partner violence in the United States—2010.* Atlanta, GA: National Center for Injury Prevention and Control, Centers for Disease Control and Prevention.

Breiding, M. J., Smith, S. G., Basile, K. C., Walters, M. L., Chen, J., & Merrick, M. T. (2014). Prevalence and characteristics of sexual violence, stalking, and intimate partner violence victimization—National Intimate Partner and Sexual Violence Survey, United States, 2011. Centers for Disease Control and Prevention, 63(SS08), 1–18. Retrieved from http://www.cdc.gov/mmwr/preview/mmwrhtml/ss6308a1.htm?s_cid=ss6308a1_e

Breslau, N. (2009). The epidemiology of trauma, PTSD, and other posttrauma disorders. *Trauma, Violence, & Abuse. 10*(3), 198–210. doi: 10.1177/1524838009334448

Bretherton, I. (1995). A communication perspective on attachment relationships and internal working models. *Monographs of the Society for Research in Child Development, 60*, 310–329.

Bretherton, I., & Waters, E. (1985). Growing points in attachment theory. *Monographs of the Society for Research in Child Development, 50* (12, Serial No. 209).

Bretherton, I., McNew, S., & Beeghly-Smith, M. (1981). Early person knowledge as expressed in gestural and verbal communications. In M. Lamb, & L Sherrod (Eds.), *Infant social cognition.* Hillsdale, NJ: Erlbaum.

Bridge, J. A., McBee-Strayer, S. M., & Cannon, E. A. (2012). Impaired decision-making in adolescent suicide attempters. *Journal of the American Academy of Child and Adolescent Psychiatry, 51*(4), 394–403.

Bridges, L. J., Grolnick, W. A., & Connell, J. P. (1997). Infant emotion regulation with mothers and fathers. *Infant Behavior and Development, 20*, 47–57.

Bridle, C., Spanjers, K., Patel, S., Atherton, N. M., & Lamb, S. E. (2012). Effect of exercise on depression severity in older people: Systematic review and meta-analysis of randomized controlled trials. *British Journal of Psychiatry, 201*, 180–185.

Briggs, W. P., Magnus, V. A., Lassiter, P., Patterson, A., & Smith, L. (2011). Substance use, misuse, and abuse among older adults: Implications for clinical mental health counselors. *Journal of Mental Health Counseling, 33*, 112–127.

Brindle, A. (2015). Waali plural formation: A preliminary study on variation in noun class realization. *Journal of African Languages and Linguistics, 36*(2), 163–192.

Briones, T. L., Klintsova, A. Y., & Greenough, W. T. (2004). Stability of synaptic plasticity in the adult rat visual cortex induced by complex environment exposure. *Brain Research, 1018*, 130–135.

Brislin, R., & Yoshida, T. (1994). *Intercultural communication training: An introduction.* Thousand Oaks, CA: Sage.

Brody, E. M. (1990). *Women in the middle: Their parent-care years.* New York, NY: Springer.

Brody, E. M., Litvin, S. J., Albert, S. M., & Hoffman, C. J. (1994). Marital status of daughters and patterns of parent care. *Journal of Gerontology, 49*, S95-S103.

Brody, E. M., Morton, H. K., Johnsen, P. T., Hoffman, C., & Schoonover, C. B. (1987). Work status and parent care: A comparison of four groups of women. *The Gerontologist, 27*, 201–208.

Brody, G. H., & Flor, D. L. (1997). Maternal psychological functioning, family processes, and child adjustment in rural, single-parent African American families. *Developmental Psychology, 33*, 1000–1011.

Brody, G. H., & Flor, D. L. (1998). Maternal resources, parenting practices, and child competence in rural, single-parent African American families. *Child Development, 69*, 803–816.

Brody, G. H., Graziano, W. G., & Musser, L. M. (1983). Familiarity and children's behavior in same-age and mixed-age peer groups *Developmental Psychology, 19*, 569–576.

Brody, G. H., Stoneman, Z., Flor, D. L., McCrary, C., Hastings, L., & Conyers, O. (1994). Financial resources, parent psychological functioning, parent co-caregiving, and early adolescent competence in rural two-parent African American families. *Child Development, 65*, 590–605.

Brody, G. H., Stoneman, Z., McCoy, J. K., & Forehand, R. (1992). Contemporary and longitudinal associations of sibling conflict with family relationship assessments and family discussions about sibling problems. *Child Development, 63*, 391–400.

Brody, J. E. (1993, February 10). Adult years bring new afflictions for DES "babies." *New York Times*, p, C–12.

Brondel, L., Romer, M. A., Nougues, P. M., Touyarou, P., & Davenne, D. (2010). Acute partial sleep deprivation increases food intake in healthy men. *American Journal of Clinical Nutrition, 91*(6), 1550–1559.

Bronfenbrenner, U. (1989). Ecological systems theory. In R. Vasta (Ed.), *Annals of child development: Vol. 6. Six theories of child development: Revised formulations and current issues.* Greenwich, CT: JAI Press.

Bronfenbrenner, U. (2000). Ecological theory. In A. Kazdin (Ed.), *Encyclopedia of psychology.* Washington, DC: American Psychological Association.

Bronfenbrenner, U. (Ed.) (2005). *Making human beings human: Bioecological perspectives on human development.* Thousand Oaks, CA: Sage.

Bronner, F. (Ed.) (1997). *Nutrition policy in public health.* New York, NY: Springer.

Bronstein, P. (1988). Marital and parenting roles in transition. In P. Bronstein, & C. P. Cowan (Eds.), *Fatherhood today: Men's changing role in the family* (pp. 3–12). New York, NY: Wiley.

Brooks-Gunn, J., & Warren, M. (1989). Biological and social contributions to negative affect in young adolescent girls. *Child Development, 60*, 40–55.

Brooten, D. (Ed.) (1992). *Low-birth-weight neonates.* Philadelphia: Lippincott.

Brophy, J. (1983). Research on the self-fulfilling prophecy and teacher expectations. *Journal of Educational Psychology, 75*, 631–666.

Broughton, D., Eisner, E., & Ligtvoet, J. (Eds.) (1996). *Evaluating and assessing the visual arts in education.* New York, NY: Teachers College Press.

Brown B. B. (1990). Peer groups and peer cultures. In S. S. Feldman & G. R. Elliot (Eds.), *At the threshold: The developing adolescent* (pp. 171–196). Cambridge, MA: Harvard University Press.

Brown, B. B., & Huang, B. (1995). Examining parenting practices in different peer contexts: Implications for adolescent trajectories. In L. J. Crockett, A. C. Crouter, et al. (Eds.) (1995). *Pathways through adolescence: Individual development in relation to social contexts: The Penn State series on child & adolescent development* (pp. 151–174). Mahwah, NJ: Lawrence Erlbaum Associates.

Brown, B. B., Mounts, N., Lainborn, S. D., & Steinberg, L. (1993). Parenting practices and peer group affiliation in adolescence. *Child Development, 64*, 467–482.

Brown, G. L., Mangelsdorf, S. C., & Neff, C. (2012). Father involvement, paternal sensitivity, and father–child attachment security in the first 3 years. *Journal of Family Psychology, 26*(3), 421.

Brown, G. L., McBride, B. A., Shin, N., & Bost, K. K. (2007). Parenting predictors of father-child attachment security: Interactive effects of father involvement and fathering quality. *Fathering: A Journal of Theory, Research, and Practice about Men as Fathers, 5*(3).

Brown, J. R., & Dunn, J. (1992). Talk with your mother or your sibling? Developmental changes in early family conversations about feelings. *Child Development, 63*, 336–349.

Brown, L., & Gilligan, C. (1992). *Meeting at the crossroads: Women's psychology and girls' development.* Cambridge, MA: Harvard University Press.

Brown, L. H., & DeRycke, S. B. (2010). The kinkeeping connection: Continuity, crisis and consensus. *Journal of Intergenerational Relationships, 8*, 338–353.

Brown, R. (1973). *A first language: The early stages.* Cambridge, MA: Harvard University Press.

Brown, S. C., & Greene, J. A. (2009). The Wisdom Development Scale: Further validity investigations. *International Journal of Aging and Human Development, 68*, 289–320.

Brown, S. L., & Lin, I. F. (2012). The gray divorce revolution: Rising divorce among middle-aged and older adults, 1990–2010. *Journals of Gerontology Series B: Psychological Sciences and Social Sciences, 67*, 731–741.

Brownell, C. A., Nichols, S. R., & Svetlova, M. (2010). Toddlers' understanding of peers' emotions. *Journal of Genetic Psychology, 171*, 35–53.

Brubaker, E., & Brubaker, T. H. (1995). Critical policy issues. In G. C. Smith, S. S. Tobin, E. A. Robertson-Tchabo, & P. W. Power (Eds.), *Strengthening aging families: Diversity in practice and policy* (pp. 235–247). Thousand Oaks, CA: Sage.

Brubaker, T. H. (1985). *Later life families.* Beverly Hills, CA: Sage.

Brubaker, T. H., & Kiusel, B. (1988). Who is responsible for household tasks in long-term marriages of the young old elderly? In L. Ade-Ridder, & C. Hennon (Eds.), *Lifestyles of the elderly: Diversity in relationships, health, and caregiving.* New York, NY: Human Sciences Press.

Bruchmüller, K., Margraf, J., & Schneider, S. (2012). Is ADHD diagnosed in accord with diagnostic criteria? Overdiagnosis and influence of client gender on diagnosis. *Journal of Consulting and Clinical Psychology, 80*(1), 128–138.

Bruner, J. (1996). *The culture of education.* Cambridge, MA: Harvard University Press.

Bryan, E. (1995). The death of a twin. *Palliative Medicine, 9*, 187–192.

Bryant, B. K. (1985). The neighborhood walk: Sources of support in middle childhood. *Monographs of the Society for Research on Child Development, 50* (3, No. 210).

Bryant, B. K. (1994). How does social support function in childhood? In F. Nestmann, & K. Hurrelmann (Eds.). *Social networks and social support in childhood and adolescence. Prevention and intervention in childhood and adolescence, 16* (pp. 23–35). Berlin, Germany: Walter De Gruyter.

Bryant, C., Bei, B., Gilson, K., Komiti, A., Jackson, H., & Judd, F. (2012). The relationship between attitudes to aging and physical and mental health in older adults. *International Psychogeriatrics, 24*, 1674–1683.

Bryant, C. D. (2003). *Handbook of death and dying* (Vol. 2, pp. 611–693). Thousand Oaks, CA: Sage Publications.

Bryant, G. A., & Barrett, H. C. (2007). Recognizing intentions in infant-directed speech: Evidence for universals. *Psychological Science, 18*, 746–751.

Buchmann, C., & DiPrete, T. A. (2006). The growing female advantage in college completion: The role of family background and academic achievement. *American Sociological Review, 71*(4), 515–541.

Buckley, K., & Kulb, N. (Eds.). (1983). *Handbook of maternal-newborn nursing.* New York, NY: Wiley.

Bugental, D. B., Ellerson, P. C., Lin, E. K., Rainey, B., Kokotovic, A., & O'Hara, N. (2010). A cognitive approach to child abuse prevention. *Journal of Family Psychology, 15*(3), 243–258.

Buhrmester, D. (1990). Intimacy of friendship, interpersonal competence, and adjustment during preadolescence and adolescence. *Child Development, 61*, 1101–1111.

Buhrmester, D., & Furman, W. (1990). Perceptions of sibling relationships during middle childhood and adolescence. *Child Development, 61*, 1387–1398.

Bukowksi, W. M., Newcomb, A. F., & Hartup, W. W. (1996). *The company they keep: Friendship in childhood, and adolescence.* New York, NY: Cambridge University Press.

Bukowski, W. M., & Hoza, B. (1989). Popularity and friendship: Issues in theory, measurement, and outcome. In T. J. Berndt, & G. W. Ladd (Eds.), *Peer relationships in child development* (pp. 15–45). New York, NY: Wiley.

Bulcroft, R., & Bulcroft, K. (1991). The nature of the function of dating in later life. *Research on Aging, 13*(2), 244–260.

Bumpass, L. L., Sweet, J. A., & Cherlin, A. (1991). The role of cohabitation in declining rates of marriage. *Journal of Marriage and the Family, 53*, 913–927.

Burd, L., Blair, J., & Dopps, K. (2012). Prenatal alcohol exposure, blood alcohol concentrations and elimination rates for the mother, fetus and newborn. *Journal of Perinatology, 32*, 652–659.

Burdette, H. L., Whitaker, R. C., Hall, W. C., & Daniels, S. R. (2006). Maternal infant-feeding style and children's adiposity at 5 years of age. *Archives of Pediatrics & Adolescent Medicine, 160*(5), 513–520.

Bureau of Labor Statistics, U. S. Department of Labor. (2015). Time spent working by full- and part-time status, gender, and location in 2014. *The Economics Daily.* Retrieved from http://www.bls.gov/opub/ted/2015/time-spent-working-by-full-and-part-time-status-gender-and-location-in.htm

Burke, T., Marwald, R., McHill, A., Chinoy, E., Snider, J., Bessman, S., ... & Wright, K. (2015). Effects of caffeine on the human circadian clock in vivo and in vitro. *Science Translational Medicine, 7*, 305ra146. doi: 10.1126/scitranslmed.aac5125.

Burnett, P., Middleton, W., Raphael, B., Dunne, M., Moy-lan, A., & Martinek, N. (1994). Concepts of normal bereavement. *Journal of Traumatic Stress, 7*, 123–128.

Burns, B. J., Phillips, S. D., Wagner, H. R., Barth, R. P., Kolko, D. J., Campbell, Y., & Landsverk, J. (2004). Mental health need and access to mental health services by youths involved with child welfare: A national survey. *Journal of the American Academy of Child & Adolescent Psychiatry, 43*(8), 960–970.

Burrus-Bammel, L. L., & Bammel, G. (1985). Leisure and recreation. In J. E. Birren, & K. W. Schaie (Eds.), *Handbook of the psychology of aging* (2nd ed., pp. 848–863). New York, NY: Van Nostrand Reinhold.

Burton, L. M. (1992). Families and the aged: Issues of complexity and diversity. *Generations, 17*(3), 5–6.

Burton, L. M. (1996). Age norms, the timing of family roles transitions, and intergenerational caregiving among aging African American women. *The Gerontologist, 36*, 199–208.

Burton, L. M., & DeVries, C. (1992). Challenges and rewards: African American grandparents as surrogate parents. *Generations, 17*(3), 51–54.

Burton, L. M., Dilworth-Anderson, P., & Merriwether-de-Vries, C. (1995). Context and surrogate parenting among contemporary grandparents. (Single parent families: Diversity, myths and realities, part 2). *Marriage & Family Review, 20*, 349–366.

Bury, M. (1997). *Health and illness in a changing society.* New York, NY: Routledge.

Bushman, B. J., & Huesmann, L. R. (2006). Short-term and long-term effects of violent media on aggression in children and adults. *Archives of Pediatrics & Adolescent Medicine, 160*(4), 348–352.

Buss, A. H. (1986). *Social behavior and personality.* Hillsdale, NJ: Erlbaum.

Buss, A. H., & Plomin, R. (1984). *Temperament: Early developing personality traits.* Hillsdale, NJ: Erlbaum.

Buss, K. A., & Goldsmith, H. H. (1998). Fear and anger regulation in infancy: Effects on the temporal dynamics of affective expression. *Child Development, 69*, 359–384.

Busse, E. W., & Maddox, G. L. (1985). *The Duke longitudinal studies of normal aging, 1955–1980: Overview of history, design, and findings.* New York, NY: Springer.

Butler, R. N. (1975). *Why survive? Being old in America.* New York, NY: Harper & Row.

Butler, R. N. (1993). Dispelling ageism: The cross-cutting intervention. *Generations, 17*(2), 75–78.

Butler, R. N. (1997). Living longer, contributing longer. *Journal of the American Medical Association, 278*(16), 1372–1373.

Butler, S. S. (2008). Gay, lesbian, bisexual, and transgender (LGBT) elders: The challenges and resilience of this marginalized group. *Journal of Human Behavior in the Social Environment, 9*, 25–44.

Buyse, E., Verschueren, K., & Doumen, S. (2011). Preschoolers' attachment to mother and risk for adjustment problems in kindergarten: Can teachers make a difference? *Social Development, 20*(1), 33–50.

Byard, R., & Cohle, S. (1994). *Sudden death in infants, children, and adolescents.* New York, NY: Cambridge University Press.

Bye, D., Pushkar, D., & Conway, M. (2007). Motivation, interest, and positive affect in traditional and nontraditional undergraduate students. *Adult Education Quarterly, 57*(2), 141–58.

Byne, W. (1994, May). The biological evidence challenged. *Scientific American*, pp. 50–55.

Byrne, A., & Carr, D. (2005). Caught in the cultural lag: The stigma of singlehood. *Psychological Inquiry, 16*(2–3), 84–90.

C

Cain, K. M., & Dweck, C. S. (1995). The relation between motivational patterns and achievement cognitions through the elementary school years. *Merrill-Palmer Quarterly, 41*, 35–52.

Caine, D., Maffulli, N., & Caine, C. (2008). Epidemiology of injury in child and adolescent sports: Injury rates, risk factors, and prevention. *Clinics in Sports Medicine, 27*(1), 19–50.

Calabrese, R. L., & Noboa, J. (1995). The choice for gang membership by Mexican-American adolescents. *High School Journal*, 226–235.

Calasanti, T., & Kiecolt, K. J. (2012). Intersectionality and aging families. In R. Blieszner, & V. H. Bedford (Eds.), *Handbook of families and aging* (pp. 263–286). Santa Barbara, CA: Praeger.

Calderon-Margalit, R., Friedlander, Y., Yanetz, R., Kleinhaus, K., Perrin, M. C., Manor, O., ... & Paltiel, O. (2009). Cancer risk after exposure to treatments for ovulation induction. *American Journal of Epidemiology, 169*(3), 365–375.

Caldwell, J. C., & Caldwell, P. (1990). High fertility in sub-Saharan Africa. *Scientific American, 262*(5), 118–125.

Calhoun, D. A., & Harding, S. M. (2010). Sleep and hypertension. *Chest, 138*, 434–443. doi:10.1378/chest.09-2954

Calhoun, L., Tedeschi, R., Cann, A., & Hanks, E. (2010). Positive outcomes following bereavement: Paths to posttraumatic growth. *Psychologica Belgica, 50*(1–2).

Caliso, J., & Milner, J. (1992). Childhood history of abuse and child abuse screening. *Child Abuse and Neglect, 16*, 647–659.

Call, K. T., Mortimer, J. T., & Shanahan, M. J. (1995). Helpfulness and the development of competence in adolescence. *Child Development, 66*, 129–138.

Callahan, J. J., Jr. (1992). Aging in place. *Generations, 16*(2), 5–6.

Calvert, S. L. (2008). Media and early development. In K. McCartney, & D. Phillips (Eds.), *Blackwell handbook of early childhood development* (pp. 508–529). Malden, MA: Blackwell Publishing.

Camacho, T. C., Roberts, R. E., Lazarus, N. B., Kaplan, G. A., & Cohen, R. D. (1991). Physical activity and depression: Evidence from the Alameda County study. *American Journal of Epidemiology, 134*, 220–231.

Campbell, M. D., Wilson, L. G., & Hanson, G. R. (1980). *The invisible minority: A study of adult university students* (Final report submitted to the Hogg Foundation for Mental Health). Austin, TX: Office of the Dean of Students, University of Texas.

Campion, M. J. (1993). Childbearing with a disability In B. K. Rotliman (Ed.), *The encyclopedia of childbearing*. New York, NY: Henry Holt.

Campos, A. P. (1990). Social work practice with Puerto Rican terminally ill clients and their families. In J. K. Parry (Ed.), *Social work practice with the terminally ill: A transcultural perspective* (pp. 129–143). Springfield, IL: Charles C Thomas.

Campos, R., Raffaelli, M., Ude, W., Greco, M., Ruff, A., Rolf, J., Antunes, C. M., Halsey, N., Greco, D., & Street Youth Study Group. (1994). Social networks and daily activities of street youth in Belo Horizonte, Brazil *Child Development, 65,* 319–330.

Camras, L. A., Sullivan, J., & Michel, G. (1993). Do infants express discrete emotions? Adult judgments of facial, vocal, and body actions., *Journal of Nonverbal Behavior, 17,* 171–186.

Cancian, F. M. (1986). The feminization of love *Signs: Journal of Women in Culture and. Society, 11,* 692–709.

Canella, G. (1997). *Deconstructing early childhood education.* New York, NY: Peter Lang.

Canfield R., Smith, E., Brezsnyak, M., & Snow, K. (1997). Information processing through the first year of life: A longitudinal study using the visual expectation paradigm. *Monographs of the Society for Research in Child Development, 62* (2, Serial No. 250).

Canfield, R., & Smith, E. (1996). Number-based expectations and sequential enumeration by 5-month-old-infants. *Developmental Psychology, 32,* 269–279.

Cannella, G. (1997). *Deconstructing early childhood education: Social justice and revolution.* New York, NY: Peter Lang Publishers.

Cantor, M. H. (1992). Families and caregiving in an aging society. *Generations, 16*(3), 67–70.

Cantos, A. L., Neidig, P. H., & O'Leary, K. D. (1994). Injuries of women and men in a treatment program for domestic violence. *Journal of Family Violence, 9*(2), 113–124.

Capaldi, D. M., Knoble, N. B., Shortt, J. W., & Kim, H. K. (2012). A systematic review of risk factors for intimate partner violence. *Partner Abuse, 3*(2), 231–280.

Cappuccio, F. P., D'Elia, L., Strazzullo, P., & Miller, M. A. (2010) Sleep duration and all-cause mortality: A systematic review and meta-analysis of prospective studies. *Sleep, 33,* 585–592.

Cappuccio, F. P., Taggart, F. M., Kandala, N., Currie, A., Peile, E., Stranges, S., & Miller, M. A. (2008). Meta-analysis of short sleep duration and obesity in children and adults. *Sleep, 31*(5), 619–626.

Card, N. A., Stucky, B. D., Sawalani, G. M., & Little, T. D. (2008). Direct and indirect aggression during childhood and adolescence: A meta-analytic review of gender differences, intercorrelations, and relations to maladjustment. *Child Development, 79*(5), 1185–1229.

Carlin, D. B., & Winfrey, K. L. (2009). Have you come a long way, baby? Hillary Clinton, Sarah Palin, and sexism in 2008 campaign coverage. *Communication Studies, 60,* 326–343.

Carlo, G., McGinley, M., Hayes, R., Batenhorst, C., & Wilkinson, J. (2007). Parenting styles or practices? Parenting, sympathy, and prosocial behaviors among adolescents. *Journal of Genetic Psychology, 168*(2), 147–176.

Carlo, G., Mestre, M. V., Samper, P., Tur, A., & Armenta, B. E. (2011). The longitudinal relations among dimensions of parenting styles, sympathy, prosocial moral reasoning, and prosocial behaviors. *International Journal of Behavioral Development, 35*(2), 116–124.

Carlson, C. I., Cooper, C. R., & Spradling, V. Y. (1991). Developmental implications of shared versus distinct perceptions of the family in early adolescence. *New Directions for Child Development, 51,* 13–32.

Carlson, E. A., Jacobvitz, D., & Sroufe, A. L. (1995). A developmental investigation of inattentiveness and hyperactivity. *Child Development, 66,* 37–54.

Carlson, S. M., & Beck, D. M. (2009). Symbols as tools in the development of executive function. In A. Winsler, C. Fernyhough, & I. Montero (Eds.), *Private speech, executive functioning, and the development of verbal self-regulation* (pp. 163–175). Cambridge University Press.

Carney, S. S., Rich, C. L., Burke, P. A., & Fowler, R. C. (1994). Suicide over 60: The San Diego study. *Journal of the American Geriatric Society, 42,* 174–180.

Carp, F. M. (1978/1979). Effects of the living environment on activity and the use of time. *International Journal of Aging and Human Development, 9,* 74–91.

Carp, F. M. (1997). Retirement and women. In J. M. Coyle (Ed.), *Handbook on woman and aging* (pp. 112–128), Westport, CT: Greenwood.

Carpenter, C. L., Yan, E., Chen, S., Hong, K., Arechiga, A., Kim, W. S., ... & Heber, D. (2013). Body fat and body-mass index among a multiethnic sample of college-age men and women. *Journal of Obesity,* 2013, 1–7.

Carr, D., Freedman, V. A., Cornman, J. C., & Schwarz, N. (2014). Happy marriage, happy life? Marital quality and subjective well-being in later life. *Journal of Marriage and Family, 76,* 930–948. doi: 10.1111/jomf.12133

Carroll, J., & Siska, E. (1998). SIDS: Counseling parents to reduce the risk. *American Family Physician,* 57(9) [On-line]. Available: www.sids.org.

Carskadon, M. A. (1990). Patterns of sleep and sleepiness in adolescents. *Pediatrician, 17*(1), 5–12.

Carskadon, M. A., Acebo, C., & Jenni, O. G. (2004). Regulation of adolescent sleep: Implications for behavior. *Annals of the New York Academy of Sciences, 1021*(1), 276–291.

Carskadon, M. A., Wolfson, A. R., Acebo, C., Tzischinsky, O., & Seifer, R. (1998). Adolescent sleep patterns, circadian timing, and sleepiness at a transition to early school days. *Sleep, 21,* 871–881.

Carstensen, L. L. (1992). Social and emotional patterns in adulthood: Support for socioemotional selectivity theory. *Psychology and Aging, 7,* 331–338.

Carstensen, L. L., Gottman, J. M., & Levenson, R. W. (1995). Emotional behavior in long-term marriage. *Psychology and Aging, 10,* 140–149.

Casarett, D. J. (2011). Rethinking hospice eligibility criteria. *JAMA, 305*(10), 1031–1032.

Case, R. (1991a). *The mind's staircase: Exploring the conceptual underpinnings of children's thought and knowledge* Hillsdale, NJ: Erlbaum.

Case, R. (1991b). General and specific views of the mind, its structure, and its development. In R. Case (Ed.), *The mind's staircase (pp. 3–16).* Hillsdale, NJ: Erlbaum.

Case, R. (1991c). A neo-Piagetian approach to the issue of cognitive generality and specificity. In R. Case (Ed.), *The mind's staircase* (pp. 17–36). Hillsdale, NJ: Erlbaum.

Case, R. (1991d). Advantages and limitations of the neo-Piagetian position. In R. Case (Ed.), *The mind's staircase* (pp. 37–51). Hillsdale, NJ: Erlbaum.

Case, R. (1992). Neo-Piagetian theories of intellectual development. In H. Beilin, & P. Pufall (Eds.), *Piaget's theory: Prospects and possibilities.* Hillsdale, NJ: Erlbaum.

Case, R. (1998, April). *Fostering the development of number sense in the elementary and middle grades.* Paper presented at the annual meeting of the American Educational Research Association, San Diego.

Case, R., & Edelstein, W. (1993). *The new structuralism in cognitive development: Theory and research on individual pathways,* New York, NY: Karger.

Casey, B. J., Jones, R. M., & Hare, T. A. (2008). The adolescent brain. *Annals of the New York Academy of Sciences, 1124,* 111–126.

Casey, B. J., Tottenham, N., Liston, C., & Durston, S. (2005). Imaging the developing brain: What have we learned about cognitive development? *Trends in Cognitive Science, 9,* 104–110.

Caspi, A., & Silva, P. A. (1995). Temperamental qualities at age 3 predict personality traits in young adulthood: Longitudinal evidence from a birth cohort. *Child development, 66,* 486–498.

Caspi, A., Elder, G. H., Jr., & Bern, D. J. (1988). Moving away from the world: Life-course patterns of shy children. *Developmental Psychology, 24,* 824–831.

Caspi, A., Henry, B., McGee, R., Moffitt, T., & Silva, P. (1995). Temperamental origins of child and adolescent behavior problems: From age 3 to age 15. *Child Development, 66,* 55–68.

Cassel, C. K., & Meier, D. E. (1990). Morals and moralism in the debate over euthanasia and assisted suicide. *New England Journal of Medicine, 323,* pp. 750–752.

Cassell, D. (1994). *Encyclopedia of obesity and eating disorders.* New York, NY: Facts on File Press.

Cassidy, J., Kirsh, S. J., Scolton, K. L., & Parke, R. D. (1996). Attachment and representations of peer relationships. *Developmental Psychology, 32,* 892–904.

Cassidy, S. B. (1995). Uniparental disomy and genomic imprinting as causes of human genetic disease. *Environmental and Molecular Mutagenesis, 25,* 13–20.

Castañeda, D. M. (1993). The meaning of romantic love among Mexican-Americans. *Journal of Social Behavior and Personality, 8,* 257–272.

Caterall, J. (1998). Risk and resilience in student transitions to high school. *American Journal of Education, 106*(2), 302–333.

Cattell, R. B. (1963). Theory of fluid and crystallized intelligence: A critical experiment. *Journal of Educational Psychology, 54,* 1–22.

Cauley, J. A. (2011). Defining ethnic and racial differences in osteoporosis and fragility fractures, *Clinical Orthopaedics and Related Research, 469,* 1891–1899.

Cazden, C. (1988). *Classroom discourse.* Portsmouth, NH: Heinemann.

Cazenave, N. A., & Straus, M. A. (1990). Race, class network embeddedness, and family violence: A search for potent support systems. In M. A. Straus & R. J. Gelles, with C. Smith (Eds.), *Physical violence in American families: Risk factors and adaptations to violence in 8,145 families* (pp. 321–339). New Brunswick, NJ: Transaction.

Centers for Disease Control and Prevention. (1992, January 3). Sexual behavior among high school students—United States, 1990. *Morbidity and Mortality Weekly Report, 40,* 885–888.

Centers for Disease Control and Prevention. (1998). *National vital statistics report, 47(4).* Bethesda, MD: National Center for Health Statistics.

Centers for Disease Control and Prevention (CDC). (2000). *2 to 20 years: Boys stature-for-age and weight-for-age percentiles.* Retrieved from http://www.cdc.gov/growthcharts/data/set1clinical/cj41l021.pdf

Centers for Disease Control and Prevention (CDC). (2000). *2 to 20 years: Girls stature-for-age and weight-for-age percentiles.* Retrieved from http://www.cdc.gov/growthcharts/data/set1clinical/cj41l022.pdf.

Centers for Disease Control and Prevention (CDC). (2005). *Deaths by place of death, age, race, and sex: United States, 2005.* Retrieved from http://www.cdc.gov/nchs/data/dvs/Mortfinal2005_worktable_309.pdf.

Centers for Disease Control and Prevention (CDC). (2005). *Web-based Injury Statistics Query and Reporting System (WISQARS).* Available from www.cdc.gov/ncipc/wisqars/default.htm

Centers for Disease Control and Prevention (CDC). (2008, January 11). Update on overall prevalence of major birth defects—Atlanta, Georgia, 1978–2005. *Morbidity and Mortality Weekly Report, 57,* 1–5.

Centers for Disease Control and Prevention (CDC). (2010). *10 leading causes of death by age group, United States—2010.* Retrieved from https://www.cdc.gov/injury/wisqars/pdf/10lcid_all_deaths_by_age_group_2010-a.pdf

Centers for Disease Control and Prevention—Division of Reproductive Health. (2011a). *2009 assisted reproductive technology success rates: National summary and fertility clinic reports.* Atlanta, GA: U.S. Department of Health and Human Services.

Centers for Disease Control and Prevention (CDC). (2011b). *Facts about Down syndrome.* Retrieved from http://www.cdc.gov/ncbddd/birthdefects/downsyndrome.html.

Centers for Disease Control and Prevention (CDC). (2011c). Quitting smoking among adults—United States, 2001–2010. *Morbidity and Mortality Weekly Report, 60*(44), 1513.

Centers for Disease Control and Prevention (CDC). (2012a). *National vital statistics reports, 61* (No. 6). Hyattsville, MD: National Center for Health Statistics. Retrieved from http://www.cdc.gov/nchs/data/nvsr/nvsr61/nvsr61_06.pdf

Centers for Disease Control and Prevention (CDC) – Office of Surveillance, Epidemiology, and Laboratory Services (2012b). *Morbidity and mortality weekly report: Abortion surveillance—United States 2009, 61* (No. SS-8).

Centers for Disease Control and Prevention (CDC). (2012c). Youth Risk Behavior Surveillance, United States, 2011. *Morbidity and Mortality Weekly Report, 61*(4), 10–12. Retrieved from http:// http://www.cdc.gov/HealthyYouth/yrbs/index.htm?s_cid=tw_cdc16.

Centers for Disease Control and Prevention (CDC). (2013a). *Breast cancer.* Retrieved from http://www.cdc.gov/cancer/breast/statistics/race.htm

Centers for Disease Control and Prevention (CDC) – Division of STD Prevention. (2013b). *Sexually transmitted disease surveillance 2012.* Atlanta, GA: U.S. Department of Health and Human Services.

Centers for Disease Control and Prevention (CDC). (2014a). *Breast cancer rates by race and ethnicity.* Retrieved from http://www.cdc.gov/cancer/breast/statistics/race.htm

Centers for Disease Control and Prevention (CDC). (2014b). *Prostate cancer rates by race and ethnicity.* Retrieved from http://www.cdc.gov/cancer/prostate/statistics/race.htm

Centers for Disease Control and Prevention (CDC). (2014c). *Summary health statistics: National Health interview survey, 2014.* Retrieved from http://ftp.cdc.gov/pub/Health_Statistics/NCHS/NHIS/SHS/2014_SHS_Table_C-5.pdf

Centers for Disease Control and Prevention (CDC). (2015a). *Childhood obesity facts.* Atlanta, GA. Retrieved from http://www.cdc.gov/healthyschools/obesity/facts.htm

Centers for Disease Control and Prevention (CDC). (2015b). *Infertility.* Retrieved from http://www.cdc.gov/nchs/fastats/infertility.htm

Centers for Disease Control and Prevention (CDC). (2015c). *Insufficient sleep is a public health problem.* Retrieved from http://www.cdc.gov/features/dssleep/

Centers for Disease Control and Prevention (CDC). (2016a). *Attention-deficit/hyperactivity disorder (ADHD) symptoms and diagnosis.* Retrieved from http://www.cdc.gov/ncbddd/adhd/diagnosis.html

Centers for Disease Control and Prevention (CDC). (2016b). *HIV/AIDS: HIV among youth.* Retrieved from http://www.cdc.gov/hiv/group/age/youth/

Centers for Disease Control and Prevention (CDC). (2016c). *HIV in the United States: At a glance.* Retrieved from http://www.cdc.gov/hiv/statistics/overview/ataglance.html

Centers for Disease Control and Prevention (CDC). (2016d). *Smoking & tobacco use: Current cigarette smoking among adults in the United States.* Retrieved from http://www.cdc.gov/tobacco/data_statistics/fact_sheets/adult_data/cig_smoking/

Centers for Disease Control and Prevention (CDC) – National Center for Health Statistics. (2016e). *Obesity and overweight.* Retrieved from http://www.cdc.gov/nchs/fastats/obesity-overweight.htm

Centers for Disease Control and Prevention – Division of Reproductive Health. (2016f). *Reproductive health: Infertility FAQs.* Atlanta, GA: U.S. Department of Health and Human Services. Retrieved from http://www.cdc.gov/reproductivehealth/infertility/

Centers for Disease Control and Prevention (CDC). (2016g). *Youth and tobacco use.* Retrieved from http://www.cdc.gov/tobacco/data_statistics/fact_sheets/youth_data/tobacco_use/

Central Intelligence Agency. (2013). *The world factbook, 2013–14.* Washington, DC: Author. Retrieved from https://www.cia.gov/library/publications/the-world-factbook/docs/contributor_copyright.html

Cervantes, C. A., & Callanan, M. A. (1998). Labels and explanations in mother-child emotion talk: Age and gender differentiation *Developmental Psychology, 34,* 88–98.

Chadwick, A., Hay, D. F., & Payne, A. (2004). Peer relations in childhood. *Journal of Child Psychology and Psychiatry, 45,* 84–108.

Chafel, J. (1993). *Child poverty and public policy.* Washington, DC: The Urban Institute.

Chakravarty, E. F., Hubert, H. B., Krishnan, E., Bruce, B. B., Lingala, V. B., & Fries, J. F. (2012). Lifestyle risk factors predict disability and death in healthy aging adults. *American Journal of Medicine, 125,* 190–197. doi: 10.1016/j.amjmed.2011.08.006

Chambré, S. M. (1993). Volunteerism by elders: Past trends and future prospects. *Gerontologist, 33,* 221–228.

Chan, S. (1991). *Asian Americans: An interpretive history.* Boston: Twayne Publishers.

Chandra, A., Copen, C. E., & Stephen, E. H. (2013). Infertility and impaired fecundity in the United States, 1982–2010: Data from the National Survey of Family Growth. *National Health Statistics Reports, 67,* 1–19.

Chang, A., Aeschbach, D., Duffy, J., & Czeisler, C. (2015). Evening use of light-emitting eReaders negatively affects sleep, circadian timing, and next-morning alertness. *Proceedings of the National Academy of Sciences, 112,* 1232–1237.

Chao, R. K. (1994). Beyond parental control and authoritarian parenting style: Understanding Chinese parenting through the cultural notion of training. *Child Development, 65,* 1111–1119.

Chapleau, K. M., Oswald, D. L., & Russell, B. L. (2008). Male rape myths: The role of gender, violence, and sexism. *Journal of Interpersonal Violence, 23*(5), 600–615. doi: 10.1177/0886260507313529

Chapman, B., Fiscella, K., Duberstein, P., Kawachi, I., & Muennig, P. (2014). Measurement confounding affects the extent to which verbal IQ explains social gradients in mortality. *Journal of Epidemiology and Community Health, 68*(8), 728–733.

Chappell, N. C. (1990). Aging and social care. In R. H. Binstock, & L. K. George (Eds.), *Handbook of aging and the social sciences* (3rd ed., pp. 438–454). San Diego: Academic Press.

Charmaz, K. (1980). *The social reality of death.* Reading, MA: Addison-Wesley.

Chase-Lansdale, P. L., Brooks-Gunn, J., & Zamsky, E. S. (1994). Young African-American multigenerational families in poverty: Quality of mothering and grandmothering. *Child Development, 65,* 373–393.

Chatters, L. M., Taylor, R. J., & Jayakody, R. (1994). Fictive kinship relations in Black extended families. *Journal of Comparative Family Studies, 25,* 297–312.

Cheatham, H. E., & Berg-Cross, L. (1992). College student development: African Americans reconsidered. Special issue: College student development. *Journal of College Student Psychotherapy, 6*(3–4), 167–191.

Cheek, D. (1974). Body composition, hormones, nutrition and growth. In M. Grumbach, G. Grave, & F. Mayer (Eds.), *Control of the onset of puberty.* New York, NY: Wiley.

Chen, P. S. D., Lambert, A. D., & Guidry, K. R. (2010). Engaging online learners: The impact of Web-based learning technology on college student engagement. *Computers & Education, 54*(4), 1222–1232.

Chen, X., Beydoun, M. A., & Wang, Y. (2008). Is sleep duration associated with childhood obesity? A systematic review and meta-analysis. *Obesity, 16*(2), 265–274.

Cheng, Y. W., Shaffer, B. L., Nicholson, J. M., & Caughey, A. B. (2014). Second stage of labor and epidural use: A larger effect than previously suggested. *Journal of Obstetrics and Gynecology, 123,* 527–535.

Cherkas, L. F., Aviv, A., Valdes, A. M., Hunkin, J. L., Gardner, J. P., Surdulescu, G. L., … & Spector, T. D. (2006). The effects of social status on biological aging as measured by white-blood-cell telomere length. *Aging Cell, 5,* 361–365.

Cherkas, L. F., Hunkin, J. L., Kato, B. S., Richards, J. B., Gardner, J. P., Surdulescu, G. L., … & Aviv, A. (2008). The association between physical activity in leisure time and leukocyte telomere length. *Archives of Internal Medicine, 168,* 154–158.

Cherkes-Julkowski, M., Sharp, S., & Stolzenberg, J. (1997). *Rethinking ADHD.* Cambridge, MA: Brookline Books.

Cherry, F. (1995). *"Stubborn particulars" of social psychology: Essays on the research process.* New York, NY: Routledge.

Chervin, R. D., Bassetti, C., Ganoczy, D. A., & Pituch, K. J. (1997). Pediatrics and sleep symptoms of sleep disorders, inattention, and hyperactivity in children. *Sleep, 20*(12), 1185–1192.

Chesters, J. (2012). Gender attitudes and housework: Trends over time in Australia. *Journal of Comparative Family Studies, 43,* 511–526.

Chi, M., Glaser, R., & Farr, M. (1989). *The nature of expertise.* Hillsdale, NJ: Erlbaum.

Children's Defense Fund. (1992). *The state of America's children, 1992.* Washington, DC: Author.

Children's Defense Fund. (1993). *Progress and peril: Black children in America: A fact book and action primer.* Washington, DC: Author.

Children's Defense Fund. (2012). *The state of America's children handbook.* Washington, DC: Author.

Chiriboga, D. A. (1989). Mental health at the midpoint: Crisis, challenge, or relief? In S. Hunter, & M. Sundel (Eds.), *Midlife myths* (pp. 116–144), Newbury Park, CA: Sage.

Chodorow, N. (1978). *The reproduction of mothering.* Berkeley: University of California Press.

Chomsky, N. (1994). *Language and thought.* Wakefield, RI: Moyer Bell Publishers.

Chornokur, G., Dalton, K., Borysova, M. E., & Kumar, N. B. (2011). Disparities at presentation, diagnosis, treatment, and survival in African American men, affected by prostate cancer. *Prostate, 71,* 985–997. doi: 10.1002/pros.21314

Chosak, R. (1998). Personal communication.

Choudhury, S., Blakemore, S. J., & Charman, T. (2006). Social cognitive development during adolescence. *Social Cognitive and Affective Neuroscience, 1*(3), 165–174.

Christakis, D. A., & Zimmerman, F. J. (2007). Violent television viewing during preschool is associated with antisocial behavior during school age. *Pediatrics, 120*(5), 993–999.

Christensen, K. Y., Maisonet, M., Rubin, C., Holmes, A., Flanders, W. D., Heron, J., ... & Marcus, M. (2010). Progression through puberty in girls enrolled in a contemporary British cohort. *Journal of Adolescent Health, 47*, 282–289.

Chung, A. E., Perrin, E. M., & Skinner, A. C. (2013). Accuracy of child and adolescent weight perceptions and their relationships to dieting and exercise behaviors: A NHANES study. *Academic Pediatrics, 13*(4), 371–378.

Cicchetti, D., & Olson, K. (1990). The developmental psychopathology of child maltreatment. In M. Lewis, & S. Miller (Eds.), *Handbook of development psychopathology*. New York, NY: Plenum Press.

Cicchetti, D., & Toth, S. L. (1998). The development of depression in children and adolescents. *American Psychologist, 53*, 221–241.

Cicirelli, V. G. (1992). Siblings as caregivers in middle and old age. In J. W. Dwyer, & R. T. Coward (Eds.), *Gender, families, and elder care* (pp. 84–101). Newbury Park, CA: Sage.

Cicirelli, V. G. (1994). Sibling relationships in cross-cultural perspective. *Journal of Marriage and the Family, 56*, 7–20.

Cicirelli, V. G. (1995). *Sibling relationships across the life span*. New York, NY: Plenum.

Cicirelli, V. G. (1997). Relationship of psychosocial and background variables to older adults' end-of-life decisions. *Psychology and Aging, 12*, 72–83.

Cillessen, A. H. N., & Bellmore, A. D. (2011). Social skills and social competence in interactions with peers. In P. K. Smith, & C. H. Hart (Eds.), *The Wiley-Blackwell handbook of childhood social development* (2nd ed., pp. 393–412). Malden, MA: Blackwell Publishing.

Cinamon, R. G., Weisel, A., & Tzuk, K. (2007). Work–family conflict within the family crossover effects, perceived parent–child interaction quality, parental self-efficacy, and life role attributions. *Journal of Career Development, 34*(1), 79–100.

Clark, D. O., Maddox, G. L., & Steinhauser, K. (1993). Race, aging, and functional health. *Journal of Aging and Health, 5*, 536–553.

Clark, R., Hyde, J. S., Essex, M. J., & Klein, M. H. (1997). Length of maternity leave and quality of mother-infant interaction. *Child Development, 68*, 363–383.

Clarke, A. T., & Kutz-Costes, B. (1997). Television viewing, educational quality of the home environment, and school readiness. *Journal of Educational Research, 90*, 279–285.

Clarke-Stewart, K. A. (1989). Daycare: Maligned or malignant? *American Psychologist, 44*, 266–273.

Clarke-Stewart, K. A., & Allhusen, V. D. (2002). Nonparental caregiving. In M. Bornstein (Ed.), *Handbook of parenting: Vol. 3: Being and becoming a parent* (2nd ed., pp. 215–252). Mahwah, NJ: Lawrence Erlbaum Associates.

Clarke-Stewart, K. A., Gruber, C. P., & Fitzgerald, L. M. (1994). *Children at home and in day care*. Hillsdale, NJ: Lawrence Erlbaum Associates.

Clarke-Stewart, K. A., & Hayward, C. (1996). Advantages of father custody and contact for the psychological well-being of school-age children. *Journal of Applied Developmental Psychology, 17*, 239–270.

Clay, D., Vignoles, V. L., & Dittmar, H. (2005). Body image and self-esteem among adolescent girls: Testing the influence of sociocultural factors. *Journal of Research on Adolescence, 15*(4), 451–477.

Clopton, N. A., & Sorell, G. T. (1993). Gender differences in moral reasoning: Stable or situational, *Psychology of Women Quarterly, 17*, 85–101.

Clouston, S. A., Kuh, D., Herd, P., Elliott, J., Richards, M., & Hofer, S. M. (2012). Benefits of educational attainment on adult fluid cognition: International evidence from three birth cohorts. *International Journal of Epidemiology, 41*, 1729–1736. doi: 10.1093/ije/dys148

Coakley, J. (1996). Socialization through sports. In O. Bar-Or (Ed.), *The child and adolescent athlete* (pp. 353–363). London: Blackwell Science.

Coates, E., & Coates, A. (2006). Young children talking and drawing. *International Journal of Early Years Education, 14*(3), 221–241.

Coates, J. (1993). *Women, men, and communication* (2nd ed.), New York, NY: Longman.

Coates, J. (2015). *Women, men and language: A sociolinguistic account of gender differences in language*. Routledge.

Cobb, P., Gravemeijer, K., Yackel, E., McClain, K., & Whitenack, J. (1997). Mathematizing and symbolizing: The emergence of chains of signification in one first-grade classroom. In D. Kirschner, & J. Witson (Eds.), *Situated cognition: Social, semiotic, and psychological perspectives* (pp. 151–234). Mahwah, NJ: Erlbaum.

Cogan, R. (1980). Effects of childbirth preparation. *Clinical Obstetrics and Gynecology, 23*, 1–14.

Cohen E. (1994). *Designing group work: Strategies for the heterogeneous classroom* (2nd ed.), New York, NY: Teachers College Press.

Cohen, E., & Latan, R. (Eds.). (1997). *Working for equity in heterogeneous classrooms*. New York, NY: Teachers College Press.

Cohen, M. (1998). *The attention zone: Parents' guide to ADHD*. Washington, DC: Brunner/Mazel;

Cohen, N. (1997). *The development of memory in childhood*. Hove, UK: Psychology Press.

Cohen, S., Doyle, W. J., Alper, C. M., Janicki-Deverts, D., & Turner, R. B. (2009). Sleep habits and susceptibility to the common cold. *Archives of Internal Medicine, 169*(1), 62–67.

Cohn, D., Livingston, G., & Wang, W. (2014). *Pew Research Center social and demographic trends: After decades of decline, a rise in stay-at-home mothers*. Retrieved from http://www.pewsocialtrends.org/2014/04/08/after-decades-of-decline-a-rise-in-stay-at-home-mothers/

Coie, J. D., Dodge, K. A., & Coppotelli, H. (1982). Dimensions and types of social status: A cross-age perspective. *Developmental Psychology, 18*, 557–570.

Coie, J. D., Dodge, K. A., Terry, R., & Wright, V. (1991). The role of aggression in peer relations: An analysis of aggression episodes in boys' play groups. *Child Development, 62*, 812–826.

Coiro, M. (1994). *Health of our nation's children*. Hyattsville, MD: United States Department of Health and Human Services.

Colby, A., & Damon, W. (1992). *Some do care: Contemporary lives of moral commitment*. New York, NY: Free Press.

Colby, A., & Kohlberg, L. (1987). *The measurement of moral judgment*. New York, NY: Cambridge University Press.

Colby, A., Kohlberg, L., Gibbs, J., & Lieberman, M. (1983). A longitudinal study of moral development. *Monographs of the Society for Research on Child Development, 48* (1–2), Serial No. 200.

Colditz, G. A., Hankinson, S. E., Hunter, D. J., Willett, W. C., Manson, J. E., Stampfer, M. J., Hennekens, C., Rosner, B., & Speizer, F. E. (1995). The use of estrogens and progestins and the risk of breast cancer in postmenopausal women. *New England Journal of Medicine, 332*, 1589–1593.

Coldren, J., & Colombo, J. (1994). The nature and process of preverbal learning. *Monographs of the Society for Research in Child Development, 59*(2, Serial No. 241), 1–75.

Cole, E., & Rothblum, E. (1991). Lesbian sex at menopause: As good or better than ever. In B. Sang, A. Smith, & J. Warshow (Eds.), *Lesbians at midlife: The creative transition* (pp. 184–193). San Francisco: Spinsters Book Company.

Cole, M. (1990). Cultural psychology. In J. Berman (Ed.), *Nebraska symposium on motivation, 1989: Cross-cultural psychology* (pp. 279–336). Lincoln, NE: University of Nebraska Press.

Cole, M. G., & Dendukuri, N. (2003). Risk factors for depression among elderly community subjects: A systematic review and meta-analysis. *American Journal of Psychiatry, 160*(6), 1147–1156.

Cole, S. Z., & Lanham, J. S. (2011). Failure to thrive: An update. *American Family Physician, 83*, 829–834.

Coleman, J. (1988). Social capital in the creation of human capital. *American Journal of Sociology, 94*, 95–120.

Coles, R. (1992). *Their eyes meeting the world: Drawings and paintings of children*. Boston: Houghton Mifflin.

Coles, R., & Stokes, G. (1985). *Sex and the American teenager*. New York, NY: Harper & Row.

Coley, R. L. (1998). Children's socialization experiences and functioning in single-mother households: The importance of fathers and other men. *Child Development, 69*, 219–230.

Coley, R. L., & Chase-Lansdale, P. L. (1998). Adolescent pregnancy and parenthood: Recent evidence and future directions. *American Psychologist, 53*, 152–166.

Coll, C. G., Lamberty, G., Jenkins, R., McAdoo, H. P., Crnic, K., Wasik, B. H., & Garcia, H. V. (1996). An integrative model for the study of developmental competencies in minority children. *Child Development, 67*, 1891–1914.

College Board/National Journal. (2014). *Next America poll, spring 2014*. Retrieved from http://www.corpsnetwork.org/sites/default/images/blog%20posts/2014/2014%20April/College%20Board_next%20america%20poll_2.pdf

Collins, W. A. (1991). Shared views and parent-adolescent relationships. *New Directions for Child Development, 51*, 103–110.

Collins, W. A., & Steinberg, L. (2006). Adolescent development in interpersonal context. In W. Dammon, & N. Eisenberg (Eds.), *Handbook of child psychology: Vol. 4. Socioemotional processes* (pp. 1003–1067). New York, NY: Wiley.

Comer, J. P., & Poussaint, A. F. (1992). *Raising black children*. New York, NY: Plume.

Comstock, F. (1991). *Television and the American child*. San Diego: Academic Press.

Condry, J. (1993, Winter). Thief of time, unfaithful servant: Television and the American Child. *Daedalus, 122*, 259–278.

Cong, X., Hashemi, F., & Ludington-Hoe, S. M. (2002). Infant crying: Nature, physiologic consequences, and select interventions. *Neonatal Network: The Journal of Neonatal Nursing, 21*, 29–36.

Conger, R. D., & Chao, W. (1996). Adolescent depressed mood. In R. L. Simons et al. (Eds.), *Understanding differences between divorced and intact families: Stress, interaction, and child outcome* (pp. 81–93). Thousand Oaks, CA: Sage.

Conklin, H. M., Luciana, M., Hooper, C. J., & Yarger, R. S. (2007). Working memory performance in typically developing children and adolescents: Behavioral evidence of protracted frontal lobe development. *Developmental Neuropsychology, 31*(1), 103–128.

Connell, S. L., Lauricella, A. R., & Wartella, E. (2015). Parental co-use of media technology with their young children in the USA. *Journal of Children and Media, 9*(1), 5–21.

Connelly, K., & Forssberg, H. (Eds.) (1997). *Neurophysiology and neuropsychology of motor development*. London: MacKeith Press.

Connidis, I. A. (1992). Life transitions and the sibling tie: A qualitative study. *Journal of Marriage and the Family, 54*, 972–982.

Connidis, I. A., & Campbell, L. D. (1995). Closeness, confiding, and contact among siblings in middle and late adulthood. *Journal of Family Issues, 16*, 722–745.

Connidis, I. A., & Davies, L. (1990). Confidants and companions in later life: The place of family and friends. *Journal of Gerontology: Social Sciences, 45*, S141–149.

Connidis, I. A., & Kemp, C. L. (2008). Negotiating actual and anticipated parental support: Multiple sibling voices in three-generation families. *Journal of Aging Studies, 22*, 229–238.

Connidis, I. A., Rosenthal, C. J., & McMullin, J. A. (1996). The impact of family composition on providing help to older parents. *Research on Aging, 18*, 402–429.

Connolly, J., White, D., Stevens, R., & Burstein, S. (1987). Adolescent self-reports of social activity: Assessment of stability and relations to social adjustment. *Journal of Adolescence, 10*, 83–95.

Connolly, S., Paikoff, R., & Buchanan, C. (1996). Puberty: The interplay of biological and psychosocial processes in adolescence. In G. Adams, R. Montemayor, & T. Gullotta (Eds.), *Psychosocial development during adolescence* (pp. 259–299). Thousand Oaks, CA: Sage.

Connor, J. (2016). Alcohol consumption as a cause of cancer. *Addiction.* doi: 10.1111/add.13477

Connor, S. R., Teno, J., Spence, C., & Smith, N. (2005). Family evaluation of hospice care: Results from voluntary submission of data via website. *Journal of Pain and Symptom Management, 30*(1), 9–17.

Conwell, Y., & Thompson, C. (2008). Suicidal behavior in elders. *Psychiatric Clinics of North America, 31*(2), 333–356.

Conwell, Y., Van Orden, K., & Caine, E. D. (2011). Suicide in older adults. *Psychiatric Clinics of North America, 34*(2), 451–468.

Cook, A., & Glass, C. (2014a). Above the glass ceiling: When are women and racial/ethnic minorities promoted to CEO? *Strategic Management Journal, 35*, 1080–1089. doi: 10.1002/smj.2161

Cook, A., & Glass, C. (2014b). Women and top leadership positions: Towards an institutional analysis. *Gender, Work & Organization, 21*(1), 91–103.

Cook, J. (1988). Who "mothers" the chronically mentally ill? *Family Relations, 37*, 42–49.

Cooksey, E. C., Menaghan, E. G., & Jekielek, S. M. (1997). Life course effects of work and family circumstances on children. *Social Forces, 761*, 637–667.

Cooney, T. M. (1994). Young adults' relations with parents: The influence of recent parental divorce. *Journal of Marriage and the Family, 56*, 45–56.

Cooney, T. M., & Kurz, J. (1996). Mental health outcomes following recent parental divorce: The case of young adult offspring. *Journal of Family Issues, 17*, 495–213.

Cooney, T. M., & Smith, L. A. (1996). Young adults' relations with grandparents following recent parental divorce. *Journals of Gerontology, Series B, 51*, S91–S95.

Cooney, T. M., & Uhlenberg, P. (1990). The role of divorce in men's relations with their adult children after mid-life. *Journal of Marriage and the Family, 52*, 677–688.

Cooper, K. L., & Gutman, D. L. (1987). Gender identity and ego mastery style in middle-aged, pre- and post-empty nest women *The Gerontologist, 27*, 347–352.

Cooper, L. A., Roter, D. L., Carson, K. A., Beach, M. C., Sabin, J. A., Greenwald, A. G., & Inui, T. S. (2012). The associations of clinicians' implicit attitudes about race with medical visit communication and patient ratings of interpersonal care. *American Journal of Public Health, 102*, 979–987. doi: 10.2105/AJPH.2011.300558

Cooper, M. H. (1994). Regulating tobacco. *CQ Researcher.* 4(36), 844–858.

Copeland, L. (2013, April, 17). Most teen-drinking deaths aren't traffic related. *USA Today.* Retrieved from http://www.usatoday.com/story/news/nation/2013/04/17/underage-drinking-madd-alcohol/2070405/

Copen, C. E., Daniels, K., & Mosher, W. D. (2013). First premarital cohabitation in the United States: 2006–2010 national survey of family growth. *National Health Statistics Reports, 64*, 1–16. Retrieved from http://www.cdc.gov/nchs/data/nhsr/nhsr064.pdf

Copen, C. E., Daniels, K., Vespa, J., & Mosher, W. D. (2012). First marriages in the United States: Data from the 2006–2010 National Survey of Family Growth. *National Health Statistics Reports, 49*, 1–22. Retrieved from http://www.cdc.gov/nchs/data/nhsr/nhsr049.pdf#x2013;2010%20National%20Survey%20of%20Family%20Growth%20[PDF%20-%20419%20KB%3C/a%3E

Copple, C., & Bredekamp, S. (Eds.) (1997). *Developmentally appropriate practice in early childhood programs serving children from birth through age 8* (3rd ed.), Washington, DC: National Association for the Education of Young Children.

Coren, S. (1996). *Sleep thieves.* New York, NY: Free Press.

Corley, C. J., & Smitherman, G. (1994). Juvenile justice: Multicultural issues. In J. E. Hendricks, B. Byers, et al. (Eds.), *Multicultural perspectives in criminal justice and criminology.* (pp. 259–290). Springfield, IL: Charles C. Thomas.

Corman, C. (1995). Treatments for a puzzling disease. In M. L. Ballweg & The Endometriosis Association (Eds.), *The endometriosis sourcebook* (pp. 237–247). Chicago, IL: Contemporary Books.

Cornelius, S. W. (1990). Aging and everyday cognitive abilities. In T. M. Hess (Ed.), *Aging and cognition: Knowledge, organization, and utilization* (pp. 411–459). Amsterdam: North-Holland/Elsevier.

Corr, C. A. (1993). Coping with dying: Lessons what we should and should not learn from the work of Elisabeth Kübler-Ross. *Death Studies, 17*, 69–83.

Corr, C. A., & Corr, D. M. (2003). Death education. In C. D. Bryant (Ed.) *Handbook of death and dying* (Vol. 1, pp. 292–301). Thousand Oaks, CA: Sage Publications.

Corr, C. A., Nabe, C. M., & Corr, D. M. (1996). *Death and dying: Life and living.* Pacific Grove, CA: Brooks Cole.

Corra, M., Carter, S. K., Carter, J. S., & Knox, D. (2009). Trends in marital happiness by gender and race, 1973 to 2006. *Journal of Family Issues.* doi: 10.1177/0192513x09336214

Corsini, N., Slater, A., Harrison, A., Cooke, L., & Cox, D. N. (2013). Rewards can be used effectively with repeated exposure to increase liking of vegetables in 4–6-year-old children. *Public Health Nutrition, 16*(05), 942–951.

Costa, A., Hernández, M., & Sebastián-Gallés, N. (2008). Bilingualism aids conflict resolution: Evidence from the ANT task. *Cognition, 106*(1), 59–86.

Costa, P. T., Jr., & McRae, R. R. (1997). Longitudinal stability of adult personality. In R. Hogan, J. A. Johnson, & S. R. Briggs (Eds.), *Handbook of personality psychology* (pp. 269–290). San Diego: Academic Press.

Costa, P. T., Jr., McCrae, R. R., Zonderman, A. B., Bar-bano, H. E., Lebowitz, B., & Larson, D. M. (1986). Cross-sectional studies of personality in a national sample: 2. Stability in neuroticism, extraversion, and openness. *Psychology and Aging, 1.* 144–149.

Costa, P. T., Jr., Metter, E. J., & McCrae, R. R. (1994). Personality stability and its contribution to successful aging. *Journal of Geriatric Psychiatry, 27*(1), 41–59.

Côté, S., Vaillancourt, T., LeBlanc, J. C., Nagin, D. S., & Tremblay, R. E. (2006). The development of physical aggression from toddlerhood to pre-adolescence: A nation wide longitudinal study of Canadian children. *Journal of Abnormal Child Psychology, 34*(1), 68–82.

Cotman, C. W., Berchtold, N. C., & Christie, L. A. (2007). Exercise builds brain health: Key roles of growth factor cascades and inflammation. *Trends in Neurosciences, 30*(9), 464–472.

Cotman, C. W., & Neeper, S. (1996). Activity-dependent plasticity and the aging brain. In E. L. Schneider, & J. W. Rowe (Eds.), *Handbook of the biology of aging* (pp. 283–299). San Diego: Academic Press.

Coudin, G., & Alexopoulos, T. (2010). "Help me! I'm old": How negative aging stereotypes create dependency among older adults. *Aging and Mental Health, 14*, 516–523.

Cousineau, T. M., & Domar, A. D. (2007). Psychological impact of infertility. *Best Practice & Research Clinical Obstetrics & Gynaecology, 21*(2), 293–308.

Couturier, J., Kimber, M., & Szatmari, P. (2013). Efficacy of family-based treatment for adolescents with eating disorders: A systematic review and meta-analysis. *International Journal of Eating Disorders, 46*(1), 3–11.

Covey, H. (1988). Historical terminology used to represent older people. *The Gerontologist, 28*, 291–297.

Cowan, C., Cowan, P., Heming, G., & Miller, N. (1991). Becoming a family: Marriage, parenting, and child development. In P. Cowan, & M. Hetherington (Eds.), *Family transitions* (pp. 79–110). Hillsdale, NJ: Erlbaum.

Cowan, G. (1984). The double standard in age discrepant relationships. *Sex Roles, 11*, 17–24.

Cowan, N. (Ed.). (1997). *Development of memory in childhood.* Hove: Psychology Press.

Cowan, P. A. (1990). Beyond meta-analysis: A plea for a family systems view of attachment. *Child Development, 68*, 571–591.

Cowan, P. A., & Cowan, C. P. (1988). Changes in marriage during the transition to parenthood: Must we blame the baby? In G. Y. Michaels, & W. A. Goldberg (Eds.), *The transition to parenthood: Current theory and research* (pp. 114–154). Cambridge, UK: Cambridge University Press.

Coward, R. T., & Dwyer, J. W. (1990). The association of gender, sibling network composition, and patterns of parent care by adult children. *Research on Aging, 12*, 158–181.

Cox, M., & Harter, K. S. M. (2003). Parent-child relationships. In M. H. Bornstein, L. Davidson, C. L. M. Keyes, K. A. Moore, & The Center for Child Well-being (Eds.), *Well-being: Positive development across the life course* (pp. 191–204). Mahwah, NJ: Lawrence Erlbaum.

Cox, M. J., Owen, M. T., Henderson, V. K., & Margand, N. A. (1992). Prediction of infant-father and infant-mother attachment *Developmental Psychology, 28*, 474–483.

Coyne, S. M., Linder, J. R., Rasmussen, E. E., Nelson, D. A., & Collier, K. M. (2014). It's a bird! It's a plane! It's a gender stereotype!: Longitudinal associations between superhero viewing and gender stereotyped play. *Sex Roles, 70*(9–10), 416–430.

Coyne, S. M., Nelson, D. A., & Underwood, M. (2011). Aggression in children. In P. K. Smith, & C. H. Hart (Eds.), *The Wiley-Blackwell handbook of childhood social development* (2nd ed., pp. 491–509). Malden, MA: Blackwell Publishing.

Cramer, P. (2003). Personality change in later adulthood is predicted by defense mechanism use in early adulthood. *Journal of Research in Personality, 37*, 76–104.

Cramer, P. (2011). Narcissism through the ages: What happens when narcissists grow older? *Journal of Research in Personality, 45*, 479–492.

Creasey, G. L., Jarvis, P. A., & Berk, L. E. (1998). Play and social competence. In O. N. Saracho & B. Spodek, et al. (Eds.), *Multiple perspectives on play in early childhood education.* SUNY series. *Early Childhood Education: Inquiries and Insights* (pp. 116–143). Albany, NY: State University of New York Press.

Crick, N. R. (1997). Engagement in gender normative versus nonnormative forms of aggression: Links to social-psychological adjustment. *Developmental Psychology, 33*, 610–617.

Crick, N. R. (1997). The role of overt aggression, relational aggression, and prosocial behavior in the prediction of children's future social adjustment. *Child Development, 67,* 2317–2327.

Crick, N. R., & Grotpeter, J. K. (1995a). Relational aggression, gender, and social-psychological adjustment. *Child Development, 66,* 710–722.

Crick, N. R., & Grotpeter, J. K. (1995b). Relational aggression, overt aggression, and friendship: Victims of relational and overt aggression. *Development & Psychopathology, 8,* 367–380.

Crick, N. R., Casas, J. F., & Mosher, M. (1997). Relational and overt aggression in preschool. *Developmental Psychology, 33,* 579–588.

Criqui, M. H., & Ringel, B. L. (1994). Does diet or alcohol explain the French paradox? *Lancet (North American Edition), 344* (8939–8940), 1719–1723.

Crockenberg, S. B., & Litman, C. (1990). Autonomy and competence in 1-year-olds: Maternal correlates of child defiance, compliance, and self-assertion. *Developmental Psychology, 26,* 961–971.

Crockenberg, S. B., & McCluskey, K. (1986). Change in maternal behavior during the baby's first year of life. *Child Development, 57,* 746–753.

Crockett, L. J., Raffaelli, M., & Moilanen, K. L. (2006). Adolescent sexuality: Behavior and meaning. In G. R. Adams, & M. D. Berzonsky (Eds.), *Blackwell handbook of adolescence* (pp. 371–392). Malden, MA: Blackwell Publishing.

Crosby, F. J. (1991). *Juggling: The unexpected advantages of balancing career and home for women and their families.* New York, NY: The Free Press.

Crowl, A. L., Ahn, S., & Baker, J. (2008). A meta-analysis of developmental outcomes for children of same-sex and heterosexual parents. *Journal of GLBT Family Sciences, 4*(3), 385–407.

Crowther, M. R., Huang, C. H., & Allen, R. S. (2014). Rewards and unique challenges faced by African-American custodial grandmothers: The importance of future planning. *Aging & Mental Health, 19*(9), 844–852.

Cuffaro, H. (1991). A view of materials as the texts of the early childhood curriculum. In B. Spodek, & O. Saracho (Eds.), *Issues in early childhood curriculum* (pp. 64–85). New York, NY: Teachers College Press.

Cui, M., & Donnellan, M. B. (2009). Trajectories of conflict over raising adolescent children and marital satisfaction. *Journal of Marriage and Family, 71,* 478–494.

Cummings, E., & Henry, W. E. (1961). *Grown old: The process of disengagement.* New York, NY: Basic Books.

Cummings, E. M., & Cummings, J. L. (1988). A process-oriented approach to children's coping with adults' angry behavior, *Developmental Review, 8,* 296–321.

Currie, J., & Widom, C. S. (2010). Long-term consequences of child abuse and neglect on adult economic well-being. *Child Maltreatment, 15*(2), 111–120.

Curry, G. D., & Spergel, I. (1988). Gang homicide, delinquency, and community. *Criminology, 26,* 381–05.

Curtin, S. C., Warner, M., & Hedegaard, H. (2016). *Suicide rates for females and males by race and ethnicity: United States, 1999 and 2014.* Retrieved from http_www.cdc.gov/nchs/data/hestat/suicide/rates_1999_2014.pdf

Cushman, P. (1991). Ideology obscured: Political uses of the self in Daniel Stern's infant. *American Psychologist, 46,* 206–219.

Cutler, S. J., & Hendricks, J. (1990). Leisure and time use across the life course. In R. H. , & L. K. George (Eds.), *Handbook of aging and the social sciences* (3rd ed., pp. 169–185). San Diego: Academic Press.

Cutler, S. J., & Hodgson, L. G. (1996). Anticipatory dementia: A link between memory appraisals and concerns about developing Alzheimer's disease. *The Gerontologist, 36,* 657–664.

D

Dalglish, P. (1998). *The courage of children: My life with the world's poorest kids.* New York, NY: HarperCollins.

D'Alton, M. E., & DeCherney, A. H. (1993). Prenatal diagnosis. *New England Journal of Medicine, 32,* 114–120.

Dalton, S. (Ed.) (1997). *Overweight and weight management,* Gaithersburg, MD: Aspen Publishers.

Damon, W. (1983). *Social and personality development: Infancy through adolescence.* New York, NY: Norton.

Damon, W. (1988). *The moral child.* New York, NY: Cambridge University Press.

Damon, W. (1996). The lifelong transformation of moral goals through social influence. In P. , & U. Staudinger (Eds.), *Interactive minds: Lifespan perspectives on social foundations of cognition* (pp. 198–221). New York, NY: Cambridge University Press.

Damon, W. (2008). The moral north star. *Educational Leadership, 66,* 8–12.

Damon, W., & Hart, D. (1988). *Self-understanding in childhood and adolescence,* New York, NY: Cambridge University Press.

Damon, W., & Hart, D. (1992). Self-understanding and its role in social and moral development. In M. C. Bornstein, & M. E. Lamb (Eds.), *Developmental psychology: An advanced textbook* (3rd ed., pp. 421–164). Hillsdale, NJ: Erlbaum.

Dane, B. O. (1989). Middle-aged adults mourning the death of a parent. *Journal of Gerontological Social Work, 14*(3/4), 75–89.

Daniels, P., & Weingarten, K. (1982). *Sooner or later: The timing of parenthood in adult lives.* New York, NY: Norton.

Danner, F., & Phillips, B. (2008). Adolescent sleep, school start times, and teen motor vehicle crashes. *Journal of Clinical Sleep Medicine: JCSM: Official Publication of the American Academy of Sleep Medicine, 4*(6), 533.

Darling, C. A., Davidson, J. K., & Passarello, L. C. (1992). The mystique of first intercourse among college youth: The role of partners, contraceptive practices, and psychological reactions. *Journal of Youth and Adolescence, 21,* 97–117.

Darling, N., & Steinberg, L. (1993). Parenting style as context: An integrative model. *Psychological Bulletin, 113,* 487–496.

Darling-Hammond, L. (1997). *The right to learn.* San Francisco: Jossey-Bass.

Darwin, C. (1877). A biographical sketch of an infant. *Mind, 2,* 286–294.

Datar, A., & Jacknowitz, A. (2009). Birth weight effects on children's mental, motor and physical development: Evidence from twins data. *Maternal and Child Health Journal, 13,* 780–794.

Dattell, A. R., & Neimeyer, R. A. (1990). Sex differences in death anxiety: Testing the emotional expressiveness hypothesis. *Death Studies, 14,* 1–11.

Davajan, V., & Israel, R. (1991). Diagnosis and medical treatment of infertility. In A. L. Stanton, & C. Dunkel-Schetter (Eds.), *Infertility.* (pp. 17–28). New York, NY: Plenum.

Davies, B. (1991). Accomplishment of genderedness in preschool children. In L. Weis, P. Altbach, G. Kelly, & H. Petrie (Eds.), *Critical perspectives in early childhood education.* Albany, NY: State University of New York Press.

Davies, B. (1995). Sibling bereavement research: State of the art. In I. B. Corless, B. B. Germino, & M. A. Pittman (Eds.), *A challenge for living: Dying, death, and bereavement,* Boston: Jones and Bartlett Publishers.

Davis, E. (1993). Common complaints of pregnancy. In B. K. Rothman (Ed.), *The encyclopedia of childbearing,* New York, NY: Henry Holt.

Davis, E. (1997). *Heart and hands: A midwife's guide to pregnancy and birth.* Berkeley, CA: Celestial Arts.

Davis, J. N., Ventura, E. E., Cook, L. T., Gyllenhammer, L. E., & Gatto, N. M. (2011). LA Sprouts: A gardening, nutrition, and cooking intervention for Latino youth improves diet and reduces obesity. *Journal of the American Dietetic Association, 111*(8), 1224–1230.

Davis, K., Christodoulou, J., Seider, S., & Gardner, H. (2011). The theory of multiple intelligences. *The Cambridge handbook of intelligence,* 485–503.

Davis, M. (2003). Factors related to bridge employment participation among private sector early retirees. *Journal of Vocational Behavior, 63,* 55–71.

Davis-Floyd, R. E. (1986). Birth as an American rite of passage. In K. L. Michaelson (Ed.), *Childbirth in America: Anthropological perspectives,* South Hadley, MA: Bergin & Garvey.

Davis-Kean, P. E. (2005). The influence of parent education and family income on child achievement: The indirect role of parental expectations and the home environment. *Journal of Family Psychology, 19*(2), 294–304.

Deater-Deckhard, S., Dodge, K. A., Bates, J. E., & Pettit, G. S. (1996). Physical discipline among African-American and European-American mothers: Links to children's externalizing behavior. *Developmental Psychology, 32,* 1065–1072.

DeCasper, A. J., & Spence, M. J. (1986). Prenatal maternal speech influences newborns, perception of speech sounds. *Infant Behavior and Development, 9,* 133–150.

DeCasper, A. J., Lecanuet, J. P., Busnel, M. C., & Granier-Deferre, C. (1994). Fetal reactions to recurrent maternal speech. *Infant Behavior and Development, 17,* 159–164.

Deci, E. L., & Ryan, R. M. (1987). The support of autonomy and the control of behavior. *Journal of Personality and Social Psychology, 56,* 1024–1037.

De Civita, M., Pagani, L., Vitaro, F., & Tremblay, R. E. (2004). The role of maternal educational aspirations in mediating the risk of income source on academic failure in children from persistently poor families. *Children and Youth Services Review, 26*(8), 749–769.

Declercq, E. (2011). Trends in midwife-attended births in the United States, 1989–2009. *Journal of Midwifery & Women's Health, 57,* 321–326.

Deeg, D. J. H., Kardaun, J. W. P. F., & Fozard, J. L. (1996). Health, behavior, and aging. In J. E. Birren, & K. W. Schaie (Eds.), *Handbook of the psychology of aging* (pp. 129–149). San Diego: Academic Press.

De Goede, I. H., Branje, S. J., Delsing, M. J., & Meeus, W. H. (2009). Linkages over time between adolescents' relationships with parents and friends. *Journal of Youth and Adolescence, 38*(10), 1304–1315.

DeJong, W. (1993). Obesity as a characterological stigma: The issue of responsibility and judgments of task performance. *Psychological Reports, 73,* 963–970.

De Jong Gierveld, J., & Peeters, A. (2003). The interweaving of repartnered older adults' lives with their children and siblings. *Ageing & Society, 23,* 187–205.

DeKlyen, M., Biernbaum, M. A., Speltz, M. L., & Greenberg, M. T. (1998). Fathers and preschool behavior problems. *Developmental Psychology, 34,* 264–275.

Delamont, S. (1996), *Women's place in education.* Brookfield, MA: Avebury Publishers.

Del Guidice, M., Manera, V., & Keysers, C. (2009). Programmed to learn? The ontogeny of mirror neurons. *Developmental Science, 12,* 350–363.

DeLisi, M., & Vaughn, M. G. (2014). Foundation for a temperament-based theory of antisocial behavior and criminal justice system involvement. *Journal of Criminal Justice, 42*(1), 10–25.

Dembe, A. E., & Yao, X. (2016). Chronic disease risks from exposure to long-hour work schedules over a 32-year period. *Journal of Occupational & Environmental Medicine/American College of Occupational and Environmental Medicine.* doi: 10.1097/JOM.0000000000000810

Demetriou, A., Christou, C., Spanoudis, G., & Platsidou, M. (2002). The development of mental processing: Efficiency, working memory, and thinking. *Monographs for the Society of Research in Child Development, 67*(1, Serial No. 268).

Demo, D. H., & Acock, A. C. (1996). Family structure, family process, and adolescent well-being. *Journal of Research on Adolescence, 6*, 457–488.

Dendinger, V. M., Adams, G. A., & Jacobson, J. D. (2005). Reasons for working and their relationship to retirement attitudes, job satisfaction and occupational self-efficacy of bridge employees. *International Journal of Aging and Human Development, 61*, 21–35.

Denham, S., Warren, H., von Salisch, M., Benga, O., Chin, J., & Geangu, E. (2011). Emotions and social development in childhood. In P. K. Smith, & C. H. Hart (Eds.), *The Wiley-Blackwell handbook of childhood social development* (2nd ed., pp. 413–433). Malden, MA: Blackwell Publishing.

Denney, N. W. (1989). Everyday problem solving: Methodological issues, research findings, and a model. In L. W. Poon, D. C. Rubin, & B. A. Wilson (Eds.), *Everyday cognition in adulthood and late life* (pp. 330–351). Cambridge, UK: Cambridge University Press.

Dennis, S. (1992). Stage and structure in the development of children's spatial reasoning. In R. Case (Ed.), *The mind's staircase* (pp. 229–245). Hillsdale, NJ: Erlbaum.

Denson, N. (2009). Do curricular and cocurricular diversity activities influence racial bias? A meta-analysis. *Review of Educational Research, 79*(2), 805–838.

Der-McLeod, D., & Hansen, J. C. (1992). On Lok: The family continuum. *Generations, 16*(3), 71–72.

Dermer, A. (2001). A well-kept secret: Breastfeeding's benefits to mothers. *New Beginnings, 18*(4), 124–127.

DeRosier, M. E., Cillessen, A. H. N., Coie, J. D., & Dodge, K. A. (1994). Group social context and children's aggressive behavior. *Child Development, 65*, 1068–1079.

Desiderato, L. L., & Crawford, H. J. (1995). Risky sexual behavior in college students: Relationships between number of sexual partners, disclosure of previous risky behavior, and alcohol use. *Journal of Youth & Adolescence, 24*, 55–68.

DeSilver, D. (2013). *Pew Research Center: Many states already bar workplace discrimination against gays.* Retrieved from http://www.pewresearch.org/fact-tank/2013/11/06/many-states-already-bar-workplace-discrimination-against-gays/

DeSpelder, L. A., & Strickland, A. L. (1996). *The last dance: Encountering death and dying.* Mountain View, CA: Mayfield.

DeStefano, L., & Colasanto, D. (1990). The gender gap in America: Unlike 1975, today most Americans think men have it better. *Gallup Poll News Service, 54*(37), 1–7.

Detering, K. M., Hancock, A. D., Reade, M. C., & Silvester, W. (2010). The impact of advance care planning on end of life care in elderly patients: Randomised controlled trial. *BMJ, 340*, c1345.

DeVita, V., Hellman, S., & Rosenberg, S. (Eds.) (1997). *AIDS: Etiology, diagnosis, treatment, and prevention* (4th ed.). Philadelphia: Lippincott-Raven.

DeVries, B., Lana, R. D., & Falck, V. T. (1994). Parental bereavement over the life course: A theoretical intersection and empirical review. *Omega, 29*(1), 47–69.

de Vries, B., Mason, A. M., Quam, J., & Acquaviva, K. (2009). State recognition of same-sex relationships and preparations for end of life among lesbian and gay boomers. *Sexuality Research & Social Policy, 6*, 90–101.

Dewilde, C., & Uunk, W. (2008). Remarriage as a way to overcome the financial consequences of divorce—A test of the economic need hypothesis for European women. *European Sociological Review, 24*(3), 393–407.

DeWolff, M. S., & van IJzendoorn, M. H. (1997). Sensitivity and attachment: A meta-analysis on parental antecedents of infant attachment. *Child Development, 68*, 571–591.

D'Hondt, E., Deforche, B., Gentier, I., De Bourdeaudhuij, I., Vaeyens, R., Philippaerts, R., & Lenoir, M. (2013). A longitudinal analysis of gross motor coordination in overweight and obese children versus normal-weight peers. *International Journal of Obesity, 37*(1), 61–67.

Diamant, A., & Cooper, H. (1991). *Living a Jewish life*, New York, NY: HarperPerennial.

Diamond, E. L., Jernigan, J. A., Moseley, R. A., Messina, V., & McKeown, R. A. (1989). Decision-making ability and advance directive preferences in nursing home patients and proxies. *The Gerontologist, 29*, 622–626.

Diamond, J. (1989, February). Blood, genes, and malaria. *Natural History*, 8–18.

Diamond, L. M., & Dubé, E. M. (2002). Friendship and attachment among heterosexual and sexual-minority youths: Does the gender of your friend matter? *Journal of Youth and Adolescence, 31*(2), 155–166.

Diamond, L. M., & Savin-Williams, R. C. (2006). The intimate relationships of sexual-minority youths. In G. R. Adams, & M. D. Berzonsky (Eds.), *Blackwell handbook of adolescence* (pp. 371–392). Malden, MA: Blackwell Publishing.

Diamond, M. C. (1988). *Enriching heredity: The impact of the environment on the anatomy of the brain.* New York, NY: The Free Press.

Diamond, M. C. (1993). An optimistic view of the aging brain, *Generations, 16*(1), 31–33.

Dickey, G. (2012). Survey of homophobia: Views on sexual orientation from certified nurse assistants who work in long-term care. *Research on Aging, 35*, 563–570.

Dickinson, G. E. (1992). First childhood death experiences, *Omega, 25*, 169–182.

Dickstein, S., & Parke, R. D. (1988). Social referencing in infancy: A glance at fathers and marriage. *Child Development, 59*, 506–511.

Diehl, M., Chui, H., Hay, E. L., Lumley, M. A., Gruhn, D., & Labouvie-Vief, G. (2014). Changes in coping and defense mechanisms across adulthood: Longitudinal findings in a European American sample. *Developmental Psychology, 50*, 634–648.

Dietrich, J., & Salmela-Aro, K. (2016). Emerging adults and work: A model of phase-adequate engagement. In J. J. Arnett (Ed.), *The Oxford handbook of emerging adulthood* (pp. 334–345). New York, NY: Oxford University Press.

Dinsa, G. D., Goryakin, Y., Fumagalli, E., & Suhrcke, M. (2012). Obesity and socioeconomic status in developing countries: A systematic review. *Obesity Reviews, 13*(11), 1067–1079.

Dishion, T. J., Andrews, D. W., & Crosby, L. (1995). Antisocial boys and their friends in early adolescence: Relationship characteristics, quality, and interactional process. *Child Development, 66*, 139–151.

Dishion, T. J., Reid, J. R., & Patterson, G. R. (1988). Empirical guidelines for a family intervention for adolescent drug use. *Journal of Chemical Dependency Treatment, 1*, 181–216.

Divisi, D., Di Tommaso, S., Salvemini, S., Garramone, M., & Crisci, R. (2006). Diet and cancer. *Acta Biomedica-Ateneo Parmense, 77*(2), 118.

Division of Global HIV/AIDS (DGHA) – Centers for Disease Control and Prevention. (2013). *Strategy for an AIDS-free generation.* Retrieved from http://www.cdc.gov/globalaids/global-hiv-aids-at-cdc/interventions.html

Dodge, H. H. (1995). Movements out of poverty among elderly widows. *Journal of Gerontology, Social Sciences, 50*, S240–S249.

Dodge, K. A. (1986). A social information processing model of social competence in children. In M. Perlmutter (Ed.), *Minnesota symposia on child psychology: Vol. 18.* Hillsdale, NJ: Erlbaum.

Dodge, K. A., & Coie, J. D. (1987). Social-information-processing factors in reactive and proactive aggression in children's peer groups. *Journal of Personality and Social Psychology, 53*, 1146–1158.

Dodge, K. A., Coie, J. D., Pettit, G. S., & Price, J. M. (1990). Peer status and aggression in boys' groups: Developmental and contextual analysis. *Child Development, 61*, 1289–1309.

Dodge, K. A., Pettit, G. S., & Bates, J. E. (1994). Socialization mediators of the relationship between socioeconomic status and child conduct problems. *Child Development, 65*, 649–665.

Doherty, D. (Ed.). (1996). *Measurement in pediatric exercise science.* Champaign, IL: Human Kinetics Press.

Doka, K. J. (2003). The death awareness movement: Description, history, and analysis. In C. D. Bryant (Ed.), *Handbook of death and dying* (Vol. 1, pp. 50–56). Thousand Oaks, CA: Sage Publishing.

Doka, K. J., & Mertz, M. E. (1988). The meaning and significance of great-grandparenthood. *Gerontologist, 28*(2), 192–197.

Dollinger, S. M. C., & Hoyer, W. J. (1996). Age and skill differences in the processing demands of visual inspection. *Applied Cognitive Psychology, 10*(3), 225–239.

Donati, T. (1995). Single parents and wider families in the new context of legitimacy. *Marriage & Family Review, 20*(1–2), 27–42.

Dorfman, L. T. (2013). Leisure activities in retirement. In M. Wang (Ed.), *The Oxford handbook of retirement* (pp. 339–353). New York, NY: Oxford University Press.

Dorius, G. L., Heaton, T. B., & Steffen, P. (1993). Adolescent life events and their association with the onset of sexual intercourse. *Youth and Society, 25*, 3–23.

Doty, R. L., Shaman, P., Applehaum, S. L., Giberson, R., Sikosorski, L., & Rosenberg, L. (1984). Smell identification ability: Changes with age. *Science, 226*, 1441–1443.

Douglas, J. D. (1990/1991). Patterns of change following parent death in midlife adults. *Omega, 22*(2), 123–137.

Downey, G., & Coyne, J. C. (1990). Children of depressed parents: An integrative review. *Psychological Bulletin, 108*, 50–76.

Draper, P., & Keith, J. (1992). Cultural contexts of care: Family caregiving for elderly in America and Africa. *Journal of Aging Studies, 6*, 113–134.

Drew, L. M., & Silverstein, M. (2004). Inter-generational role investments of great-grandparents: Consequences for psychological well-being. *Ageing and Society, 24*(1), 95–111.

Dreyer, P. H. (1982). Sexuality during adolescence. In B. B. Wolman (Ed.), *Handbook of developmental psychology.* Engle-wood Cliffs, NJ: Prentice-Hall.

Dubois, D. L., & Hirsch, B. J. (1990). School and neighborhood friendship patterns of blacks and whites in early adolescence. *Child Development, 61*, 524–536.

DuBois, D. L., & Hirsch, B. J. (1993). School/nonschool friendship patterns in early adolescence. *Journal of Early Adolescence, 13*, 102–122.

Duck, S., & Wright, P. H. (1993). Reexamining gender differences in same-gender friendships: A close look at two kinds of data. *Sex Roles, 28*, 709–727.

Dudley, J. R. (1991). Increasing our understanding of divorced fathers who have infrequent contact with their children. *Family Relations, 40*, 279–285.

Dufour, A., & Candas, V. (2007). Ageing and thermal responses during passive heat exposure: Sweating and sensory aspects. *European Journal of Applied Physiology, 100*, 19–26.

Dugan, A. (2015). *In U.S., support up for doctor-assisted suicide.* Retrieved from http://www.gallup.com/poll/183425/support-doctor-assisted-suicide.aspx

Duncan, D. T., & Hatzenbuehler, M. L. (2014). Lesbian, gay, bisexual, and transgender hate crimes and suicidality among a population-based sample of sexual-minority adolescents in Boston. *American Journal of Public Health, 104*(2), 272–278.

Duncan, L. E., & Agronick, G. S. (1995). The intersection of life stage and social events: Personality and life outcomes. *Journal of Personality and Social Psychology, 69*, 558–568.

Dunkel-Schetter, C., & Lobel, M. (1991). Psychological reactions to infertility. In A. L. Stanton, & C. Dunkel-Schetter (Eds.), *Infertility* (pp. 29–57). New York, NY: Plenum.

Dunkle, C. E., & Anthis, K. S. (2001). The role of possible selves in identity formation: A short-term longitudinal study. *Journal of Adolescence, 24*, 765–776.

Dunn, J. (1985). *Sisters and brothers,* Cambridge, MA: Harvard University Press.

Dunn, J. (1988). Connections between relationships: Implications of research on mothers and siblings. In R. A. Hinde, & J. Stevenson-Hinde (Eds.), *Relationships within families: Mutual influences.* Oxford: Clarendon Press.

Dunn, J., & Shatz, M. (1989). Becoming a conversationalist despite (or because of) having an older sibling. *Child Development, 60*, 399–10.

Dunn, J., Slomkowski, C., & Beardsall, L. (1994). Sibling Relationships from the preschool period through middle childhood and early adolescence. *Developmental Psychology, 30*, 315–324.

Dunphy, D. C. (1963). The social structure of urban adolescent peer groups. *Sociometry, 26*, 230–246.

Dupont, R. L. (1988). The counselor's dilemma: Treating chemical dependence at college. In T. M. Rivinus (Ed.), *Alcoholism/chemical dependency and the college student* (pp. 41–61). New York, NY: Haworth Press.

Durbin, D. L., Darling, N., Steinberg, L., & Brown, B. B. (1993). Parenting style and peer group membership among European-American adolescents. *Journal of Research on Adolescence, 3*, 87–100.

Durlak, J. A., & Riesenberg, L. A. (1991). The impact of death education. *Death Studies, 15*, 39–58.

Dusek, J. B. (1991). *Adolescent development and behavior* (2nd ed.), Englewood Cliffs, NJ: Prentice-Hall.

Dusek, J. B. (Ed.) (1985). *Teacher expectancies,* Hillsdale, NJ: Erlbaum.

Duursma, E., Romero-Contreras, S., Szuber, A., Proctor, P., Snow, C., August, D., & Calderón, M. (2007). The role of home literacy and language environment on bilinguals' English and Spanish vocabulary development. *Applied Psycholinguistics, 28*(01), 171–190.

Dweck, C. S., & Leggett, E. L. (1988). A social-cognitive approach to motivation and personality. *Psychological Review, 95*, 256–273.

Dyregrov, K., & Dyregrov, A. (2005). Siblings after suicide—"The forgotten bereaved". *Suicide and Life-Threatening Behavior, 35*(6), 714–724.

E

Eagle, M. (1984). *Recent developments in psychoanalysis: A critical evaluation.* New York, NY: McGraw-Hill.

Eakins, P. S. (1993, September). Obstetric outcomes at the birth place in Menlo Park: The first seven years. *Birth, 16,* 123–129.

Earnshaw, V. A., Bogart, L. M., Dovidio, J. F., & Williams, D. R. (2013). Stigma and racial/ethnic HIV disparities: Moving toward resilience. *American Psychologist, 68*(4), 225.

East, P. (1998). Racial and ethnic differences in girls' sexual marital, and birth expectations. *Journal of Marriage and the Family, 60,* 150–162.

East, P. (2009). Adolescents' relationships with siblings. In R. Learner, & L. Steinberg (Eds.), *Handbook of adolescent psychology* (3rd ed., pp. 43–73). New York, NY: Wiley.

Easterlin, R. A., Schaeffer, C. M., & Macunovich, D. J. (1993). Will the baby boomers be less well off than their parents? Income, wealth and family circumstances over the life cycle in the United States. *Population and Development Review, 19,* 497–523.

Ebbeling, C. B., Pawlak, D. B., & Ludwig, D. S. (2002). Childhood obesity: Public-health crisis, common sense cure. *Lancet, 360*(9331), 473–482.

Eccles, J., Lord, S., & Buchanan, C. (1996). School transitions in early adolescence: What are we doing to our young people? In J. Graber, J. Brooks-Gunn, & A. Petersen (Eds.), *Transitions through adolescence* (pp. 251–284). Mahwah, NJ: Erlbaum.

Eccles, J. S. (1993). Development during adolescence: The impact of stage-environment fit on young adolescents' experiences in schools and families. *American Psychologist, 48,* 90–101.

Eccles, J. S., Midgley, C., Wigfeld, A., Buchanan, C. M., Reuman, D., Flanagan, C., & MacIver, D. (1993). Development during adolescence: The impact of stage-environment fit on young adolescents' experiences in schools and families. *American Psychologist, 48,* 90–101.

Eckerman, C. O., Davis, C. C., & Didow, S. M. (1989). Toddlers' emerging ways of achieving social coordinations with a peer. *Child. Development, 60,* 440–453.

Eckstein, D., Aycock, K. J., Sperber, M. A., McDonald, J., Van Wiesner, V., Watts, R. E., & Ginsburg, P. (2010). A review of 200 birth-order studies: Lifestyle characteristics. *Journal of Individual Psychology, 66*(4), 408–434.

Edenfield, T. M., & Blumenthal, J. A. (2011). Exercise and stress reduction. In R. Contrada, & A. Baum (Eds.), *The handbook of stress science: Biology, psychology, and health* (pp. 301–319). New York, NY: Springer.

Edmondson, B., Waldrop, J., Crispell, D., & Jacobsen, L. (1993). Single parents. *American Demographics, 15*(12), 36–37.

Edwards, C., Gandini, L., & Furman, G. (Eds.) (1993). *The hundred languages of children.* Norwood, NJ: Ablex.

Edwards, C. P., & Kutaka, T. S. (2015). Diverse perspectives of parents, diverse concepts of parent involvement and participation: Contrasts between Italy and the United States. Chapter prepared for S. M. Sheridan, & E. M. Kim (Eds.), *Foundational Aspects of Family-School Partnerships* (pp. 35–54).

Egeland, B. (1988). The consequences of physical and emotional neglect on the development of young children. In A. Cowan (Ed.), *Child neglect,* Washington, DC: National Center on Child Abuse and Neglect.

Eggenberger, E., Heimerl, K., & Bennett, M. I. (2013). Communication skills training in dementia care: A systematic review of effectiveness, training content, and didactic methods in different care settings. *International Psychogeriatrics, 25*(03), 345–358.

Ehrensaft, M. K., Moffitt, T. E., & Caspi, A. (2006). Is domestic violence followed by an increased risk of psychiatric disorders among women but not among men? A longitudinal cohort study. *American Journal of Psychiatry, 163,* 885–892.

Eisenberg, N., & Fabes, R. A. (1992). Emotion, self-regulation, and social competence. In M. Clark (Ed.), *Review of personality and social psychology, Vol. 14: Emotion and social behavior* (pp. 119–150). Newbury Park, CA: Sage.

Eisenberg, N., & Mussey, P. H. (1989). *The roots of prosocial behavior in children.* Cambridge: Cambridge University Press.

Eisenberg, N., Fabes, R. A., Murphy, B., Maszk, P., Smith, M., & Karbon, M. (1995). The role of emotionality and regulation in children's social functioning: A longitudinal study. *Child Development, 66,* 1360–1384.

Eisenberg, N., Fabes, R. A., Nyman, M., Bernzweig, J., & Pinuelas, A. (1994). The relations of emotionality and regulation to children's anger-related reactions. *Child Development, 65,* 109–128.

Eisenberg, N., Fabes, R. A., Schaller, M., & Miller, P. (1989). Sympathy and personal distress: Development, gender differences, and interrelations of indices. In N. Eisenberg (Ed.), *Empathy and related emotional responses: New directions for child development* (pp. 107–126). San Francisco: Jossey-Bass.

Eisenberg, N., Fabes, R. A., Shepard, S. A., Murphy, B. C., Guthrie. I. K., Jones. S., Friedman, J., Poulin, R., & Maszk, P. (1997), Contemporaneous and longitudinal production of children's social functioning from regulation and emotionality. *Child Development, 68,* 642–664.

Eisenberg, N., Hertz-Lazarowitz, B., & Fuchs, I. (1990). Prosocial moral judgment in Israeli kibbutz and city children: A longitudinal study. *Merrill Palmer Quarterly, 36,* 273–285.

Eisenbruch, M. (1984). Cross-cultural aspects of bereavement. II: Ethnic and cultural variations in the development of bereavement practices. *Culture, Medicine & Psychiatry, 8,* 315–347.

Elbers, E., Wiegersma, S., Brand, N., & Vroon, P. (1991), Response alternation as an artifact in conservation research. *Journal of Genetic Psychology, 152,* 47–56.

Elder, G. H., Jr. (1988). The life course as developmental theory. *Child Development, 69,* 1–12.

Elderhostel. (n.d.) Retrieved from http://www.roadscholar.org/

El-Dib, M., Massaro, A. N., Glass, P., & Aly, H. (2012). Neurobehavioral assessment as a predictor of neurodevelopmental outcome in preterm infants. *Journal of Perinatology, 32,* 299–303.

Elias, M. F., Elias, J. W., & Elias, P. K. (1990). Biological and health influences on behavior. In J. E. Birren, & K. W. Schaie (Eds.), *Handbook of the psychology of aging* (3rd ed., pp. 79–102). San Diego: Academic Press.

Elizabeth Glaser Pediatric AIDS Foundation (EGPAF). (2013). *HIV and AIDS in the U.S.* Retrieved from http://www.pedaids.org/What-We-re-Doing/Public-Policy-Advocacy/Domestic-Policy

Elkind, D. (1985). Egocentrism redux. *Developmental Review, 5,* 218–226.

Elkind, D. (1994a). *A sympathetic understanding of the child* (3rd ed.). Boston: Allyn & Bacon.

Elkind, D. (1994b). *Ties that stress: The new family imbalance.* Cambridge, MA: Harvard University Press.

Elliot, A. J., & Dweck, C. S. (Eds.). (2013). *Handbook of competence and motivation.* Guilford Publications.

Ellis, S., Rogoff, B., & Cromer, C. (1981). Age segregation in children's social interactions. *Developmental Psychology, 17,* 399–407.

Elzinga, C. H., & Liefbroer, A. C. (2007). De-standardization of family-life trajectories of young adults: A cross-national comparison using sequence analysis. *European Journal of Population/Revue européenne de Démographie, 23*(3–4), 225–250.

Emery, R. E. (1989). Family violence. *American Psychologist, 44,* 321–328.

Emes, C. E. (1997). Is Mr. Pac Man eating our children? A review of the effect of video games on children. *Canadian Journal of Psychiatry, 42,* 409–114.

Emmerich, W., & Sheppard, K. (1982). Development of sex-differentiated preferences during late childhood and adolescence. *Developmental Psychology, 18,* 407–417.

Endeshaw, Y. W. (2006). Clinical characteristics of obstructive sleep apnea in community-dwelling older adults. *Journal of the American Geriatrics Society, 54,* 1740–1744.

Endeshaw, Y. W., Bloom, H. L., & Bliwise, D. L. (2008). Sleep-disordered breathing and cardiovascular disease in the Bay Area Sleep Cohort. *Sleep, 31,* 563–568.

Endres, J., & Rockwell, R. (1993). *Food, nutrition, and the young child* (4th ed.), Columbus, Ohio: Merrill.

Engle, J. M., Lasky, N., & McElwain, N. L. (2011). Presence and quality of kindergarten children's friendships: Concurrent and longitudinal associations with child adjustment in the early school years. *Infant and Child Development, 20*, 365–386.

English, T., & Carstensen, L. L. (2014). Selective narrowing of social networks across adulthood is associated with improved emotional experience in daily life. *International Journal of Behavioral Development, 38*, 1–8.

Engstrom, M., Greene, R., & O'Connor, M. C. (1993). Adult daycare for persons with dementia: A viable community option. *Generations, 17(1)*, 75–76.

Enriquez, E., Duncan, G. E., & Schur, E. A. (2013). Age at dieting onset, body mass index, and dieting practices. A twin study. *Appetite, 71*, 301–306.

Erdley, C. A., Cain, K. M., Loomis, C. C., Dumas-Hines, F., & Dweck, C. S. (1997). Relations among children's social goals, implicit personality theories, and responses to social failure. *Developmental Psychology, 33*, 263–272.

Erel, O., Margolin, G., & John, R. S. (1988). Observed sibling interaction: Links with marital and mother-infant relationship. *Developmental Psychology, 34*, 268–298.

Ericsson, K. A., & Charness, N. (1994). Expert performance: Its structure and acquisition. *American Psychologist, 49*, 725–747.

Ericsson, K. A., & U Charness, N. (1997). Cognitive and developmental factors in expert performance. In P. J. Feltovich, K. M. Ford, R. R. Hoffman (Ed.), *Expertise in context: Human and machine* (pp. 3–11). Cambridge, MA: MIT Press.

Erikson, E. H. (1982). *The life cycle completed: A review.* New York, NY: Norton.

Erikson, E. H. (1963). *Childhood and society* (2nd ed.). New York, NY: Norton.

Erikson, E. H. (1968). *Identity, youth and crisis.* New York, NY: Norton.

Erikson, E. H. (1975). "Identity Crisis" in autobiographical perspective. In E. Erikson, *Life history and the historical moment.* New York, NY: Norton.

Erikson, E. H., & Erikson, J. M. (1981). Generativity and identity. *Harvard Educational Review, 51*, 249–269.

Erikson, E. H., Erikson, J. M., & Kivnick, H. Q. (1986). *Vital involvement in old age.* New York, NY: Norton.

Essex, M. J., & Nam, S. (1987). Marital status and loneliness among older women: The differential importance of close family and friends. *Journal of Marriage and the Family. 49*, 93–106.

Ettelbrick, P. (1991). Legal protections for lesbians. In B. Sang, J. Warsbow, & A. J. Smith (Eds.), *Lesbians at midlife: A creative transition* (pp. 258–264). San Francisco: Spinsters Book Company.

Evans, C. A., & Porter, C. L. (2009). The emergence of mother-infant co-regulation during the first year: Links to infants' developmental status and attachment. *Infant Behavior & Development, 32*, 147–158.

Evans, E., Hawton, K., Rodham, K., & Deeks. J. (2005). The prevalence of suicidal phenomena in adolescents: A systematic review of population-based studies. *Suicide and Life Threatening Behavior, 35(3)*, 239–252.

Eveleth, P., & Tanner, J. (1990). *Worldwide variation in human growth* (2nd ed.), New York, NY: Cambridge University Press.

Ewing, A. T., Andre, J., Blair-Broeker, C. T., Fineburg, A. C., Henderson Daniel, J., Higa, J. J., & Weaver, K. A. (2010). When and where people learn psychological science: The sun never sets. In D. F. Halpern (Ed.), *Undergraduate education in psychology: A blueprint for the future of the discipline* (pp. 81–93). Washington, DC: American Psychological Association.

Eysenck, H. J. (1990). Type A behavior and coronary heart disease: The third stage. *Journal of Social Behavior and. Personality*, 5, 25–44.

Eysenck, H. J. (1994). Smoking, personality and stress as risk factors for cancer and coronary heart disease.

Eysenck, H. J. (1996). Personality and cancer. In G. L. Cooper (Ed.), *Handbook of stress, medicine, and health* (pp. 193–215), Boca Raton, FL: CRC Press.

F

Faber, N. B. (1991). The process of pregnancy resolution among adolescent mothers. *Adolescence, 26*, 697–716.

Fabes, R. A., & Eisenberg, N. (1992). Young children's coping with interpersonal anger. *Child Development, 63*, 116–128.

Fabes, R. A., Eisenberg, N., McCormick, S. E., & Wilson, M. S. (1988). Preschoolers' attributions of the situational determinants of others' naturally occurring emotions. *Developmental Psychology, 24*, 376–385.

Fabiano, G. A., Pelham, W. E., Gnagy, E. M., Burrows-MacLean, L., Coles, E. K., Chacko, A., ... & Robb, J. A. (2007). The single and combined effects of multiple intensities of behavior modification and methylphenidate for children with attention deficit hyperactivity disorder in a classroom setting. *School Psychology Review, 36(2)*, 195–216.

Fabrikant, G. (1996). The young and restless audience: Computers, cable and videos cut into children's TV-watching time. In press.

Facio, E. (1997). Chicanas and aging; Toward definitions of womanhood. In J. M. Coyle (Ed.), *Handbook on women and aging* (pp. 335–350). Westport, CT: Greenwood Press.

Fagot, B. I. (1982). Adults as socializing agents. In T. Field, A. Huston, H. Quay, L. Troll, & G. Finley (Eds.), *Review of human development.* New York, NY: Wiley.

Fagot, B. I. (1994). Peer relations and the development of competence in boys and girls. In C. Leaper (Ed.), *Childhood gender segregation: Causes and consequences: New directions for child development* (pp. 53–66). San Fiancisco: Jossey-Bass.

Fagot, B. I., & Hagan, R. (1991). Observations of parent reactions to sex-stereotyped behaviors: Age and sex effects, *Child Development, 62*, 617–628.

Fagot, B. I., & Leinbach, M. D. (1989). The young child's gender schema: Environmental input, internal organization. *Child Development, 60*, 663–672.

Fagot, B. I., Leinbach, M. D., & O'Boyle, C. (1992). Gender labeling, gender stereotyping, and parenting behaviors. *Developmental Psychology, 28*, 225–230.

Fagot, B. (1997). Attachment, parenting, and peer interactions of toddler children. *Developmental Psychology, 33*, 489–499.

Fairburn, C., & Wilson, T. (Eds.). (1993). *Binge eating.* Guilford, CT: Guilford Press.

Falbo, T. (1992) Social norms and the one-child family: Clinical and policy implications. In F. Boer, J. Dunn, et al. (Eds.), *Children's sibling relationships* (pp. 71–82). Hillsdale, NJ: Erlbaum.

Falbo, T. (2012). Only children: An updated review. *Journal of Individual Psychology, 68(1)*, 38–49.

Famighetti, R. (1996). *World almanac and book of facts 1997.* Mahwah, NJ: World Almanac Book.

Fangos, J. H., & Nickerson, B. G. (1991). Long-term effects of sibling death during adolescence. *Journal of Adolescent Research, 6*, 70–82.

Fantz, R. (1963). Pattern vision in newborn infants. *Science, 140* 296–297.

Farrangy, P., Steele, H., & Steele, M. (1991). Maternal representations of attachment during pregnancy predict the organization of infant-mother attachment at one year of age. *Child Development, 62*, 891–905.

Farrant, B. M., Devine, T. A., Maybery, M. T., & Fletcher, J. (2012). Empathy, perspective taking and prosocial behaviour: The importance of parenting practices. *Infant and Child Development, 21(2)*, 175–188.

Farrell, D. (1997). Psychopharmacological treatment of unipolar depression within the elderly: A discussion paper. *Counseling Psychology Quarterly, 10*, 229–235.

Farver, J. A. M., & Shin, Y. L. (1997). Social pretend play in Korean- and Anglo-American preschoolers. *Child Development, 68*, 544–556.

Farver, J. M., & Branstetter, W. H. (1994). Preschoolers' prosocial responses to their peers' distress. *Developmental Psychology, 30*, 334–341.

Faulkner, R. A., Davey, M., & Davey, A. (2005). Gender-related predictors of change in marital satisfaction and marital conflict. *American Journal of Family Therapy, 33*, 61–83.

Fedele, N. M., Golding, E. R., Grossman, F. K., & Pollack, W. S. (1988). Psychological issues in adjustment to first parenthood. In G. Y. Michaels, & W. A. Goldberg (Eds.), *The transition to parenthood: Current theory and research* (pp. 85–113), Cambridge, UK: Cambridge University Press.

Federal Bureau of Investigation. (2013). *Easy access to FBI arrest statistics: 1994–2012.* Washington, DC: U.S. Department of Justice.

Federal Interagency Forum on Aging-Related Statistics. (2012). *Older Americans 2010: Key indicators of well-being.* Retrieved from http://www.agingstats.gov/Main_Site/Data/2012_Documents/docs/EntireChartbook.pdf

Feeney, J., & Noller, P. (1996). *Adult attachment.* Thousand Oaks, CA: Sage.

Feifel, H. (1990). Psychology and death: Meaningful rediscovery. *American Psychologist, 45*, 537–543.

Feinberg, M. E. (2003). The internal structure and ecological context of coparenting: A framework for research and intervention. *Parenting: Science and Practice, 3*, 95–131.

Feinbloom, R. I. (2000). *Pregnancy, birth and the early months (3rd ed.): The thinking woman's guide.* Cambridge, MA: Da Capo Press.

Feld, S., Ruhland, D., & Gold, M. (1979). Developmental changes in achievement motivation. *Merrill-Palmer Quarterly, 25*, 43–60.

Feldman, H. A., Longcope, C., Derby, C. A., Johannes, C. B., Araujo, A. B., Coviello, A. D., ... & McKinlay, J. B. (2002). Age trends in the level of serum testosterone and other hormones in middle-aged men: Longitudinal results from the Massachusetts male aging study. *Journal of Clinical Endocrinology & Metabolism, 87*, 589–598.

Feldman, S. S., & Quatman, T. (1988). Factors influencing age expectations for adolescent autonomy: A study of early adolescents and parents *Journal of Early Adolescence, 8*, 325–343.

Ferber, R., & Kryger, M. (Eds.). (1995). *Principles and practice of sleep medicine in the child* Philadelphia: Saunders.

Ferholt, J. B. (1991). Psychodynamic parent psychotherapy: Treating the parent-child relationship. In M. Lewis (Ed.), *Comprehensive textbook of child psychiatry.* New York, NY: Saunders.

Ferketich, S. L., & Mercer, R. T. (1995). Paternal-infant attachment of experienced and inexperienced fathers during infancy. *Nursing Research, 44*, 31–37.

Fernald, A., & Kuhl, P. (1987). Acoustic determinants of infant preference for motherese speech. *Infant Behavior and Development, 10*, 279–293.

Fernandez, J. P. (1988). Human resources and the extraordinary problems minorities face. In M. London, & E. M. Mone (Eds.), *Career growth and human resource strategy* (pp. 227–239). New York, NY: Quorum.

Fernandez, R. M., & Campero, S. (2012). Gender sorting and the glass ceiling in high tech. MIT Sloan Research Paper No 4989-12. doi: 10.2139/ssrn.2067102

Ferrie, J. E., Shipley, M. J., Akbaraly, T. N., Marmot, M. G., Kivimaki, M., & Singh-Manoux, A. (2011). Change in sleep duration and cognitive function: Findings from the Whitehall II Study. *Sleep, 34*, 565–573.

Fetveit, A. (2009). Late-life insomnia: A review. *Geriatric Gerontology International, 9,* 220–234.

Field, D. (1987). A review of preschool conservation training. *Developmental Review, 7,* 210–251.

Field, D., & Millsap, R. E. (1991). Personality in advanced old age: Continuity or change? *Journal of Gerontology: Psychological Sciences, 46,* 299–308.

Field, J. (1987). Development of auditory-visual localization in infants. In B. McKenzie, & R. Day (Eds.), *Perceptual development in early infancy* (pp. 175–198). Hillsdale, NJ: Erlbaum.

Field, S., Sarver, M. D., & Shaw, S. F. (2003). Self-determination a key to success in postsecondary education for students with learning disabilities. *Remedial and Special Education, 24*(6), 339–349.

Field, T., & Roopnarine, J. (1982). Infant-peer interactions In T. Field (Ed.), *Review of human development.* New York, NY: Wiley.

Field, T., Miller, J., & Field, T. (1994). How well preschool children know their friends. *Early Child Development and Care, 100,* 101–109.

Fifer, W. P., Byrd, D. L., Kaku, M., Eigsti, I. M., Isler, J. R., Grose-Fifer, J., ... & Balsam, P. D. (2010). Newborn infants learn during sleep. *Proceedings of the National Academy of Sciences, 107*(22), 10320–10323.

Figueredo, A. J., Sefcek, J. A., & Jones, D. N. (2006). The ideal romantic partner personality. *Personality and Individual Differences, 41*(3), 431–441.

Fildes, A., van Jaarsveld, C. H., Wardle, J., & Cooke, L. (2014). Parent-administered exposure to increase children's vegetable acceptance: A randomized controlled trial. *Journal of the Academy of Nutrition and Dietetics, 114*(6), 881–888.

File, T., & Ryan, C. (2014). *Computer and internet use in the United States: 2013.* Retrieved from https://www.census.gov/history/pdf/2013computeruse.pdf

Finch, B. K. (2003). Early origins of the gradient: The relationship between socioeconomic status and infant mortality in the United States, *Demography, 40,* 675–699.

Finders, M. (1997). *Just girls: Hidden literacies and life in junior high.* New York, NY: Teachers College Press.

Fine, G. A. (1982). Friends, impression management, and preadolescent behavior. In S. Asher, & J. Gottman (Eds.), *The development of children's friendships.* New York, NY: Cambridge University Press.

Fine, M., & Kurdek, L. A. (1992). The adjustment of adolescents in stepfather and stepmother families. *Journal of Marriage and the Family, 54,* 725–736.

Fingerhut, A. W., & Maisel, N. C. (2010). Relationship formalization and individual and relationship well-being among same-sex couples. *Journal of Social and Personal Relationships, 27,* 956–969.

Finkel, E. J., Eastwick, P. W., Karney, B. R., Reis, H. T., & Sprecher, S. (2012). Online dating: A critical analysis from the perspective of psychological science. *Psychological Science in the Public Interest, 13*(1), 3–66.

Finkelhor, D. (1995). The victimization of children: A developmental perspective. *American Journal of Orthopsychiatry, 65,* 177–193.

Fischer, D. H. (1977). *Growing old in America.* New York, NY: Oxford University Press.

Fischer, K. (1980). A theory of cognitive development: The control and construction of hierarchies of skills. *Psychological Review, 87,* 477–531.

Fischer, K., & Pipp, S. L. (1984a). The process of stage transition: A neo-Piagetian view. In R. Sternberg (Ed.), *Mechanisms of cognitive development.* San Francisco: Freeman.

Fischer, K., & Pipp, S. L. (1984b). Processes of cognitive development: Optimal level and skill acquisition. In R. J. Sternberg (Ed.), *Mechanisms of cognitive development* (pp. 45–90). New York, NY: Freeman.

Fischer, K., Shaver, P., & Carnochan, P. (1990). How emotions develop and how they organize development. *Cognition and Emotion, 4,* 81–127.

Fischer, L. R., Mueller, D. P., & Cooper, P. W. (1991). Older volunteers: A discussion of the Minnesota Senior Study. *The Gerontologist, 31,* 183–194.

Fischer, M., & Barkley, R. A. (2007). The persistence of ADHD into adulthood: (Once again) it depends on whom you ask. *ADHD Report, 15*(4), 7–16.

Fish, M., Stifter, C. A., & Belsky, J. (1993). Early patterns of mother-infant dyadic integrations: Infant, mother, and family demographic antecedents. *Infant Behavior and Development, 16,* 1–18.

Fisher, C. B., & Lerner, R. M. (Eds.) (1994). *Applied developmental psychology.* New York, NY: McGraw Hill.

Fiske, A., Ciliberti, C. M., Gould, C. E., Nadorff, D. K., Nadorff, M. R., Nazem, S., ... & Clegg-Kraynok, M. M. (2012). Mental health and aging. In J. E. Maddux, & B. A. Winstead (Eds.), *Psychopathology: Foundations for a Contemporary Understanding* (3rd ed., pp. 399–428). New York, NY: Routledge.

Fiske, A., & O'Riley, A. A. (2016). Toward an understanding of late life suicidal behavior: The role of lifespan developmental theory. *Aging & Mental Health, 20*(2), 123–130.

Fitzgerald, H., Lester, B., & Zuckerman, B. (1994). *Children of poverty: Research, health, and policy issues.* New York, NY: Garland.

Fivush, R. (1989). Exploring sex differences in emotional content of mother-child conversations about the past. *Sex Roles, 20,* 675–691.

Flaks, D. K., Ficher, I., Materpasqua, F., & Joseph, G. (1995). Lesbians choosing motherhood: A comparative study of lesbian and heterosexual parents and their children *Developmental Psychology, 31,* 105–114.

Flanagan, C. A. (1990). Change in family work status: Effects on parent-adolescent decision making. *Child Development, 61,* 163–177.

Flanders, J. L., Leo, V., Paquette, D., Pihl, R. O., & Seguin, J. R. (2009). Rough-and-tumble play and the regulation of aggression: An observational study of father–child play dyads. *Aggressive Behavior, 35*(4), 285–295.

Flavell, J. H., Miller, P. H., & Miller, S. A. (1993). *Cognitive development* (3rd ed.). Englewood Cliffs, NJ: Prentice-Hall.

Fleming, R., Leventhal, H., Glynn, K., & Ershler, J. (1989). The role of cigarettes in the initiation and progression of early substance use. *Addictive Behaviors, 14,* 261–272.

Fletcher, A. C., Darling, N. E., Steinberg, L., & Dornbusch, S. M. (1995). The company they keep: Relation of adolescents' adjustment and behavior to their friends' perceptions of authoritative parenting in the social network. *Developmental Psychology, 31,* 300–310.

Flint, M., & Samil, R. S. (1990). Cultural and subcultural meanings of the menopause. In M. Flint, F. Kronenberg, & W. Utian (Eds.), *Annals of the New York Academy of Sciences,* 592 (pp. 134–148). New York, NY: New York Academy of Sciences.

Flippen, C., & Tienda, M. (2000). Pathways to retirement: Patterns of labor force participation and labor market exit among the pre-retirement population by race, Hispanic origin, and sex. *Journal of Gerontology: Social Sciences, 55,* s14–27.

Flom, R., & Pick, A. D. (2012). Dynamics of infant habituation: Infants' discrimination of musical excerpts. *Infant Behavior and Development, 35,* 697–704.

Flory, J., Young-Xu, Y., Gurol, I., Levinsky, N., Ash, A., & Emanuel, E. (2004). Place of death: U.S. trends since 1980. *Health Affairs, 23*(3), 194–200.

Floyd, M. F., Shinew, K. J., McGuire, F. A., & Noe, F. P. (1994). Race, class, and leisure activity preferences: Marginality and ethnicity revisited. *Journal of Leisure Research, 26,* 158–173.

Fomon, S. J., & Nelson, S. E. (2002). Body composition of the male and female reference infants. *Annual Review of Nutrition, 22,* 1–17.

Forrest-Pressley, D., Mackinnon, G., and Waller, T. (1985). *Metacognition, cognition and human performance.* Orlando: Academic Press.

Fowler, C., & Dillow, M. R. (2011). Attachment dimensions and the four horsemen of the apocalypse. *Communication Research Reports, 28*(1), 16–26.

Fowler, J. W. (1986). Faith and the structuring of meaning. In C. Dykstra, & S. Parks (Eds.), *Faith development and Fowler* (pp. 15–42). Birmingham, AL: Religious Education Press.

Fowler, J. W. (1991). *Stages of faith and religious development.* New York, NY: Crossroads Press.

Fox, K. (Ed.) (1997). *The physical self: From motivation to well-being.* Champaign, IL: Human Kinetics.

Fox, N. A., Kimmerly, N. L., & Schafer, W. D. (1991). Attachment to mother/attachment to father: A meta-analysis. *Child Development, 62,* 210–225.

Frank, M., & Zigler, E. F. (1996). Family leave: A developmental perspective. In E. F. Zigler, S. L. Hagan, et al. (Eds.), *Children, families and government: Preparing for the Twenty-First Century* (pp. 117–131). New York, NY: Cambridge University Press.

Frank, T., Turenshine, H., & Sullivan, S. J. (2010). *The effect of birth order on personality, intelligence and achievement.* Paper presented at the 118th Annual Convention of the American Psychological Convention, San Diego, CA.

Franklin, A., Pilling, M., & Davies, I. (2005). The nature of infant color categorization: Evidence from eye movements on a target detection task. *Journal of Experimental Child Psychology, 91,* 227–248.

Fransson, P., Skiold, B., Engstrom, M., Hallberg, B., Mosskin, M., Aden, U., ... & Blennow, M. (2009). Spontaneous brain activity in the newborn brain during natural sleep—an fMRI study in infants born at full term. *Pediatric Research, 66,* 301–305.

Franz, W., & Reardon, D. (1992). Differential impact of abortion on adolescents and adults. *Adolescence, 27,* 161–172.

Franzini, L., Ribble, J. C., & Keddie, A. M. (2001). Understanding the Hispanic paradox. *Ethnicity & Disease, 11,* 496–518.

Fraser, A. M., Brochert, J. E., & Ward, R. H. (1995). Association of young maternal age with adverse reproductive outcomes. *New England journal of Medicine, 332,* 113.

Frech, A., & Williams, K. (2007). Depression and the psychological benefits of entering marriage. *Journal of Health and Social Behavior, 48*(2), 149–163.

Freedman, V. A. (1993). Kin and nursing home lengths of stay: A backward recurrence time approach. *Journal of Health and Social Behavior, 34,* 138–152.

Freedman, V. A., Cornman, J. C., & Carr, D. (2014). Is spousal caregiving associated with enhanced well-being? New evidence from the panel study of income dynamics. *Journal of Gerontology Series B, Psychological Sciences and Social Science.* 1–9. doi: 10.1093/geronb/gbu004

French, D. C. (1984). Children's knowledge of the social functions of younger, older, and same-aged peers. *Child Development, 55,* 1429–1433.

French, J., & Rhodes, C. (1992). *Teaching thinking skills: Theory and practice* (2nd ed.), New York, NY: Garland.

Freud, S. (1983). *A general introduction to psychoanalysis* (rev. ed.), New York, NY: Washington Square Press.

Freund, A. M., & Baltes, P. B. (1998). Selection, optimization, and compensation as strategies of life management: Correlations with subjective indicators of aging. *Psychology and Aging, 13,* 531–543.

Freund, H., Sabel, B., & Witte, O. (Eds.) (1997). *Brain plasticity.* Philadelphia: Lippincott-Raven.

Frezza, M., DiPadova, C., Pozzato, G., Terpin, M., Baraona, E., & Lieber, C. S. (1990). High blood alcohol levels in women. *New England Journal of Medicine, 322*(2), 95–99.

Friedman, G. D., Tekawa, I., Klatsky, A. L., Sidney, S., & Armstrong, M. A. (1991). Alcohol drinking and cigarette smoking: An exploration of the association in middle-aged men and women. *Drug and Alcohol Dependence, 27,* 283–290.

Friedmann, H., & Kohn, R. (2008). Mortality, or probability of death, from a suicidal act in the United States. *Suicide and Life-Threatening Behavior, 38,* 287–301.

Friedman, H. S., Tucker, J. S., Schwartz, J. E., Tomlinson-Keasy, C., Martin, L. R., Wingard, D. L., & Criqui, M. H. (1995). Psychosocial and behavioral predictors of longevity: The aging and death of the "Termites." *American Psychologist, 50,* 69–78.

Fries, J. F. (1996). Physical activity, the compression of morbidity, and the health of the elderly. *Journal of the Royal Society of Medicine, 89(2),* 64–68.

Fries, J. F., & Crapo, L. M. (1981). *Vitality and aging.* San Francisco: Freeman.

Frieze, I., Francis, W., & Hanusa, B. (1981). Defining success in classroom settings. In J. Levine, & M. Wang (Eds.), *Teacher and student perceptions.* Hillsdale, NJ: Erlbaum.

Frisco, M. L., & Williams, K. (2003). Perceived housework equity, marital happiness, and divorce in dual-earner households. *Journal of Family Issues, 24,* 51–73.

Froberg, K., & Lammert, O. (1996). Development of muscle strength during childhood. In O. Bar-Or (Ed.), *The child and adolescent athlete* (pp. 25–41). London: Blackwell Science.

Frontera, W. R., & Meredith, C. N. (1989). Strength training in the elderly. In R. Harris, & S. Harris (Eds.), *Physical activity, aging and sports* (pp. 319–331). Albany, NY: Center for the Study of Aging.

Fry, C. L. (1996). Age, aging, and culture. In R. H. Binstock, & L. K. George (Eds.), *Handbook of aging and the social sciences* (pp. 117–136). San Diego: Academic Press.

Fry, J. (1974). *Common diseases: Their nature, incidence, and care,* Philadelphia: Lippincott.

Fry, R. (2009). *College enrollment hits all-time high, fueled by community college surge.* Pew Research Center. Retrieved from http://www.pewsocialtrends.org/files/2010/10/college-enrollment.pdf

Fuhrman, T., & Holmbeck, G. N. (1995). A contextual-moderator analysis of emotional autonomy and adjustment in adolescence. *Child Development, 66,* 793–811.

Fuligni, A. J., & Eccles, J. S. (1993). Perceived parent-child relationships and early adolescent's orientation toward peers. *Developmental Psychology, 29,* 622–632.

Fulkerson, J. A., Kubik, M. Y., Rydell, S., Boutelle, K. N., Garwick, A., Story, M., ... & Dudovitz, B. (2011). Focus groups with working parents of school-aged children: What's needed to improve family meals? *Journal of Nutrition Education and Behavior, 43*(3), 189–193.

Fullmer, E. M. (1995). Challenging biases against families of older gays and lesbians. In G. C. Smith, S. S. Tobin, E. A. Robertson-Tchabo, & P. W. Power (Eds.), *Strengthening aging families: Diversity in practice and policy* (pp. 99–119). Thousand Oaks, CA: Sage.

Fumagalli, M., Ferrucci, R., Mameli, F., Marceglia, S., Mrakic-Sposta, S., Zago, S., ... & Cappa, S. (2010). Gender-related differences in moral judgments. *Cognitive Processing, 11*(3), 219–226.

Furman, W. (1982). Children's friendships. In T. Field (Ed.), *Review of human development.* New York, NY: Wiley.

Furman, W. (1989). The development of children's social networks. In D. Belle (Ed.), *Children's social networks and social supports.* New York, NY: Wiley.

Furman, W., & Bierman, K. L. (1983). Developmental changes in young children's conceptions of friendship. *Child Development, 54,* 549–556.

Furman, W., & Bierman, K. L. (1984). Children's conceptions of friendship: A multidimensional study of developmental changes. *Developmental Psychology, 20,* 925–931.

Furman, W., & Buhrmester, D. (1992). Age and sex differences in perceptions of networks of personal friendships. *Child-Development, 63,* 103–115.

Furstenberg, F. F., Jr., Brooks-Gunn, J., & Chase-Lansdale, L. (1989). Teenaged pregnancy and childbearing. *American Psychologist, 44,* 313–320.

Furstenberg, F. F., Jr., & Cherlin, A. J. (1991). *Divided families: What happens to children when parents part?* Cambridge, MA: Harvard University Press.

Futagi, Y., Toribe, YH., & Suzuki, Y. (2009). Neurological assessment of early infants. *Current Pediatric Reviews, 5,* 65–70.

G

Gaesser, G. (1996). *Big fat lies.* New York, NY: Fawcett-Columbine Books.

Galambos, N. L., & Maggs, J. L. (1991). Out-of-school care of young adolescents and self-reported behavior. *Developmental Psychology, 27,* 644–655.

Galassi, J., Gulledge, S., & Cox, N. (1997). Middle school advisories: Retrospect and prospect. *Review of Educational Research, 67*(3), 301–338.

Galenkamp, H., Huisman, M., Braam, A. W., & Deeg, D. J. H. (2012). Estimates of prospective change in self-rated health in older people were biased owing to potential recalibration response shift. *Journal of Clinical Epidemiology, 65,* 978–988.

Galinsky, E. (1987). *The six stages of parenthood.* Reading, MA: Addison-Wesley.

Gallagher, J. (1993). Comments on McDaniel's "Education of the Gifted and the Excellence-Equity Debate." In J. Maker (Ed.), *Programs for the gifted in regular classrooms* (pp. 19–22). Austin, TX: Pro-Ed Publishers.

Gallagher, J., & Gallagher, S. (1994). *Teaching the gifted child* (4th ed.). Boston: Allyn & Bacon.

Gallagher, M. (1996). *Turning points in middle schools.* Thousand Oaks, CA: Corwin Press.

Gallagher, S. K., & Gerstel, N. (1993). Kinkeeping and friend keeping among older women: The effect of marriage. *The Gerontologist, 33,* 675–681.

Gallagher-Thompson, D., Futterman, A., Farberow, N., Thompson, L. W., & Peterson, J. (1993). The impact of spousal bereavement on older widows and widowers. In M. S. Stroebe, W. Stroebe, & R. O. Hansson (Eds.), *Handbook of bereavement: Theory, research, and intervention* (pp. 227–254). Cambridge, UK: Cambridge University Press.

Gallant, M. P., Spitze, G., & Grove, J. G. (2010). Chronic illness self-care and the family lives of older adults: A synthetic review across four ethnicities. *Journal of Cross Cultural Gerontology, 25,* 21–43.

Gallaway, C., & Richards, B. (1994). *Input and interaction in language acquisition.* New York, NY: Cambridge University Press.

Gallup. (2016). *Marriage.* Retrieved from http://www.gallup.com/poll/117328/marriage.aspx

Galotti, K. M. (1989). Gender differences in self-reported moral reasoning: A review and new evidence. *Journal of Youth and Adolescence, 18,* 475–488.

Galtry, J., & Callister, P. (2005). Assessing the optimal length of parental leave for child and parental well-being: How can research inform policy? *Journal of Family Issues, 26*(2), 219–246.

Galvan, A., Hare, T. A., Parra, C. E., Penn, J., Voss, K., Glover, G., & Casey, B. J. (2006). Earlier development of the accumbens relative to orbitofrontal cortex might underlie risk taking behavior in adolescents. *Journal of Neuroscience, 26,* 6885–6892.

Gándara, P., & Hopkins, M. (Eds.) (2010). *Forbidden language: English learners and restrictive language policies.* New York, NY: Teachers College Press.

Ganguli, M., Snitz, B. E., Lee, C. W., Vanderbilt, J., Saxton, J. A., & Chang, C. C. H. (2010). Age and education effects and norms on a cognitive test battery from a population-based cohort: The Monongahela–Youghiogheny Healthy Aging Team. *Aging and Mental Health, 14*(1), 100–107.

Gannon, L. R. (1985). *Menstrual disorders and menopause.* New York, NY: Praeger.

Ganong, L. H., & Coleman, M. (1993a). A meta-analytic comparison of the self-esteem and behavior problems of stepchildren to children in other family structures. *Journal of Divorce & Remarriage, 19(3–4),* 143–163.

Ganong, L. H., & Coleman, M. (1993b). An exploratory study of stepsibling subsystems. *Journal of Divorce & Remarriage, 19(3–4),* 125–141.

Ganong, L. H., Coleman, M., & Maples, D. (1990). A meta-analytic review of family structure stereotypes. *Journal of Marriage and the Family, 52,* 287–297.

Garand, L., Lingler, J. H., Deardorf, K. E., DeKosky, S. T., Schulz, R., Reynolds III, C. F., & Dew, M. A. (2012). Anticipatory grief in new family caregivers of persons with mild cognitive impairment and dementia. *Alzheimer Disease and Associated Disorders, 26*(2), 159–165.

Garbarino, J. (1982). Sociocultural risk: Dangers to competence. In C. Kopp, & J. Krakow (Eds.), *Child development in a social context.* Reading, MA: Addison-Wesley.

Garbarino, J. (1992a). *Children and families in the social environment* (2nd ed.), New York, NY: Aldine de Gruyter.

Garbarino, J. (1992b). *Children in danger.* New York, NY: Jossey-Bass.

Garbarino, J. (1993). Reinventing fatherhood. *Families in Society, 74,* 52–54.

Garbarino, J., & Kostelny, K. (1996). The effects of political violence on Palestinian children's behavior problems: A risk accumulation model. *Child Development, 67,* 33–45.

Garbarino, J., Kostelny, K., & Dubrow, N. (1991). What children can tell us about living in danger. *American Psychologist, 46,* 376–383.

Garber, C. E., Blissmer, B., Deschenes, M. R., Franklin, B. A., Lamonte, M. J., Lee, I. M., ... & Swain, D. P. (2011). American College of Sports Medicine position stand. Quantity and quality of exercise for developing and maintaining cardiorespiratory, musculoskeletal, and neuromotor fitness in apparently healthy adults: Guidance for prescribing exercise. *Medicine and Science in Sports and Exercise, 43*(7), 1334–1359.

Garcia, F., & Gracia, E. (2009). Is always authoritative the optimum parenting style? Evidence from Spanish families. *Adolescence, 44*(173), 101–131.

Gardiner, H. W., Mutter, J. D., & Kosmitzki, C. (1998). *Lives across cultures: Cross-cultural human development.* Boston: Allyn & Bacon.

Gardner, H. (1993a). *Frames of mind: The theory of multiple intelligences* (2nd rev. ed.), New York, NY: Basic Books.

Gardner, H. (1993b). *Multiple intelligences: Theory in practice.* New York, NY: Basic Books.

Gardner, H. (1997). *Extraordinary minds: Portraits of exceptional individuals and an examination of our extraordinariness.* New York, NY: Basic Books.

Gardner, H. (2006). *Multiple intelligences: New horizons in theory and practice.* New York, NY: Basic Books.

Garland, A. F., & Zigler, E. (1993). Adolescent suicide prevention: Current research and social policy. *American Psychologist, 48,* 169–182.

Garner, P. W., Jones, D. C., & Palmer, D. J. (1994). Social cognitive correlates of preschool children's sibling caregiving behavior. *Developmental Psychology, 30,* 906–911.

Garrison, M. E. B., Blalock, L. B., Zarski, J. J., & Merritt, P. B. (1997). Delayed parenthood: An exploratory study of family functioning. *Family Relations, 46,* 281–290.

Gartrell, N. K., Bos, H. M., & Goldberg, N. G. (2011). Adolescents of the U. S. National Longitudinal Lesbian Family Study: Sexual orientation, sexual behavior, and sexual risk exposure. *Archives of Sexual Behavior, 40*(6), 1199–1209.

Gates, G. J., & Newport, F. (2012, October). *Special report: 3.4% of U.S. adults identify as LGBT.* Gallup. Retrieved from http://www.gallup.com/poll/158066/special-report-adults-identify-lgbt.aspx

Gathercole, S. E., Pickering, S. J., Ambridge, B., & Wearing, H. (2004). The structure of working memory from 4 to 15 years of age. *Developmental Psychology, 40*, 177–190.

Gatz, M., Kasl-Godley, J. E., & Karel, M. J. (1996). Aging and mental disorders. In J. E. Birren, & K. W. Schaie (Eds.), *Handbook of the psychology of aging* (pp. 365–382). San Diego: Academic Press.

Gatz, M., Mortimer, J. A., Fratiglioni, L., Johansson, B., Berg, S., Andel, R., ... & Pederson, N. L. (2007). Accounting for the relationship between low education and dementia: A twin study. *Physiology and Behavior, 92*, 232–237.

Gatz, M., Reynolds, C. A., Fratiglioni, L., Johansson, B., Mortimer, J. A., Berg, S., ... & Pederson, N. L. (2006). The role of genes and environments for explaining Alzheimer's disease. *Archives of General Psychiatry, 63*, 168–174.

Gavin, L., & Furman, W. (1989). Age differences in adolescents' perceptions of their peer groups. *Developmental Psychology, 25*, 827–834.

Gaziano, J. M., Gaziano, T. A., Glynn, R. J., Sesso, H. D., Ajani, U. A., Stampfer, M. J., Manson, J. E., ... & Buring, J. E. (2000). Light-to-moderate alcohol consumption and mortality in the physicians' health study enrollment cohort. *Journal of American College of Cardiology, 35*, 96–105.

Ge, X., Best, K. M., Conger, R. D., & Simons, B. L. (1996). Parenting behaviors and the occurrence and co-occurrence of adolescent depressive symptoms and conduct problems. *Developmental Psychology, 32*, 717–731.

Geary, D. C. (2004). Mathematics and learning disabilities. *Journal of Learning Disabilities, 37*(1), 4–15.

Gecas, V., & Seff, M. A. (1990). Families and adolescents: A review of the 1980s. *Journal of Marriage and the Family, 52*, 941–958.

Geddes, J. K. The secret life of kids online: What you need to know. *Parenting*. Retrieved from http://www.parenting.com/article/kids-social-networking

Gee, E. M. (1991). The transition to grandmotherhood: A quantitative study. *Canadian Journal on Aging, 10*, 254–270.

Gee, J., & Green, J. (1998). Discourse analysis, learning, and social practice: A methodological study. In D. Pearson, & A. Iran-Nejad (Eds.), *Review of research in education* (Vol. 23, pp. 119–170), Washington, DC: American Educational Research Association.

Geiger, B. (1996). Fathers as primary caregivers. Westport, CT: Greenwood Press/Greenwood Publishing Group.

Gelles, R. (1998, August). Violence and pregnancy: Are pregnant women at greater risk of abuse? *Journal of Marriage and the Family, 50*, 841–847.

Gelles, R. J., & Cornell, C. P. (1983). *International perspectives on family violence.* Lexington, MA: D. C. Heath.

Gelman, C. R., Tompkins, C. J., & Ihara, E. S. (2014) The complexities of caregiving for minority older adults: Rewards and challenges. In K. E. Whitfield, & T. A. Baker (Eds.), *Handbook of minority aging* (pp. 313–328). New York, NY: Springer Publishing.

Gentile, D. A., Coyne, S., & Walsh, D. A. (2011). Media violence, physical aggression, and relational aggression in school age children: A short-term longitudinal study. *Aggressive Behavior, 37*(2), 193–206.

Gentile, D. A., Nathanson, A. I., Rasmussen, E. E., Reimer, R. A., & Walsh, D. A. (2012). Do you see what I see? Parent and child reports of parental monitoring of media. *Family Relations, 61*(3), 470–487.

Gentile, M., & Fello, M. (1990). Hospice care for the 1990s: A concept coming of age. *Journal of Home Health Care Practice, 3*, 1–15.

George, C., Kaplan, N., & Main, M. (1985). *The Adult Attachment Interview.* Unpublished manuscript, University of California at Berkeley, Department of Psychology.

George, T. P., & Hartiman, D. P. (1996). Friendship networks of unpopular, average, and popular children. *Child Development, 67*, 2310–2316.

Gerbasi, M. E., Richards, L. K., Thomas, J. J., Agnew-Blais, J. C., Thompson-Brenner, H., Gilman, S. E., & Becker, A. E. (2014). Globalization and eating disorder risk: Peer influence, perceived social norms, and adolescent disordered eating in Fiji. *International Journal of Eating Disorders, 47*(7), 727–737.

Gerbner, G., Gross, L., Signorielli, N., & Morgan, M. (1986). *Television's world: Violence profile No. 14-15.* University of Pennsylvania, Annenberg School of Communications, Philadelphia.

Gershoff, E. T., Grogan-Kaylor, A., Lansford, J. E., Chang, L., Zelli, A., Deater-Deckard, K., & Dodge, K. A. (2010). Parent discipline practices in an international sample: Associations with child behaviors and moderation by perceived normativeness. *Child Development, 81*(2), 487–502.

Gerson, M., Berman, L. S., & Morris, A. M. (1991). The value of having children as an aspect of adult development. *Journal of Genetic Psychology, 152*(3), 327–339.

Gerst-Emerson, K., & Burr, J. A. (2014). The demography of minority aging. In K. E. Whitfield, & T. A. Baker (Eds.), *Handbook of minority aging* (pp. 387–403). New York, NY: Springer Publishing.

Gerstorf, D., Ram, N., Hoppmann, C., Willis, S. L., & Schaie, K. W. (2011). Cohort differences in cognitive aging and terminal decline in the Seattle Longitudinal Study. *Developmental Psychology, 47*, 1026–1041.

Gesell, A. (1926). *The mental growth of the preschool child* (2nd ed.), New York, NY: Macmillan.

Gestwicki, C. (1995). *Developmentally appropriate practice: Curriculum and development in the early years.* Albany, NY: Delmar.

Gholson, B. (1994). Cognitive processes explain learning across the life span: Infants and toddlers are people too. *Monographs of the Society for Research in Child Development, 59* (4, Serial No. 241), 76–89.

Gianino, A., & Tronick, E. Z. (1988). The mutual regulation model: The infant's self and interactive regulation coping and defense. In T. Field, P. McCabe, & N. Schneiderman (Eds.), *Stress and coping* (pp. 47–68). Hillsdale, NJ: Erlbaum.

Gibbs, J. C., Basinger, K. S., Grime, R. L., & Snarey, J. R. (2007). Moral judgment development across cultures: Revisiting Kohlberg's universality claims. *Developmental Review, 27*(4), 443–500.

Gibbs, J. T. (1997). African American suicide: A cultural paradox. *Suicide and Life-Threatening Behavior, 27*(1), 68–79.

Gibeau, J. L., & Anastas, J. (1989). Breadwinners and caregivers: Interviews with working women *Journal of Gerontological Social Work, 14*, 19–40.

Gibson, R. C. (1993). The black American retirement experience. In J. S. Jackson, L. M. Chatters, & R. J. Taylor (Eds.), *Aging in black America.* Newbury Park, CA: Sage.

Gibson, R. C., & Burns, C. J. (1991). The health, labor force, and retirement experiences of aging minorities. *Generations, 15*(4), 31–35.

Gibson, E., & Walk, R. (1960). The visual cliff. *Scientific American, 202*, 64–71.

Giedd, J. N. (2004). Structural magnetic resonance imaging of the adolescent brain. *Annals of the New York Academy of Science, 1021*, 77–85.

Gilbert, A. N., & Wysocki, C. J. (1987). The results: Smell survey. *National Geographic, 172*, 514–525.

Gilbert, S. (1998, May 19). Benefits of assistant for childbirth go far beyond the birthing room. *New York Times*, p. F-7.

Gilbert, S. P., & Weaver, C. C. (2010). Sleep quality and academic performance in university students: A wake-up call for college psychologists. *Journal of College Student Psychotherapy, 24*(4), 295–306.

Gillies, R. M., & Boyle, M. (2010). Teachers' reflections on cooperative learning: Issues of implementation. *Teaching and Teacher Education, 26*(4), 933–940.

Gilligan, C. (1982). *In a different voice: Psychological theory and women's development.* Cambridge, MA: Harvard University Press.

Gilligan, C. (1987). Adolescent development reconsidered. In C. Irwin (Ed.), *Adolescent social behavior and health.* San Francisco: Jossey-Bass.

Gilligan, C., & Attanucci, J. (1988). Two moral orientations: Gender differences and similarities. *Merrill-Palmer Quarterly, 34*, 223–237.

Gilligan, C., & Wiggins, G. (1987). The origins of morality in early childhood relationships. In J. Kagarr, & S. Lamb (Eds.), *The emergence of morality in young children* (pp. 277–305). Chicago: University of Chicago Press.

Ginsburg, H. P., Cannon, J., Eisenband, J., & Pappas, S. (2008). Mathematical thinking and learning. In K. McCartney, & D. Phillips (Eds.), *Blackwell handbook of early childhood development* (pp. 208–230). Malden, MA: Blackwell Publishing.

Ginsburg, G. S., & Bronstein, P. (1993). Family factors related to children's intrinsic/extrinsic motivational orientation in academic performance. *Child Development, 64*, 1461–1474.

Giordano, P. C., Cernkovich, S. A., & Demaris, A. (1993). The family and peer relations of black adolescents. *Journal of Marriage and the Family, 55*, 277–287.

Glaser, R., Rice, J., Speicher, C. E., Stout, J. C., & Kiecolt-Glaser, J. K. (1986). Stress depresses interferon production by leukocytes concomitant with a decrease in natural killer cell activity. *Behavioral Neuroscience, 100*, 675–678.

Glaser, R., Thorn, B. E., Tarr, K. L., Kiecolt-Glaser, J. K., & D'Ambrosio, S. M. (1985). Effects of stress on methyltransferase synthesis: An important DNA repair enzyme. *Health Psychology, 4*, 403–412.

Glasgow, K. L., Dornbusch, S. M., Troyer, L., Steinberg, L., & Ritter, P. L. (1997). Parenting styles, adolescents' attributions, and educational outcomes in nine heterogeneous high schools. *Child Development, 68*, 507–529.

Glass, D. C., Neulinger, J., & Brim, O. C. (1974). Birth order, verbal intelligence, and educational aspiration. *Child Development, 45*, 807–811.

Glass, J. C., Jr. (1990). Changing death anxiety through education in the public schools. *Death Studies, 14*, 31–52.

Glass, J. C., Jr. (1991). Death, loss, and grief among middle school children: Implications for the school counselor. *Elementary School Guidance and Counseling, 26*, 139–148.

Glauser, B. (1997). Street children: Deconstructing a construct, In A. James, & A. Prout (Eds.), *Constructing and reconstructing childhood* (2nd ed., pp. 145–164). Washington, DC: Falmer.

Glendenning, F. (1995). Education for older adults: Lifelong learning, empowerment, and social change. In J. F. Nussbaum, & J. Coupland (Eds.), *Handbook of communication and aging research* (pp. 467–498) Mahwah, NJ: Erlbaum.

Glick, P. C., & Lin, S. L. (1986). More young adults are living with their parents: Who are they? *Journal of Marriage and the Family, 48*, 107–112.

Glick, P. C., & Lin, S. (1987). Remarriage after divorce: Recent changes and demographic variations. *Sociological Perspectives, 30*, 162–179.

Gluszek, A., & Dovidio, J. F. (2010). The way they speak: A social psychological perspective on the stigma of non-native accents in communication. *Personality and Social Psychology Review, 14*(2), 214–237.

Go, A. S., Mozaffarian, D., Roger, V. L., Benjamin, E. J., Berry, J. D. Blaha, M. J., ... & Turner, M. B. (2014). Heart disease and stroke statistics—2014 update: A report from the American Heart Association, *Circulation, 129*, e28-e292.

Godfrey, K. M., & Barker, D. J. P. (2001). Fetal programming and adult health. *Public Health Nutrition 4*, 611–624.

Goggin, J. M. (1992). Elderhostel: The next generation. *Aging Today, 13(2)*, 8.

Gogtay, N., Giedd, J. N., Lusk, L., Hayashi, K. M., Greenstein, D., Vaituzis, A. C., ... & Toga, A. W. (2004). Dynamic mapping of the human cortical development during childhood through early adulthood. *Proceedings National Academy of Sciences, USA, 101(PART 21)*: 8174–8179.

Gold, D. T. (1990). Late-life sibling relationships: Does race affect typological distribution? *The Gerontologist, 30*, 741–748.

Gold, J. M., Bubenzer, D. L., & West, J. D. (1993). Differentiation from ex-spouses and stepfamily marital intimacy. *Journal of Divorce & Remarriage, 19(3–4)*, 83–95.

Goldberg, A. E., & Allen, K. R. (2013). Same-sex relationship dissolution and LGB stepfamily formation: Perspectives of young adults with LGB parents. *Family Relations, 62*(4), 529–544.

Golden, C. (1996). Relational theories of white women's development. In J. C. Chrisler, C. Golden, & P. D. Rozee (Eds.), *Lectures on the psychology of women* (pp. 229–242). New York, NY: McGraw Hill.

Goldin-Meadow, S. (2008). How children learn language: A focus on resilience. In K. McCartney, & D. Phillips (Eds.), *Blackwell handbook of early childhood development* (pp. 252–273). Malden, MA: Blackwell Publishing.

Goldman, L. (1998). *Children's play: Mime, mimesis, and make-believe.* New York, NY: Oxford.

Goldman, S. E., Urbano, R. C., & Hodapp, R. M. (2011). Determining the amount, timing, and causes of mortality among infants with Down syndrome. Journal of Intellectual Disability Research, *55*, 85–94.

Goldscheider, F. K. (1997). Family relationships and life course strategies for the 21st century. In S. Dreman (Ed.), *The family on the threshold of the 21st century: Trends and implications* (pp. 73–85). Mahwah, NJ: Erlbaum.

Goldscheider, F. K., & DaVanzo, J. (1986). Semiautonomy and transition to adulthood. *Social Forces, 65*, 187–201.

Goldson, E. (1992). The longitudinal study of very low birth-weight infants and its implications for interdisciplinary research and public policy. In C. Greenbaum, & J. Auerbach (Eds.), *Longitudinal studies of children at psychological risk: Cross-national perspectives* (pp. 43–64). Norwood, NJ: Ablex.

Goldspink, D. F., George, K. P., Chantler, P. D., Clements, R. E., Sharp, L., Hodges, G., ... & Cable, N. T. (2009). A study of presbycardia with gender differences favoring ageing women. *International Journal of Cardiology, 137*, 236–245.

Goldsteen, K., & Ross, C. E. (1989). The perceived burden of children. *Journal of Family Issues, 10*, 504–526.

Goldstein, A. P., & Soriano, F. I. (1994). Delinquent gangs. In L. Eron, & J. Gentry (Eds.), *Violence and youth: Psychology's response: Vol II Papers of the American Psychological Association on Violence and Youth.* Washington, DC: American Psychological Association.

Goldstein, S., Field, T., & Healy, B. T. (1989). Concordance of play behavior and physiology in preschool friends. *Journal of Applied Developmental Psychology. 10*, 3337–3351.

Goleman, D. (1994, April 26). Mental decline in aging need not be inevitable. *New York Times*, pp. C1, C10.

Golombok, S., & Fivush, R. (1994). *Gender development.* New York, NY: Cambridge University Press.

Golombok, S., & Tasker, F. (1996). Do parents influence the sexual orientation of their children? Findings from a longitudinal study of lesbian females. *Developmental Psychology, 32*, 3–11.

Golombok, S., MacCallum, F., Murray, C., Lycett, E., & Jadva, V. (2006). Surrogacy families: Parental functioning, parent-child relationships and children's psychological development at age 2. *Journal of Child Psychology and Psychiatry, 47*, 213–222.

Goniewicz, M. L., Knysak, J., Gawron, M., Kosmider, L., Sobczak, A., Kurek, J., ... & Jacob, P. (2014). Levels of selected carcinogens and toxicants in vapour from electronic cigarettes. *Tobacco Control, 23*(2), 133–139.

Gonzaga, G. C., Turner, R. A., Keltner, D., Campos, B., & Altemus, M. (2006). Romantic love and sexual desire in close relationships. *Emotion, 6*(2), 163–179.

Gonzalez, A. L., & Wolters, C. A. (2006). The relation between perceived parenting practices and achievement motivation in mathematics. *Journal of Research in Childhood Education, 21*(2), 203–217.

Gonzalez, C. A., & Riboli, E. (2010). Diet and cancer prevention: Contributions from the European Prospective Investigation into Cancer and Nutrition (EPIC) study. *European Journal of Cancer, 46(1*4), 2555–2562.

Goodnow, J. (1996). Collaborative rules: How are people supposed to work with one another? In P. Baltes, & U. Staudinger (Eds.), *Interactive minds: Lifespan perspectives on social foundations of cognition* (pp. 163–197). New York, NY: Cambridge University Press.

Goodnow, J. J. (1976). The nature of intelligent behavior: Questions raised by cross-cultural studies. In L. B. Resnick (Ed.), *The nature of intelligence.* Hillsdale, NJ: Erlbaum.

Goodnow, J. J. (1996). From household practices to parents' ideas about work and interpersonal relationships. In S. Harkness, & C. Super (Eds.), *Parents' cultural belief systems: Their origins, expressions, and consequences.* New York, NY: Guildford Press.

Goodnow, J. J., Miller, P. M., & Kessel, F. (Eds.) (1995). Cultural practices as contexts for development. *New directions for child development:* No. 67. San Francisco: Jossey-Bass.

Goosens, F. A., & van IJzendoorn, M. H. (1990). Quality of infants' attachments to professional caregivers: Relation to infant-parent attachment and day-care characteristics. *Child Development, 61*, 832–837.

Gopaul-McNicol, S., & Thomas-Presswood, T. (1998). *Working with linguistically and culturally different children.* Boston: Allyn and Bacon.

Gorchoff, S. M., John, O. P., & Helson, R. (2008). Contextualizing change in marital satisfaction during middle age: An 18-year longitudinal study. *Psychological Science, 19*, 1194–1200.

Gordon, S., Benner, P., & Noddings, N. (1996). *Caregiving: Readings in knowledge, practice, ethics, and politics.* Philadelphia: University of Pennsylvania Press.

Gordon, T. H., & Conger, R. D. (1997). Marital conflict and adolescent distress: The role of adolescent awareness. *Child Development, 68*, 333–350.

Gorman, C. (1993, June 13). Thalidomide's return. *Time*, June 13, p. 67.

Gorsuch, N. (1998). Time's winged chariot: Short-term psychotherapy in later life. *Psychodynamic Counseling, 4*, 191–202.

Gortmaker, S. L., Must, A., Perrin, J. M., Sobol, A. M., & Dielz, W. H. (1993). Social and economic consequences of overweight in adolescence and young adulthood. *New England Journal of Medicine, 329*, 1008–1012.

Gose, B. (1995, November 10). A new approach to mortuary science. *The Chronicle of Higher Education*, p. A7.

Gosselink, C. A., Cox, D. L., McClure, S. J., & De Jong, M. L. (2008). Ravishing or ravaged: Women's relationships with women in the context of aging and western beauty culture. *International Journal of Aging and Human Development, 66*, 307–321.

Gottesman, I. I. (1963). Heritability of personality: A demonstration. *Psychological Monographs, 77*(Whole No. 572).

Gottfried, A. E., Bathurst, K., & Gottfried, A. W. (1994). Role of maternal and dual-earner employment status in children's development: A longitudinal study from infancy through early adolescence. In A. E. Gottfried, A. W. Gottfried, et al. (Eds.), *Redefining families: Implications for children's development* (pp. 55–97). New York, NY: Plenum Press.

Gottlieb, D. J., Redline, S., Nieto, F. J., Baldwin, C. M., Newman, A. B., Resnick, H. E., & Punjabi, N. M. (2006). Association of usual sleep duration with hypertension: The Sleep Heart Health Study. *SLEEP, 29*(8), 1009–1014.

Gottman, J. M. (1994). *What predicts divorce?* Hillsdale, NJ: Lawrence Erlbaum.

Gottman, J. M., Coan, J., Carrere, S., & Swanson, C. (1998). Predicting marital happiness and stability from newlywed interactions. *Journal of Marriage and the Family, 60*, 5–22.

Gottman, J. M., & Levenson, R. W. (2000). The timing of divorce: Predicting when a couple will divorce over a 14-year period. *Journal of Marriage and Family, 62*(3), 737–745.

Gottman, J. M., Levenson, R. W., Swanson, C., Swanson, K., Tyson, R., & Yoshimoto, D. (2003). Observing gay, lesbian, and heterosexual couples' relationships: Mathematical modeling of conflict interaction. *Journal of Homosexuality, 45*(1), 65–91.

Gottman, J., & Parkhurst, J. (1980). A developmental theory of friendship and acquaintanceship. In A. Collins (Ed.), *Minnesota symposia on child psychology: Vol. 13.* Hillsdale, N. J: Erlbaum.

Gould, D., & Eklund. (1996). Emotional stress and anxiety in the child and adolescent athlete. In O. Bar-Or (Ed.), *The child and adolescent athlete* (pp. 383–398). Oxford, UK: Blackwells.

Gould, R. L. (1978). *Transformations: Growth and change in adult life.* New York, NY: Simon & Schuster.

Government of the Netherlands. (n.d.). *Euthanasia, assisted suicide and non-resuscitation on request.* Retrieved from https://www.government.nl/topics/euthanasia/contents/euthanasia-assisted-suicide-and-non-resuscitation-on-request

Grabe, S., Ward, L. M., & Hyde, J. S. (2008). The role of the media in body image concerns among women: A meta-analysis of experimental and correlational studies. *Psychological Bulletin, 134*(3), 460.

Graber, J., Brooks-Gunn, J., & Petersen, A. (1996). *Transitions through adolescence: Interpersonal domains and context.* Mahwah, NJ: Erlbaum.

Grabowski, J., & Frantz, T. T. (1993). Latinos and Anglos: Cultural experiences of grief intensity. *Omega, 26*(4), 273–285.

Gralinski, J. H., & Kopp, C. (1993). Everyday rules for behavior: Mothers' requests to young children. *Developmental Psychology, 29*, 573–584.

Grand, A., Grand-Filaire, A., & Pous, J. (1995). Aging couples and disability management. In J. Hendricks (Ed.), *The ties of later life* (pp. 55–72). Amityville, NY: Baywood.

Granier-Deferre, C., Bassereau, S., Ribereiro, A., Jacquet, A., & DeCasper, A. J. (2011). A melodic contour repeatedly experienced by human near-term fetuses elicits a profound cardiac reaction one month after birth. *PLoS ONE, 6*, 1–10.

Granrud, C. (Ed.) (1993). *Visual perception and cognition in infancy.* Englewood Cliffs, NJ: Erlbaum.

Granrud, C. (2006). Size constancy in infants: 4-month-olds' responses to physical versus retinal image size. *Journal of Experimental Psychology: Human Perception and Performance, 32,* 1398–1404.

Green, J. A., Gustafson, G. E., & McGhie, A. C. (1998). Changes in infants' cries as a function of time in a cry bout. *Child Development, 69,* 271–279.

Green, M. (1994). *Sigh of relief: A first-aid handbook for childhood emergencies.* New York, NY: Bantam Books.

Green, R. (1987). *The "sissy boy" syndrome and the development of homosexuality.* New Haven, CT: Yale University Press.

Greenberg, R. A., Haley, N. J., Etzel, R. A., & Loda, F. A. (1984). Measuring the exposure of infants to tobacco smoke. *New England Journal of Medicine, 310,* 1075–1078.

Greenberger, E., O'Neill, R., & Nagel, S. K. (1994). Linking workplace and homeplace: Relations between the nature of adults' work and their parenting behaviors. *Developmental Psychology, 30,* 990–1002.

Greene, B. (1994). Lesbian and gay sexual orientations: Implications for clinical training, practice, and research. In B. Greene, & G. M. Herek (Eds.), *Lesbian and gay psychology: Theory, research, and clinical applications* (pp. 1–24). Thousand Oaks, CA: Sage.

Greenfield, P. (1994). Independence and interdependence as developmental scripts: Implications for theory, research, and practice. In P. Greenfield, & R. Cocking (Eds.), *Cross-cultural roots of minority child development* (pp. 1–40). Hillsdale, NJ: Erlbaum.

Greenfield, P. (1995, March 30). *Independence and interdependence in school conferences between Anglo teachers and Hispanic parents.* Paper presented at the biennial meeting of the Society for Research on Child Development, Indianapolis.

Greenhaus, J. H. (1988). Career exploration. In M. London, & E. M. Mone (Eds.), *Career growth and human resource strategy* (pp. 17–30). New York, NY: Quorum.

Greenhaus, J. H., & Powell, G. N. (2006). When work and family are allies: A theory of work-family enrichment. *Academy of Management Reviews, 31,* 72–92.

Gregg, M., & Leinhardt, C. (1995). Mapping out geography: An example of epistemology and education. In *Review of Educational Research, 64*(2), 311–361.

Greil, A. L. (1993). Infertility: Overview. In B. K. Rothman (Ed.), *The encyclopedia of childbearing.* New York, NY: Henry Holt.

Grimby, G. (1988). Physical activity and effects of muscle training in the elderly. *Annals of Clinical Research, 20,* 62–66.

Grimes, D. A., Benson, J., Singh, S., Romero, M., Ganatra, B., Okonofua, F. E., & Shah, I. H. (2006). *Unsafe abortion: The preventable pandemic* (World Health Organization journal paper). Retrieved from http://www.who.int/reproductivehealth/topics/unsafe_abortion/article_unsafe_abortion.pdf

Grodstein, F., Stampfer, M. J., Manson, J. E., Colditz, G. A., Willett, W. C., Rosner, B., Speizer, F. E., & Hennekens, C. H. (1996). Postmenopausal estrogen and progestin use and the risk of cardiovascular disease. *New England Journal of Medicine, 335*(18), 1406.

Grolinck, W. S., Bridges, L. J., & Connell, J. P. (1996). Emotional regulation in two-year-olds: Strategies and emotional expression in four contexts. *Child Development, 67,* 928–941.

Gross, R., Spiker, D., & Haynes, C. (1997). *Helping low-birth-weight, premature babies.* Stanford, CA: Stanford University Press.

Grossarth-Maticek, R., & Eysenck, H. J. (1996). Psychological factors in the treatment of cancer and coronary heart disease. In Editorial Board of Hatherleigh Press (Eds.), *The Hatherleigh guide to issues in modern therapy. The Hatherleigh guides series. Vol. 4* (pp. 53–68). New York, NY: Hatherleigh Press.

Grossmann, K., Grossmann, K., Spangler, G., Suess, G., & Unzner, L. (1985). Maternal sensitivity and newborns' orientation responses as related to quality of attachment in northern Germany. In I. Bretherton, & E. Waters (Eds.), *Growing points of attachment theory and research. Monographs of the Society for Research on Child Development, 50,* 233–256.

Grossmann, K. E., & Grossmann, K. (1990). The wider concept of attachment in cross-cultural research. *Human Development, 33,* 31–47.

Grossmann, T. (2010). The development of emotion perception in face and voice during infancy. *Restorative Neurology and Neuroscience, 28,* 219–236.

Grotpeter, J. K., & Crick, N. R. (1996). Relational aggression, overt aggression, and friendship. *Child Development, 67,* 2328–2338.

Grotpeter, J. K., & Crick, N. R. (1996). *Second chances: Men, women and children a decade after divorce.* Boston: Houghton Mifflin.

Grubb, A., & Turner, E. (2012). Attribution of blame in rape cases: A review of the impact of rape myth acceptance, gender role conformity and substance use on victim blaming. *Aggression and Violent Behavior, 17*(5), 443–52.

Grühn, D., Gilet, A. L., Studer, J., & Labouvie-Vief, G. (2011). Age-relevance of person characteristics: Persons' beliefs about developmental change across the lifespan. *Developmental Psychology, 47,* 376–387.

Grundy, A. M., Gondoli, D. M., & Salafia, E. H. B. (2010). Hierarchical linear modeling analysis of change in maternal knowledge over the transition to adolescence. *Journal of Early Adolescence, 30*(5), 707–732.

Grundy, E., & Henretta, J. C. (2006). Between elderly parents and adult children: A new look at the intergenerational care provided by the 'sandwich generation'. *Ageing and Society, 26,* 707–722.

Grunloh, R. L. (1978, January). To die in Cuaxomulco. *America: Magazine of the Organization of American States.*

Grusec, J. E. (1991). Socializing concern for others in the home. *Developmental Psychology, 27,* 338–342.

Grusec, J. E., Goodnow, J. J., & Cohen, L. (1996). Household work and the development of concern for others. *Developmental Psychology, 32,* 999–1007.

Grusec, J. E., Rudy, D., & Martini, T. (1997). Parenting cognition and child outcomes: An overview of implications for children's internalization of values. In J. E. Grusec, L. Kuczynski, et al. (Eds.), *Parenting and the internalization of values: A handbook of contemporary theory* (pp. 259–282). New York, NY: Wiley.

Grzywacz, J. G., & Butler, A. B. (2005). The impact of job characteristics on work-to-family facilitation: Testing a theory and distinguishing a construct. *Journal of Occupational Health Psychology, 10*(2), 97.

Guarda, A. S. (2008). Treatment of anorexia nervosa: Insights and obstacles. *Physiology & Behavior, 94*(1), 113–120.

Guardo, C., & Bohan, J. (1971). Development of a sense of self-identity in children. *Child Development, 42,* 1909–1921.

Guiaux, M., van Tilburg, T., & van Groenou, M. B. (2007). Changes in contact and support exchange in personal networks after widowhood. *Personal Relationships, 13,* 457–473.

Gunnar, M. R., Proter, F. L., Wolf, C. M., Rigatuso, J., & Larson, M. C. (1995). Neonatal stress reactivity; Predictions of later emotional temperament. *Child Development, 66,* 1–13.

Gunnarsdottir, I., & Thorsdottir, I. (2003). Relationship between growth and feeding in infancy and body mass index at the age of 6 years. *International Journal of Obesity and Metabolic Disorders, 27,* 1523–1527.

Gunner, M. R., Larson, M. C., Hertsgaard, L., Harris, M. L., & Bodersen, L. (1992). The stressfulness of separation among nine-month-old infants: Effects of social context variables and infant temperament. *Child Development, 63,* 290–303.

Guo, S. S., Zeller, C., Chumlea, W. C., & Siervogel, R. M. (1999). Aging, body composition, and lifestyle: The Fels Longitudinal Study. *American Journal of Clinical Nutrition, 70*(3), 405–411.

Gupta, N. D., Smith, N., & Verner, M. (2008). The impact of Nordic countries' family friendly policies on employment, wages, and children. *Review of Economics of the Household, 6*(1), 65–89.

Guralnick, M. J. (2008). Family influences on early development: Integrating the science of normative development, risk and disability, and intervention. In K. McCartney, & D. Phillips (Eds.), *Blackwell handbook of early childhood development* (pp. 44–61). Malden, MA: Blackwell Publishing.

Gurin, P. (1981). Labor market experiences and expectancies, *Sex Roles, 7*(11), 1079–1092.

Gurung, R. A., Taylor, S. E., & Seeman, T. E. (2003). Accounting for changes in social support among married older adults: Insights from the MacArthur Studies of Successful Aging, *Psychology and Aging, 18,* 487–496.

Gutman, S. (1996, June 24). Death and the maiden. *The New Republic,* p. 20.

Guttmacher, A., & Kaiser, I. (1984). *Pregnancy, birth, and family planning.* New York, NY: Signet.

Guttmacher Institute. (2002). Teen pregnancy trends and lessons learned. *The Guttmacher Report on Public Policy, 5*(1). Retrieved from http://www.guttmacher.org/pubs/tgr/05/1/gro50107.html

Guttmacher Institute. (2012). *Facts on induced abortion worldwide.* Retrieved from http://www.who.int/reproductivehealth/publications/unsafe_abortion/induced_abortion_2012.pdf

Guttmacher Institute. (2013a). *Counseling and waiting periods for abortion.* Retrieved from http://www.guttmacher.org/statecenter/spibs/spib_MWPA.pdf

Guttmacher Institute. (2013b). *Facts on American teens sexual and reproductive health.* Retrieved from http://www.guttmacher.org/pubs/FB-ATSRH.html.

Guttman, A. (1996). *The erotic in sports.* New York, NY: Columbia University Press.

H

Haan, N. (1989). Personality in midlife. In S. Hunter, & M. Sundel (Eds.), *Midlife myths* (pp. 145–156). Newbury Park, Cal: Sage.

HackeL L. S., & Ruble, D. N. (1992). Changes in the marital relationship after the first baby is born: Predicting the impact of expectancy disconfirmation. *Journal of Personality & Social Psychology, 62,* 944–957.

Hagerman, R. J. (1996). Biomedical advances in developmental psychology: The case of fragile-x syndrome. *Developmental Psychology, 32,* 416–424.

Haith, M., Wass, T., & Adler, S. (1997). Infant visual expectations: Advances and issues. *Monographs of the Society for Research in Child Development, 62* (2, Serial No 250).

Häkkinen, I., Kirjavainen, T., & Uusitalo, R. (2003). School resources and student achievement revisited: New evidence from panel data. *Economics of Education Review, 22*(3), 329–335.

Halim, M. L., & Ruble, D. (2010). Gender identity and stereotyping in early and middle childhood. In J. C. Chrisler & D. R. McCreary (Eds.), *Handbook of gender research in psychology* (pp. 495–525). New York, NY: Springer.

Hall, D. T., & Rabinowitz, S. (1988). Maintaining employee involvement in a plateaued career. In M. London, & E. M. Mone (Eds.), *Career growth and human resource strategy* (pp. 67–80). New York, NY: Quorum.

Hall, G. C. N., & Barongan, C. (1997). Prevention of sexual aggression. Sociocultural risk and protective factors. *American Psychologist, 52*, 5–14.

Halliday, J. L., Watson, L. F., Lumley, J., Danks, D. M., & Sheffield, L. S. (1995). New estimates of Down syndrome risks of chorionic villus sampling, amniocentesis, and live birth in women of advanced maternal age from a uniquely defined population. *Prenatal Diagnosis, 15*, 455–465.

Hallinan, M. T., & Williams, R. A. (1989). Interracial friendship choices in secondary schools. *American Sociological Review, 54*, 67–78.

Hallinan, M., & Teixeira, R. (1987). The stability of students' interracial friendships. *American Sociological Review, 52*, 653–664.

Hallowell, E., & Ratey, J. (1994). *Driven to distraction: ADHD children as adults*. New York, NY: Pantheon Books.

Halperin, J. M., Trampush, J. W., Miller, C. J., Marks, D. J., & Newcorn, J. H. (2008). Neuropsychological outcome in adolescents/young adults with Childhood ADHD: Profiles of persisters, remitters and controls. *Journal of Child Psychology and Psychiatry, and Allied Disciplines, 49*(9), 958–966.

Hamann, K., Warneken, F., & Tomasello, M. (2012). Children's developing commitments to joint goals. *Child Development, 83*(1), 137–145.

Hamarta, E., Deniz, M., & Saltali, N. (2009). Attachment styles as a predictor of emotional intelligence. *Educational Sciences: Theory and Practice, 9*(1), 213–229.

Hamburg, D. (1997). Towards a strategy for healthy adolescent development. *American Journal of Psychiatry, 154*(6), 7–12.

Hamburg, D. A. (1994). *Today's children: Creating a future for a generation of crisis*. New York, NY: Times Books.

Hamilton, B. E., Martin, J. A., & Osterman, M. J. K. (2016, June). Births: Preliminary data for 2015. *National Vital Statistics Reports, 65*(3), 1–15. Retrieved from http://www.cdc.gov/nchs/data/nvsr/nvsr65/nvsr65_03.pdf

Hamilton, N. G. (1989). *Self and others: Object relations in theory and practice*. Northvale, NJ: Jason Aronson.

Hamilton, P. M. (1984). *Basic maternity nursing* (5th ed.), St. Louis: Mosby.

Hanash, S. M., Baik, C. S., & Kallioniemi, O. (2011). Emerging molecular biomarkers—Blood-based strategies to detect and monitor cancer. *Nature Reviews Clinical Oncology, 8*, 142–150.

Harada, M. (1994). Early and later life sport participation patterns among the active elderly in Japan. *Journal of Aging and Physical Activity, 2*, 105–114.

Harding, S. R., Flannelly, K. J., Weaver, A. J., & Costa, K. G. (2005). The influence of religion on death anxiety and death acceptance. *Mental Health, Religion & Culture, 8*(4), 253–261.

Hardy, J. (1994). Alzheimer's disease: Clinical molecular genetics. *Clinical Geriatric Medicine, 10*(2), 239–247.

Hardy, J. B. (1991). Pregnancy and its outcome. In W. R. Hendee (Ed.), *The health of adolescents: Understanding and facilitating biological, behavioral, and social development* (pp. 250–281). San Francisco: Jossey-Bass.

Hardy, S. E., & Studenski, S. A. (2008). Fatigue predicts mortality in older adults. *Journal of the American Geriatrics Society, 56*, 1910–1914.

Hare-Mustin, R. T., & Marecek, J. (1988). The meaning of difference: Gender theory, postmodernism, and psychology. *American Psychologist, 43*, 455–64.

Hareven, T. (1986). Historical changes in the family and the life course: Implications for child development. In A. Smuts, & H. Ha-gen (Eds.), *History and research in child development. Monographs of the Society for Research on Child Development, 50* (4–5, Serial No. 211).

Harkness, S., & Keefer, C. (1995, February). *Cultural influences on sleep patterns in infancy and early childhood*. Paper presented at the annual meeting of the American Association for the Advancement of Science, Atlanta.

Harkness, S., & Super, C. (1992). Parental ethnotheories in action. In I. Sigel, A. McGillicuddy-DeLisi, & J. Goodnow (Eds.), *Parent belief systems: The psychological consequences for children* (2nd ed., pp. 373–392). Hillsdale, NJ: Erlbaum.

Harkness, S., Super, C., & Keefer, C. (1992). Learning to be an American parent: How cultural models gain directive force. In R. D'Andrade, & C. Strauss (Eds.), *Human motives and cultural models* (pp. 163–178). New York, NY: Cambridge University-Press.

Harlan, L., Brawley, O., Pommerenke, F., Wali, P., & Kramer, B. (1995). Geographic, age, and racial variation in the treatment of local/regional carcinoma of the prostate. *Journal of Clinical Oncology, 13*, 93–100.

Harley, C. B. (1997). Human aging and telomeres. *Ciba Foundation Symposium, 211*, 129–144.

Harold, G. T., & Conger, R. D. (1997). Marital conflict and adolescent distress: The role of adolescent awareness. *Child Development, 68*, 333–350.

Harrawood, L. K., White, L. J., & Benshoff, J. J. (2009). Death anxiety in a national sample of United States funeral directors and its relationship with death exposure, age, and sex. *OMEGA—Journal of Death and Dying, 58*(2), 129–146.

Harrell, R. (2011). *Housing for older adults: The impacts of the recession*. Insight on the Issues. Washington, DC: AARP Public Policy Institute.

Harrington, J. W., Nguyen, V. Q., Paulson, J. F., Garland, R., Pasquinelli, L., & Lewis, D. (2010). Identifying the "tipping point" age for overweight pediatric patients. *Clinical Pediatrics, 49*, 638–643.

Harris, M. (2007). *Grave matters: A journey through the modern funeral industry to a natural way of burial*. New York, NY: Scribner.

Harris, P. (1983). Infant cognition. In Paul Mussen (Ed.), *Handbook of child psychology: Vol. 4*. New York, NY: Wiley.

Harrison, A. O., Wilson, M. N., Pine, C. J., Chan, S. Q., & Buriel, R. (1990). Family ecologies of ethnic minority children. *Child Development, 61*, 347–362.

Harrison, D., Bueno, M., Yamada, J., Adams-Webber, T., & Stevens, B. (2010). Analgesic effects of sweet-tasting solutions for infants: Current state of equipoise. *Pediatrics, 126*, 894–902.

Hart, B. (1991). Input frequency and children's first words. *First Language, 11*, 289–300.

Hart, C. H., DeWolf, D. M., Wozniak, P., & Burts, D. C. (1992). Maternal and paternal disciplinary styles: Relations with preschoolers' playground behavioral orientations and peer status. *Child Development, 63*, 879–892.

Hart, C. H., Ladd, G. W., & Burleson, B. R. (1990). Children's expectations of the outcomes of social strategies; Relations with socioeconomic status and maternal disciplinary styles. *Child. Development, 61*, 127–137.

Hart, C. H., Nelson, D. A., Robinson, C. C., Olsen, S. F., & McNeilly-Chocque, M. K. (1998). Overt and relational aggression in Russian nursery-school-age children: Parenting style and marital linkages. *Developmental Psychology, 34*, 687–697.

Hart, H., Radua, J., Nakao, T., Mataix-Cols, D., & Rubia, K. (2013). Meta-analysis of functional magnetic resonance imaging studies of inhibition and attention in attention-deficit/hyperactivity disorder: Exploring task-specific, stimulant medication, and age effects. *JAMA Psychiatry, 70*(2), 185–198.

Harter, S. (1977). A cognitive-developmental approach to children's expression of conflicting feelings and a technique to facilitate such expression in play therapy. *Journal of Consulting and Clinical Psychology, 45*, 417–432.

Harter, S. (1983). Developmental perspectives on self-system. In E. M. Hetherington (Ed.), *Handbook of child psychology: Vol. 4. Socialization, personality, and social development* (4th ed., pp. 275–285). New York, NY: Wiley.

Harter, S. (1989). Processes underlying adolescent self-concept formation. In R. Montemayor (Ed.), *Advances in adolescent development: Vol 2. Transition from childhood to adolescence*. New York, NY: Russell Sage Foundation.

Harter, S., & Barnes, R. (1983). *Children's understanding of parental emotions: A developmental study*. Unpublished paper, 1981. Cited in S. Harter, Developmental perspectives on the self-system. In P. Mussen (Ed.), *Handbook of child psychology: Vol. 4*. New York, NY: Wiley.

Harter, S., & Monsour, A. (1992). Developmental analysis of conflict caused by opposing attributes in the adolescent self-portrait. *Developmental Psychology, 28*, 251–260.

Harter, S., Marold, D. B., Whitescll, N. R., & Cobbs, G. (1996). A model of the effects of perceived parent and peer support on adolescent false self behavior. *Child Development, 67*. 360–374.

Hartup, W. W. (1983). Peer relations. In P. Mussen (Ed.), *Handbook of child psychology: Vol. 4*. New York, NY: Wiley.

Hartup, W. W. (1989). Social relationships and their developmental significance. *American Psychologist, 44*, 120–126.

Hartup, W. W. (1996). The company they keep: Friendships and their developmental significance. *Child Development, 67*, 1–13.

Hartup, W. W. (1997). The company they keep: Friendships and adaptation in the life course. *Psychological Bulletin, 121*, 355–370.

Hartup, W. W., & Stevens, N. (1997). Friendships and adaptation in the life course. *Psychological Bulletin, 121*, 335–370.

Hasan, Y., Bègue, L., Scharkow, M., & Bushman, B. J. (2013). The more you play, the more aggressive you become: A long-term experimental study of cumulative violent video game effects on hostile expectations and aggressive behavior. *Journal of Experimental Social Psychology, 49*, 224–227.

Haslett, B. (1997). *Children communicating: The first 5 years*. Mahwah, NJ: Erlbaum.

Hastings, P. D., & Grusec, J. E. (1998). Parenting goals as organizers of responses to parent-child disagreement. *Developmental Psychology, 34*, 465–479.

Hatch, L. R. (1995). Gray clouds and silver linings: Women's resources in later life. In J. Freeman (Ed.), *Women: A feminist perspective* (5th ed., pp. 182–196). Mountain View, CA: Mayfield.

Hatch, L. R., & Bulcroft, C. (1992). Contact with friends in later life: Disentangling the effects of gender and marital stability. *Journal of Marriage and the Family, 54*, 222–232.

Hatzimouratidis, K., Amar, E., Eardley, I., Giuliano, F., Hatzichristou, D., Montorsi, F., ... & Wespes, E. (2010). Guidelines on male sexual dysfunction: Erectile dysfunction and premature ejaculation. *European Urology, 57*(5), 804–814.

Haug, M. R., Akiyama, H., Tryban, G., Sonoda, K., & Wykle, M. (1991). Self-care: Japan and U.S. compared. *Social Science and Medicine, 33*, 1011–1022.

Havekes, E., Bader, M., & Krysan, M. (2016). Realizing racial and ethnic neighborhood preferences? Exploring the mismatches between what people want, where they search, and where they live. *Population Research and Policy Review, 35*(1), 101–126.

Havighurst, R. J., Neugarten, B. L., & Tobin, S. S. (1968). Disengagement and patterns of aging. In B. L. Neugarten (Ed.), *Middle age and aging* (pp. 161–173). Chicago: University of Chicago Press.

Hawkins, J. D., Graham, J. W., Maguin, E., Abbott, R., Hill, K. G., & Catalano, R. F. (1997). Exploring the effects of age of alcohol use initiation and psychosocial risk factors on subsequent alcohol misuse. *Journal of Studies on Alcohol, 58*, 280–290.

Hay, P. (2013). A systematic review of evidence for psychological treatments in eating disorders, 2005–2012. *International Journal of Eating Disorders, 46*(5), 462–469.

Hayenga, A. O., & Corpus, J. H. (2010). Profiles of intrinsic and extrinsic motivations: A person-centered approach to motivation and achievement in middle school. *Motivation and Emotion, 34*(4), 371–383.

Hayes, C. (1987). *Risking the future: Adolescent sexuality, pregnancy and childbearing.* Washington, DC: National Academy Press.

Hayflick, L. (1994). *How and why we age.* New York, NY: Ballantine.

Hayne, H., Rovee-Collier, C., & Borza, M. (1991). Infant memory for place information. *Memory and Cognition, 19*. 378–386.

Hayslip, B., & Hansson, R. O. (2003). Death awareness and adjustment across the life span. In C. D. Bryant (Ed.), *Handbook of death and dying* (Vol. 1, pp. 437–447). Thousand Oaks, CA: Sage Publications.

Hayslip, B., & Page, K. S. (2012). Grandparenthood: Grandchild and great-grandchild relationships. In R. Blieszner, & V. H. Bedford (Eds.), *Handbook of families and aging* (pp. 183–212). Santa Barbara, CA: Praeger.

Hayslip, B., Sewell, K. W., & Riddle, R. B. (2003). The American funeral. In C. D. Bryant (Ed.), *Handbook of death and dying* (Vol. 2, pp. 587–597). Thousand Oaks, CA: Sage Publications.

Hazen, C., & Shaver, P. (1987). Romantic love conceptualized as an attachment process. *Journal of Personality and Social Psychology, 53*, 511–524.

Hazen, C., & Shaver, P. (1990). Love and work: An attachment-theoretical perspective. *Journal of Personality and Social Psychology, 59*, 270–290.

Heal, D. J., Smith, S. L., & Findling, R. L. (2011). ADHD: Current and future therapeutics. In C. Stanford, & R. Tannock (Eds.), *Behavioral neuroscience of attention deficit hyperactivity disorder and its treatment* (pp. 361–390). Berlin: Springer-Verlag Berlin Heidelberg.

Heath, S. (1993). *Identity and inner-city youth: Beyond ethnicity and gender.* New York, NY: Teachers' College Press.

Heath, S., Mangolia, L., Schlecter, S., & Hull, G. (Eds.). (1991). *Children of promise: Literate activity in linguistically and culturally diverse classrooms.* Washington, DC: National Education Association.

Hebblethwaite, S., & Norris, J. (2011). Expressions of generativity through family leisure: Experiences of grandparents and adult grandchildren. *Family Relations, 60*, 121–133.

Heckhausen, J., & Krueger, J. (1993). Developmental expectations for the self and most other people: Age-grading in three functions of social comparison. *Developmental Psychology, 29*, 539–548.

Heckhausen, J., Dixon, R. A., & Baltes, P. B. (1989). Gains and losses in development throughout adulthood as perceived by different adult age groups. *Developmental Psychology, 25*, 109–121.

Hegewisch, A., & Gornick, J. C. (2011). The impact of work-family policies on women's employment: A review of research from OECD countries. *Community, Work & Family, 14*(2), 119–138.

Hegewisch, A., Leipmann, H., Hayes, J., & Hartmann, H. (2010). *Separate and not equal? Gender segregation in the labor market and the gender wage gap.* Institute for Women's Policy Research, Washington, DC. Retrieved from http://www.iwpr.org/publications/pubs/separate-and-not-equal-gender-segregation-in-the-labor-market-and-the-gender-wage-gap

Heidrich, S. M., & Denney, N. W. (1994). Does social problem solving differ from other types of problem solving during the adult years? *Experimental Aging Research, 20*(2), 105–126.

Heikamp, T., Trommsdorff, G., Druey, M. D., Hübner, R., & Suchodoletz, A. V. (2013). Kindergarten children's attachment security, inhibitory control, and the internalization of rules of conduct. *Frontiers in Psychology, 4*, 1–11.

Helfer, M. E., Kempe, R. S., & Krugman, R. D. (Eds.) (1997). *The battered child.* Chicago: University of Chicago Press.

Helfer, R. E., & Kempe, R. S. (Eds.). (1987). *The battered child* (4th ed.), Chicago: University of Chicago Press.

Helson, R., & McCabe, L. (1994). The social clock project in middle age. In B. F. Turner, & L. E. Troll (Eds.), *Women growing older: Psychological perspectives* (pp. 68–93). Thousand Oaks, CA: Sage.

Helson, R., & Wink, P. (1992). Personality change in women from the early 40s to the early 50s. *Psychology & Aging, 7*, 46–55.

Helson, R., Pals, J., & Solomon, M. (1997). Is there adult development distinctive to women? In R. Hogan, J. A. Johnson, & S. R. Briggs (Eds.), *Handbook of personality psychology.* (pp. 291–314). San Diego: Academic Press.

Helton, A., McFarlane, J., & Anderson, E. T. (1987). Battered and pregnant: A prevalence study. *American Journal of Public Health, 77*, 1337–1339.

Hendler, M., & Weisberg, P. (1992). Conservation acquisition, maintenance, and generalization by mentally retarded children using equality-rule training. *Journal of Experimental Child Psychology, 53*, 258–276.

Hendrick, H. (1997). Constructions and reconstructions of British childhood: An interpretative survey, 1800 to the present. In A. James, & A. Prout (Eds.), *Constructing and reconstructing childhood* (pp. 34–62). London, UK: Falmer.

Henriksson, A., Carlander, I., & Årestedt, K. (2015). Feelings of rewards among family caregivers during ongoing palliative care. *Palliative and Supportive Care, 13*(06), 1509–1517.

Henry, B., Caspi, A., Moffitt, T. E., & Silva, P. A. (1996). Temperamental and familial predictors of violent and nonviolent criminal convictions: Age 3 to age 18. *Developmental Psychology, 32*, 614–623.

Herbenick, D., Reece, M., Schick, V., Sanders, S. A., Dodge, B., & Fortenberry, J. D. (2010). Sexual behavior in the United States: Results from a national probability sample of men and women ages 14–94. *Journal of Sexual Medicine, 7*(s5), 255–265.

Hergenrather, J. R., & Rabinowitz, M. (1991). Age-related differences in the organization of children's knowledge of illness, *Developmental Psychology, 27*, 952–959.

Herman, J. (1992). *Trauma and recovery: The aftermath of violence: From domestic abuse to political terror.* New York, NY: Basic Books.

Hernandez, D. J. (1997). Child development and the social demography of childhood. *Child Development, 68*, 149–169.

Hernandez, H. (1997). *Teaching in multilingual classrooms.* Upper Saddle River, NJ: Merrill.

Heron, M., US Department of Health and Human Services, Centers for Disease Control and Prevention, National Center for Health Statistics, and National Vital Statistics System. (2013). *Deaths: Leading causes for 2010.* (NVSS Volume 62, Number 6).

Herrenkohl, R. C., Egolf, B. P., & Herrenkohl, E. C. (1997). Preschool antecedents of adolescent assaultive behavior. A longitudinal study. *American Journal of Orthopsychiatry, 67*, 422–32.

Hershberger, S. L., & D'Augelli, A. R. (1995). The impact of victimization on the mental health and suicidality of lesbian, gay, and bisexual youths. *Developmental Psychology, 31*, 65–74.

Hespos, S. J., & Baillargeon, R. (2001). Infants' knowledge about occlusion and containment events: A surprising discrepancy. *Psychological Science, 12*, 141–147.

Hesse-Biber, S. (1996). *Am I think enough yet? The cult of thinness and commercialization of identity.* New York, NY: Oxford University Press.

Hetherington, E. M. (2005). Divorce and the adjustment of children. *Pediatrics In Review, 26*(5), 163–169.

Hetherington, E. M., Bridges, M., & Insabella, G. M. (1998). What matters? What does not? Five perspectives on the association between marital transitions and children's adjustment. *American Psychologist, 53*, 167–184.

Hetherington, E. M., Henderson, S. H., Reiss, D., Anderson, E. R., Bridges, M., Chan, R. W., ... & O'Connor, T. G. (1999). Adolescent siblings in stepfamilies: Family functioning and adolescent adjustment. *Monographs of the Society for Research in Child Development, 64*, Serial No. 259.

Hildick-Smith, G. J., Pesko, M. F., Shearer, L., Hughes, J. M., Chang, J., Loughlin, G. M., & Ipp, L. S. (2015). A practitioner's guide to electronic cigarettes in the adolescent population. *Journal of Adolescent Health, 57*(6), 574–579.

Hill, R., & Ruptic, C. (1994). *Practical aspects of authentic assessment.* Norwood, MA: Christopher-Gordon Publishers.

Hill, T. D., Burdette, A. M., & Idler, E. L. (2011). Religious involvement, health status, and mortality risk. In R. A. Settersten, & J. L. Angel (Eds.), *Handbook of sociology of aging* (pp. 533–546). New York, NY: Springer Publishing.

Hills, A. P., King, N. A., & Armstrong, T. P. (2007). The contribution of physical activity and sedentary behaviours to the growth and development of children and adolescents. *Sports Medicine, 37*(6), 533–545.

Hinde, R. A. (1989). Ethological relationships and approaches. In R. Vasta (Ed.), *Anna's of Child Development: Six theories of child development–Revised formulations and current issues.* Greenwich, CT: JAI Press.

Hinkley, T., Crawford, D., Salmon, J., Okely, A. D., & Hesketh, K. (2008). Preschool children and physical activity: A review of correlates. *American Journal of Preventive Medicine, 34*(5), 435–441.

Hirayama, T. (1981). Non-smoking wives of heavy smokers have a higher risk of lung cancer: A study from Japan. *Journal of Behavioral Medicine, 12*, 39–54.

Ho, D. (1994). Cognitive socialization in Confucian heritage cultures. In P. Greenfield, & R. Cocking (Eds.), *Cross-cultural roots of minority child development* (pp. 285–314). Hillsdale, NJ: Erlbaum.

Ho, E. S. (2010). Measuring hand function in the young child. *Journal of Hand Therapy, 23*, 323–328.

Ho, S. C., Chan, A., Woo, J., Chong, P., & Sham, A. (2009). Impact of caregiving on health and quality of life: A comparative population-based study of caregivers for elderly persons and noncaregivers. *Journals of Gerontology Series A: Biological Sciences and Medical Sciences*, glp034.

Hoare, C. H. (1994). Psychosocial identity development in United States society: Its role in fostering exclusion of cultural others. In E. P. Salett, & D. R. Koslow (Eds.), *Race, ethnicity and self: Identity in multicultural perspective.* Washington, DC: National Multicultural Institute.

Hochschild, A. (1989). *The second shift: Working parents and the revolution at home.* New York, NY: Viking.

Hodgson, L. G. (1995). Adult grandchildren and their grandparents: The enduring bond. In J. Hendricks (Ed.), *The ties of later life* (pp. 155–170). Amityville, NY: Baywood.

Hodnett, E. D., Gates, S., Hofneyr, G. J., & Sakala, C. (2007). Continuous support for women during childbirth. *Cochrane Database of Systematic Reviews, 3*.

Hoeve, M., Dubas, J. S., Eichelsheim, V. I., Van der Laan, P. H., Smeenk, W., & Gerris, J. R. (2009). The relationship between parenting and delinquency: A meta-analysis. *Journal of Abnormal Child Psychology, 37*(6), 749–775.

Hoff, E. (2008). Language experience and language milestones during early childhood. In K. McCartney, & D. Phillips (Eds.), *Blackwell handbook of early childhood development* (pp. 233–251). Malden, MA: Blackwell Publishing.

Hoff-Ginsberg, E. (1997). *Language development.* Pacific Grove, CA: Brooks/Cole.

Hoff-Ginsberg, E., & Krueger, W. (1991). Older siblings as conversational partners. *Merrill-Palmer Quarterly, 37,* 465–482.

Hoffman, L. W. (1983). Increased fathering: Effects on the mother. In M. Lamb, & A. Sagi (Eds.), *Fatherhood and family policy.* Hillsdale, NJ: Erlbaum.

Hoffman, L. W. (1984a). Maternal employment and the young child. In M. Perlmutter (Ed.), *The Minnesota symposium on child psychology: Vol. 17.* Hillsdale, NJ: Erlbaum.

Hoffman, L. W. (1984b). Work, family, and the socialization of the child. In R. Parke (Ed.), *Review of child development research: Vol. 7.* Chicago: University of Chicago Press.

Hoffman, L. W. (1989). Effects of maternal employment in the two-parent family. *American Psychologist, 44,* 283–292.

Hoffnung, A. (1992). *Shoeshine boys of Cuenca, Ecuador.* Unpublished paper, Reed College, Portland.

Hoffnung, M. (1992). *What is a mother to do? Conversations on work and family.* Pasadena, CA: Trilogy Books.

Hoffnung, M. (1995). Motherhood: Contemporary conflict for women. In J. Freeman (Ed.), *Women: A feminist perspective* (5th ed., pp. 162–181). Palo Alto, CA: Mayfield.

Hoffnung, M. (1998, November). Women's changing attitudes toward work and family. Paper presented at the Conference on Work and Family: Today's Realities and Tomorrow's Visions, Boston, MA.

Hofland, B. F. (1994). When capacity fades and autonomy is constricted: A client-centered approach to residential care. *Generations, 18*(4), 31–35.

Hogan, N. S., & DeSantis, L. (1992). Adolescent sibling bereavement: An ongoing attachment. *Qualitative Health Research. 2,* 159–177.

Hogan, R., Kim, M., & Perrucci, C. C. (1997). Racial inequality in men's employment and retirement earnings. *Sociological Quarterly, 38*(3), 431–438.

Hoge, D., Johnson, B., & Luidens, D. A. (1993). Determinants of church involvement of young adults who grew up in Presbyterian churches. *Journal for the Scientific Study of Religion, 32,* 242–255.

Hogenkamp, P. S., Nilsson, E., Nilsson, V. C., Chapman, C. D., Vogel, H., Lundberg, L. S., ... & Dickson, S. L. (2013). Acute sleep deprivation increases portion size and affects food choice in young men. *Psychoneuroendocrinology, 38*(9), 1668–1674.

Holahan, C. J., Schutte, K. K., Brennan, P. L., North, R. J., Holahan, C. K., Boos, B. S., & Moos, R. H. (2012). Wine consumption and 20-year mortality among late-life moderate drinkers. *Journal of Studies on Alcohol and Drugs, 73,* 80–88.

Holden, C. (1986). Youth suicide: New research focuses on growing social problem. *Science, 233,* 839–841.

Hollis, J. F., Carmody, T. P., Connor, S. L., Fey, S. G., & Malarazzo, J. D. (1986). The nutrition attitude survey: Associations with dietary habits, psychological and physical well-being, and coronary risk factors. *Health Psychology, 5,* 359–374.

Holmbeck, G., & O'Donnell, K. (1991). Discrepancies between perceptions of decision making and behavioral autonomy. In R. Paikoff (Ed.), *Shared views of the family during adolescence* (pp. 51–70). San Francisco: Jossey-Bass.

Holmes, B. M., & Johnson, K. R. (2009). Adult attachment and romantic partner preference: A review. *Journal of Social and Personal Relationships, 26*(6–7), 833–852.

Holmes, L. J. (1993). Midwives, southern black. In B. K. Rothman (Ed.), *The encyclopedia of childbearing.* New York, NY: Henry Holt.

Hong, J. S., & Garbarino, J. (2012). Risk and protective factors for homophobic bullying in schools: An application of the socio-ecological framework. *Educational Psychology Review, 24*(2), 271–285.

Hooyman, N. R. (1992). Social policy and gender inequalities in caregiving. In J. W. Dwyer, & R. T. Coward (Eds.), *Gender, families, and elder care* (pp. 181–201). Newbury Park, CA: Sage.

Hooyman, N. R., & Kiyak, H. A. (1993). *Social gerontology.* Boston: Allyn & Bacon.

Horgan, J. (1993, June). Eugenics revisited. *Scientific American,* 120–128.

Horn, J. L. (1970). Organization of data on life-span development of human abilities. In L. R. Goulet, & P. B. Baltes (Eds.), *Life-span developmental psychology: Research and theory* (pp. 424–466). New York, NY: Academic Press.

Horn, J. L., & Donaldson, G. (1976). On the myth of intellectual decline in adulthood. *American Psychologist, 31,* 701–719.

Horn, J. L., & Donaldson, G. (1977). Faith is not enough: A response to the Baltes-Schaie claim that intelligence does not wane. *American Psychologist, 32,* 369–373.

Horn, J. L., & Hofer, S. M. (1992). Major abilities and development in the adult period. In R. J. Sternberg, & C. A. Berg (Eds.), *Intellectual development* (pp. 44–99). New York, NY: Cambridge University Press.

Hornor, G. (2010). Child sexual abuse: Consequences and implications. *Journal of Pediatric Health Care, 24*(6), 358–364.

Horvath, T. B., & Davis, K. L. (1990). Central system disorders in aging. In E. L. Schneider, & J. W. Rowe (Eds.), *Handbook of the biology of aging* (3rd ed., pp. 306–329). San Diego: Academic Press.

Horwitz, A. V., & White, H. R. (1998). The relationship of cohabitation and mental health: A study of a young adult cohort. *Journal of Marriage and the Family, 60,* 505–514.

House, S. J., Landis, K. R., & Umberson, D. (1988). Social relationships and health. *Science, 241,* 540–544.

Howe, N., Petrakos, H., & Rinaldi, C. M. (1998). "All the sheeps are dead. He murdered them": Sibling pretense, negotiation, internal state language, and relationship quality. *Child Development, 69,*182–191.

Howe, N., Ross, H. S., & Recchia, H. (2011). Sibling relations in early and middle childhood. In P. K. Smith, & C. H. Hart (Eds.), *The Wiley-Blackwell handbook of childhood social development* (2nd ed., pp. 356–372). Malden, MA: Blackwell Publishing.

Howes, C. (1988). Peer interaction of young children. *Monographs of the Society for Research in Child Development, 53*(Serial No. 2170), 1–78.

Howes, C. (1996). The earliest friendships. In W. M. Bukowski, A. F. Newcomb, et al. (Eds.), *The company they keep: Friendship in childhood and adolescence. Cambridge Studies in Social and Emotional Development* (pp. 66–86). New York, NY: Cambridge University Press.

Howes, C., & Matheson, C. C. (1992). Sequences in the development of competent play with peers: Social and social pretend play. *Developmental Psychology, 28,* 961–972.

Howes, C., & Wu, F. (1990). Peer interactions and friendships in an ethnically diverse school setting. *Child Development, 61,* 537–541.

Howes, C., Hamilton, C. E., & Matheson, C. C. (1994). Children's relationships with peers: Differential associations with aspects of the teacher-child relationship. *Child Development, 65,* 253–263.

Howes, C., Hamilton, C. E., & Philipsen, L. C. (1998). Stability and continuity of child-caregiver and child-peer relationships. *Child Development, 69,* 418–426.

Hoyer, W. J., & Rybash, J. M. (1994). Characterizing adult cognitive development. *Adult Development, 1,* 7–12.

Hoyer, W. J., & Touron, D. R. (2003). Learning in adulthood. In J. Demick, & C. Andreoletti (Eds.), *Handbook of adult development* (pp. 23–41). Springer.

Hoyert, D. L. (1991). Financial and household exchange between generations. *Research in Aging, 13,* 205–225.

Hu, J. M., Wechter, M. E., Geller, E. J., Nguyen, T. V., & Visco, A. G. (2007). Hysterectomy rates in the United States, 2003. *Obstetrics and Gynecology, 110,* 1091–1095.

Huang, L., & Ying, Y. (1989). Chinese-American children and adolescents. In J. Gibbs, & L. Huang (Eds.), *Children of color* (pp. 30–66). San Francisco: Jossey-Bass.

Hubbard, R. (1993). Genetics. In B. K. Rothman (Ed.), *The encyclopedia of childbearing.* New York, NY: Henry Holt.

Hudley, C., & Graham, S. (1993). An attributional intervention to reduce peer-directed aggression among African-American boys. *Child Development, 64,* 124–138.

Hughes, F. P. (1991). *Children, play and development.* Boston: Allyn & Bacon.

Hughes, M. E., & Waite, L. J. (2009). Marital biography and health at mid-life. *Journal of Health and Social Behavior, 50,* 344–358.

Hughes, M. S. (1987). Black students' participation in higher education. Special issue: Blacks in U.S. higher education. *Journal of College Student Personnel, 28*(6), 532–545.

Hunt, C. (Ed.). (1992). *Apnea and SIDS.* Philadelphia: Saunders.

Hunt, E. (1993). What we need to know about aging. In J. Cerella, J. Rybash, W. Hoyer, & M. L. Commons (Eds.), *Adult information processing: Limits on loss* (pp. 587–589). San Diego: Academic Press.

Hunt, M. E., & Ross, L. (1990). Naturally-occurring retirement communities: A multiattribute examination of desirability factors. *The Gerontologist, 30,* 667–674.

Hunt, W., & Zakhari, S. (1995). *Stress, gender, and alcohol-seeking behavior.* Bethesda, MD: National Institutes of Health/National Institute of Alcohol Abuse and Alcoholism.

Hunter, M. S., Gentry-Maharaj, A., Ryan, A., Burnell, M., Lanceley, A., Fraser, L., ... & Menon, U. (2012). Prevalence, frequency and problem rating of hot flushes persist in older postmenopausal women: Impact of age, body mass index, hysterectomy, hormone therapy use, lifestyle and mood in a cross-sectional cohort study of 10,418 British women aged 54–65. *BJOG: An International Journal of Obstetrics & Gynecology, 119,* 40–50. doi: 10.1111/j.1471-0528.2011.03166.x

Hurrelmann, K. (1994). *International handbook of adolescence.* Westport, CT: Greenwood Press.

Huston, A. C. (1994). *Children in poverty: Designing research to affect policy.* Social policy report, vol. 8(2). Ann Arbor, MI: Society for Research on Child Development.

Huston, A. C., & Wright, J. C. (1996). Television and socialization of young children. In T. M. MacBeth et al. (Eds.), *Tuning in to young viewers: Social science perspectives on television* (pp. 37–60). Thousand Oaks, CA: Sage.

Huston, A. C., Watkins, B., & Kunkel, D. (1989). Public policy and children's television. *American Psychologist, 44,* 424–433.

Huston, A. C., Wright, J. C., Rice, M. L., Kerkman, D., & St. Peters, M. (1990). Development of television viewing patterns in early childhood: A longitudinal investigation. *Developmental Psychology, 26,* 409–420.

Hwang, J., & Rothbart, M. K. (2002). Measuring infant temperament. *Infant Behavior & Development, 25*, 113–116.

Hyde, J. S., Essex, M. J., Clark, R., Klein, M. H., & Byrd, J. E. (1996). Parental leave: Policy and research. *Journal of Social Issues 56*, 91–109.

Hyman, J. P. (1995). Shifting patterns of fathering in the first year of life: On intimacy between fathers and their babies. In J. L. Shapiro, M. J. Diamond, & M. Greenberg (Eds.), *Becoming a father: Contemporary, social, developmental, and clinical perspectives.* (pp. 256–267). New York, NY: Springer.

Hymel, S., Closson, L. M., Caravita, S. C. S., & Vaillancourt, T. (2011). Social status among peers: From sociometric attraction to peer acceptance to perceived popularity. In P. K. Smith, & C. H. Hart (Eds.), *The Wiley-Blackwell handbook of childhood social development* (2nd ed., pp. 375–322). Malden, MA: Blackwell Publishing.

I

Ianni, F., & Orr, M. (1996). Dropping out. In J. Graber, J. Brooks-Gunn, & A. Petersen (Eds.), *Transitions through adolescence* (pp. 285–322). Mahwah, NJ: Erlbaum.

Ikels, C. (1993). Chinese kinship and the states: Shaping policy for the elderly. In G. L. Maddox, & M. P. Lawton (Eds.), *Annual review of gerontology and geriatrics: Focus on kinship, aging and social change* (pp. 123–146). New York, NY: Springer.

Ilmarinen, J. (2002). Physical requirements associated with the work of aging workers in the European Union. *Experimental Aging Research, 28*(1), 7–23.

Ingersoll, B. (1998). *Daredevils and daydreamers: New perspectives on ADHD.* New York, NY: Doubleday.

Inhelder, B., & Piaget, J. (1958). *The growth of logical thinking from birth to adolescence.* New York, NY: Basic Books.

Innamorati, M., Sarracino, D., & Dazzi, N. (2010). Motherhood constellation and representational change in pregnancy. *Infant Mental Health Journal, 31*, 379–396.

Insana, S. P., & Montgomery-Downs, H. E. (2013). Sleep and sleepiness among first-time postpartum parents: A field-and laboratory-based multimethod assessment. *Developmental Psychobiology, 55*(4), 361–372.

Institute of Medicine. (2002). *Reducing suicide: A national imperative.* Washington, DC: National Academies Press.

Institute of Medicine. (2009). *Weight gain during pregnancy: Reexamining the guidelines.* Washington, DC: National Academies Press.

Irion, P. E. (1990/1991). Changing patterns of ritual response to death. *Omega, 22*(3), 159–172.

Isabella, R. A., & Belsky, J. (1991). Interactional synchrony and the origins of infant-mother attachment: A replication study. *Child Development, 62*, 373–384.

Isaksson, K. (1997, January). Patterns of adjustment to early retirement. Reports from the Department of Psychology, University of Stockholm, No. 828, 1–13.

Iso, A., Seppo, E., Jackson, E., & Dunn, E. (1994). Starting, ceasing, and replacing leisure activities over the life-span. *Journal of Leisure Research, 26*(3), 227–249.

It's not working. (1986). *American Demographics, 8*(12), p. 13.

Iyer, S. N., & Oiler, D. K. (2008). Prelinguistic vocal development in infants with typical hearing and infants with severe-to-profound hearing loss. *Volta Review, 108*, 115–138.

Izard, C. E. (1982). *Measuring emotions in infants and children.* New York, NY: Cambridge University Press.

Izard, C. E. (1994). Innate and universal facial expressions: Evidence from developmental and cross-cultural research. *Psychological Bulletin, 115*, 288–299.

Izard, C. E., & Malatesta, C. (1987). Perspectives on emotional development: I. Differential emotions theory of early emotional development. In J. Osofsky (Ed.), *Handbook of infant development* (2nd ed., pp. 494–554). New York, NY: Wiley.

J

Jaccard, J., Dittus, P. J., & Gordon, V. V. (1998). Parent-adolescent congruency in reports of adolescent sexual behavior and in communications about sexual behavior. *Child Development, 69*, 247–261.

Jacket, L. S., & Ruble, D. N. (1992). Changes in the marital relationship after the first baby is born: Predicting the impact of expectancy disconfirmation. *Journal of Personality & Social Psychology, 62*, 944–957.

Jackson, D. D. (1996). People say, you poor thing, and I'm thinking, I have four healthy kids. *Smithsonian, 27*(6), 30–39.

Jackson, J. S., Antonucci, T. C., & Gibson, R. C. (1990). Cultural, racial, and ethnic minority influences on aging. In J. E. Birren, & K. W. Schaie (Eds.), *Handbook of the psychology of aging* (3rd ed., pp. 103–123). San Diego: Academic Press.

Jackson, P. (1986). *The practice of teaching.* Chicago: University of Chicago Press.

Jackson, M. F., Barth, J. M., Powell, N., & Lochman, J. E. (2006). Classroom contextual effects of race on children's peer nominations. *Child Development, 77*(5), 1325–1337.

Jacob, B. A. (2002). Where the boys aren't: Non-cognitive skills, returns to school and the gender gap in higher education. *Economics of Education Review, 21*, 589–598.

Jacob, V., Chattopadhyay, S. K., Hopkins, D. P., Morgan, J. M., Pitan, A. A., Clymer, J. M., & Community Preventive Services Task Force. (2016). Increasing coverage of appropriate vaccinations: A community guide systematic economic review. *American Journal of Preventive Medicine, 50*(6), 797–808.

Jacobvitz, D. B., & Bush, N. F. (1996). Reconstructions of family relationships: Parent-child alliances, personal distress, and self-esteem. *Developmental Psychology, 32*, 732–743.

Jadack, R., Hyde, J., Moore, C., & Keller, M. (1995). Moral reasoning about sexually transmitted diseases. *Child Development, 66*, 167–177.

Jaffee, S. R., Bowes, L., Ouellet-Morin, I., Fisher, H. L., Moffitt, T. E., Merrick, M. T., & Arseneault, L. (2013). Safe, stable, nurturing relationships break the intergenerational cycle of abuse: A prospective nationally representative cohort of children in the United Kingdom. *Journal of Adolescent Health, 53*(4), S4–S10.

Jaffee, S. R., Caspi, A., Moffitt, T. E., Polo-Tomas, M., Price, T. S., & Taylor, A. (2004). The limits of child effects: Evidence for genetically mediated child effects on corporal punishment but not on physical maltreatment. *Developmental Psychology, 40*(6), 1047.

Jaggars, S. S., & Bailey, T. (2010). Effectiveness of fully online courses for college students: Response to a Department of Education meta-analysis. *Community College Research Center, Columbia University.*

Jain, A., Belsky, J., & Crnic, K. (1996). Beyond fathering behaviors: Types of dads. *Journal of Family Psychology, 10*, 431–442.

James, J., Ellis, B. J., Schlomer, G. L., & Garber, J. (2012). Sex-specific pathways to early puberty, sexual debut, and sexual risk taking: Tests of an integrated evolutionary–developmental model. *Developmental Psychology, 48*(3), 687–02.

James, T., & Countryman, J. (2012). Psychiatric effects of military deployment on children and families: The use of play therapy for assessment and treatment. *Innovations in Clinical Neuroscience, 9*(2), 16.

James, W. (1890). *The principles of psychology.* Boston: Henry Holt.

Jansson, U. B., Hanson, M., Sillén, U., & Hellström, A. L. (2005). Voiding pattern and acquisition of bladder control from birth to age 6 years—A longitudinal study. *Journal of Urology, 174*(1), 289–293.

Jeffries, S., & Konnert, C. (2002). Regret and psychological well-being among voluntarily and involuntarily childless women and mothers. *International Journal of Aging and Human Development, 54*(2), 89–106.

Jensen, L. A., & Arnett, J. J. (2012). Going global: New pathways for adolescents and emerging adults in a changing world. *Journal of Social Issues, 68*(3), 473–492.

Jetter, K. M., & Cassady, D. L. (2006). The availability and cost of healthier food alternatives. *American Journal of Preventive Medicine, 30*(1), 38–44.

Jimenez, R., Garcia, G., & Pearson, D. (1995). Three children, two languages, and strategic reading: Case studies in bilingual/monolingual reading. *American Educational Research Journal, 32*(1), 67–97.

Jin, M. K., Jacobvitz, D., Hazen, N., & Jung, S. H. (2012). Maternal sensitivity and infant attachment security in Korea: Cross-cultural validation of the Strange Situation. *Attachment & Human Development, 14*(1), 33–44.

Johnson, C. L. (1985). *Growing up and growing old in Italian-American families.* New Brunswick, NJ: Rutgers University Press.

Johnson, C. L., & Barer, B. M. (1990). Families and networks among older inner-city blacks. *The Gerontologist, 30*, 726–733.

Johnson, D., & Johnson, P. (1994). *Learning together and alone* (4th ed.). Boston: Allyn and Bacon.

Johnson, D. W., Johnson, R. T., & Maruyama, G. (1984). Goal interdependence and interpersonal attraction in heterogeneous classrooms: A meta-analysis. In N. Miller, & M. B. Brewer (Eds.), *Groups in contact: The psychology of desegregation.* New York, NY: Academic Press.

Johnson, F. B., Marciniak, R. A., & Guarente, L. (1998). Telomeres, the nucleolus and aging. *Current Opinion in Cell Biology, 10*(3), 332–338.

Johnson, F. L. (1996). Friendships among women: Closeness in dialogue. In J. T. Wood (Ed.), *Gendered relationships* (pp. 79–94). Mountain View, CA: Mayfield.

Johnson, M. (1995). Patriarchal terrorism and common couple violence: Two forms of violence against women. *Journal of Marriage and the Family, 57*, 283–295.

Johnson, M. J., Jackson, N. C., Arnette, J. K., & Koffman, S. D. (2005). Gay and lesbian perceptions of discrimination in retirement care facilities. *Journal of Homosexuality, 49*(2), 83–102.

Johnson, R. (Ed.). (1995). *African-American voices: African-American health educators speak out.* New York, NY: National League for Nursing.

Johnson, R., & Swain, M. (Eds.). (1997). *Immersion education: International perspectives.* New York, NY: Cambridge University Press.

Johnson, W. (2010). Understanding the genetics of intelligence: Can height help? Can corn oil? *Current Directions in Psychological Science, 19*, 177–182.

Johnston, L., O'Malley, P., & Bachman, J. (1992). *Drug use among American high school students, college students and other young adults: National trends through 1991.* Rockville, MD: National Institute on Drug Abuse.

Johnston, L. D., O'Malley, P. M., Bachman, J. G., Schulenberg, J. E. & Miech, R. A. (2014). *Monitoring the future—National survey results on drug use, 1975–2013: Volume I, Secondary school students.* Ann Arbor, MI: Institute for Social Research, The University of Michigan.

Johnston, L. D., O'Malley, P. M., Bachman, J. G., & Schulenberg, J. E. (2012). *Monitoring the future—National results on adolescent drug use: Overview of key findings, 2011.* Ann Arbor, MI: Institute for Social Research, The University of Michigan.

Jondrow, J., Brechling, F., & Marcu, A. (1987). Older workers in the market for part-time employment. In S. H. Sandell (Ed.), *The problem isn't age: Work and older Americans.* New York, NY: Praeger.

Jones, B. A., Kasl, S. V., Curnen, M. G., Owens, P. H., & Dubrow, R. (1995). Can mammography screening explain the race difference in stage at diagnosis of breast cancer? *Cancer, 75,* 2103–2113.

Jones, P. S., & Martinson, I. M. (1992). The experience of bereavement in caregivers of family members with Alzheimer's disease. *Image: Journal of Nursing Scholarship, 24*(3), 172–176.

Jordan, J. V., Kaplan, A. G., Miller, J. B., Stiver, I. P., & Surrey, J. L. (1991). *Women's growth in connection: Writings from the Stone Center.* New York, NY: Guilford.

Jose, P. E., & Bellamy, M. A. (2011). Relationships of parents' theories of intelligence with children's persistence/learned helplessness: A cross-cultural comparison. *Journal of Cross-Cultural Psychology,* 1–19

Joseph, K. S., Allen, A. C., Dodds, L., Turner, L. A., Scott, H., & Liston, R. (2005). The perinatal effects of delayed childbearing. *Obstetrics & Gynecology, 105,* 1410–1418.

Joshi, M., & MacLean, M. (1994). Indian and English children's understanding of the distinction between real and apparent emotion. *Child Development, 65,* 1372–1384.

Josselson, R. (1977). Adolescence in the life cycle. *Journal of Youth and Adolescence, 6*(1), 103–105.

Josselson, R. (1980). Ego development in adolescence. In J. Adelson (Ed.), *Handbook of adolescent psychology.* New York, NY: Wiley.

Josselson, R. (1996). *Revising herself: The story of women's identity from college to midlife.* New York, NY: Oxford University Press.

Joung, I. M. A., Stronks, K., van de Mheen, H., van Poppel, F. W. A., van der Meer, J. B. W., & Mackenbach, J. P. (1997). The contribution of intermediary factors to marital status differences in self-reported health. *Journal of Marriage and the Family, 59,* 476–490.

Julian, T. W., & McKenry, P. C. (1993). Mediators of male violence toward female intimates. *Journal of Family Violence, 8*(1), 39–56.

Junaid, K. A., & Fellowes, S. (2006). Gender differences in the attainment of motor skills on the movement assessment battery for children. *Physical & Occupational Therapy in Pediatrics, 26*(1–2), 5–11.

Jung, C. G. (1933). *Modern man in search of a soul* (W. S. Dell & C. F. Baynes, Trans.). New York, NY: Harcourt Brace Jovanovich.

K

Kaestle, C. E., & Halpern, C. T. (2005). Sexual activity among adolescents in romantic relationships with friends, acquaintances, or strangers. *Archives of Pediatrics & Adolescent Medicine. 159*(9), 849–853.

Kagan, J. (1998). *The Gale encyclopedia of childhood and adolescence: Puberty* (pp. 521–523). Detroit: Gale Research.

Kagan, J., Arcus, D., Snidman, N., Feng, W. Y., Handler, J., & Greene, S. (1995). Reactivity in infants: A cross-national comparison. *Developmental Psychology, 30,* 342–345.

Kagan, J., & Snidman, N. (1991). Temperamental factors in human development. *American Psychologist, 46,* 856–862.

Kagan, S. (1983). Children, families, and government: Preparing for the 21st century. In E. Zigler, S. Kagan, & E. Klugman (Eds.), *Children, families, and government* (p. 117–131). New York, NY: Cambridge University Press.

Kaijura, H., Cowart, B. J., & Beauchamp, G. K. (1992). Early developmental change in bitter taste responses in human infants. *Developmental Psychobiology, 25,* 375–386.

Kaitz, M., Meschulach-Sarfaty, O., Auerbach, J., & Eidelman, A. (1988). A re-examination of newborns' ability to imitate facial expressions. *Developmental Psychology, 24,* 3–7.

Kamsa-Ard, S., Promthet, S., Lewington, S., Burret, J. A., Sherliker, P., Kamsa-Ard, S., ... & Parkin, D. M. (2014). Alcohol consumption and mortality, The Kohn Kaen cohort study, Thailand. *Journal of Epidemiology, 24,* 154–160.

Kalish, R. A. (1985). *Death, grief, and caring relationships* (2nd ed.). Monterey, CA: Brooks/Cole.

Kalish, R. A., & Reynolds, D. K. (1981). *Death and ethnicity: A psychocultural study.* Farmingdale, NY: Baywood.

Kallman, D. A., Plato, C. C., & Tobin, J. D. (1990). The role of muscle loss in the age-related decline of grip strength: Cross-sectional and longitudinal perspectives. *Journal of Gerontology: Medical Sciences, 45,* M82–88.

Kalverboer, A., Hopkins, B., & Geuze, R. (1993). *Motor development in early infancy and late childhood.* New York, NY: Cambridge University Press.

Kamii, C. (1994). *Young children continue to reinvent arithmetic* (3rd ed.), New York, NY: Teachers College Press.

Kantor, G. K., & Straus, M. A. (1990). The "drunken bum" theory of wife beating. In M. A. Straus & R. J. Gelles, with C. Smith (Eds.), *Physical violence in American families: Risk factors and adaptations to violence in 8,145 families* (pp. 203–224). New Brunswick, NJ: Transaction.

Kao, G. (1995). Asian-Americans as model minorities? A look at their academic performance. *American Journal of Education, 103,* 121–159.

Kaplan, H. (1979). *Disorders of sexual desire.* New York, NY: Brunner/Mazel.

Kaplan, K., & Wadden, T. (1986). Childhood obesity and self-esteem. *Journal of Pediatrics, 109,* 367–370.

Kaplan, L. (1995). *No voice is ever wholly lost.* New York, NY: Simon & Schuster.

Kaplan, M. S., Adamek, M. E., & Johnson, S. (1994). Trends in firearm suicide among older American males: 1979–1988. *The Gerontologist, 34,* 59–65.

Karam, R. G., Breda, V., Picon, F. A., Rovaris, D. L., Victor, M. M., Salgado, C. A. I., ... & Caye, A. (2015). Persistence and remission of ADHD during adulthood: A 7-year clinical follow-up study. *Psychological Medicine, 45*(10), 2045–2056.

Kåreholt, I., Lennartsson, C., Gatz, M., & Parker, M. G. (2011). Baseline leisure time activity and cognition more than two decades later. *International Journal of Geriatric Psychiatry, 26,* 65–74.

Karoly, L. A. (2009). The future at work: Labor-market realities and the transition to adulthood. In I Schoon, & R. K. Silbersen (Eds.), *Transitions from school to work: Globalization, individualization, and patterns of diversity* (pp. 352–384). Cambridge, UK: Cambridge Books Online.

Karpov, Y. V., & Haywood, H. C. (1998). Two ways to elaborate Vygotsky's concept of mediation: Implications for instruction. *American Psychologist, 53,* 27–36.

Kashani, I. A., Langer, R. D., Criqui, M. H., Nader, P. R., Rupp, J., Sallis, J. F., & Houghton, R. (1991). Effects of parental behavior modification on children's cardiovascular risks. *Annals of the* New York, NY: *Academy of Sciences, 623,* 447–449.

Kastenbaum, R. (1985). Dying and death: A life-span approach. In J. E. Birren, & K. W. Schaie (Eds.), *Handbook of the psychology of aging* (2nd ed., pp. 619–643). New York, NY: Van Nostrand Reinhold.

Kastenbaum, R. (1992a). Death, suicide and the older adult. *Suicide and Life-Threatening Behavior, 22,* 1–14.

Kastenbaum, R. (1992b). *The psychology of death.* New York, NY: Springer-Verlag.

Kastenbaum, R., & Normand, C. (1990). Deathbed scenes imagined by the young and experienced by the old. *Death Studies, 14,* 201–217.

Kates, E. (1995). Escaping poverty: The promise of higher education. *Social Policy Report 9*(1). Ann Arbor, MI: Society for Research on Child Development.

Katzel, L. I., & Steinbrenner, G. M. (2012). Physical exercise and health. In S. Krauss Whitbourne, & M. J. Sliwinski (Eds.), *Adulthood and Aging* (pp. 97–117). Malden, MA: Blackwell Publishing.

Katz-Wise, S. L., Priess, H. A., & Hyde, J. S. (2010). Gender-role attitudes and behavior across the transition to parenthood. *Developmental Psychology, 46*(1), 18–28.

Kaufert, P. A., & McKinlay, S. M. (1985). Estrogen-replacement therapy: The production of medical knowledge and the emergence of policy. In E. Lewis, & V. Olesen (Eds.), *Women, health and healing: Toward a new perspective* (pp. 113–138). London: Tavistock.

Kaufman, G., & Elder, G. H. (2003). Grandparenting and age identity. *Journal of Aging Studies, 17,* 269–282.

Kaufman, J. M., & Vermeulen, A. (1997). Declining gonadal function in elderly men. *Baillieres Clinical Endocrinology & Metabolism, 11*(2), 289–309.

Kaufman, M. (2008). Adolescent sexual orientation. *Paediatrics & Child Health, 13*(7), 619–623.

Kavanaugh, R. D., & Engel, S. (1998). The development of pretense and narrative in early childhood. In O. Saracho, B. Spodek, et al. (Eds.), *Multiple perspectives on play in early childhood education.* SUNY series, *Early Childhood Education: Inquiries and Insights* (pp. 80–99). Albany, NY: State University of New York Press.

Kavanaugh, T., & Shephard, R. J. (1990). Can regular sports participation slow the aging process? *Physician and Sportsmedicine, 18,* 94–104.

Kawaguchi, D., & Miyazaki, J. (2009). Working mothers and sons' preferences regarding female labor supply: Direct evidence from stated preferences. *Journal of Population Economics, 22*(1), 115–130.

Kazdin, A. E. (1994). *Behavior modification in applied settings* (5th ed.), Pacific Grove, CA Brooks/Cole.

Keating, D. (2011). Cognitive and brain development. In R. Learner, & L. Steinberg (Eds.), *Handbook of adolescent psychology* (2nd ed.). New York, NY: Wiley.

Keating, D., & Sasse, D. (1996). Cognitive socialization in adolescence: Critical period for a critical habit of mind. In G. Adams, R. Montemayor, & T. Gullotta (Eds.), *Psychosocial development during adolescence* (pp. 232–258). Thousand Oaks, CA: Sage.

Keefe, J., & Walberg, H. (Eds.) (1992). *Teaching for thinking.* Reston, VA: National Association of Secondary School Principals.

Keesee, N. J., Currier, J. M., & Neimeyer, R. A. (2008). Predictors of grief following the death of one's child: The contribution of finding meaning. *Journal of Clinical Psychology, 64*(10), 1145–1163.

Kehl, K. A. (2006). Moving toward peace: An analysis of the concept of a good death. *American Journal of Hospice and Palliative Medicine, 23*(4), 277–286.

Keith, J., Fry, C. L., Glascock, A. P., Ikels, C., Dickerson-Putman, J., Harpending, H. C., & Draper, P. (1994). *The aging experience: Diversity and commonality across cultures.* Thousand Oaks, CA: Sage.

Keith, P. M. (1982). Perceptions of time remaining and distance from death. *Omega, 12,* 307–318.

Keith, P. M., & Schafer, R. B. (1991). *Relationships and well-being over the life stages.* New York, NY: Praeger.

Keller, J. W. (1985). Career changes: A logical phenomenon. *Journal of College Student Personnel, 26*(3), 249–251.

Keller, M., & Wood, P. (1989). Development of friendship reasoning: A study of interindividual differences and intraindividual change. *Developmental Psychology, 25,* 820–826.

Kellman, P. J., & Arterberry, M. E. (2006). Infant visual perception. In W. Damon, & R. M. Lerner (Eds.), *Handbook of child psychology: Vol. 2. Cognition, perception, and language* (6th ed.). Hoboken, NJ: Wiley.

Kelly, J. R. (Ed.) (1993). *Activity and aging.* Newbury Park, CA: Sage.

Kelly, J. R., Steinkamp, M. W., & Kelly, J. R. (1987). Later-life satisfaction: Does leisure contribute? *Leisure Sciences, 9,* 189–200.

Kelly, M. (2009). Women's voluntary childlessness: A radical rejection of motherhood? *WSQ: Women's Studies Quarterly, 37*(2), 157–172.

Kelly, M. P., Strassberg, D. S., & Kircher, J. R. (1990). Attitudinal and experiential correlates of anorgasmia. *Archives of Sexual Behavior, 19,* 165–177.

Kendall-Tackett, K. A., Williams, L. M., & Finkelhor, D. (1993). Impact of sexual abuse on children: A review and synthesis of recent empirical studies. *Psychological Bulletin, 113,* 164–180.

Kendig, H. L. (1990). Comparative perspectives on housing, aging, and social structure. In R. H. Binstock, & L. K. George (Eds.), *Handbook of aging and the social sciences* (3rd ed., pp. 288–306). San Diego: Academic Press.

Kendler, H., & Kendler, T. (1962). Vertical and horizontal processes in problem solving. *Psychological Review, 69,* 1–16.

Kenkel, W. F., & Gage, B. A. (1983). The restricted and gender-typed occupational aspirations of young women: Can they be modified? *Family Relations: Journal of Applied Family & Child Studies, 32*(1) 129–138.

Kenney, G., Alker, J., Anderson, N., McMorrow, S., Long, S., Wissoker, D., ... & Brooks, T. (2014). *A first look at children's health insurance coverage under the ACA in 2014.* Health Reform Monitoring Survey. Retrieved from http://hrms.urban.org/briefs/Childrens-Health-Insurance-Coverage-under-the-ACA-in-2014.html

Kenny, G. P., Yardley, J. E., Martineau, L., & Jay, O. (2008). Physical work capacity in older adults: Implications for the aging worker. *American Journal of Industrial Medicine, 51*(8), 610–625.

Kermoian, R., & Campos, J. (1988). Locomotor experience: A facilitator of spatial cognitive development. *Child Development, 59,* 908–917.

Kerns, K. A., & Brumariu, L. E. (2014). Is insecure parent–child attachment a risk factor for the development of anxiety in childhood or adolescence? *Child development perspectives, 8*(1), 12–17.

Kerpelman, J. L., Pittman, J. F., Saint-Eloi Cadely, H., Tuggle, F. J., Marinda Harrell-Levy, M. K., & Adler-Baeder, F. M. (2012). Identity and intimacy during adolescence: Connections among identity styles, romantic attachment and identity commitment. *Journal of Adolescence, 35,* 1427–1439.

Kerr, M., Lambert, W. W., & Bern, D. J. (1996). Life course sequel of childhood shyness in Sweden: Comparison with the United States. *Developmental Psychology, 32,* 1100–1105.

Kerr, M., Lambert, W. W., Stattin, H., & Klackenberg-Larsson, I. (1994). Stability of inhibition in a Swedish longitudinal sample. *Child Development, 65,* 138–146.

Kidder, T. (1993). *Old friends.* Boston: Houghton Mifflin.

Kiefer, C. W. (1987). Care of the aged in Japan. In E. Norbeck, & M. Lock (Eds.). *Health, illness, and medical care: Cultural and social dimensions* (pp. 89–109). Honolulu: University of Hawaii Press.

Kilty, K. M., & Behling, J. H. (1985). Predicting the retirement intentions and attitudes of professional workers, *journal of Gerontology, 40,* 219–227.

Kim, J. Y., McHale, S. M., Crouter, A. C., & Osgood, D. W. (2007). Longitudinal linkages between sibling relationships and adjustment from middle childhood through adolescence. *Developmental Psychology, 43*(4), 960.

Kim, S. K., & Jang, Y. (2010). The effect of children's temperament, parenting behavior and parenting stress on preschool children's prosocial behavior. *Korean Journal of Community Living Science, 21*(4), 605–618.

Kimlin, M. G., & Guo, Y. (2012). Assessing the impacts of lifetime sun exposure on skin damage and skin aging using a non-invasive method. *Science of the Total Environment, 425,* 35–41. doi: 10.1016/j.scitotenv.2012.02.080

Kimmel, D. C. (1988). Ageism, psychology, and public policy. *American Psychologist, 43,* 175–178.

Kimmel, D. C. (1992). The families of older gay men and lesbians. *Generations, 17*(3), 37–38.

Kindermarnn, T. (1993). Natural peer groups as contexts for individual development: The case of children's motivation in school. *Developmental Psychology, 29,* 979–977.

King, A. C., Taylor, C. B., & Haskell, W. L. (1993). Effects of differing intensities and formats of 12 months of exercise training on psychological outcomes in older adults. *Health Psychology, 12,* 292–300.

King, P., & Kitchener, K. (1994). *Developing reflective judgment.* San Francisco: Jossey-Bass.

King, P. M., & Kitchener, K. S. (2004). Reflective judgment: Theory and research on the development of epistemic assumptions through adulthood. *Educational Psychologist, 39*(1), 5–18.

King, P. M., & Kitchener, K. S. (2016). Cognitive development in the emerging adult: The emergence of complex cognitive skills. In J. J. Arnett (Ed.), *The Oxford handbook of emerging adulthood* (pp. 105–125). New York, NY: Oxford University Press.

King, V. (2006). The antecedents and consequences of adolescents' relationships with stepfathers and nonresident fathers. *Journal of Marriage and Family, 68*(4), 910–928.

King, V. (2007). When children have two mothers: Relationships with nonresident mothers, stepmothers, and fathers. *Journal of Marriage and Family, 69*(5), 1178–1193.

Kinsella, K., & Phillips, P. (2005). Global aging: The challenges of success. *Population Bulletin, 1.* Washington, DC: Population Reference Bureau.

Kinsey, A. C., Pomeroy, W. B., & Martin, C. E. (1948). *Sexual behavior in the human male.* Philadelphia: Saunders.

Kirby, D. (2007). *A matrix of risk and protective factors affecting teen sexual behavior, pregnancy, childbearing, and sexually transmitted diseases.* Retrieved from http://thenationalcampaign.org/resource/matrix-risk-and-protective-factors

Kirby, D., & Laris, B. A. (2009). Effective curriculum-based sex and STD/HIV education programs for adolescents. *Child Development Perspectives, 3*(1), 21–29.

Kirschner, D. (1997). The situated development of logic in infancy: A case study. In D. Kirschner, & J. Whitson (Eds.). *Situated cognition: Social, semiotic, and psychological perspectives* (pp. 83–96). Mahwah, NJ: Erlbaum.

Kirschner D., & Whitson, J. (Eds.) (1997). *Situated cognition: Social, semiotic, and psychological perspectives* Mahwah, NJ: Erlbaum.

Kirsh, S. J. (2006). Cartoon violence and aggression in youth. *Aggression and Violent Behavior, 11*(6), 547–557.

Kisilevsky, B. S., & Muir, D. W. (1984). Neonatal habituation and dishabituation to tactile stimulation during sleep. *Developmental Psychology, 20,* 367–373.

Kisilevsky, B. S., Muir, D. W., & Low, J. A. (1992). Maturation of human fetal responses to vibroacoustic stimulation. *Child Development, 63,* 1497–1508.

Kitchener, K. S., & King, P. M. (1990). The reflective judgment model: Ten years of research. In M. Common, C. Armon, L. Kohlberg, F. Richards, T. Grotzer, & J. Sinnott (Eds.), *Adult development: Models and methods in the study of adolescent and adult thought.* New York, NY: Praeger.

Kite, M. E., Deaux, K., & Haines, E. L. (2008). Gender stereotypes. In F. Denmark, & M. A. Pauldi (Eds.), *Psychology of women: A handbook of issues and theories* (pp. 205–236). Westport, CT: Greenwood Publishing Group.

Kitzinger, J. (1997). Who are you kidding? Children, power and the struggle against sexual abuse. In A. James, & A. Prout (Eds.), *Constructing and reconstructing childhood* (pp. 165–189). London, UK: Falmer.

Klahr, D. (1989). Information processing approaches. In R. Vasta (Ed.), *Annals of child development: Vol. 6. Six theories of child development* (pp. 133–187). Greenwich, CT: JAI Press.

Klahr, D., Triona, L. M., & Williams, C. (2007). Hands on what? The relative effectiveness of physical versus virtual materials in an engineering design project by middle school children. *Journal of Research in Science Teaching, 44*(1), 183–203.

Klappcr, J., Moss, S., Moss, M., & Rubinstein, R. L. (1994). The social context of grief among adult daughters who have lost a parent. *Journal of Aging Studies, 8*(1), 29–43.

Klassen, P. (1983/1984). Changes in personal orientation and critical thinking among adults returning to school through weekend college: An alternative evaluation. *Innovative Higher Education, 8,* 55–67.

Klein, H. (1995). Urban Appalachian children in northern schools: A study in diversity. *Young Children, 50*(3), 10–16.

Kleinsorge, C., & Covitz, L. M. (2012). Impact of divorce on children: Developmental considerations. *Pediatrics in Review, 33*(4), 147–155.

Kleitman, N., & Engelmann, T. G. (1953). Sleep characteristics of infants. *Journal of Applied Physiology, 6*(5), 269–282.

Kligman, A. M., Grove, G. L., & Balin, A. K. (1985). Aging of human skin. In C. E. Finch, & E. L. Schneider (Eds.), *Handbook of the biology of aging* (pp. 820–841). New York, NY: Van Nostrand Reinhold.

Klimes-Dougan, B., & Kistner, J. (1990). Physically abused preschoolers' responses to peers' distress. *Developmental Psychology, 26,* 599–602.

Klinnert, M. D., Emde, R. N., Butterfield, P., & Campos, J. J. (1986). Social referencing: The infant's use of emotional signals from a friendly adult with mother present. *Developmental Psychology, 22,* 427–432.

Knafo, A., & Schwartz, S. H. (2003). Parenting and adolescents' accuracy in perceiving parental values. *Child Development, 74*(2), 595–611.

Knox, G. W. (1991). *An introduction to gangs.* Berrien Springs, MI: Vande Vere.

Knutson, K. L., Van Cauter, E., Rathouz, P. J., Yan, L. L., Hulley, S. B. Liu, K., & Lauderdale, D. S. (2009). Association between sleep and blood pressure in midlife: The CARDIA sleep study. *Archives of Internal Medicine, 169,* 1055–1061.

Koball, H. L., Moiduddin, E., Henderson, J., Goesling, B., & Besculides, M. (2010). What do we know about the link between marriage and health? *Journal of Family Issues,* 1–22. doi: 10.1177/0192513x10365834

Koch, P. B. (1988). The relationship of first intercourse to later sexual functioning concerns of adolescents. *Journal of Adolescent Research, 3,* 345–362.

Kochanska, C., Casey, R. J., & Fukumoto, A. (1995). Toddlers' sensitivity to standard violations. *Child Development, 66,* 643–656.

Kochanska, G. (1992). Children's interpersonal influence with mothers and peers. *Developmental Psychology, 28,* 491–499.

Kochanska G. (1997). Mutually responsive orientation between mothers and their young children: Implications for early socialization. *Child Development, 68,* 94–112.

Kochanska, G., Coy, K. C., Tjebkes, T. L., & Husarek, S. J. (1998). Individual differences in emotionality in infancy. *Child Development, 64,* 375–390.

Kodner, D. L. (2006). Whole-system approaches to health and social care partnerships for the frail elderly: An exploration of North American models and lessons. *Health & Social Care in the Community, 14*(5), 384–390.

Koenig, H. G. (1995). Religion and health in later life. In M. A. Kinble, S. H. McFadden, J. W. Ellor, & J. J. Seeber (Eds.), *Aging, spirituality, and religion: A handbook* (pp. 9–29). Minneapolis: Fortress Press.

Koenig, H. G., & Blazer, D. G. (1992). Mood disorders and suicide. In J. E. Birren, R. B. Sloane, & G. D. Cohen (Eds.), *Handbook of mental health and aging* (2nd ed., pp. 379–407). San Diego: Academic Press.

Kogan, N. (1979). A study of age categorization. *Journal of Gerontology, 34,* 358–367.

Kogan, N. (1990). Personality and aging. In J. E. Birren, & K. W. Schaie (Eds.), *Handbook of the psychology of aging* (3rd ed., pp. 330–346). San Diego: Academic Press.

Kogan, N., & Mills, M. (1992). Gender influences on age cognitions and preferences: Sociocultural or sociobiological? *Psychology & Aging, 7,* 98–106.

Kohlberg, L. (1958). *The development of modes of thinking and choices in years 10 to 16.* (Doctoral Dissertation), University of Chicago, Chicago, IL.

Kohlberg, L. (1963). The development of children's orientations toward a moral order: I. Sequence in the development of moral thought. *Vita Humana, 6,* 11–33.

Kohlberg, L., & Hersh, R. H. (1977). Moral development: A review of the theory. *Theory Into Practice, 16,* 53–61.

Kohlberg, L., Levine, C., & Hewer, A. (1983). *Moral stages: A current formulation and a response to critics.* New York, NY: Karger.

Kohler, P. K., Manhart, L. E., & Lafferty, W. E. (2008). Abstinence-only and comprehensive sex education and the initiation of sexual activity and teen pregnancy. *Journal of Adolescent Health, 42*(4), 344–351.

Kohn, M. L. (1969). *Class and conformity: A study in values,* Homewood, IL: Dorsey Press.

Kohn, M. L., Slomczynski, K. M., & Schoenbach, C. (1986). Social stratification and the transmission of values in the family: A cross-national assessment. *Sociological Forum, 1,* 73–102.

Kokko, K., Pulkkinen, L., & Mesiäinen, P. (2009). Timing of parenthood in relation to other life transitions and adult social functioning. *International Journal of Behavioral Development,* 1–10.

Kolak, A. M., & Volling, B. L. (2010). Sibling jealousy in early childhood: Longitudinal links to sibling relationship quality. *Infant and Child Development, 20,* 213–226.

Kooij, D. T., De Lange, A. H., Jansen, P. G., Kanfer, R., & Dikkers, J. S. (2011). Age and work-related motives: Results of a meta-analysis. *Journal of Organizational Behavior, 32,* 197–225.

Kooij, D., & Van De Voorde, K. (2011). How changes in subjective general health predict future time perspective, and development and generativity motives over the lifespan. *Journal of Occupational and Organizational Psychology, 84*(2), 228–247.

Kool, R., & Lawver, T. (2010). Play therapy: Considerations and applications for the practitioner. *Psychiatry, 7*(10), 19–24.

Kopp, C. (1982). Antecedents of self-regulation: A developmental perspective. *Developmental Psychology, 18,* 199–214.

Kopp, C. (1989). Regulation of distress and negative emotions: A developmental view. *Developmental Psychology, 25,* 343–354.

Koralek, D., Colker, L., & Dodge, D. (1993). *The what, why, and how of high-quality early childhood education: A guide for on-site supervision.* Washington, DC: National Association for the Education of Young Children.

Korbin, J. E. (Ed.). (1981). *Child abuse and neglect: Cross-cultural perspectives.* Berkeley, CA: University of California Press.

Korbin, J. E. (1987). Child abuse and neglect: The cultural context. In R. E. Heifer & R. S. Kemp (Eds.), *The battered child* (4th ed.). Chicago: University of Chicago Press.

Korbin, J. E. (1991). Cross-cultural perspectives and research dilutions for the 21st century. *Child Abuse and Neglect, 15,* 67–77.

Kordi, A., & Baharudin, R. (2010). Parenting attitude and style and its effect on children's school achievements. *International Journal of Psychological Studies, 2*(2), 217.

Koretz, D. (2008). The pending reauthorization of NCLB: An opportunity to rethink the basic strategy. In G. L. Sunderman (Ed.), *Holding NCLB accountable: Achieving accountability, equity, and school reform.* Thousand Oaks, CA: Corwin Press.

Korman, A. K. (1988). Career success and personal failure: Mid-to late-career feelings and events. In M. London & E. M. Mone (Eds.), *Career growth and human resource strategy* (pp. 81–94). New York, NY: Quorum.

Koropeckyj-Cox, T., Pienta, A. M., & Brown, T. H. (2007). Women of the 1950s and the "Normative" life course: The implications of childlessness, fertility timing, and marital status for psychological well-being in late midlife. *International Journal of Aging and Human Development, 64,* 299–330.

Korte, J., Bohlmeijer, E. T., Westerhof, G. J., & Pot, A. M. (2011). Reminiscence and adaptation to critical life events in older adults with mild to moderate depressive symptoms. *Aging and Mental Health, 15,* 638–646.

Kosciw, J. G., Greytak, E. A., Diaz, E. M., & Bartkiewicz, M. J. (2010). *The 2009 National School Climate Survey: The experiences of lesbian, gay, bisexual and transgender youth in our nation's schools.* New York, NY: Gay, Lesbian Straight Education Network.

Koss, M. P., Heise, L., & Russo, N. F. (1994). The global health burden of rape. *Psychology of Women Quarterly, 18,* 509–537.

Kotchen, T. A., & McCarron, D. A. (1998). Dietary electrolytes and blood pressure: A statement for healthcare professionals from the American Heart Association Nutrition Committee. *Circulation, 98,* 613–617.

Kotelchuck, M. (1976). The infant's relationship to the father: Experimental evidence. In M. E. Lamb (Ed.), *The role of the father in child development,* New York, NY: Wiley.

Kotloff, L. (1993). Fostering cooperative group spirit and individuality: Examples from a Japanese preschool. *Young Children, 48*(3), 17–24.

Kovacs, D. M., Parker, J. G., & Hoffman, L. W. (1996). Behavioral, affective and social correlates of involvement in cross-sex friendships in elementary school. *Child Development, 67,* 2269–2286.

Kozlowski, L. T., Wilkinson, D. A., Skinner, W., Kent, C., Franklin, T., & Pope, M. (1989). Comparing tobacco cigarette dependence with other drug dependencies: Greater or equal "difficulty quitting" and "urges to use," but less "pleasure" from cigarettes. *Journal of the American Medical Association, 261,* 898–901.

Kozol, J. (1991). *Savage inequalities: Children in America's schools,* New York, NY: Crown.

Kozol, J. (1995). *Amazing grace: The lives of children and the conscience of the nation,* New York, NY: Crown.

Kramer, D. A. (1989). Development of an awareness of contradiction across the life span and the question of post formal operations. In M. L. Commons, J. D. Sinnott, F. A. Richards, & C. Armon (Eds.), *Adult development: Vol. 1. Comparisons and applications of developmental models* (pp. 133–159). New York, NY: Praeger.

Krans, E. E., & Davis, M. M. (2014). Strong start for mothers and newborns: Implications for prenatal care delivery. *Current Opinion in Obstetrics & Gynecology, 26*(6), 511–515.

Krause, N. (1991). Stress, religiosity, and abstinence from alcohol. *Psychology and Aging, 6,* 134–144.

Kreider, R. M., & Ellis, R. (2001). *Number, timing, and duration of marriages and divorces: 2009.* US Census Bureau. Retrieved from http://www.census.gov/prod/2011pubs/p70-125.pdf

Kreider, R. M., & Ellis, R. (2011). Living arrangements of children: 2009. *Current population reports* (pp. 70–126). Washington, DC: U.S. Census Bureau.

Krieger, N., Waterman, P. D., Hartman, C., Bates, L. M., Stoddard, A. M., Quinn, M. M., ... & Barbeau, E. M. (2006). Social hazards on the job: Workplace abuse, sexual harassment, and racial discrimination—A study of black, Latino, and white low-income women and men workers in the United States. *International Journal of Health Services, 36*(1), 51–85.

Kristofferzon, M. L., Lindqvist, R., & Nilsson, A. (2010). Relationships between coping, coping resources, and quality of life in patients with chronic illness: A pilot study. *Scandinavian Journal of Caring Sciences, 25,* 476–483.

Kroeger, R. A., & Smock, P. J. (2014). Cohabitation: Recent research and implications. In J. Treas, J. Scott, & M. Richards (Eds.), *The Wiley-Blackwell companion to the sociology of families* (pp. 217–235). Hoboken, NJ: Wiley.

Kroger, J. (1995). The differentiation of "firm" and "developmental" foreclosure identity statuses: A longitudinal study. *Journal of Adolescent Research, 10,* 317–337.

Kroger, J. (2007). *Identity development: Adolescence through adulthood.* Thousand Oaks: Sage Publications.

Kroger, J., & Green, K. E. (1996). Events associated with identity status change. *Journal of Adolescence, 19*(5), 477–491.

Kroger, J., & Marcia, J. E. (2011). The identity statuses: Origins, meanings, and interpretations. In S. J., Schwartz, K., Luyczk, & V. L. Vignoles (Eds.), *Handbook of identity theory and research.* New York, NY: Springer.

Krueger, J., & Heckhausen, J. (1993). Personality development across the adult life span: Subjective conceptions vs. cross-sectional contrasts. *Journal of Gerontology, 48,* 100–108.

Kübler-Ross, E. (1969). *On death and dying,* New York, NY: Macmillan.

Kübler-Ross, E. (1981). *Living with dying,* New York, NY: Macmillan.

Kuczynski, L., & Kochanska, G. (1995). Function and content of maternal demands: Developmental significance of early demands for competent action. *Child Development, 66,* 616–628.

Kuhn, D. (2008). Formal operations from a twenty-first century perspective. *Human Development, 51 (Special Issue: Celebrating a Legacy of Theory with New Directions for Research on Human Development),* 48–55.

Kuhn, D. (2009). Adolescent thinking. In R. M. Lerner & L. Steinberg (Eds.), *Handbook of adolescent psychology, Vol. 1: Individual bases of adolescent development* (3rd ed., pp. 152–186). Hoboken, NJ: Wiley.

Kulkarni, A. D., Jamieson, D. J., Jones Jr, H. W., Kissin, D. M., Gallo, M. F., Macaluso, M., & Adashi, E. Y. (2013). Fertility treatments and multiple births in the United States. *New England Journal of Medicine, 369*(23), 2218–2225.

Kunitz, S. J., & Levy, J. E. (1989). Aging and health among Navajo Indians. In K. S. Markides (Ed.), *Aging and health: Perspectives on gender, race, ethnicity and class* (pp. 211–245). Newbury Park, CA: Sage.

Kunitz, S. J., & Levy, J. E. (1994). *Drinking careers: A twenty-five year study of three Navajo populations,* New Haven, CT: Yale University Press.

Kurdek, L. A. (1991). The relations between reported well-being and divorce history, availability of a proximate adult, and gender. *Journal of Marriage and the Family, 53,* 71–78.

Kurdek, L. A. (1994). The nature and correlates of relationship quality in gay, lesbian, and heterosexual cohabiting couples: A test of the individual difference, interdependence, and discrepancy models. In B. Greene & G. M. Herek (Eds.), *Lesbian and gay psychology: Theory, research, and clinical applications* (pp. 133–155). Thousand Oaks, CA: Sage.

Kurdek, L. A. (2005). What do we know about gay and lesbian couples? *Current Direction in Psychological Science, 14,* 251–254. doi: 10.1111/j.0963-7214.2005.00375.x

Kushi, L. H., Fee, R. M., Folsom, A. R., Mink, P. J., Anderson, K. E., & Sellers, T. A. (1997). Physical activity and mortality in postmenopausal women. *Journal of the American Medical Association, 277,* 1287–1292.

Kushi, L. H., Lenart, E. B., & Willett, W. C. (1995). Health implications of Mediterranean diets in light of contemporary knowledge: 2. Meat, wine, fats, and oils. *American Journal of Clinical Nutrition, 61*(SUPPL. 6), 1416S–1427S.

Kutner, L. (1989, March 16). Parent and child: Responding to aggressive behavior. *New York Times,* p. C–1.

Kuyper, L., & Fokkema, T. (2010). Loneliness among older lesbian, gay, and bisexual adults: The role of minority stress. *Archives of Sexual Behavior, 39,* 1171–1180.

Kwak, M., Ingersoll-Dayton, B., & Kim, J. (2012). Family conflict from the perspective of adult child caregivers: The influence of gender. *Journal of Social and Personal Relationships, 29,* 470–487.

Kyoko, T., Melby, M. K., Kronenberg, F., Kurzer, M. S., & Messina, M. (2012). Extracted or synthesized soybean isoflavones reduce menopausal hot flash frequency and severity: Systematic review and meta-analysis of randomized controlled trials. *Menopause, 19,* 776–790. doi: 10.1097/gme.0b013e3182410159

L

Labouvie-Vief, G. (1985). Intelligence and cognition. In J. E. Birren & K. W. Schaie (Eds.), *Handbook of the psychology of aging* (2nd ed., pp. 500–539). New York, NY: Van Nostrand Reinhold.

Labouvie-Vief, G. (1992). A neo-Piagetian perspective on adult cognitive development. In R. J. Sternberg & C. A. Berg (Eds.), *Intellectual development,* New York, NY: Cambridge University Press.

Labouvie-Vief, G., & Hakim-Larson, J. (1989). Developmental shifts in adult thought. In S. Hunter & M. Sundel (Eds.), *Midlife myths* (pp. 69–96). Newbury Park, CA: Sage.

Lachman, M. E. (2004). Development in midlife. *Annual Review of Psychology, 55,* 305–331.

Lachman, M. E., & Agrigoroaei, S. (2011). Promoting functional health in midlife and old age: Long-term effects of control beliefs, social support, and physical exercise. *PloS ONE, 5,* e13297. doi: 10.1371/journal.pone.0013297

Lackey, C., & Williams, K. R. (1995). Social bonding and the cessation of partner violence across generations. *Journal of Marriage and the Family, 57,* 295–305.

LaCroix, A. Z., & Haynes, S. G. (1987). Gender differences in health effects of workplace. In R. C. Barnett, L. Biener, & G. K. Baruch (Eds.), *Gender and stress* (pp. 96–121). New York, NY: The Free Press.

Ladd, G. W., & Hart, C. H. (1992). Creating informal play opportunities: Are parents' and preschoolers' initiations related to children's competence with peers? *Developmental Psychology, 28,* 1179–1187.

Lakatta, E. G. (1990). Heart and circulation. In E. L. Schneider & J. W. Rowe (Eds.), *Handbook of the biology of aging* (3rd ed., pp. 181–216). San Diego: Academic Press.

Lakoff, G. (1994). What is a conceptual system? In W. Overton & D. Palermo (Eds.), *The nature and ontogenesis of meaning* (pp. 41–90). Hillsdale, NJ: Erlbaum.

La Leche League International. (1991). *The womanly art of breastfeeding* (5th ed.), New York, NY: Plume Books.

Lamaze, F. (1970). *Painless childbirth: Psychoprophylactic method.* Chicago: Henry Regnery.

Lamb, M. (1977a). The development of mother-infant and father-infant attachments in the second year of life. *Developmental Psychology, 13,* 637–648.

Lamb, M. (1977b). Father-infant and mother-infant interactions in the first year of life. *Child Development, 48,* 167–181.

Lamb, M., & Roopnarine, J. (1979). Peer influences on sex-role development in preschoolers. *Child Development, 50,* 1219–1222.

Lamb, M. E. (1997). The development of father-infant relationships. In Michael E. Lamb (Ed.), *The role of the father in child development* (3rd ed., pp. 104–120). New York, NY: Wiley.

Lamb, M. E., Keterlinus, R. D., & Fracasso, M. P. (1992). Parent-child relationships. In M. H. Bornstein & M. E. Lamb (Eds.), *Developmental psychology: An advanced textbook* (pp. 465–518). Hillsdale, NJ: Erlbaum.

Lamb, M. E., & Lewis, C. (2003). Fathers' influences on children's development: The evidence from two-parent families. *European Journal of Psychology of Education, 18,* 211–228.

Lamborn, S. D., Dornbusch, S. M., & Steinberg, L. (1996). Ethnicity and community context as moderators of the relations between family decision making and adolescent adjustment. *Child Development, 67,* 383–301.

Lamke, L. K. (1982a). Adjustment and sex-role orientation. *Journal of Youth and Adolescence, 11,* 247–259.

Lamke, L. K. (1982b). The impact of sex-role orientation on self-esteem in early adolescence. *Child Development, 53,* 1530–1535.

Lamport, M. A. (1993). Student-faculty informal interaction and the effect on college student outcomes: A review of the literature. *Adolescence, 28*(112), 971–990.

Langer, N. (1995). Grandparents and adult grandchildren: What do they do for one another? In J. Hendricks (Ed.), *The ties of later life* (pp. 171–179). Amityville, NY: Baywood.

Lansford, J. E. (2009). Parental Divorce and Children's Adjustment. *Perspectives on Psychological Science, 4*(2), 140–152.

Lanz, M., & Tagliabue, S. (2007). Do I really need someone in order to become an adult? Romantic relationships during emerging adulthood in Italy. *Journal of Adolescent Research, 22*(5), 531–549.

Lapsley, D. (1991). Egocentrism theory and the "new look" at the imaginary audience and personal fable. In R. Lerner, A. Petersen, & J. Brooks-Gunn (Eds.), *Encyclopedia of adolescence: Vol 1* (pp. 281–286). New York, NY: Garland.

LaRossa, R. (1992). Fatherhood and social change. In M. S. Kimmel & M. A. Messner (Eds.), *Men's lives* (2nd ed., pp. 521–535). New York, NY: Macmillan.

Larrabee, M. (1993). *An ethic of care: Feminist and Interdisciplinary perspectives.* New York, NY: Routledge.

Larson, R. W., & Ham, M. (1993). Stress and "storm and stress" in early adolescence: The relationship of negative events with dysphoric affect. *Developmental Psychology, 29,* 130–140.

Larson, R. W., & Richards, M. H. (1994). *Divergent realities: The emotional lives of mothers, fathers and adolescents.* New York, NY: Basic Books.

Larson, R. W. (1997). The emergence of solitude as a constructive domain of experience in early adolescence. *Child Development, 68,* 80–93.

Larson, R. W., & Richards, M. H. (1994). *Emergent Realities.* New York, NY: Basic Books.

Larson, R. W., Richards, M. H., Moneta, G., Holmbeck, G., & Duckett, E. (1996). Changes in adolescents' daily interaction with their families from ages 10–18: Disengagement and transformation. *Developmental Psychology, 32,* 744–54.

Larson, R., Zuzanek, J., & Mannell, R. (1985). Being alone versus being with people: Disengagement in the daily experience of older adults. *Journal of Gerontology, 40,* 375–381.

LaRue, A., Dessonville, C., & Jarvik, L. F. (1985). Aging and mental disorders. In J. E. Birren & K. W. Schaie (Eds.), *Handbook of the psychology of aging* (2nd ed., pp. 664–702). New York, NY: Van Nostrand Reinhold.

Larzelere, R. E. (1986). Moderate spanking: Model or deterrent of children's aggression in the family? *Journal of Family Violence, 1,* 27–37.

Lasley, J. R. (1992). Age, social context, and street gang membership. *Youth and Society, 23,* 434–451.

Latack, J. C., & Kaufman, H. G. (1988). Termination and outplacement strategies. In M. London & E. M. Mone (Eds.), *Career growth and human resource strategies* (pp. 289–313). New York, NY: Quorum Books.

Lauer, R. H., Lauer, J. C., & Kerr, S. T. (1995). The long-term marriage: Perceptions of stability and satisfaction. In J. Hendricks (Ed.), *The ties of later life* (pp. 35–41). Amityville, NY: Baywood.

Laughlin, L. (2013). Who's minding the kids? Child care arrangements: Spring 2011. *Current population reports* (pp. 70–135). Washington, DC: U.S. Census Bureau.

Lave, J. (1997). The culture of acquisition and the practice of understanding. In D. Kirschner & J. Whitson (Eds.), *Situated cognition: Social, semiotic, and psychological perspectives* (pp. 17–36). Mahwah, NJ: Erlbaum.

Lavner, J. A., & Bradbury, T. N. (2010). Patterns of change in marital satisfaction over the newlywed years. *Journal of Marriage and Family, 72*(5), 1171–1187.

Lawrence, E., Jeglic, E. L., Matthews, L. T., & Pepper, C. M. (2006). Gender differences in grief reactions following the death of a parent. *OMEGA—Journal of Death and Dying, 52,* 323–337.

Lawrence, E., Rothman, A. D., Cobb, R. J., Rothman, M. T., & Bradbury, T. N. (2008). Marital satisfaction across the transition to parenthood. *Journal of Family Psychology, 22*(1), 41.

Lawson, A., & Rhode, D. L. (1993). *The Politics of Pregnancy: Adolescent Sexuality and Public Policy,* New Haven, CT: Yale University Press.

Lawson A. E., & Wollman, W. T. (2003). Encouraging the transition from concrete to formal operations. An experiment. *Journal of Research in Science Teaching, 40*(Supplemental), S33–S50.

Lawton, M. P. (1985). Activities and leisure. In M. P. Lawton & G. L. Maddox (Eds.), *Annual Review of Gerontology and Geriatrics,* Volume 5, 127–164. New York, NY: Springer.

Laybourn, A. (1990). Only children in Britain: Popular stereotype and research evidence. *Children and Society, 4,* 386–400.

Lazarus, R. S. (1993). From psychological stress to the emotions: A history of changing outlooks. *Annual Review of Psychology, 44,* 1–21.

Leadbetter, B. (1991). Relativistic thinking in adolescence. In R. Lerner, A. Petersen, & J. Brooks-Gunn (Eds.), *Encyclopedia of adolescence: Vol. 1* (pp. 921–925). New York, NY: Garland.

Leaper, C. (Ed.). (1994). *Childhood gender segregation: Causes and consequences* (pp. 7–18). San Francisco: Jossey-Bass.

Leaper, C., Anderson, K. J., & Sanders, P. (1998). Moderators of gender effects on parents' talk to their children: A meta-analysis. *Developmental Psychology, 34,* 3–27.

Leary, W. E. (1995, January 31). Sickle cell trial called success, halted early. *The New York Times,* p. C–1.

Leckman, J., & Mayes, L. C. (1998). Understanding developmental psychopathology: How useful are evolutionary concepts? *Journal of the American Academy of Child and Adolescent Psychiatry, 37,* 1011–1021.

Lee, C. (1992). Gender-related motivational differences in participation in an organized seniors fitness program: Moving beyond sex-role stereotypic motives. *Psychological Reports, 71,* 1085–1086.

Lee, C. Y. S., & Doherty, W. J. (2007). Marital satisfaction and father involvement during the transition to parenthood. *Fathering, 5*(2), 75.

Lee, D. J., & Markides, K. S. (1990). Activity and mortality among aged persons over an eight-year period. *Journal of Gerontology, 45,* S39–42.

Lee, F. R. (1995, May 9). For women with AIDS, anguish of having babies. *The New York Times,* pp. A1–B6.

Lee, G. R., Peek, C. W., & Coward, R. T. (1998). Race differences in filial responsibility expectations among older parents. *Journal of Marriage and the Family, 60,* 404–412.

Lee, J. S., & Bowen, N. K. (2006). Parent involvement, cultural capital, and the achievement gap among elementary school children. *American Educational Research Journal, 43*(2), 193–218.

Lee, S. H., & Im, E. O. (2010). Ethnic differences in exercise and leisure time physical activity among midlife women. *Journal of Advanced Nursing, 66,* 814–827.

Lee, S. J., Bartolic, S., & Vandewater, E. A. (2009). Predicting children's media use in the USA: Differences in cross-sectional and longitudinal analysis. *British Journal of Developmental Psychology, 27*(1), 123–143.

Lee, T. S., Goh, S. J. A., Quek, S. Y., Phillips, R., Guan, C., Cheung, Y. B., ... & Krishnan, K. R. R. (2013). A brain-computer interface based cognitive training system for healthy elderly: A randomized control pilot study for usability and preliminary efficacy. *PLoS ONE, 8,* e79419.

Lee, V. E., Mackie-Lewis, C., & Marks, H. M. (1993). Persistence to the baccalaureate degree for students who transfer from community college. *American Journal of Education, 102*(1), 80–114.

Lee, V., Croninger, R., Linn, E., & Chen, X. (1996). The culture of sexual harassment in secondary schools. *American Educational Research Journal, 33*(2), 383–418.

Lee, Y. J., & Aytac, I. A. (1998). Intergenerational financial support among whites, African Americans, and Latinos. *Journal of Marriage and the Family, 60,* 426–441.

Leeies, M., Pagura, J., Sareen, J., & Bolton, J. M. (2010). The use of alcohol and drugs to self-medicate symptoms of posttraumatic stress disorder. *Depression and Anxiety, 27*(8), 731–736.

Lehman, D. R., & Nisbett, R. E. (1990). A longitudinal study of the effects of undergraduate training on reasoning. *Developmental Psychology, 26,* 952–960.

Leidy, M. S., Guerra, N. G., & Toro, R. I. (2012). Positive parenting, family cohesion, and child social competence among immigrant Latino families. *Journal of Latina/o Psychology, 1,* 3–13.

Leigh, B. C. (1989). Reasons for having sex: Gender, sexual orientation, and relationship to sexual behavior. *Journal of Sex Research, 26,* 199–209.

Leigh, B. C., & Stall, R. (1993). Substance use and risky sexual behavior for exposure to HIV: Issues of methodology, interpretation, and prevention. *American Psychologist, 10,* 1035–1045.

Leming, M. R., & Dickinson, G. E. (1994). *Dying, death, and bereavement* (3rd ed.). New York, NY: Holt, Rinehart & Winston.

Lentz, E., & Allen, T. D. (2009). The role of mentoring others in the career plateauing phenomenon. *Group & Organization Management, 34,* 358–384. doi: 10.1177/1059601109334027

Leon, A. S. (1983). Exercise and coronary heart disease. *Hospital Medicine, 19,* 38–59.

Leon, A. S., & Fox, S. M., III. (1981). Physical fitness. In E. L. Wynder (Ed.), *The book of health* (pp. 283–341). New York, NY: Franklin Watts.

Leonard, L. G., & Denton, J. (2006). Preparation for parenting multiple birth children. *Early Human Development, 82*(6), 371–378.

Leor, J., Poole, W. K., & Kloner, R. A. (1996). Sudden cardiac death triggered by an earthquake. *New England Journal of Medicine, 334,* 413–419.

Lepage, J. F., & Théoret, H. (2007). The mirror neuron system: Grasping others' actions from birth? *Developmental Science, 10,* 513–524.

LePort, A. K., Mattfeld, A. T., Dickinson-Anson, H., Fallon, J. H., Stark, C. E., Kruggel, F., ... & McGaugh, J. L. (2012). Behavioral and neuroanatomical investigation of highly superior autobiographical memory (HSAM). *Neurobiology of Learning and Memory, 98*(1), 78–92.

Lerner, J. (1993). *Learning disabilities* (6th ed.). Boston: Houghton Mifflin.

Lerner, R. M. (1996). Relative plasticity, integration, temporality, and diversity in human development: A developmental contextual perspective about theory, process, and method. *Developmental Psychology, 32,* 781–786.

Letourneau, N., Watson, B., Duffett-Leger, L., Hegadoren, K., & Tryphonopoulos, P. (2011). Cortisol patterns of depressed mothers and their infants are related to maternal-infant interactive behaviours. *Journal of Reproductive and Infant Psychology, 29,* 439–459.

LeVay, S., & Hamer, D. H. (1994, May). Evidence for a biological influence in male homosexuality. *Scientific American,* 44–49.

Levene, I., & Parker, M. (2011). Prevalence of depression in granted and refused requests for euthanasia and assisted suicide: A systematic review. *Journal of Medical Ethics, 37*(4), 205–211.

Levenson, R. W., Carstensen, L. L., & Gottman, J. M. (1993). Long-term marriage: Age, gender, and satisfaction. *Psychology and Aging, 8,* 301–313.

Levine, G., & Parkinson, S. (1994). *Experimental methods in psychology.* Hillsdale, NJ: Erlbaum.

LeVine, R. (1994). *Child care and culture: Lessons from Africa,* New York, NY: Cambridge University Press.

Levinson, D. J. (1978). *The seasons of a man's life,* New York, NY: Knopf.

Levinson, D. J. (1986). A conception of adult development. *American Psychologist, 41,* 1–13.

Levinson, D. J. (1996). *The seasons of a woman's life,* New York, NY: Knopf.

Levitt, M. J., Guacci-Franco, N., & Levitt, J. L. (1993). Convoys of social support in childhood and early adolescence: Structure and function. *Developmental Psychology, 29,* 811–818.

Levitt, M. J., Weber, R. A., & Guacci, N. (1993). Convoys of social support: An intergenerational analysis. *Psychology & Aging, 8*(3), 323–326.

Levy, B. R., Slade, M. D., Kunkel, S. R., & Stanislav, K. V. (2002). Longevity increased by positive self-perceptions of aging. *Journal of Personality and Social Psychology, 83,* 261–270. doi: 10.1037/0022-3514.83.2.261

Levy-Shiff, R. (1994). Individual and contextual correlates of marital change across the transition to parenthood. *Developmental Psychology, 30,* 591–601.

Lewis, C. T. (1993). Prenatal care in the United States. In B. K. Rothman (Ed.), *The encyclopedia of childbearing,* New York, NY: Henry Holt.

Lewis, J. M. (1993). Childhood play in normality, pathology and therapy. *American Journal of Orthopsychiatry, 63,* 6–15.

Lewis, M. (1992). *Shame: The exposed self,* New York, NY: The Free Press.

Lewis, M., & Brooks-Gunn, J. (1979a). *Social cognition and the acquisition of self,* New York, NY: Plenum Press.

Lewis, M., & Brooks-Gunn, J. (1979b). Toward a theory of social cognition: The development of the self. In I. Uzgiris (Ed.), *Social interaction and communication during infancy.* San Francisco: Jossey-Bass.

Lewis, M., Brooks-Gunn, J., & Jaskir, J. (1985). Individual differences in visual self-recognition as a function of mother-infant attachment relationship. *Developmental Psychology, 21,* 1181–1187.

Liao, W., Li, C., Lin, Y., Wang, C., Chen, Y., Yen, C., ... & Lee, M. (2011). Healthy behaviors and onset of functional disability in older adults: Results of a national longitudinal study. *Journal of the American Geriatric Society, 59,* 200–206.

Lichten, E. (2003). Children and the death of a parent. In C. D. Bryant (Ed.), *Handbook of death and dying* (Vol. 2, pp. 871–879). Thousand Oaks, CA: Sage Publications.

Liebmann-Smith, J. (1993). Infertility: Overview. In B. K Rothman (Ed.), *The encyclopedia of childbearing.* New York, NY: Henry Holt.

Lickona, T. (1991). Moral development in the elementary school classroom. In W. Kurtines & J. Gewirtz (Eds.), *Handbook of moral behavior and development: Vol. 3* (pp. 143–162). Hillsdale. NJ: Erlbaum.

Lieberman, M. A. (1993). Bereavement self-help groups: A review of conceptual and methodological issues In M. S. Stroebe, W. Stroebe, & R. O. Hansson (Eds.), *Handbook of bereavement: Theory, research, and intervention* (pp. 411–426). Cambridge, UK: Cambridge University Press.

Liebert, R. M., & Sprafkin, J. (1988). *The early window: Effects of television on children and youth* (3rd ed.). New York, NY: Pergamon Press.

Liem, D. G., & Mennella, J. A. (2002). Sweet and sour preferences during childhood: Role of early experiences. *Developmental Psychology, 41,* 388–395.

Liem, R., & Liem, J. H. (1988). Psychological effects of unemployment on workers and their families. *Journal of Social Issues, 44,* 87–105.

Lightfoot, C. (1997). *The culture of adolescent risk-taking.* New York, NY: Guilford Press.

Lightfoot, S. L. (1983). *The good high school: Portraits of character and culture.* New York, NY: Basic Books.

Lillard, A. S. (2012). Preschool children's development in classic Montessori, supplemented Montessori, and conventional programs. *Journal of School Psychology, 50*(3), 379–401.

Lillard, A. S., & Peterson, J. (2011). The immediate impact of different types of television on young children's executive function. *Pediatrics, 128*(4), 644–649.

Lin, F. R., Thorpe, R., Gordon-Salant, S., & Ferrucci, L. (2011). Hearing loss prevalence and risk factors among older adults in the United States. *Journal of Gerontology, 66A,* 582–590. doi: 10.1093/gerona/glr002

Lin, I. F. (2008). Consequences of parental divorce for adult children's support of their frail parents. *Journal of Marriage and Family, 70,* 113–28.

Lindblad-Goldberg, M. (1989). Successful minority single-parent families. In L. Combrinck-Graham (Ed.), *Children in family contexts* (pp. 116–134). New York, NY: Guilford.

Lindell, S. G. (1988). Education for childbirth: A time for change. *Journal of Obstetrics, Gynecology, and Neonatal Nursing, 17,* 108–112.

Lindau, S. T., & Gavrilova, N. (2010). Sex, health, and years of sexually active life gained due to good health: Evidence from two US population based cross sectional surveys of ageing. *BMJ, 340,* c810.

Lin Gomez, S., Quach, T., Horn-Ross, P. L., Pham, J. T., Cockburn, M., Chang, E. T., ... & Clarke, C. A. (2010). Hidden breast cancer disparities in Asian women: Disaggregating incidence rates by ethnicity and migrant status. *American Journal of Public Health, 100,* S125–S131. doi: 10.2105/AJPH.2009.163931

Linn, S., Lieverman, E., Schoenbaum, S. C., Monson, R. R., Stubblefield, P. G., & Ryan, K. (1988). Adverse outcomes of pregnancy in women exposed to diethylstilbestrol in utero. *Journal of Reproductive Medicine, 33,* 3–7.

Linney, J. A., & Seidman, E. (1989). The future of schooling. *American Psychologist, 44,* 336–340.

Lipman, B., Lubell, J., & Salomon, E. (2012). *Housing an aging population: Are we prepared?* Center for Housing Policy. Retrieved from http://www.nhc.org/media/files/AgingReport2012.pdf

Lips, H. M. (1993). *Sex & gender* (2nd ed.). Mountain View, CA: Mayfield.

Lipsitt, L. (1990). Learning and memory in infants. *Merrill-Palmer Quarterly, 35,* 53–66.

Lipsitt, L., & Kaye, H. (1964). Conditioned sucking in the newborn. *Psychonomic Science, 1,* 29–30.

Lisitsa, E. (2013). *The four horsemen: The antidotes.* The Gottman Institute. Retrieved from https://www.gottman.com/blog/the-four-horsemen-the-antidotes/

Lister, L. (1991). Men and grief: A review of research, *Smith College Studies in Social Work, 61(3),* 220–235.

Little, J. T., Reynolds, C. F., 3rd, Dew, M. A., Frank, E., Begley, A. E., Miller, M. D., Cornes, C., Mazumdar, S., Perel, J. M., & Kupfer, D. J. (1998). How common is resistance to treatment in recurrent, nonpsychotic geriatric depression? *American Journal of Psychiatry, 155,* 1035–1038.

Little, T. D., Mroczek, D. K., & Shiner, R. L. (2006). *Handbook of personality development.* Mahwah, NJ: Lawrence Erlbaum Associates.

Littleton, H. L., Bye, K., Buck, K., & Amacker, A. (2010). Psychosocial stress during pregnancy and perinatal outcomes: A meta-analytic review. *Journal of Psychosomatic Obstetrics & Gynecology, 31,* 219–228.

Litwin, H., & Shiovitz-Ezra, S. (2006). The association between activity and well-being in later life: What really matters? *Ageing and Society, 26,* 225–242.

Liu, H., Bravata, D. M., Olkin, I., Nayak, S., Roberts, B., Garber, A. M., & Hoffman, A. R. (2007). Systematic review: The safety and efficacy of growth hormone in the healthy elderly. *Annals of Internal Medicine, 146,* 104–115.

Liu, H., & Umberson, D. J. (2008). The times they are a changin': Marital status and health differentials from 1972 to 2003. *Journal of Health and Social Behavior, 49(3),* 239–253.

Liu, R. T., & Mustanski, B. (2012). Suicidal ideation and self-harm in lesbian, gay, bisexual, and transgender youth. *American Journal of Preventive Medicine, 42(3),* 221–228.

Liu, Y., Arai, A., Obayashi, Y., Kanda, K., Boostrom, E., Lee, R., & Tamashiro, H. (2013). Trends of gender gaps in life expectancy in Japan, 1947–2012: Associations with gender mortality ration and a social development index. *Geriatrics & Gerontology, 13,* 792–797. doi: 10.111/ggi.12001

Livingston, G. (2014a). *Pew Research Center social and demographic trends: Growing number of dads home with the kids.* Retrieved from http://www.pewsocialtrends.org/2014/06/05/growing-number-of-dads-home-with-the-kids/

Livingston, G. (2014b, December). *Fewer than half of U.S. kids today live in a 'traditional' family.* Pew Research Center. Retrieved from http://www.pewresearch.org/fact-tank/2014/12/22/less-than-half-of-u-s-kids-today-live-in-a-traditional-family/

Livingston, G., & Cohn, D. (2010). *Childlessness up among all women; down among women with advanced degrees.* Pew Research Center. Retrieved from http://www.pewsocialtrends.org/2010/06/25/childlessness-up-among-all-women-down-among-women-with-advanced-degrees/

Livingston, G., Parker, K., & Rohal, M. (2014). Four-in-ten couples are saying "I do" again: Growing number of adults have remarried. Pew Research Center. Retrieved from http://www.pewsocialtrends.org/files/2014/11/2014-11-14_remarriage-final.pdf

Livingston, M. (1993a). Read method: Natural childbirth In B. K. Rothman (Ed.), *The encyclopedia of childbearing.* New York, NY: Henry Holt.

Livingston, M. (1993b). Psychoprophylactic method (Lamaze). In B. K. Rothman (Ed.), *The encyclopedia of childbearing.* New York, NY: Henry Holt.

Livingston, M. (1993e). Bradley method: Husband-coached childbirth. In B. K. Rothman (Ed.), *The encyclopedia of childbearing* New York, NY: Henry Holt.

Livson, N., & Peskin, H. (1981a). Perspectives on adolescence from longitudinal research. In J. Adelson (Ed.), *Handbook of adolescent psychology.* New York, NY: Wiley.

Livson, N., & Peskin, H. (1981b). Psychological health at 40: Predictions from adolescent personality. In D. Eichorn, J. Clausen, N. Haan, M. Honzik, & P. Mussen (Eds.), *Present and past in middle life.* New York, NY: Academic Press.

Lobo, R. A. (1995). Benefits and risks of estrogen replacement therapy. *American Journal of Obstetrics and Gynecology, 173,* 982–989.

Lock, M. (1993). *Encounters with aging: Mythologies of menopause in Japan and North America.* Berkeley, CA: University of California Press.

Lock, M. (1996). Death in technological time: Locating the end of meaningful life. *Medical Anthropology Quarterly, 10,* 575–600.

Lockery, S. A. (1991). Family and social supports: Caregiving among racial and ethnic minority elders. *Generations, 15(4),* 58–62.

Loeb, R. C., Horst, L., & Horton, P. J. (1980). Family interaction patterns associated with self-esteem in preadolescent girls and boys. *Merrill-Palmer Quarterly, 26,* 203–217.

Loeber, R., Menting, B., Lyman, D. R., Moffitt, T. E., Southamer-Loeber, M., Stallings, R., Farrington, D. P., & Pardini, D. (2012). Findings from the Pittsburgh Youth Study: Cognitive impulsivity and intelligence as predictors of the age-crime curve. *Journal of the American Academy of Child and Adolescent Psychiatry, 51(11),* 1136–1149.

Loeber, R., & Stouthamer-Loeber, M. (1998). Development of juvenile aggression and violence: Some common misconceptions and controversies. *American Psychologist, 53,* 242–259.

Lohnes, K. L., & Kalter, N. (1994). Preventative intervention groups for parentally bereaved children. *American Journal of Orthopsychiatry, 64,* 594–603.

Londerville, S., & Main, M. (1981). Security of attachment, compliance, and maternal training methods. *Developmental Psychology, 17,* 289–299.

Long, H. B., & Zoller-Hodges, D. (1995). Outcomes of Elder-hostel participation. *Educational Gerontology, 21,* 113–127.

Longino, C. F., Soldo, B. J., & Manton, K. G. (1990). Demography of aging in the United States. In K. Ferraro (Ed.), *Gerontology issues and perspectives.* New York, NY: Springer.

Loomis, D., & Richardson, D. (1998). Race and the risk of fatal injury at work. *American Journal of Public Health, 88(1),* 40–44.

Lopata, H. (1984). The widowed. In E. Palmore (Ed.) *Handbook on the aged in the United States* (pp. 109–124). Westport, CT: Greenwood Press.

Lopata, H. Z. (1993). The role of social support in bereavement. In M. S. Stroebe, W. Stroebe, & R. O. Hansson (Eds.), *Handbook of bereavement: Theory, research, and. intervention* (pp. 381–396). Cambridge, UK: Cambridge University Press.

Lopez, M. H., & Gonzalez-Barrera, A. (2014). *Women's college enrollment gains leave men behind.* Pew Research Center. Retrieved from http://www.pewresearch.org/fact-tank/2014/03/06/womens-college-enrollment-gains-leave-men-behind/

Loprinzi, P. D., & Trost, S. G. (2010). Parental influences on physical activity behavior in preschool children. *Preventive Medicine, 50(3),* 129–133.

Lothian, J., & DeVries, C. (2005). *The official Lamaze guide: Giving birth with confidence.* Minnetonka, MN: Meadowbrook Press.

Louis, K., Marks, H., & Kruse, S. (1996). Teachers' professional community in restructuring schools. *American Educational Research Journal, 33(4),* 757–800.

Love, J. M., Banks Tarullo, L., Raikes, H., & Chazan-Cohen, R. (2008). Head Start: What do we know about its effectiveness? What do we need to know? In K. McCartney, & D. Phillips (Eds.), *Blackwell handbook of early childhood development* (pp. 549–575). Malden, MA: Blackwell Publishing.

Love, J. M., Kisker, E. E., Ross, C., Raikes, H., Constantine, J., Boller, K., ... & Fuligni, A. S. (2005). The effectiveness of early head start for 3-year-old children and their parents: Lessons for policy and programs. *Developmental Psychology, 41(6),* 885.

Lozoff, B. (1989). Nutrition and behavior. *American Psychologist, 44,* 231–236.

Lucas, R. E., Clark, A. E., Georgellis, Y., & Diener, E. (2003). Reexamining adaptation and the set point model of happiness: Reactions to changes in marital status. *Journal of Personality and Social Psychology, 84,* 527–539.

Lucas-Thompson, R. G., Goldberg, W. A., & Prause, J. (2010). Maternal work early in the lives of children and its distal associations with achievement and behavior problems: A meta-analysis. *Psychological Bulletin, 136(6),* 915.

Lucile Packard Children's Hospital at Stanford (LPCH). (2013). *Down syndrome (trisomy 21).* Retrieved from http://www.lpch.org/DiseaseHealthInfo/HealthLibrary/genetics/downs.html

Luna, B., Paulson, D. J., Padmanabhan, A., & Geier, C. (2013). The teenage brain: Cognitive control and motivation. *Current Directions in Psychological Science, 22,* 94–100.

Lund, D. A., Caserta, M. S., & Dimond, M. F. (1993). The course of spousal bereavement in later life. In M. S. Stroebe, W. Stroebe & R. O. Hansson (Eds.), *Handbook of bereavement: Theory, research, and intervention* (pp. 240–254). Cambridge, UK: Cambridge University Press.

Lundy, B. L. (2002). Paternal socio-psychological factors and infant attachment: The mediating role of synchrony in father-infant interactions. *Infant Behavior & Development, 25,* 221–236.

Luo, S., & Zhang, G. (2009). What leads to romantic attraction: Similarity, reciprocity, security, or beauty? Evidence from a speed-dating study. *Journal of Personality, 77(4),* 933–964.

Luria, A. R. (1976). *Cognitive development: Its cultural and social foundations.* Cambridge, MA: Harvard University Press.

Luster, T., & McAdoo, H. (1996). Family and child influences on educational attachment: A secondary analysis of the High/Scope Perry Preschool data. *Developmental Psychology, 32,* 26–35.

Lustig, M., & Koester, J. (1993). *Intercultural competence: Interpersonal communication across cultures.* New York, NY: Harper-Collins.

Lynch, B., & Bonnie, R. (Eds.). (1994). *Growing up tobacco free.* Washington, DC: National Academy Press.

Lynch, J. S., & van den Broek, P. (2007). Understanding the glue of narrative structure: Children's on-and off-line inferences about characters' goals. *Cognitive Development, 22*(3), 323–340.

Lyon, G. (1993). *Better understanding learning disabilities: New views for research and. their implications for education and public policy.* Baltimore: Paul Brookes.

Lyons-Ruth, K., & Block, D. (1996). The disturbed caregiving system: Conceptualizing the impact of childhood trauma on maternal caregiving behavior during infancy. *Infant Mental Health Journal, 17*, 257–275.

Lyons-Ruth, K., Easterbrooks, M. A., & Cibelli, C. D. (1996). Infant attachment strategies, infant mental lag, and maternal depressive symptoms: Predictors of internalizing and externalizing problems at age 7. *Developmental Psychology, 33*, 681–692.

Lytton, H., & Romney, D. M. (1991). Parents' sex-related differential socialization of boys and girls: A meta-analysis *Psychological Bulletin, 109*, 267–296.

M

Maab, W. (2011). The elderly and the Internet: How senior citizens deal with online privacy. In S. Trepte, & L. Reinecke (Eds.), *Privacy Online* (pp. 235–249). Berlin, Germany: Springer Publishing.

MacCallum, F., Golombok, S., & Brinsden, P. (2007). Parenting and child development in families with a child conceived through embryo donation. *Journal of Family Psychology, 21*, 278–287.

Maccoby, E. E. (1995). The two sexes and their social systems. In P. Moen, G. Elder, & K. Luscher (Eds.), *Examining lives in context: Perspectives on the ecology of human development* (pp. 347–364). Washington, DC: American Psychological Association.

Maccoby, E. E. (1980). *Social development, psychological growth, and parent-child relations.* New York, NY: Harcourt Brace Jovanovich.

Maccoby, E. E. (1990). Gender and relationships: A developmental account. *American Psychologist, 45*, 513–520.

Maccoby, E. E., & Jacklin, C. (1980). Sex differences in aggression: A rejoinder and reprise. *Child Development, 48*, 964–980.

Maccoby, E. E., & Martin, J. A. (1983). Socialization in the context of the family: Parent-child interaction In E. M. Hetherington (Ed.), *Handbook of child psychology: Vol. 4. Socialization, personality, and social development* (4th ed., pp. 1–101). New York, NY: Wiley.

MacDorman, M. F., Anderson, R. N., & Strobino D. M. (1997). Annual summary of vital statistics–1996. *Pediatrics, 100*(6), 905–918.

Mackenbach, J. P. (2012). The persistence of health inequalities in modern welfare states: The explanation of a paradox. *Social Science & Medicine, 75*, 761–769. doi: 10.1016/j.socscimed.2012.02.031

MacKinnon-Lewis, C., Starnes, R., Volling, B., & Johnson, S. (1997). Perceptions of parenting as predictors of boys' sibling and peer relations. *Developmental Psychology 33*, 1024–1031.

MacKinnon-Lewis, C., Volling, B. L., Lamb, M. E., Dechman, K., Rabiner, D., & Curtner, M. E. (1994). A cross-contextual analysis of boys' social competence: From family to school. *Developmental Psychology, 30*, 325–33.

MacNeil, S., & Byers, E. S. (1997). The relationships between sexual problems, communication, and sexual satisfaction. *Canadian Journal of Human Sexuality, 6*, 277–283.

Macrae, C., Stangar, C., & Hawthorne, M. (1996). *Stereotypes and stereotyping* Guilford. CT: Guilford Press.

Madden, M. (2010). *Older adults and social media.* Pew Research Center. Retrieved from http://www.pewinternet.org/2010/08/27/older-adults-and-social-media/

Madden, M., Lenhart, A., Cortesi, S., Gasser, U., Duggan, M., Smith, A., & Beaton, M. (2013). *Teens, social media and privacy.* Pew Research Internet Privacy. Retrieved from http://www.pewinternet.org/2013/05/21/teens-social-media-and-privacy.

Madnawat, A. S., & Kachhawa, P. S. (2007). Age, gender, and living circumstances: Discriminating older adults on death anxiety. *Death Studies, 31*(8), 763–769.

Magistro, D., Liubicich, M. E., Candela, F., & Ciairano, S. (2013). Effects of ecological walking training in sedentary elderly people: Act on aging study. *The Gerontologist.* Advance online publication. doi: 10.1093/geront/gnt039

Maguire, M. D., & Dunn, J. (1997). Friendships in early childhood and social understanding. *International Journal of Behavioral Development, 21*, 669–686.

Mahler, M., Pine, F., & Bergman, A. (1975). *The psychological birth of the human infant: Symbiosis and individuation.* New York, NY: Basic Books.

Mahoney, J. L., & Cairns, R. B. (1997). Do extracurricular activities protect against early school dropout? *Developmental Psychology, 33*(2), 241.

Mahoney, J. L., Parente, M. E., & Lord, H. (2007). After-school program engagement: Links to child competence and program quality and content. *Elementary School Journal, 107*(4), 385–04.

Main, M. (1995). Recent studies in attachment: Overview, with selected implications for clinical work. In S. Goldberg, R. Muir, & J. Kerr (Eds.), *Attachment theory: Social, developmental, and clinical perspectives* (pp. 407–470). Hillsdale, NJ: Analytic Press.

Main, M., & George, C. (1985). Responses of abused and disadvantaged toddlers to distress in agemates: A study in the day care setting. *Developmental Psychology, 21*, 407–412.

Main, M., & Goldwyn, R. (1989). Predicting rejection of her infant from mother's representation of her own experience: Implications for the abused-abusing intergenerational cycle. *Child Abuse and Neglect, 8*, 203–217.

Main, M., & Solomon, J. (1990). Procedures for identifying infants as disorganized/disoriented during the Ainsworth Strange Situation. In M. Greenberg, D. Cicchetti, & E. M. Cummings (Eds.), *Attachment in the preschool years: Theory, research and intervention* (pp. 121–160). Chicago: University of Chicago Press.

Main, M., Kaplan, N., & Cassidy, J. (1985). Security in infancy, childhood and adulthood: A move to the level of representation. In I. Bretherton & E. Waters (Eds.), *Growing points in attachment. Monographs of the Society for Research in Child Development, 50*(1–2), 66–104.

Maker, J. (Ed.) (1993). *Programs for the gifted in regular classrooms.* Austin, TX: Pro-Ed Publishers.

Maldonado, D. (1995). Religion and racial/ethnic minority elderly populations. In M. A. Kimble, S. H. McFadden, J. W. Ellor, & J. J. Seeber (Eds.), *Aging, spirituality, and religion: A handbook*, Minneapolis: Fortress Press.

Malina, R. M. (1990). Physical growth and performance during the transition years (9–16). In R. Montemayor, G. R. Adams, & T. P. Gullotta (Eds.), *From childhood to adolescence: A transitional period?* (pp. 41–62). Newbury Park, CA: Sage.

Malinosky-Rummell, R., & Hansen, D. J. (1993). Long-term consequences of childhood physical abuse. *Psychological Bulletin, 114*, 68–79.

Mallinckrodt, B., & Fretz, B. R. (1988). Social support and the impact of job loss on older professionals. *Journal of Counseling Psychology, 35*(3), 281–286.

Mallory, G., & New, R. (Eds.). (1994). *Diversity and develop-mentally appropriate practice. Challenges for early childhood education.* New York, NY: Teachers' College Press.

Malone, J. C., Cohen, S., Liu, S. R., Vaillant, G. E., & Waldinger, R. J. (2013). Adaptive midlife defense mechanisms and late life health. *Personality and Individual Differences, 55*, 85–89.

Maluf, S. W., Marroni, N. P., Heuser, V. D., & Pra, D. (2013). DNA damage and oxidative stress in human disease. *Biomedical Research International, 2013*, 696104. doi: 10.1155/2013/696804

Mandel, D. R., Jusczyk, P. W., & Pisoni, D. B. (1995). Infants' recognition of the sound patterns of their own names. *Psychological Science, 6*, 314–317.

Mangelsdorf, S. C., Shapiro, J. R., & Marxolf, D. (1995). Developmental and temperamental differences in emotion regulation in infancy. *Child Development, 66*, 1817–1828.

Marcia, J. (1980). Identity in adolescence. In J. Adelson (Ed.), *Handbook of adolescent psychology.* New York, NY: Wiley.

Marcia, J. E. (1966). Development and validation of ego identity status. *Journal of Personality and Social Psychology, 3*, 551–558.

Marcia, J. E. (1993). The relational roots of identity. In J. Kroger (Ed.), *Discussions on ego identity* (pp. 101–120), Hillsdale, NJ: Erlbaum.

Marcia, J. E., Waterman, A. S., Matteson, D. R., Archer, S. L., & Osofsky, J. L. (1993). *Ego Identity: A handbook for psychosocial research.* New York, NY: Springer-Verlag.

Marcus, D., & Overton, W. (1978). The development of cognitive gender constancy and sex role preferences. *Child Development, 49*, 434–444.

Marcus, G., Pinker, S., Ullman, M., Hollander, M., Rosen, T., & Xu, F. (1992). Overregularization in language acquisition. *Monographs of the Society for Research on Child Development, 57*(4, Serial No. 228).

Margolin, L. (1994). *Goodness personified: The emergence of gifted children.* New York, NY: Aldine de Gruyter.

Markides, K. S. (1990). Risk factors, gender, and health. *Generations, 14*(3), 17–21.

Markides, K. S., & Black, S. A. (1996). Race, ethnicity, and aging: The impact of inequality. In R. H. Binstock & L. K. George (Eds.), *Handbook of aging and the social sciences* (pp. 143–170). San Diego: Academic Press.

Markides, K. S., & Krause, N. (1986). Older Mexican Americans (family relationships). *Generations, 10*(4), 32–35.

Markiewicz, D., Lawford, H., Doyle, A. B., & Haggart, N. (2006). Developmental differences in adolescents' and young adults' use of mothers, fathers, best friends, and romantic partners to fulfill attachment needs. *Journal of Youth and Adolescence, 35*(1), 121–134.

Markman, H. J., & Kadushin, F. S. (1986). Preventive effects of Lamaze training for first-time parents: A short-term longitudinal study. *Journal of Consulting and Clinical Psychology, 54*, 872–874.

Marlowe, B. (1998). *Creating and sustaining the constructivist classroom* Thousand Oaks, CA: Corwin Press.

Marschark, M. (1993). *Psychological development of deaf children.* New York, NY: Oxford.

Marsella, A. J. (1998). Urbanization, mental health, and social deviancy: A review of issues and research. *American Psychologist, 53*, 624–634.

Marshall, E. A., & Butler, K. (2016). School-to-work transitions in emerging adulthood. In J. J. Arnett (Ed.), *The Oxford handbook of emerging adulthood* (pp. 316–333). New York, NY: Oxford University Press.

Marshall, V. W. (1996). The state of theory in aging and the social sciences. In R. H. Binstock & L. K George (Eds.), *Handbook of aging and the social sciences* (pp. 12–30). San Diego: Academic Press.

Marshall, V. W., & Levy, J. (1990). Aging and dying. In R. H. Binstock & L. K. George (Eds.), *Handbook of aging and the social sciences* (3rd ed., pp. 245–260). San Diego: Academic Press.

Martens, A., Greenberg, J., Schimel, J., & Landau, M. J. (2004). Ageism and death: Effects of mortality salience and perceived similarity to elders on reactions to elderly people. *Personality and Social Psychology Bulletin, 30*, 1524–1536.

Martin, B. (1975). Parent-child relations. In F. Horowitz (Ed.), *Review of child development research: Vol. 4*. Chicago: University of Chicago Press.

Martin, C. L., & Ruble, D. N. (2010). Patterns of gender development. *Annual Review of Psychology, 61*, 353.

Martin, C. L., Wood, C. H., & Little, J. K. (1990). The development of gender stereotype components. *Child Development, 61*, 1891–1904.

Martin, J. A., Hamilton, B. E., Ventura, S. J., Osterman, M. J. K., & Matthews, T. J. (2013). Births: Final data for 2011. *National Vital Statistics Reports, 62*. Retrieved from http://www.cdc.gov/nchs/data/nvsr/nvsr62/nvsr62_01.pdf

Martin, J. A., Hamilton, B. E., Ventura, S. J., Oserman, M. J. K., Wilson, E. C., & Mathews, T. J. (2012). Births: Final data for 2010. *National Vital Statistics Reports, 61*(1), 1–72. Retrieved from http://www.cdc.gov/nchs/data/nvsr61/nvsr61_01.pdf

Martinez, G., Copen, C. E., & Abma, J.C. (2011). Teenagers in the United States: Sexual activity, contraceptive use, and childbearing, 2006–2010 National Survey of Family Growth. *National Center for Health Statistics. Vital Health Statistics, 23*(31).

Martinez, I. L., Crooks, D., Kim, K. S., & Tanner, E. (2011). Invisible civic engagement among older adults: Valuing the contributions of informal volunteering. *Journal of Cross Cultural Gerontology, 26*, 23–37.

Marx, K. H. (1991). Mutation identified as a possible cause of Alzheimer's disease. *Science, 251*, 867–877.

Mason, A. W., Hitch, J. E., Kosterman, R., McCarty, C. A., Herrenkohl, T. I., & Hawkins, J. D. (2010). Growth in adolescent delinquency and alcohol use in relation to young adult crime, alcohol use disorders, and risky sex: A comparison of youth from low-versus middle income backgrounds. *Journal of Child Psychology and Psychiatry, 51*(12), 1377–1385.

Mason, C. A., Cauce, A. M., Gonzales, N., & Hiraga, Y. (1996). Neither too sweet nor too sour: Problem peers, maternal control, and problem behavior in African American adolescents. *Child Development, 67*, 2115–2130.

Masotti, P. J., Fick, R., Johnson-Masotti, A., & MacLeod, S. (2006). Healthy naturally occurring retirement communities: A low-cost approach to facilitating healthy aging. *American Journal of Public Health, 96*, 1164–1170.

Masten, A. S., & Coatsworth, J. D. (1998). The development of competence in favorable and unfavorable environments. *American Psychologist, 53*, 205–220.

Masters, W. H., & Johnson, V. E. (1966). *Human sexual response* Boston: Little, Brown.

Masters, W. H., Johnson, V. E., & Kolodny, R. C. (1992). *Human sexuality* (4th ed.). Boston: Little, Brown.

Masters, W. H., Johnson, V. E., & Kolodny, R. C. (1994). *Heterosexuality*. New York, NY: HarperCollins.

Matas, L., Arend, R. A., & Sroufe, L. A. (1978). Continuity of adaptation in the second year. The relationship between quality of attachment and later competence. *Child Development, 49*, 547–555.

Mathews, T. J., & Hamilton, B. E. (2016). Mean age of mothers is on the rise: United States, 2000–2014. *NCHS data brief, no 232*. Hyattsville, MD: National Center for Health Statistics. Retrieved from http://www.cdc.gov/nchs/products/databriefs/db232.htm

Matos, K. (2015). *Modern families: Same-and different-sex couples negotiating at home*. Retrieved from http://www.familiesandwork.org/downloads/modern-families.pdf

Matthews, D., & Kitchen, J. (2007). School-within-a-school gifted programs perceptions of students and teachers in public secondary schools. *Gifted Child Quarterly, 51*(3), 256–271.

Matthews, S. H., & Rosner, T. T. (1988). Shared filial responsibility: The family as the primary caregiver. *Journal of Marriage and the Family, 50*, 185–195.

Mazur, J. (1994). *Learning and behavior* (3rd ed.), Englewood Cliffs, NJ: Erlbaum.

McAdams, D. P., de St. Aubin, E., & Logan, R. L. (1993). Generativity among young, midlife, and older adults. *Psychology and Aging, 8*, 221–230.

McAuley, E., Jerome, G. J., Elvasky, S., Marquez, D. X., & Ramsey, S. N. (2003). Predicting long-term maintenance of physical activity in older adults. *Preventative Medicine, 37*, 110–118.

McCall, G. J. (1995). Juvenile delinquency in Germany, South Africa, and America: Explorations in national character. In J. Braun, et al. (Eds.). *Social pathology in comparative perspective: The nature and psychology of civil society*. (pp. 117–132). Westport, CT: Praeger Publishers/Greenwood Publishing Group.

McCall, R. (1981). Nature-nurture and the two realms of development: A proposed integration with respect to mental development. *Child Development, 52*, 1–12.

McCall, R., & Kagan, J. (1967). Stimulus schema discrepancy and attention in the infant. *Journal of Experimental Child Psychology, 5*, 381–390.

McCloyd, V. C. (1998). Socioeconomic disadvantage and child development. *American Psychologist, 53*, 185–204.

McCrae, R. R. (Ed.). (1992). The five-factor model: Issues and applications [Special issue]. *Journal of Personality, 60*(2).

McCrae, R. R., & Costa, P. T., Jr. (1993). Psychological resilience among widowed men and women: A 10-year follow-up of a national survey. In M. S. Stroebe, W. Stroebe, & R. O. Hansson (Eds.), *Handbook of bereavement: Theory, research, and intervention* (pp. 196–207). Cambridge, UK: Cambridge University Press.

McCrea, R. R., & John, O. P. (1992). An introduction to the five-factor model and its applications. *Journal of Personality, 60*, 175–216.

McCurdy, K., Gorman, K. S., Kisler, T. S., & Metallinos-Katsaras, E. (2012). Maternal mental health and child health and nutrition. In V. Maholmes & R. B. King (Eds.), *The Oxford handbook of poverty and child development* (pp. 124–144). New York, NY: Oxford University Press.

McDaniel, D., McKee, C., & Smith, H. (1996). *Methods of assessing children's syntax* Cambridge, MA: MIT Press.

McDonald, M., Sigman, M., Espinosa, M., & Neumann, C. (1994). Impact of a temporary food shortage on children and their mothers. *Child Development, 65*, 404–415.

McDonald, T. W., Chown, E. L., Tabb, J. E., Shaeffer, A. K., & Howard, E. K. M. (2013). The impact of volunteering on seniors' health and quality of life: An assessment of the Retired and Senior Volunteer Program. *Psychology, 4*, 283–290.

McElhaney, L. J. (1992). Dating and courtship in the later years: A neglected topic of research. *Generations, 17*(3), 21–23.

McFadden S. H. (1996). Religion, spirituality, and aging. In J. E. Birren & K. W. Schaie (Eds.), *Handbook of the psychology of aging* (162–177). San Diego: Academic Press.

McFadden, S. H., & Gerl, R. (1990). Approaches to understanding spirituality in the second half of life. *Generations, 14*(3), 35–38.

McGinnis, J. M., & Foege, W. H. (1993). Actual causes of death in the United States. *Journal of the American Medical Association 270*, 2207–2212.

McGinnis, M., Richmond, J. B., Brandt, E. N., Windom, R. E., & Mason, J. O. (1992). Health progress in the United States: Results of the 1990 objectives for the nation. *Journal of the American Medical Association, 268*, 2545–2552.

McGoldrick, M., Pearce, J. K., & Giordano, J. (Eds.). (1982). *Ethnicity and family therapy*. New York, NY: Guilford.

McHale, S. M., Corneal, D., Crouter, A., & Birch, L. (2001). Gender and weight concerns in early and middle adolescence: Links with well-being and family characteristics. *Journal of Clinical Child Psychology, 30*, 338–348.

McHale, S. M., Crouter, A. C., & Tucker, C. J. (2001). Free-time activities in middle childhood: Links with adjustment in early adolescence. *Child Development, 72*(6), 1764–1778.

McIntosh, J. L., & Drapeau, C. W. (for the American Association of Suicidology). (2014, June 19). *U.S.A. suicide 2011: Official final data*. Washington, DC: American Association of Suicidology. Retrieved from http://www.suicidology.org

McKay, M. M. (1994). The link between domestic violence and child abuse: Assessment and treatment considerations. *Child Welfare, 73*, 29–39.

McKay, S. (1993). Labor: Overview. In B. K. Rothman (Ed.), *The encyclopedia of childbearing*. New York, NY: Henry Holt.

McKinlay, S. M., Brambilla, D. J., & Posner, J. G. (1992). The normal menopause transition. *American Journal of Biology, 4*, 37–46.

McKnight-Eily, L. R., Eaton, D. K., Lowry, R., Croft, J. B., Presley-Cantrell, L., & Perry, G. S. (2011). Relationships between hours of sleep and health-risk behaviors in US adolescent students. *Preventive Medicine, 53*(4), 271–273.

McKussick, V. A. (1995). *Mendelian inheritance in man: Catalogues of autosomal dominant, autosomal recessive, and X-linked phenotypes* (10th ed.). Baltimore: Johns Hopkins University Press.

McLoyd, V. C. (1990). The impact of economic hardship on Black families and children: Psychological distress, parenting and socioemotional development. *Child Development, 61*, 311–346.

McLoyd, V. C. (1998). Socioeconomic disadvantage and child development. *American Psychologist. 53*. 185–204.

McNamara, T., Miller, D., & Bransford, J. (1991). Mental models and the construction of meaning. In P. Pearson (Ed.), *Handbook of reading research: Vol. 2* (pp. 490–511). New York, NY: Longman.

McQuoid, Joan. (1996). The ISRD Study: Self-report findings from N. Ireland. *Journal of Adolescence, 19*, 95–98.

McWilliams, S., & Barrett, A. E. (2014). Online dating in middle and later life: Gendered expectations and experiences. *Journal of Family Issues, 35*, 411–436.

Measor, L., & Sykes, P. (1992). *Gender and schools* New York, NY: Cassell.

Medicaid. (2014). *Medicaid.gov: Keeping America healthy*. Retrieved from https://www.medicaid.gov/chip/reports-and-evaluations/reports-and-evaluations.html

Meehan, P. J., Lamb, J. A., Saltzman, L. E., & O'Carroll, P. W. (1992). Attempted suicide among young adults: Progress toward a meaningful estimate of prevalence. *American Journal of Psychiatry, 149*, 41–44.

Meilman, P. (1979). Cross-sectional age changes in ego identity status during adolescence. *Developmental Psychology, 15*, 230–231.

Meins, E. (1997). *Security of attachment and the social development of cognition*. Hove: Psychology Press.

Mela, D., & Roberts, P. (1998). *Food, eating, and obesity: Psychobiological basis of appetite and weight control* New York, NY: Chapman and Hall.

Meltzer, L. J., & Mindell, J. A. (2006). Sleep and sleep disorders in children and adolescents. *Psychiatric Clinics of North America, 29*(4), 1059–1076.

Meltzoff, A., & Kuhl, P. (1994). Faces and speech: Intermodel processing of biologically relevant signals in infants and adults. In D. Lewkowicz & R. Lickliter (Eds.), *The development of intersensory perception* (pp. 335–370). Hillsdale, NJ: Erlbaum.

Meltzoff, A., Kuhl, P., & Moore, M. K. (1991). Perception, representation, and control of action in newborns and young infants. In M. Weiss & P. Zelazo (Eds.), *Newborn attention: Biological constraints and the influence of experience* (pp. 377–411). Norwood, NJ: Ablex.

Mendelson, B., & White, D. (1995). Children's global self-esteem predicted by body-esteem but not by weight. *Perceptual & Motor Skills, 80,* 97–98.

Mendes de Leon, C. F., Kasl, S. V., & Jacobs, S. (1994). A prospective study of widowhood and changes in symptoms of depression in a community sample of the elderly. *Psychological Medicine, 24,* 613–624.

Mendoza, J. A., Zimmerman, F. J., & Christakis, D. A. (2007). Television viewing, computer use, obesity, and adiposity in US preschool children. *International Journal of Behavioral Nutrition and Physical Activity, 4*(1), 1.

Menkes, J. (1994). *Textbook of child neurology* (5th ed.). Philadelphia: Williams and Wilkins.

Mennuti, R. B., & Creamer, D. G. (1991). Role of orientation, gender, and dilemma content in moral reasoning. *Journal of College Student Development, 32,* 241–248.

Mercer, C. H., Fenton, K. A., Johnson, A. M., Wellings, K., Macdowall, W., McManus, S., ... & Erens, B. (2003). Sexual function problems and help seeking behaviour in Britain: National probability sample survey. *British Medical Journal, 327,* 426–427.

Mercer, C. H., Tanton, C., Prah, P., Erens, B., Sonnenberg, P., Clifton, S., ... & Copas, A. J. (2013). Changes in sexual attitudes and lifestyles in Britain through the life course and over time: Findings from the National Surveys of Sexual Attitudes and Lifestyles (Natsal). *Lancet, 382*(9907), 1781–1794.

Mercer, P. W., Merritt, S. L., & Cowell, J. M. (1998). Differences in reported sleep need among adolescents. *Journal of Adolescent Health, 23*(5), 259–263.

Meredith, H. (1981). Body size and form among ethnic groups of infants, children, youth, and adults. In R. Munroe, R. Munroe, and B. Whiting (Eds.), *Handbook of cross-cultural human development.* New York, NY: Garland Press.

Merenstein, G., Kaplan, D., & Rosenberg, A. (1997). *Handbook of pediatrics* (18th ed.). Norwalk, CT: Appleton and Lange.

Merriam, S. B. (1993). Race, sex, and age-group differences in the occurrence and uses of reminiscence. *Activities, Adaptation and Aging, 18*(1), 1–18.

Merriam, S. B., & Kee, Y. (2014). Promoting community wellbeing: The case for lifelong learning for older adults. *Adult Education Quarterly.* Advance online publication. doi: 10.1177/0741713613513633

Mersky, J. P., Topitzes, J., Reynolds, & Arthur J. (2012). Unsafe at any age: Linking childhood and adolescent maltreatment to delinquency and crime. *Journal of Research in Crime and Delinquency, 49*(2), 295–318.

Messer, D. (1994). *The development of communication: From social interaction to language.* New York, NY: Wiley.

Messinger, D. S. (2002). Positive and negative: Infant facial expressions and emotions. *Current Directions in Psychological Science, 11,* 1–6.

Messner, M., and Sabo, D. (1994). *Sex, violence, and power in sports* Freedom, CA: Crossing Press.

Metz, K. (1995). Reassessment of developmental constraints on children's science instruction. *Review of Educational Research, 65*(2), 93–128.

Michelsson, K., Rinne, A., & Paajanen, S. (1990). Crying, feeding and sleeping patterns in 1 to 12-month-old infants. *Child: Care, health and development, 116,* 99–111.

Mickelson, K. D., Kessler, R. C., & Shaver, P. R. (1997). Adult attachment in a nationally representative sample. *Journal of Personality and Social Psychology, 73,* 1092–1106.

Mikaye, K., Chen, S., & Campos, J. (1985). Infant temperament, mother's mode of interaction, and attachment in Japan. In I. Bretherton & E. Waters (Eds.), Growing points of attachment theory and research. *Monographs of the Society for Research on Child Development. 50*(209).

Milevsky, A., Schlechter, M., Netter, S., & Keehn, D. (2007). Maternal and paternal parenting styles in adolescents: Associations with self-esteem, depression and life-satisfaction. *Journal of Child and Family Studies, 16*(1), 39–47.

Miller, B. (1987). Gender and control among spouses of the cognitively impaired: A research note. *The Gerontologist, 27,* 447–453.

Miller, B. (1990). Gender differences in spouse caregiver strain: Socialization and role explanations. *Journal of Marriage and the Family, 52,* 311–321.

Miller, I. J. (1988). Human taste bud density across adult age groups. *Journal of Gerontology, 43,* B26–30.

Miller, P. (2011). *Theories of developmental psychology* (5th ed.). New York, NY: W. H. Freeman.

Miller, P., & Simon, W. (1980). The development of sexuality in adolescence. In J. Adelson (Ed.), *Handbook of adolescent psychology.* New York, NY: Wiley.

Miller, R. H., Edwards, W. B., Brandon, S. C. E., Morton, A. M., & Leduzio, K. J. (2013). Why don't most runners get knee osteoarthritis? A case for per-unit-distance loads. *Medicine & Science in Sports & Exercise, 46*(3), 572–579. doi: 10.1249/MSS

Miller, T., & Winston, R. (1990). Assessing development from a psychosocial perspective. In D. Creamer & associates (Eds.), *College student development: Theory and practice for the 1990s* (Media Publication No. 49). Alexandria, VA: American College Personnel Association.

Miller, W. B. (1990). Why the United States has failed to solve its youth gang problem. In C. R. Huff (Ed.), *Gangs in America* (pp. 263–287). Newbury Park, CA: Sage.

Millstein, S. G. (1989). Adolescent health: Challenges for behavioral scientists. *American Psychologist, 44,* 837–842.

Milner, J. S., Thomsen, C. J., Crouch, J. L., Rabenhorst, M. M., Martens, P. M., Dyslin, C. W., ... & Merrill, L. L. (2010). Do trauma symptoms mediate the relationship between childhood physical abuse and adult child abuse risk? *Child Abuse & Neglect, 34*(5), 332–344.

Milteer, R. M., Ginsburg, K. R., Mulligan, D. A., Ameenuddin, N., Brown, A., Christakis, D. A., ... & Levine, A. E. (2012). The importance of play in promoting healthy child development and maintaining strong parent-child bond: Focus on children in poverty. *Pediatrics, 129*(1), e204–e213.

Milunsky, A. (1992). *Heredity and your family's health.* Baltimore: Johns Hopkins University Press.

Minagawa-Kawai, Y., van der Lely, H., Ramus, F., Sato, Y., Mazuka, R., & Dupoux, E. (2011). Optical brain imaging reveals general auditory and language-specific processing in early infant development. *Cerebral Cortex, 21,* 254–261.

Minino, A. M. (2010). Mortality among teenagers aged 12–19 years: United States, 1999–2006. *NCHS Data Brief, 37.* Retrieved from http://www.cdc.gov/nchs/data/databriefs/db37.

Minnotte, K. L., Minnotte, M. C., Pedersen, D. E., Mannon, S. E., & Kiger, G. (2010). His and her perspectives: Gender ideology, work-to-family conflict, and marital satisfaction. *Sex Roles, 63,* 425–438.

Miramontes, O., Nadeau, A., & Commins, N. (1997). *Restructuring schools for linguistic diversity.* New York, NY: Teachers College Press.

Mirecki, R. M., Chou, J. L., Elliott, M., & Schneider, C. M. (2013). What factors influence marital satisfaction? Differences between first and second marriages. *Journal of Divorce & Remarriage, 54*(1), 78–93.

Mishna, F. (2003). Learning disabilities and bullying double jeopardy. *Journal of Learning Disabilities, 36*(4), 336–347.

Mitchell, V., & Helson, R. (1990). Women's prime of life: Is it the 50s? Special issue: Women at midlife and beyond. *Psychology of Women Quarterly, 14,* 451–170.

Mitford, J. (1963). *The American way of death.* New York, NY: Simon & Schuster.

Moen, P., Dempster-McClain, D., & Williams R. M. (1989). Social integration and longevity: An event history analysis of women's roles and resilience. *American Sociological Review, 54,* 635–647.

Mogford, K. (1993). Language development in twins. In D. Bishop & K. Mogford (Eds.), *Language development in exceptional circumstances* (pp. 80–95). Hillsdale, NJ: Erlbaum.

Mohlman, J. (2012). A community based survey of older adults' preferences for treatment of anxiety. *Psychology and Aging, 27,* 1182–1190.

Monk, T. H., Essex, M. J., Smider, N. A., Klein, M. H. (1996). The impact of the birth of a baby on the time structure and social mixture of a couple's daily life and its consequences for well-being. *Journal of Applied Social Psychology, 26,* 1237–1258.

Montemayor, R. (1983). Parents and adolescents in conflict: All families some of the time and some families most of the time. *Journal of Early Adolescence, 9,* 417–428.

Montessori, M. (1964). *The Montessori method.* New York, NY: Schocken Books.

Montgomery, M. J., & Côté, J. E. (2003). College as a transition to adulthood. In G. R. Adams & M. D. Berzonsky (Eds.), *Blackwell handbook of adolescence.* Malden, MA: Blackwell.

Montgomery, M. J., & Sorell, G. T. (1997). Differences in love attitudes across family life stages. *Family Relations, 46,* 55–61.

Montgomery, R. J. (1992). Gender differences in patterns of child-parent caregiving relationships. In J. W. Dwyer & R. T. Coward (Eds.), *Gender, families, and elder care* (pp. 65–83). Newbury Park, CA: Sage.

Montgomery-Downs, H. E., Insana, S. P., Clegg-Kraynok, M. M., & Mancini, L. M. (2010). Normative longitudinal maternal sleep: The first 4 postpartum months. *American Journal of Obstetrics and Gynecology, 203*(5), 465-e1.

Moody, H. R. (1994a). *Aging: Concepts and controversies.* Thousand Oaks, CA: Pine Forge Press.

Moody, H. R. (1994b). Should people have the choice to end their lives? In H. R. Moody (Ed.), *Aging: Concepts and controversies* (pp. 99–107). Thousand Oaks, CA: Pine Forge Press.

Moore, C., & Dunham, P. (1995). *Joint attention: Its origins and role in development.* Hillsdale, NJ: Erlbaum.

Moore, D. (1984). Parent-adolescent separation: Intrafamilial perceptions and difficulty separating from parents. *Personality and Social Psychology Bulletin, 10,* 611–619.

Moore, D. (1987). Parent-adolescent separation: The construction of adulthood by late adolescents. *Developmental Psychology, 23,* 298–307.

Moore, K., & Persaud, T. (1998). *The developing human: Clinically oriented embryology* (6th ed.). Philadelphia: Saunders.

Moore, S., Rosenthal, D., & Mitchell, A. (1996). *Youth, AIDS, and sexually transmitted diseases,* London: Routledge.

Moorehouse, M. J. (1991). Linking maternal employment patterns to mother-child activities and children's school competence. *Developmental Psychology, 27,* 295–303.

Moorman, S. M., Booth, A., & Fingerman, K. L. (2006). Women's romantic relationships after widowhood. *Journal of Family Issues, 27,* 1281–1304.

Moos, R. H., Shutte, K. K., Brennan, P. L., & Moos, B. S. (2009). Older adults' alcohol consumption and late-life drinking problems: A 20-year perspective. *Addiction, 104,* 1293–1302.

Moran, E. G. (1993). Domestic violence and pregnancy. In B. K. Rothman (Ed.), *The encyclopedia of childbearing.* New York, NY: Henry Holt.

Morell, V. (1995). Attacking the causes of "silent" infertility. *Science 269*(5225), 775–777.

Morgan, J. P., & Roberts, J. E. (2010). Helping bereaved children and adolescents: Strategies and implications for counselors. *Journal of Mental Health Counseling, 32*(3), 206.

Morin, R. (2013). *Study: Opposition to same sex marriage is likely to be understated in public opinion polls.* Pew Research Center. Retrieved from http://pewresearch.org/fact-tank/2013/09/30/opposition-to-same-sex-marriage-may-be-understated-in-public-opinion-polls

Morris, J. N., & Morris, S. A. (1992). Aging in place: The role of formal services. *Generations, 16*(2), 41–48.

Morrison, E. H. (1998). Common peripartum emergencies. *American Family Physician, 58*, 1593–1604.

Morrongiello, B. (1994). Effects of colocation on auditory-visual interactions and cross-modality perception in infants. In D. Lewkowicz & R. Lickliter (Eds.), *The development of intersensory perception* (pp. 235–264). Hillsdale, NJ: Erlbaum.

Morrow, L. (1996). *Motivating reading and writing in diverse classrooms: Social and physical contexts in a literature-based program.* Urbana, IL: National Council of Teachers of English.

Mortimer, J., & Finch, M. (Eds.). (1996). *Adolescents, work, and family.* Thousand Oaks, CA: Sage.

Mortimer, J., Shanahan, M., & Ryu, S. (1994). The effects of adolescent employment on school-related orientation and behavior. In R. Silbereisen & E. Todt (Eds.), *Adolescence in context: The interplay of family, school, peers, and work in adjustment* (pp. 304–326). New York, NY: Springer-Verlag.

Morton, R. A., Jr. (1994). Racial differences in adenocarcinoma of the prostate in North American men. *Urology, 44*, 637–645.

Moser, C., Spagnoli, J., & Santos-Eggimann, B. (2011). Self-perception of aging and vulnerability to adverse outcomes at the age of 65–70 years. *Journals of Gerontology Series B: Psychological Sciences and Social Sciences, 66*, 675–680.

Mottaz, C. J. (1987). Age and work satisfaction. *Work & Occupations, 14*(3) 387–409.

Moyer, M. S. (1992). Sibling relationships among older adults. *Generations, 17*(3), 55–58.

Muehlenhard, C., & Linton, M. (1987). Date rape. *Journal of Counseling Psychology, 34*, 186–196.

Mullan, J. T., Pearlin, L. I., & Skaff, M. M. (1995). The bereavement process: Loss, grief, recovery. In I. B. Corless, B. B. Germino, & M. A. Pittman (Eds.). *A challenge for living: Dying, death, and bereavement* Boston: Jones and Bartlett Publishers.

Munroe, R., Munroe, R., & Whiting, J. (1981). Male sex-role resolutions. In *Handbook of cross-cultural human development*, New York, NY: Garland.

Muraco, A. (2006). Intentional families: Fictive kin ties between cross-gender, different sexual orientation friends. *Journal of Marriage and Family, 68*(5), 1313–1325.

Muraco, A., & Fredriksen-Goldsen, K. (2011). "That's what friends do": Informal caregiving for chronically ill midlife and older lesbian, gay, and bisexual adults. *Journal of Social and Personal Relationships, 28*, 1073–1092.

Murphy, J. M., & Gilligan, C. (1980). Moral development in late adolescence and adulthood: A critique and reconstruction of Kohlberg's theory. *Human Development, 23*, 77–104.

Murphy, L. (1937). *Social behavior and child personality.* New York, NY: Columbia University Press.

Murray, C., Luckey, M., & Meier, D. (1996). Skeletal integrity. In E. L., Schneider & J. W. Rowe (Eds.), *Handbook of the biology of aging* (pp. 431–444). San Diego: Academic Press.

Murry, V. M., Bynum, M. S., Brody, G. H., Willert, A., & Stephens, D. (2001). African American single mothers and children in context: A review of studies on risk and resilience. *Clinical Child and Family Psychology Review, 4*(2), 133–155.

Murstein, B. I. (1988). A taxonomy of love. In R. J. Stemberg & M. L. Brown (Eds.), *The psychology of love.* New Haven, CT: Yale University Press.

Museus, S. D., & Quaye, S. J. (2009). Toward an intercultural perspective of racial and ethnic minority college student persistence. *Review of Higher Education, 33*(1), 67–94.

Myers, J. (1993). Curricular designs that resonate with adolescents' ways of knowing. In R. Lerner (Ed.), *Early adolescence: Perspectives on research, policy, and intervention* (pp. 191–206). Hillsdale, NJ: Erlbaum.

Myers, S. A. (2011). "I have to love her, even if sometimes I may not like her": The reasons why adults maintain their sibling relationships. *North American Journal of Psychology, 13*, 51–62.

Myhill, D., & Jones, S. (2006). "She doesn't shout at no girls": Pupils' perceptions of gender equity in the classroom. *Cambridge Journal of Education, 36*(1), 99–113.

N

Nagata, D. K., Cheng, W. J., & Tsai-Chae, A. H. (2010). Chinese American grandmothering: A qualitative exploration. *Asian American Journal of Psychology, 1*(2), 151–161.

Nagy, Z., Takacs, A., Filkorn, T., & Sarayba, M. (2009). Initial clinical evaluation of an intraocular femtosecond laser in cataract surgery. *Journal of Refractive Surgery, 25*, 1053–1060.

National Alliance for Caregiving. (2009). *Caregiving in the U.S., 2009.* Retrieved from http://www.caregiving.org/data/Caregiving_in_the_US_2009_full_report.pdf.

National Cancer Institute. (1990). *Cancer statistics review, 1973–87.* (NCI, NIH Pub. No. 90-2789.) Bethesda, MD: U.S. Government Printing Office.

National Cancer Institute. (2011). *Surveillance, epidemiology, and end results program: Turning cancer data into discovery.* Retrieved from http://seer.cancer.gov/faststats/selections.php?series=age

National Center for Education Statistics (NCES). (1997). *Digest of education statistics, 1997.* Washington, DC: U.S. Department of Education, Office of Educational Research and Improvement.

National Center for Education Statistics (NCES). (2010). *Digest of education statistics.* Retrieved from http://nces.ed.gov/programs/digest/d12/tables/dt12_486.asp

National Center for Health Statistics. (1993). Advance report of final mortality statistics, 1990. *Monthly Vital Statistics Report, 41*(7) (Supp.). Hyattsville, MD: U.S. Department of Health and Human Services, Public Health Service, Centers for Disease Control and Prevention.

National Center for Health Statistics. (2013). *Health, United States, 2012: With special feature on emergency care.* Hyattsville, MD: Public Health Service.

National Heart, Lung, and Blood Institute (NHLBI). (2012a). *Morbidity & mortality: 2012 chart book on cardiovascular, lung, and blood diseases.* Retrieved from https://www.nhlbi.nih.gov/files/docs/research/2012_ChartBook_508.pdf

National Heart, Lung, and Blood Institute (NHLBI). (2012b). *Sickle cell anemia.* Retrieved from http://www.nhlbi.nih.gov/health/health-topics/topics/sca/

National Human Genome Research Institute (NHGRI). (2010). *Learning about fragile X syndrome.* Retrieved from http://www.genome.gov/19518828

National Institute of Child Health and Human Development (NICHD). (2012). *Klinefelter syndrome: Condition information.* Retrieved from https://www.nichd.nih.gov/health/topics/klinefelter/conditioninfo/

National Institute of Mental Health (NIMH). (2007). Suicide in the U.S.: Statistic and prevention. Retrieved from http://www.nimh.nih.gov/health/publications/suicide-in-the-us-statistics-and-prevention/index.shtml#CDC-Web-Tool

National Institute on Aging. (2013). *Age page: Menopause.* Retrieved from http://www.nia.nih.gov/sites/default/files/menopause_2.pdf

National Institute on Alcohol Abuse and Alcoholism. (1997, July). Youth drinking: Risk factors and consequences. *Alcohol Alert*, 37.

National Institute on Alcohol Abuse and Alcoholism. (2006). *Alcohol alert: Young adult drinking.* Retrieved from http://pubs.niaaa.nih.gov/publications/aa68/aa68.htm

National Institute on Alcohol Abuse and Alcoholism. (2016). *Alcohol facts and statistics.* Retrieved from https://www.niaaa.nih.gov/alcohol-health/overview-alcohol-consumption/alcohol-facts-and-statistics

National Institutes on Health. (2008). *Menopausal symptoms and complementary health practices.* Retrieved: http://nccam.nih.gov/health/menopause/menopausesymptoms

National Resource Center for Health and Safety in Child Care. (2013). *Choosing child care.* Retrieved from http://childcareaware.org/parents-and-guardians/child-care-101/choosing-child-care

National Science Foundation. (n.d.) *Chore wars: Men, women, and housework.* Retrieved August 12, 2016, from https://www.nsf.gov/discoveries/disc_images.jsp?cntn_id=111458

National Sleep Foundation. (2015). *National Sleep Foundation recommends new sleep durations.* Washington, DC. Retrieved from https://sleepfoundation.org/media-center/press-release/national-sleep-foundation-recommends-new-sleep-times

National Sleep Foundation. (n.d.) *Healthy sleep habits.* Retrieved from https://sleepfoundation.org/excessivesleepiness/sleep-tools-tips/healthy-sleep-tips

Neal, J. W. (2009). Social aggression and social position in middle childhood and early adolescence: Burning bridges or building them? *Journal of Early Adolescence*, 1–16.

Nelson, A. I., & Neinstein, L. S. (2008). Contraception. In L. S. Neinstein, C. M. Gordon, D. K. Katzman, & D. S. Rosen (Eds.), *Handbook of adolescent health care.* Philadelphia, PA: Lippincott, Williams & Wilkins.

Nelson, K. (1996). *Language in cognitive development: Emergence of the mediated mind.* New York, NY: Cambridge University Press.

Neugarten, B. L. (1967). The awareness of middle age. In R. Owen (Ed.), *Middle age.* London: British Broadcasting Company.

Neugarten, B. L. (1968). Adult personality: Toward a psychology of the life cycle. In B. L. Neugarten (Ed.), *Middle age and aging: A reader in social psychology* (pp. 137–147). Chicago: University of Chicago Press.

Neugarten, B. L. (1968). The awareness of middle age. In B. L. Neugarten (Ed.), *Middle age and aging: A reader in social psychology* (pp. 93–98), Chicago: University of Chicago Press.

Neugarten, B. L. (1977). Personality and aging. In J. E. Birren & K. W. Schaie (Eds.), *Handbook of the psychology of aging* (pp. 626–649). New York, NY: Van Nostrand Reinhold.

Neugarten, B. L., & Neugarten, D. A. (1986, Winter). Age in the aging society. *Daedalus*, 31–49.

Neugarten, B. L., & Neugarten, D. A. (1987). The changing meanings of age. *Psychology Today, 21*(5), 29–33.

Neulinger, J. (1981). *The psychology of leisure.* Springfield, IL: Charles C Thomas.

Newman, D. L., Caspi, A., Moffitt, T. E., & Silva, P. A. (1997). Antecedents of adult interpersonal functioning: Effects of individual differences in age 3 temperament. *Developmental Psychology, 33*, 203–217.

Newman, F., & Holzman, L. (1993). *Lev Vygotsky: Revolutionary scientist.* New York, NY: Routledge.

Newman, K. (1996). Working poor: Low-wage employment in the lives of Harlem youth. In J. Graber, J. Brooks-Gunn, & A. Petersen (Eds.), *Transitions through adolescence* (pp. 323–344), Mahwah, NJ: Erlbaum.

Newman, R. S. (2005). The cocktail party effect in infants revisited: Listening to one's own name in noise. *Developmental Psychology, 41*, 352–362.

Newton, N. J., & Stewart, A. J. (2012). Personality development in adulthood. In S. K. Whitbourne, & M. J. Sliwinski (Eds.), *The Wiley-Blackwell handbook of adulthood and aging* (pp. 211–235). Malden, MA: Blackwell Publishing.

Newtson, R. L., & Keith, P. M. (1997), Single women in later life. In J. M. Coyle (Ed.), *Handbook on women and aging* (pp. 385–399). Westport, CT: Greenwood Press.

Nic Gabhainn, S., Baban, A., Boyce, W., & Godeau, E. (2009). How well-protected are sexually active 15-year-olds? Cross national patterns in condom and contraceptive pill use 2002–2006. *International Journal of Public Health, 54,* 209–215.

NICHD Early Child Care Research Network. (1997). The effects of infant child care on infant-mother attachment security: Results of the NICHD study of early child care. *Child Development.* 68, 860–879.

Nichojs, J., Nelson, J., & Gleaves, K. (1995). Learning "facts" versus learning that most questions have many answers: Student evaluations of contrasting curricula. *Journal of Educational Psychology, 87(2),* 253–260.

Nicholson, L., & Zeece, P. D. (2008). Grandparents in the lives of young children. In M. R. Jalongo (Ed.), *Enduring bonds: The significance of interpersonal relationships in young children's lives.* New York, NY: Springer.

Nickerson, A. B., & Nagle, R. J. (2005). Parent and peer attachment in late childhood and early adolescence. *Journal of Early Adolescence, 25,* 223–249.

Nicol-Smith, L. (1996). Causality, menopause, and depression: A critical review of the literature. *British Medical Journal, 313*(7067), 1229–1232,

Noam, G., & Wren, T. (1993). *The moral self.* Cambridge, MA: MIT Press.

Noble, V. (1992). *Shakti woman.* San Francisco: Harper.

Noble, K. D., & Drummond, J. E. (1992). But what about the prom? Students' perceptions of early college entrance. Special issue: Challenging the gifted: Grouping and acceleration. *Gifted Child Quarterly, 36(2),* 106–111.

Nock M K., & Mendes W. B. (2008). Physiological arousal, distress tolerance, and social problem-solving deficits among adolescent self-injurers. *Journal of Consulting Clinical Psychology, 76,* 28–38.

Noel-Miller, C. M. (2011). Partner caregiving in older cohabitating couples. *Journal of Gerontology: Psychological Sciences and Social Sciences, 66B,* 341–353.

Noh, S., Dumas, J. E., Wolf, L. C., & Fisman, S. (1989). Delineating sources of stress in parents of exceptional children. *Family Relations, 38,* 456–461.

Nolen-Hoeksema, S., Wolfson, A., Mumme, D., & Guskin, K. (1995). Helplessness in children of depressed and nondepressed mothers. *Developmental Psychology, 31,* 377–387.

Noller, P. (2005). Sibling relationships in adolescence: Learning and growing together. *Personal Relationships, 12,* 1–22.

Noppe, I. C., Noppe, L. D., & Hughes, F. P. (1991). Stress as a predictor of the quality of parent-infant interactions, *Journal of Genetic Psychology, 152,* 17–28.

Noppe, L., & Noppe, I. (1996). Ambiguity in adolescent understandings of death. In C. Corr & D. Balk (Eds.), *Handbook of adolescent death and bereavement* (pp. 25–41). New York, NY: Springer Publishing.

Norbeck, J. S., & Tilden, V. P. (1983). Life stress, social support, and emotional disequilibrium in complications of pregnancy: A prospective, multivariate study. *Journal of Health and Social Behavior, 24,* 30–46.

Norcross, W. A., Ramirez, C., & Palinkas, L. A. (1996). The influences of women on the health care-seeking behavior of men. *Journal of Family Practice, 43,* 475–480.

Norman, C. (1988). Math education: A mixed picture. *Science, 241,* 408–409.

Norman, R. E., Byambaa, M., De, R., Butchart, A., Scott, J., & Vos, T. (2012). The long-term health consequences of child physical abuse, emotional abuse, and neglect: A systematic review and meta-analysis. *PLoS Med, 9*(11), e1001349.

Norris, J. E., & Tindale, J. A. (1994). *Among generations: The cycle of adult relationships.* New York, NY: Freeman.

Northrup, C. (1994). *Women's bodies, women's wisdom.* New York, NY: Bantam.

Notelovitz, M. (1997). Estrogen therapy and osteoporosis: Principles & practice, *American Journal of the Medical Sciences, 313*(1), 2–12.

Notman, M. T. (1990). Varieties of menopausal experience. In R. Formanek (Ed.), *The meanings of menopause* (pp. 239–254). Hillsdale, NJ: Analytic Press.

Nucci, L., & Turiel, E. (1993). God's word, religious rules, and their relation to Christian and Jewish children's concepts of morality. *Child Development, 64,* 1475–1491.

Nunes-Costa, R. A., Lamela, D. J., & Figueiredo, B.F. (2009). Psychosocial adjustment and physical health in children of divorce. *Journal of Pediatrics, 85*(5), 385–396.

O

Öberg, M., Jaakkola, M. S., Woodward, A., Peruga, A., & Prüss-Ustün, A. (2011). Worldwide burden of disease from exposure to second-hand smoke: A retrospective analysis of data from 192 countries. *Lancet, 377*(9760), 139–146.

O'Brien, R. W., Smith, S. A., Bush, P. J., & Peleg, E. (1990). Obesity, self-esteem, and health locus of control in black youths during transition to adolescence. *American Journal of Health Promotion, 5*(2), 133–139.

O'Brien, S. F., & Bierman, K. L. (1988). Conceptions and perceived influence of peer groups: Interviews with preadolescents and adolescents. *Child Development, 59,* 1360–1365.

O'Callaghan, F. V., O'Callaghan, M., Najman, J. M., Williams, G. M., & Bor, W. (2007). Prenatal alcohol exposure and attention, learning and intellectual ability at 14 years: A prospective longitudinal study. *Early Human Development, 83,* 115–123.

O'Connell, E., Boat, T., & Warner K. E. (Eds). (2009). *Preventing mental, emotional, and behavioral disorders among young people.* Washington, DC: National Academies Press.

O'Connor, C. (1997). Dispositions toward (collective) struggle and educational resilience in the inner city: A case analysis of six African-American high school students. *American Educational Research Journal, 34*(4), 593–629.

O'Connor, D. M. (1987). Elders and higher education: Instrumental or expressive goals? *Educational Gerontology, 13*(6) 511–519.

O'Connor, G. T., Hennekens, C. H., Willett, W. C., Goldhaber, S. Z., Paffenbarger, R. S., Jr., Breslow, J. L., Lee, I. M., & Buring, J. E. (1995). Physical exercise and reduced risk of nonfatal myocardial infarction. *American Journal of Epidemiology, 142,* 1147–1156.

O'Connor, M., & Michaels, S. (1996). Shifting participant frameworks: Orchestrating thinking practices in group discussions. In D. Hicks (Eds.), *Discourse, learning, and schooling* (pp. 63–103). New York, NY: Cambridge University Press.

O'Connor, P. (1992). *Friendships between women.* New York, NY: Harvester Wheatshaft.

O'Donnell, J., Hawkins, J. D., Catalano, R. F., Abbott, R. D., & Day, L. E. (1995). Preventing school failure, drug use bind delinquency among low-income children: Long-term intervention in elementary schools. *American Journal of Orthopsychiatry, 65,* 87–100.

OECD. (2013, January). *Cohabitation rate and prevalence of other forms of partnership.* Retrieved from http://www.oecd.org/els/soc/SF3_3_Cohabitation_rate_and_prevalence_of_other_forms_of_partnership_Jan2013.pdf

OECD. (2015). *Education at a glance 2015: OECD indicators.* OECD Publishing. Retrieved from http://dx.doi.org/10.1787/eag-2015-en

Ofcom. (2014). *Children and parents: Media use and attitudes report.* Retrieved from http://stakeholders.ofcom.org.uk/binaries/research/media-literacy/media-use-attitudes-14/Childrens_2014_Report.pdf

Offer, D., & Schonert-Reichl, K. A. (1992). Debunking the myths of adolescence: Findings from recent research. *Journal of the American Academy of Child and Adolescent Psychiatry, 31,* 1003–1014.

Office for National Statistics. (2012). *Statistical bulletin: Divorces in England and Wales: 2012.* Retrieved from http://www.ons.gov.uk/peoplepopulationandcommunity/birthsdeathsandmarriages/divorce/bulletins/divorcesinenglandandwales/2014-02-06#age-at-divorce

O'Hara-Devereaux, M., & Johansen, R. (1994). *Globalwork: Bridging distance, culture, and time.* San Francisco: Jossey-Bass.

Ohayon, M. M., Carskadon, M. A., Guilleminault, C., & Vitiello, M. V. (2004). Meta-analysis of quantitative sleep parameters from childhood to old age in healthy individuals: Developing normative sleep values across the human lifespan. *Sleep, 27,* 1255–1273.

O'Keeffe, G. S., & Clark-Pearson, K. (2011). The impact of social media on children, adolescents, and families. *Pediatrics 127(*4). 800–805.

O'Keefe, M. (Ed.). (1998). *Brady emergency care* (8th ed.). Upper Saddle River, NJ: Prentice-Hall.

Okun, M. A., Yeung, E. W., & Brown, S. (2013). Volunteering by older adults and risk of mortality: A meta-analysis. *Psychology and Aging, 28,* 564–577.

Oldehinkel, A. J., Verhulst, F. C., & Ormel, J. (2011). Mental health problems during puberty: Tanner stage-related differences in specific symptoms. The TRAILS study. *Journal of Adolescence, 34,* 73–85.

Olds, D. L. (1997). The prenatal/early infancy project: Fifteen years later. In G. Albee, & T. Gullotta (Eds.), *Issues in children's and families' lives: Primary prevention works* (pp. 41–68). Thousand Oaks, CA: Sage Publications.

Olsen, J. P., Parra, G. R., Cohen, R., Schoffstall, C. L., & Egli, C. J. (2012). Beyond relationship reciprocity: A consideration of varied forms of children's relationships. *Personal Relationships, 19*(1), 72–8.

Olshansky, S. J., Carnes, B. A., & Cassel, C. (1990). In search of Methuselah: Estimating the upper limits to human longevity. *Science, 250,* 634–640.

Olshansky, S. J., Passaro, D. J., Hershow, R. C., Layden, J., Carnes, B. A., Brody, J., ... & , D. S. (2005). A potential decline in life expectancy in the United States in the 21st century. *New England Journal of Medicine, 352,* 1138–1145.

Olson, M. R., & Haynes, J. A. (1993). Successful single parents. *Families in Society: The Journal of Contemporary Human Services, 74*(5), 259–267.

Onwuteaka-Philipsen, B. D., Rurup, M. L., Pasman, H. R. W., & van der Heide, A. (2010). The last phase of life: Who requests and who receives euthanasia or physician-assisted suicide? *Medical Care, 48*(7), 596–603.

Oppenheim, D., Emde, R. N., & Warren, S. (1997). Preschoolers face moral dilemmas: A longitudinal study of acknowledging and resolving internal conflict. *International Journal of Psychoanalysis, 78,* 943–957.

Orathinkel, J., & Vansteenwegen, A. (2007). Do demographics affect marital satisfaction? *Journal of Sex & Marital Therapy, 33,* 73–85.

Ordúñez-García, P. O., Espinosa-Brito, A. D., Cooper, R. S., Kaufman, J. S., & Nicto, F. J. (1998). Hypertension in Cuba: Evidence of a narrow black-white difference. *Journal of Human Hypertension, 12*(2), 111–116.1998.

Orland-Barak, L., & Yinon, H. (2007). When theory meets practice: What student teachers learn from guided reflection on their own classroom discourse. *Teaching and Teacher Education, 23*(6), 957–969.

Orzech, K., Grandner, M., Roane, B., & Carskadon, M. (2016). Digital media use in the 2 h before bedtime is associated with sleep variables in university students. *Computers in Human Behavior, 55*, 43–50.

Oshio, T., Nozaki, K., & Kobayashi, M. (2013). Division of household labor and marital satisfaction in China, Japan, and Korea. *Journal of Family and Economic Issues, 34*(2), 211–223.

Oster, H., Hegley, D., & Nagel, L. (1992). Adult judgments and fine-grained analysis of infant facial expressions: Testing the validity of a priori coding formulas. *Developmental Psychology, 28*, 1115–1131.

Oswald, R. F., & Masciadrelli, B. P. (2008). Generative ritual among nonmetropolitan lesbians and gay men: Promoting social inclusion. *Journal of Marriage and Family, 70*, 1060–1073.

Otis, N., Grouzet, F. M. E., & Pelletier, L. G. (2005). Latent motivational change in an academic setting: A three-year longitudinal study. *Journal of Educational Psychology, 97*, 170–183.

Overman, J. J., & Carmichael, S. T. (2014). Plasticity in the injured brain: More than molecules matter. *Neuroscientist, 20*, 15–28.

Owen, M. T., & Cox, M. J. (1997). Marital conflict and the development of infant-parent attachment relationships. *Journal of Family Psychology, 11*, 152–164.

Owens, D. (2008). Recognizing the needs of bereaved children in palliative care. *Journal of Hospice and Palliative Nursing, 10*, 14–16.

Owens, J. A., Belon, K., & Moss, P. (2010). Impact of delaying school start time on adolescent sleep, mood, and behavior. *Archives of Pediatrics & Adolescent Medicine, 164*(7), 608–614.

P

Packman, W., Horsley, H., Davies, B., & Kramer, R. (2006). Sibling bereavement and continuing bonds. *Death Studies, 30*(9), 817–841.

Padilla-Walker, L. M. (2016). Moral development during emerging adulthood. In J. J. Arnett (Ed.), *The Oxford handbook of emerging adulthood* (pp. 449–463). New York, NY: Oxford University Press.

Page, D. C. Mosher, R., Simpson, E. M., Fisher, E. M., Mardon, G., Pillack, J., McGillivray, B., de la Chapelle, A., & Brown, L. G. (1987). The sex-determining region of the human Y chromosome encodes a finer protein. *Cell, 51*, 1091–1104.

Page, H. (1989). Estimation of the prevalence and incidence of infertility in a population: A pilot study. *Fertility and Sterility, 51*, 571–577.

Pager, D., & Shepherd, H. (2008). The sociology of discrimination: Racial discrimination in employment, housing, credit, and consumer markets. *Annual Review of Sociology, 34*, 181–209.

Pager, D., & Western, B. (2012). Identifying discrimination at work: The use of field experiments. *Journal of Social Issues, 68*, 221–237. doi: 10.1111/j.1540-4560.2012.01746.x

Pagliaro, A., & Pagliaro, L. (1996). *Substance abuse among children and adolescents: Nature, extent, and effects from conception to adulthood*. New York, NY: Wiley.

Pakiz, B., Reinherz, H. Z., & Giaconia, R. M. (1997). Early risk factors for serious antisocial behavior at age 21: A longitudinal community study. *American Journal of Orthopsychiatry, 67*, 92–101.

Pallock, L. L., & Lamborn, S. D. (2006). Beyond parenting practices: Extended kinship support and the academic adjustment of African-American and European-American teens. *Journal of Adolescence, 29*(5), 813–828.

Paniagua, F. A. (2005). *Assessing and treating culturally diverse clients: A practical guide*. Thousand Oaks, CA: Sage.

Pannese, E. (2011). Morphological changes in nerves cells during normal aging. *Brain Structure and Function, 216*, 85–89.

Pappert, A. (1993). Preimplantation diagnosis. In B. K. Rothman (Ed.), *The encyclopedia of childbearing*. New York, NY: Henry Holt.

Paquette, D. (2004). Theorizing the father-child relationship: Mechanisms and developmental outcomes. *Human Development, 47*, 193–219.

Paquette, D., Carbonneau, R., Dubeau, D., Bigras, M., & Tremblay, R. E. (2003). Prevalence of father-child rough-and-tumble play and physical aggression in preschool children. *European Journal of Psychology of Education, 18*, 171–189.

Parke, R. D., Burks, V. M., Carson, J. L., Neville, B., & Boyum, L. A. (1994). Family-peer relationships. A tripartite model. In R. D. Parke & S. G. Kellam (Eds.), *Exploring family relationships with other social constructs* (pp. 115–146). Hillsdale, NJ: Erlbaum.

Parke, R. D., MacDonald, K. B., Beitel, A., & Bhavnagri, N. (1988). The role of the family in the development of peer relationships. In R. Peters & R. J. McMahan (Eds.), *Marriages and families: Behavioral treatment and processes*. New York, NY: Brunner/Mazel.

Parker, R. G. (1995). Reminiscence: A community theory framework. *Gerontologist, 35*, 515–525.

Parker, S. E., Mai, C. T., Canfield, M.A., et al. (2010). Updated national birth prevalence estimates for selected birth defects in the United States, 2004–2006. *Birth Defects Research: A Clinical Molecular Teratology, 88*, 1008–1016.

Parmelee, A. H., Wenner, W. H., & Schulz, H. R. (1964). Infant sleep patterns: From birth to 16 weeks of age. *Journal of Pediatrics, 65*(4), 576–582.

Parmelee, P. A., Katz, I. R., & Lawton, M. P. (1992). Depression and mortality among institutionalized aged. *Journal of Gerontology, 47*, P3–10.

Parsons, C. E., Young, K. S., Kumari, N., Stein, A., & Kringelbach, M. L. (2011). The motivational salience of infant faces is similar for men and women. *PloS ONE, 6*(5), e20632.

Parten, M. (1932). Social play among preschool children. *Journal of Abnormal and Social Psychology, 27*, 243–269.

Pascarella, E. T., & Terenzini, P. T. (1991). *How college affects students: Findings and insights from twenty years of research*. San Francisco: Jossey-Bass.

Pasley, K., & Moorefield, B. S. (2004). Stepfamilies: Changes and challenges. In M. Coleman & L. H. Ganong (Eds.), *Handbook of contemporary families* (pp. 317–330). Thousand Oaks, CA: Sage.

Pasterski, V., Golombok, S., & Hines, M. (2011). Sex differences in social behavior. In P. K. Smith, & C. H. Hart (Eds.), *The Wiley-Blackwell handbook of childhood social development* (2nd ed., pp. 281–298). Malden, MA: Blackwell Publishing.

Pasupathi, M., Carstensen, L. L., & Tsai, J. L. (1995). Ageism in interpersonal settings. In B. Lott & D. Maluso, *The social psychology of interpersonal discrimination*. New York, NY: Guilford Press.

Patchin, J. W., & Hinduja, S. (2006). Bullies move beyond the schoolyard: A preliminary look at cyberbullying. *Youth Violence and Juvenile Justice, 4*(2), 148–169.

Patel, C. J., Govender, V., Paruk, Z., & Ramgoon, S. (2006). Working mothers: Family-work conflict, job performance and family/work variables. *SA Journal of Industrial Psychology, 32*(2).

Patterson, C. J. (1995). Sexual orientation and human development: An overview. *Developmental Psychology, 31*, 3–11.

Patterson, C. J. (1997). Children of lesbian and gay parents. In T. H. Ollendick & R. J. Prinz (Eds.), *Advances in clinical child psychology* (Vol. 19, pp. 235–282). New York, NY: Plenum.

Patterson, C. J. (2006). Children of lesbian and gay parents. *Current Directions in Psychological Science, 15*(5), 241–44.

Patterson, G. R. (1982). *Coercive family processes*. Eugene, OR: Castilia Press.

Patterson, G. R. (1985). *A social learning approach to family intervention: Vol. 1. Families with aggressive children*. Eugene, OR: Castilia Press.

Patterson, G. R., & Dishion, T. J. (1985). Contributions of families and peers to delinquency. *Criminology, 23*, 63–79.

Patterson, M. L., & Werker, J. F. (2002). Infants' ability to match dynamic phonetic and gender information in the face and voice. *Journal of Experimental Child Psychology, 81*, 93–115.

Paulston, C. (1992). *Linguistic and communicative competence: Topics in ESL*. Philadelphia, PA: Multilingual Matters Ltd.

Paus, T. (2009). Brain development. In R. Lerner & L. Steinberg (Eds.), *Handbook of adolescent psychology* (3rd ed., Vol. 1, pp. 95–115). New York, NY: Wiley.

Payer, L. (1992). *Discase-mongers: How doctors drug companies and insurers are making you feel sick*. New York, NY: John Wiley.

Payne, B. P., & McFadden, S. H. (1994). From loneliness to solitude: Religious and spiritual journeys in late life. In L. E. Thomas & S. A. Eisenhandler (Eds.), *Aging and the religious dimension* (pp. 13–27). Westport, CT: Auburn House.

Pease-Alvarez, L. (1993). *Moving in and out of bilingualism: Investigating native language maintenance and shift in Mexican-descent children*. Santa Cruz, CA: National Center for Research on Cultural Diversity, University of California.

Peets, K., Hodges, E. V., Kikas, E., & Salmivalli, C. (2007). Hostile attributions and behavioral strategies in children: Does relationship type matter? *Developmental Psychology, 43*(4), 889.

Peipert, J. F., Madden, T., Allsworth, J. E., & Secura, G. M. (2012). Preventing unintended pregnancies by providing no-cost contraception. *Obstetrics and Gynecology, 120*(6), 1291–1297.

Pelaez, M., Virues-Ortega, J., & Gewirtz, J. L. (2012). Acquisition of social referencing via discrimination training in infants. *Journal of Applied Behavior Analysis, 45*(1), 23–36.

Pellegrini, A. D., & Smith, P. K. (1998). Physical activity play: The nature and function of a neglected aspect of play. *Child Development, 69*, 577–598.

Penner, S. (1987). Parental responses to grammatical and un-grammatical child utterances. *Child Development, 58*, 376–384.

Peplau, L. A., & Cochran, S. D. (1990). A relationship perspective on homosexuality. In D. P. McWhirter, S. A. Sanders, & J. M. Reinisch (Eds.), *Homosexuality/heterosexuality: Concepts of sexual orientation* (pp. 321–349). New York, NY: Oxford University Press.

Peplau, L. A., & Fingerhut, A. W. (2007). The close relationships of lesbians and gay men. *Annual Review of Psychology, 58*, 405–424.

Perkins, H. W., & Harris, L. B. (1990). Familial bereavement and health in adult life course perspective. *Journal of Marriage and the Family, 52*, 233–241.

Perrin, A. J., Cohen, P. N., & Caren, N. (2013). Are children of parents who had same-sex relationships disadvantaged? A scientific evaluation of the no-differences hypothesis. *Journal of Gay & Lesbian Mental Health, 17*(3), 327–336.

Perry, W. G. (1970). *Forms of intellectual and ethical development in the college years*. New York, NY: Holt.

Pesonen, A. K., Räikkönen, K., Keltikangas-Järvinen, L., Strandberg, T., & Järvenpää, A. L. (2003). Parental perception of infant temperament: Does parents' joint attachment matter? *Infant Behavior and Development, 26*(2), 167–182.

Peters, E., Riksen-Walraven, J. M., Cillessen, A. H., & de Weerth, C. (2011). Peer rejection and HPA activity in middle childhood: Friendship makes a difference. *Child Development, 82*(6), 1906–1920.

Petersen, A. C., Compas, B. E., Brooks-Gunn, J., Stemmler, M. E., & Grant, K. E. (1993). Depression in adolescence. *American Psychologist, 48*, 155–168.

Peterson, P., McCarthey, S., & Elmore, R. (1996). Learning from school restructuring. *American Educational Research Journal, 33*(1), 119–153.

Peterson, R. L., & Pennington, B. F. (2012). Developmental dyslexia. *Lancet, 379*(9830), 1997–2007.

Petlichkoff, L. (1996). The drop-out dilemma in youth sports. In O. Bar-Or (Ed.), *The child and adolescent athlete* (pp. 418–432). Oxford, UK: Blackwell.

Pettit, G. S., Bates, J. E., & Dodge, K. A. (1997). Supportive parenting, ecological context, and children's adjustment: A seven-year longitudinal study. *Child Development, 68*, 908–923.

Pettit, G., Dodge, K., & Brown, N. (1988). Early family experience, social problem solving patterns, and children's social competence. *Child Development, 59*, 107–120.

Pettito, L., & Marentette, P. (1991). Babbling in the manual code: Evidence for the ontogeny of language. *Science, 251*, 1493–1496.

Philadelphia Child Guidance Center. (1994). *Your child's emotional health: The middle years*. New York, NY: Macmillan.

Philippe, F. L., & Vallerand, R. J. (2008). Actual environments do affect motivation and psychological adjustment: A test of self-determination theory in a natural setting. *Motivation and Emotion, 32*, 81–89.

Phinney, J. S. (1989). Stages of ethnic identity development in minority group adolescents. *Journal of Early Adolescence, 9*, 34–49.

Phinney, J. S., Dennis, J., & Osorio, S. (2006). Reasons to attend college among ethnically diverse college students. *Cultural Diversity and Ethnic Minority Psychology, 12*(2), 347–366.

Phinney, J. S., Ferguson, D. L., & Tate, J. D. (1997). Intergroup attitudes among ethnic minority adolescents: A causal model. *Child Development, 68*, 955–969.

Piaget, J. (1952). *The child's conception of number*. New York, NY: Norton.

Piaget, J. (1962). *Play, dreams, and imitation in childhood*. New York, NY: Norton.

Piaget, J. (1963). *The origins of intelligence in children*. New York, NY: Norton.

Piaget, J. (1964). *The moral development of the child* New York, NY: Free Press.

Piaget, J. (1965). *The child's conception of the world*. Totowa, NJ: Littlefield, Adams.

Piaget, J. (1983). Piaget's theory. In P. Mussen (Ed.), *Handbook of child psychology: Vol. 1*, New York, NY: Wiley.

Piaget, J., & Inhelder, B. (1967). *The child's conception of space*. New York, NY: Norton.

Pianta, R., Egeland, B., & Erikson, M. (1989). The effects of maltreatment on the development of young children. In D. Cicchetti & V. Carlson (Eds.), *Child Maltreatment*. New York, NY: Cambridge University press.

Piazza, J. R., & Charles, S. T. (2012). Affective disorders and age. In S. K. Whitbourne, & M. J. Sliwinski (Eds), *The Wiley-Blackwell handbook of adulthood and aging* (pp. 275–292). Malden, MA: Blackwell Publishing.

Picot, S. J., Debanne, S. M., Namazi, K. H., & Wykle, M. L. (1997). Religiosity and perceived rewards of black and white caregivers, *Educational Research, 37*, 89–101.

Piercy, K. W. (1998). Theorizing about family caregiving: The role of responsibility. *Journal of Marriage and the Family, 20*, 109–118.

Pike, A., Coldwell, J., & Dunn, J. F. (2005). Sibling relationships in early/middle childhood: Links with individual adjustment. *Journal of Family Psychology, 19*(4), 523–532.

Pillemer, K., & Suitor, J. J. (1991). "Will I ever escape my child's problems?" Effects of adult children's problems on elderly parents. *Journal of Marriage and the Family, 53*, 585–594.

Pinquart, M., & Sörensen, S. (2000). Influences of socioeconomic status, social network, and competence in later life: A meta-analysis. *Psychology and Aging, 15*, 187–224.

Pinquart, M., & Sörensen, S. (2003). Differences between caregivers and noncaregivers in psychological health and physical health: A meta-analysis. *Psychology and Aging, 18*(2), 250–267.

Pinquart, M., & Sörensen, S. (2006). Gender differences in caregiver stressors, social resources, and health: An updated meta-analysis. *Journal of Gerontology: Psychological Sciences, 61*, P33–P45.

Pinquart, M., & Sörensen, S. (2011). Spouses, adult children, and children-in-law as caregivers of older adults: A meta-analytic comparison. *Psychology and Aging, 26*, 1–14.

Piotrowski, C. (1997). Rules of everyday family life: The development of social rules in mother-child and sibling relationships. *International Journal of Behavioral Development, 21*, 571–598.

Piran, N. (1997). Prevention of eating disorders; Directions for future research. *Psychopharmacology Bulletin, 33*, 419–423.

Pittard, W. B., Laditka, J. N., & Laditka, S. B. (2008). Associations between maternal age and infant health outcomes among Medicaid-insured infants in South Carolina: Mediating effects of socioeconomic factors. *Pediatrics, 122*(1), e100–e106.

Pittman, T., & Kaufman, M. (1994). *All shapes and sizes: Promoting fitness and self-esteem in your overweight child*. Toronto: Harper Perennial Books.

Pitts, D. G. (1982). Visual acuity as a function of age. *Journal of the American Optometric Association, 53*, 117–124.

Plante, T. G., & Rodin, J. (1990). Physical fitness and enhanced psychological health. *Current Psychology: Research and Reviews, 9*, 3–24.

Plomin, R. (1989). Environment and genes: Determinants of behavior. *American Psychologist, 44*, 105–111.

Plomin, R. (1990). *Nature and nurture: An introduction to human behavioral genetics*. Pacific Grove, CA: Brooks/Cole.

Plomin, R., Owen, M. J., & McGuffin, p. (1994). The genetic basis of behavior. *Science, 264*, 1733–1739.

Pollitt, E. (Ed.). (1995). *The relationships between undernutrition and behavioral development in children*. Washington, DC: American Institute of Nutrition.

Pollock, M. L., Foster, C., Knapp, D., Rod, J. L., & Schmidt, D. H. (1987). Effect of age and training on aerobic capacity and body composition of master athletes. *Journal of Applied Physiology, 62*, 725–731.

Pomerantz, E. M., Ruble, D. N., Frey, K. S., & Greulich, F. (1995). Meeting goals and confronting conflict: Children's changing perceptions of social comparison. *Child Development, 66*, 723–738.

Porter, R. H., & Reiser, J. J. (2005). Retention of olfactory memories by newborn infants. In R. T. Mason, P. M. LeMaster, & D. Müller-Schwarze (Eds.), *Chemical Signals in Vertebrates*. New York, NY: Springer.

Portrie, T., & Hill, N. R. (2005). Blended families: A critical review of the current research. *Family Journal, 13*(4), 445–451.

Posada, G., & Kaloustian, G. (2010). Attachment in infancy. In J. G. Bremner, & T. D. Wachs (Eds.), *The Wiley-Blackwell handbook of infant development* (pp. 483–509). Malden, MA: Wiley-Blackwell Publishing.

Posner, J. K., & Vandell, D. L. (1994). Low-income children's after-school care: Are there beneficial effects of after-school programs? *Child Development, 65*, 440–456.

Potter, D. (2012). Same-sex parent families and children's academic achievement. *Journal of Marriage and Family, 74*(3), 556–571.

Poulin, F., & Chan, A. (2010). Friendship stability and change in childhood and adolescence. *Developmental Review, 30*(3), 257–272.

Powell, M. (1991). The psychosocial impact of sudden infant death syndrome on siblings. *Irish Journal of Psychology, 12*, 235–247.

Power, H., & Everly, G. S. (1988). Psychological factors in preterm labor: Critical review and theoretical synthesis. *American Journal of Psychiatry, 145*, 1507–1513.

Power, T. G. (2011). Social play. In P. K. Smith, & C. H. Hart (Eds.), *The Wiley-Blackwell handbook of childhood social development* (2nd ed., pp. 455–471). Malden, MA: Blackwell Publishing.

Pownall, T., & Kingerlee, S. (1993). *Seeing, reaching, and touching: Relationships between vision and touching in infants*. New York, NY: Harvester and Wheatsheaf.

Pratt, L. V. (1981). Business temporal norms and bereavement behavior. *American Sociological Review, 46*, 317–333.

Prayson, R. A., & Estes, M. L. (1994). The search for diagnostic criteria in Alzheimer's disease: An update. *Cleveland Clinical Journal of Medicine, 61*(2), 115–122.

Price, R. H. (1992). Psychosocial impact of joblessness on individuals and families. *Current Directions in Psychological Science, 1*, 9–11.

Primeau, M. R. (1993). Fetal movement. In B. K. Rothman (Ed.), *The encyclopedia of childbearing*. New York, NY: Henry Holt.

Prinstein, M. J. (2008). Introduction to the special section on suicide and non-suicidal self-injury: A review of the unique challenges and important directions for self-injury science. *Journal of Consulting and Clinical Psychology, 76*(1), 1–8.

Prinz, P., & Prinz, E. (1979). Simultaneous acquisition of ASL and spoken English. *Sign Language Studies, 25*, 283–296.

Pritchett, L. (1993). *Wealthier is healthier*. Washington, DC: The World Bank.

Proctor, C. P., Dalton, B., & Grisham, D. L. (2007). Scaffolding English language learners and struggling readers in a universal literacy environment with embedded strategy instruction and vocabulary support. *Journal of Literacy Research, 39*(1), 71–93.

Prohaska, T. R., Leventhal, E. A., Leventhal, H., & Keller, M. L. (1985). Health practices and illness cognition in young, middle aged, and elderly adults. *Journal of Gerontology, 40*, 569–578.

Pryor, D. W., & McGarell, E. F. (1993). Public perceptions of youth gang crime: An exploratory analysis. *Youth and Society, 24*, 399–418.

Pudrovska, T., Schieman, S., & Carr, D. (2006). Strains of singlehood in later life: Do race and gender matter? *Journal of Gerontology: Psychological Sciences and Social Sciences, 61*, S315–S322.

Puhl, R. M., & King, K. M. (2013). Weight discrimination and bullying. *Best Practice & Research Clinical Endocrinology & Metabolism, 27*(2), 117–127.

Pulakos, J. (1989). Young adult relationships: Siblings and friends. *Journal of Psychology, 123*(3), 237–244.

Purhonen, M., Kilpeläinen-Lees, R., Valkonen-Korhonen, M., Karhu, J., & Lehtonen, J. (2004). Cerebral processing of mother's voice compared to unfamiliar voice in 4-month old infants. *International Journal of Psychophysiology, 52*, 257–266.

Putney, N. M., & Bengston, V. L. (2001). Families, intergenerational relationships, and kin-keeping in midlife. In M. E. Lachman (Ed.), *Handbook of Midlife Development* (pp. 528–570). New York, NY: Wiley.

Pynoos, J., & Golant, S. (1996). Housing and living arrangements for the elderly. In R. H. Binstock & L. K. George (Eds.), *Handbook of aging and the social sciences* (pp. 303–324). San Diego: Academic Press.

Q

Quadagno, J., & Hardy, M. (1996). Work and retirement. In R. H. Binstock & L. K. George (Eds.), *Handbook of aging and the social sciences* (pp. 325–345). San Diego: Academic Press.

Quadrel, M. J., Fischoff, B., & Davis, W. (1993). Adolescent (in) vulnerability. *American Psychologist, 48*, 102–116.

Quam, J. K., & Whitford, G. S. (1992). Adaptation and age-related expectations of older gay and lesbian adults. *The Gerontologist, 32*, 367–374.

Quan, J., Bureau, J. F., Yurkowski, K., Moss, E., & Pallanca, D. (2013). The association between time spent in daycare and preschool attachment to fathers and mothers: An exploration of disorganization. *International Journal of Arts and Sciences, 6*(2), 415–422.

Queen, P., & Lang, C. (1993). *Handbook of pediatric nutrition.* Gaithersburg, MD: Aspen Publishers.

Quinlan, J. D., & Hill, D. A. (2003). Nausea and vomiting of pregnancy. *American Family Physician, 68*, 121–128.

Quinn, P. C., Kelly, D. J., Kang, L., Pascalis, O., & Slater, A. M. (2008). Preference for attractive faces in human infants extends beyond conspecifics. *Developmental Science, 11*, 76–83.

Quinn, P. K., & Reznikoff, M. (1985). The relationship between death anxiety and the subjective experience of time in the elderly. *The International journal of Aging and Human Development, 21*, 197–210.

Quintana, S. M. (2011). Ethnicity, race, and social development. In P. K. Smith, & C. H. Hart (Eds.), *The Wiley-Blackwell handbook of childhood social development* (2nd ed., pp. 299–318). Malden, MA: Blackwell Publishing.

Quirouette, C., & Gold, D. P. (1995). Spousal characteristics as predictors of well-being in older couples. In J. Hendricks (Ed.), *The ties of later life* (pp. 21–33). Amityville, NY: Baywood.

R

Raabe, T., & Beelmann, A. (2011). Development of ethnic, racial, and national prejudice in childhood and adolescence: A multinational meta-analysis of age differences. *Child Development, 82*, 1715–1737.

Rabins, P. (1992). Prevention of mental disorder in the elderly: Current perspectives and future prospects. *Journal of the American Geriatrics Society, 40*, 727–733.

Raby, K. L., Steele, R. D., Carlson, E. A., & Sroufe, L. A. (2015). Continuities and changes in infant attachment patterns across two generations. *Attachment & Human Development, 17*(4), 414–428.

Radke-Yarrow, M., Nottelmann, E., Belmont, B., & Welsh, J. D. (1993). *Journal of Abnormal Child Psychology, 21*, 683–695.

Radke-Yarrow, M., & Zahn-Waxler, C. (1987). Roots, motives, and patterns in children's prosocial behavior. In J. Reykowski, J. Karylowski, D. Bar-Tal, & E. Staub (Eds.), *Origins and maintenance of prosocial behaviors.* New York, NY: Plenum Press.

Radmacher, K., & Azmitia, M. (2006). Are there gendered pathways to intimacy in early adolescents' and emerging adults' friendships? *Journal of Adolescent Research, 21*(4), 415–448.

Rakowski, W., Julius, M., Hickey, T., Verbrugge, L. M., & Halter, J. B. (1988). Daily symptoms and behavioral responses results of a health diary with older adults. *Medical Care, 26*(3). 278–297.

Raloff, J. (2015). The dangers of vaping: Teens are falling for flavored e-cigs, but the vapors they inhale may be toxic. *Science News, 188*(1), 18–21.

Ralston, P. A. (1997). Midlife and older black women. In J. M. Coyle (Ed.), *Handbook on women and aging* (pp. 273–289). Westport, CT: Greenwood.

Rambachan, A. (2003). The Hindu way of death. In C. D. Bryant (Ed.), *Handbook of death and dying* (Vol. 2, pp. 640–648). Thousand Oaks, CA: Sage Publications.

Ramirez, O. (1998). Mexican-American children and adolescents. In J. Gibbs & L. Huang (Eds.), *Children of color: Psychological interventions with culturally diverse youth* (2nd ed.) (pp. 215–239). San Francisco: Jossey-Bass.

Ramsey, P. (1995). Changing social dynamics in early childhood classrooms. *Child Development, 66*, 764–773.

Ramu, G. N. (1991). Changing family structure and fertility patterns: An Indian case. *Journal of Asian and African Studies, 26*(3–4), 189–206.

Raphael, B., Middleton, W., Martinek, N., & Misso, V. (1993). Counseling and therapy of the bereaved. In M. S. Stroebe, W. Stroebe, & R. O. Hansson (Eds.), *Handbook of bereavement: Theory, research, and intervention* (pp. 427–453). Cambridge, UK: Cambridge University Press.

Raphael, D. (1993). Doula. In B. K. Rothman (Ed.), *The encyclopedia of childbearing.* New York, NY: Henry Holt.

Ratcliff, K. S., & Bogdan, J. (1988). Unemployed women; When social support is not supportive. *Social Problems, 35*, 54–63.

Ratner, P. A. (1998). Modeling acts of aggression and dominance as wife abuse and exploring their adverse health effects, *Journal of Marriage and the Family, 60*, 453–465.

Raver, C. C. (1996). Relations between social contingency in mother-child interaction and two-year-old's social competence. *Developmental Psychology, 32*, 850–859.

Rawlins, W. K. (1992). *Friendship matters: Communication, dialectics, and the life course.* New York, NY: Aldine DeGruyter.

Rawson, N. (2003). Age-related changes in perception of flavor and aroma. *Generations, 27*, 20–26.

Rawson, N. E., Gomez, G., Cowart, B. J., Kriete, A., Pribitkin, E., & Restrepo, D. (2012). Age-associated loss of selectivity in human olfactory sensory neurons. *Neurobiology of Aging, 33*, 1913–1919. doi: 10.1016/j.neurobiolaging.2011.09.036

Reaves, J., & Roberts, A. (1983). The effect of type of information on children's attraction to peers. *Child Development, 54*, 1024–1031.

Reccio Adrados, J. L. (1995). The influence of family, school, and peers on adolescent drug misuse. *International Journal of the Addictions, 30*, 1407–1423.

Recker, R. R., Davies, K. M., Hinders, S. M., Heaney, R. P., Stegman, M. R., & Kimmel, D. B. (1992). Bone gain in young adult women. *Journal of the American Medical Association, 268.* 2403–2408.

Reed, S. D., Lampe, J. W., Qu, C., Gundersen, G., Fuller, S., Copeland, W. K., & Newton, K. M. (2013). Self-reported menopausal symptoms in a racially diverse population and soy food consumption. *Maturitas, 75*, 152–158. doi: 10.1016/j.maturitas.2013.03.003

Reeder, K. (Ed.). (1996). *Literate apprenticeships: The emergence of language and literacy in the preschool years.* Norwood, NJ: Ablex.

Reese, H. W., & Rodeheaver, D. (1985). Problem solving and complex decision making. In J. E. Birren & K. W. Schaie (Eds.), *Handbook of the psychology of aging* (2nd ed., pp. 474–499). New York, NY: Van Nostrand Reinhold.

Rege, M., Telle, K., & Votruba, M. (2011). Parental job loss and children's school performance. *Review of Economic Studies, 78*, 1462–1489.

Reiche, E. M. V., Nunes, S. O V., & Morimoto, H. K. (2004). Stress, depression, the immune system and cancer. *Lancet Oncology, 5*, 617–625.

Reichstadt, J., Sengupta, G., Depp, C., Palinkas, L., & Jeste, D. (2010). Older adults' perspectives on successful aging: Qualitative interviews. *American Journal of Geriatric Psychiatry, 18*, 567–575. doi: 10.1097/JGP.0b013e3181e040bb

Reid, M., Landesman, S., Treider, R., & Jaccard, J. (1989). "My family and friends": Six- to twelve-year-old perceptions of social support. *Child Development, 60*, 896–910.

Reif, J. S., Bruns, C., & Lower, K. S. (1998). Cancer of the nasal cavity and paranasal sinuses and exposure to environmental tobacco smoke in pet dogs. *American Journal of Epidemiology, 147*(5), 488–492.

Reif, J. S., Dunn, K., Ogilvie, G. K., & Harris, C. K. (1992). Passive smoking and canine lung cancer risk. *American Journal of Epidemiology, 135*, 234–239.

Reilly, R. R., Brown, B., Blood, M. R., & Malatesta, C. Z. (1981). The effects of realistic previews: A study and discussion of the literature. *Personnel Psychology, 34*, 832–834.

Remafedi, G. (2007). Adolescent homosexuality. In R. M. Kliegman, R. E. Behrman, J. B. Jenson, & B. F. Stanton (Eds.), *Nelson textbook of pediatrics* (pp. 67–68). Philadelphia, PA: WB Saunders Company.

Remafedi, G., Resnick, M., Blum, R., & Harris, L. (1992). Demography of sexual orientation in adolescents. *Pediatrics, 89*, 714–721.

Reno, V. P., & Vehte, B. (2011). Economic status of the elderly. In R. H. Binstock & L. K. George (Eds.), *Handbook of aging and the social sciences* (pp. 175–191). San Diego, CA Academic Press.

Renzulli, J. (1994). *Schools for talent improvement.* Mansfield Center, CT: Creative Learning Press.

Reuter, M. A., & Conger, R. D. (1995). Antecedents of parent-adolescent disagreements. *Journal of Marriage and the Family, 57*, 435–448.

Rey-Lopez, J. P., Vicente-Rodríguez, G., Biosca, M., & Moreno, L. A. (2008). Sedentary behaviour and obesity development in children and adolescents. *Nutrition, Metabolism and Cardiovascular Diseases, 18*(3), 242–251.

Reynolds, A. J., & Temple, J. A. (1998). Extended early childhood intervention and school achievement: Age thirteen findings from the Chicago Longitudinal Study. *Child Development, 69*, 231–246.

Reynolds, K., Lewis, L. B., Nolen, J. D., Kinney, G. L., Sathya, B., & He, J. (2003). Alcohol consumption and risk of stroke: A meta-analysis. *Journal of the American Medical Association, 289*, 579–588.

Richards, M., & Wadsworth, M. E. J. (2004). Long term effects of early adversity on cognitive function. *Archives of Disease in Childhood, 89*, 922–927.

Richards, M. H., Crowe, P. A., Larson, R., & Swarr, A. (1998). Developmental patterns and gender differences in the experience of peer companionship during adolescence. *Child Development, 69*, 154–163.

Richardson, V., & Kilty, K. M. (1992). Retirement intentions among black professionals: Implications for practice with older black adults. *The Gerontologist, 32*, 7–16.

Richio, L. J., Phipps, M. G., & Raker, C. A. (2010). Repeat teen birth: Does delivery mode make a difference? *American Journal of Obstetrics and Gynecology, 203*, 453–458.

Richter, P. (1993). HIV and pregnancy. In B. K. Rothman (Ed.), *The encyclopedia of childbearing.* New York, NY: Henry Holt.

Ricketts, S., Klingler, G., & Schwalberg, R. (2014). Game change in Colorado: Widespread use of long-acting reversible contraceptives and rapid decline in births among young, low-income women. *Perspectives on Sexual and Reproductive Health, 46*(3), 125–132.

Rickman, M. D., & Davidson, R. J. (1995). Personality and behavior in parents of temperamentally inhibited and uninhibited children. *Developmental Psychology, 30,* 346–354.

Rideout, V. J., Foehr, U. G., & Roberts, D. F. (2010). Generation M^2: Media in the lives of 8-to 18-year-olds. *Henry J. Kaiser Family Foundation.* Retrieved from http://files.eric.ed.gov/fulltext/ED527859.pdf

Rieck, T., Jackson, A. W., Martin, S. B., Petrie, T. A., & Greenleaf, C. A. (2013). Relation between depression and physical fitness of middle school students. *Medicine & Science in Sport & Exercise, 45*(6), 1083–1088.

Riggle, E. D., Rotosky, S. S., & Riggle, S. G. (2010). Psychological distress, well-being, and legal recognition in same-sex couple relationships. *Journal of Family Psychology, 24*(1), 82–86.

Rigsby, D. C., Macones, G. A., & Driscoll, D. A. (1998). Risk factors for rapid repeat pregnancy among adolescent mothers: A review of the literature. *Journal of Pediatric and Adolescent Gynecology, 11*(3), 115–126.

Riley, E. P., Infante, M. A., & Warren, K. R. (2011). Fetal alcohol spectrum disorders: An overview. *Neuropsychology Review, 21,* 73–80.

Rivkees, S. A. (2003). Developing circadian rhythmicity in infants. *Pediatrics, 112,* 373–381.

Roberto, K. A., & Stroes, J. (1995). Grandchildren and grandparents: Roles, influences, and relationships. In J. Hendricks (Ed.), *The ties of later life* (pp. 142–153). Amityville, NY: Baywood.

Roberts, B. W., & Mroczek, D. (2008). Personality trait change in adulthood. *Current Directions in Psychological Science, 17,* 31–35.

Roberts, P., & Newton, P. M. (1987). Levinsonian studies of women's adult development. *Psychology and Aging, 2,* 154–163.

Roberts, R. E. Kaplan, G. A., Shema, S. J., & Strawbridge, W. J. (1997). Does glowing old increase the risk for depression? *American Journal of Psychiatry, 154,* 1384–1390.

Roberts, R. E. L., & Bengston, V. L. (1996). Affective ties to parents in early adulthood and self-esteem across 20 years. *Social Psychology Quarterly, 59,* 96–106.

Roberts, W., & Strayer, J. (1996). Empathy, emotional expressiveness, and prosocial behavior. *Child Development, 67,* 449–470.

Robertson, M. (1992). *Starving in the silences.* New York, NY: New York University Press.

Robin, A. L., & Foster, S. L. (1989). *Negotiating parent-adolescent conflict: A behavioral family systems approach.* New York, NY: Guilford Press.

Robin, A. L., Koepke, T., & Moye, A. (1990). Multidimensional assessment of parent-adolescent relations. *Psychological Assessment: A Journal of Consulting and Clinical Psychology, 2*(4), 451–459.

Robins, R. W., & Trzesniewski, K. H. (2005). Self-esteem development across the lifespan. *Current Directions in Psychological Science, 14*(3), 158–162.

Rochat, P. (2003). Five levels of self-awareness as they unfold early in life. *Consciousness and Cognition, 12*(4), 717–731.

Roche, K. M., Ensminger, M. E., & Cherlin, A. J. (2007). Variations in parenting and adolescent outcomes among African American and Latino families living in low-income, urban areas. *Journal of Family Issues, 28*(7), 882–909.

Rodeheaver, D., & Stobs, J. (1991). The adaptive misperception of age in older women: Sociocultural images and psychological mechanisms of control. *Educational Gerontology, 17,* 141–156.

Rodgers, J. L., & Rowe, D. C. (1993). Social contagion and adolescent sexual behavior: A developmental EMOSA model. *Psychological Review, 100,* 479–510.

Rodin, G. M., Chmara, J., Ennis, J., Fenton, S., Locking, H., & Steinhouse, K. (1981). Stopping life-sustaining medical treatment: Psychiatric considerations in the termination of renal dialysis. *Canadian Journal of Psychiatry, 26,* 540–544.

Rodin, J. (1986). Aging and health: The effects of the sense of control. *Science, 233,* 1271–1276.

Rodkin, P. C., Ryan, A. M., Jamison, R., & Wilson, T. (2013). Social goals, social behavior, and social status in middle childhood. *Developmental Psychology, 49*(6), 1139.

Roelofs, J., Meesters, C., ter Huurne, M., Bamelis, L., & Muris, P. (2006). On the links between attachment style, parental rearing behaviors, and internalizing and externalizing problems in non-clinical children. *Journal of Child and Family Studies, 15*(3), 319–332.

Roerecke, M., & Rehm, J. (2012). The cardioprotective association of average alcohol consumption and ischaemic heart disease: A systematic review and meta-analysis. *Addiction, 107*(7), 1246–1260.

Rogers, L. P., & Markides, K. S. (1989). Well-being in the postparental stage in Mexican-American women. *Research on Aging, 11,* 508–516.

Roggman, L. A., Langlois, J. H., Hubbs-Tait, L., & Rieser-Danner, L. A. (1994). Infant day-care, attachment, and the "file drawer problem." *Child Development, 65,* 1429–1443.

Rogoff, B. (1990). *Apprenticeship in thinking.* New York, NY: Oxford University Press.

Rogoff, B., & Chavajay, P. (1995). What's become of research on the cultural basis of cognitive development? *American Psychologist, 50,* 859–877.

Rogoff, B., Mistry, J., Goncu, A., & Mosler, C. (1993). Guided participation in cultural activity by toddlers and caregivers. *Monographs of the Society for Research in Child Development, 58*(8, Serial No. 236).

Roisman, G. I., Clausell, E., Holland, A., Fortuna, K., & Elieff, C. (2008). Adult romantic relationships as contexts of human development: A multimethod comparison of same-sex couples with opposite sex dating, engaged, and married dyads. *Developmental Psychology, 44,* 91–101.

Roland, A. (1988). *In search of self in India and Japan: Toward a cross-cultural psychology.* Princeton, NJ: Princeton University-Press.

Romaine, S. (1995). *Bilingualism* (2nd ed.). Oxford, UK: Black-wells.

Romig, D. A., Cleland, C., & Romig, J. (1989). *Juvenile delinquency: Visionary approaches* Columbus, Ohio: Merrill.

Rooks, J. P., et al. (1989, December). Outcomes of care in birth centers. *New England Journal of Medicine, 321,* 1801–1822.

Room, R. (2004). Smoking and drinking as complementary behaviors. *Biomedicine and Pharmacotherapy, 58,* 111–115. doi: 10.1016/j.biopha.2003.12.003

Roopnarine, J. L., Johnson, J. E., & Hooper, F. H. (Eds.), (1994). *Children's play in diverse cultures.* Albany, NY: State University of New York Press.

Rose, J., & Gamble, J. (1993). *Human walking* (2nd ed.). Baltimore: Williams and Williams.

Rosemary, S. L., Arbeau, K. A., Lall, D. I., & De Jaeger, A. E. (2010). Parenting and child characteristics in the prediction of shame in early and middle childhood. *Merrill-Palmer Quarterly, 56*(4), 500–528.

Rosenberg, B. G., & Hyde, J. S. (1993). The only child: Is there only one kind of only? *Journal of Genetic Psychology, 154,* 269–282.

Rosenberg, M. S. (1979). *Conceiving the self.* New York, NY: Basic Books.

Rosenberg, M. S., & Repucci, N. D. (1985). Primary prevention of child abuse. *Journal of Consulting and Clinical Psychology, 53,* 576–585.

Rosenblatt, P. C. (1993). Grief: The social context of private feelings. In M. S. Stroebe, W. Stroebe, & R. O. Hansson (Eds.), *Handbook of bereavement: Theory, research, and intervention* (pp. 102–111). Cambridge, UK: Cambridge University Press.

Rosenblatt, P. C., Walsh, R. P., & Jackson, D. A. (1976). *Grief and mourning in cross-cultural perspective.* New Haven. CT: Human Relations Area Files Press.

Rosenfeld, E., Shemesh, G., & Kurtz, S. (2012). The efficacy of selective laser trabeculoplasty versus argon laser trabeculoplasty in pseudophakic glaucoma patients. *Clinical Ophthalmology, 6,* 1935–1940.

Rosenfeld, M. J., & Thomas, R. J. (2012). Searching for a mate: The rise of the internet as a social intermediary. *American Sociological Review, 77*(4), 523–547.

Rosenheim, M. K., & Testa, M. F. (Eds.). (1992). *Early parenthood and coming of age in the 1990's.* New Brunswick, NJ: Rutgers University Press.

Ross, C. E., Mirowsky, J., & Goldsteen, K. (1990). The impact of the family on health: A decade in review. *Journal of Marriage and the Family, 52,* 1059–1078.

Ross, H. M. (1994). Societal/cultural views regarding death and dying. In G. E. Dickinson, M. R. Lerning, & A. C. Mermann (Eds.), *Dying, death, and bereavement* (2nd ed., pp. 83–90) Guilford, CT: Dushkin Publishing Group.

Ross, H., Tesla, C., Kenyon, B., & Lollis, S. (1990). Maternal intervention in toddler peer conflict: The socialization of principles of justice. *Development Psychology, 26,* 994–1003.

Ross, J., & Kahan, J. P. (1983). Children by choice or by chance: The perceived effects of parity. *Sex Roles, 9,* 69–77.

Ross, P. (1993). *National excellence: The case for developing A*merica*'s talent.* Washington, DC: United States Department of Education.

Rossell, C. H. (1988). How effective are voluntary plans with magnet schools? *Educational Evaluation and Policy Analysis, 10,* 325–342.

Rossi, A. S. (1982). Transition to parenthood. In L. R. Allman & D. T. Jaffe (Eds), *Readings in adult psychology: Contemporary perspectives* (2nd ed., pp. 263–275). New York, NY: Harper & Row.

Rossi, A. S., & Rossi, P. H. (1990). *Of human bonding: Parent child relations across the life course* New York, NY: Aldine de Gruyter.

Rossi, G. (1997). The nestlings: Why young adults stay at home longer. The Italian case. *Journal of Family Issues, 18,* 627–644.

Rostila, M., & Saarela, J. M. (2011). Time does not heal all wounds: Mortality following the death of a parent. *Journal of Marriage and Family, 73,* 236–249.

Rothbart, M. (1989). Temperament in childhood: A framework, In G. Kohnstamm, J. Bates, & M. Rothbart (Eds), *Temperament in childhood (*pp 59–73) New York, NY: Wiley.

Rothbart, M. K. (2007). Temperament, development, and personality. *Current Directions in Psychological Science, 16*(4), 207–212.

Rothbart, M. K., & Ahadi, S. (1994). Temperament and the development of personality *Journal of Abnormal Psychology, 103,* 55–66.

Rothbart, M. K., Hanley, D., & Albert, M. (1986). Gender differences in moral reasoning. *Sex Roles, 15,* 645–653.

Rothman, K. J. (2008). BMI-related errors in the measurement of obesity. *International Journal of Obesity, 32,* S56–S59.

Rounds, J. B., & Zevon, M. A. (1993). Cancer stereotypes: A multidimensional scaling analysis *Journal of Behavioral Medicine, 16,* 485–496.

Rourke, B., & Del Dotto, J. (1994). *Learning disabilities: Neuropsychological perspectives.* Thousand Oaks, CA: Sage.

Routledge, C., & Juhl, J. (2010). When death thoughts lead to death fears: Mortality salience increases death anxiety for individuals who lack meaning in life. *Cognition and Emotion, 24*(5), 848–854.

Rowe, J. W., & Kahn, R. L. (1987). Human aging: Usual and successful. *Science, 237,* 143–149.

Rowe, J. W., & Kahn, R. L. (1997). Successful aging. *Gerontologist, 37,* 433–440.

Rowe, M. L., Levine, S. C., Fisher, J. A., & Goldin-Meadow, S. (2009). Does linguistic input play the same role in language learning for children with and without early brain injury? *Developmental Psychology, 45,* 90–102.

Rowland, T. (1993). The physiological impact of intensive training on the prepubertal athlete. In B. Cahill and A. Pearl (Eds.), *Intensive participation in children's sports* (pp. 167–194). Champaign, IL: Human Kinetics Press.

Royce, J. M., Hymowitz, N., Corbett, K., Hartwell, T. D., & Orlandi, M. A. (1993). Smoking cessation factors among African Americans and whites. *American Journal of Public Health, 83*(2), 220–226.

Rozee, P. D. (1996). Freedom from fear of rape: The missing link in women's freedom. In J. C Chrisler, C. Golden, & P. D. Rozee (Eds.), *Lectures on the psychology of women* (pp. 309–322). New York, NY: McGraw Hill.

Rubenstein, J. L., & Howes, C. (1976). The effects of peers on toddler interaction with mother and toys. *Child Development, 47*, 597–605.

Rubenstein, J. L., & Howes, C. (1983). Social-emotional development of toddlers in day care: The role of peers and of individual differences. *Advances in Early Education and Day Care, 3*, 13–45.

Rubenstein, J. L., Halton, A., Kasten, M. A., Rubin, C., & Stechler, G. (1998). Suicidal behavior in adolescents: Stress and protection in different family contexts. *American Journal of Orthopsychiatry, 68*, 274–284.

Rubenstein, J. L., Heeren, T., Housman, D., Rubin, C., & Stechler, G. (1989). Suicidal behavior in "normal" adolescents: Risk and protective factor's. *American Journal of Orthopsychiatry, 59*, 59–71.

Rubin, K., Fredstrom, B., & Bowker, J. (2008). Future directions in... Friendship in childhood and early adolescence. *Social Development, 17*(4), 1085–1096.

Rubin, K. H., Coplan, R. J., & Bowker, J. C. (2009). Social withdrawal in childhood. *Annual Review of Psychology, 60*, 141.

Rubin, K. H., & Krasnor, L. (1980). Changes in the play behaviors of preschoolers: A short-term longitudinal investigation. *Canadian Journal of Behavioral Science, 12*, 278–282.

Rubin, L. B. (1979). *Women of a certain age: The midlife search for self.* New York, NY: Harper & Row.

Rubin, S. S. (1993). The death of a child is forever: The life course impact of a child loss. In M. S. Stroebe, W. Stroebe, & R. O. Hansson (Eds.), *Handbook of bereavement: Theory, research., and intervention* (pp. 285–299). Cambridge, UK: Cambridge University Press.

Rubinstein, R. L., Alexander, B. B., Goodman, M., & Luborsky, M. (1991). Key relationships of never married, childless older women: A cultural analysis. *Journal of Gerontology, 46*, S270–277.

Ruble, D. N. (1988). Sex-role development. In M. H. Bornstein & M. E. Lamb (Eds.), *Developmental psychology: An advanced textbook* (2nd ed., pp. 411–460). Hillsdale, NJ: Erlbaum.

Ruble, D. N., Martin, C. L., & Berenbaum, S. (2006). Gender development. In W. Damon, & R. M. Lerner (Series Eds.), & N. Eisenberg (Vol. Ed.), *Handbook of child psychology: Vol. 3. Social, emotional and personality development* (6th ed.). Hoboken, NJ: Wiley.

Rudman, D., Feller, A. G., Nagraj, H. S., Gergans, G. A. Lalitha, P. Y., Goldberg, A. F., ... & Mattson, D. E. (1990). Effects of human growth hormone in men over 60 years old. *New England Journal of Medicine, 323*, 1–6.

Rudowitz, R., Artiga, S., & Arguello, R. (2014). *Children's health coverage: Medicaid, CHIP, and the ACA.* Retrieved from http://kff.org/health-reform/issue-brief/childrens-health-coverage-medicaid-chip-and-the-aca/

Rudy, D., & Grusec, J. E. (2006). Authoritarian parenting in individualist and collectivist groups: Associations with maternal emotion and cognition and children's self-esteem. *Journal of Family Psychology, 20*(1), 68–78.

Rueter, M. A., & Conger, R. D. (1995). Interaction style, problem solving behavior, and family problem-solving effectiveness. *Child Development, 66*, 98–115.

Ruhm, C. J. (1997). The Family and Medical Leave Act. *Journal of Economic Perspectives, 11*, 175–186.

Ruhm, C. J. (2000). Parental leave and child health. *Journal of Health Economics, 19*(6), 931–960.

Ruiz, S. A., & Silverstein, M. (2007). Relationships with grandparents and the emotional well-being of late adolescent and young adult grandchildren. *Journal of Social Issues, 63*, 793–808.

Ruiz-Primo, M. A. (2011). Informal formative assessment: The role of instructional dialogues in assessing students' learning. *Studies in Educational Evaluation, 37*(1), 15–24.

Russ, S. W., & Dillon, J. A. (2011). Changes in children's pretend play over two decades. *Creativity Research Journal, 23*(4), 330–338.

Russell, K., & Ludwig, B. (2015). *Smoking is out; vaping is in. The rise of e-cigarettes among US youth.* Retrieved from http://jdc.jefferson.edu/cgi/viewcontent.cgi?article=1952&context=hpn

Russell, R. M. (1992). Nutrient requirements. In J. B. Wyngaarden, L. H. Smith, & J. C Bennett (Eds.), *Cecil textbook of medicine, Vol. 2* (19th ed., pp. 1147–1151). Philadelphia: Saunders.

Rutter, M. (1995). *Psychosocial disturbances in young people.* New York, NY: Cambridge University Press.

Ruzek, V. L. (1997). Women, personal health behavior, and health promotion. In S. B. Ruzek, V. L. Olesen, & A. E Clarke (Eds.), *Women's health: Complexities and differences* (pp. 118–153). Columbus: Ohio State University Press.

Ryan, A. (2012). Exercise in aging: Its important role in mortality, obesity, and insulin resistance. *Aging Health, 6*, 551–563. doi: 10.2217/ahe.10.46

Ryan, J. (1995). *Little girls in pretty boxes: The making and breaking of elite gymnasts and figure skaters.* New York, NY: Double-day.

Rybash, J. M., Hoyer, W. J., & Roodin, P. A. (1986). *Adult cognition and aging: Developmental changes in processing, knowing and thinking.* Elmsford, NY: Pergamon Press.

Rybash, J. M., Roodin, P. A., Hoyer, W. J. (1995). *Adult development and aging (3rd ed.)* Madison: Brown & Benchmark.

S

Saad, L. (2013). *Gallup politics: Majority of Americans still support Roe v. Wade decision.* Retrieved from http://www.gallup.com/poll/160058/majority-americans-support-roe-wade-decision.aspx

Saad-Lessler, J., Ghilarducci, T., & Richman, K. (2014). Work and retirement. In K. E. Whitfield, & T. A. Baker (Eds.), *Handbook of Minority Aging.* New York, NY: Springer Publishing.

Saarelainen, S., Vasankari, T., Jousilahti, P., Heistaro, S., Heliovaara, M., Luukkaala, & T. Paavilainen, E. (2010). COPD, chronic bronchitis and capacity for day-to-day activities: Negative impact of illness on the health-related quality of life. *Chronic Respiratory Disease, 7*, 207–215.

Sachs, J. S. (1995, October). Worrying yourself sick: Alzheimer's anxiety can hit anyone. *Longevity*, pp. 68, 76.

Safety-belt use and motor-vehicle-related injuries–Navajo Nation, 1988–1991. (1992, September 25). *Morbidity and Mortality Weekly Report, 41*(38), 705.

Sagi, A., van Ijzendoorn, M. H., Aviezer, O., Donnell, F., & Mayseless, O. (1994). Sleeping out of home in a kibbutz communal arrangement: It makes a difference for infant-mother attachment. *Child Development, 65*, 992–1004.

Sagi-Schwartz, A. (2008). The well being of children living in chronic war zones: The Palestinian—Israeli case. *International Journal of Behavioral Development, 32*(4), 322–336.

Sakraida, T. J. (2008). Stress and coping of midlife women in divorce transition. *Western Journal of Nursing Research, 30*, 869–887.

Salcido, R. M. (1990). Mexican-Americans: Illness, death and bereavement. In J. K. Parry (Ed.), *Social work practice with the terminally ill: A transcultural perspective* (pp. 99–112). Springfield, IL: Charles C Thomas.

Sale, C., & Addington-Hall, J., & McCarthy, M. (1997). Awareness of dying: Prevalence, causes and consequences. *Social Science & Medicine, 45*, 477–484.

Saler, L., & Skolnick, N. (1992). Childhood parental death and depression in adulthood: Roles of surviving parent and family environment. *American Journal of Orthopsychiatry, 62*, 504–516.

Salguero, A., Gonzalez-Boto, R., Tuero, C., & Marquez, S. (2003). Identification of dropout reasons in young competitive swimmers. *Journal of Sports Medicine and Physical Fitness, 43*(4), 530.

Salisbury, C., & Robertson, C. (2013). Maternal nutrition: Building foundations of long-term good health. *Nutrition Bulletin, 38*, 249–253.

Salomon, G., & Perkins, D. (1998). Individual and social aspects of learning. In P. D. Pearson & A. Iran-Nejad (Eds.), *Review of research in education* (Vol. 23, pp. 1–24). Washington, DC: American Educational Research Association.

Salthouse, T. A. (1984). Effects of age and skill in typing. *Journal of Experimental Psychology: General, 113*, 345–371.

Samter, W., & Haslett, B. (1997). Family influences on communicative and social development. In B. Haslett & W. Samter (Eds.), *Children communicating: The first five years* (pp. 160–191). Mahwah, NJ: Erlbaum.

Samuel-Hodge, C. D., Garcia, B. A., Johnston, L. F., Gizlice, Z., Ni, A., Cai, J., ... & Keyserling, T. C. (2013). Translation of a behavioral weight loss intervention for mid-life, low-income women in local health departments. *Obesity, 21*, 1764–1773. doi: 10.1002/oby.20317

Samuels, C. A. (2005). Special educators discuss NCLB effect at national meeting. *Education Week, 24*, 12.

Samuelsson, I. P., & Carlsson, M. A. (2008). The playing learning child: Towards a pedagogy of early childhood. *Scandinavian Journal of Educational Research, 52*(6), 623–641.

Sanders, C. M. (1993). Risk factors in bereavement outcome In M. S. Stroebe, W. Stroebe, & R. O. Hansson (Eds.), *Handbook of bereavement: Theory, research, and intervention* (pp. 255–267). Cambridge, UK: Cambridge University Press.

Sanders, S. A., Graham, C. A., & Milhausen, R. R. (2008). Predicting sexual problems in women: The relevance of sexual excitation and sexual inhibition. *Archives of Sexual Behavior, 37*(2), 241–251.

Sandler, I. N., Ma, Y., Tein, J. Y., Ayers, T. S., Wolchik, S., Kennedy, C., & Millsap, R. (2010). Long-term effects of the family bereavement program on multiple indicators of grief in parentally bereaved children and adolescents. *Journal of Consulting and Clinical Psychology, 78*(2), 131–143.

Sandnabba, N. K., & Ahlberg, C. (1999). Parents' attitudes and expectations about children's cross-gender behavior. *Sex Roles, 40*(3–4), 249–263.

Sanfilippo, J., Finkelstein, J., & Styne, D. (Eds.) (1994). *Medical and gynecological endocrinology* Philadelphia: Hanley and Belfus.

Sankar, A. (1991). *Dying at home: A guide for family caregivers* Baltimore: Johns Hopkins University Press.

Sankar, A. (1993). Images of home death and the elderly patient: Romantic versus real. *Generations, 16*(2), 59–63.

Santrock, J., & Sitterle, K. (1987). Parent-child relationships in stepmother families. In K. Pasley & M. Ihinger-Tallman (Eds.), *Remarriage and stepparenting: Current research and theory,* New York, NY: Guilford Press.

Saracho, O. N., & Spodek, B. O. (1998). A historical overview of theories of play. In O. N. Saracho & B. Spodek, et al. (Eds.), *Multiple perspectives on play to early childhood education*. SUNY series, *Early Childhood Education: Inquiries and Insights* (pp. 1–10). Albany, NY: State University of New York Press.

Sarafino, E., & Armstrong, J. (1986). *Child and adolescent development*. New York, NY: West.

Sato, D. (1993). DES: Diethylstilbestrol. In B. K. Rothman (Ed.), *The encyclopedia of childbearing*. New York, NY: Henry Holt.

Saucier, M. G. (2004). Midlife and beyond: Issues for aging women. *Journal of Counseling and Development, 82*, 420–425.

Sault, N. (Ed.). (1994). *Many mirrors: Body image and social relations*. New Brunswick, NJ: Rutgers University Press.

Saunders, P. A., Copeland, J. R. M., Dewey, M. E., Davidson, I. A., McWilliam, C., Sharma, V. K., Sullivan, C., & Voruganti, L. N. P. (1989). Alcohol use and abuse in the elderly: Findings from the Liverpool longitudinal study of continuing health in the community. *International Journal of Geriatric Psychiatry, 4*, 103–108.

Sautter, J. M., Thomas, P. A., Dupre, M. E., & George, L. K. (2012). Socioeconomic status and the black-white mortality crossover. *American Journal of Public Health, 102*, 1566–1571.

Savelsbergh, G. (1993). *Development of coordination in infancy*. New York, NY: North-Holland.

Savin-Williams, R. C. (1995). An exploratory study of pubertal maturation timing and self-esteem among gay and bisexual male youths. *Developmental Psychology, 31*, 56–64.

Savin-Williams, R. C., & Berndt, T. (1990). Peer relations during adolescence. In S. Feldman & G. Elliot (Eds.), *At the threshold: The developing adolescent*. Cambridge, MA: Harvard University Press.

Sawin, D. (1979). Assessing empathy in children: A search for an elusive construct. Paper presented at the meeting of the Society for Research on Child Development, San Francisco.

Scanzoni, J., Polonko, K., Teachman, J., & Thompson, L. (1989). *The sexual bond: Rethinking families and close relationships*. Newbury Park, CA: Sage.

Scarr, S. (1998). American child care today. *American Psychologist, 53*, 95–108.

Schaefer, J. A., & Moos, R. H. (1992). Life crisis and personal growth. In B. N. Carpenter (Ed.), *Personal coping, theory, research, and application* (pp. 149–170). Westport. CT: Praeger.

Schafer, W. (1987). *Stress management for wellness*. New York, NY: Holt, Rinehart and Winston.

Schaie, K. W. (1977/1978). Toward a stage theory of adult cognitive development. *Journal of Aging and Human Development., 5*(2), 129–138.

Schaie, K. W. (1988). Ageism in psychological research. *American Psychologist, 43*, 179–183.

Schaie, K. W. (1990). Intellectual development in adulthood. In J. E Birren & K. W. Schaie (Eds.), *Handbook of the psychology of aging* (3rd ed., pp. 291–309). San Diego: Academic Press.

Schaie, K. W. (1994). The course of adult intellectual development. *American Psychologist, 49*, 304–313.

Schaie, K. W. (1996). Intellectual developments. In J. E. Birren & K. W. Schaie (Eds.), *Handbook of the psychology of aging* (pp. 266–286). San Diego: Academic Press.

Schaie, K. W. (2005). *Developmental influences on adult intelligence: The Seattle longitudinal study*. New York, NY: Oxford University Press.

Schaie, K. W. (2008). A lifespan developmental perspective of psychological ageing. In K. Laidlaw & B. Knight (Eds.), *Handbook of emotional disorders in later life: Assessment and treatment* (pp. 3–32). New York, NY: Oxford University Press.

Schaie, K. W. (2010). Adult intellectual abilities. In I. B. Weiner & W. E. Craigshead (Eds.), *Corsini encyclopedia of psychology* (4th ed., vol. 1, pp. 36–37). Hoboken, NJ: Wiley.

Schaie, K. W. (2013). *Developmental influences on adult intelligence: The Seattle longitudinal study* (2nd ed.). New York, NY: Oxford University Press.

Schaie, K. W. (2014). *About the Seattle Longitudinal Study*. Retrieved from https://sharepoint.washington.edu/uwsom/sls/about/Pages/default.aspx.

Schaie, K. W., & Strother, C. R. (1968). A cross-sequential study of age changes in cognitive behavior. *Psychological Bulletin, 70*, 671–680.

Scharlach, A. E. (1991). Factors associated with filial grief following the death of an elderly parent. *Journal of Orthopsychiatry, 61* (2), 307–313.

Scharlach, A. E., & Boyd, S. (1989). Caregiving and employment: Results of an employee survey. *The Gerontologist, 29*. 382–387.

Scharlach, A. E., & Fredriksen, K. I. (1993). Reactions to the death of a parent during midlife. *Omega, 27*(4), 307–319.

Scharlach, A. E., & Fuller-Thomson, E. (1994). Coping strategies following the death of an elderly parent. *Journal of Gerontological Social Work, 21*(3/4), 85–100.

Scherder, E., Scherder, R., Verburgh, L., Konigs, M., Blom, M., Kramer, A. F., & Eggermont, L. (2013). Executive functions of sedentary elderly may benefit from walking: A systematic review and meta-analysis. *American Journal of Geriatric Psychiatry, 22*(8):782–791 doi: 10.1016/j.jagp.2012.12.026

Schick, V., Herbenick, D., Reece, M., Sanders, S. A., Dodge, B., Middlestadt, S. E., & Fortenberry, J. D. (2010). Sexual behaviors, condom use, and sexual health of Americans over 50: Implications for sexual health promotion for older adults. *Journal of Sexual Medicine, 7*, 315–329.

Schiller, B. (2004). *The economics of poverty and discrimination* (9th ed.). Upper Saddle River, NJ: Pearson Prentice Hall.

Schlegel, A., & Barry, H. (1991). *Adolescence: An anthropological inquiry* (pp. 133–156). New York, NY: Free Press.

Schmid, S. M., Hallschmid, M., Jauch-Chara, K., Born, J., & Schultes, B. (2008). A single night of sleep deprivation increases ghrelin levels and feelings of hunger in normal-weight healthy men. *Journal of Sleep Research, 17*(3), 331–334.

Schneider, J., Jock, S. S., & Meier, C. R. (2009). Risk of gynecological cancers in users of estradiol/dydrogesterone or other HRT preparations. *Climacteric, 12*, 514–524.

Schneidman, E. (1992). *Death: Current perspectives* (3rd ed.). Mountain View, CA: Mayfield.

Schoenborn, C. A., & Danchik, K. M. (1980, November). Health practices among adults. *Advance data, vital health statistics*, No. 64, November 4.

Schoklitsch, A., & Baumann, U. (2012). Generativity and aging: A promising future research topic? *Journal of Aging Studies, 26*, 262–272.

Schoppe-Sullivan, S. J., & Mangelsdorf, S. C. (2013). Parent characteristics and early coparenting behavior at the transition to parenthood. *Social Development, 22*, 363–383.

Schrader, D. (Ed.). (1990). *The legacy of Lawrence Kohlberg (New Directions in Child Development, No. 47)*. San Francisco: Jossey-Bass.

Schulenberg, J., Maggs, J., and Hurrelmann, K. (Eds.). (1997). *Health risks and developmental transitions during adolescence*. New York, NY: Cambridge University Press.

Schulman, E. P., Steinberg, L., & Piquero, A. R. (2013). The age-crime curve in adolescence and early adulthood is not due to age differences in economic status. *Journal of Youth and Adolescence, 42*, 848–860.

Schulz, R. (1978). *The psychology of death, dying, and bereavement*. Reading, Mass: Addison-Wesley.

Schutzer, K. A., & Graves, B. S. (2004). Barriers and motivations to exercise in older adults. *Preventative Medicine, 39*, 1056–1061.

Schwartz, D., Dodge, K. A., Pettit, G. S., & Bates, J. (1997). The early socialization of aggression and bullying *Child Development, 68*, 665–675.

Schweinhart, L., Barnes, H., & Weikart, D. (1993). Significant benefits: The High/Scope Perry Preschool Study through age 27. (*Monographs of the High/Scope Educational Research Foundation*, No. 10). Ypsilanti, MI: High/Scope Press.

Schweinhart, L., & Weikart, D. (1992). The High/Scope Perry Preschool Study, similar studies, and their implications for public policy in the United States. In D. Slegelin (Ed.), *Early childhood education: Policy issues for the 1990's* (pp. 67–88). Norwood, NJ: Ablex.

Schweinhart, L., & Weikart, D. (1999). The advantages of High/Scope: Helping children lead successful lives. *Educational Leadership, 57*, 76–77.

Schweinle, A., & Wilcox, T. (2004). Intermodal perception and physical reasoning in young infants. *Infant Behavior and Development, 27*, 246–265.

Scollon, R., & Scollon, S. (1994). *Intercultural communication: A discourse approach*. Oxford, UK: Blackwell.

Scott, K. D., Klaus, P. H., & Klaus, M. H. (1999). A comparison of intermittent and continuous support during labor: A meta-analysis. *Journal of Women's Health & Gender-Based Medicine, 8*, 1257–1264.

Scraton, S. (1992). *Shaping up to womanhood: Gender and girls' physical education*. Philadelphia: Open University Press.

Seale, C., & Addington-Hall, J. (1994). Euthanasia: Why people want to die earlier. *Social Science & Medicine, 39*, 647–654.

Seale, C., & Kelly, M. (1997a). A comparison of hospice and hospital care for people who die: Views of the surviving spouse. *Palliative Medicine, 11*, 93–100.

Seale, C., & Kelly, M. (1997b). A comparison of hospice and hospital care for the spouses of people who die: *Palliative Medicine, 11*, 101–106.

Seale, C., Addington-Hall, J., & McCarthy, M. (1997). Awareness of dying: Prevalence, causes and consequences. *Social Science & Medicine, 45*, 477–484.

Sears, S. F., Urizar, G. G., & Evans, G. D. (2000). Examining a stress-coping model of burnout and depression in extension agents. *Journal of Occupational Health Psychology, 5*, 56–62.

Seccombe, K. (1991). Assessing the costs and benefits of children: Gender comparisons among childfree husbands and wives. *Journal of Marriage and the Family, 53*, 191–202.

Seccombe, K. (1992). Employment, the family, and employer-based policies. In J. W. Dwyer & R. T. Coward (Eds.), *Gender, families, and elder care* (pp. 165–180). Newbury Park, CA: Sage.

Sedgh, G., Finer, L. B., Bankole, A., Eilers, M. A., & Singh, S. (2015). Adolescent pregnancy, birth, and abortion rates across countries: Levels and recent trends. *Journal of Adolescent Health, 56*(2), 223–230.

Seidel, H., Rosenstein, B., & Pathak, A. (Eds.). (1997). *Primary care of the newborn* (2nd ed.). St. Louis: Mosby.

Seidman, S. N., & Rieder, R. O. (1994). A review of sexual behavior in the United States. *American Journal of Psychiatry, 151*, 330–341.

Seidner, L. B., Stipek, D. J., & Feshbach, N. D. (1988). A developmental analysis of elementary school-aged children's concepts of pride and embarrassment. *Child Development, 59*, 367–377.

Seifer, R., Sameroff, A. J., Barrett, L. C., & Krafechuk, E. (1994). Infant temperament measured by multiple observations and mother reports. *Child Development, 65*, 1478–1490.

Seifert, K. (1993). Cognitive development in early childhood. In B. Spodek (Ed.), *Handbook of research on the education of young children* (3rd ed., pp. 7–40). New York, NY: Macmillan.

Seifert, K. (2000). Uniformity and diversity in everyday views of "the" child. In S. Harkness (Ed.), *New directions in child development: Parental belief systems in cultural context*. San Francisco: Jossey-Bass.

Seiffge-Krenke, I. (2010). Predicting the timing of leaving home and related developmental tasks: Parents' and children's perspectives. *Journal of Social and Personal Relationships, 27*(4), 495–518.

Seiffge-Krenke, I. (2016). Leaving home: Antecedents, consequences, and cultural patterns. In J. J. Arnett (Ed.), *The Oxford handbook of emerging adulthood* (pp. 177–189). New York, NY: Oxford University Press.

Seitz, V., & Apfel, N. (1994). Parent-focused intervention: Diffusion effects on siblings. *Child Development, 65*(2), 677–683.

Seleen, D. R. (1982). The congruence between actual and desired use of time by older adults: A predictor of life satisfaction. *The Gerontologist, 22*, 995–99.

Selekman, J. (1993). Update: New guidelines for the treatment of infants with sickle cell disease. *Pediatric Nursing, 19*, 800–809.

Selman, R. (1980). *The growth of interpersonal understanding,* New York, NY: Academic Press.

Selman, R. (1981). The child as friendship philosopher. In S. Asher & J. Gottman (Eds.), *The development of children's friendships.* New York, NY: Cambridge University Press.

Seltzer, M. M., Greenberg, J. S., Floyd, F. J., Pettee, Y., & Hong, J. (2001). Life course impacts of parenting a child with a disability. *American Journal on Mental Retardation, 106*, 265–286.

Selye, H. (1985). History and present status of the stress concept. In A. Monat and R. Lazarus (Eds.), *Stress and coping.* New York, NY: Columbia University Press.

Selzer, R. (1993). *Mortal lessons* New York, NY: Touchstone.

Shafer, M. B., & Moscicki, A. (1991). Sexually transmitted diseases. In W.R. Hendee (Ed.), *The health of adolescents: Understanding and facilitating biological, behavioral, and social development* (pp. 211–249). San Francisco: Jossey-Bass.

Shapiro, A. F., Gottman, J. M., & Carrere, S. (2000). The baby and the marriage: Identifying factors that buffer against decline in marital satisfaction after the first baby arrives. *Journal of Family Psychology, 14*, 59–70.

Shapiro, J. P. (1993). *No pity: People with disabilities forging a new civil rights movement.* New York, NY: Random House.

Shaughnessy, L., Doshi, S. R., & Everett Jones. (2004). Attempted suicide and associated health risk behaviors among Native American high school students. *Journal of School Health, 74*, 177–182.

Shaw, B. A., Liang, J., Krause, N., Gallant, M., & McGeever, K. (2010). Age differences and social stratification in the long-term trajectories of leisure-time physical activity. *Journals of Gerontology Series B: Psychological Sciences and Social Sciences, 65*, 756–766.

Sheehan, M. J., & Watson, M. W. (2008). Reciprocal influences between maternal discipline techniques and aggression in children and adolescents. *Aggressive Behavior, 34*(3), 245–255.

Sheldon, S., Spire, J., & Levy, H. (1992). *Pediatric sleep medicine.* Philadelphia: Saunders.

Shenk, D., & Achenbaum, A. (1993). Introduction: Changing perceptions of the aging and the aged *Generations,* 17(2), 5–8.

Shephard, R. J. (1987). *Physical activity and aging.* Rockville, MD: Aspen Publishers.

Shepherd-Look, D. (1982). Sex differentiation and the development of sex roles. In B. Wolman (Ed.), *Handbook of developmental psychology.* Englewood Cliffs, NJ: Prentice-Hall.

Shiao, R., Tao, X., McLeskey, S., Bano, M., Khera, S., Kern, F., Freter, C., & Vincent, T. (1995). Over-expression of' TL–6 in MCF-7 breast cancer cells results in increased tumorigenicity in nude mice. *Proceedings of the American Association for Cancer Research Annual Meeting, 36*, 255.

Ship, J. A., Pearson, J. D., Cruise, L. J., Brant, L. J., & Metter, E. J. (1996). Longitudinal changes in smell identification, *Journal of Gerontology: Series A, Biological Sciences & Medical Sciences, 51*(2), M86–91.

Short, J. E. (2015). *How much media? 2015 report on American consumers.* Retrieved from http://www.marshall.usc.edu/faculty/centers/ctm/research/how-much-media

Shrum, W., Cheek, N. H., & Hunter, S. M. (1988). Friendship in school: Gender and racial homophily. *Sociology of Education, 61*, 227–239.

Shu, C., Hummel, T., Lee, P., Chiu, C., Lin, S., & Yuan, B. (2009). The proportion of self-rated olfactory dysfunction does not change across the life span. *American Journal of Rhinology and Allergy, 23*, 413–416.

Shuchter, S. T., & Zisook, S. (1993). The course of normal grief. In M. S. Stroebe, W. Stroebe, & R. O. Hansson (Eds.), *Handbook of bereavement: Theory, research, and intervention* (pp. 23–43). Cambridge, UK: Cambridge University Press.

Shulman, S., & Connolly, J. (2016). The challenge of romantic relationships in emerging adulthood. In J. J. Arnett (Ed.), *The Oxford handbook of emerging adulthood* (pp. 230–244). New York, NY: Oxford University Press.

Shultz, S., & Vouloumanos, A. (2010). Three-month-olds prefer speech to other naturally occurring signals. *Language Learning and Development, 6*, 241–257.

Shure, M. B., & Spivak, G. (1988). Interpersonal cognitive problem solving. In R. II. Price, W. L. Cowen, R. P. Lorion, & J. Ramos-McKay (Eds.), *14 ounces of prevention: A casebook for practitioners* (pp. 69–82). Washington, DC: American Psychological Association.

Siebens, J. (2013). Extended measures of well-being: Living conditions in the United States, 2011. Retrieved from https://www.census.gov/prod/2013pubs/p70-136.pdf

Siegel, J. M., & Kuykendall, D. H. (1990). Loss, widowhood, and psychological distress among the elderly. *Journal of Consulting and Clinical Psychology, 58*, 519–524.

Sigelman, C., Maddox, A., Epstein, J., & Carpenter, W. (1993). Age differences in understandings of disease causality: AIDS, colds and cancer. *Child Development, 64*, 272–284.

Silber, S. J. (1991). *How to get pregnant with the new technology.* New York, NY: Warner Books.

Silveira, M. J., Kim, S. Y., & Langa, K. M. (2010). Advance directives and outcomes of surrogate decision making before death. *New England Journal of Medicine, 362*(13), 1211–1218.

Silverman, P. R., Nickman, S., & Worden, J. W. (1992). Detachment revisited: The child's reconstruction of a dead patent. *American Journal of Orthopsychiatry, 62*, 494–505.

Silverman, P., & Worden, J. (1993). Children's reactions to the death of a parent. In M. Stroebe, W. Stroebe, & R. Hansson (Eds.), *Handbook of bereavement: Theory, research, and intervention* (pp 300–315). Cambridge: Cambridge University Press.

Silverstein, L. B. (1991). Transforming the debate about child care and maternal employment. *American Psychologist, 46*, 1025–1032.

Simkin, P. (2007). *The birth partner, third edition: A complete guide to childbirth for dads, doulas, and all other labor companions.* Boston, MA: Harvard Common Press.

Simonds, W. (1993). Politics of abortion. In B. K. Rothman (Ed.), *The encyclopedia of childbearing.* New York, NY: Henry Holt.

Simone, P. M., & Haas, A. L. (2013). Frailty, leisure activity and functional status in older adults: Relationship with subjective well being. *Clinical Gerontologist, 36*, 275–293.

Simons, R. L., & Beaman, J. (1996). Fathers' parenting. In R. L. Simons et al. (Eds.), *Understanding differences between divorced and intact families: Stress, interaction and child outcome* (pp. 94–103). Thousand Oaks, CA: Sage.

Simons, R. L., & Chao, W. (1996). Conduct problems. In R. L. Simons et al. (Eds.), *Understanding differences between divorced and intact families: Stress, interaction, and child outcome* (pp. 81–93). Thousand Oaks, CA: Sage.

Simons, R. L., & Johnson, C. (1996). Mothers' parenting. In R. L. Simons et al. (Eds.), *Understanding differences between divorced and intact families: Stress, interaction and child outcome* (pp. 81–93). Thousand Oaks, CA: Sage.

Simonton, D. K. (1990). Creativity and wisdom in aging. In J. E. Birren & K. W. Schaie (Eds.), *Handbook of the psychology of aging* (3rd ed. , pp. 320–329). San Diego: Academic Press.

Simpson, J. A., Collins, W. A., Tran, S., & Haydon, K. C. (2007). Attachment and the experience and expression of emotions in romantic relationships: A developmental perspective. *Journal of Personality and Social Psychology, 92*(2), 355–367.

Simpson, J. L., Holzgreve, W., & Driscoll, D.A. (2012). Genetic counseling and genetic screening. In S. G. Gabbe, J. R. Niebyl, & J. L. Simpson (Eds.), *Obstetrics: Normal and problem pregnancies* (6th ed.). Philadelphia, PA: Elsevier Churchill Livingstone.

Sinclair, D. (1990). *Human growth after birth* (5th ed.). New York, NY: Oxford University Press.

Singer, J. L. (1995). Imaginative play in childhood: Precursor of subjunctive thought, daydreaming, and adult pretending games, In A. D. Pellegrini (Ed.), *The future of play theory: A multidisciplinary inquiry into the contributions of Brian Sutton-Smith.* SUNY series, *Children's Play in Society* (pp. 187–219). Albany, NY: State University of New York Press.

Singh, G. K., & Siahpush, M. (2006). Widening socioeconomic inequalities in the US life expectancy, 1980–2000. *International Journal of Epidemiology, 35*, 969–979.

Sinnott, J. D. (1998). *The development of logic in adulthood: Postformal thought and its applications.* New York, NY: Plenum.

Sinnott, J. D. (1989). Life-span relativistic postformal thought: Methodology and data from everyday problem-solving studies. In M. L. Commons, J. D. Sinnott, F. A. Richards, & C. Armon (Eds.), *Adult development: Vol. 1. Comparisons and applications of developmental models* (pp. 239–265). New York, NY: Praeger.

Sinnot, J. D. (2003). Postformal thought and adult development. In J. Demick & C. Andreoletti (Eds.), *Handbook of adult development.*(pp. 221–238). New York, NY: Springer.

Sipe, B., & Hall, E. J. (1996). *I am not your victim.* Newbury Park, CA: Sage.

Sizer, T. (1996). *Horace's hope* Boston: Houghton Mifflin.

Skinner, B. F. (1957). *Verbal behavior.* New York, NY: Appleton-Century-Crofts.

Skinner, J. H. (1992). Aging in place: The experience of African American and other minority elders. *Generations, 16*(2), 49–51.

Skolnick, A., & Skolnick, J. (1989). *Families in transition: Rethinking marriage, sexuality, child-rearing and family organization* (6th ed.). New York, NY: Scott Foresman.

Skoog, I. (1994). Bisk factors for vascular dementia: A review. *Dementia, 5*(3–4), 137–144.

Slade, A. (1987). Quality of attachment and early symbolic play. *Developmental Psychology, 23*, 78–85.

Slater, A., Bremner, G., Johnson, S. P., Sherwood, P., Hayes, R., & Brown, E. (2000). Newborn infants' preference for attractive faces: The role of internal and external facial features. *Infancy, 1*, 265–274.

Slater, A., & Morrison, V. (1991). Visual attention and memory at birth. In M. Weiss & P. Zelazo (Eds.), *Newborn attention: Biological constraints and the influence of experience* (pp. 256–277). Norwood, NJ: Ablex.

Slater, S. (1995). Lesbians and generativity: Not everyone waits for midlife. *Work in Progress, No. 72* Wellesley, MA: The Stone Center Working Paper Series.

Slavin, R. (1996). Research on cooperative learning and achievement: What we know, and what we need to know. *Contemporary Educational Psychology, 21*, 43–69.

Slavin, R. (Ed.). (1998). *Show me the evidence: Promising programs for American schools*. Thousand Oaks, CA: Corwin Press.

Slavin, R. E. (1995). *Cooperative learning* (2nd ed.) Boston: Allyn & Bacon.

Slaughter, V. (2005). Young children's understanding of death. *Australian Psychologist, 40*(3), 179–186.

Slaughter, V., & Griffiths, M. (2007). Death understanding and fear of death in young children. *Clinical Child Psychology and Psychiatry, 12*(4), 525–535.

Slochower, J. A. (1993). Mourning and the holding function of shiva. *Contemporary Psychoanalysis, 29*, 352–367.

Slomin, M. (1991). *Children, culture, and ethnicity: Evaluating and understanding the impact*. New York, NY: Garland.

Sloper, P., Turner, S., Knussen, C., & Cunningham, C. C. (1990). Social life of school children with Down's syndrome. *Child Care, Health, and Development, 16*, 235–251.

Slusher, M. P., Mayer, C. J., & Dunkle, R. E. (1996). Gays and lesbians older and wiser (GLOW): A support group for older gay people. *Gerontologist, 36*, 118–123.

Small, S. A., & Kearns, D. (1993). Unwanted sexual activity among peers during early and middle adolescence: Incidence and risk factors. *Journal of Marriage and the Family, 55*, 941–952.

Smetana, J. G. (1995). Parenting styles and conceptions of parental authority during adolescence. *Child Development, 66.* 299–316.

Smetana, J. G., Killen, M., & Turiel, E. (1991). Children's reasoning about interpersonal and moral conflicts. *Child Development, 62*, 629–644.

Smilansky, S. (1968). *The effects of sociodramatic play on disadvantaged preschool children*. New York, NY: Wiley.

Smith, A. (1996). Rehabilitation of children following sport- and activity-related injuries. In O. Bar-Or (Ed.), *The child and adolescent athlete* (pp. 224–244). Oxford, UK: Blackwells.

Smith, A. D. (1996). Memory. In J. E. Birren & K. W. Schaie (Eds.), *Handbook of the psychology of aging* (pp. 236–250). San Diego: Academic Press.

Smith, C. J., Alexander, L. M., & Kenney, W. L. (2013). Nonuniform, age-related decrements in regional sweating and skin blood flow. *American Journal of Regulatory, Integrative and Comparative Physiology, 205*, R877–R885.

Smith, D. (1998). *Inclusion: Schools for all students*. Belmont. CA: Wadsworth.

Smith. D. E., & Blinn Pike, L. (1994). Relationship between Jamaican adolescent's drinking patterns and self-image: A cross-cultural perspective. *Adolescence, 29*, 429–437.

Smith, G. R., Williamson, G. M., Miller, L. S., & Schulz, R. (2011). Depression and quality of informal care: A longitudinal investigation of caregiving stressors. *Psychology and Aging, 26*, 584–591.

Smith, J., & Baltes, P. B. (1990). Wisdom-related knowledge: Age/cohort differences in response to life-planning problems. *Developmental Psychology, 26*, 494–505.

Smith, J. F., Eisenberg, M. L., Glidden, D., Millstein, S. G., Cedars, M., Walsh, T. J., ... & Katz, P. P. (2011). Socioeconomic disparities in the use and success of fertility treatments: Analysis of data from a prospective cohort in the United States. *Fertility and Sterility, 96*(1), 95–101.

Smith, K. R., Zick, C. D., & Duncan, G. J. (1991). Remarriage patterns among recent widows and widowers. *Demography, 28*, 361–374.

Snarey, J. R. (1985). Cross-cultural universality of social-moral development: A critical review of Kohlbergian research. *Psychological Bulletin, 97*, 202–232.

Snowling, M., & Stackhouse, J. (1996). *Dyslexia, speech, and language: A practitioner's handbook*. San Diego: Singular Publishers Group.

Soldier, L. (1993). Working with Native-American children, *Young Children, 47*(6), 15–21.

Soley, G., & Hannon, E. E. (2010). Infants prefer the musical meter of their own culture: A cross-cultural comparison. *Developmental Psychology, 46*, 286–292.

Solfrizzi, V., Scafato, E., Capurso, C., D'Introno, A., Colacicco, A. M., Frisardi, V., ... & Panza, F. (2010). Metabolic syndrome and the risk of vascular dementia: The Italian Longitudinal Study on Ageing. *Journal of Neurology, Neurosurgery, and Psychiatry, 81*, 433–440.

Soltis, J. (2004). The signal functions of early infant crying. *Behavioral and Brain Sciences, 27*, 443–490.

Somers, M. D. (1993). A comparison of voluntarily childfree adults and parents. *Journal of Marriage and the Family, 55*, 643–650.

Sommerville, J. (1990). *The rise and fall of childhood* (2nd ed.). New York, NY: Vintage Books.

Sood, A. B., Razdan, A., Weller, E. B., & Weller, R. A. (2006). Children's reactions to parental and sibling death. *Current Psychiatry Reports, 8*(2), 115–120.

Sorenson, S., & Bowie, P. (1994). Vulnerable populations: Girls and young women. In L. Eron & J. Gentry (Eds.), *Violence and youth: Psychology's response: Vol. II. Papers of the American Psychological Association on Violence and Youth*. Washington, DC: American Psychological Association.

Sorkhabi, N., & Mandara, J. (2013). Are the effects of Baumrind's parenting styles culturally specific or culturally equivalent? In R. E. Larzelere, A. S. Morris, & A. W. Harrist (Eds). *Authoritative parenting: Synthesizing nurturance and discipline for optimal child development* (pp. 113–135). Washington, DC: American Psychological Association.

Soto, L. (1997). *Language, culture, and power: Bilingual families and the struggle for quality education*. Albany, NY: State University of New York Press.

Sousa, C., Herrenkohl, T. I., Moylan, C. A., Tajima, E. A., Klika, J. B., Herrenkohl, R. C., & Russo, M. J. (2011). Longitudinal study on the effects of child abuse and children's exposure to domestic violence, parent-child attachments, and antisocial behavior in adolescence. *Journal of Interpersonal Violence, 26*(1), 111–136.

Spaccarelli, S. (1994). Stress, appraisal, and coping in child sexual abuse: A theoretical and empirical review. *Psychological Bulletin, 116*, 340–362.

Spassov, L., Curzi-Dscalovi, L., Clairambuait, J., Kauffman, F., Eiselt, M., Medigue, C., & Peirano, P. (1994). Heart rate and heart-rate variability during sleep in small-for-gestational-age newborns. *Pediatric Research, 35*, 500–505.

Speece, M. W., & Brent, S. B. (1984). Children's understanding of death: A review of three components of the death concept. *Child Development, 55*, 1671–1686.

Spencer, S. M., & Patrick, J. H. (2009). Social support and personal mastery as protective resources during emerging adulthood. *Journal of Adult Development, 16*(4), 191–198.

Spencer, T. J., Faraone, S. V., Biederman, J., Lerner, M., Cooper, K. M., Zimmerman, B., & Concerta Study Group. (2006). Does prolonged therapy with a long-acting stimulant suppress growth in children with ADHD? *Journal of the American Academy of Child & Adolescent Psychiatry, 45*(5), 527–537.

Spetner, N., & Olsho, L. (1990). Auditory frequency resolution in human infants. *Child Development, 61*, 632–652.

Spirito, A., Stark, L., Fristad, M., Hart, K., & Owens-Stively, J. (1989). Adolescent suicide attempters hospitalized on a pediatric unit. In S. Chess, A. Thomas, & M. E. Hertzig (Eds.), *Annual progress in child psychiatry and child development*. New York, NY: Brunner/Mazel.

Spitze, G., & Logan, J. R. (1990). Sons, daughters, and inter-generational support. *Journal of Marriage and the Family, 52*, 420–430.

Spitze, G., & Logan, J. R. (1992). Helping as a component of parent-adult child relations. *Research on Aging, 14*, 291–312.

Spodek, B., & Saracho, O. (Eds.). (1993). *Language and literacy in early childhood education*. New York, NY: Teachers' College Press.

Sponseller, D., & Jaworski, A. (1979). *Social and. cognitive complexity in young children's play*. Paper presented at the annual meeting of the American Educational Research Association, San Francisco.

Spurrier, N. J., Magarey, A. A., Golley, R., Curnow, F., & Sawyer, M. G. (2008). Relationships between the home environment and physical activity and dietary patterns of preschool children: A cross-sectional study. *International Journal of Behavioral Nutrition and Physical Activity, 5*(1), 31.

Sroufe, L. A. (1979). The coherence of individual development: Early care, attachment, and subsequent developmental issues. *American Psychologist, 34*, 834–841.

Sroufe, L. A., Fox, N., & Pancake, V. (1983). Attachment and dependency in developmental perspective. *Child Development, 54*, 1615–1627.

St. James-Roberts, I. (2007). Helping parents to manage infant crying and sleeping: A review of the evidence and implications for services. *Child Abuse Review, 16*, 47–69.

St. James-Roberts, I., & Halil, T. (1991). Infant crying patterns in the first year: Normal community and clinical findings. *Journal of Child Psychology and Psychiatry, 32*, 951–968.

St. James-Roberts, I., Harris, G., & Messer, D. (Eds.). (1993). *Infant crying, feeding, and sleeping: Development, problems, and treatments*. New York, NY: Harvester Wheatsheaf.

St. Jeor, S. (Ed.). (1997). *Obesity assessment: Tools, methods, interpretations*. New York, NY: Chapman & Hall.

St. Peters, M., Fitch, M., Huston, A. C., Wright, J .C., & Eakins, D. J. (1991). Television and families: What do young children watch with their parents? *Child Development, 62*, 1409–1423.

Stack, C. B. (1981). Sex roles and survival strategies in an urban black community. In F. C. Steady (Ed.), *The black woman cross-culturally* (pp. 349–367). Cambridge, MA: Shinkman.

Stack, C. B. (1993). The culture of gender: Women and men of color. In M. J. Larrabee (Ed.), An *ethic of care: Feminist and interdisciplinary perspectives* (pp. 108–111). New York, NY: Routledge.

Stack, S., & Eshleman, J. R. (1998). Marital status and happiness: A 17-nation study. *Journal of Marriage and the Family, 60*, 527–536.

Stake, J. E. (1997). Integrating expressiveness and instrumentality in real-life settings: A new perspective on the benefits of androgyny. *Sex Roles, 37*, 541–564.

Stander, V., & Jensen, L. (1993). The relationship of value orientation to moral cognition: Gender and cultural differences in the United States and China explored. *Journal of Cross-Cultural Psychology, 24*, 42–52.

Stanford, E. P., & DuBois, B. (1992). Gender and ethnicity patterns. In J. E. Birren, R. B. Sloane, & G. D. Cohen (Eds.), *Handbook of mental health and aging* (2nd ed., pp. 99–115). San Diego: Academic Press.

Stanger-Hall, K. F., & Hall, D. W. (2011). Abstinence-only education and teen pregnancy rates: Why we need comprehensive sex education in the US. *PLoS ONE, 6*(10), e24658.

Stathopoulou, G., Powers, M. B., Berry, A. C., Smits, J. A., & Otto, M. W. (2006). Exercise interventions for mental health: A quantitative and qualitative review. *Clinical Psychology: Science and Practice, 13*(2), 179–193.

Staudinger, U. M., Smith, J., & Baltes, P. B. (1992). Wisdom-related knowledge in a life review task: Age differences and the role of professional specialization. *Psychology and Aging, 2,* 271–281.

Steele, H., Steele, M., & Fonagy, P. (1996). Associations among attachment classifications of mothers, fathers, and their infants. *Child Development, 67,* 541–555.

Steiger, C. (1993). Midwifery: Overview. In B. K. Rothman (Ed.), *The encyclopedia of childbearing.* New York, NY: Henry Holt.

Stein, P. N., Gordon, W. A., Hibbard, M. R., & Sliwinski, M. J. (1992). An examination of depression in the spouses of stroke patients. *Rehabilitation Psychology, 37,* 121–130.

Steinberg, L., Lamborn, S. D., Darling, N., Mounts, N. S., & Dornbusch, S. M. (1994). Over-time changes in adjustment and competence among adolescents from authoritative, authoritarian, indulgent, and neglectful families. *Child. Development, 65,* 754–770.

Steinberg, L. D. (1986). Latchkey children and susceptibility to peer pressure: An ecological analysis. *Developmental Psychology, 22,* 433–439.

Steinberg, L. D. (2004). Risk taking in adolescence: What changes, and why? In R. E. Dahl & L. P. Spear (Eds.), *Adolescent brain development: Vulnerabilities and opportunities* (Vol. 1021, pp. 51–58), New York, NY: New York Academy of Sciences.

Steinberg, L. D., Lamborn, S. D., Dornbusch, S. M., & Darling, N. (1992). Impact of parenting practices on adolescent achievement: Authoritative parenting, school involvement, and encouragement to succeed. *Child Development, 63,* 1266–1281.

Steinberg, L. D., & Levine, A. D. (1990). *You and your adolescent: A parent's guide to development from 10 to 20.* New York, NY: Harper & Row.

Steinberg, L. D., Mounts, N. S., Lamborn, S. D., & Dornbusch, S. M. (1991). Authoritative parenting and adolescent adjustment across varied ecological niches. *Journal of Research in Adolescence, 1,* 19–36.

Steiner, G. (1987). Spatial reasoning in small-size and large-size environments; In search of early prefigurations of spatial cognition in small-size environments. In B. Inhelder, D. de Caprona, & A. Wells (Eds.), *Piaget today.* Hillsdale, NJ: Erlbaum.

Steiner, H., McQuivey, R. W., Pavelski, R., Pitts, T., & Kraemer, H. (2000). Adolescents and sports: Risk or benefit? *Clinical Pediatrics, 39*(3), 161–166.

Steiner, J. E., Glasser, D., Hawilo, M. E., & Berridge, I. C. (2001). Comparative expression of hedonic impact: Affective reactions to taste by human infants and other primates. *Neuroscience & Biobehavioral Reviews, 25,* 53–74.

Steinglass, P., & Gerrity, E. (1990). Natural disasters and posttraumatic stress disorder: Short-term versus long-term recovery in two disaster-affected communities. *Journal of Applied Social Psychology, 20,* 1746–1765.

Stephenson, J. S. (1985). *Death, grief, and mourning: Individual and social realities.* New York, NY: The Free Press.

Steptoe, A., Peacey, V., & Wardle, J. (2006). Sleep duration and health in young adults. *Archives of Internal Medicine, 166*(16), 1689–1692.

Stern, D. N. (1992). *Diary of a baby.* New York, NY: Basic Books.

Stern, D. N. (1995). *The motherhood constellation: A unified view of parent-infant psychotherapy* New York, NY: Basic Books.

Stern, D. N. (2004). The motherhood constellation: Therapeutic approaches to early relational problems. In A. J. Sameroff, S. C. McDonough, & K. L. Rosenblum (Eds.), *Treating parent-infant relationship problems: Strategies for intervention* (pp. 29–42). New York, NY: Guilford Press.

Sternberg, R. J. (1987). *The triangle of love: Intimacy, passion, commitment.* New York, NY: Basic Books.

Sternberg, R. J. (1988). *The triarchic mind: A new theory of human intelligence.* New York, NY: Penguin Books.

Sternberg, R. J. (1992). Intellectual development: A satiric fairy tale. In R. J. Sternberg & C. A. Berg (Eds.), *Intellectual development* (pp. 381–394). New York, NY: Cambridge University Press.

Sternberg, R. J. (1994). *Thinking and problem solving.* San Diego: Academic Press.

Sternberg, R. J. (1997). *Thinking styles.* New York, NY: Cambridge University Press.

Sternberg, R. J. (1998). Abilities are forms of developing expertise. *Educational Researcher, 27*(3), 11–21.

Sternberg, R. J. (2006). The nature of creativity. *Creativity Research Journal, 18*(1), 87–98.

Sternberg, R. J., & Wagner, R. (Eds.). (1994). *Mind in context: Interactionist perspectives on human intelligence.* New York, NY: Cambridge University Press.

Stets, J. E. (1990). Verbal and physical aggression in marriage. *Journal of Marriage and the Family, 52,* 501–514.

Stevenson, H. W., & Lee, S. Y. (1990). Contexts of achievement: A study of American, Chinese, and Japanese children. *Monographs of the Society for Research in Child Development, 55.*

Stevenson, H. W., Chen, C., & Uttal, D. H. (1990). Beliefs and achievement: A study of black, white and Hispanic children, *Child Development, 61,* 508–523.

Stevenson-Hinde, J. (1998). Parenting in different cultures: Time to focus, *Developmental Psychology, 34,* 698–700.

Stevenson-Hinde, J., & Verschueren, K. (2002). Attachment in childhood. In P. K. Smith, & C. H. Hart (Eds.), *Blackwell handbook of childhood social development* (pp. 182–204). Oxford: Blackwell.

Stuart, G. L., Meehan, J. C., Moore, T. M., Morean, M., Hellmuth, J., & Follansbee, K. (2006). Examining a conceptual framework of intimate partner violence in men and women arrested for domestic violence. *Journal of Studies on Alcohol, 67*(1), 102–112.

Stuart, G. L., Temple, J. R., Follansbee, K. W., Bucossi, M. M., Hellmuth, J. C., & Moore, T. M. (2008). The role of drug use in a conceptual model of intimate partner violence in men and women arrested for domestic violence. *Psychology of Addictive Behaviors, 22*(1), 12–24.

Stewart, R. B., Mobley, L. A., Van Tuyl, S. S., & Salvador, M. A. (1987). The firstborn's adjustment to the birth of a sibling: A longitudinal assessment. *Child Development, 58,* 341–355.

Stickgold, R. (2005). Sleep-dependent memory consolidation. *Nature, 437*(7063), 1272–1278.

Stifter, C. A., Coulehan, C. M., & Fish, M. (1993). Linking employment to attachment: The mediating effects of maternal separation anxiety and interactive behavior. *Child Development, 64,* 1451–1460.

Stiles, J., & Jernigan, T. L. (2010). The basics of brain development. *Neuropsychology Review, 20,* 327–348.

Stillion, J. M. (1985). *Death and the sexes: An examination of differential longevity, attitudes, behaviors, and coping skills.* Washington, DC: Hemisphere.

Stipek, D. J., Gralinski, H., & Kopp, C. B. (1990). Self-concept development in the toddler years. *Developmental Psychology, 26,* 972–977.

Stocker, C. (1994). Children's perceptions of relationship with siblings, friends and mothers: Compensatory processes and links with adjustment. *Journal of Child Psychology and Psychiatry, 35,* 1447–1459.

Stokes, G. (1985). The social profile. In R. Coles & G. Stokes (Eds.), *Sex and the American teenager* (pp. 31–144). New York, NY: Harper & Row.

Stolberg, A. L., & Walsh, P. (1988). A review of treatment methods for children of divorce. In S. A. Wolchik & P. Karoly (Eds.), *Children of divorce* (pp. 299–321). New York, NY: Gardner Press.

Stoller, E. P. (1992). Gender differences in the experiences of caregiving spouses. In J. W. Dwyer & R. T. Coward (Eds.), *Gender, families, and elder care* (pp. 49–64). Newbury Park, CA: Sage.

Stoller, E. P., & Cutler, S. J. (1992). The impact of gender on configurations of care among married elderly couples. *Research on Aging, 14,* 313–330.

Stoller, E. P., & Pugliesi, K. L. (1989). Other roles of caregiver: Competing responsibilities or supportive resources. *Journal of Gerontology: Social Sciences, 44,* 231–238.

Stone, M. R., Brown, B. B. (1998). In the eye of the beholder: Adolescents' perceptions of peer crowd stereotypes. In R. E. Muuss, H. D. Porton, et al. (Eds). *Adolescent behavior and society; A book of readings* (5th ed.). (pp. 158–169). New York, NY: McGraw Hill.

Stone, R., Cafferata, G. L., & Sangl, J. (1987). Caregivers of the frail elderly: A national profile. *The Gerontologist, 27,* 616–626.

Stones, M. J., & Kozma, A. (1996). Activity, exercise, and behavior. In J. E. Birren, & K. W. Schaie (Eds.), *Handbook of the psychology of aging* (338–352.) San Diego: Academic Press.

Stoppa, T. M., & Lefkowitz, E. S. (2010). Longitudinal changes in religiosity among emerging adult college students. *Journal of Research on Adolescence, 20*(1), 23–38.

Stout, B. C. (1993). Thalidomide. In B. K. Rothman (Ed.), *The encyclopedia of childbearing.* New York, NY: Henry Holt.

Stratford, B. (1994). Down syndrome is for life. *International Journal of Disability, Development and Education, 41,* 3–13.

Straub, R. O. (2014). *Health Psychology* (4th ed.). New York, NY: Worth.

Straus, M. A., & Smith, C. (1990). Violence in Hispanic families in the United States: Incidence rates and structural interpretations. In M. A. Straus & R. J. Gelles, with C. Smith (Eds.), *Physical violence in American families: Risk factors and adaptations to violence in 8,145 families* (pp. 341–367). New Brunswick, NJ: Transaction.

Straus, M. A., Gelles, R. J., & Steinmetz, S. (1980). *Behind closed doors: Violence in the American family.* Garden City, NY: Anchor.

Streissguth, A. P., Barr, H. M., Sampson, P. D., Darby, B. L., & Martin, D. C. (1989). IQ at age 4 in relation to maternal alcohol use and smoking during pregnancy. *Developmental Psychology, 25,* 3–11.

Streissguth, A. P., Bookstein, F. L., Sampson, P., & Barr, H. (1995). Attention: Prenatal alcohol and continuities of vigilance and attentional problems from 4 through 14 years. *Development and Psychopathology, 7,* 419–446.

Strickland, B. R. (1988a). Menopause. In E. A. Blechman & K. D Brownell (Eds.), *Handbook of behavioral medicine for women* (pp. 41–48). New York, NY: Pergamon.

Strickland, B. R. (1988b). Sex-related differences in health and illness. *Psychology of Women Quarterly, 12,* 381–399.

Striegel-Moore, R. H. (1997). Risk factors for eating disorders, In M. S. Jacobson, J. M. Rees, N. H. Golden, & C. E. Irwin (Eds.), Adolescent nutritional disorders: Prevention and treatment. *Annals of the New York Academy of Sciences, 817,* pp. 98–109.

Striegel-Moore, R. H., & Bulik, C. M. (2007). Risk factors for eating disorders. *American Psychologist, 62*(3), 181–198.

Striegel-Moore, R., & Smolak, L. (1996). The role of race in the development of eating disorders. In L. Smolak, M. P. Levine, & R. Striegel-Moore (Eds.), *The developmental psychopathology of eating disorders: Implications for research, prevention, and treatment* (pp. 259–284). Mahwah, NJ: Erlbaum.

Stringhini, S., Dugravot, A., Shipley, M., Goldberg, M., Zins, M., Kivimaki, M., ... & Singh-Manoux, A. (2011). Health behaviours, socioeconomic status, and mortality: Further analyses of the British Whitehall II and the French GAZEL prospective cohorts. *PLoS Medicine, 8,* e1000419. doi: 10.1371/journal.pmed.1000419.

Stroebe, M., Schut, H., & Stroebe, W. (2007). Health outcomes of bereavement. *Lancet, 370*, 1960–1973.

Stroebe, M. S., & Stroebe, W. (1993). The mortality of bereavement: A review. In M. S. Stroebe, W. Stroebe, & R. O. Hansson (Eds.), *Handbook of bereavement: Theory, research, and intervention* (pp. 175–195). Cambridge, UK: Cambridge University Press.

Stroebe, M. S., Stroebe, W., & Hansson, R. O. (1993). Bereavement theory and research: An introduction to the handbook. In M. S. Stroebe, W. Stroebe, & R. O. Hansson (Eds.), *Handbook of bereavement: Theory, research, and intervention* (pp. 3–19). Cambridge, UK: Cambridge University Press.

Stroebe, W., & Stroebe, M. S. (1993). Determinants of adjustment to bereavement in younger widows and widowers. In M. S. Stroebe, W. Stroebe, & R. O. Hansson (Eds.), *Handbook of bereavement: Theory, research, and intervention* (pp. 208–226). Cambridge, UK: Cambridge University Press.

Strom, R., & Strom, S. (1995). Raising expectations for grandparents: A three generational study. In J. Hendricks (Ed.), *The ties of later life* (pp. 133–139). Amityville, NY: Baywood.

Stutzer, A., & Frey, B. S. (2006). Does marriage make people happy, or do happy people get married? *Journal of Socio-Economics, 35*(2), 326–347.

Suarez, E., & Gadalla, T. M. (2010). Stop blaming the victim: A meta-analysis on rape myths. *Journal of Interpersonal Violence, 25*(11), 2010–2035.

Subramanian, S. V., Elwert, F., & Christakis, N. (2008). Widowhood and mortality among the elderly: The modifying role of neighborhood concentration of widowed individuals. *Social Science & Medicine, 66*, 873–884.

Sue, D. W., & Sue, D. (2012). *Counseling the culturally diverse: Theory and practice* (6th ed.). Hoboken, NJ: John Wiley & Sons.

Sue, S. (1998). In search of cultural competence in psychotherapy and counseling. *American Psychologist, 53*, 440–448.

Sue, S., & Zane, N. (1987). The role of culture and cultural techniques in psychotherapy: A critique and reformulation. *American Psychologist, 42*, 37–45.

Sue, S., Zane, N., & Young, W. (1994). Research on psychotherapy with culturally diverse populations. In A. E. Bergin & S. L. Garfield (Eds.), *Handbook of psychotherapy and behavior change* (4th ed., pp. 783–820). New York, NY: Wiley.

Suitor, J. J. (1991). Marital quality and satisfaction with the division of household labor across the family life cycle. *Journal of Marriage and the Family, 53*, 221–230.

Sullivan, H. (1953). *The interpersonal theory of psychiatry*. New York, NY: Norton.

Sullivan, J. L. (2003). Prevention of mother-to-child transmission of HIV—What next? *Journal of Acquired Immune Deficiency Syndrome, 34*, S67–S72.

Sullivan, K., & Sullivan, A. (1980). Adolescent-parent separation. *Developmental Psychology, 16*, 93–99.

Sultan, D. H. (2003). The Muslim way of death. In C. D. Bryant (Ed.), *Handbook of death and dying* (Vol. 2, pp. 649–655). Thousand Oaks, CA: Sage Publications.

Sun, Q., Townsend, M. K., Okereke, O. I., Rimm, E. B., Hu, F. B., Stampfer, M. J., & Grodstein, F. (2011). Alcohol consumption at midlife and successful ageing in women: A prospective cohort analysis in the Nurses' Health Study. *PloS ONE, 8*, e1001090. doi: 10.1371/journal.pmed.1001090

Sunderman, G. L. (Ed.) (2008). *Holding NCLB accountable: Achieving accountability, equity, and school reform*. Thousand Oaks, CA: Corwin Press.

Super, C. M., & Harkness, S. (2010). Culture and infancy. In J. G. Bremner, & T. D. Wachs (Eds.), *The Wiley-Blackwell handbook of infant development* (pp. 623–649). Malden, MA: Wiley-Blackwell Publishing.

Susa, A. M., & Benedict, J. O. (1994). The effects of playground design on pretend play and divergent thinking. *Environment and Behavior, 26*, 560–579.

Swain, R. A., Harris, A. B., Weiner, E. C., Dutka, M. V., Morris, H. D., Theien, B. E., ... & Greenough, W. T. (2003). Prolonged exercise induces angiogenesis and increases cerebral blood volume in primary motor cortex of the rat. *Neuroscience, 117*, 1037–1046.

Swanson, H., Cooney, J., & Brock, S. (1993). The influence of working memory and classification ability on children's word problem solution. *Journal of Experimental Child Psychology, 55*, 374–395.

Swanson, S. A., Crow, S. J., Le Grange, D., Swendsen, J., & Merikangas, K. R. (2011). Prevalence and correlates of eating disorders in adolescents. Results from the national comorbidity survey replication adolescent supplement. *Archive of General Psychiatry, 68*(7), 714–723.

Swinburn, B. A., Sacks, G., Hall, K. D., McPherson, K., Finegood, D. T., Moodie, M. L., & Gortmaker, S. L. (2011). The global obesity pandemic: Shaped by global drivers and local environments. *Lancet, 378*(9793), 804–814.

Syed, M. (2016). Emerging adulthood: Developmental stage theory, or nonsense? In J. J. Arnett (Ed.), *The Oxford handbook of emerging adulthood* (pp. 11–25). New York, NY: Oxford University Press.

T

Taber-Thomas, B., & Perez-Edgar, K. (2016). Emerging adulthood brain development. In J. J. Arnett (Ed.), *The Oxford handbook of emerging adulthood* (pp. 126–141). New York, NY: Oxford University Press.

Taffel, S. M. (1993). Cesarean birth: Social and political aspects, In B. K. Rothman (Ed.), *The encyclopedia of childbearing*. New York, NY: Henry Holt.

Takahasbi, K. (1990). Are the key assumptions of the "Strange Situation" procedure universal? A view from Japanese research. *Human Development, 33*, 23–30.

Takanishi, R. (1993). The opportunities of adolescence–Research, interventions, and policy: Introduction to the special issue *American Psychologist, 48*, 85–88.

Takanishi, R., & Hamburg, D. (Eds.). (1997). *Preparing adolescents for the 21st century*. New York, NY: Cambridge University Press.

Takata, S., & Zevitz, R. (1990). Divergent perceptions of group delinquency in a midwestern community: Racine's gang problem. *Youth and Society, 21*, 282–305.

Takei, W. (2001). How do deaf infants attain first signs? *Developmental Science, 4*, 71–78.

Tandon, P. S., Zhou, C., Lozano, P., & Christakis, D. A. (2011). Preschoolers' total daily screen time at home and by type of child care. *Journal of Pediatrics, 158*(2), 297–300.

Tannen, D. (1990). *You just don't understand*. New York, NY: Morrow.

Tannenbaum, C., & Frank, B. (2011). Masculinity and health in late life men. *American Journal of Men's Health, 5*, 243–254. doi: 10.1177/1557988310384609

Tanner, J. L. (2006). Recentering during emerging adulthood: A critical turning point in life span human development. In J. J. Arnett & J. L. Tanner (Eds.), *Emerging adults in America: Coming of age in the 21st century* (pp. 21–55). Washington, DC: American Psychological Association.

Tanner, J. L. (2016). Mental health in emerging adulthood. In J. J. Arnett (Ed.), *The Oxford handbook of emerging adulthood* (pp. 499–520). New York, NY: Oxford University Press.

Tanner, J. M. (1981). Growth and maturation during adolescence. *Nutrition Review, 39*, 43–55.

Tanner, J. M. (1990). *Fetus into man. Physical growth from conception to maturity* (rev. ed.). Cambridge, MA: Harvard University Press.

Tardiff, T., Fletcher, P., Liang, W., Zhang, Z., Kaciroti, N., & Marchman, V. (2008). Baby's first 10 words. *Developmental Psychology, 44*, 929–938.

Task Force on Pediatric AIDS. (1989). Pediatric AIDS and human immunodeficiency virus infection: Psychological issues. *American Psychologist, 44*, 258–264.

Tasker, F. L., & Golombok, S. (1997). *Growing up in a lesbian family*. New York, NY: Guilford.

Taylor, C. A., Manganello, J. A., Lee, S. J., & Rice, J. C. (2010). Mothers' spanking of 3-year-old children and subsequent risk of children's aggressive behavior. *Pediatrics, 125*(5), e1057–e1065.

Taylor, J., Gilligan, C., & Sullivan, A. (1995). *Between voice and silence: Women and. girls, race and relationship*. Cambridge, MA: Harvard University Press.

Taylor, M. J. (2006). Neural bases of cognitive development. In E. Bialystok & F. I. M. Craik (Eds.), *Lifespan cognition: Mechanisms of change*. New York, NY: Oxford University Press.

Taylor, P., Cohn, D., Livingston, G., Wang, W., & Dockterman, D. (2010). *The new demography of American motherhood*. Pew Research Center. Retrieved from http://www.pewsocialtrends.org/files/2010/10/754-new-demography-of-motherhood.pdf

Taylor, S. E. (1998). *Health psychology*. New York, NY: McGraw Hill.

Teaff, J., & Johnson, D. (1983). Pre-retirement education. A proposed bill for tuition credit. *Educational Gerontology, 9*, 31–36.

Telama, R., Yang, X., Viikari, J., Välimäki, I., Wanne, O., & Raitakari, O. (2005). Physical activity from childhood to adulthood: A 21-year tracking study. *American Journal of Preventive Medicine, 28*(3), 267–273.

Telkemeyer, S., Rossi, S., Kock, S. P., Nierhaus, T., Steinbrink, J., Poeppel, D., Obrig, H., & Wartenburger, I. (2010). Sensitivity of newborn auditory cortex to the temporal structure of sounds. *Journal of Neuroscience, 29*, 14726–14733.

Teno, J. M., Gruneir, A., Schwartz, Z., Nanda, A., & Wetle, T. (2007). Association between advance directives and quality of end-of-life care: A national study. *Journal of the American Geriatrics Society, 55*(2), 189–194.

Teno, J. M., Gozalo, P. L., Bynum, J. P. W., Leland, N. E., Miller, S. C., Moden, N. E., ... & Mor, V. (2013). Change in end-of-life care for Medicare beneficiaries: Site of death, place of care, and health care transitions in 2000, 2005, and 2009. *JAMA, 309*(5), 470–477.

Terenzini, P. T., Pascarella, E., & Blinding, G. S. (1996). Students' out-of-class experiences and their influence on learning and cognitive development: A literature review. *Journal of College Student Development, 37*, 149–162.

Tesman, J., & Hills, A. (1994). Developmental effects of lead exposure in children. *Social Policy Report: Society for Research on Child Development, 8*(3).

Teti, D. M. (1992). *Sibling interaction*. New York, NY: Plenum Press.

Thomas, A., & Chess, S. (1977). *Temperament and development*. New York, NY: Bruner/Mazel.

Thomas, A., & Chess, S. (1981). The role of temperament in the contributions of individuals to their development. In R. Lerner & N. Busch-Rossnagle (Eds.), *Individuals as producers of their development: A life-span perspective*. New York, NY: Academic Press.

Thomas, J. L. (1995). Gender and perceptions of grandparenthood. In J. Hendricks (Ed.), *The ties of later life* (pp. 181–193). Amityville, NY: Baywood.

Thomas, L. E. (1991). Dialogues with three religious renunciates and reflections on wisdom and maturity. *International Journal of Aging and Human Development, 32*(3), 211–227.

Thomas, L. E. (1994). The way of the religious renouncer. In L. E. Thomas & S. A. Eisenhandler (Eds.), *Aging and the religious dimension* (pp. 51–64). Westport, CT: Auburn House.

Thompson, R. A. (1990). On emotion and self-regulation. In R. A. Thompson (Ed.), *Nebraska symposium on motivation: Vol. 36* (pp. 383–483). Lincoln, NE: University of Nebraska Press.

Thomson, E., & Colella, U. (1992). Cohabitation and marital stability: Quality or commitment? *Journal of Marriage and the Family, 54,* 259–267.

Thornborrow, N. M., & Sheldon, M. B. (1995). Women in the labor force. In J. Freeman (Ed.), *Women: A feminist perspective* (5th ed., pp. 197–219). Mountain View, CA: Mayfield.

Thornton, W. L., Paterson, T. S., & Yeung, S. E. (2013). Age differences in everyday problem solving: The role of problem context. *International Journal of Behavioral Development, 37,* 13–20.

Thorson, J. A., & Powell, F. C. (1988). Elements of death anxiety and meanings of death. *Journal of Clinical Psychology, 44,* 691–701.

Tidwell, N. D., Eastwick, P. W., & Finkel, E. J. (2013). Perceived, not actual, similarity predicts initial attraction in a live romantic context: Evidence from the speed-dating paradigm. *Personal Relationships, 20*(2), 199–215.

Tilcsik, A. (2011). Pride and prejudice: Employment discrimination against openly gay men in the United States. *American Journal of Sociology, 117,* 586–626.

Tillman, P. (1992). *Adolescent alcoholism.* Bethesda, MD: U.S. Department of Health and Human Services.

Tobin, S. S. (1991). *Personhood in advanced old age: Implications for practice.* New York, NY: Springer.

Tobin, S. S., Fullmer, E. M., & Smith, G. C. (1994). Religiosity and fear of death in non-normative aging. In L. E. Thomas & S. A. Eisenbandler (Eds.), *Aging and the religious dimension* (pp. 183–202). Westport, CT: Auburn House.

Tobin-Richards, M. H., Boxer, A. M., & Petersen, A. C. (1983). The psychological significance of pubertal change: Sex differences in perceptions of self during early adolescence. In J. Brooks-Gunn & A. C. Petersen (Eds.), *Girls at puberty: Biological and psychological perspectives* (pp. 127–154). New York, NY: Plenum.

Tolson, T., & Wilson, M. (1990). The impact of two- and three-generational black family structure on perceived family climate. *Child Development, 61,* 416–428.

Tonti, M. (1988). Relationships among adult siblings who care for their aged parents. In M. D. Kahn & K. G. Lewis (Eds.), *Siblings in therapy: Life span and clinical issues* (pp. 417–434). New York, NY: Norton.

Topa, G., Moriano, J. A., Depolo, M., Alcover, C. M., & Morales, J. (2009). Antecedents and consequences of retirement planning and decision-making: A meta-analysis and model. *Journal of Vocational Behavior, 75,* 38–55.

Tornstam, L. (1992). The quo vadis of gerontology: On the scientific paradigm of gerontology. *The Gerontologist, 32,* 318–326.

Torres, S. J., & Nowson, C. A. (2007). Relationship between stress, eating behavior, and obesity. *Nutrition, 23*(11), 887–894.

Tortolero, S. R., Markham, C. M., Peskin, M. F., Shegog, R., Addy, R. C., Escobar-Chaves, S. L., & Baumler, E. R. (2010). It's your game: Keep it real: Delaying sexual behavior with an effective middle school program. *Journal of Adolescent Health, 46*(2), 169–179.

Toth, K., Dawson, G., Meltzoff, A. N., Greenson, J., & Fein, D. (2007). Early social, imitation, play, and language abilities of young non-autistic siblings of children with autism. *Journal of Autism and Developmental Disorders, 37*(1), 145–157.

Tough, P. (2012). *How children succeed: Grit, curiosity, and the hidden power of character.* Boston: Houghton Mifflin Harcourt.

Townshend, J. M., Kambouropoulos, N., Griffin, A., Hunt, F. J., & Milani, R. M. (2014). Binge drinking, reflection impulsivity, and unplanned sexual behavior: Impaired decision-making in young social drinkers. *Alcoholism: Clinical and Experimental Research, 38*(4), 1143–1150.

Trainor, L. J., & Heinmiller, B. M. (1998). The development of evaluative responses to music: Infants prefer to listen to consonance over dissonance. *Infant Behavior & Development, 21,* 77–88.

Trautman, P. D., & Shaffer, D. (1989). Pediatric management of suicidal behavior. *Pediatric Annals, 18,* 134–143.

Trawick-Smith, J., & Dziurgot, T. (2011). 'Good-fit' teacher–child play interactions and the subsequent autonomous play of preschool children. *Early Childhood Research Quarterly, 26*(1), 110–123.

Trends in prostate cancer–United States. (1992, June 12). *Morbidity and Mortality Weekly Report,* pp. 41, 401–404.

Trent, K., & Spitze, G. D. (2011). Growing up without siblings and adult sociability behaviors. *Journal of Family Issues, 32*(9), 1178–1204.

Trinke, S., & Bartholomew, K. (1997). Hierarchies of attachment relationships in young adulthood. *Journal of Social and Personal Relationships, 14,* 603–625.

Troll, L. E. (1994). Family connectedness of old women: Attachments in later life. In B. F. Turner & L. E. Troll (Eds.), *Women growing older: Psychological perspectives* (pp. 169–201). Thousand Oaks, Cal: Sage.

Trommsdorff, G., Friedlmeier, W., & Mayer, B. (2007). Sympathy, distress, and prosocial behavior of preschool children in four cultures. *International Journal of Behavioral Development, 31*(3), 284–293.

Tronick, E. Z. (1989). Emotions and emotional communication in infants. *American Psychologist, 44,* 112–119).

Tronick, E. Z., Morelli, G. A., & Ivey, P. K. (1992). The Efe forager infant and toddler's pattern of social relationships: Multiple and simultaneous. *Developmental Psychology, 28,* 568–577.

Tropp, L. R., & Prenovost, M. A. (2008). The role of intergroup contact in predicting children's interethnic attitudes: Evidence from meta-analytic and field studies. In S. R. Levy & M. Killen (Eds.), *Intergroup attitudes and relations in childhood through adulthood* (pp. 236–248). New York, NY: Oxford University Press.

Turkheimer, E., & Gottesman, I. I. (1991). Individual differences and the canalization of human behavior. *Developmental Psychology, 27,* 18–22.

Turner, E. A., Chandler, M., & Heffer, R. W. (2009). The influence of parenting styles, achievement motivation, and self-efficacy on academic performance in college students. *Journal of College Student Development, 50*(3), 337–346.

Tylanda, C. A., & Baum, B. J. (1988). Oral physiology and the Baltimore Longitudinal Study of Aging. *Gerontology, 7,* 5–9.

U

Uddin, M., Sipahi, L., Li, J., & Koenen, K. C. (2013). Sex differences in DNA methylation may contribute to risk of PTSD and depression: A review of existing evidence. *Depression and Anxiety, 30*(12), 1151–160.

Ullal-Gupta, S., Vanden Bosch der Nederlanden, C., Tichko, P., Lahav, A., & Hannon, E. (2013). Linking prenatal experience to the emerging musical mind. *Frontiers in Systems Neuroscience, 7,* 1–7.

Umberson, D. (1987). Family status and health behaviors: Social control as a dimension of social integration. *Journal of Health and Social Behavior, 38,* 306–319.

Umberson, D. (1989). Relationships with children: Explaining patents' psychological well-being. *Journal of Marriage and the Family, 51,* 999–1012.

Umberson, D., Anderson, K., Glick, J., & Shapiro, A. (1998). Domestic violence, personal control, and gender. *Journal of Marriage and the Family, 60,* 442–452.

Umberson, D., Crosnoe, R., & Reczek, C. (2010). Social relationships and health behavior across life course. *Annual Review of Sociology, 36,* 139–157.

Umberson, D., Pudrovska, T., & Reczek, C. (2010). Parenthood, childlessness, and well-being: A life course perspective. *Journal of Marriage and Family, 72,* 612–629.

Umberson, D., Workman, C. B., & Kessler, R. C. (1992). Widowhood and depression: Explaining long-term gender differences in vulnerability. *Journal of Health and Social Behavior, 33,* 10–24.

UNICEF Office of Research. (2013). Child well-being in rich countries: A comparative overview, *Innocenti Report Card 11,* UNICEF Office of Research. Florence, IT: Author.

United Health Foundation. (2016). *America's health rankings: Infant mortality rates.* Retrieved from http://www.americashealthrankings.org/MS/IMR.

United Nations International Children's Emergency Fund (UNICEF). (1993). *The state of the world's children, 1992.* New-York: Oxford University Press.

United Nations International Children's Emergency Fund (UNICEF). (1995). *The slate of the world's children, 1995.* New York, NY: Oxford University Press.

United Nations International Children's Emergency Fund (UNICEF). (1998). *State of the world's children, 1997.* New York, NY: Oxford University Press.

United Nations International Children's Emergency Fund (UNICEF). (2009). *The state of the world's children: Maternal and newborn health, 2009.* Retrieved from http://www.unicef.org/sowc09/index.php

United Nations Statistics Division. (2008) *Demographics yearbook.* Retrieved from http://unstats.un.org/unsd/demographic/products/dyb/dyb2008htm

Updegraff, K. A., McHale, S. M., Killoren, S. E., & Rodriguez, S. A. (2011). Cultural variations in sibling relationships. In J. Caspi (Ed.), *Sibling development: Implications for mental health practitioners.* New York, NY: Springer.

U.S. Bureau of the Census. (1990a). *Statistical abstract of the United States* (110th ed.). Washington, DC: U.S. Government Printing Office.

U.S. Bureau of the Census. (1990b). *Who's minding the kids? Current population reports* (Series P-70, No. 20.). Washington, DC: U.S. Government Printing Office.

U.S. Bureau of the Census. (1991). *Statistical abstract of the United States* (111th ed.). Washington, DC: U.S. Government Printing Office.

U.S. Bureau of the Census. (1992). Marital status and living arrangements: March 1991. *Current Population Reports,* Series P-20, No. 461. Washington, DC: U.S. Government Printing Office.

U.S. Bureau of the Census. (1992a). *Statistical abstract of the United States, 1992* (112th ed.). Washington, DC: U.S. Government Printing Office.

U.S. Bureau of the Census. (1992b). *Poverty in the United States, 1991.* Washington, DC: U.S. Government Printing Office.

U.S. Bureau of the Census. (1994). *Statistical abstract of the United States: 1993* (113th ed.). Washington, DC: U.S. Government Printing Office.

U.S. Bureau of the Census. (1994). *Statistical abstract of the United States: 1994* (114th ed.) Washington, DC: U.S. Government Printing Office.

U.S. Bureau of the Census. (1995a). Live births, deaths, marriages, and divorces: 1900–1994. *Statistical abstract of the United States* (115th ed.). Washington, DC: U.S. Government Printing Office.

U.S. Bureau of the Census. (1995b). Employment status of and presence and age of children: 1960–1994. *Statistical abstract of the United States* (115th ed.). Washington, DC: U.S. Government Printing Office.

U.S. Bureau of the Census. (2006). Grandparents living with grandchildren by race and sex: 2006. *Statistical abstract of the United States: 2006.* Washington, DC: U.S. Government Printing Office.

U.S. Bureau of the Census. (2008). *Nearly half of preschoolers receive child care from relatives.* Retrieved from http://www.census.gov/newsroom/releases/archives/children/cb08-31.html

U.S. Bureau of the Census. (2010). *America's families and living arrangements: 2010.* Retrieved from https://www.census.gov/population/www/socdemo/hh-fam/cps2010.html

U.S. Bureau of the Census. (2012a). Births, deaths, marriages, and divorces. *Statistical abstract of the United States: 2012.* Retrieved from https://www.census.gov/prod/2011pubs/12statab/vitstat.pdf

U.S. Bureau of the Census. (2012b). *Marital status of the population 55 and over by sex and age: 2012.* Current Population Survey, Annual Social and Economic Supplement. Retrieved from http://www.census.gov/population/age/data/2012.html

U.S. Bureau of the Census. (2012c). *Projections of the Population by selected age groups and sex for the United States: 2015–2060.* Retrieved from http://www.census.gov/population/projections/data/national/2012/summarytables.html

U.S. Bureau of the Census. (2012d). *Statistical abstract of the United States: 2012.* Retrieved from https://www.census.gov/compendia/statab/2012/tables/12s0010.pdf

U.S. Bureau of the Census. (2013) *Labor force participation and work status of people 65 years and older.* Retrieved from http://www.census.gov/prod/2013pubs/acsbr11-09.pdf.

U.S. Bureau of the Census. (2015a). *Current population survey, March and annual social and economic supplements, 2015 and earlier.* Retrieved from http://www.census.gov/hhes/families/files/ms2.csv

U.S. Bureau of the Census. (2015b). *Detailed languages spoken at home and ability to speak English for population 5 years and over: 2009–2013.* Retrieved from http://www.census.gov/data/tables/2013/demo/2009-2013-lang-tables.html

U.S. Bureau of the Census. (2015c). *Families and living arrangements.* Retrieved from http://www.census.gov/hhes/families/data/marital.html

U.S. Bureau of the Census. (2015d). *Families and living arrangements: Children.* Retrieved from http://www.census.gov/hhes/families/data/cps2015C.html

U.S. Bureau of Labor Statistics. (1995). Bulletin 2307.

U.S. Bureau of Labor Statistics and the Census Bureau. (2013). *Current population survey, 2013 annual social and economic supplement.* Retrieved from http://www.census.gov/hhes/www/cpstables/032013/pov/pov01_100.htm.

U.S. Congress, Office of Technology Assessment. (1988). *Infertility: Medical and social choices* (OTA-BA-358). Washington, DC: U.S. Government Printing Office.

U.S. Congressional Budget Office. (1993). *Trends in health spending.* Washington, DC: Author.

U.S. Department of Commerce. (1995). *Statistical abstract of the United States, 1994.* Washington, DC: U.S. Government Printing Office.

U.S. Department of Commerce. (1998). *Statistical abstract, of the United States, 1997.* Washington, DC: U.S. Government Printing Office.

U.S. Department of Education. (1997). *Digest of education statistics, 1997.* Washington, DC: National Center for Education Statistics.

U.S. Department of Education. (2014). *The condition of education, 2014.* Washington, DC: National Center for Education Statistics.

U.S. Department of Education. (2015). Every Student Succeeds Act (ESSA), *2015.* Retrieved from http://www.ed.gov/essa

U.S. Department of Education, National Center for Education Statistics. (2016a). Undergraduate retention and graduation rates. *The condition of education 2016.* Retrieved from https://nces.ed.gov/programs/coe/indicator_ctr.asp

U.S. Department of Education, National Center for Education Statistics. (2016b). *Digest of education statistics.* Retrieved from https://nces.ed.gov/programs/digest/d14/tables/dt14_311.15.asp?current=yes

U.S. Department of Health and Human Services. (1993). *Health United States, 1992.* (DHHS Pub. No. (PHS) 93-1232). Washington, DC: U.S. Government Printing Office.

U.S. Department of Health and Human Services. (1994). *Preventing tobacco use among young people* Washington, DC: Author.

U.S. Department of Health and Human Services. (1993). *Talking to children about death.* Washington, DC: U.S. Government Printing Office.

U.S. Department of Health and Human Services (HHS; National Toxicology Program). (2005). *Thalidomide.* Retrieved from http://ntp.niehs.nih.gov/

U.S. Department of Health and Human Services (HHS; Maternal and Child Health Bureau). (2009). *Child health USA 2008–2009.* Rockville MD: U.S. Department of Health and Human Services.

U.S. Department of Health and Human Services (HHS; Maternal and Child Health Bureau). (2011). *Child health USA 2011.* Rockville, MD: U.S. Department of Health and Human Services.

U.S. Department of Health and Human Services (HHS; Administration on Aging). (2012). *A profile of older Americans: 2012.* Rockville, MD: U.S. Department of Health and Human Services.

U.S. Department of Health and Human Services. (2014). *National vital statistics reports: United States life tables 2009.* Retrieved from http://www.cdc.gov/nchs/data/nvsr/nvsr62/nvsr62_07.pdf

U.S. Department of Health and Human Services. (2015). *Child maltreatment 2013: Summary of key findings.* Retrieved from https://www.childwelfare.gov/pubPDFs/canstats.pdf

U.S. Department of Justice (Bureau of Justice Statistics). (2013). *Female victims of sexual violence, 1994–2010.* Retrieved from http://www.bjs.gov/content/pub/pdf/fvsv9410.pdf

U.S. Department of Labor. (2014). *Earnings.* Washington, DC: Women's Bureau. Retrieved from https://www.dol.gov/wb/stats/earnings_2014.htm#Ratios

U.S. Department of Labor. (2015). *Women of working age.* Washington, DC: Women's Bureau. Retrieved from https://www.dol.gov/wb/stats/latest_annual_data.htm#labor

U.S. Department of Labor. (n.d.). *Funeral leave.* Retrieved from https://www.dol.gov/general/topic/benefits-leave/funeral-leave

U.S. Department of Labor (Bureau of Labor Statistics). (2013, October). *Marriage and divorce: Patterns by gender, race, and educational attainment.* Retrieved from http://www.bls.gov/opub/mlr/2013/article/marriage-and-divorce-patterns-by-gender-race-and-educational-attainment.htm

U.S. Department of Labor (Bureau of Labor Statistics). (2016, July). *Labor force statistics from the current population survey.* Retrieved from http://www.bls.gov/web/empsit/cpsee_e16.htm

U.S. Equal Employment Opportunity Commission. (n.d.). *Sexual harassment charges EEOC & FEPAs combined: FY 1997–2011.* Retrieved August 7, 201 from https://www.eeoc.gov/eeoc/statistics/enforcement/sexual_harassment.cfm

U.S. Equal Employment Opportunity Commission. (2013). *Charge statistics FY 1997 through FY 2013.* Retrieved http://eeoc.gov/eeoc/statistics/enforcement/charges.cfm

U.S. General Accounting Office. (1993). *Preventive home care for children: Experience from select foreign countries.* Washington, DC: Author.

U.S. National Center for Health Statistics. (1991). *Vital statistics of the United States.* Washington, DC: U.S. Government Printing Office.

U.S. National Library of Medicine (USNLM). (2011). *Age-appropriate diet for children.* Retrieved from http://www.nlm.nih.gov/medlineplus/ency/article/002455.htm

U.S. National Library of Medicine (USNLM). (2012). *Genetics home reference: Cystic fibrosis.* Retrieved from http://ghr.nlm.nih.gov/condition/cystic-fibrosis

U.S. National Library of Medicine (USNLM). (2012). *Placenta previa.* Retrieved from http://www.ncbi.nlm.nih.gov/pubmedhealth/PMH0001902/

U.S. National Library of Medicine (USNLM). (2013). *Fetal electrocardiogram (ECG) for fetal monitoring during labor.* Retrieved from http://www.ncbi.nlm.nih.gov/pubmedhealth/PMH0010486/

U.S. National Library of Medicine (USNLM). (2013). *Genetics home reference: Huntington disease.* Retrieved from http://ghr.nlm.nih.gov/condition/huntington-disease

U.S. Select Committee on Children, Youth, and Families. (1992). *Health care reform: How do women, children, and teens fare?* Washington, DC: U.S. Government Printing Office.

U.S. Senate Special Committee on Aging. (1990). *Developments in aging: 1989* (Vol. 1.) Washington, DC: U.S. Government Printing Office.

U.S. Senate Special Committee on Aging. (1991). *Aging America: Trends and projections.* Washington, DC: U.S. Department of Health and Human Services.

U.S. Senate Special Committee on Aging. (1992). *Aging America: Trends and. projections.* Washington, DC: U.S. Department of Health and Human Services.

V

Vaidya, V., Partha, G., & Karmakar, M. (2012). Gender differences in utilization of preventive care services in the United States. *Journal of Women's Health, 21,* 140–145. doi: 10.1089/jwh.2011.2876

Vaillant, C. O., & Vaillant, G. E. (1993). Is the U-curve of marital satisfaction an illusion? A 40-year study of marriage. *Journal of Marriage and the Family, 55,* 230–239.

Vaillant, G. E. (1977). *Adaptation to life.* Boston: Little, Brown.

Vaillant, G. E., & McArthur, C. C. (1972). Natural history of male psychological health: I. The adult life cycle from 18–50. *Seminars in Psychiatry, 4(4),* 415–427.

Vaillant, G. E., & Vaillant, C. O. (1990). Natural history of male psychological health, XII: A 45-year study of predictors of successful aging at age 65. *American Journal of Psychiatry, 147(1),* 31–37.

Vallerand, R. J., O'Connor, B. P., & Blais, M. R. (1989). Life satisfaction of elderly individuals in regular community housing, in low-cost community housing, and high and low self-determination nursing homes. *International Journal of Aging and Human Development, 28(4),* 277–283.

Valvanne, J., Juva, K., Erkinjuntti, T., & Tilvis, R. (1996). Major depression in the elderly: A population study in Helsinki. *International Psychogeriatrics, 8(3),* 437–443.

van den Boom, D. C., & Hoeksma, J. B. (1994). The effect of infant irritability on mother-infant interaction: A growth-curve analysis. *Developmental Psychology, 30,* 581–590.

van der Horst, K., Ferrage, A., & Rytz, A. (2014). Involving children in meal preparation. Effects on food intake. *Appetite, 79,* 18–24.

van der Voort, T. H. A., & Valkenburg, P. M. (1994). Television's impact on fantasy play: A review of research. *Developmental Review, 14,* 227–251.

Van Doorn, M. D., Branje, S. J. T., & Meeus, W. H. J. (2011). Developmental changes in conflict resolution styles in parent-adolescent relationships: A four-wave longitudinal study. *Journal of Youth and Adolescence, 40,* 97–107.

van Hasselt, M., Kruger, J., Han, B., Caraballo, R. S., Penne, M. A., Loomis, B., & Gfroerer, J. C. (2015). The relation between tobacco taxes and youth and young adult smoking: What happened following the 2009 US federal tax increase on cigarettes? *Addictive Behaviors, 45,* 104–109.

Van Houtven, C. H., Coe, N. B., & Skira, M. M. (2013). The effect of informal care on work and wages. *Journal of Health Economics, 32,* 240–252.

van IJzendoorn, M. H. (1992). Review. Intergenerational transmission of parenting: A review of studies in nonclinical populations. *Developmental Review, 12,* 76–99.

van IJzendoorn, M. H. (1995). Adult attachment representations, parental responsiveness, and infant attachment: A metaanalysis on the predictive validity of the adult attachment interview. *Psychological Bulletin, 117,* 387–403.

van IJzendoorn, M. H., & Bakermans-Kranenburg, M. J. (1997). Intergenerational transmission of attachment: A move to the contextual level. New York, NY: Guilford Press.

van IJzendoorn, M. H., & de Wolff, M. S. (1997). In search of the absent father—meta-analysis of infant-father attachment: A rejoinder to our discussants. *Child Development, 68,* 604–609.

van IJzendoorn, M. H., & Kroonenberg, P. M. (1988). Cross-cultural patterns of attachment: A meta-analysis of the Strange Situation. *Child Development, 59,* 147–156.

van Ravesteyn, N., Schechter, C. ., Near, A. M., Heijnskijk, E. A. M., Stoto, M. A., Draisma, G., ... & Mandelblatt, J. S. (2011). Race-specific impact of natural history, mammography screening, and adjuvant treatment on breast cancer mortality rates in the United States. *Cancer Epidemiology, Biomarkers, and Prevention, 20,* 112–122. doi: 10.1158/1055-9965.EPI-10-0944

van Reek, J., Adrizaanze, H., & Knibbe, R. (1994). Alcohol consumption and correlates among children in the European Community. *International Journal of Addictions, 29,* 15–21.

van Sleuwen, B. E., Engelberts, A. C., Boore-Boonekamp, M. M., Wietse, K., Schulpen, T. W. J., & L'Hoir, M. P. (2007). Swaddling: A systematic review. *Pediatrics, 120,* 1097–1106.

Vandell, D. L. (1980). Sociability with peers and mothers in the first year. *Developmental Psychology, 16,* 355–361.

Vandell, D. L., & Ramanan, J. (1991). Children of the national longitudinal survey of youth: Choices in after-school care and child development. *Developmental Psychology, 27,* 637–643.

Vandell, D. L., Hyde, J. S., Plant, E. A., & Essex, M. J. (1997). Fathers and "others" as infant-care providers: Predictors of parents' emotional well-being and marital satisfaction. *Merrill-Palmer Quarterly, 43,* 361–385.

Vanderlinden, J. (1997). *Trauma, dissociation, and impulse dyscontrol in eating disorders.* Bristol, PA: Brunner/Mazel.

Vandewater, E. A., Rideout, V. J., Wartella, E. A., Huang, X., Lee, J. H., & Shim, M. S. (2007). Digital childhood: Electronic media and technology use among infants, toddlers, and preschoolers. *Pediatrics, 119*(5), e1006–e1015.

Vansteenkiste, M., Lens, W., & Deci, E. L. (2006). Intrinsic versus extrinsic goal contents in self-determination theory: Another look at the quality of academic motivation. *Educational Psychologist, 41*(1), 19–1.

VanTassel-Baska, J. (2006). A content analysis of evaluation findings across 20 gifted programs: A clarion call for enhanced gifted program development. *Gifted Child Quarterly, 50*(3), 199–215.

Varni, J. W., Setoguchi, Y., Rappaport, L. R., & Talbot, D. (1992). Psychological adjustment and perceived social support in children with congenital/acquired limb deficiencies. *Journal of Behavioral Medicine, 15,* 31–44.

Veevers, J. E. (1980). *Childless by choice.* Toronto: Butterworth.

Ventura, A. K., & Worobey, J. (2013). Early influences on the development of food preferences. *Current Biology, 23*(9), R401–R408.

Ventura, S. J., & Hamilton, B. E. (2011). U.S. teenage birthrate resumes decline. *NCHS Data Brief,* No. 58. Hyattsville, MD: National Center for Health Statistics.

Ventura, S. J., Martin, J. A., Curtin, S. C., & Mathews, T. J. (1997). Report of final natality statistics, 1995. *Monthly Vital Statistics Report, 45*(11, Suppl. 2). Hyattsville, MD: National Center for Health Statistics.

Vera, M. (2003). Social dimensions of grief. In C. D. Bryant (Ed.), *Handbook of death and dying* (Vol. 2, pp. 838–846). Thousand Oaks, CA: Sage Publications.

Verbrugge, L. M. (1982). Women's social roles and health. In P. W. Berman & E. R. Ramey (Eds.), *Women: A developmental perspective* (pp. 49–78). Bethesda, MD: U. S. Department of Health and Human Services.

Verbrugge, L. M. (1989a). Gender, aging and health. In K. S. Markides (Ed.), *Aging and health: Perspectives on gender, race, ethnicity and class* (pp. 23–78). Newbury Park, CA: Sage.

Verbrugge, L. M. (1989b). The twain meet: Empirical explanations of sex differences in health and mortality. *Journal of Health and Social Behavior, 30,* 282–304.

Verbrugge, L. M., & Patrick, D. L. (1995). Seven chronic conditions: Their impact on US adults' activity levels and use of medical services. *American Journal of Public Health, 85*(2), 173–182.

Verma, S., Turbey, B., Muradyan, N., Rajesh, A., Cornud, F., Haider, M., ... & Harisinghani, M. (2012). Overview of dynamic contrast-enhanced MRI in prostate cancer diagnosis and management. *Journal of Roentgenology, 198,* 1277–1288.

Vianna, F. S. L., Lopex-Camelo, J. S., Leite, J. C. L., Sanseverina, M. T., V., Dutra, M. G. D., Castilla, E. E., & Schuler-Faccini, L. (2011). Epidemiological surveillance of birth defects compatible with thalidomide embryopathy in Brazil. *PLos ONE, 6.* Retrieved from http://www.ncbi.nlm.nih.gov/pmc/articles/PMC3130769/

Victor, S. B., & Fish, M. C. (1995). Lesbian mothers and their children: A review for school psychologists. *School Psychology Review, 24,* 456–479.

Vigilant, L. G., & Williamson, J. B. (2003). To die, by mistake: Accidental deaths. In C. D. Bryant (Ed.), *Handbook of death and dying* (Vol. 1, pp. 211–222). Thousand Oaks, CA: Sage Publications.

Vignoles, V. L., Regalia, C., Manzi, C., Golledge, J., & Scabini, E. (2006). Beyond self-esteem: Influence of multiple motives on identity construction. *Journal of Personality and Social Psychology, 90*(2), 308.

Viinamaki, H., Koskela, K., Niskanen, L., Arnkill, R., & Tikkanen, J. (1993). Unemployment and mental well-being: A factory closure study in Finland. *Acta Psychiatrica Scandinavia, 88,* 429–433.

Vissing, Y. (1996). *Out of sight, out of mind: Homeless children and families in small-town America.* Lexington, KY: University Press of Kentucky.

Vita, A. J., Terry, R. B., Herbert, H. B., & Fries, J. F. (1998). Aging, health risks, and cumulative disability. *New England Journal of Medicine, 338*(15), 1035–1041.

Vitaro, F., Barker, E. D., Boivin, M., Brendgen, M., & Tremblay, R. E. (2006). Do early difficult temperament and harsh parenting differentially predict reactive and proactive aggression? *Journal of Abnormal Child Psychology, 34*(5), 681–691.

Vitaro, F., Tremblay, R. E., Kerr, M., Pagani, L., & Bukowski, W. M. (1997). Disruptiveness, friends' characteristics, and delinquency in early adolescence: A test of two competing models of development. *Child Development, 68,* 676–689.

Volling, B. L., & Belsky, J. (1992). Contribution of mother-child and father-child relationships to the quality of sibling interaction: A longitudinal study. *Child Development, 63,* 1209–1222.

Volling, B. L., & Belsky, J. (1992). Infant, father, and marital antecedents of infant-father attachment security in dual-earner and single earner families. *Journal of Behavioral Development, 15,* 83–100.

Volling, B. L., Youngblade, L. M., & Belsky, J. (1997). Young children's social relationships with siblings and friends. *American Journal of Orthopsychiatry, 67,* 102–111.

Vosler, N. R., & Proctor, E. K. (1991). Family structure and stressors in a child guidance clinic population. *Families in Society: The Journal of Contemporary Human Services, 72*(3), 164–174.

Vygotsky, L. (1997). *Educational psychology.* Boca Raton, FL: St. Lucie Press.

Vygotsky, L. S. (1967). Play and its role in the mental development of the child. *Soviet Psychology, 12,* 62–76.

Vygotsky, L. S. (1978). *Mind in society: The development of higher psychological processes.* Cambridge, MA: Harvard University Press.

W

Wadden, T. A., & Stunkard, A. J. (1985). Social and psychological consequences of obesity. *Annals of Internal Medicine, 106,* 1062–1067.

Wadden, T. A., Brown, G., Foster, G. D., & Linowitz, J. R. (1991). Salience of weight-related worries in adolescent males and females. *International Journal of Eating Disorders, 10,* 407–414.

Wadsworth, B. (1996). *Piaget's theory of cognitive and affective development: Foundations of constructivism.* 5th ed. White Plains, NY: Longman.

Wadsworth, M. (1986). Serious illness in childhood and its association with later-life achievement. In R. Wilkinson (Ed.). *Class and health: Research and longitudinal data.* London: Tavistock.

Wagner, R. M. (1993). Psychosocial adjustments during the first year of single parenthood: A comparison of Mexican-American and Anglo women. *Journal of Divorce and Remarriage, 19*(1–2), 12–33.

Wahistrom, K. (2002). Changing times: Findings from the first longitudinal study of later high school start times. *NASSP Bulletin, 86*(633), 3–21.

Wainright, J. L., & Patterson, C. J. (2006). Delinquency, victimization, and substance use among adolescents with female same-sex parents. *Journal of Family Psychology, 20*(3), 526–530.

Waite, E. B., Shanahan, L., Calkins, S. D., Keane, S. P., & O'Brien, M. (2011). Life events, sibling warmth, and youths' adjustment. *Journal of Marriage and Family, 73,* 902–912.

Waite, L. J., Laumann, E. O., Das, A., & Schumm, L. P. (2009). Sexuality: Measures of partnerships, practices, attitudes, and problems in the National Social Life, Health, and Aging Study. *Journal of Gerontology, 64B,* i56–i66.

Waite-Stupiansky, S. (1997). *Building understanding together: A constructivist approach to early childhood education.* Albany, NY: Delmar.

Wakschlag, L. S., Chase-Landsdale, P. L., & Brooks-Gunn, J. (1996). Not just "ghosts in the nursery": Contemporaneous intergenerational relationships and parenting in young African-American families. *Child Development, 67,* 2131–2147.

Walden, T. A., & Kim, G. (2005). Infants' social looking toward mothers and strangers. *International Journal of Behavioral Development, 29*(5), 356–360.

Waldman, S. (1993). Contraception: Defining terms, In B. K. Rothman (Ed.), *The encyclopedia of childbearing*. New York, NY: Henry Holt.

Waldrop, D. P. (2007). Caregiver grief in terminal illness and bereavement: A mixed-methods study. *Health & Social Work, 32*(3), 197–206.

Walker, J. M. (2008). Looking at teacher practices through the lens of parenting style. *Journal of Experimental Education, 76*(2), 218–240.

Walker, K. (1994). Men, women, and friendship: What they say, what they do. *Women and Gender, 8*, 246–265

Walker, S. N., Sechrist, K. R., & Pender, N. J. (1987). The health-promoting lifestyle profile: Development and psychometric characteristics. *Nursing Journal, 36*, 76–81.

Walker, S. N., Volkan, K., Sechrist, K. R., & Pender, N. (1988). Health-promoting life styles of older adults: Comparisons with young and middle-aged adults, correlates and patterns. *Advanced Nursing Science, 11*, 76–90.

Walkerdine, V. (1997). Redefining the subject in situated cognition theory. In D. Kirschner & J. Whitson (Eds.), *Situated cognition: Social, semiotic, and psychological perspectives* (pp. 57–70). Mahwah, NJ: Erlbaum.

Walter, J. L., & Burnaford, S. M. (2006). Developmental changes in adolescents' guilt and shame: The role of family climate and gender. *North American Journal of Psychology, 8*(2).

Walters, M. L., Chen, J., & Greiding, M. J. (2013, January). The national intimate partner and sexual violence survey (NISVS): 2010 findings on victimization by sexual orientation. Atlanta, GA: Centers for Disease Control and Prevention. Retrieved from https://www.cdc.gov/violenceprevention/pdf/nisvs_sofindings.pdf

Walton, G. M., & Cohen, G. L. (2007). A question of belonging: Race, social fit, and achievement. *Journal of Personality and Social Psychology, 92*(1), 82–96.

Walton, G. M., & Cohen, G. L. (2011). A brief social-belonging intervention improves academic and health outcomes of minority students. *Science, 331*(6023), 1447–1451.

Wandersman, A., & Nation, M. (1998). Urban neighborhoods and mental health: Psychological contributions to understanding toxicity, resilience, and interventions. *American Psychologist, 53*, 647–656.

Wang, M. (2012). Retirement: An adult development perspective. In S. K. Whitbourne, & M. J. Sliwinski (Eds.), *The Wiley-Blackwell handbook of adulthood and aging* (pp. 416–432). Malden, MA: Wiley Blackwell.

Wang, M. T., & Fredricks, J. A. (2014). The reciprocal links between school engagement, youth problem behaviors, and school dropout during adolescence. *Child Development, 85*(2), 722–737.

Wang, J.-J., & Kaufman, A. S. (1993). Changes in fluid and crystallized intelligence across the 20- to 90-year age range on the K-BIT. *Journal of Psychoeducational Assessment, 11*, 29–37.

Wang, V., & Marsh, F. H. (1992). Ethical principles and cultural integrity in health care delivery: Asian ethnocultural perspectives. *Journal of Genetic Counseling, 1*, 81–92.

Wang, W., & Parker, K. (2014, September). *Record share of Americans have never married*. Pew Research Center Social and Demographic Trends. Retrieved from http://www.pewsocialtrends.org/2014/09/24/record-share-of-americans-have-never-married/

Wang, Y., & Zhang, Q. (2006). Are American children and adolescents of low socioeconomic status at increased risk of obesity? Changes in the association between overweight and family income between 1971 and 2002. *American Journal of Clinical Nutrition, 84*(4), 707–716.

Wansink, B., Painter, J. E., & North, J. (2005). Bottomless bowls: Why visual cues of portion size may influence intake. *Obesity Research, 13*(1), 93–101.

Ward, R. A. (1993). Marital happiness and household equity in later life. *Journal of Marriage and the Family, 55*, 427–438.

Wardle, F. (1995). Alternatives . . . Bruderhof education: Outdoor school. *Young Children, 50*(3), 68–74.

Warneken, F., & Tomasello, M. (2007). Helping and cooperation at 14 months of age. *Infancy, 11*(3), 271–294.

Warnock, F., & Sandrin, D. (2004). Comprehensive description of newborn distress behavior in response to acute pain (newborn male circumcision). *Pain, 107*, 242–255.

Warren, S. N., Gartstein, V., Kligman, A. M., Montagna, W., Allendorg, R. A., & Ridder, G. M. (1991). Age, sunlight, and facial skin: A histologic and quantitative study. *Journal of the American Academy of Dermatology, 25*, 751–760.

Warshow, J. (1991). Eldercare as a feminist issue. In B. Sang, J. Warshow, & A. J. Smith (Eds.), *Lesbians at midlife: A creative transition* (pp. 65–72). San Francisco: Spinsters Book Company.

Waterman, A. S. (1982). Identity development from adolescence to adulthood: An extension of theory and a review of research. *Developmental Psychology, 18*, 341–358.

Waterman, A. S. (1985). Identity in the context of adolescent psychology. *New Directions for Child Development, 39*, 5–24.

Webb, N. (Ed.) (1993). *Helping bereaved children: A handbook for practitioners*. New York, NY: Guilford Press.

Wechsler, H., Davenport, A., Dowdall, G., Moeykens, B., & Castillo, S. (1994). Health and behavioral consequences of binge drinking in college: A national survey of students on 140 campuses. *Journal of the American Medical Association, 272*, 1672–1677.

Wechsler, H., Rigotti, N. A., Gledhill-Hoyt, J., & Lee, H. (1998). Increased levels of cigarette use among college students: A cause for national concern. *Journal of the American Medical Association, 280*, 1673–1678.

Weinberg, M. K., & Tronick, E. Z. (1994). Beyond the face: The empirical study of infant affective configurations of facial, vocal, gestural, and regulatory behaviors. *Child Development, 65*, 1503–1515.

Weisner, T. S., & Wilson-Mitchell, J. E. (1990). Nonconventional family life-styles and sex typing in six-year-olds. *Child Development, 61*, 1915–1933.

Weiss, D., & Lang, F. R. (2012). "They" are old but "I" feel younger: Age-group dissociation as a self-protective strategy in old age. *Psychology and Aging, 27*, 153–164.

Weiss, G., & Hechtman, L. (1993). *Hyperactive children grown up* (2nd ed.). New York, NY: Guilford Press.

Weiss, L. H., & Schwarz, C. (1996). The relationship between parenting types and older adolescents' personality, academic achievement, adjustment, and substance abuse. *Child Development, 67*, 2101–2114.

Weiss, R. W. (1993). Loss and recovery. In M. S. Stroebe, W. Stroebe, & R. O. Hansson (Eds.), *Handbook of bereavement: Theory, research, and intervention* (pp. 271–284). Cambridge, UK: Cambridge University Press.

Weizman, S. G., & Kamm, P. (1985). *About mourning*. New York, NY: Human Sciences Press.

Welch, R. D., & Houser, M. E. (2010). Extending the four-category model of adult attachment: An interpersonal model of friendship attachment. *Journal of Social and Personal Relationships, 27*(3), 351–366.

Wellman, B. (1990). The place of kinfolk in personal community networks. *Marriage and Family Review, 15*, 195–221.

Wellman, H., & Hickling, A. (1994). The mind's "I": Children's conception of the mind as an active agent. *Child Development, 65*(6), 1564–1581.

Wenger, G. C., Dykstra, P. A., Melkas, T., & Knipscheer, K. (2007). Social embeddedness and late-life parenthood: Community activity, close ties, and support networks. *Journal of Family Issues, 28*, 1419–1456.

Werner, E. (1991). Grandparent-grandchild relationships amongst U.S. ethnic groups. In P. Smith (Ed.), *The psychology of grand-parenthood* (pp. 68–84). London: Routledge.

Wertsch, J. V. (1985). *Vygotsky and the social formation of mind*. Cambridge, MA: Harvard University Press.

Wertsch, J. V. (1989). A socio-cultural approach to mind. In W. Damon (Ed.), *Child development today and tomorrow* (pp. 14–33). San Francisco: Jossey-Bass.

Wertsch, J. V., del Rio, P., & Alvarey, A. (1995). *Sociocultural studies of mind*. New York, NY: Cambridge University Press.

West, L., Anderson, J., & Duck, S. (1996). Crossing the barriers to friendships between men and women. In J. T. Wood (Ed.), *Gendered relationships* (pp. 111–127). Mountain View, CA: Mayfield.

Whitbourne, S. K. (1985). *The aging body: Physiological changes and psychological consequences*. New York, NY: Springer-Verlag.

Whitbourne, S. K. (2001). The physical aging process in midlife: Interactions with psychological and sociocultural factors. In M. E. Lachman (Ed.), *Handbook of Midlife Development* (pp. 109–155). New York, NY: Wiley.

White, B. (1975). Critical influences in the origins of competence. *Merrill-Palmer Quarterly, 21*, 243–266.

White, B. (1993). *The first three years of life* (Rev. ed.). New York, NY: Simon & Schuster.

White, J. W., & Kowalski, R. M. (1998). Male violence toward women: An integrated perspective. In R. Green & E. Donnerstein (Eds.), *Human aggression: Theories, research, and implications for policies*. New York, NY: Academic Press.

White, L. K., & Edwards, J. N. (1990). Emptying the nest and parental well-being: An analysis of national panel data. *American Sociological Review, 55*, 235–242.

White, L. K., & Riedmann, A. (1992). Ties among adult siblings. *Social Forces, 71*, 85–102.

White, L. K., & Rogers, S. J. (1997). Strong support but uneasy relationships: Coresidence and adult children's relationships with their parents. *Journal of Marriage and the Family, 59*, 62–76.

White, R. D. (1999). Are women more ethical? Recent findings on the effects of gender on moral development. *Journal of Public Administration Research and Theory, 3*, 459–471.

White, S. D., & DeBlassie, R. R. (1992). Adolescent sexual behavior. *Adolescence, 27*, 183–191.

Whitehurst, G., Epstein, J., Angell, A., Payne, A., Crone, D., & Fischel, J. (1994). Outcomes of an emergent literacy intervention in Head Start. *Journal of Educational Psychology, 86*(4), 542–555.

Whiteman, S. D., McHale, S. M., & Soli, A. (2011). Theoretical perspectives on sibling relationships. *Journal of Family Theory & Review, 3*(2), 124–139.

Whiting, B. B., & Edwards, C. P. (1988). *Children of different worlds*. Cambridge, MA: Harvard University Press.

Whiting, B. B., & Whiting, J. (1975). *Children of six cultures: A psychocultural analysis*. Cambridge, MA: Harvard University Press.

Whiting, J. W. M. (1981). Environmental constraints on infant care practices. In R. Munroe, R. H. Monroe, & B. B. Whiting (Eds.), *Handbook of cross-cultural development*. New York, NY: Garland Press.

Whittemore, A. S., Wu, A. H., Kolonel, L. N., John, E. M., Gallagher, R. P., Howe, G. R., West, D. W., Teh, C. Z., & Stamey, T. (1995). Family history and prostate cancer risk in black, white, and Asian men in the United States and Canada. *American Journal of Epidemiology, 141*, 732–740.

Widom, C. S., Czaja, S. J., Bently, T., & Johnson, M. S. (2012). A prospective investigation of physical health outcomes in abused and neglected children: New findings from a 30-year follow-up. *American Journal of Public Health, 102*, 1135–1144.

Wieacker, P., & Steinhard, J. (2010). The prenatal diagnosis of genetic diseases. *Deutsches Arzteblatt International, 107*, 857–862.

Wigfield, A., Eccles, J., & Rodriguez, D. (1998). The development of children's motivation in school contexts. In P. Pearson & A. Iran-Nejad (Eds.), *Review of research in education* (Vol. 23, pp. 73–118.) Washington, DC: American Educational Research Association.

Wight, R. G., LeBlanc, A. J., & Badgett, M. V. L. (2013). Same-sex legal marriage and psychological well-being: Findings from the California Health Interview Survey. *American Journal of Public Health, 103*, 339–346.

Wijngaards-de Meij, L., Stroebe, M., Schut, H., Stroebe, W., van den Bout, J., van der Heijden, P., & Dijkstra, I. (2005). Couples at risk following the death of their child: Predictors of grief versus depression. *Journal of Consulting and Clinical Psychology, 73*(4), 617.

Wilcox, A. J., Weinberg, C. R., & Baird, D. (1995). Timing of sexual intercourse in relation to ovulation: Effects on the probability of conception, survival of the pregnancy, and sex of the baby. *New England Journal of Medicine, 333*, 1517–1519.

Wilcox, S. (1997). Age and gender in relation to body attitudes: Is there a double standard of aging? *Psychology of Women Quarterly, 21*, 549–566.

Wilfley, D. E., Schreiber, G. B., Pike, K. M., & Striegel-Moore, R. H. (1996). Eating disturbance and body image: A comparison of a community sample of adult Black and White women. *International Journal of Eating Disorders, 20*(4). 377–387.

Wilkinson, L., & Marrett, C. (Eds.) (1985). *Gender influences in classroom interaction*. Orlando, FL: Academic Press.

Wilkinson, R. (1996). *Unhealthy societies: The afflictions of inequality*. New York, NY: Routledge.

Willcox, S. M., Himmelstein, D. U., & Woolhandler, S. (1994). Inappropriate drug prescribing for the community-dwelling elderly. *Journal of the American Medical Association, 272*, 292–296.

Williams, A., Khattak, A. Z., Garza, C. N., & Lasky, R. E. (2009). The behavioral pain response to heelstick in preterm neonates studied longitudinally: Description, development, determinants, and components. *Early Human Development, 85*, 369–374.

Williams, A. L., & Merten, M. J. (2009). Adolescents' online social networking following the death of a peer. *Journal of Adolescent Research, 24*(1), 67–90.

Williams, C., & Kimm, S. (1993). *Prevention and treatment of childhood obesity*. New York, NY: New York Academy of Sciences.

Williams, J. D., & Jacoby, A. P. (1989). The effects of premarital heterosexual and homosexual experience on dating and marriage desirability. *Journal of Marriage and the Family, 51*, 489–497.

Williams, K., & Dunne-Bryant, A. (2006). Divorce and adult psychological well-being: Clarifying the role of gender and child age. *Journal of Marriage and Family, 68*, 1178–1196.

Williams, P. M., Goodie, J., & Motsinger, C. D. (2008). Treating eating disorders in primary care. *American Family Physician, 77*(2), 187–195.

Willis, D. J., Holden, E. W., & Rosenberg, M. S. (Eds.). (1992). *Prevention of child maltreatment: Developmental and ecological perspectives*. New York, NY: Wiley.

Willis, S. L. (1989). Adult intelligence. In A. Hunter & M. Sundel (Eds.), *Midlife myths: Issues, findings, and practice implications*. Newbury Park, CA: Sage.

Willis. S.L. (1996). Everyday problem solving. In I. E. Buren & K. W. Schaie (Eds.), *Handbook of the psychology of aging* (287–307). San Diego: Academic Press.

Willis, S. L., & Dubin, S. (Eds). (1990). *Maintaining professional competence*. San Francisco: Jossey Bass.

Wilsgaard, T., Emaus, N., Ahmed, L. A., Grimnes, G., Joakimsen, R. M., Omsland, T. K., & Berntsen, G. R. (2009). Lifestyle impact on lifetime bone loss in women and men. *American Journal of Epidemiology, 196*, 877–886.

Wilson, M. R. (1989). Glaucoma in Blacks: Where do we go from here? *Journal of the American Medical Association, 26*, 281–282.

Wilson, W. J. (1996). *When work disappears: The world of the new urban poor*. New York, NY: Knopf.

Winfree, L. T., Backstrom, T. V., & Mays, G. L. (1994). Social learning theory, self-reported delinquency, and youth gangs. *Youth and Society, 26*, 147–177.

Wingard, D. L. (1997). Patterns and puzzles: The distribution of health and illness among women in the United States. In S. B. Ruzek, V. L. Olesen, & A. E. Clarke (Eds.), *Women's health: Complexities and differences* (pp. 29–45). Columbus: Ohio State University Press.

Wink, P., & Helson, R. (1993). Personality change in women and their partners. *Journal of Personality & Social Psychology, 65*, 597–605.

Winkler, I., Haden, G. P., Ladinig, O., Sziller, I., & Honing, H. (2009). Newborn infants detect the beat in music. *Proceedings of the National Academy of Science, 106*, 2468–2471.

Winter, L., Gitlin, L. N., & Dennis, M. (2011). Desire to institutionalize a relative with dementia: Quality of premorbid relationship and caregiver gender. *Family Relations, 60*, 221–230.

Winters, K. C., & Arria, A. (2011). Adolescent brain development and drugs. *Prevention Researcher. 18*(2), 21–25.

Wiseman, A. D. (1972). *On dying and denying*. New York, NY: Behavioral Publications.

Witherington, D. C., Campos, J. J., Harriger, J. A., Bryan, C., & Margett, T. E. (2010). Emotion and its development in infancy. In J. G. Bremner, & T. D. Wachs (Eds.), *The Wiley-Blackwell handbook of infant development* (pp. 568–591). Malden, MA: Wiley-Blackwell Publishing.

Wolf, D. (1993). There and then, intangible and internal: Narratives in early childhood. In B. Spodek (Ed.), *Handbook of research on the education of young children* (pp. 42–56). New York, NY: Macmillan.

Wolf, N. (1997). *The beauty myth*. New York, NY: Vintage Books.

Wolfe, D. A., McMahon, R. D., & Peters, R. D. (Eds.). (1997). *Child abuse: New directions in prevention and treatment across the lifespan*. Thousand Oaks, CA: Sage.

Wolff, P. (1966). The causes, controls, and organization of behavior in the neonate. *Psychological Issues, 5*, 1–105.

Wolfson, A. R., & Carskadon, M. A. (1998). Sleep schedules and daytime functioning in adolescents. *Child Development, 69*, 875–887.

Wolock, I. (1998). Beyond the battered child *Readings: A Journal of Reviews and Commentary in Mental Health*, 4–9.

Wood, E., Senn, C. Y., Desmarais, S., Park, L., & Verberg, N. (2002). Sources of information about dating and their perceived influence on adolescents. *Journal of Adolescent Research, 17*(4), 401–417.

Woodburn, J. (1982). Social dimensions of death in four African hunting and gathering societies. In M. Bloch & J. Parry (Eds.). *Death and the regeneration of life* (pp. 187–210). Cambridge, UK: Cambridge University Press.

Woolfolk, A. (2013). *Educational psychology*. Upper Saddle River, NJ: Pearson.

Woolston, J. (1993). *Eating and growth disorders*. Philadelphia: Saunders.

Wootan, M., & Liebman, B. (1998). Ten steps to a healthy 1998. *Nutrition Action Health Letter, 25*(1), 1, 6–10.

Worden, J. W. (1996), *Children and grief*. New York, NY: Guilford.

World Bank. (1997). *Confronting AIDS: Public priorities in a global epidemic*. New York, NY: Oxford University Press.

World Health Organization (WHO). (2005). *WHO multi-country study on women's health and domestic violence against women*. Retrieved from http://apps.who.int/iris/bitstream/10665/43310/1/9241593512_eng.pdf

World Health Organization (WHO). (2011). *WHO recommendations for induction of labour*. Retrieved from http://whqlibdoc.who.int/publications/2011/9789241501156_eng.pdf

World Health Organization (WHO). (2013). *Treatment of children living with HIV*. Retrieved from http://www.who.int/hiv/topics/paediatric/en/index.html

Wortman, C. B., Silver, R. C., & Kessler, R. C. (1993). The meaning of loss and adjustment to bereavement. In M. S. Stroebe, W. Stroebe, & R. O Hansson (Eds.), *Handbook of bereavement: Theory, research, and intervention* (pp. 349–366). Cambridge, UK: Cambridge University Press.

Wozniak, R., & Fischer, K. (1993). *Development in context: Acting and thinking in specific environments*. Hillsdale, NJ: Erlbaum.

Wright, A. A., Zhang, B., Ray, A., Mack, J. W., Trice, E., Balboni, T., ... & Prigerson, H. G. (2008). Associations between end-of-life discussions, patient mental health, medical care near death, and caregiver bereavement adjustment. *JAMA, 300*(14), 1665–1673.

Wright, D. J. (1987). Minority students: Developmental beginnings. *New Directions for Student Services, 38*, 5–21.

Wright, J. C., Huston, A. C., Truglio, R., Fitch, M., Smith, E., & Piemyat, S. (1995). Occupational portrayals on television: Children's role schemata, career aspirations, and perceptions of reality. *Child Development, 66*, 1706–1718.

Wright, J. D., & Hamilton, R. F. (1978). Work satisfaction and age: Some evidence for the job change hypothesis. *Social Forces. 56*, 1140–1158.

Wright, J. L., Neushouser, M. L., Lin, D. W., Kwon, E. M., Feng, Z., Ostrander, E. A., & Stanford, J. L. (2011). AMACR polymorphisms, dietary intake of red meat and dairy and prostate cancer risk. *Prostate, 71*, 498–506. doi: 10.1002/pros.21267

Wright, K. (2000). Computer-mediated social support, older adults, and coping. *Journal of Communication, 50*, 100–118.

Wright, P. H. (1988). Interpreting research on gender differences in friendship: A case for moderation and a plea for caution. *Journal of Social and Personal Relationships, 5*, 367–373.

Wu, F. C., Tajar, A., Beynon, J. M., Pye, S. R., Silman, A. J., Finn, J. D., ... & Huhtaniemi, I. T. (2010). Identification of late-onset hypogonadism in middle-aged and elderly men. *New England Journal of Medicine, 363*, 123–135.

Wyatt, L. G. (2011). Nontraditional student engagement: Increasing adult student success and retention. *Journal of Continuing Higher Education, 59*, 10–20.

Wykle, M. L., & Musil, C. M. (1993). Mental health of older persons: Social and cultural factors *Generations, 17*(l), 7–12.

Y

Yacker, N., & Weinberg, S. L. (1990). Care and justice moral orientation: A scale for its assessment. *Journal of Personality Assessment, 56*, 18–27.

Yale School of Medicine. (2013). *Achondroplasia*. Retrieved from http://www.yalemedicalgroup.org/stw/

Yang, S., Yang, H., & Lust, B. (2011). Early childhood bilingualism leads to advances in executive attention: Dissociating culture and language. *Bilingualism: Language and Cognition, 14*(03), 412–422.

Yap, S. C., Anusic, I., & Lucas, R. E. (2012). Does personality moderate reaction and adaptation to major life events? Evidence from the British Household Panel Survey. *Journal of Research in Personality, 46*, 477–488.

Yarrow, M., & Waxler, C. (1978). The emergence and functions of prosocial behavior in young children. In M. Smart & R. Smart (Eds.), *Infants, development and relationships.* New York, NY: Macmillan.

Yavorsky, J. E., Kamp Dush, C. M., & Schoppe-Sullivan, S. J. (2015). The production of inequality: The gender division of labor across the transition to parenthood. *Journal of Marriage and Family, 77*(3), 662–679.

Yee, B. W. K. (1992). Gender and family issues in minority groups. In L. Glasse & J. Hendricks (Eds.), *Gender and aging* (pp. 69–77). Amityville, NY: Baywood.

Yeh, H. C., Lorenz, F. O., Wickrama, K. A. S., Conger, R. D., & Elder, G. H. (2006). Relationships among sexual satisfaction, marital quality, and marital instability at midlife. *Journal of Family Psychology, 20*, 339–343.

Yeh, S. S. (2008). High stakes testing and students with disabilities: Why federal policy needs to be changed. In E. L. Grigorenko (Ed.), *Educating individuals with disabilities: IDEIA 2004 and beyond.* New York, NY: Springer.

Yeung, W. J., Sandberg, J. F., Davis-Kean, P. E., & Hofferth, S. L. (2001). Children's time with fathers in intact families. *Journal of Marriage and Family, 63*, 136–154.

Yllo, K., & Bogard, M. (1988). *Feminist perspectives on wife abuse.* Newbury Park, CA: Sage.

Yoder, P., & Warren, S. (1993). Can developmentally delayed children's language development be enhanced through prelinguistic intervention? In A. Kaiser & D. Gray (Eds.), *Enhancing children's communication: Vol. 2* (pp. 35–62). Baltimore, MD: Paul Brookes.

Yonas, A. (1988). *Perceptual development in infants. Minnesota Symposium on Child Psychology: Vol. 20.* Minneapolis: University of Minnesota Press.

Yoshikawa, H., Aber, J. L., & Beardslee, W. R. (2012). The effects of poverty on the mental, emotional, and behavioral health of children and youth: Implications for prevention. *American Psychologist, 67*(4), 272.

Youlden, D. R., Cramb, S. M., Dunn, N. A. M., Muller, J. M., Pyke, C. M., & Baade, P. D. (2012). The descriptive epidemiology of female breast cancer: An international comparison of screening, incidence, survival and mortality. *Cancer Epidemiology, 36*, 237–248.

Youniss, J. (1980). *Parents and peers in social development: A Sullivan-Piaget perspective.* Chicago: University of Chicago Press.

Youniss, J., & Smollar, J. (1985). *Adolescent relations with mothers, fathers, and friends.* Chicago: University of Chicago Press.

Yousefi, M., Karmaus, W., Zhang, H., Roberts, G., Matthews, S., Clayton, B., & Arshad, S. H. (2013). Relationships between age of puberty onset and height at age 18 years in girls and boys. *World Journal of Pediatrics, 9*(3), 230–238.

Yu, J. (2012). A systematic review of issues around antenatal screening and prenatal diagnostic testing for genetic disorders: Women of Asian origin in western countries. *Heath and Social Care in the Community, 20*, 329–346.

Yuan, A. S. V. (2012). Perceived breast development and adolescent girls' psychological well-being. *Sex Roles, 66*, 790–806.

Z

Zahn-Waxler, C., Radke-Yanow, M., & King, R. A. (1979). Child rearing and children's prosocial initiations toward victims of distress. *Child Development, 50*, 319–330.

Zahn-Wexler, C., Radere-Yanow, M. Wagner, E., & Chapman, M. (1992). Development of concern for others. *Developmental Psychology, 28*, 126–136.

Zampi, C., Fagioli, I., & Salzarulo, P. (2002). Time course of EEG background activity level before spontaneous awakening in infants. *Journal of Sleep Research, 11*, 283–287.

Zani, B. (1993). Dating and interpersonal relationships in adolescence. In S. Jackson, & H. Rodriguez-Tome (Eds.), *Adolescence and its social worlds* (pp. 95–119). Hillsdale, NJ: Lawrence Erlbaum.

Zarbatany, L., Hartmann, D. P., & Rankin, D. B. (1990). The psychological functions of preadolescent peer activities. *Child Development, 61*, 1067–1080.

Zarit, S. H., & Reamy, A. M. (2013). Developmentally appropriate long-term care for people with Alzheimer's disease and related disorders. In S. H. Zarit, & R. C. Talley (Eds.), *Caregiving for Alzheimer's disease and related disorders: Research, practice, policy* (pp. 51–69). New York, NY: Springer Publishing.

Zarit, S. H., & Zarit, J. M. (2007). *Mental disorders in older adults* (2nd ed.). New York, NY: Guilford Press.

Zeitz, G. (1990). Age and work satisfaction in a government agency: A situational perspective. *Human Relations, 43*(5), 419–438.

Zeleznik, J. (2003). Normative aging of the respiratory system. *Clinics in Geriatric Medicine, 19*, 1–18.

Zerbe, K. (1993). *The body betrayed: Women, eating disorders. and treatment.* Washington, DC: American Psychiatric Press.

Zhang, J., Himes, J. H., Guo, Y., Jiang, J., Yang, L., Lu, Q., Ruan, H., & Shi, S. (2013). Birth weight, growth and feeding pattern in early infancy predict overweight/obesity status at two years of age: A birth cohort study of Chinese infants. *PLoS ONE, 8*, 1–8.

Zigler, E. F., Taussig, C., & Black, K. (1992). Early childhood intervention: A. promising preventative for juvenile delinquency, *American Psychologist, 47*, 997–1006.

Zilbergeld, B., & Ellison, C. R. (1980). Desire discrepancies and arousal problems in sex therapy. In S. R. Leiblum & L. A. Pervin (Eds.). *Principle and practice of sex therapy.* New York, NY: Guilford Press.

Zimmer-Gembeck, M. J., & Helfand, M. (2008). Ten years of longitudinal research on U.S. adolescent sexual behavior: Developmental correlates of sexual intercourse, and the importance of age, gender and ethnic background. *Developmental Review, 28*(2), 153–224.

Zimmerman, L., & McDonald, L. (1995). Emotional availability in infants' relationships with multiple caregivers. *American Journal of Orthopsychiatry, 65*, 147–152.

Zimprich, D., & Martin, M. (2002). Can longitudinal changes in processing speed explain longitudinal age changes in fluid intelligence? *Psychology and Aging, 17*, 690–695.

Zipfel, S., Wild, B., Groß, G., Friederich, H. C., Teufel, M., Schellberg, D., ... & Burgmer, M. (2014). Focal psychodynamic therapy, cognitive behaviour therapy, and optimised treatment as usual in outpatients with anorexia nervosa (ANTOP study): Randomised controlled trial. *Lancet, 383*(9912), 127–137.

Zsembik, B. A., & Singer, A. (1990). The problem of defining retirement among minorities: The Mexican Americans. *The Gerontologist, 30*, 749–757.

Zuo, J. (1992). The reciprocal relationship between marital interaction and marital happiness: A three-wave study. *Journal of Marriage and the Family, 54*, 870–878.

Zweig, J. M., Dank, M., Yahner, J., & Lachman, P. (2013). The rates of cyber dating abuse among teens and how it relates to other forms of teen dating violence. *Journal of Youth and Adolescence, 42*, 1063–1077.

Author/Name Index

Aaron, J., 659
Abel, E., 669
Aber, J. L., 310
Abma, J. C., 403
Aboraya, A., 603
Abukabar, A., 120
Abu-Raiya, H., 318
Acebo, C., 348
Achenbaum, A., 610
Acock, A. C., 391
Acquaviva, K., 565
Adachi, P. J., 233
Adair, L., 183
Adamchak, D. J., 610
Adamek, M. E., 666
Adams, G. A., 616
Adams, R. G., 633
Adams, S. G., Jr., 583
Adams, S. L., 588
Addington-Hall, J., 659
Ade-Ridder, L., 620
Adlercreutz, H., 513
Adler, S., 424, 432, 437
Adler, T., 16
Adolph, K. E., 117
Agras, W. S., 429
Agrigoroaei, S., 507
Agronick, G. S., 540
Ahadi, S., 159
Ahlberg, C., 246
Ahn, J., 244
Ahn, S., 494
Aiken, L., 280
Ainlay, S. C., 645
Ainsworth, M., 141, 162
Ainsworth, M. S., 50, 160, 161
Akande, A., 166
Akbaraly, T. N., 507
Åkerstedt, T., 435
Albert, M., 452
Albert, M. S., 599
Alberts, A., 364
Aldous, M. B., 550
Alegria, M., 430
Alexander, A. W., 275
Alexander, F., 588
Alexander, G. M., 315
Alexander, K. L., 303
Alexander, L. L., 425, 426
Alexander, L. M., 579
Alexandersen, P., 515
Alfonso, M., 455
Allaire, J. C., 526
Allen, J. P., 376, 384
Allen, K. R., 485
Allen, R. S., 556
Allen, S. M., 622
Allen, T. D., 531
Allhusen, V. D., 155
Altenbaugh, R., 371
Alvarado, K. A., 661
Amacker, M. K., 495
Amato, P. R., 306–307, 484–485, 549
Ambry, M. K., 495
Ames, L., 213
Amott, T., 461
Anastasi, A., 281
Anastas, J., 533
Ancoli-Israel, S., 587–588
Anderson, A. M., 149
Anderson, B., 169

Anderson, J., 233
Anderson, L. M., 233
Anderson, S., 534
Anderson, S. A., 547
Andrien, M., 184
Angier, N., 68
Anglin, J., 277
Annear, M. J., 564
Anson, O., 474
Anthis, K. S., 379, 396
Anthony, J. C., 603
Antonucci, T. C., 472, 474, 554, 628, 629
Anusic, I., 623
Apfel, N., 11, 407
Apgar, V., 105
Aquilino, W. S., 553
Arbeau, K. A., 298
Archer, J., 106
Archer, S. L., 379, 380
Archibald, A. B., 338
Architti, J., 140
Arditti, J. A., 307
Arenberg, D., 525
Arend, R., 693
Årestedt, K., 670
Arguello, R., 186
Ariès, P., 11, 656
Arliss, L., 208
Armenta, B. E., 227
Armour, S., 400
Armstead, C. A., 591
Armstrong, J., 429
Armstrong, T. P., 429
Arnett, J. J., 335, 378, 382, 388, 396, 417, 466
Arria, A., 352
Arterberry, M. E., 114
Arthur-Banning, S., 264
Artiga, S., 186
Asendorpf, J. B., 173
Ashley, K. B., 403
Aslanian, C. B., 528, 529
Ata, R. N., 350
Atchley, R. C., 556, 557, 614, 617, 618, 623, 628, 632, 638, 643, 645
Attanucci, J., 451
Aureli, T., 151
Aviezer, O., 164
Avioli, P. S., 558, 630
Avis, N. E., 514
Ayers, B., 513
Ayers, T. S., 327
Ayscue, J. B., 317
Aytac, I. A., 551
Azmitia, M., 311, 312, 474

Bachman, J. G., 373
Bachmann, G. A., 515
Backx, F., 262
Bader, M., 316
Badgett, M. V. L., 459, 484, 548
Bagwell, C. L., 319, 344, 392
Baharudin, R., 300
Baik, C. S., 592
Baile, W. F., 659
Bailey, J. M., 245, 402
Bailey, T., 455
Baillargeon, R., 134, 135, 136
Baird, P., 68
Baker, B. L., 264
Baker, C., 206

Baker, J., 494
Baker, J. E., 324
Baker, L. A., 556
Bakermans-Kranenburg, M. J., 170
Balantekin, K. N., 261
Baldwin, D. A., 172
Balk, D., 341, 342
Balter, M., 402, 403
Baltes, B. B., 563, 616
Baltes, M. A., 300
Baltes, M. M., 615, 643
Baltes, P. B., 16, 563, 594, 595, 596, 615, 616, 643
Bamford, F., 112
Bammel, G., 563
Bandura, A., 42, 43, 56, 231, 437
Bank, L., 224
Banks Tarullo, L., 213
Barbaresi, W. J., 266
Barber, B. K., 304, 311
Barber, C. F., 482
Barber, E., 96
Barer, B. M., 622, 629, 630, 632, 646
Barker, D. J. P., 88
Barker, E. D., 229
Barkley, R. A., 267
Barlow, D. H., 171
Barnes, G. M., 432
Barnes, R., 297
Barness, L., 348
Barnett, R., 436
Barnett, R. C., 552
Barrett, A. E., 625
Barrett, H. C., 141
Barrett, K. C., 156
Barr, H. M., 84
Barr, R. G., 156
Barry, C. M., 474, 475
Barry, H., 389
Barth, J. M., 288, 317
Barthlen, G. M., 588
Bartholomew, J. B., 426, 427
Bartholomew, K., 170
Bartick, M., 167
Bartolic, S., 232
Barton, E. E., 239
Bartoshuk, L. M., 582
Bartsch, K., 355
Baruch, G., 436
Baruch, G. K., 552
Basinger, K. S., 451
Bat-Chava, Y., 380
Batenhorst, C., 227
Bates, J. E., 304
Baumrind, D., 221, 384, 385
Bausell, R. B., 584
Baxter, J., 489
Baydar, N., 223
Bayley, N., 519
Beale, E. A., 659
Beaman, J., 307
Bean, R. A., 304, 305, 311
Beardsall, L., 224
Beardslee, W. R., 310
Beauchamp, G. K., 115
Bechara, A., 422
Beck, D. M., 197
Becker, A., 261
Becker, A. E., 261

Bedford, V. H., 630
Beelmann, A., 317
Bègue, L., 19, 21
Behling, J. H., 565
Behrens, K. Y., 163
Behrman, J., 186
Behrman, R., 186
Belenky, M. F., 449, 450, 455
Bellamy, M. A., 300
Bell, K., 372, 627
Bellmore, A. D., 319
Bellugi, U., 210
Belon, K., 348
Belsky, J., 150, 152, 153, 156, 166, 168, 169, 170, 248, 249, 491
Bem, S. L., 246, 247
Benatov, J., 318
Bender, K. A., 618
Benedict, J. O., 239
Benenson, J. F., 241
Bengtson, V. L., 554, 555, 557, 622
Benner, A. D., 369
Benner, P., 361
Bennett, K. M., 623
Bennett, M. I., 670
Bennett, T., 610
Benoit, D., 171
Benshoff, J. J., 661
Benson, J., 646
Benson, P., 646
Berchtold, N. C., 426
Berg, E. C., 308
Berger, A., 157, 441
Berger, R., 318
Berger, R. M., 626
Berko, J., 204
Berlin, J. E., 283
Berlucchi, G., 599
Berman, L. S., 495
Berndt, T., 401
Berndt, T. J., 314
Bernhardt, J. S., 86
Bertakis, K. D., 590
Bertrand, K., 347
Bertrand, M., 459, 532
Besedovsky, L., 425
Best, S., 579
Beydoun, M. A., 260
Bhavnagri, N., 244
Bialystok, E., 278
Bianchi, S. M., 490, 555
Bierman, K. L., 314, 318
Bingham, C. R., 399, 400
Birch, L., 260, 261
Bird, G., 480
Birditt, K. S., 621
Birenbaum, L. K., 323
Biringen, Z., 160, 161
Birren, J. E., 525
Biosca, M., 429
Black, M., 249
Black, M. C., 401
Black, M. M., 120
Black, S. A., 511, 575, 576, 577
Blackburn, J. A., 445, 446
Blackman, J. A., 84, 86
Blair, J., 84
Blair, S. N., 587
Blais, M. R., 640
Blakemore, S. J., 314, 334, 351, 352
Blanchett, W. J., 283

Blanck, G., 48
Blashill, A. J., 339
Blazer, D. G., 664
Bleakley, A., 234
Blier, M. J., 478
Blier-Wilson, L. A., 478
Blinn Pike, L., 388
Bliwise, D. L., 587
Bloch, M., 647
Block, D., 163, 165
Bloom, D. A., 187
Bloom, H. L., 587
Bloom, L., 140
Blumenthal, J. A., 507
Boat, T., 347
Bock, R. D., 303
Boergers, J., 348
Bogart, L. M., 434
Bogdan, J., 475
Bogdon, J. C., 91
Bohan, J., 296
Bohn, A., 296
Boivin, M., 229
Bojko, M., 317
Bolger, K. E., 310
Bollerud, K., 360
Bolton, J. M., 435
Bonanno, G. A., 647
Bond, J. T., 490
Bonnie, R., 347
Bonoti, F., 662
Bookwala, J., 552
Boone-Heinonen, J., 426
Boonen, S., 515
Booth, A., 488, 624
Booth, D. A., 115
Booth, J. R., 272
Boquet, J. R., 632
Bornstein, M. H., 222
Borysova, M. E., 511
Bos, H. M., 494
Bosman, E. A., 527
Botwinick, J., 519, 520, 525
Bouchard, C., 505
Bowen, N. K., 302, 303
Bowers, R., 363
Bowker, J., 314
Bowker, J. C., 319
Bowlby, J., 50, 160, 161, 248
Boyle, M., 290
Boyle, P. J., 623
Bradbury, T. N., 484
Bradley, M., 410
Bradsher, J. E., 623
Brady, E. M., 644
Braithwaite, R. L., 577
Branje, S. J., 314
Branstetter, W. H., 227
Brazelton, T. B., 106
Bredekamp, S., 213
Breiding, M. J., 401, 482
Brendgen, M., 229
Brent, S. B., 326
Breslau, N., 437
Bretherton, I., 164, 166, 172
Brickell, H. M., 528, 529
Bridges, L., 152
Bridle, C., 606
Briggs, W. P., 589
Brim, O. C., 108
Brindle, J. A., 204
Brinsden, P., 72

Briones, T. L., 598
Brislin, R., 370
Brody, E. M., 558, 559
Brody, G. H., 304, 305, 312, 315, 558
Brody, J. E., 84
Brondel, L., 422
Bronfenbrenner, U., 7, 8, 48, 389, 409
Bronner, F., 121
Bronstein, P., 149, 299
Brooks-Gunn, J., 173, 295, 335
Brooten, D., 122
Broughton, D., 190
Brown, B., 312, 394, 398
Brown, B. B., 394, 398
Brownell, C. A., 157
Brown, G. L., 166
Brown, J. R., 224
Brown, L., 27
Brown, L. H., 555
Brown, R., 202
Brown, S., 643
Brown, S. C., 596
Brown, S. L., 548
Brown, T. H., 547
Brubaker, T. H., 619, 622, 626
Bruce, B. B., 507, 582
Bruchmüller, K., 266
Brumariu, L. E., 165
Bruner, J., 207
Bruns, C., 431
Bryan, E., 658
Bryant, B. K., 311, 312
Bryant, C., 610
Bryant, C. D., 656
Bryant, G. A., 141
Bubenzer, D. L., 486
Buchmann, C., 457
Buck, K., 89
Buckley, K., 94
Bugental, D. B., 251
Buhrmester, D., 314, 315, 392
Bukowski, W. M., 313, 318, 319, 392
Bulcroft, C., 624
Bulcroft, K., 632, 633
Bulcroft, R., 624
Bulik, C. M., 430
Bumpass, L. L., 548
Burdette, A. M., 645
Burdette, H. L., 429
Burd, L., 84
Burke, T., 348
Burnaford, S. M., 298
Burnett, P., 676
Burns, B. J., 251
Burns, C. J., 618
Burr, J. A., 572
Burrus-Bammel, L. L., 563
Burton, L. M., 554, 555, 556
Bury, M., 186
Bushman, B. J., 19, 21
Bush, N. F., 409
Buss, A. H., 227, 319
Buss, K. A., 157
Butler, A. B., 308, 309
Butler, K., 458
Butler, R., 610, 647
Butler, R. N., 610, 646
Butler, S. S., 627
Buyse, E., 170
Byard, R., 110
Bye, D., 456
Bye, K., 89
Byers, E. S., 440, 517
Byne, W., 402
Byrne, A., 486

Cafferata, G. L., 638
Caillaud, C., 579
Caine, C., 262
Caine, D., 262, 263
Caine, E. D., 664
Cain, M., 299
Cairns, R. B., 371
Calabrese, R. L., 389
Calasanti, T., 557, 558
Calderon-Margalit, R., 443

Calhoun, D. A., 507
Calhoun, L., 682
Caliso, J., 249
Calkins, S. D., 225
Callahan, J. J., Jr., 635
Callanan, M. A., 246
Callister, P., 167
Call, K. T., 397, 399
Calvert, S. L., 232, 233, 234
Camacho, T. C., 606
Campbell, L. D., 558, 630
Campbell, M. D., 529
Campero, S., 533
Campos, A. P., 681
Campos, J., 128
Campos, R., 18, 239
Camras, L. A., 156
Cancian, F. M., 474, 178
Candas, V., 579
Canfield R., 128
Cann, A., 682
Cannella, G., 12, 195
Cannon, J., 199
Cantor, M. H., 670
Cantos, A. L., 482
Capaldi, D. M., 482
Cappuccio, F. P., 507
Caravita, S. C. S., 318
Card, N. A., 228, 229, 320
Caren, N., 494
Carlander, I., 670
Carlin, J. B., 625
Carlo, G., 227
Carlson, C. I., 381, 384
Carlson, E. A., 159
Carlson, S. M., 197
Carlsson, M. A., 270
Carmichael, S. T., 600
Carney, S. S., 665
Carpenter, C. L., 421
Carp, F. M., 617, 642
Carr, D., 486, 548, 620, 622, 628
Carrere, S., 485
Carroll, J., 111
Carskadon, M. A., 348, 587
Carstensen, L. L., 544, 547, 548, 628
Carter, J. S., 483
Carter, S. K., 483
Casarett, D. J., 670
Case, R., 45, 136, 189, 199, 201, 271
Casey, B. J., 352, 422
Caspi, A., 157, 159, 229, 482
Cassady, D. L., 426
Cassel, C. K., 672
Cassidy, J., 156
Cassidy, S. B., 65
Castañeda, D. M., 479
Caterall, J., 371
Cattell, R. B., 522
Caughey, A. B., 94
Cauley, J. A., 579
Cazden, C., 322
Cazenave, N. A., 482
Cervantes, C. A., 246
Chadwick, A., 155
Chafel, J., 11
Chakravarty, E. F., 507
Chambrè, S. M., 643
Chan, A., 242, 243, 244, 313, 315, 317
Chandler, M., 300
Chandra, A., 442
Chang, A., 348
Chan, S., 74
Chao, R. K., 219, 222
Chao, W., 391
Chapleau, K. M., 438
Chapman, B., 208
Chappell, N. C., 619, 621
Charles, S. T., 646
Charman, T., 314
Charmaz, K., 667
Charness, N., 527, 528
Chase-Landsdale, P. L., 87, 399, 404, 405, 406, 407
Chatters, L. M., 634
Chavajay, P., 45, 49

Chazan-Cohen, R., 213
Cheatham, H. E., 457
Cheek, D., 338
Cheng, W. J., 219
Cheng, Y. W., 94
Chen, J., 401, 482
Chen, P. S. D., 455
Chen, Y., 260
Cherkas, L. F., 578
Cherkes-Julkowski, M., 266
Cherlin, A. J., 222, 485, 549
Cherry, F., 17
Chervin, R. D., 266, 267
Chess, S., 158
Chesters, J., 481, 531
Chi, M., 47
Chiriboga, D. A., 538, 542
Chomsky, N., 206
Chornokur, G., 511
Choudhury, S., 314
Chou, J. L., 486
Christakis, D. A., 231, 233, 239, 429
Christakis, N., 623
Christensen, K. Y., 337
Christiansen, C., 505, 515, 516, 579, 588, 599
Christie, L. A., 426
Christodoulou, J., 284
Chumlea, W. C., 421
Chung, A. E., 261
Cibelli, C. D., 832
Cicchetti, D., 249, 409
Ciccolo, J. T., 426
Cicirelli, V. G., 152, 557, 558, 631, 659, 660
Cillessen, A. H., 244
Cillessen, A. H. N., 319
Cinamon, R. G., 309
Clark, D. O., 577
Clark-Pearson, K., 395, 396
Clark, R., 167
Clausell, E., 548
Clay, D., 421
Clinchy, B. M., 449
Closson, L. M., 318
Clouston, S. A., 529
Coakley, J., 338
Coan, J., 485
Coates, A., 189
Coates, E., 189
Coates, J., 208
Coatsworth, J. D., 299, 300, 318, 319, 320
Cobb, P., 200
Cobb, R. J., 547
Cochran, S. D., 483
Coe, N. B., 533
Cogan, R., 93
Cohen, E., 288
Cohen, G. L., 457
Cohen, P. N., 494
Cohen, S., 425
Cohle, S., 110
Cohn, D., 301, 302, 493
Coie, J. D., 230, 318, 319
Coiro, M., 264
Colby, A., 15, 359, 361
Colditz, G. A., 515
Coldwell, J., 312
Cole, E., 517
Colella, U., 488
Cole, M., 49
Cole, M. G., 679, 682
Coleman, J., 385
Coleman, M., 493
Cole, M. G., 679, 682
Coles, E. K., 189
Cole, S. Z., 212
Coley, R. L., 87, 305, 399, 404, 405, 406
Coll, C. G., 48
Collier, K. M., 233
Collins, W. A., 381, 384
Comer, J. P., 231, 232
Comstock, F., 234
Condry, J., 232
Conger, R. D., 390, 391, 551
Cong, X., 156
Conklin, H. M., 272

Connell, S. L., 234
Connelly, K., 118
Connidis, I. A., 555, 557, 558, 559, 630, 632, 634
Connolly, J., 394, 475
Connolly, S., 339, 341
Connor, S. R., 672
Conway, M., 456
Conwell, Y., 664
Cook, A., 459, 533
Cooke, L., 184
Cook, J., 546
Cooksey, E. C., 310
Cooney, T. M., 549, 550, 631
Cooper, H., 680
Cooper, K. L., 551
Cooper, L. A., 510
Cooper, P. W., 643
Cooper, R. S., 512
Copeland, L., 346
Copen, C. E., 301, 403, 405, 442, 487
Coplan, R. J., 319
Copple, C., 213
Coren, S., 111
Corley, C. J., 388
Corman, C., 443
Corneal, D., 248
Cornelius, S. W., 526
Cornman, J. C., 548, 620, 622
Corpus, J. H., 299
Corra, M., 483
Corr, C. A., 341, 342, 659, 663, 666, 667, 677
Corr, D. M., 663
Corsini, N., 184
Costa, A., 278
Costa, K. G., 661
Costa, P. T., Jr., 538, 542, 543, 611, 612, 623, 624
Côté, J. E., 455
Côté, S., 320
Cotman, C. W., 426, 427
Countryman, J., 236
Cousineau, T. M., 443
Covey, H., 600
Covitz, L. M., 388, 390
Cowan, C., 149, 491
Cowan, C. P., 491
Cowan, G., 625
Cowan, P., 491
Cowan, P. A., 170, 272, 491
Coward, R. T., 558
Cowell, J. M., 348
Cox, N., 166, 167, 170
Coyne, J. C., 409
Coyne, S., 231
Coyne, S. M., 233, 247, 320, 321
Cramer, P., 51, 612
Crane, D. R., 304, 311
Crapo, L. M., 422
Crawford, H. J., 432
Crawford, S., 514
Creamer, D. G., 450
Creasey, G. L., 235
Crick, N. R., 228, 229, 320
Criqui, M. H., 432
Crnic, K., 152
Crockenberg, S. B., 159, 174
Crockett, L. J., 399, 400, 401
Crosby, F. J., 531
Crosnoe, R., 474
Crouter, A., 248
Crouter, A. C., 311
Crowl, A. L., 494
Crow, S. J., 349
Crowther, M. R., 556
Cuffaro, H., 212
Cummings, E. M., 390
Cummings, J. L., 390
Currie, J., 251
Currier, J. M., 676
Curry, G. D., 412
Curtin, S. C., 664, 665
Cushman, G., 564
Cutler, S. J., 563, 564, 602, 615, 622, 625, 642, 643
Czaja, S. J., 251

Dalglish, P., 19
Dalton, B., 207
Dalton, K., 511
D'Alton, M. E., 73
Dalton, S., 259
Damon, W., 14, 15, 295, 296, 297, 321, 377, 392
Danchik, K. M., 586
Dane, B. O., 560
Daniels, K., 301, 487
Daniels, P., 489
Daniels, S. R., 429
Danner, F., 348
Darling, N., 219, 221
Darwin, C., 12
Datar, A., 122
Dattell, A. R., 661
D'Augelli, A. R., 403
Davajan, V., 442
DaVanzo, J., 551
Davey, A., 548
Davey, M., 548
Davidson, R. J., 159
Davies, B., 191, 323
Davies, I., 114
Davies, L., 632, 634
Davis, E., 80, 93
Davis-Floyd, R. E., 97
Davis, J. N., 260
Davis, K., 284
Davis-Kean, P. E., 454
Davis, M., 616
Davis, M. M., 186
Dawson, G., 206
Deater-Deckhard, S., 230
Deaux, K., 191
DeBlassie, R. R., 401
DeCasper, A. J., 80, 149
DeCherney, A. H., 73
Deci, E. L., 299, 300
De Civita, M., 302, 303
Declercq, E., 94
Deeg, D. J. H., 589
De Goede, I. H., 314
DeGrace, A., 474
De Jaeger, A. E., 298
De Jong Gierveld, J., 558
DeJong, W., 349
DeKlyen, M., 229
Delamont, S., 288
Del Dotto, J., 274
Del Guidice, M., 138
D'Elia, S., 507
DeLisi, M., 229
Delsing, M. J., 314
Dembe, A. E., 437
Demetriou, A., 365
Demo, D. H., 391
Dendinger, V. M., 616
Denham, S., 311, 314
Deniz, M., 163
Denney, N. W., 455, 525, 526, 527
Dennis, J., 455
Dennis, M., 622
Dennis, S., 201
Denson, N., 288
Denton, J., 444
Depp, C., 502
Der-McLeod, D., 671
Dermer, A., 120
DeRycke, S. B., 555
de St. Aubin, E., 540
DeSantis, L., 659
Desiderato, L. L., 432
DeSilver, D., 533
DeSpelder, L. A., 656, 657, 667, 670, 673
DeStefano, L., 481
Detering, K. M., 668
de Vries, B., 565
DeVries, B., 675
DeVries, C., 93, 556
de Weerth, C., 244
Dewilde, C., 303
DeWolff, M. S., 165
D'Hondt, E., 191
Diamant, A., 680
Diamond, E. L., 565
Diamond, J., 67, 70

Diamond, L. M., 402, 403, 475
Diamond, M. C., 597, 598
Dickey, G., 627
Dickinson, G. E., 673, 677
Dickstein, S., 161
Diehl, M., 613
Dietrich, J., 458
Dikkers, J. S., 532
Dillon, J. A., 238, 334, 335
Dillow, M. R., 306
Dinsa, G. D., 429
DiPrete, T. A., 457
Dishion, T. J., 394, 395, 411
Dittmar, H., 421
Divisi, D., 425
Dodge, H. H., 624
Dodge, K. A., 229, 230, 232, 249, 304, 318
Doherty, D., 183
Doherty, W. J., 490
Doka, K. J., 632, 657
Dollinger, S. M. C., 527
Domar, A. D., 443
Donaldson, G., 522, 524
Donati, T., 492
Dorfman, L. T., 642, 644
Dorius, C., 306, 307
Dorius, G. L., 400
Dornbusch, S. M., 387
Doshi, S. R., 577
Doty, R. L., 582
Douglas, J. D., 561
Doumen, S., 170
Dovidio, J. F., 279, 434
Downey, G., 409
Doyle, A. B., 474
Drapeau, C. W., 664
Draper, P., 555
Drew, L. M., 632
Driscoll, D. A., 71
Druey, M. D., 219
Drummond, J. E., 456
Dubè, E. M., 475
Duberstein, P., 208
Dubin, S., 529
DuBois, B., 604, 605
Dubois, D. L., 317, 394
Duck, S., 475
Dudley, J. R., 549
Duff, R. W., 588
Dufour, A., 579
Dugan, A., 659
Duncan, D. T., 410
Duncan, G. E., 261
Duncan, L. E., 540
Dunham, P., 151
Dunkel-Schetter, C., 442
Dunkle, C. E., 379, 396
Dunne-Bryant, A., 548, 549
Dunn, J., 152, 224, 238, 244, 312
Dunn, J. F., 312
Dupont, R. L., 431
Durand, V. M., 171
Durbin, D. L., 394
Durlak, J. A., 657
Dusek, J. B., 392
Duursma, E., 224
Dweck, C. S., 299
Dwyer, J. W., 558
Dyregrov, A., 323
Dyregrov, K., 323
Dziurgot, T., 239

Eakins, P. S., 92
Earnshaw, V. A., 434
Easterlin, R. A., 502
East, P., 224, 468
Eastwick, P. W., 479
Ebbeling, C. B., 260
Eccles, J. S., 303, 335, 369, 381, 385, 409
Eckerman, C. O., 240
Eckstein, D., 225
Edelstein, W., 271
Edenfield, T. M., 507
Edmondson, B., 492, 548
Edmonson, M. B., 550
Edwards, C. P., 213, 214, 227
Edwards, J. N., 552

Egeland, B., 249
Eggenberger, E., 670
Ehrensaft, M. K., 482
Eisenband, J., 199
Eisenberg, N., 157, 226, 227, 228, 229
Eisenbruch, M., 681
Eklund, R. C., 289
Elbers, E., 198
Elder, G. H., 48, 49, 53, 554
El-Dib, M., 115
Elias, J. W., 601
Elias, M. F., 601
Elias, P. K., 601
Elieff, C., 548
Elkin, C., 646
Elkind, D., 270, 335, 363, 364
Elliot, A. J., 299
Elliott, M., 486
Ellison, C. R., 439
Ellis, R., 152, 543
Ellis, S., 312, 315
Elwert, F., 623
Elzinga, C. H., 468
Emery, R. E., 231
Emes, C. E., 233
Emmerich, W., 245
Endeshaw, Y. W., 587
Endres, J., 184
Engelmann, T. G., 111
Engel, S., 184, 238, 259
Engle, J. M., 156
English, T., 628
Engstrom, M., 640
Ennett, S. T., 347
Enriquez, E., 261
Ensminger, M. E., 222
Entwisle, D. R., 303
Erdley, C. A., 299
Erel, O., 224
Ericsson, K. A., 527, 528
Erikson, E. H., 37, 38, 148, 171, 175, 298, 335, 377, 378, 382, 613
Erikson, J. M., 613
Eshleman, J. R., 483, 484
Estes, M. L., 600
Ettelbrick, P., 565
Evans, C. A., 151
Evans, E., 410
Evans, G. D., 531
Eveleth, P., 183
Everett Jones, 577
Everly, G. S., 89
Ewing, A. T., 679
Eysenck, H. J., 591, 592, 621

Fabes, R. A., 228, 229
Fabiano, G. A., 266, 267
Facio, E., 632
Fagioli, I., 113
Fagot, B. I., 155, 208, 245, 246, 247
Fairburn, C., 350
Falbo, T., 225
Fangos, J. H., 323
Fantz, R., 127
Farrangy, P., 248
Farrant, B. M., 174
Farrell, D., 603, 606
Farver, J. A. M., 239
Farver, J. M., 227
Faulkner, R. A., 548
Fedele, N. M., 490
Feeney, J., 628
Feifel, H., 657
Feinberg, M. E., 150
Feinbloom, R. I., 68, 71, 73, 94, 95
Fein, D., 206
Feldman, H. A., 516
Feld, S., 299
Fello, M., 670
Fellowes, S., 190
Fell, R. F., 670
Feng, Z., 623
Ferber, R., 112
Ferholt, J. B., 149, 248
Ferketich, S. L., 166
Fernald, A., 114
Fernandez, J. P., 533
Fernandez, R. M., 533

Ferrage, A., 184
Ferrie, J. E., 507
Ferrucci, L., 506
Fetveit, A., 587, 588
Field, D., 612, 613
Field, J., 152
Field, S., 277
Field, T., 244
Fifer, W. P., 41
Figueredo, A. J., 479
Fildes, A., 184
File, T., 232
Finch, B. K., 123
Finch, M., 372, 599
Finders, M., 369
Findling, R. L., 266
Fine, G. A., 321
Fine, M., 551
Fingerhut, A. W., 548, 626, 627
Fingerman, K. L., 624
Finkel, E. J., 479, 480
Finkelhor, D., 248, 251
Fiscella, K., 208
Fischer, K., 45, 201, 296
Fischer, L. R., 643
Fischer, M., 267
Fish, M., 151
Fish, M. C., 494
Fiske, A., 588, 600, 602, 603, 606, 665
Fitzgerald, H., 186, 265
Fivush, R., 315
Flaks, D. K., 494
Flanagan, C. A., 383
Flanders, J. L., 237
Flannelly, K. J., 661
Flavell, J.H., 356
Fletcher, A. C., 385, 398
Flippen, C., 617
Flom, R., 129
Flor, D. L., 304, 305
Flory, J., 669
Floyd, M. F., 564
Foehr, U. G., 233
Fokkema, T., 627
Fomon, S. J., 107
Forrest-Pressley, D., 47
Forshaw, M., 513
Forssberg, H., 118
Fortuna, K., 548
Foster, S. L., 383
Fowler, C., 306
Fowler, J. W., 453, 646
Fox, K., 339
Fox, N., 166
Fox, S. M. III, 427
Frank, B., 509
Franklin, A., 114
Frank, M., 167
Fransson, P., 111
Frantz, T. T., 681
Franzini, L., 575
Fraser, A. M., 87
Frech, A., 483
Fredricks, J. A., 371
Fredriksen-Goldsen, K., 627, 634
Fredriksen, K. I., 561, 564
Fredstrom, B., 314
Freedman, V. A., 548, 620, 622
Freedman, V. A., 548, 620, 622
French, D. C., 315
French, J., 368
Fretz, B. R., 534
Freud, S., 35, 298
Freund, A. M., 108, 616
Frey, B. S., 481, 483
Frezza, M., 432
Friedlmeier, W., 227
Friedman, G. D., 508
Friedman, H. S., 483
Friedman, J., 54, 55
Friedmann, H., 664
Fries, J. F., 422, 507, 589
Frieze, I., 299
Frisco, M. L., 547
Froberg, K., 338
Frontera, W. R., 587
Fry, C. L., 555
Fry, J., 341
Fry, R., 454

Fuligni, A. J., 385
Fulkerson, J. A., 260
Fuller-Thomson, E., 560, 561, 562
Fullmer, E. M., 627, 661
Fumagalli, E., 429
Fumagalli, M., 452
Furman, W., 312, 314, 315, 318
Furstenberg, F. F., Jr., 405, 549
Futagi, Y., 114

Gable, C. J., 348
Gadalla, T. M., 438
Gaesser, G., 260
Gains, J., 610
Galambos, N. L., 311
Galassi, J., 369
Galenkamp, H., 590
Galinsky, E., 149
Gallagher, J., 282
Gallagher, M., 372
Gallagher, S., 282, 644
Gallagher, S. K., 283
Gallagher-Thompson, D., 646
Gallant, M. P., 623, 639, 645
Gallaway, C., 141
Galotti, K. M., 452
Galtry, J., 167
Galvan, A., 422
Gamble, J., 188
Ganguli, M., 455
Gannon, L. R., 514
Ganong, L. H., 486, 493
Garand, L., 677
Garbarino, J., 7, 8, 152, 249, 320, 409
Garber, C. E., 426
Garcia, F., 222
Garcia, G., 27
Gardner, H., 73, 283, 284, 367
Garland, A. F., 410
Garner, P. W., 224
Garrison, M. E. B., 550
Gartrell, N. K., 494
Gates, G. J., 480
Gathercole, S. E., 364
Gatz, M., 534, 588, 602, 603, 604
Gavrilova, N., 517
Gaziano, J. M., 588
Geary, D. C., 273, 274
Gecas, V., 550
Geddes, J. K., 396
Gee, E. M., 554
Gee, J., 286
Geiger, B., 152
Geller, E. J., 515
Gelman, C. R., 622, 623
Gentile, D. A., 231, 234
Gentile, M., 670
George, C., 170, 227
George, T. P., 313, 512
Gerbasi, M. E., 261
Gerbner, G., 233
Gerrity, E., 437
Gershoff, E. T., 172
Gerson, M., 495
Gerstel, N., 644
Gerst-Emerson, K., 572
Gerstorf, D., 520, 522
Gesell, A., 12, 13
Gestwicki, C., 213
Ge, X., 384
Ghilarducci, T., 616, 617
Gianino, A., 157
Gibbs, J. C., 451
Gibbs, J. T., 665
Gibeau, J. L., 533
Gibson, E., 127
Gibson, R., 554
Gibson, R. C., 616, 618
Gidlow, B., 564
Giedd, J. N., 351, 352
Gilbert, A. N., 582
Gilbert, S. P., 425
Gilbert, S., 94
Gilet, A. L., 539
Gilligan, C., 27, 358, 360, 361, 362, 380, 450, 451
Ginsburg, G. S., 299, 300

Ginsburg, H. P., 199, 201
Giordano, P. C., 394
Gitlin, L. N., 622
Glaser, R., 592
Glasgow, K. L., 384, 386
Glass, C., 459, 533
Glass, D. C., 108
Glass, J. C., Jr., 323, 661
Glauser, B., 12, 18, 19
Glendenning, F., 529
Glick, P. C., 553
Gluszek, A., 279
Go, A.S., 590
Godfrey, K. M., 88
Goggin, J. M., 644
Gogtay, N., 352
Golant, S., 635, 636
Goldberg, A. E., 485
Goldberger, N. R., 449
Goldberg, N. G., 494
Gold, D. P., 619
Gold, D. T., 630
Goldin-Meadow, S., 210
Gold, J. M., 486
Goldman, L., 197
Goldman, S. E., 68
Goldscheider, F. K., 551, 555
Goldsmith, H. H., 157
Goldson, E., 122
Goldspink, D. F., 580
Goldsteen, K., 546
Goldstein, A. P., 411
Goldstein, S., 242
Goldwyn, R., 248
Golledge, J., 295
Golombok, S., 72, 314, 315, 402, 494
Gomez, G., 506
Gondoli, D. M., 312
Goniewicz, M. L., 430
Gonzaga, G. C., 479
Gonzalez, A. L., 300
Gonzalez-Barrera, A., 456
Gonzalez-Boto, R., 289
Gonzalez, C. A., 425
Goodie, J., 430
Goodnow, J., 15, 49, 214
Goosens, F. A., 170
Gopaul-McNicol, S., 208, 211, 214
Gorchoff, S. M., 547
Gorman, C., 83
Gorman, K. S., 185
Gornick, J. C., 308, 309
Gordon, S., 361
Gordon-Salant, S., 506
Gorsuch, N., 606
Gortmaker, S. L., 349
Goryakin, Y., 429
Gose, B., 649
Gosselink, C. A., 624
Gottesman, I. I., 72, 73
Gottesman, I. L., 72, 73
Gottfried, A. W., 309, 310
Gottlieb, D. J., 425
Gottman, J. M., 241, 306, 481, 485, 547, 548
Gould, D., 289
Gould, R. L., 541
Govender, V., 309
Graber, J., 338, 349, 351
Grabe, S., 421
Grabowski, J., 381
Gracia, E., 222
Graham, C. A., 441
Graham, S., 321, 369
Gralinski, H., 174
Grand, A., 622
Granier-Deferre, C., 149
Granrud, C., 127
Graves, B. S., 587
Greenberger, E., 221, 309, 386
Greenberg, J., 610
Greenberg, R. A., 431
Greene, B., 480
Greene, J. A., 596
Greenfield, P., 16, 142
Greenhaus, J. H., 309, 458, 469
Green, J., 286
Green, J. A., 156
Greenleaf, C. A., 350

Greenough, W. T., 598
Green, R., 402
Greenson, J., 206
Gregg, M., 366
Griffiths, M., 326
Grimby, G., 580
Grime, R. L., 451
Grisham, D. L., 207
Grodstein, F., 515
Grolinck, W. S., 157
Grossarth-Maticek, R., 621
Grossmann, K., 164
Grossmann, K. E., 164
Grossmann, T., 157
Gross, R., 122
Grotpeter, J. K., 229, 320
Grove, J. G., 623, 639, 645
Grubb, A., 438
Gruhn, D., 539
Grundy, A. M., 312
Grundy, E., 550
Grunloh, R. L., 678
Grusec, J. E., 219, 222, 226, 304, 305, 384, 397, 399
Grzywacz, J. G., 308, 309
Guacci-Franco, N., 474
Guacci, N., 474
Guarda, A. S., 430
Guardo, C., 296
Guerra, N. G., 219
Guidry, K. R., 455
Guilleminault, C., 587
Gunnar, M. R., 159, 162
Gunnarsdottir, I., 121
Guo, S. S., 421
Guo, Y., 504
Gupta, N. D., 308
Guralnick, M. J., 200
Gurin, P., 461
Gurung, R. A., 619
Gutman, D. L., 551
Guttmacher, A., 81
Guttman, A., 351

Haan, N., 542
Haas, A. L., 642, 643
Hagan, R., 246
Hagerman, R. J., 67, 76
Haggart, N., 474
Haines, E. L., 191
Haith, M., 128
Hakim-Larson, J., 446
Häkkinen, I., 302, 303
Hakuta, K., 278
Halil, T., 156
Halim, M. L., 245, 246, 316
Hall, D. T., 531
Hall, D. W., 343
Halliday, J. L., 68, 69
Hallinan, M. T., 393
Hall, W. C., 429
Halperin, J. M., 267
Hamann, S., 226
Hamarta, E., 163
Hamburg, D. A., 335, 347, 412
Hamer, D. H., 402
Hamilton, B. E., 404, 425, 489, 493
Hamilton, R. F., 532
Ham, M., 335
Hanash, S. M., 592
Hancock, A. D., 668
Hanks, E., 682
Hanley, D., 452
Hannon, E. E., 129
Hansen, D. J., 250
Hanson, M., 187
Hansson, R. O., 659, 663
Harada, M., 587
Harding, S. M., 507
Harding, S. R., 661
Hardy, J., 602
Hardy, J. B., 408
Hardy, M., 534
Hardy, S. E., 587
Hare-Mustin, R. T., 247
Hareven, T., 12
Harkness, S., 112, 164, 214
Harlan, L., 511

Harley, C. B., 578
Harold, G. T., 390, 391
Harrawood, L. K., 661
Harrington, J. W., 121
Harris, L., 562
Harris, M., 679
Harris, M. L., 509
Harrison, A. O., 380
Harrison, D., 114
Harris, P., 78, 79
Hart, B., 377
Hart, C. H., 221, 227, 230, 385
Hart, D., 238, 295, 296, 297, 377
Harter, S., 175, 296, 297, 377
Hart, H., 266
Hartmann, H., 460
Hartup, W. W., 155, 159, 243, 244, 312, 313, 314, 318, 392
Hasan, Y., 19, 20, 21
Haslett, B., 141, 142
Hastings, P. D., 304, 305
Hatch, L. R., 617, 632, 633
Hatzenbuehler, M. L., 410
Hatzimouratidis, K., 441
Havekes, S., 316
Havighurst, R. J., 614
Hayenga, A. O., 299
Hayes, J., 460
Hayes, R., 227
Hayflick, L., 575, 577, 578, 579
Hayne, H., 125
Haynes, J. A., 492
Haynes, M., 489
Haynes, S. G., 437
Haynie, D., 400
Hay, P., 350
Hayslip, B., 554, 555, 556, 659, 663, 677
Hayward, C., 307
Haywood, H. C., 48
Hazen, C., 382, 472, 550, 628
Heal, D. J., 266
Heath, S., 208, 281
Hebblethwaite, S., 631
Hechtman, L., 267
Heckhausen, J., 538, 594
Hedegaard, H., 664, 665
Heffer, R. W., 300
Hegewisch, A., 308, 309, 460, 461
Hegreness, R., 264
Heidrich, S. M., 455
Heikamp, T., 219
Heimerl, K., 670
Heinmiller, B. M., 129
Helfand, M., 399, 401
Hellström, A. L., 187
Helson, R., 539, 543, 547, 551, 561
Hendler, M., 269
Hendrick, H., 12
Hendricks, J., 563, 564, 615, 642, 643
Hennessy, M., 234
Henretta, J. C., 550
Henriksson, A., 670
Henry, B., 229
Henry, W. E., 614
Herbenick, D., 439
Herman, J., 437
Hernandez, D. J., 48
Hernandez, H., 279
Hernández, M., 278
Heron, J., 591
Herrenkohl, E. C., 229, 249
Herrenkohl, R. C., 229, 249
Hershberger, S. L., 403
Hersh, R. H., 358
Hespos, S. J., 134
Hesse-Biber, S., 350, 351
Hesse, E., 163
Hesser, J., 311, 312
Hetherington, E. M., 11, 237, 303, 305, 306, 308, 383, 388, 389, 390, 391
Hewitt, B., 489
Hildick-Smith, G. J., 347
Hill, D. A., 80
Hill, N. R., 493
Hill, R., 271
Hills, A., 186
Hills, A. P., 429

Hill, T. D., 645
Hinde, R. A., 163
Hinduja, S., 396
Hines, M., 314, 315
Hinkley, T., 191
Hirayama, T., 431
Hirsch, B. J., 317, 394
Hoare, C. H., 297
Hochschild, A., 481
Ho, D., 142, 459
Hodapp, R. M., 68
Hodges, E. V., 230
Hodgson, L. G., 602, 631
Hodnett, E. D., 92
Ho, E. S., 117
Hoeve, M., 221, 223, 229
Hofer, S. M., 518, 522, 523, 524
Hoff, E., 203, 206, 207, 208
Hoff-Ginsberg, E., 207, 224
Hoffman, L. W., 168, 309, 310, 316
Hoffnung, A., 239
Hoffnung, M., 93, 490, 493, 632, 678
Hofland, B. F., 642
Hogan, N. S., 659
Hogan, R., 617
Hoge, D., 454
Hogenkamp, P. S., 425
Hohmann-Marriott, B., 485
Holahan, C. J., 588
Holden, C., 410
Holland, A., 548
Hollis, J. F., 426
Holmbeck, G., 381
Holmes, B. M., 479
Holmes, L. J., 94
Holzgreve, W., 71
Holzman, L., 200
Hooper, C. J., 272
Hooyman, N. R., 573, 582, 618
Hoppmann, C., 520
Horgan, J., 69, 76
Hornor, G., 251
Horn, J. L., 518, 522, 523, 524, 525
Horsley, H., 323
Horwitz, A. V., 487
Ho, S. C., 670
Houser, M. E., 244
House, S. J., 474
Howe, N., 224, 311
Howes, C., 155, 156, 238, 239, 241, 242, 244, 317
Hoyert, D. L., 557
Hoyer, W. J., 445, 524, 527
Hoza, B., 313
Huang, B., 398
Huang, C. H., 556
Huang, L., 219
Hubbard, R., 71
Hubert, H. B., 507
Hudley, C., 321
Huesmann, L. R., 231
Hughes, G. M., 623
Hughes, M. E., 548
Hughes, M. S., 457
Hughes, F. P., 240
Hunt, C., 110
Hunt, E., 524
Hunter, M. S., 513, 514
Hunt, M. E., 636
Hurrelmann, K., 335
Huston, A. C., 231, 233, 234, 245
Hyde, J. S., 167, 225, 421, 491
Hyman, J. P., 149, 152
Hymel, S., 318

Ianni, F., 371
Idler, E. L., 645
Ihara, E. S., 622
Ikels, C., 555
Ilmarinen, J., 422
Im, E. O., 564
Infante, M. A., 84
Ingersoll-Dayton, B., 560
Inhelder, B., 197, 198, 354
Innamorati, M., 149
Insabella, G. M., 160
Insana, S. P., 111, 112
Irion, P. E., 677, 678, 679
Isaksson, K., 618

Iso, A., 563
Israel, R., 442
Iyer, S. N., 140
Izard, C. E., 156, 157

Jaccard, J., 405
Jacklin, C., 315
Jacknowitz, A., 122
Jackson, A. W., 350
Jackson, D. A., 679
Jackson, D. D., 444
Jackson, J. S., 554, 564, 576
Jackson, M. F., 288, 317
Jackson, P., 322
Jacob, B. A., 456, 457
Jacobson, J. D., 616
Jacob, V., 186
Jacobvitz, D. B., 409
Jacoby, A. P., 402
Jadack, R., 360
Jaggars, S. S., 455
Jain, A., 152
James, J., 401
James, T., 236
James, W., 113
Jang, Y., 227
Jansson, U. B., 187
Jaworski, A., 237
Jay, O., 422
Jeffries, S., 496
Jenni, O. G., 348
Jensen, L. A., 378, 382, 388, 396, 450, 451
Jernigan, T. L., 108
Jeste, D., 502
Jetter, K. M., 426
Jimenez, R., 27, 278
Jin, M. K., 164
Johansen, R., 272
John, O. P., 543, 547, 551
Johnson, B., 454
Johnson, F. B., 578
Johnson, C., 630
Johnson, C. L., 622, 629, 630, 632, 646
Johnson, D., 288, 565
Johnson, D. W., 318
Johnson, E., 488
Johnson, F. L., 474
Johnson, K. R., 479
Johnson, M., 265
Johnson, M. J., 627
Johnson, M. S., 251
Johnson, P., 288
Johnson, R., 279, 482
Johnson, R. T., 318
Johnson, V. E., 306, 438, 439, 483
Johnson, W., 108
Johnston, L. D., 335, 344, 345, 346, 347
Jondrow, J., 618
Jones, B. A., 510
Jones, D. N., 288, 479
Jones, P. S., 677
Jordan, A. B., 234
Jordan, J. V., 470
Jose, P. E., 300
Joseph, K. S., 550
Joshi, M., 22
Josselson, R., 341, 376
Joung, I. M. A., 484
Juhl, J., 661
Julian, T. W., 482
Junaid, K. A., 190
Jung, C. G., 539
Jusczyk, P. W., 129

Kachhawa, P. S., 661
Kadushin, F. S., 93
Kaestle, C. E., 343
Kagan, J., 125, 158, 159, 337, 339
Kahan, J. P., 493
Kahn, R. L., 610
Kaijura, H., 115
Kaiser, I., 81
Kaitz, M., 138
Kalish, R. A., 646, 661, 671, 681
Kallioniemi, O., 592
Kallman, D. A., 503
Kaloustian, G., 165, 166, 170, 171

Kalter, N., 326, 327
Kalverboer, A., 187, 190
Kamii, C., 270
Kamm, P., 561
Kamp Dush, C. M., 481
Kamsa-Ard, S., 588
Kanfer, R., 532
Kantor, G. K., 482
Kao, G., 26
Kaplan, H., 439
Kaplan, K., 620
Kaplan, L., 110
Kaplan, M. S., 605, 666
Karam, R. G., 267
Kåreholt, I., 564, 643
Karmakar, M., 509
Karoly, L. A., 458
Karpov, Y. V., 48
Karsdal, M. A., 515
Kashani, I. A., 507
Kasl, S. V., 502
Kastenbaum, R., 657, 661, 664, 665, 667
Katzel, L. I., 503, 505, 578, 579
Katz-Wise, S. L., 306
Kaufert, P. A., 515
Kaufman, A. S., 524
Kaufman, G., 554
Kaufman, H. G., 534
Kaufman, J. M., 516
Kaufman, M., 260, 402
Kavanaugh, R. D., 238
Kavanaugh, T., 504
Kawachi, I., 208
Kawaguchi, D., 310
Kaye, H., 41
Kazdin, A. E., 266
Keane, S. P., 225
Keating, D., 271, 353, 367
Keddie, A. M., 575
Keefe, J., 368
Keefer, C., 112
Keehn, D., 221
Keesee, N. J., 676
Kee, Y., 645
Kehl, K. A., 663
Keith, J., 555, 628, 633
Keith, P. M., 481, 545, 547, 551, 659
Keller, M., 314
Keller, M. L., 458, 585
Kellman, P. J., 114
Kelly, J. H., 642, 643
Kelly, M., 495, 672
Kelly, M. P., 441, 563
Kemp, C. L., 559
Kendall-Tackett, K. A., 250, 251
Kendig, H. L., 637
Kenney, G., 185
Kenney, W. L., 579
Kenny, G. P., 422
Kermoian, R., 128
Kerns, K. A., 165, 401
Kerr, M., 159
Kessler, R. C., 683
Keysers, C., 138
Kidder, T., 642
Kiecolt-Glaser, J. K., 557, 558
Kiecolt, K. J., 557, 558
Kikas, E., 230
Kilty, K. M., 565
Kimber, M., 430
Kim, G., 173
Kim, H. K., 482, 560
Kim, J. Y., 311, 312
Kimlin, M. G., 504
Kimmel, D. C., 610, 626
Kimm, S., 121
Kim, S. K., 227
Kim, S. Y., 565, 659
King, A. C., 507
King, K. M., 349
King, N. A., 429
King, P., 368, 446, 529
King, V., 308
Kinsella, K., 635
Kirby, D., 343, 404
Kirjavainen, T., 302
Kirschner, D., 199

I-4 Author/Name Index

Kirsh, S. J., 233
Kisilevsky, B. S., 80, 125
Kisler, T. S., 185
Kistner, J., 249
Kitchener, K., 368, 446, 529
Kitchen, J., 282
Kite, M. E., 191
Kitzinger, J., 12
Kivimaki, M., 507
Kivnick, H. Q., 613
Kiyak, H. A., 506, 573, 582, 618
Klahr, D., 45, 270
Klassen, P., 529
Klaus, M. H., 94
Klaus, P. H., 94
Kleinsorge, C., 388, 390
Kligman, A. M., 579
Klimes-Dougan, B., 249
Klinnert, M. D., 173
Klintsova, A. Y., 598
Knafo, A., 321
Knoble, N. B., 482
Knox, D., 483
Knox, G. W., 412
Knutson, K. L., 507
Koball, H. L., 483
Kobayashi, M., 481
Kochanska, C., 173
Kochanska, G., 157, 219, 221
Kodner, D. L., 671
Koenen, K. C., 437
Koenig, H. G., 645, 664
Koester, J., 370
Kogan, N., 624
Kohlberg, L., 358, 359, 360, 450
Kohler, P. K., 343
Kohn, M. L., 309, 386
Kohn, R., 664
Kokko, K., 468
Kolak, A. M., 152
Kolodny, R. C., 483
Konnert, C., 496
Kooij, D. T., 532, 659
Kool, R., 236
Kopp, C., 157, 174
Korbin, J. E., 250
Kordi, A., 300
Koretz, D., 369
Korman, A. K., 531
Koropeckyj-Cox, T., 547
Korte, J., 647
Kosciw J. G., 402
Koss, M. P., 438
Kostelny, K., 320
Kotchen, T. A., 579
Kotloff, L., 213
Kovacs, D. M., 316
Kowalski, R. M., 461
Kozlowski, L. T., 431
Kozma, A., 587
Kozol, J., 19, 320
Kramer, D. A., 445
Kramer, R., 323
Krans, E. E., 186
Krasnor, L., 238
Krause, N., 588
Kreider, R. M., 543
Krieger, N., 459
Kriete, A., 506
Kringelbach, M. L., 192
Krishnakumar, A., 249
Kristofferzon, M. L., 621
Kroeger, R. A., 488
Kroger, J., 378
Kroonenberg, P. M., 163
Krueger, J., 538, 594
Krueger, W., 224
Kryger, M., 112
Krysan, M., 316
Kübler-Ross, E., 666, 667
Kuczynski, L., 221
Kuhl, P., 114, 138
Kuhn, D., 353, 365
Kulb, N., 94
Kulkarni, A. D., 444
Kumari, N., 192
Kumar, N. B., 511
Kunitz, S. J., 577
Kunkel, S. R., 502
Kuper-smidt, J. B., 320

Kurdek, L. A., 481, 486, 548, 551
Kurtz, S., 581
Kurz, J., 549
Kushi, L. H., 432, 587, 588
Kutaka, T. S., 213, 214
Kutner, L., 231, 232
Kutz-Costes, B., 231
Kuykendall, D. H., 647
Kuyper, L., 627
Kwak, M., 560
Kyoko, T., 514

Labouvie-Vief, G., 446, 455, 524, 539
Lachman, M. E., 507, 542
LaCroix, A. Z., 437
Ladd, G. W., 227, 238
Laditka, J. N., 405
Laditka, S. B., 406
Lafferty, W. E., 343
Lakatta, E. G., 581, 586
Lakoff, G., 356
Lall, D. I., 298, 350
Lally, M. M., 350
Lamaze, F., 92
Lambert, A. D., 455
Lamb, M. E., 152, 166, 221, 222, 247
Lamborn, S. D., 384, 387
Lamke, L. K., 247
Lammert, O., 338
Lamport, M. A., 455
Landau, M. J., 610
Langa, K. M., 565, 659
Lang, C., 119
Langer, N., 632
Lange, T., 425
Lang, F. R., 539
Lanham, J. S., 122
Lanz, M., 473
Lapsley, D., 364
Laris, B. A., 343
LaRosa, J. H., 425, 426
LaRossa, R., 491
Larrabee, M., 362
Larson, R., 24, 312, 335, 381, 382, 384, 614
LaRue, A., 603
Larzelere, R. E., 231
Lasley, J. R., 411
Latack, J. C., 534
Latan, R., 288
Lauer, R. H., 545, 547
Laughlin, L., 154
Laumann, E. O., 400
Lauricella, A. R., 234
Lave, J., 199, 285
Lavner, J. A., 484
Lawford, H., 473
Lawrence, E., 490, 491, 547, 561, 562
Lawson, A., 87
Lawton, M. P., 563
Lawver, T., 236
Laybourn, A., 225
Lazarus, R. S., 435
Leadbetter, B., 355
Leaper, C., 246, 288
LeBlanc, A. J., 548
Leckman, J., 50
Lee, C., 507
Lee, C. Y. S., 490
Lee, D. J., 615
Lee, F. R., 86
Lee, G. R., 639
Leeies, M., 435
Lee, J. S., 302, 303
Lee, S. H., 564
Lee, S. J., 231, 232
Lee, S. Y., 300
Lee, T. S., 599
Lee, V., 369
Lee, Y. J., 551
Lefkowitz, E. S., 453, 454
Leggett, E. L., 299
Lehman, D. R., 455
Leidy, M. S., 219, 220
Leigh, B. C., 401, 432
Leinbach, M. D., 245

Leinhardt, C., 366
Leming, M. R., 677
Lennartsson, C., 564
Lens, W., 299
Lentz, E., 531
Leonard, L. G., 444
Leon, A. S., 427
Leondari, A., 662
Leor, J., 437
Leo, V., 237
Lepage, J. F., 138
Lerner, J., 273
Lerner, R. M., 53
Lester, B., 707
Letourneau, N., 151
LeVay, S., 402
Levene, J., 672
Levenson, R. W., 306, 547, 548, 619
Leventhal, E. A., 584
Leventhal, H., 585
Levine, A. D., 396
Levine, G., 17
LeVine, R., 118
Levinson, D. J., 51, 470, 542
Levitt, J. L., 394
Levitt, M. J., 474
Levy, B. R., 502
Levy, J., 657, 659, 667, 678
Levy, J. E., 577
Levy-Shiff, R., 149, 150
Lewis, C., 87, 152
Lewis, J. M., 236
Lewis, M., 39, 157, 171, 173, 295, 320
Liao, W., 584, 585, 587
Lichten, E., 663, 673
Lickona, T., 360
Lieberman, M., 682
Liebert, R. M., 234
Liebman, B., 121
Liebmann-Smith, J., 72
Liefbroer, A. C., 468
Liem, D. G., 115
Liem, J. H., 310
Liem, R., 310
Lightfoot, C., 340, 342
Li, J., 437
Lillard, A. S., 212, 233
Lindau, S. T., 517
Lindblad-Goldberg, M., 220
Lindell, S. G., 93
Linder, J. R., 233
Lindqvist, R., 621
Lingala, V. B., 507
Lin Gomez, S., 509
Lin, F. R., 506
Lin, I. F., 548, 549
Linney, J. A., 322
Linn, S., 84
Lin, S. L., 553
Lipman, B., 635, 636, 637, 638
Lips, H. M., 461
Lipsitt, L., 41
Lisitsa, E., 485
Lister, L., 646, 647
Litman, C., 174
Little, J. T., 606
Little, T. D., 159, 228, 320
Littleton, H. L., 89
Litwin, H., 615
Liu, H., 260, 484, 578
Liu, Y., 509
Livingston, G., 301, 302, 486, 492, 493
Livingston, M., 92, 93
Livson, N., 339
Lobel, M., 442
Lobo, R. A., 580
Lochman, J. E., 288, 317
Lockery, S. A., 623
Lock, M., 513, 515
Loeber, R., 321, 411
Loeb, R. C., 222
Logan, J. R., 551, 557
Logan, R. L., 540
Lohnes, K. L., 326, 327
Londerville, S., 163
Long, H. B., 644

Longino, C. F., 592, 619
Loomis, D., 512
Lopata, H., 623
Lopata, H. Z., 647
Loprinzi, P. D., 191
Lord, H., 310
Lorenz, F. O., 106
Lothian, J., 93
Louis, K., 370
Love, J. M., 170
Lower, K. S., 431
Lozano, P., 239
Lozoff, B., 88
Lubell, J., 535
Lucas, R. E., 623
Lucas-Thompson, R. G., 170
Luciana, M., 272
Ludden, A. B., 350
Ludwig, B., 347
Ludwig, D. S., 260
Luidens, D. A., 454
Luna, B., 351, 365
Lund, D. A., 647
Lundy, B. L., 152
Luo, S., 479
Luria, A. R., 49
Lust, B., 278
Luster, T., 412
Lustig, M., 370
Lynch, B., 347
Lynch, J. S., 273
Lyon, G., 275
Lyons-Ruth, K., 163, 165
Lythcott, N., 577
Lytton, H., 246

Maab, W., 634
Maccoby, E. E., 219, 222, 246, 288, 315, 316
MacKinnon-Lewis, C., 320
MacLean, M., 22
MacNeil, G., 440, 517
Madden, M., 395, 396, 590, 634
Madnawat, A. S., 661
Madsen, S. D., 474
Maffulli, N., 262
Maggs, J. L., 311
Magistro, D., 579
Maguire, M. D., 244
Mahler, M., 160, 166
Mahoney, J. L., 310, 371
Main, M., 160, 163, 165, 170, 227, 248
Maisel, N. C., 626, 627
Maker, J., 283
Malatesta, C., 157
Malina, R. M., 337, 338
Malinosky-Rummell, R., 250
Mallinckrodt, B., 534
Mallory, C., 484
Mallory, G., 484
Malone, J. C., 611
Maluf, S. W., 592
Mandara, J., 219
Mandel, D. R., 129
Manera, V., 138
Manganello, J. A., 231
Mangelsdorf, S. C., 150, 161, 166
Manhart, L. E., 343
Mannell, R., 614
Manzi, C., 295
Marcia, J. E., 378, 379, 380
Marcus, D., 296
Marcus, G., 203, 204
Marecek, J., 247
Marentette, P., 140
Margolin, L., 282
Margraf, J., 266
Marini, M. E., 261
Markides, K. S., 508, 511, 551, 575, 576, 577, 615
Markiewicz, D., 473
Markman, H. J., 93
Marlowe, B., 212
Marmot, M. G., 507
Marquez, S., 289
Marrett, C., 288
Marschark, M., 140, 209
Marsella, A. J., 320

Marshall, E. A., 458
Marshall, V. W., 615, 657, 659, 661
Marsh, F. H., 74
Martens, A., 610
Martin, B., 230
Martin, C. E., 87, 96, 350
Martin, C. L., 219, 246, 247
Martineau, L., 422
Martinez, G., 403, 405
Martin, J. A., 492, 493
Martin, M., 525
Martinson, I. M., 677
Masciadrelli, B. P., 540
Mason, A., 565
Mason, A. M., 385, 565
Mason, C. A., 385
Masotti, P. J., 637
Masten, A. S., 299, 300, 318, 319, 320
Masters, W. H., 438, 439, 483, 517
Mastora, A., 662
Mataix-Cols, D., 266
Matas, L., 163
Matheson, C. C., 238, 239, 241
Mathews, T. J., 489
Matos, K., 481
Matthews, D., 282
Matthews, S., 559
Mayer, B., 227
Mayes, L. C., 50
Mazur, J., 125
McAdams, D. P., 540
McAdoo, H. P., 412
McArthur, C. C., 541
McAuley, E., 587
McCabe, L., 543
McCall, G. J., 338
McCall, R., 81, 125
McCarron, D. A., 579
McCloyd, V. C., 320, 380
McCluskey, K., 159
McCrae, R. R., 538, 542, 611, 612, 623, 624
McCurdy, K., 185
McDaniel, D., 204
McDonald, L., 170
McDonald, M., 185
McDonald, T. W., 643
McElhaney, L.J., 625
McFadden S. H., 645
McGarell, E. F., 411
McGinley, M., 227
McGinnis, J. M., 432
McGuffin, P., 64
McGuire, E. J., 187
McHale, S. M., 153, 248, 311
McIntosh, J. L., 664
McKay, M. M., 482
McKay, S., 91
McKenry, P. C., 482
McKinlay, S. M., 514, 515
McKussick, V. A., 62, 65
McLoyd, V. C., 383
McNamara, T., 273
McQuoid, Joan., 389
McWilliams, S., 625
Measor, L., 288
Meehan, P. J., 410
Meier, C. R., 515
Meier, D. E., 672
Meilman, P., 379
Meins, E., 141
Mela, D., 349
Meltzer, L. J., 267
Meltzoff, A. N., 134, 138, 206
Melville, K., 480
Mendes de Leon, C. F., 623
Mendoza, J. A., 429
Menkes, J., 115
Mennella, J. A., 115
Mennuti, R. B., 450
Mercer, C. H., 440
Mercer, P. W., 348
Mercer, R. T., 166
Meredith, H., 586
Merenstein, G., 335, 337
Merriam, S. B., 644, 645, 647
Merten, M. J., 455
Mertz, M. E., 632

Author/Name Index I-5

Mesiäinen, P., 468
Messer, D., 205, 207
Messinger, D. S., 156
Messner, M., 264
Mestre, M. V., 227
Metallinos-Katsaras, E., 185
Metz, K., 271
Michaels, S., 287
Michelsson, K., 109
Mickelson, K. D., 170
Mikaye, P., 164
Milevsky, A., 221, 222, 223
Milhausen, R. R., 441
Miller, B., 411, 420, 622
Miller, I. J., 582
Miller, M. A., 507
Miller, P., 38, 43, 102
Miller, R. H., 593
Millsap, R. E., 612–613
Mills, M., 334, 612–613
Milner, J. S., 249
Milteer, R. M., 239
Milunsky, A., 66
Minagawa-Kawai, Y., 129
Mindell, J. A., 267
Minino, A. M., 342
Minnotte, K. L., 547
Miramontes, O., 208
Mirecki, R. M., 486
Mishna, F., 277
Mitchell, V., 316
Mitford, J., 678
Miyazaki, J., 310
Moen, P., 436
Moffitt, T. E., 482
Mogford, K., 206
Mohlman, J., 610
Moilanen, K. L., 401
Monk, T. H., 149
Monsour, A., 377
Montemayor, R., 383
Montessori, M., 212
Montgomery-Downs, H. E., 111, 112, 557
Montgomery, M. J., 455
Moody, H. R., 565, 659, 672
Moore, C., 151
Moore, D., 382
Moore, E. G. J., 303
Moorefield, B. S., 308
Moorehouse, M. J., 310, 316
Moore, K., 118
Moore, S., 343
Moorman, S. M., 624
Moos, B. S., 588
Moos, R. H., 588, 621
Morell, V., 434
Moreno, L. A., 429
Morgan, J. P., 663
Morimoto, H. K., 592
Morin, R., 480
Morris, A. M., 495
Morris, J. N., 637
Morrison, D., 426
Morrison, E. H., 96
Morris, S. A., 637
Morrongiello, B., 129
Morrow, L., 212
Mortimer, J., 372, 397
Morton, R. A., Jr., 511
Moscicki, A., 343
Moser, C., 539
Moses, L. J., 172
Mosher, W. D., 301, 487
Moss, M., 677
Moss, M. B., 599
Moss, P., 348
Moss, S., 677
Motsinger, C. D., 430
Mottaz, C. J., 532
Moyer, M. S., 629–630
Mroczek, D. K., 543
Mueller, D. P., 643
Muennig, P., 208
Mullainathan, S., 459, 532
Munroe, R., 118
Muraco, A., 474, 475, 627, 634
Murphy, J. M., 450
Murphy, L., 226
Murray, C., 579

Murstein, B. I., 479
Museus, S. D., 457
Musil, C. M., 604
Myers, J., 355
Myers, S. A., 630
Myhill, D., 288

Nagata, D. K., 219
Nagle, R. J., 349
Nagy, Z., 581
Nakao, T., 266
Nathanson, A. I., 234
Nation, M., 320
Neal, J. W., 318, 588, 616
Neeper, S., 598, 600
Neff, C., 166
Neimeyer, R. A., 661, 676
Neinstein, L. S., 343
Nelson, D. A., 233, 320
Nelson, A. I., 343
Nelson, K., 197
Nelson, S. E., 107
Netter, S., 221
Neugarten, B. L., 13, 52, 467, 506, 539, 614
Neugarten, D. A., 468
Neulinger, J., 108, 563
Newcomb, A. F., 319, 392
Newman, D. L., 159
Newman, F., 200
Newman, K., 372
Newman, R. S., 129
Newport, F., 480
New, R., 214
Newton, N. J., 554, 613
Newton, R. L., 628
Nezworski, T., 169
Nguyen, V. Q., 515
Nic Gabhainn, S., 343
Nichojs, J., 170
Nicholson, J. M., 94
Nicholson, L., 153
Nichols, S. R., 368
Nickerson, A. B., 349
Nickerson, B. G., 323
Nicol-Smith, L., 513
Nilsson, A., 621
Nisbett, R. E., 455
Noam, G. J., 358
Noble, V., 456
Noboa, J., 389
Noddings, N., 361
Noel-Miller, C. M., 626
Noh, S., 546
Nolen-Hoeksema, S., 151
Nolen, J. D., 151
Noller, P., 152, 628
Noppe, I. C., 152
Noppe, L. D., 152
Norbeck, J. S., 89
Norcross, W. A., 590
Norman, C., 302
Normand, C., 667
Norman, R. E., 250
Norris, J., 548, 550, 551, 554, 631
North, J., 260
Northrup, C., 513, 514, 518
Notelovitz, M., 515
Notman, M. T., 513
Nowson, C. A., 435
Nozaki, K., 481
Nucci, L., 360
Nugent, J., 106
Nunes-Costa R. A., 390
Nunes, S. O. V., 592

Obayashi, Y., 481
Öberg, M., 431
O'Brien, M., 225
O'Brien, S. F., 225
O'Callaghan, F. V., 84
O'Callaghan, M., 84
O'Conner, T. G., 474
O'Connor, B. P., 640
O'Connor, C., 372
O'Connor, D. M., 456
O'Connor, M., 287, 505
O'Connor, P., 474
O'Connor, T. G., 287, 505
O'Donnell, J., 321

O'Donnell, K., 381
Offer, D., 381
O'Hara-Devereaux, M., 370
O'Hara, N., 370
Ohayon, M. M., 587
Oiler, D. K., 140
O'Keefe, M., 194
O'Keeffe, G. S., 395, 396
Oldehinkel, A. J., 335
Olds, D. L., 87, 408
Olsen, J. P., 319
Olshansky, S. J., 575
Olsho, L., 129
Olson, K., 249
Olson, M. R., 492
Onwuteaka-Philipsen, B. D., 660
Oppenheim, D., 219
Orfield, G., 317
O'Riley, A. A., 665
Orland-Barak, L., 287
Ormel, J., 335
Orr, M., 371
Orzech, K., 348, 425
Osgood, D. W., 311
Oshio, T., 481
Osorio, S., 455
Osterman, M. J. K., 493
Oswald, R. F., 438, 540
Otis, N., 369
Overman, J. J., 600
Overton, W., 296
Owen, M. J., 64
Owen, M. T., 167, 170
Owens, D., 323
Owens, J. A., 348
Owens, P. H., 348

Packman, W., 323
Padilla-Walker, L. M., 450
Pagani, L., 302
Page, D. C., 64
Page, K. S., 554, 555, 556
Pager, D., 459, 532
Pagura, J., 435
Pakiz, B., 321
Palinkas, L. A., 502, 590
Pallock, L. L., 223
Paniagua, F. A., 74
Pannese, E., 579
Papalia, D. E., 445, 446
Pappas, S., 199
Pappert, A., 71
Paquette, D., 152, 237
Parente, M. E., 310
Parke, R. D., 152, 155, 161, 244
Parker, G., 486
Parker, J. G., 316
Parker, K., 171, 480, 487
Parker, M., 672
Parker, M. G., 554
Parker, R. G., 647
Parkhurst, J., 241
Parkinson, S., 17
Parmelee, A. H., 604
Parsons, C. E., 192
Parten, M., 239–240, 253
Partha, G., 509
Paruk, Z., 309
Pascarella, E., 455, 529
Pasley, K., 308
Pasman, H. R. W., 660
Pasterski, V., 314, 315, 316
Pasupathi, M., 610
Patchin, J. W., 396
Patel, C. J., 309
Patrick, D. L., 589, 590, 593
Patrick, J. H., 455
Patterson, C. J., 402, 494
Patterson, G. R., 221, 232, 235, 395
Patterson, M. L., 130
Paulston, C., 370
Paus, T., 422
Pavilanis, R., 239
Pawlak, D. B., 260
Payer, L., 515
Payne, B. P., 645
Peacey, V., 424
Pearson, D., 27

Pease-Alvarez, L., 278
Peeters, A., 558
Peets, K., 230, 232
Peipert, J. F., 405
Pelaez, M., 172
Pender, N., 584
Penner, S., 205
Pennington, B. F., 274, 275
Peplau, L. A., 483, 548
Perez-Edgar, K., 422
Perkins, D., 286, 289
Perkins, H. W., 562
Perrin, A. J., 494
Perrin, E. M., 261
Perry, W. G., 448, 449, 450, 455
Persaud, T., 118
Peskin, H., 339
Pesonen, A. K., 170
Peters, E., 244
Peterson, J., 233, 409
Peterson, R. E., 529
Peterson, R. L., 274, 527
Petlichkoff, L., 263, 289
Petrie, T. A., 350
Pettit, G., 221, 304
Pettito, L., 140
Philippe, F. L., 641
Phillips, B., 348
Phillips, K., 635
Phinney, J. S., 380, 394, 455
Phipps, M. G., 405
Piaget, J., 13, 34, 42, 43, 44–45, 47, 49, 56, 58, 130–137, 138, 182, 195–199, 201, 237–238, 268–271, 276, 313, 329, 353–356, 358, 445–447
Pianta, R., 249
Piazza, J. R., 646
Pick, A. D., 129
Picot, S. J., 622
Pienta, A. M., 547
Piercy, K. W., 632
Pihl, R. O., 237
Pike, A., 312
Pike, B., 388
Pillemer, K., 546
Pilling, M., 114
Pinquart, M., 620, 622, 623, 670
Piotrowski, C., 218
Pipp, S. L., 45
Pisoni, D. B., 129
Pittard, W. B., 406
Pittman, T., 260
Pitts, D. G., 423
Plante, T. G., 427
Plato, C. C., 503
Plomin, R., 159, 227
Pollitt, E., 120
Pollock, M. L., 504–505
Pomerantz, E. M., 300
Porter, C. L., 209
Porter, R. H., 115
Portrie, T., 493
Posada, G., 165, 166, 170, 171
Posner, J. K., 310
Potter, J., 494
Poulin, F., 242, 243, 244, 313, 315, 316, 317, 318
Poussaint, A. F., 231, 232
Powell, F. C., 661
Powell, G. N., 309, 317
Powell, M., 323
Powell, N., 288
Power, T. G., 235, 237, 238, 240, 241, 244, 246
Pownall, T., 117
Pratt, C. L. V., 657
Prause, J., 170
Prayson, R. A., 600
Prenovost, M. A., 317
Presaghi, F., 151
Pribitkin, E., 506
Price, R. H., 310
Priess, H. A., 491
Primeau, M. R., 80
Prinstein, M. J., 410
Prinz, R., 210
Prinz, P., 210
Pritchett, L., 123
Proctor, C. P., 207

Proctor, E. K., 492, 493
Prohaska, T. R., 584
Pryor, D. W., 411
Pudrovska, T., 554, 628, 634
Pugliesi, K. L., 533
Puhl, R. M., 349
Pulakos, J., 474
Pulkkinen, L., 468
Purhonen, M., 148
Pushkar, D., 456
Putney, N. M., 554, 556
Pynoos, J., 635, 637

Quam, J. K., 565, 626, 627
Quan, J., 169
.Quaye, S. J., 457
Queen, P., 119
Quinlan, J. D., 80
Quinn, P. K., 661
Quintana, S. M., 316
Quirouette, C., 619

Raabe, T., 317
Raab, G. M., 623
Rabinowitz, S., 531
Rabins, P., 603
Raby, K. L., 171
Radmacher, K., 474
Radua, J., 266
Raffaelli, M., 401
Raikes, H., 213
Raker, C. A., 405
Rakowski, W., 474
Raloff, J., 347
Ralston, P. A., 616, 632
Ramanan, J., 311
Rambachan, A., 667
Ramgoon, S., 309
Ramirez, C., 590
Ramirez, O., 153, 220
Ram, N., 520
Ramos, K. D., 382
Ramsey, P., 208
Ramu, G. N., 555
Raphael, B., 94, 682
Rasmussen, E. E., 233, 234
Ratcliff, K. S., 475
Ratner, P. A., 482
Raver, C. C., 151
Rawlins, W. K., 313, 314, 392, 474, 475
Rawson, N. E., 506, 583
Razdan, A., 658
Reade, M. C., 668
Reamy, A. M., 639, 642
Reaves, J., 118
Recchia, H., 224, 311
Recker, R. R., 421
Reczek, C., 474, 554, 634
Reeder, K., 207
Reed, S. D., 303, 513, 514
Reese, H. W., 455
Regalia, C., 295
Rege, M., 310
Rehm, J., 432
Reiche, E. M. V., 592
Reichstadt, J., 502
Reid, M., 392
Reif, J. S., 431
Reilly, K. R., 458
Reimer, R. A., 234
Reinhold, A., 167
Reiser, J. J., 115
Remafedi, G., 402
Reno, V. P., 573
Restrepo, D., 506
Reuter, M. A., 551
Rey-Lopez, J. P., 429
Reynolds, A. J., 300
Reynolds, C., 646
Reynolds, D. K., 681
Reynolds, K., 508
Reznikoff, M., 661
Rhode, D. L., 87
Rhodes, C., 368
Ribble, J. C., 575
Riboli, E., 425
Rice, J. C., 231
Richards, B., 141
Richards, M., 24, 109, 393

I-6   Author/Name Index

Richards, M. H., 381, 384
Richardson, D., 512
Richardson, V., 565
Richio, L. J., 405
Richman, K., 616, 617
Richter, P., 86
Rickman, M. D., 159
Riddle, R. B., 677
Rideout, V. J., 233
Rieck, T., 350
Riedmann, A., 630, 634, 664
Riesenberg, L. A., 657
Riggle, E. D., 481
Riggle, S. G., 481
Rigsby, D. C., 405
Riksen-Walraven, J. M., 244
Riley, E. P., 84
Ringel, B. L., 432
Ritchey, M. L., 187
Rivers, C., 436
Rivkees, S. A., 112
Roberto, K. A., 619, 631, 632, 633
Roberts, A., 318
Roberts, B. W., 543
Roberts, D. F., 233
Roberts, J. E., 663
Roberts, P., 349
Roberts, R., 554
Roberts, R. E., 604
Roberts, R. E. L., 320
Robin, A. L., 381, 383
Robinson, J. P., 490
Robins, R. W., 175
Rochat, P., 173
Roche, K. M., 222
Rockwell, R., 184
Rodeheaver, D., 455, 539
Rodin, G. M., 665
Rodin, J., 427, 641
Rodkin, P. C., 313, 314, 318
Roelofs, J., 311
Roerecke, M., 432
Rogers, L. P., 551
Rogers, S. J., 552, 554
Roggman, L. A., 169
Rogoff, B., 45, 48, 49, 199
Rohal, M., 486
Roisman, G. I., 548
Roland, A., 74, 297
Romaine, S., 277
Romig, D. A., 411
Romney, D. M., 246
Roodin, P. A., 445
Rooks, J. P., 92
Room, R., 508
Roopnarine, J. L., 239, 247
Rose, J., 188
Rosemary, S. L., 298
Rosenberg, B. G., 225
Rosenberg, M. S., 251, 296
Rosenblatt, P. C., 679
Rosenfeld, E., 480, 581
Rosenheim, M. K., 404
Rosner, T. T., 559
Ross, C. E., 483, 484, 546
Rossell, C. H., 317
Ross, H. S., 224, 311
Rossi, A. S., 489, 551, 556
Rossi, G., 488
Rossi, P. H., 551, 556
Ross, J., 493
Ross, L., 636
Ross, P. M., 282
Rostila, M., 562
Rothbart, M., 158, 452
Rothbart, M. K., 159, 229
Rothblum, E., 517
Rothman, K. J., 427, 547
Rotosky, S. S., 481
Rounds, J. B., 621
Rourke, B., 274
Routledge, C., 661
Rovine, M., 169, 491
Rowe, J. W., 610
Rowe, M. L., 109
Rowland, T., 263
Royce, J. M., 430
Rozee, P. D., 438

Rubenstein, J. L., 155, 410
Rubia, K., 266
Rubin, K. H., 238, 315, 317, 319
Rubin, L. B., 661
Rubin, S. S., 647
Rubinstein, R. L., 677
Ruble, D., 245, 246, 247, 316
Ruble, D. N., 489, 490, 491
Rudman, D., 577
Rudowitz, R., 186
Rudy, D., 222
Ruhm, C. J., 167
Ruiz-Primo, M. A., 271
Ruiz, S. A., 631
Ruptic, C., 271
Rurup, M. L., 660
Russell, B. L., 438
Russell, K., 347
Russell, R. M., 347
Russ, S. W., 238
Rutter, M., 266
Ruzek, V. L., 512
Ryan, A. M., 313
Ryan, C., 232
Ryan, J., 351
Ryan, R. M., 300
Rybash, J. M., 423, 445, 524, 525, 527
Rytz, A., 184

Saad-Lessler, J., 616, 617
Saarelainen, S., 589
Saarela, J. M., 560, 562, 589
Sabo, D., 264
Sachs, J. S., 602
Sadovnick, A. D., 68
Sagi, A., 164, 170
Sagi-Schwartz, A., 320
St. James-Roberts, I., 137, 156
Sakraida, T. J., 548
Salafia, E. H. B., 312
Salcido, R. M., 681
Saler, L., 326
Salguero, A., 289
Salisbury, C., 87, 88
Salmela-Aro, K., 458
Salmivalli, C., 230
Salomon, E., 635
Salomon, G., 286, 289
Saltali, N., 163
Salthouse, T. A., 527
Salzarulo, P., 113
Salzman, C., 587
Samper, P., 227
Samter, W., 142
Samuel-Hodge, C. D., 507
Samuels, C. A., 369
Samuelsson, I. P., 270
Sanders, C. M., 647
Sanders, S. A., 441
Sandler, I. N., 327
Sandnabba, N. K., 246
Sandrin, D., 114
Sanfilippo, J., 183
Sangl, J., 638
Sankar, A., 669, 670
Santos-Eggimann, B., 539
Santrock, J., 308
Saracho, O., 207, 235
Sarafino, E., 411
Sareen, J., 435
Sarver, M. D., 277
Sasse, D., 353
Sato, D., 84
Saucier, M. G., 624, 625
Sault, N., 261
Sautter, J. M., 577
Savage, J. S., 261
Savelsbergh, G., 117
Savin-Williams, R. C., 401, 402, 403
Sawalani, G. M., 228, 320
Sawin, D., 226
Scabini, E., 295
Scanzoni, J., 481
Scarr, S., 154, 169
Schaefer, J. A., 621
Schafer, R. B., 481, 545, 547, 551
Schafer, W., 551

Schaie, K. W., 23
Scharkow, M., 19, 21
Scharlach, A. E., 560, 561, 562, 564
Scherder, E., 579
Schick, V., 517
Schieman, S., 628
Schiller, B., 532
Schimel, J., 610
Schlecter, S., 221
Schlegel, A., 389
Schmid, S. M., 425
Schneider, C., 515
Schneider, C. M., 486
Schneider, S., 266
Schneidman, E., 681
Schoklitsch, A., 540
Schonert-Reichl, K. A., 381
Schoppe-Sullivan, S. J., 150, 481
Schrader, D., 358
Schulz, R., 564
Schur, E. A., 261
Schut, H., 546
Schutzer, K. A., 587
Schwalberg, R., 405
Schwartz, D., 230
Schwartz, S. H., 321
Schwarz, C., 384
Schwarz, N., 548
Schweinhart, L., 22, 212
Schweinle, A., 130
Scollon, R., 370
Scollon, S., 370
Scott, K. D., 94
Seale, C., 659, 668, 672
Sears, B., 459
Sears, S. F., 531
Sebastián-Gallés, N., 278
Seccombe, K., 495
Sechrist, K. R., 551, 553, 554, 557, 584
Sedgh, G., 404
Seeley, W. W., 187
Seeman, T. E., 619
Sefcek, J. A., 479
Seff, M. A., 550
Seguin, J. R., 237
Seidel, H., 13
Seider, S., 284
Seidman, E., 322
Seidman, S. N., 399, 403
Seidner, L. B., 297
Seifer, R., 159
Seifert, K., 3, 12, 45, 270
Seiffge-Krenke, I., 473
Seitz, V., 11
Seleen, D. R., 564
Selekman, J., 67, 70
Selman, R., 296, 313, 314
Seltzer, M. M., 546
Selye, H., 434, 435
Sengupta, G., 502
Sewell, K. W., 677
Shafer, M. B., 343
Shanahan, L., 225
Shanahan, M., 397
Shapiro, A. F., 149, 150
Shatz, M., 224
Shaughnessy, L., 577
Shaver, P., 382, 472, 550, 628
Shaw, S. F., 277
Sheehan, M. J., 232
Sheldon, M. B., 458, 461
Sheldon, S., 111
Shemesh, G., 581
Shenk, D., 610
Shephard, R. J., 422, 504, 505
Shepherd, H., 459
Shepherd-Look, D., 244
Sheppard, K., 245
Shiao, R., 510
Shin, Y. L., 239
Shiovitz-Ezra, S., 615
Ship, J. A., 506, 582
Shipley, M. J., 507
Short, J. E., 232
Shortt, J. W., 482
Shrum, W., 315, 316, 317
Shu, C., 582
Shuchter, S. T., 646, 676

Shulman, S., 475
Shultz, S., 114
Shure, M. B., 321
Siahpush, M., 573
Siebens, J., 232
Siervogel, R. M., 421
Silber, S. J., 72
Sillén, U., 187
Silva, P. A., 159
Silveira, M. J., 565, 659
Silverman, P., 663
Silverman, P. R., 326
Silver, R. C., 683
Silverstein, L. B., 168
Silverstein, M., 556, 631, 632
Silvester, W., 668
Simkin, P., 92
Simone, P. M., 642, 643
Simons, R. L., 307, 391
Simonton, D. K., 596
Simpson, J. A., 170
Simpson, J. L., 71
Sinclair, D., 336
Singer, A., 617
Singer, J. L., 238
Singh, G. K., 573
Singh-Manoux, A., 507
Sinnott, J. D., 355, 445
Sipahi, L., 437
Siska, E., 111
Sitterle, K., 308
Sizer, T., 372
Skinner, A. C., 261
Skinner, B. F., 41, 205
Skinner, J. H., 635, 637, 639
Skira, M. M., 533
Skolnick, A., 219
Skolnick, J., 219
Skolnick, N., 326
Skoog, I., 601
Slade, A., 163
Slade, M. D., 502
Slater, A., 127
Slaughter, V., 326
Slavin, R., 290, 318, 372
Slavin, R. E., 368
Slinger-Constant, A. M., 275
Slochower, J. A., 680
Slomin, M., 153
Slomkowski, C., 224
Sloper, P., 68
Slusher, M. P., 627
Small, S. A., 401
Smetana, J. G., 382, 383, 385
Smilansky, S., 237
Smith, A. D., 593
Smith, C., 482
Smith, C. J., 579
Smith, D. E., 388
Smith, D. R., 645
Smith, E., 128, 631
Smitherman, G., 388
Smith, G. C., 661
Smith, G. R., 443, 620
Smith, J., 594, 595, 596
Smith, K. R., 624
Smith, L. A., 262, 550
Smith, N., 308, 623, 672
Smith, P. K., 192, 236
Smith, P. T., 623
Smith, S. L., 266
Smock, P. J., 488
Smolak, L., 430
Snarey, J. R., 450, 451
Snidman, N., 158, 159
Snowling, M., 274
Soley, G., 129
Solfrizzi, V., 601
Soli, A., 153
Solomon, J., 163, 165
Soltis, J., 156
Somers, M. D., 493, 495, 496
Sommerville, J., 12
Sood, A. B., 658
Sorensen, S., 620, 622, 623, 670
Soriano, F. I., 411
Sorkhabi, N., 219
Soto, L., 279
Sousa, C., 249

Spaccarelli, S., 251
Spagnoli, J., 539
Spassov, L., 113
Speece, M. W., 326
Spence, C., 672
Spence, M. J., 149
Spencer, S. M., 475
Spencer, T. J., 266
Spergel, I., 412
Spetner, N., 129
Spitze, G., 551, 557, 623, 639, 645
Spitze, G. D., 225
Spivak, G., 321
Spodek, B., 207
Spodek, B. O., 235
Sponseller, D., 237
Sprafkin, J., 234
Spurrier, N. J., 191
Sroufe, L. A., 165
Stacey, N., 186
Stackhouse, J., 274
Stack, S., 483, 484
Stake, J. E., 248
Stall, R., 432
Stander, V., 450, 451
Stanford, E. P., 604, 605
Stanger-Hall, K. F., 343
Stathopoulou, A., 426, 427
Staudinger, U. M., 16, 594, 595, 596
Steele, H., 171
Steiger, C., 91, 93, 94
Stein, A., 192
Steinberg, L., 219, 221, 311, 352, 381, 384, 385, 386, 387, 396
Steinbrenner, G. M., 503, 505, 578, 579
Steiner, G., 197
Steiner, H., 263
Steiner, J. E., 115
Steinglass, P., 437
Steinhard, J., 73
Stein, P. N., 621
Stephen, E. H., 442
Stephenson, J. S., 679
Steptoe, A., 424, 425
Sternberg, R. J., 73, 281, 282, 284, 366, 445, 475, 476, 477, 478
Stern, D. N., 148, 149, 151, 166, 248
Stets, J. E., 899
Stevens, N., 243, 244, 313, 314
Stevenson-Hinde, J., 163, 222
Stevenson, H. W., 300, 302, 303
Stewart, A. J., 554, 613
Stewart, B., 482
Stewart, R. B., 152
Stickgold, R., 425
Stifter, C. A., 168
Stiles, J., 108
Stipek, D. J., 173, 299
Stocker, C., 219
Stokes, G., 402
Stolberg, A. L., 306
Stoller, E. P., 533, 619, 620, 622
Stone, M. R., 394
Stones, M., 587
Stoppa, T. M., 453, 454
Stout, B. C., 83
Stouthamer-Loeber, M., 321, 411
Stratford, B., 67, 68
Straub, R. O., 509, 591
Straus, M. A., 482
Strayer, J., 320
Strazzullo, P., 507
Streissguth, A. P., 84
Strickland, A. L., 656, 657, 667, 670, 673
Strickland, B. R., 591
Striegel-Moore, R. H., 430
Stringhini, S., 584, 586
Stroebe, M. S., 646, 647, 675
Stroebe, W., 646, 647
Stroes, J., 631
Strom, R., 153, 546
Strom, S., 153, 546
Strother, C. R., 521
Stucky, B. D., 228, 320
Studenski, S. A., 587

Studer, J., 539
Stutzer, A., 481, 483
Suarez, E., 438
Subramanian, S. V., 623
Suchodoletz, A. V., 219
Sue, D., 74
Sue, D. W., 74
Sue, S., 74
Suhrcke, M., 429
Suitor, J. J., 481, 546
Sullivan, A., 361, 382
Sullivan, H., 313
Sullivan, J. L., 86
Sullivan, K., 382
Sullivan, S. J., 108
Sultan, D. H., 667
Sunderman, G. L., 369
Sun, Q., 508
Super, C. M., 164, 214
Susa, A. M., 239
Suzuki, Y., 114
Swain, M., 279
Swain, R. A., 598
Swanson, C., 485
Swanson, H., 273
Swanson, S. A., 349
Sweet, J. A., 548
Swendsen, J., 349
Swinburn, B. A., 260
Syed, M., 468
Sykes, P., 288
Szatmari, P., 430

Taber-Thomas, B., 422
Tadmor, C. T., 318
Taffel, S. M., 96
Tagliabue, S., 473
Takanishi, R., 342
Takata, S., 411
Takei, W., 140
Tandon, P. S., 239
Tannenbaum, C., 509
Tannen, D., 479
Tanner, J. L., 472
Tanner, J. M., 183, 338
Tardiff, T., 141
Tarule, J. M., 449
Tasker, F., 402
Tasker, F. L., 494
Taylor, C. A., 231
Taylor, J., 27, 361, 362
Taylor, M. J., 109
Taylor, P., 493
Taylor, S. E., 425, 426, 429, 431, 507, 589, 591, 619, 621
Teaff, J., 565
Tedeschi, R., 682
Teixeira, R., 317
Telama, R., 426
Telkemeyer, S., 140
Telle, K., 310
Temple, J. A., 300
Teno, J. M., 659, 669, 672
Terenzini, P. T., 455, 529
Tesman, J., 186
Testa, M. F., 404
Teti, D. M., 152
Théoret, H., 138
Thomas, A., 158
Thomas, J. L., 556
Thomas, L. E., 613, 667
Thomas-Presswood, T., 208, 211, 214
Thomas, R. J., 480
Thompson, C., 664
Thompson, M., 579
Thompson, R. A., 29
Thomson, E., 488
Thornborrow, N. M., 458, 461
Thornton, W. L., 527
Thorpe, R., 506
Thorsdottir, I., 121
Thorson, J. A., 661
Tidwell, N. D., 479
Tienda, M., 617

Tilcsik, A., 533
Tilden, V. P., 89
Tillman, P., 346
Tindale, J. A., 548, 550, 551, 554
Tobin, J. D., 503
Tobin-Richards, M. H., 339
Tobin, S. S., 614, 659, 661, 662, 663
Tolson, T., 220
Tomasello, M., 226, 227
Tompkins, C. J., 622
Tonti, M., 559
Topa, G., 565
Toribe, Y. H., 114
Tornstam, L., 610
Toro, R. I., 219
Torres, S. J., 435
Tortolero, S. R., 343
Toth, K., 206
Toth, S. L., 409
Tough, P., 367
Touron, D. R., 524, 527
Townshend, J. M., 432
Trainor, L. J., 129
Trawick-Smith, J., 239
Tremblay, R. E., 229, 302
Trent, K., 225
Trinke, S., 170
Triona, L. M., 270
Troll, L. E., 628
Trommsdorff, G., 219, 227
Tronick, E. Z., 157, 170
Tropp, L. R., 317
Trost, S. G., 191
Trzesniewski, K. H., 175
Tsai-Chae, A. H., 219
Tuero, C., 289
Tur, A., 227
Turenshine, H., 108
Turiel, E., 360
Turkheimer, E., 72, 73
Turner, E., 438
Tylanda, C. A., 582
Tzuk, K., 309

Uddin, M., 437
Uhlenberg, P., 549
Ullal-Gupta, S., 80
Umberson, D. J., 474, 482, 484, 546, 554, 624
Underwood, M., 320
Updegraff, K. A., 152
Urbano, R.C., 68
Urbina, S., 281
Urizar, G. G., 531
Uunk, W., 303
Uusitalo, R., 302

Vaidya, V., 509
Vaillant, C. O., 51, 469, 470, 541, 547, 611
Vaillant, G. E., 51, 469, 547, 611
Valkenburg, P. M., 239
Vallerand, R. J., 640, 641
Valvanne, J., 603
Vandell, D. L., 149, 150, 310, 311
van den Boom, D. C., 159, 165
van den Broek, P., 273
van der Heide, A., 660
van der Horst, K., 184
Van De Voorde, L., 659
Vandewater, E. A., 232, 234
Van Doorn, M. D., 381
Van Houtven, C. H., 533
van IJzendoorn, M. H., 151, 163, 164, 165, 166, 170
van Jaarsveld, C. H., 184
Van Orden, K., 664
van Ravesteyn, N., 510, 511
van Reek, J., 388
van Sleuwen, B. E., 118
Vansteenkiste, M., 299, 300
Vansteenwegen, A., 619
VanTassel-Baska, J., 283
Varni, J. W., 621

Vaughn, M. G., 229
Veevers, J. E., 495
Ventura, A. K., 184
Ventura, S. J., 404
Vera, M., 679, 681
Verbrugge, L. M., 436, 509, 587, 589, 590, 593
Verhulst, F. C., 335
Verma, S., 511
Vermeulen, A., 516
Verner, M., 308
Verschueren, K., 163, 170
Vespa, J., 301
Vianna, F. S. L., 83
Victoria, C., 11
Victor, S. B., 494
Vigilant, L. G., 659
Vignoles, V. L., 295, 421
Visco, A. G., 515
Vissing, Y., 19
Vita, A. J., 426, 507, 572, 584
Vitaro, F., 229, 230, 302, 394, 395
Volkan, K., 584
Volling, B. L., 152, 153, 166, 224
Vosler, N. R., 492, 493
Votruba, M., 310
Vouloumanos, A., 114
Vygotsky, L. S., 48, 49, 50, 56, 200, 212, 238, 285, 286, 314, 315, 322

Wadsworth, B., 195, 268, 269
Wadsworth, M. E. J., 109
Wagner, R., 282
Wagner, R. M., 492
Wahistrom, K., 378
Wainright, J. L., 494
Waite, E. B., 225
Waite, L. J., 548, 583, 621
Waite-Stupiansky, S., 270
Wakschlag, L. S., 407
Walberg, H., 368
Walden, T. A., 173
Waldrop, D. P., 677
Walkerdine, V., 211
Walker, J. M., 322
Walker, K., 475
Walker, S. N., 584, 585
Walk, R., 127
Walsh, D. A., 231, 234
Walsh, P., 306
Walsh, R. P., 679
Walter, J. L., 298
Walters, M. L., 482
Walton, G. M., 457
Wandersman, A., 320
Wang, J.-J., 524
Wang, M., 616, 617, 618
Wang, M. T., 371
Wang, V., 74
Wang, W., 301, 480, 487
Wang, Y., 260, 429
Wardjiman, E., 621
Wardle, J., 184, 425
Ward, L. M., 421
Ward, R. A., 619
Ward, R. H., 87
Warneken, F., 226, 227
Warner, K. E., 347
Warner, M., 664
Warnock, F., 114
Warren, K. R., 84
Warren, M., 335
Warren, R., 422, 504
Warren, S., 142
Warshow, J., 558
Wartella, E., 234
Waskel, S. A., 588
Waterman, A. S., 379, 380
Waters, E., 164
Watson, M. W., 232
Waxler, C., 226
Weaver, A. J., 661
Weaver, C. C., 425
Webb, N., 662
Weber, R. A., 474

Wechter, M. E., 515
Weiffenbach, J. M., 582
Weikart, D., 412
Weinberg, M. K., 157
Weinberg, S. L., 452
Weingarten, K., 489
Weisberg, P., 269
Weisel, A., 309
Weisner, T. S., 316
Weiss, D., 539
Weiss, G., 267
Weiss, L. H., 384
Weiss, R. W., 263, 673, 674, 382
Weizman, S. G., 561
Welch, R. D., 244
Weller, E. B., 658
Weller, R. A., 658
Wells, M. S., 264
Wenger, G. C., 634
Werker, J. F., 130
Werner, E., 153
Wertsch, J. V., 48, 49, 285
Western, B., 532
West, J. D., 486
West, L., 475
Whitaker, R. C., 429
Whitbourne, S. K., 423, 504
White, B., 141, 174, 175
White, H. R., 487
White, J. W., 461
White, L. J., 661
White, L. K., 552, 554, 630, 634
Whiteman, S. D., 153
White, R. D., 362
White, S. D., 401
Whitford, G. S., 626, 627
Whiting, B. B., 227, 239
Whiting, J., 239
Whiting, J. W. M., 118
Whitson, J., 199
Whittemore, A. S., 510
Widom, C. S., 251
Wigfield, A., 288, 322
Wiggins, G., 362
Wight, R. G., 548, 627
Wijngaards-de Meij, L., 676
Wilcox, A. J., 77
Wilcox, S., 624, 625
Wilcox, T., 130
Wilfley, D. E., 430
Wilhelm, S., 339
Wilkinson, J., 227
Wilkinson, L., 288
Wilkinson, R., 185, 186
Willcox, S. M., 589
Williams, A. L., 114, 659
Williams, C., 121, 270
Williams, D. R., 434
Williams, J. D., 402
Williams, K., 483, 547, 548, 549
Williamson, J. B., 659
Williams, P. M., 430
Williams, R. M., 317, 393
Willis, D. J., 251
Willis, S. L., 519, 520, 529, 593
Willoughby, T., 233
Wilsgaard, T., 579
Wilson, M., 220
Wilson-Mitchell, J. E., 316
Wilson, M. R., 478, 581
Wilson, T., 313, 350
Wilson, W. J., 404
Winefield, A. H., 534
Winfree, L. T., 411, 412
Winfrey, K. L., 625
Winkler, I., 129
Winston, R., 420
Winter, L., 622
Winters, K. C., 352
Wiseman, A. D., 659, 667
Witherington, D. C., 172, 173
Wolf, D., 272
Wolfe, D. A., 251
Wolfson, A. R., 348
Wolock, I., 248

Wolters, C. A., 300
Wood, E., 401
Wood, P., 314
Woolfolk, A., 366
Woolston, J., 122
Wootan, M., 121
Worden, J. W., 657, 658, 662, 663, 673, 675, 678, 682
Worobey, J., 184
Wortman, C. B., 646, 683
Wozniak, R., 201
Wren, T., 358
Wright, A. A., 659
Wright, D. J., 457
Wright, J. C., 233, 234
Wright, J. D., 532
Wright, J. L., 511
Wright, K., 590, 634
Wright, P. H., 475
Wu, F., 317
Wu, F. C., 516
Wyatt, L. G., 526
Wykle, M. L., 604
Wysocki, C. J., 582

Yacker, N., 452
Yang, H., 278
Yang, S., 278
Yao, X., 437
Yap, S. C., 623
Yardley, J. E., 422
Yarger, R. S., 272
Yarrow, M., 226
Yavorsky, J. E., 481
Yee, B. W. K., 632
Yeh, H. C., 564
Yeh, S. S., 369
Yeung, E. W., 643
Yeung, S. E., 527
Yeung, W. J., 152
Ying, Y., 219
Yinon, H., 287
Yoder, P., 142
Yonas, A., 127
Yoshida, T., 370
Yoshikawa, H., 310
Youlden, D. R., 592
Youniss, J., 313, 314, 392
Yousefi, M., 183
Yuan, A. S. V., 338, 339
Yu, J., 74

Zahn-Waxler, C., 157, 226, 227
Zampi, C., 113
Zane, N., 74
Zani, B., 401
Zarbatany, L., 314
Zarit, J. M., 601, 603, 604
Zarit, S. H., 601, 603, 604, 639, 642
Zeitz, G., 532
Zeleznik, J., 581
Zeller, C., 421
Zerbe, K., 351
Zevitz, R., 411
Zevon, M. A., 621
Zhang, G., 479
Zhang, J., 121
Zhang, Q., 429
Zhou, C., 239
Zigler, E., 410
Zigler, E. F., 167, 412
Zilbergeld, B., 439
Zimmer-Gembeck, M. J., 399, 401
Zimmerman, F. J., 429
Zimmerman, L., 170, 231, 233
Zimprich, D., 525
Zipfel, S., 43
Zisook, S., 646, 676
Zoller-Hodges, D., 644
Zsembik, B. A., 617
Zucker, K. J., 245, 402
Zuo, J., 547
Zuzanek, J., 614
Zweig, J. M., 401

Subject Index

Accommodation, 45, 132
Achievement motivation, 299
Achievement test, 280
Achieving stage, 447
Acquaintance rape, 438
Acquisitive stage, 447
Active euthanasia, 672
Activity competence, 642
Activity settings, 199
Activity theory, 614–615
Adaptation, 45
Adaptive mechanisms, 469
Adolescence
    brain development, 350–353
    clique, 395
    cognitive development, 353–373
    crowd, 395
    description of, 334
    displaced homemaker, 391
    health in, 341–350
        alcohol and tobacco, 346–347
        death, causes of, 341–342
        drug use, 343–346
        eating disorders, 349–350
        nutritional problems, 347–349
        sexually transmitted infections, 343
        sleep, 347–348
    homophobia, 402
    identity diffusion, 378
    identity status, 379
    identity *versus* role confusion, 377
    individuation, 376
    information processing of thoughts, 364–366
    juvenile delinquency, 410
    moral development, 357–364
        ethics of care, 362–363
        Gilligan's ethics of care, 361–362
        justice, issues in, 360
        Kohlberg's six stage of moral judgment, 358–360
        negative identity, 378
    operational thinking, 353–357
        formal thought, 355
        implications, 356–357
        logical combination of ideas, 355
        possibilities *vs.* realities, 354
        scientific reasoning, 354
    physical development, 333–352
        height and weight, 335–336
        psychological effects, 339–341
        puberty, 337–339
    psychosocial development in. *See* Psychosocial development, adolescence
    school, influence of, 367–373
        cognitive effects, 367–369
        social effects, 369–373
    social cognition, development of, 363–364
    socioeconomic status (SES), 386
Adolescent children, 550–551
Adolescent egocentrism, 363
Adolescent pregnancy and parenthood, 403–408
Adoption study, 74
Adulthood theories
    coping styles (Vaillant), 51
    lives seasons (Daniel), 51–52
    normative-crisis model, 51
    timing-of-events model, 52–54
Adult learner
    education, 528–529
    returning to college, 529–531

Advance directive, 565
Ageism, 610
Aggression, 228
    child-rearing styles, 229–230
    media influences, 230–231
    peer influences, 229–230
    positive behavior methods, 232
    spanking and punishment, 231–232
    temperamental differences, 229
Alcohol
    in adolescence, 346–347
    in early adulthood, 431–432
Allele, 62
Alzheimer's disease, 601–602
American Sign Language (ASL), 209
Amniotic sac, 79
Androgyny, 247
Anorexia nervosa, 349
Anticipatory grief, 677
Anxious-avoidant attachment, 163
Anxious-resistant attachment, 163
Apgar Scale, 105
Assessment, 288
Assimilation, 44, 132
Assisted living, 637
Assisted reproductive technology (ART), 72
Assisted suicide, 672–673
Athletics, middle childhood and, 260–264
    physical effects of, 262–263
    psychological effects of, 263–264
Attachment, 40
Attention deficit/hyperactivity disorder (ADHD), 265
Attitudinal independence, 382
Authoritarian parenting, 221
Authoritative parenting, 219

Babbling, 140
Balanced bilingual, 278
Basic dualism, 448
Beanpole family structure, 555
Behavioral learning theories
    classical conditioning (Pavlov), 40–41
    lifespan applications, 43
    operant conditioning (Skinner), 41–42
Behavior modification, 43, 266
Bereavement, 560–562, 673
    funeral rituals, 677–679
    grief, 673–677
    mourning, 679–681
    recovery, 682–683
    support group, 681–682
Bilingualism, middle childhood and
    cognitive effects of bilingualism, 278
    social effects of, 278–279
Binge eating disorder, 349
Biographical method, 470
Birth
    childbirth settings and methods, 91–94
    family and, 97
    faulty passenger, 95–97
    fetal presentation (or orientation), 89–90
    problems during labor and delivery, 94–95
    stages of labor, 90–91
Blended family, 308
Brain development
    adolescence, 350–353
    early adulthood, 421–422
Bronfenbrenner's ecological systems
    chronosystem, 8–9
    exosystem, 8–9
    macrosystem, 8–9

mesosystem, 8–9
microsystem, 8–9
Bulimia nervosa, 349
Burnout, 531

Canalization, 81
Career consolidation, 469
Caregiver-infant synchrony, 151
Caring for dying, 668–673
Cellular theories, 576
Cephalocaudal principle, 115
Child abuse and maltreatment, 248–251
Child maltreatment
    causes of, 248–249
    consequences of, 249–251
    cultural differences and, 250
    overview of, 248
    punishment and, 231
    treatment and prevention of, 251
Children's growth, impact on adults
    appearance effects, 192
    family settings, 194–195
    motor skills effect, 192–193
Child's weight problem, guidelines for responding, 260
Chromosome, 60
Circular reaction, 132
Classical conditioning, 40–41
Climacteric, 512–513
Clique, 395
Cognitive development
    description of, 5
    domain of, 5–6
    preschool children
        activity settings, 199
        conceptual development, 197–199
        early education, 211–215
        egocentrism, 197
        neostructuralist theory, 201
        preoperational stage, 195–196
        from preschooler to child, 215
        situated cognition, 199
        social constructivism, 199
        symbolic thought, 196–197
        zone of proximal development (ZPD), 200
Cognitive development, middle childhood
    conservation, 268–270
    information processing skills, 271–277
        learning disabilities, 273–277
        memory capacity, 271–273
    intelligence, defining and measuring, 279–286
        Gardner's theory, 284–285
        information processing approaches, 281–286
        psychometric approaches, 280–281
        sociocultural approaches, 285–286
        triarchic theory, 281–284
    language development, 277–279
        cognitive effects of bilingualism, 278
        social effects of bilingualism, 278–279
    Piaget's theory and, 268–270
        assessment of student's progress, 271
        curriculum content, 270–271
        teaching methods, 270
    school influences, 286–290
        biases the affect learning, 288
        impact of assessment, 288–290
        participation structures, 286–288
Cognitive developmental theories
    information-processing theory, 45–47

    lifespan applications, 47
    Neo-Piagetian, 45
    Piaget's, 44–45
Cognitive mechanics, 594
Cognitive pragmatics, 595–597
Cohabitation, 487
Cohort, 22
Communicable diseases, 656
Competence, 174
Conception, 76
Concrete operations, 268
Conflictual independence, 382
Congregate housing, 637
Conservation, 268
Constructive play, 238
Contextual developmental theories, 48–50
Contextual relativism, 448
Control group, 21
Control talk, 287
Coparenting, 150
Correlation, 25
Crisis theory
    Erikson's, 471
    Grant/Vaillant, 468–470
    Levinson's, 470
Critical period, 82
Critical thinking, 367
Cross-sectional study, 22
Crowd, 395
Crystallized intelligence, 522–523

Death
    attitude towards, 656–658
    facing one's own, 658–659
Death acceptance
    differences in death anxiety, 661–663
    end-of-life choices, 659–661
Death awareness movement, 657
Degenerative diseases, 656
Delayed parenthood, 550
Dependent variable, 20
Development
    description of, 6
    ecological systems of, 8–9
    ethical constraints on studying, 27–29
    selected landmarks of, 6
Developmental studies
    benefits, 10
    early precursors, 12
    ethical concerns, 27–29
    modern, 12–13
Developmental theories
    active or passive, 34
    classification, 33
    comparison, 54–57
    continuous or discontinuous, 33–34
    ideas and beliefs, 32
    maturation or experience, 33
    qualities, 32–33
Diet
    in early adulthood, 425–426
    in late adulthood, 584–586
    pregnancy and, 87–88
Discourse, 286
Discrimination, 458
Disengagement theory, 614–615
Displaced homemaker, 391
Divorce
    custody arrangements and, 306–308
    impact on adolescence, 388–391
    impact on children, 302–308
Domain, 5
Dominant gene, 62

I-9

Down syndrome, 68
Drug abuse
　in adolescence, 343–346
　in young adulthood, 431–432
Durable power of attorney for health care, 565
Dying process, 666–667

Early adulthood, 444–462
　adult moral reasoning, 450–454
　choices, 444
　cognitive development, 444–462
　　adult moral reasoning, 450–454
　　college, 454–457
　　context and moral orientation, 452–453
　　contextual relativism, 448–450
　　contextual thinking, 446–450
　　formal operations, critiques of, 445–446
　　Fowler's faith-knowing system, 453
　　growth and change, 462
　　occupational segregation, 460
　　postformal thought, 445–446
　　Schaie's stages of adult thinking, 447–448
　　sexual harassment, 461
　　work, 457–462
　college, 454–457
　context and moral orientation, 452–453
　contextual relativism, 448–450
　contextual thinking, 446–450
　formal operations, critiques of, 445–446
　Fowler's faith-knowing system, 453
　growth and change, 462
　health in, 424–434
　　alcohol and drug abuse, 431–432
　　diet, 425–426
　　eating disorders, 429–430
　　exercise, 426–427
　　sleep, 424–425
　　smoking and tobacco use, 430–431
　　unsafe sex, 432–434
　　weight control, 427–429
　occupational segregation, 460
　physical development, 420–442
　　age-related changes, 422–423
　　brain development, 421–422
　　height and weight, 420–421
　　strength, 421–422
　postformal thought, 445–446
　psychosocial development. See Psychosocial development, early adulthood
　Schaie's stages of adult thinking, 447–448
　sexual and reproduction, 438–444
　　attitudes and behaviors, 439–440
　　infertility, 442–443
　　reproductive technologies, 443–444
　　sexual dysfunction, common, 440–441
　　sexual response cycle, 438–439
　sexual harassment, 461
　stress, 434–438
　　experience of, 435–437
　　and health, 435
　　rape and, 438
　　societal, 437
　work, 457–462
Early articulator, 495
Eating disorders
　in adolescence, 349–350
　adolescence and, 349–350
　in early adulthood, 429–430
　female athletes and, 351
Ego, 35
Egocentrism, 197
Embryonic stage, 76
Emotional independence, 382
Empathy, 226
Employment
　career stages and, 458
　gender, race and SES and, 458–459
　maternal, 167–168
　overview of, 457
　sexual harassment and, 461
Equal-partner relationship, 481
Erikson's theory, 34, 37–40, 171, 467
Estrogen, 338
Estrogen replacement therapy (ERT), 515

Ethics of care, 362–363
Ethnicity and community, in family decision making, 387
Ethological theory, 50
Executive stage, 448
Experimental group, 21
Expertise, 366, 525

Failure to thrive, 122
Family life cycle, 545–548
Fetal alcohol syndrome (FAS), 84
Fetal presentation, 89
Fetal stage, 76
Fictive kin, 474, 633–634
Fluid intelligence, 523–525
Formal operational thought, 353
Fowler's faith-knowing system, 453
Freudian Theory, 35–37
Friendship, adolescence and, 391–394
Functional independence, 382
Functional play, 237
Funeral rituals, 677–679

Games with rules, 238
Gardner's theory of multiple intelligences, 284–285
Gender, 244
Gender-role stereotypes, 245
Gene, 60
General adaptation syndrome, 434
Generativity versus stagnation, 540
Genetic abnormalities
　chromosome disorders, 65–70
Genetic counseling, 70–71
Genetic imprinting, 64
Genetics, 59–60
Genetic transmission
　meiosis, 60–61
　mitosis, 61
　role of DNA, 60
Genotype, 62
Germinal stage, 76
Gilligan's ethics of care, 361–362
Glass ceiling, 532
Good death, 667
Grandparenting, 554–556
Grief, 673–683
Grief reactions, 561–562
Grief work, 669
Growth spurt, 335

Habituation, 125
Health-compromising behaviors, 424
Heredity, 71–76
Holographic speech or telegraphic speech, 203
Homophobia, 402, 480
Hormone replacement therapy (HRT), 515
Hospice, 670–672
Hostile attribution bias, 230
Hyperactivity, 265
Hypertrophy, 516
Hypokinesia, 587
Hypothesis, 17
Hysterectomy, 515

Id, 35
Identity development, theories of, 376–381
Identity diffusion, 378
Identity status, 379
Identity versus role confusion, 377
Imaginary audience, 363
Independent variable, 20
Individual genetic expression
　dominant gene, 62
　genotype, 62
　phenotype, 62
　polygenic transmission, 64
　recessive gene, 62
　sex determination, 64–65
　transmission of multiple variations, 62–64
Individuation, 376
Industry versus inferiority, 298
Infant-directed speech, 141, 207
Infant mortality rate, 123
Infants. See also Stage theory (Piaget)
　anticipation of visual events, 128
　arousal, 111–113
　attachment formation, 160–161
　auditory acuity, 114
　auditory perception, 128–129

autonomy, 171–175
behavioral learning theory, 136–138
brain growth, 107–109
breast milk versus formula, 119–120
cognitive development, 123–126
depth perception, 127–128
early social relationships, 148–156
emotions and temperament, 156–160
failure to thrive, 122–123
language acquisition, 138–144
lifespan themes, 175–176
low-birth-weight infants, 121–122
mortality rate, 123
motor development, 115–119
object perception, 127
olfactory acuity, 114–115
overnutrition, 121
physical growth, 106–107
poor nutrition, 120
sensory information, 129–130
sleep, 109–112
tactile, 114–115
taste, 114–115
visual acuity, 113–114
visual perception, 126–127
Infants, attachment
　day care, effects on, 169–170
　definition, 160
　disorganized-disoriented attachment, 163
　father's role, 166–167
　intergenerational effects, 170–171
　long-term effects, 170–171
　maternal employment, 167–168
　mother's role, 165–166
　multiple caregivers, 169–170
　patterns, 163–165
　secure attachment, 162
　strange situation (SS), 170–171
　working models, 160–161
Infants, autonomy
　competence, 174–175
　emergence, 171–172
　emotional response to wrongdoing, 173
　observational learning, 172
　operant conditioning, 172
　self-awareness, 173
　self-description, 173
　self-esteem, 174–175
　self-evaluation, 173
　self-recognition, 173
　social referencing, 172–173
Infertility, 442
Information-processing theory
　definition, 45
　developmental changes, 46–47
　key principles, 45
Informed consent, 28
Integrity versus despair, 613
Intelligence, 279
Intelligence, middle childhood and, 279–286
　Gardner's theory, 284–285
　information processing approaches, 281–283
　psychometric approaches, 280–281
　sociocultural approaches, 285–286
　triarchic theory, 281–284
Intermodal perception, 130
Interviews, 27
Intimacy versus isolation, 471

Juvenile delinquency, 410
Juvenile period, 313

Kohlberg's six stages of moral judgment, 358–360

Labouvie-Vief's theory intrasystemic thought, 446
Language acquisition and variations, preschool children
　deaf and hearing impaired, 209–210
　deficits and differences, 210–211
　duos and telegraphic speech, 202–203
　gender differences, 208
　imitation and practice, 205–206
　infer grammatical relationships, 204
　language acquisition device (LAD), 206–207
　overgeneralizations, 203
　parent-child interactions, 207

regularities, 203
reinforcement, 204–205
socioeconomic differences, 208–209
syntactic rules, 204
syntax rules, 202
Late adulthood, 564–565
　aging and ageism, 610
　aging brain, 599–603
　alcoholism, 588–589
　arthritis, 593
　behavior slows, 579
　cancer, 591–593
　cardiovascular disease, 590–591
　cardiovascular system changes, 580–581
　chronic illness, 589–590
　cognitive development, 593–599
　diet, 584–586
　exercise, 586–587
　family and friends, 628–634
　gender differences, 590
　interests and activities, 642–648
　longevity, 572–578
　marriage, 619–628
　mental health, 603–606
　personality development, 610–616
　prescription drugs, 589
　problems of living, 634–642
　respiratory system changes, 581
　retirement, 606, 616–619
　sensory system changes, 581–583
　sexual functioning, 583–584
　skin, bone, and muscle changes, 579–580
　sleep, 587–588
　work, 606
Late-life suicide, 664–666
Latency, 298
Learning disability, 273–277
Learning orientation, 299
Legacy-creating stage, 448
Leisure, 562–565
Life expectancy, 502
Life review, 647–648
Lifespan development, 4
　changing meanings, 15
　continuity within change, 13–14
　diversity, 16
　lifelong growth, 14–15
　strength and limitations, 29
　vantage points, 15
Lifespan psychology
　case studies, 27
　experimental study, 19–21
　naturalistic studies, 24–27
　quasi-experimental studies, 21–24
　scientific methods, 17–19
Living will, 565
Longitudinal study, 22
Long-term care, 638–640
Long-term memory (LTM), 272
Low birth weight, 121

Marcia's theory of identity status, 379
Marital conflict, 390
Marriage, early adulthood
　cohabitation, 487–488
　divorce, 484–485
　equal partnerships, 481
　marital satisfaction, 481–484
　remarriage, 485–486
　singlehood, 486–487
Menarche, 337
Menopause, 513
Metacognition, 47
Metalinguistic awareness, 278
Middle adulthood
　aging, 502–504
　aging parents, 556–558
　breast cancer, 509–510
　cardiovascular changes, 504–505
　cognitive development, 518
　health in, 506–509
　intelligence in, 519–528
　male climacteric, 516–517
　marriage, 543–550
　menopause, 513–516
　physical development, 502
　prostate cancer, 510–511
　psychosocial development, 537–567
　reproductive change, 512
　respiratory system changes, 505

sensory system changes, 505–506
sexuality, 517–518
siblings, 558–560
socio economic status, impact on health, 511–512
strength, 503
work in, 531–534
Middle childhood
   and athletics, 260–264
      physical effects of, 262–263
      psychological effects of, 263–264
   cognitive development. *See* Cognitive development, middle childhood
   health and illness, 264–267
      attention deficit hyperactivity disorder, 265–267
      sleep, 267
      social influence on, 265
   height and weight, trends and variations in, 259–260
   and motor development, 260–264
   physical development, 258
   psychosocial development. *See* Psychosocial development, middle childhood
Middle school, 369
Midlife crisis
   era of middle adulthood, 542
   Harvard Grant study, 541
   UCLA study, 541
Midlife divorce, 548–550
Midwife, 91
Morality, 357
Morbidity, 506
Mortality, 264, 506
Motor development, middle childhood and, 260–264
Motor skill development
   catching, 189
   definition, 115
   drawing, 189–190
   jumping, 188
   running, 188
   throwing, 189
   variations, 191–192
   walking, 188
Mourning, 679–681
Multi-infarct neurocognitive disorder, 600–601
Multiple intelligences, 284
Myelination, 109

Naturally occurring retirement communities (NORCs), 636–637
Negative identity, 378
Neonate, 105
Neostructuralist theory, 201
Neurocognitive disorders (NCD), 600–601
Neurons, 108
Newborn, physical development
   Apgar Scale, 105–106
   first few hours, 105
   size and bodily proportions, 106
Non-normative life event, 540
Non-REM sleep, 109
Normative crisis model, 51, 541–542
Normative life event, 540
Normative personality change, 543
Norms, 13
Nutritional problems, adolescence and, 347–349

Obesity, 260
Object permanence, 133
Observational learning, 42, 43
Occupational segregation, 460
Oophorectomy, 515
Operant conditioning, 41, 43
Organ reserve, 422, 503
Osteoporosis, 515
Overgeneralizations, 204
Overnutrition, 121
Overt aggression, 228
Ovum, 60

Palliative care, 671
Parent-child relationships
   authoritarian parenting, 221–222
   authoritative parenting, 219–221

change over time, 223
indifferent parenting, 222–223
permissive parenting, 222
preschool years, 218–219
Parenthood, early adulthood and
   child free, 493–496
   single, 492
   stepparent/blended families, 492–493
   transition to, 489–491
Participation structures, 286
Passive euthanasia, 672
Pathological aging, 424
Peer groups, adolescence and, 394–397
Peer relationships, middle childhood and, 312–323
Peers, definition, 294
Perceived popularity, 318
Perception, 123
Performance orientation, 299
Permissive parenting, 222
Personal fable, 364
Phenotype, 62
Phonemes, 140
Physical activity play, 236
Physical development
   in adolescence, 335–336
   description, 5
   domains, 5
   early adulthood, 420–442
      age-related changes, 422–423
      brain development, 421–422
      height and weight, 420–421
      strength, 421–422
   early childhood, 182–184
   first two years, 105–106
   late adulthood, 572–578
   middle adulthood, 502
   middle childhood, 258
Piaget's preoperational stage, 195
Piaget's stage theory, 130
Piaget's theory, concrete operational skills, 268
Piaget's theory, middle childhood and, 268–270
   assessment of student's progress, 271
   curriculum content, 270–271
   education, influence on, 270–271
   teaching methods, 270
Piaget's theory of cognition, 44–45, 51
Piaget's theory of education, 270–271
Piaget's theory of infant cognition, 134
Placenta, 78
Plasticity, 108, 597
Plateauing, 531
Play
   cognitive theory, 237
   constructive, 238
   ethological theory, 236–237
   functional, 237
   games with rules, 238
   learning theory, 236
   nature of, 235
   other influences, 238–239
   pretend, 238
   psychoanalytic theory, 235–236
   social levels, 239–241
Postconventional moral judgment, 360
Postformal thought, 445
Postponer, 495
Posttraumatic stress disorder (PTSD), 437
Practical intelligence, 525
Prenatal development, 76–81
Prenatal diagnosis, 70–71
Prenatal influences on the child, 81–89
Preoperational stage, 196
Prepared childbirth, 92
Preschool children
   bladder control, 185–187
   classification skills, 197–198
   cognitive development, 195–201
   concept of numbers, 199
   conservation task, 198–199
   egocentrism, 197
   gender differences, physical development, 190–191
   genetic background, 183
   growth measurement, 182–183
   impact of children's growth on adults, 192–195

language acquisition and variations, 201–211
nutritional needs, 184
reversibility, 198
socioeconomic status, 184–185
Preschoolers
   effects of media, 232–234
   friendships, 241–244
   gender influences, 244–248
   play activities, 234–241
Pretend play, 238
Primary aging, 503
Primary sex characteristics, 337
Programming structures, 577–578
Proximodistal principle, 116
Psychodynamic developmental theories
   Erikson's, 37–40
   Freudian, 35–37
   lifespan applications, 40
Psychometric approach to intelligence, 280
Psychosocial development, adolescence, 375–414
   family relationships, 381–391
      divorce, remarriage, and single parenthood, 388–391
      with parents, 381–387
   identity development, theories of, 376–381
   sexuality, 399–403
      and everyday life, 403
      sexual experience, 399–401
      sexual orientations, 402–403
   social relationships, 391–398
      friendship, 391–394
      peer groups, 394–397
   special problems, 403–412
      adolescent pregnancy and parenthood, 403–408
      juvenile delinquency, 410–412
      teenage depression and suicide, 408–410
Psychosocial development, description, 6
Psychosocial development, early adulthood
   adult development, theories of, 466–472
      Daniel Levinson's seasons of adult lives, 470–471
      Erik Erikson's intimacy *versus* isolation, 471–472
      George Vaillant and Grant study, 468–470
      social clocks, 467–468
   intimate relationships, 472–480
      friendship, 473–475
      love, 475–479
      mate selection, 479–480
   marriage, divorce, remarriage, and singlehood, 480–488
      cohabitation, 487–488
      divorce, 484–485
      equal partnerships, 481
      marital satisfaction, 481–484
      remarriage, 485–486
      singlehood, 486–487
   parenthood, 488–496
      child free, 493–496
      single, 492
      stepparent/blended families, 492–493
      transition to, 489–491
Psychosocial development, early childhood
   child abuse and maltreatment, 248–251
   gender development, 244–248
      androgyny, 247–248
      concept, 244–245
      gender-role stereotypes, 245
      influences, 246–247
      learning gender schema, 245–246
   play in
      cognitive theory, 237
      constructive, 238
      ethological theory, 236–237
      functional, 237
      games with rules, 238
      learning theory, 236
      nature of, 235
      other influences, 238–239
      pretend, 238
      psychoanalytic theory, 235–236
      social levels, 239–241
   relationships with family

attachment relationships, 218–219
authoritarian parenting, 221–222
authority parenting, 219–221
authority patterns, 219
changes over time, 223
indifferent parenting, 222–223
only children, 225
permissive parenting, 222
relationships with siblings, 223–225
social world
   aggression, 228–232
   effects of media, 232–234
   empathy, 226
   prosocial behavior, 226–228
Psychosocial development, first two years
   attachment formation, 160–171
   autonomy, emergence of, 171–175
   early social relationships, 148–156
   emotions and temperament, 156–159
Psychosocial development, late adulthood
   aging and ageism, 610
   dating and remarriage, 624–626
   ever-single older adults, 627–628
   interests and activities
      activity competence, 642
      community involvement, 643–645
      religion and spirituality, 645–648
   marriage, 619–623
   older lesbians and gay men, 626–628
   personality development, 610–616
   problems of living, 610–616
      assisted living, 637–638
      control over living conditions, 640–642
      independent living, 635–637
      long-term care, 638–640
   relationships with family and friends
      adult grandchildren, 631–632
      childlessness, 634
      fictive kin, 633–634
      friends, 632–633
      great-grandchildren, 632
      Internet and social media use, 634
      retirement, 616–618
      siblings, 629–631
      widowhood, 623–624
Psychosocial development, middle adulthood
   bereavement, 560–562
   crisis or no crisis, 539–543
   family relationships, 550–560
   leisure, 562–564
   marriage and divorce, 543–550
   multiplicity of images, 538–539
   preparing for late adulthood, 564–565
Psychosocial development, middle childhood, 293–329
   age of industry and achievement, 298–300
   challenges, 294–295
   death, loss, and grieving during school, 323–327
   family relationships, 300–311
   peer relationships, 312–323
   sense of self, 295–298
   social support, sources of, 311–312
Psychosocial moratorium, 378
Puberty, 337
Punishment, 42

Random sample, 20
Range of reaction, 72
Recall memory, 272
Recentering, 472
Recessive gene, 62
Recognition memory, 272
Reflex, 115
Reinforcement, 41
Reintegrative stage, 448
Relational aggression, 228
Reminiscence, 646–648
REM sleep, 109
Resilience, 371
Responsible stage, 448
Retirement planning, 565
Right to die, 673

Same-sex marriage, 548
Sample, 26
Sandwich generation, 550

Subject Index I-11

Schaie's stage theory, 447
Scheme, 44, 131
Secondary aging, 503
Secondary sex characteristics, 337
Selective attention, 272
Selective optimization with compensation (SOC), 615–616
Self-constancy, 296
Self-esteem, 175
Semantics, 140
Senescence, 576
Sense of self, 295
Sensorimotor intelligence, 130
Sequential study, 23
Serial monogamy, 475
Sex-linked recessive traits, 64
Sexual dysfunction, 440
Sexual harassment, 461
Sexuality
    in adolescence, 399–403
    in early adulthood, 438–444
        attitudes and behaviors, 439–440
        infertility, 442–443
        reproductive technologies, 443–444
        sexual dysfunction, common, 440–441
        sexual response cycle, 438–439
    in late adulthood, 583–584
    in middle adulthood, 517–518
Sexually transmitted infections, adolescence and, 343

Siblings relationships, 223–225
Sickle-cell disease, 70
Situated cognition, 199
Sleep, adolescence and, 347–348
Sleep, early adulthood, 424–425
Smoking and tobacco use, early adulthood, 430–431
Social clock, 467
Social clock projects, 539
Social cognition, 363
Social cognitive learning theory, 42–43
Social constructivism, 199
Social conventions, 360
Social convoy, 628–629
Social referencing, 172
Social relationships
    caregiver-infant synchrony, 150–151
    coparenting, 150
    father-infant interactions, 152
    grandparents, 153
    infants, 148–149
    interactions with peers, 154–156
    interactions with siblings, 152–153
    with nonparental caregivers, 153–154
    transition to parenthood, 149–151
Social relationships, adolescence and, 391–398
Social trajectory, 48
Social world behavior
    aggression, 228–232
    conflicts, 228

    empathy, 226
    prosocial behavior, 226–227
Sociocultural perspective on intelligence, 285
Socioeconomic status (SES), 386
Sociometric popularity, 318
Sperm, 60
Stage theory (Piaget), 130–136
Sternberg's theory of love, 478, 481
Stranger rape, 438
Stress
    in early adulthood, 434–438
        experience of, 435–437
        and health, 435
        rape and, 438
        societal, 437
    in pregnancy, 88–89
Stunting, 120
Successful aging, 613
Sudden infant death syndrome (SIDS), 110
Superego, 35
Survey, 26
Symbolic thought, 196
Synaptic pruning, 108
Synaptogenesis, 108
Syntax, 202–205, 208, 209

Teenage depression and suicide, 408–410
Temperament, 158
Teratogen, 82
Terminal care alternatives, 669–671
Testosterone, 338

Timing-of-events model, 52–54
Trait, 542
Transient exuberance, 108
Triarchic theory of intelligence, 281–284
Twin adoption study, 75
Twin study, 75

Umbilical cord, 79
Unsafe sex, early adulthood, 432–434

Validity, 21
Vascular neurocognitive disorder, 600–601
Visual cliff, 127–128

Weight control, early adulthood, 427–429
Wisdom, 594–599

Young adult children, 549, 551–554
Young children
    developmentally appropriate practices, 213
    fine motor coordination, 189–190

Zone of proximal development (ZPD), 48, 200, 207
Zygote, 60